Yearbook of International Humanitarian Law

Yearbook of International Humanitarian Law

Timothy L.H. McCormack
General Editor

Avril McDonald
Managing Editor

Volume 7

2004

T·M·C·Asser press

Published by T.M.C.ASSER PRESS,
P.O. Box 16163, 2500 BD The Hague, The Netherlands
www.asserpress.nl

T.M.C.ASSER PRESS English language books are distributed exclusively by:

Cambridge University Press, The Edinburgh Building, Shaftesbury Road,
Cambridge CB2 2RU, UK,
or
for customers in the USA, Canada and Mexico:
Cambridge University Press, 100 Brook Hill Drive, West Nyack, NY 10994-2133, USA

www.cambridge.org

Cover photograph: Sudan – Darfur-Chad Border – Sudanese Rebels

ISBN 90-6704-224-2
ISBN 978-90-6704-224-6
ISSN 1389-1359

T.M.C. Asser Instituut – Institute for Private and Public International Law, International Commercial Arbitration and European Law
Institute Address: R.J. Schimmelpennincklaan 20-22, The Hague, The Netherlands; Mailing Address: P.O. Box 30461, 2500 GL The Hague, The Netherlands; Tel.: (31-70)3420300; Fax: (31-70)3420359; Internet: www.asser.nl.
Over thirty years, the T.M.C. Asser Institute has developed into a leading scientific research institute in the field of international law. It covers private international law, public international law, including international humanitarian law, the law of the European Union, the law of international commercial arbitration and increasingly, also, international economic law and the law of international commerce.
Conducting scientific research, either fundamental or applied, in the aforementioned domains, is the main activity of the Institute. In addition, the Institute organizes congresses and postgraduate courses, undertakes contract-research and operates its own publishing house.
Because of its inter-university background, the Institute often cooperates with Dutch law faculties as well as with various national and foreign institutions. The Institute organizes *Asser College Europe*, a project in cooperation with East and Central European countries whereby research and educational projects are organized and implemented.

CORRESPONDENTS

The Yearbook of International Humanitarian Law *extends its sincere thanks and appreciation to its correspondents, without whose assistance the compilation of this volume would not have been possible:*

Africa
Professor Kamel Filali, *Algeria*
Dr Jose Doria, *Angola*
Mr Adel Maged, *Egypt*
Dr. Kithure Kindiki, *Kenya*
Professor Khadija Elmadmad, *Morocco*
Mr Benson Chinedu Olugbuo, *Nigeria*
Mr Abdul Tejan-Cole, *Sierra Leone*
Dr Phenyo Keising Rakate, *South Africa*
Dr Khoti Kamanga, *Tanzania*
Mr Emmanuel Kasimbazi, *Uganda*

Asia-Pacific
Professor Tim McCormack, *Australia*
Mr David Boyle, *Cambodia*
General Nilendra Kumar, *India*
Professor Hideyuki Kasutani, *Japan*
Professor Seigo Iwamoto, *Japan*
Ms Dana Zhandayeva, *Kazakhstan*
Ms Treasa Dunworth, *New Zealand*
Mr Soliman M. Santos Jr., *The Philippines*
Dr Djura Inomzoda, *Tajikistan*

Europe
Dr Thomas Desch, *Austria*
Mr Peter Kustor, *Austria*
Mr Munir Mammadov, *Azerbaijan*
Mr Oleg Starovoitov, *Belarus*
Professor Eric David, *Belgium*
Mr Jan Hladik, *Czech Republic/Slovakia*
Mr Peter Otken, *Denmark*
Mr Tanel Kerikmäe, *Estonia*
Mr Andres Parmas, *Estonia*
Professor Paul Tavernier, *France*
Mr Gregor Schotten, *Germany*
Dr Maria Gavouneli, *Greece*
Professor Péter Kovács, *Hungary*
Mr Ray Murphy, *Ireland*
Dr Giovanni Carlo Bruno, *Italy*
Dr Valentina Della Fina, *Italy*
Dr Rosa Dinuzzi, *Italy*
Dr Ornella Ferrajola, *Italy*
Dr Amina Maneggia, *Italy*
Professor Sergio Marchisio, *Italy*
Dr Fabio Raspadori, *Italy*
Dr Guilliano Salberini, *Italy*
Professor Gedimanos Mesonis, *Lithuania*
Mr Rytis Satkauskas, *Lithuania*
Professor Nico Keijzer, *The Netherlands*
Dr. Elies van Sliedregt *The Netherlands*
Professor Elzbieta Mikos-Skuza, *Poland*
Professor Miodrag Starčević, *Serbia and Montenegro*
Mr Michael Hartmann, *Serbia and Montenegro (Kosovo)*
Professor Antoni Pigrau Solé, *Spain*
Mr Peter Hostettler, *Switzerland*
Mr A.P.V. Rogers, *United Kingdom*

Middle East
Mr Mehrdad Molaei, *Iran*
Professor Djamchid Momtaz, *Iran*
Professor Yuval Shany, *Israel*
Dr Mustafa Mari, *Occupied Palestinian Territories*

North America
Professor René Provost, *Canada*
Mr Joseph Rikhof, *Canada*
Mr Burrus M. Carnahan, *USA*

Central and South America
Professor José Alejandro Consigli, *Argentina*
Mr Gabriel Valladares, *Argentina*
Professor Carlos Dettleff Beros, *Chile*
Professor Hernan Salinas Burgos, *Chile*
Professor Rafael Prieto Sanjuán, *Colombia*
Dr José A. Guevara, *Mexico*
Ms Fatima Andrada, *Paraguay*
Professor Alfonso Velázquez, *Paraguay*

TABLE OF CONTENTS

ABBREVIATIONS

Abl.	Amtsblatt
AC	Appeal Cases
ACTR	Australian Capital Territory Reports
AD	Annual Digest of Public International Law Cases
Adelaide LR	Adelaide Law Review
ADF	Australian Defence Force
AFDI	Annuaire français de droit international
African JI & CL	African Journal of International and Comparative Law
Air Force LR	Air Force Law Review
AJIL	American Journal of International Law
Albany LR	Albany Law Review
All ER	All England Law Reports
ALR	Australian Law Reports
Amer. Univ. JIL & Pol.	American University Journal of International Law and Policy
Amer. Univ. ILJ	American University International Law Journal
Amer. Univ. ILR	American University International Law Review
AP	Additional Protocol
AP	Associated Press
APL(s)	Anti-personnel landmine(s)
ARABSAT	Arab Satellite Communications Organization
Arizona JI & CL	Arizona Journal of International and Comparative Law
ASEAN	Association of South East Asian Nations
ASIL Proc	American Society of International Law Proceedings
ATCA	Alien Tort Claims Act (USA)
Australian YIL	Australian Yearbook of International Law
Austrian JPIL	Austrian Journal for Public International Law
Austrian Rev. Int. & Eur. L	Austrian Revue of International and European Law
AVM	Anti-vehicle landmine
Berkeley JIL	Berkeley Journal of International Law
B.O.	Boletín Oficial de la República Argentina
BGBl	Bundesgesetzblatt
BGH	Bundesgerichtshof
Boston Univ. ILJ	Boston University International Law Journal
Boston College Int. & Comp. LR	Boston College International and Comparative Law Review
BTF	Balkans Task Force
BverfGE	Bundesverfassungsgericht
BYIL	British Yearbook of International Law
Calif. Western ILJ	California Western International Law Journal
Can. JL & Jur.	Canadian Journal of Law and Jurisprudence
Canadian YIL	Canadian Yearbook of International Law
Case Western Reserve JIL	Case Western Reserve Journal of International Law
Catholic Univ. LR	Catholic University Law Review

CCW	Convention on Certain Conventional Weapons
CD	Conference on Disarmament
CENTCOM	Central Command
CHR (UN)	Centre for Human Rights
CIA	Central Intelligence Agency
CICC	Coalition for the International Criminal Court
CICR	Comité International de la Croix Rouge
CID	Criminal Investigation Division
CIS	Commonwealth of Independent States
CIVPOL	Civilian Police
CLA	Chief Legal Advisor
CLJ	Criminal Law Journal
CLR	Commonwealth Law Reports
CMAC	Court Martial Appeal Court
Cmnd.	Command Paper
Columbia HRLR	Columbia Human Rights Law Review
Columbia JTL	Columbia Journal of Transnational Law
Cornell ILJ	Cornell International Law Journal
Cr. App. R	Criminal Appeals Reports
CRC	Convention on the Rights of the Child
Criminal LF	Criminal Law Forum
Criminal LR	Criminal Law Review
CSP	Conference of States Parties
CTBT	Comprehensive Test Ban Treaty
CTS	Commonwealth Treaty Series
CWC	Chemical Weapons Convention
Dalhousie LJ	Dalhousie Law Journal
Denver JIL & Pol.	Denver Journal of International Law and Policy
DLR	Dominian Law Reports
DMU	Detainee Management Unit
DoD	Department of Defense (USA)
Duke JCIL	Duke Journal of Comparative and International Law
ECCAS	Economic Community of Central African States
ECHR Rep.	European Convention on Human Rights Reports
ECHR	European Convention on Human Rights
ECOMOG	ECOWAS Monitoring Group
ECOSOC	United Nations Economic and Social Council
ECOWAS	Economic Community of West African States
EECC	Eritrea-Ethiopia Claims Commission
EHRR	European Human Rights Reports
Emory ILR	Emory International Law Review
EJIL	European Journal of International Law
ERW	Explosive Remnants of War
EU	European Union
Eur. Ct. HR	European Court of Human Rights
Eur. Comm. HR	European Commission of Human Rights

Eur. J. Crime, Crim. L & Crim. Jus.	European Journal of Crime, Criminal Law and Criminal Justice
Ex D	Exchequer Digest
F	Federal
F Supp.	Federal Supplement
FCJ	Federal Court of Justice (Canada)
FCR	Federal Court Reports
FDC	Force Detention Centre
FDTL	East Timorese Defence Force
Fed. Rep.	Federal Reporter
Finnish YIL	Finnish Yearbook of International Law
Fordham ILJ	Fordham International Law Journal
FRETILIN	Frente Revolucionaria Timor Lest Independence
FRY	Federal Republic of Yugoslavia
GA	General Assembly (United Nations)
GA Res.	General Assembly Resolution (United Nations)
GAOR (United Nations)	General Assembly Official Records
GC	Geneva Conventions
Georgetown Int. Environ. LR	Georgetown International Environmental Law Review
Georgia JI & Comp. L	Georgia Journal of International and Comparative Law
GW JIL and Econ.	The George Washington Journal of International Law and Economics
GU	Gazzetta Ufficiale (Italian Official Gazette)
GYIL	German Yearbook of International Law
Hague YIL	Hague Yearbook of International Law
Harvard ILJ	Harvard International Law Journal
HCJ	High Court of Justice
HRLJ	Human Rights Law Journal
HRQ	Human Rights Quarterly
I/A Court HR	Inter-American Court of Human Rights
I/A Comm. HR	Inter-American Commission on Human Rights
ICA	International Council on Archives
ICBL	International Campaign to Ban Landmines
ICBS	International Committee of the Blue Shield
ICC	International Criminal Court
ICCPR	International Covenant on Civil and Political Rights
ICCROM	International Centre for the Study of the Preservation and Restoration of Cultural Property
ICJ	International Court of Justice
ICJ Rep.	International Court of Justice Reports
ICLR	International Criminal Law Review
ICLQ	International and Comparative Law Quarterly
ICOM	International Council of Museums
ICOMOS	International Council on Monuments and Sites
ICRC	International Committee of the Red Cross
ICTR	International Criminal Tribunal for Rwanda

ICTY	International Criminal Tribunal for the former Yugoslavia
IFLA	International Federation of Library Association and Institutions
IFOR	Implementation Force
IHL	International Humanitarian Law
IJRL	International Journal of Refugee Law
ILAS JI & Comp. L	ILAS Journal of International and Comparative Law
ILC Yearbook	Yearbook of the International Law Commission
ILM	International Legal Materials
ILR	International Law Reports
IMT	International Military Tribunal (in Nuremberg)
IMTFE	International Military Tribunal for the Far East (in Tokyo)
Indian JIL	Indian Journal of International Law
INTELSAT	International Telecommunications Satellite Organization
Int. LF	International Law Forum
INTERFET	International Force in East Timor
IRA	Irish Republican Army
IRRC	International Review of the Red Cross
ISAF	International Security Assistance Force
Israel LR	Israel Law Review
Israel YB	Israel Yearbook
Israel YB HR	Israel Yearbook on Human Rights
J Armed Conflict L	Journal of Armed Conflict Law
JICL	Journal of International and Comparative Law
JIL & Prac.	Journal of International Law and Practice
J Int. Criminal Justice	Journal of International Criminal Justice
JPI	Judicial Police Inspectors
J Trans. L & Pol.	Journal of Transnational Law & policy
KFOR	Kosovo Force
LAS	League of Arab States
Leiden JIL	Leiden Journal of International Law
LNTS	League of Nations Treaty Series
LOAC	Law of Armed Conflicts
Loy. LA I & CLJ	Loyola of Los Angeles International and Comparative Law Journal
Loyola I & CLJ	Loyola International and Comparative Law Journal
LQR	Law Quarterly Review
Maryland JIL & T	Maryland Journal of International Law and Trade
MCC	Military Criminal Code
Melbourne JIL	Melbourne Journal of International Law
Melbourne Univ. LR	Melbourne University Law Review
Mich. JIL	Michigan Journal of International Law
Mich. LR	Michigan Law Review
Mil. LR	Military Law Review
MLR	Modern Law Review
MNF	Multinational Force
Monash LR	Monash Law Review

Moscow JIL	Moscow Journal of International Law
MPYBUNL	Max Planck Yearbook of United Nations Law
MPYIL	Max Planck Yearbook of International Law
NATO	North Atlantic Treaty Organisation
Naval LR	Naval Law Review
NCOs	Non-Commissioned Officers
New England LR	New England Law Review
NGO	Non-Governmental Organisation
NILR	Netherlands International Law Review
NJ	Nederlandse Jurisprudentie
NLR	Naval Law Review
Nordic JIL	Nordic Journal of International Law
Northwestern Univ. LR	Northwestern University law Review
Notre Dame JL	Notre Dame Journal of Law
NPC	New Penal Code
NQHR	Netherlands Quarterly of Human Rights
NY Univ. JIL & Pol.	New York University Journal of International Law and Politics
NY Univ. LR	New York University Law Review
NYIL	Netherlands Yearbook of International Law
NZLR	New Zealand Law Review
ÖAD	Österreichische Außenpolitische Dokumentation
OAS	Organization of American States
OECS	Organization of Eastern Caribbean States
ONU	Organisation des Nations Unies
ONUC	United Nations Force in the Congo
OPCW	Organisation for the Prohibition of Chemical Weapons
OSA	Operational Support Arrangement
OTP	Office of the Prosecutor (of the ICTR and/or ICTY)
Palestine YIL	Palestine Yearbook of International Law
PD	Probate Division, English Law Reports
Penn. State ILR	Pennsylvania State International Law Review
PKF	Peace Keeping Force
PMG	Peace Monitoring Group
POW	Prisoner of War
Proc. ASIL	Proceedings of the American Society of International Law
QB	Queen's Bench
RBDI	Revue Belge de droit international
RDI	Rivista di diritto internazionale
RDPC	Revue de droit pénal et de criminologie
Recueil des Cours	Collected Courses of the Hague Academy of International Law
RGDIP	Revue générale de droit international public
RIAA	Reports of International Arbitral Awards
RICR	Revue International de la Croix Rouge
RQDI	Revue Québécoise de Droit International

RSC	Rules of the Supreme Court
RSCDPC	Revue de science criminelle et de droit pénal comparé
RSDIE	Revue Suisse de droit international et de droit européen
SADC	South African Development Community
SASC	South African Security Council
SC	Security Council
SC Res.	Security Council Resolution
SCOR (United Nations)	Security Council Official Records
SCR	Supreme Court Reports
SCU	Serious Crimes Unit
SFOR	Stabilization Force
SFRY	Socialist Federal Republic of Yugoslavia
SG	Secretary-General
SIPRI	Stockholm International Peace Research Institute
SOFA	Status of Force Agreement
South Texas LR	South Texas Law Review
Stanford JIL	Stanford Journal of International Law
Syracuse JIL & Com.	Syracuse Journal of International Law & Commerce
SZIER	Schweizerische Zeitschrift für internationales und europäisches Recht
Texas ILJ	Texas International Law Journal
Texas LR	Texas Law Review
Tilburg For. LR	Tilburg Foreign Law Review
TLPS	Timorese Police Force
Transn. L & Contemp. Probs.	Transnational Law and Contemporary Problems
TRC Report (South African)	Truth and Reconciliation Commission Report
Tulsa J Comp. & IL	Tulsa Journal of Comparative and International Law
UNAMA	United Nations Assistance Mission in Afghanistan
UNAMET	United Nations Mission in East Timor
UNAMIR	United Nations Assistance Mission for Rwanda
UNAMSIL	United Nations Mission in Sierra Leone
UNCHR	United Nations Commission on Human Rights
UNCHS	United Nations Centre for Human Settlements
UNCIVPOL	United Nations Civilian Police
UNCTAD	United Nations Conference on Trade and Development
UN Doc.	United Nations Documents Series
UNDP	United Nations Development Programme
UNEF	United Nations Emergency Force (in the Sinai)
UNEP	United Nations Environment Programme
UNESCO	United Nations Educational, Scientific and Cultural Organisation
UNFICYP	United Nations Force in Cyprus
UNGCI	United Nations Guards Contingent in Iraq
UNHCR	United Nations High Commissioner for Refugees
UNHFOR	United Nations Human Rights Field Office in Rwanda
UNICEF	United Nations (International) Children's (Emergency) Fund

UNIDIR	United Nations Institute for Disarmament Research
UNIFIL	United Nations Interim Force in Lebanon
UNIIMOG	United Nations Iran/Iraq Military Observer Group
UNIKOM	United Nations Iraq/Kuwait Observer Mission
UNITAF	United Nations Unified Task Force
UNITAF	United Nations Task Force (in Somalia)
UNMIS	United Nations Mission in Sudan
UNOMIG	United Nations Observer Mission in Georgia
UNOMSIL	United Nations Observer Mission in Sierra Leone
UNOSOM	United Nations Operation in Somalia
UNPF	United Nations Peacekeeping Force
UNPROFOR	United Nations Protection Force (in Bosnia and Herzegovina)
UNTAC	United Nations Transitional Authority in Cambodia
UNTAET	United Nations Transitional Authority in East Timor
UNTS	United Nations Treaty Series
UNWCC	United Nations War Crimes Commission
USAFA JLS	USAFA Journal of Legal Studies
Vanderbilt JTL	Vanderbilt Journal of Transnational Law
Virginia JIL	Virginia Journal of International Law
Virginia LR	Virginia Law Review
Wake Forest LR	Wake Forest Law Review
WCR	War Crimes Reports
WHO	World Health Organisation
Whittier LR	Whittier Law Review
WLR	Weekly Law Reports
Yale HR & Dev. LJ	Yale Human Rights & Development Law Journal
Yale JIL	Yale Journal of International Law
Yale LJ	Yale Law Journal
Yb Eur. Conv. HR	Yearbook of the European Convention of Human Rights
Yb ILC	Yearbook of the International Law Commission
YIHL	Yearbook of International Humanitarian Law
Yug. Rev. IL	Yugoslav Review of International Law
ZaöRV	Zeitschrift für ausländisches öffentliches Recht und Völkerrecht
ZöR	Zeitschrift für öffentliches Recht

ARTICLES

UNEQUAL COMBAT AND THE LAW OF WAR[1]

A.P.V. Rogers[2]

---

2. Yorke Distinguished Visiting Fellow of the Faculty of Law, University of Cambridge; Fellow, Lauterpacht Centre for International Law, University of Cambridge; former Director of Army Legal Services, United Kingdom; author of the prize-winning book, *Law on the Battlefield* (Manchester, Manchester University Press 1996). This article is based on lectures given at the International Institute of Humanitarian Law in the early 1980s, at the Bruges Colloquium of the College of Europe in 2002, at the Lauterpacht Centre in 2004 and to NATO legal officers at Mönchengladbach in 2005.

Yearbook of International Humanitarian Law
Volume 7 - 2004 - pp. 3-34 DOI 10.1017/S1389135904000030

1. INTRODUCTION

Unequal combat, more usually called asymmetric warfare,[3] describes the situation where regular, well-armed and well-trained and disciplined forces, duty bound to act lawfully, are opposed by irregular forces that are lightly armed, more loosely structured and for whom respect for the law is not important.[4] While countless examples of unequal combat can be given, the operations by US and Iraqi-government forces against armed opposition groups in Fallujah in November 2004 provide a good, recent case study.

Unequal combat is not, of course, a new phenomenon. It is something powerful armies have experienced over the centuries: no doubt those of Rome and, more recently, those of Napoleon or Prussia and Germany. Other armed forces are not in a position to defeat them. Faced with such overwhelming opposition, opponents have adopted another approach: to wear down the opposition by lots of small-scale operations. To do so, they take advantage of local knowledge and any environmental factors that work to their advantage: mountains, marshland, woodland

3. A recent article that addresses this issue is T. Pfanner, 'Asymmetrical warfare from the perspective of humanitarian law and humanitarian action', 87 *IRRC* (2005) pp. 149-174. This looks at the problem from the perspective of the ICRC.

4. Though it might be called in aid to avoid conviction in a criminal trial. In his fascinating article, 'International humanitarian law and irregular warfare', 82 *IRRC* (2000) p. 941, J.C. Lacavo states that 'Guerrilla movements in fact invent their own rules of humanitarian conduct and do not act, as States do, on the basis of their knowledge of the law, but rather as a matter of political expediency'. The author cites the case of Nicaragua, one of only two in Latin America where insurgents succeeded in gaining power, as vindicating their approach of 'implacable in combat, generous in victory', which involved respect for what would be recognised as norms of international humanitarian law.

and jungle, towns and cities and the creation of areas where they can operate safely with local support.

Generally speaking, armed opposition groups are not able to win a direct confrontation with the regular armed forces because they lack firepower but they can win small, local engagements, keep large numbers of regular forces tied up and, perhaps, prevent control by the armed forces of the whole territory. Such operations place a severe strain on the rule of law. In this article, it is their impact on the law of war that is examined, but it will be done from the perspective of the regular armed forces.[5] In this respect, it should be noted that the law has been laid down by just those powerful states and it may be that insufficient provision is made in the law for that type of combat. If it is to stand any hope of being complied with, the law must be realistic. That applies with greater force to unequal combat.

2. THE PROBLEM OF UNEQUAL COMBAT

It is not surprising that, if they are to survive, armed opposition groups tend to adopt tactics of a hit and run nature. They use clandestine methods, seeking shelter and intelligence from sympathisers. They do not have sophisticated logistics and will rely on foreign supplies or captured stocks for weapons and ammunition. When possible, they will concentrate their efforts against enemy armed forces' weak points, such as the supply chain, soft-skinned vehicles or low-flying aircraft, with surprise ambush or sabotage operations, or they will exploit the vulnerability of modern society to disruption. Because the armed forces are well armed and their locations strongly guarded, armed opposition groups tend to turn their attention to intimidating the civilian population, with attacks against officials and collaborators or against the civilian population itself, in the hope of provoking a heavy-handed response and invoking international sympathy. All this may be coupled with political activity and propaganda.

In conventional armed conflict, members of the opposing armed forces usually wear uniform or combat gear that distinguishes them from members of the civilian population. In a situation of unequal combat, both sides may be less keen to operate in uniform: members of armed opposition groups for fear that they will be identified and attacked or captured; members of the regular armed forces for concern about the vulnerability to attack of single soldiers or small groups, especially when deployed in areas where armed opposition groups operate or are known to have local support.

The regular armed forces will have a difficult decision to make: whether to take a hard line or to try to win the 'hearts and minds' of the population. That decision will affect the choice of means and methods: soldiers on foot patrol in berets and armed with rifles; or soldiers in armoured vehicle patrols with combat helmets, body armour and heavy weapons. A lot will depend on whether the purpose of the

---

5. The author has dealt with the wider legal implications in 'Asymmetric warfare: some personal reflections', 27 *Collegium* (published by the College of Europe) (Spring 2003) at p. 15.

patrols is to get in touch with local people and gather information or whether it is to show a strong presence. If the former, there is the immediate problem of the difficulty of communicating with the local population from the relative safety of armoured vehicles. The same is true when the armed forces adopt a 'fort mentality', operating only from strongholds. In tackling the armed opposition groups they need to be able to identify and isolate the troublemakers both physically and morally. Initially this may necessitate the adoption of undercover tactics and the infiltration of armed groups. The aim will be to arrest individuals or to surround and storm them where a sufficient concentration of the opposition makes this worthwhile. Since the latter operation may have adverse consequences for civilians, their evacuation from the area needs to be considered but any advance warning is likely to lead to the members of the opposition group just slipping away. If the latter stay to fight, there are dangers of high civilian casualties in this type of warfare, especially if fought in urban areas. Even if the armed opposition groups are defeated or evicted from an area, the problem remains of maintaining control there. Evacuation of civilians to enable the armed forces better to tackle the armed opposition groups brings with it serious logistic and welfare problems, for which careful planning is needed. The internment of members of armed opposition groups to prevent them from operating requires the allocation of sufficient resources and manpower and legal procedures equal to the task. Internment is usually seen as an extraordinary measure, legally tolerated only in time of armed conflict or serious national danger. When a sense of frustration about dealing with armed opposition groups starts to creep in, members of the armed forces must resist the temptation to resort to unlawful measures, such as torture or coercion to obtain information or reprisals against those sympathetic to the opposition.

Caught in the middle between the armed forces and the armed opposition groups are the civilians. Among these may be foreign civilians, such as aid workers, who have been sent to the country to alleviate suffering. Both sides need civilian help and support. Civilians suffer double jeopardy, as they are likely to have information of value to both sides. They are vulnerable to hostage taking and intimidation and may be caught in the crossfire or subjected to a high risk of becoming collateral casualties if heavy weapons are deployed.

3. LAW AND PRACTICE IN UNEQUAL COMBAT

When considering the phenomenon of unequal combat there can be a complete cycle of operations: armed conflict, defence against invasion, a *levée en masse*, surrender and the question of whom it binds,[6] occupation, resistance to occupation, liberation of territory, resumption of armed conflict. So what law applies, and when?

---

6. Local surrender, general armistice, resistance, effect of violation of armistice, mobilisation of whole population, government in exile, free forces.

3.1 Applicability of the law of war

The legal regime is similarly complicated. Applicable law includes the domestic law of the place where the conflict takes place; the domestic law of the state where individuals affected by the conflict happen to find themselves; and international law relating to, for example, genocide, torture, crimes against humanity, human rights law[7] and, if the situation amounts to an armed conflict, the law of war.

3.1.1 *What constitutes an armed conflict?*

For the law of war to apply, there must be an armed conflict or an occupation. The term 'armed conflict' is not defined in treaty law, though that contains some indication of situations that do not amount to armed conflict. Use of armed force by criminals, street rioting or even well organised terrorist activity is not an armed conflict to which international law applies. Protocol II of 1977 additional to the Geneva Conventions of 1949 (hereinafter, Protocol II), which deals with non-international armed conflicts, does not apply to internal disturbances and tensions, such as riots, isolated and sporadic acts of violence and other acts of a similar nature. Protocol II does not apply unless dissident armed forces or other organised armed groups are under responsible command, exercise control over part of a state's territory and carry out sustained and concerted military operations, and comply with the law of war.

Of course, Protocol II applies on its own terms. However, there can be an armed conflict to which international law, in the shape of common Article 3 to the Geneva Conventions of 1949 (hereinafter, common Art. 3) and customary law, applies in other situations as well. Various factors may be of importance in determining whether the situation is one of armed conflict, for example whether armed groups have territorial control, an organisation having the characteristics of a state, properly structured armed forces, show respect for the law of war, or their belligerent status has been recognised.[8] There must also be a certain level of intensity of the conflict to distinguish between armed conflict and internal security operation.[9]

---

7. There are some limitations as to the applicability of the European Convention on Human Rights outside the territory of the contracting state. For example, in the case of *Banković* v. *Belgium and others*, 123 *ILR* (2003) p. 94, it was held, in effect, that it was not applicable to the results of the NATO bombing campaign relating to Kosovo. In the UK Divisional Court judgment in *R (Al Skeini and Others)* v. *Secretary of State* [2004] EWHC 2911 of 14 December 2004, it was held that outside the regional sphere of the convention it only applied in exceptional and limited cases such as embassies, consulates, vessels and aircraft and, as in the *Al Skeini* case, in British military prisons.

8. See J. S. Pictet, *Commentary on the First Geneva Convention* (Geneva, ICRC 1952) pp. 49-50.

9. See Y. Sandoz, C. Swinarski and B. Zimmermann, *Commentary on the Additional Protocols* (Geneva, ICRC 1987) para. 4438; P.K. Rakate, 'The shelling of Knin by the Croation Army in August 1995: a police operation or a non-international armed conflict', 82 *IRRC* (2000) p. 1037, concludes that the operation in Knin amounted to an armed conflict. This assessment seems to be based on intensity. It seems that artillery and tanks were used.

There can be an armed conflict between opposing factions within a state.[10] In the context of unequal combat, it is worth observing also that a non-international armed conflict may become international if any of the armed groups involved is under the overall control of an outside state.[11]

Questions were asked in 1999 by the Crimes of War Project team[12] about whether the conflict then raging in Chechnya amounted to an armed conflict. In the opinion of the author, once heavy armour, artillery and ground attack aircraft had been deployed in action, it was clear that the intensity threshold had been crossed and that common Article 3 applied. There is an argument that Protocol II, to which Russia is a party,[13] also applied. That would depend on a factual analysis of the situation to ascertain whether the Chechen forces were properly organised and commanded, whether they controlled territory and were able to carry out sustained and concerted military operations and comply with the law of war. In the latter respect one would be looking for evidence that these forces operated in uniform, respected civilian immunity and treated captured members of the Russian armed forces humanely.

Another example of a non-international armed conflict was the situation in Kosovo before the NATO intervention in 1999. Was this an internal security operation governed by domestic law or a non-international armed conflict to which the law of war applied? In dealing with this question, one needs to consider the factors set out above. There is also the jurisprudence of the Yugoslav Tribunal, notably in the *Tadić* case. However, the definition of armed conflict in that case[14] is not all that helpful, its emphasis (at least as far as a non-international armed conflict is concerned) being on the protracted nature of the armed violence. The reference by the Appeals Chamber to large-scale violence raises another, and perhaps in the context more relevant, factor: the severity or the intensity of the armed conflict. This is important because one has to make a distinction between armed police action, perhaps against organised crime, which could be protracted, and armed conflict. Even if the armed forces are called out to assist the police, this may not be enough to convert the situation into an armed conflict. When referring to state practice, it is noteworthy that the United Kingdom government consistently denied

---

10. *Prosecutor* v. *Duško 'Dule' Tadić*, Case No. IT-94-1, Decision on the Defence Motion for Interlocutory Appeal on Jurisdiction (Jurisdiction)(Appeals Chamber), 105 *ILR* (1997) p. 419, at p. 488.

11. *Prosecutor* v. *Aleksovski*, Case No. IT-95-14/1-A, Judgement, (Appeals Chamber) 24 March 2000, paras. 134, 145.

12. See <http://www.crimesofwar.org/expert/chechnya.html>.

13. The USSR ratified both Protocol I and Protocol II on 29 September 1989. On 13 January 1992 the Russian Federation declared that it continued to perform the rights and fulfil the obligations following from the international agreements signed by the USSR, see A. Roberts and R. Guelff, *Documents on the Laws of* War, 3rd edn. (Oxford, Oxford University Press 2000) p. 497. The Constitutional Court of the Russian Federation, in a judgement of 31 July 1995, recognised the applicability of Protocol II to the conflict in Chechnya at that stage in the conflict, see 17 *Human Rights Law Journal* (1996) Nos. 3-6, at p. 133.

14. See 105 *ILR* (1997) pp. 419 at 488: 'an armed conflict exists whenever there is a resort to armed force between States or protracted armed violence between governmental authorities and organized armed groups or between such groups within a State'.

the existence of an armed conflict in Northern Ireland since 1969, even though large numbers of troops were stationed there in support of the civil authorities. It is of interest that the government tried to deal with the situation under the ordinary law, even though this meant introducing substantial amounts of emergency legislation. That leads one to another relevant factor: whether there has been a declaration of a state of emergency, state of siege, or state of martial law, with control effectively passed to the military. In that case it would be difficult for the state concerned to deny that an armed conflict existed. Another possible consideration might be the size and scale of any refugee problem connected with the conflict, as large-scale movement of civilians away from the fighting is often a feature of armed conflict. In the Kosovo case, of course, it may be possible to argue that the refugee problem was caused not by the intensity of the conflict but by the policy of 'ethnic cleansing'.

The question of the organisation of the forces in conflict is a relevant consideration because this helps to distinguish between criminal or terrorist activity and armed conflict. If armed opposition groups control territory, are structured on military lines and conduct operations wearing something recognisable as a form of military uniform, there is a strong case for saying that there is an armed conflict. But that is not all because Protocol I of 1977 additional to the Geneva Conventions of 1949 (hereinafter, Protocol I), for example, in Article 44(3), recognises that there are, even in international armed conflict, situations that preclude the wearing of uniform. In those situations, carrying arms openly during deployments and engagements is the minimum requirement.

It seems more important, in the Kosovo case, to establish what sort of operations were being conducted on both sides during the relevant period, in particular the composition of the forces deployed, on the Serb side whether it was the special police or the armed forces, the nature of their missions, the type of weapons used and casualty figures, both civilian and military. For example, the use of assault rifles and rocket-propelled grenades would not necessarily point to the existence of an armed conflict unless, as in Somalia or Iraq, these are the only weapons available to insurgents or fighters. If tanks, artillery other than mortars, and attack helicopters are actually used in attacks,[15] even if only on one side, this would tend to point to the existence of an armed conflict.

Another example is the fighting in Iraq in late 2004 when the apparent sovereign authority in Iraq was the interim Iraqi administration. One expert wrote of the alleged murder of an insurgent by a US marine:

> 'The legal basis for the Fallujah operation … is far from clear. What is happening in Iraq is unlikely to be international armed conflict (although that is how the war started 20 months ago). But it could be classed as internal armed conflict, and therefore still subject to the provisions of the 1949 Geneva Conventions. Those conventions say that a combatant who has surrendered or is rendered *hors de combat* by sickness, wounds or any other cause must be treated humanely and is protected, in particular, against

15. As opposed to merely being in the equipment tables of the units concerned.

"murder of all kinds". If that is the case, whatever the mitigating circumstances, the marine could be tried for a war crime.'[16]

The reference here to the Geneva Conventions is, no doubt, to common Article 3 of those conventions.

3.1.2 *What law applies?*

Since treaty law is essentially contractual, it is not too difficult, when a conflict between states occurs, to work out which treaties are binding on the parties. The situation becomes more complicated if states not party to the treaties, national liberation or resistance movements become involved.[17]

The author takes the view that the law of international armed conflict applied in Iraq from the beginning of hostilities on 20 March 2003 until the end of the occupation period on 30 June 2004.[18] After that, a non-international armed conflict continued between the Interim Government and later the Government of Iraq, supported by coalition forces, on one side and insurgent groups on the other. However, persons who, before that date, acquired protection under the law of war, for example, as prisoners of war or internees, would continue to benefit from that protection until final release or repatriation. Military operations meet the intensity requirement. In the action in Fallujah, 51 US soldiers and eight Iraqi government soldiers were reported killed as well as an estimated 1,200 insurgents[19] and, possibly, as many as 800 civilians.[20] The provisions of common Article 3 as well as those of customary law apply to the conflict.[21]

---

16. C. Bellamy, professor of military science and doctrine at Cranfield University, 'The Americans are sowing dragons' teeth in Iraq', *The Independent*, 17 November 2004.

17. An attempt to resolve these difficulties was made in the Certain Conventional Weapons Convention of 1980, Art. 7(1), which avoids the non-participation clause found, for example, in the Hague Conventions of 1907. Under the 1907 Conventions, if a state not party becomes involved in an armed conflict, the States Parties are absolved from compliance. Under the Weapons Convention, however, parties will always be bound as between themselves. They are not, however, bound as regards states not party unless the non-party accepts and applies the convention and notifies the depositary of its intention to do so. Art. 7(4) deals with the complicated situation where a war of national liberation is going on. If the State Party involved in the liberation conflict is a party to both Protocol I and the Geneva Conventions, the Weapons Convention will apply provided the authority representing the liberation movement has undertaken to apply all three of those treaties. If, however, the State Party involved in the liberation conflict is not a party to Protocol I but is a party to the Geneva Conventions of 1949, the Weapons Conventions applies provided the authority representing the liberation movement undertakes to apply both the Geneva Conventions and the Weapons Convention.

18. See Common Art. 2 to the Geneva Conventions of 1949 (hereinafter, GC). Persons protected by the Geneva Conventions continue to be protected until their final release or repatriation.

19. 'Troops storm major Baghdad mosque', BBC News Online of 19 November 2004, quoting Lt Gen Sattler, the US commander.

20. See A. Buncombe, 'Fears mount for families inside Fallujah', *The Independent*, 17 November 2004.

21. For an exposition of the rules on the conduct of combat in internal armed conflicts, see Rogers, *supra* n. 2, ch. 9.

3.2 Principle of distinction

3.2.1 *The general rule*

The whole of the law of war is built on the propositional foundation that armed conflict is a contest between the opposing armed forces. That means that members of the armed forces have the right to fight but may be attacked; and that civilians do not have the right to fight but are protected from attack. This edifice, therefore, is dependent on a clear distinction being made between members of the armed forces, known as combatants, and civilians. Even though combatant status is not addressed in the treaty rules governing non-international armed conflict, the application of those rules does require a distinction to be made in practice between those who take a direct part in the fighting and those who do not.[22]

The general rule is that combatants must distinguish themselves from the civilian population while they are engaged in an attack or in a military operation preparatory to an attack.[23] It has been customary for members of the armed forces to distinguish themselves by wearing military uniform and for irregular armed groups to do so by wearing a 'fixed distinctive emblem, recognizable at a distance',[24] perhaps on an armband.[25] The reality of unequal combat is such, however, that members of armed opposition groups wear combat fatigues or a recognisable emblem if they consider it safe to do so, perhaps in interviews before the camera or in territory that they control.

However, uniform and distinctive signs are not the only ways for combatants to demonstrate their status. What is important is 'whether members of the adversary forces are able to recognize the person concerned as a combatant, and therefore a legitimate target, rather than a civilian who is protected under international law'.[26] It would be a legitimate ruse of war, though, for a combatant to camouflage himself by wearing foliage to blend into a woodland background, because he would not be feigning civilian, and therefore protected, status by doing so.

3.2.2 *The exception to the general rule*

The general rule is fine for traditional conflicts, such as the Falklands conflict of 1982, between regular armed forces fighting by the rules.[27] It does not sit happily with cases of guerrilla warfare, especially during non-international armed conflict,

---

22. See further, ibid., pp. 222-228.

23. Protocol I of 1977 (hereinafter, AP I), Art. 44(3). This means during combat and in military operations prior to combat, for example, when deploying for, manoeuvring in connection with or withdrawing from an attack, see ICRC Manual, *Fight it Right* (Geneva, ICRC 1999) (hereafter, ICRC Manual), para. 603.1.

24. Art. 1 of the Hague Regulations of 1907 (hereinafter, HR).

25. The question of uniform or distinguishing emblems is examined in more detail in *Rogers*, *supra* n. 2. pp. 38-42, 223.

26. UK Ministry of Defence, *The Manual of the Law of Armed Conflict* (Oxford, Oxford University Press 2004) (hereinafter, UK Manual) para. 4.4.2.

27. In this case, the parties were the United Kingdom and Argentina.

where members of armed groups may well prefer not to advertise their membership of those groups by wearing uniform thus easing their opponents' task of identifying and arresting them. In drafting treaty rules, it would have been possible for the international community to take a strict view, maintain the classical rule of distinction and, in effect, label guerrillas as war criminals. But, at least in the case of international armed conflicts, it was decided to alter the law to make allowance for this type of warfare. The result was the exception to be found in Article 44 of Protocol I. This recognises that there are situations in international armed conflicts where, owing to the nature of the hostilities, an armed combatant cannot distinguish himself. In those cases, he retains his combatant status so long as he carries his arms openly (a) during each military engagement, and (b) while visible to the enemy when deploying for an attack in which he is going to take part.[28]

On ratification of the protocol, a number of states made statements of understanding to the effect that this exceptional rule could only apply in occupied territory or in wars of national liberation.[29] This seems to the author to be an unduly narrow interpretation since the exception would also be of use to special forces conducting long-range patrols in enemy-held territory. States also made interpretative statements, for example, that 'deployment' meant any individual or collective movement towards a position from which an attack was to be launched; and that 'visible' included visibility due to electronic or other forms of surveillance.[30] That would include binoculars and night sights.[31]

The level at which a decision is taken to take advantage of the exception is not laid down in the protocol. Because it is an exception to the normal rule, non-distinction should be of the shortest possible duration and not become standard procedure.[32]

---

28. Art. 44(3) AP I.

29. The United Kingdom made a declaratory statement on ratification of the protocol about the interpretation of this provision: (a) deployment means any movement towards a place from which an attack is to be launched and (b) that the exceptional circumstances can only occur in occupied territory or during wars of national liberation. The inference is that, in other situations, the rule of distinction would invariably apply. In the UK Manual it is stated, at para. 4.5.1, that 'wide application of this special rule would reduce the protection of civilians to vanishing point. Members of the opposing armed forces would come to regard every civilian as likely to be a combatant in disguise and, for their own protection, would see them as proper targets for attack. The special rule is thus limited to those exceptional situations where a combatant is truly *unable* to operate effectively whilst distinguishing himself in accordance with the normal requirements'.

30. See the declarations made on ratification of AP I by Belgium and New Zealand respectively, as set out in Roberts and Guelff, *supra* n. 13, pp. 501, 508.

31. According to the UK Manual, para. 4.5.3, 'visible' means visible in a broad sense, including with the aid of infrared or image intensification devices.

32. The ICRC Manual, para. 604.4, states as follows, that the 'level at which the decision to take advantage of the exception is not laid down but it is recommended that it be made at a high level, certainly above the level of commanding officer. Non distinction should be of the shortest duration. There can be no justification for regarding it as anything other than a highly exceptional measure. Exceptions to the rule of distinction are most likely to be encountered in guerrilla warfare.'

3.2.3 *Effect of failure to comply with the rule of distinction*

What are the consequences for individuals who fail to distinguish themselves? Do they forfeit prisoner of war status? Article 44(4) of Protocol I provides that people captured in these circumstances are entitled to protection equivalent in all respects to that accorded to prisoners of war. What does this mean? Can it be argued by reference to Article 44(6) of Protocol I that persons coming within Article 4 of the Geneva Prisoner of War Convention of 1949 are entitled as of right to prisoner-of-war status?

Protocol I does not 'repeal' the Hague Regulations of 1907, nor the Geneva Prisoner of War Convention; it is an attempt at rationalisation. If a person qualifies as a prisoner of war under the Convention, then it seems to the author that he must be accorded prisoner-of-war status even if he has not complied with Article 44 of Protocol I.[33] So a member of the special forces operating behind enemy lines, even if he does not carry his weapons openly in deployments and engagements, is entitled to prisoner-of-war status. However, he would be criminally responsible for any war crimes he may have committed in the process.

The situation is different for irregular armed groups in international armed conflict. They have to do more to convince the outside world that they are genuine combatants and not just criminals or thugs: compliance with the law of war and particularly the requirement to distinguish themselves from civilians and strict compliance with the conditions for the exception. The question of whether by failing to do so they commit a punishable act is addressed below under 'unprivileged belligerency'.[34]

---

33. The ICRC Manual, para. 604.6, states as follows: 'Since the rules in Geneva Protocol I about combatant status are expressed to be without prejudice to the generally accepted practice of states that members of the regular armed units wear uniform and without prejudice to entitlement to prisoner of war status under the Geneva Prisoner of War Convention, that must mean that members of the regular armed forces who do not wear uniform or carry their arms openly when involved in deployments or engagements do not forfeit prisoner of war status, but are punishable as war criminals. Regular armed units in this context cannot have the narrow meaning which, in some countries, separates regular from reserve forces. The rule is probably intended to encompass all units belonging to a High Contracting Party. It is not clear if it includes *ad hoc* units belonging to a movement not qualifying as a state in international law because there is a distinction between "regular armed forces" and "armed forces" in the treaty text. It is recommended that if guerrillas qualify as armed forces, the saving for regular armed forces should be applied to them too.'

34. The UK Manual, para. 4.6, is as follows: 'The position of a person who takes a direct part in hostilities while failing to comply with the rule of distinction is as follows. If he falls into the power of the enemy while engaged in an attack or a military operation preparatory to an attack, and is not at that time complying with the requirements of the general rule (or, where applicable, the special rule set out above), he forfeits his combatant status and may be tried and punished for unlawful participation in hostilities. If he has disguised himself as a civilian, he will also be guilty of perfidy if he kills, injures or captures an adversary by resort to that disguise. He also forfeits his right to be treated as a prisoner of war unless, in spite of the circumstances, he still falls within one of the categories entitled to prisoners of war status under Geneva Convention III. He must, however, be accorded treatment equivalent to that of a prisoner of war, so that he is entitled, for example, to the protection afforded to prisoners of war at his trial. If he falls into the power of the adversary while he is not engaged in a military engagement or in a military operation preparatory to an attack, he does not forfeit his rights to be a combatant

3.3 Combatant status

3.3.1 *The rules*

Since combatants have specific rights and duties under the law of war, it is necessary to be able to establish who they are. Under the Hague Regulations of 1907, it was open to a state to decide which members of its army were combatants and which were non-combatants. Combatant status was also available to (a) members of militia and volunteer forces under responsible command and having a fixed distinctive emblem recognisable at a distance and (b) members of a *levée en masse*. Both categories had to carry their arms openly and respect the law of war.

The effect of Article 4 of the Geneva Prisoner of War Convention was to extend the militia and volunteer force category to organised resistance movements.

Under Protocol I, however, all members of the armed forces of a party to the conflict (except medical personnel and chaplains) are combatants. Armed forces of a party to the conflict are defined as: 'all organized armed forces, groups and units which are under a command responsible to the Party to the conflict for the conduct of its subordinates, even if that Party is represented by a government or an authority not recognised by an adverse Party. Such armed forces shall be subject to an internal disciplinary system which, *inter alia*, shall enforce compliance with the rules of international law applicable in armed conflict.'[35]

In trying to deal with the phenomenon of guerrilla warfare and defining what is meant by armed forces, Article 43 of Protocol I assimilates regular and irregular forces. Emphasis is now on organisation. Members of the armed forces are combatants and have a right to participate in hostilities.[36] They are also entitled to prisoner of war status.

The actual composition of the armed forces is a matter for the state or faction concerned. Their components may be regular units, reservists, territorial defence units, citizens called up for part-time service or full-time soldiers, as long as the conditions set out above are fulfilled. However, if a paramilitary or armed law enforcement agency, such as gendarmerie or police, is incorporated into the armed forces, the other parties to the conflict must be notified.[37] It is normal for members of the armed forces to have ranks, the more senior ranks having power to give orders to and exercise discipline over their subordinates. Although the point is not specifically addressed in the treaties, membership of the armed forces must require a certain level of formality both in terms of joining and being discharged from those forces. One would expect proper procedures to obtain in the armed forces of

---

or a prisoner of war by virtue of his past activities, though he remains liable to trial in respect of those activities, if they were unlawful. Any person who has taken part in hostilities but who is not entitled to prisoner of war status, and does not benefit from more favourable treatment as a civilian in the hands of a party to the conflict, is nevertheless entitled to certain basic humanitarian guarantees.'

35. Art. 43(1) AP I.

36. The ICRC Manual, para. 601.1 explains that 'taking a direct part in hostilities' means 'engaging in hostile action against enemy armed forces but not assisting in the general war effort'.

37. Art. 43(3) AP I.

states in any event, but that should also be the case with irregular armed groups. It is a matter of organisation and discipline, which goes to the root of the definition of armed forces.[38]

Whether the head of state is a member of the armed forces will depend on whether he has, in reality, powers of command over the armed forces rather than being merely a titular or honorary head of those forces.[39]

Irregular fighters, or even civilians, are legitimate objects of attack when they take a direct part in hostilities, whether or not they distinguish themselves from ordinary civilians.

In the case of non-international armed conflict, no provision is made in treaty law or by customary usage for combatant or prisoner-of-war status to be bestowed unless either belligerency has been recognised or the parties to the conflict have agreed to apply treaty law, for example, the Hague Regulations and Geneva Conventions. An agreement is more likely to be successfully negotiated in cases such as those of a federal state where the elements of that state are in conflict or where the parties to the conflict control definable portions of territory. In those cases, the parties will probably have a degree of autonomy and separate structures. In the absence of recognition or agreement, members of armed opposition groups are simply subject to the domestic law of the state concerned and answerable for any violations of that law that they may have committed. Any claim that they are combatants legitimately engaged in an armed conflict will provide no defence unless the domestic law so provides.

3.3.2 *Jurisprudence*

Two cases on combatant status were decided in 1968 by the Privy Council, in this context the supreme appellate court for Commonwealth cases. In the first case, the accused was a Malaysian national in the Indonesian armed forces operating in Malaysia. It was held that he was not entitled to prisoner-of-war status as he owed allegiance to the detaining power and that he could be tried for an offence against the security laws of Malaysia.[40] In the second case, the accused was a member of the Indonesian armed forces. While wearing civilian clothes he committed sabotage in an office building in Singapore, killing three civilians. It was held that, as he was not operating as a member of the Indonesian armed forces at the time and did not comply with the requirements of Article 4(A)(2) of the Third Geneva Convention, he had neither combatant nor prisoner-of-war status and could be tried for murder under Malaysian domestic law.[41] While the second case turned on its facts, the first case seems objectionable under international law since the prisoner of war convention does not make a distinction according to the nationality of the captured

38. The ICRC Manual, para. 602.2 states that persons 'cannot acquire and divest themselves of combatant status at will. Once they have become combatants, they remain combatants until the close of hostilities unless they are properly demobilized'.

39. ICRC Manual, para. 602.3.

40. *Public Prosecutor* v. *Koi*, [1968] All ER 419.

41. *Mohammed Ali* v. *Public Prosecutor*, [1968] All ER 488.

person. The case would probably be decided differently in a conflict to which Protocol I applied, so that prisoner of war status would be accorded. Nevertheless, even though entitled to prisoner of war status, the accused was, as a Malaysian national, susceptible to trial before the Malaysian courts for offences under Malaysian domestic law.

3.3.3 *Failure to comply with the law of war*

Before Protocol I, it was a condition of qualification for combatant status that militia, volunteer and resistance fighters had to comply with the law of war.[42] This differed from the position of members of the regular armed forces. If the latter failed to comply with the law they were punishable but did not lose combatant status.

In international armed conflict the position has now been regularised by Protocol I. Now neither regulars nor irregulars lose combatant status if they violate the law unless they fail to carry their arms openly during engagements and deployments.[43] But this is not solely a matter of individual responsibility since regular violations by an armed force would have consequences for the force as a whole.

A disciplinary system that ensures compliance with the law of war is an essential requirement for legitimate armed forces. Violators of the law of war should be tried and punished. If members of an armed group consistently violate the law of war and are not punished, that is strong evidence that the group does not qualify as 'armed forces', since it fails to meet the criterion of an internal disciplinary system. That means that its members would not have combatant status.

In non-international armed conflicts that are not liberation conflicts governed by Protocol I,[44] the old differences between regulars and irregulars are still maintained. One of the conditions for applicability of Protocol II is that the dissident forces implement that Protocol.[45]

In these conflicts, therefore, compliance with the law of war is a condition for recognition of the armed opposition groups as a party to the conflict. While this might confer some political benefit, in practice armed opposition groups are likely to take advantage of the law if they are in sufficient strength or can benefit from advantageous terrain or safe areas; they are unlikely to do so if they are weak, operate in areas controlled by the opposing armed forces or have negligible local support. In the latter circumstances, they may prefer to take the chance that they will be considered as criminals under domestic law.

3.3.4 *Special missions and airborne troops*

The exception to the rule of distinction was incorporated into the law of war to make provision for guerrilla operations, especially in occupied territory and con-

---

42. Art. 1 Hague Regulations; Art. 4 GC III.
43. Art. 44(2) AP I.
44. Art. 1(4) has the effect of turning these into international conflicts.
45. Art. 1 AP II.

flicts of national liberation, but there is no reason why regular armed forces should not take advantage of it too in those situations and also in connection with operations behind enemy lines, such as long-range reconnaissance patrols.[46]

3.3.5 *Child soldiers*

In the past, states usually specified a minimum age for recruitment into their armed forces. Some younger people managed to enlist by lying about their age. In the closing weeks of the Second World War, children were often recruited into German territorial defence units.[47] But these cases tended to be exceptions. Many conflicts in recent years, though, have been blighted by the practice of the leaders of opposing factions of recruiting children to fight on their behalf.

Protocols I and II seek to address the problem. Parties to an international armed conflict are required to take all feasible measures to ensure that children who have not attained the age of 15 years do not take a direct part in hostilities. They must refrain from recruiting such children into their armed forces. In recruiting children aged 15 and over but under 18, the oldest are to be recruited first.[48] If captured, under-aged members of the armed forces are entitled to be treated as prisoners of war, but are also entitled to the special protection afforded to children.[49]

While recruitment of children might be a breach of the law of war, the rules on combatant status apply equally to adults and children. If children are combatants, they may be targeted. It is only on capture that special rules for their treatment apply.[50]

---

46. According to the UK Manual, para. 4.7, 'members of armed forces on hostile missions behind enemy lines, whether conveyed to enemy or enemy occupied territory by air, land or water and also airborne troops whether landed by parachute or aircraft (even if they are operating by highly skilled methods of surprise and combat) retain their combatant status, whether operating alone or in company. As is true for all uniformed forces, they must comply with the law of war including distinguishing themselves from the civilian population ... These provisions are equally applicable to members of armed forces on sabotage missions. The earlier rules, which equated saboteurs with spies, have been superseded.'

47. Many found their way into the *Volkssturm*, made up of old men and boys, see I. Matanle, *World War II* (Godalming, Colour Library Books 1989) p. 360, or into anti-aircraft units. Members of the Hitler Youth were recruited into bicycle companies equipped with anti-tank launchers and trained to fight Soviet T-34 tanks at close quarters, see A. Beevor, *Berlin, the Downfall 1945* (London, Viking 2002) especially pp. 74, 126, 181-182, 235.

48. Art. 77(2) AP I; Art. 4(3)(c) AP II, applicable to certain non-international armed conflicts, is even stricter: 'children who have not attained the age of fifteen years shall neither be recruited in the armed forces or groups nor allowed to take part in hostilities'. It is noteworthy, too, that that the prohibition in AP II is wider reaching because it does not use the usual formula 'take a direct part in hostilities', but uses the broader formula 'take part in hostilities'.

49. Art. 77(3) AP I; Art. 4(3)(d) AP II. In 2000 an Optional Protocol, on the involvement of children in armed conflict (39 *ILM* (2000) 1285), to the Convention on the Rights of the Child 1989 was adopted. It entered into force on 12 February 2002. It raises the age to 18, at which persons may be permitted to take a direct part in hostilities.

50. See e.g., Arts. 77 and 78 AP I.

3.3.6 *Effect of surrender on combatant status*

Combatants who surrender are *hors de combat* and must stop fighting. That includes all members of units or formations that have surrendered. A local armistice would affect only the soldiers surrendering. A general armistice would bind the army surrendering or even the state, depending on the level of ratification. If binding on the state, further fighting would then be inadmissible. If part only of the territory is occupied by the enemy, or part only of its forces surrender, the armistice should be limited to that part so that the fight can be carried on elsewhere. Where the whole of the state is occupied and government and free forces are in exile and the armistice binds the state as a whole, members of the free forces would have to enlist in the forces of an ally if they wanted legitimately to carry on fighting.

3.4 **Civilian status**

3.4.1 *The rule*

In contrast to combatants, civilians are not permitted to take a direct part in hostilities and are immune from attack so long as they refrain from doing so.[51] A civilian is any person who is not a member of the armed forces of a party to the conflict.[52]

3.4.2 *Position of the civilian population*

During an armed conflict, the civilian population may lawfully support their local armed forces,[53] for example, by providing billets or material aid, so long as this support falls short of taking a direct part in hostilities. The only case where the law permits civilians to take a direct part in hostilities is the case of the *levée en masse*. In that case they become combatants.

Even after effective occupation, members of the armed forces that have not surrendered, members of organised resistance movements and members of internationally recognised liberation movements may continue the fight. Members of the civilian population are likely in practice to be involved in supporting the resistance movement by providing information or material, assisting escape, hiding weapons, or undertaking more positive acts such as civil disobedience, sabotage or riot. As before, if they take a direct part in hostilities, they lose their immunity. Their activities may be punished if they amount to a war crime or if they contravene any laws or regulations passed by the occupying power for the security of its forces. Collective action against the civilian population to redress the activities of unprivileged belligerents would be unlawful as loss of non combatant immunity applies to the civilian who takes a direct part in hostilities, not to the civilian population at large. Once captured, any civilian liable to trial would be entitled to the protection of the

51. Art. 51(2) and (3) AP I.
52. Art. 50(1) AP I.
53. Even if they are taking advantage of the exception to the rule of distinction, see ICRC Manual, para. 610(2).

Geneva Civilian Convention of 1949 and Protocol I,[54] although the right of communication may be suspended in the case of spies if necessary for security reasons.

It is important, therefore, to be able to establish what is meant by taking a direct part in hostilities.

3.4.3 *Taking a direct part in hostilities*

The author takes the view that 'taking a direct part in hostilities' should be interpreted narrowly, otherwise the rule of distinction and civilian immunity generally would be put in serious jeopardy.[55] The term means, in essence, taking part in activity that would normally be undertaken only by members of the armed forces, that is combat-related activities:[56] attacks with roadside bombs on military patrols, sabotage of military communications installations, electronic interference with weapons systems or capturing members of the armed forces. Support activities, such as provision of supplies and services, do not amount to taking a direct part in hostilities. Even if there is doubt about whether a civilian driving a truck with ammunition from a munitions factory to a military storage facility would be taking a direct part in hostilities, there is no doubt that the truck would be a military objective and liable to attack.[57]

There is certainly a case for arguing that a person who becomes a member of a guerrilla group or armed faction that is involved in attacks against enemy armed forces forfeits his protected status for so long as he participates in the activities of the group. The case of children throwing petrol bombs or stones at enemy military patrols is more difficult – is this just criminal activity or is it a forfeiture of civilian immunity? A lot will depend on the precise circumstances of the case, but the members of the patrol would be entitled to use necessary force in self-defence.

---

54. See the restrictions in Arts. 5, 35, 42 and 78 GC IV and the minimum standards laid down in Art. 75 AP I.

55. See Rogers, *supra* n. 2, pp. 10-12. The subject was examined by Gehring some years ago. He also believes that 'hostilities' should be given a narrow interpretation, equivalent to military or combatant activity. He concludes that shooting enemy soldiers, sabotage and setting free prisoners of war would be direct participation but that manufacturing or transporting supplies would not, at least so long as it is not carried out behind enemy lines or after territory has been effectively occupied. He also considers that loss of protection is personal to the civilian committing the hostile act, not the civilian population as a whole. See R. W. Gehring, 'Loss of civilian protection under the fourth Geneva Convention and Protocol I', 19 *Military Law and Law of War Review* (1980) p. 11.

56. The ICRC Manual, para. 601(2) and 601(3) gives the following examples. 'It would be prohibited for civilians to: a. engage in combat activity such as shooting at enemy soldiers, sabotaging military installations or setting free prisoners of war; b. act as members of gun crews, artillery spotters or as drivers delivering ammunition to firing positions; c. gather military intelligence in enemy controlled territory'; but the following would not amount to taking a direct part in hostilities: 'a. indirect action such as manufacturing or transporting military equipment so long as it is not done behind enemy lines, in the contact zone or in areas where occupation has become effective; b. supporting a resistance movement by providing information or materials, assisting escape, hiding weapons, or more positive acts such as civil disobedience; c. the employment of civilians in indirect support of the armed forces, such as work in rear areas in defence plants, the distribution or storage of military supplies or the maintenance of military aircraft and communications equipment'.

57. See the discussion in Rogers, *supra* n. 2, pp. 9-12.

One has to be able to differentiate between public and private activities. Erection of road blocks to facilitate armed robbery or assaults on off-duty soldiers in bars are more likely to fall into the private law, rather than international law, domain.

The mere fact that a civilian carries a weapon, especially in countries where this is the normal practice, is not of itself conclusive evidence that the person has forfeited his civilian status. It is not illegal for civilians to carry arms to protect their families.[58]

In non-international armed conflicts, the law of the place where the conflict takes place continues to apply. International law gives nobody a licence to kill. If a dissident kills a member of the security forces, he commits the offence of homicide for which he can be prosecuted. If a member of the security forces kills a civilian, he is also liable to be tried before the courts for homicide and will have to justify his actions according to the law. If a member of dissident forces is captured, he is not entitled to prisoner-of-war status. He may be dealt with according to the law of the state for any offences he may have committed. If a member of the security forces is captured by dissidents, he is also not a prisoner of war. He may take such legal action to secure his release as is permitted by the law of the state. International law simply does not provide for prisoner of war status in internal armed conflicts; it endeavours to ensure that the basic human rights of those involved are respected.

3.4.4 *Offences of a private law nature*

Reference has been made above to the need to distinguish between acts directed against the armed forces as such and privately motivated criminal offences. This is a problem that members of regular armed forces may meet and they need to be trained and equipped to deal with the situation. A recent phenomenon has been that of looting by civilians. In both Somalia and Iraq, soldiers had to deal with civilians entering unit lines with a view to stealing supplies. The informal 'punishments' imposed on persons captured in those circumstances had no basis in law, and several military personnel faced trial by court martial as a result.[59] Similarly, coalition forces were criticised for their failure to stop widespread looting in Iraq in April 2003.

The law of war has little to say on the subject. An occupying power may introduce laws for its security and for the administration of occupied territory, but that requires a proper legal infrastructure, including occupation courts. In cases where that has not been done or that fall short of occupation, it is a question that may be addressed in a status of forces agreement between the troop-sending state and the host country. For example, such agreements commonly provide that acts done in

---

58. The ICRC Manual, para. 603(3) states that this is not illegal 'provided that they only use their weapons in self-defence, but they run the risk of being mistaken for combatants. The wearing of military-type clothing by civilians should be actively discouraged.'

59. It has been reported that four British soldiers are to face manslaughter charges after allegations that a suspected looter was forced into the Shatt al-Basra canal and drowned, see B. Russell, 'First British soldiers face charges for war crimes', *The Independent*, 20 July 2005.

the course of official duty are outside the jurisdiction of the courts of the host nation and so liable to trial according to the military law of the sending state.[60] In the absence of a status of forces agreement, basic legal principles would surely permit the use of the minimum necessary and proportionate force to prevent looting or other criminal activities, to arrest offenders and hand them over to the local civil authorities (if they exist) for further action. If, in a collapsed state, there is no proper civil infrastructure for dealing with offences, the problem is more acute, especially with repeated offenders who ignore previous warnings. It may be that one would be justified in detaining them for a longer period as a preventative measure but they should be treated humanely, with consideration and respect, and in conditions no less than those laid down for civilian internees by the Geneva Civilian Convention.

3.5 Hybrid categories

3.5.1 *Civilians who accompany the armed forces*

Civilians who are authorised to accompany the armed forces, such as military aircraft technicians, war correspondents, welfare personnel or the staff of military canteens, are entitled to prisoner of war status on capture and are required to carry a special identity card confirming their status. Otherwise they are in the same position as other civilians in that they must not take a direct part in hostilities and are protected from direct attack, though they share the dangers of war to the same extent as the armed forces they accompany because the places where these civilians work are likely to be military objectives. The treaties are silent about whether they may wear uniform or carry arms. It is probably better if they do not wear uniform and any arms should be for personal self-defence and this should be reflected in the training and rules of engagement of such personnel.[61]

3.5.2 *Spies*

One of the curiosities of the law of war is that it makes allowance for military reconnaissance and does not render unlawful the practice of spying but it does make life difficult for spies.[62] They are not entitled to treatment as prisoners of war

60. For more on visiting forces law, see D. Fleck, ed., *Handbook of the Law of Visiting Forces* (Oxford, Oxford University Press 2001).

61. See ICRC Manual, para. 611.

62. Maj. R.R. Baxter (then of the US Army JAG Corps), 'So-called 'unprivileged belligerency': spies, guerrillas, and saboteurs', 28 *BYIL* (1951) p. 323. The UK Manual, para. 4.9.3, states that 'the obtaining of intelligence about the enemy is an important military activity. It can be done in many ways, from monitoring signal traffic to reconnaissance by satellites and drones. Sometimes long-range patrols or agents have to deploy behind enemy lines. The Hague Regulations formally sanctioned the employment of measures necessary for the obtaining of intelligence in enemy-held territory. The collection of such information *openly* by combatants wearing uniform is a recognized branch of the art of warfare. The obtaining of such information by *secret* methods is governed by different rules. Thus it is lawful to employ spies and secret agents but the fact that these methods are lawful under

and are subject to the full force of the domestic law of the capturing power. Spies are defined as persons who, acting clandestinely or under false pretences, gather information in the territory of a belligerent with intent to communicate it to the enemy. Their only safeguard is that, if captured, they may not be punished without trial.

If members of the armed forces take part in intelligence gathering activities in enemy occupied territory, they may not be treated as spies so long as they are in uniform. That is because, when in uniform, they are not acting clandestinely. It follows that soldiers on a reconnaissance patrol who are in uniform and driving in a military vehicle at the time of capture, as in the case of the US soldiers captured in the former Yugoslavia in 1999, would not have been acting clandestinely.[63] Even if not in uniform, members of the armed forces who were involved in spying cease to be spies as soon as they return to their own lines. If subsequently captured, they cannot be punished for their previous spying activities.[64] The law also makes an exception for a member of the armed forces who is resident in an area occupied by the adversary. If he gathers, or attempts to gather, military information in that area, he is guilty of spying only if he does so through an act of false pretences or deliberately in a clandestine manner.[65] Here there is no requirement to wear uniform and there must be a positive act of deception to render the person a spy. Unless that happens, he remains entitled to prisoner of war status.

If captured, spies may not be punished without proper trial[66] and they must be treated with the minimum standards of humanity, known as fundamental guarantees, to which everybody is entitled.[67] As spying is not a war crime, it would seem to the author that any trial would have to be for any violation that may have been committed of any law enforceable in the courts of the place of trial.

3.5.3 *Subcontractors and mercenaries*

There is increasing use these days of private security and logistic companies to support the armed forces. Their personnel are civilians to whom the normal rules of civilian status apply. So long as they do not take a direct part in hostilities, they do not lose their civilian status. There is nothing in law that would prevent them from being armed with light, personal weapons for their own self-defence or the defence of those they are protecting. However, it is important that they do not dress like members of the armed forces and are clearly distinguishable from them and that they do not engage in combat-related activities, otherwise they run the risk, if captured by the enemy, of being accused of perfidy, unprivileged belligerency or,

---

international law does not prevent the punishment under domestic or occupation law of individuals who are engaged in procuring intelligence in other than an open manner'.

63. Rogers, *supra* n. 2, p. 43.
64. Art. 46(4) AP I.
65. Art. 46(3) AP I.
66. Art. 30 Hague Regulations.
67. Art. 75 AP I.

more likely, of being mercenaries and subject to the rigours of the domestic law of the capturing power.

Mercenaries are illegal combatants who do not qualify as prisoners of war because they are not members of the armed forces and, essentially, sell their services for money. According to Protocol I, a person is a mercenary only if all the following conditions are fulfilled:

a. He is recruited abroad or locally to fight in an armed conflict;
b. He takes a direct part in hostilities;
c. He does so for private gain;
d. He is promised compensation exceeding that earned by members of the armed forces alongside whom he fights;
e. He is not a national of a party to the conflict nor a resident of territory controlled by a party to the conflict;
f. He is not a member of the armed forces of a party to the conflict;
g. He is not sent by a non-belligerent state on official duty as a member of the armed forces of that non-belligerent.[68]

That would exclude from mercenary status persons enlisting in the French Foreign Legion or the Brigade of Gurkhas or military personnel sent by a state to advise a party to the conflict about military matters.[69] In any event, a person only becomes a mercenary if he has taken a direct part in hostilities. If so, he may also have committed offences against the domestic law of the capturing power, or war crimes. It is arguable that acting as a mercenary is a war crime (see unprivileged belligerency below). Like spies, however, mercenaries are entitled to proper trial and fundamental guarantees.[70]

In the case of non-international armed conflict, no provision is made for mercenaries. That means that foreign fighters are subject to the domestic law of the state in which they operate.

3.5.4 *Resistance movements*

In recognition of the widespread activities of resistance movements in occupied territory during the Second World War, the Third Geneva Convention specifically confers on members of the fighting arm of those movements the same privilege as that accorded to members of militias and volunteer corps: entitlement to prisoner of war status.[71] However, the conditions for entitlement are also the same: respon-

---

68. Art. 47 AP I. This summary of Art. 47 is based on the ICRC Manual, para. 607.
69. The UK Manual, para. 4.10.4, states that 'when Iraqi armed forces invaded Kuwait in 1990, members of the British armed forces seconded to the Kuwaiti armed forces as the Kuwait Liaison Team were captured by the Iraqis. They were not mercenaries because they were members of the British armed forces. Indeed, they were not prisoners of war because, at that stage, the United Kingdom was not involved in an armed conflict with Iraq. Their status was that of civilian protected persons and they were eventually released.'
70. Art. 75 AP I.
71. Art. 4(A)(2) GC III.

sible command; fixed distinctive emblem recognisable at a distance; the carrying of arms openly; and compliance with the law of war. Although Protocol I does not refer by name to resistance movements, it is reasonable to suppose that members of armed groups belonging to resistance movements are entitled to combatant and prisoner of war status provided they fulfil the conditions laid down in Articles 43 and 44 of the Protocol.[72]

Again no provision is made for resistance movements in the law relating to non-international armed conflict.

3.6 Unprivileged belligerency

Combatants who take part in attacks or military operations preparatory to attacks without distinguishing themselves from civilians lose their combatant status and forfeit their entitlement to prisoner of war status, though they are entitled to equivalent protection.[73] That subtle distinction between combatants who distinguish themselves and those who do not must mean that, on capture, the latter may be tried for the war crime of violating the principle of distinction but otherwise must be treated as if they were prisoners of war. This 'equivalent protection' clause must relate to persons who in all other respects qualify as combatants. Civilians who take a direct part in hostilities lose their protection from attack but if captured are usually protected under the Geneva Civilian Convention. Any captured person is entitled as a minimum to the protection afforded by Article 75 of Protocol I.

The interesting issue, highlighted by the plight of the inmates of Guantanamo Bay, is the position of a captured person who neither qualifies as a combatant nor benefits from equivalent protection.[74] A tribunal dealing with his status would have to look at numerous questions. For example, he might be a protected person under the Geneva Civilian Convention but, if he is a national of a state that is not a party to the armed conflict, he might fall outside the ambit of that convention.[75] Or he might be a spy or mercenary. Or he may have taken part in an attack while dressed

---

72. The UK Manual, para. 4.3.3, states: 'However, particularly in the case of resistance movements in occupied territory, formal state recognition is not essential and an organization may be formed spontaneously and appoint its own officers. The essential feature of the requirement is that the commander should accept responsibility for the acts of his subordinates and equally his responsibility to, and his duty of obedience to the orders of, the power or authority upon which he depends. Partisans or paramilitary forces acting on their own initiative do not comply with that requirement and so are not members of an armed force.'

73. Art. 44(4) AP I.

74. There have been some interesting recent articles on the subject: J. P. Bialke, 'Al-Qaeda and Taliban unlawful combatant detainees, unlawful belligerency and the international laws of armed conflict', 55 *Air Force LR* (2004) pp. 16-49 is a spirited defence of the US position; S. Borelli, 'Casting light on the legal black hole: international law and detentions abroad in the war on terror', 87 *IRRC* (2005) pp. 39-68 is critical of the US position and argues the humanitarian approach to these problems; see also K. Watkin, 'Warriors without rights? Combatants, unprivileged belligerents and the struggle over legitimacy', Harvard University Program on Humanitarian Policy and Conflict research, Occasional Paper No. 2 (Winter 2005).

75. See Art. 4 GC IV.

as a civilian, when it would be for consideration whether he committed the war crime of perfidy. If, however, deploying for an attack on the security forces, he carried his AK 47 rifle openly, did not act in a clandestine manner and nobody was killed or injured as a result of his actions because he was captured before he could use his rifle, it would be necessary to consider whether mere unprivileged belligerency is a war crime. A more extreme example would be where he was arrested at his home, following a tip-off that he was a member of an armed group. There is still controversy about whether membership of the armed group could be construed as taking a direct part in hostilities.

3.6.1 *Is unprivileged belligerency a war crime?*

The old textbooks suggest that if civilians commit hostile acts they are not entitled to the rights of prisoners of war and are liable to execution as war criminals.[76] This approach seems to have been adopted by the US Supreme Court in the case of *Ex Parte Quirin et al.*[77] This was a case of eight German saboteurs, apparently belonging to the German Marine Infantry, who, after war had been declared on Germany, were landed by submarine in the United States with instructions to carry out the destruction of war facilities and who were captured while dressed in civilian clothes. The court, considering an application for *habeas corpus*, commented:

> 'The spy who secretly and without uniform passes the military lines of a belligerent in time of war, seeking to gather military information and communicate it to the enemy, or an enemy combatant who without uniform comes secretly through the lines for the purpose of waging war by destruction of life or property, are familiar examples of belligerents who are generally deemed not to be entitled to the status of prisoners of war, but to be offenders against the law of war subject to trial and punishment by military tribunals.'[78]

However, Baxter, writing in 1951, regarded this view of the law as erroneous and that the correct view was that hostilities by civilians 'merely deprive such individuals of a protection they might otherwise enjoy under international law and place them virtually at the power of the enemy'.[79] Stone, writing in 1954, took a similar view, saying that 'guerrillas, even when they are unprivileged belligerents, are (like spies) merely left by international law to punishment by the enemy State under its own law, or that of the occupied territory, and are not criminals under international law'.[80] So, more recently, has Dinstein.[81]

---

76. E.g., J.E. Edmonds and L. Oppenheim, *The Laws and Usages of War on Land* (London, H.M. S.O., 1914) paras. 19, 441, 444; United Kingdom, *The Law of War on Land* (London, H.M.S.O., 1958) (written by H. Lauterpacht and G. Draper) paras. 88, 634.
77. 10 (1941-2) *Annual Digest* p. 564.
78. At p. 571.
79. Baxter, *supra* n. 62, p. 343.
80. J. Stone, *Legal Controls of International Conflict* (London, Stevens 1954) at p. 567.
81. Y. Dinstein, *The Conduct of Hostilities under the Law of International Armed Conflict* (Cambridge, Cambridge University Press 2004) at pp. 29-31. Greenspan, however, still referred to such

While one might have some sympathy for the argument that spying, *per se*, is not a war crime, the argument is less convincing in respect of people who have taken a direct part in hostilities without having lawful combatant status. It is true that the US military tribunal in *The Hostages Trial*[82] equated actions by guerrillas with those of spies, saying that:

> 'By the law of war it is lawful to use spies. Nevertheless, a spy, when captured, may be shot because the belligerent has the right, by means of an effective deterrent punishment, to defend against the grave dangers of enemy spying. The principle therein involved applies to guerrillas who are not lawful belligerents.'[83]

However, the tribunal went on to say:

> 'We think the rule is established that a civilian who aids, abets or participates in the fighting is liable to punishment as a war criminal under the laws of war. Fighting is legitimate only for the combatant personnel of a country. It is only this group that is entitled to treatment as prisoners of war and incurs no liability beyond detention after capture or surrender.'[84]

While the law of war does not render spying illegal, it makes it clear that the rights of war apply only to the armed forces, organised militia and volunteer corps and resistance movements, and to members of a *levée en masse*.[85] The principle of distinction goes to the very root of the law of war. This is not just for the protection of members of the armed forces; it is fundamental to the protection of the civilian population. The importance of this principle is such that one cannot lightly conclude that a violation of the principle is not a war crime. It seems to this author, at least, that any individual or group not belonging to these categories that takes a direct part in hostilities commits a war crime by violating the laws and customs of war.

Unprivileged belligerents may be entitled to the protection of the Geneva Civilian Convention and Protocol I, although the right of communication may be suspended in the case of spies if it is necessary to do so for security reasons.

3.7 Determination of status

The status of a captured person is an important matter because it determines the body of law that protects him. An unscrupulous capturing power might feel inclined to use legal arguments to put a person into a category that provides the least

---

activity as a war crime in 1959: M. Greenspan, *The Modern Law of Land Warfare* (Berkeley and Los Angeles, University of California Press 1959) at pp. 53, 465.

82. *Trial of Wilhelm List and Others*, VIII WCR 34.

83. Ibid., at p. 58.

84. Ibid.

85. HR, Arts. 1 and 2; GC III, Art. 4; AP I, Arts. 43 and 44.

protection.[86] However, the law militates against this by making presumptions in favour of the detainee, such as the presumption of prisoner of war status where there is any doubt about the status of a captured person who has committed a belligerent act and until that doubt is resolved by a competent tribunal.[87] Of course, there may be a situation where the detainee claims prisoner of war status but the commandant denies it on the grounds that he has no doubt on the evidence that the detainee is an unprivileged belligerent and, therefore, there is no need for a tribunal to determine the question. In cases where Protocol I applies[88] that loophole has been closed because prisoner of war status must be bestowed on a person who claims that status until such time as a competent tribunal determines his status.[89]

3.8 Discussion of recent practice

3.8.1 *Urban fighting*

If unequal combat places strains on the law of war, these strains are exacerbated, almost to breaking point, by unequal combat in an urban setting. The concentration of civilians and civilian property makes heavy incidental loss and damage an inevitable consequence of normal military tactics, especially when heavy weapons and mortars are deployed. For the armed opposition groups for whom compliance with the law is not a high priority, however, a built-up area provides an ideal operating environment: plenty of cover for hiding and clandestine operations, ability to deploy their light weapons effectively at short range[90] and, usually, better knowledge of local geography and good local information networks that are not dependent on, for example, traceable mobile telephone communications. The regular armed forces generally would prefer not to operate in populated areas for two main reasons. First, they cannot deploy their heavy weapons effectively and are much more susceptible to ambush and sabotage and, second, the proportionality of incidental civilian deaths and property damage is always going to be called into question by the world's media. Despite their reluctance to go into a town, the regular forces may be obliged to do so because the armed opposition groups will have seized the initiative by installing themselves there and using it as a base for their operations.

---

86. Even the US authorities have been criticised by the English Court of Appeal for interning people at Guanatanamo Bay, where they seemed to be in a 'legal black hole', out of the reach of judicial review, see *R (Abbasi and Anor)* v. *Secretary of State* [2002] EWCA Civ 159, though there have been welcome signs of judicial activity since then following the US Supreme Court decision in *Rasul* v. *Bush* 124 S Ct. 2686 (28 June 2004).

87. Art. 5 GC III.

88. The USA is not, of course, a party to AP I.

89. Art. 45(1) AP I.

90. US officer, Captain R. Bodisch, reported that during the Fallujah operation, 'A man pulled out from behind a wall and fired an RPG at my tank.' K. Sengupta, 'US 'pacifies' city but rebels take violence to rest of country', *The Independent*, 10 November 2004.

There are interesting parallels in this respect between the Israeli incursion into the Palestinian settlement of Jenin in 2002 and the US-led incursion into Fallujah in 2004.

Jenin and the adjacent refugee camp were entered by Israeli armed forces on 3 April 2002 in a counter-terrorism operation against Palestinian militants. The Israeli army met with stiff resistance. On the basis of media reports, this author, and probably other observers too, was left with the impression that there had been serious loss of life and destruction in the course of this operation. Palestinian officials claimed that a massacre had occurred in Jenin. Israel denied it.[91] Amnesty International called for a full investigation, having found evidence of war crimes.[92] It was important, therefore, to establish the facts.

The UN set up a fact-finding team comprising Martti Ahtisari, Cornelio Sommaruga and Sadeko Ogata.[93] However, a failure to agree terms for a visit by the team and the pressure of time meant that the team did not, in fact, visit Jenin and was disbanded. So the Secretary-General's report was compiled from information from secondary sources.[94] The report confirmed that the refugee camp housed some 14,000 persons, including about 200 armed militants; at least 52 Palestinians, half of whom may have been civilians, and 23 Israeli soldiers died during the fighting; 150 buildings were destroyed; and 450 families were rendered homeless. The report mentions that, following an ambush in which 13 Israeli soldiers were killed, there seemed to be a change of tactics from house-to-house searches and destruction of homes of well-known militants to wider bombardment with tanks and missiles.[95] Every casualty of war is a tragedy but in this case the casualty figures themselves do not point to a massacre but more to the effects of fighting in an urban environment. However, the impression caused by the initial media reports tends to be the one that lingers in the memory.

In the case of Fallujah, the author has not seen any report from official sources, so this passage is based on media reports, which are often inaccurate or exaggerated but will suffice for the purpose of the discussion of legal principles. A lot of civilians left Fallujah before the assault started, but many remained and some became casualties of the fighting as well as suffering the deprivations of lack of food, power,[96] water and treatment for wounds or disease.[97] Iraqi people claimed that the US response was often disproportionate, with tank rounds being used to dislodge snipers and devastate buildings, something denied by the US military

---

91. J. Huggler, 'UN issues 'seriously flawed' report on Jenin killings', *The Independent*, 2 August 2002.

92. *Israel and the Occupied Territories, shielded from scrutiny: IDF violations in Jenin and Nablus*, Amnesty International, November 2002 (AI Index: MDE 15/143/2002).

93. Report of the Secretary General prepared pursuant to GA Res. ES 10/10, para. 3, <http://www.un.org/peace/jenin/index.html>.

94. Report of the Secretary-General paras. 4-7.

95. Para. 59.

96. K. Sengupta and S. Khan, 'Civilians suffer consequences of Fallujah's 'liberation'', *The Independent*, 10 November 2004

97. M. Georgy and K. Sengupta, 'A city lies in ruins, along with the lives of the wretched survivors', *The Independent*, 15 November 2004.

authorities.[98] One reporter described the aftermath as: 'a shattered landscape of gutted buildings, crushed cars and charred bodies ... with concrete houses flattened, mosques in ruins, telegraph poles down, power and phone lines hanging slack and rubble and human remains littering the empty streets.'[99]

The US forces are reported to have subjected the Jolan district of Fallujah, difficult terrain because of its narrow alleys, to intense bombardment from artillery and tanks. Bombardment of Fallujah was carried out by artillery, aeroplanes (dropping 500lb bombs) and helicopter gunships.[100] One assumes that they were bombarding military objectives. It was alleged that air raids destroyed a clinic and a nearby medical warehouse in the centre of Fallujah, causing loss of life.[101]

Booby-trapped buildings or cars make life difficult for soldiers trying to establish or re-establish control. House to house searches are time-consuming and dangerous, with attendant problem of dealing with booby-traps and clearing cellars. Even if a warning is shouted before a hand grenade is lobbed in, the occupants may not understand or may be too scared to come out.

The Iraqi Red Crescent organisation was unable to gain access to Fallujah, being prevented by the Iraqi and US authorities, but a spokesman for the US military authorities said they were taking their own supplies into the city, the implication being that they had the necessary resources to treat the wounded and sick.[102] Traditionally, the parties to the conflict have not been under any obligation to allow the distribution of humanitarian aid while the fighting is actually going on.[103] In any event, it was probably not safe to enter Fallujah in the immediate aftermath of the operation and it was later reported that the ICRC was negotiating with the US forces to open a 'humanitarian corridor' into the city.[104]

3.8.2 *Perfidy*

Members of armed opposition groups will, no doubt, claim that they have to resort to unorthodox tactics if they are to succeed and that is in the nature of unequal combat. If they go about their business dressed in uniform and carrying their weapons openly, they are easily spotted and attacked or captured. They have to be able to get as close as possible to the enemy before showing themselves and opening fire if they are to have any chance of success. The classic case is that of apparent farm workers in the fields who, at the last minute, pick up hidden weapons and fire at column of occupying troops. They would, no doubt, claim legitimacy of circum-

---

98. Ibid.

99. Ibid.

100. K. Sengupta and J. Huggler, 'Battle for Fallujah rages', *The Independent*, 9 November 2004.

101. *Supra* n. 103; K. Sengupta, 'US claims militants are trapped as air strike hits clinic', *The Independent*, 11 November 2004.

102. K. Sengupta, 'Fallujah situation 'disastrous', charity says', *The Independent*, 13 November 2004; and A. Buncombe, 'Families trapped in Fallujah', *The Independent*, 17 November 2004; Anon., 'Battle 'nearing end' in Fallujah', BBC News Online, 14 November 2004.

103. Art. 70 AP I makes the distribution of relief supplies 'subject to the agreement of the Parties concerned in such relief actions'.

104. Anon., 'Fallujah assault 'breaks' rebels', BBC News Online, 19 November 2004.

stances, but the law makes no allowance for them. If, in such a case, the occupying troops are killed or injured, the farm workers' actions would amount to the war crime of perfidy.[105]

Since the end of active coalition military operations in Iraq, we have seen attacks on coalition forces, usually by mortar against their bases or by ambushing patrols using wire-controlled roadside bombs,[106] rocket-propelled grenades or suicide attacks. The insurgents usually melt away in the face of a serious assault before gradually re-infiltrating 'liberated' areas.[107] None of these tactics is perfidious in itself, provided those employing them do not feign protected, for example, civilian, status to achieve their objective. The misuse of white flags, for example, to entice enemy forces to reveal their position would be potentially perfidious as a misuse of protected status.

3.8.3 *Humane treatment of persons captured by armed groups*

In Iraq there have been many cases of foreign civilians being captured and held as hostages. Hostage taking is clearly contrary to the current law of war and a war crime, even in a non-international armed conflict.[108] Some of the hostages have been executed; others released. Some of those released have complained about mistreatment. That is not only the case with foreigners. Al-Jazeera television, reporting on the capture of Iraqi government soldiers by militants, said that militants had promised not to kill the prisoners shown on a videotape but would kill others captured in the future.[109] Of course, because of the type of operations conducted by irregulars, a proper system of handling prisoners of war is difficult to achieve, and prisoner-of-war status is not recognised in non-international armed confict. But humane treatment of captured persons is a legal necessity.

3.8.4 *Protection of civilians during the fighting*

Other tactics of armed opposition groups also show scant regard for the law of war. There has been the deliberate targeting of civilians, for example, attacks on police posts or army recruiting offices with car bombs. Civilian contractors or aid workers have been taken hostage and have been shown on television pleading for their lives. This kind of activity is unlikely to result in the withdrawal of troops by the armed forces and is more likely to provoke an angry response. In practice it may, however, result in ransoms being paid to secure their release.

---

105. Art. 23(b) Hague Regulation; Art. 37 AP I; Art. 8(2)(b)(xi) ICC Statute.

106. Pte. Tukutukuwaqa of the Black Watch was killed in this way, J. Brown, 'Fijian solder serving as sniper with Black Watch is fifth victim', *The Independent*, 10 November 2004.

107. It is reported that despite attempts by the US to pacify Samarra in October, the militants were back in November as 34 people died in a wave of car bombings, J. Huggler, 'A brutal assault that was rendered inevitable by the mistakes made earlier in the campaign', *The Independent*, 10 November 2004.

108. Art. 8(2)(c)(iii) ICC Statute.

109. Sengupta, *supra* n. 101.

3.8.5 *Protection of medical facilities*

During the Fallujah operation, it was reported that US and Iraqi government forces captured a hospital and detained patients of military age to determine whether they were insurgents.[110] Iraqi President Allawi said that four foreigners were captured and 38 persons killed and that they had been stationed at the hospital to carry out terrorist actions. The director of the hospital, however, said: 'The American troops' attempt to take over the hospital was not right because they thought they would halt medical assistance to the resistance. But they did not realize that the hospital did not belong to anybody, especially the resistance.'[111] This is the sort of case where an inquiry by an international fact-finding commission to establish the facts would be useful.[112]

3.8.6 *Misuse of cultural property*

It was reported that while US troops made loudspeaker calls to the insurgents to lay down their arms, clerics made calls from mosques urging the population to join the *mujahedin* and defy the invaders.[113] One US objective was said to be the al-Hidra mosque, a weapons dump and planning centre for the militants.[114] The legal position is that civilian property is normally protected from attack or from being made the subject of military operations, this protection being underlined in the case of cultural property such as places of worship. However, protection is lost if property is used for military purposes such as storage of weapons or military planning.

3.8.7 *Treatment of those* hors de combat

It was reported that video footage had been taken by war correspondents – now known, for some reason, as 'embedded' journalists,[115] – of the shooting of an unarmed Iraqi insurgent in questionable circumstances. According to this report, he was shot because he was feigning death. He was one of five Iraqis wounded in fighting the previous day and left at a mosque.[116] The incident is described thus: 'A frightened, tired and shell-shocked young US marine, concerned that a wounded Iraqi left behind in a mosque might be lying on a compression mine, clutching a hand grenade or concealing a pistol, makes a split-second decision and allegedly shoots him in the head. The marines have lost many people to insurgents feigning death or surrender in this way.'[117]

---

110. Sengupta and Huggler, *supra* n. 100.
111. Ibid.
112. Such a commission has been established under Art. 90 of AP I, but has never been used.
113. Sengupta and Huggler, *supra* n. 100.
114. Sengupta, *supra* n. 90.
115. War correspondents accompany the armed forces, see Geneva Convention III of 1949, Art. 4 A (4); other journalists reporting on armed conflict do not, see Protocol I, Art. 79.
116. A. Buncombe, 'Video shows US soldier killing wounded insurgent in cold blood', *The Independent*, 16 November 2004.
117. Bellamy, *supra* n. 16.

The US Marines were reported to be investigating this incident.[118] What are the relevant factors? Can the operational background be taken into account?

US military lawyers say that the marine's actions must be judged in the light of the enemy's actions: hiding behind civilians, taking over places of worship, booby-trapping corpses[119] and feigning surrender as a means to attack. Non-military lawyers seem to take a different view, saying that unlawful enemy tactics and battlefield stress are not sufficient justification for killing, that fear and frustration cannot be considered mitigating and that is difficult to see how shooting the body protects you from a booby-trap.[120]

Anybody wounded in the fighting, whether civilian or soldier, who has been rendered *hors de combat* by his wounds may not be attacked. But in the case of a soldier or fighter, he must either have surrendered or have been rendered unconscious or incapacitated to be regarded as *hors de combat*.[121] There are two possible charges in a case of killing somebody *hors de combat*: the grave breach of wilfully killing a wounded member of an enemy militia or resistance movement or a civilian protected person;[122] or the war crime of killing a combatant who, having laid down his arms or having no longer means of defence, has surrendered at discretion.[123]

In the case of the grave breach charge, the defence could argue that, given the operational background, the soldier acted reasonably in his own defence or that of his comrades,[124] and in the case of the war crimes charge that the insurgent had not surrendered.

4. PRACTICAL GUIDELINES

Compliance with the law of war results from good training, clear and lawful orders, a sense that compliance is part of a soldier's professional duty and firm action if violations occur. Perfect compliance is hard to achieve at the best of times, though it should always be the aim; it may, for the reasons outlined in this article, be more difficult to achieve in conditions of unequal combat. Thus, commanders need to be aware of factors that can lead to violations of the law of war being committed by soldiers under their command and take corrective action whenever the symptoms appear. Apart from anything else, those symptoms may

---

118. A. Buncombe, 'Marines will investigate claims of war crimes', *The Independent*, 17 November 2004 and 25 February 2005.

119. Prohibited under Art. 6(1)(b)(ii) of Protocol II to the Conventional Weapons Convention of 1980, but anyway perfidious, under Art. 23(b) Hague Regulations, if it results in killing or wounding.

120. B. Bender, 'Marines defend actions of an accused comrade', *International Herald Tribune*, 18 November 2004.

121. Art. 23 Hague Regulations; Art. 8(a) AP I.

122. Art. 23 Hague Regulations; Arts. 13, 50 GC I; Arts. 4, 27, 147; GC IV; Art. 8(2)(a)(i) ICC Statute.

123. Art. 8(2)(b)(vi) ICC Statute.

124. See Art. 31(1)(c) ICC Statute.

indicate a breakdown in discipline or a drop in morale, with adverse consequences either way for the operational effectiveness of military units.

Common reasons why things go wrong are:

1. A sense of frustration among soldiers because of apparently consistent violations of the law by the enemy and a feeling that only extreme measures will put a stop to them.[125]
2. If things are going badly a sense of hopelessness can creep in when soldiers see little point in upholding standards.
3. A misguided sense that military necessity somehow overrules the law of war so that, for example, soldiers think it is right to torture detainees to obtain timely military intelligence.
4. A sense that enemy nationals are somehow inferior and not deserving of care or respect. To prevent this, officers should ensure that disrespectful language and behaviour is not tolerated from the outset, so that such attitudes do not take root.
5. Lack of proper supervision. Over the years very many war crimes have been committed that involve the ill-treatment of detainees. Often abuses have been carried out at a low level by inexperienced or poorly trained soldiers who have not been adequately supervised by experienced non-commissioned officers or officers. It is important that frequent and unannounced checks are carried out in detention centres, that regular medical checks are undertaken and that a system by which detainees can make complaints to a responsible and independent officer is put in place. Higher military authorities have an important role to play here and cannot leave everything to the commander of the place of detention.
6. Creation, by words or deeds, by unit or sub-unit commanders of a climate of disrespect for the law or that minor violations will be tolerated is likely to lead to the commission of war crimes and is unacceptable.
7. Issuing staff with unclear or ambiguous orders, such as to 'give them a hard time' or to 'soften them up for interrogation', is dangerous and inadequate. Staff must know precisely what their powers and duties are with regard to persons held for interrogation. This is so important that the policy must be approved at the highest level of command and promulgated in such a way that there is no room for misinterpretation.
8. Failure of commanders at all levels to anticipate events and issue appropriate instructions. This is often due to a lack of imagination.
9. Especially in cases of unequal combat, it is dangerous to rely on uncorroborated local intelligence. People often have scores to settle and make use of the armed forces as their executioners in their webs of deceit.
10. Above all, the successful waging of unequal combat requires wise and experienced heads with good training. Eighteen to twenty year old conscripts or

---

125. ICRC Manual, para. 606(1), states that 'commanding officers should be aware that the sense of frustration felt by members of the regular forces when dealing with guerrillas is dangerous since it may lead to the commission of atrocities. They are put under a special obligation to lay down and enforce proper professional standards of conduct, including clear principles for the treatment of the civilian population and rules of engagement for dealing with the guerrillas.'

young officers just out of training are not suitable for the difficult tasks and decisions facing them unless they are firmly under the control of seasoned superiors. Careful decisions need to be made about the manning levels and force structures to be used. Experience of Iraq before and since the end of active military operations shows that successful war fighting forces may not be ideal for carrying out the duties of an occupying force.

5. CONCLUSIONS

It seems to the author that the law relating to international armed conflict does provide adequate protection for the victims of war, even in cases of unequal combat. Departures from the law caused by the strains of unequal combat are due less to inadequacies of the law than to failures of a practical nature on the part of those concerned. This may be due to deliberate 'bending' of the rules or, more usually, to a surprising inability of personnel to apply basic principles sensibly to cases where the law is silent or ambiguous. If the factors listed in part 4 of this article are taken into account by commanding officers and commanders, one might hope for some improvement in compliance even in cases of unequal combat.

Of course, the law relating to non-international armed conflict is far from comprehensive, protection of the victims of civil war being left chiefly to domestic and human rights law. Nevertheless, there is a respectable body of law – to be found in basic principles such as military necessity, humanity, distinction and proportionality, in common Article 3 and in the war crimes provisions of the Rome Statute of the International Criminal Court[126] – that provides some level of protection in the conduct of combat. The biggest discrepancy between the legal regimes for international and non-international armed conflict is the lack of combatant and prisoner-of-war status in the latter. Perhaps, if this were to be introduced into the law, there might be hope for better compliance overall and especially in cases of unequal combat. The negotiating history of Protocol II, however, does not give cause for optimism. States appear reluctant to allow further intrusion by international law into what they consider to be their internal affairs and reluctant to any kind of legitimacy to armed opposition groups that resort to tactics such as detonating bombs in congregations of civilians. It is a vicious circle that is well-nigh impossible to break. In the meantime one can only exhort the parties to a non-international armed conflict to apply the existing rules in good faith.

---

126. This is examined more fully in Rogers, *supra* n. 2, ch. 9.

MILITARY OBJECTIVE AND COLLATERAL DAMAGE: THEIR RELATIONSHIP AND DYNAMICS[1]

Joseph Holland[2]

2. Lieutenant-Colonel Joseph Holland is a member of the Office of the Judge Advocate General, Canadian Forces, presently posted as a Legal Officer with the Office of the Legal Advisor, Supreme Headquarters Allied Powers Europe (SHAPE) Casteau, Belgium. This article is based on a portion of a thesis submitted as part of the Master of Laws requirements of the 50th Judge Advocate Officer Graduate Course, The Judge Advocate General's School, United States Army, Charlottesville, VA, USA.

 DOI 10.1017/S1389135904000352

1. INTRODUCTION

Grisly images of dead or injured civilians vie with 'morbidly spectacular film of PGM (precision guided munition) strikes'.[3] These phenomena, like this article, focus attention on the two most basic law of targeting components, that of military objective and that of incidental civilian losses. The latter component, being incidental civilian loss, injury and damage, also known as collateral damage, is one side of the proportionality 'equation'. Expected incidental civilian losses (which term will be used interchangeably with collateral damage) are balanced against the anticipated military value of the strike. This balancing, i.e., proportionality, is one of the major factors in the law of targeting. The concepts examined are two of the most dramatic aspects of targeting. Is there any relationship between military objective and incidental civilian losses? If so, what is the linkage? If one concept expands or contracts what happens to the other? This relationship may have important implications for the type of expertise required to make legal targeting decisions. The type of expertise required would indicate who is best placed to make such targeting decisions and what sorts of errors such decision makers are prone to make and thus must particularly strive to avoid.

Military objective and collateral damage are the law of targeting's very core. While certainly some situations require consideration of other matters, many targeting decisions can be confined to the following two 'simple' issues: is the proposed target a lawful military objective and is there an unacceptable risk of disproportionate collateral damage?[4]

---

3. M.N. Schmitt, 'Bellum Americanum: The U.S. Views of Twenty-First Century War and Its Possible Implications for the Law of Armed Conflict', 19 *Michigan JIL* (1998) pp. 1051, 1081. PGM are precision-guided munitions.

4. See e.g., Protocol Additional to the Geneva Conventions of 12 August 1949, and Relating to the Protection of Victims of International Armed Conflicts, 12 December 1977, [hereinafter, Protocol I] 1125 *UNTS* (1977) p. 3; Art. 54 (protecting objects indispensable to the survival of the civilian population) and Art. 56 (protecting certain works and installations containing dangerous forces). F. Kalsho-

A recent trend in modern warfare indicates that a focussed consideration of military objective and proportionality is particularly useful. Soldiers, sailors and airmen have always had to make many combat decisions in seconds or minutes. Modern warfare is placing even more emphasis on quick decision-making, particularly those decisions related to targeting. There is every indication that the trend toward very rapid targeting decisions will continue or even accelerate.[5] In such an environment, any useful legal rules will have to be simple if they are to be effective.[6] Those tasked with making or advising on targeting determinations may have time to consider only the most basic of issues. Military objective and collateral damage are such basic legal issues.

Any in-depth analysis of the law of war requires a determination of the basic purpose of this peculiar body of law. The purpose of the law of war, also called the law of armed conflict or international humanitarian law, is to balance military necessity and humanitarian concerns: 'The law of armed conflict rests upon a judicious balance between military operational needs and humanitarianism.'[7] Military necessity and humanity have been called 'primary concepts' underlying the law of armed conflict.[8] Most commentators expressly accept the tension or balance between these sometimes opposing needs.[9]

---

ven,'Remarks in a Panel on Implementing Limitations on the Use of Force: The Doctrine of Proportionality and Necessity', *Amer. Soc. IL Proc.* (1992) pp. 39, 41; C. Greenwood, 'Customary International Law and the First Geneva Protocol of 1977 in the Gulf Conflict', in P. Rowe, ed., *The Gulf War 1990-91 in International and English Law*, (London, Sweet & Maxwell 1993) pp. 63, 69.

5. United States Air Force, *Air Force Basic Doctrine* (1997) p. 32 [hereinafter, USAF Basic Doctrine] (setting the goal of being able to 'react to a situation and make accurate decisions more rapidly than the enemy' and improve 'the speed and quality of our observe-orient-decide-act loop'); Schmitt, *supra* n. 3, at p. 1057 (foreseeing warfare that is 'fast-paced, mobile, and highly lethal'), 1062-1063 (forecasting 'access to on-demand real-time information will allow real-time planning, rather than the current practice of executing plans developed in advance'); V. Loeb and T.E. Ricks, '1's and 0's replacing bullets in U.S. arsenal', *The Washington Post*, 2 February 2002 at A1 (citing 'the real-time value of being able to target rapidly', 'the American approach to combat increasingly focuses on how to get information, move it and act on it quickly' and 'instantaneous targeting'); B. Rolfsen, 'Air Force learned lessons in Kosovo, but problems remain', *Air Force Times*, 4 February 2002, p. 15 (citing the United States Air Force goal 'of reducing the sensor-to-shooter timeline to fewer than 10 minutes'.).

6. USAF Basic Doctrine, *supra* n. 5, at p. 21 (citing simplicity as one of the principles of war, i.e., the need to avoid 'unnecessary complexity' in military operations); L. Doswald-Beck, 'Implementation of International Humanitarian Law in Future Wars', 52 *Naval War College Review* (1999) pp. 24, 34 (stating 'the more complex the rules, the less likely it is that they will be followed accurately'.).

7. L.C. Green, *The Contemporary Law of Armed Conflict*, 2nd edn. (Manchester, Manchester University Press 2000) p. 353.

8. W.J. Fenrick, 'The Rule of Proportionality and Protocol I in Conventional Warfare', 98 *Mil. LR* (1982) pp. 91, 93 (setting out three such concepts being military necessity, humanity and chivalry).

9. Commentary on the Additional Protocols of 8 June 1977 to the Geneva Conventions of 12 August 1949, para. 1389 (Y. Sandoz et al., eds., 1987) [hereinafter, the ICRC Commentary] ('The law of armed conflict is a compromise based on a balance between military necessity, on the one hand, and the requirements of humanity, on the other.'); P. Rowe, *Defence: The Legal Implications* (London, Brassey's Defence Publishers 1987) p. 150 (quoting Draper: 'The essential balance in the Law of War has probably swung too far in the direction of humanitarianism. Insufficient attention has been paid to the nature of warfare and what commanders are trained to do.'); F.J. Hampson, 'Means and Methods of Warfare in the Conflict in the Gulf', in Rowe, ibid., pp. 89, 91; O. Bring, 'Collateral Damage and Military Objectives: A Point of View de lege ferenda after Kosovo', in *Colloquium: Legal and Ethical*

Interestingly, the most recent label for this area of law, international humanitarian law, can actually obscure this dynamic.[10] The term risks over emphasising but one of the pillars upon which the entire edifice of the law of war is built. It may skew analysis of specific issues by explicitly giving priority only to humanitarian factors while ignoring military factors. It may mislead some into thinking that the sole purpose of this discipline is to protect humanitarian values. In fact, the purpose of the law of armed conflict is to balance humanitarian and military factors in an acceptable fashion. This label also invites confusion with the field of human rights law, a related but distinct discipline.[11]

That said, it is critical to note that military necessity is not an over-ride that can be used to ignore humanitarian factors. Where a rule, whether based on treaty or customary international law, exists it cannot be ignored based on alleged military necessity. Indeed such is the power of these rules that a United States tribunal found that: 'Military necessity or expediency do not justify a violation of the positive rules …. The rules must be followed even if it results in the loss of a battle or even a war.'[12]

In any disciplined analysis, neither principle should be over emphasised. Some law of war debates will be settled by military factors, others by humanitarian considerations. It is legally wrong and intellectually dishonest to accord either principle automatic primacy in interpretation or analysis. Therefore, where the law of armed conflict is unclear or requires interpretation or analysis beyond the words at issue, one should balance the basic principles of military necessity and humanity.

The purposes of this article are threefold. Firstly, it will examine the relationship between two key law of targeting concepts, military objective and collateral damage. As a necessary preliminary to that examination it will briefly discuss military objective and collateral damage. Secondly, it will seek to validate the proposed relationship by suggesting a method to test its validity. Thirdly, it will examine

---

Lessons of NATO's Kosovo Campaign, Aug. 8-10, 2001 (held at the United States Naval War College, Newport, Rhode Island) (hereinafter, Colloqium) (Newport Rhode Island, United States Naval War College 2001) p. 11; S. A. Egorov, 'The Kosovo Crisis and the Law of Armed Conflicts', 82 *IRRC* (2000) pp. 183, 188 (citing as one of the main characteristics of the law of armed conflict 'the confrontation between the principle of humanity and that of military expediency'.); R. Normand and C.A. F. Jochnick, 'The Legitimation of Violence: A Critical Analysis of the Gulf War', 35 *Harvard ILJ* (1994) pp. 387, 389 (citing as the law of war's goal 'a reasonable balancing of military necessity and humanity' in a very sceptical analysis of the current law of armed conflict regime).

10. W. Hays Parks, 'Air War and the Law of War', 32 *Air Force LR* (1990) pp. 1, 72 fn. 245; A. Roberts, 'The Laws of War: Problems of Implementation in Contemporary Conflicts', 6 *Duke JC & IL* (1995) pp. 11, 14.

11. Advisory Opinion on the Legality of the Threat or Use of Nuclear Weapons, International Court of Justice, 35 *ILM* (1996) p. 809, at para. 25 [hereinafter, *Nuclear Weapons* case] (finding that that the International Covenant of Civil and Political Rights, a human rights treaty, has limited direct application in armed conflict situations but rather such rights in an armed conflict are decided by reference to armed conflict's *lex specialis*, i.e., the law of war).

12. *United States* v. *Wilhelm List, et al.* (*The Hostage* case), reprinted in XI *Trials of War Criminals Before the Nuremberg Military Tribunals* (Washington, United States Government Printing Office 1947-48) pp. 759, 1256, 1272.

some of the potential implications of the proposed relationship between these two key concepts.

2. MILITARY OBJECTIVE

2.1 Introduction and history

The concept of military objective is critical because without that concept one of the absolute bedrocks of the law of war will not function. That bedrock is the principle of distinction.[13] Distinction demands that: 'The Parties to the conflict shall at all times distinguish between the civilian population and combatants and between civilian objects and military objectives and accordingly shall direct their operations only against military objectives.'[14] Obviously, one cannot confine one's attacks to military objectives unless one knows what they are.[15] Distinction's importance cannot be over-stated. 'Distinction provides the main line of defence against methods of barbarism in warfare.'[16] It is the 'very heart and soul of the law of war'.[17] It illustrates the basic law of war purpose set out earlier. Military targets may be engaged, thus accommodating military necessity, but civilians and civilian objects must be spared, thus giving humanity its due.

Therefore, it is somewhat surprising that such a critical concept as military objective was not successfully codified until 1977 in the Protocol Additional to the Geneva Conventions of 12 August 1949, and Relating to the Protection of Victims of International Armed Conflict (Protocol I).[18] The term 'military objective' and the initial attempt to codify it arose in the 1922-1923 Hague Rules of Air Warfare

---

13. *Nuclear Weapons* case, *supra* n. 11, para. 78; GA Res. 2444, UN GAOR, 23rd Sess., Supp. No. 18, at 164, UN Doc. A/7218 (1968) para. 1(c), 19 December 1968, reprinted in,D. Schindler and J. Toman, eds., *The Laws of Armed Conflicts*, 3rd edn. (Dordrecht, Martinus Nijhoff Publishers 1988) p. 263; GA Res. 2675, UN GAOR, 25th Sess., Supp. No. 28, at p. 76, UN Doc. A/8028 (1970) para. 2, 9 December 1970, ibid. 267; International Criminal Tribunal for the former-Yugoslavia, Final Report to the Prosecutor by the Committee Established to Review the NATO Bombing Campaign Against the Federal Republic of Yugoslavia para. 29 (20 June 2000) [hereinafter, ICTY Committee Report]; Parks, *supra* n. 10, at p. 4 (using the equivalent term 'discrimination'); H.B. Robertson, Jr., 'The Principle of the Military Objective in the Law of Armed Conflict', in M.N. Schmitt, ed., *The Law of Military Operations: liber amicorum professor Jack Grunawalt* (Newport RI, United States Naval War College 1998) p. 197; Hampson, *supra* n. 9, at p. 89.

14. Protocol I, *supra* n. 4, Art. 48.

15. ICRC Commentary, *supra* n. 9, para. 1994; Greenwood, *supra* n. 4, at p. 71.

16. Prof. Y. Dinstein, 'Legitimate Military Objectives Under the Current Jus in Bello', in Colloquium, *supra* n. 9, at p. 41.

17. W. Hays Parks, 'The Protection of Civilians from Air Warfare', 27 *Israel YB HR* (1998) pp. 65, 72.

18. Protocol I, *supra* n. 4, Art. 5(2) (stating in part 'military objectives are limited to those objects which by their nature, location, purpose or use make an effective contribution to military action and whose total or partial destruction, capture or neutralization, in the circumstances ruling at the time, offers a definite military advantage'.).

(1923 Hague Air Rules).[19] However, those rules as such were never adopted in any treaty. Nevertheless, as Horace Robertson recounts in his excellent article on military objective, the 1923 Hague Air Rules term eventually bore fruit in Protocol I after having been further developed in a series of intermediate documents and processes.[20]

2.2 Conventional international law definition of military objective

Military objectives are defined in Protocol I Article 52(2) as 'those objects which by their nature, location, purpose or use make an effective contribution to military action and whose total or partial destruction, capture or neutralization, in the circumstances ruling at the time, offers a definite military advantage'. This definition is a two-stage test. The objective in question must simultaneously meet both the following criteria: firstly, its nature, location, purpose or use must make an effective contribution to military action; and secondly, its total or partial destruction, capture or neutralisation, in the circumstances ruling at the time must offer a definite military advantage.[21] Read literally, this definition is limited to objects only, i.e., it does not deal with armed forces' personnel. However, there is no doubt that such personnel are legitimate targets and, absent being *hors de combat* due to injury, illness or surrender, may be lawfully attacked at any time.[22]

The 'nature' of the objects set out in the article refers to those things used directly by armed forces, e.g., weapons, military vehicles, barracks, fortifications, military headquarters, etc.[23] 'Location' refers to a geographic site of military importance. Such areas inherently may have no military value but in the circumstances ruling at the time, they have become militarily important.[24] Examples of such areas might include a mountain pass, a ford in a river or other 'specific area of land'.[25] 'Purpose' refers to the intended future use of an object.[26] Thus, trucks in a civilian factory in a country at war, which is acquiring a substantial number of such vehicles for its armed forces, are legitimate military objectives despite the fact they belong to the civilian factory owner and are at the time of attack part of an at least temporary civilian pool. 'Use' refers to the object's present function aside

19. Robertson, *supra* n. 13, at p. 199; Hague Rules of Air Warfare, reprinted in Schindler and Toman, *supra* n. 13, p. 207.

20. Ibid., at pp. 199-201 (including the International Committee of the Red Cross (ICRC) 1956 Draft Rules for the Limitation of the Dangers Incurred by the Civilian Population in Time of War (1956 ICRC Draft Rules), a further 1965 ICRC Vienna conference, a 1968 Teheran International Conference on Human Rights, 1968 and 1970 United Nations General Assembly resolutions and a resolution from a 1969 Edinburgh meeting of the Institute of International Law).

21. ICRC Commentary, *supra* n. 9, para. 2018; M. Bothe et al., *New Rules for Victims of Armed Conflicts* (The Hague, Martinus Nijhoff 1982) p. 323.

22. ICRC Commentary, *supra* n. 9, paras. 1951, 2017.

23. Ibid., para. 2020.

24. Ibid., para. 2021.

25. Office of the Judge Advocate General, Canadian Forces, The Law of Armed Conflict at the Operational and Tactical Level 4-1 (1999).

26. ICRC Commentary, *supra* n. 9, para. 2022.

from its nature.[27] Thus, if a hotel is being used to house soldiers or a military headquarters it is a military objective.[28] Likewise, use of Paris taxis by the French in the opening stages of the Great War to transport troops to the front is another example of how current usage can bring normally civilian objects within the ambit of military objective.

The object under consideration must 'make an effective contribution to military action'. For example, even if a bridge might normally be a military objective,[29] a bridge in a very remote area far from the military confrontation is unlikely to make an effective contribution to the military action. However, the contribution of an object to military action need not directly relate to combat activity. Thus, if a military commander had to destroy some houses to permit large armoured vehicles to transit a village with narrow streets, the destruction of those houses may be legitimate.

Additionally, the destruction, capture or neutralisation must offer a *definite* military advantage, i.e., the military advantage must be 'concrete and perceptible'.[30] The word 'definite' is a word of limitation meaning the advantage cannot be merely hypothetical or speculative.[31] During negotiations, this adjective was the subject of extensive discussion with the terms 'distinct', 'clear', 'immediate', 'obvious', 'specific' and 'substantial' being considered but rejected for no readily apparent reasons.[32]

A further important consideration in the conventional definition of military objective is the temporal requirement. The destruction, capture or neutralisation must offer the requisite definite military advantage 'in the circumstances ruling at the time'.[33] Does this mean all potential targets of only future military utility are excluded by this definition? Any competent military commander legitimately considers the future and its possibilities. Article 52(2) Protocol I's reference to the 'purpose' of an object logically includes its intended future usage thereby incorporating certain objects of only future military utility. However, there is a limit to how remote the future possibilities can be and still render the object a legitimate military objective. Also, this temporal requirement means that there are some situations in which certain previously legal targets can cease to be valid military objectives. Targets and target lists must be re-examined periodically to ensure those objects have retained the characteristics that rendered them lawful military objectives initially.

In order to properly judge if any given object is a military objective, it is important to realise that it is not at the stage of determining military objective status that any balancing of collateral damage factors is done. This definitional phase is conceptually distinct from the proportionality balancing. Article 52(2) 'does not deal

---

27. Ibid.
28. Ibid.
29. See *infra* Part 5-8.
30. Bothe, *supra* n. 21, at p. 326.
31. Ibid.
32. Ibid., at pp. 325-326.
33. Protocol I, *supra* n. 12, Art. 52(2).

with the question of collateral damage'.[34] The determination of military objective is a threshold issue only. If the preceding criteria are met as to effective contribution to military action and destruction, etc., offering a definite military advantage, then the object is a military objective. Military objective determination simply requires that a certain standard be met.[35]

If that standard is not met then the object is, in law, a civilian object and may not be attacked. This exempt status is affected by Article 52(1), which provides: 'Civilian objects are all objects which are not military objectives as defined in paragraph 2.' A further treaty presumption as to civilian status for objects of normally purely civilian usage is set out in Article 52(3) which states: 'In case of doubt whether an object which is normally dedicated to civilian purposes, such as a place of worship, a house or other dwelling or a school, is being used to make an effective contribution to military action, it shall be presumed not to be so used.' This presumption does not apply to dual military-civilian usage objects.[36]

Drafters of the above standard of military objective intended military personnel to be able to use this standard in combat to guide their decision-making. Its guidance is valuable but commentators recognise that it will not always be easy to apply.[37] It contains many subjective elements. Certainly, no 'bright line rule'[38] is provided nor will there always be a 'fixed borderline'[39] between civilian and military objectives. Not all determinations will be obvious. Decision-makers must exercise discretion and caution. Thus, the onus on these soldiers, sailors and air personnel is a heavy one.

However, it is not an unreasonable burden.[40] The standards by which military personnel with these duties will be judged are those of simple reasonableness and honesty.[41] Aside from the law, similar dilemmas and duties with equal levels of difficulty are imposed on military professionals every day by their internal requirements to instil weapons discipline, maintain order, and prevent wastage of critical resources such as ammunition, plus a myriad of other responsibilities. Effectively, the law of war only requires military personnel to fight with the same restraint and caution they would use if they were recapturing their own village and liberating their own countrymen.

---

34. Bothe, *supra* n. 21, at p. 322.

35. F.J. Hampson, Remarks in a Panel on Implementing Limitations on the Use of Force: The Doctrine of Proportionality and Necessity, *Amer. Soc. IL Proc.* (1992) pp. 39, 49.

36. Bothe, *supra* n. 21, at p. 326.

37. ICRC Commentary, *supra* n. 9, para. 2016.

38. D. Fleck, 'Strategic Bombing and the Definition of Military Objectives', 27 *Israel YB HR* (1998) pp. 41, 47.

39. A. Randelzhofer, 'Civilian Objects', in R. Bernhardt, ed.,1 *Encyclopedia of Public International Law* (1992) pp. 603, 604 .

40. Bothe, *supra* n. 21, at p. 326.

41. Ibid.

2.3 Customary international law definition of military objective

The primary debate concerning the customary international law definition of military objective is whether the customary international law definition is more expansive than that set out in Protocol I. The purpose of this article in setting out the controversy is not to offer an opinion on that question but only to discern if the debate itself tells us something about whether the concept of military objective is changing; i.e., what does it tell us about any possible evolution in the concept of military objective.

'Customary international law is that law which has evolved from the practice or customs of states.'[42] It results 'from a general and consistent practice of states followed by them from a sense of legal obligation'.[43] It and conventional international law, i.e., that international law derived from treaties, are the two main sources of international law. Customary international law is the source of international law that provides the definition of military objective for those few countries not directly bound by Protocol I.[44]

Based on those requirements of customary international law, the definition of military objective found in Protocol I has probably become the customary international law definition binding on non-parties to Protocol I. Most international legal scholars agree. Non-American commentators are convincingly unanimous.[45] A representative statement in this regard is that of Professor Yoram Dinstein, who, while not always enthusiastic about Protocol I,[46] states: 'There is no doubt that, irrespective of objections to sundry other stipulations of Protocol I, 'the principle of the military objective has become a part of customary international law for armed conflict whether on land, at sea or in the air.'[47] A nuance to this chorus is provided by Professor Fausto Pocar, a Judge for the International Criminal Tribunal for the former Yugoslavia (ICTY). While he concludes that Article 52(2) en-

42. M. Dixon, *Textbook on International Law* (London, Blackstone 1990) p. 21.

43. Restatement (Third) of the Foreign Relations Law of the United States §102 (2).

44. International Committee of the Red Cross, International Humanitarian Law, <http://www.icrc.org/eng> (IHL Database/States Parties to the Geneva Conventions and their Additional Protocols) (indicating that as of 5 January 2005, 162 countries are bound by Protocol I and 31 are not).

45. Greenwood, *supra* n. 4, at pp. 75, 88 (stating, 'the definition of a military objective in Article 52 (2) was accepted as declaratory of custom during the Gulf conflict' and 'The definition of a military objective in Article 52(2) is generally regarded as declaratory of customary law', respectively); Kalshoven, *supra* n. 4, at p. 43 (referring to Protocol I Art. 52(2), states 'this provision is widely regarded as proper law, both within and outside the United States'); W.J. Fenrick, 'The law applicable to targeting and proportionality after Operation Allied Force: A view from the outside', 3 *YIHL* (2000) pp. 53, 57 (stating 'the Protocol I definition of military objective is the definition generally accepted today'.); Hampson, *supra* n. 35, at p. 50 (stating: 'The definition of a military objective found in Protocol I seems to be recognized as representing customary international law.'); Bring, *supra* n. 10, at p. 2 (stating: 'The Protocol's definition of military objectives has often been perceived as a codification of traditional customary law … This perception is probably correct').

46. Y. Dinstein, 'Comments on Protocol I', 37 *IRRC* (1997) p. 515 (stating 'And from the viewpoint of implementation, assessed in the light of 20 years of experience, it is evident that the Protocol has been a failure.').

47. Dinstein, *supra* n. 16, at p. 1.

capsulates existing principles of customary international law, he opines that there is still room for interpretation and clarification of the terms used in Article 52(2).[48]

Also telling is the work of the Committee Established to Review the NATO Bombing Campaign Against the Federal Republic of Yugoslavia for the Prosecutor for the International Criminal Tribunal for the former Yugoslavia (ICTY Committee). The ICTY Committee, in its final report of 8 June 2000, stated: 'The most widely accepted definition of "military objective" is that found in Article 52 of Additional Protocol I.'[49] This committee was examining a bombing campaign in which American aircraft carried out the majority of missions.[50] It is telling that the United States does not appear to have objected to having its actions assessed against this standard.

Many American international lawyers and sources agree that this definition either was or has become customary international law.[51] In 1987 one said: 'The definition of military objectives in Article 52 has already been incorporated in some military manuals, as well as in treaties other than the protocol; it almost certainly represents customary international law.'[52] Several are of the same opinion as Professor Pocar that Protocol I Article 52(2) accurately states the principles of customary law but disagreement as to how they are interpreted remains.[53]

However, some American commentators differ. They hold that the customary international law definition of military objective encompasses more than is set out in Protocol I. The Protocol I definition is said to be too restrictive.[54] The primary addition proposed to the objects legitimately subject to attack seems to be those that go to a 'war sustaining capability'.[55] This position seems to have arisen within the last ten years or so. In 1995 wording to reflect this possibly expanded defini-

---

48. F. Pocar (now Vice-President of the ICTY's Judges Chambers), 'To What Extent is Protocol I Customary International Law?', in Colloquium, *supra* n. 9, p. 8.

49. ICTY Committee Report, *supra* n. 13, para. 35, see also para. 42.

50. US DoD, Report to Congress, Kosovo/Operation Allied Force After-Action Report 78 (31 January 2000) (stating that the US' NATO allies flew about 39 percent of the sorties during Operation Allied Force).

51. Robertson, *supra* n. 13, at p. 204; C.J. Dunlap, Jr., 'The End of Innocence: Rethinking Noncombatancy in the Post-Kosovo Era', 9 *Strategic Review* (2000) pp. 9, 13 fn. 21 (accepting that the Protocol I definition of military objective is 'considered part of customary international law').

52. B.M. Carnahan, 'Remarks in a Panel on Customary Law and Additional Protocol I to the Geneva Conventions for Protection of War Victims: Future Directions in Light of the U.S. Decision not to Ratify', *Amer. Soc. IL Proc.* (1987) pp. 26, 37: B.M. Carnahan, 'Remarks in a Panel on Customary International Law Relative to the Conduct of Hostilities and the Protection of the Civilian Population in International Armed Conflict', 2 *Amer. Univ. JIL & Pol.* (1987) pp. 497 (making a statement to the same effect).

53. See e.g., M.N. Schmitt, 'The Principle of Discrimination in 21st Century Warfare', 2 *Yale HR & DLJ* (1999) p. 143, para. 13.

54. J.M. Meyer, 'Tearing Down the Façade: A Critical Look at the Current Law on Targeting the Will of the Enemy and Air Force Doctrine', 51 *Air Force LR* (2001) pp. 143, 144 and 164 (arguing that Protocol I Art. 52(2)'s definition of military objective is, or is being interpreted in a manner, inconsistent with the customary international law definition of military objective).

55. See e.g., ibid., at p. 172.

tion was added to the most recent American military manual, *The Commander's Handbook on the Law of Naval Operations (The 1995 Commander's Handbook).*[56]

This matter is settled by the initial position taken by the United States around the time of the negotiations of Protocol I and in the decade thereafter. In 1976, before Protocol I was signed, the United States Air Force defined military objectives in virtually the same words as Article 52(2).[57] In that same year, the United States Army adopted Protocol I's definition of military objective verbatim.[58] Further, in 1987, Michael J. Matheson, Deputy Legal Advisor with the United States Department of State, spoke expressly 'on the United States position concerning the relation of customary international law to the 1977 Protocols Additional to the 1949 Geneva Conventions'.[59] He dealt with American objections to various portions of Protocol I at some length. There was no objection to the definition of military objective. Rather he stated 'the United States has no great concern over the new definition of "military objective" set forth in Article 52(2) of Protocol I'.[60]

However, what is the legal effect of what appear to be second thoughts, i.e., the recent effort evidenced by the expanded definition of military objective in the United States Navy manual? *The 1995 Commander's Handbook* adds significantly to the Protocol I definition of military objective. The earlier United States Air Force and Army manuals had accepted Article 52(2)'s definition as a comprehensive statement of the customary international law definition of military objective. A judgment of the International Court of Justice (ICJ) seems to provide a logical and authoritative answer, albeit concerning a different treaty. If 'an interested State, which was not a party to the Convention, formally recorded its view that the Convention was an expression of generally applicable international law. This view being perfectly well founded, that State is not now in a position to escape the authority of the Convention.'[61] Thus, the United States is bound by its earlier ac-

---

56. US Dept. of Navy, The Commanders Handbook on the Law of Naval Operations (1995) § 8.1.1 [hereinafter, 1995 Commanders Handbook]; see also US Dept. of Navy, Annotated Supplement to the Commanders Handbook on the Law of Naval Operations (1997) § 8.1.1), adding the concept of 'war-sustaining capability' to the Protocol I definition of military objective); Schmitt, supra n. 3, at p. 1076 for a concise and helpful outline of this issue. The US Dept. of Defense is planning to publish an all services law of war manual. The date of issue is unknown. This publication should settle for American forces what appears to be a disagreement between the latest Navy manual, which expands the Protocol I definition of military objective, and the earlier Air Force and Army manuals which take the Protocol I definition of military objective as a complete encapsulation of the customary international law definition of military objective.

57. US Dept. of Air Force, Pam. 110-31, International Law – *The Conduct of Armed Conflict and Air Operations*, para. 5-3 (b)(1) (19 November 1976).

58. US Dept. of Army, Pam. 27-10, *The Law of Land Warfare Change 1*, para. 40 (c) (July 1956 with 15 July 1976 Change No. 1).

59. M.J. Matheson, 'Session One: The United States Position on the Relation of Customary International Law to the 1977 Protocols Additional to the 1949 Geneva Conventions', 2 *Amer Univ. JIL & Pol.* (1987) p. 419.

60. Ibid., at p. 436.

61. *North Sea Continental Shelf* cases (*Federal Republic of Germany* v. *Denmark.*; *Federal Republic of Germany* v. *the Netherlands*), *ICJ Rep.* (1969) p. 4, dissenting opinion of Judge ad hoc Sørensen, reprinted in D.J. Harris, *Cases and Materials on International Law*, 4th edn. (London,

ceptance of the Protocol I definition of military objective as the complete customary international law definition.

Professor Dinstein is of the same view on substantive grounds. He says that: 'an American attempt … to substitute the words 'military action' by the idiom 'war-fighting or war-sustaining capability' goes too far. The 'war-fighting' limb can pass muster, since it may be looked upon as equivalent to military action. But the 'war-sustaining' portion is too broad.'[62]

3. COLLATERAL DAMAGE/PROPORTIONALITY

3.1 Introduction and history

Incidental civilian losses are one of the two components in the balancing calculus mandated by the concept of proportionality. Proportionality is the legal rule that requires that there be an acceptable relationship between the military advantage anticipated from a military action and the expected incidental harm to civilians and civilian property.[63] In this article the term 'civilian losses' encompasses 'loss of civilian life, injury to civilians, damage to civilian objects, or a combination thereof'.[64]

Proportionality never permits a deliberate attack on civilians. This concept is a prime illustration of the basic purpose underlying the law of war, as proportionality expressly balances military necessity and humanity.[65] It permits attacks on military objectives even where incidental civilian losses are inevitable, but only where such expected losses are not disproportionate to the military advantage anticipated.

The major practical and conceptual difficulty with this rule is that it requires that two very unlike values be weighed[66] and balanced[67] and a judgment rendered as to which of them is to be preferred. The first value is the composite of the loss of civilian life, civilian injury and damage to civilian objects expected from the attack. The second value is the concrete and direct military advantage anticipated from the target's destruction. There simply is no objective method to compare two

---

Sweet & Maxwell 1991) p. 39. The reasons for which this opinion was a dissent do not affect the statement cited.

62. Dinstein, *supra* n. 16, at p. 8; see also F. Kalshoven, 'Noncombatant Persons: A Comment to Chapter 11 of the Commanders Handbook on the Law of Naval Operations', *64 International Legal Studies* (1991) pp. 300, 310 (warning that 'To add "war-sustaining effort" is going too far … as this might easily be interpreted to encompass virtually every activity in the enemy country'.).

63. See e.g., W.J. Fenrick, 'Attacking the Enemy Civilian as a Punishable Offence', *7 Duke JC & IL* (1997) pp. 539, 545.

64. Protocol I, *supra* n. 4, Arts. 51(5)(b), 57(2)(a)(iii), 57(2)(b).

65. A.V.P. Rogers, *Law on the battlefield* (Manchester, Manchester University Press 1996) p. 14; Doswald-Beck, *supra* n. 7, at p. 28 (stating 'The law of proportionality … is an excellent example of compromise between military and humanitarian needs'); Fenrick, *supra* n. 9, at p. 94.

66. ICRC Commentary, *supra* n. 9, para. 2208; Schmitt, *supra* n. 54, para. 16.

67. Y. Dinstein, 'The Laws of Air, Missile and Nuclear Warfare', 27 *Israel YB HR* (1997) pp. 1, 15.

such disparate notions. Obviously, any such weighing has to be extremely subjective,[68] which aspect will be considered further in a later section.

In addition to the major difficulty set out above, at least three further sub-questions arise in proportionality dilemmas.[69] William Fenrick sets out all four questions, the first being the dilemma of unlike values referred to above:

> '1) What are the relative values to be assigned to the military advantage gained and the injury to non-combatants and or the damage to civilian objects?
> 2) What do you include or exclude in totalling your sums?
> 3) What is the standard of measurement in time and space?, and
> 4) To what extent is a military commander obligated to expose his own forces to danger in order to limit civilian casualties or damage to civilian objects?'[70]

The dilemma posed by the first question has already been outlined. The second question can relate to a number of factors but the most obvious ones relate to how incidental losses are calculated. Hays Parks demonstrates that not all is what it might at first seem in tabulating incidental losses.[71] In fact, responsibility for collateral damage is often shared between the attacker and the defender.[72] Many questions about responsibility for incidental civilian losses arise. A sample of those raised by Hays Parks illustrates the inherent complexity of this issue. Do you include civilians killed by their own anti-aircraft forces, e.g., by falling debris? Do you count civilians killed by bombs that are forced off course by miscellaneous defensive measures? Do you include those deliberately not evacuated by their own government? Clearly, one cannot always attribute every civilian death after an attack to the attacker. Indeed, to do so would be misleading and potentially dishonest. One cannot assess incidental civilian losses for which the attacker is responsible by simply conducting a body count. Such an oversimplification is as superficial as assessing the quality of a hospital by only counting the bodies in its morgue.

There is a further complication in addressing the problem of incidental civilian losses, especially when considering the public reaction to such events. It is related to the different nature of the effects balanced by the concept of proportionality. Collateral civilian losses are often concrete, dramatic and emotive. They lend themselves to powerful pictures and strong reactions. The contrasting value, military advantage, is usually very abstract. It cannot generally be photographed. It tends to have at most a muted emotional impact. Undervaluing expected incidental civilian losses often results in gory pictures. Undervaluing anticipated military ad-

---

68. Ibid., at p. 8; Middle East Watch, *Needless Deaths in the Gulf War* (1991) pp. 19, 43 [hereinafter 'Needless Deaths']; Doswald-Beck *supra* n. 6, at p. 34; ICRC Commentary, *supra* n. 9, para. 2208.

69. ICTY Committee Report, *supra* n. 13, para. 49; Fenrick, *supra* n. 45, at p. 75; Fenrick, *supra* n. 63, at p. 546.

70. Fenrick, *supra* n. 45, at p. 75; Fenrick, *supra* n. 63, at p. 546; The issue of time is dealt with at *infra* pp. 48 et seq.

71. Parks, *supra* n. 10, at pp. 194-197 (setting out a theoretical scenario in which a substantial number of civilian casualties turn out upon analysis to not be attributable necessarily to the attacker.).

72. See Protocol I, *supra* n. 4, Arts. 51(7), 58; Parks, *supra* n. 10, at pp. 153-154.

vantage usually results in simply a missed targeting opportunity of which the public will likely be unaware.[73] The public is generally going to react much more strongly to collateral damage than to forgone targets. Feeding this asymmetrical public response to such issues are the often-unrealistic public expectations when it comes to the accuracy of PGM.[74] The public expects not only smart weapons but infallible weapons.[75]

William Fenrick's third question refers to the measure of time as it pertains to the military advantage anticipated.[76] When balancing civilian losses should the military commander be considering the military advantage of the destroyed bridge over the next day? Week? Month? Year? Likewise, over what time are the civilian losses to be calculated? The attacking military commander may be in a very poor position to judge how quickly the enemy can repair the electrical grid for at least emergency purposes. He usually cannot know with any reasonable degree of certainty the enemy's resources, even less the enemy's priorities.

How, then, is this difficult, highly charged concept to be applied? Is it so inherently flawed that is cannot usefully be employed? Not at all. Obviously and despite the mathematical terms used earlier, there is no mathematical formula to balance expected incidental civilian losses and anticipated military advantage. Even less will there be a 'proportionometer' to assist commanders and others tasked with these difficult decisions. The military member (and it will be military personnel along with the occasional politician who inserts him or herself in the targeting process)[77] will have to make a good faith,[78] honest and competent[79] decision as a 'reasonable military commander'.[80] As has been pointed out, such judgments by

---

73. See contra Ricks, *supra* n. 5. That article started: 'As many as 10 times over the last six weeks, the Air Force believed it had top Taliban and al Qaeda members in its cross hairs but was unable to receive clearance to fire in time to hit them .' Such missed opportunities are seldom made public.

74. A.P.V. Rogers, 'Zero-Casualty Warfare', 82 *IRRC* (2000) pp. 165, 169 (stating that the public's shock at images of civilian dead 'is probably exacerbated by their unduly high expectations of the accuracy of smart weapons').

75. M. Cernetig, 'Civilian deaths anger moderate Muslims', *The Globe and Mail* (Toronto), 15 October 2001, p. A4 (quoting one Pakistani on the US bombing of Afghanistan: 'How can a laser bomb miss its target and kill poor farmers?' and another: 'How can their computers make so many mistakes?', both of whom attributed resulting civilian deaths to deliberate targeting of civilians).

76. This question has occurred to others. See e.g., Rogers, *supra* n. 65, at p. 18 (stating: 'Another problem is whether the humanitarian and military limbs of the proportionality rule must be looked at in the longer or the shorter term.').

77. P. Rowe, 'Kosovo 1999: The Air Campaign – Have the Provisions of Additional Protocol I Withstood the Test?', (837-31 March 2000) *IRRC* (2000) pp. 147, 157-158 (quoting the British Secretary of State for Defence: 'I personally approve some of the targets, but for most, I have now delegated the decisions to the operational commanders.'); Press Release, US DoD, Joint Statement on the Kosovo After Action Review, (14 October 1999) <http://www.defenselink.mil/news/Oct1999/b10141999_bt478-99.html> (stating: 'For selected categories of targets, for example, targets in downtown Belgrade or targets likely to involve high collateral damage, NATO reserved approval for higher political authorities.').

78. Needless Deaths, *supra* n. 68, at p. 45; ICRC Commentary, *supra* n. 9, para. 1978; Dinstein, *supra* n. 67, at p. 8.

79. Bothe, *supra* n. 21, at p. 310.

80. ICTY Committee Report, *supra* n. 13, para. 50.

experienced combat commanders are not likely to be the same as those made by human rights lawyers.[81] Nor should they be. The combat commander has a wide range of responsibilities including, but not limited to, the successful execution of his mission and adherence to the law of armed conflict. So subjective are proportionality decisions that different reasonable experienced combat commanders are likely to differ on occasion.[82]

This subjectivity is widely recognised.[83] The various enforcement mechanisms related to punishing breaches of the proportionality standard effectively acknowledge this subjectivity as well. Article 85 of Protocol I deals with grave breaches of Protocol I more specifically in paragraph 3, for that of causing excessive civilian losses. Causing excessive civilian losses is made a grave breach but only when committed *wilfully* and when death or serious injury result and when committed '*in the knowledge* that such attack will cause excessive loss'.

The same recognition is even stronger for the permanent International Criminal Court (ICC). Causing excessive incidental civilian losses only comes within the jurisdiction of the ICC where such damage is *clearly* excessive in relation to the concrete and direct military advantage anticipated.[84] The addition of the word 'clearly' means that the evidence of a disproportionate attack is going to have to be very strong before a prosecution before the ICC is warranted. Reinforcing this is the ICC's Finalized Draft Text of the Elements of the Crimes for the war crime of excessive incidental death, injury or damage (Draft Text of the Elements).[85] One of the requisite elements for that crime is that '[t]he perpetrator *knew* that the attack would cause' the prohibited degree of loss, i.e., clearly excessive collateral damage. Those extra elements in the grave breach portion of Protocol I, the statute of the ICC and its related documents are evidence that the drafters of those instruments recognise that determinations as to proportionality are so subjective that they are only internationally criminalised when such decisions are very obviously

---

81. Ibid.; Fenrick, *supra* n. 63, at p. 546; Fenrick, *supra* n. 45, at p. 75.

82. Greenwood, *supra* n. 4, at p. 78 (citing as an example of professional military differences, the British air commander during the Gulf War declining two targets assigned to him by his US counterparts because in his assessment the risk of collateral damage was too great). Although proportionality decisions are not mathematical, an example using concrete numbers illustrates both the inherent subjectivity and the limits of that subjectivity in proportionality questions. For the destruction of a given military objective, one reasonable military commander may judge that at most 25 incidental civilian deaths were not disproportionate. A second equally reasonable commander may judge that 40 incidental civilian deaths was the upper limit. One probably cannot say that either is wrong. However, both may agree that 400 incidental civilian fatalities caused to destroy that particular target would be disproportionate.

83. Rogers, *supra* n. 65, at p. 58; Dinstein, *supra* n. 67, at p. 8; Needless Deaths, *supra* n. 67, at p. 43.

84. Rome Statute of the International Criminal Court, 17 July 1998, Art. 8(b)(iv) as corrected by the *procès-verbaux* of 10 November 1998 and 12 July 1999, 30 November 1999 and 8 May 2000, reprinted in W.A. Schabas, *An Introduction to the International Criminal Court* (Cambridge, Cambridge University Press 2001) pp. 167, 172: See Rogers, *supra* n. 74, at p. 180.

85. United Nations Preparatory Commission for the International Criminal Court, Report of the Preparatory Commission for the International Criminal Court, Addendum, Part II, Finalized Draft Text of the Elements of Crimes Art. 8(2)(b)(iv) War Crime of Excessive Incidental Death, Injury, or Damage (2 November 2000) [hereinafter, Draft Text of the Elements].

wrong. In reality, before any commander is prosecuted for a grave breach in this regard, the attack will likely have to be so disproportionate as to amount to a deliberate attack on the civilian population.

3.2 Conventional international law rule of proportionality

The conventional rule concerning proportionality in the law of armed conflict is set out in the negative three times in Protocol I at Articles 51(5)(b), 57(2)(a)(iii) and 57(2)(b). In all three provisions, a disproportionate attack is defined as an 'attack which may be expected to cause incidental loss of civilian life, injury to civilians, damage to civilian objects, or a combination thereof, which would be excessive in relation to the concrete and direct military advantage anticipated'.

While civilian losses are to be absolutely avoided if all possible,[86] it is recognised that this will often not be possible. 'Not all civilian deaths in wartime are unlawful.'[87] The general immunity that civilians enjoy is not absolute[88] in the sense that civilian deaths in an attack on a legitimate military objective not involving disproportionate losses are permitted. Even critics of what they feel is too aggressive military action concede that the law of war does not prohibit all civilian casualties.[89]

The standard set out in Protocol I is clearly prospective, i.e., it is intended to serve as a guide to those planning an attack. The *expected* civilian losses must be compared to the *anticipated* concrete and direct military advantage.[90] Any such plans are necessarily based on expectations as to how the future will unfold. As such, it is an activity fraught with real uncertainty. Thus, in addition to all its other challenges, proportionality requires a weighing of disparate *future* predicted events.

---

86. Protocol I, *supra* n. 4, Art. 57(2)(ii).

87. Amnesty International Report, NATO/Federal Republic of Yugoslavia, 'Collateral Damage' or Unlawful Killings, Violations of the Laws of War by NATO during Operation Allied Force (2000) p. 6 [hereinafter, Collateral Damage].

88. The general protection offered by Protocol I Art. 51(1), *supra* n. 4, is just that general. It provides in part, 'The civilian population and individual civilians shall enjoy general protection against dangers arising from military operations.' Incidental civilian casualties are clearly contemplated by the three repeated proportionality formulations, see sources cited *infra* n. 92, more specifically by Art. 57 (2)(ii) wherein attackers are required to take all feasible precautions 'with a view to avoiding, and in any event minimizing' civilian losses.

89. Needless Deaths, *supra* n. 68, at pp. 42-47 (accepting implicitly the legality of at least some incidental civilian casualties in some circumstances.); Normand and Jochnick, *supra* n. 9, at pp. 2, 11 (citing 'a reasonable balancing of military necessity and humanity' as the desired goal of the law of armed conflict and that this law 'limits the right of belligerents to massacre civilians under an overly broad definition of military necessity', both of which imply an acceptance of some civilian casualties in some circumstances).

90. Protocol I, *supra* n. 4, Arts. 51(5)(b), 57(2)(a)(iii), 57(2)(b).

3.3 Customary international law rule of proportionality

Like the treatment of the customary international law definition of military objective, the purpose of this discussion of the customary international law formulation of the rule of proportionality, including its incidental civilian losses component, is not to settle any controversy. The main goal is to determine what if anything this debate tells us about the dynamics of proportionality and collateral damage. This dynamic will be used to shed light on the relationship between military objective and incidental civilian losses.

The primary debate about proportionality and Protocol I is whether the rule as formulated in Protocol I sets out the customary international law rule on proportionality or not. That there is a rule of proportionality in customary international law is not in real dispute. This possible customary, as opposed to conventional, rule has been phrased in a number of fashions. A judgment of the ICJ stated it as the rule that 'even a legitimate target may not be attacked if the collateral civilian casualties would be disproportionate to the specific military gain from the attack'.[91]

Among those who believe that Protocol I sets out the customary rule is Christopher Greenwood, who, after acknowledging the pre-Gulf War debate and contradictory American statements in these regards, finds: 'The principle of proportionality laid down in Articles 51 (5) (b) and 57 (2) (a) (iii) is generally accepted as part of customary law … .'[92] Professors Françoise Hampson and Ove Bring, Lieutenant Colonel Corn and Brigadier General Charles Dunlap concur.[93] As pointed out by Greenwood, this was also the position taken in the 1976 change to the United States Department of the Army Field Manual *The Law of Land Warfare* FM 27-10 and the 1989 United States Navy *Annotated Supplement to the Commander's Handbook on the Law of Naval Operations*.[94] Again, note that the above Army manual version preceded finalisation of Protocol I.

The ICTY Committee set out a similar position. It held that 'in combat military commanders are required … when directing their operations against military objectives, to ensure that the losses to the civilian population and the damage to civilian property are not disproportionate to the concrete and direct military advantage anticipated'.[95] This wording is so close to that in Protocol I as to amount to the same rule.

As with the definition of military objective, the initial American position on the relationship of Protocol I to the United States' view of proportionality in customary international law was set out in 1987 by Mr Matheson of the Department of State. He said: 'We support the principle … that attacks not be carried out that

---

91. *Nuclear Weapons* Advisory Opinion, *supra* n. 11, dissenting opinion of Judge Higgins, para. 20.

92. Greenwood, *supra* n. 4, at p. 88.

93. Hampson, *supra* n. 35, at p. 46; Bring, *supra* n. 9, at p. 4; then Major Corn, 'International and Operational Law Note Principle 3: Endeavor to Prevent or Minimize Harm to Civilians, The Army Lawyer', October 1998 (The Judge Advocate General's School, United States Army, Charlottesville, VA) at p. 57; Dunlap, *supra* n. 51, at p. 11.

94. Greenwood, *supra* n. 4, at p. 76.

95. ICTY Committee Report, *supra* n. 13, para. 28.

would clearly result in collateral civilian casualties disproportionate to the expected military advantage.'[96] In the context of this debate, this statement is somewhat ambiguous. One can argue that the formulation Matheson used is so close to the Protocol I definition of proportionality as to amount to an endorsement of the conventional definition. Alternatively, the fact that he bothered to reformulate the conventional proportionality rule, unlike his explicit endorsement of the Protocol I definition of military objective, is some evidence that he was deliberately setting out a somewhat differently worded rule.

At the very least, Matheson's statement strongly indicates that some customary international law rule of proportionality exists. Also supporting the view that the customary international law rule of proportionality exists even if its exact formulation is open to debate is Professor Dinstein. He states: 'But whatever its correct formulation, the principle of proportionality ... can be viewed by now as an integral part of customary international law.'[97] The United States Department of Defense, in its Final Report to Congress after the Gulf War, said that there was an *uncodified* principle of proportionality in customary international law that 'prohibits military action in which the negative effects (such as collateral civilian casualties) clearly outweigh the military gain'.[98]

Virtually nothing important hinges on the above debate. Both the formulation of the rule of proportionality in Protocol I and whatever formulation is used for the customary international law rule, assuming for the sake of argument the two differ, are so flexible, and subjective that it is pointless to quibble about exact terminology.[99] In practice, they will be the same rule.

4. RELATIONSHIP AND DYNAMIC OF MILITARY OBJECTIVE TO COLLATERAL DAMAGE/PROPORTIONALITY

4.1 Inherent relationship

There is an inherent relationship between military objective and proportionality as revealed by certain common wording or terminology.[100] Both concepts incorporate the common term 'military advantage'. That term as used regarding military objec-

---

96. Matheson, *supra* n. 59, at p. 426.

97. Dinstein, *supra* n. 67, at p. 7 (citing Greenwood, *supra* n. 4, at p. 77).

98. US DoD, Conduct of the Persian Gulf War: Final Report to Congress, app. at O-10 (April 1992) [hereinafter, Final Report].

99. Ibid., (setting out the United States' position, which leaves the exact formulation of the customary international law rule on proportionality uncertain. This position is not without risks for the United States. See Parks, *supra* n. 10, at p. 169. He takes a critical position in relation to Protocol I but admits: 'There is value in codifying proportionality, if for no other reason than to define a concept that has been badly abused in the past.') Fenrick, *supra* n. 8, at p. 125.

100. Hampson, *supra* n. 35, at pp. 50-51. Hampson also expressly dealt with the relationship of military objective and proportionality. However, her treatment of this issue centres on a perceived gap between the incidental civilian losses calculated on an individual target basis and the truer long-term and aggregated effects on the civilian population.

tive in Article 52(2) is also logically linked to the related term 'effective contribution to military action' in that same paragraph. Concrete and direct military advantage factors into the proportionality equation by being balanced against expected incidental civilian losses.

Therefore, both military objective and proportionality require a consideration of military advantage. This commonality of military advantage has implications for whom should make targeting decisions in light of that advantage, or at least what type of expertise is required to make those assessments. Those implications will be dealt with later. This commonality of the concept of military advantage in both military objective and proportionality also means that there should be a general tendency for both concepts to move in the same direction, i.e., the more military advantage associated with an object the more collateral damage is legally permissible in an attack. While this is hardly surprising, this basic analysis has determined that the mechanism for this linkage is the common term 'military advantage'.

However, anyone applying either or both concepts – and, as noted earlier, all targeting decisions must involve, at a minimum, consideration of both concepts – must quickly move beyond the common element of military advantage and examine where military advantage in both these contexts diverge. The adjective modifying 'military advantage' in the concept of military objective is 'definite'. The adjectives modifying 'military advantage' in proportionality are 'concrete and direct'. Concrete and direct is a higher requirement that merely definite.[101] This is logical given that the first usage is concerned only with military objectives in isolation but the second is concerned with military objectives attacks upon which entail a risk of incidental civilian losses, i.e., collateral damage. A higher level of military advantage is required where collateral damage is anticipated.

There is a further difference between the term 'military advantage' as set out in these two concepts. That further point of divergence is temporal, i.e., the point in time at which military advantage must be considered. The military advantage within the concept of military objective is that ruling in the circumstances at the time. This implies a requirement to assess military advantage in relatively immediate terms. However, the military advantage assessed in proportionality situations is that advantage 'anticipated', i.e., something of a future military advantage. Likewise, the civilian losses in proportionality calculations are those 'expected', another future oriented term.

It might be thought that the immediacy of the military advantage required by the definition of military objective would pose a targeting problem for a realistic military commander. In fact, this immediacy requirement is not as stringent as it might at first appear. Article 52(2)'s definition of military objective includes those objects that by their 'purpose' make an effective contribution to military action. As mentioned earlier,[102] purpose can include intended *future* use. Thus, logical future possibilities can be integrated into the legal definition of military objective. Obviously,

---

101. Bothe, *supra* n. 21, at p. 365.
102. See *supra* section 2.2 n. 26, p. 40.

the other targeting strictures as to definiteness, circumstances ruling at the time, etc., also still apply. These further requirements place a good faith, common sense limitation on future possibilities and prevent objects being targeted for fanciful or remote future possibilities.

The degree of subjectivity in both these concepts also implies something about their relationship. The definition of the concept of military objective contains many subjective elements. The words 'effective' and 'definite' lack objective content, thus requiring a subjective, albeit good faith, application.

Yet, proportionality adds several layers of subjectivity on top of those in the definition of military objective. Proportionality assumes that a military objective has been identified so all those objective and non-objective assessments have been made. Then proportionality requires additional subjective judgments from targeters. Such personnel must quantify (in a sense) the military advantage anticipated so they can balance the value of that military objective against the expected incidental civilian losses. Any such quasi-quantification is inherently very subjective. Expected civilian losses also require subjective judgments.[103] The subjectivity of 'excessive' is self-evident. Likewise, anticipated military advantage is a somewhat more elastic concept than present tense military advantage. Assessments of anticipated military advantage can be very different from one reasonable commander to another based upon, among other factors, their relative levels of optimism.[104]

What does all this additional subjectivity in the concept of proportionality imply for its relationship to military objective? This subjectivity in general and the differing levels of subjectivity in particular mean that any linkage between these concepts is going to be weak and sporadic. That is to say, when one concept is changed the effect on the other is going to be very difficult to discern given the intervening subjectivity, i.e., the effect of all the unpredictable individualised variables.

In summary, the common linkage of military advantage in both military objective and the proportionality equation, of which collateral damage is a part, is greatly affected by:

1) different adjectives, being 'definite' for military objective and 'concrete and direct' in the proportionality calculus;

2) different temporal elements, albeit this difference is not as great as it might at first appear, being the relatively immediate 'in the circumstances ruling at the time' for military objective and the future oriented 'expected' incidental civilian losses and 'anticipated' military advantage for proportionality;

3) different applications, being a threshold determination for military objective and a balancing for proportionality; and

---

103. Rowe, *supra* n. 77, at p. 160 (highlighting the inherent subjectivity of proportionality especially as attacks are being planned. 'At this stage of military operations those planning the attack are at their most optimistic and civilians most at risk.'

104. Despite this subjectivity, the conventional definition of proportionality at least provides some guidance, albeit subjective, and is better than no guidance at all on such a crucial concept. See ICRC Commentary, *supra* n. 9, paras. 2210, 2219.

4) different degrees of subjectivity, being fairly subjective for military objective determinations and extremely subjective for proportionality calculations.

The effect of these divergent modifications of the concept of military advantage in military objective and in collateral damage should be to weaken any dynamic between these two terms.

4.2 Dynamic

For the purposes of this analysis, there are four broad likely alternatives as to the dynamic between military objective and the collateral damage component of proportionality. Firstly, there may be no dynamic between these two terms. Secondly, there may be an inverse dynamic. In this dynamic, as the field or scope of military objective widens that of proportionality narrows. This means that the amount of legally permissible collateral civilian damage becomes less. For example, in an inverse dynamic, an increase in the number or type of military objectives is acceptable if the amount of collateral damage is reduced. Thirdly, there may be a complementary dynamic. In a complementary dynamic the same pressures that restrict the concept of military objective may lessen the amount of tolerable incidental civilian losses. An equally complementary dynamic, albeit one that works in the opposite direction, is one in which the same pressures to expand the list of legitimate military objectives are at work to increase the quantum of legitimate incidental civilian damage. Lastly, there may be some other dynamic entirely

Despite the apparent inclusiveness of these four alternatives, the dynamic of military objective and the incidental civilian losses component of proportionality may not be amenable to this form of analysis or in these terms. Regardless of this potential shortcoming, this examination of a potential dynamic may shed light on both concepts and their relationship.

5. TESTING THE RELATIONSHIP OF MILITARY OBJECTIVE AND COLLATERAL DAMAGE/PROPORTIONALITY

5.1 Introduction

All too often, debate and academic discussion of law of armed conflict controversies appears to be a simple 'exchange of broadsides' at best and a series of simultaneous monologues at worst. Proponents simply set out their sometimes policy-based arguments. There appears to be little attempt at resolution or objective consideration of competing views or objective testing of one's own conclusions.

This part explores the possibility that there might be a somewhat more objective way to measure the merits of an argument, position or proposition in this area. It is this author's theory that the fact of certain controversies, initiatives or developments in the law of war points to general trends in international humanitarian law. Current concerns being raised indicate the law of war's basic direction, i.e., where the current legal regime might be changing. It further supposes that positions, arguments and proposals consistent with those trends are more likely to prevail over the longer term. Even if mistaken, should this article merely provoke other attempts to find a less sterile approach to advancing the academic and practical application of the law of armed conflict it will have been worthwhile.

To discern the dynamics that might be at play in the terms military objective and collateral damage, this part examine a range of controversies, proposals and developments pertaining to targeting. After outlining each issue and in some cases offering an opinion on it, an attempt is made to specifically look for what that issue might tell us about the relationship between military objective and collateral damage. The objective is not necessarily to decide which point of view in any controversy is legally correct or if the reform proposal is worthwhile. Rather the objective is to determine what the controversies or initiatives themselves tell us about the law of armed conflict as it pertains to the definition of military objective and incidental civilian losses within the rule of proportionality.

5.2 General public concern for collateral damage

There is one phenomenon relating to proportionality that is particularly significant, namely, the dramatically decreased public tolerance for collateral damage. This phenomenon is of such strength that it may outweigh all the others. Yet, comparatively speaking, the two conflicts this article primarily uses have caused remarkably few direct civilian losses. [105]

The phenomenon of a greatly increased sensitivity to collateral damage may say two alternative things about the relationship between military objective and incidental civilian losses. Concern about collateral damage may be so heightened that it restricts the numbers and types of objects considered lawful targets. This would imply that there is a complementary dynamic, i.e., the same pressures at work to decrease the amount of lawful incidental civilian damage are also at work to reduce the number and type of permitted military objectives. Alternatively, the concern about collateral damage may be so focused on purely civilian effects that if civilian losses are eliminated or kept very low, the number and type of lawful military objectives will be a matter of indifference. This would to lead to an expansion of the concept of military objective. This latter possibility implies an inverse dynamic between these two terms. Given these contradictory alternatives, this debate neither confirms nor contradicts any relationship between military objective and collateral damage.

---

105. Being the 1991 Gulf War and the 1999 NATO bombing of Serbia (Operation Allied Force) see e.g., Fenrick, *supra* n. 45 (using the figures from Parks, *supra* n. 10, at p. 154 with Operation Allied Force figures added). The comparable figures for the 2001 bombing of Afghanistan may not yet be reliable but preliminary indications are they are not dramatically different in relative scale from the 1991 Gulf conflict or the 1999 Serbia bombing. See M. Campbell, 'Afghanistan civilian toll notably high', *The Globe and Mail* (Toronto), 19 January 2001, at A11 (citing a Project on Defense Alternatives estimate of 1,000-1,300 Afghan civilian deaths between 7 October 2001 and 10 December 2001 caused by United States bombing).

5.3 Difference in customary and conventional definitions of military objective

Regardless of the merits of the argument that the customary international law definition of military objective is broader than the conventional definition, what does the fact that this argument is being made say about the dynamics of the concept of military objective? To the extent an expanded definition has merit, it argues for an obvious and significant enlargement of the number of objects considered lawful military objectives. However, the fact that the proposed customary international law definition of military objective would have a tendency to expand the category of lawful military objectives as compared to the conventional definition says nothing necessarily about the relationship of military objective to incidental civilian losses.

5.4 Difference in customary and conventional rules of proportionality

The implications of the analogous debate regarding proportionality are even less clear-cut. Given the conclusion that the customary and conventional formulations of the rule are to all practical effect indistinguishable, no conclusion as to the dynamics of the rule of proportionality can be drawn from this debate. To the extent that Hays Parks' arguments about the real complexity of the collateral damage question and the shared responsibility of the attacker and defender for such losses are part of this issue,[106] they imply a somewhat increased tolerance for what would otherwise be viewed as incidental civilian losses. However, this phenomenon does not seem to have any implications for the concept of military objective. Therefore, this debate tells us nothing about the relationship between military objective and collateral damage.

5.5 Civilian morale

The legitimacy of attacking the enemy's civilian morale, as such, has been questioned in recent conflicts, most sharply in the context of the NATO bombing of Serbia.[107] To a lesser extent, it also arose in the Coalition attack on Iraq in 1991. This part only considers the legality of an attack on an abstract concept, i.e., civilian morale. The concrete way in which this is done may be by attacking media outlets; the objects proposed by Brigadier General Dunlap;[108] or perhaps electrical systems or other physical objects. Thus, this analysis will necessarily blend somewhat with the later consideration of certain of those other concrete objectives.

The controversy arises over whether civilian morale *per se* is a military objective within the meaning of Article 52(2). Does destruction of or diminution of an opponent's civilian morale offer a definite military advantage? It would be pedan-

---

106. Parks, *supra* n. 10, at pp. 149-168.

107. The targets most closely associated with civilian morale were the media outlets and the electrical systems.

108. See *infra* Section 5.9.

tic to argue that civilian morale does not qualify as a physical object. Civilian morale certainly does make an effective contribution to military action.[109] But are such strategic psychological goals illegitimate targets?[110]

There is an historical context for attacks on civilian morale and that history is relevant to this discussion. The background of such attacks is perhaps most dramatically illustrated by the Second World War attacks on enemy morale by strategic aerial bombardment.[111] The efficacy of such attacks is far from clear. There is at least some evidence that those attacks were counter-productive, either not affecting morale in any significant way or perhaps even strengthening the will to resist.[112] What are not in doubt are the tens if not hundreds of thousands of civilian casualties resulting from such bombing.[113] It seems likely that bloody history was at least part of the reason for the current prohibition on indiscriminate area bombardment or deliberate terrorisation of the civilian population found in Article 51(5)(a) and (2), respectively.[114]

Recent justification for attacks on civilian morale, in the sense of the enemy civilian population's support for the war effort, is rooted in sophisticated modern strategic bombing theory. Proponents hold that it is obvious that wars are not fought for their own sakes. Colonel John Warden, an influential strategic theoretician of air warfare states: 'We don't go to war merely to have a nice fight; rather,

---

109. USAF Basic Doctrine, *supra* n. 5, at p. 6 (stating 'While physical factors are crucial in war, the national will and the leadership's will are also critical components of war. The will to prosecute or the will to resist can be decisive elements.'). See also B. Brodie, 'Tet Offensive, in Decisive Battles of the Twentieth Century', N. Frankland and C. Dowling, eds. (London, Sidgwick & Jackson 1976) pp. 321, 334 (concluding that in his 1968 offensive North Vietnamese General Giap 'expected his offensive to have a great shock effect on the South Vietnamese and especially the Americans, and it most certainly did'. Such was the shock that 'it was probably unique in that the side that lost completely in the tactical sense came away with an overwhelming psychological and hence political victory. And there can be no question of its decisiveness.').

110. Parks, *supra* n. 10, at p. 141 (arguing they are not).

111. Parks, *supra* n. 17, at pp. 77-87.

112. Fleck, *supra* n. 38, at p. 50 n.22.

113. It is difficult, if not impossible, to calculate the civilian casualties in the Second World War caused by attacks specifically directed against civilian morale versus more traditional military objectives. What is clear is that at least for the Royal Air Force civilian morale was a significant bombing objective either primarily or secondarily. See generally W.A. Jacobs, 'The British Strategic Air Offensive Against Germany in World War II', in *Case Studies in Strategic Bombardment* (Washington, Air Force History and Museum Program 1998) pp. 91, 92, 121 (summarising the February 1942 Air Ministry directive to Bomber Command to 'destroy large urban areas with the aim of undermining the morale of the German industrial work force'. Just one such attack, in July 1943 against Hamburg, killed 50,000 and left nearly 1,000,000 people homeless.).

114. Protocol I, *supra* n. 4, Art. 51(5)(a) states concerning prohibited indiscriminate attacks: 'Among others, the following types of attacks are to be considered as indiscriminate: (a) an attack by bombardment by any method or means which treats as a single military objective a number of clearly separated and distinct military objectives located in a city, town, village or other area containing a similar concentration of civilians or civilian objects ...' and Art. 51(2), which states: 'The civilian population as such, as well as individual civilians, shall not be the object of attack. Acts or threats of violence the primary purpose of which is to spread terror among the civilian population are prohibited.'

we go to war to attain something of political value to our organization.'[115] To obtain those objectives it is most efficient to attack the enemy's centres of gravity. Speaking of the future, Michael Schmitt says: 'The goal will still be to strike decisively at an enemy's center of gravity … .'[116] Centres of gravity are '[t]hose characteristics, capabilities, or localities from which a military force derives its freedom of action, physical strength, or will to fight.'[117]

Often those centres of gravity will include the enemy civilian support for its government's war effort. Such support may be the enemy's critical weakness. Eroding that support might be the quickest and most efficient way to prevail over an enemy.

This possibility has led the United States Air Force to conclude that proper air warfare strategy 'place(s) maximum stress on both enemy defences and the enemy society as a whole'.[118] Further, '[s]trategic attack objectives often include producing effects to demoralize the enemy's leadership, military forces, and population, thus affecting an adversary's capability to continue the conflict'.[119] Confirming the centrality of such a psychological approach is one assessment of the 1999 NATO bombing campaign as 'an exercise in coercive diplomacy designed to change one man's mind'.[120]

Despite the historic ambiguity of the effectiveness of attacking enemy civilian morale, there is some indication it can be effective at least in some circumstances. The North Vietnamese re-commenced negotiations after 1971 United States' bombing intended to have exactly that effect.[121] Serbia's leader, Slobodan Milošević, did eventually agree to NATO's demands after a bombing campaign that targeted certain objects intended to affect civilian morale.[122] Not targeting such civilian morale-related targets might even have the effect of prolonging a war, resulting in many more military and collateral civilian casualties.

Conventional attacks on civilian morale require the striking of actual physical targets,[123] examples of which are media outlets and in a less clear-cut sense, electrical generating/distribution facilities. However, because civilian morale can only be physically struck by attacks on such targets, this article examines media strikes

115. J.A. Warden, III, 'The Enemy as a System', 1 *Airpower Journal* (1995) pp. 40, 43.

116. Schmitt, *supra* n. 13, at p. 1055.

117. USAF Basic Doctrine, *supra* n. 5, at p. 79. This concept is obviously based on that set out by Carl von Clausewitz. See Carl von Clausewitz, *On War* (Princeton, Princeton University Press, 1976) p. 595 (M. Howard and P. Paret, eds. and trans.) (defining the term in stating 'one must keep the dominant characteristics of both belligerents in mind. Out of these characteristics a certain center of gravity develops, the hub of all power and movement, on which everything depends. That is the point against which all our energies should be directed.').

118. Ibid., at p. 24.

119. Ibid., at p. 51.

120. Michael Ignatieff, *Virtual War* (New York, Henry Holt 2000) p. 110.

121. Parks, *supra* n. 10, at pp. 142-143. The bombing campaign presumably hit military objectives but the motivation in hitting those military objectives was not the defeat of military forces but a change in enemy government policy. This is a legitimate use of military force. War always has a political motivation. Motivation and the objective characteristics of the targets must not be confused.

122. Meyer, *supra* n. 54, at p. 176.

123. Cyber warfare is beyond the scope of this article and will not be considered.

and certain aspects of attacks against electricity related facilities as representative morale targets to discern what if anything these controversies reveal about the relationship of military objective and the incidental civilian losses component of proportionality. Attacks on the abstract of civilian morale will not be separately considered regarding the relationship between these two terms.

5.5.1 *Electrical systems*

Significant targeting controversies have arisen concerning the legality of targeting an enemy's national electrical generating and distribution system. In the 1991 Gulf War the Coalition allegedly 'virtually destroyed Iraq's electrical system'.[124] The longer-term effect of this damage in a country with Iraq's climate was the main point of contention. Likewise, NATO targeted Serbia's electrical capacity in its 1999 bombing campaign.[125] The collateral civilian effects of these attacks generated much controversy.[126]

Of course, destroying or even interrupting a nation's electrical system is going to be immediately and dramatically apparent to civilians in any moderately developed country. There are obvious effects on civilian morale. In 1999 NATO alluded to the morale effects of such strikes. It was part of NATO's motivation for targeting the electrical system.[127]

They were also very effective in this regard. Michael Ignatieff writes of the attacks on Serbia's electrical transformer yards: 'Hitting these yards turned out to be the single most effective military strike of the campaign … After the grid was destroyed, both the political elite and the people knew that NATO had secured control of the regime's central nervous system.'[128] However, such targeting is only legitimate if the objects or capability attacked meets the threshold military objective test. Those criteria being met, the effect on civilian morale may legitimately either be a bonus from or even the main motivation for such strikes. The motiva-

124. Needless Deaths, *supra* n. 68, at p. 9; Rogers, *supra* n. 65, at p. 45 (stating that Coalition attacks eventually made 88 percent of Iraq's pre-war electrical power unavailable. Rogers disagrees with other higher figures.).

125. Meyer, *supra* n. 54, at p. 178.

126. Egorov, *supra* n. 9, at p. 185; W.A. Arkin, Greenpeace International, *Gulf War Effects and Laws of War Briefing, For Meeting of Experts on the Protection of the Environment in Time of Armed Conflict*, International Committee of the Red Cross (ICRC), Geneva, 27-29 April 1992 (copy on file with author). It is interesting to note neither Amnesty International at Collateral Damage, *supra* n. 87, nor Human Rights Watch at Human Rights Watch Report, Civilian Deaths in the NATO Air Campaign (2000) [hereinafter, Civilian Deaths] in their respective reports mentioned the electrical systems as *per se* illegal targets.

127. Lieutenant General M. Short, Interview, Morning Edition, National Public Radio broadcast, 15 September 1999, (during which Lieutenant General Short, one of NATO's air commanders during its 1999 bombing of Serbia said: 'There can be no doubt in your mind that with the power down … and the refrigerator not running and no water in your house and the public transportation system in Belgrade not running and no street lights, that the war was brought home, not just to the ruling elite, but to the average Serb on the street.').

128. Ignatieff, *supra* n. 120, at pp. 107-108.

tion for an attack may legitimately be much broader than the strict military advantage anticipated but only as long as the threshold military objective criteria are met.

However, having decided that electrical systems will generally be legitimate military objectives does not end even a basic targeting analysis. Proportionality must also be addressed. Immediate proportionality concerns in targeting electrical facilities would involve any incidental civilian casualties in the attacks themselves. More significantly for these types of target sets are likely to be the secondary or reverberating effects.

For some, 'the cost to the civilian population of these attacks on the electrical system was severe' in Iraq in 1991.[129] Others went further. 'Evidence suggests that the Coalition's overall campaign against Iraq's electrical system provided negligible military gains relative to the amount of civilian suffering it caused.'[130] These effects were felt through the interruption or complete stoppage of electrical power to water plants, sewage facilities, hospitals, refrigeration equipment and irrigation capability. Such effects in the *immediate* aftermath of an attack are a necessary collateral damage consideration for any commander contemplating such military action.

Yet, it is with the later secondary or reverberating effects of such attacks that a more contentious debate begins. How far into the future must the attacking military commander project collateral civilian damage from his or her strikes? This issue of remoteness, particularly, but not exclusively, in the context of attacks on electrical grids, is obvious, real and recognised.[131] Further, the potential for such longer term secondary incidental civilian effects is likely to grow, given modern societies' increasingly inter- and intra-connectivity.

Any determination of how far into the future commanders must project collateral damage has to acknowledge some very real world limitations. How is a commander supposed to know what resources the enemy has to repair damage? How should the attacking commander guess how the enemy will priorise his repair and re-building resources? Perhaps the enemy should get hospitals' power restored but he may choose to channel the power to his air defence facilities. This cannot be the attacker's responsibility. Exactly how the war will turn out even if victory is assured (and often it is not) is not infrequently an open question. How much freedom will either party have to affect events during and after the conflict? Will the post-conflict government receive assistance? How will the defending government allocate scarce resources? There are simply too many variables over which the military commander can have no influence. 'It would be wholly unreasonable to expect a commander to take into account actions over which he had no control.'[132] These

---

129. Needless Deaths, *supra* n. 68, at p. 9.

130. Normand and Jochnick, *supra* n. 9, at p. 7.

131. Greenwood, *supra* n. 5, at p. 79; Hampson, *supra* n. 36, at p. 51.

132. Hampson, *supra* n. 9, at p. 93; contra J.W. Crawford, 'The Law of Noncombatant Immunity and the Targeting of National Electrical Power Systems', 21 *Fletcher Forum of World Affairs* (1997) pp. 101-102. Crawford argues that objections to consideration of relatively remote effects on the basis they are 'theoretical scholastic postulation' and 'insincere'. However, Crawford ignores the real world limits of knowledge and predictive accuracy. At a certain point such predictive activities become so unreliable and speculative as to be meaningless. There is something of a contradiction in the require-

practical limitations mean an attacking commander legally need only project incidental civilian damage into the immediate but not indefinite future. Although very fact dependent, a generally reasonable standard would be days and weeks but not months and years.

The criticism of the Coalition for the post-war effects of its attacks on the Iraqi electrical system seems particularly overblown.[133] The real problem appears to be either the effect of ongoing sanctions, the responsibility for which arguably did not rest outside Iraq or the Iraqi government's priorities and competence. As A.P.V. Rogers points out, while Iraqi power was reduced to 12 percent of its pre-war level by the end of the war, within three months it was at 23 percent of pre-war levels and was at 90 percent within 18 months.[134] Even a 12 percent figure should have permitted most emergency power to water, sewage and hospital facilities.

In conclusion, in the vast majority of cases such attacks on an enemy nation's electrical generating and distributions system are legitimate. The nature of national power grids means the entire system becomes a valid military objective. If the threshold military objective test is met and the incidental civilian losses are not disproportionate, such attacks are legitimate even if the main motivation for such strikes is to affect civilian morale.[135] Proportionality must be considered but only over the relatively short term, perhaps days and weeks. More remote effects will generally be beyond the attacking commander's ability to reliably predict and are probably within the defenders' control. Thus, they are not the attacker's legal responsibility.

The fact of the controversy over the targeting of enemy civilian electrical systems demonstrates a decreased tolerance of collateral damage. To the extent this controversy will have an effect, it would also expand the concept of incidental civilian losses in a temporal sense, i.e., make the attacker consider the longer-term effects of such targeting than heretofore. It would also require attackers to assess much more indirect and remote collateral damage than has traditionally been the case. The effect would also be to render civilian electrical systems unlawful military objectives much more often than has been the recent historical practice, i.e., to decrease the scope of lawful military objective. Since the tendency of this issue is to reduce both acceptable levels of collateral damage and range of military objective, it evidences a complementary dynamic between collateral damage and military objective.

---

ment for military advantage to be considered in the relatively immediate 'in the circumstances ruling at the time' but for incidental civilian losses to be projected into the relatively indefinite future.

133. Needless Deaths, *supra* n. 68, at pp. 9-11; Arkin, *supra* n. 126.

134. Rogers, *supra* n. 65, at pp. 45-46.

135. Of course, it is human tendency to allow one's motivations to colour one's objective judgment. The danger here is that in deciding if an attack on a legitimate military objective (but having a high-civilian-morale impact) is proportionate, one might be tempted to exaggerate the anticipated military advantage so as to permit the attack despite incidental civilian losses that would not be justified based on the strictly military advantage involved. Like many other difficult law of war decisions the only real guide and protection is the good faith and moral character of the decision maker.

5.5.2 *Media outlets*

Attacks on media outlets, more particularly a specific 1999 NATO strike on the Serb Radio and Television (RTS) facilities in Belgrade, have caused a great deal of controversy.[136] While some mention was made of targeting telecommunications infrastructure during the 1991 Gulf War,[137] the prominence of this one incident in the criticism of NATO's 1999 bombing campaign was extraordinary. The ICTY Committee devotes more space to its analysis of this attack than any other strike. It was the first incident referred to by Amnesty International in its *Collateral Damage* Report,[138] which had a picture of the RTS attack's aftermath on its cover.[139] It was the only specific target mentioned in Amnesty International's response to the report of the ICTY Committee.[140] Likewise, Human Rights Watch listed the RTS attack first in its complaint about NATO's allegedly illegitimate targeting of non-military targets.[141]

The objections to this strike were two-fold. Critics maintain the RTS facility was not a military objective and that, in any event, the collateral damage, being 16 civilian RTS workers killed, was disproportionate.[142]

Attacks upon the media are only justified if the facility in question meets the conventional definition of military objective. Television broadcasting facilities, given their instant utility to the military as potential backup communication systems, will virtually always be such objectives. However, attacks cannot be justified based solely on the facility's transmission of enemy propaganda. Yet, if the physical infrastructure of a propaganda outlet simultaneously meets the separate definition of military objective then it might be attacked. There may be a separate category of lawful target for broadcasters of incitement to genocide-like crimes.[143]

In this regard, it is interesting to note that Canadian aircraft were assigned to attack the television station in Novi Sad during NATO's bombing of Serbia. That attack apparently caused no incidental civilian casualties and attracted no criticism.[144] This incident is a very slight indication of an inverse dynamic between military objective and collateral damage, i.e., the target set was arguably expanded without apparent concern, presumably because incidental civilian losses were avoided.

---

136. See e.g., Egorov, *supra* n. 9, at p. 185.

137. Greenwood, *supra* n. 4, at p. 73.

138. Collateral Damage, *supra* n. 87, in the summary at the third paragraph and in the introduction, p. 2.

139. Ibid., cover.

140. Public Statement, Amnesty International, Amnesty International's Initial Comments on the Review by the International Criminal Tribunal for the Former Yugoslavia of NATO's Operation Allied Force (13 June 2000) (on file with author).

141. Civilian Deaths, *supra* n. 126, at summary 1.

142. Collateral Damage, *supra* n. 87, at pp. 43, 45; Civilian Deaths, *supra* n. 126, at summary 7; T. Voon, 'Pointing the Finger: Civilian Casualties of NATO Bombing in the Kosovo Conflict', 16 *Amer. Univ. ILR.* (2001) pp. 1083, 1107; Bring, *supra* n. 10, at p. 3.

143. See e.g., ICTY Committee Report, *supra* n. 14, paras. 47 and 76.

144. B. Wallace, 'Canadian aces over Kosovo', *Maclean's* (27 March 2000) at p. 21.

The critics of strikes against media outlets and the proponents of such attacks in a civilian morale-attacking sense share a similar view of the dynamic between military objective and proportionality. Both groups believe, or at least their positions imply, that the dynamic between these concepts is complementary. Critics are pushing for a restricted view of military objective and, at the same time, a restricted view of what is lawful collateral damage.[145] Proponents of such strikes who believe that civilian morale is a lawful target are proposing an expansive view of military objective and an expanded view of lawful incidental civilian effects, i.e., including the effect on civilian morale.[146] Therefore, this debate evidences a complementary dynamic between the two terms under consideration.

5.6 Bridges

The destruction of bridges in the NATO campaign against Serbia caused a certain amount of adverse comment.[147] NATO's 1999 strikes were moderately effective against Serbia's bridges, destroying 70 percent of the Danube road bridges and 50 percent of such railway bridges.[148] To a lesser extent, concerns were expressed about such targets in the 1991 Gulf War.

A major complaint against NATO's strikes on Serbian bridges was that, in the context of NATO's war against Serbia, 'bridges (had) become irrelevant for the military effort'.[149] In a similar vein, Human Rights Watch complained about attacks against 'seven bridges that were neither on major transportation routes nor had other military functions'.[150] A more nuanced general criticism of such targeting is that which holds that bridges cannot be treated as military objectives *per se*. In this view 'the status of bridges ... depends entirely on the situation'.[151]

Bridges, like electrical systems, would appear to warrant such a conditional status. The 1956 ICRC Draft Rules permits targeting those 'lines and means of communication (railway lines, roads, bridges, tunnels and canals) which are of fundamental military importance'.[152] United States military authorities conceded this very point in the 1991 Gulf War by targeting only those 'railroads and bridges

---

145. Collateral Damage, *supra* n. 87, at pp. 43, 45 (stating respectively that the attack on RTS facilities 'stretches the meaning of 'effective contribution to military action' and 'definite military advantage' beyond the acceptable bounds of interpretation', and 'even if that building could have been properly considered a military objective ... that attack would have violated the rule of proportionality').

146. See e.g., Dunlap, *supra* n. 51, p. 17.

147. See e.g., Egorov, *supra* n. 9, at p. 185.

148. A.H. Cordesman, *The Lessons and Non-Lessons of the Air and Missile Campaign in Kosovo* (Westport CT, Praeger 2001) pp. 156, 184 , citing US DoD estimates).

149. Bothe, *supra* n. 21, at para. 3.

150. Civilian Deaths, *supra* n. 126, at summary 1.

151. Kalshoven, *supra* n. 4, at p. 42; Hampson, *supra* n. 35, at p. 49 (offering the same opinion, although Hampson seems to find bridges meet the threshold of military objective without undue analysis).

152. Draft Rules for the Limitation of the Dangers Incurred by the Civilian Population in Time of War, International Committee of the Red Cross 1956, reprinted in Schindler and Toman, *supra* n. 13, page? The annex referred to in Art. 7 of the 1956 ICRC Draft Rules is reprinted in the ICRC Com-

connecting Iraqi military forces with logistical support centres'.[153] NATO's attacks on Serbia's infrastructure, specifically including bridges, 'degraded the ability of the FRY military to perform command and control and to resupply or reconstitute its forces',[154] thus providing the requisite definite military advantage.

In many senses, militaries are systems of systems. There are built in redundancies and deliberate synergistic relations are created. These links and connections apply within the military and can apply between the military and its supporting civil society. By way of example, the military may have an actual back up plan or at least a ready capability to use the civilian telephone or television system if its own communications are destroyed. Military units far from the battle and apparently of no immediate military utility may be part of a reserve. Depriving the enemy of the ability to move such reserves apparently unconnected to any immediate concrete and direct military advantage by destroying bridges (or even delaying them by destroying only some bridges) deprives the enemy of potentially valuable options and flexibility. In arguing for excessively strict definitions of military objective, many critics ignore these effects. A modicum of analysis reveals that such redundant resources, military or civilian, do make an effective contribution to military action and their destruction can offer the requisite definite or even concrete and direct military advantage.

As Dinstein points out, bridges qualify under at least three if not all four of the initial criteria for a military objective under Article 52(2) of Additional Protocol I, being: nature; location; purpose; and use making an effective contribution to military action.[155] His conclusion that 'bridges are among the clearest of military targets' seems only logical.[156] Even if bridges are not automatic military objectives, there is a strong presumption that bridges are military objectives absent an unusual fact pattern. These conclusions are supported by the absence of questioning of the status of bridges as military objectives by Middle East Watch and the ICTY Committee despite this issue being raised with both.[157]

---

mentary, *supra* n. 9, para. 2002 n. 3. The term 1956 ICRC Draft Rules used hereafter in this article refers to the annex to those rules.

153. US DoD, Conduct of the Persian Gulf Conflict: An Interim Report to Congress 4-2 (July 1991).

154. Press Release, US DoD, Joint Statement on the Kosovo After Action Review, (14 October 1999), <http://www.defenselink.mil/news/Oct1999/b10141999_bt478-99.html>.

155. Dinstein, *supra* n. 16, at p. 15.

156. Y. Dinstein, 'The Thirteenth Waldemar A. Solf Lecture in International Law', 166 *Mil. LR* (2000) pp. 93, 107 . Professor Dinstein's opinion is reflected in the public's intuitive acceptance of bridges as legitimate targets as witnessed by a series movies accepting the military importance of bridges: The Bridge over the River Kwai (Columbia Pictures 1957); A Bridge Too Far (United Artists 1977); The Bridge at Remagen (United Artists 1969); The Bridges at Toko-Ri (Paramount Pictures 1955).

157. Needless Deaths, *supra* n. 68, at pp. 8-14; ICTY Committee Report, *supra* n. 13, para. 6 (citing both Civilian Deaths, *supra* n. 126, Collateral Damage, *supra* n. 87 raising this issue but not dealing with it in the ICTY Committee analysis of military target paras. 35-47).

Critics of targeting bridges are also concerned about the direct, and to a lesser extent, the longer-term collateral damage.[158] Middle East Watch criticised 1991 strikes against Iraqi bridges only in the context of the timing of the attacks. It believed that daylight bombing increased the number of civilians killed during the attacks.[159] Likewise, Amnesty International was more concerned about the civilians killed during the attacks on Serbian bridges than questioning the attacks on the bridges *per se*.[160] As argued above, bridges are generally military objectives. Thus, the concern in most cases is collateral damage. This conclusion is buttressed by the nature of the concerns expressed by Middle East Watch et al. These concerns imply that the less incidental civilian damage caused in striking any given bridge, the more likely the bridge was to be a lawful target. However, certain commentators do argue for a strict interpretation of military objective in relation to bridges.[161] Thus, this issue evidences a decreased tolerance for collateral damage and a concurrent tendency to reduce the scope of military objective. Therefore, it indicates a complementary dynamic between collateral damage and military objective.

5.7 Retreating forces

There is no legal controversy regarding the legitimacy of attacking a retreating enemy. Retreating enemy forces, absent surrender or being otherwise *hors de combat*, are clearly lawful targets. The primary incident that brought out this legal non-controversy was the Coalition attacks at the end of the 1991 Gulf War on Iraqi forces retreating from Kuwait along the road to Basra.[162]

This controversy is interesting in that it is from such non-legal, non-military motivations, that other law of armed conflict norms have on occasion emerged. Prohibitions on poison, chemical warfare, lasers and anti-personnel landmines are examples of such norms. This concern also evidences a potential resurrection of some notion of chivalry.

This incident gave rise to a suggestion that 'soldiers retreating in disarray – as epitomized by the Iraqi land forces during the 1991 Gulf War ... should not be further attacked'.[163] Hampson, while conceding the complete lawfulness of such targets, questions the wisdom and morality of such 'turkey shoots'.[164] Recognising the practical difficulties, she suggests a new principle, being that of targeting in the context of war aims to deal with such situations.[165]

---

158. Some concern has been expressed about targeting bridges as such apparently aside from collateral damage issues. See Egorov, *supra* n. 9, at p. 185; Bring, *supra* n. 9, at pp. 3-4; Bothe, *supra* n. 21, para. 3.

159. Needless Deaths, *supra* n. 68, at pp. 4-5.

160. See e.g., Collateral Damage, *supra* n. 87, at pp. 2-3; see also Civilian Deaths, *supra* n. 126, at p. 5.

161. Bring, *supra* n. 9, at pp. 3-4.

162. Hampson, *supra* n. 35, at pp. 53-54.

163. Dinstein, *supra* n. 16, at p. 18.

164. Hampson, *supra* n. 9, at p. 107; Hampson, *supra* n. 35, at pp. 53-54.

165. Hampson, *supra* n. 9, at p. 107; see also *infra* Section 5.10.

It is noteworthy that United States authorities while strongly, and in legal terms very convincingly, defending the attacks on the retreating Iraqis sounded somewhat defensive. They mentioned their warnings to Iraqi soldiers 'that their tanks and other vehicles were subject to attack, but that Iraqi soldiers would not be attacked if they abandoned their vehicles'.[166] They referred to their attempts to minimise Iraqi military casualties. The law of war requires neither warnings to the enemy military nor minimisation of enemy military casualties. These explanations implicitly recognised that factors other than those related to current law of armed conflict norms were at play.

The issue of the appropriateness of attacking military forces retreating in disarray is a subset of the public's decreased tolerance of casualties unrelated to obvious military benefit. This controversy indicates that, to some, even military casualties are acceptable only if linked to very immediate and concrete military advantage. The public uneasiness with seemingly needless enemy combatant casualties implies there is a clearly complementary dynamic between military objective and the public's view of acceptable collateral damage. Both the level of acceptable collateral damage and the range of acceptable military objectives are shrinking in the views of those so concerned.

5.8 **Listing military objectives**

The current definition of military objective in both customary international law and in the treaty is a generic one. No lists or even examples are given. It is an abstract concept that users, in theory at least, must apply to every proposed target. As Kalshoven says, this means targeters must not rely 'exclusively on abstract categorizations in the determination of whether specific objects constitute military objectives'.[167]

Some critics of the current definition of military objective believe this definition is too subjective and leaves too much discretion to the military personnel making the targeting decisions. Other critics feel that the current definition is too unclear, offers inadequate guidance and leads only to controversy and the injection of non-legal and non-military considerations. One possible solution for both groups of critics is to move from an abstract generic definition to a more concrete listing of legitimate military objectives.

The 1923 Hague Air Rules attempted to formulate a comprehensive list of military objectives in the context of aerial bombardment.[168] The exclusive listing never became effective in the sense of being considered exhaustive. It was thought to be too restrictive.[169] The desire for more precision and certainty continued with the

166. Final Report, *supra* n. 98, app. at O-34.

167. F. Kalshoven, 'Reaffirmation and Development of International Humanitarian Law Applicable in Armed Conflicts: The Diplomatic Conference, Geneva, 1974-1977, Part II, 9 *NYIL* (1978) pp. 107, 111.

168. 1923 Hague Air Rules, *supra* n. 19, Art. 24 (2).

169. Fleck, *supra* n. 38, at p. 46.

1954 Hague Convention on Cultural Property[170] and the 1956 ICRC Draft Rules.[171] Significantly, this was not the approach taken by the drafters of Protocol I. Their rejection of such a list-definition in favour of a generic description is strong evidence that a list of military objectives was either not practical or not desirable.[172] However, the drive for more precision continued. In the drafting of the 1994 *San Remo Manual on International Law Applicable to Armed Conflicts at Sea* (San Remo Naval Manual), the merits of the two types of definitions were debated and a combination definition was finally used.[173]

Professor Dinstein has also proposed a list of military objectives. He finds 'Article 52 (2)'s definition leaves a lot to be desired. Its language is abstract and generic, and no list of specific military objectives is provided (if only on an illustrative, non-exhaustive, basis). ... The text lends itself to "divergent interpretations".'[174] He believes that only 'an abstract statement with a non-exhaustive catalogue of concrete illustrations – can effectively avoid vagueness'.[175] On another occasion, he elaborated that 'no abstract definition of military targets can be fully satisfactory without an accompanying (and agreed upon) list itemising at least prime objectives laid bare to attack'.[176] He admits this is an ambitious task. 'A useful list of military targets must be quite elaborate, but ... it should leave a margin of appreciation for the commander on the spot.'[177]

The pressure to list military objectives is going to have a tendency to decrease the number of military objectives or at least prevent any expansion of the range of military objectives. Proponents of such an initiative may deny this. They may even advocate listing as a way to preserve discretion to target militarily relevant objects.[178] However, even when the proposed list includes a general definition and is expressly non-exhaustive, the practical effect will be to tend to limit the permitted targets to those specified. Any targeting outside the specified list will require an extra justification, and critics will argue that anything not obvious enough to be listed should not be considered a target. Such lists, being extremely controversial, will not be readily revised and will tend to become out-dated. Inclusion or exclusion on the list will inevitably involve considerations of how much danger to the civilian population will result from targeting such objects.

---

170. Convention for the Protection of Cultural Property in the Event of Armed Conflict, The Hague, 14 May 1954, Art. 8(1)(a), reprinted in Schindler and Toman, *supra* n. 13, p. 741.

171. 1956 ICRC Draft Rules, *supra* n. 152.

172. A review of the relevant portions of the ICRC Commentary, *supra* n. 9, paras. 1994-2038, and Bothe, *supra* n. 21, at pp. 318-327, fails to reveal any consideration of a listing of specific military objectives. Likewise, H.S. Levie, *Protection of War Victims: Protocol 1 to the 1949 Geneva Conventions* (Dobbs Ferry NY, Oceana Publications 1980) pp. 176-194 is silent in this regard save for a single suggestion that 'it might be useful to supply a list of examples of military objectives which, though not exhaustive, might serve as a guide to those concerned'.

173. Fleck, *supra* n. 38, at pp. 48-49.

174. Dinstein, *supra* n. 16, at p. 4.

175. Ibid., (citation omitted).

176. Dinstein, *supra* n. 67, at p. 5.

177. Ibid.

178. See Dinstein, *supra* n. 156, at p. 107.

Thus, this proposal implies a complementary dynamic between military objective and proportionality, i.e., the same pressures at work to decrease the lawful range of military objectives will be at work to decrease the quantum of acceptable collateral damage. The same complementary dynamic is evident even if this initiative should result in an increased range of lawful military objectives. As that range grows, an increase in acceptable collateral damage will have to be accepted.

5.9 Partial abandonment of the military connection in military objective

Brigadier General Dunlap has proposed a radical change in targeting. He suggests a 'revolutionary re-interpretation of 'military objective' so as to de-link the now required nexus to a contribution to a specific military action, and to explicitly include those civilian objects whose loss weakens the nation's collective will to continue the conflict'.[179] While still protecting those objects necessary for the civilian population's physical survival, he suggests that other 'personal property of the sentient, adult population' and 'things such as banks and financial institutions. Factories, plants, stores, and shops that produce, sell, or distribute luxury products' become lawful targets.[180] The motivation of the proposal is consistent with the very basic purpose of the law of war, i.e., how can a state impose its political-military will on its opponent with a minimum of true human suffering.

Brigadier General Dunlap's proposal to dramatically increase the range of lawful military objectives demonstrates a clearly complementary dynamic between military objective and the collateral damage aspect of proportionality. This proposal accepts a much greater range of lawful targets and lawful civilian effects than the current legal regime. Indeed, the change proposed intends to cause these wider, albeit non-lethal, civilian effects.

5.10 Military objectives in the context of explicit war aims

Françoise Hampson has proposed the addition of a new element in the definition of military objective. It would impose a mixed functional/proportionality test. The proposed additional requirement is that 'the destruction etc. of the objective is necessary to the achievement of the war aim'.[181] In another forum she said:

> '[W]hat is needed is a qualification to the definition of military objectives. Either it should require the likely cumulative effect on the civilian population of attacks against such targets be taken into account, or the same result might be achieved by requiring that the destruction of the object offers a definite military advantage in the context of the war aim.'[182]

---

179. Dunlap, *supra* n. 51, at p. 17.
180. Ibid., at p. 14.
181. Hampson, *supra* n. 35, at p. 51.
182. Hampson, *supra* n. 9, at p. 100.

This new element would apply to civilians, civilian objects or military personnel.[183] It would be a restrictive extra criteria to avoid the obviously detrimental effects of making legitimate any objective simply because it advanced a party's war aims.

Hampson intended this new rule to address the sorts of problems she saw with the onerous effects on the Iraqi people of the Coalition's destruction, albeit lawful, of Iraq's electrical supply system during the 1991 Gulf War. She also saw it limiting what were, in her view, unnecessary casualties visited on Iraqi armed forces by some of the Coalition's 1991 attacks.[184]

The proposal to require an additional element in the targeting process so that the targets' destruction is necessary in the context of the attacker's war aims is expressly designed to limit collateral damage. In itself, and particularly when married with Hampson's related proposal to integrate an element of collateral damage into the definition of military objective, this will also have the effect of substantially narrowing the definition of military objective. Thus, it demonstrates a complementary dynamic between military objective and incidental civilian losses, i.e., acceptable collateral damage is decreased and the acceptable range of military objectives tends to decrease. Indeed, this proposal demonstrates an even more dramatic complementary dynamic between these concepts, in that it could effectively expand the term collateral damage to encompass certain enemy combatants, i.e., those whose destruction did not directly advance the attacker's war aim.

5.11 Addition to the 1981 Conventional Weapons Convention

Peter Rowe has proposed an addition to the 1981 Conventional Weapons Convention to protect concentrations of civilians from air-delivered PGM:

> 'It is prohibited to make any military objective located within a concentration of civilians the object of attack, except when such military objective is clearly separated from the concentration of civilians, and all feasible precautions are taken with a view to limiting the effects of the attack to the military objective and to avoiding, and in any event to minimizing, incidental loss of civilian life, injury to civilians and damage to civilian objects.'[185]

This would impose a threshold burden not any balancing requirement. He intends all feasible precautions to include consideration of: weapon malfunction, tactics such as the height at which the attack is carried out, attacker air crew risk not automatically taking priority over incidental civilian losses, and the effect of defensive measures. Arguably, this is a more onerous burden for attackers than the current law in Protocol I.

---

183. Ibid., at p. 107.
184. Fenrick, *supra* n. 63, at p. 544 (alluding to this proposal).
185. Rowe, *supra* n. 77, at p. 162.

Rowe's proposal is expressly designed to protect civilians.[186] Targeters are to explicitly apply its protections before any balancing of proportionality factors. It is a proposed additional precaution in the attack. Thus, its effect is to exclude certain objects from the range of lawful military objectives before any consideration of proportionality. It thus exhibits a tendency to narrow the range of military objectives and decrease the level of acceptable incidental civilian losses, i.e., it indicates a complementary dynamic between the concept of military objective and collateral damage.

5.12 **Increased use of PGM**

The vastly increased use of PGM has the general effect of reducing collateral damage. Indeed, PGM might be credited with the historically low levels of incidental civilian losses in the conflicts referred to in this article.[187] At the same time, the use of PGM may have a tendency to increase the range and scope of things that will be considered lawful military objectives. If certain decision-makers feel they may be able to destroy a civilian object with no or little civilian death or injury, they may be tempted to ignore traditional distinction criteria at least as that doctrine relates to objects. Certainly, the use of PGM will not in itself restrict the range or scope of the concept of military objective. Thus, this development demonstrates a potentially inverse dynamic between military objective and incidental civilian loss, i.e., a possible increase in the scope of military objective is made more acceptable by the decrease in collateral damage.

5.13 **Summary of conclusions as to relationship revealed by dynamics**

My conclusions as to the dynamics of military objective and incidental civilian losses can be summarised in the following chart.

The overall conclusion about the dynamic between military objective and incidental civilian losses that can be drawn from examining these controversies and proposals is that there is a general but sporadic tendency for these two terms to have a complementary dynamic. The tenuous nature of the relationship is confirmed by the 12 situations examined. Eight exhibited a complementary or strongly complementary dynamic. In three cases the dynamic could not be determined and, in the final situation, a potentially inverse dynamic was detected between military objective and collateral damage.

Thus, the dynamic of military objective and collateral damage as determined by this examination of a representative sample of current proposals and controversies confirms the analysis of the inherent nature of the relationship discussed in Section 4.2.

186. Ibid., at p. 161.

187. Fenrick, *supra* n. 45, at p. 65 (using the figures in Parks, *supra* n. 10, at p. 154 plus his own from Operation Allied Force to demonstrate a general dramatic downward trend in deaths per ton of bombs dropped from 1937 to 1999).

	LOAC Issue	Tendency Effect on Collateral Damage	Tendency Effect on Range of Military Objectives	Type of Dynamic Implied
5.2	General public concern for collateral damage	Decreased	Increased or decreased	?
5.3	Military objective: customary – conventional difference	Unknown	Increased	?
5.4	Proportionality: customary – onventional difference	Possibly Increased	Unknown	?
5.5	Civilian morale	Considered with Electrical Systems and Media Outlets		
5.5.1	Electrical xystems	Decreased	Decreased	Complementary
5.5.2	Media outlets	Increased / Decreased	Increased / Decreased	Complementary
5.6	Bridges	Decreased	Decreased	Complementary
5.7	Retreating forces	Decreased	Decreased	Strongly Complementary
5.8	Listing military objectives	Possibly decreased / increased	Decreased / Increased	Complementary
5.9	Partial abandonment of military connection	Increased	Increased	Complementary
5.10	Military objectives in context of war aims	Decreased	Decreased	Strongly complementary
5.11	Addition to 1981 CWC	Decreased	Possibly decreased	Complementary
5.12	PGM trend	Decreased	Possibly increased	Potentially inverse

6. IMPLICATIONS OF RELATIONSHIP OF MILITARY OBJECTIVE TO COLLATERAL DAMAGE/PROPORTIONALITY

The relationship between military objective and incidental civilian losses is mediated by the common element of military advantage. This strongly implies that for the most part the decision-makers in this regard must be military commanders or at least military personnel. The determination of military objective requires an ability to recognise military advantage. This is obvious. What is somewhat less obvious is that proportionality also requires an ability to recognise and value military advantage because it is military advantage ('the concrete and direct military advantage anticipated') that must be weighed against the expected civilian losses.

Certainly, these decisions can sometimes be so critical that non-military persons might play some role before, during and after the targeting process. However, such non-military persons should have a reasonable appreciation of the military factors if their input or review is to be of real value. This conclusion accords with the basic purpose of the law of war outlined at the beginning of this article that set out a fundamental balancing of military and humanitarian factors. Anyone seriously interested in applying or analysing the law of armed conflict must properly consider both its military and humanitarian dimensions. Such balancing is specifically required in the proportionality calculus.

The general practical necessity for military targeting decision-makers has led most commentators to assess the legality of various law of armed conflict decisions from the point of view of the 'reasonable military commander'.[188] However, does not an emphasis on military decision-making risk upsetting the required balance in the law of war between military factors and humanity in favour of the former? It might, unless the central place of morality in the law of armed conflict is recognised. Fortunately, such recognition is long standing. One example is found in the 1863 Lieber Code. 'Men who take up arms against one another in public war do not cease on this account to be moral beings, responsible to one another and to God.'[189] In more modern times, '[t]here is in other words a moral basis for the rules of war.'[190] and '[i]t must never be forgotten that the law of war ... began mainly as a matter of religion and ethics.'[191] Thus, the law of war's role is to 'reinforce and particularize individual morality'.[192] This is what is behind various commentators' exhortations to good faith application of the rules. Calls for good faith are essentially appeals to the individual morality of those charged with making critical law of war decisions.

---

188. ICTY Committee Report, *supra* n. 13, para. 50; Fenrick, *supra* n. 63, at p. 5; Fenrick, *supra* n. 45, at p. 75. However, at least one commentator takes some issue with this standard. M. Bothe, 'The Protection of the Civilian Population and NATO Bombing on Yugoslavia: Comments on a Report to the Prosecutor of the ICTY', 12 *EJIL* (2001) pp. 531, 535. In Bothe's opinion, such a military decision maker must be defined in 'civilian terms' which he expressly assumes is democratic. He says these military decision makers should reflect societal civilian norms. He assumes this would produce decisions that are more humane. This view might be superficially attractive to some. However, it ignores the situation of military decision makers in non-democratic regimes. Obviously, the law of armed conflict aspires to universality. As such, it must be applicable across a range of political systems. It is unrealistic to expect military decision-makers in autocratic regimes to reflect democratic norms. The non-democratic leadership of those military decision makers likely would not support such democratically informed choices. A better, i.e., more universal basis for such decisions is one premised upon a basic individual moral code grounded in the law of war. It is a more practical guide across a broader spectrum of societies with varying degrees of democratic values.

189. General Orders No. 100 (Lieber Code), Art. 15, reprinted in Schindler and Toman, *supra* n. 10, p. 6.

190. T. Nagel, 'War and Massacre', 1 *Philosophy & Public Affairs* (1972) p. 123

191. Geoffrey Best, *War and Law Since 1945* (Oxford, Clarendon Press 1994) p. 289.

192. Fenrick, *supra* n. 63, at p. 18.

This means that military commanders making targeting and other law of war decisions must be moral human beings. Many of the most difficult targeting decisions, i.e., proportionality, will require a decision that is in essence a moral one. This implies that military commanders should be selected, at least in part, for their moral sense. The callous and self-serving should not be selected for advancement. The 'hard-nosed' should be scrutinised to ensure that their firmness of mind is properly based. Those without an adequate moral base will not have the tools with which to make proper law of war decisions (or indeed many other non-law of war decisions required of such leaders). Technical ability, even mastery of the legal rules, will be insufficient. This moral requirement also implies that training for military officers, including senior officers, should include studies in ethics and morality. Advanced academic study for such officers should include the humanities and not simply the sciences and administration.

None of these recommendations, even in combination, will guarantee an ethical and moral officer corps capable of properly applying the laws of war. However, such initiatives will foster a group that is much more likely to comply with the laws of armed conflict. They will be more likely to recognise moral dilemmas and to have developed an ability to properly analyse and resolve them.

The phenomenon of civilian political leaders participating in at least certain targeting decisions is particularly problematic. This analysis indicates that such individuals must have at least some familiarity with the 'military art'. An appreciation of the law of armed conflict would also be important for politicians who might insert themselves in such decisions. NATO's political leaders,[193] presumably including American and certainly British government officials, involved themselves in some of the targeting decisions during the NATO bombing campaign against Serbia.[194] Such involvement, at least in sensitive cases, can be expected in the future. The risks involved with uneducated part-time potential targeters are great. '[T]here can be no nastier a militarist than a civilian one'.[195] Such officials have usually not devoted their professional lives to matters military. This combined with their perhaps over-sensitivity to short term political considerations could make for disastrous or illegal targeting decisions.

The relationship between military objective and incidental civilian losses is also a legal one. This fact of a legal relationship implies a need for the availability of legal advice. This is one of the reasons that Protocol I contains a requirement for the parties to that treaty to 'ensure that legal advisers are available, when necessary, to advise military commanders at the appropriate level on the application of the Conventions and this Protocol'.[196] Future trends are only likely to 'increase the importance of the role of legal advisers'.[197]

---

193. Press Release, *supra* n. 77.
194. Rowe, *supra* n. 77, at p. 157-158.
195. G. Best, *Humanity in Warfare* (New York, Columbia University Press 1980) p. 27.
196. Protocol I, *supra* n. 4, Art. 82.
197. Schmitt, *supra* n. 3, at p. 1087.

The role of legal advisers in the targeting process includes training and advising the appropriate military personnel.[198] Such advice may include the legal aspects of specific targeting decisions. On occasion, such advice will bring to the recipient's attention a wider scope of legal discretion than the recipient assumed he or she had. It is not unknown for operational personnel to think they face a legal constraint when in law no such constraint operates. In other circumstances, legal advisers can point out possible alternatives to legally accomplish the desired effect.

However, there will be times when the legal adviser's role will be to restrain the targeting decision-makers. One Canadian pilot flying in the NATO campaign against Serbia said: 'The pilots would push and the lawyers would hold us back.'[199] Legal constraints in NATO's bombing of Serbia resulted in very strict rules of engagement.[200] In 2001, during the United States bombing of Afghan targets, at least one legal adviser was reportedly required to exert such a moderating influence.[201] While remaining advocates, especially in public, legal advisers inside the targeting process must exhibit strength of personal and professional character to offer accurate, practical and, if the situation demands, firm counsel.[202]

While the role of legal adviser is important and occasionally critical, one must recognise the limitations of that advice. Legal advisers are just that, advisers. In most military systems they have no or very limited command authority. Legal considerations are often only one of many at play in any given targeting decision. In many of the subjective decisions required in the targeting process, the legal advisers' views may be no more and often less authoritative than the operational personnel's. Nevertheless, military legal advisers are often in an ideal position to properly navigate the laws of armed conflict given their dual status as lawyers and military personnel. This duality matches the twin nature of the law of war that is apparent even from its name being the 'law' of 'war'.

However, a fundamental limitation on the role legal advisers can play is simply the practical limits of law in warfare. 'Increasing the number of lawyers specializ-

---

198. F. Green, 'Remarks in a Panel on Implementing Limitations on the Use of Force: The Doctrine of Proportionality and Necessity', *Amer. Soc. Int'l L. Proc.* (1992) pp. 39, 64 (describing legal advisers' roles in the 1991 Gulf War); Final Report, *supra* n. 98, app. at O-3-O-4 (describing legal advisers' roles in the 1991 Gulf War); J.A. Burger, 'International Humanitarian Law and the Kosovo Crisis: Lessons Learned or to be Learned', 82 *IRRC* (2000) p. 129 (describing legal advisers' roles in the 1999 NATO Bombing of Serbia); T. Montgomery, 'Operation Allied Force Targeting: Perspective from the EUCOM Targeting Cell, in Colloquium, *supra* n. 9, p. 37 (describing legal advisers' roles in the 1999 NATO Bombing of Serbia); Ignatieff, *supra* n. 120, at pp. 100-101 (describing legal advisers' roles in the 1999 NATO Bombing of Serbia); Ricks, *supra* n. 5 (describing anecdotally a legal adviser's role in the 2001 bombing of Afghanistan).

199. Wallace, *supra* n. 144, at p. 21.

200. Ignatieff, *supra* n. 120, at p. 101.

201. Ricks, *supra* n. 5 (stating: 'When clearance was sought, officials said, (the legal adviser) frequently would ask, "Are you sure?" When faced with that question, the officials said, (the commander) would then turn to his top intelligence officer … who tended to say they did not have total certainty about the target.'). Remarkably, the tenor of the article was somewhat critical of the legal officer. Any targeting process that cannot withstand the scrutiny of a simple question, 'Are you sure?' is not worthy of a military professional.

202. Fleck, *supra* n. 38, pp. 63-64.

ing in a subject does not necessarily mean that more heed will be given to humanitarian values.'[203] Michael Ignatieff expresses a similar sensible scepticism. 'The real problem with the entry of lawyers into the prosecution of warfare is that it encourages the illusion that war is clean if the lawyers say so.'[204] Over-emphasis on legality ignores both the fundamentally violent nature of war and the fundamentally moral basis for international humanitarian law. Too much can be expected of the law. While the 'Western military's response to sharpened moral and political exposure has been to call in the lawyers',[205] the law and lawyers can seldom provide the moral or political comfort sought.

This examination of the inherent and other relationship indicia between military objective and collateral damage reveals a basically complementary dynamic. This makes sense given the common element of military advantage. The greater the military advantage an object represents the more likely it is to be a target and the more collateral damage it will legally justify, assuming such collateral damage is unavoidable. Certainly, the military objective assessment is based on a threshold test and the proportionality calculus is a balancing but the tendency for the two terms to move in tandem remains.

This dynamic is logical but does have within it some potential dangers. Objects of great military advantage might well justify considerable incidental civilian losses. However, there is a danger that targeters seeing an opportunity to achieve a great military advantage will ignore, downplay or give insufficient weight to collateral damage concerns.[206] Such a danger is heightened when time pressures mount. The quite legitimate military utility in reducing targeting decision times is exactly the sort of pressure that will increase this danger. The solution to the danger posed by under-emphasising incidental civilian losses due to the temptingly high value of certain military objectives is to rigidly adhere to the two-phase legal targeting scheme suggested earlier. All targeting opportunities must be analysed by asking at least these two separate questions: Is the target a military objective? And if collateral damage is unavoidable, is there an unacceptable risk of disproportionate incidental civilian losses?

As noted above, the combined effect of the various modifying factors is to render the complementary dynamic between military objective and incidental civilian losses somewhat indirect and sporadic. The weakness of this relationship means that there will on occasion be pressure to adopt an inverse dynamic between military objective and incidental civilian losses. An example of such pressure is the temptation to strike an object that is not a military object, e.g., a civilian morale target such as a television studio just because there is no or limited collateral damage anticipated.[207] These pressures should be resisted. Not only is it legally

203. Fenrick, *supra* n. 45, at p. 80.

204. Ignatieff, *supra* n. 120, at p. 200. See generally ibid., at pp. 197-200 (describing 'The Legal War' aspect of NATO's 1999 bombing).

205. Ibid., at p. 197.

206. Rowe, *supra* n. 77, at p. 160.

207. Transmission facilities are a different issue. See *supra* Section 5.5.2.

wrong,[208] it risks a gradual or not so gradual erosion of the bedrock law of war principle, i.e., that of distinction. Artificial or not on occasion, victory delaying or not on occasion, the bright line rule of distinction is of such a critical nature that any weakening of its authority must be resisted.

7. CONCLUSION

Different concepts in the law of armed conflict may be connected to each other in unexpected ways. Even if the relationship between concepts is obvious, the mechanism effecting the relationship may not be readily apparent or may operate in a significant manner. In addition, there may be potentially significant implications arising from the relationships of different concepts, the mechanisms affecting the relationships or the dynamics of these relationships.

The academic and intellectual discipline surrounding the law of armed conflict can be somewhat sterile. Much of the debate in this area is inconclusive. The law of armed conflict would benefit greatly if attempts to find more objective criteria and methodologies upon which to settle or at least advance the debate of issues inherent in this important and controversial field were successful.

Regarding the specific concepts examined in this article, the concept of military objective in conventional international law is set out in Article 52(2) of Protocol I. That definition involves a two stage test requiring that an object by its nature, location, purpose or use make an effective contribution to military action and, separately, that the destruction, capture or neutralisation of the object offer a definite military advantage in the circumstance ruling at the time. The customary international law definition of military objective has become the same as the treaty-based one.

The conventional international law definition of (dis)proportionality is found in three places in Protocol I, being Articles 51(5)(b), 57(2)(a)(iii) and 57(2)(b). It requires a balancing of expected civilian losses against anticipated military advantage. The customary international law definition of proportionality may be somewhat different but the effects of any such difference are negligible.

The inherent linkage between these two terms implies a complementary dynamic between military objective and collateral damage. That linkage is 'military advantage'. Because of various modifying factors, including the adjectives used, the time periods considered, the nature of the assessments and the degree of subjectivity, this linkage tends to be indirect and sporadic. The dynamics of the possible customary international law variations from the treaty-based terms, plus various other controversies, initiatives and proposals, confirms the very general but not universal complementary dynamic between military objective and the collateral damage part of proportionality.

---

208. ICRC Commentary, *supra* n. 9, para. 1979; Kalshoven, *supra* n. 4, p. 41; Hampson, *supra* n. 35, at p. 49 (stating 'the mere fact that an attack against a particular target does not cause excessive civilian casualties does not mean that the attack was lawful').

The major implications of this relationship are that military expertise is generally required to make targeting decisions and there are dangers in ignoring this. However, the central role of morality in such military decisions can never be neglected and indeed must be fostered. Pressures to adopt any weapon, target, strategy or tactic based on an inverse dynamic should be resisted. Such developments are dangerous because of the peril they pose for the civilian population through a diminution of the fundamental law of armed conflict principle of distinction.

APPLYING THE RULE OF PROPORTIONALITY: FORCE PROTECTION AND CUMULATIVE ASSESSMENT IN INTERNATIONAL LAW AND MORALITY[1]

Noam Neuman[2]

Our current obsession with zero casualties leads to ludicrous results like a joint force commander starting in the first sentence of his commander's intent 'Force protection is my top priority,' or a senior commander telling the assembled officers of his several multinational flying squadrons, 'There's not one thing here worth dying for.'[3]

---

2. Lieutenant Colonel Noam Neuman is Head of the Security and Foreign Relations Branch, International Law Department, Military Advocate General's Corps, Israel Defense Forces. LL.M., 2004, the Judge Advocate General's Legal Center and School, U.S. Army; M.A. Philosophy (with honours), 2000, Bar-Ilan University, Ramat-Gan, Israel; LL.B 1994, Bar-Ilan University, Ramat-Gan, Israel. The opinions and conclusions in this paper do not necessarily represent the views of the IDF or the Government of Israel. I would like to thank Major Derek Grimes, USAF and Mr Roy Schondorf, JSD candidate, New York University School of Law, for their comments on an earlier draft.

3. Lieutenant Colonel Jeffery K. Walker, 'The demise of the nation-state, the dawn of new paradigm warfare, and a future for the profession of arms', 51 *Air Force LR* (2001) pp. 323, 336.

Yearbook of International Humanitarian Law
Volume 7 - 2004 - pp. 79-112 DOI 10.1017/S1389135904000790

1. INTRODUCTION

After a wave of Palestinian terror attacks directed against Israeli civilians, in which hundreds of them were murdered,[4] Israel launched Operation 'Defensive Shield'. The operation was launched on 29 March 2002 in order to eradicate the Palestinian terrorist infrastructure and prevent further terrorist attacks.[5] In the context of this operation, on 3 April 2002 the Israel Defence Forces (IDF) entered the refugee camp of Jenin, 'the capital of the suicide bombers',[6] from which a terror infrastructure – unprecedented in scope – had perpetrated a large number of terror attacks.[7] It soon became obvious that the Palestinian militants intended to defend the refugee camp using every means they had.[8] These conditions created a real dilemma for the IDF – which approach should be selected to fight the enemy, considering the required mission, the safety of the soldiers and the need to minimise injury to innocent civilians?[9]

The planners of 'Defensive Shield' decided to use infantry forces that would progress through the camp in a gradual and cautious manner on a house-to-house basis.[10] The planners knew that there were other modes of military action that could have accomplished the mission more expediently and with minimal risk for the soldiers' lives – such as the use of aircraft or artillery.[11] However, these alternatives were rejected because of the desire to minimise collateral damage among the civilian population.[12]

The IDF infantry forces that entered Jenin encountered harsh resistance from militants, who used all available means to fight the IDF. These means included

---

4. This wave of Palestinian terror attacks began in September 2000, and grew in severity, reaching a peak in March 2002. During the latter month, 780 terrorist attacks were perpetrated in which 135 Israelis were killed and another 670 were injured. See The Battle in Jenin, the Israel Defense Forces response to the report by Amnesty International 2002 (on file with the author) at p. 5. See also HCJ 3278/02, *The Center for the Defense of the Individual* v. *Commander of the IDF forces in the West Bank*: 'Beginning in September of 2000, there was an increase in Palestinian terrorist activity against the Jewish community in Judea and Samaria, the Gaza Strip, and within Israel itself. Hundreds were killed and died … Terrorist activity intensified in the beginning of 2002. In March of that year there was an increase of Palestinian terrorist activity. Approximately one hundred and twenty Israeli civilians were killed and hundreds were wounded.' <http://elyon1.court.gov.il/files_eng/02/780/032/a06/02032780.a06.pdf>.

5. See HCJ 3278/02, ibid.: 'In response to the terrorist activity, the government decided, on 29.03.2002, to carry out a large-scale military operation. The goal of the operation, Operation Defensive Wall, was to destroy the Palestinian terrorist infrastructure.'

6. A report of the Fatah, dated 25 September 2001, which the IDF seized during Operation Defensive Shield, stated: '[the Jenin refugee camp] is characterized by an outstanding presence of young fighters and provocateurs working [for] the national activity. Nothing will overcome them and nothing worries them. Therefore, it is not strange, that Jenin [is called] the capital of the suicide bombers.' See The Battle in Jenin, *supra* n. 4, at p. 6.

7. Ibid.

8. See *infra* n. 14.

9. The Battle in Jenin, *supra* n. 4, at p. 9.

10. Ibid.

11. Ibid.

12. Ibid.

operating from civilian houses and using innocent Palestinian civilians as human shields.[13] Additionally, the terrorists planted thousands of booby-traps and explosive charges all over the refugee camp[14] and used ambulances to execute terrorist activities.[15]

During the later stages of the battle, after the fighting had become drawn out and inflicted a heavy price on the IDF, the commanders increased the use of bulldozers in those areas where fighting was most difficult. Once again, the means chosen were designed to minimise the possibility of causing harm to civilians.[16]

The fighting in Jenin inflicted a heavy death toll upon the IDF – 23 soldiers were killed. The loss set forth a flurry of emotions in Israel regarding the question of whether it was justified to risk the soldiers' lives in order to minimise the possibility of injuring innocent Palestinian civilians.

This battle illustrates one of the most central legal and moral dilemmas a commander has to face during modern armed conflicts. It forms a backdrop of reality against which the foreground of the law should be viewed when trying to assess the meaning and effectiveness of the law of armed conflict[17] in general and the rule of proportionality in particular.[18]

---

13. Ibid, pp. 17-18.

14. Ramadan Shelah, the Secretary General of the Palestinian Islamic Jihad, said in an interview to the Al-Khieyat daily on 4 April 2002: 'The mujahadeen in Jenin prepared themselves ... and they prepared large amounts of explosives ... [the fighters] places explosive charges in different places in the streets, such as in dustbins and cars ... They placed booby traps in their houses ... on the doors or inside, even in the furniture, in closets or even in the books ...' Ibid., p. 7.

15. Ibid., p. 1. See also HCJ 2936/02, *Physicians for Human Rights* v. *The Commander of the IDF forces in the West Bank*: 'The state claims, however, that this situation [free movement of ambulances in the context of Operation Defensive Shield] is the result of the fighting itself, in the context of which it became clear that in a number of cases explosives were transported via ambulances and wanted terrorists found shelter in hospitals.' <http://elyon1.court.gov.il/files_eng/02/360/029/l02/02029360.l02.pdf>.

16. The method was designed to minimise civilian casualties by calling on inhabitants to leave their houses, prior to entering them or using bulldozers. See The Battle in Jenin, *supra* n. 4, at p. 59. In a petition to the Supreme Court of Israel, the petitioners argued that a massacre had taken place in the Jenin refugee camp. Israeli authorities responded to the petition, explaining that it is impossible to talk of a 'massacre' in a situation in which Israel had made its best efforts to avoid causing harm to the innocent by choosing to fight from house-to-house and not by way of aerial bombardments. Indeed, the court held that '... massacre is one thing. A difficult battle is another'. See HC 3114/02, *Barake* v. *Minister of Defence and others*, <http://elyon1.court.gov.il/files_eng/02/140/031/a02/02031140.a02.pdf>.

17. In this paper I prefer to use the term 'law of armed conflict' instead of the term 'law of war', since the application of the law of armed conflict does not depend upon the recognition of the existence of a formal 'state of war' but comprehends situations of armed conflict. For this reason, many treaties concluded since the Second World War refer to 'armed conflict' rather than 'war'. See e.g., A. Roberts and R. Guelff, *Documents on the Law of War*, 3rd. edn. (Oxford, Oxford University Press 2000) p. 2; C. Greenwood, 'The concept of war in modern international law', 36 *ICLQ* (1987) pp. 208, 303-305; I. Detter, *The Law of War*, 2nd edn. (Cambridge, Cambridge University Press 2000) pp. 3-26.

18. Although the armed conflict in Jenin was not an 'international armed conflict', since an international armed conflict can only take place between states, Israel has characterised the war against the Palestinian terror as an 'armed conflict short of war'. Accordingly, Israel does apply the relevant provisions of the law of armed conflict, while interpreting them as appropriate for dealing with the

The law of armed conflict is concerned in part with the question of how to balance humanitarian concerns with the practical inevitabilities of warfare.[19] To do this, it accepts the possibility of collateral damage when military operations are directed against military objectives.[20] However, it also establishes the rule of proportionality, which prohibits such attacks if the collateral civilian damage is assessed to be excessive in relation to the anticipated military advantage to be gained from the attack.[21]

This paper explores two issues concerning the way the rule of proportionality should be applied during armed conflict. The paper first addresses the amount of risk the law of armed conflict expects a commander to take in order to decrease the risk to civilians.[22] The paper then addresses how to assess military advantage while applying the proportionality test – must the military advantage be assessed in relation to each individual attack, or can it be assessed on a cumulative basis, taking into account the contribution of the attack to the belligerent's overall strategy?[23]

The paper is divided into five parts. Part 2 starts with a historical background of the development of the rule of proportionality from the Christian theory of 'just war' to Additional Protocol I to the Geneva Conventions.[24] Part 2 then presents the role and the importance of the rule of proportionality in protecting the civilian population. Part 3 continues by analysing the relevant Protocol I provisions, based on the commentaries, the *travaux préparatoires* and scholars' writings. It argues that Protocol I does not require a commander to risk his soldiers' lives in order to

---

present type of conflict. See the response of the Government of the State of Israel to the report of the UN High Commissioner for Human Rights § 28 (29 November 2000), available at <http://www.mfa.gov.il/mfa/go.asp?mfah0jik0)>: 'Israel is engaged in an armed conflict short of war. This is not a civilian disturbance or a peaceful demonstration or a riot.' J.N. Kendall, 'Recent development: Israeli counter-terrorism: 'targeted killing' under international law', 80 *North Carolina LR* (2002) pp. 1069, 1069-1070, nn.3-6; HC 3451/02, *Almandi* v. *The Minister of Defense and Others*: 'Israel finds itself in the middle of difficult battle against a furious wave of terrorism ... This combat is not taking place in a normative void. It is being carried out according to the rules of international law, which provide principles and rules for combat activity.' <http://elyon1.court.gov.il/files_eng/02/510/034/a06/02034510.a06.pdf>.

19. See e.g., W.J. Fenrick, 'The rule of proportionality and Protocol I in conventional warfare', 98 *Mil. LR* (1982) pp. 91, 92.

20. In this paper, the term 'collateral damage' will be used in relation to the incidental loss of civilian life, injury to civilians, damage to civilian objects, or a combination thereof, when military operations are directed against military objectives. See Protocol Additional to the Geneva Conventions of 12 August 1949, and Relating to the Protection of Victims of International Armed Conflict (Protocol I), 8 June 1977, Arts. 51(5)(b), 57(2)(a)(iii), 1125 *UNTS.* 3-608, 16 *ILM* 1391-441 [hereinafter Protocol I], reprinted in D. Schindler and J. Toman, *The Laws of Armed Conflicts*, 3rd. edn., (Dordrecht, Nijhoff 1988) p. 621.

21. Protocol I, ibid., Arts. 51(5)(b), 57(2)(a)(iii).

22. In relation to the battle of Jenin, the issue is whether the IDF had a legal obligation to conduct a house-to house fight, despite the risk to the soldiers, or whether they could have used aircraft, artillery or bulldozers from the beginning.

23. In relation to the battle of Jenin, the question is whether the planners of the operation, while applying the proportionality test, could have taken into account the overall picture, to include considerations of whether the method used might prevent similar battles in the future. Or could they have taken into account only the anticipated direct result of each individual attack?

24. Protocol I, *supra* n. 20.

reduce civilian casualties. However, it is also submitted that it is possible to interpret Protocol I in a way that will establish such an obligation, in situations where a moral basis exists. Part 3 argues that the standard for measuring 'military advantage' in Protocol I is the advantage anticipated from the military campaign, of which the attack is part, as a whole, and not only from isolated or particular parts of that campaign or operation. Part 4 addresses the moral aspects of the rule of proportionality, and their possible implications. It is submitted that the moral arguments regarding the innocence of non-combatants, the obligation to spare them as much as possible, and the 'principle of double effect' underpin the rule of proportionality. Part 4 continues by analysing the moral aspects of the aforementioned issue, arguing that occasionally a commander has a moral duty to risk his soldiers in order to save civilians' lives. Morally, a cumulative analysis of military advantage should be preferred within a broader combination of both cumulative and case-by-case analyses. Part 5 concludes that 'military advantage' must be assessed within a broader combination of both the tactical aspects of the operation and the strategic aspects of the overall operational plan or war strategy.

2. THE ORIGINS OF THE PROPORTIONALITY DOCTRINE

The idea of proportionality was part of the Christian theory of Just War.[25] According to this theory, before starting a war, a state had to assess whether the overall evil the war would cause was balanced by the good that would be achieved. However, the emphasis of the theory was on the requirement of a just cause rather than on the manner in which the war would be conducted.[26] Moreover, there was no independent doctrine of the *jus in bello* of the type that exists in international law today.[27] Once the cause of a war was considered just, almost any methods or means used to win it were considered permissible.[28]

---

25. J.G. Gardam, 'Proportionality and force in international law', 87 *AJIL* (1993) pp. 391, 394-395; M.C. Bonafede, 'Here, there, and everywhere: assessing the proportionality doctrine and US uses of force in response to terrorism after the September 11 attacks', 88 *Cornell LR* (2002) pp. 155, 163-164. For full description of just war theory see Y. Melzer, *Concepts of Just War* (Leiden, Sijthoff 1975); P. Christopher, *The Ethics of War and Peace: An Introduction to Legal and Moral Issues*, 3rd edn. (Upper Saddle River NJ, Pearson Prentice Hall 2004) pp. 7-64.

26. Gardam, ibid., at p. 395. See also G. Van Damme and N. Fotion, 'Proportionality', in B. Coppieters and N. Fotion, eds., *Moral Constraints on War* (Lanham MD, Lexington 2002) pp. 129, 131, arguing that, as a principle, proportionality in the just war theory will be best applied in the extremes.

27. The *jus ad bellum* deals with the right of states to resort to force. The *jus in bello* deals with the conduct of war. See Detter, *supra* n. 17, at pp. 156-158; C. Greenwood, 'Jus ad bellum and jus in bello in the Nuclear Weapons Advisory Opinion', in L. Boisson de Chazournes and P.J. Sands, eds., *International Law, The International Court of Justice and Nuclear Weapon* (Cambridge, Cambridge University Press 1999) pp. 247-266; S.R. Ratner, 'Note and comment: jus ad bellum and jus in bello after September 11', 96 *AJIL* (2002) pp. 905, 905-906; Gardam, *supra* n. 25, at pp. 391-394; M. Sassoli and A.A. Bouvier, *How Does Law Protect in War?* (Geneva, ICRC 1999) pp. 83-85.

28. R.W. Stone, 'Protecting civilians during Operation Allied Force: The enduring importance of the proportionality response and NATO's use of armed force in Kosovo', 50 *Catholic Univ. LR* (2001) pp. 501, 506; Gardam, *supra* n. 25, at p. 395.

In the period of the Thirty Years War (1618-1648), one of the founding scholars of international law, Hugo Grotius, attempted to transform the Just War principles from a set of moral principles into positive international law.[29] In relation to *jus in bello*, Grotius' main contribution was in developing the distinction between combatants and non-combatants and the prohibition against harming non-combatants when there was no justification for such harm.[30] However, Grotius did not explicitly recognise the rule of proportionality in the *jus in bello* sense of the word.[31] In his analysis, proportionality remained a main component of the legal justification, in the *jus ad bellum* sense.[32] Even so, we can find seeds of this rule in his recognition that some civilian casualties must be tolerated as a consequence of military action,[33] and, in those circumstances, we must 'beware of what happens, and what we foresee may happen, beyond our purpose, unless the good which our action has in view is much greater than the evil which is feared, or, unless the good and the evil balance, the hope of good is much better than the fear of the evil'.[34]

In the nineteenth century, the Just War theory was abandoned for new theories[35] that emphasised the concept of war as an instrument of national policy.[36] Those

---

29. See B. Coppieters and B. Kashnikov, 'Right intentions', in Coppieters and Fotion, *supra* n. 26, at pp. 59, 64; E. Rindskopt Parker, 'Five wars of globalization: Comment on the Grotius lecture by Moises Naim', 18 *Amer. Univ. ILR* (2002) pp. 19, 19-20.

30. He also developed the hypothesis that the rules concerning the conduct of war binds all parties, regardless of the justice of a party's resort to war. See Hugo Grotius, *The Law of War and Peace 1625* (Indianapolis Bobbs-Merill 1925) p. 599: 'We have considered both those who wage war and on what grounds war may be waged. It follows that we should determine what is permissible in war, also to what extent, and in what ways, it is permissible;' B. Kingsbury and A. Roberts, 'Introduction: Grotian thought in international relations', in H. Bull, B. Kingsbury and A. Roberts, eds., *Hugo Grotius and International Relations* (Oxford, Clarendon 1992) pp. 1, 20-21.

31. Gardam, *supra* n. 25, at p. 396.

32. Ibid. See Christopher, *supra* n. 25, at pp. 82-91.

33. For example, 'we may bombard a ship full of pirates, or a house full of brigands, even if there are within the same ship or house a few infants, women, and other innocent persons who are thereby endangered'. See Grotius, *supra* n. 30, at p. 601.

34. Ibid.

35. However, even after that era, the just war theory was not totally abandoned. See e.g., J.Bethke Elshtain, 'Conference: The Third Annual Grotius Lecture: just war and humanitarian intervention', 17 *Amer. Univ. ILR* (2001) pp. 1, 14, arguing that Geneva Protocol I (1977) codifies just war thinking on civilian and nonmilitary targeting. We can also find in that era that leaders use just war argument to justify their actions. For instance, during the American Civil War, General Sherman ordered the forced evacuation and burning of Atlanta. When he was accused by General Hood that 'those measures transcend, in studied and ingenious cruelty, all acts ever before in the dark history of war,' he used just war arguments to support his actions, by saying that the war was entirely the crime of those who began it – the Confederate leaders, and therefore he can never be blamed for anything he did to bring victory. See M.L. Walzer, *Just and Unjust Wars: a moral argument with historical illustrations,* 3rd edn. (New York NY, Basic Books 2000) pp. 32-33. About the compliance of General Sherman's tactics with the law of war, see T.G. Robisch, 'General William T. Sherman: would the Georgia campaigns of the First Commander of the modern era comply with current law of war standards?', 9 *Emory ILR* (1995) p. 459, arguing that General Sherman would need to modify his tactics greatly in order to attain compliance with the current law of war.

36. The roots for this view may be found in Clausewitz's famous description of war as a continuation of politics by other means. See C. von Clausewitz, *On War* (1832) (Harmondsworth, Penguin 1968). However, later on international law reached the position where it outlaws war as such, as an

theories developed into the modern law of armed conflict, culminating in the adoption of the 1899 and 1907 Hague Conventions[37] and, later on, the 1949 Geneva Conventions.[38] This developing law of armed conflict was underpinned by three main principles. First, belligerents do not have an unlimited choice of means to achieve victory;[39] the only legitimate object which states should endeavour to accomplish during war is to weaken the military force of the enemy.[40] Second, international law protects the civilian population and civilian objects; soldiers are required to distinguish between combatants and non-combatants and between

---

instrument of international policy. The 1928 General Treaty for the Renunciation of War (Kellogg-Briand Pact) first reflected this position by condemning 'recourse to war for the solution of international controversies,' setting out various undertakings to renounce 'war as an instrument of national policy.' See Treaty Between the United States and Other Powers Providing for the Renunciation of War as an Instrument of National Policy, August 27, 1928, Art. 1, 46 stat. 2343, 2345, 94 *LNTS* 57, 59. This prohibition of threat or use of force was repeated in Art. 2(4) of the United Nations Charter. See UN Charter (enter into force 24 October 1945), Art. 2, para. 4 (stating that 'all members shall refrain ... from the threat or use of force against the territorial or political independence of any state.')

37. Convention with Certain Powers Respecting the Laws and Customs of War on Land, July 29, 1899, 32 stat. 1803 (1903), t.s. No. 403; Convention with Other Powers Respecting the Laws and Customs of War on Land, October 18, 1907, 36 stat. 2277, T.S. No. 539.

38. Geneva Conventions of 1949 for the Protection of War Victims, August 12, 1949, 6 *UST* 3114, 75 *UNTS* 3. For the treaties the Geneva Conventions consists of, see *infra* n. 54. Pictet divided the law of war into two branches: 'the law of the Hague,' which 'determines the rights and duties of belligerents in the conduct of operations and limits the choice of the means of doing harm,' and the 'law of Geneva,' which is 'intended to safeguard military personnel placed *hors de combat*, and persons not taking part in hostilities.' See J. Pictet, *Humanitarian Law and the Protection of War Victims* (Leiden, Sijthoff 1975) p. 31. See also Detter, *supra* n. 17, at pp. 158-159; H. Reinhold, 'Target lists: A 1923 idea with application for the future', 10 *Tulsa J Comp. & IL* (2002) pp. 1, 7-8.

39. This principle was first found at the Declaration Renouncing the Use, in Time of War, of Explosive Projectiles Under 400 Gram Weight, signed at St. Petersburg, 29 November/11 December, 1868 [hereinafter St. Petersburg Declaration], reprinted in Schindler and Toman, *supra* n. 20, at p. 101, and is the basis for many prohibitions in international law, such as the prohibition on weapons causing unnecessary suffering. See Gardam, *supra* n. 25, at pp. 395-397; Bonafede, *supra* n. 25, at p. 164; H. McCoubrey and N.D. White, *International Law and Armed Conflict* (Aldershot, Dartmouth 1992) pp. 209-223.

40. St. Petersburg Declaration, *supra* n. 39. This rule is often referred to as the principle of military necessity. According to this principle, a belligerent is justified in using force of any kind to the extent necessary for the realization of the purpose of war, which is the partial or complete submission of the enemy at the earliest possible moment. See Francis Lieber, Instructions for the Government of Armies of the U.S. in the field, issued as Gen. Orders No. 100 by Pres. Lincoln, 24 April 1863, Art. 14 [hereinafter Lieber Code], reprinted in Schindler and Toman, *supra* n. 20, at pp. 3-23; Detter, *supra* n. 17, at pp. 393-398; Reinhold, *supra* n. 38, at pp. 8-9.

military and civilian objects.[41] Third, it is prohibited to cause unnecessary suffering to combatants.[42]

During the nineteenth century, war was conducted mostly between professional armies, and the civilian population was not involved to a great extent.[43] Therefore, no general and consistent state practice existed in relation to the principle of proportionality.[44] Consequently, proportionality did not exist in that era as a norm of customary international law.[45] Likewise, state practice in World War I confirms that although some attempts were made by aircrews to avoid directly targeting civilians, in many cases bombardment was indiscriminate and attacks on military targets did not take collateral casualties into account.[46] Nevertheless, as armed con-

41. This rule is often referred to as the principle of discrimination. This principle is the most important restriction on damage to civilian and civilian property. One of the main provisions regarding this principle is Art. 23(g) to the Hague Convention No. IV, Convention Respecting the Laws and Customs of War on Land, opened for signature 18 October 1907, 36 stat. 2277 [hereinafter Hague Convention], reprinted in Schindler and Toman, *supra* n. 20, at 69, which states that 'it is especially forbidden to destroy or seize the enemy's property, unless such destruction or seizure be imperatively demanded by the necessities of war'. See also Lieber Code, *supra* n. 40, Arts. 19, 25, 35; Legality of the Use by a State of Nuclear Weapons in Armed Conflict, Advisory Opinion, 1996 *ICJ Rep.* 226 para. 78 (July 8) (response to request of UN General Assembly) [hereinafter GA Advisory Opinion on the Use of Nuclear Weapon]; Reinhold, *supra* n. 38, at pp. 8-9; A.P.V. Rogers, *Law on the Battlefield* (Manchester, Manchester University Press 1996) at pp. 7-9.

42. This rule is often referred to as the principle of unnecessary suffering. One of the main provisions regarding this principle is Art. 23(e) to the Hague Convention, *supra* n. 41, which states that 'it is especially forbidden to employ arms, projectiles, or material of a nature to cause superfluous injury'. See also GA Advisory Opinion on the Use of Nuclear Weapon, *supra* n. 41, para. 78.

43. See A.P. Higgins, *Non-Combatants and the War* (Oxford, Oxford University Press 1914) p. 15; Bonafede, *supra* n. 25, at pp. 164-165; Gardam, *supra* n. 25, at p. 397.

44. The rule of proportionality deals with the relation between military necessity and civilian casualties. Since civilians were not involved to a great extent in armed conflicts during that era, there was no state practice which can serve as a basis for a creation of customary norms to govern this rule. See also R.A. Ramey, 'Armed conflict on the final frontier: The law of war in space', 48 *Air Force LR* (2000) pp. 1, 4, stating that at the time of world war I one could hardly establish firm legal principles with respect to air warfare, in the absence of state practice.

45. For a rule to be considered as 'customary international law', there must exist extensive and uniform state practice flowing from a sense of legal obligation (*opinio juris*). See *North Sea Continental Shelf Cases, ICJ Rep.* (1969) 4, paras. 73-81; *Continental Shelf* (Libyan Arab Jamahiriya/Malta), *ICJ. Rep.* (1985) 29, para. 27; GA Advisory Opinion on the Use of Nuclear Weapons, *supra* n. 41, para. 64. For a general discussion of 'Customary International Law', see e.g., American Law Institute, Restatement (Third) of the Foreign Relations Law of the United States (1987).

46. Y. Dinstein, *The Conduct of Hostilities Under the Law of International Armed Conflict* (Cambridge, Cambridge Univ. Press 2004), at p. 119 ('in the past, once an attack was directed at an indisputable military objective, any unavoidable injury or damage caused to civilians or civilian objects was accepted as "collateral damage"'.); M. Lippman, 'Aerial attack on civilians and the humanitarian law of war: Technology and terror from World War I to Afghanistan', 33 *Calif. Western ILJ* (2002) pp. 1, 9; Gardam, *supra* n. 25, at p. 401; M.W. Lewis, 'The law of aerial bombardment in the 1991 Gulf War', 97 *AJIL* (2003) pp. 481, 482 ('parties on both sides seldom honored these provisions during World War I. They not only bombarded cities and towns of no military value, but even declared that the purpose of aerial bombardment was to undermine civilian morale by killing civilians and destroying their cities'.)

flicts increasingly affected civilians, the rule of proportionality became an important and crucial issue.[47]

The first written provisions that specifically recognised the rule of proportionality were drafted by the Commission of Jurists, which met in The Hague in 1922 with the task of examining the partial revision of the Rules of Air Warfare. Article 24(4) of the second draft of those rules states that:

> 'In the immediate neighborhood of the operations of the land forces, the bombardment of cities, towns, and villages, dwelling or building is legitimate provided there exists a reasonable presumption that the military concentration is sufficiently important to justify such bombardment, having regard to the danger thus caused to the civilian population.'[48]

Those rules were never adopted by states. However, as Lauterpacht states, 'they are important as an authoritative attempt to clarify and formulate rules of law governing the use of aircraft in war and they will doubtless prove a convenient starting-point for any future steps in this direction'.[49]

The 1938 resolution of the League of Nations Assembly concerning protection of the Civilian Population Against Bombing From Air in Case of War also reflects a similar approach, by stating that: 'Any attack on legitimate military objectives must be carried out in such a way that civilian populations in the neighbourhood are not bombed through negligence.'[50] However, the exact meaning of this paragraph is unclear because it may contain either an absolute prohibition on civilian casualties or an approach rooted in proportionality.[51]

---

47. The civilian population was involved to great extent especially during World War I (1914-1918) and the Spanish Civil War (1936-1939), in which aerial bombardment became a method of warfare. See Lippman, *supra* n. 46, at pp. 9, 13; Gardam, *supra* n. 25, at p. 399; *Prosecutor* v. *Tadić*, Case No. IT-94-1-AR72 (decision on the defense motion for interlocutory appeal on jurisdiction) (ICTY Appeals Chamber 2 October 1995), para. 102, reprinted in 35 *ILM* (1996) p. 32.

48. Hague Rules of Air Warfare, drafted by a Commission of Jurists at the Hague, December 1922 – February 1923, reprinted in Schindler and Toman, *supra* n. 20, at p. 207 (emphasis added). See Lippman, *supra* n. 46, at pp. 9-12; Reinhold, *supra* n. 38, at pp. 12-14; M. Greenspan, *The Modern Law of Land Warfare* (Berkeley, University of California Press 1959) at p. 351.

49. L. Oppenheim, *International Law: A Treatise*, H. Lauterpacht, ed., 7th edn.(London, Longmans 1952) p. 519. See also Lippman, *supra* n. 46, at 12 (arguing that the central provisions of the instrument are recognized as a component of customary law); Greenspan, *supra* n. 48, at 352 (noting that since the Hague Rules of Air Warfare, 1923, constitutes the chief existing guide to the rules of air warfare, it has strong persuasive authority).

50. League of Nations, OJ Spec. Supp. (1938) pp. 183, at 135-136, reprinted in Schindler and Toman, *supra* n. 20, at p. 162. The British Prime Minister Neville Chamberlain proposed this statement just before World War II. The League of Nations adopted Chamberlain's proposal in a non-binding resolution. See Lippman, *supra* n. 46, at pp. 12-15; Reinhold, *supra* n. 38, at p. 14; *Prosecutor* v. *Tadić*, *supra* n. 47, para. 101.

51. Fenrick, *supra* n. 19, at p. 96. See also Lippman, *supra* n. 46, at p. 14.

During the Second World War, aerial attacks on civilian cities caused substantial civilian casualties.[52] This clearly shows that states paid almost no heed to the rule of proportionality.[53] The high number of civilian casualties led to a great concern for the need to apply the rule of proportionality in operations against military targets in which massive collateral damage to civilians was likely to be caused. However, the 1949 Geneva Conventions contain no provisions regarding the rule of proportionality.[54]

3. PROTOCOL I PROVISIONS AND ANALYSIS

3.1 **Protocol I provisions**

With the adoption in 1977 of Protocol I to the Geneva Convention, after three years of deliberations, proportionality became a conventional rule, to be applied in all international armed conflicts.[55] Part IV of Protocol I sets forth a detailed set of rules for protection of the civilian population from the effect of hostilities,[56] in which it explicitly recognises and codifies the rule of proportionality as part of *jus in bello*[57] with regard to international armed conflict.[58] This part of the Protocol

---

52. For a description of aerial attacks during the World War II and the justifications given at that time see B. Johnson and D. Johnson, *Rights in Air Space* (Manchester, Manchester University Press 1965) pp. 44-55. See also Detter, *supra* n. 17, at pp. 284-285.

53. Lippman, *supra* n. 46, at pp. 15-31 (2002); Gardam, *supra* n. 25, at p. 401; Fenrick, *supra* n. 19, at pp. 96-97.

54. Geneva Conventions, *supra* n. 38. The Geneva Conventions consist of four treaties: Geneva Convention for the Amelioration of the Condition of the Wounded and Sick in Armed Forces in the Field, 12 August 1949, 6 *UST* 3114, 75 *UNTS* 31; Geneva Convention for the Amelioration of the Condition of the Wounded, Sick and Shipwrecked Members of the Armed Forces at Sea, 12 August 1949, 6 *UST* 3217, 75 *UNTS* 85; Geneva Convention Relative to the Treatment of Prisoners of War, 12 August 1949, 6 *UST* 3316, 75 *UNTS* 135; Geneva Convention Relative to the Protection of Civilian Persons in Time of War, 12 August 1949, 6 *UST* 3516, 75 *UNTS* 287. None of these treaties contain provisions about the rule of proportionality. See H. Mccoubrey, *International Humanitarian Law: The Regulation of Armed Conflicts* (Aldershot, Dartmouth 1990) p. 14, stating that the Geneva Conventions are now believed to have reached a reasonable satisfactory state so far as 'textbook' conventional warfare is concerned, except in the case of civilian protection, which remain very limited.

55. Although some states, including the United States and Israel, have not ratified Protocol I, the rule of proportionality, as it is codified in Protocol I, is considered to possess the character of customary international law. Therefore, it should be applied in all international armed conflicts (for an explanation of when a rule is considered to be customary international law, see *supra* n. 45). See Dinstein, *supra* n. 46, at 120; C. Greenwood, 'Customary law status of the 1977 Additional Protocols', in A.J. M. Delissen and G.J. Tanja, eds., *Humanitarian Law of Armed Conflict Challenges Ahead: Essays in Honour of Frits Kalshoven* (Dordrecht, Nijhoff 1991) pp. 93, 102-104; T. Meron, *Human Rights and Humanitarian Norms as Customary Law* (Oxford, Oxford University Press 1989); 'Report of the Swedish International Humanitarian Law Committee, 1984', in Sassoli and Bouvier, *supra* n. 27, at p. 153.

56. Arts. 48-67 Additional Protocol I.

57. Ibid., Arts. 51(5)(b), 57(2).

58. The Geneva Conventions and Protocol I apply only in international armed conflict. See Geneva Conventions, *supra* n. 38, Art. 2. The expression 'international armed conflict' is not defined in the

contains the three main principles relevant to this paper. The first one is the general protection of the civilian population against dangers arising from military operations and the affirmation of the distinction between combatants and non-combatants.[59] The second is the rule of proportionality, which states that an attack will be considered indiscriminate, and therefore prohibited, if the attack is expected to cause collateral civilian damage that would be excessive in relation to the concrete and direct military advantage anticipated.[60] The third principle refers to a situation where a choice is possible between several military objectives for obtaining a similar military advantage. In this case, the military objective the attack on which may be expected to cause the least danger to civilian lives and to civilian objects should be selected.[61]

The articles from Protocol I stating these principles raise numerous interpretive questions, of which this paper will address two:[62]

Protocol, but it is considered to describe any engagement of regular armed forces with the regular armed forces of a foreign state. Protocol I, *supra* n. 20, Art. 1(4), also includes within the meaning of international armed conflict, 'armed conflict in which peoples are fighting against racist regimes in the exercise of their right of self-determination.' See W.J. Fenrick, *supra* n. 19, at p. 98. See also Detter, *supra* n. 17, at pp. 51-53 (Detter argues that Art. 1(4) does not alter the nature of the conflict from non-international armed conflict to international armed conflict, but only equates the rights of the peoples who fight against racist regimes for self-determination with the rights of other belligerents under Protocol I).

59. Ibid., Arts. 48, 51. Art. 48 states: 'in order to ensure respect for and protection of the civilian population and civilian objects, the parties to the conflict shall at all times distinguish between the civilian population and combatants and between civilian objects and military objectives and accordingly shall direct their operations only against military objectives.' Art. 51(1) states, inter alia: 'the civilian population and individual civilians shall enjoy general protection against dangers arising from military operations.'

60. Ibid., Arts. 51(5), 57. Art. 51(5) states: Among others, the following types of attacks are to be considered as indiscriminate: … (b) an attack which may be expected to cause incidental loss of civilian life, injury to civilians, damage to civilian objects, or combination thereof, which would be excessive in relation to the concrete and direct military advantage anticipated.
Art. 57 establishes the procedures by which the standard set forth in Art. 51 is to be accomplished. According to it: 2. With respect to attacks, the following precautions shall be taken: (a) those who plan or decide upon an attack shall … (iii) refrain from deciding to launch any attack which may be expected to cause incidental loss of civilian life, injury to civilians, damage to civilian objects, or a combination thereof, which would be excessive in relation to the concrete and direct military advantage anticipated (b) an attack shall be cancelled or suspended if it becomes apparent that the objective is not a military one or is subject to special protection or that the attack may be expected to cause incidental loss of civilian life, injury to civilians, damage to civilian objects, or a combination thereof, which would be excessive in relation to the concrete and direct military advantage anticipated.

61. Ibid., Art. 57(3).

62. In relation to the principle of proportionality, the main question is what criteria should be used to determine if the anticipated civilian casualties will not be excessive in relation to the military advantage anticipate. Are there any objective criteria to the term 'may be expected to cause'? Is this balancing test subjective one, per se? Are there, at least, any guidelines that might help the commander decide in this issue? The difficulty in doing this balancing test in a real case, based on the fact that the values being measured – civilian casualties and military advantage – are from different kind, and therefore it is very hard to establish a formula that will help us conclude the exact proportionality between them. The text raises other questions, such as the meaning of the word 'feasible' in Art. 57 (2)(a) and who is required to take the executive action required by Art. 57(2)(b). However, these questions are beyond the scope of this paper.

1) What is a 'similar military advantage' for the purpose of Article 57(3)?
2) What is the standard for measuring 'concrete and direct military advantage anticipated' in Articles 51(5)(b) and 57(2)?

These two interpretive questions must be resolved in accordance with the 1969 Vienna Convention on the Law of Treaties.[63] According to this convention, 'a treaty shall be interpreted in good faith in accordance with the ordinary meaning of the terms in their context and in light of its object and purpose'.[64] Additionally, the Vienna Convention states that when there is doubt about the proper interpretation of a treaty, supplementary means of interpretation such as the *travaux préparatoires* may be used.[65] Therefore, the meaning of Protocol I text has to be analysed, *inter alia,* on the basis of its object and purpose, which is to reaffirm and develop the rules for the protection of the civilian population,[66] and also on the basis of its preparatory work.

3.2 **'Similar military advantage'**

Article 57(3) to Protocol I states that: 'when a choice is possible between several military objectives for obtaining a similar military advantage, the objective to be selected shall be that the attack on which may be expected to cause the least danger to civilian lives and to civilian objects'.[67] The question is how to apply this provision in a situation where a commander has two military objectives with equal military value in relation to the enemy, where one is more risky to her soldiers and less

63. Vienna Convention on the Law of Treaties, May 23, 1969, 1155 *UNTS* 331, 8 *ILM* 679 (1969) (entered into force 27 January 1980) [hereinafter Vienna Convention]. See also D.N. Hylton, 'Default breakdown: The Vienna Convention on the Law of Treaties inadequate framework on reservation', 27 *Vanderbilt JTL* (1994) pp. 419, 424 (noting that the Vienna convention was attempt to bring certainty to international law); P.C. Maki, 'Interpreting GATT using the Vienna Convention on the Law of Treaties: A method to increase the legitimacy of the Dispute Settlement System', 9 *Minnesota Journal of Global Trade* (2000) 343, 350-352 (noting that also Arts. 31 and 32 to Vienna Convention prefer the objective, textualist school of interpretation over the parties' intent, it is still justified to advocate a variety of interpretive techniques.)

64. Vienna Convention, *supra* n. 63, Art. 31(1).

65. Ibid. Art. 32. Art. 32 states: 'Recourse may be had to supplementary means of interpretation, including the preparatory work of the treaty and the circumstances of its conclusion, in order to confirm the meaning resulting from the application of article 31, or to determine the meaning when the interpretation to article 31: (a) leaves the meaning ambiguous or obscure; or (b) leads to a result which is manifestly absurd or unreasonable.'

66. The primary purpose of Protocol I in relation to the doctrine of proportionality, is the safety of the civilian population. See Commentary on the Additional Protocols of 8 June 1977 to the Geneva Conventions of 12 August 1949, [hereinafter Protocols Commentary] (Y. Sandoz et al. eds.,Geneva, ICRC 1987) § 2024, 2037. This aim is stated at the preamble to Protocol I, *supra* n. 20: 'believing it is necessary nevertheless to reaffirm and develop the provisions protecting the victims of armed conflicts and to supplement measures intended to reinforce their application.' See also Vienna Convention, *supra* n. 63, Art. 31(2) (the interpretation of a treaty includes its preamble and annexes); Protocols Commentary, § 2037 (noting that in case of a doubt about the meaning and application of the protocol provisions, the general aim of the protocol should be borne in mind, i.e., the protection of the civilian population).

67. Protocol I, *supra* n. 20, Art. 57(3).

dangerous to the civilians and the second is less risky to her soldiers, but more dangerous to the civilians. Are they both considered as giving a 'similar military advantage' – pursuant to which the commander will have the legal obligation to risk her soldiers in order to spare civilian lives, in accordance with the Article 57 (3) provision? Or could she consider the operation that puts her soldiers at higher risk as one that gives her less of a 'military advantage'?

The exact meaning of the term 'similar military advantage' was not discussed in the negotiation history of Article 57(3).[68] The Commentary to Protocol I does not discuss the exact meaning of this term either.[69] The Commentary describes it as 'the lesser of two evils', and gives an example in which it is possible to launch an attack against enemy road or rail traffic.[70] In this example, both attacks give the same military advantage. Therefore, the commander must launch an attack against the road and not against the rail traffic, in order to minimise civilian casualties.[71] However, it does not refer to a situation in which attacking the road is more dangerous to the offensive force than attacking the rail traffic.

Nevertheless, the term 'military advantage' relates to the principle of 'military necessity', which justifies a belligerent in applying compulsion and force of any kind that is not prohibited by law, to the extent necessary for the realisation of the purpose of war.[72] The object of war is to ensure the submission of the enemy at the earliest possible moment with the least possible expenditure of men and resources.[73] Therefore, the term 'military advantage', should be interpreted in this context – as an advantage that will help a commander reach the goal of submission of the enemy at the earliest possible moment with the least possible expenditure of men and resources. When interpreting the term 'similar military advantage', in this context, it seems obvious that the lives of the soldiers must be taken into account, and that an operation in which some soldiers will die will give the commander less military advantage, because he would be left with less soldiers for subsequent operations than an operation that will do the same to the enemy with no casualties to his soldiers.[74]

---

68. H.S. Levie, *Protection of War Victims: Protocol I to the 1949 Geneva Convention* (Dobbs Ferry NY, Oceana 1980) pp. 309-338.
69. Protocols Commentary, *supra* n. 66, § 2226-2228.
70. Ibid., § 2227.
71. Ibid., § 2227-2228.
72. See *supra* n. 40.
73. Rogers, *supra* n. 41, at p. 5.
74. See also M. Bothe et al., *New Rules for Victims of Armed Conflict: commentary on the Two 1977 Protocols Additional to the Geneva Conventions of 1949* (The Hague, Nijhoff 1982) p. 324 ('the term military advantage involves a variety of considerations, including the security of the attacking force.'); International and Operational Law Dept., The Judge Advocate General Legal Center and School, US Army, JA 422, Operational Law Handbook (2004) 14-15 [hereinafter: Operational Law Handbook] ('[the proportionality balancing test] may involve a variety of considerations, including the security of the attacking force'); Rogers, *supra* n. 41, at p. 17 ('it is suggested, however, that the risk to the attacking forces is a factor to be taken into consideration when applying the proportionality rule'); Field-Manual (FM) 3-06.11 (FM 90-10-1), Combined Arms Operations in Urban Terrain, Washington DC Headquarters, Department of the Army, 28 February, 2002, at pp. 1-6 ('a condition that commanders and leaders will be required to confront during urban operations will be minimizing

In scholarly writings there is almost no reference to this issue. There are numerous articles discussing the application of the rule of proportionality in recent armed conflicts, such as the Gulf War,[75] the 1999 NATO air strikes against the Federal Republic of Yugoslavia[76] and the 2001 Operation Enduring Freedom against Afghanistan.[77] However, there are almost no discussions of the extent to which a military commander is obligated to expose his own forces to increased risk in order to limit civilian casualties or damage to civilians. As will be noted below, some scholars indeed refer to this issue, but only tangentially, without discussing it to a great extent or fully supporting their arguments.

Professor Judith Gardam has referred to this issue, arguing briefly that, 'the proportionality equation, as it currently stands in International Humanitarian Law (IHL), does not deal with the extent to which a military commander must assume a higher level of risks for his own combatants in order to protect the civilian population of the opposing side'.[78] However, she does not explain her argument nor mention what are the practical implications of such a 'legal void'.[79]

Another scholar who has referred to this issue is Professor Michael Reisman, who argues, in one sentence, that 'no rule requires a combatant otherwise in compliance with the law of armed conflict to choose a course of conduct that is more, rather than less, dangerous to itself'.[80] However, he too does not articulate the rationale for this argument, nor support it in any other way.

---

collateral damage and non-combatant casualties. This will have to be balanced with mission accomplishment and the requirement to provide force protection'.) These statements express the same view that the security of the attacking force is part of the 'military advantage' assessment.

75. See e.g., F.J. Hampton, 'Comdr. Charles A. Allen, Panel discussion, Implementing limitation on the use of force: the doctrine of proportionality and necessity', 86 *ASIL Proc.* (1992) pp. 39, 45-46 (Panelist F. Hampton discussing the proportionality principle and the conditions under which bridges in the Gulf War may be attacked); Lippman, *supra* n. 46, at 40-48; Lewis, *supra* n. 46; O. Medenica, 'Protocol I and Operation Allied Forces: Did NATO Abide by Principles of Proportionality?' 23 *Loy. LA I & CLR* (2001) pp. 329, 372-374.

76. See e.g., Medenica, *supra* n. 75, at pp. 372-374; Stone, *supra* n. 28, at pp. 524-525; Lippman, *supra* n. 46, at pp. 48-56; D. Wippman, 'Kosovo and the limits of international law', 25 *Fordham IlJ* (2001) p. 129.

77. See e.g., Lippman, *supra* n. 46, at pp. 56-65; F. Biggio, 'Neutralizing the threat: Reconsidering existing doctrines in the emerging war on terrorism', 34 *Case Western Reserve JIL* (2002) pp. 1, 23-24; B. Feinstein, 'Operation enduring freedom', 11 *J Transn. L & Pol.* (2002) pp. 201, 289-293; M.A. Drumbl, 'Victimhood in our neighborhood: Terrorist crime, Taliban guilt, and the asymmetries of the international legal order', 81 *North Carolina LR* (2002) pp. 1, 45-48.

78. J. Gardam, 'Proportionality as a restraint on the use of force', 20 *Australian YIL* (1999) pp. 161, 171.

79. It is not necessarily clear that if there is no specific prohibition in the law of armed conflict to do something, the act is permitted. See e.g., O. Spiermann, 'Lotus and the double structure of international legal argument', in Boisson de Chazournes and Sands, *supra* n. 27, pp. 131, 137-143; H. Thirlway, 'The Nuclear Weapons Advisory Opinions: The Declarations and Separate and Dissenting Opinions', in Boisson de Chazournes and Sands, *supra* n. 27, at pp. 390, 406-414.

80. W.M. Reisman, 'NATO's Kosovo intervention: Kosovo's antinomies', 93 *AJIL* (1999) pp. 860, 861.

William J. Fenrick has also referred to this issue, highlighting the difficulty in determining the obligations on a commander to expose his forces to risk.[81] In his analysis, he uses the rule of proportionality to determine if a commander has such an obligation. According to his view, a willingness to risk soldiers in order to protect civilians may indicate a greater desire to comply with the rule of proportionality. However, in my view, the rule of proportionality provides little assistance on this issue. The reason for that is because the question concerning the extent to which a military commander is obliged to expose his own forces to danger in order to limit civilian casualties arises when there is more than one military option which complies with the rule of proportionality. The only difference is that one will limit civilian casualties at the price of increasing the risk to the attacking soldiers. In this case, the rule of proportionality cannot help us since all the military options comply with it, and there is no requirement, under the law of armed conflict, to compare between them in order to determine which military option is 'more proportionate' than the others.

Let me explain this point with an example. Suppose that the US Army has just received information that Osama Bin Laden is currently present in a certain area. Suppose further that the US Army can bomb the place where Osama Bin-Laden is currently located, or send infantry units that will capture or kill him. The commander assesses that in both options, Bin Laden will not be able to escape. He further assesses that if they bomb the area, hundreds of civilians will be killed. Still, the target value is so high that the rule of proportionality would permit bombing because collateral damage will not be excessive in relation to the anticipated military advantage. If they send in infantry troops, the risk to the men is greater than from aerial bombardment. In this case, the rule of proportionality cannot help us in determining which alternative to choose, since both military options comply with it.

Professor George Wright argues that Protocol I does not explicitly acknowledge the issue, nor does it explicitly adopt a strict liability standard or a subjective and reasonable good faith standard.[82] He gives an example in which a commander

---

81. W.J. Fenrick, 'Justice in cataclysm criminal trials in the wake of mass violence: Attacking the enemy civilian as a punishable offense', 7 *Duke J Comp. & IL* (1997) pp. 539, 548-549.: 'Determining the extent to which a military commander is obliged to expose his own forces to danger in order to limit civilian casualties or damage to civilian object is almost impossible. Strictly speaking, resolution of the proportionality equation requires a determination of the relative worths of military advantage gained by one side and the civilian casualties or damage to civilian objectives incurred in areas in the hand of the other side. Military casualties incurred by the attacking side are not a part of the equation. A willingness to accept some own-side casualties in order to limit civilian casualties may indicate a greater desire to ensure compliance with the principle of proportionality. Military commanders do, however, also have a duty to limit casualties to their own forces.' in my view military casualties incurred by the attacking side can be part of the proportionality equation. That is because 'military advantage' is part of the proportionality equation, and it includes force protection.'

82. R.G. Wright, 'Combating civilians casualties: Rules and balancing in the developing law of war', 38 *Wake Forest LR* (2003) 129, 138-39. Wright's argument that Protocol I does not explicitly adopt a reasonable good-faith standard is not clear of doubt. One can argue that according to the Vienna Convention, *supra* n. 63, Art. 26, 'every treaty in force is binding upon the parties to it and must be performed by them in good faith'. This 'good faith' standard must be applied in all kinds of military operations, even if the protocol text does not explicitly require choosing a course of action

wants to bomb a target. The higher the altitude at which bombing occurs, the greater the inaccuracy and the greater the number of inadvertent civilian casualties, but the fewer the military casualties of the attacker. In this case, Wright argues, Protocol I text does not require choosing a course of conduct that is more dangerous to the attacking force. However, he too did not articulate his argument nor explain the consequences of such a 'legal void'.[83]

A similar case was scrutinised by a committee established by the Prosecutor of the International Criminal Tribunal for the Former Yugoslavia. The committee examined, *inter alia*, allegations that North Atlantic Treaty Organization (NATO) aircraft operated at heights that enabled them to avoid attack by Yugoslav defences and, consequently, made it impossible to properly distinguish between military and civilian objects on the ground.[84] Regarding this allegation, the committee agreed that NATO aircraft operated at heights that made it difficult to distinguish between military and civilians on the ground. However, the committee determined that there is nothing inherently unlawful about flying at such heights in order to avoid attack by enemy air defences.[85]

The British Manual of the Law of Armed Conflict expresses the same approach, stating that:

> '[T]he application of the proportionality principle is not always straight-forward. Sometimes a method of attack that would minimize the risk to civilians may involve increased risk to the attacking forces. The law is not clear as to the degree of risk that the attacker

---

that is more dangerous to the attacking power. See also Protocols Commentary, *supra* n.66, § 2198; H. Parks, 'The protection of civilians from air warfare', 27 *Israel YB HR* (1997) pp. 65, 70: 'the law of war historically has been grounded in its consistency with military efficiency and good faith implementation by states parties'.

83. See *supra* n. 79.

84. International Criminal Tribunal for the Former Yugoslavia (ICTY): 'Final Report to the Prosecutor by the Committee Established to Review the NATO Bombing Campaign Against the Federal Republic of Yugoslavia', 39 *ILM* 1257 para. 2 (2000) <http://www.un.org/icty/pressreal/nato061300.htm>.

85. Ibid., paras. 56, 69: 'The committee agrees there is nothing inherently unlawful about flying above the height which can be reached by enemy air defences ... It is the opinion of the committee that civilians were not deliberately attacked in this incident. While there is nothing lawful about operating at a height above Yugoslav air defences, it is difficult for any aircrew flying at several hundred miles an hour and at a substantial height to distinguish between military and civilian vehicles in a convoy. In this case, most of the attacking aircraft were F16s with a crew of one person to fly the aircraft and identify the target. As soon as the crews of the attacking aircraft became aware of the presence of civilians, the attack ceased.' But see A. Laursen, 'NATO, the war over Kosovo, and the ICTY investigation', 17 *Amer. Univ. ILR* (2002) pp. 765, 808-809 (arguing that one may read that report as an implicit confirmation that NATO violated Art. 57 of Protocol I, but that the mens rea failed to qualify the violation for prosecution); T. Voon, 'Pointing the finger: Civilian casualties of NATO bombing in the Kosovo conflict', 16 *Amer. Univ. ILR* (2001) pp. 1083, 1099 (arguing that in several cases NATO's attacks were difficult to justify under the laws of armed conflict. In addition, the civilian toll may have been relatively low, but the absence of single allied casualty is even more striking.); Elshtain, *supra* n. 35, at pp. 16-17 (suggesting that the manner in which the Kosovo War was conducted violated the norm of discretion by devising a new criterion: 'combatant immunity,' as our combatants ranked higher as a consideration than did non-combatants immunity for Serbian civilians.).

must accept. The proportionality principle does not itself require the attacker to accept increased risk. Rather, it requires him to refrain from attacks that may be expected to cause excessive collateral damage.'[86]

The body of literature represented here shares the idea that the law of armed conflict in general, and Protocol I in particular, do not oblige military commanders to expose their forces to danger in order to limit civilian casualties. However, this literature notwithstanding, it is possible to develop an argument which derives such an obligation, in certain circumstances, from the principles and purpose of the law of armed conflict. Such an argument might be based on the so called 'Martens Clause', which prescribes that in cases not covered by treaties and traditional customary international law, 'civilians and combatants remain under the protection and authority of the principles of international law derived from established custom, from the principles of humanity and from the dictates of public conscience'.[87]

The Martens Clause acts as an embedded moral code in the law of armed conflict because it provides an objective means of determining the presence of natural law in international law.[88] As such, it has significance as a 'built-in mechanism [that] fill[s] in the *lacuna* existing in the law of war at any particular time'.[89] As

---

86. UK Ministry of Defence, *The Manual of the Law of Armed Conflict*, para. 2.7.1 (Oxford, Oxford University Press 2004) [hereinafter: The British Manual].

87. This clause appears in the preambles of Hague Convention No. IV of 1907, *supra* n. 41, and in Protocol I, *supra* n. 20, Art. 1(2). According to it, even when there is no specific prohibition, an act might still be unlawful in war. The Martens clause appears consistently in every major instrument through the development of the law of armed conflict, and it is recognized as belonging to customary international law. Its importance has also been recognized in international case law – *United States* v. *Krupp*, 9 Trials War Crim. (Nur. Mil. Tri. 1949) pp. 1327, 1341: '[the clause] is much more than a pious declaration. It is a general clause, making the usage established among civilized nations, the laws of humanity, and the dictates of public conscience into the legal yardstick to be applied if and when the specific provisions of the [Hague] Convention and the Regulations annexed to it do not cover specific cases occurring in wartime, or concomitant to warfare'.
See also Protocols Commentary, *supra* n. 66, at pp. 38-39; Detter, *supra* n. 17, at pp. 375-377 (noting that the Martens Clause covers the most basic rights, even if these have not been incorporated or clearly spelt out in the texts. Through the Martens Clause it may be that an underlying obligation is derived from international law in general); GA Advisory Opinion on the Use of Nuclear Weapons, *supra* n. 41, para. 87 ('the court points to the martens clause, whose continuing existence and applicability is not to be doubted, as an affirmation that the principles and rules of humanitarian law apply to nuclear weapons'); Greenspan, *supra* n. 48, at p. 155; Sassoli and Bouvier, *supra* n. 27, at p. 113; Mccoubrey, *supra* n. 54, at pp. 190-191; T. Meron, 'The humanization of humanitarian law', 94 *AJIL* (2000) pp. 239, 245; R.D. Glick, 'Lip service to the laws of war: Humanitarian law and United Nations Armed Forces', 17 *Michigan JIL* (1995) p. 53 n.17.

88. See M.H. Sperber, 'John Walker Lindh and Yaser Esam Hamdi: Closing the loophole in international humanitarian law for American nationals captured abroad while fighting with enemy forces', 40 *Amer. Crim. LR* (2003) pp. 159, 187. But see T. Meron, 'The Martens Clause, principles of humanity, and dictates of public conscience', 94 *AJIL* (2000) pp. 78, 88 ('nevertheless, the Martens Clause does not allow one to build castles of sand. Except in extreme cases, its references to principles of humanity and dictates of public conscience cannot, alone, delegitimize weapons and methods of war, especially in contested cases').

89. E.K. Kwakwa, *The International Law of Armed Conflict: Personal and Material Fields of Application* (Dordrecht, Kluwer International Law 1992) p. 13.

will be argued in the next section, there are situations in which there is a moral obligation to risk soldiers' lives in order to reduce risk to civilians. If this view is accepted, the Martens Clause will provide the mechanism to interpret the law of armed conflict in such a way such that no contradiction will exist between the current law of armed conflict and the moral aspects underpinning it.

3.3 **'Concrete and direct military advantage anticipated'**

The rule of proportionality prohibits an attack if the probable collateral civilian damage is expected to be disproportionate in relation to the concrete and direct military advantage anticipated from the attack.[90] The question is, what is the standard for measuring 'concrete and direct military advantage anticipated'? Should the military advantage be measured based on the specific tactical objective of a particular action ('case by case' basis), or should it be measured on a 'cumulative' basis, taking into account the contribution of the attack to the belligerent's overall strategic goals?[91]

The most famous example of this dilemma in modern warfare is the nuclear bombing of Hiroshima and Nagasaki by the United States in 1945. The Americans adopted the cumulative approach and argued that the military advantage gained from the bombing was not just the destruction of the Japanese war industry, but also the surrender of Japan. The Japanese surrender eliminated the necessity of an Allied invasion of Japan, which would have significantly increased the number of casualties on both sides. The Japanese took the other approach, arguing that the attack was disproportionate since 'aerial bombardment with an atomic bomb, even if its target is confined to military objectives, brings about the same result as blind aerial bombardment because of the tremendous destructive power of the bomb'.[92]

According to the Commentary, 'concrete and direct' was intended to indicate that the advantage sought should be 'substantial' and 'relatively close', as opposed to advantages that are 'hardly perceptible' and 'would only appear in the long-

90. Protocol I, *supra* n. 20, Arts. 51(5)(b), 57(2)(a)(iii), 57(2)(b). See *supra* n. 60.

91. See e.g., B.L. Brown, 'The proportionality principle in humanitarian law of warfare: recent efforts at codification', 10 *Cornell ILJ* (1977) pp. 134 , 141.

92. Brown, *supra* n. 91, at p. 141. The issue of the legality of the use of nuclear weapons was brought before the International Court of Justice (ICJ) in the request from the United Nations General Assembly for advisory opinions on the legality of the use of nuclear weapons. The court gave an advisory opinion in the request from the General Assembly, on 8 July 1996, ruling by the narrowest of majorities that the threat or the use of nuclear weapons: 'Would generally be contrary to the rules of international law applicable in armed conflict, and in particular the principles and rules of humanitarian law; however, in view of the current state of international law, and of the elements of fact at its disposal, the court cannot conclude definitively whether the threat or use of nuclear weapons would be lawful or unlawful in an extreme circumstance of self-defence, in which the very survival of a state would be at stake.'
See GA Advisory Opinion on the Use of Nuclear Weapons, *supra* n. 41, paras. 97, 105.
Proportionality and, to a much more limited extent, necessity, were integral components of the court's reasoning. However, the court did not refer to the meaning of the words 'concrete and direct military advantage.' See also Judith Gardam, 'Necessity and proportionality in Jus Ad Bellum and Jus In Bello', in Coppieters and Fotion, *supra* n. 27, at p. 275.

term'.[93] Accordingly, the 'military advantage' should be measured based on the specific tactical objective of a particular action, given that 'military advantage' under the cumulative approach will be, at least in most cases, 'hardly perceptible' and 'only appear in the long term'.[94]

However, as Rogers points out, the Commentary explanation of the words 'concrete and direct' does not accord with ordinary English usage.[95] The meaning of the word 'concrete' is not 'predicted' but 'specific' or 'perceptible' (rather than general) and the meaning of the word 'direct' is not 'relatively close' but 'without intervening condition of agency'.[96]

The approach that we should interpret the term 'concrete and direct military advantage' on a 'case by case' basis was also adopted by Brown, who argues that the Diplomatic Conference appeared to favour this approach, as is indicated by the use of the phrase 'concrete and direct military advantage'.[97] He adds that this approach is more consistent with the Conference's desire to strengthen the protection accorded to civilians.[98] Therefore, he concludes, 'both policy factors and language of the Conference's articles support a "case-by-case" interpretation of "military advantage"'.[99]

Brown is seemingly incorrect, both in his assumption that adopting the 'case by case' approach will necessarily strengthen the protection provided to civilians, and in his claim that the Diplomatic Conference appears to favour this approach.

---

93. Protocols Commentary, *supra* n. 66, § 2209. The commentary also states that the words 'concrete and direct' impose stricter conditions on the attacker than those implied by the criteria defining military objectives in Art. 52(2). See ibid. § 2218.

94. Ibid.

95. Rogers, *supra* n. 41, at pp. 59-60.

96. Ibid.

97. Brown, *supra* n. 91, at p. 142. Gardam, Schmidt, Stone and Colangelo hold the same view as Brown. See Gardam, *supra* n. 25, at p. 407: 'it appears from the word 'concrete and direct' that the protocol requires that proportionality be assessed in relation to each individual attack, rather on cumulative basis'; Michael N. Schmitt, 'The principle of discrimination in 21st century warfare', 2 *Yale HR & Dev. LJ* (1999) pp. 143, 150; Antony J. Colangelo, 'Manipulating international criminal procedures: The decision of the ICTY office of the independent prosecutor not to investigate NATO bombing in the Former Yugoslavia', 97 *Northwestern Univ. LR* (2003) pp. 1393, 1416-1417; Stone, *supra* n. 28, at pp. 524-525, 537 ('the current trend of accepting a cumulative analysis of military advantage, within a broader combination of both cumulative and case-by-case analyses, fails to meet the standard set forth by the protocol. This combination deprives civilians of the most protection during wartime.').

98. Brown, *supra* n. 91, at p. 142.

99. Ibid. In relation to the bombing of Hiroshima and Nagasaki, Brown added that it is extremely unlikely that the bombings would be legitimate military acts under those provisions, regardless of their cumulative military advantage. He acknowledges the fact that the 'cumulative' approach has been defended on the basis that taking civilians lives now will save more lives later, but he asserts that this approach 'would greatly weaken the specific protections accorded civilians under the law of warfare', and that 'the standard for measuring the legality of an act would become vague and elusive, due to the difficulty of assessing how, if at all, an act prevented undesirable future events and of determining how serious the adverse consequences would have been.' See also A. Raby, 'Bombardment of land targets – Military necessity and proportionality interpellated' (1968) 70 n. 184 (unpublished LL M. Thesis, The Judge Advocate General's School; on file with the Judge Advocate General's Legal Center and School Library) (defending the atomic bombing of Hiroshima and Nagasaki).

First, adopting the 'case by case' basis approach will not necessarily strengthen the protection accorded to civilians. For example, a commander considers destroying a dual-use facility, such as a power station, because it supports the enemy's army. In this case, if he assesses this target individually he might conclude that the military advantage justifies the collateral damage. However, if he adopts the cumulative approach he might notice that the enemy can get power from another power station, and therefore, based on the 'big picture', the military advantage will not be proportionate to the civilian casualties, unless the attack is against a substantial number of power stations.[100]

Second, even if we accept the argument that by adopting a 'case by case' basis approach we will strengthen the protection provided to civilians, this would not be true in the short term. Over the long term, adopting this approach might significantly increase the number of civilian casualties on both sides.[101]

Third, the negotiation history of Protocol I leads to the conclusion that the Diplomatic Conference favoured the 'cumulative' approach over the 'case-by-case' one. At some points in the negotiations of Protocol I's articles concerning the rule of proportionality, several states expressed their opinions that the reference to 'direct military advantage anticipated' from an attack was intended to refer to the advantages anticipated from the attack *considered as a whole*, and not just from isolated or particular parts of the attacks.[102] There were no objections to these statements.[103]

---

100. See H. Shue and D. Wippman, 'Limiting attacks on dual-use facilities performing indispensable civilian functions', 35 *Cornell ILJ* (2002) pp. 559, 571.

101. For example, in the case of the bombing of Hiroshima and Nagasaki, the Americans argued that the nuclear bombardment was justified, although a lot of civilians died as a result, since it eliminated the necessity of an Allied invasion of Japan, which would have significantly increased the number of casualties on both sides. Therefore, in the long term, adopting the cumulative approach saved very many lives on both sides.

102. The states that express that view, using almost the same words, were the United Kingdom, Belgium, Canada, the Federal Republic of Germany, the Netherlands, Italy, Spain and the United Sates of America. See Levie, *supra* n. 68, at pp. 165, 169, 171, 331-132, 334 and 336-137; M.A. Drumbl, 'International human rights, international humanitarian law, and environmental security: can the ICC bridge the gaps?', 6 *ILAS JI & Comp. L*, p. 305 n. 61, International Law Weekend Proceedings: stating that the governments of Belgium, Canada, Germany, Italy, the Netherlands and Spain hold the same position as Great Britain in regard to this issue; D. Fleck, ed., *The Handbook of Humanitarian Law in Armed Conflict* (Oxford, Oxford University Press 1995) p. 456; Statement made in the final plenary session on the adoption of the two protocols (9 June 1977), quoted in United States Delegation to the Diplomatic Conference on the Reaffirmation and Development of International Humanitarian Law Applicable in Armed Conflicts, Report, App. C (8 September 1977) stating that during the negotiation of Protocol I, the representatives of the United States held the same position that military advantages anticipated from an attack is intended to refer to the advantage anticipated from the attack considered as a whole.

103. See also Bothe, *supra* n.74, at p. 311 The term 'concrete and direct military advantage' as used in this article [Art. 51(5)(b)] and Art. 57, refers to the advantage anticipated from the specific military operation of which the attack is a part taken as a whole and not from isolated or particular parts of that operation. It would obviously be impossible to apply this balancing requirement to each individual act of violence which takes place during the course of a battle.The authors of this book participated as members of the delegations of their countries in the Diplomatic Conference from 1974 until 1977. After the Conference closed they decided to write this book in order to make a personal

Likewise, the United Kingdom has placed on record an understanding that 'military advantage anticipated from an attack' is 'intended to refer to the advantage anticipated from the attack considered as a whole and not only from isolated or particular parts of the attack'.[104] Several additional army manuals also express this approach.[105] For example, the US Army Operational Law Handbook expresses the view that, 'military advantage' is not restricted to tactical gains, but is linked to the full context of war strategy. Balancing between collateral damage to civilian objects and collateral civilian casualties may be done on a target-by-target basis ... but also may be weighed in overall terms against campaign objectives.'[106] Likewise, the Canadian Manual expresses the view that 'the military advantage at the time of the attack is that advantage anticipated from the military campaign of which the attack is part, considered as a whole, and not only from isolated or particular parts of that campaign or operation'.[107] As seen above, the British manual expresses the same view.[108]

The committee established to review the NATO bombing campaign against the Federal Republic of Yugoslavia also held the 'cumulative approach' view. One of the allegations brought before the committee was that the bombing by NATO of the Serbian TV and Radio station was disproportionate. In response, the committee concluded that the casualties 'do not appear to be clearly disproportionate'.[109] They explained this conclusion by clarifying that the proportionality rule does not apply to specific incidents, but rather to the 'overall assessment of the totality of civilian victims as against the goals of the military campaign'.[110]

The cumulative approach could be derived from the International Criminal Court [ICC] Statute as well, which includes as a war crime 'intentionally launching an attack in the knowledge that such attack will cause incidental loss of life or injury to civilians or damage to civilian objects or widespread, long-term and

---

contribution by writing commentary on the new law. For that reason, it seems that their interpretation represents the common view in the conference.

104. See Schindler and Toman, *supra* n. 20, at p. 717.

105. Military manuals serve as evidence of state *opinio juris*, and it might serve a limited lawmaking rule as well. In addition, given sufficient uniformity, principles of law articulated in law of war manuals could be viewed as 'general principles of law recognized by civilized nations,' and thus a formal source of international law. See Ramey, *supra* n. 44, at pp. 140-141; W.M. Reisman and W.M. Leitzau, 'Moving international law from theory to practice: the role of military manuals in effecting the law of armed conflict', in H.B. Robertson, ed., *The Law of Naval Operations* (Newport RI, Naval War College Press 1991) Series *International Law Studies* Vol. 64, p. 8: 'because international law notoriously lacks its own enforcement system, national implementation is often a critical factor in successful international lawmaking ... Certainly, both the absence of a manual or the use of manuals whose content does not include the relevant norms would strongly suggest that those norms have not been adopted'; Stat. of the ICJ, 26 June 1945, 59 stat. 1031 (entered into force 24 October 1945), Art. 38(1)c.

106. Operational Law Handbook, *supra* n.74, at pp. 14-15.

107. Canadian Manual, Art. 20, cited in *Israel Defense Forces' School of Military Law, a Comparative Manual to LOAC* (2003) p. 171 (on file with the author).

108. The British Manual, *supra* n. 86, para. 5.33.4.

109. Final Report to the Prosecutor by the Committee Established to Review the NATO Bombing Campaign Against the Federal Republic of Yugoslavia , *supra* n. 84, para. 77.

110. Ibid., para. 52

severe damage to the natural environment which would be clearly excessive in relation to the concrete and direct *overall* military advantage anticipated'.[111] Adding the word 'overall' to the term 'concrete and direct military advantage' clearly indicates that the military advantage can be assessed on a cumulative basis, taking into account the overall operational plan or war strategy. As a commentator notes: 'The word 'overall' somewhat broadens the scope of military advantages which may be taken into account to the effect that a broader range of advantages may be considered on the basis of the military situation taken as a whole, not only for particular point where the attack is launched.'[112]

Therefore my conclusion is that based on the Protocol I text, the negotiation history, military manuals and the ICC Statute, the standard for measuring 'concrete and direct military advantage anticipated' in Protocol I is the advantage anticipated from the military campaign, of which the attack is part, as a whole, and not only from isolated or particular parts of that campaign or operation. Therefore, while conducting the proportionality balancing test, a commander has to take into account both the tactical aspects of the attack and the strategic aspects of the overall operational plan or war strategy.

4. THE MORAL ASPECTS OF THE RULE OF PROPORTIONALITY

To understand the current law of proportionality, one must also look to history and philosophy. Admittedly, controversy exists as to the extent to which the law of armed conflict is linked to moral or religious beliefs regarding the justifiability of actions undertaken in war.[113] However, the close link between the positive law of armed conflict and traditional moral and religious principles is inescapable, and the doctrine of proportionality can only be understood by reference to its roots in moral and religious teachings.[114]

---

111. Rome Statute of the International Criminal Court, United Nations Diplomatic Conference of Plenipotentiaries on the Establishment of an International Criminal Court, 52d Sess., Annex II, UN Doc. A/CONF.183/9 (1998), reprinted in M. Cherif Bassiouni ed., *The Statute of the International Criminal Court: A Documentary History* (Ardsley NY, Transnational Pub. 1998) Art. 8, para. 2(b)(iv) (emphasis added).

112. A. Cassese et al., eds., *The Rome Statue of the International Criminal Court: A Commentary*, Vol. I, (Oxford, Oxford University Press 2002) at p. 399.

113. R.G. Wright, 'Non-combatant immunity: A case study in the relation between international law and morality', 67 *Notre Dame LR* (1991) pp. 335, 339. See also R.L. Holmes, *On War and Morality* (Princeton NJ, Princeton University Press 1989) p. 153; S.M. Cohen, *Arms and Judgment: Law, Morality and the Conduct of War in the Twentieth Century* (Boulder CO, Westview Press 1989) pp. 7-10.

114. Wright, ibid., at pp. 339-340. See e.g., Elshtain, *supra* n. 35, at p. 14: arguing that Additional Protocol I (1977) codifies just war thinking on civilian and non-military targeting; R.S. Hartigan, 'Saint Augustine on war and killing: The problem of the innocent', 27 *Journal of the History of Ideas* (1966) p. 195, 195, arguing that the international law adopted religious doctrine of civilian immunity from intentional killing; W.V. O'Brien, 'The jus in bello in revolutionary war counterinsurgency', 18 *Virginia JIL* (1978) pp. 193, 209, noting that 'proportionality and discrimination are principles of both natural law recognized by just war doctrine and positive international law'; Raby, *supra* n. 99, at p. 83, noting that 'the most important aspect of the doctrine of proportionality is its moral element'; T.

Examining the moral doctrine regarding the rule of proportionality might help at least in two different aspects. First, the negotiation history of the rule of proportionality reveals that there was disagreement about the subjective content of the rule.[115] Eventually the rule was codified with no objective definition, with 'a hope that such open-textured rule can be progressively interpreted more demandingly over time'.[116] Therefore, examining the moral arguments underpinning the rule might help us interpret and implement this rule, and give it content based on the moral principles underpinning it.

Second, a moral requirement might be embedded in the law of armed conflict, through the Martens Clause.[117] Therefore, it is crucial to examine the moral aspects underpinning these issues in order to determine the need for further restrictions. Eventually, if countries recognise such moral demands, and follow them under the belief that the law of armed conflict requires compliance with them, these moral requirements might hopefully become part of the customary international law.[118]

4.1 The rule of proportionality – moral analysis

The moral issue in relation to the rule of proportionality is under what circumstances, if any, innocent persons may be killed or injured in order to achieve some military objective.[119] By asking that question, we assume that human beings have a *prima facie* obligation not to intentionally harm innocent persons.[120] Therefore, the question arises as to when military necessity overrides this obligation.

The criminal analogy is of little help here. War as an activity has no equivalent in a settled civil society – killing someone else because of his status (combatant) is never accepted in a civilised society.[121] Likewise, in criminal law an actor is presumed to have intended the expected natural and probable consequences of her actions.[122] However, in the context of the law of armed conflict, a commander

---

Nagel, *Moral Questions* (Cambridge, Cambridge University Press 1979) p. 53 'there is, in other words, a moral basis for the rules of war, even though the conventions now officially in force are far from giving it perfect expression'.

115. See Levie, *supra* n. 68, at pp. 309-338; Protocols Commentary, *supra* n. 66, at pp. 623-626; Fenrick, *supra* n. 19, at pp. 98-112.

116. Wright, *supra* n. 82, at 139.

117. See *supra* nn. 87-89 and the accompanying text.

118. For an explanation of when a rule is considered to be customary international law, see *supra* n. 45.

119. Conceptually it is clearer to ask under what circumstances it is morally justified to kill innocents, than to ask what should be the proportion between anticipated military necessity and probable civilian casualties in order that an action will be morally justified. The reason is that we should try to avoid, as far as we can, presuppositions such as that there are cases in which the rule of proportionality can legitimately overrule the Principle of Discrimination.

120. Virtually all ethical constructs, whether they are deontological, consequential, or virtue based, have this proscription against taking innocent human life. See e.g., Christopher, *supra* n. 25, at p. 151.

121. Walzer, *supra* n. 35, at pp. 127-128.

122. Courts typically held that a defendant might be 'presumed to have intended the natural and probable consequences of what he knowingly did.' See e.g., *Grubal* v. *United States*, 264 F 44 (8th Cir. 1920); *Fontana* v. *United States*, 262 F 283 (8th Cir. 1919); *Shilter* v. *United States*, 257 F 724 (9th Cir. 1919).

who targets military objectives in which there are incidental civilian casualties will not be considered as one who intended to kill civilians, although the civilians' deaths were the probable consequence of her action.[123]

A moral analysis must always begin with the fundamental distinction in the law of armed conflict between combatants and non-combatants, giving the non-combatant segment of the population a moral immunity from being intentionally targeted.[124] Although the explanation for this distinction causes some controversy among scholars,[125] for the purpose of moral analysis we adopt what is fairly characterised as the majority view, which is that civilians are considered 'innocent' because they are not participating in the actual hostilities.[126] Therefore, it is forbidden to intentionally target them, as opposed to combatants.

As stated above, the law of armed conflict recognises cases in which it will be lawful to cause collateral damage, as long as the collateral damage is not excessive in relation to the anticipated military advantage.[127] In making this determination, the commander is faced with two moral duties she has to choose between: (1) moral duty 1 (MD1): it is wrong to intentionally harm innocent persons (a soldier must refrain from intentionally harming the non-combatants of the enemy); and (2) moral duty 2 (MD2): a commander has a duty to protect her soldiers to the extent

---

123. See Walzer, *supra* n. 35, at pp. 348-349.

124. Any member of the armed forces is a combatant. Civilians might lose their immunity if they take part in hostilities. See e.g., Detter, *supra* n. 17, at pp. 316-320; Sassoli and Bouvier, *supra* n. 27, at pp. 116-118; Wright, *supra* n. 113 at p. 335; L.L. Turner and L.G. Norton, 'Civilians at the tip of the spear', 51 *Air Force LR* (2001) pp. 1, 28-30: 'customary international law does not recognize the ability of an unlawful combatant to regain the protections of his civilian status. However, a controversial provision of Additional Protocol I allows the civilian to regain his protection from attack when he ceases direct participation in hostilities'.; Rogers, *supra* n. 41, at p. 8: 'only combatants are permitted to take a direct part in hostilities. It follows that they may be attacked. Civilians may not take a direct part in hostilities and for so long as they refrain from doing so are protected from attack'.

125. The explanation for the distinction between combatant and non-combatant is controversial among scholars. Walzer thinks that civilians who do not fight are, in a certain way, innocent, and therefore they are entitled to a kind of moral immunity that soldiers do not get. See Walzer, *supra* n. 35, at pp. 138-159. Norman thinks that from the moral point of view there is no difference between the moral guilt of soldiers and civilians. However, killing civilians shows disrespect to human lives that is very serious. Therefore, the distinction between combatant and non-combatant attempts to reduce, as far as possible, the de-humanisation and de-personalisation that are part of each war. See R. J. Norman, *Ethics, Killing and War* (Cambridge, Cambridge University Press 1995) pp. 159-206. Mavrodes agrees that there is no moral basis to the claim that civilians, in contrast to soldiers, are innocent. However, the basis for distinction is the common desire of the parties to minimise the killing and destruction and to put minimal limitations on their possibility to fight. See G.I. Mavrodes, 'Conventions and the morality of war', 4 *Philosophy and Public Affairs* (1975) p. 117. See also R.K. Fullinwider, 'War and innocence', 5 *Philosophy and Public Affairs* (1975) p. 90, explaining the justification to kill combatant and not to kill non-combatant from the point of view of self-defence; L.A. Alexander, 'Self-defense and the killing of non-combatants: A reply to Fukkinwider', *Philosophy and Public Affairs* (1975) p. 408, rejects the self-defence argument, since being a cause of danger does not mark the distinction between combatant and non-combatant.

126. See also Nagel, *supra* n. 114, at p. 70: 'according to an absolutist position, deliberate killing of the innocent is murder, and in warfare the role of the innocent is filled by non-combatants'.

127. See *supra* n. 60 and the accompanying text.

possible (commanders have a duty to endanger themselves and their comrades only to the extent required to carry out the mission).

In making a proportionality determination, the commander faces a moral dilemma, in which no matter what her decision will be, it will be inconsistent with one of her moral duties.[128] For instance, in the Osama Bin Laden example[129] a commander has to decide whether to bomb the place Osama Bin Laden is currently at, or send soldiers who will capture or kill him. If the commander decides to bomb the target, she will inflict harm on peaceful members of the civilian population, and therefore violate MD1. However, if she does not bomb the target, and instead sends infantry units to achieve the mission, she will fail to protect the members of her force and therefore violate MD2.

One of the most widely recognised ethical paradigms is the duty-based theory of Immanuel Kant.[130] Kant thought that a dilemma like the one described above is insoluble, because there is a moral imperative stating that human beings are equal in value, and every person must be treated as having her own value and being an end in herself.[131] However, duty-based approaches, like Kant's, are problematic in discussing proportionality where much of the determination depends on the outcome of the act, since duty-based approaches are based on the idea that moral duties are absolute.[132] This idea contradicts our strong intuition and our personal experience that in extreme cases the duties, even those impacting human life, can be overridden.[133] There is a prohibition to kill innocents, but for those who are not

---

128. A moral dilemma is a situation in which there is a clash between different values, and no matter what the decision will be it will be inconsistent with the obligations and values of the man facing the dilemma. See D. Statman, *Moral Dilemmas* (Amsterdam, Rodopi 1995) pp. 5-28. See also J. Raz, *The Morality of Freedom* (Oxford, Clarendon Press 1986) pp. 359-360, 'most, if not all, the cases used as examples of moral dilemmas are cases of a choice between evils. They are cases of being in a situation in which whatever one does either one will wrong people, or one will fail in some binding duty'.

129. See *infra* at section 3.2.

130. See e.g., B. Orend, 'Kant on international law and armed conflict', 11 *Can. J L & Jur.* (1998) pp. 329, 330-337.

131. Immanuel Kant, *Fundamental Principles of the Metaphysics of Ethics*, translated by M. Shefi (Jerusalem, Magnes Press 1973) pp. 108-109.

132. The assumption that moral prohibitions are absolute is based on Kant's posture that the moral obligations are formulations of what he calls the 'categorical imperative', the foremost norm of practical reason, as opposed to 'hypothetical imperative.' the difference between the categorical imperative and the hypothetical one is that hypothetical imperative is conditional on the agent's desiring the end in question, while the categorical imperative is unconditional – it stipulates the adoption of certain intentions and actions, regardless of whether or not the agent desires to conform by them. In Kant's view, wilful adherence to the dictates of the categorical imperative is essential for progress towards moral justice in our world. For example, Kant argues that we must always tell the truth, regardless of the consequences (even in the case that lying will save the life of our innocent friend from those who want to kill him). See Immanuel Kant, 'On a Supposed Right to Lie from Altruistic Motives', in L.W. Beck, ed. and transl., *Critique of Practical Reason and Other Writings in Moral Philosophy* (Chicago, University of Chicago Press 1963) p. 346; T. Hill, Jr., 'Making exception without abandoning the principle: Or how a Kantian might think about terrorism', in R.G. Frey and C.W. Morris, *Violence, Terrorism and Justice* (Cambridge, Cambridge University Press 1991) pp. 220-224.

133. See also E. Gross, 'Use of civilians as human shield: What legal and moral restrictions retain to a war waged by a democratic state against terrorism?', 16 *Emory ILR* (2002) pp. 445, 463. Gross

pacifists and know the modern reality of war, it will be difficult to claim that the prohibition on killing innocents is an absolute duty.[134] A commander has a duty to command and protect her soldiers, but if her children are in danger she might be able to morally justify abandoning her soldiery duties and going and defending her children, even though this might cause some of her fellow citizens and soldiers to be harmed. Therefore, if we agree that these moral duties are not absolute, we have to determine which approach should be used to decide which moral obligation governs.

The moral philosophical 'principle of double effect', which is widely considered to be the moral foundation for the rule of proportionality,[135] provides an answer to this dilemma, by building upon the possibility that our actions may have more or less probable consequences apart from those consequences we intend.[136] According to this principle, actions with the same consequences – such as killing the non-combatant – may be judged differently depending upon whether the consequences are intended, as an end or a means, or were merely foreseen.[137]

Classical formulations of the principle of double effect require four conditions to be met if the action in question is to be morally permissible:

---

argues that Kant's absolute approach is a problematic one, because 'if the value of human life always prevailed in any clash … people would not die in road accidents because the state would provide authorities with the entire budget necessary to minimize traffic accident fatalities. Reality urges us to refrain from absolute concepts and exercise discretion within the decision making process. On occasion, other considerations outweigh the value of human life.'

134. Some scholars state that even Kant, as an 'extremely cultivated and informed thinker' must have known that civilian casualties are part and parcel of the war process, and even tough war can be sometimes justly fought. See e.g., Orend, *supra* n. 130, at pp. 372-373.

135. See e.g., Walzer, *supra* n. 35, at pp. 151-159; S. Hoffmann, *Duties Beyond Borders: On the Limits and Possibilities of Ethical International Politics* (Syracuse NY, Syracuse University Press 1981) p. 48; C. McKeogh, *Innocent Civilians: The Morality of Killing in War* (Basingstoke, Palgrave 2002) pp. 64-65; Wright, *supra* n. 113, at 340-344; Orend, *supra* n. 130, at 372-373; Gross, *supra* n. 133, at 486-491; J. Gordon, 'When intent makes all the difference in the world: economic sanctions on Iraq and the accusation of genocide', 5 *Yale HR & DLJ* pp. 57, 64-65; A. Moseley, 'Just War Theory, in the Internet Encyclopedia of Philosophy', <http://www.utm.edu/research/iep/j/justwar.htm>; M.J. Garcia, 'A necessary response: The lack of domestic and international constraints upon a U.S. nuclear response to terrorist attack', 1 *Georgtown JL & Pub. Pol.* (2003) pp. 515, 542-543; P.W. Kahn, 'Nuclear weapons and the rule of law', 31 *NY Univ. JIL & Pol.* (1999) pp. 349, 351-352.

136. The principle of 'double effect' was a basic principle of Catholic moral reasoning. The initial Christian response to war was fundamentally pacifist. This response, however, was based more on a desire to 'total[ly] disengage from statecraft and from the things of this world generally,' than on a reasoned opposition to warfare. During the fourth century, however, the Roman Empire first began to tolerate Christianity and finally recognized it as the legally preferred faith. As a result of this reversal, Christianity became responsible for affairs of state and suddenly became aware of the need to reconcile faith with political realities. Augustine was the seminal figure in this reconciliation. Part of this reconciliation was the recognition of the principle of double effect as a moral principle, which justifies collateral damage in certain circumstances. See C.J. Reid, 'Robert L. Philips' war and justice', 34 *Catholic Univ. LR* (1985) pp. 1173, 1174-1176 (book review); McKeogh, *supra* n. 135, at p. 64.

137. See e.g., Wright, *supra* n. 113, at p. 341; Walzer, *supra* n. 35, at pp. 152-153; Christopher, *supra* n. 25, at pp. 92-93; McKeogh, *supra* n. 135, at pp. 64-65.

1) The action contemplated should be in itself either morally good or morally indifferent, which means, for our purposes, that it is a legitimate act of war;
2) The direct effect is morally acceptable – the destruction of military supplies, for example, or the killing of enemy soldiers;
3) The intention of the actor is good, that is, he aims narrowly at the acceptable effect; the evil is not one of his ends, nor is it a means to his ends; and
4) The good effect is sufficiently good to compensate for allowing the evil effect.[138]

When all of these conditions are met, the action under consideration is morally permissible despite the bad result.

In relation to the law of armed conflict, it will be morally justified to target a military object, even if the commander anticipates that civilians will probably die during the attack, if and only if:

1) The operation is itself morally good, i.e., a legitimate act of war;
2) The direct effect – destruction of military objective or killing the enemy soldiers, for example – is morally acceptable;
3) The intention of the actor is good. He aims only at the acceptable effect. Collateral damage is not one of her aims, nor is it a means to her end; and
4) The good effect – destroying the military objective – is sufficiently good to compensate for allowing the bad effect – causing collateral damage.

Interpreted this way, the principle of double effect provides a moral framework for the doctrine of proportionality. Just as the law of armed conflict prohibits operations in which the collateral civilian damage is excessive in relation to the anticipated military advantage, so does the principle of double effect.

4.2 Military necessity and reducing risks – moral analysis

The issue is whether a commander has a moral duty to expose her own soldiers to danger in order to limit civilian casualties.

The four conditions of the principle of double effect do not require, by themselves, to risk the soldiers' lives in order to decrease the risk to the adversary's civilians. If the act is a legitimate act of war, the direct effect is morally acceptable, the civilian casualties are not one of the commander's ends nor are they means to her ends, and the military advantage is sufficiently good to compensate for allowing the civilian casualties, the commander is permitted to perform such act and there are no further moral requirements.

Nonetheless, Professor Michael Walzer argues that, morally, soldiers have to worry about civilian deaths even if they are unintended:

---

138. Walzer, *supra* n. 35, at p. 153.

> '[W]e have to worry, I think, about all those unintended but foreseeable deaths, for their number can be large; and subject only to the proportionality rule – a weak constraint – double effect provides a blanket justification. The principle for that reason invites an angry or a cynical response: what difference does it make whether civilian deaths are a direct or an indirect effect of my actions? It can hardly matter to the dead civilians, and if I know in advance that I am likely to kill so many innocent people and go ahead anyway, how can I be blameless?'[139]

Therefore, Walzer suggests correcting the principle of double effect by adding a demand that not only the bad result not be directly intended, but the agent should seek to minimise the bad result by accepting costs to herself.[140]

To illustrate his argument, Walzer describes an event in the Korean War, in which automatic fire was directed toward American troops.[141] In response, the American troops called several fighter planes, which bombed the area from which the fire was coming. This bombardment killed some enemy soldiers, as well as civilians who were nearby.[142] In this case, 'it was not the intention of the officers who called in the artillery and planes to kill civilians; they were acting out of a concern for their own men. And that is legitimate concern. No one would want to be commanded in wartime by an officer who did not value the lives of his soldiers.'[143] Still, Walzer argues that the commander must not save her soldiers by killing innocent people, even if such killing is unintended and proportional:

> 'Even if the proportions work out favorably, in particular cases or over a period of time, we would still want to say, I think, that the patrol must be sent out, the risk accepted, before the big guns are brought to bear . . . What we look for in such cases is some sign of a positive commitment to save civilian lives. Not merely to apply the proportionality rule and kill no more civilians than is militarily necessary – that rule applies to soldiers as well; no one can be killed for trivial purposes. Civilians have a right for something more. And if saving civilian lives means risking soldiers' lives, the risk must be accepted. But there is a limit to the risk that we require. These are, after all, unintended deaths and legitimate military operations, and the absolute rule against attacking civilians does not apply. War necessarily places civilians in danger; that is another aspect of its hellishness. We can only ask soldiers to minimize the dangers they impose.'[144]

However, Walzer recognises that it is difficult to determine how much risk soldiers must assume to save civilians, and that 'the degree of risk that is permissible is going to vary with the nature of the target, the urgency of the moment, the avail-

---

139. Walzer, *supra* n. 35, at p. 153.

140. The third of the conditions listed above, therefore, should be restated as: '(3) the intention of the actor is good, that is, he aims narrowly at the acceptable effect; the evil effect is not one of his ends, nor is it a means to his ends, and, aware of the evil involved, he seeks to minimize it, accepting costs to himself.' Ibid., at pp. 155-156.

141. Ibid., at p. 154.

142. Ibid., at pp. 154-155.

143. Ibid., at p. 155.

144. Ibid., at pp. 155-156.

able technology, and so on'.[145] Therefore, he concludes that it is best to say simply 'that civilians have a right that "due care" be taken'.[146] This definition might be equivalent to 'recognizing their rights as best we can in the context of the war'.[147]

Professor Sheldon Cohen thinks that Walzer asks far more of soldiers than the law of armed conflict,[148] and there is no moral reason for that.[149] Therefore, he suggests the following as a reasonable account of the limits on soldiers:

> 'Innocents have certain moral rights, and it would be immoral for a rifleman who has an infant in his sights to gun the child down. But the rights of innocents are defeasible. If the indiscriminate shelling or bombing of a town is an attack on innocents, then armies are not under a moral obligation, in assaults, not to attack innocents. The rule is, I suggest, that the attacker may, given the presence of innocents in a combat zone, do anything that it would be permissible to do if there were no innocents there – subject to the restrictions entailed by the principle of proportionality ... This rules out discriminate (selective) attacks on innocents but allows the indiscriminate shelling or bombing of defended areas containing innocents ... The rights of innocents are defeasible when honoring those rights would push the soldiers' risks beyond what it is reasonable to expect any group to endure.'[150]

On the other hand, Professor Paul Christopher objects to Cohen's approach, on the ground that it does not acknowledge that part of what it means to be a soldier is taking risks:

> 'While all widely accepted moral theories require some degree of impartiality or objectivity in choosing among alternatives, the risk to lives of combatants should not be weighed equally against the risk to the lives of non-combatants, because it is in the nature of the soldier to take risks – risking one's life is part of what it means to be a soldier. Taking the position that minimizing the risks to soldiers is the basis for choosing among alternatives undermines the very notion of distinguishing between combatant

---

145. Ibid., at p. 156.

146. Ibid.

147. B. Orend, *Michael Walzer on War and Justice* (Cardiff, University of Wales Press 2000) p. 120.

148. See Cohen, *supra* n. 113, at p. 28: 'Walzer was also right in saying that the use of mortar, artillery, or air strikes causes civilian casualties that would be avoided if, instead of calling in artillery fire, rifleman crawled up and fired only at the observed enemy troops. But the law of war does not require this: it allows troops under fire to fire back without ascertaining that there are no civilians mingled with the troops who are firing upon them. It allows troops under fire to fire back even if they know civilians are mingled with the enemy.'
See also ibid., at p. 33: 'the law of armed conflict implies that soldiers are not obliged to raise their already high risks to even higher levels in order to lower further the risk to innocents in combat zones.'

149. Ibid., at p. 32: 'It seems unlikely that it was morally permissible for the Allies to attempt to defeat the Germans, but morally impermissible to employ the means that had to be used if the war was to be won. The notion of 'military necessity' lends itself to abuse, but every use of it is not abusive. It is not being abused if the alternative is to ask more of troops than we have any right to ask of anyone or than anyone can deliver.'

150. Ibid., at p. 33.

> and non-combatant. An analogous domestic example might be to hire a police officer to prevent crime and limit her duty to times or places where there was little crime so that she would not be put in risk.'[151]

Christopher's argument is not fully persuasive for two reasons. First, Christopher does not convincingly support his argument that soldiers have a moral duty to risk their lives in order to limit the enemy's civilian casualties. One can successfully claim that soldiers have to assume great personal risk in the performance of their duty – weakening the military force of the enemy, defending their country and assisting their comrades when they need their help. However, no equivalent requirement exists in relation to the enemy civilians.[152] Second, as I mentioned before,[153] the criminal or the domestic analogy is inapt, since war, as an activity, has no equivalent in settled civil society. Therefore, the analogy he made between the police officer's duties and the soldier's duties is problematic.

Still, there is logic to the view that sometimes a commander has a moral obligation to expose his soldiers to danger in order to limit civilian casualties. Let me go back to the Osama Bin Laden example. Suppose that the commander assesses that if he bombs the place where Osama Bin Laden is currently located, hundreds of citizens will be killed. He assesses further that if he sends infantry units some of them might die but they will be able to catch or kill Bin Laden with much less collateral damage. In this scenario, there is a strong sense that the commander has a moral duty to expose his soldiers to risk in order to prevent such high civilian casualties, because mission success is assumed in either case and the increased risk to the enemy's civilians if the bombardment option is adopted is much higher than the increased risk to the soldiers if the other option is adopted.

Let me develop this point a little further. The law of armed conflict prohibits the deliberate killing of non-combatants, even in cases of extreme necessity, such as when the killing of non-combatants would be the only way to enable a military force to escape from deadly danger.[154] However, if the deaths of the civilians are not intended, but are collateral damage from attacking a military objective, then they are permitted if they are not excessive in relation to the military advantage. In our case, we have two options to achieve the mission. One of the alternatives will prevent killing civilians but will expose the soldiers to higher risk. In this scenario, are there good moral reasons not to require soldiers to accomplish the mission without killing the civilians?[155] Does the mere fact that the killing of civilians is

---

151. Ibid., at p. 155.

152. In other words, a soldier has no positive moral duty to defend the enemy civilians. The only duty he has is not to intentionally harm them (MD1). However, he has a positive moral duty to protect the citizens of his country (MD2). Therefore, the comparison between these two moral duties is inadequate.

153. See *supra* nn. 121-123 and the accompanying text.

154. See e.g., Protocol I, *supra* n. 20, Art. 51(2); G. Von Glahn, *Law Among Nations: An Introduction to Public International Law*, 6th edn. (New York, Macmillan 1992) p. 697; Detter, *supra* n. 17, at pp. 316-320; McCoubrey, *supra* n. 54, at pp. 113-118.

155. See also Walzer, *supra* n. 35, at p. 157: 'Even if the target is very important, and the number of innocent people threatened relatively small, they must risk soldiers before they kill civilians.'

not intended, but is a probable consequence of the military action, make all the difference?[156] Will the answer to these questions be the same even if civilians will surely die as a result of the attack, but the military force might be able to achieve the same mission without casualties? [157]

I suggest accepting Walzer's approach that civilians have a right that 'due care' be taken.[158] Additionally, I suggest accepting the idea that when a choice is possible between several military objectives, and one of them will be more dangerous to the soldiers, the commander must make a good faith estimate of what will be the price of reducing risks to civilians, in terms of exposing his soldiers to danger. Based on that analysis, the commander has to decide if the amount of increased risk to the civilians is proportionate to the amount of decreased risk to his soldiers.[159] By honestly engaging in this analysis, a military commander can undertake aggressive combat operations without violating minimum humanitarian requirements.

4.3 The method to assess military necessity – moral analysis

The issue is what method should be morally used to assess the military advantage while carrying out the proportionality balancing test: must the assessment be in

156. For the importance of intent in international law and morality see e.g., Gordon, *supra* n. 135. See also McKeogh, *supra* n. 135, at p. 169 'The conclusion must be that the principle of double effect is unconvincing in its application to the 'collateral' killing of civilians in war. The attempt to apply it to the collateral killing of civilians in war reveals only the weaknesses of the principle and its openness to abuse. We are responsible not only for that which we directly intend; we are culpable also for our negligence and for the foreseeable avoidable consequences of our acts.'

157. Walzer describes a case from the Second World War, where a heavy water plant at Vermok needed to be destroyed. It was vitally important to stop the production of heavy water so as to delay the development of an atomic bomb by German scientists. British and Norwegian officials debated whether to make the attempt from the air or from the ground and choose the latter approach because it was less likely to injure civilians. But it was very dangerous to commandos. The first attempt failed, and 34 men were killed in its course; the second attempt, by a smaller number of men, succeeded without casualties. See ibid., at pp. 157-58.

158. See *supra* n. 146 and the accompanying text. It is worth noting that Christopher thinks that the United States seems to have adopted a like approach. See Christopher, *supra* n. 25, at p. 92: 'In its military operations, the United States seems to have adopted a modification to the doctrine of double effect so that one may undertake military operations aimed at legitimate objectives or targets, even though the operations will also have foreseeable "bad" consequences. Such operations become permissible when they meet the following necessary criteria: (1) the bad effect is unintended; (2) the bad effect is proportional to the desired military objective; (3) the bad effect is not a direct means to the good effect (e.g., bomb cities to encourage peace talks); and (4) actions are taken to minimize the foreseeable bad effects, even if it means accepting an increased risk to combatants.'

159. However, if the civilians were given an advance warning to leave the place, but refuse to do so – the commander, arguably, will no longer be required to risk his soldiers lives for those civilians who intentionally decide to be in danger. See Gross, *supra* n. 133, at 477-478. See also W. Hays Parks, 'Air war and the law of war', 32 *Air Force LR* (1990) pp. 1, 55, 'noting that "the primary responsibility for protection of the civilian population rested squarely with the defender", and that civilians working in industries directly related to the war effort should not be regarded as collateral casualties and, therefore, should not be taken into account when applying the proportionality rule'.

relation to each individual attack, or can it be done on a cumulative basis, taking into account the overarching operational plans?[160]

The principle of double effect is of little help here. The fourth condition demands that the good effect is sufficiently good to compensate for allowing the bad effect, but it gives no method to assess the 'military necessity', i.e., the good effect. However, some scholars adopt the cumulative approach by focusing on the ultimate objective: winning the war.

Henry Sidgwick, for example, asserts that in the conduct of hostilities it is not permissible to do 'any mischief which does not tend materially to the end [of victory], nor any mischief of which the conduciveness to the end is slight in comparison with the amount of the mischief'.[161] Accordingly, the military necessity assessment should be made in relation to the victory in war. As Walzer states, 'any act of force that contributes in a significant way to winning the war is likely to be called permissible'.[162]

Van Damme and Fotion agree with this conclusion, claiming that in assessing whether a particular military operation is moral or not, one must include in the calculation both its immediate anticipated consequences and anticipated consequences of how this operation might help to end a war more quickly.[163] Therefore, they conclude that the principle of proportionality favours 'a more holistic approach in measuring consequences over a more particularistic one. The principle favors the 'big picture' approach rather than one that views the battle scene narrowly.'[164]

Moreover, we, as moral agents, have a duty to maximise good and minimise evil.[165] When, in our ordinary life, we face moral dilemmas, we determine what will be the result of doing one thing and not the other, based on all we know and all the foreseeable consequences of our actions. The same criteria should be ap-

---

160. See e.g., Bothe, *supra* n. 74, at p. 325, 'Prior to the 1944 cross channel operation, the Allies attacked a large number of bridges, fuel dumps, airfields and other targets in the Pas de Calais. These targets made an effective contribution to German military action in that area. The primary military advantage of these attacks anticipated by the Allies, however, was not to reduce German military strength in that area, but to deceive the Germans into believing that the Allied amphibious assault would occur in the Pas de Calais instead of the beaches of Normandy. Therefore, the military advantage expected from these air raids was not related to their value to the adverse party.'

161. H. Sidgwick, *The Elements of Politics* (London, Macmillan 1891) p. 254.

162. Walzer, *supra* n. 35, at p. 129.

163. Van Damme and Fotion, *supra* n. 26, at p. 131.

164. Ibid., at p. 132.

165. This approach is based on utilitarianism, which says that one should try to maximise good and minimise evil, and that if faced with the possibility of preventing great evil by producing a lesser evil, one should choose the lesser evil. Also there are some problems about the formulation of utilitarianism, and much has been written about it; its intent is morally transparent. See Nagel, *supra* n. 114, at p. 55. However, even absolutists will share the idea that in this case we have a moral duty to maximize good and minimize evil, since this does not require us to violate an absolute prohibition. See Nagel, ibid., at p. 58, 'An absolutist can be expected to try to maximize good and minimize evil, so long as this does not require him to transgress an absolute prohibition like that against murder', and at p. 59, 'There could not, for example, without coherence, be an absolute prohibition against bringing about the death of an innocent person. For one may find oneself in a situation in which, no matter what one does, some innocent people will dic as a result.'

plied here. There is no moral reason why a commander who conducts the proportionality balancing test should not consider all the relevant information he has, for the short term and for the long term, including the context of the overall operational plan or war strategy.

Therefore, I suggest accepting a cumulative analysis of military advantage, within a broader combination of both cumulative and case-by-case analysis. Consequently, the assessment of collateral civilian casualties and damage to civilian objects during the proportionality balancing test has to be done both on a case-by-case basis and in light of the overarching operational plan and war strategy.

5. CONCLUSION

In the future, it is likely that many battles will be fought in an urban environment, much like the battle of Jenin.[166] In such battles, the risk both to the civilian population and to the attacking soldiers increases drastically.[167] As a result, commanders will certainly face the very difficult dilemma of determining the amount of danger to which they will expose their forces to limit civilian casualties. Additionally, they will be required to determine their course of conduct, based on tactical and strategic considerations. In these circumstances, these issues become extremely important.

In relation to the first issue – the extent to which a military commander is obligated to expose her soldiers to risk in order to limit civilian casualties – the current law of armed conflict in general, and Protocol I in particular, do not explicitly require a commander to risk her soldiers' lives in order to reduce civilian casualties. However, there are moral reasons to accept such obligation in certain situations. Hence, states should accept Walzer's approach that civilians have a right that 'due care' be taken. Consequently, when a choice is possible between several military objectives, all of which comply with the rule of proportionality but some of which will cause more collateral damage than others, commanders will have an obligation to make a good faith estimate of what will be the price of reducing risks

---

166. See e.g., Field-Manual (FM) 3-06.11 (FM 90-10-1), 'Combined Arms Operations in Urban Terrain, Washington DC: Headquarters, Department of the Army', 28 February 2002, at 1-1, 'it is estimated that by the year 2010, seventy-five percent of the world's population will live in urban areas. Urban areas are expected to be the future battlefield and combat in urban areas cannot be avoided'.

167. Any urban operation requires the infantryman, and many of them, not only to clear buildings and fight the fight, one room at a time, but to secure buildings already taken and to guard precarious lines of communication that can be cut by a determined enemy squad. In such conditions, the risk to the civilian population increases drastically, and the commanders must face very difficult moral dilemmas. See G.J. Mordica II, 'It's a dirty business, but somebody has to do it (urban combat)', US Army Center for Army Lessons Learned (CALL), <http://www.globalsecurity.org/military/library/report/1999/99-16/chap1.htm>; M.C. Waxman, *International law and the politics of urban air operations* (Santa Monica CA, Rand 2000) p. 18, 'the structure and organization of urban centers pose special problems for compliance with the principles of discrimination and proportionality ... The collocation of military civilian assets in urban environments multiplies the chances that military attacks will cause unintended, and perhaps disproportionate, civilian damage'.

to civilians, in terms of exposing their soldiers to danger. Based on that analysis, they have to decide if the amount of increased risk to the civilians is proportionate to the amount of decreased risk to their soldiers. This requirement might be embedded in the law of armed conflict through interpretation of current provisions[168] or through the Martens Clause.

In relation to the second issue – how 'military assessment' must be measured – both international law and morality require that the assessment be made within a broader combination of both cumulative and case-by-case analyses. Hence, a commander must take into account, while conducting the proportionality balancing test, both the tactical aspects of the operation and the strategic aspects of the overall operational plan or war strategy.

As modern warfare continues to exact tolls on civilians, it is crucial that nations continue to look for ways to strengthen the role of the law of armed conflict as a means of mitigating human suffering during armed conflicts. It is hoped that the discussion provided in this paper will help to facilitate this task, by illuminating and strengthening the role of the law of armed conflict as a means of minimising civilian suffering.

---

168. Such an approach could be based, for example, on an interpretation of the proportionality rule, in a way that requires comparison between alternative methods. See for example, the finding of the Israeli Supreme Court in its security fence decision, in which the court concludes, based, *inter alia*, on Israeli administrative law, that: '[I]t is also possible to apply the test of proportionality in the narrow sense in a "relative manner." According to this approach, the administrative act is tested *vis-à-vis* an alternate act, whose benefit will be somewhat smaller than that of the former one. The original administrative act is disproportionate in the narrow sense if a certain reduction in the advantage gained by the original act – by employing alternate means, for example – ensures a substantial reduction in the injury caused by the administrative act.' HCJ 2056/04, *Beit Sourik Village Council* v. *The Government of Israel*, para. 41, <http://elyon1.court.gov.il/files_eng/04/560/020/a28/04020560.a28.pdf>.

JUS IN BELLO IN THE TWENTY FIRST CENTURY: REAPING THE BENEFITS AND FACING THE CHALLENGES OF MODERN WEAPONRY AND MILITARY STRATEGY[1]

David D. Jividen[2]

2. LL.M Harvard Law School, 1997, J.D, University of Cincinnati Law School 1986. David D. Jividen is a Lieutenant Colonel in the US Air Force assigned to the Pentagon, Joint Staff, Strategy and Policy (J-5), in the International Negotiations and Multilateral Affairs Deputy Directorate, Nuclear Arms Control Branch. The views presented are those of the author and do not necessarily reflect the views of the Department of Defense or any of its components.

Yearbook of International Humanitarian Law
Volume 7 - 2004 - pp. 113-152 DOI 10.1017/S1389135904001138

1. INTRODUCTION

The relentless modernisation of weaponry, the transformation of military strategy, and recent conflicts incorporating both these trends, especially in response to the War on Terror (WOT), have affected *jus in bello* in ways that legal practitioners are just beginning to discern four years into the twenty-first century.[3] Two critical questions relevant to the *jus in bello* are posed by these changes. First, does the almost exponential increase in the use of modern weaponry and commensurate changes in military strategies foster compliance with *jus in bello* or, alternatively, does it make its observance less likely, especially in light of belligerents resorting to asymmetrical warfare? Second, is *jus in bello* in danger of becoming increasingly irrelevant in the era of modern and asymmetrical warfare, and if so, should it be modified to meet these new challenges?

In answering these two questions, this article describes *jus in bello* law, reviews how advances in weapon technology have been reflected in recent military operations, reviews some *jus in bello* issues that have arisen in these recent conflicts, surveys changes in US military strategies, and identifies future weapon modernisation efforts. Because the United States (US) has been the most robust military player on the world stage since the end of the Cold War, and has had the largest military budget, this article will draw mostly on US examples and perspectives – with the knowledge that similar changes have occurred, and will continue to occur, in other nations.[4] The article concludes by noting that weapon modernisation and new military strategies have thus far proceeded within the parameters of *jus in bello*, and have fostered its observance. This trend will assist *jus in bello* in fulfilling its *raison d'être* of ensuring distinction between combatants and noncombatants in order to protect civilian populations, thereby ensuring it will survive the unique challenges to its continued vitality posed by non-conforming terrorists and belligerent states.

---

3. *Jus in bello* refers to the use of force 'in war' during the armed conflict and stands in contrast to *jus ad bellum*, which refers to the law relating to the 'resort to force' in the conduct of international relations. See generally, H. McCoubry and N. White, *International Law and Armed Conflict* (Aldershot, Dartmouth Publishing Co. 1992) pp. 1, 17, 189.

4. US military expenditures, calculated at market exchange rates for the base year of 2000, accounted for 47 percent of the world total military expenditure in 2003. Stockholm International Peace Research Institute, *The Major Spenders in 2003* (Stockholm, Stockholm International Peace Research Institute), <http://www.sipri.org/contents/milap/milex/mex_trends.html>. The next four in order are Japan, the UK, France and China. Ibid. Countries have adopted and improved upon US military technologies in the past. For example, a mere 15 years after the Wright brothers' first flight, 'the air forces of every other major nation that participated in the First World War were numerically and technically superior' to those of the US, while the United Kingdom adopted the Caterpillar track invention of the US inventor Benjamin Holt – which had been developed for farm machinery – for armoured vehicle use, creating the tank. J. Hyten and R. Uy, 'Moral and ethical decisions regarding space warfare', 18 *Air and Space Power Journal* (2004) pp. 51, 55. The inevitability of technological diffusion is recognised by the US. Noting that the 'global proliferation of a wide range of technology and weaponry will affect the character of future conflicts', the National Military Strategy of the United States (hereinafter, NMS) notes that this technological diffusion and access to advanced weapons and delivery systems have significant implications for military capabilities. US Joint Chiefs of Staff, National Military Strategy of the United States of America (13 May 2004) p. 6.

2. MODERN WEAPONRY AND *JUS IN BELLO*

Current *jus in bello* governing the use of force in war consists of positive treaty law and customary law. The main treaty law in this are the Hague and Geneva codifications, as well as the two Additional Protocols to the 1949 Geneva Conventions (AP I and II) and the 1954 Hague Convention for the Protection of Cultural Property in the Event of Armed Conflict and its 1954 and 1999 Protocols.[5] *Jus in bello* treaty law includes other treaties that regulate and limit specific aspects of a country's potential or actual defence arsenal, including nuclear, chemical and biological weaponry.[6] Customary laws arise primarily from the general practice of states accepted as law.[7] Moreover, customary international law overlaps and incorporates other sources.[8] *Jus in bello* issues raised by modern military strategy, weapon sys-

---

5. The Geneva Conventions focus on the victims of armed conflict and on the amelioration of their conditions while 'Hague Law' limits the means and methods of warfare which may legitimately be used in armed conflict. McCoubry and White, *supra* n. 3, at p. 257. Specifically, the 1949 Conventions consist of four treaties: Geneva Convention for the Amelioration of the Condition of the Wounded and Sick in Armed Forces in the Field, 6 *UST* 3114, 75 *UNTS* 31; Geneva Convention for the Amelioration of the Condition of Wounded, Sick and Shipwrecked Members of Armed Forces at Sea; 6 *UST* 3217, 75 *UNTS* 85; Geneva Convention Relative to the Treatment of Prisoners of War; 6 *UST* 3316, 75 *UNTS* Geneva Convention Relative to the Protection of Civilian Persons in Time of War, 6 *UST* 3516, 75 *UNTS* 287. The Additional Protocols to the Geneva Convention are: Protocol Additional to the Geneva Conventions of 12 August 1949, and Relating to the Protection of Victims of International Armed Conflicts (AP I), adopted 8 June 1977, 1125 *UNTS* 1, and Protocol Additional to the Geneva Conventions of 12 August 1949, and Relating to the Protection of Victims of Non-International Armed Conflicts (AP II), 1125 *UNTS*. The Hague Conventions of 1907 include: the Hague Convention III Relative to the Opening of Hostilities of 1907, 36 *Stat.* 2259; the Hague Convention IV Respecting the Laws and Customs of War on Land, 36 *Stat.* 2277; the Hague Convention V Respecting the Rights and Duties of Neutral Powers and Persons in Case of War on Land , 36 *Stat.* 2310; the Hague Convention IX Concerning Bombardment by Naval Forces in Time of War of 1907, 36 *Stat.* 2351; and the Hague Convention X for the Adaptation to Maritime Warfare of the Principles of the Geneva Convention of 1906, 36 *Stat.* 237. Cultural treasures are protected in the Convention for the Protection of Cultural Property in the Event of Armed Conflict of 1954, 249 *UNTS* 240 and its two Protocols, Protocol for the Protection of Cultural Property in the Event of Armed Conflict of 1954 and Second Protocol to the Hague Convention of 1954 for the Protection of Cultural Property in the Event of Armed Conflict of 1999.

6. See e.g., Convention on the Prohibition of the Development, Production, Stockpiling and Use of Chemical Weapons and on Their Destruction of 1993, S. Treaty Doc. No. 103-21 (1993), 1975 *UNTS* 469; Convention on the Prohibition of the Development, Production and Stockpiling of Bacteriological (Biological) and Toxin Weapons and on their Destruction, 10 April 1972, 26 *UST* 583, 1015 *UNTS* 163; Treaty on the Non-Proliferation of Nuclear Weapons, 1 July 1968, 21 *UST* 483, 729 *UNTS* 161; Protocol for the Prohibition of the Use in War of Asphyxiating, Poisonous or Other Gases and of Bacteriological Methods of Warfare, Signed at Geneva of 1925, 26 *UST* 571, 94 *LNTS* 65.

7. See Statute of the International Court of Justice, 26 June 1945, Art. 38, 59 *Stat.* 1055, *T.S.* 993. The Third Restatement of International Law defines international customary law as resulting 'from a general and consistent practice of states which is followed by them from a sense of legal obligation'. Restatement (Third) of Foreign Relations Law of the United States (1987) § 102(2).

8. See e.g., the recognition by the Secretary-General of the United Nations in a report to the UN Security Council prior to the establishment of the International Criminal Court for the Former Yugoslavia, that:
'The part of conventional international humanitarian law which has beyond doubt become part of international customary law is the law applicable in armed conflict as embodied in: the Geneva Con-

tems and targeting fall into two general categories. The first category is whether the weapon itself is violative of *jus in bello* and thus illegal under international law.[9] This legal standard for weapons is found in the general sense in Article 22 of Hague Convention IV, and, more specifically in Articles 51(4)(b) and (c) and 35(2) of AP I, which prohibit indiscriminate weapons, namely weapons that cannot be directed at a specific military objective or that have effects that cannot be limited, and weapons that cause superfluous injury or unnecessary suffering.[10]

The second *jus in bello* issue with regard to modern weapon systems is whether the employment of the weapon system violates *jus in bello* with regard to attacks against particular targets or objects. These prohibitions proscribe attacks that violate the principles of distinction. Currently, a party to a conflict violates the principle of distinction either through the employment of a weapon system to directly target a non-military objective, or when a weapon is used in an indiscriminate fashion, i.e., when not aimed at a military objective or when its use results in collateral damage to civilian property or incidental injury to civilians that is excessive in relation to the concrete and direct military advantage anticipated.[11] Attacks that

---

ventions of 12 August 1949 for the Protection of War Victims; the Hague Convention (IV) Respecting the Laws and Customs of War on Land and the Regulations annexed thereto of 18 October 1907; the Convention on the Prevention and Punishment of the Crime of Genocide of 9 December 1948; and the Charter of the International Military Tribunal of 8 August 1945.'

Report of the Secretary-General Pursuant to Paragraph 2 of United Nations Security Council Resolution 808 (1993), adopted on 22 February 1993 (S/25704) para. 35 (3 May 1993)(footnotes omitted), approved and adopted by UN SCOR 827, 3217th mtg., S/Res/827 (1993). The International Court of Justice has similarly held common Art. 1 of the 1949 Geneva Conventions, stating that the Parties to the Geneva Conventions 'undertake to respect and ensure respect for the present Convention in all circumstances', to be declaratory of customary law. See *Case Concerning Military and Paramilitary Activities in and against Nicaragua* (*Nicaragua* v. *US*), Merits, *ICJ Rep.* (1986) pp. 14, 114.

9. One author has opined that the *jus in bello* norms rendering some weapons illegal *per se* stems from three ideas. The first of these ideas is that the weapon is treacherous or violates the idea of fair play, second, that some suffering can be characterized as 'unnecessary,' and third, the fear forces have towards the use of a particular mutilating weapon. See F.J. Hampson, 'Means and methods of warfare in the conflict in the Gulf', in P. Rowe, ed., *The Gulf War 1990-91 in International and English Law* (London, Routledge 1993) pp. 89, 101.

10. Art. 22 Hague IV, *supra* n. 5 ('The right of belligerents to adopt means of injuring the enemy is not unlimited'); Art. 51(4)(b) AP I, ibid., n. 5 (prohibiting method or means of combat, the effects of which cannot be directed at a specific military objective); and Art. 35(2) AP I, ibid., n. 3 (prohibiting weapons that cause superfluous injury or unnecessary suffering).

11. See Art. 48 AP I, ibid., (prohibiting the failure to distinguish between the civilian population and combatants and between civilian objects and military objectives); Art. 51 (prohibiting targeting of civilians not participating in hostilities); Art. 51(4)(a) (prohibiting attacks not directed at specific military objectives); Art. 52(1) (prohibiting targeting of civilian objects); Art. 51(5)(b) and (c)(prohibiting attacks which may be expected to cause incidental loss of civilian life, injury to civilians, damage to civilian objects, or a combination thereof, which would be excessive in relation to the concrete and direct military advantage anticipated. The US has specifically affirmed it 'supported' the following Articles of AP I: 5, 10, 11, 12-20, 21-23, 24-31, 32, 33, 34, 35(1)(2), 37, 38, 44 (a few parts), 45, 51 (except para. 6), 52, 54, 57-60, 62, 63, 70, 73, 74, 75, 76, 77, 78, 79, 80-85, and 86-89, while specific objections have been made by government officials with respect to Arts. 1(4), 35(3), 39(2), 47, 55, and 56. H.S. Levie, 'The 1977 Protocol I and the United States', 38 *St. Louis LJ* (1994) pp. 469, fn. 4. See also M.J. Matheson, 'The United State's position on the relation of customary Law to the 1977 Protocol Additional to the 1949 Geneva Conventions', 2 *Amer. Univ. JIL & Pol.* (1987) pp. 419, 420.

fail to include sufficient precautions to preclude or minimise collateral damage or incidental injury are also prohibited.[12]

Underlying these rules is the protection of non-combatants and the prevention of attacks not directed at a specific 'military objective', a term whose contours are not definitely or equally defined by states under international law.[13] Moreover, a definitive listing of military objectives is not realistic because the determination of whether an object is a valid 'military objective' is situationally dependent on whether the object, in the context of a particular attack, can meet a two part test: first, are they items which by their 'nature location, purpose or use' make them a military objective and, second, would the 'total or partial destruction, capture, or neutralisation of the object' at the time offer a definitive military advantage.[14]

These basic *jus in bello* concepts have arisen in discourse regarding recent conflicts featuring modern weaponry. Reviewing this discourse is possible in part through highlighting US and Allied military operations, since, for domestic, legal and policy reasons, these are the countries, in contrast to their opponents, who strive to comport with *jus in bello*. Indeed, as noted *infra*, US and Allied adversaries have violated *jus in bello* law before and after the end of the Cold War in order to seek a military advantage.[15] Among other egregious violations occurring since the 1980s, Iraqi, Serb and Taliban troops have all used churches, mosques,

12. See AP I *supra* n. 5, at Art. 57 (requiring attackers to take all feasible precautions in the choice of means and methods of attack with a view to avoiding, and in any event to minimising, incidental loss of civilian life, injury to civilians and damage to civilian objects).

13. As one author pointed out, efforts to clarify the terms 'military objective' and 'military necessity' have not been successful, as States have historically defined these terms themselves. *See* N.A. Canestaro, 'Legal and policy constraints on the conduct of aerial precision warfare', 37 *Vanderbilt JTL* (2004) pp. 431, 455. Nevertheless, a workable core definition of the term 'military objective' can be found in AP I, *supra* n. 5, at Art. 52, which defines military objective as 'limited to those objects which, by their nature, location, purpose, or use make an effective contribution to military action and whose total or partial destruction, capture or neutralization in the circumstances ruling at the time, offers a definite military advantage'. See D. Kaye, 'Book Review: the ethics of destruction: norms and the use of force in international relations', 97 *AJIL* (2003) pp. 229, 232 (asserting that there exists a widely-accepted rule on the definition of military objectives – although it remains subject to substantial interpretation). The US, for example, defines as valid military objectives 'combatants and those objects, which, by their nature, location, purpose, or use, effectively contribute to the enemy's war-fighting or war-sustaining capability and whose total or partial destruction, capture, or neutralization would constitute a definite military advantage to the attacker under the circumstances at the time of the attack'. US Navy, *Commander's Handbook on the Law of Naval Operations*, para. 8.1.1 in *Annotated Supplement* (Rhode Island, Naval War College International Studies 1997). The difference between the US and Art. 52 AP I definitions of 'military objective' in the opinion of one author can be distilled to the 'war sustaining' aspect of the US definition, and close comparison with Art. 52's definition and the San Remo Manual's definition of armed conflicts at sea reveals that the differences are merely limited to whether exports that may be the source or principle source of financial resources for a belligerent's continuation of its war effort are military objectives. See H.B. Robertson, Jr., 'The principle of the military objective in the law of armed conflict', 8 *USAFA Journal of Legal Studies* (1997/1998) at pp. 35, 51. See also M.N. Schmitt, 'The impact of high and low-tech warfare on the principle of distinction', Working Paper, International Humanitarian Law Research Initiative (Harvard University November 2003) <http://ihlresearch.org/portal/ihli/alabama.php> p. 2.

14. See Art. 52 AP I, *supra* n. 5.

15. See discussion in Canestaro, *supra* n. 13, at p. 481.

hospitals and schools to shelter military equipment and personnel from military attack.[16]

3. RECENT CONFLICTS

3.1 **Iraq I (Operation Desert Storm)**

Operation Desert Storm was the first conflict in which air power almost exclusively decided the outcome.[17] It also saw the first calculated and indiscriminant use of 'Scud' missiles against the US.[18] The US's and other coalition forces' use of airpower was intensive – the US flew more than 112,000 individual sorties, dropping an estimated 250,000 individual bombs and missiles.[19] Navy weapon platforms also fired Tomahawk cruise missiles targeting Iraq, the first time the Tomahawk was used in conflict.[20] Facing this coalition onslaught was an Iraqi air defence 'twice as dense as eastern Europe during the cold war', a state-of-the-art air defence radar net, the sixth largest air force in the world, and with over 700,000 personnel, the fourth largest army in the world equipped with biological weapons and possessing ballistic missiles.[21]

The modern weaponry that, rightly or wrongly, came to symbolise Operation Desert Storm around the world were Precision-Guided Munitions (PGM).[22] PGM, also known as smart bombs, are weapons that use a seeker to detect electromagnetic energy reflected from a target or reference point, and, through processing,

---

16. Ibid., at p. 481. See also R.A. Baily, 'Why do states violate the law of war? A comparison of Iraqi violations in two Gulf Wars', 27 *Syracuse JIL & Com.* (2000) p. 103; J.H. McNeill, 'Iraqi war crimes', 34 *Virginia JIL* (1994) p. 283. See also *infra* n. 229 and accompanying text for further discussion of *jus in bello* violations.

17. D.L. Infeld, 'Note: precision-guided munitions demonstrated their pinpoint accuracy in desert storm: but is a country obligated to use precision technology to minimize collateral civilian injury and damage?' 26 *GW JIL and Econ.* (2004) pp. 109, 127 at 109. Some still argue that air power was 'irrelevant to the defeat of the Iraqi army', in the Gulf War, but others concede that, at minimum, the use of stealth technology and PGMs during Operation Desert Storm point to a greater strategic role for aviation in future conflicts. M.E. Lewis, 'The law of aerial bombardment in the 1991 Gulf War', 97 *AJIL* (2003) pp. 481, 486.

18. The Scud ballistic missile is incapable of accuracy that would allow the proper selection of military targets over the civilian population – its circular error of probability (CEP), where the bomb is over 50 percent likely to hit within a desired radius, is sufficiently large to make any degree of discrimination effectively impossible. Scuds were used by the Iraqis to attack Israel in the 1991 Gulf War. Canestaro, *supra* n. 13, at n. 181. See *infra* nn. 119, 174 and accompanying text for blast radius comparison with other weapons. During the Iran-Iraq War, especially in 1988, Scuds with improved range were used against Iran, even reaching Tehran. Iraq is believed to have fired about 500 scuds during this conflict with Iraq. BCC News, 'Scud: Iraq's ballistic missile', 18 November 2002, <http://news.bbc.co.uk/1/hi/world/middle_east/2462583.stm>.

19. Infeld, *supra* n. 17, at p. 127.

20. Ibid., at p. 130.

21. C.B. Shotwell, 'Economy and humanity in the use of force: a look at the aerial rules of engagement in the 1991 Gulf War', 4 *USAFA Journal of Legal Studies* (1993) p. 15.

22. M.N. Schmitt, 'Future war and the principle of discrimination', *Israel YB HR* (1999) pp. 28 at 74 (opining that Operation Desert Storm was inaccurately hailed as the first smart war).

provide guidance commands to a control system that guides these weapons to their target.[23] They are variants of the first prototype munitions used in the Vietnam War.[24] Since that war, the US has developed and acquired over 20 types of PGM, at a cost of over forty billion dollars.[25] In general, there are two types of PGM. Laser-Guided Bombs (LGB) glide to their aim points by locating and locking onto a laser beam to reach their target point.[26] Global Positioning System (GPS) guided munitions use GPS satellites to guide themselves to their aim points.[27] Other than Tomahawk Land-Attack Missiles (TLAM), GPS munitions, as noted below, were not used until Kosovo's Operation Allied Force.[28]

During Operation Desert Storm, an estimated 22,000 PGM were used.[29] This amounted to approximately eight percent of the bombs used during that war.[30] Tomahawk cruise missiles were also used during Operation Desert Storm. Launched from navy ships and submarines in the Persian Gulf and the Red Sea, 282 of 288 Tomahawks (98 percent) were successfully launched. At $1.35 million dollars each, they were also some of the most expensive munitions in the US inventory. General purpose conventional, or gravity, bombs, including napalm, fuel-air explosives, cluster bombs and air to surface missiles, were also used by coalition forces during Operation Desert Storm.[31] Delivery systems for these munitions

---

23. Joint Chiefs of Staff, Department of Defense, *Dictionary of Military and Associated Terms*, Joint Publication 1-02, 12 April 2001 (as Amended 7 October 2004) at p. 417. For a description of current PGMs in the US inventory see Air Force Link, Library, Fact Sheets, <http://www.af.mil/factsheets>.

24. Infeld, *supra* n. 17, at p. 127.

25. Canestaro, *supra* n. 13, at p. 450.

26. S. Belt, 'Missiles over Kosovo, lex lata, of a customary norm requiring the use of precision munitions in urban areas', 47 *Naval LR* (2000) pp. 115, 120.

27. M. Rip and J. Hasik, *The Precision Revolution: GPS and the Future of Aerial Warfare*, (Annapolis MD, Naval Institute Press 2002) p. ix. Among GPS guided munitions are the Joint Stand-Off Weapon (JSOW), the Tomahawk Land Attack Missile (TLAM) and the Joint Direct Attack Munition (JDAMs). JSOWs, like the AGM-154 JSOW are precision-attack glide bombs. See description at Strategic Air Command, SAC Aircraft Launched Missiles, Raytheon AGM-154 JSOW, <http://www.strategic-air-command.com/missiles/Aircraft-Launched_Missiles/Agm-154_JSOW_missile.htm>.
TLAMs are designed to fly at extremely low altitudes at high subsonic speeds, and are piloted over an evasive route by several mission tailored guidance systems. United States Navy Fact File, *Tomahawk Cruise Missile* (11 August 2003) at <http://www.chinfo.navy.mil/navpalib/factfile/missiles/wep-toma.html>. JDAMS are guidance kits that convert existing unguided free-fall bombs into accurate, adverse weather 'smart' bombs. Their tail section contains an inertial navigation system (INS) and a global positioning system (GBS). Air Force Link, Library, Fact Sheets, *Joint Direct Attack Munitions Gbu 31/3* at <http://www.af.mil/factsheets>. (Air Force Link – JDAMS) See also *supra* n. 20 and *infra* nn. 35-36, p. 117 and accompanying text for a further description of their use in combat.

28. See United States General Accounting Office (GAO) Report to Congressional Committees, Military Operations: *Recent Campaigns Benefited from Improved Communications and Technology, but Barriers to Continued Progress Remain* (GAO-04-547 June 2004) (GAO Military Operations Report) at Appendix II for descriptions and pictures of DoD Reconnaissance Aircraft, Precision Weapons, and Other Technologies Used in Recent Operations.

29. Infeld, *supra* n. 17, at p. 127.

30. GAO Military Operations Report, *supra* n. 28, at p. 9.

31. Hampson, *supra* n. 9, at p. 104.

varied and were mixed and matched depending on the target, with the goal of minimising civilian damage and casualties.[32]

The targeting strategy in Desert Storm, especially in relation to the use of air power, its prevailing campaign, can be best described as 'utility targeting', epitomised by Colonel John Warden's 'five-ring' theory.[33] With targets drawn from Saddam Hussein's 'vital centres' or 'centres of gravity', coalition attacks focused on those targets most likely to impede the enemy's ability to conduct military operations. These targets consisted of four of Colonel Warden's theoretical five strategic rings, and they were, in order of importance: central command leadership, essential war-related production, infrastructure and fielded military force.[34]

In 1998, following Desert Storm, the US conducted a four-day, intensive bombing campaign, Desert Fox, against Iraq in order to induce it to allow UN inspectors to re-enter the country after being expelled.[35] Using predominately PGM, 650 sorties were flown against 100 targets, including warhead development facilities, air defence sites, Special Republican Guard Barracks, Baath Party and Intelligence Headquarters in Baghdad and a presidential palace near Samarra. Only 200 dumb bombs were used, in contrast to the 300 laser-guided bombs, 330 TLAM and 90 Air Force delivered cruise missiles.[36] Not only was this operation a milestone, being the first time PGM were predominately used to accomplish bombing missions, it also demonstrated for the first time that carriers were able to hit targets with PGM by equipping F-18s with self-lasing capability.[37]

3.1.1 Jus in bello *weaponry issues in Operation Desert Storm*

The nature of Operation Desert Storm raised *jus in bello* issues surrounding the use of PGM and collateral damage. The illegality of individual weapon systems, *per se*, was, for the most part, not at issue during Operation Desert Storm. However,

---

32. See Infeld, *supra* n. 17, at p. 129. At a briefing on 27 January 1991, General H. Norman Schwarzkopf stated:
'I think we've stated all along that we're being absolutely as careful as we can not only in the way we are going about executing our air campaign, but in the type of armament we're using. We're using the appropriate weapon against the appropriate targets. We're being very, very careful in our direction of attacks to avoid damage of any kind to civilian installations.' Ibid.

33. P.R. Kan, 'What should we bomb? Axiological targeting and the abiding limits of airpower theory', 18 *Air and Space Power Journal* (Spring 2004) p. 25. Colonel Warden, subsequently wrote that, to think strategically, a warfighter 'must think of the enemy as a system composed of numerous subsystems' which would give one 'a better chance forcing or inducing him to make our objectives his objectives and doing so with minimum effort and the maximum chance of success.' J.A. Warden, 'The enemy as a system', 9 *Airpower Journal* (Spring 1995) pp. 40, 41. He identified the enemy's systems as its leadership, organic essentials, infrastructure, population, and fighting mechanism. Ibid., at Table 1. Opposing Colonel Warden's strategy was Lieutenant General Horner, the Ninth Air Force Commander, who believed the primary use of conventional air power was to support campaigns waged on the ground, an air/land battle concept. See Lewis, *supra* n. 17, at pp. 484-485.

34. Shotwell, *supra* n. 21, at pp. 21-22.

35. M.L. Cornell, 'Decade of Failure: The Legality and Efficacy of United Nations Actions in the Elimination of Iraqi Weapons of Mass Destruction', 16 *Connecticut JIL* (2001) pp. 325, 339.

36. Belt, *supra* n. 26, at p. 132.

37. Ibid.

some have implied that conventional ordnance use was illegal, given the presence of PGM in coalition arsenals.[38] According to this view, a military power with smart bomb capability is required to use such a technology over more conventional bombs in urban areas.[39] Advocates of this position point to the accuracy of PGM, which have a circular error probable (CEP) – the radius of a circle within which 50 per cent of the weapons will strike.[40] They then contrast the PGM's accuracy with conventional bombs to imply that conventional bombs are hopelessly and illegally indiscriminate.[41] This position effectively would render less accurate conventional ordnance illegal should a party have access to PGM. This allegation has rightly been rejected as inconsistent with international law, ill-informed as to the nature of targeting, and implausible due to the expense and limited availability of smart bombs, both for US and foreign use.[42]

The use of PGM in Operation Desert Storm was subject to several allegations of *jus in bello* violations with regard to resultant collateral damage. One illustrative example of this is the controversy surrounding the coalition attack on the Al-Firdus

---

38. Human Rights Watch (HRW), Middle East Watch, *Needless Deaths In The Gulf War, Civilian Casualties During the Air Campaign and Violations of the Laws of War* (1991) at Chapter Three: The Means and Methods of Attack, <http://www.hrw.org/reports/1991/gulfwar/> (Needless Deaths)(asserting that it was impossible to assess the Allies' compliance with the laws of war without knowing the percent of attacks in proximity to civilian areas executed with dumb bombs in relation to PGMs).

39. Infeld, *supra* n. 17, at p. 133. See also Needless Deaths ibid. (stating that if munitions clearly known to be inaccurate in relation to PGMs were deliberately used than the resulting deaths, injuries and damages were potentially avoidable – given the alternative and more accurate means and methods of attack).

40. Shotwell, *supra* n. 21, at p. 28. As much as 85 percent of PGMs reportedly hit within ten feet of their aim points, while unguided bombs hit the target only 25 percent of the time. Canestaro, *supra* n. 13, at p. 451.

41. See e.g., M. Lippman, 'Aerial attacks on civilians and humanitarian law of war: technology and terror from World War I to Afghanistan', 33 *Calif. Western ILJ* (2002) pp. 1, 40 (citing the 'War Crimes Tribunal' a private group alleging that the US engaged in 'indiscriminate deployment of weapons of mass destruction', referencing the fact only seven percent of the bombs utilised were smart bombs).

42. *See* Infeld, *supra* n. 17, at pp.132-33 (observing that the use of PGMs was not mandatory under international law, and that adverse weather can deteriorate the PGMs' accuracy and cause more collateral civilian injury than a conventional bomb). See also Shotwell, *supra* n. 21, at p. 28 (noting that no law requires combatants to use only PGMs, and that the limited supply of PGMs are the only effective ordnance and are required to be used against specific targets); Hampson, *supra* n. 9, at p. 104 (stating that there is no legal obligation for states to deploy PGMs in preference to other less accurate weapons). Interestingly, at least one author has argued, following a 'normative relativism' approach, that *jus in bello* proportionality requirements prohibit the use of non-precision-guided technology in urban areas by advanced nations. Belt, *supra* n. 26, at p. 18. The key to this argument requiring the use of precision weapons is the proposition that the practice of states, from the conclusion of Desert Storm to the conclusion of Operation Allied Force, establishes a 'not uniform world-wide' but 'generally recognised' practice that unguided, gravity bombs are not employed in densely populated, urban areas; instead, when targets are identified in urban areas, precision-guided weapons are to be used. Belt, ibid. Upon examination, this argument is at odds with positive treaty law, customary law, and *opinio juris*, and it furthermore confuses the choice of precision weapons by states as legally compelled, rather than being used for other reasons. See also *supra* n. 63 and *infra* nn. 51, 116-117, 170-171, 202-203 and 221, 226 and accompanying text regarding political and strategic reasons for the US to avoid collateral deaths and damage.

bunker (or Al-'Amariyah 'shelter') on 13 February 1991, resulting in the death of 200 to 300 civilians, which gave rise to the allegation that the United States failed to meet AP I obligations to avoid civilian casualties.[43] The bunker was classified as a secondary command and control bunker before Operation Desert Storm began, and was placed on the target list after it was activated by the Iraqis as a command and control centre.[44] The allegation that the US failed to abide by its AP I obligations revolved around the alleged US failure to take feasible precautions to avoid civilian casualties, such as warning Iraq about the addition of the bunker to the coalition target list, providing notice that the US no longer considered the shelter as used for civilian defence purposes, and the failure to acquire morning reconnaissance photographs, which might have shown civilians leaving the bunker.[45]

This criticism is undercut by the facts and the law. The presence of civilians in the bunker was not known by the US, and although originally constructed during the Iran-Iraq war as an air raid shelter, it had been converted to a military command and control bunker.[46] Its appearance was also inconsistent with that of an air raid shelter: it was surrounded by barbed wire, its entrances were secured to prevent unauthorised access, armed guards were posted and it was covered with camouflage.[47] Moreover, there is no requirement in international law to provide a target list to the other party in a conflict, nor must adequate legal precautions, at minimum, include repeated reconnaissance of a target.[48] In short, there is no reason to believe the US knew the civilians were there, and even had they known, the bunker was a valid military target even with the presence of civilians.[49] A party to a conflict that places its own citizens in danger accepts the responsibility of an otherwise legal attack upon a valid military objective, since Article 51(7) AP I prohibits the use of 'human shields', codifying the principle of 'chivalry' which prohibits ruses and the deliberate abuse of protected status entities.[50] Politically, moreover, had the US known of the presence of civilians, the attack would not have not taken place, in accordance with the policy enunciated by the President at the beginning of the

43. Needless Deaths, *supra* n. 38, at pp.140-43.

44. Lewis, *supra* n. 17 at p. 503, Shotwell, *supra* n. 21, at p. 33.

45. See Needless Deaths, *supra* n. 38, at ibid. HRW's Middle East Watch highlighted the fact that Article 65 of AP I provides that civil-defence structures lose their protected status only after a warning has been given setting, whenever appropriate, a reasonable time-limit, and after such warning has remained unheeded. Ibid. see also Lewis, *supra* n. 17, at p. 502; Shotwell, *supra* n. 21, at p. 33. Not addressed in *Needless Deaths* is its inference that a protected site 'carries over' its protective status into a second conflict if it is obvious that the function of the status was not consistent with its status since before the onset of the second war.

46. US Dept. of Defense, 'Conduct Of The Persian Gulf War: Final Report To Congress', Pursuant To Title V of the Persian Gulf Conflict Supplemental Authorization and Personnel Benefits Act Of 1991, App. O, at p. 615 (1992 (Final Report to Congress).

47. Final Report to Congress ibid., at p. 615; Shotwell, *supra* n. 21, at p. 33.

48. Lewis, *supra* n. 17, at p. 504.

49. The Final Report to Congress noted that the Al-Firdus bunker, since it was being used as an Iraqi command and control centre, was a legitimate military target and as such, even with the presence of civilians, there was no obligation to refrain from attacking it. Final Report to Congress, *supra* n. 46, at p. 33.

50. AP I, *supra* n. 5, Art 51(7).

campaign to limit civilian casualties.[51] This focus on civilian casualties was also evident in the debate over the number of civilian casualties inflicted by the war beyond those that died directly from a weapon's destruction of a military objective. Thus, some calculated the number of civilians killed as including not only those who perished directly during an attack, but also those who died from indirect causes attributed to the war.[52]

The *jus in bello* issues raised in the aftermath of Operation Desert Storm: use of conventional weapons instead of PGM, the failure to take all feasible precautions prior to an attack, and the proper calculation of collateral casualties and damage, were ones that were destined to be raised in future military conflicts. This was the case, as noted below, in Operations Allied Force, Enduring Freedom, and Iraqi Freedom, even though technology and weapons modernisation continued at a relentless pace. As US military intelligence, surveillance and reconnaissance (ISR) abilities improve, along with its ability to collect, process and act on intelligence information, tragedies such as the civilian deaths at Al-Firdus will likely decrease in number, although unintentional deaths due to intelligence errors will not be totally eliminated. As Operation Allied Force was soon to illustrate after Operation Desert Storm, collateral damage and death due to attacks based on faulty intelligence kept the issue of whether all feasible precautions were taken prior to an attack in the forefront of these *jus in bello* inquires.

3.2 Kosovo (Operation Allied Force)

Operation Allied Force was the NATO operation that terminated the regime of Slobodan Milošević in the Federal Republic of Yugoslavia. Thirteen of NATO's 19 members took part in this operation.[53] The air campaign was the primary factor leading to Milošević's surrender, to an even greater extent than the corresponding air campaign had led to victory in Operation Desert Storm.[54] From the beginning of the conflict on 24 March 1999 to its suspension on 10 June 1999, NATO planes made approximately 38,000 sorties, dropping 23,614 bombs, of which approximately 30 percent were PGM.[55] These PGM struck 64 percent of their targets.[56] Approximately 500 Yugoslavian civilians were killed during Operation Allied

51. Lewis, *supra* n. 17, at p. 503. One US general stated unequivocally that 'had we known that there were civilians in the bunker, it never would have been attacked'. Ibid.

52. A controversial Commerce Department analyst eventually fixed the number of those civilians killed in Operation Desert Storm and the post-Cold War period as 205,500, including in this figure deaths resulting from war-related damage to medical facilities and supplies, the electric power grid, and the water system. B. Osborne, 'Toting the casualties of war', *Business Week Online*, 6 February 2003, <http://www.businessweek.com>.

53. T. Voon, 'Pointing the finger: civilian casualties of NATO bombing in the Kosovo conflict', 16 *Amer. Univ. ILR* (2001) pp. 1083, 1084.

54. J. Gordon IV and J. Sollinger, 'The Army's dilemma', 34 *Parameters* (Summer 2004) pp. 33, 35.

55. Canestaro, *supra* n. 13, at p. 451; GOA Military Operations Report *supra* n. 28, at p. 9.

56. Canestaro, ibid.

Force, with two-thirds of these killed in only 12 incidents.[57] Operation Allied Force saw the début of the GBU-31 Joint Direct Attack Munition (JDAM). A JDAM can be released up to 15 miles from target and from altitudes exceeding 35,000 feet, thereby protecting pilots from air defences.[58] Moreover, JDAMs are moderately priced from as little as $18,000 a bomb, permitting the military to purchase them in large numbers.[59]

The targeting strategy used in Operation Allied Force was more axiological than Operation Desert Storm's utility-based targeting. In axiological targeting, airpower is used to force an adversary to accept the demands of the attacker, and, as such, attempts to identify the correct target set within an adversary's centre of gravity to modify an enemy's behaviour and attitude.[60] This was critical in Operation Allied Force as, early on, NATO excluded the use of any ground troops'.[61] The goals of Operation Allied Force were coercive: 'to demonstrate the seriousness of NATO's purpose so that Serbian leaders understand the imperative of reversing course, to deter an even bloodier offensive against innocent civilians in Kosovo, and if necessary, to seriously damage the Serb military capacity to harm the people of Kosovo'.[62] As a coercive operation, the air campaign initially had only a very limited target base, with symbolic air strikes and some conventional utility targets, but eventually targeting shifted to include institutions that Milošević used to maintain his rule, i.e., 'everything that kept the Serb leadership in power and comfort'.[63] A complete analysis was performed on all potential targets, including consideration of their location, military significance, possible collateral damage, and potential risk if the weapon missed the target, an analysis repeated for 'different types of weapons' in the search for the 'specific type of weapon and warhead size that would destroy the target and have the least adverse impact elsewhere'.[64]

3.2.1 Jus in bello *weaponry issues in Operation Allied Force*

Operation Allied Force *jus in bello* issues were highlighted even before the termination of the conflict, since the International Criminal Tribunal for the Former Yugoslavia (ICTY) previously received several requests to investigate NATO's conduct. In response, the Chief Prosecutor set up a committee on 14 May 1999 to evaluate the accusations and to recommend whether a formal investigation was

---

57. A. Laursen, 'NATO, the war over Kosovo, and the ICTY investigation', 17 *Amer. Univ. ILR* (2002) pp. 765, 767.

58. See Air Force Link – JDAMS *supra* n. 27; Canestaro, *supra* n. 13, at pp. 451-452.

59. Canestaro, *supra* n. 13, at p. 452.

60. Kan, *supra* n. 33, at p. 26.

61. Ibid., at p. 28.

62. Ibid. See also Canestaro, *supra* n. 13, at p. 472 (noting that Operation Allied Force was intended purely as a coercive operation with the implied goal of merely inflicting enough pain to convince Milošević to capitulate).

63. Kan, *supra* n. 33, at p. 28.

64. See also Canestaro, *supra* n. 13, at pp. 473-474.

required.[65] On 2 June 2000 Carla del Ponte, the Chief Prosecutor, accepted the recommendation in the committee's report (hereinafter, ICTY Report) not to initiate a formal investigation.[66] The ICTY's informal report thereby reviews contemporaneous *jus in bello* concerns raised by Operation Allied Force. Additionally, one human rights organisation, Human Rights Watch (HRW), sent a letter to NATO Secretary General Javier Solana expressing concern about the 'mounting civilian casualties in NATO's air war against Yugoslavia', and 'raising serious concern about whether NATO is targeting civilian objects or objects that, if attacked, would cause disproportionate harm to civilians', as well as asking 'whether, in attacking legitimate military targets, NATO is taking all feasible precautions to avoid harm to civilians'.[67]

As was the case in Operation Desert Storm, the legality of individual weapon systems was not an overriding issue during Operation Allied Force. However, cluster munitions or bombs concerned HRW and were addressed in the ICTY report, although they were used in greater numbers during Operation Desert Storm without serious controversy, as were depleted uranium shells.[68]

Cluster bombs best illustrate the temptation faced to leap ahead of existing international law to arrive at a desired conclusion, although this same phenomenon is present regarding the issue of uranium bombs.[69] Cluster munitions, also referred to as Cluster Bomb Units (CBU), are dropped together from aircraft and are designed to explode at or near impact.[70] CBUs, by falling for a specific amount of time or distance prior to the opening of their dispensers, permit their submunitions to cover a wide area target.[71] Some CBU are precision weapons, with each 'sensor fused weapon' consisting of 40 individually targeted bomblets that hone in on a vehicle's infrared signature, while others are deployed by a 'wind corrected munitions dispenser' that makes the cluster bomb canister accurate to within 30 feet.[72] Combined Effects Munition CBU provide anti-armour, incendiary and fragmentation effects for use against light armour and personnel, making their use a significant

---

65. See 'Final Report to the Prosecutor by the Committee Established to Review NATO Bombing Campaign against the Federal Republic of Yugoslavia', paras. 2-3 (2000) (ICTY Report) at <http://www.un.org/icty/pressreal/NATO061300.htm>.

66. Laursen, *supra* n. 57, at p. 769.

67. HRW, 'Growing Concern about NATO Violating the Laws of War' (13 May 1999) at <http://hrw.org/english/docs/1999/05/13/serbia914.htm>.

68. See ICTY Report, *supra* n. 65, paras. 26-27; HRW, 'Ticking Time Bombs: NATO's Use of Cluster Munitions in Yugolavia' (June 1999) <http://www.hrw.org/reports/1999/nato2/> (hereinafter, Ticking Time Bombs). In Desert Storm 61,000 cluster bombs were dropped, compared to the 1,632 cluster bombs dropped during Operation Allied Force. T.J. Herthel, 'On the chopping block: cluster munitions and the law of war', 51 *Air Force LR* (2001) pp. 229, 239-240.

69. The ICTY Report noted that the use of depleted uranium projectiles was simply not prohibited by a specific treaty ban or by 'a consensus view' that use of these projectiles violates general principles of the laws of armed conflict, presumably referring to customary international law. See ICTY Report, *supra* n. 65, at para. 26.

70. Herthel, *supra* n. 68, at pp. 234-235.

71. P.S. Meilinger, 'Precision aerospace power, discrimination, and the future of war', 15 *Aerospace Power Journal* (Fall 2001) pp. 12, 16.

72. Ibid. The wind correction dispenser was used for the first time in Operation Enduring Freedom. See *infra* accompanying text at n. 104.

military necessity.[73] Although critics of cluster bombs are hard-pressed to make the case that they are illegal *per se*, since neither customary or treaty law bans their possession or use, some attacked their method of employment during Allied Force.[74] Specifically, during and following Operation Allied Force, critics charged that cluster munitions are incapable of being accurately controlled due to the large area covered by the weapon, and that they are 'indiscriminate' due to malfunctioning units, or 'duds', which transform them into virtual landmines, incapable of distinguishing between civilians and lawful combatants, allegations, which, if true, would violate Article 51 AP I.[75]

The ICTY report reached three conclusions regarding Operation Allied Force's use of cluster munitions. First, the report logically found that cluster bombs are not illegal weapons *per se*, as 'there is no specific treaty provision which prohibits or restricts the use of cluster bombs'.[76] Second, the report found individual unexploded bombs from a cluster bomb are not legally comparable to landmines, stating 'there is no general legal consensus that cluster bombs are, in legal terms, equivalent to antipersonnel mines'.[77] This comports with customary law. As one author notes, 'even landmines, *designed* to lay dormant and detonate later in time are not considered *per se* indiscriminate by the world community . . . at Ottawa, it took a consensus of nations to determine, that as a matter of policy and/or domestic law, they chose to refrain from using landmines in the future. Customary international law, however, still recognises their legality.'[78] Third, the ICTY report found that cluster bombs were not used indiscriminately; contrasting NATO's use of cluster munitions with the illegal use of cluster munitions in the *Martić* case, where they were intentionally used in an Orkin rocket targeted against civilians in Zagreb, the Croatian capital.[79] The ICTY Report thus logically focused on whether Allied Force planners used cluster munitions illegally by employing them in an

73. Ibid., at p. 235. In addition to their use against light armour and personnel, cluster munitions are effective against AAA and SAM sites and artillery vehicles, while minimising the risk and exposure of aircrews to enemy fire because they facilitate striking a target with a single sortie rather than by flying multiple aircraft over the same target a number of times, and may reduce collateral damage by preventing the use of high explosive ordnance to accomplish the military goal. Ibid., at pp. 258-259.

74. See e.g., T.M. McDonnell, 'Cluster bombs over Kosovo: a violation of international law?' 44 *Arizona LR* (2002) pp. 3, 73-74 for an admission by a cluster bomb critic that cluster bombs are not illegal *per se*. See also Herthel, *supra* n. 68, at p. 259 (noting that 'on balance, it is impossible to objectively say that cluster munitions cause unnecessary suffering or superfluous injury as a matter of law'.).

75. See Ticking Time Bombs, *supra* n. 68 (asserting that because of the high failure rate, submunitions in cluster bombs effectively become antipersonnel landmines, unable to distinguish between combatants and innocent civilians and ready to detonate on contact); See also Herthel, *supra* n. 68, at pp. 263-266; McDonnell, *supra* n. 74, at pp. 79-87.

76. See ICTY Report, *supra* n. 65, at para. 27. See *supra* n. 72, and infra nn. 75-78 and accompanying text for a discussion of how cluster munitions are not illegal *per se*.

77. ICTY Report, ibid.

78. Herthel, *supra* n. 68, at p. 265.

79. ICTY Report, *supra* n. 65, at para. 27. The ICTY Report specifically noted that 'the rocket was inaccurate, it landed in an area with no military objectives nearby, it was used as an antipersonnel weapon launched against the city of Zagreb and the accused indicated he intended to attack the city as such.' Ibid.

indiscriminate manner, and not on the mere fact that, as with all ordnance, some unintentionally malfunction and become duds. Because cluster munitions were subject to the same painstaking analysis where their expected collateral damage was balanced against the concrete and direct military value anticipated, there was no violation of *jus in bello* with regard to their use in Operation Allied Force.[80]

The ICTY Report also reviewed the Allied Forces target selection process and focused on five individual attacks: the attack on the passenger train at Grdelica Gorge, the attack on the Djakovica Convoy, the attack on the Serbian Radio and Television Station, the attack on the Chinese Embassy, and the attack on Korisa Village. The issue in the Grdelica Gorge incident involved whether the object destroyed, a bridge, illegally resulted in civilian casualties due to a failure to take all feasible precautions prior to the attack. Specifically, at Grdelica Gorge, a train was destroyed by two laser-guided bombs released at two different times, which were aimed at a bridge over the Juzna Morava river, killing at least ten people and injuring 15.[81] The ICTY Report found that the bridge was a legitimate target, and the passenger train was apparently not deliberately targeted, so its initial destruction was not illegal.[82] Unlike the release of the first bomb, where the committee found no issues or facts to initiate an investigation, the committee was divided on whether the release of the second bomb indicated an 'element of recklessness on the part of the pilot or WSO [weapons system officer]'.[83] Although the second bomb incident was not recommended for investigation, at least some on the committee apparently rejected General Wesley Clark's (NATO's Supreme Allied Commander for Europe) explanation that the second impact on the train was caused by a second 'uncanny accident' resulting when the pilot, who was endeavouring to complete his mission by striking the other side of the bridge, hit parts of the train that had slid forward.[84]

The Serbian Radio and Television Station incident and the attacks on the Djakovica Convoy, Korisa Village and the Chinese Embassy, unlike the previous Grdelica Gorge incident, involved deliberate targeting and destruction of an intended object that was subsequently alleged to be immune from any attack under the *jus in bello*.[85] Two of these targets, the Serbian TV and Radio Station and the buildings in Korisa, were defended by NATO as valid and legitimate targets, while the Chinese Embassy and the Djakovica convoy incidents were conceded by NATO as being tragic mistakes.

With regard to the Serbian TV and Radio Station attack, which killed between ten and 17 people, the committee found that although the attack on the station, if premised solely by reference to its propaganda value, could be legally questioned:

80. Herthel, *supra* n. 68, at p. 267 (noting that cluster munitions were subject to the same laborious process involving lawyers, targeteers and intelligence analysts who were charged with reworking all attack plans for any target where more than 20 civilians might be killed.)

81. ICTY Report, *supra* n. 65, at para. 58.

82. Ibid., para. 62.

83. Ibid.

84. Ibid., para. 58.

85. The embassy and the civilian convoys, as non-military objectives, were protected from attack by, *inter alia*, Art. 51 AP I, *supra* n. 5.

'NATO targeting of the RTS building for propaganda purposes was an incidental, (albeit complementary) aim of its primary goal of disabling the Serbian military command and control system and to destroy the nerve system and apparatus that keeps Milosevic in power.'[86] The report also found that 'the attack on the RTS must therefore be seen as forming part of an integrated attack against numerous objects, including transmission towers and control buildings of the Yugoslav relay network which were "essential to Milosevic's ability to direct and control the repressive activities of his army and special police forces in Kosovo"'.[87]

In the Korisa Village incident, NATO attacked a Serbian military and command post which was located near the village, resulting in 87 civilian casualties and approximately 60 wounded. The ICTY Report noted that the military revetments were identified as such immediately preceding the attack, 'there were never any doubts' as to the validity of this target, and that NATO knew nothing 'of the presence of civilians and that none were observed immediately prior to the attack'.[88] The committee concluded that although there was some information that displaced Kosovar civilians were forcibly concentrated within a military camp in the village of Lorisa as human shields, the available information was in conflict, and Yugoslavian forces were at least partially responsible for the deaths there.[89] The ICTY Report concluded that there was insufficient evidence to show that the aircrew or their superiors committed a crime in the Korisa Village incident, and accordingly recommended no further investigation into this incident.[90]

With regard to the Chinese embassy incident, the ICTY prosecutors found that the aircrew and senior leaders should not be assigned any responsibility for the attack that killed three and wounded 15 Chinese citizens.[91] In its review of the embassy incident, the ICTY report noted that the air crew were given the wrong target and information regarding the building, by officials of another agency, namely, NATO forces mistakenly thought the Chinese Embassy building housed the Yugoslav Federal Directorate for Supply and Procurement.[92] Regarding the Djakovica convoy, the convoy was mistakenly identified as attacking Yugoslav Special Police Forces. Specifically, NATO pilots, flying at 15,000 feet and viewing the targets with the naked eye rather than remotely, thought Yugoslav Forces were conducting ethnic cleansing operations in the area by burning Kosovar Albanian villages.[93] The ICTY Report found that civilians were not deliberately attacked,

---

86. ICTY Report, *supra* n. 65, para. 76.

87. Ibid., para. 78. The ICTY report, in reaching this conclusion, highlighted the fact that the 'proportionality or otherwise of an attack should not necessarily focus exclusively on a specific incident'. Ibid., apparently relying on its recognition that 'today's technological society has given rise to many dual use facilities and resources', and that 'military objectives are often located in densely populated areas and fighting occasionally occurs in such areas'. Ibid., at p. 51. For a critique of this approach taken by the ICTY Report, see Laursen, *supra* n. 57, at pp. 789-793.

88. ICTY Report, *supra* n. 63, at paras. 86-88.

89. Ibid., paras. 88-89.

90. Ibid., para. 89.

91. Ibid., para. 85.

92. Ibid.

93. Ibid., para. 64.

and that although the aircrews 'could have benefited from lower altitude scrutiny of the target at an early stage . . . neither the aircrew nor their commanders displayed the degree of recklessness in failing to take precautionary measures which would sustain criminal charges'.[94]

These *jus in bello* issues arising from Operation Allied Force, highlighted in part by the ICTY report, continued the focus on whether combatants took all feasible measures prior to an attack causing collateral damage. Despite calls for repeated intelligence reconnaissance, like those critical of the Al-Firdus bunker and Korisa village incidents, it is doubtful that particular preferenced actions to avoid and minimise civilian casualties beyond that generally found in Article 57(2) of AP I gain traction in the military community. [95] Due to the fact specific nature of every attack, attempting to pre-identify acts with particularity would give the misimpression these were feasible acts that would definitively establish compliance with Article 57(2) of AP I. Collateral casualties and damage will likely never be eliminated: war, by definition, is messy and unpredictable. Technology, however, could help dissipate some of this 'fog of war', but unfortunately, some level of collateral damage will be present. Intelligence failures, for example, might not be considered or identified as such before a mishap despite excellent assets. Additionally, repeated reconnaissance and other verification might not have prevented Chinese embassy-type incidents, but correct intelligence might have. In other instances, intelligence might be accurate but only certain types and amounts of reconnaissance could avoid collateral damage, reconnaissance that might or might not be feasible.

Moreover, identifying particular measures as essential to accomplishing everything feasible prior to an attack is not needed to motivate compliance with *jus in bello's* admonition that attackers must take all feasible measures. Strategic political reasons, as well as military ones, compel US political leaders and military targeteers to want to 'get it right the first time', and not waste political capital and military assets on non-military objectives.[96] Additionally, as discussed below, ascribing criminal liability to those acting on faulty intelligence or other types of unintentional errors would be counterproductive and damaging to *jus in bello*.[97] Nevertheless, it is conceivable that Intelligence, Surveillance and Reconnaissance (ISR) systems, and aviation technology will increase to the point where mistakenly identifying a target from high altitudes by merely using the naked eye could lend support to a finding of recklessness under current *jus in bello* law, especially should a pilot have modern capabilities for remote identification of ground targets in a high tech environment.[98] Mistakenly destroying civilian targets under those

---

94. Ibid., paras. 69-71, 80, 86.

95. See *supra* n. 45 and *infra* n. 203 and accompanying text for examples of some of the feasibility measures suggested for the US and its Allies prior to an attack.

96. See *infra* nn. 117-118, 170-171, 202, 204 and 221 and accompanying text for discussion of strategic and political motivations for the US to abide by *jus in bello* law and keep civilian casualties to a minimum.

97. See *infra* nn. 203-208 and accompanying text for a discussion of the consequences of separating the *mens rea* element from *jus in bello* legal norms.

98. In fact, these types of improper identification mistakes have decreased since Operation Allied Force. HRW has noted that 'it appears that US air forces learned some lessons from the problems

circumstances would be more difficult to defend as not reckless and less palatable to a public believing in computer-assisted precision.

3.3 Afghanistan (Operation Enduring Freedom)

Following the 11 September 2001 terrorist attacks on its soil, the US soon found itself at war within Afghanistan, pursuing the Al Qaeda terrorist network. Starting on 7 October 2001 and lasting until 6 December 2001, when Khandahar fell ending the Taliban regime, this campaign spanned just 49 days.[99] During that period, the United States and its allies dropped approximately 12,000 bombs, of which 6,700, or 56 percent, were smart.[100] JDAM use in Afghanistan expanded, as half of the smart bombs dropped were JDAMs.[101] JDAM delivery platforms increased from the sole B-2 platform in Operation Allied Force to Navy and Air Force fighters to all three types of bombers (B-1, B-2, and B-52s), resulting in a 24 hour-precision strike capability in all types of weather.[102]

Operation Enduring Freedom also unveiled the lethality of unmanned aerial vehicles (UAVs), which were used for the first time to strike at targets with precision and accuracy, in addition to their previous Operation Allied Force-assigned role of observing and tracking.[103] Also employed for the first time in Operation Enduring Freedom was the wind-corrected munitions (bomblet) dispenser (WCCMD), which was usable in bad weather to a far greater extent than laser-guided weapons.[104] In addition, the Allied military campaign was, for the first time in history, able to maintain 24/7 airborne surveillance, imposing substantial pressure on the enemy with the goal of being able to hit a moving target within five minutes of identifying it.[105] This unprecedented situational awareness was created in part by combining Predator UAV video feeds, Global Hawk surveillance information and direct input from US Special Operations Forces on the ground.[106] As noted by the director of the Pentagon's Intelligence, Surveillance and Reconnaissance systems, the US found out in Afghanistan that 'ISR is all about targeting'.[107]

---

encountered with emerging targets in recent conflicts ... in Yugoslavia, US aircraft bombed many civilian convoys after mistakenly them for military targets ... in Iraq, there was only one reported case of a civilian vehicle being mistakenly targeted by aircraft. HRW, 'Off Target: The Conduct of the War and Civilian Casualties in Iraq' (2003) p. 21, <http://www.hrw.org/reports/2003/usa1203/usa1203.pdf> (hereinafter, Off Target).

99. C.J. Werenskjold, *The Effect of Unmanned Aerial Vehicle Systems on Precision Engagement*, Thesis (Monterey CA, Naval Post-Graduate School 2002) p. 21.

100. N. Friedman, *Terrorism, Afghanistan, and America's New Way of War* (Annapolis MD, Naval Institute Press 2003) p. 168. Of all the ordnance delivered, 60 percent were precision-guided, as opposed to 30 percent in Kosovo and eight percent in the Gulf War. GAO Report on Military Operations, *supra* n. 28, at p. 9.

101. Friedman, *supra* n. 100, at p. 167.

102. R. Grant, 'The war nobody expected', 85 *Air Force Magazine* (April 2002) p. 4.

103. Werenskjold, *supra* n. 99, at p. 22.

104. Friedman, *supra* n. 100, at p. 166.

105. Ibid.

106. Grant, *supra* n. 102, at p. 5.

107. Werenskjold, *supra* n. 99, at p. 23.

In contrast to Operation Desert Storm, the lines of operation during the Operation Enduring Freedom campaign were conducted simultaneously, rather than sequentially.[108] Specifically, instead of attacking targets sequentially in order to 'roll back' the enemy as a prelude to a land invasion, the modern air strategy used in Operation Enduring Freedom was effects-based, concurrently targeting military objectives such as 'air defenses, command and control centers, leadership sites and telephone and electricity grids'.[109] Modern effects-based targeting is accordingly technologically-based on 'understanding the effect' desired on the battlefield, thereby creating that effect more efficiently, more effectively, striking fewer targets, using fewer weapons and, quite frankly, mitigating or easing the potential for collateral damage and civilian casualties'.[110] In Afghanistan, this strategy translated into an air campaign aimed at degrading Taliban military effectiveness by striking at emergent targets that would enable the Northern Alliance to move and take territory, since bombing high-value, fixed targets was not an option.[111] In fact, strikes on pre-planned targets designed to take down Afghan air defences gave way within days to the vast majority of sorties committed to striking emerging targets.[112]

Operation Enduring Freedom's effects-based, time-sensitive target strategy had several ramifications on military tactics. For example, battlespace coverage, rather than relative percentage of missions flown or ordnance dropped, became a critical metre of operational success. Thus, from the Combined Air Operations Center (CAOC) perspective, the high number of emerging targets meant the real value of employing strike aircraft was in having them constantly available to attack resistance on the ground.[113] Additionally, the previously venerable air warfare doctrine of 'centralized control, decentralized execution' was strained by the close-hold held by Washington over target selections.[114] Decision bottlenecks occurred when guidance regarding rapidly emergent targets was hung up in higher headquarters as strategic and operational perspectives clashed.[115]

---

108. Grant, *supra* n. 102, at p. 5.

109. N. Cook, 'Combat operations: missions over Iraq, new high speed satellite networks bring pinpoint targeting', *The Financial Times*, 16 June 2003, at p. 5.

110. Ibid.

111. Grant, *supra* n. 102, at p. 23 (noting the Secretary of Defense recalled that 'there were not a lot high-value targets').

112. Ibid. One figure establishes that within days, as many as 90 percent of the sorties were striking emergent targets.

113. Ibid. The CAOC integrated mobility, space, and information operations, along with strike operations, into the actual master attack-planning cell. Plans, operations and intelligence reported directly to the CAOC commander, without 'stovepipes', that is, without intervening command structures. Ibid.

114. For additional discussion regarding the increasing centralisation of the execution of operations, see *infra* n. 227 and accompanying text.

115. Grant, *supra* n. 102, at p. 7. According to some sources, an opportunity to target Mullah Mohammad Omar, the leader of the Taliban and the second most-wanted man after Osama bin Laden, was allowed to lapse due to the initial hesitancy of CENTCOM legal advisors. Ibid. The objections evidently stemmed from concern that longstanding policy against attacking foreign heads of state applied to Mullah Omar. Friedman, *supra* n. 100, at p. 175.

As in prior conflicts, criteria for targets went beyond mere *jus in bello* constraints, encompassing the consequences of any attack on the reconstruction effort. This led to one senior judge advocate to comment, 'things like transportation infrastructure very often are *bona fide* legal targets, but we look for ways of minimizing that damage because we're always thinking about what's the next step going to be. What are we going to do after the conflict is over?'[116] Senior officers were accordingly forbidden to attack sensitive or political infrastructure, such as electrical power systems, roads, industry and mosques, without approval from Washington, even if they were being used for military purposes and were legitimate targets under *jus in bello*.[117]

3.3.1 Jus in bello *weaponry issues in Operation Enduring Freedom*

Unlike the ICTY Report, there was no preliminary third party review of alleged *jus in bello* violations by the Coalition regarding Operation Enduring Freedom. There were reports, similar to those aired during Operation Allied Force, of civilian casualties due to collateral damage or malfunctioning ordnance as well as some coalition casualties due to 'friendly fire' incidents. In one example regarding the latter, during the Al Qaeda prison revolt in Mazar el Sharif, a controller called in a JDAM which exploded only 50 feet away, probably due to erroneous coordinates entered in by the pilot.[118] With regard to the former, critical news organisations and advocacy groups reported several instances of collateral casualties. Some criticised the number of collateral victims, laying the blame on 'reliance on high-altitude aerial bombardment, rather than ground forces', and 'methods of attack which, when combined with faulty intelligence, created an enhanced risk of the accidental and incidental civilian injury and loss of life'.[119] These methods of attack included cluster bombs, which led HRW to call for a suspension of cluster bomb use 'until the initial dud rate can be reduced dramatically', and for 'militaries to consider the long-term effects of cluster bombs in areas to which civilians may return or in environments that increase the dud rate, such as soft terrain'.[120] Estimates of civilian causalities during Operation Enduring Freedom range from the Afghan government's estimate of fewer than 500, the US aid group Global Exchange's estimate of at least 800, to the Project on Defense Alternatives' approximations of between

---

116. Canestaro, *supra* n. 13, at p. 475.

117. Ibid.

118. Friedman, *supra* n. 100, at p. 167. JDAM bombs can have a personnel incapacitation (PI) radius of between 500 meters for large 2,000 lb bombs and 435 meters for laser-guided 500 lb bombs. See Air Force Link – JDAMS, *supra* n. 27.

119. Lippman, *supra* n. 41, at p. 64 (providing a laundry list of examples of collateral damage during Enduring Freedom prior to linking precision air combat with causing terrorism, suggesting that the 'contemporary terrorist assault on civilians' is merely 'an extension of the lack of regard and respect for' noncombatants in contemporary arial warfare).

120. 'Fatally Flawed: Cluster Bombs and Their Use by the Untied States in Afghanistan' (December 2002) p. 4, <http://hrw.org/reports/2002/us-afghanistan/Afghan1202.pdf> (hereinafter, Fatally Flawed).

1,000 and 1,300.[121] Despite these fatalities, and their accompanying inevitable criticism, casualty rates likely would have been much greater should a ground invasion have been launched or absent the US use of precision weaponry, which increased bombing accuracy. One study found that the percentage of attacks resulting in damage or destruction to fixed targets increased by 12 percentage points from Operations Allied Force to Enduring Freedom, while the percentage of attacks resulting in damage or destruction to mobile targets increased by 21 percentage points.[122] This debate over the propriety of collateral damage in Afghanistan was quickly eclipsed by the preparations for, and execution of, Operation Iraqi Freedom.

3.4 **Iraq II (Operation Iraqi Freedom)**

Iraq's alleged chemical, biological and nuclear weapons programs, as well as its long-range missile development and support for terrorism, led to Operation Enduring Freedom, which started on 19 March 2003 with offensive operations in the form of air strikes against Iraqi leadership positions.[123] In contrast with Operation Desert Storm, Operation Iraqi Freedom was characterised by a simultaneous air and ground offensive. Iraqi resistance was sporadic and incohesive, with coalition forces pursuing a strategy of rapid advance, bypassing urban centres when possible, and pausing when encountering Iraqi resistance.[124] Oil and port facilities were secured with few oil wells set afire and no widespread environmental sabotage.[125] Special Operations Forces, cooperating with Kurdish irregulars, seized Mosul,

---

121. 'Afghans Defense US Air Strikes', South Asia Section *BBC News*, 21 July 2002, <http://news.bbc.co.uk/1/hi/world/south_asia/2142899>; C. Conetta, 'Operation Enduring Freedom: Why a Higher Rate of Civilian Bombing Causalities', Briefing Report 1, Project on Defense Alternatives, <http://www.comw/org/pda/0201oef.html>.

122. GAO Report on Military Operations, *supra* n. 28, at p. 18. Similar analysis regarding success rates for Operation Iraqi Freedom has yet to be undertaken. Ibid. See *infra* nn. 36-54 and *supra* n. 38-67 and accompanying discussion for a description of how civilian casualties and damage were reflected in media reports and other public discourse following Operation Iraqi Freedom.

123. S. Bowman, 'Iraq: US Military Operations, CRS Report for Congress 1' (2 October 2003); Evidence indicating strong links between Saddam Hussein and terrorism includes the fact that the following individuals fled to Saddam's Iraq for medical care and or sanctuary: Palestinian terrorist Abu Nidal, whose terrorist organisation killed or maimed more than 1,200 people in 20 countries; Abu Abbas, who hijacked the Italian cruise ship Achille Lauro in 1985 and killed wheelchair-bound Leon Klinghoffer; Abu Musab al Zarqawi, who ran an Islamist terrorist training camp in Afghanistan; and Abdul Rahman Yasin, indicted for mixing chemicals in the 1993 World Trade Center bombing and on the FBI's Most Wanted Terrorist List, as well as others. See e.g., P. Crispo, 'Evidence supports that Hussein had strong links with terrorists', *The Miami Herald*, 1 June 2004, Sec. A, p. 19. According to the US State Department, 'the terrorists whom Hussein backed had killed or injured more than 3,500 civilians outside Iraq', leading to the conclusion that Hussein failed to follow UN SC Res. 687, para. 32 (the 1991 Iraq disarmament resolution) which 'called on Hussein to renounce terrorism'. Ibid. For additional evidence and discussion regarding the links between Saddam and terrorism see also S. F. Hayes and T. Joscelyn, 'The mother of all connections', 10 *The Weekly Standard*, 18 July 2005; S. Hayes, 'Case closed', 9 *The Weekly Standard*, 24 November 2003; 'Saddam's link with terrorists', *The Scotsman*, 15 October 2004.

124. Ibid., at p. 3.

125. Ibid.

Kirkuk and Tikrit.[126] Within 25 days of offensive operations, coalition forces had relative control of all major Iraqi cities, including Baghdad and Basra.[127] During the period 19 March through 18 April 2003, US and coalition forces expended 29,239 munitions, 19,948, or approximately 68 percent, of which were PGM.[128] Significant from the standpoint of ordnance flexibility, the mix of PGM missiles changed over the course of the last few conflicts: although from Operations Allied Force to Enduring Freedom the use of GPS bombs increased 45 percent and laser-guided PGM munitions decreased 32 percent, this trend was reversed in Operation Enduring Freedom, where the use of laser-guided bombs increased ten percent and the use of GPS bombs decreased about 13 percent.[129]

Effects-based targeting was the norm in Operation Iraqi Freedom, just as it was during Operation Enduring Freedom, with planners taking advantage of the lessons learned in the Afghan campaign.[130] Building on the 'embryonic network-centric' infrastructure, noted above, that was developed in Afghanistan, military planners in Operation Iraqi Freedom were able to develop 'a comprehensive image of the Iraqi order of battle' and 'formulate a list of priority targets' from the CAOC at Prince Sultan Air Base, and respond rapidly to changing battlefield developments.[131] One key target was Iraqi satellite communications, and in particular Iraqi state-run television, to prevent Saddam Hussein from communicating instructions to his forces, and propaganda to the world. Having watched Allied Force operations, the Iraqis had built redundancy into their communications, including their satellite ground infrastructure, to defeat attempts to shut down their communications.[132] Consequently, a 25 March direct hit on a satellite TV dish by a laser-guided hellfire missile launched by an unmanned Predator failed to keep Iraqi TV off the air.[133] The Iraqis also attempted to defend against PGM attacks and to force Allied troops to use less effective missiles by jamming the GPS signal used by PGM, the first time in history a belligerent during conflict attempted to do so.[134] All jammers, however, were easily identified and destroyed by Allied forces.[135]

---

126. Ibid.

127. Ibid.

128. United States Air Force, CENTAF (Assessment and Analysis Division) 'Operation Iraqi Freedom: By the Numbers' (30 April 2003) p. 11; see also GAO Report on Military Operations, *supra* n. 30, at p. 9.

129. GAO Report of Military Operations, *supra* n. 28, at p. 17. This illustrates the fact that both types of these PGMs fill a need in modern warfare; GPS bombs provide an all-weather capability enabled by satellite navigation, while laser-guided bombs, which, as noted *supra*, follow a narrow beam of pulsed energy trained on a target by an aircraft or ground operators, are more precise and have a capacity for attacks on moving targets that GPS-guided bombs do not. Ibid., at p. 16.

130. Cook, *supra* n. 109, at p. 5.

131. Ibid.

132. Hyten and Uy, *supra* n. 4, at pp. 56-57.

133. Ibid., at p. 56.

134. Ibid., at p. 57.

135. Ibid.

3.4.1 Jus in bello *weaponry issues in Operation Iraqi Freedom*

As in Operation Enduring Freedom, the most publicised *jus in bello* issue arising out of Operation Iraqi Freedom was whether collateral civilian casualties, estimated at 1,000 to 3,240 during major combat operations, exceeded the constraints of international law.[136] This was not unanticipated, and the close scrutiny public interest and advocacy groups continually gave this issue, no doubt further encouraged the US to continue to take all feasible measures to avoid and minimise civilian deaths and property damage.[137] These efforts were generally effective, a fact the US underscored for the nation and the world in President Bush's historic speech aboard the *USS Abraham Lincoln* at the conclusion of major combat operations in Iraq.[138] 'In defeating Nazi Germany and Imperial Japan', he recalled, 'Allied Forces destroyed entire cities, while enemy leaders who started the conflict were safe until the final days … with new tactics and precision weapons, [the US] can achieve military objectives without directing violence against civilians.'[139]

Following a five-week investigation in Iraq, HRW praised the military's efforts in a report that concluded, 'coalition air strikes on pre-planned fixed targets apparently caused few civilian casualties … and air forces generally avoided civilian infrastructure'.[140] Nevertheless, HRW also alleged that military planners 'failed in the conduct of the air war that led to the loss of civilian life or to other civilian harm … the most egregious was the flawed targeting of Iraqi leadership … the US and UK air forces also used some cluster bombs in or near populated areas'.[141] With respect to the use of cluster bombs, this issue was a continuation of the debate, noted above, that arose in Operations Allied Force and Enduring Freedom. Critics alleged that the military too often 'used cluster bombs when faced with enemy fire', thereby 'pushing the risk to Iraq civilians'.[142] Military planners countered by pointing out that, of the approximately 1,500 cluster bombs used in the

---

136. M. Farley, 'Report note toll of cluster bombs, strikes in Iraq', *The Los Angeles Times*, 12 December 2003 at p. A15. A *Los Angeles Times* article placed the number of noncombatant deaths at 1,700 during the five weeks of active combat. Ibid. HRW notes, however, 'a complete accounting of civilian casualties may not be possible', due to the varying quality of hospital records, the Muslim custom of burying the dead almost immediately, and, sometimes, due to the few remains by which to identify the dead. Off Target, *supra* n. 98, at p. 13.

137. A spokesman for US Central Command noted:
'The military applied precise methodology and extreme caution in a meticulous process when choosing valid military targets and munitions, including cluster bombs … US Central Command understands that various private and international organizations are very concerned with civilian casualties resulting from decisive combat operations in Operation Iraqi Freedom. While any civilian casualties of war are a tragedy, coalition forces have taken extreme care in Operation Iraqi Freedom in limiting needless loss of life and collateral damage.' Farley, *supra* n. 136, at p. A15.

138. See CNN Transcript, 'Bush makes historic speech aboard warship', 1 May 2003, <http://www.cnn.com/2003/US/05/01/bush.transcript/>.

139. Ibid.

140. Off Target, *supra* n. 98, at p. 6; See also B. Rolfsen, 'Group says haste made for civilian casualties', *Air Force Times*, 22 December 2003, at p. 21.

141. J. Darman, 'How many is too many', Newsweek Web Exclusive (11 December 2003), International Section, <http://msnbc.msn.com/id/3693864/site/newsweek>.

142. Ibid.

war, only 26 fell in civilian areas, and these were used only when it was deemed a military necessity, which unfortunately was where 'the Iraqi regime placed military targets near civilians'.[143]

With regard to targets of opportunity, critics complained that attempts to target Iraqi leaders, or other targets of opportunity, caused 'excessive civilian casualties'.[144] HRW in this regard noted that the two unsuccessful attempts to kill Saddam Hussein, and other failed leadership decapitation attacks, such as on 'Chemical Ali', killed and injured dozens of civilians.[145] This was due to the fact that the signals emitted by these leaders' Thuraya satellite telephones were used by the military, along with other intelligence, to target them through the GPS, a methodology labelled 'flawed' by HRW.[146] Asserting that this targeting 'turned a precision weapon into a potentially indiscriminate weapon', HRW pointed out that these signals can only pinpoint a location within a 100 metre (328-foot) radius, sweeping in residents of neighbourhoods sheltering these leaders within that radius and thereby making them collateral victims of the attacks.[147]

From Operations Desert Storm to Iraq Freedom, the number of precision weapons utilised by the United States increased, as noted above, from eight to 68 percent, while military strategy evolved from an emphasis on linear sequential attacks to effects-based simultaneous attacks on emergent targets. The *jus in bello* issues, however, remained relatively constant, focused on identifying civilian collateral damage and casualties, and determining if these casualties stemmed from an alleged failure to take all feasible precautions prior to an attack or through the improper selection of weapons systems. Although issues of collateral death and damage issues raised by these military operations are usually framed using *jus in bello* terminology, many do not, or even try to, establish even a *prima facie* case that collateral death and damage violated the relevant proportionality and direct targeting *jus in bello* tests. As noted by HRW in *Off Target*, it 'does not assess the military advantage of any particular attack it describes'.[148] This omission is critical, especially if the public or media tend to equate criticisms such as that from HRW

143. G. Miller, 'Head of joint chiefs defends use of cluster bombs in Iraq; Myers says few fell in populated areas, but reports of casualties from duds persist', *The Los Angeles Times*, 26 April 2003, Part 1, p. 8.

144. Off Target, *supra* n. 98, at p. 20.

145. Ibid., at pp. 21, 26.

146. Ibid. at p. 24; See also Farley, *supra* n. 136, at p. A15.

147. Off Target, *supra* n. 98, at pp. 24-25. Nowhere does HRW explain how the a radius of one-hundred meters is 'indiscriminate' *in se,* especially in light of disclaiming any effort to analyze the military advantages expected from the attacks, a key aspect of the proportionality test in *jus in bello*. AP I, *supra* n. 5, at Art. 51(5)(b). Moreover, assertions of excessive casualties notwithstanding, HRW evidently used *ex post facto* reasoning to dismiss the validity of intelligence used to corroborate these strikes on Iraqi leadership due to their failure and the fact they resulted in collateral death and damage. *Off Target*, *supra* n. 98, at pp. 25, 26 (stating both that 'although the US undoubtedly attempted to use corroborating sources for satellite phone coordinates ... *based on the results,* however, accurate corroborating information must have been difficult if not impossible to come by and additional methods of tracking the Iraqi leadership just as unreliable as satellite phones' and '*given the lack of success*, it seems human intelligence was completely unreliable.' (emphasis added)).

148. Off Target, *supra* n. 98, at p. 12.

and other groups with establishing whether or not the US is complying with *jus in bello*, since the military advantage anticipated is a key component of that law's proportionality test.[149] As precision weaponry continues to increase in reliability, the need to factor in the military advantage sought in an attack into any *jus in bello* judgments on collateral death and damage is necessary for a fair and credible legal assessment of the military operation.

As noted above, in Operation Desert Storm the Al-Firdus bunker was grist for numerous complaints that the US and its Coalition partners failed to take adequate measures prior to the attack. In Operations Allied Force, Enduring Freedom and Iraqi Freedom, collateral civilian deaths and damage, along with the use of cluster munitions, gave rise to further issues involving the failure to take all feasible measures to avoid collateral deaths and damage from the attack. The common motivating thread behind these proposed complaints was not a proven failure by the US to abide by *jus in bello*, rather it was the failure of certain incidents to pass a 'CNN-factor' pseudo litmus test for collateral damage, where public officials are sometimes forced to react to issues and pressure resulting from issues or events in the media spotlight.[150] As HRW admitted, although it 'neither has the information nor is in a position to evaluate the military advantages expected from the cluster bomb attacks … ', it 'is nevertheless concerned about the significant civilian casualties these attacks caused'.[151] Aside from the few unsuccessful ideological attempts to use judicial systems to bring civil and criminal charges against US and coalition pilots and military leaders, however, this increased critical focus by groups on the diminishing numbers of civilian casualties is not a totally adverse development.[152] As discussed earlier, it helps military and public officials remain focused on this issue, and has unintentionally highlighted one ironic public affairs dilemma that military high tech nations must address. As countries publicise, and media celebrate, precision weaponry, many in the general public tend to erroneously assume that no modern ordnance impacts a target unintentionally. When, invariably, one does, causing tragic yet permissible *jus in bello* collateral damage, victims and groups sometimes assume it was intentional or avoidable. As one survivor whose family were collateral casualties during Operation Iraqi Freedom stated, 'the Americans said no civilians were targeted, I don't understand how this could

149. AP I, *supra* n. 5, at Art. 51(5)(b).

150. See *infra* nn. 203-210 and accompanying text for discussion regarding the pseudo CNN-litmus test.

151. Off Target, *supra* n. 98, at p. 62.

152. See Phillip Meilinger, 'Air-ground cooperation perspectives', 83 *Military Review* (1 November 2003) p. 50 at n. 14 (noting that civil charges against US pilots and commanders, 'can only add to concerns over battlespace awareness, which, in turn might elongate the decision cycle'); See A. Evans-Pritchard, 'Belgium restricts war crime law', *The Daily Telegraph*, 24 June 2003, at p. 14; C.S. Smith, 'Belgium plans to amend law on war crimes', *The New York Times*, 23 June 2003, at Sec. A, p. 9 for reports on how Belgium's war crimes legislation was politically abused by organisations who charges leading political figures from the UK and the US with 'war crimes'.

happen'.[153] How these assumptions are addressed in the future could impact the short-, or even long-term, success of the US and Allied strategic goals.[154]

4. PRESENT AND FUTURE MILITARY STRATEGIES

As detailed above in the survey of recent conflicts, modern weapon innovations have been introduced into combat during each conflict since the end of the Cold War. These changes were fuelled by the latest revolution in military affairs (RMA) generated by 'technological advances and a dramatically altered geopolitical environment'.[155] The explosion of computer-driven information-handling technology is one key aspect of the technical revolution, while the geopolitical change can be attributed to the increased need for deterrence against terrorist organisations post-9/11.[156]

The evolution in US military strategy at the end of the Cold War was first clearly evident in the Pentagon's *Joint Vision 2010*, a 1996 document setting out official military strategy.[157] One author noted that this first post-Desert Storm document was 'particularly applicable to a new world of precision warfare'.[158] This joint vision strategy helped resolve the issue of how the military could harness 'network centric warfare', by its transformation to 'fully exploit the new power of computers'.[159] As President Bush spelled out, 'this transformed military force would be defined less by size and more by mobility and swiftness, one that is easier to deploy and sustain'.[160] In particular, instead of destroying massed forces and industrial assets, heretofore thought of as the path to victory, *Joint Vision 2010* envisioned the transformed force finding and destroying the 'center of gravity' of the enemy in the most precise manner possible.[161] In so doing, Joint Vision 2010 emphasised that the US will strive to attain 'full spectrum dominance' and 'greater situational awareness'.[162] As noted above, this strategy was the foundation of the effects-based air campaigns in Operations Enduring Freedom and Iraqi Freedom.[163]

The Pentagon's current *Joint Vision 2020* 'builds upon and extends the conceptual template' of Joint Vision 2010 and continues this approach to military strategy,

---

153. Off Target, *supra* n. 98, at p. 32.

154. Darmen, *supra* n. 141, at p. 14.

155. Schmitt, *supra* n. 22, at p. 28.

156. Friedman, *supra* n. 100, at pp. 87, 107. In addition to the information handling/global information network aspects of the current RMA, technologies of long-ranged aviation, and radar-evading stealth, are also redefining war. See Rip and Hasik, *supra* n. 27, at p. ix.

157. US Joint Chiefs of Staff, *Joint Vision 2010* (1996) at pp. 21-22.

158. Friedman, *supra* n. 100, at p. 111.

159. Ibid.

160. Remarks by President at US Naval Academy Commencement (25 May 2001), <http://www.whitehouse.gov/news/releases/2001/05/20010525-1.html>.

161. Friedman, *supra* n. 100, at p. 111.

162. Schmitt, *supra* n. 22, at p. 25.

163. See *supra* n. 121-152 and accompanying text for discussion of Operation Iraqi Freedom.

including its emphasis on precision engagement for effects-based operations.[164] This strategic approach to warfare was also confirmed in a 2003 White Paper entitled *An Evolving Joint Perspective: US Joint Warfare and Crisis Resolution in the 21st Century* (hereinafter, 2003 White Paper), and in the recently released *National Military Strategy of the United States of America* 2004 (hereinafter, 2004 NMS).

In the 2003 White Paper the Joint Chiefs of Staff furthered defined 'full spectrum dominance' as 'the decisive defeat of any adversary or control of any situation across the full range of military operations'.[165] The White Paper also recognised the need for the US to '*leverage* US asymmetric advantages in the ever-changing, strategic and operational environments US forces will face', and highlighted how knowledge superiority, manoeuver and precision fire work together to 'help minimize casualties and shorten the conflict'.[166] Conversely, in the 2004 NMS, the US recognised how adversaries will *seek* asymmetric capabilities and 'will avoid US strengths like precision strike and seek to counter US power projection capabilities by creating an anti-access environment. Such adversaries will target civilian populations, economic centers and symbolic locations as a way to attack US political will and resolve.'[167]

The emphasis in the 2004 NMS on how the adversary may fight, rather than where and when they might fight, has forced the US to carefully analyse potential crises and to commit a fully effective, properly tailored and fully integrated joint task force in as short a period as possible, in order to be prepared for any eventuality. Accordingly, US Defense Planning Guidance for fiscal year 2004 directs regional commanders to create a standing joint force headquarters by fiscal year 2005, one which would serve as a full-time core of functionally organised and skilled joint planners.[168] This standing force would provide decision superiority for effects-based operations through 'development of an operational net assessment based on a political, military, economic, social, infrastructure and information analysis of the enemy'.[169] The 2004 NMS also touches on *jus in bello* issues. It warns military commanders to become cognisant of collateral damage resulting from their effects-based targeting by cautioning:

> 'While US Armed Forces will continue to emphasize precision, speed, lethality and distributed operations, commanders must expect and plan for the possibility that their operations will produce unintended 2nd- and 3rd-order effects. For example, US forces can precisely locate, track, and destroy discrete targets to reduce collateral damage and conclude operations as quickly as possible. Operations that rely on precision may result in large elements of an adversary's military remaining intact and segments of the popula-

164. US Joint Chiefs of Staff, *Joint Vision 2020*, (2000) at pp. 27-28.

165. US Joint Chiefs of Staff, *An Evolving Joint Perspective: US Joint Warfare and Crisis Resolution in the 21st Century* (2003) at p. 7.

166. Ibid., at pp. 7, 31 (emphasis added).

167. NMS, *supra* n. 4, at p. 5.

168. S.E. Jasper, 'Transforming joint warfighting capabilities', 35 *Joint Force Quarterly* (2004) pp. 69, 71.

169. Ibid., at p. 71.

> tions unaffected. Commanders must prepare to operate in regions where pockets of resistance remain and there exists the potential for continued combat operations amidst a large number of non-combatants.'[170]

The topics addressed in this segment of the 2004 NMS – the unintended 2nd and 3rd order effects: increased precision targeting, reduced collateral damage, and urban warfare in the midst of a large number of combatants – are evidence of the relevance of *jus in bello* in US military strategy, and are the legal impetus for weapons modernisation programs.

5. FUTURE WEAPONS

Changing military strategies and the global war on terror have been catalysts for weapon modernisation plans and programming. These include both the traditional lethal categories, in which weapons are made even more precise and lethal, as well as a burgeoning non-lethal category as well.

Regarding traditional weapons modernisation programs, some of the most interesting research in precision warfare most relevant to *jus in bello* concerns involves efforts to reduce collateral damage. For example, the US Air Force has modified the F-16 Block 30 Fighting Falcon multi-role fighter to permit it to carry the 500lb GBU-38 JDAM, instead of the 2,000lb variant of the JDAM, in order to reduce collateral damage during anti-insurgency operations.[171] In addition, even smaller, more precise bombs are in development. A small diameter bomb (SDB), a 250-pound, 71-inch long bomb with fold-out wings and advanced, jam-resistant, GPS-Inertial Navigation System (GPS-INS) guidance, is being developed to allow a tactical aircraft to attack more than a dozen targets and a B-1B bomber to attack up to 96 targets, with a stand-off distance of more than 40 miles and with less risk of collateral damage.[172] The SDB lowers collateral damage because it has a blast radius of only 26 feet.[173] This lowered blast radius is due to the fact that the warhead's skin, unlike traditional warheads, is comparatively thin and most of its weight is in its explosive content.[174] Within its intended radius it is quite effective, but outside of this area 'the lethality drops off to near-zero'.[175] According to

170. NMS, *supra* n. 4, at p. 5.

171. M. Sirak, 'US Air Force increases strike punch of F-16s', *Jane's Defense Weekly*, 25 August 2004, p. 24.

172. Ibid.

173. R. Wall and D. Barrie, 'Making an impact', 44 *Aviation Week & Space Technology*, 17 May 2004, p. 16. This warhead is 'just what you want in an urban environment', according to the Director of the Engineering and Technical Management Directorate in the Air Armaments Center at Eglin Air Force Base, Florida. M. Sirak, 'US pursues low collateral damage warhead', *Jane's Defense Weekly*, 7 April 2004, p. 10.

174. Ibid.

175. Ibid.

Representative Duncan Hunter, chairman of the House Armed Services Committee, this precision weapon is 'the wave of the future'.[176]

Somewhat counter-intuitively, collateral damage may be also reduced by developing a larger bomb designed to attack deeply buried bunkers containing underground targets such as weapons of mass destruction, alleviating the need for massive and continued bombardment to neutralise these weapons caches. Drawing on experience gained by developing the GPS-guided 21,000 lb GBU-43/B Massive Ordnance Air Burst Bomb (MOAB) designed for combat operations in Iraq but never deployed, current research centres on devising a Massive Ordnance Penetrator (MOP).[177] The MOP is intended to weigh more and have a thicker steel casing, in order to achieve the desired penetration, but would be filled with a smaller amount of explosives.[178]

Research into how to further exploit UAVs also continues, with a heavy emphasis on network centric warfare.[179] The Pentagon's Joint Unmanned Combat Air Systems (J-UCAS) office is working on developing a UAV common operating system (COS) and two new UAVs by 2007, spending about $4.2 billion on this effort between 2004 and 2009.[180] The COS would enable 'unprecedented levels of autonomy with the air vehicle operations', including stealthy UAV missions 'like strike, long-range surveillance, suppression of enemy air defenses and electronic attack while flying over hostile airspace and in concert with manned assets'.[181] In fact, earlier this year, a UAV, flying at 700 kilometres per hour (442 mph) at 10,670 metres (35,000 feet) under human supervision 130 kilometres (80 miles) away dropped an inert 114-kilogram (250 lb) GPS-guided bomb at the Naval Warfare Center Weapons Division range in China Lake, California, and then landed.[182] The bomb struck within several inches of its target, a truck.[183] The Defense Advanced Research Projects Agency (DARPA) is also working on developing a UAV that is only 22 inches in height and less than five pounds, in order to enable it to 'dart behind enemy lines, take photographs, and get back home without human intervention', as well as on micro-UAVs, which are only a few inches long, which can be launched in a variety of modes, and would have the ability to fly behind buildings, trees and hills without a large auxiliary power source.[184] DARPA, moreover,

---

176. Sirak, *supra* n. 171, at p. 24. Representative Hunter also noted that 'the idea of leveraging our stealth aircraft combined with precision munitions is one of America's great advantages'. Ibid.

177. R. Wall and D. Barrie, 'Bunker "plinking"', 48 *Aviation Week & Space Technology*, 17 May 2004, p. 49.

178. Ibid.

179. B. Sweetman, 'In the tracks of predator: combat UAV programs are gathering speed', 37 *Jane's International Defense Review*, August 2004, p. 48.

180. M. Sirak, 'US shapes unmanned combat aircraft project', *Jane's Defense Weekly*, 20 October 2004, p. 12.

181. Ibid.

182. 'Robot plane drops bomb in test,' Associated Press, 19 April 2004, <http://www.msnbc.msn.com/id/4779727)>.

183. Ibid. The chief operator for the mission and the UAV's operator noted that the test was 'a huge step forward for us. It shows the capability of an unmanned airplane to carry weapons.' Ibid.

184. J.B. Alexander, *Winning The War, Advanced Weapons, Strategies, And Concepts For The Post – 9/11 World* (New York, St. Martin's Press 2003) p. 51.

is developing an Unmanned Combat Armed Rotorcraft (UCAR) for the US Army.[185]

At the level of the individual soldier, the US is seeking technology advances aimed at reducing collateral damage caused by ground troops engaged in urban combat. The US military is, accordingly, in discussions with a Norwegian company seeking possible use of its reduced ricochet range (R3) ammunition.[186] These rounds are comprised of a steel tube wrapped around a metal rod, with an aluminum nose cap, which produces high-drag fragments as ricochets which do not fly as far as ricochets associated with standard rounds.[187] These types of bullets would be 'a boost for forces that are engaged in Iraq-type of environments in which ground troops are facing a constant threat from insurgent attacks', but in which, simultaneously, it is paramount to win the 'hearts and minds' of the local population.[188]

The transformation of military forces in order to meet the political and technical challenges posed by the WOT has also been the catalyst for the development of non-lethal weapon systems. These weapons systems are defined by the Pentagon as those 'that are explicitly designed and primarily employed so as to incapacitate personnel or materiel, while minimising fatalities, permanent injury to personnel, and undesired damage to property and the environment'.[189] These non-lethal weapons thus attempt to 'significantly reduce [fatalities or permanent injuries] as compared with physically destroying the same target', rather than having a 'zero probability' of such a result.[190] Moreover, some non-lethal weapons may be, and have been, reviewed by DoD lawyers for conformity with *jus in bello*, while other non-lethal systems may not be since they may not be considered 'weapons' for review purposes.[191] Still others, due to their chemical makeup or affects on humans, implicate the provisions of other treaties and should be analysed to ensure compliance.[192]

Since Operation United Shield, when the US military that provided security for a UN withdrawal from Somalia was equipped for the first time with non-lethal weapons, the US has actively sought, acquired, trained with and deployed non-lethal weapons systems for use for mission accomplishment on the battlefield.[193]

---

185. Sweetman, *supra* n. 179, at p. 48.

186. J.J. Lok, 'US looking at reduced ricochet rounds for use in urban combat', *Jane's International Defense Review*, November 2004, at p. 29.

187. Ibid.

188. Ibid.

189. E. Nutley, 'Non-lethal weapons: setting our phasers on stun? Potential strategic blessing and curses of non-lethal weapons on the battlefield', 2 Occasional Paper No. 34 Center for Strategy and Technology, Air War College (August 2003) citing US Department of Defense (DoD) Policy Directive 300.3, *Policy for Non-lethal Weapons*, 9 July 1996, para. 3.1.

190. Ibid.

191. Nutley, *supra* n. 189, at pp. 38-41.

192. Ibid., at p. 39 (Table 4).

193. J.C. Duncan, 'A primer on the employment of non-lethal weapons', 45 *Naval L R* (1998) p. 1. The Commanding General, Lt. Gen Anthony Zinni, was provided with 'off-the-shelf' technologies, such as low-impact 12 gauge shotgun shells, sticky and aqueous foams, and a low-energy laser system, to intimidate suspected snipers. Nutley, *supra* n. 189, at p. 3.

Indeed, the Pentagon's Joint Non-Lethal Weapons Directorate (JNLWD), which has served as the focal point for all DoD non-lethal weapons matters since it was first established in 1997, has screened over 100 different non-lethal technologies resulting in the approval of 14 separate multiservice programs.[194] Non-lethal weapon technologies can be categorised into those that are counter-personnel and those that are counter-materiel, and, within these categories, a DoD working group found, the technologies with the greatest potential for application include electromagnetic systems, chemical-based substances, mechanical and kinetic devices, and enabling technologies.[195]

One example of emerging non-lethal weaponry is the Active Denial System (ADS). The ADS is a millimetre-wave device that projects a short wavelength beam that results in pain caused by its effect on the pain receptors near the surface of the skin.[196] Other anti-personnel non-lethal weapons that are being developed include newer models of the M-26 TASER, which employ electro-muscular disruption technology that brings a target down immediately, and PepperBall Systems, a product of PepperBall Tactical Systems, which shoot frangible plastic marble-sized projectiles filled with powdered Oleoresin Capsicum (pepper spray), creating a triple combination of effects: the physical shock of being shot, the kinetic pain of the projectile impact, and the irritant effects of the chemical agent.[197] These non-lethal technologies, along with others not surveyed here, are particularly relevant in facing the 'operational realities and highly political nature of the war on terrorism', as noted by one author.[198] Especially due to the 'CNN-factor', non-lethal weapons which minimise or eliminate casualties, particularly collateral damage among non-combatants and their property, are an 'extremely valuable' tool in the US's arsenal.

Research into how to bring these new weapons and capabilities, lethal and non-lethal, to bear on an enemy in an effective, timely and precise fashion by further developing and exploiting network-centric warfare is also proceeding. The US, for example, is developing a Global Information Grid (GIG) to combine information processing, storing, disseminating and managing capabilities throughout the US Department of Defense into an integrated network.[199] This would create, in effect, what the DOD's Chief Information Officer has described as 'a private military version of the World Wide Web'.[200] US military policy on the GIG dictates that it will support 'all DoD missions with information technology . . . that offers the most effective, efficient, and assured information handling capabilities available,

---

194. Duncan, *supra* n. 193, at p. 14.
195. Nutley, *supra* n. 189, at p. 15.
196. Alexander, *supra* n. 184, at pp. 14-15; See also USAF, Air Force Research Laboratory Fact Sheet, Active Denial System: Advance Concept Technology Demonstration (February 2003), <http://www.de.afrl.af.mil/factsheets/activedenial.html>.
197. Ibid., at pp. 18, 24.
198. Nutley, *supra* n. 189, at p. 49.
199. GAO Report on Military Operations, *supra* n. 28, at p. 22.
200. Ibid.

consistent with national military strategy, operational requirements, and best value enterprise-level business practices'.[201]

6. RECENT CONFLICTS, MODERN STRATEGY AND WEAPONS AND THEIR AFFECT ON *JUS IN BELLO*

As noted above, the US has fought its conflicts, fashioned its military strategies, and formulated its weapons modernisation programs with an eye towards *jus in bello*, not only due to the law's legal proscriptions but also due to the ubiquitous 'CNN-factor'. In so doing, the US has striven to avoid adverse publicity and to secure domestic and political support. Indeed, both of these considerations have made the use of precision weaponry in modern conflicts a given, rather than a luxury. These legal and strategic political considerations have spurred the US into developing and fielding better precision weapons, more efficient and functional UAVs, low collateral damage bombs, non-lethal weapons, and network-centric technologies for increased situational awareness. Uniting these elements in a strategy that is collateral damage adverse, these trends will likely continue, and in so doing, continue to affect *jus in bello*.[202]

Specifically, a review of the *jus in bello* issues raised in recent conflicts reveal three factors that have largely affected *jus in bello's* distinction and proportionality tests. First, modern weaponry's increased accuracy have led some to suggest that the rules requiring distinction and proportionality are violated whenever collateral damage involving civilian casualties results from an attack, effectively creating a 'CNN-factor' pseudo-litmus test for the legal propriety of collateral damage.[203]

---

201. DoD Directive 8100.1, Global Information Grid (GIG) Overreaching Policy (19 September 2002) (certified current as of 31 November 2003).

202. Modern weaponry's affect on *jus in bello* is to be expected. As one writer noted, 'since evolution in the conduct of warfare affects the individuals and objects which humanitarian law seeks to shelter, it is not surprising that law has proven responsive, both proactively and reactively, to warfare's changing nature'. Schmitt, *supra* n. 22, at p. 53.

203. The ICTY Report noted this tendency when it commented that many of the materials submitted to the Office of the Prosecutor for the ICTY 'consisted of reports that civilians have been killed and inviting the conclusion to be drawn that crimes have therefore been committed.' ICTY Report, *supra* n. 65, at para. 51. Even in a clear-cut case such as the attack on Korisa Village, in which, as noted *supra*, the ICTY Report found no evidence to contradict NATO's assertion that the military objectives were legal targets and that no civilians were illegally targeted, one critic charged that NATO somehow likely violated *jus in bello* law to 'avoid targeting civilians' and comply with the rule of distinction apparently because there were unintended civilian casualties. See Voon, *supra* n. 51, at pp. 1110-1112; see also Lippman, *supra* n. 41, at p. 50. These critics, using 20/20 hindsight and disregarding applicable *jus in bello* standards (see e.g., *supra* nn. 220-223 and accompanying text) assert that NATO and the US should have continually ensured that information and targets were accurate, and requested additional information when needed, thereby inferring that these were all feasible, attainable and timely actions that would have prevented collateral casualties. *Supra* n. 53, at p. 1112; Lippman, *supra* n. 41, at p. 64. For example, one author noted that NATO should have somehow 'confirmed that the target remained legitimate' and opined that the attack should have been conducted 'in daylight' and more updated intelligence should have been obtained, and the attack should have been made from a lower altitude.' Voon, *supra* n. 53, at p. 1112. Additionally, one critic, when dis-

Second, and related to this pseudo-litmus test, is if and how secondary or tertiary effects of an attack factor into the required proportionality calculation as relevant collateral damage when assessing an attack's legality. Third, and also aligned to concerns over increased collateral damage and death relevant to the proportionality test, recent conflicts have also served as a catalyst in exposing the fissures in the legal community over what constitutes a valid military objective in *jus in bello.* In particular, the confluence of precision weaponry with increasingly interdependent modern societies have created issues involving the legitimacy of targeting constitutive elements of the modern state such as dual use facilities.

With regard to modern communications' first affect on *jus in bello's* distinction and proportionality tests, in which the legitimacy of collateral damage is subject to a 'CNN factor' pseudo-litmus test, political and military leaders should resist the temptation of substituting or confusing the legal requirements of distinction and proportionality with the unabashedly political requirement at the heart of this pseudo-litmus test.[204] Although, as noted *supra*, the US is keenly aware of the need to go beyond minimum legal requirements and avoid as much collateral damage as possible for political and strategic reasons, such as the need for post-conflict reconstruction, these two imperatives should never be confused. At the heart of Article 52(1) AP I's legal prescription, for example, is the moral element consisting of the warfighter's intent, namely: civilian objects shall not be the 'object' of an attack.[205] Similarly, the state of mind of an attacker with regard to a violation of Article 52(4) and 52(5)'s prohibition against indiscriminate attacks, as noted above with regard to the discussion in the ICTY Report on NATO's attack on Grdelica Gorge and the Djakorica convoy, is whether the war fighter acted with 'reckless disregard' as to where a strike will fall.[206] Severing the moral element of

---

cussing a hypothetical based on the Grdelica Gorge train incident, described *supra* at nn. 79-82 and accompanying pages, in relation to 'precautionary measures', the lack of which would make an attack with collateral damage illegal, even complained that insufficient precautions could be found where the attacker failed to consult 'the train schedule' prior to attacking a railroad bridge, evidently discounting the fact the trains might not be running on time in a country at war or that they might be purposely not following a schedule. Laursen, *supra* n. 57, at p. 807.

204. This distinction is one found in customary law. *See* Infeld *supra* n. 17, at p. 114. Moreover, confusing the political and the moral not only leads to incoherence (*see infra* n. 207) it leads to the wholesale jettisoning of *jus in bello* as a normative force, substituting customary law with post-modern political agendas. For example, one writer, disregarding *jus in bello's* historical customary and codified strictures against indiscriminate weapons, chalks up the characterisation of Scud missile attacks as illegal, and cruise missiles as surgical, to 'the tendency to humanize technologically-advanced weaponry at the expense of more primitive implements of warfare', and to 'bias in favor of sophisticated technologies'. G.J. Simpson, 'War crimes: A critical introduction', in T.LH. McCormack and G.J. Simpson, eds., *The Law of War Crimes: National and International Approaches* (The Hague, Kluwer Law International 1997) pp. 7, 10-11; G.J. Simpson, 'Conceptualizing violence: present and future developments in international law: panel I: adjudicating violence: problems confronting international law and policy on war crimes and crimes against humanity: didactic and dissident histories in war crimes trials', 60 *Albany LR* (1997) pp. 801, 814.

205. Art. 52(1) AP I, *supra* n. 5.

206. Art. 51(4) and (5) AP I, ibid. See *supra* nn. 98-104 and accompanying text for a discussion of NATO's attack on Grdelica Gorge and the Djakorica convoy. See also M.N. Schmitt, 'Precision in aerial warfare and the law of international armed conflict', Unpublished manuscript in possession of

intent from these legal norms – by condemning as 'illegal' any collateral (and thus unintended) casualties, or casualties due to weapon malfunctions, intelligence errors or human mistakes rather than keeping this and similar *jus in bello* prescriptions limited to the intentional or culpably negligent targeting of civilians – is akin to cutting the moral element from the heart of *jus in bello.* This excision removes incentives for its observance, its moral significance, and ultimately its normative value.[207] This would be especially ironic, since precision weaponry has enhanced US efforts to avoid collateral damage and civilian casualties to the point that, in the future, 'significant collateral damage and incidental injury will be the exception, not the rule', in the words of one expert commentator.[208] Disregarding a war fighter's intent, and, moreover, totally eviscerating the preservation of one's own forces as a calculable military advantage in the proportionality calculation, all in the haste to condemn non-intentional collateral damage and casualties as illegal, would tragically remove this legal incentive to continue the trend toward precision warfare and weaken *jus in bello's* normative force.[209] By effectively lowering the moral bar

---

the author, Marshall Center, Garmisch, Germany, at p. 20, citing Y. Dinstein, *The Conduct of Hostilities under the Law of International Armed Conflict* (Cambridge, Cambridge University Press 2004) p. 117

207. This moral element is particularly true with regard to the laws of war, as noted by one expert, '[w]hat is legal is not necessarily moral and what is moral is not always legal, but particularly with regard to the law of war, the two are inextricably intertwined.' S. Murray, *The Moral and Ethical Implications of Precision Guided Munitions*, Thesis (Alabama, School of Advanced Air and Space Studies, Air University, Maxwell AFB June 2003) at p. 46, quoting from law of war expert; W. Hayes Parks, 'Air war and the law of war', 32 *Air Force LR* (1990) pp. 7, 8. Separating the legal from the moral leads to confusion with regard to both. The inability to legally and morally distinguish between deaths intended in an attack and those that are not intended but merely foreseeable is evident in one article that argues the following points: that any non-combatant deaths should be condemned as immoral, now that the 'age of segregated battlefields has all but vanished'; that non-combatant lives should be preserved, 'even if significantly increasing the risk to [a commander's] own soldiers'; and that unintended, yet foreseeable deaths, differ 'only in degree' in being just as morally condemnable as terrorist targeting innocents'. See M. Carline, 'The moral limits of strategic attack', *Parameters* (2002) pp. 15-27. See also Lippman, *supra* n. 41 at p. 67 (confusing 'foreseeable' collateral injuries and deaths under the *jus in bello* proportionality test with 'intended' casualties reached as a 'result of a rational calculus').

208. Schmitt, *supra* n. 22, at p. 79.

209. See e.g., Schmitt, *supra* n. 13, at pp. 10, 12 (noting both that critics, alleging that disproportionate collateral damage results from US planes improperly operating beyond the range of air defences, wrongful exclude the preservation of one's own forces as an important military advantage to be considered when conducting proportionality calculations, and that states will seldom bind themselves through humanitarian law when they perceive that it excessively limits their military options). See generally, D. Kaye, 'Book Review: The Ethics of Destruction: Norms and Force in International Relations, by W. Thomas', 97 *AJIL* (2003) pp. 229, 230 (describing the potential differences between norms and laws and explaining how 'the more directly a norm reflects the interests of strong states, the stronger the norm will be'). Although strategic and policy rationales likely would continue to mitigate in favour of increased precision weaponry, budget constraints and potential shifts in budgetary priorities to an area such as self defence would no longer be further constrained by a legal argument in favour of precision if any and all collateral damage is indictable. Policy makers, especially those from developed countries, also face a frustrating *mens rea* catch-22 situation regarding this pseudo-litmus test, which would serve only to lessen respect for *jus in bello,* and thus its normative value as it would fuel illegality allegations that could undermine domestic support and ultimately affect their ability to conduct military operations. Specifically, although warfighters would not be able to establish a *non-*

for culpability by condemning as illegal any collateral damage that fails to pass the 'CNN factor' pseudo-litmus test would also create an environment that would promulgate the idea that civilian deaths and collateral damage equates somehow to 'losing the war', a proposition that even the senior military advisor to Human Rights Watch has characterised as 'quite dangerous'.[210]

Similarly, modern weaponry and strategy has raised a second issue concerning *jus in bello*'s distinction and proportionality test: the issue whether secondary or tertiary effects of an attack, especially those creating long-term casualties, can or should be factored into the required proportionality calculation as relevant collateral damage. One commentator has adroitly noted that this phenomenon is a natural consequence of modernization; 'as first-tier collateral damage and incidental injury (i.e., damage and injury directly caused by the kinetic force of the attack) become rarer, it is probable that humanitarian attention will increasingly dwell on subsequent-tier, or reverberating, effects'.[211] Legally, however, the significant issue in determining if these secondary or tertiary effects are properly calculable into the *jus in bello* proportionality equation is not predicated on the degree of its current interest to commentators or humanitarian activists; rather, it is and remains whether or not an attack would be '*expected to cause* incidental loss of civilian life, injury to civilians, damage to civilian objects, or a combination thereof, which would be excessive in relation to the concrete and definite military advantage anticipated'. (Emphasis added).[212] Accordingly, the 'expected to cause' language in this legal test provides a commander with a 'fairly broad margin of judgment', one which serves as a 'universally recognized guideline'.[213] The warfighter, thus, is legally required to use his or her discretion, using 'common sense and good faith', to do everything 'feasible' to obtain information to determine the incidental collateral

---

criminal state of mind by the act of using precision weapons, having to face allegations of illegality for any collateral damage, *regardless* of intent, they would nevertheless be subject to the inference of *criminal intent,* e.g., violating the all 'feasible precautions' clause in Art. 57 AP I, or not abiding by an alleged customary law for bombing urban areas, by the mere use of non-precise weaponry. See c.f., Belt, *supra* n. 26, at pp. 148-149, 164; containing an illustrative example alleged illegality based on the failure to use 'all feasible precautions' during Allied Force. Similarly, others would argue that any use of dumb bombs is illegal *per se* regardless of the circumstances surrounding the utilisation of dumb ordnance or the *mens rea* of the war fighter. As noted above, *supra* n. 42 and accompanying text, there is no legal basis for these positions.

210. Transcript, Talk of the Nation, 'Aerial warfare and precision bombing', PBS, 24 July 2002. This same note of caution against equating civilian deaths as a measure of assessing a military operation was reflected by many participants in a 2003 'Understanding collateral damage' workshop held at Harvard's John F. Kennedy's School of Government. They deemed this approach as 'fundamentally flawed.' Report, Understanding Collateral Damage Workshop, Project on the Means of Intervention, Carr Center for Human Rights Policy, John F. Kennedy School of Government, Harvard University (4-5 June 2002) at p. 4.

211. Schmitt, *supra* n. 22, at pp. 79-80.

212. See Art. 51(5) AP I *supra* n. 5, where the relevant element related to determining incidental loss calculations is the casualties and damage the attack is 'expected to cause' and Art. 57 AP I, stating that 'everything feasible' must be done to obtain information regarding this expected incidental loss.

213. E.T. Jensen, 'Unexpected consequences from knock-on effects: a different standard for computer networks operations?' 18 *Amer. Univ. ILR* (2003) pp. 1145, 1180-1181.

losses of any attack.[214] In short, if the secondary and tertiary effects can be characterised as expected as a result of an attack, they should be factored into the required proportionality calculation as relevant collateral damage and weighed to determine if they are excessive relative to the concrete and definite military advantage anticipated from the attack.

The relevant issue is, thus, not if secondary or tertiary effects resulting from an attack on a legitimate military objective *should* be calculated, but rather, *can* a military commander in good faith reasonably calculate the effect of the damage. This question is the one that should be answered, despite the difficulty it poses.[215] In fact, as observed by one author, 'US targeting has overtly adopted this approach'.[216] As technology increases, the ability to more readily identify and calculate an attack's 'expected' effects will likely also increase, be they primary, secondary or tertiary, and be they the result of attacking a dual-use facility or another modern technologically-interconnected facility. Future commanders will have more information at their disposal for this proportionality calculation although, as one progresses from first- tier to third- tier effects, the damage 'expected' from the attack becomes increasingly attenuated.[217] This increase in collateral damage information does not, it should be stressed, necessarily equate to placing more targets legally off-limits. The military significance of attacking, kinetically or otherwise, an enemy's increasingly interconnected communication or command nodes, for example, could increase the clearly articulated, non-speculative, anticipated military advantage to the point where it exceeds the increased second or third tier col-

---

214. Ibid. This legal requirement to give 'consideration to all factors and existing possibilities', found in the 'Rendulic Rule' and emphasised in the Commentary to AP I, is balanced with the overarching constraint of taking facts as they appear at the time of the decision, since the commander need not 'remain in inaction until he feels he has turned over every stone in search of that least shred of information concerning all factors and possibilities that might affect his decision.' Ibid., at p. 1183.

215. See C. Greenwood, 'Customary international law and the first Geneva Protocol of 1977', in P. Rowe, ed., *The Gulf War 1990-91 In International And English Law* (London, Routledge 1993) pp. 63, 79 (noting that indirect effects may be difficult to predict and difficult to separate from other contributing factors, such as the effect of economic sanctions and decisions taken by the government of the state subject to attack).

216. Schmitt, *supra* n. 13, at p. 9 citing Joint Chiefs of Staff, Joint Doctrine for Targeting (Joint Publication 3-60), 17 January 2002, at p. I-7 (stating that 'sound planning should allow for consideration of the risks of unintended second- and third-order consequences').

217. See *supra* nn. 213-215 discussing the difficulty of assessing indirect effects. These first to third tier concepts were summarised in the following way in a seminar report after a recent international legal conference:

' … identifying effects-based collateral damage is a difficult endeavor, but not impossible in some cases. Intelligence should be used to identify critical nodes of a civilian community, such as communication, transportation, or health systems and using statistical analytical techniques, attempt to assess and perhaps reduce the primary damage to these facilities as a result of an effects-based attack. At some point however, the group noted that such an analysis becomes progressively more difficult as the effects analysis proceeds to the secondary and tertiary effects. The group noted that perhaps the international legal community could import concepts found in civil law to determine at what point responsibility of an effects-based attack would end. 'Reasonable foreseeability' is one such concept identified by the group.'

D.D. Jividen, 'Targeting norms and international humanitarian law', 9 *Peacekeeping: The Yearbook of International Peace Operations* (2005) pp. 229, 232.

lateral damage, thereby permitting the attack under *jus in bello's* proportionality test.[218]

The third *jus in bello* issue raised by modern weaponry and military strategy noted above involves identifying legitimate military objectives in technologically advanced, increasingly interdependent societies. Extracting effects-based targeting from legal and moral norms and extrapolating this strategy to its outer limits, some have approached this modern conundrum by positing that modern warfare has rendered obsolete the immunity provided *by jus in bello* to civilian property.[219] Aside from the practical difficulty of protecting innocent civilians while destroying civilian infrastructure, these proposals are a moral step backwards in terms of *jus in bello's* humanitarian *raison d'être* and should be resisted. Others, alleging that 'relatively little attention is paid to the long-term, indirect harm to civilians from attacks on dual-use facilities and infrastructure', have argued for the ratification of a higher *jus in bello* standard for attacks on dual-use facilities 'indispensable to the survival of the civilian population', namely, rendering these types of targets impermissible unless 'the expected incidental civilian harm would not be excessive in relation to an anticipated military advantage that was compelling, not simply concrete and direct'.[220] Although a laudable humanitarian impulse, this proposal effectively disregards the fact, noted *supra,* that nations adhering to *in bello* law, unlike their opponents, are extremely wary of destroying indispensable dual-use facilities. Indeed, as noted above, a modern strategy has highlighted the need for modern warfighters to ensure that second- and third- tier effects are considered by commanders, and that they should be cognisant of the political ramifications resulting from their attacks. In light of these existent sensitivities, granting dual use facilities a higher level of legal immunity, *ab initio,* would excessively limit permissible military options in the rare case that the potent strategic reasons for limiting their damage would be overruled, a comfort that an actual or potential opponent should not be provided with.[221] More significantly, adopting these types of proposals

---

218. See e.g., H. Shue and D. Wippman, 'Limiting attacks on dual use facilities performing indispensable civilian functions', 35 *Cornell ILJ* (2002) pp. 559, 574 (conceding that the *jus in bello* proportionality test 'as currently constituted, nor the restrictions on attacking indispensable objects, provides much protection for civilian function of dual-use facilities'). See also Jensen, *supra* n. 213 at p. 12 (concluding that the permissibility of computer network attacks can be analysed with reference to *jus in bello* principles).

219. C. Dunlap Jr., 'The end of innocence: Rethinking noncombatancy in the Post-Kosovo era', 28 *Strategic Review* (2000) pp. 9, 14.

220. H. Shue and D. Wippman, *supra* n. 218, at p. 574 (urging a modification of the proportionality test to permit attacks on 'indispensable objects, including qualifying dual-use facilities', only in the event the anticipated military advantage was 'compelling', rather than 'simply concrete and direct').

221. As discussed *supra* in n. 87, the ICTY prosecutors conducting the informal investigation of NATO's bombing campaign during Operation Allied Force recognised the reality that dual use facilities arising from today's technology are often located in densely-populated areas, making them valid military objectives. Additionally, as evident in the allegations by some, noted *supra* at nn. 132, 211, 217 and accompanying text, even attacks fulfilling proposed higher 'compelling' standards would not be immune from criticism and attack by advocacy groups. Indeed, some who propose a strict international code of 'personal accountability' by military and other decision-makers for any collateral damage (unintentionally belying their own assertions that any collateral damage is already illegal under humanitarian law) likely have an agenda aimed at thwarting the success of military operations,

would, at minimum, detract from the non-compulsory exploration of other options that would create the same effect yet not achieve the same level of destruction.[222]

A *via media* between the extremes of partially jettisoning the legal element of distinction, one of the cornerstones of *jus in bello*, and seeking to impose a higher legal standard on high tech nations while their opponents regularly violate the *jus in bello*, is to strive instead to apply current *jus in bello* concepts to new, technologically-advanced societies and commensurate targets. Illustrative of this approach is the discussion over the legitimacy of 'information warfare' targets as military objectives during an armed conflict.[223] Applying *jus in bello* described above, including the legal requirements for defining an object as a military objective, proportionality and precautions, these *via media* authors systematically analyse the propriety of an attack without seeking to diminish the protection afforded by, or increasing the burden on military operations imposed by, humanitarian law.[224] Proposed manual provisions also assist in clarifying the *application* of *jus in bello* to evolving weapon systems and military strategies, rather than making changes in *jus in bello's* substance.[225] It is these efforts, clarifying how *jus in bello* is applicable to new challenges posed by modern technology and strategies, that best preserve and increase its relevance. This is especially true since further *jus in bello* proscriptions will fall on the nations committed to abiding by the law, rather than on those bent on its violation.

---

rather than upholding and strengthening humanitarian norms. See e.g., Lippman, *supra* n. 41, at p. 65 (noting that since Taliban extremists and Al Qaeda terrorist forces seek safety and security from high tech warfare through integration into the indigenous population, should any collateral, and thus, illegal, casualties occur during combat to these now indigenous forces, the attacker's only legal options are to 'limit its operations or withdraw from the country in whole or in part').

222. Even proponents of higher standards for dual-use facilities recognise alternative methods to neutralise sensitive dual-function facilities exist: 'there are many ways to skin a cat'. See Shue and Wippman, *supra* n. 218, at p. 578. Some of these alternative methods were utilised during modern conflicts such as Operations Allied Force and Desert Storm. Ibid., at pp. 565-566 (recalling that the use of special carbon-graphic filaments used to temporarily disrupt power in Yugoslavia, and attacking switching stations rather than generating stations in Iraq to enable repair of the electrical system after the war).

223. Information operations (IO) are broadly defined by the Joint Chiefs of Staff as 'actions taken to affect adversary information and information systems while defending one's own information and information system', while information warfare (IW) is IO 'conducted in times of crisis or conflict to achieve or promote specific objectives over a specific adversary or adversaries.' Joint Chiefs of Staff, Department of Defense, Dictionary of Military and Associated Terms, Joint Publication 1-02, 12 April 2001 (as Amended 7 October 2004) at p. 257. Targets of IW accordingly can include dual-use facilities such as airports, rail systems, road, communications, satellites and factories. See M.N. Schmitt, Background Paper, 'Computers and war: the legal battlespace', International Humanitarian Law Research Initiative: Reaffirmation and Development of IHL (Harvard University's Program on Humanitarian Law and Conflict Research at Harvard University (Nov 2003) at <http://www.ihlresearch.org/portal/ihli/alabama.php> at p. 7.

224. See e.g., Schmitt, *supra* n. 231; Jensen, *supra* n. 221.

225. See Schmitt, *supra* n. 214, at pp.30-32, (proposing clarifying language for, *inter alia*, the San Remo Manual to address issues raised by precision doctrine and technology).

7. CONCLUSION

Weapon modernisation, new military strategies and recent conflicts (at least from the US and Allied side) have all marched forward taking into account *jus in bello*, thereby strengthening its global normative value. In particular, as discussed above, the emphasis on precision warfare and sensitivities towards collateral damage; changes in military strategy highlighting the need for knowledge superiority; manoeuvre and precision fire to work together to help minimise casualties and shorten a conflict; US awareness of, and attempts to, identify and account for second- and third- tier effects in attacks; increased research and development of more precise, collateral damage diminishing, and less lethal modern weaponry; and development of systems to improve situational awareness, are all indicative of how *jus in bello* has retained and strengthened its normative value among the US and its allies. In fact, although the US has specifically recognised in its NMS 2004 that its adversaries will violate *jus in bello* norms, it continues to shape its force and doctrine within the parameters of the law. Even those suspicious of US and allied commitment to legal norms in the face of asymmetric attacks cannot easily disregard the fact that strategic political pressures on the US and its Allies to abide by *jus in bello* are potent and irresistible, especially since the contrast between US and Allied adherence to *jus in bello,* and their foes' utter disregard of that law, presents a powerful illuminating lesson for the international community, as well as one that contributes to motivating, forming and maintaining the WOT alliance.[226]

These overall trends fostering compliance with *jus in bello* will continue, in spite of, and impervious to, belligerents resorting to asymmetrical warfare.[227] The cynical disregard and abuse of humanitarian law has been, and will continue to be, the *sine qua non* of terrorist organisations and many dictatorial belligerents. These belligerents have in the past and likely will continue to abysmally disregard *jus in*

---

226. In fact, one author, writing before the events of 9/11, made an observation regarding the ramifications of *jus in bello* violations on the world politic, one equally applicable to the WOT. In a discussion of *jus in bello* enforcement mechanisms, his article notes:
'One other powerful instrument of enforcement is neglected in most discussions of the subject. Sometimes illegal conduct by a belligerent, including the commission of atrocities, may contribute to the formation of an international military coalition against the offending state, and may influence the coalition's willingness to use force. Such conduct has been a significant element in the building of many coalitions, including the Allied alliance in World War II, the international coalition against Iraq in 1990-91, the intervention in Somalia in December 1992, and the decision by the North Atlantic Treaty Organization and the United Nations to initiate 'Operation Deliberate Force' in Bosnia-Herzegovina on August 30, 1995. Even the possibility of such a process is almost entirely neglected in the relevant legal literature.'
A. Roberts, 'The laws of war: problems of implementation in contemporary conflicts', 6 *Duke JC & IL* (1995) pp. 11, 20.

227. For example, increases in network-centric operations will continue to increase battlefield awareness and centralise command and control, ultimately increasing the involvement of senior leaders in more operational details of a campaign. See GAO Military Operations report, *supra* n. 28, at pp. 32-33. This heightened scrutiny of military operations, including 'lawyers, and senior civilian and military leaders at headquarters', will invariable involve target selection, sensitive issues and other operational details, thereby increasing the opportunity to ensure complete adherence to *jus in bello* law. Ibid.

bello for reasons not related to technological gaps in military precision capabilities or the lack of a level military playing field.[228] Accordingly, anxiety over whether precision weaponry and the asymmetrical gap in warfighting capabilities will drive nations or groups away from following *jus in bello* principles is likely misplaced.[229] Indeed, the very fact that *jus in bello* adherence in this modern era serves not only a normative role, but also a differentiating, motivating and symbolic one as well, is a testament to its continued vitality for the international community, even in the face of the threats posed by terrorism and other asymmetric challenges. As such, the effects of modern weaponry and military strategy on *jus in bello* provide affirmation for thoughts expressed by the winner of a 1973 University of Arizona graduate essay contest, who, in the midst of the Cold War, and before the computer technology explosion, pondered *jus in bello's* future in his tract, *Modern War and the Laws of War*.[230] There, in a rejoinder to 'technological fatalists' predicting that modern military technology will 'slip from human control', make persons 'prisoners of their own creation', and invite 'dull, throbbing terror', he responded with his own future vision:

> 'It is conceivable that future military technology may very well introduce elements of precision (perhaps a laser system) which would again make it possible to revolutionize warfare in a positive direction (assuming it will not be abolished). Under such circumstances it would surely be possible to talk of discriminate usage, and thus a return to the Classical Tradition of the international laws of war. Precision weapons would mean that the devastation of large geographical areas would be militarily unnecessary, and thus criminal.'[231]

At the beginning of the twenty-first century, it is apparent that his dream is slowly becoming a welcome and much needed reality.

---

228. Indeed, *jus in bello* violations occurred in the Iraq-Iran war, where an asymmetrical technological gap akin to that between US and Allied forces' and their recent foes did not exist. In particular, although the main treaties of the laws of war were 'incontestably applicable', they were not adhered to by either side, with 'violations of fundamental rules in such matters as the treatment of prisoners, the use of gas, and attacks on neutral shipping'. Roberts, *supra* n. 226, at pp. 45-46. Horrifying violations of the minimal levels of protection of humanitarian law is also all too common in intra-state conflicts, such as in the Former Yugoslavia, Somalia, and Rwanda, again indicating that equalising asymmetric warfighting capabilities would likely not change terrorist strategies such as targeting innocent civilians for atrocities and death. See generally ibid., at pp. 56-66.

229. See Schmitt, *supra* n. 13, at pp. 12-13 (discussing the stress on humanitarian law presented by asymmetric warfare, including the possibility that high tech nations could 'ignore or dismantle legal architecture' by, *inter alia*, authorising reprisals, or unlawful *proportionate* acts, against enemy civilians and objects for the limited purpose of compelling the other side to desist in its pre-existing unlawful activities).

230. R.E. Moffit, *Modern War and the Laws of War*, Research Series No.17, Institute of Government Research, University of Arizona (Tucson, Arizona 1973).

231. Ibid., at pp. 34-35.

THE PROSECUTION OF UNLAWFUL ATTACK CASES BEFORE THE ICTY[1]

William J. Fenrick[2]

2. Dalhousie University Law School, formerly Senior Legal Adviser, Office of the Prosecutor, International Criminal Tribunal for the former Yugoslavia. The views expressed in the article are solely those of the author.

 DOI 10.1017/S1389135904001539

1. INTRODUCTION AND GENERAL LEGAL CONSIDERATIONS

The prohibition of attacks directed against civilians and civilian objectives is a logical implication of the principle of distinction and an essential component of international humanitarian law (IHL). There is a dearth of war crimes cases focusing on unlawful attacks, perhaps because such cases have been regarded as simply too difficult to prosecute.[3] Recently, the Office of the Prosecutor (OTP) of the International Criminal Tribunal for the former Yugoslavia (ICTY) has conducted such prosecutions.[4] Unlawful attack charges have been or are being considered by the ICTY in five cases to date.

In *Prosecutor* v. *Tihomir Blaškić*[5] and in *Prosecutor* v. *Dario Kordić and Mario Čerkez*,[6] the accused were Bosnian-Croat leadership figures and the cases revolved around several incidents in the Lasva River Valley in Bosnia, in particular the Ahmici massacre in which many of the inhabitants of a small Bosnian Muslim village were killed when it was overrun by Bosnian-Croat forces. *Blaškić* was the first case before the ICTY to address unlawful attack charges. At trial, Blaškić was found guilty of the crime against humanity of persecution and of the war crime of unlawful attacks, among other charges and sentenced to 45 years' imprisonment.[7] The Trial Chamber decision contained very little legal analysis and what there was focused primarily on the crime against humanity of persecution.[8] A substantial amount of new evidence was considered in the *Blaškić* Appeal Decision with the result that the findings were reversed on several counts and the accused's sentence was reduced to nine years' imprisonment, that is, in substance, the time he had served at the date of judgement.[9] Both Kordić and Čerkez were convicted at trial of a number of counts related to persecutions, unlawful attacks and other crimes and sentenced to 25 years' imprisonment and 15 years' imprisonment respectively, although Čerkez was acquitted in respect of charges related to the Ahmici massacre.[10] As with *Blaškić*, the *Kordić and Čerkez* Trial Chamber decision contained

---

3. In the only marginally relevant World War II war crimes decision, it was considered lawful to direct fire at civilians attempting to flee a besieged area in order to keep them within the besieged area where they might drain the resources available to the besieged forces. The German High Command Trial, 12 *LRTWC* (1948) pp. 1, 84.

4. Unlawful attack charges have been considered in the following ICTY cases: *Prosecutor* v. *Tihomir Blaškić*, Case No. IT-95-14-T, Judgement 3 March 2000 and Case No. IT-95-14-A, Appeals Judgement 29 July 2004; *Prosecutor* v. *Dario Kordić and Mario Čerkez*, Case No. IT-95-14/2, Judgement 26 February 2001 and Case No. IT-95-14/2-A, Appeals Judgement 17 December 2004; *Prosecutor* v. *Stanislav Galić*, Case No. IT-98-29-T, Judgement 5 December 2003; and *Prosecutor* v. *Pavle Strugar*, Case No. IT-01-42-T, Judgement 31 January 2005. They are also being considered in *Prosecutor* v. *Slobodan Milošević*, Case No. IT-02-54-T. This article will focus primarily on the *Galić* and *Strugar* cases as these are the two in which, to date, issues related to unlawful attack have been addressed and discussed in the most elaborate fashion.

5. *Supra* n. 4.

6. Ibid.

7. *Blaškić*, Trial Judgement, Part VI.

8. W.J. Fenrick, 'A first attempt to adjudicate conduct of hostilities offences: comments on aspects of the ICTY Trial Decision in the Prosecutor v. Tihomir', 13 *Leiden JLI* (2000) pp. 931-947.

9. Appeal Judgement, Part XIII.

10. *Kordić and Čerkez*, Trial Judgement, Part V.

very little legal analysis related to unlawful attacks.[11] Kordić's sentence was affirmed on appeal and that of *Čerkez* was reduced to six years' imprisonment.

In the *Galić* case,[12] General Galić was the commander of the Bosnian Serb Army (RSK) Sarajevo Romanija Corps, the force surrounding Sarajevo, from 10 September 1992 to 10 August 1994. He was charged with individual criminal responsibility for inflicting terror on the civilian population of Sarajevo, for attacking civilians and for the crimes against humanity of murder and causing inhumane acts. The underlying basis for the charges were alleged protracted sniping and shelling campaigns upon the civilian population during which large numbers of civilians were killed or wounded. General Galić was convicted of ordering the infliction of terror and the crimes against humanity and given a sentence of 20 years' imprisonment.[13] The unlawful attack counts were dismissed because they were regarded as being assimilated into the infliction of terror count.[14] A strong dissenting opinion was filed by Judge Nieto-Navia.[15] The decision, which is currently under appeal[16] for, among other reasons, those referred to in the dissenting opinion, contains a thorough analysis of the law relating to unlawful attacks and to the infliction of terrorism and also addresses how one must prove the existence of a sustained campaign.[17]

The *Strugar* case[18] revolves primarily around the events of a single day although evidence of what happened before and after is essential to appraising culpability for these events. General Strugar, Commander of the JNA 2nd Operational Group (2 OG) which surrounded the Croatian city of Dubrovnik, was charged with responsibility for the unlawful attacks on civilian and civilian objects in the Old Town of Dubrovnik on 6 December 1991. In brief, in the early morning of 6 December a small unit of the JNA attempted to capture a strong point at Srd a hill above Dubrovnik. Croatian forces in and around Dubrovnik responded and the attacking JNA unit became bogged down and began taking casualties. JNA mortars, recoilless guns and wire guided rockets were fired at Dubrovnik and a large number of these munitions landed in the Old Town of Dubrovnik, a distinct area adjacent to the rest of Dubrovnik which contained nothing but specially protected civilian objects and civilians, causing death or injury to civilians and substantial damage to several specially protected civilian structures. Initially, four persons were indicted in connection with the incident, Army Captain Kovačević, who commanded the Third Battalion of the 472nd Motorized Brigade (3/472 mtbr), the unit principally responsible for the unlawful attack; Admiral Jokić, who was Captain Kovačević's superior and commanded the Ninth Military Naval Sector (9VPS); Naval Captain Zec, who was Admiral Jokić's Chief of Staff; and General Strugar,

11. Ibid., paras. 321-328.
12. *Supra* n. 4.
13. *Galić*, Trial Judgement, Part VI.
14. Ibid., para. 752.
15. Ibid., Separate and Partially Dissenting Opinion of Judge Nieto-Navia.
16. Case No. IT-98-29-A.
17. *Galić*, Trial Judgement, paras. 13-138, 582-594; D. Kravetz, 'The protection of civilians in war: the ICTY's Galić case', 17 *Leiden JIL* (2004) pp. 521-536.
18. *Prosecutor* v. *Pavle Srugar*, Case No. IT-01-42-T, Judgement 31 January 2005.

who commanded the 2 OG and was Admiral Jokić's superior. Charges were withdrawn without prejudice against Naval Captain Zec. Army Captain Kovačević was the subject of the Prosecutor's Rule 11 *bis* motion for referral of the indictment to another court. Admiral Jokić submitted a guilty plea and was sentenced to seven years' imprisonment,[19] and the trial of General Strugar proceeded with Admiral Jokić as one of the main witnesses against him. General Strugar was found guilty of attacks on civilians and of destruction or willful damage to protected buildings on the basis of command responsibility and sentenced to eight years' imprisonment.[20] Although the court found that all of the elements of the other counts, including attacks on civilian objects, had been established, it considered the offences for which it did make a guilty finding to most accurately encapsulate the criminal conduct.[21]

The *Strugar* Trial Decision is currently under appeal.[22] It is worth noting that during the course of the trial, the Defence moved to terminate proceedings against General Strugar on the basis of fitness. A full evidentiary hearing was held to determine fitness to stand trial and the Trial Chamber found General Strugar fit and, of great precedential note, served to set the standard for fitness in the ICTY.[23]

The trial of Slobodan Milošević, the former President of Serbia and of the Federal Republic of Yugoslavia was still continuing at the time of writing. The indictment against the accused included counts alleging higher level responsibility for the events in Dubrovnik and in Sarajevo.[24]

A review of the law concerning unlawful attacks considered in a military context together with a discussion of the experience of the OTP in conducting such prosecutions is intended to provide guidance for those involved in such prosecutions in future before international or national tribunals and to serve as an aid for those involved in advising military forces or evaluating military operational conduct.

Combat involves both lawful and unlawful killing, injury and destruction. Lawful killing or destruction occurs when military operations are directed against military objectives in circumstances where it is reasonably anticipated that the unintended death or injury inflicted on civilians or the unintended damage caused to civilian objects will not be excessive (disproportionate) in relation to the concrete and direct military advantage anticipated from the attack. Unlawful attacks are those which are:

---

19. *Prosecutor* v. *Miodrag Jokić*, Sentencing Judgement Case No. IT-01-42/1-S, 18 March 2004. The sentence was upheld on Appeal Case No. IT-01-42/1-S, 30 August 2005.

20. *Strugar*, Judgement, paras. 477-483.

21. Ibid., paras. 447-455; F.L. Pola and E.C. Rojo, The Strugar case before the International Criminal Tribunal for the former Yugoslavia, 18 *Journal of International Law of Peace and Armed Conflict* (2005) pp. 139-145.

22. Case No. IT-01-42-A.

23. *Prosecutor* v. *Pavle Strugar*, Decision Re the Defense Motion to Terminate Proceedings, Case No. IT-01-42-T 26 May 2004.

24. Case No. IT-02-54-T.

(i) directed against civilians or civilian objects
(ii) indiscriminate; or
(iii) directed against military objectives in circumstances where it can be reasonably anticipated that excessive (disproportionate) death or injury will be inflicted on civilians and/or excessive (disproportionate) damage will be caused to civilian objects.[25]

Proof that an unlawful attack occurred is a prerequisite for determining whether or not other offences also occurred in a combat situation. Where the crime base consists of shelling or sniping incidents in a combat environment, it must first be proved that death, injury or damage was caused by an unlawful attack, that is, one directed against civilians or civilian objects or one directed against a military objective which may be expected to cause disproportionate incidental losses, before moving on to determine whether the additional elements necessary to establish the commission of other offences have also been established. If the attack was not unlawful then the resultant death, injury or damage cannot be unlawful as it is the result of a lawful act of war. If a civilian is killed or injured during an attack on a military objective which was not reasonably expected to result in civilian casualties or damage to civilian objects disproportionate to the expected military advantage, then no crime has been committed because, once again, it is a lawful act of war. This is so even if there is an expectation that, unfortunately, some civilians may be killed or injured during the attack. There is no basis for a crime against humanity charge because the attack was directed against a military objective, not against civilians or civilian objects. There is no basis for a war crimes charge of murder because the *mens rea* is lacking. The intent was to perform a lawful act. The unlawful attack foundation is essential to the assessment of legality even if there is no unlawful attack charge relating to a particular combat related incident. The issue cannot be avoided by simply avoiding the charge. Quite clearly there can be some incidents in which it is so clear that the attack is directed against civilians that one can proceed with a persecution count or a war crime or crime against humanity count of murder. Even in such circumstances, however, it is essential that the prosecutor in making charging decisions and the court in assessing the facts take into account the unlawful attack elements, at least implicitly, before coming to the conclusion that counts charged have been proven.

The *Galić* Trial Chamber, seemingly without enthusiasm, accepted and applied the OTP submission that proof of an unlawful attack was a prerequisite for proof of other offences related to shelling or sniping:

> 'The Prosecution submits that, in the context of an armed conflict, the determination that an attack is unlawful in light of treaty and customary international law with respect to the principles of distinction and proportionality is critical in determining whether the

---

25. Arts. 51, 52, 1977 Geneva Protocol I Additional to the Geneva Conventions of 12 August 1949, and Relating to the Protection of Victims of International Armed Conflicts (AP I), and Art. 13, 1977 Geneva Protocol II Additional to the Geneva Conventions of 12 August 1949, and Relating to the Protection of Victims of Non-International Armed Conflicts (AP II).

> general requirements of Article 5 have been met. Otherwise, according to the Prosecution, unintended civilian casualties resulting from a lawful attack on legitimate military objectives would amount to a crime against humanity under Article 5 and lawful combat would, in effect, become impossible. It therefore submits that an accused may be found guilty of a crime against humanity if he launches an unlawful attack against persons taking no active part in the hostilities when the general requirements of Article 5 have been established. The Trial Chamber accepts that when considering the general requirements of Article 5 (crimes against humanity), the body of laws of war plays an important part in the assessment of the legality of the acts committed in the course of an armed conflict and whether the population may be said to have been targeted as such.'[26]

In determining whether or not an attack is unlawful, it is essential to distinguish between motive and intent. An attack directed against a military objective which is not expected to cause disproportionate/excessive civilian casualties or damage to civilian objects is a lawful attack. If that lawful attack is directed by a commander to enable others to commit crimes such as ethnic cleansing (persecution) in the area overrun by the attack, it is possible that the commander or others might be held liable for aiding and abetting ethnic cleansing (persecution) or for some other mode of participation but the attack itself does not become an unlawful attack. Any alternative broader approach would erode the credibility of IHL. If normally lawful combat activities are converted into crimes because of someone's alleged motive, all the soldiers on the offending side may be converted into criminals in any event and there is no incentive for soldiers on that side to comply with the law. Indeed, if persons on both sides are engaging in ethnic cleansing then the broader approach might, inadvertently, convert all the soldiers of both sides into criminals. A domestic legal example might clarify this matter. If A drives B to the airport where B kills C, then A may, depending on his mental state, bear some criminal responsibility for the killing of C. A's act of driving B to the airport does not, however, become unlawful driving.

1.1 Undefended or open towns

It is also essential to distinguish between an attack on an undefended town or village as referred to in Article 3(c) of the ICTY Statute and an unlawful attack. In brief, an attack on an undefended town or village is a subset of the more general category of unlawful attacks but the criteria for such attacks are very restrictive.

As indicated in the 1958 British Manual on the Law of Land Warfare, drafted by Sir Hersch Lauterpacht:

> 'An undefended or "open" town is a town which is so completely undefended from within or without that the enemy can enter and take possession of it without fighting or

26. *Prosecutor* v. *Stanislav Galić*, Case No. IT-98-29-T, Judgement and Opinion 5 December 2003, para. 144.

incurring casualties. It follows that no town behind the immediate front line can be open or undefended for the attacker must fight his way to it …'[27]

Article 59 of Additional Protocol I sets out conditions under which appropriate authorities of a party to a conflict may declare an area a non-defended locality if it is in or near a zone where armed forces are in contact and it is open for occupation by the adverse party. The locality must meet the following conditions:

(a) all combatants, as well as mobile weapons and mobile military equipment must have been evacuated;
(b) no hostile use shall be made of fixed military installations or establishments;
(c) no acts of hostility shall be committed by the authorities or by the population; and
(d) no activities in support of military operations shall be undertaken.[28]

As is obvious, these conditions are difficult to meet. The OTP has not, to date, made a charge under Article 3(c).

2. MILITARY CONSIDERATIONS

Parties to an armed conflict are required, to the maximum extent feasible, to remove civilians and civilian objects under their control from the vicinity of military objectives and to avoid locating military objectives within or near densely populated areas.[29] These obligations notwithstanding, peacetime economic development and urban planning are rarely conducted paying particular heed to the potential but presumably remote requirements of IHL. When an armed conflict does occur, civilians, civilian objects, combatants and material military objectives will frequently be intermingled. When combat occurs in a given area, it may be extremely difficult to determine whether deaths, injuries or property damage are the result of lawful or unlawful acts without an in-depth assessment of the context. The collaboration of military experts, either from the staff of the prosecution office or retained from outside, is vital for the analysis, development and presentation of an unlawful attack case. Notwithstanding this collaboration, it must be emphasised that it is the *Prosecutor* who directs all members of the team to build the case in accordance with the overall theory of the case and within the parameters of the governing rules of procedure and evidence of the particular jurisdiction or tribunal. The overarching concern is analysing the impact of any act or omission on civilians or civilian objects and keeping the investigation and prosecution focused accordingly. It is essential to develop an accurate and sufficiently comprehensive moving picture of what has happened in order to determine what happened and why. Among other things, it will be necessary to learn where personnel and equip-

---

27. 1958 *British Manual on the Law of Land Warfare*, para. 290.
28. Art. 59(2), AP I.
29. Art. 58, AP I.

ment of the relevant armed forces were deployed, how the armed forces were structured and controlled (command and control), how the armed forces conduct operations (doctrine), what constituted a military objective in the area where munitions landed, the capabilities of weapons available to either side, and the military operations which were planned or underway in or close to the area where injury or damage occurred. For some matters, it will be appropriate to rely on experts familiar with how armed forces in general operate. For others, it may be necessary to use experts who are familiar with particular national armed forces or the components of armed forces. The purpose of this part of the Article is to introduce readers to some of the ideas and concepts with which it will be necessary to become familiar while preparing or presenting a case.[30] It is not a substitute for expert advice.

Armed forces are organised on a hierarchical basis, meaning commanders at a higher level issue orders or directions to commanders at a lower level. Commanders at a higher level may exercise command over specific units or formations which are subordinated to them or over all units or formations which are present in a specific geographic area. Above the lowest level, commanders are assisted by staff officers who, usually, act as advisers to the commander without command authority over lower level units and formations unless they are authorised to act on behalf of the commander. Each nation or military alliance will have its own command and control vocabulary. There may be national variances. As examples, however, here are some of the expressions used by the US armed forces, together with partial definitions:

(i) 'command – the authority that a commander in the Armed Forces lawfully exercises over subordinates by virtue of rank or assignment. Command includes the authority and responsibility for effectively using available resources and for planning the employment of, organizing, directing, coordinating, and controlling military forces for the accomplishment of assigned missions …

(ii) control – authority that may be less than full command exercised by a commander over part of the activities of subordinate or other organisations … (control normally involves a degree of authority to move units or assign missions)

(iii) operational control – … operational control includes authoritative direction over all aspects of military operations and joint training necessary to accomplish missions assigned to the command. Operational control should be exercised through the commanders of subordinate organizations. … it does not, in and of itself, include authoritative direction for logistics or matters of administration, discipline, internal organization, or unit training …'[31]

The commander of a multinational force would normally exercise operational control over subordinate formations because he or she would have no disciplinary

30. A much more elaborate attempt to introduce United States Air Force lawyers to air operations is R. Coe and M. Schmitt, 'Fighter ops for shoe clerks', 47 *Air Force LR* (1997) p. 49. There is no equivalent for land or sea operations.

31. *United State Department of Defense Dictionary of Military and Associated Terms*, JP 1-02 as amended through 9 May 2005.

authority over members of units from another country. The nature of the command or control relationship exercised by a particular superior over subordinate units or formations must be assessed as part of the process to determine potential criminal culpability, in particular under the doctrine of command responsibility. It is also necessary to be aware of particular practical command concepts, such as commander's intent and command climate. Commander's intent is essentially self-explanatory. What does a commander intend to do in the near term or long term future? Generally speaking, subordinates should be well aware of their commander's intent and they should be expected to govern their conduct in accordance with it. General Pringle, one of the Prosecution's expert witnesses on command and control in the *Strugar* case, explained the concept of command climate as follows:

> 'And from the moment he walks into his office on first appointment he is beginning to set that climate, and it reflects the way he is, the way he acts, what he says, what his views are, how he executes command, how he deals with problems. All of that goes to create a climate. What he does when something goes right, what he does when something goes wrong, what action he takes. Does he take a blind eye to certain events or does he – is he a rigid disciplinarian? All of that encapsulates what we call the command climate.'[32]

One should also be aware of the style of command that prevails in a given armed force. Is the armed force orders driven or mission driven? In an orders driven army, as was the Yugoslav People's Army (JNA) for example, everything is driven from the top down. Admiral Miodrag Jokić, co-accused of General Strugar,[33] testified on behalf of the Prosecution in the *Strugar* case and described this approach as follows:

> '... the soldiers need much more detailed orders and much more detailed supervision ... the onus lies on the commanders to execute a tighter form of command with constant supervision, direction and redirection as required.'[34]

In a mission driven armed force, on the other hand, subordinates are given more general assigned tasks or missions and it is up to them to determine how to accomplish the mission. Much more initiative is expected of subordinates. Generally speaking, in order to ensure command and control functions are effectively carried out, military forces must maintain good channels of communication and retain comprehensive records of operational decision making. Documents such as communications logs and war diaries are compiled to assist in the conduct of operations but they may also be of considerable assistance later on when one is trying to reconstruct what happened for historical or judicial purposes. During cross examination of a defence witness in the *Strugar* trial, the OTP demonstrated that com-

---

32. General Andrew Pringle, *Strugar*, Transcript at T. 1565.
33. Co-accused Jokić plead guilty in August 2003 and was sentenced to a term of seven years imprisonment.
34. Admiral Jokić, *Strugar*, Transcript at T. 4422.

manders seeking to avoid criminal culpability may even alter or be complicit in the alteration of such documents in an attempt to cover up actual events. In the *Strugar* judgement, the Trial Chamber concluded that a document introduced by a military defence witness had been deliberately falsified after the event.[35]

When ground forces carry out attacks they may use small arms, such as pistols, rifles and machine guns, or heavier weapons, such as mortars, guns, howitzers and rockets. With small arms, the fire is directed at a target which can be seen from the firing position. With heavier weapons, the fire may be direct fire if it can be seen from the firing position or indirect fire if fire is directed at a target that cannot be seen from the firing position. With indirect fire, aim is taken indirectly with the aid of an auxiliary targeting point and the results of fire are observed from an observation point, if at all. Small arms munitions have an effect when they hit something or someone. Most other weapons have an effective zone, that is an area around the landed munition within which it may cause death or injury. For example, the evidence was that 120 mm mortar munitions fired by JNA forces in and around Dubrovnik had an effective zone of 60 metres.[36] The effective zone of various munitions can be determined by consulting the appropriate national military manual for the weapon system concerned.

Further, unfortunately, with rare exceptions, persons firing weapons cannot expect the munitions they fire to hit precisely the point which they intend to hit. Generally speaking, munitions from anything other than small arms can, at best, be expected to land within a particular area of the point at which they are aimed. This area is given various names in different armed forces, such as Circular Error Probable (CEP) or Error Ellipse. The expression is used to indicate the percentage of munitions fired from a particular type of weapon system, for example an 82 mm or 120 mm mortar, which can be expected to land within a given area of the aiming point. For example, for a 82 mm mortar fired using charge A at an aim point B metres from the firing position, one can expect X percent of the projectiles to land within an Error Ellipse of Y by Z metres around the aim point.[37] Munitions land around instead of on the aim point because of a variety of factors. For munitions fired from tubes, these include: ambient temperature, wind conditions, quality and temperature of the propellant used in the charge, errors in laying the weapon on target, and the condition of the barrel. There are manuals for each type of weapon system which contain tables which can be used by a weapons expert to predict the size of the Error Ellipse in different circumstances. The same types of manuals contain weapon expenditure norms which will indicate how many munitions of a certain type must be fired at a particular military objective in order to achieve an assurance of destroying or neutralising the objective. In the case of mortars, which are area weapons, these figures can be extremely high. For example, evidence was

35. *Strugar*, Trial Judgement, paras. 96-97.

36. Ibid., Exhibit P 184, Expert Report of Jožef Poje, p. 13.

37. Ibid., Exhibit P 184, Poje Expert Report gives several examples of Error Ellipses for the types of projectiles used in the shelling of Dubrovnik.

given in the *Strugar* case that to achieve 80 percent neutralisation of a dug in platoon of mortars, 2,160 rounds of 120 mm mortar shells should be fired.[38]

Generally speaking, artillery doctrine requires the use of a methodical and deliberate targeting process for the use of artillery. A list of targets giving detailed co-ordinates and target descriptions will be drawn up. Fire plans will be produced orchestrating firing units to a given time schedule with an allocation of ammunition. Battlefield Damage Assessment (BDA) should be conducted after the attack and re-attack options will frequently be considered in advance. Fire support coordination measures listing 'no fire areas' should be designated. Munitions fired should be listed in a log. Further, there are targeting techniques which can be used when targets are located close to 'no fire areas'. For example, the normal approach to targeting would involve bracketing, that is firing a round over the expected target location then another under the location then firing a series of rounds at the centred target. When the target is close to a 'no fire area' the preferred approach would be to use an aim point clearly some distance away from that area and then fire rounds directed precisely at the target. A review of plans and logs after the event should assist in determining whether specific targets were deliberately attacked and whether these targets were military objectives. The review should be conducted bearing in mind specific questions such as: was the type of weapons system and munition selected appropriate for the target; was the effect limited to that necessary to do the job; and was a BDA actually conducted. It should be remembered, however, that an artillery commander will have a limited choice of weapons systems to use and he or she may have to rely on one which is not the most appropriate. It must also be remembered that an attack which is conducted in accordance with military doctrine, that is, using the appropriate number of munitions in accordance with weapons expenditure norms to achieve a desired effect on a given target, may, nevertheless, be unlawful if, in the circumstances, it is indiscriminate or is expected to cause excessive collateral injury to civilians or damage to civilian objects. For example, military doctrine may prescribe or permit the use of mortars in built up areas but their use may be unlawful in a given case if excessive collateral damage or injury might be expected.

In *Strugar*, where most of the projectiles were fired from 82 mm or 120 mm mortars, the Prosecution expert was an experienced Slovenian Army artillery officer, Lieutenant Colonel Jožef Poje, with many years as an artillery instructor, including instruction on the use of mortars. The Defence, on the other hand, retained a ballistics expert, Janko Viličić, Ph.D., with experience in weapon and ammunition design but much less practical experience using the weapons under discussion. The end result was that the Prosecution argued that the Error Ellipses were relatively small with the result that projectiles which landed in the Old Town of Dubrovnik must have been wilfully so directed. The Defence argued that the Error Ellipses were in fact much bigger for complicated scientific reasons and the projectiles landing in the Old Town were in fact aimed at military objectives located too close to the Old Town. In the end result, the *Strugar* Trial Chamber paid little

38. Ibid., Transcript, J. Poje, T. 6306.

heed to the defence expert and some heed to the Prosecution expert but, even where the Prosecution expert was concerned, the Chamber was of the view that the expert paid insufficient heed to factors such as weather conditions.[39] One might conclude from this experience that experts with a great amount of practical experience might be preferable to those with a strong theoretical basis where use of artillery is the issue. It is, however, neccessary, to ensure that the court is made aware of all relevant factors having an impact on weapon accuracy in a given case.

3. LEGAL BASIS FOR UNLAWFUL ATTACK CHARGES

Unlawful attacks are not enumerated offences in the ICTY Statute. Before the ICTY, therefore, unlawful attacks must be charged as unenumerated offences under Article 3 of the Statute, which is concerned with violations of the laws or customs of war. As a result of the *Tadić* Jurisdiction Appeal Decision, all unenumerated offences must meet the following four general criteria:

(i) The violation must constitute an infringement of a rule of international humanitarian law.
(ii) The rule must be customary in nature or, if it belongs to treaty law, the treaty must
(a) bind the parties at the time of the offence (including being applicable to the type of conflict in which the incident occurred), and
(b) not be in conflict with or derogate from a peremptory norm of international law.
(iii) The violation must be "serious", that is to say, it must constitute a breach of a rule protecting important values, and the breach must involve grave consequences for the victim.
(iv) The violation of the rule must entail the individual criminal responsibility of the person breaching the rule.[40]

The potential legal sources for the unlawful attack offences were customary international law, the APs[41] and the Statute of the International Criminal Court (ICC Statute).[42] Since the ICC Statute was not adopted until 1998, well after most of the offences within the jurisdiction of the ICTY were committed, and since that Statute (i) applies only to crimes committed after it came into force (Art. 11), and (ii) formulates unlawful attack offences in a way which might be more restrictive than customary law or pre-existing treaty law, the OTP relied upon customary law and the APs to provide the legal basis for its unlawful attack charges.

---

39. Ibid., Judgement, paras. 203-211.
40. *Prosecutor* v. *Duško Tadić,*Case No. IT-94-1-AR72, Decision on the Defence Motion for Interlocutory Appeal on Jurisdiction, 2 October 1995, paras. 94, 143.
41. *Supra* n. 4.
42. 1998 Rome Statute of the International Criminal Court.

The OTP charged unlawful attacks in the *Strugar* case using the following representative formulations and these formulations were upheld by the Appeals Chamber:[43]

(i) Attacks on civilians, a Violation of the Laws or Customs of War, as recognised by Article 51 of Additional Protocol I and Article 13 of Additional Protocol II to the Geneva Conventions of 1949, punishable under Articles 3 and 7(1) and 7(3) of the Statute of the Tribunal.

(ii) Unlawful attacks on civilian objects, a violation of the Laws or Customs of War, as recognised by Article 52 of Additional Protocol I to the Geneva Conventions of 1949, and customary law, punishable under Articles 3 and 7(1) and 7(3) of the Statute of the Tribunal.

Although these formulations were upheld, bearing in mind the precise wording of the Appeals Chamber in the *Strugar* Jurisdiction Decision, in future it might be preferable: (a) to include a reference to customary law before the reference to Article 51 in the attack on civilians charge because of the importance of customary law to underpin the offence, and (b) to delete 'unlawful' from the formulation of the attack on civilian objects charge as all attacks on civilian objects are unlawful. In accordance with the *Galić* Trial Judgement, these formulations embrace direct, indiscriminate and disproportionate attacks.[44] It should be noted that the *Blaškić* Trial Chamber considered in its judgement the duration of the unlawful attack (the overrunning of small villages in that case) to include actions which occurred while control over the villages was still in dispute.

The Appeals Chamber held in the *Strugar* Jurisdiction Decision that attacks on civilians and on civilian objects were prohibited under customary law and, although the Chamber was less explicit than one might prefer, it would appear the customary law prohibition applies in all conflicts:

> 'Articles 51 and 52 of Additional Protocol I and, to a lesser extent, Article 13 of Additional Protocol II consists of a number of provisions focusing on but not limited to the prohibition of attacks on civilians and civilian objects cited in the relevant counts of the Indictment. ... the Trial Chamber did not pronounce on the legal status of the whole of the relevant Articles, as, having found that they did not form the basis of the charge against the Appellant, it was not obliged to do so. It rather examined "whether the *principles contained in* the relevant provisions of the Additional Protocols have attained the status of customary international law" (emphasis added), and in particular the principles explicitly stated in the Indictment: the prohibition of attacks on civilians and of unlawful attacks on civilian objects. It held that they had attained such a status, and in this it was correct ...

---

43. *Prosecutor* v. *Pavle Strugar*, Case No. IT-01-42-AR72, Decision on Interlocutory Appeal, 22 November 2002.

44. *Galić*, Trial Judgement, paras. 57-61.

> (T)he Trial Chamber made no error in its finding that, as the Appeals Chamber understood it, the principles prohibiting attacks on civilians and unlawful attacks on civilian objects stated in Article 51 and 52 of Additional Protocol I and Article 13 of Additional Protocol II are principles of customary international law. Customary international law establishes that a violation of these principles entails individual criminal responsibility ....'[45]

The *Tadić* Jurisdiction Appeal Decision has provided the OTP with the basis for arguing that certain offences have a substantially similar legal content in both international and internal conflicts.[46] The OTP has, therefore, developed and defended the practice of alleging unlawful attack charges which are common to all conflicts. In order to evade the conflict classification issue, the ICTY OTP has rooted its unlawful attack on civilians charges in identically worded provisions of AP I (which applies to international conflicts) and AP II (which applies to internal conflicts). Both Article 51(2) of AP I and Article 13(2) of AP II state in part: 'The civilian population as such, as well as individual civilians, shall not be the object of attack.' AP I, however, goes on to refer to other forms of unlawful attack. In particular, Article 51 refers to indiscriminate attacks, including disproportionate attacks, and refers to five forms of indiscriminate attack, all of which are prohibited. In addition, Article 85 contains grave breach provisions relating to unlawful attacks. By contrast, AP II has no provisions related to unlawful attacks on civilians beyond the single sentence in Article 13(2) quoted earlier. ICTY OTP practice has been to focus on the common sentence in Article 51(2) of AP I and Article 13(2) of AP II and to argue that proof of the occurrence of the various types of indiscriminate attacks, including disproportionate attacks, may provide an evidentiary basis for the Trial Chamber to draw an inference that the attacks were, in substance, directed against the civilian population. In other words, the OTP has argued that the essential substance of the detailed AP I provisions concerning unlawful attacks applicable to international conflicts is also contained in the single relevant sentence in AP II which is applicable to internal conflicts. This is a conscious effort on the part of the OTP, successful to date, to argue that the law concerning unlawful attacks against civilians is, in substance, the same in both international and internal conflicts. An essentially similar approach has been accepted in the International Committee of the Red Cross (ICRC) Customary International Humanitarian Law Study.[47]

The basis for the unlawful attack against civilian objects charge is a bit different. Article 52(1) of AP I states in part: 'Civilian objects shall not be the object of

---

45. *Strugar*, Jurisdiction Interlocutory Appeal Decision, paras. 9-10, 13. The Trial Chamber in its subsequent Judgment explicitly concluded that the general rule prohibiting attacks on civilian objects applied to internal conflicts as a matter of customary law notwithstanding the absence of an Article in AP II similar to Art. 52 of AP I. See para. 224.

46. *Prosecutor* v. *Tadić*, Case No. IT-94-1-AR 72, Decision on the Defence Motion for Interlocutory Appeal on Jurisdiction 2 October 1995, paras. 96-127.

47. J-M. Henckaerts and L. Doswald-Beck, *Customary International Humanitarain Law*, Vol. I-Rules (Cambridge, Cambridge University Press, ICRC 2005) sec Rulcs 1, 11-14 at pp. 3-8, 37-50.

attack or reprisals. Civilian objects are all objects which are not military objectives …' There is no similar general provision in AP II although there are prohibitions on attacking specific civilian objects, including objects indispensable to the survival of the civilian population (Art. 14), works and installations containing dangerous forces (Art. 15), and cultural objects and places of worship (Art. 16). In addition, the UN General Assembly adopted Resolution 2675 on 9 December 1970 on Basic Principles for the Protection of the Civilian Population. These Principles include: '(3) In the conduct of military operations, every effort should be made to spare civilian populations from the ravages of war, and all necessary precautions should be taken to avoid injury, loss or damage to civilian populations', and '(5) Dwellings and other installations that are used only by civilian populations should not be the object of military operations.' UN GA Res 2675 applies to all armed conflicts. As indicated in the *Tadić* Jurisdiction Appeal Decision, these resolutions were 'declaratory of the principles of customary international law regarding the protection of civilian populations and property in armed conflicts of any kind …'[48] Once again, the ICRC customary law study adopts a similar approach.[49]

As indicated above, the OTP has rooted its unlawful attack charges in customary law and in the APs and not in the ICC Statute where the wording is somewhat different. The APs were initially adopted in 1977 and have a firmer customary law basis than the 1998 ICC Statute. The ICC Statute contains different enumerated lists of war crimes for international conflicts (Art. 8(2)(a) and (b)) and for internal conflicts (Art. 8(2)(c) and (e)). Unenumerated offences may not be charged under the ICC Statute. The relevant ICC offences include: (1) for international conflicts – intentional attacks on civilians (Art. 8(2)(b)(i)), intentional attacks on civilian objects (Art. 8(2)(b)(ii)), and intentionally launching attacks which are expected to cause disproportionate incidental civilian losses or damage (Art. 8(2)(b)(iv); and (2) for internal conflicts – intentional attacks on civilians (Art. 8(2)(d)(i)). Reliance on the ICC Statute, if the OTP could do so – which is debatable because it was not drafted until after most of the offences within the ICTY's jurisdiction were committed – would be helpful because proof of the effect of the unlawful attack (death or injury to civilians, damage to civilian objects) is not an element of the offence. As a purely practical matter, however, it would be unlikely that the offence would ever be charged unless the effect occurred and it would usually be necessary to prove the effect as part of the circumstantial evidence for proof of the mental element. The OTP has utilised the grave breach provisions of Article 85(3) of AP I in developing its elements and AP I does require proof of effect. There are, however, aspects of the ICC unlawful attack offences which are not helpful. In particular, (1) the OTP uses the AP I mental element of wilful, which includes a degree of recklessness, while the ICC mental element is intention, which may not include a degree of recklessness; (2) the OTP uses the AP I formulation for proportionality which is 'excessive' while the ICC formulation is 'clearly excessive', which may be higher, and (3) the ICC Statute prohibits a narrower range of attacks in internal

---

48. *Tadić*, Jurisdiction Appeal Decision, paras. 111-112.
49. Henckaerts and Doswald-Beck, *supra* n. 47, Rules 7-10, at pp. 25-36.

conflicts than the OTP, relying on the *Tadić* Jurisdiction decision, has been able to prosecute.

4. ELEMENTS OF UNLAWFUL ATTACK CHARGES

For cases before the ICTY, the elements for the unlawful attacks on civilians charge are as indicated in the *Galić* Trial Judgement (subject to the modification of the *mens rea* element required by the *Blaškić* Appeal Judgement). In *Galić,* the Trial Chamber accepted that the mental element for the offence of unlawful attack was 'wilful' and accepted that the approach taken in the grave breach provisions of AP I was appropriate. Specifically, it held:

> '... The Commentary to Article 85 of Additional Protocol I explains the term as follows:
>
> *wilfully*: the accused must have acted consciously and with intent, *i.e.,* with his mind on the act and its consequences, and willing them ('criminal intent' or 'malice aforethought'); this encompasses the concepts of 'wrongful intent' or 'recklessness', viz., the attitude of an agent who, without being certain of a particular result, accepts the possibility of it happening; on the other hand, negligence or lack of foresight is not covered, i.e., when a man acts without having his mind on the act or its consequences.
>
> The Trial Chamber accepts this explanation, according to which the notion of "wilfully" incorporates the concept of recklessness, while excluding mere negligence. The perpetrator who recklessly attacks civilians acts "wilfully".'[50]

The approach to the concept of recklessness must, however, be modified as a result of the holding of the Appeal Chamber in *Blaškić* to the effect that the knowledge of any sort of risk is not sufficient for the imposition of criminal responsibility and that an accused must be aware of the 'substantial likelihood' that the *actus reus* of the crime will occur.[51]

The *Galić* Trial Chamber then went on to decide that the elements for the charge are the elements common to all unenumerated offences under Article 3 of the ICTY Statute and also the following specific elements:

1. Acts of violence directed against the civilian population or individual civilians not taking direct part in hostilities causing death or serious injury to body or health within the civilian population.
2. The offender wilfully made the civilian population or individual civilians not taking direct part in hostilities the object of those acts of violence.[52]

---

50. *Galić*, Trial Judgement, para. 54, quoting the ICRC Commentary, para. 3474.
51. *Prosecutor* v. *Tihomir Blaškić*, Case No. 95-14-A, Appeal Judgement, 29 July 2004, paras. 41-42.
52. *Galić*, Trial Judgement, para. 56.

It adds that 'indiscriminate attacks, that is to say, attacks which strike civilians or civilian objects and military objectives without distinction, may qualify as direct attacks against civilians'.[53] Further, the Trial Chamber considered that 'certain apparently disproportionate attacks may give rise to the inference that civilians were actually the object of attack. This is to be determined on a case-by case basis in light of the available evidence'.[54] Further, '[t]o establish the *mens rea* of a disproportionate attack the Prosecution must prove … that the attack was launched wilfully and in knowledge of circumstances giving rise to the expectation of excessive civilian casualties.'[55] The Trial Chamber went on to observe that the failure of a party to comply with its obligation to remove civilians, to the maximum extent feasible, from the vicinity of military objectives did not 'relieve the attacking party of its duty to abide by the principles of distinction and proportionality when launching an attack'.[56] The Trial Chamber did allude in passing to the possibility that proof of results was not an element of the offence of unlawful attack on civilians.[57] The Appeals Chamber, in the *Kordić* Judgement issued after the *Galić* Trial Judgement, reviewed the state of the law concerning the requirement for proof of results and concluded that there was such a requirement under customary law at the time of the offence.[58] In a corrigendum to the same judgement, the Appeals Chamber corrected an error made in earlier trial judgements which appeared to hold that civilians or civilian objects could be attacked if justified by military necessity and held 'the prohibition against attacking civilians and civilian objects may not be derogated from because of military necessity'.[59]

The specific elements for the unlawful attacks on civilian objects charge are, *mutatis mutandis*, the same as those for unlawful attacks on civilians spelled out in the *Galić* Trial Judgement:

1. Acts of violence directed against civilian objects causing damage to civilian objects; and
2. The offender wilfully made civilian objects the object of these acts of violence.[60]

Wilful has the same meaning as it does for attacks on civilians.

Generally speaking, although the elements for the analogous ICC offences do not require proof of results (with the exception of Art. 8(2)(b)(iv) (war crime of

53. Ibid., para. 57.

54. Ibid., para. 60.

55. Ibid., para. 59. This particular finding is criticized in D. Kravetz, 'The protection of civilans in war: the ICTY's Galić Case', 17 *Leiden JIL* (2004) pp. 521-536 at 532 as, in that author's view, disproportionate attacks should not come within the definition of the crime of attack on civilians.

56. *Galić*,Trial Judgement, para. 61.

57. Ibid., para. 43.

58. *Prosecutor* v. *Dario Kordić and Mario Čerkez*, Case No. IT-95-14/2, Judgement 17 December 2004, paras. 55-68.

59. *Kordić*, Appeal Judgment, para. 54, corrigendum issued 26 January 2005.

60. *Prosecutor* v. *Pavle Strugar*, Case No. IT-01-42-T, Judgment 31 January 2005, para. 280. The Trial Chamber indicated that it was unclear whether the damage to civilian objects must be extensive but noted that, in any event, the damage was extensive in the particular case.

excessive incidental death, injury, or damage)), the ICC offences appear to be narrower than the ICTY offences prosecuted to date as the ICTY has prosecuted for unlawful attacks against civilian objects in all conflicts and narrower than the offences set forth in the APs as they appear to have a narrower *mens rea*, intention in lieu of willfulness.

5. MILITARY OBJECTIVES

Military objectives, that is, persons and objects subject to attack, are:

(i) combatants;[61]
(ii) civilians taking a direct part in hostilities;[62] and
(iii) in so far as objects are concerned, those objects which by their nature, location, purpose or use make an effective contribution to military action and whose total or partial destruction, capture or neutralisation in the circumstances ruling at the time, offers a definite military advantage.[63]

In so far as people are concerned, military objectives are combatants and civilians directly participating in hostilities. Combatants are members of the armed forces of a Party to a conflict other than medical personnel and chaplains.[64] Combatants have the right to participate directly in hostilities (shoot at the enemy) at any time and, for that reason, they may also be attacked at any time, sleeping, eating, and marching to the rear, unless they have surrendered or are injured and have ceased to take part in hostilities. Wounded combatants who continue to fight may be lawfully attacked. Although, strictly speaking, the concept of combatant status is legally relevant only during international armed conflicts, as is the related concept of prisoner of war status, the concept is applicable by analogy to internal conflict. As a result, the members of the armed forces of all parties to an internal conflict (other than medical personnel and chaplains) would also be subject to lawful attack at all times unless they have surrendered or are injured and have ceased to take part in hostilities. The ICTY Appeals Chamber has explicitly addressed the situation of members of a Territorial Defence (TO) organisation in the territory of the former Yugoslavia and whether they are to be considered combatants at all times during a conflict or only when they directly take part in hostilities. It concluded 'members of the armed forces residing in their homes in the area of the conflict, as well as members of the TO residing in their homes, remain combatants whether or not they are in combat, or for the time being armed'.[65]

The concept of civilians directly participating in hostilities is much more contentious and also much more complicated. Armed forces of many western states in

---

61. Arts. 43, 48, AP I.
62. Art. 51(3), AP I.
63. Art. 52(2), AP I.
64. Art. 43(2), AP I.
65. *Kordić*, Appeal Judgement, para. 51.

particular have begun to outsource to meet many of their requirements so that private contractors may provide both specialist services (such as technical representatives for the maintenance of complicated weapons systems) and more routine services (logistical support and provision of food services) which had previously been provided by military personnel. After a fashion, this is a return to the beginning of the modern period when specialists, even artillery personnel, were civilians. Further, quite clearly, some key civilian personnel, defence scientists for example, may be much more important to the war effort than most military personnel. In the territory of the former Yugoslavia an additional complicating factor was the fact that, at least in the early stages, new states were emerging and these were required to create new armed forces as the conflict went on. Although the matter is not beyond dispute, it is submitted that the concept of civilians participating directly in hostilities should be narrowly construed. Hostile acts 'should be understood to be acts which by their nature and purpose are intended to cause actual harm to the personnel and equipment of the armed forces'.[66] 'Direct participation in hostilities implies a direct causal relationship between the activity engaged in and harm done to the enemy at the time and place where the activity takes place.'[67] 'There should be a clear distinction between direct participation in hostilities and participation in the war effort. The latter is often required from the population as a whole to various degrees. Without such a distinction the efforts made to reaffirm and develop international humanitarian law could become meaningless.'[68] Civilians are military objectives only while they are taking a direct part in hostilities, not before or after. When making targeting decisions, in case of doubt whether a person is a civilian, that person shall be considered to be a civilian. The above comments reflect customary law and are codified in AP I.[69] Essentially the same standard applies to internal conflicts as a result of Article 13 of AP II and Article 3 common to the four Geneva Conventions of 1949 although the latter uses the expression 'persons taking no active part in hostilities' which, it is submitted, is synonymous with taking no direct part in hostilities.

The direct participation in hostilities issue was addressed, but not in depth, in the *Strugar* Judgement. Civilian Mato Valjalo, who was wounded in the shelling of the Old Town of Dubrovnik, was a driver for the Dubrovnik Municipal Crisis Staff. The Chamber concluded without analysis that there was nothing in the evidence to suggest that, as a driver, he was taking an active part in hostilities.[70]

Article 52(2) of AP I states in part:

> 'In so far as objects are concerned, military objectives are limited to those objects which by their nature, location, purpose or use make an effective contribution to military action

---

66. Y. Sandoz et al, eds., *Commentary on the Additional Protocols of 8 June 1977 to the Geneva Conventions of 12 August 1949* (ICRC, Geneva 1987) p. 618 (para. 1942).
67. Ibid., p. 516 (para. 1679).
68. Ibid., p. 619 (para. 945).
69. AP 1 Arts. 50(1), 51(2) and (3), and 43(1).
70. *Strugar*, Judgement, para. 274.

> and whose total or partial destruction, capture or neutralization, in the circumstances ruling at the time, offers a definite military advantage.'

Paragraph 3 of the Article goes on to indicate that in case of doubt whether an object which is normally dedicated to civilian purposes is being used to make an effective contribution to military action, it shall be presumed not to be so used. The definition has two elements:

> (a) That the nature, location, purpose or use of the object must make an effective contribution to military action; and
> (b) That the total or partial destruction, capture or neutralisation of the object must offer a definite military advantage in the circumstances ruling at the time.

States which have ratified AP I and most other states would accept the AP I definition of military objective as a reasonably accurate definition applicable as a matter of customary law to all conflicts.[71] The definition is supposed to provide a means whereby informed objective observers (and decision makers in a conflict) can determine whether or not a particular object constitutes a military objective. It accomplishes this purpose in simple cases. Everyone will agree that a munitions factory is a military objective and an unoccupied church is a civilian object. When the definition is applied to dual-use objects which have some civilian uses and some actual or potential military uses (communications systems, transportation systems, petrochemical complexes, manufacturing plants of some types), opinions may differ. The application of the definition to particular objects may also differ depending on the scope and objectives of the conflict. Further, the scope and objectives of the conflict may change during the conflict. Although representatives of the United States government have at times indicated that the AP I definition of military objective does reflect customary law,[72] it should be noted that the United States appears to have adopted a substantially broader definition of military objective for its Military Commission Instructions:

> '"Military objectives" are those potential targets during an armed conflict which by their nature, location, purpose, or use, effectively contribute to the opposing force's war-fighting or war-sustaining capability and whose total or partial destruction, capture, or neutralization would constitute a military advantage to the attacker under the circumstances at the times of the attack.'[73]

Certainly the reference to 'war-sustaining capability' appears to be an extension beyond the AP I definition.

A number of issues remain unresolved in connection with the scope of the military objective concept, including:

---

71. Henckaerts and Doswald-Beck, *supra* n. 47, Rule 8, pp. 29-32.
72. Ibid., Vol. II Pt I – Practice, pp. 187-188.
73. Art. 5D, Military Commission Instruction No. 2, US Department of Defence, 30 April 2003.

(1) Should more or fewer things be regarded as military objectives by the intervening side during a humanitarian intervention or by the 'good' side during an international armed conflict?[74]
(2) Is civilian morale a military objective?[75]
(3) Is the political leadership a legitimate target?[76]

To a considerable extent, the debate concerning what should constitute a military objective has yet to be commenced and it clearly will be when and if a case concerning air bombardment is prosecuted. Cases brought before the ICTY to date have been concerned primarily with ground combat, and identification of military objectives has tended to be a relatively simple task since the objectives are usually troop concentrations or weapons emplacements.[77]

Civilians who take up arms to defend themselves and others may retain their protected status and not be regarded as taking a direct part in hostilities in certain limited circumstances although, as a purely practical matter, they may increase the risk they will be attacked by mistake by combatants on the opposing side. If civilians arm themselves to protect themselves or their families against an attacking force, do they automatically become subject to attack? The question is one of degree. If a group of Hutu civilians in Rwanda defended themselves with sticks and stones against Interahamwe militia (also equipped with sticks and stones) who were coming to kill them, it is submitted that the Hutu civilians would not be converted into armed fighters whom the Interahamwe were entitled to kill. They would simply be acting in self-defence. Somewhat similarly, if troops attack a village with a clear intent to kill all the inhabitants and the male inhabitants take up arms to save themselves and their families, it is submitted the armed male inhabitants are not converted into 'civilians taking a direct part in hostilities' whom the attackers are entitled to regard as lawful military objectives. A similar type of argument was made in the UNSCR 780 Commission of Experts Report.[78] That report is, however, the only published document that indicates there should be some limited scope for individual self defence in a conduct of hostilities situation.

---

74. The author tends to be a bit reluctant to distinguish between the good and the bad side for the purposes of applying IHL. But see C.J. Dunlap, 'The end of innocence: rethinking non-combatancy in the post-Kosovo era', 28 *Strategic Review* (Summer 2000) p. 4.

75. For a vigorous statement of the view that enemy civilian moral has traditionally been a legitimate military objective and that the AP I definition of military objective should be interpreted to encompass attacks on morale targets, see J.M. Meyer, 'Tearing down the façade: a critical look at the current law on targeting the will of the enemy and air force doctrine', 51 *Air Force LR* (2001) p. 143.

76. See extended discussion of practical aspects of targeting Saddam Hussein in Human Rights Watch, 'Off Target: the conduct of the war and civilian casualties in Iraq', (2004) pp. 21-40.

77. The one exception to this rule, which in the event did not involve litigation, was the ICTY: 'Final Report to the Prosecutor by the Committee Established to Review the NATO Bombing Campaign Against the Federal Republic of Yugoslavia (8 June 2000)', 39 *ILM* (2000) p. 1257. See in particular the contentious discussion of the NATO attack on the headquarters and studios of Serbian State Television and Radio (RTS) in central Belgrade on 23 April 1999.

78. UN Doc. S/1994/674 (1994) 'Final Report of the Commission of Experts established pursuant to Security Council Resolution 780 (1992)', para 78.

The 'individual self defence' concept must, however, be very rigidly confined or it will undermine all of IHL. An appropriate set of boundaries would be something like the following: an individual civilian who takes up arms on an *ad hoc* basis to defend himself or another person against an unlawful immediate risk to life posed by enemy combatants does not thereby become a 'civilian taking a direct part in hostilities' whom enemy combatants may lawfully attack. Any extension beyond narrow boundaries such as these would pose extreme problems. If we apply the individual self defence concept more widely so that, for example, individual civilians may take up arms in self defence on an ad hoc basis to defend themselves or those under their protection from ethnic cleansing then, in a conflict such as the recent one in Bosnia where all sides practice ethnic cleansing, all civilians could take up arms in self defence and, simultaneously, be immune from attack themselves and allowed to use force against attacking forces.

6. PROPORTIONALITY

Where unlawful attacks are concerned, proportionality is the ratio between the concrete and direct military advantage anticipated and the incidental loss of civilian life, injury to civilians, and damage to civilian objects anticipated from an attack directed against a military objective.

The concept of proportionality is linked to the principle of distinction which is the fundamental legal principle underlying combat activities. Although the concept has been a part of IHL for a long time, it did not appear in treaty texts until the development of AP I in 1974-7. The concept is important because military objectives, civilians and civilian objectives are too frequently located in the same area. Civilians and civilian objects do not have absolute immunity from the effects of combat. Attacks directed against military objectives are lawful unless they are anticipated to cause disproportionate civilian losses. It is not practicable to determine whether civilian casualties are lawful or unlawful until there have been prior determinations of whether the attack which caused the civilian casualties was directed against a military objective and whether, if the answer was yes, disproportionate civilian casualties were anticipated. If disproportionate civilian casualties are caused, that may provide the basis for an inference that such casualties were anticipated. The word proportionality is not used in AP I but it is implicitly contained in several of its provisions,[79] all of which refer to a prohibition on attacks 'which may be expected to cause incidental loss of civilian life, injury to civilians, damage to civilian objects or a combination thereof, which would be *excessive* in relation to the concrete and direct military advantage anticipated'. 'Excessive', considered in context, is synonymous with 'disproportionate'.[80] In the context of the law related to unlawful attacks, proportionality is relevant simply for assessing the relative values of two essentially unlike concepts, notions or entities, military advantage

79. See Arts. 51(5)(b), 57(2)(a)(iii), 57(2)(b), and 85(3)(c).
80. Art. 8(2)(b)(iv) of the ICC Statute contains an analogous expression 'clearly excessive'.

and civilian losses. Since the relative values are of essentially unlike concepts, precise valuation is difficult. It is not a simple accounting exercise. The best one can say is that if similar things are being measured, such as human lives, usually each life must be given a similar value.

Proportionality is not a legally relevant concept for other measurements of combat activity. The word 'proportionality' may be used in various other contexts, such as disproportionate use of force when one side has or uses more military resources in a particular situation. Use of the expression may be factually accurate but it is also legally irrelevant. There is nothing unlawful about using more or better equipment or troops than an opponent. Armed conflict is not a sporting contest. The rules must be obeyed but there is no legal requirement to have a level playing field. Military forces strive to have a technological advantage and to inflict more combatant casualties than the other side. Measuring own side casualties against civilian losses on the other side is also of no legal significance. Compliance or non compliance with weapon expenditure norms is equally irrelevant. If military doctrine prescribes the use of X number of projectiles of certain type to neutralise a military objective to Y extent, whether or not an attacker uses all the projectiles authorised by doctrine to neutralise the objective may be interesting from the point of view of doctrine. It is of no significance, however, when attempting to assess whether or not civilian losses are disproportionate relative to military advantage.

Although, unfortunately, it is not possible to provide simple answers concerning the application of the concept of proportionality to concrete military situations because of a lack of examples in legal decisions or legal literature, the following provides a rough frame of reference. First, who decides whether an action is disproportionate? The *Galić* Trial Chamber held that the decision maker should be regarded as 'a reasonably well-informed person in the circumstances of the actual perpetrator, making reasonable use of the information available to him or her'.[81] Second, what is compared? The comparison is between the *anticipated* concrete and direct military advantage and the *anticipated* incidental loss of civilian life, injury to civilians, damage to civilian objects, or a combination thereof. The actual results of the attack may assist in inferring the intent of the attacker as he or she launched the attack but what counts is what was in the mind of the decision maker when the attack was launched. Third, what is the standard? The attack is prohibited if it is anticipated it will result in *excessive* civilian losses. Fourth, what is the scope of 'concrete and direct military advantage anticipated'? The *Galić* Trial Chamber referred to several sources in addressing this point:

> 'The *travaux préparatoires* of Additional Protocol I indicate that the expression "concrete and direct" was intended to show that the advantage must be "substantial and relatively close" and that "advantages which are hardly perceptible and those which would only appear in the long term should be disregarded." ICRC Commentary para. 2209. The Commentary explains that "a military advantage can only consist in ground

81. *Prosecutor* v *Galić*, Case No. IT-98-29-T, Judgement and Opinion, 5 December 2003, para. 58.

gained or in annihilating or in weakening the enemy armed forces". ICRC Commentary, para. 2218.'[82]

The military advantage gained by a successful attack on a military objective may vary somewhat depending on circumstances. For example, a successful attack on a military objective such as an artillery emplacement always gives the attacker a military advantage but the extent of the direct and concrete direct military advantage gained may vary depending on factors such as location of the objective and its current or potential use.

Fifth, what scale should be used in assessing proportionality? Should proportionality be assessed on the basis of an attack on a single military objective, on the basis of a battle, a campaign or a war? Several states made statements of understanding concerning the application of 'military advantage' considered in the context of Articles 51, 52, and 57 when ratifying or acceding to AP I.[83] The Statement by Canada is representative:[84]

> 'It is the understanding of the Government of Canada in relation to Articles 51(5)(b), 52 (2), and 57(2)(a)(iii) that the military advantage anticipated from an attack is intended to refer to the advantage anticipated from the attack considered as a whole and not from isolated or particular parts of the attack.'

These Statements of Understanding notwithstanding, it is suggested that proportionality can be determined using a variety of scales ranging from the tactical (military objective by military objective) level to a much bigger scale as long as the more general context is also taken into account.[85] For example, if it is essential to block military traffic across a river and the enemy forces may use three bridges to cross the river, it may well be permissible to inflict greater collateral losses for destroying the last bridge because of the resultant greater military advantage. The military objective scale is commonly used in modern state practice, particularly in

---

82. *Galić*, Trial Judgement, para. 58, n. 106.

83. See for example, Statements of Interpretation by Belgium, Canada, Germany, Italy, Netherlands, New Zealand, Switzerland, and the United Kingdom, in A. Roberts and R. Guelff, *Documents on the Laws of War*, 3rd. edn. (Oxford, Oxford University Press 2000) pp. 499-512.

84. Ibid., p. 503.

85. In an earlier article, W.J. Fenrick, 'The rule of proportionality and Protocol I in conventional warfare', 98 *Mil. LR* (1982) pp. 91-127 at 112, the author expressed the view that the AP I proportionality provisions would probably not be applicable below a divisional level attack. The earlier view was premised on the assumption that there could be such a thing as an attack which was disproportionate but which was not , in substance, directed against civilians or civilian objects. Whether or not that assumption was valid, in the cases which have been prosecuted to date a de facto higher threshold has been used and the argument advanced has been that the attack was so disproportionate that it must be regarded as directed against civilians or civilian objects.

assessing the legitimacy of aerial attacks.[86] It was also used by the *Galić* Trial Chamber.[87]

No tribunal to date has ever explicitly determined in a well articulate manner that disproportionate damage was caused when assessing an incident in which the disproportionate impact of the attack was not blatant or conspicuous. The *Galić* Trial Chamber was, however, compelled to grapple with the issue in its discussion of one shelling incident, the shelling of the Dobrinje football tournament on 1 June 1993. In that incident, about 200 spectators, including women and children, were watching a football game in the corner of a parking lot which was bounded on three sides by 6-storey apartment blocks and on the fourth by a hill. Two shells exploded in the parking lot killing between 12 and 16 persons and wounding between 80 and 140 persons. The players and many of the spectators were military personnel and, as such, military objectives. The Commander of the Army of Bosnia and Herzegovina (ABiH) 5th Motorized Dobrinja Brigade, to which the soldiers belonged, filed a report indicating there were 11 killed and 87 wounded (6 combatants killed and 55 wounded, 5 civilians killed and 32 wounded).[88] Although assessing proportionality is not a simple exercise in number crunching, it would be difficult to conclude that, in this incident, there were disproportionate civilian casualties unless one makes the arbitrary determination that civilian lives count for more than military lives. The majority of the chamber finessed a requirement to assess the proportionality of the result by focusing on the *mens rea* of the perpetrators and on the fact that civilian casualties were caused:

> '… Although the number of soldiers present at the game was significant, an attack on a crowd of approximately 200 people, including numerous children, would clearly be expected to cause incidental loss of life and injuries to civilians excessive in relation to the direct and concrete military advantage anticipated …'[89]

7. RELEVANT MODES OF INDIVIDUAL CRIMINAL RESPONSIBILITY

The three most likely modes of individual criminal responsibility for senior military personnel involved in unlawful attacks are: ordering, aiding and abetting, and command responsibility. All three modes of liability are referred to in the Statutes of the ICTY (Art. 7) and the ICC (Arts. 25 and 28). Unless the evidence unequivocally supports a conclusion concerning one particular mode of liability, preferred prosecution practice would be to introduce evidence which provides as detailed a

86. J.E. Baker, 'Judging Kosovo: the legal process, the Law of Armed Conflict, and the Commander in Chief', in A.E. Wall, ed., *Legal and Ethical Lessons of NATO's Kosovo Campaign* (Newport RI, Naval War College 2002) pp. 7-18; and the various incident studies referred to in International Criminal Tribunal for the former Yugoslavia (ICTY), *supra* n. 77.

87. *Galić*, Trial Judgement, para. 387.

88. Ibid., para. 377.

89. Ibid., para. 387.

picture as possible of the involvement of the accused in the offence and to argue that the accused may be held liable on the basis of any of a number of modes of liability. As examples, a failure to prevent during an extended period of time or a repeated failure to prevent or punish may be categorised as aiding and abetting in lieu of command responsibility or the circumstantial evidence which is introduced to indicate the state of knowledge of an accused for command responsibility may also substantiate a conclusion the accused must have ordered the act.

Circumstantial evidence will usually be essential to proving responsibility for superiors. Both the *Blaškić* and *Čelebići* Trial Chambers endorsed a non-exclusive list of factors to establish actual knowledge:

> 'the number, type and scope of the illegal acts; the time during which the illegal acts occurred; the number and type of troops involved; the logistics involved, if any, the geographical location of the acts; the widespread occurrence of the acts; the speed of the operations; the *modus operandi* of similar illegal acts; the officers and staff involved; and the location of the commander at the time.'[90]

The same kinds of factors might also be used to establish had 'reason to know' or, for that matter, that the accused had actually ordered commission of the illegal acts.

In order to determine the potential culpability of a superior, evidence should be collected on the following points, among others:

1. the commission of the offence;
2. the nature of the superior-subordinate relationship between the accused and the perpetrators (military, paramilitary, other), (direct superior in chain of command, superior in rank only), (executive authority, staff officer);
3. the means available to the accused to exercise control over the perpetrators (authority to issue binding orders, authority to take or recommend disciplinary measures, types of disciplinary measures available);
4. the state of knowledge of the accused before, during, and after offences were committed;
5. the routine or extraordinary systems available to provide information to the accused, effectiveness of systems and relevant information provided;
6. the notice of alleged offenses provided to the accused by external sources – NGOs, U.N., press, other;
7. the measures taken by the accused to prevent commission of an offence or to punish those responsible; and
8. the extent of the accused's participation in the commission of the offence. Did he or she plan, instigate, order, commit or otherwise aid and abet in the planning, preparation or execution of the offence?

---

90. *Blaškić*, Trial Judgement, para. 307, *Prosecutor* v. *Zejnil Delalić et al* (*Čelebići* case), Case No. IT-96-21-T, Trial Judgement 16 November 1998, para. 386. Appeal Judgement, Case No. IT-96-21-A 20 February 2001.

7.1 Ordering

Ordering incurs criminal responsibility under Article 7(1) of the ICTY Statute and Article 25(3)(b) of the ICC Statute. In the *Blaškić* decision, the ICTY Appeals Chamber held:

> 'a person who orders an act or omission with the awareness of the substantial likelihood that a crime will be committed in the execution of that order, has the requisite *mens rea* for establishing liability under Article 7(1) pursuant to ordering. Ordering with such awareness has to be regarded as accepting that crime.'[91]

The accused must possess authority to issue binding orders to the perpetrator although there need not be a formal superior-subordinate relationship in existence. The order may be given indirectly and it need not be in any particular form.[92] There must be a causal link between the act of ordering and the physical perpetration of the crime.[93] There is no relevant litigation under the ICC Statute to date but one might expect the ICC to pay due regard to ICTY decisions on this mode of liability.

7.2 Aiding and abetting

Aiding and abetting incurs criminal responsibility under Article 7(1) of the ICTY Statute and Article 25(3)(c) of the ICC Statute although the ICC formulation is a bit broader and more elaborate: 'For the purpose of facilitating the commission of such a crime, aids, abets, or otherwise assists in its commission or attempted commission, including providing the means for its commission.' The ICTY Appeals Chamber has reaffirmed the *actus reus* and *mens rea* for aiding and abetting under its statute as:

> '(i) The aider and abettor carries out acts specifically directed to assist, encourage or lend moral support to the perpetration of a specific crime…, and this support has a substantial effect upon the perpetration of the crime…
> (ii)… the requisite mental element is knowledge that the acts performed by the aider and abettor assist (in) the commission of the specific crime of the principal.'[94]

An omission may constitute the *actus reus* for aiding and abetting.[95] 'Trial Chambers have held that this is the case, for example, if a person with superior authority is present at the crime scene, provided that his presence had a significant encouraging effect on the principal offender, or if there was an explicit duty to act.'[96] The

---

91. *Blaškić*, Appeals Judgement, para. 42.
92. *Strugar*, Trial Judgement, para. 331.
93. Ibid., para. 332.
94. *Blaškić*, Appeal Judgement, para. 45.
95. Ibid., para. 47.
96. *Strugar*, Trial Judgement, para. 349.

actus reus may occur before, during or after the principal crime has been perpetrated and in a location removed from the location of the principal crime.[97] The aider and abettor need not know the precise crime which was intended and which, in the event, was committed. It is sufficient if he or she is aware that one of a number of crimes will probably be committed and one of these crimes is in fact committed.[98]

7.3 Command responsibility

The doctrine of command responsibility is incorporated into the law applicable before the ICTY by Article 7(3) of the ICTY Statute:

> 'The fact that any of the acts referred to in Articles 2 to 5 of the present Statute was committed by a subordinate does not relieve his superior of criminal responsibility if he knew or had reason to know that the subordinate was about to commit such acts or had done so and the superior failed to take the necessary and reasonable measures to prevent such acts or to punish the perpetrators thereof.'

Treaty law provisions referring to the doctrine of command responsibility are Articles 86 and 87 of AP I and Article 28 of the ICC Statute. AP I, which was in force in the former Yugoslavia throughout the various conflicts, applies to international conflicts only and the ICC Statute is prospective and came into force in July 2002. Article 28 of the ICC Statute distinguishes two groups of superiors: a) military commanders or persons effectively acting as military commanders, and b) other superiors. The issue of whether or not the doctrine of command responsibility applied to internal conflicts during and since 1991, the period during which the ICTY has temporal jurisdiction, was recently considered by the Appeals Chamber in *Prosecutor* v. *Hadžihasanović et al.* The Appeals Chamber issued a decision affirming the application of the doctrine to internal conflicts as a matter of customary international law.[99] In the same decision it also held that a superior could not be held responsible for the acts of his subordinates which were committed before he became their superior.[100]

> 'The essential elements of command responsibility for failure to act are:
> (i) the existence of a superior-subordinate relationship
> (ii) the superior knew or had reason to know that the criminal act was about to be or had been committed; and

---

97. *Blaškić*, Appeal Judgement, para. 48.
98. Ibid., para. 48.
99. *Prosecutor* v. *Enver Hadžihasanović et al.*, Decision on Interlocutory Appeal Challenging Jurisdiction in Relation to Command Responsibility, Case No. IT-01-47-AR72, 16 July 2003, paras. 11-37.
100. Ibid., para. 51.

(iii) the superior failed to take the necessary and reasonable measures to prevent the criminal act or punish the perpetrator thereof.'[101]

Concerning the superior-subordinate relationship, the *Čelebići* trial decision addresses the applicability of the doctrine of command responsibility to military and to non-military superiors at paragraphs 354-78. These state in part:

> '377. While it is, therefore, the Trial Chamber's conclusion that a superior, whether military or civilian, may be held liable under the principle of superior responsibility on the basis of his *de facto* position of authority, the fundamental considerations underlying the imposition of such responsibility must be borne in mind. The doctrine of command responsibility is ultimately predicated upon the power of the superior to control the acts of his subordinates. A duty is placed upon the superior to exercise this power so as to prevent and repress the crimes committed by his subordinates, and a failure by him to do so in a diligent manner is sanctioned by the imposition of individual criminal responsibility in accordance with the doctrine. It follows that there is a threshold at which persons cease to possess the necessary powers of control over the actual perpetrators of offences and, accordingly, cannot properly be considered their "superiors" within the meaning of Article 7(3) of the Statute. While the Trial Chamber must at all times be alive to the realities of any given situation and be prepared to pierce such veils of formalism that may shield those individuals carrying the greatest responsibility for heinous acts, great care must be taken lest an injustice be committed in holding individuals responsible for the acts of others in situations where the link of control is absent or too remote.
>
> 378. Accordingly, it is the Trial Chamber's view that, in order for the principle of superior responsibility to be applicable, it is necessary that the superior have effective control over the persons committing the underlying violations of international humanitarian law, in the sense of having the material ability to prevent and punish the commission of those offences. With the caveat that such authority can have a *de facto* as well as a *de jure* character, the Trial Chamber accordingly shares the view expressed by the International Law Commission that the doctrine of superior responsibility extends to civilian superiors only to the extend that they exercise a degree of control over their subordinates which is similar to that of military commanders.'

There is no legal requirement that the superior-subordinate relationship be direct or immediate. The subordinate perpetrators may be several levels below the superior held responsible as long as the superior exercises effective control over them.[102]

Concerning the meaning of 'knew or had reason to know', knew is self explanatory. Actual knowledge can be established by direct or circumstantial evidence.

101. *Čelebići*, Trial, para. 346.
102. *Strugar*, Trial Judgement, para. 366.

The *Čelebići* Appeals Chamber[103] upheld the following interpretation of 'had reason to know' by the *Čelebići* Trial Chamber:

> '393...a superior can be held criminally responsible only if some specific information was in fact available to him which would provide notice of offences committed by his subordinates. This information need not be such that it by itself was sufficient to compel the conclusion of the existence of such crimes. It is sufficient that the superior was put on further inquiry by the information, or, in other words, that it indicated the need for additional investigation in order to ascertain whether offences were being committed or about to be committed by his subordinates.'

Concerning the meaning of necessary and reasonable measures to prevent or punish, the *Čelebići* Trial Chamber held:

> '394. The legal duty which rests upon all individuals in positions of superior authority requires them to take all necessary and reasonable measures to prevent the commission of offences by their subordinates or, is such crimes have been committed, to punish the perpetrators thereof. ...any evaluation of the action taken by a superior to determine whether this duty has been met is so inextricably linked to the facts of each particular situation that any attempt to formulate a general standard *in abstracto* would not be meaningful.
>
> 395. It must, however, be recognised that international law cannot oblige a superior to perform the impossible. Hence, a superior may only held criminally responsible for failing to take such measures that are within his powers. The question then arises of what actions are to be considered to be within the superior's powers in this sense. As the corollary to the standard adopted by the Trial Chamber with respect to the concept of superior, we conclude that a superior should be held responsible for failing to take such measures that are within his material possibility....'[104]

In assessing potential liability in *Strugar,* the Trial Chamber, among other factors, considered:

> 'whether specific orders prohibiting or stopping the criminal activities were issued; what measures to secure the implementation of these orders were taken; what other measures were taken to secure that the unlawful acts were interrupted and whether these measures were reasonably sufficient in the specific circumstances; and, after the commission of the crime, what steps were taken to secure an adequate investigation and to bring the perpetrators to justice.'[105]

---

103. *Čelebići*, Appeals Judgement, para. 241.
104. Ibid., paras. 394-395.
105. *Strugar*, Trial Judgement, para. 378.

8. INVESTIGATIVE ISSUES

The investigation of shelling incidents and of sniping incidents each require that a range of specific questions be addressed. Sniping, for the purposes of this Article, is understood to be the 'direct targeting of individuals at a distance using any type of small caliber weapon'.[106]

8.1 Investigative checklist for shelling incidents

The following questions might be asked during the course of the investigation of a shelling incident:

A. Investigation where the projectile landed:

1. Where did the projectile land?
2. What damage did the projectile cause? Death or injury (identify victims and provide proof of death or injury)? Damage or destruction of property (how much damage or destruction was caused and to what kinds of structures, e.g., generic civilian objects, objects under additional special protection such as hospitals, institutions dedicated to religion, charity, education, Articles and sciences, historic monuments and works of Article and science)? Precisely where, when and how was death, injury, damage or destruction caused? What prior investigations, if any, have been conducted in relation to the incident? Obtain copies of relevant prior reports.
3. Was this damage or injury done to military objectives (including combatants or civilians taking a direct part in hostilities), to civilians or to civilian objects? If the damage was done to military objectives only then it is not unlawful. If damage was done to military objectives and civilians or civilian objects then an assessment must be made whether or not the damage to civilians or civilian objects was 'excessive/disproportionate' in relation to the military advantage gained by the attack. If the damage was not excessive or disproportionate then, once again, it is not unlawful.
4. If both military objectives and civilians and/or civilian objects were hit, in what order were they hit?
5. What other military objectives were located relatively close to the area of impact (50 metres, 100 metres, 200 metres, 500 metres) at the time of impact or shortly beforehand (shoot and scoot mortars for example)?
6. What other projectiles landed relatively close to the area of impact (50 metres, 100 metres, 200 metres, 500 metres) at or about the time of the incident?
7. What kinds of projectiles were used?
8. Where were projectiles landed from (using crater analysis and other techniques if available)?
9. When (time and day) did the incident occur and what was the weather like?

---

106. *Galić*, Trial Judgement, para. 184.

10. In general terms, what else was occurring in the battle (particularly fairly close by) on the day and particularly about the time when the incident occurred?

B. Investigation where the projectile was launched from:

11. Where is the launch site located and how far was the weapon from the point of impact of the projectile? It is important to establish that the weapon had a range which would enable a projectile fired from it to reach the point of impact.
12. Was the point of impact of the projectile visible to those firing or directing the firing of the weapon? Vision may be obscured by, among other things, weather, foliage, buildings and smoke.
13. What were those firing the projectile or their superiors actually aiming at?
14. What was the firing protocol process? Who or what aimed the weapon? Who gave the order to fire and who implemented it? What kind of spotting process was there?
15. What measures were taken to eliminate or minimise civilian casualties, such as intelligence gathering and assessment?
16. What were the applicable rules of engagement and/or firing orders?
17. What was the applicable doctrine of artillery generally and for use of this type of weapon? What are the characteristics of this type of weapon, in particular those concerning range and accuracy?
18. Who controlled use of the weapon and allocation of projectiles to it?
19. What (other) weapons systems were available to the attacking commander?
20. What unit actually conducted the firing and what was its chain of command to the potential accused?

8.2 Investigative checklist for sniping incidents

The following questions might be asked during the investigation of a sniping incident:

1. What is the status of the victim? If the victim was a civilian not taking a direct part in hostilities, an offence may have been committed. If the victim was a combatant or a civilian taking a direct part in hostilities, an unlawful act has not been committed.
2. Where was the victim hit?
3. Was the victim killed or wounded (identify victim and provide proof of death or injury)? What prior investigations, if any, have been conducted in relation to the incident? Obtain copies of relevant prior reports.
4. What type of weapon (calibre, manufacturer, etc.) was used?
5. Where is the most likely source of fire?
6. How far was the location of the incident from the most likely source of fire?
7. Was the victim within the unobstructed line of sight from the most likely source of fire?

8. When (time and day) did the incident occur and what was the weather like? Was there daylight when the incident occurred?
9. At the time of the incident, how did the victim appear as to age, gender and clothing? Was the victim carrying any weapons openly?
10. At the time of the incident, what activity did the victim appear to be engaged in?
11. What military objectives, if any, were located close to the location and at the time of the incident? Were there a large number of troops present in the area?
12. How far was the location of the incident from the nearest confrontation line?
13. In general terms, what else was occurring in the battle (particularly fairly close by) on the day and particularly about the time when the incident occurred?

9. CASE PRESENTATION ISSUES

The prosecutor must strive to develop and present a complete picture, both static and moving of what was present in and around the area of the alleged unlawful attack and of what occurred during the period of the attack. An assessment of the military capabilities of all parties to the conflict with respect to weaponry and troops must be undertaken. It is expected that these capabilities will be raised during some part of the defence case and the prosecution must know in advance how to meet and neutralise any negative inferences which might be drawn to the detriment of the prosecution's case. The prosecution may anticipate relying on a wide variety of evidence. Document exploitation should be undertaken. As a practical matter, it may not be feasible to secure certain documents from the opposing party's military archives due to claims – whether or not valid – as to national security. Document exploitation of the side against which the unlawful attacks are alleged to have taken place may also be a source of relevant information as to the command structure and military capabilities of the accused's side. Witness statements, including 'insider' witnesses from the same military as the accused, expert witnesses on command and control issues as well as artillery or weapons issues, maps made at the time or afterwards, if their accuracy can be confirmed, photographs, films, computer graphics and site visits, sometimes referred to as 'crime scene visits', may be used in support of the prosecution's case. In the experience of the ICTY OTP, the use of open source material such as newspapers containing accounts tracking the gains and casualties of both sides, but particularly of the accused, may provide potential evidence or leads thereto as to the commission of unlawful attacks. These open sources can provide a basis for refining further requests to the military archives for documents. Open source material may also be useful for cross-examination. Media interviews of an accused or subordinates have, where appropriate, been used in cross examination. As evidenced by the aforementioned checklist, the prosecutor must know and be prepared to adduce evidence, among other things, as to where munitions landed, the effects of the munitions, where actual or potential military objectives were located, where civilians or civilian objects were located, how the defending force conducted operations, how the attacking forces conducted operations, the effects of relevant weapons systems, how the relevant armed forces were commanded and controlled, and what was the precise role of the accused. It is insufficient to merely introduce evidence that forces under the command of an accused caused death or injury to civilians or damage to civilian objects without introducing relevant evidence of surrounding circumstances. The circumstances and context often provide the key to allow the prosecutor to argue in support of an inference that an attack was unlawful. Circumstantial evidence is frequently relied upon. In the *Strugar* case, the prosecution relied on all of the above types of evidence and witnesses to create its picture. In the author's view, particularly effective use was made of testimony by Admiral Jokić, a co-accused who had submitted a guilty plea, in order to create a picture of how the attacking force conducted operations, as well as that of the chief of artillery of the defending forces in order to show where and how the defenders conducted operations. The Prosecution moved for a site visit to assist the Trial Chamber in the *Strugar* case, which took place between filing the closing briefs and closing arguments where the Trial Chamber had the entire range of evidence at its disposal to apply to the evidence it gathered by visiting the site in the Dubrovnik area. In the *Galić* case, particular use was made of computer graphics and of 360 degree panoramic pictures and films to indicate what probably happened during sniping incidents. Evidence as to cause of death or serious injury may vary depending on the availability of documentation or witness testimony concerning same.

It is essential that the prosecution develop as clear, simple and coherent a theory of the prosecution case as possible while leaving open its options concerning modes of liability and modes for commission of the offence. For example, focusing exclusively on the unlawful attack issue, it may be said that the prosecution theory in the *Strugar* case included, *inter alia*, the following propositions: civilians and civilian objects were unlawfully attacked (directly or as a result of an indiscriminate or disproportionate attack) in the Old Town of Dubrovnik on 6 December 1991 by forces under the command of General Strugar, and General Strugar was responsible for the attacks because he ordered them or ratified an order for them or aided and abetted those who committed them or was responsible on the basis of the doctrine of command responsibility. It must, of course, be expected that the defence will also develop a theory of the case sometimes leaving open a number of options depending on developments during the prosecutor's case. From the defense submissions and presentation, one might surmise that the defence theory in the *Strugar* case appeared to include, *inter alia*, the following propositions: (i) no injury or damage was caused to civilians or civilian objects during the attack; (ii) if injury or damage was caused it was not inflicted by the JNA; (iii) if damage or injury was inflicted by the JNA it was lawful because it was proportionate to the advantage gained by an attack directed against military objectives; (iv) if the attack was unlawful, General Strugar was not responsible for it because he did not order it or aid and abet the perpetrators and he did not exercise command responsibility over the perpetrators (trying to assert that he was a strategic level command commander with no responsibility for day to day operations as these were the responsibility of Admiral Jokić, his immediate subordinate who had earlier submitted a guilty plea). Indeed, as the defence case evolved in *Strugar*, the defence introduced several witnesses and documents as part of its strategy to attempt to shift responsibility from General Strugar to Admiral Jokić.

9.1 Establishing the big picture

Since, generally speaking, unlawful attack counts will require reference to multiple incidents and it would be impracticable to introduce detailed evidence concerning each incident, it will be necessary to develop a way for getting from the micro to the macro level in presenting the case.

In the *Galić* case, hundreds of civilians were killed or wounded in Sarajevo by shelling or sniping during the period covered by the indictment, 1992-1994. It would be impracticable to treat each incident of killing as a separate murder case. Some way had to be developed to get from the specific incident at the micro level to what was alleged to be an unlawful shelling or sniping campaign at the macro level. Indeed, the link from the micro to the macro level was essential to that case. If, for example, the prosecution could prove with a degree of precision in a manageable time that 20 sniping incidents have occurred over a two year period when the accused is responsible for 15,000 soldiers in the front lines, in the absence of direct evidence of relevant orders being given, would a reasonable court conclude that the commander bears command responsibility for the sniping or that he must have ordered such acts? On the other hand, if the prosecutor could establish both the occurrence of the 20 incidents and an adequate link to what appears to be a much broader crime base, it might be much easier for the court to reach such conclusions.

Presumably the preferred approach would be to determine in some scientifically valid fashion the entire apparent crime base, for example, it appears from sound medical evidence that 1000 civilians have been killed by sniper fire from forces under the command of X, and then to pick a statistically valid sample on something like a random numbers basis for more detailed examination. Detailed evidence concerning all cases in the sample group would then be put before the court. If that was done, or if the prosecutor made the court aware of incidents or situations in the sample group which do not indicate unlawful acts occurred, then, perhaps, the court could conclude, for example, that 70 percent of the cases in the sample group constituted crimes therefore 70 percent of the larger group also constituted crimes and therefore a campaign of unlawful sniping occurred.

Desirable as the mathematical/scientific approach might be, it is not always practicable. The *Galić* prosecution team listed scheduled sniping and shelling incidents as 'representative allegations' in annexes to the indictment. The prosecution also introduced evidence of unscheduled incidents, survey or impressionistic evidence, and solid demographic evidence which could adequately establish cause of death or injury but which did not, in and of itself, establish whether the death or injury was the result of unlawful acts.

The majority in the Trial Chamber held that a campaign of military actions in the area of Sarajevo involving widespread or systematic shelling and sniping of civilians resulting in civilian death or injury existed together with a lawful military campaign directed against military objectives.[107] Civilians were directly or indiscriminately attacked and, at a minimum, hundreds of civilians were killed and thousands of others were injured.[108] The reasons for this finding included:

(a) No civilian activity and no areas of Sarajevo held by the ABiH seemed to be safe from sniping or shelling attacks from SRK-held territory;[109]
(b) Indeed, specific areas of the city became notorious as sources of sniper fire directed at civilians;[110]
(c) Although civilians adapted to the environment by taking precautionary measures, they were still not safe from deliberate attack;[111]
(d) The evidence of residents of Sarajevo and of victims was supported by the evidence of international military personnel;[112]
(e) Although there was some evidence that ABiH forces attacked their own civilians to attract the attention of the international community, that stray bullets may have struck some civilians, and that some civilians were shot in the honest belief they were combatants, evidence in the Trial Record conclusively establishes that the pattern of fire throughout the city of Sarajevo was that of indiscriminate or direct fire at civilians in ABiH-held areas of Sarajevo from SRK-controlled territory not that of combat fire where civilians were accidentally hit;[113] and
(f) Fire into ABiH-held areas of Sarajevo followed a temporal pattern.[114]

10. CONCLUSION

International humanitarian law is primarily a body of preventive law. To the extent it purports to regulate combat situations, it should be applied by military commanders on the advice of legal advisers during the conduct of military operations. If the objective of IHL, the reduction of net human suffering during armed conflict, is to be achieved, what counts most is compliance. Litigation is a device to enhance the likelihood of compliance and it may also assist in clarifying certain aspects of the law. The part of IHL which regulates combat situations is usually articulated at a high level of generality. It focuses on general concepts such as proportionality, indiscriminateness, military necessity, and military objective. Subject to certain qualifications, the adjudication of specific cases applying the law to particular instances may flesh out the law. The qualifications are that the number of decided cases will always be quite small as such cases are difficult to prosecute, that, inevitably, prosecutors will consider themselves obligated to choose cases in which it is

---

107. Ibid., paras. 582-583.
108. Ibid., para. 591.
109. Ibid., para. 584.
110. Ibid., para. 585.
111. Ibid., para. 586.
112. Ibid., para. 587.
113. Ibid., para. 589.
114. Ibid., para. 590.

most easy to establish that an offence has been committed (prosecution involves trying to put people in jail, it is not an intellectual exercise), and that prosecutors will prefer to retain the maximum number of options concerning both modes of committing the offence and modes of individual criminal responsibility.

In the course of assisting with the *Strugar* case the author engaged in extensive discussions with military lawyers and combat arms officers from several countries concerning the application of the principle of proportionality and the meaning of 'excessive' in particular cases. It was his conclusion, and one which he did not desire to reach, that there did not appear to be a general and reasoned understanding concerning the application of the principle. It is possible there is such general agreement in military circles but it is not disclosed to outsiders. It is, however, his view that a generally agreed open source detailed analysis of the meaning of excessive/disproportionate linked to a number of illustrative case studies (hypothetical or historical as there is no sufficient body of usable judicial decisions at present) would be extremely beneficial to military commanders, their legal advisers, and those involved in the adjudication of unlawful attack cases. The absence of such analysis leaves the field open to polemicists who simply assert, with ever increasing volume, that a particular act was 'obviously' legal or illegal. This is not good for the law or for those armed forces which take their legal obligations seriously.

Unlawful attacks are crimes and unlawful attack charges must be adjudicated in criminal proceedings. The only such proceedings to date have been before the ICTY, a tribunal made up of judges whose appointments do not require them to have direct military experience. It is occasionally suggested by military personnel that only those with combat experience can judge combat conduct or that only military courts are competent to evaluate military conduct. The author disagrees with such suggestions. Due regard must be paid to military factors, to the realities of combat, and to the opinions of military experts when prosecuting unlawful attack cases. All concerned in such proceedings must bring themselves adequately up to speed on the relevant military issues. That being said, as the experience of the ICTY, particularly in the *Galić* and *Strugar* cases, indicates, competent prosecution, defence and adjudication of unlawful attack cases is not beyond the practical competence of non-specialist tribunals.

USES AND EFFECTS OF DEPLETED URANIUM MUNITIONS: TOWARDS A MORATORIUM ON USE[1]

Owen Thomas Gibbons[2]

2. LL.M. Graduate of the School of Law, University of Nottingham. This paper is based upon the author's dissertation submitted for the LL.M.

DOI 10.1017/S1389135904001916

1. INTRODUCTION

Depleted Uranium (DU) munitions were first used operationally by US and British coalition forces during *Operation Desert Storm* in 1991 to eject Iraqi forces from Kuwait.[3] Since that time, concerns have been raised in various quarters regarding the possible adverse effects DU may have on human health and the environment. In particular, it has been suggested that the reported 'explosion of childhood cancer in southern Iraq'[4] and so-called Gulf War[5] and Balkans[6] Syndromes may be attributable to combat uses of DU in the Middle East and, more recently, in Bosnia in the mid 1990s. Such concerns,[7] however, appear not to have impeded either the proliferation or continued use of DU munitions, such as in Kosovo and Serbia in 1999, in Afghanistan in 2001 and in *Operation Iraqi Freedom* in 2003.[8] It is

3. Ministry of Defence, *DU in the Gulf War (90-91)* (London, MoD 2003) <http://www.mod.uk/issues/depleted_uranium/gulf_1.htm>; See also J. Pilger, *Hidden Agendas* (London, Vintage 1998) p. 56.

4. R. Fisk, 'The hidden war', in A. Arnove, ed., *Iraq Under Siege: The Deadly Impact of Sanctions and War* (London, Pluto Press 2000) pp. 93-107; see also R. Fisk 'The deadly cost of a degrading act', *The Independent*, 18 December 1998, p. 5 and R. Fisk 'The evidence is there – we caused cancer in the Gulf', *The Independent*, 16 October 1998, p. 4. See also, more recently, A. Barnett 'Army shells pose cancer risk in Iraq', in *The Observer*, 14 December 2003, <http://www.guardian.co.uk/Iraq/story/0,2763,1106687,00.html>; P. Brown 'Uranium hazard prompts cancer check on troops', *The Guardian*, 25 April 2003, <http://www.guardian.co.uk/uranium/story/0,7369,943340,00.html>. More generally, see P. Bennis and M. Moushabeck, *Beyond the Storm: A Gulf Crisis Reader* (New York, Olive Branch Press 1991), <http://www.iacenter.org>.

5. The existence of 'gulf war syndrome' is disputed, as are its multifarious symptoms. The UK Ministry of Defence (MoD) has denied it exists in veterans of the 1990-91 Gulf War. However, on June 2003 the High Court upheld the findings of an earlier tribunal that the syndrome does exist, *Secretary of State for Defence* v. *Rusling*, *EWHC* 1359 (2003). More recently, a recent UK independent public inquiry into Gulf War Illnesses by former Lord Lloyd of Berwick stated that Gulf War Syndrome does exist and that many veterans of the campaign 'are ill because they served in the Gulf', see The Rt. Hon. Lord Lloyd of Berwick, *Independent Public Inquiry on Gulf War Illnesses*, (London, The Lloyd Inquiry 2004) also available online at <http://www.lloyd-gwii.com/report.asp>; see also World Health Organisation, *Health Conditions of the Population in Iraq Since the Gulf Crisis*, (Geneva, World Health Organization Resource Centre 1996), <http://www.who.int>.

6. European Parliament, 'Use of depleted uranium in Bosnia and Kosovo (Balkan syndrome)', text adopted by the parliament on 17 January 2001, <http://www.europarl.eu.int/omk/omnsapir.so/pv2>; see also A. Kirby, 'Depleted Uranium "threatens Balkan cancer epidemic"', on BBC News Online, 30 July 1999, <http://news.bbc.co.uk/1/hi/sci/tech/408122.stm>; AFP, 'Euro parliament calls for moratorium on use of depleted uranium rounds (2001)', <http://www.balkanpeace.org/hed/archive/jan01/hed2447.shtml>.

7. See Royal Society, *The Health Hazards of Depleted Uranium Munitions: Part 1*, Policy Document 6/01, (London, The Royal Society 2001), p. 1; see also Royal Society, *The Health Hazards of Depleted Uranium Munitions: Part 2*, Policy Document 5/02, (London, The Royal Society 2002); and Royal Society, *The Health Hazards of Depleted Uranium Munitions: Summary*, Policy Document 6/02, (London, The Royal Society 2002).

8. Ministry of Defence (UK), *supra* n. 3, confirms the use by UK forces of DU in Iraq in 2003; regarding US use of the munitions, see also BBC News Online, *US to use depleted uranium*, 18 March 2003, <http://news.bbc.co.uk/2/hi/in_depth/2860759.stm>. N.B. The operation conducted in Iraq in 2003 was known as *Operation Iraqi Freedom* by the USA, *Operation Telic* by the UK and *Operation Falconer* by Australia. For the purposes of this paper, *Operation Iraqi Freedom* is used for ease of reference, and as a reflection of the overall operational command of the United States.

thought that, in addition to the US and the UK, a growing number of other countries have DU munitions in their arsenals.[9]

Since concerns over DU weapons[10] first emerged in the 1990s, the debate surrounding the effects, and thus the legality of their continued use, has not abated. The argument of this paper is not so much concerned with the objective or subjective integrity of the claims and concerns regarding DU munitions, or the effects of their use *per se*. Rather, the paper suggests that, in light of the fundamental principles of international humanitarian law (hereinafter IHL) evaluated, it is possible to construct a legal case for a moratorium on the use of weapons whilst serious concerns persist regarding the effects of their use. From the outset, therefore, it should be noted that the paper presents a fundamentally *humanitarian* argument for a moratorium on the use of DU munitions. Throughout this paper the term 'international humanitarian law' (IHL) is preferred to 'law of international armed conflict' (LOIAC), or the more old-fashioned 'Hague Law' and Geneva Law'. Though the author concedes the argument of Yoram Dinstein that the term IHL tends to create the impression that the rules which it defines *must* be truly humanitarian in nature, the fundamental argument of the paper suggests that the humanitarian dimension of the laws that govern the conduct of hostilities should gain the 'benefit of the doubt' over the dimension of military necessity in cases where there is serious doubt over the safety of weapons.[11]

The evaluation of concerns over the impact depleted uranium may have on the natural environment will primarily be concerned with any consequential detrimental effects this may have on human health such as through agricultural processes.[12] This is not to say that environmental concerns regarding DU are of secondary importance, only that they do not fit so concordantly with the humanitarian logic of the argument proposed. After all, the principles of IHL with which this paper is concerned exemplify the *raison d'être* of the discipline, and pre-date the more

9. D. Fahey, 'Depleted uranium weapons: lessons from the 1991 Gulf War', in Laka Foundation, eds., *Depleted Uranium: A Post-War Disaster for Environment and Health* (Amsterdam, 1999) p.13, <http://www.laka.org/teksten/Vu/hap-99/2.html>; US Army Environmental Policy Institute cited in A. McDonald, *Use of Depleted Uranium as a War Crime* (International Association of Lawyers Against Nuclear Arms (IALANA), 2000) p. 4; N.H. Harley et al., *A Review of the Scientific Literature As It Pertains to Gulf War Illnesses*, (Washington DC, National Defense Research Institute/RAND 1999) p. 1; D. Fahey, *Science or Science Fiction: Facts, Myths and Propaganda in the Debate over Depleted Uranium Weapons* (2003) <http://www.antenna.nl/wise/uranium/pdf/dumyths.pdf> notes: although it is thought that Bahrain, Egypt, France, Greece, Iraq, Israel, Kuwait, Pakistan, Russia, Saudi Arabia, Taiwan, Thailand, Turkey, UK and USA possess DU munitions, the true number of states possessing weapons utilising DU is not known.

10. In this paper, the terms 'weapons', 'munitions' and 'ammunition' will be used interchangeably. Concerning whether DU munitions are 'weapons' or 'enablers', see A. McDonald, *Depleted Uranium as a New Weapon* (IALANA 2000) <http://www.ialana.net/deplited_uranium.htm>.

11. Y. Dinstein, *The Conduct of Hostilities under the Law of International Armed Conflict* (Cambridge, Cambridge University Press 2004) pp. 12-13.

12. For environmental assessments of recent combat use of DU in the Balkans, see United Nations Environment Program reports and, regarding the obligation to protect the environment and use of DU, see R. Desgagné, *The Use of Depleted Uranium and the Protection of the Environment* (IALANA 2000) <http://www.ialana.net/deplited_uranium.htm>.

contemporary – though, in the view of the author, equally valid – concerns over the effects of combat on the natural environment.

The paper will initially examine the nature and uses of DU munitions, including addressing why DU is used. Secondly, it will be necessary to briefly examine the nature of concerns over the effects that the use of DU munitions may have on human health. However, the purpose of the paper is not to determine the validity of such concerns, but to illustrate that such concerns – and particularly their gravity and persistence – in themselves should be sufficient to prompt restrictions on use. Thirdly, the relevant sources of international law which may relate to the development and use of these and other weapons will be discussed. It will then be necessary to distinguish DU munitions in order to inform the argument as to why these weapons should receive different treatment from other conventional weapons. In so doing, it will thus be possible to consider such responses as may include a moratorium on the continued use of DU weapons.

2. THE NATURE AND USES OF DEPLETED URANIUM

In order to appreciate the argument concerning the possible dangers posed by DU to human health, a brief introduction to its origins, chemical properties and behaviour is necessary. Depleted Uranium is a by-product of the process of enriching natural uranium in order to extract the more valuable, fissionable isotope, uranium-235, primarily for use in the manufacture of nuclear fuel rods and nuclear weapons.[13] This enrichment process leaves several less radioactive, non-fissionable isotopes of uranium, consisting of approximately 99.8 percent uranium-238, which is thus termed 'depleted' uranium.[14] The International Atomic Energy Agency (IAEA) defines DU as a Low Specific Activity Material[15] meaning that it is only weakly radioactive.[16] The density of DU is 1.7 times that of lead,[17] and its abundance has provided developers of weapons with a plentiful and inexpensive supply

---

13. Royal Society, *supra* n. 7, p. 2; Harley et al., *supra* n. 9, p. xiii and p. 1; For an explanation of the technical process see P. Diehl, 'Depleted Uranium: a by-product of the Nuclear Chain', in Laka Foundation, *supra* n. 9; see also IAEA website <http://www.iaea.org/>; see also BBC News Online web pages on DU at <http://news.bbc.co.uk/1/shared/spl/hi/world/02/military_fact_files/du/html/flash.stm>.

14. See 'What is Depleted Uranium', advice pages of the National Radiological Protection Board at <http://www.nrpb.org/faq/du/du2.htm>; IAEA, *supra* n. 13; M. Zwanenburg, *Depleted Uranium and the Prohibition of Weapons of a Nature to Cause Superfluous Injury or Unnecessary Suffering* (IALANA 2000) <http://www.ialana.net/deplited_uranium.htm> p. 9; Laka Foundation, *supra* n. 9.

15. The lowest category used by the IAEA. See <http://www.iaea.org/worldatom/Press/Focus/DU/du_qaa.shtml#q1>.

16. The specific activity of DU is 14.8 becquerels per milligram (Bq/mg) compared with 25.4 Bq/mg for natural uranium and 2.3 million Bq/mg for plutonium-239. Becquerels are the SI unit used to measure the radioactivity of a substance. An activity of one becquerel means that one radioactive decay takes place every second. Therefore using the example above, in 1mg of depleted uranium, approximately 15 units of radioactive decay will be emitted per second.

17. DU has a density of $19 g/cm^3$, Harley et al., *supra* n. 9, p. 6; IAEA (2003).

of material for use in the manufacture of armour piercing rounds.[18] Indeed a cynic may suggest that one reason DU is reused in various ways is to solve the problem states would otherwise face in disposal or storage of such radioactive, toxic material.[19]

However, though only mildly radioactive, DU is, nonetheless, a toxic heavy metal.[20] With uranium-235 accounting for approximately two percent[21] of the radioactivity of naturally occurring uranium in around one percent of the total matter, the depleted element retains 60 percent of the radioactivity of natural uranium. DU produces approximately 15 percent less gamma radiation than naturally occurring uranium though equivalent amounts of alpha and beta radiation.[22] There is, however, no difference in chemical behaviour or toxicity between uranium and DU.[23]

It must be emphasised, however, that regardless of their radioactive properties, munitions utilising DU are not 'nuclear weapons' in any sense of how that term is commonly understood. In its 1996 Advisory Opinion on the Legality of the Threat or Use of Nuclear Weapons (hereinafter, the *Nuclear Weapons* Advisory Opinion), the International Court of Justice provided a definition of the types of weapons that fall within this category:

> '...[The Court] notes that nuclear weapons are explosive devices whose energy results from the fusion or fission of the atom. By its very nature, that process, in nuclear weapons as they exist today, releases not only immense quantities of heat and energy, but also powerful and prolonged radiation. ... The destructive power of nuclear weapons cannot be contained in either space or time. They have the potential to destroy all civilization and the entire ecosystem of the planet.
>
> ...
>
> The radiation released by a nuclear explosion would affect health, agriculture, natural resources and demography over a very wide area. Further, the use of nuclear weapons would be a serious danger to future generations. Ionizing radiation has the potential to damage the future environment, food and marine ecosystem, and to cause genetic defects and illness in future generations.'[24]

---

18. Royal Society (2001), *supra* n. 7, p. 2; Fahey (2003) *supra* n. 9, p. 3.
19. See Campaign Against Depleted Uranium (2003) <http://www.cadu.org.uk/intro.htm>; Fahey (2003), *supra* n. 9, p. 3 and p. 6.
20. Royal Society (2001), *supra* n. 7, p. 1; V.S. Zajic, *Review of the Radioactivity, Military Use, and Health Effects of Depleted Uranium* (Ratical 1999) <www.ratical.org/radiation/vzajic>. 'Heavy metals' are dense metals that are toxic to humans (e.g., *inter alia*, uranium, tungsten, cadmium and lead).
21. Harley et al., *supra* n. 9, p. 57; IAEA, *supra* n. 13.
22. Fahey (2003), *supra* n. 9, p. 11; IAEA, *supra* n. 13.
23. Royal Society (2001) *supra* n. 7, p. 2; DU is chemically identical to uranium, Harley et al., *supra* n. 9 , p. 57; IAEA, *supra* n. 13.
24. *ICJ Rep.* (Advisory Opinion), *Legality of the Threat or Use of Nuclear Weapons*, 1996; 35 *ILM* (1997) p. 809.

From the comprehensive description above, the only similarities between nuclear weapons and DU munitions are that they both generate ionising radiation, yet the extent of this also differs by a significant degree. Therefore, references to depleted uranium munitions as 'weapons of mass destruction'[25] emotively confuses the issue of how DU weapons are to be conceptualised in law.[26] The mere use of 'uranium' (both the word and the element itself) must not confuse the legal regime concerning DU weapons with that concerning so-called 'weapons of mass destruction'.[27] This point can be emphasised by reference to further comments in the ICJ Advisory Opinion that 'there is a qualitative as well as quantitative difference between nuclear weapons and all conventional arms'.[28] Thus, DU munitions are correctly categorised as conventional weapons and, accordingly, the legal 'regime' governing nuclear weapons does not apply.[29]

Depleted Uranium has both civilian and military uses.[30] As only limited concerns exist relating to effects of civilian uses,[31] this paper will concern itself solely with military uses of DU. An understanding of why and how DU munitions are used is essential to any further reasoning concerning the effects of such weapons. So, why use DU in munitions as opposed to any other substance? The main military uses of DU take advantage of both its physical and chemical properties.[32] Depleted Uranium, often alloyed with a small proportion of titanium, is utilised either as a hardened tip for missiles and ammunition or in kinetic energy (KE) [33] rounds, such as tank-fired Armour Piercing Fin Stabilised Discarding Sabot (APFSDS) rounds incorporating a 'penetrator' of Depleted Uranium.[34] The ten-

---

25. Written statement by International Educational Development/Humanitarian Law Project to the UN Commission on Human Rights (1999), 53rd Session, p. 1.

26. A sub-commission of the United Nations Commission on Human Rights appointed a 'rapporteur' to investigate the use of depleted uranium weapons among other types of weapons, after passing a resolution which categorised depleted uranium weapons alongside nuclear, chemical and biological weapons, napalm, and cluster bombs as a 'weapon of indiscriminate effect'. See United Nations Commission On Human Rights, *Depleted Uranium Munitions: The Use of Radiological Weapons as a Violation of Human Rights*, written statement from the International Peace Bureau and International Educational Development, (UN 1999), <http://hlp.home.igc.org/docs/depleteduranium.htm>.

27. J. Beckett, *Interim Legality: A Mistaken Assumption?* (1999) unpublished manuscript; copy on file with author, p. 6.

28. *ICJ Rep.* (Advisory Opinion), *supra* n. 24, para. 86.

29. To the extent that it could be argued that a separate legal regime exists for nuclear weapons. See for example, Y. Dinstein, *supra* n. 11, p. 77.

30. See for example IAEA at <http://www.iaea.org/worldatom/press/Focus/DU/du_qaa.shtml>; also Laka Foundation, *supra* n. 9; Zajic (1999), *supra* n. 20.

31. Possibly with the notable exception of concerns over the effects of DU caused by the crash of a Boeing 747 aircraft in Amsterdam on 4th October 1992 and in Tenerife, Canary Islands in March 1977 when two Boeing 747s crashed. DU has been used extensively in aircraft manufacture as a counterweight. See generally The Laka Foundation at <http://www.antenna.nl/wise/uranium/>; also Royal Society (2001), *supra* n. 7, p. 3.

32. Beckett, *supra* n. 27, p. 6; J.K. Kleffner, *The Use of DU and the Prohibition of Indiscriminate Attacks*' (IALANA 2000), <http://www.ialana.net/deplited_uranium.htm>.

33. Munitions that combine high velocity and density to destroy a target.

34. Armour Piercing Fin-Stabilised Discarding Sabot (APFSDS) rounds are a type of tank-fired munition without an explosive charge but combining a penetrator with a sabot that falls away from

dency of DU penetrators to 'sharpen' upon impact[35] with a hard target, due in part to its high density and pyrophoric[36] properties, has proven it to be a most efficient and destructive penetrator of armour such that it has become the armour-piercer of choice for the armed forces of many states. US and UK officials have often claimed the military necessity of DU by reference to its superior effectiveness when compared to other available penetrators such as tungsten alloy.[37]

Approximately 9,500 APFSDS main battle tank rounds were fired in *Operation Desert Storm* in 1991.[38] Each of these munitions typically contain approximately 4.5 kilograms of depleted uranium in the penetrator rod,[39] which translates to nearly 44,000 kilograms of DU expended in Kuwait, southern Iraq and on firing ranges in the Saudi Arabian desert. In total, approximately 260,000 kilograms of DU was fired in *Operation Desert Storm* and 11,250 kilograms in the Balkans.[40] Upon striking a hard target, the pyrophoric properties of DU cause a proportion of it to become aerosol and suspend in the air as uranium oxide dust.[41] It is estimated that around 20 percent of the DU penetrator is 'aerosolised' in this way.[42] The dust created may be ingested or inhaled either by combatants who survive the strike, or by other people entering the target area.[43] Around 90 percent of the uranium oxide dust created following a strike against a hard target falls to the ground within 50

---

the penetrator soon after leaving the barrel. See also Royal Society (2001), *supra* n. 7, p. 2; Fahey (2003), *supra* n. 9, p. 8, also notes the use of DU in the casing for 'bunker busting' bombs.

35. Royal Society (2001), *supra* n. 7, p. 2; H. Beach, 'The Military Hazards of Depleted Uranium', Abridged version, ISIS Policy Paper No. 78 (2001), available online at <http://www.isisuk.demon.co.uk/0811/isis/uk/regpapers/no78.html> – unabridged report cited by Fahey, *supra* n. 9, p. 1; Beckett, *supra* n. 27; See also Ministry of Defence (UK) *Depleted Uranium: The Facts* (London, MOD 2003) <http://www.mod.uk/issues/depleted_uranium/facts.htm>.

36. Fine particles can ignite spontaneously in air following frictional decay upon impact with a hard target, Harley et al., *supra* n. 9, p. 6; Kleffner, *supra* n. 32 , pp. 3-4. The fireball created can generate temperatures in the range of 200-400 degrees centigrade, Bertell in Laka Foundation, *supra* n. 9; IAEA, *supra* n. 13.

37. Fahey, *supra* n. 9, pp. 25-26 citing B. Rostker, US DoD, 'DU did have an effect on the battlefield: It undoubtedly saved thousands of American lives', 23 March 1998; Government Response to the House of Commons Defence Select Committee's Report on Gulf Veterans Illnesses, cited by Zwanenburg, *supra* n. 14, p. 10. See also Ministry of Defence (UK), *Memorandum: Gulf War Illnesses*, (London, MOD 1991) provided to the House of Commons Defence Select Committee on 26 April 2001, (London, HMSO 2001).

38. Royal Society (2001), *supra* n. 7, p. 3.

39. Ibid., p. 3.

40. Ibid., (the figure for the Balkans includes both Bosnia and Kosovo); Beckett, *supra* n. 27, p. 9; Fahey, *supra* n. 9, p. 3 suggests that the A-10 'Tank buster' aircraft has fired over 85 percent of DU ammunition in warfare.

41. Royal Society (2001), *supra* n. 7, p. 2; Zajic, *supra* n. 20.

42. Fahey, *supra* n. 9, notes that though typically between 10 percent and 35 percent of the penetrator oxidises into dust, the figure can be as high as 70 percent, yet 20 percent is the most commonly used estimate for the amount of dust created by an impact with a hard target; Harley et al., *supra* n. 9, pp. 6, 9.

43. Royal Society (2001), *supra* n. 7, p. 4; See also Ministry of Defence (UK), *Safety Instructions – Hazard Management of Depleted Uranium on Operations – Version for Open Publication*, (London, MOD 2003), <http://www.mod.uk/issues/depleted_uranium/gulf_safety_instructions.htm>.

metres of the site of impact.[44] The dust is also readily re-suspended in the air by disturbance such as by military personnel or civilians entering a target area during 'clean up' operations or to salvage re-usable equipment; by children playing in and around destroyed armour; or by environmental factors.[45]

However, as noted by Beach, it has been estimated that only 20 percent of the DU fired during *Operation Desert Storm* in 1991 struck a hard target.[46] It would also appear from UNEP investigations in the Balkans that the 'hit rate' in the operations in Bosnia and Kosovo was little improved.[47] Thus it is reasonable to assume that the majority of DU expended in combat remains either 'intact' or as fragments upon the battlefield.[48]

3. CONCERNS OVER THE USE OF DEPLETED URANIUM MUNITIONS

Depleted Uranium has a half-life of some 4.4 billion years.[49] Although total figures have not yet been released detailing the amount of DU fired in *Operation Iraqi Freedom*,[50] it is reasonable to suggest that the populations of those areas where DU has been used, are living in the midst of many tonnes of DU dust or other debris. Due to the dry conditions in the deserts of Iraq, Kuwait and Saudi Arabia, DU dust has not been leached into the soil as it has been in Kosovo but has remained to be easily resuspended by wind and human activity. This dust can be

---

44. US Army Center for Health Promotion and Preventative Medicine, No.26-MF-7555-00D cited by Fahey, *supra* n. 9, p. 9. The UK suggests that DU particulate fragments remain "highly localised to the points of impact" with a hard target, Ministry of Defence (UK), *The Misconceptions*, (London, MOD 2003), <http://www.mod.uk/issues/depleted_uranium/misconceptions.htm>. However, this opinion is somewhat contradicted by the UNEP (2002) Report which suggested that five sites investigated in Serbia and Montenegro had 'wide-spread, but low-level DU contamination', although 'wide-spread' was not quantified. See United Nations Environment Programme, 'UN Environment Programme Confirms Low-Level Depleted Uranium Contamination in Serbia and Montenegro, Urges Precautionary Measures', Press Release UNEP/105, 27 March 2002, <http://www.un.org/News/Press/docs/2002/unep105.doc.htm>.

45. Royal Society (2001), *supra* n. 7, p. 4, p. 21; United Nations Environment Programme, 'Depleted Uranium in Bosnia and Herzegovina: Post Conflict Environmental Assessment', (Geneva, UNEP 2003) p. 34; United Nations Environment Programme, *Depleted Uranium in Kosovo: Post Conflict Environmental Assessment* (Geneva, UNEP 2001) p. 31; See also comments on clearing Iraqi armour in Iraq by A. Hopkins and Capt. P. Ballard, interviewed on BBC Radio 4, 'File on 4: Depleted Uranium Fears, Programme No. 03VY3022LHO', reporter: J. Cuffe, broadcast on 3 June 2003 (transcript on file with author).

46. See Beach, *supra* n. 35, p. 14.

47. See UNEP Reports, *supra* n. 45.

48. The Iraqi government has made little attempt to clean up DU debris in southern Iraq, Fahey, *supra* n. 9, p. 15.

49. Royal Society (2001), *supra* n. 7, p. 2; IAEA, *supra* n. 13 .The 'half-life' is the time taken for half of the atoms of radioactive substance to decay or be absorbed.

50. The UK Ministry of Defence has confirmed the use of approximately 1.9 tonnes of DU by Challenger Main Battle Tanks during '*Operation Telic*', Ministry of Defence (UK), *OP TELIC Middle East DU Brief*, (London, MOD 2003), <http://www.mod.uk/issues/depleted_uranium/index.htm>.

inhaled into the lungs or can find its way into the soil and, eventually, plant matter which itself can be ingested, and subsequently concentrated internally in both livestock and humans. DU also corrodes and may therefore enter water supplies and thus the agricultural cycle.[51]

In its Post Conflict Environmental Assessments of Kosovo and Bosnia and Herzegovina, the United Nations Environment Programme (UNEP) has suggested that if the amount of uranium leached into groundwater and soil increased 100-fold, this could imply that the concentration of uranium would exceed the WHO standards for drinking water.[52] In its Post-Conflict Assessment of Serbia and Montenegro following the NATO action in 1999, the UNEP has reported that '[DU] contamination in the targeted sites is [geographically] widespread'.[53] As noted by Kleffner, due to the long half-life of DU, once in the soil or watercourses, DU will remain until removed.[54]

3.1 The behaviour of depleted uranium in the human body

From the outset, it should be noted that scant data exists specifically examining the long-term effects of exposure to DU in humans.[55] The chemical and radiological effects of uranium have been comprehensively studied for decades through epidemiological studies of uranium miners and workers.[56] As the chemical properties of depleted uranium and 'natural' uranium are identical, such studies relating to chemical effects of DU on human health can be deduced from existing data.[57] However, the radiological properties of DU differ quite significantly from those of natural uranium suggesting that the studies carried out to date concerning radiation effects of uranium on human health may not be transferable to the radiation effects of DU. In particular, in contrast to uranium, the uranium oxide dust created when DU burns (such as in the explosion following contact with a hard target) is insoluble.[58]

---

51. Royal Society (2002), *supra* n. 7, p. 21; UNEP (2003), *supra* n. 45, pp. 30-38; UNEP, 'Depleted Uranium in Serbia and Montenegro: Post Conflict Environmental Assessment' (Geneva, UNEP 2002) p. 27, cited in Fahey, *supra* n. 9, p. 10; UNEP (2001), *supra* n. 45, pp. 27-31. See also *The Observer* (2003), *supra* n. 4, citing calls for water and milk in the Basra area of Iraq to be monitored for levels of radioactivity following the use of DU shells in *Operation Iraqi Freedom*. This precaution was also suggested by Dr Brian Spratt, chairman of the Royal Society working group on DU, see *The Guardian* (2003), *supra* n. 4.

52. UNEP, *supra* n. 51, p. 34.

53. UNEP, *supra* n. 45.

54. See Kleffner, *supra* n. 32, p. 3. See also Royal Society (2002), *supra* n. 7, regarding the environmental effects of corroding DU leaching into ground water and enduring in soil.

55. Beral and Darby in Royal Society (2001), *supra* n. 7, at Appendix III, p. 77; Harley et al., *supra* n. 9, p. 69.

56. IAEA, *supra* n. 13; See also Harley et al., *supra* n. 9.

57. See in particular, Royal Society (2001), *supra* n. 7; Royal Society (2002), *supra* n. 7; and Harley et al., *supra* n. 9.

58. Kleffner, *supra* n. 32, p. 3.

The danger to health of ionising radiation such as that found in DU is derived from the energy it dissipates to biological matter,[59] as was also recognised explicitly by the ICJ in its *Nuclear Weapons* Advisory Opinion.[60] The dominant radiation from DU consists of alpha particles, yet significant amounts of beta and gamma radiation are also present. Further, DU may also contain trace amounts of more dangerously radioactive elements such as plutonium, uranium-236 and americium from contamination during the enrichment process for nuclear fuels or weapons production.[61] However, concentrations of these elements are so small as to be largely insignificant in comparison to the DU present.[62] Though alpha radiation can be shielded by a leaf of paper and is unable to penetrate the skin, it is more harmful if internalised.[63] Highly energetic beta radiation is capable of travelling up to 1cm through skin into soft tissue,[64] and exposure to the more penetrating gamma radiation will occur even at a 'considerable distance' from the source of DU.[65]

Once in the body, as DU is insoluble, it will not pass into the urine but will instead be carried by the blood and deposited internally.[66] It will consequently irradiate surrounding tissue as it moves through the body and when concentrated in the kidneys, liver, lungs, lymph nodes and bone.[67] It has not been proven that either uranium or depleted uranium are themselves carcinogenic. Rather, it is the radioactive decay of the element that causes cell deterioration which may eventually manifest itself as cancer.[68]

3.2 Concerns over the effects on human health

Before detailing the concerns over the possible health effects of DU, it may be instructive to attempt to establish 'who' has raised such concerns. Space precludes a comprehensive investigation of this subject, suffice to say that 'concern' – of various sorts – has been registered by virtually every sector of modern society

---

59. Harley et al., *supra* n. 9, p. 4.
60. *ICJ Rep*. (Advisory Opinion), *supra* n. 24, at para. 35.
61. Royal Society (2001), *supra* n. 7, p. 3; IAEA, *supra* n. 13; See also NATO Press Statement of 18 January 2001, <http://www.nato.int/docu/pr/2001/p01-006e.htm>.
62. NATO, ibid., citing UNEP findings; IAEA, *supra* n. 13, suggests 'very low levels' of impurities have been detected in DU.
63. Royal Society (2001), *supra* n. 7, p. 11; Harley et al., *supra* n. 9, p. 4.
64. Royal Society (2001), *supra* n. 7, p. 3.
65. Ibid., although the term 'considerable distance' is not quantified.
66. Kleffner, *supra* n. 32, p. 4.
67. Harley et al., *supra* n. 9, pp. 14-18 provides a very comprehensive explanation of this process; See also Royal Society (2001), *supra* n. 7, p. 6.
68. Royal Society (2001), *supra* n. 7, p. 11.

from international organisations,[69] governments,[70] armed forces[71] and national parliaments,[72] through virtually all forms of the modern media,[73] to the general public and academia. At the same time, states have often sought to counter such concerns. The attribution of reported increases in childhood cancers and birth abnormalities in southern Iraq since 1991[74] to the effects of DU is disputed by the US and UK who maintain that, if any toxic effects are to blame for such calamities, it is more likely due to the presence of chemical plants in the south of the country.[75] Anecdotal claims of Iraqi doctors attributing incidences of poor health among the civilian population to DU[76] remain unsupported by any scientific evidence and have also been dismissed as propaganda at the instigation of the former Iraqi regime.[77] At the same time, the risks to personnel of DU, in particular, military personnel exposed to ionising radiation through handling DU munitions in storage and loading and

69. See for example, ICTY, 'Final Report to the Prosecutor by the Committee Established to Review the NATO Bombing Campaign Against the Federal Republic of Yugoslavia' (39 *ILM* (2000) p. 1257) <http://www.un.org/icty/pressreal/nato061300.htm>; 'NATO North Atlantic Military Committee/Committee of the Chiefs of the Military Medical Services in NATO (COMEDS)', <http://www.nato.int/du/docu/d010124c.htm>; See also UNEP 'Reports on Post-Conflict Environmental Assessments regarding the effects of DU', UNEP (2000), (2001) and (2002). See also *ICJ Rep.* (Request For The Indication Of Provisional Measures), *Case Concerning Legality of Use of Force (Yugoslavia* v. *United States of America)*, General List No. 114, 1999.

70. In the UK, the government has responded to 'concerns'; expressed in various quarters by establishing, *inter alia*, the Gulf War Veterans Medical Assessment Programme (GVMAP). In the USA, the Department of Defense established the Office of the Special Assistant for Gulf War Illnesses, see <http://www.gulflink.osd.mil/>; See also Ministry of Defence (UK), Proposal for a Research Programme on Depleted Uranium, (MOD 2002), <http://www.mod.uk/issues/depleted_uranium/du_research.htm>, and, more generally, Department of Defense (US) (2003) 'Depleted Uranium Information Page', <http://www.deploymentlink.osd.mil/du_library/>.

71. See for example, MOD signal of 25 February 1991, 'Advise as follows. Wear industrial type IPE [Individual Protective Equipment] with particulate RPE [Respiratory Protective Equipment], canister, gloves and overalls', Ministry of Defence (UK), 'Signal on Precautionary Measures', dated 25 February 1991 from MoD UK (Army) to Commander Medical at 1st UK Armoured Division, <http://www.mod.uk/issues/depleted_uranium/gulf_1.htm>.

72. House of Commons Foreign Affairs Committee stated that '[w]hether or not depleted uranium is lawful, it has potentially deleterious effects on the environment and human health' cited by Zwanenburg, *supra* n. 14, p. 11.; See also House of Commons Defence Select Committee (2001).

73. BBC Radio, *supra* n. 45, reported that several Italian servicemen who had served as peacekeepers in Kosovo have died of leukaemia, see n. 9; see also articles by Fisk, *supra* n. 4; The Berlin-based Depleted Uranium Centre, has suggested that the incidence of lymphoma is greater among Italian veterans of the Kosovo conflict than would be expected in a similar sized cohort of the general population. See also Laka Foundation, *supra* n. 9.

74. UNICEF/Government of Iraq, Ministry of Public Health, *Child and Maternal Mortality Survey* (Baghdad, UNICEF 1999) <http://www.unicef.org>; See also Fisk, *supra* n. 4; See also <http://www.iacenter.org>.

75. BBC Radio, *supra* n. 45; Ministry of Defence (UK) *supra* n. 50.

76. Republic of Iraq, Ministry of Higher Education and Scientific Research (2002), <http://www.idust.org/> cited by Fahey, *supra* n. 9, p. 15.

77. Fahey, ibid.; Beach, *supra* n. 35, p. 5 also cites William Arkin, Director of Military Research for Greenpeace International who noted that, 'once inside Iraq and away from the Baghdad propaganda regime, the story [of alleged effects of DU on the civilian population] simply evaporated', Arkin, 'The desert glows – with propaganda', 49 *Bulletin of Atomic Scientists* (1993) No. 4.

clean up of DU,[78] have been clearly and publicly recognised by the military in both the UK[79] and USA.[80]

Since concerns over the possible detrimental health effects of DU were first raised in the early 1990s, several attempts have been made to resolve them through the commission of independent studies to investigate the issue. In recognition of the 'persistent'[81] reports of illnesses in Gulf War veterans, and concerns linking such illnesses to the effects of DU on the environment and human health, the reports of the British-based Royal Society on the 'Health Hazards of Depleted Uranium Munitions', published in 2001 and 2002,[82] provide an independent review of the contemporary scientific knowledge regarding the health and environmental effects of DU in order to 'inform the public debate'.[83] In the United States, the seventh volume of the RAND 'Review of the Scientific Literature Pertaining to Gulf War Illnesses'[84] was commissioned by the Department for Defense following concerns that illnesses reported by veterans of *Operation Desert Storm* may be attributable to the use of depleted uranium.[85] Together, the eight RAND reviews constitute an aetiology of many factors which may have contributed to Gulf War illnesses from chemical and biological warfare agents,[86] to immunisations[87] to oil well fires.[88]

These 'official' investigations to date agree, unsurprisingly, that health concerns associated with DU are linked to its toxic and radiological effects.[89] Estimates of the toxic effects of DU have been extrapolated from previous studies of the effects

---

78. Royal Society (2001), *supra* n. 7, p. 8; Ministry of Defence (UK), *supra* n. 71; Ministry of Defence (UK) *supra* n. 43.

79. Dr Lewis Moonie; evidence to the House of Commons Defence Committee, 'Gulf Veterans Illnesses and Depleted Uranium', *Minutes of Evidence*, 9 May 2001, (London, House of Commons – The Stationery Office Limited 2001) p. 10.

80. See US DoD/Deployment Health Clinical Center, 'Depleted Uranium Information for Service Members and Their Families', Washington DC, 17 September 2004, US DoD, in particular the section entitled 'Safe Handling and Use of DU'. Also see 'Memorandum for Secretaries of the Military Departments; Chairmen of the Joint Chiefs of Staff; Under Secretary of Defense for Acquisition, Technology and Logistics; Assistant Secretary of Defense for Health Affairs; Director, Defense Research and Engineering', Washington DC, US DoD 6 February 2004 and in particular, attachment 3, 'Guidance and Procedures for Depleted Uranium (DU) Bioassay DU Urine Analysis', December 1, 2003, which states that 'Depleted Uranium is one of many potentially hazardous substances that personnel may encounter during deployment and combat operations. … there is still a theoretical risk for radiation-induced health effects from inhaling or ingesting DU aerosols or residues'.

81. Royal Society (2001), *supra* n. 7, p. 1.

82. Part I, Royal Society (2001), *supra* n. 7, deals with the amounts of DU to which combat personnel may reasonably be exposed on the battlefield and radiation doses. Part II, Royal Society (2002), *supra* n. 7, addresses the risks of toxic poisoning and environmental issues.

83. Royal Society (2001), *supra* n. 7, p. vii. and p. 1.

84. Harley et al., *supra* n. 9.

85. Ibid., p. v.

86. See RAND, Vol. 5.

87. See RAND, Vol. 3.

88. See RAND, Vol. 6.

89. Harley et al., *supra* n. 9, p. 57; see also Ministry of Defence (UK) signal, *supra* n. 71, which states that: 'Two potential health risks from DU oxide dusts exist. First, irradiation from alpha particles … second, [from] heavy metal [toxicity].'

of uranium as both substances have identical chemical properties. The effects of DU on human health due to radiation are most detrimental when it is internalised by one of three means; ingestion, inhalation or by embedded fragments (shrapnel) in wounds.[90] Studies have suggested that the body is very effective at eliminating ingested uranium through internal renal dissolution[91] yet, as was noted above, uranium oxide dust is *insoluble* and is consequently more likely to accumulate in the body. This suggests that the urine tests employed by the UK Ministry of Defence[92] and US Department of Defense[93] to determine the levels of DU exposure in Gulf War veterans may be a very crude way of determining the level of exposure as very little of the internalised DU dust will have been dissolved in the urine.[94] The Royal Society suggests that possibly the greatest risk to human health would be from lung cancer through inhaled DU dust being deposited in the soft tissue of the lungs.[95] The Royal Society study also highlighted the dangers to civilians, and children in particular, of an increased risk in skin cancers due to handling of DU fragments found on the battlefield.[96]

Part I of the Royal Society study found that exposure to 'large quantities' of DU oxide dust would be likely to cause an increase in the incidences of some cancers and, possibly, leukaemia,[97] a finding that has been reiterated by the World Health Organisation.[98] However, such large quantities are unlikely to be found on the battlefield, even in the 'worst case' scenario envisaged by the Royal Society, leading them to conclude that the actual increase in the incidence of cancers among cohorts of soldiers would be very slight.[99] Reaching a similar conclusion, the RAND study suggests that no links between DU and adverse effects on human health have been proven.[100] However, the second Royal Society report raises the possibility that certain 'hotspots of contamination' on former battlefields could lead to an increased amount of *compound* ingestion of DU by the civilian population which may have subsequent toxic effects.[101] As has been previously alluded to by reference to the dangers to children and other civilians of handling DU fragments, targets struck

---

90. Harley et al., *supra* n. 9, p. 1, p. 13; Ministry of Defence (UK), *supra* n. 43.

91. Harley et al., *supra* n. 9, p. 69.

92. See Depleted Uranium Oversight Board website at <http://www.duob.org.uk/>.

93. See US DoD 'Urine Testing for Depleted Uranium' May 2004, <https://chppm-www.apgea.army.mil/documents/UrineTesting.pdf>.

94. See Professor Albrecht Schott's contribution to the Lloyd Inquiry, *supra* n. 5, at para. 135. See also the website of the World Depleted Uranium Centre for other comments by Professor Schott, <http://www.woduc.de/Html/Frameset_EN.htm>.

95. Royal Society (2001), *supra* n. 7, p. 21.

96. Ibid., McClain et al., also suggested that children may be most susceptible to exposure to expended DU and subsequent health risks, McClain et al., *The Science of the Total Environment*, cited by Fahey, *supra* n. 9, p. 10.

97. Royal Society (2001), *supra* n. 7, p. 21.

98. World Health Organisation, *Depleted Uranium: Sources, Exposure and Health Effects* (Geneva, World Health Organisation 2001) p.84.

99. Royal Society (2001), *supra* n. 7, p. 22; Ministry of Defence (UK), *supra* n. 44. See also *The Guardian*, *supra* n. 4.

100. Harley et al., *supra* n. 9.

101. Royal Society (2002*), supra* n. 7, p. 27.

and destroyed by DU rounds in Iraq have presented a potential health hazard to the civilian population following the end of hostilities.[102] With this in mind, it should be noted that military personnel are supposedly[103] provided with safety instructions advising of precautions to be taken while handling DU and in the event of coming into contact with DU dust.[104] However, safety warnings are not routinely disseminated to the civilian population.[105] Therefore, how are children playing around burned-out tanks to know of the possible dangers of the effects of DU?

3.3 Temporal and evidential factors

Both the Royal Society and RAND studies recommend further research, including long-term epidemiological and aetiological studies of people, both military and civilian, who may have come into contact with DU.[106] Dr Brian Spratt, chair of the Royal Society panel and also a member of the UK Depleted Uranium Oversight Board, has consistently called for more research into the effects of DU.[107] Similarly, the need for long-term, comprehensive epidemiological studies into the ef-

---

102. Fahey, *supra* n. 9, p. 15. It should also be noted, however, that little in the way of objective, verifiable epidemiological studies of these groups has been undertaken.

103. However, as reported by Jenny Cuffe on BBC Radio 4, *supra* n. 45, in the recent *Operation Telic*, 'some troops were never told about DU and never given any safety instructions'. See also a report following the Kosovo crisis that briefing documents on the dangers of DU ammunition to be provided to UK troops were scrapped; see BBC News Online, '*Troops "not told" about uranium risks*', 7 February 2001, <http://news.bbc.co.uk/1/hi/uk_politics/1159218.stm>.

104. Ministry of Defence (UK), *supra* n. 43; Ministry of Defence (UK), *supra* n. 71; BBC Radio (2003), *supra* n. 45. See also letters from then Minister of State for the Armed Forces Jeremy Hanley MP which confirm that safety instructions were issued to some UK troops in the 1991 Gulf conflict yet, surprisingly, also confirm that these instructions were not disseminated to tank crews, J. Hanley , MP, *Letter to Paul Flynn Esq, MP*, dated 13 July 1993, (London, House of Commons Library) Ref. D/MIN(AF)/JH/5/3/3 and 1/1/1. See also Hansard, 20 July 1993, Col. 182, *DU Ammunition Instructions*, Written Parliamentary Question from Dr David Clark MP to Mr Jeremy Hanley MP (Minister of State for the Armed Forces), (London, Hansard 1993); Hansard, 5 July 1993, Col. 59, *DU Ammunition Instructions*, Written Parliamentary Question from Mr George Foulkes MP to Mr Jeremy Hanley MP (Minister of State for the Armed Forces) , (London, Hansard 1993); Hansard, 23 June 1993, Col. 194, *DU Ammunition Instructions*, Written Parliamentary Question from Mr Paul Flynn MP to Mr Jeremy Hanley MP (Minister of State for the Armed Forces), (London, Hansard, 1993).

105. See, however, International Committee of the Red Cross, 'Depleted Uranium Munitions: Comments of the International Committee of the Red Cross', (Geneva, ICRC 2001) <http//www.icrc.org> which requests ICRC Staff to 'to share these [safety] instructions with others, including the resident population'. 'It should be incumbent upon nations using DU munitions in future conflicts to advise the local population of the potential dangers of handling fragments of penetrators', Royal Society (2001), *supra* n. 7, 'Recommendations', p. 24; Regarding the responsibility to 'clean up' following the end of hostilities, see Ministry of Defence (UK), *supra* n. 50, which, citing 'customary understanding', suggests that the UK is under no obligation to clean up DU debris in Iraq, though acknowledges the responsibility of the US and UK forces, as occupying powers, to protect the civilian population. See also *The Observer* (2003), *supra* n. 4.

106. Royal Society (2001), *supra* n. 7, p. 23 suggests that any monitoring scheme for soldiers exposed to DU should be undertaken by a 'mechanism that is seen to be completely independent of government'; Royal Society (2002), *supra* n. 7, citing 'major uncertainties' at present, p. 26; Harley et al., *supra* n. 9.

107. BBC Radio (2003), *supra* n. 45.

fects DU and its progress through various human and environmental media has on human health in the long term has been highlighted by both studies[108] as well as being recognised by the UK Ministry of Defence.[109]

As is so often the case, both 'sides' of the debate have claimed vindication of their respective standpoints by reference to the reports conducted to date in the UK and USA. Governments have highlighted the findings that no concrete link between DU and adverse health effects has been found. For example, the Pentagon has stated that 'no cancers or leukaemia' have been identified in groups of US Balkans veterans.[110] Yet this statement has been contested due to a case of Hodgkin's lymphoma in one US veteran[111] and cases of leukaemia in Italian veterans of Kosovo.[112] Opponents of the use of DU have similarly noted the recommendations in both reports that further research be conducted before categorical conclusions are drawn.[113] In short, far from being resolved, the debate has endured. Therefore, in the light of this fact, and as noted by General Sir Hugh Beach,[114] it seems that it is difficult to be absolutely confident that DU is not responsible for any adverse health effects.

3.4 The dangers of sensationalising the debate

A US veteran of *Operation Desert Storm* in 1991, and legal adviser to other veterans, Dan Fahey, has recently attempted to inform the public debate by debunking the extremes on both sides of the DU fence so as to present a factual representation of the realities of use of the munitions.[115] Fahey is especially critical of 'anti-DU activists' whom he accuses of having mixed fact with propaganda and sometimes apocalyptic speculation which, though relatively easy to dispel due to a lack of credible evidence, has nonetheless 'stirred public concern'.[116] Yet Fahey's criticism is not limited to those campaigning against DU. Officials of the US Department of Defense have been accused of deliberately deceiving the public[117] and similarly, governments have been accused of being 'economical with the truth' over the effects of DU, and even of wilfully providing misinformation.[118] Such extremes of

---

108. Beckett, *supra* n. 27, p. 9; Harley et al., *supra* n. 9, p. 71.
109. See information on GVMAP, Ministry of Defence (UK), *supra* n. 50.
110. Dr. Michael Kilpatrick speaking at a NATO Press Briefing, Brussels, 10 January 2001 cited by Fahey, *supra* n. 9, p. 23; For a UK denial of cause and effect, see Ministry of Defence (UK), *supra* n. 50, and comments by MoD Chief Medical Advisor Sir Keith O'Nions, interviewed on BBC Radio, *supra* n. 45.
111. Fahey, *supra* n. 9, p.23.
112. BBC Radio, *supra* n. 45. See also BBC News Online, 'Italy demands answers on DU', by Ben Brown, 10 January 2001, <http://news.bbc.co.uk/1/hi/world/Europe/1109877.stm>; See also *The Observer* (2003), *supra* n. 4.
113. Harley et al., *supra* n. 9, at p. xiii.
114. Beach, *supra* n. 35, p. 12; BBC Radio, *supra* n. 45.
115. See Fahey, *supra* n. 9, in particular at p. 5.
116. Ibid., pp. 3-4.
117. Ibid., p. 3; Also Dan Fahey, interviewed on BBC Radio 4, *supra* n. 45.
118. Beach, *supra* n. 35 – unabridged report cited by Fahey, *supra* n. 9, p. 12.

opinion, often unsubstantiated by credible, objective evidence do little but polarise the debate and make objective reasoning more difficult.

It has already been noted that some references to the health effects and nature of DU munitions could be interpreted as sensationalist or alarmist. Such references to 'weapons of mass destruction'[119] and the media reporting of some postulated effects of DU are essentially detrimental to the reasoned, rational debate which has its proper place in evaluating genuine concerns. For example, in the period prior to the 1999 NATO action in Kosovo, a BBC report quoted a British scientist claiming that the 'use of depleted uranium weapons in the war with Serbia is likely to cause 10,000 extra deaths from cancer' and predicting a six month delay before the increased incidences of cancers and leukaemia manifests itself in the civilian and veteran populations.[120] Yet more than three years after the end of hostilities in Kosovo, no evidence of such an 'explosion'[121] in cancers has been found. Describing the use of DU use as a 'war crime'[122] or 'genocide'[123] is so excessively erroneous as to be far-fetched but must also surely be demeaning to such human tragedies as do warrant that title.

4. EVALUATION OF RELEVANT LAW

In contemporary international law, as determined by the will and actions of states, it must be debatable whether the maxim *hominum causa omne jus constitutum est*[124] is truly apposite. As will become clear *infra*, however, the reasoning of this part of the paper is predicated on the assumption that international humanitarian law is indeed created for the benefit of humanity.

It is further prudent to note that, for the purposes of this paper, the consideration of the law relating to the use of weapons will necessarily be confined to the laws regulating the actual conduct of hostilities – the *jus in bello*.[125] It is not within the scope of this paper to comment upon the *jus ad bellum* aspects of various conflicts in which DU was deployed, and suffice it to reiterate the finding of the ICJ in the *Nuclear Weapons* Advisory Opinion that the use of any weapon does not make it

119. See *supra* n. 26.

120. Roger Coghill quoted in a report by Alex Kirby, *supra* n. 6.

121. See, *inter alia*, media reports cited *supra* n. 4.

122. See Comments by Dr Doug Rokke, former Director of the US Army Depleted Uranium (DU) Project, <http://traprockpeace.org/depleteduranium.html>.

123. See ibid.; also J. Hasslberger, 'Depleted Uranium – Silent genocide to haunt perpetrators', <http://www.newmediaexplorer.org/sepp/2003/08/05/depleted_uranium_silent_genocide_to_haunt_-perpetratorshtm>; also R.C. Koehler, *Silent Genocide*, <http://www.informationclearinghouse.info/article5941.htm>.

124. Translation: All law is created for the benefit of mankind.

125. For example, evaluation of the law of 'new' weapons is within the *jus in bello* as noted by Y. Sandoz, C. Swinarski and B. Zimmermann, eds., *Commentary on the Additional Protocols of 8 June 1977 to the Geneva Conventions of 12 August 1949* (Geneva, Martinus Nijhoff 1987) p. 424.

lawful 'by reason of its being used for a legitimate purpose under the [United Nations] Charter'.[126]

The three fundamental principles of the *jus in bello* are; a) that a belligerent is justified in applying any amount of force necessary to achieve a specific military objective (the principle of necessity); b) all means and methods of warfare that are not necessary for achieving the military objective are not permitted (the principle of humanity); and, c) that a degree of mutual respect for the enemy should prevail and provide for fairness in the contention between belligerents (the principle of chivalry).[127] In short, therefore, within the overall regime of the principle of chivalry, the 'only' constraints to the waging of warfare are humanitarian considerations. Yet the balance to be struck between humanitarian considerations on the one side and military considerations on the other demonstrates what Kalshoven has termed the 'awkward relationship between war and humanity',[128] to which IHL attempts to provide clarity.

This part will firstly introduce the fundamental principles of international law relevant to the creation of (il)legality and a brief note on the relationship between law, ethics and morals. The chapter then continues to examine in turn the 'cardinal principles'[129] of IHL; firstly, the prohibition on causing superfluous injury or unnecessary suffering; and secondly, that of distinction. After consideration of the significance of the Martens Clause, it will be necessary to consider how the legality of 'new' weapons is determined. This part will address how the provisions concerning the legality of new weapons have been, and may yet be, applied to DU munitions.

4.1 General principles of international humanitarian law

The positivism that characterises international law dictates that state consent is ultimately required to create illegality[130] such that the legality of DU is presumed.[131] The *Lotus* case thus found that restrictions on sovereign states cannot be presumed, with the implication that that which is not subject to prohibition in law

---

126. ICJ Rep. (Advisory Opinion), *supra* n. 24, para.39. UN Charter and Statute of the ICJ (1945), <http://www.un.org/aboutun/charter/>.

127. H. Lauterpacht, ed., *International Law: A Treatise, Vol. II: Disputes, War and Neutrality*, by L. Oppenheim, 7th edn. (London, Longmans 1952) p. 227.

128. F. Kalshoven, *Constraints on the Waging of War* (Geneva, ICRC/Martinus Nijhoff 1987) p. 160; see also Zwanenburg, *supra* n. 14.

129. *ICJ Rep.* (Advisory Opinion), *supra* n. 24, para. 78. See also M. Mohr, 'Advisory Opinion of the International Court of Justice on the legality of the use of nuclear weapons under international law – 'A few thought on its strengths and weaknesses', *International Review of the Red Cross*, No. 316 (Geneva, ICRC 1997).

130. See R. Ticehurst 'The Martens Clause and the Laws of Armed Conflict', *International Review of the Red Cross*, No. 317 (Geneva, ICRC 1997) pp. 125-134; also Brierly in D.J. Harris, *Cases and Materials on International Law*, (London, Sweet & Maxwell 1998) pp. 1-5, also pp. 5-20 and pp. 47-51; J. Lau, *Brief Introduction to the* Ius in Bello *concerning Depleted Uranium Weapons* (2000), <http://www.ialana.net/breif_introduction.htm>; Sandoz et al., *supra* n. 125, p. 406; Beckett, *supra* n. 27, p. 3; International Military Tribunal, Nuremberg (1945).

131. The *nullem crimen sine lege* principle has its origins in criminal law.

must be permitted by law.[132] However, contemporary interpretation of IHL may suggest a move away from presumed legality.[133] This issue will be addressed further in the following part. A further demonstration of positivism is encapsulated in the principle of *pacta sunt servanda*[134] which, in simple terms, determines that sovereign states are bound only by those principles to which they have *agreed* to be bound.[135] International treaties expressly prohibit some means and methods of warfare, yet customary law also provides restrictions on the rights of states in their waging of war.[136] However, in the light of the emergence of increasing numbers of law-creating treaties since 1945, there often exists a contention between customary law and treaty law.[137]

As it has been consistently argued that international law has no hierarchy of sources,[138] there arises a conflict between those provisions and principles of international law by which states have consented to be bound, and those by which they are assumed to be bound by virtue of the existence of a customary rule. This contention is particularly notable where a state may have 'persistently objected' to the emergence or formation of a customary rule.[139] This should therefore be borne in mind when evaluating principles of the law, in particular those provisions provided by the 1977 Protocols Additional to the Geneva Conventions of 1949,[140] to which the USA, for one, is not a party.

Lauterpacht notes that, 'apart from those expressly prohibited by treaties or custom, all means of killing and wounding that exist, or may be invented, are lawful'.[141] However, it is possible to argue that existing, mainly customary, principles of IHL provide grounds for restrictions on the use of DU munitions. Therefore, in line with Article 38(1) of the Statute of the ICJ, in any case attempting to establish the legality of the use of a weapon, we must look to treaties and custom as the primary sources for express (or implied) prohibition.[142]

---

132. *PCIJ Rep., France* v. *Turkey* (1927), Series A, No.10; see also Beckett, *supra* n. 27, p. 12; Zwanenburg, *supra* n. 14, p. 6.

133. Beckett, *supra* n. 27, p. 36.

134. Art. 26 of the 1969 Vienna Convention on the Law of Treaties states that 'Every treaty in force is binding upon the parties to it and must be performed by them in good faith.'

135. For more information on the International Law of Treaties, see A. Aust, *Modern Treaty Law and Practice*, (Cambridge, Cambridge University Press 2000), and the 1969 Vienna Convention on the Law of Treaties.

136. Lauterpacht, *supra* n. 127, p. 340.

137. See Aust, *supra* n. 135, pp. 11-12.

138. See Art. 38(1) of the Statute of the International Court of Justice (1945); Also Schwarzenburger (1957) cited in Harris, *supra* n. 130, pp. 21-22.

139. For a more detailed explanation. See J. Charney, 'The Persistent Objector Rule and the Development of Customary International Law', 56 *BYIL* 1985, pp.1-24.

140. International Committee of the Red Cross, *Protocols of 8 June 1977 Additional to the Geneva Conventions of 12 August 1949*, (Geneva, ICRC 1996), hereafter the First Additional Protocol. See also International Committee of the Red Cross, *The Geneva Conventions of 12 August 1949*, (Geneva, ICRC 1996).

141. H. Lauterpacht, ed., *supra* n. 127, p. 340.

142. See Schwarzenberger in Harris, *supra* n. 130, pp. 21-24 and pp. 1067-1079.

It is difficult to contradict the assertion of the former UK Minister of State for Veterans Affairs that 'there is no question of these weapons being illegal'[143] due to a lack of a *lex scripta* prohibition. As was determined by the ICTY *Review of the NATO Bombing of the Federal Republic of Yugoslavia*, '[t]here is no specific treaty ban on the use of DU projectiles'.[144]

The customary[145] rule regulating the means and methods to which a belligerent may resort during warfare is Article 22 of the Hague Regulations of 1907, specifically that '[t]he right of belligerents to adopt means of injuring the enemy is not unlimited'. This principle, which some have suggested may form the entire foundation of the international humanitarian law of armed conflict,[146] has its origins in the necessity of *temperamenti belli*,[147] as postulated by Grotius[148] in the Seventeenth Century. The principle was restated in the First Additional Protocol as Article 35(1) which refines the lexicon thus: 'In any armed conflict, the right of the Parties to the conflict to choose methods or means of warfare is not unlimited,'[149] and was confirmed by the ICJ in its *Nuclear Weapons* Advisory Opinion that: 'States do not have unlimited freedom of choice of means in the weapons they use.'[150]

In reviewing the influence the principles of law evaluated below may have on DU, it is prudent to note the relationship between law, ethics and morals. Principles of humanity, ethics and morals are not merely the historical foundations of the law but rather form part of the laws of war although there is some contention regarding the 'decisive relevance' of these principles.[151] Brierly has gone so far as to suggest that 'international law should be characterised as a branch of ethics rather than law',[152] yet what is important is that our reflections on our contemporary understanding of the law should be informed by and respect their ethical and moral foundations.

4.2 The prohibition on causing superfluous injury or unnecessary suffering

In its *Nuclear Weapons* Advisory Opinion, the ICJ noted that, '... humanitarian law, at a very early stage, prohibited certain types of weapons either because of their indiscriminate effect on combatants and civilians or because of the unneces-

---

143. Dr Lewis Moonie MP, at the time Minister of State at the UK Ministry of Defence, speaking on BBC Radio 4, *supra* n. 45.

144. ICTY, *supra* n. 69, Section A, part ii.

145. Sandoz et al., *supra* n. 125, p. 391.

146. Kalshoven, *supra* n. 128, p. 29.

147. Imposing limitations on the destructive power of weapons.

148. Grotius, *De iure belli ac pacis* [The Laws of War and Peace] (1625); Sandoz et al., *supra* n. 125, p. 390.

149. ICRC, *supra* n. 140.

150. *ICJ Rep.* (Advisory Opinion), *supra* n. 24, para. 78.

151. Lauterpacht, *supra* n. 127, p. 348 and pp.350-352 with regard to the legality of atomic weapons.

152. Brierly, 'The Law of Nations' in Harris, *supra* n. 130, p. 2.

sary suffering caused to combatants, that is to say, a harm greater than that unavoidable to achieve legitimate military objectives'.[153]

Article 35(2) of the First Additional Protocol of 1977 restates the prohibition of employment of methods or means of warfare 'of a nature to cause superfluous injury or unnecessary suffering'[154] which was first recognised by States Parties to the St. Petersburg Declaration of 1868.[155] It should also be noted that, far from being an anachronism representative of an earlier era of international law, the principles encapsulated in the St. Petersburg Declaration were vociferously defended by delegates to the Lucerne conference of 1974, which was a precursor to the adoption of the 1977 Additional Protocols,[156] where it was also suggested that 'some sort of equation between, on the one hand, ... the humanitarian aspect ... and, on the other, ... the military aspect'[157] was required.

As far as the moral and legal constraints on military necessity are concerned, the defeat of the enemy is the aim of waging war, which can be achieved by killing or wounding enemy combatants, or by the taking of prisoners of war.[158] However, the St. Petersburg Declaration suggests that disablement (wounding) alone should be sufficient in the waging of war, and that in so wounding, there is a limit to the amount of suffering a combatant should endure. This suffering should not be 'unnecessary', and the injuries inflicted should not be 'superfluous'[159] to the necessities of war. The principle of proportionality is also inherently encapsulated within these provisions. As has previously been noted, the ICJ in the *Nuclear Weapons* case has confirmed the principle prohibiting superfluous injury and unnecessary suffering as an 'intransgressible principle of international customary law'.[160]

---

153. *ICJ Rep.* (Advisory Opinion), *supra* n. 24, para. 78; Lauterpacht, *supra* n. 127, p. 340, also confirms that 'all means are *unlawful* that needlessly aggravate the sufferings of wounded combatants', emphasis added.

154. Art. 35(2), Additional Protocol I (1977), *supra* n. 140. Note that the ICRC Study on Customary International Humanitarian Law suggests that, '[s]tate practice establishes this rule as a norm of customary international law applicable in both international and non-international armed conflicts', see J-M Henckaerts and L. Doswald-Beck, *Customary International Humanitarian Law, Volume 1: Rules* (Geneva, ICRC 2005) Rule 70, p. 237.

155. See Preamble to the 1868 St. Petersburg Declaration. The St. Petersburg Declaration provides the first example of the 'international community' specifically prohibiting a weapon. Though the weapon to which the declaration refers (explosive projectiles under 400 grammes in weight) ceases to be relevant in modern warfare, the principles established in the Declaration are recognised to be 'overtly humanitarian' and are thus, contemporaneously significant. See for example, McCoubrey in M.A Meyer, ed., *Armed Conflict and the New Law: Aspects of the 1977 Geneva Protocols and the 1981 Weapons Convention* (London, Chameleon Press 1989) p. 45.

156. See for example, the position of the Swedish delegate, Dr. Hans Blix in the negotiations, F. Kalshoven in M. Meyer, ed., *supra* n. 155, pp. 258-261.

157. Conference of Government Experts on the Use of Certain Conventional Weapons (1975) cited in R. Cryer, 'The Fine Art of Friendship: *Jus in Bello* in Afghanistan', 7 *JConSL* (2002) p. 57; see also Kalshoven, *supra* n. 128; Zwanenburg, *supra* n. 14.

158. L.C. Green, *The Contemporary Law of Armed Conflict*, 2nd edn. (Manchester, Manchester University Press 2000) p.349.

159. The authoritative French texts refers to '*maux superflus*' which has come to be written as 'superfluous injury' in English yet should more correctly be understood to reflect psychological as well as physical injury.

160. ICJ Rep. (Advisory Opinion), *supra* n. 24, paras. 78-79. See also ICRC Study, *supra* n. 154.

However, a problem of interpretation presented by the principle is that determination of what is 'unnecessary' or 'superfluous' is inherently subjective.[161] As queried by Kalshoven, 'how much injury is necessary [before crossing the threshold to be considered 'unnecessary'] to disable the enemy?'[162] Kalshoven notes that what is considered to be 'unnecessary' is determined by a value judgment of what is *necessary* such that suffering which cannot be 'justified by its military utility, either because such utility is entirely lacking or at best negligible'[163] is prohibited.

Consideration of this problem is to be weighed against the military advantage gained in any engagement such that, in the words of the St. Petersburg Declaration, 'necessities of war ought to yield to the requirements of humanity'. As Yoram Dinstein[164] notes, the use of the term 'of a nature' in Article 35(2) as opposed to 'calculated to' in the earlier 1907 Hague Regulations[165] suggests that it is the 'objective nature of the weapon' which is emphasised by the most contemporary framing of this principle, rather than the *intended* effects. In short, that a certain weapon has superfluously injurious effects trumps any argument that such effects were not intended. Dinstein goes on to note that, '[a] weapon is proscribed only if it causes injury or suffering that can be avoided, given the military constraints of the situation'.[166] Dinstein's interpretation would thus suggest that the tendency of DU to cause injury and/or suffering to combatants that could otherwise be avoided – for example by use of alternative munitions – are sufficient to consider them to be proscribed by Article 35(2).

A debate also exists as to whether the principle applies to weapons known to cause unnecessary suffering in the *majority* of military engagements, or whether in applies *ab initio* to all uses of a particular weapon, it having previously been determined to be so. Lauterpacht, writing in 1952, noted that the restrictions on means and methods of warfare have increasingly had to 'yield to the overriding necessities of the ultimate purpose of war'.[167] In his dissenting opinion in the *Nuclear Weapons* Advisory Opinion, Judge Shahabudeen also suggested that the

161. The SIrUS project was established by the ICRC with the intention of providing an objective definition of superfluous injury or unnecessary suffering. See also I. Daoust, 'ICRC Expert Meeting on Legal Reviews of Weapons and the SIrUS Project', 83 *International Review of the Red Cross*, No. 842 (Geneva 2001) pp. 539-542, and generally, the ICRC website <www.icrc.org>.

162. Kalshoven in Meyer, ed., *supra* n. 155, p. 261.

163. Kalshoven, *supra* n. 128, pp. 29-30. See also Scott, in Meyer, ed., *supra* n. 155, p. 275, regarding the scientific determinant of what would be 'unnecessary' as discussed at the Lucerne Conference. It had been calculated that the amount of physical force required to 'cause the centre of gravity of an upright, fully loaded German soldier to pass in front of, or behind, the point of support on the balls of his feet' was 70 lbs. Thus, any force reaching a target which exceeded this would be considered 'unnecessary'; see also Beckett, *supra* n. 26, who notes that suffering 'is not measured against a fixed external referent, but rather against a contextual military utility of the weapon (or method of attack)' employed.

164. Dinstein, *supra* n. 11, pp. 57-61, particularly for his interpretation of the significance of the wording of Art. 35 (2), and the evolution of the lexicon employed in defining this principle.

165. Hague Regulations Annexed to Hague Convention (IV) 'Respecting the Laws and Customs of Law on Land' (The Hague 1907) at pp. 75, 83.

166. Dinstein, *supra* n. 11, p. 59.

167. Lauterpacht, *supra* n. 127, p. 336.

'greater the military advantage [achieved in a particular targeting incident], the greater will be the willingness to tolerate higher levels of suffering'.[168] This view appears to be in fundamental contradiction to the logic of humanitarian law that human suffering must be alleviated to as great a degree as possible,[169] yet it demonstrates the realism in the recognition that violent conflict continues to occur and that any rules designed to regulate such conduct will necessarily have to balance humanitarian concerns with military necessity. The 'balancing test' is nonetheless constrained with regard to military necessity by the limitations of legal and moral considerations,[170] proportionality,[171] and the availability and practicality of alternatives. These things being duly considered, however, military utility alone cannot satisfy the legality of a weapon,[172] nor can it ever override conventional and customary rules.[173]

War being the contention of two political entities (states) through their armed forces, the intended 'target' is the enemy state which is to be overwhelmed by all legitimate means, yet it is the soldiers and other 'military objectives' of the state who are targeted *in reality* in attempting to achieve this aim.[174] Yet the objective of an engagement utilising DU munitions will not be combatants in the field, but 'hard targets' such as tanks. As noted by Robert Cryer, any legal appraisal of the use of weapons must not only look to proscription of use but must be contextualised by reference to the general law relating to weaponry and targeting.[175] Therefore, in order to illustrate the difficulties of balancing the principle prohibiting superfluous injury or unnecessary suffering with military necessity, it may be instructive to consider the following hypothetical scenarios.

Having established above that, in terms of the means (weapon) of warfare employed in engaging a particular target, the fulcrum that represents the legal use of a particular weapon must be positioned so as to balance military necessity with humanitarian considerations,[176] it is apparent that what *weighs* the balance are whatever limitations commanders may impose (or have imposed upon them) in achieving a military objective. Thus, imagining a legitimate target in an open space, isolated from any civilian areas or population, the means and methods of warfare available to a commander will be determined by the *nature* of the target. If the target is a soldier, and if engaging the soldier would represent a military advantage, the commander will be limited to the use of those weapons which would incapaci-

168. Dissenting Opinion of Judge Shahabudeen in *ICJ Rep.* (Advisory Opinion) *supra* n. 24, at p. 375.

169. Written Statement by New Zealand, p. 15, paras. 63-64 cited ibid., para. 86.

170. See Green, *supra* n. 158, p. 348.

171. Green in A.J.M. Delissen and G.J. Tanja, eds., *Humanitarian Law of Armed Conflict: Challenges Ahead*, (London, Martinus Nijhoff 1991) p. 286.

172. M. Sassòli and A. Bouvier, *How Does Law Protect in War?* (Geneva, ICRC 1999) p. 1563.

173. Lauterpacht, *supra* n. 127, p. 232; see also p. 126.

174. Ibid., pp. 202 and 337-338.

175. Cryer, *supra* n. 157, p. 56

176. Kalshoven, *supra* n. 128.

tate the soldier without causing him unnecessary suffering or rendering his death inevitable.[177]

Considering now that our isolated target in a field is a tank, the issue of which weapon to use such that the tank is incapacitated remains. However, it is essentially pointless applying the principle prohibiting unnecessary suffering or superfluous injury to the tank as it is a tank, and therefore will not 'suffer' or be 'injured'. General Sir Hugh Beach, who was responsible for the introduction of DU munitions into the arsenal of the UK Armed Forces, has noted that the intense heat generated when DU strikes a hard target causes the 'contents' of vehicles to 'burn up'.[178] It must surely be remembered that such 'contents' will, almost without exception, include human beings, combatants though they may be. Following the essentially civilising logic of the St. Petersburg Declaration that warfare should not cause unnecessary suffering we would concern ourselves with the fate of the military personnel *within* the tank over the 'fate' of the tank.[179] Therefore, in view of the principles discussed above, it is conceivable that the suffering caused in disabling those personnel within the tank is 'unnecessary' or that any injuries sustained would be 'superfluous'.[180] This aptly demonstrates the unacceptability to those responsible for achieving military objectives of following humanitarian or 'natural law' logic too rigorously as such reasoning would dictate that the commander could engage the tank with nothing more than those arms he would use against the soldier in the field.

Thus, with the targeting of armour, the factor ultimately determining the choice of weapon, and therefore the legality of the use thereof, appears to be military necessity not humanitarian considerations unless, as Cassese notes, it is clear that the cruelty of the weapon is so manifest as to be undeniable.[181] This is a logical inference as the invention of the tank was, in large part, necessitated by a desire to protect troops in forward positions in battle. The mere existence of the tank necessitates military means and methods for negating its existence, noting that the tank itself has not been the subject of legal proscription on the grounds that it makes battle 'unfair'!

Therefore, it is demonstrated by the practice of states that it is legal to engage a tank with rounds with consequent incendiary effects such as DU munitions, regardless of the fact that the suffering caused to those individuals inside the tank would otherwise be considered to be unnecessarily severe. Hence we return to the question of whether the contemporary aim of warfare is to kill 'efficiently' as op-

---

177. See 1868 St. Petersburg Declaration. It could be argued, however, that the commander could attempt to avoid the soldier enduring unnecessary *suffering* by killing him 'efficiently'.

178. Beach, *supra* n. 35, p. 1.

179. See similarly, Green in Delissen and Tanja, eds., *supra* n. 171, p. 275 and Green, *supra* n. 158, p. 133. Also, Zwanenburg, *supra* n. 14, pp. 10-11.

180. See R. M. Coupland and P. Herby, 'Review of the Legality of Weapons: A New Approach – The SIrUS Project', 835 *International Review of the Red Cross* (1999) pp. 583-592 where Robin Coupland, a surgeon and adviser to the ICRC Chief Medical Officer implores us to base the determination of illegality of a weapon on the nature of injuries it causes.

181. A. Cassese, *The New Humanitarian Law of Armed Conflict*, cited by Beckett, *supra* n. 27, p. 21.

posed to the 1868 standard of 'disabling the greatest number of men'. In the words of UK Minister of State for Defence, Dr Lewis Moonie concerning the use of DU, 'the purpose of using a weapon like this is to ensure that the enemy is killed and destroyed and that our people are not'.[182] Which appears to answer the question, at least from the perspective of a politician.

Turning to the question of viable alternatives, DU munitions are 'exceptionally good at their intended task'[183] of piercing armour, to the extent that the British Ministry of Defence has stated that, 'no satisfactory alternative material to DU exists to achieve the level of penetration necessary to defeat Main Battle Tanks'.[184] Yet most armies of the world use a tungsten alloy for armour piercing rounds.[185] As Green has noted, post-deployment evaluation of military necessity suggests that if states believe that a weapon will provide them with an advantage over an adversary, it will maintain that use of that weapon will be lawful.[186] This appears to be confirmed by political statements emphasising the military utility of DU from the perspective of states, as demonstrated above by Dr Moonie.

However, as far as the military establishment is concerned, both the UK and USA have recently reverted to munitions utilising tungsten. In 1989 the US Navy announced that the DU munitions it had previously been using in the *Vulcan Phalanx* Close-in-Weapon System would be replaced with tungsten rounds 'based on live fire tests showing that tungsten met … performance requirements while offering reduced probabilities of radiation exposure and environmental impact'.[187] The US Marine Corps has also announced a preference for tungsten alloy ammunition for its Amphibious Assault Vehicle 'because of the environmental problems with it [DU], be them real or perceived'.[188] Similarly, the UK Ministry of Defence announced in January 2002 that it was reverting to the use of tungsten alloy rounds for use in the Challenger II Main Battle Tank as an 'alternative to DU', although depleted uranium rounds will continue to be used in combat situations.[189] Though these decisions suggest that other effective munitions are available as a militarily feasible alternative to DU, it is not clear whether they could also readily be inter-

---

182. Dr Lewis Moonie MP, speaking on BBC Radio, *supra* n. 45.

183. Beckett, *supra* n. 27, p. 25.

184. See House of Commons (2001), *supra* n. 37.

185. Janes Defence Weekly, *Depleted Uranium – FAQs*, (London, Janes 2001), cited by Fahey, *supra* n. 9, p. 7.

186. Green in Delissen and Tanja, eds., *supra* n. 171, p. 276; Green, *supra* n. 158, p. 348. For example, The US has flatly rejected the call for restrictions on the use of DU, repeatedly denying the existence of any link between the use of the munitions and health risks, as reported by AFP (2001), *supra* n. 6.

187. Office of the Special Assistant to the Deputy Secretary of Defense for Gulf War Illnesses cited in Fahey, *supra* n. 9, p. 7. The UK MoD has also stated its intention to use tungsten rounds in its *Phalanx* systems once existing stocks of DU ammunition have been expended.

188. <http://www.usatoday.com/news/poison/2001-06-25-hotnukes-side.htm> cited in Fahey, *supra* n. 9, p. 8.

189. *The Daily Telegraph*, 10th January 2002 cited by Fahey, *supra* n. 9, pp. 7-8. See also BBC News Online, 'Uranium shell tests halted', 3 July 2001 <http://news.bbc.co.uk/1/hi/Scotland/1420916.stm> concerning the decision by the UK Ministry of Defence to suspend test firing of DU munitions at the Dundrennan firing range in Kirkcudbright, Scotland.

preted as further confirmation that serious concerns exist surrounding the use of DU even within the military establishment. It also raises the issue of whether, as suggested by Zwanenburg, the risks of DU to a state's own personnel detracts somewhat from its undeniable military utility.[190]

To conclude this part, it is the contention of this paper that a momentum has been generated in IHL (back) towards the over-riding importance of 'humanity' at the expense of military utility,[191] in part due to increased public exposure to and understanding of contemporary armed conflict, particularly through the media. This can be seen as a compelling rejection of the doctrine of *kriegsraeson*,[192] which was still advocated as recently as the last century. In essence, however, the importance of humanity over military utility had been established by the 1868 St. Petersburg Declaration, the penultimate paragraph of which establishes between the parties an obligation – legal as well as moral – to come to an 'understanding' concerning 'future improvements which science may effect in the armament of troops' such that they may 'maintain the principles which they have established, …and…conciliate the necessities of war with the rules of humanity',[193] which seems particularly poignant in relation to the current debate over DU.

The principles established in the St. Petersburg Declaration are not merely those prohibiting superfluous injury or unnecessary suffering, but are also the three preceding operative paragraphs of the Declaration pertaining to the need for the progress of civilisation to alleviate the calamities of war; that the only legitimate object states should endeavour to accomplish during conflict is to *weaken* the forces of the enemy, and that for such an objective it is necessary to limit the destructive power of warfare to the incapacitation (disablement) of the enemy forces.[194] As the Declaration's contemporary, Article 35(2) of the First Additional Protocol of 1977 suggests, these principles should be interpreted objectively, based on the actual effects of weapons, not solely on their intended effects.

4.3 The principle of distinction

The rules of IHL dealing with the protection of the civilian population are detailed in Part IV of the First Additional Protocol of 1977 and define who can and cannot

---

190. Zwanenburg, *supra* n. 14, p. 11; see also comments by Lt.Col. Ian Curry, interviewed on BBC Radio 4, *supra* n. 45.

191. T. Meron, 'The Martens Clause, Principles of Humanity and Dictates of Public Conscience', 94 *AJIL* (2000) p. 88; also Draper in Meyer, ed., *supra* n. 155, p. 18.

192. *Kriegsraeson geht vor Kriegsrecht* – the necessities of war override the laws of war, cited by Green, *supra* n. 158, p. 123; See also C. von Clausewitz translated by J.J. Graham, *On War*, (Ware, Wordsworth Editions 1997). For more on the emergence of just war doctrine in IHL, see McCoubrey in Meyer, ed., *supra* n.155, pp. 26-37.

193. See 1868 St. Petersburg Declaration.

194. The St. Petersburg Declaration asserts:

'That the only legitimate object which States should endeavour to accomplish during war is to weaken the military forces of the enemy; That for this purpose it is sufficient to disable the greatest possible number of men; That this object would be exceeded by the employment of arms which uselessly aggravate the sufferings of disabled men, or render their deaths inevitable; That the employment of such arms would, therefore, be contrary to the laws of humanity;'.

be legitimately targeted.[195] Kalshoven notes the standard to which commanders should aspire by stating that, 'total avoidance of damage to the civilian population is the *ideal* combatants should seek to realize in all cases'.[196] Article 48 of the First Additional Protocol provides the basic rule that, at all times during military engagements, commanders are required to distinguish between military and civilian objectives and must direct their operations solely against the former.[197] This principle – confirmed as a 'cardinal principle' of customary status[198] – has been observed for many centuries, and is complemented by Articles 51-60 of the First Additional Protocol of 1977.[199] In particular, Article 51(4)(b) prohibits weapons which cannot be *directed* against military objectives and Article 51(4)(c) defines indiscriminate attacks, 'those which employ a means or method of combat *the effects* of which cannot be limited by this Protocol'.[200] Article 51(5)(b) further defines and prohibits those attacks which '*may be expected* to cause incidental loss of civilian life, injury to civilians, ... which would be excessive in relation to the concrete and direct military advantage gained'.[201] As has been established *supra,* by 'means of combat' the Protocol implies, *inter alia*, 'weapons'[202] and the reference to 'concrete and direct military advantage' weighs the balance against the humanitarian considerations. Therefore, it must be asked how such limitations may apply to the use of DU munitions. In order to answer this question, I will address the two provisions above separately.

The rule provided in Article 51(4)(c) has been qualified by the question of whether the definition of 'attacks', as provided in Article 49(1),[203] must also be breached such that if the civilian population is not being 'attacked', any consequential negative *effects* of a legitimate engagement of the enemy cannot be considered to be an unlawful breach of the protection of the civilian population. This reasoning can be seen to reflect the *mens rea* element of criminal responsibility – if there is no *intent* to harm, there is no (or reduced) responsibility in law for any

195. Sassòli and Bouvier, *supra* n. 172, p. 117.

196. Kalshoven, *supra* n. 128, p. 98, emphasis added.

197. Article 48, First Additional Protocol, *supra* n. 140, provides that:
'In order to ensure respect for and protection of the civilian population and civilian objects, the Parties to the conflict shall at all times distinguish between the civilian population and combatants and between civilian objects and military objectives and accordingly shall direct their operations only against military objectives.'

198. *ICJ Rep*. Advisory Opinion, *supra* n. 24, para. 78.

199. S. Oeter considers Arts. 51-60 to represent 'established rules of traditional [sic] customary law', in D. Fleck, ed., *The Handbook of Humanitarian Law in Armed Conflicts*, (Oxford, Oxford University Press 1999), p. 109. See also Henckaerts and Doswald-Beck, *supra* n. 154, pp. 237-250.

200. Arts. 51(4)(b) and 51(4)(c) of the First Additional Protocol, *supra* n. 140, emphasis added. See also Henckaerts and Doswald-Beck, *supra* n. 154, p. 247.

201. Art. 51(5)(b), First Additional Protocol, *supra* n. 140, emphasis added. See also Kalshoven, *supra* n. 128, pp. 98-102.

202. Sandoz et al., *supra* n. 125, p. 621.

203. See Kalshoven, *supra* n. 128, pp. 86-88.

consequential harm.[204] An alternative interpretation could be that it applies to certain 'indentifiable and intrinsically indiscriminate weapons'.[205]

Essentially, this question asks whether DU can be considered to have indiscriminate effects which cannot be confined in time and space[206] such that it may have adverse effects on the civilian population.[207] This requires us to conceptualise the law with respect to the two 'stages' associated with the use of DU weapons: firstly, DU as an armour-piercing munition, and secondly, as the uranium oxide dust and DU fragments enduring in the environment of the battlefield once DU munitions have been fired.[208] It is now more straightforward to accept that DU rounds in the authority of military forces or in the barrel of tank canon will not have indiscriminate effects on civilians. In this sense, though there may still be concerns about the effect of DU munitions on combatants operating in proximity to DU, it is true to say that civilians are not being 'attacked' by its adverse effects.

However, civilians are more likely to suffer corollary consequences of the eventual use of DU munitions.[209] In a similar way to cluster bombs being considered to be 'victim-activated',[210] DU dust or fragments, unless cleared through decontamination, remain and endure in a target area after the effective cessation of hostilities and could thus be seen to be inherently indiscriminate due to their effects being unconfined within space and time.[211] This concept is effectively articulated by Doswald-Beck who notes that, in some cases, a weapon although accurately[212] and legitimately deployed, may have effects that 'take on a "life of [their] own" and affect combatants or civilians randomly to a significant degree'[213] regardless of the diligence of military planning and intended use. This may be proven to be true with regard to compound concentration of DU in human and plant tissue thus leading to further adverse health effects in the civilian population in targeted areas.[214]

With regard to Article 51(5)(b) of Additional Protocol I,[215] as has been clearly established by the scientific reports to date, DU munitions may certainly 'injure'

---

204. See for example, ICTY, *supra* n. 69, Section A, Part iv (a).

205. Kleffner, *supra* n. 32, p. 7; See also L. Doswald-Beck, 'International humanitarian law and the Advisory Opinion of the International Court of Justice on the legality of the threat or use of nuclear weapons', in *International Review of the Red Cross*, No.316, (Geneva, ICRC 1997), p. 3. Also see F. Hampson, cited in Beckett, *supra* n. 27, regarding intrinsic and inherent illegality.

206. See *ICJ Rep.* (Advisory Opinion), *supra* n. 24, para. 35; Henckaerts and Doswald-Beck, *supra* n. 154, p. 247.

207. See Dinstein, *supra* n. 11, p. 62; Kleffner, *supra* n. 32, pp. 7-8.

208. What Kleffner, idem, refers to as 'immediate and consequential effects of the use of weapons', at p. 9.

209. Beckett, *supra* n. 27, p. 28.

210. Beach, *supra* n. 35, p. 1; see also P.J. Lightfoot, 'The Landmine Review Conference: Will the Revised Landmine Protocol Protect Civilians?' in 18 *Fordham ILR* (1995), pp. 1526-1565.

211. Kleffner, *supra* n. 32, p. 10; see also Beckett, *supra* n. 27, pp. 27-32 in particular.

212. Kleffner notes that DU munitions have a "high degree of precision", *supra* n. 32, p. 12.

213. Doswald-Beck, *supra* n. 205, p. 4; also noted, by Kleffer, ibid., p. 8.

214. Ibid., p. 10.

215. Art. 51 (5) (b) establishes that, *inter alia*, an '... attack which may be expected to cause incidental loss of civilian life, injury to civilians, damage to civilian objects, or a combination thereof, which would be excessive in relation to the concrete and direct military advantage anticipated' will be considered to be indiscriminate, see *supra* n. 140.

civilians through inhalation or ingestion of uranium oxide dust, and/or by handling DU fragments. The provision also reintroduces the military necessity element into the equation such that, for the rule to be breached, it must be proven that the 'collateral damage' sustained by the civilian population is 'excessive' when compared to the military advantage gained.[216] It has been suggested by the independent studies detailed in Part 2 that the 'injuries' sustained due to the use of DU munitions may, in certain albeit extreme circumstances (or after a temporal delay) lead to loss of civilian life.

It may also be argued that *continued* use of DU, since such reports made clear these possible consequences, in itself contravenes Article 51(5)(b) as it may be more than 'expected' that civilian injury or loss of life may occur but is in fact *known* by commanders (and their political superiors) that DU munitions may have such effects. As it is inevitable that such an evaluation will reintroduce value judgements of what is 'excessive in relation to the concrete and direct military advantage gained', it must be remembered that the interests of the civilian population should prevail in cases of doubt.[217]

4.4 The Martens Clause

The Martens Clause, the text of which was first agreed at the Hague Peace Conference of 1899, has sometimes been distilled to epitomise the 'principle of humanity'. The clause has since been confirmed in contemporary IHL through Article 1(2) of the First Additional Protocol of 1977. In stating that, in cases not specifically covered by international legal instruments or agreements, 'civilians and combatants remain under the protection and authority of international law derived from established custom, from the principles of humanity and from the dictates of the public conscience', the clause is subject to both broad and narrow interpretations.[218]

Since the adoption of the Martens Clause, it has been questionable what legal effect, if any, concerns of the public should be afforded in international law. Yet at the Lucerne Conference of 1974, there was a general readiness on the part of states to acknowledge the importance of the Martens Clause.[219] To some delegations 'dictates of the public conscience' constituted a distinct legal criterion, whereas to others it represented a political rather than a legal factor.[220] It is debateable whether the ICJ affirmed the clause as a principle of customary international law[221] in the *Nuclear Weapons* Advisory Opinion. Yet it is widely accepted, and equally regret-

---

216. NB: As noted by Bothe et al., eds., pp. 309-311, this refers to the whole operation, not isolated engagements, as cited by Kleffner, *supra* n. 32, p. 11. Also noted by Kleffner, ibid., is the lack of definition in the First Additional Protocol of what is considered to be 'excessive'.

217. Sandoz et al., *supra* n. 125, pp. 625-626. Also see Arts. 57-58 of the First Additional Protocols 1977, 'Precautionary Measures', *supra* n. 140.

218. See Ticehurst, *supra* n. 130.

219. Kalshoven in Meyer, ed., *supra* n. 155, p. 263.

220. Ibid.

221. *ICJ Rep.* (Advisory Opinion), *supra* n. 24, para. 78; See also the *Krupp* case 15 Annual Digest, 620, 622, US Military Tribunal (1948) stating that the clause represents 'much more than a

table, that the Court failed to provide any clarification on its interpretation.[222] Similarly to the principles provided by the St. Petersburg Declaration, it is difficult to define how one is to evaluate such subjective criteria as a satisfactory reflection of the law.

A broad interpretation provides that conduct in armed conflicts is judged not solely by treaties and custom but by the 'principles of humanity' and the 'dictates of the public conscience'[223] such that the Clause suggests a 'fall back' for those cases not specifically codified in conventional law.[224] As Meron suggests, the Martens Clause is fundamentally based on morality, as well as law, in providing supplementary protection in such cases.[225] This would suggest that the clause contradicts the *nullem crimen sine lege* (presumed legality) principle that, absent a specific prohibition, a means or method of warfare is legal.[226] Further, in his Dissenting Opinion in the *Nuclear Weapons* Advisory Opinion, Judge Shahabudeen suggested that the clause can itself prohibit what is not otherwise proscribed by conventional or customary law stating that 'principles of humanity *could themselves exert a legal force* to govern military conduct in cases in which no relevant rule was provided by conventional law'. [227] Yet Zwanenburg suggests that, in the light of the other opinions of the judges of the ICJ in the *Nuclear Weapons* Advisory Opinion who did not appear to share Judge Shahabudeen's interpretation, the clause cannot stand alone 'but can *lend support* to humanitarian values in the interpretation … of a rule'.[228] This seems to be the view taken by ICTY Presiding Judge Cassese in the *Kupreskić* case,[229] where it was found that the clause could not be considered to have been 'elevated to the rank of independent sources of international law … [but that] … as a minimum, reference [should be made] to those principles [of humanity] and dictates [of the public conscience] any time a rule … is not sufficiently rigorous or precise: in those circumstances, the scope and purport of the rule must be defined with reference to those principles and dictates'.[230]

Therefore, as reasoned by Meron, the contemporary significance of the Martens Clause is as a 'safeguard to customary international law, and in support of the argument that what is not prohibited by treaty may not necessarily be lawful'.[231] Thus, in cases where other principles of international law are not conducive to the establishment of definitive conclusions, the Martens Clause can and does provide a fundamental reference point from which to proceed. To again quote Meron:

---

pious declaration. It is a general clause, … the legal yardstick to be applied if and when specific provisions of the Convention … do not cover specific cases …'.

222. Ticehurst, *supra* n. 130, p. 125.

223. Ibid., p. 126.

224. Ibid.; Zwanenburg, *supra* n. 14, p. 8.

225. Meron, *supra* n. 191, p. 79.

226. Ibid., p. 78 also cited in Zwanenburg, *supra* n. 14, p. 8.

227. Shahabudeen J., Dissenting Opinion, *supra* n. 168, para. 408, emphasis added.

228. Zwanenburg, *supra* n. 14, p. 9, emphasis added.

229. See International Criminal Tribunal for the Former Yugoslavia, *Prosecutor* v. *Kupreskić*, Judgement of 14 January 2000, Case IT-95-16-T, para. 525.

230. Ibid.

231. Meron, *supra* n. 191, p. 87.

'Where there already is some legal basis for adopting a *more humanitarian* position, the Martens Clause enables decision makers to take an extra step forward.'[232] It certainly appears clear from the previous chapters that the use of DU munitions challenges the 'public conscience', if not so obviously the 'principles of humanity'.

4.5 DU munitions as 'new' weapons

As provided by Article 36 of the First Additional Protocol, it is necessary for commanders to be sure that any 'new' weapon available to them conforms to the principles and provisions of IHL.[233] DU munitions are 'new' weapons for those states possessing them in their (operational) arsenals, from the time when they first acquire them.[234] This is true regardless of whether they have developed/manufactured or acquired/purchased them. Representative of customary international law as it may be, interpretation of the principle prohibiting the use of weapons of a nature to cause unnecessary suffering or superfluous injury, discussed *supra*, is not without controversy in relation to its application to 'new' weapons.[235] In particular, several states have 'expressed the conviction that the principle ... has no legal impact on new weapons'.[236] However, in the *Nuclear Weapons* Advisory Opinion, the ICJ rejected this approach when it stated that 'such a conclusion would be incompatible with the intrinsically humanitarian character of the legal principles in question which ... applies ... to all kinds of weapons, those of the past, those of the present and those of the future'.[237] The Opinion continues to assert that '[i]n this respect it seems significant that the thesis that the rules of humanitarian law do not apply to the new weaponry, because of the newness of the latter, has not been advocated in the present proceedings.'[238]

As noted by the ICRC in its Commentary, Article 36 flows from, and reflects, the basic 'humanitarian-inspired' limitations provided by Article 35.[239] Article 36 does not in itself *prohibit* the use of a weapon that may be considered illegal,[240] but obliges states to establish mechanisms to undertake a review of the legality of *all*

232. Ibid., p. 88, emphasis added.

233. Art. 36 establishes that:
'In the study, development , acquisition or adoption of a new weapon, means or method or warfare, a High Contracting Party is under an obligation to determine whether its employment would, in some or all circumstances, be prohibited by this Protocol or by any other rule of international law applicable to the High Contracting Party', see *supra* n. 140; See also Daoust et al., *supra.* n. 234.

234. McDonald, *supra* n. 10; Sandoz et al., *supra* n. 125, p. 425; See also I. Daoust, R.M. Coupland, and R. Ishoey, 'New Wars, New Weapons? The Obligation of States to Assess the Legality of Means and Methods of Warfare', 84 *IRRC* No. 846 (Geneva, ICRC 2002) p. 352.

235. Zwanenburg, *supra* n. 14, p. 4; Kalshoven, *supra* n. 128, p. 30.

236. A. Cassese, 'Weapons Causing Unnecessary Suffering: Are They Prohibited?', 58 *Rivista di Diritto Internazionale* (1975) cited by Zwanenburg, *supra* n. 14, p. 4.

237. *ICJ Rep.* (Advisory Opinion), *supra* n. 24, para. 78.

238. Ibid., para. 86.

239. Sandoz et al., *supra* n. 125, pp. 421-422.

240. Beckett, *supra* n. 27, p. 35.

'new' weapons to ensure they conform with IHL.[241] The rules established are thus designed to *prevent* the operational deployment of 'new' weapons, means or methods of warfare of a nature to cause superfluous injury or unnecessary suffering, which have indiscriminate effects or which cause widespread, long-term and severe damage to the natural environment.

The origins of Article 36 lie in the desire to retard the 'arms race' such that future weapons would not be developed with ever more devastating effects.[242] At the Diplomatic Conference at which the Additional Protocols were agreed, it was expressly noted that the aims of Article 36 were, *inter alia*, to limit the scope for development of 'radiological warfare as well as devices generating radiation'.[243] However, radioactive as DU may be, it is possibly too much to expect that this reference to 'radiological' weapons in the Commentary was intended to capture weapons emitting radiation in the same sense as DU munitions. This stems from the 'primary purpose' principle which will be addressed in greater detail *infra*. Nonetheless, Article 36 provides the sole legal framework for states to apply in determining the legality of new means and methods of warfare and must therefore be considered of the utmost importance for this reason. Further, it is also clear that failure by states to take measures in conformity with Article 36 would result in the state being responsible in international law.[244]

In considering Article 36, the questions to be addressed in assessing the legality of a new weapon are twofold: a) against what criteria is conformity with the principles of international law to be measured? and, b) who should determine conformity with such criteria, when, and how? In answering the first question, it seems clear from Article 36 that the criteria must be 'rules of international law as provided by the Protocol'[245] or 'prohibited…by any other rule of international law'.[246] This clearly encompasses the fundamental principles discussed above concerning superfluous injury or unnecessary suffering and distinction, yet, as noted in the ICRC Commentary, and Daoust et al., will apply equally to any principles established by subsequently emerging conventional and customary rules of international law.[247] As far as the timing of an Article 36 review is concerned, it is obviously desirable that this should take place before a 'new' weapon has entered into operational service.[248]

Turning to the second question, this provides the dilemma for issues such as the one at hand regarding the use of a new weapon around which a debate exists concerning its conformity with the law – a debate which has developed mainly since the combat use of a weapon. At the Diplomatic Conference which led to the 1977 Additional Protocols, it was envisaged by some negotiating states that an interna-

---

241. See ICRC Commentary, Sandoz et al., *supra* n. 125, pp. 421-428; Daoust et al., *supra* n. 234, pp. 351-352.
242. Sandoz et al., *supra* n. 125, p. 427.
243. ibid., p. 427.
244. ibid., p. 423.
245. McDonald, *supra* n. 10; Sandoz et al., *supra* n. 125, p. 423.
246. First Additional Protocol (1997), *supra* n. 140, Article 36.
247. Sandoz et al., *supra* n. 125, p. 425; Daoust et al., *supra* n. 234, pp. 349-350.
248. Sassòli and Bouvier, *supra* n. 172, p. 176; McDonald, *supra* n. 10, p. 2, 7.

tionalised procedure would be established for the review of new weapons.[249] However, it was countered that, in the interests of protecting the right to secrecy in developing new weapons, such an international control would be unpalatable to other states. The result of the discussion is that States Parties are *themselves* obliged to undertake national reviews of legality to ensure new weapons conform to international law.[250] This obligation extends to those states developing and manufacturing 'new' weapons, but also to those possessing and purchasing such weapons.[251]

In conducting a review, states are not expected to analyse or anticipate all possible misuses of a new weapon[252] but only its 'normal use' at the time of the evaluation .[253] This is a practical reality as the effects of new weapons in the battlefield are often insufficiently known.[254] However, Daoust et al have drawn attention to the need for a 'multi-disciplinary approach' which would include issues of a 'military, technical and health-related nature' as well as issues of alternatives, and the proliferation of the weapon.[255] These issues are certainly pertinent to the use of DU where the possible expansion of the use of DU munitions and armour without restrictions increases the need for a definitive review of legality.[256] Unfortunately, what is not clear from the ICRC Commentary, let alone from the wording of Article 36, is whether the process of review should be continual, such that when debates concerning the use of weapons arise, a further duty exists to suspend use of the weapon pending a review of legality in the light of such concerns. Thus, it may be reasoned that, in the same way that in conducting an evaluation states cannot be expected to predict all possible negative effects of a new weapon, should the understanding of a 'new' weapon's legality be called into question, there is a case for a re-evaluation of legality in the light of changed circumstances. This may suggest that 'new' information in the shape of 'concerns' (obviously assuming they are of sufficient gravity) may warrant a re-evaluation of the legality of the use of such weapons.

DU munitions have been the subject of two reviews by the USA;[257] the first by the Department of the Air Force in 1975,[258] and the second by the Department of the Army in 1994.[259] The 1975 review examined the prohibition on unnecessary suffering, the prohibition on use of poison and the principle of proportionality and

249. Solf in Bothe et al., eds., cited by Oeter in Fleck, ed., *supra* n. 200, p. 121; Sandoz et al., *supra* n. 125.

250. Oeter in Fleck, ed., *supra* n. 200, p. 121.

251. Sandoz et al., *supra* n. 125, p. 426; Also noted in Daoust et al., *supra* n. 234, p. 348.

252. Sandoz et al., *supra* n. 125, p. 424.

253. Ibid., pp. 423-428; Council of Europe, OR XV p. 269, CDDH/215/Rev. 1, paras. 30-31.

254. Kalshoven, *supra* n. 128, p. 81.

255. See Daoust et al., *supra* n. 234, p. 352.

256. Harley et al., *supra* n. 9, p. 72.

257. Interesting in itself as the USA is not a State Party to the Additional Protocols of 1977, nor therefore, to Art. 36.

258. See Department of the Airforce HQUSAF (JA), *Legal Memorandum* as cited by McDonald, *supra* n. 10, p. 4. For a more comprehensive evaluation of this review, see idem., pp.4-8.

259. See Memorandum for US Army Armament Research, Development and Engineering Center, *Subject M-829A2 Cartridge, 120mm APFSDS-T,* cited by McDonald, *supra* n. 10, p. 8.

indiscriminate effects, all of which constitute rules of customary international law.[260] The 1994 review, conducted at a time when 'concerns' over DU had begun to be raised and articulated, examined the superfluous injury and unnecessary suffering principle, and DU as a poison weapon. The results of both reviews found that, as far as the unnecessary suffering or superfluous injury question was concerned, DU did not fall foul of this principle as its military utility as an armour-piercing kinetic energy round was deemed to outweigh humanitarian concerns although, as noted by McDonald, the 1994 review did not present any medical or scientific evidence to justify such a finding.[261] As far as the reviews examined the prohibition on the deployment of poison weapons, the 1975 review found that this principle was not violated as the toxic and radiological effects of DU were due to the inherent chemical characteristics of the substance and were therefore not its 'intended effect'. The 1994 review cited the 1975 review and added that the post-*Desert Storm* studies into environmental and health effects had suggested no evidence that use of DU contravened this principle. These conclusions, unsubstantiated by objective medical or scientific data, and conducted by an undeniably 'interested party', cannot therefore be satisfactory, even if the review process fulfilled the requirements of Article 36 and customary international law.[262]

4.6 Summary

In order for the principle prohibiting employment of means or methods of warfare of a nature to cause unnecessary suffering or superfluous injury to apply to DU, it must be demonstrable either a) that the suffering caused to combatants is unnecessary; or b) that the injuries caused by DU are superfluous in relation to the military advantage gained in the majority of cases; or c) that the effects of the use of DU munitions are unable to distinguish between civilians and combatants.[263] As was noted *supra*, the lack of conclusive and comprehensive aetiological data on the injurious effects of DU, coupled with the possible temporal delay in the manifestation of such effects, is such that it is not yet possible to conclude that use of DU breaches this principle. However, a statement made in 1999 by the Special Rapporteur of NATO's Parliamentary Assembly Civilian Affairs Committee that, 'the lawfulness of its [DU's] use could be challenged under IHL',[264] also highlights the difficulty of drawing conclusions either way.

More problematic for states possessing DU munitions, and particularly those who have used them in combat, is the principle of distinction. The obvious question raised by the propensity for the use of DU to create uranium oxide dust that can endure in the environment, and be absorbed by and concentrated in living tissue, is whether this 'side-effect' can be said to distinguish between military and

---

260. McDonald, *supra* n. 10, p. 5.
261. Ibid., p. 8
262. Ibid., p. 10.
263. See Zwanenburg, *supra* n. 14, p. 10; Dinstein, *supra* n. 11, p. 62; Beckett, *supra* n. 27.
264. Statement by Mr Völker Kröning of 15 October 1999, para. 24, cited in Zwanenburg, *supra* n. 14, p. 11.

civilian objectives. Further, it raises the issue of whether it can continue to so distinguish following the cessation of hostilities. If we negate the assumption that the civilian population must be 'attacked' for the principle of distinction to be breached, it seems clear that the effects of DU endure long after the end of hostilities such that its effects are unable to distinguish between military and civilian objectives. The longevity of uranium oxide dust created by use of DU munitions also suggests that the effects of use are unable to be limited in space or time, as required by customary international law.

The conclusions drawn to date from the known reviews of DU, apparently under the provisions of Article 36, are based on the argument that the adverse effects of DU are merely consequential, unintended side-effects which should therefore be considered as subordinate to the 'primary purpose' of the weapon as an armour-piercing round. This will be discussed further in the following part. However, as noted by Roberts and Guelff,[265] a consensus on the law applicable to 'new' weapons has seldom been achieved and has largely neglected the more subtle humanitarian considerations in favour of military necessity. It has been suggested by Rupert Ticehurst that such positivism evident in the interpretation of both the Martens Clause – and, in the view of this author, Article 36 of the First Additional Protocol – has resulted in a situation where powerful states who possess weapons for which others are calling for restrictions on use or development, are able to influence the interpretation of the laws of armed conflict to their own advantage.[266] If Ticehurst's synopsis is true, this hardly confirms the maxim that all laws are created for the benefit of mankind, but rather for the benefit of states, at a time of their choosing, in order to protect their military advantage.[267]

Hence, the legal debate above identifies several 'grey areas' in relation to DU and demonstrates how the conflict between the intentions and the realities of armed conflict provides IHL with a vacuum of practicality between that which may be desirable through the rules and regulations created by law, and that which occurs *in fact* upon the battlefield and around the negotiating table.

5. RESPONSES TO CONCERNS

If we accept, therefore, that the preceding arguments are credible, though equally that they leave DU in a legal 'grey area', why should DU receive any more rigorous control than any other conventional weapon? Is there any reason why DU munitions should be subject to a '*lex specialis*' prohibition or restriction on use? In short, should not DU – as well as all other weapons – receive exactly the same

265. A. Roberts and R. Guelff, eds., *Documents on the Laws of War*, 3rd edn., (Oxford, Oxford University Press 2001) p. 7; Daoust et al., *supra* n. 234, also note the lack of attention afforded to Article 36 by states.

266. Ticehurst, *supra* n. 130, p. 132.

267. As noted by Schachter, '… the States that made and applied law were not governed by morality or "natural reason"; they acted for reasons of power and interest', see O. Schachter, *International Law in Theory and Practice*, (Dordrecht, Martinus Nijhoff Publishers 1991) p. 36.

degree of control, scrutiny and evaluation? To suggest that all weapons already do, in any sense more than the loose, subjective regime established by Article 36, is patently false as shown by the varying degrees of scrutiny and evaluation that exist between states.[268]

As has been demonstrated in the previous chapter, it is difficult to argue that legally-based prohibition on the use of DU munitions is already clearly established. Yet it seems apparent that this is not so much due to the lack of explicit prohibitions on the sorts of effects associated with the combat deployment of DU, but more due to an inability (or unwillingness) to 'place' DU munitions into any pre-existing categories. Arguments have been made by those seeking to ban the use of DU that it falls under the legal regimes of numerous existing conventions from the 1925 Geneva Gas Protocol,[269] to the use of poison or poisoned weapons as proscribed by Article 23(a) of the Fourth Hague Convention, to Protocol III of the Convention on Certain Conventional Weapons (CCW) of 1980 prohibiting use of incendiary weapons.[270] This chapter will examine why these existing conventions have been deemed to be largely inapplicable when arguing for a prohibition on the use of DU munitions. In light of the argument presented in the preceding chapter, the lack of existing legal restrictions might further suggest a pressing need for a moratorium on the continued use of DU munitions until such conventional proscription is debated.

5.1 The 'primary purpose' principle

It has been argued from various quarters at various times during the debate about DU that DU can be classified as a radiological, poison, incendiary, nuclear or indiscriminate weapon.[271] However, acceptance that DU falls within any conventional restrictions dealing with such weapons has been discounted based on the fact that the 'primary purpose' of DU is as an armour-piercing munition and that, therefore, any subsequent 'unintended' effects are irrelevant.[272] Indeed, as was noted in part 2, the pyrophoric nature of DU is one of its main military utilities. Yet the provisions of the Protocol to the 1980 Convention on Certain Conventional Weapons (CCW) on Prohibitions or Restrictions on the Use of Incendiary Weapons (Protocol III) are not applicable to DU munitions due to the clauses of Article

---

268. See Daoust et al., *supra* n. 234, regarding the review mechanisms of certain States; also International Committee of the Red Cross 'New Weapons', part of the *Advisory Service on International Humanitarian Law*, (2001) <http//www.icrc.org>.

269. 1925 Geneva Protocol for the Prohibition on the Use in War of Asphyxiating, Poinsonous or Other Gases, and of Bacteriological Methods of Warfare. See Roberts and Guelff, eds., *supra* n. 265, pp. 155-167.

270. See A. Schott, *Resolution on the banning of the use of depleted uranium-DU* [sic], (Berlin, World Depleted Uranium Centre 2000) claiming that use of DU contravenes, *inter alia*, the prohibition on the use of poison or poisoned weapons. See also N. Mackay, US Forces' Use of Depleted Uranium Weapons is 'Illegal', 30 March 2003 *The Sunday Herald* (Scotland) and reproduced on numerous anti-DU websites.

271. See *inter alia*, *supra* n. 26; Beach, *supra* n. 35.

272. See Beckett, *supra* n. 26, p. 15.

1(1)(b) that exclude '(i) [m]unitions which may have *incidental* incendiary effects, …'[273] and '(ii) [m]unitions designed to combine penetration, blast or fragmentation effects with an additional incendiary effect, such as armour-piercing projectiles'. It is therefore clear that Protocol III has been designed not to apply to armour-piercing incendiary rounds such as DU munitions.

Similarly, with regard to whether DU falls under the prohibition on poison as an 'analogous material or device' to poison gas, the findings of the ICJ in the *Nuclear Weapons* Advisory Opinion are particularly instructive:

> 'The Court will observe that the Regulations annexed to the Hague Convention IV do not define what is to be understood by "poison or poisoned weapons" and that different interpretations exist on the issue. Nor does the 1925 [Geneva Gas] Protocol specify the meaning to be given to the term "analogous materials or devices". The terms have been understood, through the practice of States, in their ordinary sense as covering weapons whose prime, or even exclusive, effect is to poison or asphyxiate. This practice is clear, and the parties to those instruments have not treated them as referring to nuclear weapons.'[274]

However, this is surely an error on the part of the drafters of these conventions as it would appear that, on the humanitarian basis of minimising human suffering, as argued in section 4.2 *supra*, DU munitions are exactly the sort of weapons that *should* be covered by Protocol III, if not so convincingly by the 1925 Gas Protocol. However, Kalshoven notes that the prohibitions in the CCW of 1980 and other more recent conventions represented a concession by states that some of their weaponry was *already* illegal under existing customary law.[275] It is also inevitable that the written laws of conventions are unable to keep pace with the technological (and destructive) advancements in weapons development.[276] This fact has been manifest by states wishing to define conventions prohibiting weapons in narrow terms such that as little of their arsenals as possible might be eroded by exactly the sorts of arguments as have surrounded linking DU munitions to these conventions. This may also explain the reluctance on the part of states currently possessing DU to accept anything other than conventional restrictions, which, at least in the near future, would not appear to be forthcoming.

The primary purpose principle thus belies the fact that, regardless of the intended effects of DU munitions, they do have *de facto* detrimental, and possibly very serious, side-effects which may amount to breaches of the principles evaluated above.[277] A preferable guiding principle in such a case is surely the precau-

---

273. 1980 Convention on Certain Conventional Weapons on Prohibitions or Restrictions on the Use of Incendiary Weapons (Protocol III), emphasis added.

274. *ICJ Rep.* (Advisory Opinión) *supra* n. 24, para. 55.

275. Kalshoven in Meyer, ed., *supra* n. 155, p. 257.

276. Roberts and Guelff, eds., *supra* n. 265, p. 7; However, see also R. Lloyd, 'Strengthening the Inhumane Weapons Convention: Second Review Conference of the Certain Conventional Weapons Convention', *International Security Information Service* Policy Paper No. 02, (2001) <http://www.isisuk.demon.co.uk/0811/isis/uk/>.

277. McDonald, *supra* n. 10, p. 6; Beckett, *supra* n. 27.

tionary principle[278] which, when extrapolated from its environmental law origins, would suggest that when the safety of a weapon is questionable, its use should be limited.[279] The applicability of this principle is particularly pertinent to the case of DU, not simply for consideration of the environmental impact DU dust may have, but also as it recognises both the spatial and temporal variables of the possible detrimental effects of DU. Applying this principle within the humanitarian law context suggests that, logically, whether or not a weapon was *intended* to have harmful effects upon the civilian population is subordinate to the reality that it does, in fact, have such negative effects. For states to argue purely from the 'primary purpose' standpoint, that DU as a weapon in its pre-deployment state is not intended to have chemical and radiological effects is for Aladdin to deny the existence of the genie within the lamp.

5.2 The public conscience and the threshold for action

Therefore, what essentially continues to distinguish DU munitions from other conventional weapons is the endurance of concerns over the effects of their use. As has been argued above, this has been manifest as a 'public conscience' over use of DU munitions. Yet, as has also been discussed, such a subjective, 'value judgement' of what may ultimately determine legality poses problems of credibility and interpretation, not least for states. It may therefore be necessary to consider what 'threshold' would be significant enough to warrant this being accepted as a basis for action. To simplify the question; where should the threshold be set such that the principle of the public conscience 'kicks in'? Are a 'substantial amount of public discussion'[280] or 'persistent concerns'[281] or 'consequences', in the ambiguously sanitised language of the British Ministry of Defence,[282] enough? It is probably fair to say that public concerns over DU have not yet reached the status of what Herby terms 'public abhorrence',[283] yet it is the position of this paper that the range of concerns voiced, or at least recognised by, such a broad sector of society as has been seen with the debate over DU, coupled with the longevity and consistency of the concerns, is sufficient to represent a 'public conscience'. If accepted, this would imply that the concerns themselves could act to prevent the continued use of DU munitions as provided by the Martens Clause.[284]

---

278. The 'precautionary principle' is more commonly associated with environmental law. For an explanation of the principle within the environmental law context, see W.T. Douma 'The Precautionary Principle', in 49 *Ulfjotur* [Icelandic Legal Journal] (1996) pp. 417-430, also at <http://www.eel.nl/virtue/precprin.htm>.

279. In simplified terms as provided by Douma, ibid., the 'principle indicates that it is better to be safe than sorry'; see also Beach, *supra* n. 35, p. 10.

280. Royal Society (2001), *supra* n. 7, p. vii.

281. Ibid.

282. See Ministry of Defence (UK) (2003), *supra* n. 3.

283. Herby in Coupland and Herby, *supra* n.180.

284. As Beach, *supra* n. 35, warns, continued use of DU munitions in defiance of the concerns over their use may provoke further negative public opinion.

5.3 Restrictions on the use of DU munitions

As has been noted above, there have already been some notable military moves away from use of DU munitions – especially notable as they have been made by the two states that have used DU in combat, the US and UK.[285] In January 2001, following the deaths from leukaemia of several veterans of the Italian armed forces who had served in Kosovo,[286] Italy, Belgium, Portugal, Norway and Finland requested that the European Parliament adopt a resolution calling for 'EU member states that are also NATO members to propose that a moratorium be placed on the use of depleted uranium (DU) weapons in accordance with "precautionary principles"'.[287] Consequently, the Parliament adopted a resolution which asked NATO to 'consider other types of munitions [to those containing DU] until the results of the investigations on depleted uranium are known'.[288] The result of this process appears to be that NATO has taken the decision to 'ban' DU from its arsenals.[289] However, this 'ban' does not mean that NATO Member States may not use DU, only that they may not use DU munitions whilst operating under a mandate of the organisation. The European Parliament also called for 'a thorough investigation … into all the effects of the military operations conducted during the conflicts in Bosnia and Kosovo on military personnel, the civilian population and the environment'.[290]

Since its 2001 resolution, the European Parliament further passed a resolution in 2003 in which it expressed its reaffirmation of 'the need to establish moratoriums [sic] on these types of ammunition [unexploded ordnance (landmines and cluster submunitions) and depleted uranium ammunition] pending a total ban', and called on states, *inter alia*, to 'review and monitor the design and development of weapons, ensuring that these are in line with applicable intenational law and meet the highest international standards directed against technical misuse, misdeployment, mistargeting and malfunction'.[291]

Another notable response of the international community to the concerns over DU has been the groups of experts of the UNEP sent to Bosnia and Herzegovina and Kosovo[292] to investigate the post conflict effects of DU on the environment. This could be seen as indicative of recognition by the United Nations – often seen as the representative of an 'international community' – of concerns over DU and its effects. However, with many observers predicting the increased proliferation of

---

285. Ibid., p.10. See also nn. 184-190 *supra*.

286. BBC Radio, *supra* n. 45.

287. Ibid., also reported in AFP, *supra* n. 6; see also BBC News Online, 'Europe Votes for DU Ban', 17 January 2001, <http://news.bbc.co.uk/1/hi/world/Europe/1121384>.

288. European Parliament, *supra* n. 6, operative para. 7.

289. BBC Radio, *supra* n. 45.

290. European Parliament, *supra* n. 6, preambular paragraph F.

291. European Parliament , *Unexploded ordnance and depleted uranium ammunition*, Resolution of 13 February 2003, P5_TA(2003)0062.

292. UNEP, *supra* n. 51, p. 23; UNEP, *supra* n. 45, p. 21. A team of similar size and constitution was also sent to Serbia and Montenegro in 2001-2002.

DU munitions,[293] the more important question is whether these responses are *sufficient*, which can only be measured by whether they are effective.

Absent an international agreement between states on the use of DU, the responsibility for establishing any regulation of the use of weapons ultimately lies with the UN Security Council as the international authority charged with the maintenance of international peace and security,[294] and with the upholding of the principles of international law articulated *supra*. Yet, with seemingly all of the permanent members of the Council save China possessing DU munitions, it is admittedly difficult to see how decisive action will be taken on the issue within this fora. As noted by Kalshoven, 'once States have integrated a weapon into their armaments, they will not lightly be convinced to give it up again on the mere ground that it is alleged to cause unnecessary suffering'.[295] However, this dose of realism is entirely subordinate to the argument as to whether they *should* give up such weapons – at least temporarily – in the interests of the principles of humanity and the dictates of the public conscience. Again, therefore, we return to the balance between the principles of military necessity on the one hand and humanity on the other and must argue for the latter in view of the fact that we do not yet know the true effects of DU on human health.

5.4 The necessity for further review of legality

As was discussed in the previous chapter, there is a case to be made that the concerns over DU as a 'new' weapon necessitate a re-evaluation of legality in line with the provisions of Article 36 of the First Additional Protocol. As well as the calls from the European Union noted above, the ICRC has also urged all states involved in the study, development, acquisition or possession of munitions containing depleted uranium to conduct legal reviews in line with Article 36.[296] Preferably, such a review process would be undertaken by an independent (possibly international) authority.[297] However, in the light of the culture of secrecy in military development, justified by considerations of military necessity, it may be conceded that the eventuality of independent weapons review is also difficult to imagine.

Alternatively, a compromise to the need for objective review mechanisms could be to establish an internationally recognised and accepted standardised test of legality to be undertaken 'in country' and, more importantly from a military perspective, in secret. An argument is therefore to be made for the national review bodies of States Parties to the 1977 First Additional Protocol to be as independent from the vested interests of the military (and political) establishment in those countries as possible – even to the degree that an internationally standardised code of review be accepted by all states. In this way, the cloak of secrecy could be maintained

---

293. Fahey, *supra* n. 9; Royal Society (2002), *supra* n. 7; Beach, *supra* n. 35.
294. Lauterpacht, ed., *supra* n. 127, p. 129. See also UN Charter (1945).
295. Kalshoven, *supra* n. 128, p. 81.
296. ICRC, *supra* n. 105.
297. Ibid.; Daoust et al., *supra* n. 234; McDonald, *supra* n. 10, p. 11.

whilst ensuring the conformity of weapons development and use with the principles of IHL.

5.5 Towards a moratorium on the continued use of DU munitions

Thus, it follows that the arguments as to whether DU munitions should be used pivots around the question of whether they can continue to be used at all without states reviewing their legality. Further, in view of the likelihood that states will drag their heels on the establishment of an independent review mechanisms for new weapons, it must be postulated that existing legal grounds must be invoked for immediate restrictions on the continued use of DU munitions. In such a case, it is possible to envisage a moratorium on the post-development[298] use of such weapons pending such an evaluation process. Thus the determining considerations in proposing a moratorium will not be whether the assertions that DU weapons have *in fact* caused harm to health or the environment have any significance *vis-à-vis* the law, but rather whether there already exists (or should exist) any legal impediment to their use while such concerns endure over their effects.

The serious concerns therefore form the evidence in the legal argument to be made in favour of a moratorium, and thus the essential justification for restrictions or prohibition. However, the significance of this line of reasoning is that it could then be applied to other post-development weapons or weapons systems – subject to the existence of serious concerns. The repercussions of such an argument, if accepted, would doubtless be controversial and difficult for states to accept if it implied an operational 'pause' between development and authority to deploy a weapons system.

6. CONCLUSIONS

In a statement to the ICJ in the *Nuclear Weapons* Advisory Opinion, New Zealand asserted that: 'International humanitarian law has evolved to meet contemporary circumstances, and is not limited in its application to weaponry of an earlier time. The fundamental principles of this law endure: to mitigate and circumscribe the cruelty of war for humanitarian reasons.'[299] Essentially, this paper suggests that the legal argument for accepting restrictions on the continued use of depleted uranium munitions centres not around the definitive truth of concerns as to their effects on health and the environment, but on fundamentally humanitarian justifications. Previous studies, both scientific and academic, have sought to identify the legal arguments against which the legality of the use of DU could be assessed, whilst conceding that illegality cannot be definitively proven.[300] Therefore, hu-

---

298. By 'post-development' use, the author refers to weapons or weapons systems that have been designed, developed, refined and tested and are 'ready' to enter into operational service.

299. Written Statement by New Zealand, p. 15, paras. 63-64 cited in *ICJ Rep.* (Advisory Opinion), *supra* n. 24, para. 86.

300. See in particular Zwanenburg, *supra* n. 14; McDonald, *supra* n. 10, Kleffner, *supra* n. 32.

manitarian considerations are to be coupled with reasoning that the potential seriousness of the concerns, should they be realised in time, necessitates a re-evaluation of the legality of the use of DU weapons, during which time they are not used by states which possess them or proliferated to those which do not. It is thus postulated that the only practical and effective restrictions on the use of DU munitions would be a legally-reasoned moratorium on continued use, based on ultimately humanitarian concerns, pending (preferably independent) re-evaluation of legality.

The logic of the argument is based on interpretation of 'dictates of the public conscience' in the Martens Clause which, as has been demonstrated *supra*, continues to be contemporaneously valid and instructive to cases where explicit provisions of law are absent, yet where humanitarian concerns endure. In particular, the principles of the Martens Clause provide an essential 'safety mechanism' in the process of assessing the legality of 'new' weapons due to the lack of effective, objective and independent review structures, and based on the 'new' information which 'concerns' represent. Thus, in the absence of incontrovertible evidence of the safety of DU munitions, the 'precautionary principle' should be applied such that, as Douma suggests, governments do not 'refrain from taking action against possible damages, even if the causal link between the human behaviour and those damages is not 100% clear'.[301]

Further, the humanitarian principles of the 1868 St. Petersburg Declaration complement the argument for a moratorium. Perhaps the gravity of the 1868 Declaration has been forgotten (if not ignored) as, in reality, it does appear that some of its essence has been lost to modern military requirements through such assumptions that states are free to use any weapon not specifically prohibited by convention, until illegality has been established through a sufficient weight of mutual consent, regardless of humanitarian concerns. The justification that certain effects of weapons and warfare are irrelevant to considerations of their legality, merely because such undesirable effects are not the 'primary purpose' of the weapons is surely preposterous. In the interests of protecting the principle of humanity, whether or not a certain weapon has consequential undesirable effects should be subservient to the fact that it does *in fact* have such effects. As Lauterpacht elucidated:

> '[W]e shall entirely fail to understand the true character of the law of war unless we realise that its purpose is almost entirely humanitarian in the literal sense of the word, namely, to prevent or mitigate suffering and in some cases, life, from the savagery of battle and passion. This, and not the regulation of hostilities is its essential purpose.'[302]

With regard to the humanitarian justification of the argument, the 1868 St. Petersburg Declaration has rightly been hailed as the origin of the prohibition on causing superfluous injury or unnecessary suffering to combatants. However, it may also be true that this achievement has caused scholars to overlook other fundamental elements of the Declaration which are particularly pertinent to the issue of 'new'

301. Douma, *supra* n. 278.
302. Lauterpacht, ed., cited by Draper in Meyer, ed., *supra* n. 1, p. 3.

weapons. On closer examination, the declaration embodies more than a mere prohibition of a specific weapon, but a prohibition on potential suffering and, thus, an advancement for civilisation. If we are to be so bold as to allow these principles of humanity to be reflected in our interpretation of contemporary IHL, it is not difficult to see that the law can be interpreted so as to provide a *humanitarian* constraint to the continued use of 'new' weapons and a readiness to re-evaluate their status should serious concerns be raised. It is especially difficult to refute this logic when adequate, albeit slightly inferior, alternatives are to be found.

In the light of the advances in the scientific and popular understanding of DU, it may be said that the issues raised in this paper should rightly have been addressed when concerns over DU first arose in the early 1990s. In this way, such calls for restrictions or reviews of conformity with the law, as envisaged by Article 36, may have been argued more convincingly. However, it is not possible to draw definitive conclusions with regard to either the effects or legality of use of DU munitions. Therefore, it may not be too late for states to demonstrate the 'pragmatism and conscience'[303] in support of humanitarianism by suspending their use of DU munitions in favour of alternatives until the issue of their conformity with IHL has been definitively established.

303. Beckett, *supra* n. 27, p. 36.

THE RIGHT TO EDUCATION IN OCCUPIED TERRITORIES: MAKING MORE ROOM FOR HUMAN RIGHTS IN OCCUPATION LAW[1]

Jonathan Thompson Horowitz[2]

2. Human rights officer for the United Nations Mission in Sudan (UNMIS); LL.M., International Human Right Law, University of Essex (UK); B.A., Political Science, Bates College (USA). This paper is based on the author's LL.M. dissertation, which was authored under the helpful supervision and guidance of Professor Françoise Hampson. The author is also grateful to Avril McDonald for her valuable comments and suggestions. The author takes full responsibility for the content of this paper.

Yearbook of International Humanitarian Law
Volume 7 - 2004 - pp. 233-277 DOI 10.1017/S1389135904002338

1. INTRODUCTION

In 2004 the International Court of Justice (ICJ) issued an advisory opinion stating that Occupying Powers must extend their international human rights treaty obligations to the people in the territories they occupy.[3] This finding reaffirmed what many human rights and occupation law scholars and judicial and quasi-judicial bodies have long claimed.[4] Nonetheless, while international humanitarian law and human rights law are concurrently applicable and largely compatible, tensions between the two can arise.[5] This is not surprising given the basic premises that each body of law is based upon. While occupation law largely works to restrict the occupant from tampering with the laws and institutions of the occupied territory, there are significant portions of human rights law that work hard to press states to amend or change laws and develop infrastructure to accommodate the welfare of their populations.[6] The International Covenant on Economic, Social and Cultural

---

3. *Legal Consequences of the Construction of a Wall in the Occupied Palestinian Territory,* International Court of Justice (ICJ), Advisory Opinion, 9 July 2004, paras. 111-113.

4. See *Detainees in Guantanamo Bay, Cuba: Request for Precautionary Measures*, Inter-American Commission on Human Rights (IACHR), (13 March 2002); *Banković and Others* v. *Belgium and 16 Other Contracting States*, 52207/99, European Court of Human Rights (ECtHR) (2001), para. 71; *Cyprus* v. *Turkey*, 25781/94 (2001), ECtHR (2001); *Issa and others* v. *Turkey*, 31821/96, ECtHR (2000); *Coard et al.* v. *United States*, Case 10.951 Report No. 109/99, IACHR (1999), para. 37; *Loizidou* v. *Turkey*, 40/1993/435/514, ECtHR (1996), para. 56; Human Rights Committee (HRC), General Comment 31, para. 10; For discussion on the overlap between international humanitarian law (IHL) and human rights law see, Y. Dinstein, 'Human rights in armed conflict: international humanitarian law', in T. Meron, ed., *Human Rights in International Law: Legal and Policy Issues* (Oxford, Clarendon Press 1984) pp. 345-368; Y. Dinstein, 'The International Law of Belligerent Occupation and Human Rights', Vol. 8 *Israel YB HR* (1978) p. 104-143; L. Green, 'Human Rights and the Law of Armed Conflict', Vol. 10 *Israel YB HR* (1980) pp. 9-37; T. Meron, 'Human rights in time of peace and in time of armed strife: selected problems', in T. Buergenthal, ed., *Contemporary Issues in International Law: essays in honor of Louis B. Sohn* (Kehl, Engle 1984) pp. 1-21.

5. See Dinstein, in Meron (1984), ibid., pp. 345-368; Meron, in Buergenthal, ibid, p. 17.

6. Sassòli and Bouvier have noted that: 'It is logical that the obligations of the occupying power can be summed up as permitting life in the occupied territory to continue as normally as possible. international humanitarian law is therefore strong in protecting the *status quo ante*, while weak in responding to new needs of the population of the occupied territories. The longer the occupation lasts, the more shortcomings of the regime established by international humanitarian law therefore appear.' M. Sassòli and A. Bouvier, *How Does Law Protect in War?: Cases Documents and Teaching Materials on Contemporary Practice in International Humanitarian Law* (Geneva, ICRC 2003), p. 154.

Rights (ICESCR), for example, specifically calls on States Parties to take legislative measures to meet their treaty obligations.[7]

To suggest that under occupation law prohibits the occupant from taking certain human rights actions to benefit the local population may seem antithetical to the hard fought (and won) battle waged by human rights advocates to ensure that human rights are applied extraterritorially in occupied territories. The opposite side of this coin, however, is that a state has substantial latitude under international human rights law to determine how it is allowed to meet its human rights obligations. If that discretion is not reined in, an occupant could make significant social and legal changes that masquerade as human rights initiatives but are in fact unnecessary and even used for the sole benefit of the occupant.[8]

With these thoughts in mind, this article explores the compatibilities and tensions between the human right to education and occupation law. To narrow its focus, this study looks at the extraterritorial positive human rights obligations that occupants have with regard to the primary education of children inside an occupied territory.[9] Focusing on this particular issue is deliberate, with the intention of making a modest contribution to the largely undeveloped literature in the fields of positive human rights obligations and economic, social and cultural rights in occupied territories. Moreover, this topic is not merely theoretical. It has been the case since at least World War I that occupants have taken an interest in making changes to the education of youth and educational institutions in the territory they occupy.[10]

Section 2 provides a few focused remarks about the extraterritorial application of human rights law as well as the duel obligations that an occupying power has under international humanitarian law and the human rights treaties it is a party to. Section 3 outlines the basic principles of occupation law and reviews the obligations that occupants have with respect to education under occupation law. Section 4 provides an overview of the common features of economic, social and cultural rights and recalls the basic components of the right to education. Sections 2 to 4 all provide the groundwork for Section 5, which explores the compatibility of occupation law with the core obligations of the right to education and sets out an approach that helps mediate the areas where the two are less than compatible. Section 6 discusses additional considerations to the application of the right to education in

---

7. International Covenant on Economic, Social and Cultural Rights (ICESCR), Art. 2(1).

8. M. Sassòli, 'Article 43 of the Hague Regulations and peace operations in the twenty-first century', (International Humanitarian Law Research Initiative) (Background Paper prepared for Informal High-Level Expert Meeting on Current Challenges to International Humanitarian Law, Cambridge, 25-27 June 2004) p. 14.

9. This paper does not address the issue of secondary or higher education and does not address the obligations that Occupying Powers have to the educational needs of children who are internees, detainees, or those who need to be evacuated. For provisions on these matters see 1949 Geneva Convention Relative to the Treatment of Prisoners of War (Third Geneva Convention), Art. 38; 1949 Geneva Convention Relative to the Protection of Civilian Persons in Time of War (Fourth Geneva Convention), Arts. 94 and 24(2); 1977 Protocol I Additional to the Geneva Conventions of relating to the Protection of Victims of International Armed Conflicts (Protocol I), Art. 78.

10. See the section on *State Practice* (3.2.1) below.

occupied territories that are not elaborated on in the paper. Section 7 contains concluding remarks.

2. EXTRATERRITORIAL APPLICATION OF HUMAN RIGHTS IN OCCUPIED TERRITORIES

Before entering into the specific topic of this paper, it is worth making a few basic, focused, but certainly not exhaustive, remarks about the extraterritorial application of human rights as well as the duel obligations that an occupying power has under international humanitarian law and the human rights treaties it is a party to. Firstly, the legal reasoning that supports the extraterritorial application of human rights in occupied territories is based on the general notions that 1) a state has obligations under human rights treaties to the people within its jurisdiction, 2) that the territorial jurisdiction is extended to the areas that a state has 'effective control' over, and 3) an occupied territory, as defined in Article 42 of the Hague Regulations, is under the 'effective control' of the Occupying Power.[11] Secondly, the focus of the extraterritorial applicability of human rights in court rooms and scholarly discussions has primarily been on civil and political rights. However, economic, social and cultural rights should not be excluded from these discussions. The ICJ took the view in its 2004 Advisory Opinion on the separation barrier that the Covenant on Economic, Social and Cultural Rights, as well as the Convention on the Rights of the Child, which contains economic, social and cultural rights, must be applied extraterritorially during times of occupation if the Occupying Power is a member state to those treaties. Thirdly, an Occupying Power has both positive and negative obligations under human rights treaties that are equally applicable in territory under its jurisdiction. This, as will be demonstrated by this paper, can create legal quagmires between human rights law and occupation law when an occupant asserts the broad positive obligation powers it has under its human rights treaties. In a recent case, *Ilaşcu*, the European Court of Human Rights (ECtHR) indicated that a state may not be fully responsible for all the components of each human right if it does not have full effective control over its territory.[12] This ruling manifests a tension with *Banković*, in which the court stated that the positive obligations a state has cannot be 'divided and tailored in accordance with the particular circumstances of the extra-territorial act in question'.[13] But wherever the issue may stand in the minds of the judges the court provides no support for the argument that if effective control does exist then the full set of obligations of each right are not applicable.

---

11. For an extensive discussion of domestic and Strasbourg case law on the extraterritorial application of human rights see *Al-Skeini*, EWHC 2911 (Admin), House of Lords (2004), paras. 127-243.

12. *Ilaşcu and Others* v. *Moldova and Russia*, 48787/99, (ECtHR) (2004).

13. *Banković and Others* v. *Belgium and 16 Other Contracting States*, 52207/99, (ECtHR) (2001), para. 74.

That is to say, when an occupant has effective control over a territory, it cannot pick and choose which components of a right it will have obligations to.[14]

A similar question that deals with parsing out certain rights and not others, is whether or not an occupant is responsible to the same degree to the people under its occupation compared to the people under its home territory. Generally speaking it is.[15] The Human Rights Committee stated in General Comment 31, 'the enjoyment of the Covenant rights is not limited to citizens of States Parties but must also be available to all individuals, regardless of nationality or statelessness, such as asylum seekers, migrant workers and other persons'. The General Comment goes on to say, 'this principle also applies to those within the power or effective control of the forces of a State Party acting outside its territory'. As just mentioned, the ICJ in its Advisory Opinion on the separation barrier held that this concept applies with respect to the CESCR and the CRC as well.[16] In *Al-Skeini* the Law Lords noted that even though defendants had no 'connection with the United Kingdom other than as residents of a province in a foreign country where the United Kingdom is an occupying power … we would be reluctant to distinguish their case from that of a British resident or national where Convention rights are interfered with in a narrow extra-territorial context interpreted by Strasbourg jurisprudence (itself founded in concepts of international law) to be within a state party's essentially territorial jurisdiction under Article 1'.[17]

All that being said, the content of the Convention on the Protection of the Rights of All Migrant Workers and Members of Their Families (CMW) indicates that nationality can have a dramatic impact on the obligations a state has with respect to the human rights of the people within its jurisdiction. For example, Article 43 of the CMW does not provide a 'right to education' or a 'right to health' for documented migrants as found in the ICESCR. Rather, it provides a right to 'equality of treatment with nationals of the State of employment' in such fields as education, health, vocational guidance, and housing. Additionally, the CMW distinguishes between the rights it affords to legal and illegal migrant workers, thus making another rift in the notion of human rights as being universal and equally applicable to everyone. But at this point the CMW is exceptional and has no judicial interpretations to sweep away the abovementioned judicial decisions.

A fourth point to note about the extraterritorial application of human rights in occupied territory comes from a 2004 decision of the House of Lords, *Al-Skeini*, which held that under the Human Rights Act of 1998 (which is the domestic implementation legislation for the European Convention for the Protection of Human Rights and Fundamental Freedoms) the United Kingdom as an Occupying Power

---

14. In *Skeini*, the House of Lords supported this claim. See *Al-Skeini*, *supra* n. 11, paras. 324 and 341.

15. A notable exception is Article 25 of the ICCPR, which pertains to, *inter alia*, voting rights and participation in public affairs.

16. The Court also notes that this view has been advanced by the Committee on Economic, Social and Cultural Rights. *Legal Consequences of the Construction of a Wall in the Occupied Palestinian Territory*, *supra* n. 3, paras. 112, 113 and 114.

17. *Al-Skeini*, *supra* n. 11, *para*. 302.

in Iraq was not legally accountable for violations of the Act because Iraq was not a member state of the European Convention. The Lords based this conclusion largely on the *Banković* decision handed down by the ECHR. In *Banković* the court pointed out that the Convention was essentially a regional agreement that was not meant to be enforced outside its 'legal space'.[18] The impact that this legal reasoning can have on the extraterritorial applicability of human rights is potentially significant and limiting. However, the Lords concurred that a state does have jurisdiction over certain special objects that a state has control over, such as their consulates, embassies, ships, jails or courts, regardless of their location. Thus, they ruled that the British had responsibilities under the European Convention (via the domestic Human Rights Act) to the rights of a man who died while in the custody of a British-run prison in Iraq.

Finally, it is imperative to note the ICJ's Advisory Opinion of 1996, which states that international humanitarian law is *lex specialis* to international human rights law.[19] The legal concept of *lex specialis* is critical to the topic of this essay and has the significance of potentially limiting the content of the human rights obligations an Occupying Power has. It means, essentially, that where obligations that an occupant has to human rights law and occupation law overlap, human rights obligations remain applicable but must be interpreted through international humanitarian law. This is because international humanitarian law is more appropriately tailored for the situation under inspection, namely occupation.

3. OCCUPATION LAW AND EDUCATION

3.1 **Overview of occupation law**

Before entering into the core discussion of this paper, it is helpful to understand some of the fundamental underpinnings of occupation law. Doing so draws out not only why tensions and similarities between human rights and occupation law exist, but is also helpful for thinking about how to reconcile these two bodies of law when tensions do arise. Both bodies of law have been developed over time for good reason, often shaped by the difficult lessons of history. To attempt to resolve their incompatibilities without such a basic understanding would be a mistake and would likely lead to poorly thought-out and myopic conclusions and recommendations.

3.1.1 *Fundamental principles*

The bulk of occupation law is found in the 1907 Fourth Convention Respecting the Laws and Customs of War on Land (hereafter, Hague Regulations) and the 1949

---

18. *Banković and Others* v. *Belgium and 16 Other Contracting States*, *supra* n. 13, para. 80.
19. *Legality of the Threat or Use of Nuclear Weapons*, ICJ, Advisory Opinion, 8 July 1996, para. 25.

Fourth Geneva Convention Relative to the Protection of Civilian Persons in Time of War (hereafter, Fourth Geneva Convention).[20] This body of law rests on four basic principles, the first of which is that sovereignty does not pass from the hands of the occupied state to the hands of the occupying force. This is reflected by the limited powers given to the occupant and is articulated through Article 43 of the Hague Regulations, which instructs the occupant to respect the laws in the country unless they prevent the occupant from carrying out its duty to restore and ensure 'public order and [civil life]'.[21] The 1958 International Committee of the Red Cross Commentary (ICRC Commentary) on the Fourth Geneva Convention states: 'the occupation of territory in wartime is essentially a temporary, de facto situation, which deprives the occupied Power of neither its statehood nor its sovereignty'.[22]

The second principle, common to the Hague Regulations and the Fourth Geneva Convention, is that of legal non-interference. Article 43 of the Hague Regulations states:

> 'The authority of the legitimate power having in fact passed into the hands of the occupant, the latter shall take all the measures in his power to restore, and ensure, as far as possible, public order and [civil life], *while respecting, unless absolutely prevented, the laws in force in the country.*' [emphasis added][23]

Article 64 of the Fourth Geneva Convention, an elaboration of Article 43, stays true to the principle of non-interference and the ICRC Commentary affirms that respect for the law in force is a principle that 'dominates the whole of occupation law'.[24]

The third principle of occupation law is that the occupant must not injure the local population and, additionally, must provide them with care.[25] The fourth prin-

---

20. Protocol I contains provisions concerning occupied territories as well. Also, relevant customary international law is applicable. See G. von Glahn, *Law Among Nations: An Introduction to Public International Law*, 5th edn. (New York, MacMillan 1986) pp. 683, 686.

21. Benvenisti and others have explained that it is more accurate to use 'civil life', as translated from the French text, than the word 'safety', which is found in the English text. The French version uses '*l'ordre et la vie publics*' instead of 'public order and safety'. It is only the French text that is binding. E. Benvenisti, *The International Law of Occupation* (Princeton NJ, Princeton University Press 1993) p. 2.

22. International Committee of the Red Cross (ICRC), J. Pictet, et al., eds., *Commentary on the Geneva Conventions of 12 August 1949: IV Geneva Convention Relative to the Protection of Civilian Persons in Time of War* (hereafter, Commentary Geneva IV) (Geneva, ICRC 1958) p. 275.

23. Dinstein and others have argued that the words 'absolutely prevented' in Art. 43 should not be taken literally but rather '*empechement absolu*' is the equivalent of '*necessite*' (the original of Brussels Art. 3)'. Y. Dinstein, 'The Israel Supreme Court and the law of belligerent occupation: Article 43 of the Hague Regulations,' 25 *Israel YB HR* (1995) p.6.

24. Commentary Geneva IV, *supra* n. 22, p. 290; see also the discussion on Article 43 in the section *From the Hague Regulations to the Fourth Geneva Convention* (3.1.2.).

25. See for example, 1907 Convention (IV) Respecting the Laws and Customs of War on Land and its Annex: Regulations concerning the Laws and Customs of War on Land (Hague Regulations), Art. 53 (prohibiting destruction of private property) and Fourth Geneva Convention, Arts. 50 (education), 55 (food and medical supplies) and 56 (health and hygiene).

ciple is that the occupant may not undertake activities for the sole benefit of its native state.[26] An occupant must direct its actions toward the local population or toward military necessity; actions outside those two realms are prohibited.[27]

3.1.2 *From the Hague Regulations to the Fourth Geneva Convention*

While the fundamental principles of occupation law have remained constant in the texts of the Hague Regulations and the Fourth Geneva Convention, shifts from 1907 to 1949 in the nature of war, the understanding of international law and the consideration given to humanitarian issues demanded changes to the law.[28] In World War II states, in control of territory that was not initially theirs, largely regarded the law of occupation as inapplicable to them, and did not act in accordance with it, even on a *de facto* basis, and acted only in self-interest.[29] In response to these problems, the Fourth Geneva Convention strengthened the underpinnings of occupation law with the codification of two important provisions.[30]

Article 47 strengthened the principle that sovereignty is not transferable from the conquered government to the occupant. It holds that an Occupying Power must abide by the laws of occupation without regard to

> '… any change introduced, as a result of the occupation of a territory, into the institutions or government of the said territory, nor by any agreement concluded between the authorities of the occupied territories and the Occupying Power, nor by any annexation by the latter of the whole or part of the occupied territory'.[31]

This provision has the purpose of denying a state the ability to circumvent caring for the civilian population by claiming that it is not an Occupying Power. There were instances in World War II where states invoked the rule of *debellatio* and thus regarded occupation law as inapplicable and the land open to annexation or under the sovereign control of the occupant.[32] Article 47, in turn, reflected the illegitimacy of *debellatio* in contemporary international law and represented a fundamental shift in the way international law, states and people would have to interact in future occupations. A corollary effect of this rule was that it was clearly appropriate for international law to place certain obligations on the occupant (which does

---

26. This principle is reflected in Hague Regulations, Arts. 48, 52, and 55 and Fourth Geneva Convention, Arts. 51, 52, and 57.

27. For various discussions on the relevance of military necessity in occupation law, see E. Benvenisti, 'The Applicability of Human Rights Conventions to Israel and to the Occupied Territories', 26 *Israel LR* (1992) p. 30; Dinstein, *supra* n. 23, pp. 2, 7; D. Graber, *The Development of the Law of Belligerent Occupation, 1863-1914: A Historical Survey* (New York, Columbia University Press 1949) pp. 207-208.

28. For commentary on why the Hague Regulations were formulated as they were see Benvenisti, *supra* n. 21, pp. 27-28; Dinstein, ibid., p. 15.

29. Benvenisti, *supra* n. 21, pp. 96-97.

30. Ibid., p. 98.

31. Fourth Geneva Convention, Art. 47.

32. Benvenisti, *supra* n. 21, pp. 91-96.

not have sovereign control over the people in the occupied territory) that relate to the welfare of the people under its control. Thus, Article 43 begins, 'Protected persons who are in occupied territory shall not be deprived, in any case or in any manner whatsoever, of the benefits of the present Convention …'.[33]

Article 64 further secured the principle of legal non-interference and set out a similar, though narrower, rule than Article 43 of the Hague Regulations by placing a general obligation on an Occupying Power not to suspend or repeal the penal laws in force or to impose new laws.[34] Each article, however, does permit exceptions to this rule of non-interference for reasons of the security of the occupier[35] and, to varying degrees, for the welfare of the civilian population.

It is this latter exception that is most pertinent to this essay. While Article 43 of the Hague Regulations and Article 64 of the Fourth Geneva Convention similarly allow occupants to change and introduce laws that benefit the civilian population, their terms for doing so differ substantially. Article 43 allows an occupant to introduce legislation if it is necessary for restoring and ensuring public order and civil life, though it does not define what constitutes public order and civil life. Article 64, on the other hand, is far more specific and permits the occupant to change laws to in the interests of the population and in order to fulfil its obligations under the Fourth Geneva Convention. The Commentary to the Fourth Convention points out that the interests of the population 'makes it possible to abrogate any discrimina-

---

33. Fourth Geneva Convention, Art. 47.

34. When defining the term 'laws in force', the ICRC Commentary informs that, 'The words "penal laws" mean all legal provisions in connection with the repression of offences: the penal code and rules of procedure proper, subsidiary penal laws, laws in the strict sense of the term, decrees, orders, the penal clauses of administrative regulations, penal clauses of financial laws, etc.' Commentary Geneva IV, *supra* n. 22, p. 335; Sassòli notes that 'laws in force' not only includes laws, but also refers to the constitution, decrees, ordinances, court precedents, and administrative regulations and executive orders. M. Sassòli, *supra* n. 8, p. 6.
Art. 64 reads: 'The penal laws of the occupied territory shall remain in force, with the exception that they may be repealed or suspended by the Occupying Power in cases where they constitute a threat to its security or an obstacle to the application of the present Convention.
Subject to the latter consideration and to the necessity for ensuring the effective administration of justice, the tribunals of the occupied territory shall continue to function in respect of all offences covered by the said laws.
The Occupying Power may, however, subject the population of the occupied territory to provisions which are essential to enable the Occupying Power to fulfil its obligations under the present Convention, to maintain the orderly government of the territory, and to ensure the security of the Occupying Power, of the members and property of the occupying forces or administration, and likewise of the establishments and lines of communication used by them.'

35. Art. 64 allows for changes to the 'penal laws' when they, *inter alia*, 'constitute a threat to [the Occupying Power's] security or an obstacle to the application of the present Convention'. It also allows an Occupying Power 'to subject the population of the occupied territory to provisions which are essential to enable the Occupying Power to fulfil its obligations under the present Convention, to maintain the orderly government of the territory, and to ensure the security of the Occupying Power, of the members and property of the occupying forces or administration, and likewise of the establishments and lines of communication used by them'. The degree to which the Hague Regulations allow military necessity to dictate changes in legislation has been debated. For various discussions on the relevance of military necessity in occupation law, see Benvenisti, *supra* n. 27, p. 30; Dinstein, *supra* n. 23, pp. 2, 7; Graber, *supra* n. 27, pp. 207-208.

tory measures incompatible with humane requirements'.[36] Moreover, according to the Commentary, the Occupying Power 'may promulgate provisions required for the application of the Convention in accordance with the obligations imposed on it by the latter in a number of spheres: child welfare, labour, food, hygiene and public health etc'.[37]

The precise articles in the Fourth Convention relating to education of children, food and medical supplies, and health and hygiene place precise obligations on an occupant that might otherwise rely on a narrow interpretation of what it means under the Hague Regulations to restore and ensure public safety and civil life. Article 64, in turn, serves as a provision that permits these obligations to be carried out in an effective manner. In this case, Article 64 and the welfare provisions in the Fourth Geneva Convention can only be seen as a positive contribution to occupation law. On the other hand, the specificity written into Article 64 and the welfare provisions can be a restrictive combination. For an occupant who wishes to make changes to the law for the benefit of the local population that are above and beyond the obligations included in occupation law, it can only do so if those changes can be justified by the other exception clauses, namely for purposes of maintaining an orderly government and ensuring security of the Occupying Power. While it might seem misplaced to say that such limitations do exist, given that the Fourth Geneva Convention was largely written to benefit civilians during times of armed conflict and occupation, there are important and sensible reasons why this is so, namely, to put reins on occupants that seeks to exploit the broad language of Article 43.[38]

In this discussion of the similarities and differences between the Hague Regulations and the Geneva Conventions, it is worth noting that Article 154 of the Fourth Geneva Convention makes the provisions on occupation in the Hague Regulations supplementary to the provisions on occupation in the Geneva Convention.[39] This was necessary because the Hague Regulations contains provisions that are altogether absent from the Fourth Geneva Convention. The Convention is silent on issues of taxation and levied monies, for example. It should not, however, be assumed that all of the Hague Regulations should be interpreted as they were prior to the adoption of the Fourth Geneva Convention. With due consideration of the partial eclipse that Article 64 of the Fourth Geneva Conventions has over Article 43 of the Hague Regulations, and in keeping with the principle of *lex posterior derogat priori*,[40] the ICRC Commentary correctly holds: '[i]t may therefore be concluded

---

36. Commentary Geneva IV, *supra* n. 22, p. 335.

37. Ibid., p. 337. This is a non-exhaustive list and there is no reason for 'education for children' (which also falls under 'child welfare') not to be included if the list were expanded.

38. Benvenisti has noted that while the language of 'ensure and restore public order and civil life' was initially insisted on by weaker states out of a fear that occupants would not give care to the local population, occupants used the language as 'justification for increased intervention in local affairs'. Benvenisti, *supra* n. 21, p. 10.

39. Art. 154 reads: 'In the relations between the Powers who are bound by the Hague Conventions respecting the Laws and Customs of War on Land, whether that of July 29, 1899, or that of October 18, 1907, and who are parties to the present Convention, this last Convention shall be supplementary to Sections II and III of the Regulations annexed to the above-mentioned Conventions of The Hague'.

40. Vienna Convention on the Law of Treaties, Art. 30.

that the Convention has taken from this provision of the Hague Regulations those parts essential for the protection of civilian persons. In all other respects, Article 43 of the Regulations remains valid.'[41]

The reason it is misguided to fall back on the Hague Regulations in full is illustrated by the practice of Israel's High Court of Justice. The court came to the conclusion in the case of *Abu Aita* v. *Commander of the Judea and Samaria Region* that 'restore and ensure' is the overriding principle of occupation law and anything that is done in the name of restoring and ensuring public order and civil life trumps other restrictions found in the Hague Regulations.[42] If other courts were to apply Article 43 instead of the Fourth Geneva Convention the implicit constraints that the Fourth Geneva Convention places on an Occupying Power would become effectively useless.[43]

3.2 **Education in occupation law**

Now that a basic overview of occupation law has demonstrated that the Fourth Geneva Convention attempted to, *inter alia*, codify a balance between what an occupant can and cannot do for the civilian population, we can turn to the more specific issue of the obligations an Occupying Power has with regard to education in the territory that it occupies under occupation law.

Throughout the development of modern day occupation law educational institutions have been regarded as private property and thus out of bounds to the occupant.[44] It was only with the Fourth Geneva Convention that occupants were given explicit positive duties. Until this time the positive obligations that the occupant had with respect to education could only be found through an interpretation of the '"supra"-general' phrase 'restore and ensure, as far as possible, public order and [civil life]'.[45]

The relevant provisions of Article 50(1) and (3) of the Fourth Geneva Conventions read:

---

41. Commentary Geneva IV, *supra* n. 22, p. 617.

42. This is not to suggest that the High Court took this exact approach. In this case the court did not believe that the Geneva Conventions as treaty law was applicable under its jurisdiction. In the case, *Abu Aita* v. *Commander of the Judea and Samaria Region*, the court ruled that Arts. 48 and 49 took a back seat to the duties in Art. 43. Von Glahn disputed this interpretation and though Dinstein has agreed with the logic of the court's reasoning, he has noted that there is little evidence to support it. Dinstein, *supra* n. 23, pp. 16-20.

43. The fact that the Israel High Court of Justice has taken the time to scrutinise the motives behind projects that claim to benefit the local population does help to mitigate the freedoms occupants have under Art. 43 of the Hague Regulations. See *Christian Society for the Holy Places* v. *Minister of Defense et al.*, H.C. 337/71; *Jerusalem District Electricity Company, Ltd.* v. *(a) Minister of Energy and Infrastructure, (b) Commander of the Judea and Samaria Region,* H.C. 673/81.

44. See Brussels Code (1874), Art. 8; Oxford Code (1880), Art. 53; 1907 Hague Regulations, Art. 56.

45. F. Domb, 'Judgements of the Supreme Court of Israel: *Cooperative Society Lawfully Registered in the Judea and Samaria Region* v. *Commander of the IDF Forces in the Judea and Samaria Region* H.C.393/82', 14 *Israel YB HR* (1984) p. 305.

> 'The Occupying Power shall, with the cooperation of the national and local authorities, facilitate the proper working of all institutions devoted to the care and education of children.
>
> ...
>
> Should the local institutions be inadequate for the purpose, the Occupying Power shall make arrangements for the maintenance and education, if possible by persons of their own nationality, language and religion, of children who are orphaned or separated from their parents as a result of the war and who cannot be adequately cared for by a near relative or friend.'

Article 24(1), which is also applicable in times of occupation and overlaps considerably with Article 50(3), responds to the educational needs of *all* orphans and children separated from their families as a result of war. Article 77 of 1977 Protocol I Additional to the Geneva Conventions relating to the Protection of Victims of International Armed Conflicts (Protocol I) requires states to provide children with 'the care and aid they require, whether because of their age or for any other reason'. While the language is open-ended, according to the drafting record and the ICRC Commentary Article 77 adds little to what is already included in Articles 24 and 50 of the Fourth Geneva Convention aside from importantly extending Article 50 to all children and not only to children who are protected persons in occupied territories.[46]

3.2.1 *State practice*

There has been a rich history from World War I to contemporary times of Occupying Powers making changes in the field of education, and it is clear from this history that benefits and detriments may result. During the German occupation of Belgium from 1914-1918, the Government General issued several decrees focused on education, and in 1916 the Germans made primary education compulsory.[47] But as Benvenisti points out, the German initiatives in the Flemish region of Belgium concerning education were directed at restructuring the body politic of Belgium for self-benefit.[48] Following World War II, the US took various initiatives in Italy and Germany to eliminate Fascism and Nazism from the education system. It also took an interest in ensuring that the education system was up and running. Lieutenant Colonel Gayre, referring to the US occupation of Italy, reported:

---

46. Y. Sandoz, C. Swinarski and B. Zimmermann, eds., Commentary on the Additional Protocols of 8 June 1977 to the Geneva Conventions of 12 August 1949 (hereafter, Commentary Protocol I) (Geneva, ICRC/Dordrecht, Martinus Nijhoff 1987), paras. 3173-3174; M. Bothe, K. Partsch, and W. Solf, *New Rules for Victims of Armed Conflicts: Commentary on the Two 1977 Protocols Additional to the Geneva Conventions of 1949* (The Hague, Martinus Nijhoff 1982) p. 474.

47. A. Solansky, *German Administration in Belgium* (New York, Colombia University 1928) p. 163.

48. Benvenisti, *supra* n. 21, pp. 40-43.

> 'Not only have we the physical problem of opening the actual school buildings and the big task of examining the history of each teacher so as to exclude all ardent Fascists, but we have not a single text book which can be used. Furthermore, the Italian teacher virtually cannot teach without a text book, so reliant had he become upon this method. ... Therefore it is necessary to begin working on a set of temporary text books immediately.'[49]

General Eisenhower ordered in 1944 that '[a]ll German courts and educational institutions within the occupied territories are suspended'.[50]

In East Timor, Indonesia used education as a tool for indoctrination to maintain its hold of the land.[51] It imposed on Timorese the curriculum that was in place in Indonesia. Classes were taught only in Bahasa Indonesia, the official Indonesian language, rather than the native language Tetum. When the USSR was in Afghanistan in the 1970s and 1980s it used education largely as a vehicle for advancing the 'socialist transformation of the Afghan society'.[52] It announced in three decrees a 'jihad' against illiteracy; in 1979 the budget for education increased by 30 percent; classes were taught in Russian and other foreign languages rather than languages that allowed for intertribal communication; the authorities also eliminated corporal punishment in schools.[53] In Cyprus the Turkish-Cypriot authorities vetted primary school textbooks as part of 'confidence-building measures' suggested by UNFICYP (United Nations Peacekeeping Force in Cyprus).[54] The Turkish-Cypriot authorities also abolished secondary educational facilities once available to Greek Cypriots.[55] In the Israeli Occupied Territories, the authorities reviewed textbooks to exclude anti-Israeli and anti-Semitic content. This was done with the approval of the United Nations Educational, Scientific and Cultural Organization (UNESCO).[56] In 1986 the General Assembly condemned Israel for, among other things, closing educational institutions, prohibiting the use of Syrian textbooks, and imposing courses that promoted hatred and intolerance and declared that these actions were 'in clear violation of the Geneva Convention'.[57] More recently, in the case of the occupation of Iraq, the US signed over 90 contracts aimed at renovating

---

49. H. Coles and A. Weinberg, *Civil Affairs: Soldiers Become Governors* (Washington, DC, Office of the Chief of Military History, Department of the Army 1965) p. 401. For a detailed look at the US military actions toward education and an assessment of those actions see generally, pp. 400-405.

50. Quoted in Benvenisti, *supra* n. 21, p. 91.

51. Ibid., p. 155.

52. Ibid., p. 162.

53. A. Hyman, *Afghanistan under Soviet Domination, 1964-1981* (London, MacMillan 1982) pp. 93, 94; Benvenisti, *supra* n. 21, p. 162.

54. *Cyprus* v. *Turkey*, 25781/94 (2001) para. 44.

55. Ibid., para. 275.

56. D. Shefi, 'The Reports of the U.N. Special Committees in Israeli Practices in the Territories', in M. Shamgar, ed., *Military Government in the Territories Administered by Israel 1967-1980; the legal aspects*, Vol. I (Jerusalem, Alpha Press 1982) pp. 312-313; *Report of the Commission General of United Nations Relief and Works Agency for Palestine Refugees in the Near East* (UNRWA), A/38/13 (1983).

57. GA Res.41/63 (1986), para. D(10).

schools and removing propaganda from texts, and facilitated training programs for teachers and administrators.[58]

Despite these examples, however, many of the states just mentioned were not, or did not consider themselves, bound by the occupation law of the Fourth Geneva Convention, and therefore there exists only a scant record of how occupants have sought to respect their positive obligations under Articles 24 and 50.[59] In the case of the US in Iraq, while Security Council Resolution 1483 made it clear that the US did consider itself an Occupying Power, it is unclear if the attention given to education was done for political or legal reasons, or both. Moreover, while some occupants have been criticised for their actions in relation to education under international humanitarian law as well as human rights law, these criticisms have almost exclusively been directed at the military administration in the Israeli Occupied Territories and have been based on the occupant's obstruction of the normal workings of educational institutions rather than not doing enough to make sure they were working properly.[60] This is all by way of saying that in academic and legal circles, it remains to be articulated clearly what exactly are the positive obligations that an occupant has with respect to the education of children under occupation law.

3.2.2 *Commentary by the International Committee of the Red Cross*

The ICRC Commentary to Articles 24 and 50 help to clarify some of the opaqueness by giving detailed interpretations of these provisions. While there is no explicit mention of age with regard to Article 50(1) and (3), the Commentary sets three grounds for determining what the word 'children' means in terms of age. First, by relying on other provisions in the treaty, including Article 24, the Commentary deduces that the article affords protections to 'children and younger people up to the age of fifteen'.[61] Secondly, the Commentary states that in certain circumstances it may be necessary to consider the 'degree of development of the physical and mental faculties of the persons concerned'.[62] Thus, the age limit may not strictly be 15, but higher. Finally, it recognises that the legislation of the occupied territory should be considered.[63]

---

58. See the section *Physical operation of educational institutions* (5.1.2) below.
59. SC Res. 1483, 22 May 2003.
60. See *Legal Consequences of the Construction of a Wall in the Occupied Palestinian Territory*, *supra* n. 3; Report of the Special Rapporteur on the Situation of Human Rights in the Palestinian Territories Occupied by Israel since 1967, E/CN.4/2003/30; GA Res. A/57/366 (2002); GA Res. 41/63 (1986), para. D(10); GA Res. A/RES/40/161 (1985); GA Res. A/RES/39/95, (1984); GA Res. A/RES/38/79 (1983); Committee on Economic Social and Cultural Rights (CESCR), Concluding observations (Israel), E/C.12/1/Add.90, 2003; Human Rights Watch, 'Israel's 'Separation Barrier' in the Occupied West Bank: Human Rights and International Humanitarian Law Consequences', Briefing Paper, February 2004; Save the Children, 'Education Under Occupation: Palestinian Children Talk about Life and School', 2002; *Cyprus* v. *Turkey*, 25781/94 (2001).
61. Commentary Geneva IV, *supra* n. 22, p. 285.
62. Ibid., p. 286.
63. Ibid., see also Commentary Protocol I, *supra* n. 46, para. 3179.

On the issue of 'institutions', the Commentary states that this term is purposefully broad. It lists examples but does not separate which institutions are for the 'care of children' and which are for their 'education'. The two can overlap and the Commentary groups them together to include, 'e.g., child welfare centres, orphanages, children's camps, children's homes and day nurseries, "medio-social" reception centres, social welfare services, reception centres, canteens, etc'.[64] The Commentary also notes that these institutions refer to both state run and private establishments.[65] Though the list is not exhaustive, it is unfortunate that it did not explicitly list 'schools'. There is nothing to indicate, however, that 'schools' were intentionally omitted.

The Commentary also elaborates on what it means in Article 50(1) for an occupant to work 'with the cooperation of the national and local authorities'.[66] It stresses that an occupant is not allowed to interfere with educational institutions. However, the occupant

> 'must ensure by *mutual agreement with the local authorities* that the persons concerned receive food, medical supplies and anything else necessary to enable them to carry out their task. It is in that sense that the expression "the proper working" of children's institutions should be understood'. [67] [emphasis added]

Accordingly, any action taken by the occupant to assist educational institutions must therefore be agreed upon with the national and local authorities.

This language in the Commentary begs an obvious question and reveals a understandable, but nonetheless thought provoking, presumption about the dynamic of education under occupation law. The question is: What is an Occupying Power responsible for if a 'mutual agreement' cannot be reached? Can the occupant simply walk away? The presumption that the Commentary reveals – which is inextricably linked to the question of responsibility just posed – is that the local authorities should remain in some degree of control of the education system such that they are in a position to give their 'agreement'. If this is true, then this raises potentially provocative implications about who has responsibilities for the education of children under human rights law – especially if we equate 'responsibilities' with 'legal obligations'. Does the local administration have responsibilities, does the occupant, or do both? The language in the Commentary implies, not surprisingly, that occupation law does not in fact permit an Occupying Power to assert full effective control over a territory. There are, of course, limits to what an occupant is permitted to due under international humanitarian law. However, human rights law, as it has been codified and adjudicated, has in no significant way taken into account a dynamic of cooperative power-sharing that places responsibilities on the occupant *and* the local authorities who are operating, indeed required to operate, under a state of occupation.

---

64. Commentary Geneva IV, *supra* n. 22, p. 286.
65. Ibid.
66. Fourth Geneva Convention, Art. 50.
67. Commentary Geneva IV, *supra* n. 22, p. 286.

The Final Record of the Diplomatic Conference of Geneva of 1949 (hereinafter, Final Record) and the ICRC Commentary make it clear that a main purpose of adding the language 'with the cooperation of the national and local authorities' to Article 50(1), which is also found in Article 56 (hygiene and public health), was to emphasize that the tasks in those provisions should fall firstly on existing native service providers and only where they fail should the Occupying Power work in cooperation with local and national authorities to achieve the goals of those provisions.[68] That said, remarks by the ICRC to the draft convention it submitted to the August 1948 International Red Cross Conference in Stockholm and the ICRC Commentary to Article 56 present a different understanding of the nature of 'co-operation', at least in the context of health if not education. With respect to this article the draft convention held, 'in this field, one has the right to *demand* the cooperation of national or local authorities, in the interest of their own country and of the population of the occupied territory'. [emphasis added] The ICRC Commentary to Article 56, too, notes that an Occupying Power is permitted to 'demand the co-operation not only of the national and local authorities but also of the population in the fight against epidemics'.[69]

The ICRC's interpretations of 'cooperation' in Articles 50 and 56 create an obvious discrepancy. In relation to the latter, the ICRC believed that the occupant was entitled to receive cooperation from local and national authorities. The occupant could 'demand' cooperation. But in relation to Article 50(1), the ICRC asserted that the occupant is obligated to work in cooperation with the national and local authorities. The occupant must work in 'mutual agreement'. Perhaps it is that the ICRC interpretations of 'cooperation' differed because Article 56 dealt primarily with preventing contagious diseases and epidemics, which were regarded as essential, whereas providing education was not. Whatever the reason, this still does not settle the question of what an occupant must do (or can do) if it is unable to work in mutual agreement with the national and local authorities on issues concerning education. This dilemma will be addressed in more detail in the section on *Right to Education in Occupied Territories* (5.1 and 5.2).

While the ICRC's Commentary sheds light on certain issues that are unclear in the text of the Fourth Geneva Convention, as just illustrated above, there are issues that remain untouched. Neither the Commentary to Articles 24 and 50 nor scholarly writings give a normative substantive understanding of what 'properly working' should mean. At most, the Fourth Geneva Convention demands an occupant to facilitate an unaccompanied child's education, not obstruct educational institutions from operating, assist in the operation of those institutions when needed, and not inject into a child's education 'any religious or political propaganda designed to wean children from their natural milieu'.[70] The absence of any explanation as to

68. Ibid., pp. 313-314.

69. ICRC 1948 Draft Revised or New Conventions for the Protection of War Victims, p. 177; Commentary Geneva IV, *supra* n. 22, p. 314.

70. Though not a strictly accurate term, this paper will use 'unaccompanied children' as shorthand to refer to children protected under Art. 24(1) and Art. 50(3). Commentary Geneva IV, *supra* n. 22, p. 187.

what constitutes a properly working educational institution or a proper education leaves an important question unanswered: what powers does an occupant have to make changes to an education system if it disagrees with the way the system functioned prior to the conflict or occupation? What is available from general principles of occupation law and doctrine points to allowing children to be educated as they were being educated prior to the occupation.[71] This is most clearly illustrated by Articles 24(1) and 50(3), which work to ensure that orphaned children and children who were separated from their parents and families are educated by persons of their own nationality, language, religion or a similar culture. However, when the native education system is inconsistent with right to education norms this answer raises serious concerns from a human rights perspective.

4. THE RIGHT TO EDUCATION UNDER HUMAN RIGHTS LAW

As demonstrated, occupation law provides a secure (be it at times opaque) place for the protection and facilitation of education. This is true too for human rights law. The right to education was included in the 1948 Universal Declaration of Human Rights and provisions concerning education have been included in all the major international and regional human rights treaties.[72] Of these treaties, the most developed provisions concerning education are found in the ICESCR (Arts. 13 and 14) and the Convention on the Rights of the Child (CRC) (Arts. 28 and 29).

The right to education has two general purposes. It aims to give individuals an education and it aims to ensure that that education is adequate and appropriate. The right to education is a unique human right, as it affords a right and also makes that right compulsory for certain individuals to enjoy.[73] While there may be many ways to interpret the obligations that states have with respect to the right to education, the Committee on Economic, Social and Cultural Rights (CESCR)[74] and the UN Special Rapporteur on the Right to Education, Katarina Tomaševski, have indi-

---

71. G. von Glahn, *The Occupation of Enemy Territory: A Commentary on the Law and Practice of Belligerent Occupation* (Minneapolis MN, University of Minnesota Press 1957) pp. 63-64.

72. See African Charter on Human and Peoples' Rights, Art. 17; American Convention on Human Rights, Art. 26; Convention on the Elimination of All Forms of Discrimination Against Women, Art. 10; Convention on the Elimination of All Forms of Racial Discrimination, Art. 5(e)(v); Convention on the Protection of the Rights of All Migrant Workers and Members of Their Families (CMW), Art. 30; Convention on the Rights of the Child, Art. 28; International Covenant on Civil and Political Rights (ICCPR), Art. 18; European Convention on Human Rights and Fundamental Freedoms, Protocol No.1, Art. 2; International Covenant on Economic, Social and Cultural Rights (ICESCR), Art. 13. This is not an exhaustive list of human rights provisions concerning education.

73. Art. 13(2)(a) of the ICESCR and Art. 28(a) of the CRC obligate states to work to ensure that primary education is compulsory.

74. The Committee on Economic, Social and Cultural Rights (CESCR) is the body of independent experts that monitors implementation of the International Covenant on Economic, Social and Cultural Rights by its States parties. The Committee was established under ECOSOC Res.1985/17 of 28 May 1985 to carry out the monitoring functions assigned to the United Nations Economic and Social Council (ECOSOC) in Part IV of the Covenant. This description was provided by the Office of the United Nations High Commissioners for Human Rights, <www.ohchr.org/english/bodies/cescr>.

cated that the right to education has four components: availability, accessibility, acceptability and adaptability.[75] In General Comment 13, the CESCR defined these terms:

> '(a) Availability – functioning educational institutions and programmes have to be available in sufficient quantity within the jurisdiction of the State party. What they require to function depends upon numerous factors, including the developmental context within which they operate; for example, all institutions and programmes are likely to require buildings or other protection from the elements, sanitation facilities for both sexes, safe drinking water, trained teachers receiving domestically competitive salaries, teaching materials, and so on; while some will also require facilities such as a library, computer facilities and information technology;
>
> (b) Accessibility – educational institutions and programmes have to be accessible to everyone, without discrimination, within the jurisdiction of the State party. Accessibility has three overlapping dimensions:
>
> — Non-discrimination – education must be accessible to all, especially the most vulnerable groups, in law and fact, without discrimination on any of the prohibited grounds (see paras. 31-37 on non-discrimination);
> — Physical accessibility – education has to be within safe physical reach, either by attendance at some reasonably convenient geographic location (e.g. a neighbourhood school) or via modern technology (e.g. access to a "distance learning" programme);
> — Economic accessibility – education has to be affordable to all. This dimension of accessibility is subject to the differential wording of article 13 (2) in relation to primary, secondary and higher education: whereas primary education shall be available "free to all", States parties are required to progressively introduce free secondary and higher education;
>
> (c) Acceptability – the form and substance of education, including curricula and teaching methods, have to be acceptable (e.g., relevant, culturally appropriate and of good quality) to students and, in appropriate cases, parents; this is subject to the educational objectives required by Article 13(1) and such minimum educational standards as may be approved by the State (see Art. 13(3) and (4));
>
> (d) Adaptability – education has to be flexible so it can adapt to the needs of changing societies and communities and respond to the needs of students within their diverse social and cultural settings.'[76]

The right to education, like all human rights, places 'respect', 'protect' and 'fulfil' obligations on the state. 'Respect' is to not actively violate the right. 'Protect' is to prohibit third parties from violating the right. 'Fulfil' is to actively facilitate the

---

75. *Annual Report of the Special Rapporteur on the Right to Education*, E/CN.4/2002/60, paras. 27-29; CESCR, General Comment 13, para. 6.

76. Ibid.

realisation of the right.[77] That said, the right to education, as with all rights in the ICESCR, is subject to conditional language that makes a state's obligations somewhat unclear and flexible. Article 2 of the ICESCR reads, *inter alia*:

> 'Each State Party to the present Covenant undertakes to take steps... to the *maximum of its available resources*, with a view to *achieving progressively* the full realization of the rights recognized in the present Covenant by all appropriate means, including particularly the adoption of legislative measures.' [emphasis added]

The right to education in the CRC is articulated in a similar fashion. Article 28(1) reads: 'States Parties recognize the right of the child to education, and with a view to *achieving this right progressively* and on the basis of equal opportunity they shall ... ' [emphasis added] It is largely agreed that this conditional language does not, however, give unlimited discretion to a state to progressively realise a right at the rate it wishes. The CESCR has stated:

> 'Thus while the full realization of the relevant rights may be achieved progressively, steps towards that goal must be taken within a reasonably short time after the Covenant's entry into force for the States concerned. Such steps should be deliberate, concrete and targeted as clearly as possible towards meeting the obligations recognized in the Covenant.'[78]

Article 14 of the ICESCR in fact mandates that states deal directly with these potential problems, ordering states to develop a plan of action for the progressive implementation 'of the principle of compulsory education free of charge for all'. Additionally, economic, social and cultural rights experts have worked to develop 'indicators' and 'benchmarks' to give more precision to the notion of 'progressive realisation' under the ICESCR.[79]

Legal experts and scholars on economic, social, and cultural rights also point out that every economic, social and cultural right imposes certain obligations that are to take 'immediate effect.'[80] The CESCR has pointed out that a state cannot, for example, use the language of 'progressive realization' or cite a lack of resources to

---

77. Ibid., paras. 46-47.

78. Ibid., para. 2.

79. Nowak lists several indicators that are helpful for determining if a state is meeting its right to education obligations. They include: 'literacy rates, primary, secondary and tertiary enrolment ratios, completion and drop-out rates, primary pupil-teacher ratio or public expenditure on education as a percentage of GNP or of total public expenditure or in comparison to other expenditure, for example, for military purposes'. M. Nowak, 'The Right to Education', in A. Eide, C. Krause, and A. Rosas, eds., *Economic, Social and Cultural Rights*, 2nd rev. edn., (Dordrecht, Martinus Nijhoff 2001) p. 257. In her 2002 annual report, the UN Special Rapporteur on the Right to Education, Katarina Tomaševski, provided an indicators scheme based on the four human rights components to the right to education: availability, accessibility, acceptability, and adaptability. *Annual Report of the Special Rapporteur on the Right to Education*, E/CN.4/2002/60, paras. 27-29.

80. CESCR, General Comment 3, para. 1.

exclude girls from its education system.[81] The same holds true for the prohibition on corporal punishment. More generally, there is also, as the CESCR has stated, 'a strong presumption of impermissibility of any retrogressive measures taken in relation to the right to education'.[82]

Finally, in an attempt to give even greater meaning and precision to the rights of the ICESCR, the CESCR has held that States Parties have 'core minimum obligations' to 'ensure the satisfaction of, at the very least, minimum essential levels' of each right in the covenant.[83] It lists essential foodstuffs, essential primary health care, basic housing and shelter, and the most basic forms of education as being within the scope of these obligations.[84] The committee reasoned that '[i]f the Covenant were to be read in such a way as not to establish such a minimum core obligation, it would be largely deprived of its *raison d'être*.'[85] While the committee concedes that a state may not be able to meet its minimum core obligations due to a lack of available resources, it places a heavy burden squarely on the state to prove why it cannot meet those obligations:

> 'In order for a State party to be able to attribute its failure to meet at least its minimum core obligations to a lack of available resources it must demonstrate that every effort has been made to use all resources that are at its disposition in an effort to satisfy, as a matter of priority, those minimum obligations.'[86]

The CESCR holds that the core obligations to the right to education are:
— to ensure the right of access to public educational institutions and programmes on a non-discriminatory basis;
— to ensure that education conforms to the objectives set out in Article 13(1);
— to provide primary education for all in accordance with Article 13(2)(a);
— to adopt and implement a national educational strategy which includes provision for secondary, higher and fundamental education; and to ensure free choice of education without interference from the State or third parties, subject to conformity with 'minimum educational standards' (Art. 13(3) and (4)).[87]

81. CESCR, General Comment 13, para. 31 and 43; see also P. Hunt, 'State Obligations, Indicators, Benchmarks and the Right to Education', 4 *Human Rights Law and Practices* (1998) p. 110.

82. CESCR, General Comment 13, para. 45.

83. CESCR, General Comment 3, para. 10.

84. Ibid., para. 10.

85. Ibid., para. 9.

86. Ibid., para. 10.

87. CESCR, General Comment 13, para. 57. A report by UNESCO and the special rapporteur similarly list the 'core obligations' as they relate to the availability, accessibility, acceptability, and adaptability components of the right to education. UNESCO Bangkok, *Manual on Rights Based Education: Global Human Rights Requirements Made Simple* (Bangkok, UNESCO 2004) p. 8.

5. THE RIGHT TO EDUCATION IN OCCUPIED TERRITORIES

As noted, when an Occupying Power seeks to meet its Article 24 and Article 50 Geneva IV obligations it must provide necessary assistance to facilitate the education of unaccompanied children and to facilitate the proper working of institutions devoted to the education of children. Simultaneously, when any state seeks to meet its education obligations arising under human rights law it must make considerations as to the availability, accessibility, acceptability and adaptability components of that right. But are these two obligations fully compatible? Can an Occupying Power, in the name of its human rights treaty obligations, change laws to make education compulsory and free; break zoning regulations to build new schools; legislate that pregnant girls are allowed to attend school; change the curricula and syllabi of schools and, for example, teach additional classes in math and fewer in history; change teacher salaries; replace the content of textbooks and use new teaching materials; increase the minimum number of years a child must be in school; or reorganise the municipal and national branches to make the education system work more efficiently? In particular, can it make progressive changes that are specifically designed to outlive the occupation and transform the society?

Part 4 will proceed by evaluating how well occupation law in the Hague Regulations, the Fourth Geneva Convention, and Protocol I accommodates the positive obligations that the right to education places on an occupant. It would be impossible to fit within the space of this paper a consideration of the whole of the right to education. Indeed, this is not its purpose. Instead, this paper will use as a guide for discussion the core obligations that UNESCO and the UN special rapporteur on the right to education have stated are contained within the availability, acceptability, accessibility and adaptability components of the right to education.[88]

5.1 Availability

— Obligation to ensure compulsory and free education for all children in the country within a determined age range, up to at least the minimum age of employment.

— Obligation to respect parental freedom to choose education for their children, observing the principle of the best interests of the child.[89]

---

88. Due to the evolution and progress in thinking on economic, social and cultural rights and the right to education in particular, this paper relies on the UNESCO core obligations because they were published in 2004, whereas the CESCR's General Comment on the right to education (General Comment 13) was published in 1999.

89. UNESCO Bangkok, *supra* n. 87, p. 8.

5.1.1 *Legislative requirements*

The first obligation, 'availability', has legislative and material components.[90] With respect to the former, the question must be asked: if the laws in force do not meet these standards does occupation law permit the occupant to change them?

When children are in the care of their families or parents, the Fourth Geneva Convention does not explicitly require the occupant to provide for their education. It stipulates only that the occupant must ensure the facilitation of the proper working of educational institutions.[91] As mentioned, it is reasonable to believe that at the time of drafting the term 'properly working' was to be interpreted according to the attitudes of the removed government. This would mean that an occupant's Article 50(1) obligation does not support a change in law to provide compulsory and free primary education where it did not exist previously. But this is problematic from a human rights perspective.

There are several ways around this problem. One is to expose the areas where occupation law and human rights law overlap on this issue. Article 77 of Protocol I instructs states to 'take all feasible measures in order that children who have not attained the age of fifteen years do not take a direct part in hostilities …' Making primary education compulsory could, potentially, be relied on as a tool for the occupant to use to 'ensure' that it is meeting this obligation and therefore it would be permissible.[92] As this paper will demonstrate, various human rights obligations concerning education can be accommodated by occupation law in this way.

It may also be argued that in cases where the previous government ratified a human rights treaty but did not implement it into domestic law, the occupant can change the domestic laws in force to give effect to the treaty. In this sense, the occupant would give respect to the international laws in force above and beyond the domestic laws in force.[93] Because this paper focuses on the extraterritorial application of an occupant's human rights obligations, it is not its purpose to give this

---

90. For provisions calling for legislative measures, see CRC, Arts. 3(2) and 28(1)(a) and ICESCR, Arts. 2(1) and 13(2)(a).

91. Fourth Geneva Convention, Arts. 1 and 50(1).

92. The notion that under international humanitarian law states must take positive measures to ensure their obligations will be met was articulated by Israel's High Court in 2004. Speaking to the military's obligation to ensure the welfare of the population, the court held, '[the military commander] must make prior arrangements in order to ensure there are sufficient supplies of food and water. Damage to the water supply is something that can be anticipated from the outset, and if it cannot be avoided, a solution to this problem must be prearranged'. *Physicians for Human Rights* v. *Commander of the IDF Forces in the Gaza Strip*, H.C. 4764/04, para. 68. For additional information about the notion of 'ensure' in international humanitarian law see Commentary Geneva IV, *supra* n. 22, p. 16. The Committee on the Rights of the Child has noted with disapproval, however, that schools can also be a place for recruitment of children into armed conflicts. Committee on the Rights of the Child, Concluding observations (Pakistan), CRC/C/15/Add.217, 2003, para. 62

93. Greenwood appears to support the notion that an occupant is bound to respect the native human rights obligations of the occupied territory. C. Greenwood, 'The Administration of Occupied Territory in International Law', in E. Playfair, ed., *International Law and the Administration of Occupied Territories: Two Decades of Israeli Occupation of the West Bank and Gaza Strip* (Oxford, Clarendon Press 1992) p. 248.

possibility serious consideration. It can be said, however, that this approach does sit well with the fact that domestic law cannot allow a state to evade its international legal obligations.[94]It has not, however, been studied in detail, and given the broad legislative powers and positive obligations that an occupant can draw from human rights treaties, it appears at a superficial look that states could attempt to use this approach to circumvent the requirement in Article 64 of Geneva IV that occupants can change laws only for limited reasons and only when necessary. Though written prior to the advent of a detailed international human rights system, Von Glahn noted in 1957 the limitations occupation law places on education specifically:

> 'If ... a comprehensive reorganization of an educational system were contemplated, then the limitations which at present appear to circumscribe permitted interference with education will have to be set aside.'[95]

A third approach is to say that the right to primary education is a part of customary international law and therefore the occupant could legitimately enact a law that made primary education compulsory and free. In its 2003 concluding observations to Israel, the CESCR held that, 'fundamental human rights must be respected and that basic economic, social and cultural rights, as part of the minimum standards of human rights, are guaranteed under customary international law and are also prescribed by international humanitarian law'.[96] However, this claim must have the support of sufficient state practice and *opinio juris*.[97] If, in fact, the right to education has gained the status of customary international law in occupied territories it is most likely that this is true primarily with respect to the component of the right that prohibits states from damaging and restricting access to education.[98] This was the context in which the CESCR made the above statement and it is in this context that the Israeli military government has been widely criticised.[99]

A fourth approach, the one this paper focuses on and advocates, it to read international human rights standards into relevant occupation law provisions. This could be done through the following line of interpretation: the CRC and ICESCR demonstrate that the essential purpose of primary education institutions, as a collective, is to educate *all* children. If a state does not put in place legislation to make this happen, then it is not ensuring that the institutions are working properly. If this dynamic were imported into occupation law, which also contains the concept of

---

94. 1969 Vienna Convention on the Law of Treaties, Art. 27.

95. Von Glahn, *supra* n. 71, p. 67.

96. CESCR, Concluding Observations (Israel), E/C.12/1/Add.90, 2003, para. 31; see also, O. Schachter, 'International Law in Theory and Practice', in H. Steiner and P. Alston. eds., *International Human Rights in Context: Law, Politics, Morals*, 2nd edn. (Oxford, Oxford University Press 2000) p. 231.

97. These two conditions are set out in section 102 of the *Restatement (Third), Foreign Relations Law of the United States*, and are widely accepted as indicators of customary international law. See Steiner and Alston, ibid., p. 70.

98. See also discussion on customary international law in the section *Accessibility* (5.2.) below.

99. *Supra* n. 60. These documents and criticisms alone do not, of course, prove custom.

'ensure', an occupant would then be permitted to make primary education compulsory and free without violating occupation law.[100] In doing so, it would be 'facilitat [ing] the proper working of all institutions devoted to the care and education of children'.[101]

The difference between the first approach and this fourth approach is that the latter expands the scope of occupation law so that occupants do not need to look for loopholes in occupation law each time they wish to meet their human rights obligations. The difference between the second approach (e.g., changing laws in force so an occupant can abide by the native international human rights treaty obligations) and this one is that this one allows the occupant to change laws only with respect to the human rights obligations that can be read into the provisions of the Fourth Geneva Convention. This grants the occupant freedom to provide assistance to the local population only within the scope allowed by the Convention. While this can be a hindrance in some cases, this more closely coincides with the non-interference principles of occupation law and nonetheless expands occupation law to help better accommodate the right to education.

Admittedly, there is little evidence to support this fourth approach. What does exist is scattered, untailored and speculative. Benvenisti simply notes that occupation law is the balance between military necessity and care for the local population. Of an occupant's obligations to meet the latter, he states, 'it can be generally said that occupants would be authorized to adopt measures that conform to internationally accepted standards, measures that could only increase the well-being of the occupied community'.[102] Sassòli parses his words more carefully and says an occupant has a strong argument for changing laws that are contrary to human rights but it cannot invoke a full set of legislative powers. He argues that the occupant 'must stay as close as possible to similar local standards and the local cultural, legal and economic traditions'.[103] Roberts states that in times of occupation, 'the application of international human rights standards is highly desirable'.[104]

More compelling support for this approach is found in the drafting history of the Fourth Geneva Convention and Protocol I. Records indicate that some states were willing to accept that Occupying Powers should be obligated to follow certain international standards. At the 1949 diplomatic conference Mexico made a (unsuccessful) proposal that would have allowed an occupant to modify legislation only if the legislation violated the Universal Declaration of Human Rights.[105] In the drafting of Article 55 (concerning food and medical supplies), state delegates introduced the sentence, 'If international standards of nutrition have been established, they shall be applied', to supplement the sentence that preceded it, 'The

---

100. See *supra* n. 92.

101. Fourth Geneva Convention, Art. 50(1).

102. Benvenisti, *supra* n. 27, pp. 31-32.

103. Sassòli, *supra* n. 8, p. 13-14.

104. A. Roberts, 'Prolonged Military Occupation: The Israeli-Occupied Territories since 1967', 84 *AJIL* (1990) p. 73; see also ibid., generally.

105. ICRC, 1948 Draft Revised or New Conventions for the Protection of War Victims, *supra* n. 69, p. 173; Final Record of the Diplomatic Conference of Geneva of 1949 (hereafter, Final Record) (Berne, Federal Political Department 1949), Vol. II (A), p. 671.

occupying Power is bound to assure the food supply of the civilian population.'[106] This language was unanimously rejected because, it appears, the delegates did not believe that such standards had been established.[107] Is it to be assumed that if such standards had been established then the language would have remained? If the answer is yes, and delegates were not averse to allowing existing international standards for humanitarian provisions to dictate the responsibilities of an occupant, then importing the right to education into the words 'proper working' in Article 50 (1) and 'are facilitated' in Article 24(1) Geneva IV may not be too far misplaced. Indeed, it was not an anomaly for states to agree that it was a good idea to incorporate human rights concepts and standards into international humanitarian law. State delegates that drafted Protocol I made reference to the right to freedom of religion in the UDHR and the ICCPR when they included 'religion' into Article 78(2) of the Protocol, which addresses the evacuation of children. Greece explicitly drew attention to the right to education in the ICESCR and 'suggested that paragraph 2 should be re-drafted to take account of present-day requirements'.[108]

It is also worth noting that this fourth approach helps to mitigate the restrictions that the concept of *lex specialis* could otherwise place on the obligations an Occupying Power has with regard to the right to education under international human rights law. As indicated in the beginning of this essay, the concept of *lex specialis* might be relied on to limit the right to education to the boundaries set out by occupation law. This is because occupation law is a specialised body of law that deals with a specific situation (i.e., occupation), whereas international human rights law is a more generally applicable law. Grotius, in explaining the rationale behind the concept of *lex specialis*, wrote: 'Among agreements that are equal … that should be given preference which is most specific and approaches most nearly to the subject in hand, for special provisions are ordinarily more effective than those that are general.'[109]

These restrictive boundaries that occupation law could place on the right to education exist primarily in two forms: 1) differing interpretations of the legal texts (e. g., what does it mean for an educational facility to be 'properly working' under human rights law versus occupation law), and 2) differing substantive rules (e.g., provisions to the right to education under international human rights law pertain to children under the age of 18, whereas educational institutions mentioned in occupation law refer to institutions for children who are most often under the age of 15.) By interpreting relatively vague occupation law provisions through the assistance of human rights standards, as was demonstrated above, this first boundary

---

106. ICRC, 1948 Draft Revised or New Conventions for the Protection of War Victims, ibid., p. 173; Final Record, ibid., p. 121.

107. ICRC, 1948 Draft Revised or New Conventions for the Protection of War Victims, p. 173; Final Record ibid., pp. 667, 745.

108. Official Records of the Diplomatic Conference on the Reaffirmation and Development of International Humanitarian Law Applicable in Armed Conflicts, Geneva (1974-1977) Vol. 15 (Buffalo, New York, W.S. Hein 1981) pp. 72, 75.

109. Hugo Grotius, 'De Jure belli as pacis. Libre Tres, Book II Sect. XXIX', cited in *Fragmentation of International Law: Topic (a): The function and scope of the* lex specialis *rule and the question of 'self-contained regines': an outline*, International Law Commission.

can be expanded such that the two work in cooperation rather than one suffocating the other. In this discussion of *lex specialis* it also cannot be ignored that the right to education as it exists under international human rights law is far more detailed in comparison to provisions on education under occupation law. In this sense, it is international human rights law that provides a specialised and contemporary understanding of the educational needs of a child and it is occupation law that provides the generalised rules. When observed in this way, the issue of *lex specialis* has less to do with the relationship between the specific law and the general law, and more to do with resolving tensions between two specific laws. With this in mind, this fourth approach finds its strength in its pragmatism, whereby it seeks a way for human rights law and occupation law to work together so that the specialised importance of both is maintained simultaneously.

Admittedly, and as mentioned above, it appears to be more difficult to expand the second type of boundaries, which are formed by the letter of the law and cannot be as easily stretched through interpretations of vague language. But if it were possible to do so, this would nonetheless be a serious infringement on the structure of occupation law and the consequences of such an approach should be carefully considered.

While the importing of right to education standards into occupation law is a useful step towards justifying that an occupant can change a law and make primary education compulsory and free, there are additional tensions between the right to education and occupation law that are not fully resolved by this approach. One tension is that not all children in occupied territories are 'protected persons' under Article 50. Article 50, therefore, does not justify allowing an occupant to legislate compulsory and free primary education for all children. This problem is diluted by Article 24, which calls on occupants to facilitate the education of *all* orphaned children and children separated from their families as the result of the war. But what of non-orphaned children who are not protected persons? Article 77 of Protocol I resolves this problem in full by extending the protection of Article 50 to *all* children in occupied territories, though the problem obviously remains if the Occupying Power has not ratified the Protocol.[110]

Another tension that emerges between the right to education and Article 50(1) Geneva IV is that Article 50(1), according to the ICRC, directs states to provide assistance to educational institutions for children when needed, but not to interfere. Thus, an occupant would be permitted to make a change in the law only if a law in force prevents the occupant from not interfering (e.g., a law requiring school demolitions in certain neighbourhoods) or if a law in force prevents the occupant from providing needed assistance. In addition, the ICRC Commentary states that assistance can only be given through 'mutual agreement' with the local and national authorities.[111] The positive side of these interpretations is that the notions of non-interference and cooperation dilute the ability of an occupant who operates with nefarious motives to replace the old and 'bad' education system with its new

110. Commentary Protocol I, *supra* n. 46, paras. 3173-3174.
111. Commentary Geneva IV, *supra* n. 22, p. 286.

and 'better' system under the auspices of 'assistance'. That said, this interpretation is too restrictive with respect to the international right to education standards. Imagine the case where the minimum age for employment is 15 and the national and local authorities only wish for children under the age of nine to attain a primary education. In this case the educational institutions would not be working in accordance with international standards (i.e., the upper age limit for primary education should not be below the minimum working age), and yet if the occupant sought to change that situation it would not be 'assisting' but 'interfering'. Is the occupant therefore not allowed to make such a change without the agreement of national and local authorities?

While the ICRC Commentary is the authoritative interpretation of the Geneva Conventions, it would be fruitful to tweak its interpretation of Article 50(1) in light of the immediate and long-term importance that the right to education and the continuity of education have on the welfare of children.[112] One way of doing this is to rely on the interpretation the ICRC gives to the words 'with the cooperation' in Article 56 of the Fourth Geneva Convention (hygiene and public health). As noted above in the section on *Commentary by the ICRC* (3.2.2), under this interpretation an occupant is permitted to 'demand' the cooperation of the national and local authorities to ensure that educational facilities are working properly.[113] It follows that what might be considered 'interference' by the authorities but 'assistance' by the occupant is then made permissible. This means that if an occupant seeks to require that children receive free primary education it can demand from (but must also work with the cooperation of) the local and national authorities in this endeavour even if the authorities object to such a law. This interpretation provides a solution that enables the occupant to meet its human rights obligations without being in violation of occupation law.

Though not bound by the Fourth Geneva Convention at the time, this seems to have been the approach the United States took in World War II when Colonel Charles M. Spofford, in his responsibilities as the Chief of Staff Officer to the Allied Military Government, wrote a letter to a Regional Civil Affairs Officer in Italy instructing that a *Provveditore* (provincial authority on public education) be appointed to head classes but that individual '*must agree* to assume full responsibility that [*inter alia*] there will be no Fascist or anti-ally propaganda or doctrine in the school, and no Fascist forms, ceremonies, or organizations'. [emphasis added][114]

112. See section on 'education' in C. Bruderlein and T. Stichick, 'Children Facing Insecurity: New Strategies for Survival in a Global Era' (Harvard Program on Humanitarian Policy and Conflict Research) (Policy paper produced for the Canadian Department of Foreign Affairs and International Trade) May 2001.

113. ICRC, 1948 Draft Revised ICRC 1948 Draft Revised or New Conventions for the Protection of War Victims, *supra* n. 69, p. 177.

114. Coles and Weinberg, *supra* n. 49, p. 400.

5.1.2 *Physical operation of educational institutions*

Implicit in the core obligation a state has to make education 'available' is an obligation to work to ensure that the educational institutions are open and physically operating. International human rights law has a broad interpretation of what this means. This can require supplying textbooks, desks, and chairs; it can require adequate health conditions at schools;[115] and it can necessitate teacher trainings.[116]

Overall, this human rights obligation is highly compatible with occupation law – especially if an occupant can demand the cooperation of uncooperative national or local authorities. Von Glahn notes: 'Writers … appear to agree that the occupant should see to it that schools are reopened, under supervision, as soon as conditions permit this to be done.'[117] US Colonel Spofford wrote in 1943 with regard to the US occupation of Italy:

> 'It is the policy of the Military Government to open the public schools as rapidly as is consistent with security. To wait for a general re-opening of the schools before opening schools which are ready to open now or in the near future, would cause unnecessary hardship and defeat our general purpose.'[118]

With regard to ensuring that schools are not only open but also adequately supplied, the ICRC Commentary to Article 50(1) Geneva IV states, 'when [the resources of local and national authorities] are inadequate, the Occupying Power must ensure … that the persons concerned receive food, medical supplies and anything else necessary to enable them to carry out their task'.[119] In occupied Iraq, the US sought to adequately supply schools and did so at times in cooperation with national and local authorities and residents.[120] As mentioned, it is unclear if it thought that it was acting under legal obligations or in accordance with political considerations. Nonetheless, the Occupying Power awarded over 90 contracts aimed at schools that covered everything from general renovations of schools to school computers, renovations of restrooms, and school windows and doors.[121] On 14 January 2004, the White House announced: 'More than 51 million new text-

---

115. See Committee on the Rights of the Child, *Concluding observations (Bangladesh)*, CRC/C/15/Add.211, 2003, para. 65(d).

116. See CESCR, General Comment 13, para. 6(a); Committee on the Rights of the Child, *Concluding observations (Sri Lanka)*, CRC/C/15/Add.207, 2003, para. 43(d).

117. Von Glahn, *supra* n. 71, p. 64.

118. Coles and Weinberg, *supra* n. 49, p. 400.

119. Commentary Geneva IV, *supra* n. 22, p. 286. Similarly, the commentary to Art. 55 states, 'it will be remembered that Article 55 requires the Occupying Power to import the necessary medical supplies, such as medicaments, vaccines and sera, when the resources of the occupied territory are *inadequate*'. [emphasis added].Commentary Geneva IV, *supra* n. 22, p. 314.

120. United States Agency for International Development (USAID), 'Revitalizing Iraq's Education System: Teacher Training Program', March 2004, <http://www.usaid.gov/iraq/pdf/iraq_teachertraining_0304.pdf>.

121. Coalition Provisional Authority, 'CPA-CA Register of Awards (1 Jan. 04-10 April 04)', <http://www.iraqcoalition.org/business/Awarded_Contracts.pdf>.

books – without propaganda – are being distributed.'[122] Training programs for teachers and school administrators were also put in place and reportedly instituted with some degree of cooperation of the national authorities.[123]

It is also worth stressing that while it is often said that occupation law focuses on re-establishing the status *quo ante*, the Fourth Geneva Convention codifies obligations in the field of education that focus on the quality of the working conditions of educational institutions.[124] This matches well with the right to education and is especially important in a setting such as Iraq, where an Occupying Power controlled territory where the education system was suffering prior to the conflict.[125]

5.1.3 *Adequate number of educational institutions*

In addition to schools being open and able to physically operate, states with right to education responsibilities must work to provide a sufficient number of educational institutions so that all children can attain a primary education. When occupation law was codified it did not envisage that it would require the occupant to develop educational infrastructure.[126] But what does occupation law say to an occupant that wishes to develop educational infrastructure by building new schools?

As argued above, when international right to education standards are injected into Article 50(1) Geneva IV the occupant has a duty under international human rights law that is compatible with occupation law to work to ensure that compulsory and free education is being provided. If it is necessary to change the laws in force to build schools to enable the occupant to accomplish this goal then the occupant has this freedom. It would be meaningless for occupation law to allow an occupant to make a law that caters to the need of the people but then restrict the occupant from taking actions that aim to make the purpose of that law a reality.[127] It is also conceivable that an occupant would be permitted to build new schools to

---

122. US White House, 'Education in Iraq: Iraq Fact of the Day', <http://www.whitehouse.gov/news/releases/2004/01/20040114-9.html>. For a description by USAID of the contributions it made to education in Iraq see <http://www.usaid.gov/iraq/accomplishments/education.html>.

123. USAID, 'Improving Schools with Citizen Involvement: New Parent-Teacher Association Guides Baghdad School Repairs', <http://www.usaid.gov/stories/iraq/fp_iraq_school.html>; USAID, *supra* n. 120.

124. Commentary Protocol I, *supra* n. 46, para. 582.

125. In 1995 the Ministry of Education stated that schools lacked '500,000 teaching aid units, 2 million desks, 68 million textbooks, and 15,000 computers were lacking from'. By 2003, but prior to the war, UNICEF cited a number of improvements but still found that only one in four children received primary education and 70 percent of school were, 'in dire need of renovation and repair and many of them pose health hazards to the students'. UNICEF, 'The Situation of Children in Iraq: An Assessment Based on the United Nations Convention on the Rights of the Child, Reprinted in 2003 with updated Malnutrition Information' (2003) p. 40; UNICEF, 'Iraq–Country in Crisis: Repairing Schools, Rebuilding Hope' (February 2003), <http://www.unicef.org/emerg/iraq/index_rebuild_-hopes.html>.

126. Benvenisti, *supra* n. 21, p. 105; E. Cohen, *Human Rights in the Israeli-Occupied Territories, 1967-1982* (Manchester, Manchester University Press 1985) p. 9; Sassòli and Bouvier, *supra* n. 6, p. 154.

127. M. Greenspan, *The Modern Law of Land Warfare* (Berkeley and Los Angeles, University of California Press 1959) p. 224.

take the strain off overcrowded schools so to make them function better. That said, there are a variety of safeguards that are written into occupation law that curb the apparently wide power an occupant has to develop the territory it is occupying.

First, the occupant must respect the laws in force only up to the point that they prohibit it from meeting its obligations under occupation law. The occupant must as a general rule respect the laws that shape how, when, and where schools are built. If it must change laws, then it can only change those laws where it is 'essential to enable' it to carry out its responsibilities.[128] This is true whether the Occupying Power is in control of the bodies that determine if a school can be built or if the local people administer such bodies.[129] Simply put, an occupant cannot simply build at will, but it can allow schools to be built in accordance with the law.

Second, an occupant must work with the cooperation of the national and local authorities. One might argue that because Article 50(1) places obligations on an occupant that relate only to existing educational institutions and not on the planning of new ones, that cooperation for planning new institutions is not a requirement. However, this is a petty distinction. The concept of cooperation is meant to benefit the education of children and the education institutions generally. The ICRC Commentary makes it clear that one of the over-arching principles of Article 50 is that an occupant is supposed to work with national and local authorities to ensure that education facilities are functioning properly. Practically speaking, local and national authorities will likely have important input for the planning and construction of new educational institutions that is critical for these new facilities to successfully operate during occupation as well as after.

A third safeguard is that when an occupant changes a law to carry out a task it must honestly pursue that task. For example, an occupant might deem it necessary to change laws to build schools to facilitate primary education for *all children*. But if the occupant then builds schools only in neighbourhoods of certain ethnicities even though other neighbourhoods have equal needs, then the operation would be discriminatory. In turn, it would not be acting in accordance with the stated purpose for changing the law (i.e., providing primary education for all children) and this would violate Article 64. Similarly, if an occupant gives a contract to a construction firm merely to benefit the contractor and the occupant has no intention of working to make sure children in fact attend the new schools, this too oversteps the bounds of Article 64.

Before closing on this issue it should be recognised that building permanent schools may not be necessary to remedy the problem of insufficient space for primary education. Boyden and Ryder hold that 'schools are not an essential component of an education system' in times of conflict, and have pointed out that it may be a mistake to build schools in situations where conflicts have not subsided, as they might be destroyed (illegally) or as permanent structure they might be (illeg-

---

128. Fourth Geneva Convention, Art. 64. For case law on the construction of permanent structures from Israel's High Court of Justice, see Domb, *supra* n. 45; *Beit Sourik Village Council* v. *Government of Israel*, H.C. 2056/04.

129. F. Domb, 'Judgements of the Supreme Court of Israel: *Temple Mount Faithful et al.* v. *Attorney-General et al.*, H.C. 4185/90', 30 *Israel YB HR* (2000) p. 311.

ally) used for military purposes.[130] Instead, Boyden and Ryder consider that it might be 'more appropriate to invest in portable resources' and that 'maximum use needs to be made of improvised venues and community facilities for classes'.[131] Given that occupations are envisaged to be short-term, anything the occupant does to make permanent changes to the land should have its necessity carefully assessed.[132]

5.1.4 *Respecting parental decisions*

Tomaševski, UNESCO, and the CESCR agree that a core obligation to the right to education is that states must respect the decisions that parents make about the education of their children, provided that such education meets the minimum educational standards set by the state. Parents must be allowed to choose between private, public or home schooling for their children. Parent have the right also to provide, or allow their children to receive, religious schooling.[133]

It is not difficult to imagine scenarios where an occupant would be well-justified in changing a law in force that restricts children from receiving private or home schooling. Each venue could be an effective means for easing strains on public schools and decreasing overcrowding, thus allowing the education system as a whole to function better. Private education may also increase the safety of children in times of occupation.

If right to education standards are imported into Article 24(1) Geneva IV, this provision may also permit the occupant to meet this component of the right to education – though only in relation to unaccompanied children – without violating Article 64. The ICRC Commentary to this article holds that when an occupant facilitates the education of unaccompanied children, 'they will apply the measures which seem most appropriate under the conditions prevailing in their territory'.[134] From a human rights perspective, it would always be 'most appropriate' to respect the decisions that parents would have wished to have made about their child's education, provided those decisions do not collide with other human rights protections or international humanitarian law provisions. As for accompanied children, the rights parents have with respect to the education of their children may be supported by Article 27 of Geneva IV, which calls on occupants to respect the 'family rights' and 'religious convictions and practices' of protected persons.[135]

---

130. J. Boyden and P. Ryder, Implementing the Right to Education in Areas of Armed Conflict (Oxford, 1996) <http://www.essex.ac.uk/armedcon/story_id/000021.htm>.

131. Ibid.

132. See Domb, *supra* n. 45, p. 309.

133. UNESCO Bangkok, *supra* n. 87, p. iv..

134. Commentary Geneva IV, *supra* n. 22, p. 187.

135. Admittedly, the ICRC's interpretation of 'family rights' would likely need updating for it to include allowing a parent to make decisions about the education of his or her child. The ICRC Commentary holds merely, '[r]espect for family rights implies not only that family ties must be maintained, but further that they must be restored should they have been broken as a result of wartime events.' Ibid., pp. 202-203.

Additionally, Articles 24(1) and 50(3) Geneva IV and Article 78 of Protocol I indicate (ironically) that occupation law may implicitly, and necessarily, permit an occupant to respect the wishes parents had for the education of their children when they were still in their care. These provisions aim at ensuring that children who are out of the hands of their parents or family receive an acceptable education. Articles 24(1) and 50(3) do this by pressing the occupant to entrust the education of unaccompanied children to persons of a similar nationality, language, religion and cultural tradition. If an occupant is allowed under these provisions to change a law so that persons of a similar cultural tradition or the same nationality were allowed to shape the education of children who are not theirs, then an occupant must, logically, also be allowed to change the law to accommodate the same for parents who are still in control of their children. This claim finds it strongest support in the drafting notes of Article 78 (evacuated children), which states: 'Children belong first to their parents, second to their own country and only in the last place to third countries or families.'[136]

5.2 Accessibility

- Obligation to eliminate exclusion from education based on the internationally prohibited grounds of discrimination (race, colour, sex, language, religion, opinion, origin, economic status, birth, social status, minority or indigenous status and disability).
- Obligation to eliminate gender and racial discrimination by ensuring equal enjoyment of all human rights in practice, rather than only formally prohibiting discrimination.

5.2.1 De facto *accessibility*

In states where the law does not grant primary education to, for example, girls, the question arises as to whether an occupant is allowed to change this legislation. Non-discrimination in schools is fundamental to what it means for schools to be properly functioning in accordance with the right to education. Non-discrimination is not only a core obligation but it is also an immediate obligation that states cannot refuse under any circumstances.[137] In the same sense that primary schools can only be properly functioning if students are in the classrooms, primary schools would be improperly functioning if they were only educating, say, white boys. Whether out of its obligation to make primary education 'available' to all, or out of its obligation to make primary education 'accessible' without adverse discrimination, importing the right to education into Articles 24 and 50 Geneva IV would guaran-

136. Official Records of the Diplomatic Conference on the Reaffirmation and Development of International Humanitarian Law Applicable in Armed Conflicts, *supra* n. 108, p. 74.

137. CESCR, General Comment 13, para. 31.

tee that children would not be excluded from primary education on the basis of race, colour, sex, etc.[138]

The deeply embedded principle of non-discrimination that tracks through human rights law also exists in occupation law. Article 13 Geneva IV obligates an Occupying Power not to carry out its responsibilities in Part II (which includes Article 24) with distinction based on, 'in particular ... race, nationality, religion or political opinion ...'[139] Article 27 Geneva IV, which applies to the provisions relating to occupied territories (which includes Art. 50), forbids an Occupying Power from making adverse distinctions based on such factors as 'race, religion or political opinion'.[140] While gender and other categories are conspicuously absent from Articles 13 and 27, the ICRC Commentary notes that their lists are not exhaustive. The Commentary to Article 27 Geneva IV notes that 'the criteria of language, colour, social position, financial circumstances and birth might be added. In a word, any discriminatory measure whatsoever is banned, unless it results from the application of the Convention'.[141]

In addition to prohibiting discrimination by Occupying Powers, the Final Record demonstrates that delegates agreed that an Occupying Power should be allowed to change penal laws that prohibit it from carrying out its Article 27 commitments to non-discrimination.[142] The ICRC Commentary to Article 64 states:

> 'It should be noted too that the prohibition of all adverse distinctions in the treatment given to protected persons is not merely a negative duty. It implies an active role. An occupying Power is, for example, bound to abrogate any discriminatory laws it may find in occupied territory, if they place difficulties in the way of the application of the Convention.'[143]

The US Law of Land Warfare Field Manual allows the changing of '[l]egislation the enforcement of which would be inconsistent with the duties of the occupant, such as laws establishing racial discrimination.'[144] The British military manual on the law of war on land noted approvingly of a military government order in Germany that provided that:

> '[n]o German law ... shall be applied judicially or administratively within occupied territory in any instances where such application would cause injustice and inequality

138. See Committee on the Rights of the Child, Concluding observations (Czech Republic), CRC/C/15/Add.201, 2003, para. 29; Committee on the Rights of the Child, Concluding observations (United Kingdom of Great Britain and Northern Ireland), CRC/C/15/Add.188, 2002, para. 57.

139. Fourth Geneva Convention, Art. 13.

140. Ibid., Art. 27.

141. Commentary Geneva IV, *supra* n. 22, p. 206. Art. 27, in fact, permits the occupant to make distinctions on the basis of health, age and sex. But these distinctions are meant to benefit, and not excuse, adverse discrimination.

142. ICRC, 1948 Draft Revised or New Conventions for the Protection of War Victims, *supra* n. 69, p. 173; Final Record, *supra* n. 105, p. 833.

143. Commentary Geneva IV, *supra* n. 22, p. 207.

144. *US Department of Army FM 27-10: The Law of Land Warfare* (1956), para. 371.

by discriminating against any person by reason of his race, nationality, religious belief or opposition to the National-Socialist Party or its directives'.[145]

An occupant could also justify changing adverse racially discriminatory laws on the basis of customary international law, which prohibits racial discrimination.[146] It is, however, debatable whether the discrimination has to be systematic for it to be a violation of customary international law.[147] It is also debatable whether or not customary norms prohibit other forms of discrimination. Some have posited that gender discrimination has crystallised or is in the process of crystallising.[148]

While these debates cannot be resolved here, there is strong evidence that discrimination, or at least certain forms of discrimination, is prohibited under occupation law and by customary international law. However, concerns can nevertheless be pointed to that make it beneficial to import the non-discrimination component of the right to education into occupation law. First, occupation law and customary international law are noticeably weak on gender discrimination, which the right to education explicitly prohibits. Second, it is uncertain whether the sort of discrimination that is prohibited under customary international law must be systematic. Under the right to education it need not be. Third, if Article 50 is not interpreted to allow an Occupying Power to legislate compulsory and free education for all children in a territory where an education system is discriminatory, then an occupant might not be permitted to derogate from those discriminatory laws. This is because according to the ICRC Commentary the occupant can only derogate from discriminatory laws 'if they place difficulties in the way of the application of the Convention.'[149] This latter concern is tempered, however, by additional commentary to Article 64 which states generally that it is possible for an Occupying Power to abrogate any discriminatory measure that 'adversely affect racial or religious minorities, such provisions being contrary to the Convention, which forbids *all adverse distinction* based, in particular, on race, religion or political opinion'. [emphasis added][150]

---

145. British War Office, *The Law of War on Land being Part III of the Manual of Military Law* (London: The War Office 1958) para. 510.

146. *Barcelona Traction, Light and Power Co*, ICJ, Judgement of 1970 (Second Phase), para. 34; American Law Institute, *Restatement (Third) Foreign Relations Law of the United States* (1987) Section 702.

147. Cf., para. 34 of the 1962 ICJ case, *Barcelona Traction, Light and Power Co., Ltd.*, to section 702 of the *Restatement (Third) Foreign Relations Law of the United States*. See also, C. Howland, 'The challenge of religious fundamentalism to the liberty and equality rights of women: an analysis under the United Nations Charter', 35 *Columbia JTL* (1997) p. 334.

148. American Law Institute, *supra* n. 146, Section 702; A. Cassese, *International Law* (Oxford, Oxford University Press 2001) p. 370; Howland, *supra* n. 147, pp. 334-335.

149. Commentary Geneva IV, *supra* n. 22, p. 207.

150. Ibid., p. 335.

5.2.2 De jure *accessibility*

The right to education also requires an occupant to work to ensure that children are able to physically access the primary education that has been afforded to them by law.[151] Meeting this obligation could include working with local authorities to establish 'safe routes' to schools for children, providing transportation to get children to schools, setting up monitoring programs to track whether or not students are receiving primary education, and deciding where a new school should be built.[152] There are two potential areas of tension on this issue that one could point out between occupation law and the right to education. First, one might argue that an occupant does not need to ensure children are attending school, but only ensure that the schools are functioning. As stated above, if a right to education perspective is adopted into occupation law then it is enough to say that empty schools are not functioning properly and therefore the Occupying Force is not meetings its obligations. Second, one may argue that if occupation law is not permitted to allow an Occupying Power to legislate compulsory and free primary education for all, then the Occupying Power would logically have no responsibility or authority for ensuring that education is accessible to children who are not required to attend. This problem too, is resolved with the injection of right to education standards into occupation law which would make it the duty of the Occupying Power to ensure that education is free and compulsory.

5.3 **Acceptability**

- Obligation to set minimum standards for education, including the medium of instruction, contents and methods of teaching, and to ensure their observance in all educational institutions.
- Obligation to improve the quality of education by ensuring that the entire education system conforms to all human rights.[153]

The 'acceptability' component of the right to education instructs states to set minimum standards for education. It is, however, relatively silent as to what those standards must include.[154] The right to education provides instruction on the aims of education and this does, to a degree, provide information on what must and must

151. The Committee on the Rights of the Child recommended to Spain, 'In light of articles 28 and 29 of the Convention, the Committee recommends that the State party ... [e]nsure regular attendance at schools and the reduction of truancy and drop-out rates, especially with regard to Roma children and children belonging to migrant families.' Committee on the Rights of the Child, Concluding observations (Spain), CRC/C/15/Add.185, 2002, para. 44.

152. Under the Fourth Geneva Convention the obligation an occupant has to providing security for children and teachers also falls under its more general obligations under Art. 27 as well as its Art. 64 obligations to maintain the orderly government of the territory. See also Committee on the Rights of the Child, Concluding observations (Spain), CRC/C/15/Add.185, 2002, para. 18(a).

153. UNESCO Bangkok, *supra* n. 87, p. 8.

154. Nowak points out that many question about the right to education are unsettled, such as what constitutes minimum educational standards. Nowak, *supra* n. 79, p. 268.

not be taught in educational institutions. Included in this is that hate and intolerance cannot be taught and that human rights must be taught.[155]

5.3.1 *Removing objectionable educational materials*

The obligations states have under the right to education to remove hate and intolerance from educational institutions coincides with the past practices of various occupants.[156] Von Glahn gave legal support to some of these sorts of actions, but his support did not arise out of a general disdain for the use of propaganda and the teaching of hatred.[157] His support was instead based on the ground that the changes were made out of military necessary or to ensure public order.[158] In cases where the education of youth is contributing to violence between the local population and the occupant, or causing inter-communal violence, it is perfectly acceptable for an occupant to remove the inciting content from educational institutions – whether that content takes the form of texts or teachers.[159]

The question arises, however, whether an Occupying Power can remove texts or teachers that promote hatred and intolerance when they have no bearing on the security of the occupant or public order and safety? Imagine the case where hatred in classrooms is directed not at the Occupying Power but at another country not involved in the conflict. It would appear that under occupation law, the answer is no. As Von Glahn points out:

> 'it can be affirmed (despite the silence of customary law and of the Hague Regulations) that the occupant in essence may control and supervise only such aspects of an educational system in occupied territory as affect directly the military occupation and the conduct of hostilities. Beyond this point no interference appears to be permissible'.[160]

The ICRC Commentary does note that Article 24 is 'intended to exclude any religious or political propaganda designed to wean children from their natural milieu; for that would cause additional suffering to human beings already grievously stricken by the loss of their parents'.[161] But this interpretation does little to solve this incongruity between occupation law and human rights law. Firstly, it only affects unaccompanied children. Secondly, the proscription is directed at restraining the occupant from teaching hate and not at requiring an Occupying Power to remove hatred from classrooms that existed prior to its arrival.

---

155. ICESCR, art. 13(1) and CRC, art. 29(1)(b) and (d). See also, UNESCO Bangkok, *supra* n. 87, p. 36; and CESCR, Concluding observations (Trinidad and Tobago) E/C.12/1/Add.80, 2002, para. 55. The ICRC also advocates the incorporation of international humanitarian law education into basic education. S. Tawil, 'International Humanitarian Law and Basic Education', 839 *IRRC* (2000).
156. See section on *State practice* (3.2.1) above.
157. Von Glahn, *supra* n. 71, p. 63
158. Ibid., pp. 64-67
159. Ibid., p. 63.
160. Ibid., p. 64.
161. Commentary Geneva IV, *supra* n. 22, p. 187.

This conflict between occupation law and the right to education has not gone completely unnoticed.[162] Finding a way to make the two bodies of law compatible has, however, largely been absent from the literature of occupation law and human rights scholars.[163] The methods that this paper advances for dealing with this dilemma is to read into Articles 24 and 50 Geneva IV the obligation of an occupant to ensure that children are educated in accordance with international right to education standards. If this is done, then an occupant would be allowed to remove materials from schools without citing an additional reason other than showing that they do in fact promote hatred and intolerance. In doing so, the occupant would be contributing to the proper working of educational institutions and the facilitation of a child's education as required under occupation law.

It is worth stressing that the removal of hatred and intolerance from educational materials may not be an easy task. It is possible that the national and local authorities that occupants are required to cooperate with are the ones who approved the objectionable texts in the first place. This appears to have been the case when Israel vetted textbooks in Jordan.[164] This scenario provides another important reason for pursuing an interpretation of Article 50 that permits an occupant to demand the cooperation of the national and local authorities and, in turn, allows the occupant to 'interfere'.

Another problem to resolve emerges when the national and local authorities are non-existent or refuse to abide by the demands of the occupant. The ICRC Commentary does not contemplate that cooperation by locals would be unavailable and, admittedly, throughout this paper there is the assumption that the occupant will be able to work with the national and local authorities on issues concerning education, even if those authorities would prefer not to. To settle this conflict, it is necessary to visit again the Convention's drafting history and the ICRC Commentary to Articles 50 and 56.

The language of 'with the cooperation' can be a beneficial tool for ensuring that the occupant is well informed in the ways it facilitates the proper working of educational institutions. Secondly, if any legislative changes are needed and they are done with the cooperation of national and local authorities those changes, and their corollary effects, will have a better chance of remaining in place once the occupation ends.[165] Cooperation can therefore add to the continuity of a child's education from the time prior to occupation to the time after occupation. However, it is not clear from the Final Record whether these were the main strategies for the language of 'with the cooperation'. What is clear from the ICRC Commentary is that

---

162. See for example, Cohen, *supra* n. 126, p. 223.

163. Cohen, for example, has recognised this conflict and simply cites provisions in the ICESCR to resolve the matter, as if they automatically trump occupation law. She does not, however, articulate a way to make the two bodies of law compatible. Ibid., p. 223.

164. See 'Annex V: Reply received from the Government of Jordan' (section on education), in Report of the Special Committee to Investigate Israeli Practices Affecting the Human Rights of the Population of the Occupied Territories, GA. Res.A/8089, (1970).

165. For a discussion about the post-occupation legitimacy of legislative changes an occupant made, see Dinstein, The international law, etc., *supra* n. 4, p. 142; see also, Benvenisti, *supra* n. 21, pp. 70-71.

Article 50 Geneva IV places an obligation on the national and local authorities to continue their responsibilities toward the local population and not to abandon ship. The ICRC Commentary to Article 56 Geneva IV states:

> 'The reference in the Article to "the co-operation of national and local authorities" – a formula we have already seen in Article 50 in connection with children's institutions – shows clearly that there can be no question of making the Occupying Power alone responsible for the whole burden of organizing hospitals and health services and taking measures to control epidemics. *The task is above all one for the competent services of the occupied country itself.* It is possible that in certain cases the national authorities will be perfectly well able to look after the health of the population.' [emphasis added][166]

The ICRC presents a similar attitude in its commentary to Article 50(3), placing an obligation on the occupant only when 'the local authorities have not carried out their duties and when there is no relative or friend who can provide for the maintenance and education of the children concerned'.[167]

According to these interpretations, the emphasis on cooperation places a burden on the national and local authorities to work with the occupant in order to, 'above all', benefit the civilian population.[168] Because of this, when the national and local authorities do not, or cannot, carry out their duties, a lack of cooperation should not hinder services going to civilians. Despite the use of the language 'mutual agreement' in the ICRC Commentary, an occupant should not be prohibited from addressing the needs of educational institutions when the national and local authorities refuse the demands of the occupant or are absent altogether.[169] Indeed, a more fitting interpretation of the words 'with the cooperation' in Article 50(1) would appear to be 'with the cooperation when possible'.[170]

While a relaxed interpretation of Article 50(1) can be helpful to Occupying Powers who wish to meet their right to education obligations under human rights law, it is equally important to consider if this is a wise interpretation to make in light of the fact that it can be open to abuse. It seems, however, that there are enough safeguards to avoid this. Under both regimes the occupant does not have a blank check to make educational reforms, even if it is able to demand the cooperation of national and local authorities or to implement changes on its own when those authorities are absent or uncooperative. Just as an occupant cannot build

---

166. Commentary Geneva IV, *supra* n. 22, p. 313.

167. Ibid., p. 288.

168. Ibid., p. 313.

169. The British Military Manual seems, unfortunately, to say exactly this. It instructs that schools must be permitted to continue to operate and adds, '[h]owever, *provided that* the national and local authorities co-operate, the Occupant is bound to facilitate the proper working' of institutions devoted to the education of children. [emphasis added] British War Office, *supra* n. 145, para. 537.

170. When Greenspan contemplated the absence of authorities at all levels of education, he appears to have arrived at a similar conclusion: 'Institutions devoted to religion, charity, education, science, and art must also be treated as private property, even when they belong to the state, but if those responsible for these institutions are absent, the Custodian must endeavour to preserve the properties of their contents.' Greenspan, *supra* n. 127, p. 307; see also Greenwood, *supra* n. 93, p. 256.

schools at will, an occupant is not permitted to tamper with educational materials, syllabi, curriculum, etc., that do not promote hatred and intolerance. Cohen notes that it was unacceptable for the military administration to replace textbooks in East Jerusalem and the Golan Heights with textbooks used in Arab schools in Israel when the replacement was not necessary.[171] This assessment coincides with human rights law. In the case of *Turkey* v. *Cyprus*, the European Court of Human Rights (ECtHR) accepted that schoolbooks could be vetted, but emphasised that such a process must not be unlimited. The court went on to find a violation of Article 10 (freedom of expression) 'in so far as school-books destined for use in their primary school were subject, during the period under consideration, to excessive measures of censorship'.[172]

Additionally, when an occupant does find it necessary to remove certain discriminatory materials, it must not replace old objectionable materials with new objectionable materials. Cohen approvingly notes: 'In the West Bank and Gaza Strip Israel did not substitute pro-Israeli propaganda in the old curriculum and textbooks, but merely eliminated anti-Israel and anti-Jewish propaganda.'[173]

The initiatives Israel took to make changes to textbooks in coordination with UNESCO are perhaps the best way to carry out this task.[174] Involving an impartial expert body can provide oversight of the process and illustrates a willingness on the part of the occupant to make necessary changes in good faith. That said, if expediency is required or a third party is unwilling to provide its assistance, then this may not be an option and the occupant should be allowed to perform the vetting nonetheless.

5.3.2 *Adding necessary educational materials*

Keeping in mind the restrictions that occupation law place on an Occupying Power's ability to make changes to education, it is difficult to argue that a strict interpretation of occupation law permits an occupant to add human rights education to the curriculum or syllabus. Here we see again the utility of infusing human rights standards into the interpretation of Articles 24 and 50 Geneva IV. To do so would make human rights education a fundamental component of what it means for an occupant to facilitate the education of unaccompanied children and to facilitate the proper working of educational institutions more generally.

Adding the topic of human rights to a child's education does, however, bring with it the complex issues of how human rights are taught and what is taught. Different people (lawyers, politicians, scholars, teachers, etc.) place varying degrees of importance on different human rights and interpret human rights in different ways. In certain regions of the world greater importance may be given to the human rights of men than to women. In other regions, civil and political rights may

---

171. Cohen, *supra* n. 126, p. 223.
172. *Cyprus* v. *Turkey*, 25781/94 (2001) para. 254.
173. Cohen, *supra* n. 126, p. 223.
174. Shefi, *supra* n. 56, pp. 312-313; Report of the Commission General of United Nations Relief and Works Agency for Palestine Refugees in the Near East (UNRWA), A/38/13 (1983).

be given greater importance than economic, social, and cultural rights. In her report on the situation of education in Uganda, Tomaševski wrote of the task of mainstreaming human rights and gender into education:

> 'this requires addressing difficult and controversial issues such as schoolgirl pregnancy, adaptation of the content of educational curricula and textbooks to the objective of equipping girls with the knowledge and skills necessary for them to avoid early pregnancy, and broadening the objectives and purposes of education to provide the future generations of women in Uganda with options unavailable to the past and current generations of women.'[175]

This paper does not seek to resolve this tension, which is likely to be amplified in occupied states. It merely points it out. With the ousting of a government the local population may be eager to incorporate human rights into areas of life where they were previously prohibited or absent. Or, the incorporation of human rights into the education system may be regarded as an insensitive and manipulative imposition on social norms by a foreign power. The truth will probably lie somewhere muddled in between where some are hungry for its incorporation and others are not. The perennial battle between human rights and cultural relativism is not far removed from the tension between the right to education and occupation law. In an attempt to remedy this problem to at least some degree, it is critical to scrutinise who in the occupied territory does not want human rights in the education system, or wants it taught in a certain way, and why. It would be insincere, however, to say that this is too difficult a problem to try to resolve. To do so would nullify most of this paper's purpose. When international right to education standards are reflected into the Fourth Geneva Convention, an occupant must work toward the incorporation of human rights into the local education system but will in all likelihood have to walk a thin rope of political considerations in this pursuit.

5.3.3 *Corporal punishment*

The prohibition on corporal punishment presents a clear example where the positive obligation that an occupant has to nullify a law under the right to education is fully compatible with its obligations under occupation law.[176]

5.4 **Adaptability**

— Obligation to design and implement education for children precluded from formal schooling (e.g., refuge-seeking or internally displaced children, children deprived of their liberty, or working children).

---

175. Report by the Special Rapporteur on the Right to Education: Mission to Uganda, E/CN.4/2000/6/Add.1, para. 92.

176. Fourth Geneva Convention, Art. 32 and Protocol I, Art. 75(2)(a)(iii).

— Obligation to adapt education to the best interests of each child, especially regarding children with disabilities, or minority and indigenous children.
— Obligation to apply indivisibility of human rights as guidance so as to enhance all human rights through education, such as the right to marry and raise a family, or the right to freedom from forced and child labour.[177]

The 'adaptability' component of the right to education attaches itself to every action a state takes in the field of education. This component can operate as a reactionary device to criticise actions taken by a state that are not in the best interest of the child. It is also an informative device to help instruct a state on what considerations it should make in its plans to carry out its obligations. It is akin, though broader, to the safeguards in Articles 24(1) and 50(3) Geneva IV that work to ensure that children without family or parents are protected from propaganda. In the context of occupation, it acts as a protective layer to ensure that actions taken that are permissible under occupation law are inclusive rather than exclusive and are moulded around the uniqueness of a child's situation, whether he or she is a refugee, disabled, without parents, speaks a language uncommon in the population, etc.[178] It finds its closest ally in Article 77 of Protocol I, which states: 'The Parties to the conflict shall provide [children] with the care and aid they require, whether because of their age or for *any other reason*.' [emphasis added][179] Bothe, Partsch, and Solf have interpreted 'any other reason' to include 'health, mental retardations, etc.'[180]

6. ADDITIONAL CONSIDERATIONS REGARDING THE APPLICATION OF THE RIGHT TO EDUCATION IN OCCUPIED TERRITORIES

6.1 When is an occupant allowed to interfere?

While occupation law does not restrict an occupant from cooperatively assisting the national and local authorities from working to facilitate institutions devoted to the education of children, it does seem to prohibit interference. This paper has challenged this strict interpretation and has argued that interference should be justified when the actions of the occupant are aimed at meeting international right to education standards. Indeed, from the human rights perspective this would not be interference but assistance. Nonetheless, one implication of this is that there must be a human rights violation taking place for the occupant to legitimately 'interfere'. Finding such a violation is not difficult when the national and local authorities are not meeting their 'immediate obligations', or even their 'core obligations'. How-

177. UNESCO Bangkok, *supra* n. 87, p. 8.
178. See for example, Committee on the Rights of the Child, Concluding observations (Poland), CRC/C/15/Add.194, 2003, para. 40.
179. Protocol I, Art. 77.
180. Bothe et al., *supra* n. 46, p. 476.

ever, a violation may be difficult to determine if the component of the right to education that is under review can be progressively realised. If the local authorities of a municipality are using all their available resources to realise the right to education and they do not want the occupant to interfere, under either occupation law or human rights law, can the occupant push the local authorities aside to complete the task more quickly?

The dictates of international human rights law suggest it can. The Occupying Power is the one responsible for the human rights of the local population since it has effective control. Strictly speaking, the national and local authorities cannot be held responsible for human rights violations and for that reason it would be odd to hinder the actions of the occupant because only lesser initiatives can be taken by the local authorities. To do so goes against the grain of human rights law, which holds that states with effective control are responsible for the actions of third parties and not the other way around. That said, the politics and law of occupation confuse this issue considerably. At the heart of occupation law is the notion that the occupant can interfere only when it is necessary, regardless of the resources available to the occupant. To this end, if the local and national authorities are advancing those components of the rights to education that can be progressively realised, then the right an occupant has to interfere in those advancements, even if in a positive manner, seems to be limited. This issue can by no means be resolved here, though it deserves focused attention.

6.2 Prolonged occupation

The discussion of this paper focused solely on 'regular' occupations. It should not be ignored, however, that Article 6 of Geneva IV states that occupants are subject to special conditions when occupations extend one year beyond the general close of military operations. When this happens the occupant is held only to certain provisions in the convention, namely Articles 1 to 12, 27, 29 to 34, 47, 49, 51, 52, 53, 59, 61 to 77, and 143.[181]

These Articles include the most basic of protections that the convention affords, though Articles 24 and 50 are not included.[182] The drafting history indicates that the absence of Articles 24 and 50 from Article 6 were made under the assumption that as occupations get longer and longer the national and local authorities should (re)gain increased responsibilities.[183] After one year of the general close of hostilities the drafters foresaw little reason that educational institutions could not be fully cared for by these authorities, nor did they want to place this burden on the occupant.

---

181. Fourth Geneva Convention, Art. 6.

182. Roberts notes that Art. 6 may be archaic for several reasons. Nonetheless, the ICJ made note of the provision in its 2004 advisory opinion and therefore it appears to still be relevant. Roberts, *supra* n. 104, p. 56; Legal Consequences of the Construction of a Wall in the Occupied Palestinian Territory, *supra* n. 3, para. 125.

183. ICRC 1948 Draft Revised or New Conventions for the Protection of War Victims, *supra* n. 69, p. 173; Final Record, *supra* n. 105, p. 815.

A problem arises, however, when the occupant does not hand control back to the local authorities and the institutions do not become self-sustaining. In the scenario of a prolonged occupation, Article 6 effectively grants the occupant the right to refuse to provide necessary assistance to education without violating the Fourth Geneva Convention. This situation can be mitigated by the fact that the Occupying Power could be permitted to provide assistance in so far as the assistance respects the laws in place and does not require the changing of laws. Indeed, human rights law might obligate the Occupying Power to provide such assistance. What is more worrisome is that in cases of prolonged occupation the provisions on education in the Fourth Geneva Convention would have expired and even a benevolent occupant would be limited in its ability to make positive changes in the law that are necessary to facilitate the proper working of educational institutions. These provisions were drafted with it in mind that occupations would be short lived, education should continue as it did prior to the time of occupation, and scant legal changes to the education system would be needed. From an occupation law perspective, this restriction makes perfect sense. But from the human rights perspective this reasoning is insufficient when the laws in place are contrary to the right to education. It is also problematic because the content of education and methods for teaching can change over time, and syllabi and curriculum may need to be altered accordingly.

In a case where the occupant is a State Party to Protocol I this dilemma is resolved through the application of Article 77, which provides general care for children and continues throughout times of occupation no matter how long it lasts.[184] In cases where the occupant is not bound by Protocol I, occupation law may provide little relief to solving this problem. It is hoped that, at the very least, a state would have laws in force prior to occupation that call for regular reviews of curricula and syllabi that can accommodate changes that naturally occur over time in what and how subjects are taught. If they do not, it might be beneficial for the occupant to put these procedures in place when the occupation begins so to prevent the petrification of a state's education system if the occupation becomes prolonged.

7. CONCLUSION

This paper has explored the compatibilities and tensions between occupation law and the right to education. Using as a guide the core obligations set out by

---

184. Art. 3(b) of Protocol I states that the Protocol shall cease, 'on the general close of military operations and, in the case of occupied territories, on the termination of the occupation …' Exceptions are not made for prolonged occupation.
Art. 96 of Protocol I explains the Protocol's relationship with the Geneva Conventions. The ICRC Protocol I Commentary elaborates: 'Basically the Protocol supplements the Conventions by extending the scope of their application, the categories of protected persons and objects and the protection conferred. Thus the Conventions remain and the Protocol adds to them without in principle removing anything. When the recognized rules of interpretation reveal an incompatibility on a particular point between the provisions of the Conventions and those of the Protocol, the latter take precedence. In this respect this paragraph merely repeats, succinctly, the relevant rule of the law of treaties'. Commentary Protocol I, *supra* n. 46, para. 3748.

UNESCO and the UN Special Rapporteur on the right to education, it looked at a variety of the extraterritorial positive obligations that occupants have with regard to the primary education of children inside the territories they occupy. In doing so, it has been demonstrated that while similarities between the two exist, tension do as well. The question then arises, what is the solution to this problem?[185] This paper argues for an injecting of international right to education standards into the provisions on education in occupation law, as well as reinterpretations of the ICRC Commentary. It also points out a number of safeguards that are in place to curb the abuse of this approach. In addition to the ones already mentioned, there are human rights oversight mechanisms in place today that could not have been envisaged in 1949 that work to monitor the actions of states. These include the UN Special Rapporteur on the right to education, the various human rights treaty committees, and regional human rights judicial and quasi-judicial bodies. As more states ratify human rights conventions and accept the jurisdiction of these bodies the justification for loosening the restrictions that occupation law places on human rights will become stronger. It will become stronger still when these mechanisms increasingly give attention to situations of occupation. In taking this approach, this paper seeks to make a contribution toward remedying the still relevant dilemma that Von Glahn pointed out back in 1957:

> 'The accepted rules of international law are unfortunately silent on [the extent to which an occupant could interfere legitimately with the educational system of a territory under his control] and while a very few writers on the law of nations have briefly commented on education under belligerent occupation, little has actually been contributed toward the solution of this very real and important problem in our age of ideological conflicts.'[186]

It should be noted that while this paper demonstrates a model for making various facets of the right to education compatible with occupation law, there are issues completely absent from this paper. That is, this paper is not comprehensive and the approach it advocates is by no means a panacea from a human rights perspective.

In closing, scholars have highlighted that human rights law is applicable in times of occupation. They have also noticed and begun to attempt to solve the tensions that can arise between human rights law and occupation law. This paper is an additional contribution to this growing body of work. Nonetheless, if it is true that the occupation of Iraq in 2003 'revived occupation law from its slumber' and if it is true that human rights can 'breathe new life' into occupation law, further

---

185. Scholars have made various pronouncements on this issue. See E. Benvenisti, 'The Security Council and the law on occupation: Resolution 1483 on Iraq in historical perspective', 1 *Israel Defense Forces Law Review* (2003); D. Goodman, 'The Need for Fundamental Change in the Law of Belligerent Occupation', 37 *Stanford LR* (1985) p. 1607; D. Scheffer, 'Beyond Occupation', 97 *AJIL* (2003) p. 842.

186. Von Glahn, *supra* n. 171, pp. 62-63.

detail is needed to instruct occupants how exactly they are permitted to make the two operate simultaneously.[187]

187. Benvenisti, *supra* n. 185, p. 29.

CURRENT DEVELOPMENTS

THE YEAR IN REVIEW[1]

Avril McDonald[2]

2. Dr Avril McDonald is Head of the Section of International Humanitarian Law and International Criminal Law at the TMC Asser Institute for International Law; Managing Editor of the *Yearbook of International Humanitarian Law*; Lecturer in Advanced International Law.

Yearbook of International Humanitarian Law
Volume 7 - 2004 - pp. 281-323 DOI 10.1017/S1389135904002818

1. INTRODUCTION: THE ROOTS OF MISBEHAVIOUR IN WAR

1.1 The Roots of Behaviour in War

The question of what determines the behaviour of combatants in war and influences them to respect or violate international humanitarian law was the subject of a slim but compelling publication of the International Committee of the Red Cross (ICRC) entitled *The Roots of Behaviour in War* issued in October 2004.[3] Among the authors' tentative conclusions were the following:

---

3. J.-J. Frésard and D. Muñoz-Rojas, *The Roots of Behaviour in War: A Survey of the Literature* (Geneva, ICRC 2004). The report is one of a four part research project on behaviour in war. For more information <http://www.icrc.org/Web/Eng/siteeng0.nsf/iwpList74/FC4181278BEE58FEC1256E-CA00357055>.

'Although in some cases violations may be explained by passions, pathological behaviour and stress, we consider that they are mostly the result of deliberate policies which either encourage or tolerate such behaviour. We have also taken care to point out that those who perpetrate these acts are often obeying those who instigate them, and this distinction should be borne in mind, not to absolve the perpetrators of the acts they commit but to recognize where primary responsibility for certain types of behaviour lies. This point is also made in order to emphasize that if we want to influence the perpetrators in any effective way it is often the instigators who have to be approached.'[4]

1.2 The roots of misbehaviour at Abu Ghraib

In April 2004 horrifying photographs of prisoner abuse by US soldiers, military police and contractors at Abu Ghraib prison in Iraq – just a sampler of a much wider collection[5] – flashed around the world.[6] They depicted detainees being subjected to a wide range of cruel, inhuman, humiliating and degrading treatment, in some cases amounting to torture. The mistreatment included beatings; sexual assault and humiliation; hooding; the use of stress positions; forcing prisoner to walk on all fours, sometimes on leashes, and retrieve their food from toilets; burning detainees' skin with chemicals; assembling detainees in human pyramids and other contortions; and threatening them with dogs and with electrocution.

When the story broke, a furore ensued, and the inevitable questions of how and why such terrible things could have occurred followed.[7] Scratching their heads, officials at the US Department of Defense (DoD) vowed to get to the bottom of the matter and commissioned a series of investigations into the abuses at Abu Ghraib and other Iraqi prisons. A number of reports duly followed during the year. Some were more hard-hitting than others but all reached the same basic conclusion: while some abuses had certainly taken place, at Abu Ghraib and elsewhere, they represented aberrant behaviour by low level sadistic individuals who were not following authorised interrogation techniques and Army doctrine, and not any official policy of torture or other types of coercive and inhumane interrogation methods.[8]

---

4. Ibid., p. 108.

5. More photos of prisoner abuse emerged later in the year. See K. Kiely, 'Pentagon to show senators new photos', *USA Today*, 11 May 2004; S. Higham and J. Stephens, 'New Details of Prison Abuse Emerge: Abu Ghraib Detainees' Statements Describe Sexual Humiliation And Savage Beatings', *The Washington Post*, 21 May 2004; S. Hettena, 'Navy investigating new set of Iraqi prisoner photos', Associated Press, 4 December 2004; J. Walsh, 'The Abu Ghraib files', Salon, <http://www.salon.com/news/abu_ghraib/2006/03/14/introduction/>.

6. 'Abuse of Iraqi POWs by GIs Probed', 60 Minutes II, CBS News, 28 April 2004, <http://www.cbsnews.com/stories/2004/04/27/60II/main614063.shtml>.

7. See K. Kiely and W.M. Welch, 'Abu Ghraib photos cause gasps in Congress', *USA Today*, 12 May 2004, <http://www.usatoday.com/news/world/iraq/2004-05-12-congress-abuse_x.htm>; for an analysis of media reporting on the story, see S. Ricchiardi, 'Missed signals', *American Journalism Review* (July-August 2004) <http://www.ajr.org/Article.asp?id=3716>.

8. See generally, 'General: No pattern of abuse at prisons: New Abu Ghraib images involve body', 20 May 2004; S.M. Hersh, 'Chain of command: How the Department of Defense mishandled the disaster at Abu Ghraib', *The New Yorker*, 17 May 2004.

The Mikolashek Report went the furthest in pinning the blame on a few deviants:

> 'We could not identify a systemic cause for the abuse incidents. … The DAIG [Department of the Army Inspector General] determined that incidents where detainees were allegedly mistreated occurred as isolated events. In a few incidents, higher ranking individuals up to Lieutenant Colonel were involved; however, the chain of command took action when an allegation of detainee abuse was reported.'[9]

The Fay Jones Report found that:

> 'There is no single, simple explanation for why this abuse at Abu Ghraib happened. The primary causes are misconduct (ranging from inhumane to sadistic) by a small group of morally corrupt soldiers and civilians, a lack of discipline on the part of the leaders and Soldiers of the 205th MI BDE [Military Intelligence Brigade] and a failure or lack of leadership by multiple echelons within CJTF-7 [Combined Joint Task Force]. Contributing factors can be traced to issues affecting Command and Control, Doctrine, Training, and the experience of the Soldiers we asked to perform this vital mission.'[10]

The Taguba Report blamed Brigadier General Janet Karpinski of the 800th Military Police Brigade and the dysfunctionality and lack of training of the Brigade.[11]

The most thoughtful report, by the independent panel headed by James Schlesinger, found that: 'No approved procedures called for or allowed the kinds of abuses that in fact occurred. There is no evidence of a policy of abuse promulgated by senior officials or military authorities.'[12] The report attributed the abuses mainly to

> 'the aberrant behavior of a limited number of soldiers and the predilections of the non-commissioned officers on the night shift of Tier 1 at Abu Ghraib, … commanding officers and their staffs at various levels failed in their duties and … such failures contributed directly or indirectly to detainee abuses.'[13]

Direct responsibility didn't go very far up the chain of command, however; just as far as the Commanding General of the 800th Military Police Brigade and the Com-

---

9. The Mikolashek Report, Department of the Army, The Inspector General Detainee Operations Inspection, July 2004, reprinted in K.J. Greenberg and J.L. Dratel, eds., *The Torture Papers: The Road to Abu Ghraib* (Cambridge, Cambridge University Press 2005) pp. 630 at 648.

10. The Fay-Jones Report, Investigation of Intelligence Activities at Abu Ghraib, Investigation of the Abu Ghraib Prison and 205th Military Intelligence Brigade, LTG Anthony R. Jones, Investigation of the Abu Ghraib Detention Facility and the 205th Military Intelligence Brigade, MG George R. Fay, August 2004, reprinted in Greenberg and Dratel, *supra* n. 9, pp. 987 at 989.

11. The Taguba Report, Article 15-6 Investigation of the 800th Military Police Brigade, March 2004, reprinted in Greenberg and Dratel, *supra* n. 9, pp. 405 at 432-439.

12. The Schlesinger Report, Final Report of the Independent Panel to Review DoD Detention Operations, August 2004, reprinted in Greenberg and Dratel, *supra* n. 9, pp. 908 at 909.

13. Ibid., p. 928.

manding Officer of the 205th Military Intelligence Brigade, whose weak and ineffectual leadership allowed the abuses.[14] Schlesinger conceded that there was indirect personal and institutional responsibility at higher levels: '... the abuses were not just the failure of some individuals to follow known standards, and they are more than the failure of a few leaders to enforce proper discipline.'[15] Lieutenant General [LTG] Richardo Sanchez, the commander of US ground forces in Iraq, was lightly rapped on the knuckles for not taking 'stronger action in November [2003] when he realized the extent of the leadership problems at Abu Ghraib', but no disciplinary action against him was recommended.[16] The report described in detail the DoD's interrogation policy and the sanctioning of more aggressive methods in order to satisfy the pressure for more intelligence, admitting that: 'The existence of confusing and inconsistent interrogation technique policies contributed to the belief that additional interrogation techniques were condoned.'[17] Yet it failed to make the connection between the administration's attempts to redefine torture, its authorisation of more aggressive interrogation techniques and the subsequent abuses of detainees.

The Schlesinger Report offered at least a partial psychological explanation for the Abu Ghraib abuses by reference to the so-called Stanford Prison Experiment of 1971,[18] which demonstrated the increasingly aggressive behaviour of individual volunteers acting as prison guards in an experiment.[19] One of the main findings of the experiment was that violence is situationally determined. Following the revelations about Abu Ghraib, one of the authors of the study, Philip Zimbardo, was reported as saying that his experiment foretold the abuses.[20] According to Zimbardo, the men and women who carried out the abuses at Abu Ghraib, like his 'guards', were good people reacting to the dehumanising situation they were placed in, which implicitly gave them permission to suspend their moral values. They were not rotten apples but good people corrupted by being in a bad barrel.[21] On the one hand, this seems to contradict the conclusion of the report that the abuses were the work of a few bad apples, a conclusion that is in some ways difficult to square with its other finding of institutional problems. On the other hand, the allusion to the Stanford Prison Experiment underscores the conclusion of Schlesinger and the other reports that the violence at Abu Ghraib was essentially

14. Ibid.

15. Ibid., p. 909.

16. Ibid., pp. 915; 929.

17. Ibid., p. 902.

18. Conducted by C. Haney, W.C. Banks and P. Zimbardo, 'Interpersonal dynamics in a simulated prison', 1 *International Journal of Criminology and Penology* (1973) p. 69. See generally <http://www.prisonexp.org/>.

19. See *supra* n. 12, pp. 970-975.

20. P.G. Zimbardo, 'Power turns good soldiers into 'bad apples'', *The Boston Globe*, 9 May 2004, <http://www.boston.com/news/globe/editorial_opinion/oped/articles/2004/05/09/power_turns_good_-soldiers_into_bad_apples/>.

21. See 'You can't be a sweet cucumber in a vinegar barrel', A talk with Philip Zimbardo, Edge, The Third Culture, 19 January 2005, <http://www.edge.org/3rd_culture/zimbardo05/zimbardo05_index.html>.

random, directionless and 'just for fun'.[22] Left to their own devices, without responsible leadership, institutional environments develop a life of their own. In a morally permissive environment, it becomes a race to the bottom. This removes from the picture the question of agency.

While the Stanford Prison Experiment might appear to shed light on the causes of the perpetrators' behaviour, a more apposite psychological explanation for what happened can be found in the work of another American social psychologist. As Stanley Milgram's 'electric shock' experiments demonstrated,[23] a key element in determining behaviour, particularly in an institutional setting, is obedience to or compliance with authority. It interesting that in listing some of the factors determining human aggression, the Schlesinger report omitted this one. Most people are followers and not leaders, and will go very far in obeying an authority whom they perceive to be legitimate or in doing what they think the authority wishes or expects, and those that are not compliant and that resist authority are the exception to the rule. Milgram observed that:

> 'There is a propensity for people to accept definitions of action provided by legitimate authority. That is, although the subject performs the action, he allows authority to define its meaning. It is this ideological abrogation to the authority that constitutes the principal cognitive basis of obedience.'[24]

The tendency towards obedience to authority is particularly pronounced once an individual enters a hierarchical organisation, the armed forces being a hierarchical organisation par excellence. According to Milgram, 'conscience, which regulates impulsive aggressive action, is diminished at the point of entering a hierarchical structure such that the person enters an agentic state in contrast to the usual autonomous state'.[25] He speculated that individuals would more easily be able to direct

---

22. Paul Arthur, a military investigator testifying at the court martial of Private First Class Lynddie England, one of the soldiers photographed abusing prisoners at Abu Ghrabi, stated that England told him that 'it was just for fun'. 'They didn't think it was that serious. ... They didn't think it was that big a deal. They were joking around,' Arthur said England told him.' J. Polk, 'Testimony: Abu Ghraib photos 'just for fun'', 4 August 2004, <http://www.cnn.com/2004/LAW/08/03/england.hearing/>. 'England sentenced to 3 years for prison abuse: Soldier dishonorably discharged for Abu Ghraib scandal', Associated Press, 28 September 2005, <http://www.msnbc.msn.com/id/9492624/>.

23. Wishing to see how an individual behaves when asked by someone whom he perceives as a legitimate authority to undertake coercive action against another person, in 1963 Milgram set up an experiment which involved an authority figure telling members of the public ('teachers') – who were unaware of the real nature of the experiment (they thought they were taking part in an experiment to measure the effect of punishment on memory and the learning process) – to administer what they thought were electric shocks to 'learners' (in reality, actors) every time they gave a wrong answer to a question asked. On the instructions of the authority figure, the majority of 'teachers' were prepared to administer what they thought were electronic shocks of up to 450 volts, or enough to kill somebody, despite the pleadings of the 'learners' for the experiment to stop and their feigning unconsciousness. S. Milgram, *Obedience to Authority* (New York, Harper & Row 1974).

24. Ibid., p. 145.

25. Quoted in The Root of Behaviour, Frésard and Muñoz-Rojas, *supra* n. 3, at p. 10.

violence against other persons if those individuals were denigrated by the authority in their eyes:

> 'In all likelihood, our subjects would have experienced greater ease in shocking the victim had he been convincingly portrayed as a brutal criminal or a pervert.
> ... Many subjects harshly devalue the victim as a consequence of acting against him. ... Once having acted against the victim, these subjects found it necessary to view him as an unworthy individual.'[26]

The Abu Ghraib scandal claimed a few low-ranking scalps,[27] but no senior or even mid-level commanders were prosecuted on the basis of either direct or indirect responsibility for the abuses.[28] Even Janet Karpinski, the much maligned commander of the army's 800th military police brigade, was only demoted – a year later – from Brigadier General to Colonel.[29] If Abu Ghraib was just one bad barrel and the abuses there were isolated events, this failure of senior commanders and of a Party to an armed conflict to enforce compliance with the law would be troubling enough. What makes the situation not merely troubling but truly alarming is the fact that the abuses there were part of a wider pattern of mistreatment of detainees. The widespread nature of abuses against detainees in Iraq, for example, was noted in a February 2004 Report of the International Committee of the Red Cross (ICRC) on the Treatment by the Coalition Forces of Prisoners of War and Other Protected Persons by the Geneva Conventions in Iraq During Arrest, Internment and Interrogation, which found that:

> 'ill treatment during interrogation was not systematic, except with regard to persons arrested in connection with suspected security offences or deemed to have an "intelligence" value. In those cases, persons deprived of their liberty under supervision of the Military Intelligence were at high risk of being subjected to a variety of harsh treatments ranging from insults, threats and humiliations to both physical and psychological coercion, which in some cases was tantamount to torture, in order to force cooperation with their interrogators.'[30]

Recently published books, such as Karen Greenberg and Joshua Dratel's *The Torture Papers: The Road to Abu Ghraib*,[31] Mark Danner's *Torture and Truth: America, Abu Ghraib and the War on Terror*[32] and Seymour Hersh's *Chain of Com-*

---

26. Milgram, *supra* n. 23, pp. 9-10.
27. Only one of the perpetrators of the abuses, Charles A. Graner, Jr., Lynddie England's boyfriend, was court-martialed. He received a ten year sentence. See 'Graner gets 10 years for Abu Ghraib abuse: Says he was ordered to abuse Iraqi prisoners', Associated Press, 16 January 2005. Others reached plea bargains, including Pfc England, *supra* n. 22.
28. Many, including Human Rights Watch in its annual report, called for prosecutions higher up.
29. See PBS Online News of 6 May 2005, <http://www.pbs.org/newshour/bb/military/jan-june05/abuse_5-6.html>.
30. Published in Greenberg and Dratel, *supra* n. 9, pp. 383 at 385.
31. Ibid.
32. New York, New York Review of Books 2004.

mand: The Road from 9/11 to Abu Ghraib,[33] and the diligent efforts of a number of human rights organisations[34] and sections of the media[35] have helped to shed light on the provenance of the abusive behaviour by US troops at Abu Ghraib and elsewhere. Their work, departing from the conclusions of the DoD reports, supports the theory that the abuses conform to a Milgramian rather than a Zimbardoian analysis.

The editors of *The Torture Papers*, for example, have collected together in one voluminous tome the various memoranda that were written by US legal counsel concerning the treatment of detainees in the hands of the US, including the notorious so-called 'torture memorandum' written by Assistant Attorney General Jay Bybee for the Counsel to the President Alberto R. Gonzales[36] – the latter who subsequently was elevated to the position of US Attorney General[37] – as well as a host of other documents, including all of the aforementioned official investigative reports of the US DoD. The documents contained in the book, together with the other evidence that has entered the public domain, chillingly attest to a concerted attempt at the highest government levels to deny fundamental rights to persons suspected of involvement in terrorist or hostile activity. The roots of the misbehaviour of the individuals working the night shift on Tier 1 – cast by some of the DoD investigators and parts of the media in the role of frat boys and sorority girls run amuck[38] – are revealed to be not, or not only, their personal predilection for sadistic behaviour but the policy, emanating from the highest echelons of the Bush

33. *The New Yorker* 17 May 2004.

34. Including the Center for Constitutional Rights, <http://www.ccr-ny.org/v2/home.asp>; the American Civil Liberties Union, <http://www.aclu.org>; Human Rights Watch, <http://www.hrw.org>; and Human Right First, <http://www.humanrightsfirst.org/index.asp>; and Amnesty International, <http://www.amnesty.org>.

35. A number of journalists working for print and broadcast media were instrumental in breaking the story and investigating the cause of the brutality, in particular *The New Yorker's* Seymour Hersh and *The New York Review of Book's* Mark Danner. See, *inter alia*, S.M. Hersh, 'Torture at Abu Ghraib: American soldiers brutalized Iraqis. How far up does the responsibility go?' *The New Yorker*, 10 May 2004, <http://www.newyorker.com/fact/content/?040510fa_fact>; 'The Gray Zone How a secret Pentagon program came to Abu Ghraib', *The New Yorker*, 24 May 2004; <http://www.newyorker.com/fact/content/?040524fa_fact>; M. Danner, 'Torture and Truth', '*The New York Review of Books,* 10 June 2004, <http://www.markdanner.com/nyreview/061004_Torture_Truth.htm>; 'The Logic of Torture', '*The New York Review of Books,* 24 June 2004, <http://www.markdanner.com/nyreview/062404_Road_-to_Torture.htm>; 'Abu Ghraib: The Hidden Story', *The New York Review of Books,* 7 October 2004, <http://www.markdanner.com/nyreview/100704_abu.htm>; J. Barry, M. Hirsh and M. Isikoff, 'The Roots of Torture: The road to Abu Ghraib began after 9/11, when Washington wrote new rules to fight a new kind of war', *Newsweek*, 24 May 2004 <http://www.msnbc.msn.com/id/4989422/>.

36. Memorandum for Alberto R. Gonzales Counsel to the President from Jay S. Bybee, 1 August 2002, published in Greenberg and Dratel, *supra* n. 9, p. 172. See Year in Review, 5 *YIHL* (2002) pp. 258-259.

37. On 3 February 2005. See <http://www.whitehouse.gov/government/gonzales-bio.html>.

38. James Schlesinger, presenting his report into the Abu Ghraib abuses, characterised the atmosphere on Tier One as 'Animal House' on the night shift. ' Report: Abu Ghraib was "Animal House" at night', 25 August 2006, <http://edition.cnn.com/2004/US/08/24/abughraib.report/>; 'Limbaugh returned to downplaying Abu Ghraib prisoner abuse as "hazing" and "an out-of-control fraternity prank"', Media Matters for America, 31 August 2004, <http://mediamatters.org/items/200408310002>; '*Hannity & Colmes* guest compared U.S. soldiers' maltreatment of Iraqi POWs to

administration,[39] of sanctioning interrogation techniques which either stretched the law to breaking point or went way beyond it,[40] and particularly the initial refusal to recognise the legal status and rights of the Guantanamo detainees,[41] which paved the way for the subsequent abuses of detainees there and elsewhere.[42] As the Schlesinger report noted, aggressive interrogation techniques that had been approved for Guantanamo and Afghanistan, where detainees were not considered POWs, migrated to Iraq, where many were considered to be POWs.[43] According to Schlesinger, 'techniques effective under carefully controlled conditions at Guantanamo became far more problematic when they migrated and were not adequately safeguarded'.[44] These techniques included the removal of detainees' clothes, the use of stress positions, exploiting fear of dogs, isolation and sleep and light deprivation.[45] The consequences of the sanctioning of coercive methods of interrogation in order to yield more intelligence could quickly be seen: first in Afghanistan[46] and

---

"frat hazing"', Media Matters for America, 3 May 2004, <http://mediamatters.org/items/200405030010>.

39. See J. Conason, 'Torture Begins at the Top', Salon.com, 17 December 2004; J. Barry, M. Hirsh and M. Isikoff, 'The Roots of Torture', *Newsweek,* 24 May 2006, <http://www.msnbc.msn.com/id/4989481/>; J. White, 'Abu Ghraib Tactics Were First Used at Guantanamo', *The Washington Post*, 14 July 2005, <http://www.washingtonpost.com/wp dyn/content/article/2005/07/13/AR2005071302380.html>; S. Hersch, 'The Gray Zone: How a secret Pentagon program came to Abu Ghraib', *The New Yorker,* 24 May 2004, http://www.newyorker.com/fact/content/?040524fa_fact; M. Danner, 'Abu Ghraib: The Hidden Story', *The New York Review of Books*, 7 October 2004, <http://www.markdanner.com/nyreview/100704_abu.htm>.

40. The Schlesinger report took note of the 1 August memorandum of the Office of Legal Counsel (*supra* n. 23) which held that 'only the most extreme acts, that were specifically designed to inflict severe pain and torture, would be in violation; less acts might be "cruel, inhumane, or degrading" but would not violate the Convention Against Torture or domestic statutes. The OLC memorandum went on to say, as Commander in Chief exercising his wartime powers, the President could even authorize torture, if he so decided.' *Supra* n. 9, pp. 923-924. However, it failed to make the connection between this memorandum and the abuses at Abu Ghraib.

41. See Fact Sheet: Status of Detainees at Guantanamo. White House Press Release of 7 February 2004. Reproduced in 5 *YIHL* (2002) p. 662.

42. See D. Rose, *Guantanamo: The War on Human Rights* (New York NY, New Press 2004).

43. Policy guidelines approved by Secretary Rumsfeld for use in Guantanamo, in 2 December and 16 April memoranda which authorised interrogation techniques going beyond those approved in US Army Field Manual 34-52, were imported to Iraq by Lt. General Sanchez via a memorandum dated 14 September 2003. See the Schlesinger report, *supra* n. 9, at pp. 910-912, 941 and 966 and 967. 'Policies approved for use on al Qaeda and Taliban detainees, who were not afforded the protections of the Geneva Conventions, now applied to detainees who did fall under the Geneva Conventions.' Ibid., p. 915. J. Sturcke, 'General approved extreme interrogation methods', *The Guardian*, 30 March 2005.

44. Schlesinger Report, *supra* n. 9, p. 911.

45. Ibid., at p. 967.

46. See S. Goldenberg and J. Meek, 'Papers reveal Bagram abuse', *The Guardian*, 18 February 2005, <http://www.guardian.co.uk/afghanistan/story/0,1284,1417396,00.html>; '"Enduring Freedom": Abuses by U.S. Forces in Afghanistan', Human Rights Watch, March 2004, <http://hrw.org/reports/2004/afghanistan0304>/; 'U.S.: Systemic Abuse of Afghan Prisoners', Human Rights Watch, 13 May 2004, <http://www.hrw.org/english/docs/2004/05/13/afghan8577.htm>; R. Jeffrey Smith, 'General Cites Problems at U.S. Jails in Afghanistan', *The Washington Post*, 4 December 2004, <http://www.washingtonpost.com/wp-dyn/articles/A29824-2004Dec2.html>; T. Golden, 'In U.S. Report, Brutal Details of 2 Afghan Inmates' Deaths', *The New York Times*, 20 May 2005, <http://www.nytimes.com/2005/05/20/international/asia/20abuse.html?ex=1274241600&-

at Guantanamo Bay[47] and later in Iraq, to mention just the verified loci of abuses. As Karen Greenberg writes in the Introduction to *The Torture Papers*:

> 'Ultimately, what the reader is left with after reading these documents is a clear sense of the systematic decision to alter the use of methods of coercion and torture that lay outside the accepted legal norms, a process that began early in 2002 and that was well defined by the end of that year; months before the invasion of Iraq. ... Not only did the lawyers and policy makers knowingly overstep legal doctrine, but they did so against the advice of individuals in their midst, notably Secretary of State Colin Powell and William H. Taft, Legal Advisor to the Secretary of State.'[48]

1.3 Influencing the instigators

If we accept that the violations of humanitarian law committed by US soldiers against detainees captured in the context of the GWOT are the result of deliberate policies, then the only way to stop the abuses is by influencing the instigators to desist.

Two main legal problems present themselves as far as the detainees: the indefinite detention without trial of at least some of them and the lack of any real possibility to challenge this situation and second, their ill treatment. The wellspring of the problem being the official refusal to recognise the legal status of persons detained in the context of the GWOT and its associated real wars,[49] and the authorisation in relation to them of coercive methods of interrogation which have percolated down the chin of command, it seems that it can only be remedied through a concerted effort to influence the instigators to approach the issue of detainees through the applicable international legal framework. Only through acceptance by the instigators of the abuses that detainees are entitled to status and rights can violence against detainees be avoided. Those who guard the prisons and carry out the interrogations could only be expected to stay within the law and apply it correctly if they are told that it does apply, know what it is and feel that they are expected to observe the rules on pain of sanction. They cannot be expected to work within a legal vacuum. Rendering someone a legal non-person, an individual who falls within the cracks, with no recognised rights or even sometimes existence, is a license for abuse.

International law recognises freedom from torture and cruel and humane treatment[50] as being absolute rights so anyone who engages in such practices, at any level and to whatever extent and by whichever means, should be made aware that they are breaking the law and risk being prosecuted before the courts of their own

---

en=4579c146cb14cfd6&ei=5088>; E. Bazelon, 'From Bagram to Abu Ghraib', *Mother Jones*, March-April 2005, <http://www.motherjones.com/news/feature/2005/03/03_2005_Bazelon.html>.

47. D. Rose and G. Hinsliff , 'US guards 'filmed beatings' at terror camp', *The Observer*, 16 May 2004, <http://observer.guardian.co.uk/international/story/0,6903,1217973,00.html>.

48. In Greenberg and Dratel, *supra* n. 9, pp. xvii at xix.

49. *REFS*

50. The only difference between them, as noted in an earlier 'Year in Review', is torture's purposive element. See 5 *YIHL* (2002) p. 259.

state, by another state according to the principle of universal jurisdiction or before an international criminal court with jurisdiction.

It hardly seems necessary to justify why freedom from torture should be an absolute right, as the interdiction is rooted in fundamental principles of morality and ethics. Freedom from torture must be an absolute right, however, because experience has all too often shown that once the absolute nature of the prohibition is denied, while it might technically be possible to regulate or set limits on the use of torture, either in an individual case or as a matter of policy, once the lid comes off the tendency is towards increased resorted to abusive treatment. As David Luban has observed: 'Escalation is the rule, not the aberration. Abu Ghraib is the fully predictable image of what a torture culture looks like. You cannot reasonably expect that interrogators in a torture culture will be the fastidious and well-meaning torturers that the liberal ideology fantasizes.'[51]

It seems clear that the current policy has emanated from a political clique with no regard for international law. Very many persons in the military, working in intelligence and in counter-terrorism and most right thinking people are opposed to the humiliation, ill treatment, coercion and torture of detainees. Only if those with the ability to influence the instigators use that influence to remind those in power that they do not enjoy absolute power and are not, after all, above the law and are in fact answerable for their actions is there a chance of climbing out of this moral and legal abyss and regaining the moral high ground and respect for the rule of law. This means above all other states, international organisations, the military, legislative bodies, the judiciary, democratic opposition and civil society, including NGOS and the media.

While the abuse of prisoners at Abu Ghraib or elsewhere did not by any means represent the worst violations of humanitarian law – 2004 was, after all, the year in which the crisis in Darfur was starting to be referred to as genocide, including by the US House of Representatives – they were perhaps the most significant. The fact that such abuses were attributed to a state that formerly was one of the greatest champions of human rights means that the bar was lowered for everyone. The legitimacy of the US in speaking out on humanitarian law violations elsewhere – it was one of the only states to speak out on Darfur – was eroded. And the safety of US troops, in Iraq and elsewhere, was put in jeopardy.

2. SOURCES AND GENERAL PRINCIPLES

2.1 **Geneva Law**

The Additional Protocols gained an important new adherent in 2004 when Japan acceded to both Protocols I and II on 31 August. The Protocols will enter into force

---

51. See also D. Luban, 'Liberalism, torture and the ticking bomb', *Harpers Magazine*, March 2006, pp. 11 at 16. See also D. Luban, 'Liberalism, torture and the ticking bomb', *Virginia LR* (October 2005) p. 1425.

for Japan six months after the deposit of the instruments of accession, i.e., on 28 February 2005. Upon acceding, Japan lodged a declaration, stating: 'The Government of Japan declares that it is its understanding that the situation described in the second sentence of paragraph 3 of Article 44 can exist only in occupied territory or in armed conflicts covered by paragraph 4 of Article 1. The Government of Japan also declares that the term "deployment" in paragraph 3(b) of Article 44 is interpreted as meaning any movement towards a place from which an attack is to be launched.'[52]

3. CONFLICTS, ARMED FORCES AND COMBATANTS

3.1 Types of conflict

According to the Stockholm International Peace Research Institute: 'All the 19 conflicts recorded as "major armed conflicts" in 2004 – those causing over 1000 battle-related deaths in any one year – were classified as intra-state conflicts. ... However, in a globalised world, intra-state conflicts are increasingly becoming international in nature and in effect. The complexity and diversity of these conflicts challenge the distinction between the "internal" and the "external", in turn calling into question the basis on which conflicts are classified and addressed.'[53]

4. PROTECTED PERSONS

4.1 Civilians generally

While in the past number of years the protection of civilians in armed conflict has been a prominent item on the agenda of the United Nations organisation, the plethora of reports, resolutions and declarations that its various organs have issued on the subject stand more as a testament to the failure of the international community, including the UN, to protect civilians from harm during war than as a record of its success. Although attention to the devastation wrought by the parties to armed conflict on civilian populations is necessary and may over time prompt concrete action in addressing the problem, thus far high level admonitions have yet to have any discernable effect on reality on the ground.

In May the UN Secretary-General issued his fifth report in as many years on the subject of the protection of civilians in armed conflict.[54] The report noted that: 'Stark and disturbing evidence that civilians continue to bear the brunt of armed

---

52. See <www.icrc.org>.

53. R. Dwan and C. Holmqvist, 'Major armed conflicts', Chapter 2, *SIPRI Yearbook* (2005) *Armaments, Disarmaments and International Security* (Stockholm, Stockholm International Peace Research Institute 2005) <http://yearbook2005.sipri.org/ch2/ch2>.

54. Report of the Secretary-General to the Security Council on the protection of civilians in armed conflict, United Nations S/2004/431, 28 May 2004.

conflicts has emanated from four very different types of conflict that have received increased attention over the past 18 months': the conflict in the Darfur region of the Sudan; the conflict in Côte d'Ivoire; Iraq, and Nepal.[55] In countries emerging from conflict, including Afghanistan, the Democratic Republic of the Congo and Liberia, 'many protection challenges increase rather than diminish and the continued engagement of the international community is vital in order to ensure that civilians are not denied the dividends of peace. Compliance by all parties to conflict with international humanitarian, human rights, refugee and criminal law is critical in all of these situations, whether they are situations of armed conflict, occupation or transition.'[56]

The Secretary-General gave a disheartening portrayal of a climate of long term conflict where

> 'A prevailing culture of impunity has continued to spur cycles of violence and criminality. Indiscriminate terrorist attacks and counterterrorism measures that do not always comply with international human rights norms complicate the protection environment. Finally, humanitarian actors are operating in a less secure environment where they are deliberately attacked and are no longer protected by the emblems of the United Nations and the International Federation of Red Cross and Red Crescent Societies.'[57]

The report examined the issues identified in a ten-point platform[58] on the protection of civilians in armed conflict prepared by the -Secretary-General for Humanitarian Affairs and presented by him to the Security Council in December 2003,[59] and identified specific ways in which performance could be improved.[60]

Identifying ways forward in dealing with these challenges, the Secretary-General said that: 'An even clearer agenda is needed to ensure that the implementation of agreed priorities for civilian protection is sustained in an increasingly complex and unpredictable global political context.'[61]

The report noted the need to take the protection of civilians into account in peace processes.

---

55. Ibid., para. 3.
56. Ibid.
57. Ibid., para. 4.
58. The ten areas are (a) improving humanitarian access to civilians in need; (b) improving the safety and security of humanitarian personnel; (c) improving measures to respond to the security needs of refugees and internally displaced persons; (d) ensuring that the special protection and assistance requirements of children in armed conflict are fully addressed; (e) ensuring that the special protection and assistance requirements of women in armed conflict are fully addressed; (f) addressing shortcomings in our approach to disarmament, demobilization, reintegration and rehabilitation; (g) addressing the impact of small arms and light weapons on civilians; (h) combating impunity; (i) developing further measures to promote the responsibility of armed groups and non-State actors; and (j) ensuring the provision of the necessary resources to address the needs of vulnerable populations in 'forgotten emergencies'.
59. The platform addressed many of the issues set out in the aide memoire on the protection of civilians (S/PRST/2003/27, annex).
60. SG Report, supra n. 54, para. 7.
61. Ibid., para. 46.

> '[a]t a minimum ceasefire and peace agreements must include a commitment by parties to conflict to immediately cease all attacks on civilians, to facilitate humanitarian access, to create conditions conducive to the safe and sustainable return of refugee and internally displaced persons, to ensure the safety of humanitarian personnel and to disarm and demobilize combatants. Peace agreements must also provide for the development and strengthening of national human rights protection systems. While amnesties may constitute an important measure for dealing with lesser crimes, they must never be granted for serious violations of international humanitarian and human rights law.'[62]

The Secretary-General was particularly outspoken on the subject of violations against women and children and the needs of victims:

> 'Special attention also needs to be devoted to assisting the survivors of sexual violence, and their communities. Sexual violence is one of the most complex issues confronting the international community and the time has come to address it comprehensively. . . . Processes of justice and reconciliation are critical responses to these and other grave violations of international humanitarian and human rights law and, ultimately, to sustainable peace. The need for reconciliation in post-conflict situations must be tempered with a clear commitment to ending impunity for serious violations of international humanitarian and human rights law. It has been argued that focusing on punishment for past atrocities can destabilize post-conflict situations and undermine national reconciliation. Impunity, however, can be an even more dangerous recipe for sliding back into conflict. Thus, where sustainable peace is the goal, the question is not whether to focus on accountability and justice, but rather when and how.'[63]

In concluding, the Secretary-General urged

> 'the Security Council to engage fully with these issues in order to be prepared to address important new challenges to the environment for protecting civilians. Formal military capacities, supporting multilateral peacekeeping operations and coalitions of the willing, are stretched as never before. The nature of warfare continues to change, and there are now many more actors and parties involved in conflicts. These include armed groups and militias, mercenaries, private military contractors and borderless terrorist networks. This evolving environment and the diversity of new actors creates circumstances where certain groups may evade responsibility entirely. This requires better regulation and standards of accountability for armed forces, as well as for private sector groups actively engaged with or working in support of militaries.'[64]

62. Ibid., para. 52.
63. Ibid., para. 55.
64. Ibid., para. 59.

4.2 Women

On 13 October 2004 the Secretary-General issued a report on 'Women and peace and security',[65] which identified the progress that had been made in implementing UN Security Council resolution 1325 (2000) on women and peace and security.[66] The report noted that while 'Resolution 1325 (2000) has been effectively utilized by civil society organizations as an advocacy and monitoring tool, "[d]espite significant achievements, major gaps and challenges remain in all areas, including, in particular, in relation to women's participation in conflict prevention and peace processes"; the integration of gender perspectives in peace agreements; attention to the contributions and needs of women in humanitarian and reconstruction processes; and representation of women in decision-making positions.'[67]

It found that while in the four years since the adoption of the resolution there had been some 'positive shift in international understanding of the impact of armed conflict on women and girls and the importance of women's participation as equal partners in all areas related to peace and security', these efforts had little effect on the ground. 'In no area of peace and security work are gender perspectives systematically incorporated in planning, implementation, monitoring and reporting. … In the areas of conflict prevention, peace negotiations and post-conflict reconstruction, women do not participate fully and more needs to be done to ensure that the promotion of gender equality is an explicit goal in the pursuit of sustainable peace.'[68] 'The reality on the ground is that humanitarian and human rights law are blatantly disregarded by parties to conflicts and that women and girls continue to be subject to sexual and genderbased violence and other human rights violations. Much more sustained commitment and effort, including partnerships with men and boys, is required to stop the violence, end impunity and bring perpetrators to justice.'[69]

4.3 Children

The use and abuse of children during armed conflict continued to be a grim reality during 2004. UN Security Council resolution 1539 of 22 April 2004 observed the gulf between aspiration and reality in its preamble, where it took note of 'the advances made for the protection of children affected by armed conflict, particularly in the areas of advocacy and the development of norms and standards', yet the 'lack of overall progress on the ground, where parties to conflict continue to violate with impunity the relevant provisions of applicable international law relating

---

65. United Nations S/2004/814, 13 October 2004.

66. That resolution 'reaffirmed the need to fully implement international humanitarian and human rights law to protect women and girls from human rights abuses, including gender based violence. It identified the need to mainstream gender perspectives in relation to conflict prevention, peace negotiations, peacekeeping operations, humanitarian assistance, post-conflict reconstruction and disarmament, demobilization and reintegration initiatives.' Ibid., para. 2.

67. Ibid., para. 4.

68. Ibid., para. 118.

69. Ibid., para. 118-119.

to the rights and protection of children in armed conflict'. It recalled the 'responsibilities of States to end impunity and to prosecute those responsible for genocide, crimes against humanity, war crimes and other egregious crimes perpetrated against children', and noted that 'the conscription or enlistment of children under the age of 15 or using them to participate actively in hostilities in both international and non international armed conflict is classified as a war crime' by the Statute of the International Criminal Court (ICC).

The Council called on the Secretary General to devise, preferably within three months, 'an action plan for a systematic and comprehensive monitoring and reporting mechanism', which utilises expertise from within the UN and from national governments, regional organisations, NGOs and various civil society actors in order to provide timely, objective, accurate and reliable information on the recruitment and use of child soldiers in violation of applicable international law and on other violations and abuses committed against children affected by armed conflict, for consideration in taking appropriate action.

In addition, resolution 1539 addressed other issues concerning child soldiers and children and armed conflict, including the need to include children in all DDR [Disarmament, Demobilization and Reintegration] programs.

In a Statement of the Presidency made to the SC on 20 January 2004, the EU expressed its support for the Council's work on children and armed conflict and reiterated its condemnation of the recruitment and use of children to serve during armed conflicts.[70]

5. OCCUPATION

The occupation of Iraq officially came to an end on 30 June 2004, with the handover of full authority to the Interim Iraqi Government. The UN Security Council recognised the end of the occupation as being from this date.[71] Still, there was no drawdown of US or UK troops.

6. TRUTH COMMISSIONS

The final report of the Sierra Leone Truth and Reconciliation Commission was transmitted to the President of Sierra Leone on 5 October 2004 and presented to the UN Security Council on 27 October 2004.[72]

---

70. EU Presidency Statement, Children and Armed Conflict, Statement to the Security Council of the United Nations by H.E. Ambassador Richard Ryan, Permanent Representative of Ireland to the United Nations on behalf of the European Union. Children and Armed Conflict (New York), 20 January 2004, <http://europa-eu-un.org/articles/en/article_3165_en.htm>.

71. UN SC resolution 1546 of 8 June 2004.

72. See further the Sierra Leone Report in Correspondents' Reports in this volume at p. 586. The report was partly available online at the website of the US Institute for Peace, <http://www.usip.org/library/tc/tc_regions/tc_sl.html#rep>.

7. IMPLEMENTATION OF IHL

7.1 **Military manuals**

The UK made a significant contribution to the work of dissemination of IHL and its implementation at the national level with the publication of its long-awaited military manual on 1 July 2004. The 611-page manual sets out the UK's position on all of the important aspects of land and aerial warfare. The manual as a whole applies only in international armed conflict. However, one of the manual's 16 chapters, chapter 15, deals with the law applicable in internal armed conflict.

Soldiers in the field are not expected to carry a copy of this tome in a pocket of their fatigues or even be familiar with its contents. Instead, a more user-friendly version will be developed for this purpose.[73]

7.2 **The International Humanitarian Fact-Finding Commission**

Three states recognised the competence of the International Humanitarian Fact-Finding Committee (IHFFC) during 2004, established by Article 91 of Additional Protocol I. On 16 April the government of the Republic of Korea recognised the competence of the IHFFC when it deposited its declaration of recognition with the Swiss Federal Council, the depository of the Protocols. The following month, on 24 May, Burkina Faso recognised the competence of the IHFFC, becoming the 11th African state to do so.[74] Upon its accession to Additional Protocols I and II on 31 August, Japan deposited a declaration relating to its recognition of the competence of the IHFFC, becoming the 68th state to do so.

8. INTERNATIONAL ORGANISATIONS AND INTERNATIONAL ACTIONS

8.1 **United Nations Organisation**

8.1.1 *The Security Council*

8.1.1.1 Afghanistan

Resolution 1536 of 26 March 2004 extended the mandate of the United Nations Assistance Mission in Afghanistan (UNAMA) for 12 months. Welcoming the adoption of a Constitution by the Loja Jirga on 4 January 2004, it encouraged the Afghan authorities to move towards a democratic election process. It welcomed the progress made since the commencement of the Disarmament, Demobilization

---

73. The UK Manual, and the role of manuals in generally, is discussed in more detail elsewhere in this volume. See C. Garraway, 'The use and abuse of Military Manuals', This volume AND PAGE

74. The others are Algeria, Togo, Seychelles, Rwanda, Madagascar, Guinea, Namibia, Cape Verde, the Democratic Republic of the Congo and Mali.

and Reintegration (DDR) process in October 2003, and stressed that further progress was essential. In this regard, it called upon all Afghan parties to abide by commitments made in the Bonn Agreement.

Resolution 1563 of 17 September 2004, adopted under Chapter VII, extended the authorisation of the International Security Assistance Force (ISAF), as defined in SC resolutions 1386 (2001) and 1510 (2003), for a period of 12 months beyond 13 October 2004, and authorised the Member States participating in ISAF to take all necessary measures to fulfill its mandate. Recognising the need to strengthen ISAF, the Council called upon Member States to contribute personnel, equipment and other resources to the force, and to make contributions to the Trust Fund established pursuant to resolution 1386 (2001).

8.1.1.2 Bosnia

Security Council resolution 1551 of 9 July 2004 reaffirmed the Council's support for the Peace Agreement,[75] as well as for the Dayton Agreement on implementing the Federation of Bosnia and Herzegovina of 10 November 1995 and called on all parties to strictly comply with their obligations under those Agreements. It reminded the parties of their commitment to full cooperation with all entities, including the ICTY, and emphasised the Council's full support for the continued role of the High Representative. It welcomed NATO's decision to conclude its current SFOR operation in Bosnia and Herzegovina by the end of 2004 and welcomed the EU's intention to launch an EU mission to Bosnia and Herzegovina, including a military component, from December 2004.

Resolution 1575 of 22 November 2004, adopted under Chapter VII, reaffirmed the Council's support for the Peace Agreement, as well as for the Dayton Agreement and called on the parties to comply strictly with their obligations under those Agreements. It reiterated that the primary responsibility for the further successful implementation of the Peace Agreement lies with the authorities in Bosnia and Herzegovina themselves. It reminded the parties of their commitments under the agreements, including cooperation with the ICTY. It welcomed the EU's intention to launch an EU military operation to Bosnia and Herzegovina from December 2004, and authorised the Member States to establish for an initial planned period of 12 months a multinational stabilisation force (EUFOR) under unified command and control as a legal successor to SFOR.

8.1.1.3 Burundi

Since the signing of the Arusha Peace and Reconciliation Agreement for Burundi on 28 August 2000, Burundi has been inching its way towards an end to armed conflict but the absence of Agathon Rwasa's Palipehutu-FNL's from the process has impeded a final end to hostilities. In 2004, fighting, attended by IHL violations, continued in some parts of the country. Meanwhile, there was the beginning

75. The General Framework Agreement for Peace in Bosnia and Herzegovina, <http://www.ohr.int/dpa/default.asp?content_id=380>.

of talks between the President of the Republic of Burundi, Domitien Ndayizeyé, and Palipehutu-FNL at a meeting from 18 to 21 January 2004 at Oisterwijk in the Netherlands, and at a congress held in Kigoma, Tanzania, from 18 to 21 April 2004.

The Security Council's response to the ongoing armed conflict and desperate humanitarian and economic situation in Burundi was resolution 1545 of 21 May 2004, adopted under Chapter VII. Its main purpose was to authorise the deployment for an initial six month period from 1 June 2004 of a peacekeeping operation to Burundi, to be known as the United Nations Operation in Burundi (ONUB).

ONUB was given a broad mandate, set out in detail in this lengthy resolution, and authorised to use all necessary means to carry it out. It was to be headed by the Special Representative of the Secretary-General, who chairs the Implementation Monitoring Committee for the Arusha Agreement. ONUB shall consist of a maximum of 5,650 military personnel, including 200 observers and 125 staff officers, up to 120 civilian police personnel, as well as the appropriate civilian personnel. Personnel would initially be drawn from existing troops deployed as part of African Union's African Mission in Burundi (AMIB). The Council requested the Secretary-General, acting in liaison with the African Union, to ensure the transfer of authority over AMIB to his Special Representative for Burundi.

Resolution 1545 condemned human rights and international humanitarian law violations, and noted the Council's particular concern about the increasing incidents of rapes, including mass rapes. It reaffirmed its determination to support the efforts of Burundians to bring the perpetrators of such acts and violations to justice on the basis of the rule of law and called upon the parties and transitional authorities to take all necessary measures to that end. It also noted the continued need to promote peace and national reconciliation and to foster accountability and respect for human rights in Burundi, and urged the government of Burundi, specialised agencies, other multilateral organisations, civil society and UN Member States to accelerate their efforts to establish the Truth and Reconciliation Commission for in the Arusha Agreement. With the transitional period due to end on 31 October 2004, the Council urged the transitional institutions of Burundi to enact without delay the laws and regulations required for the organisation of the electoral process under the Arusha Agreement, so that this process could take place before the expiration of the transitional period.

By Resolution 1577 of 1 December 2004, adopted under Chapter VII, the Council extended ONUB's mandate until 1 June 2005. It urged all the governments and parties concerned in the region to denounce the use of and incitement to violence, to condemn unequivocally violations of human rights and of international humanitarian law, and to actively cooperate with ONUB and MONUC and with efforts of states aimed at ending impunity.

8.1.1.4 Côte d'Ivoire

Resolution 1527 of 4 February 2004, adopted under Chapter VII, renewed the mandate of the United Nations Mission in Côte d'Ivoire (MINUCI) until 27 February 2004, and the authorisation given to Member States participating in ECOWAS forces together with French Forces until 27 February 2004.

The Council's very next resolution, 1528 of 27 February 2004, returned to the situation in Côte d'Ivoire. Adopted under Chapter VII, given the persistent challenges to the stability of Côte d'Ivoire and the fact that the situation in Côte d'Ivoire continued to pose a threat to international peace and security in the region, it established the United Nations Operation in Côte d'Ivoire (UNOCI) for an initial period of 12 months as from 4 April 2004, as requested by ECOWAS. It requested the Secretary-General to transfer authority from MINUCI and the ECOWAS forces to UNOCI on that date, and to that end, renewed MINUCI's mandate for a final period, until 4 April 2004.

UNOCI has, in addition to the appropriate civilian, judiciary and corrections component, a military strength of a maximum of 6,240 United Nations personnel, including 200 military observers and 120 staff officers, and up to 350 civilian police officers. UNOCI's mandate was set out in paragraph 6 and consists of: monitoring of the ceasefire and movements of armed groups; disarmament, demobilisation, reintegration, repatriation and resettlement; protection of United Nations personnel, institutions and civilians; support for humanitarian assistance; support for the implementation of the peace process; assistance in the field of human rights; the provision of public information; and promoting and assisting in the maintenance of law and order.

The Council called on all parties to cooperate fully in the deployment and operations of UNOCI, in particular by guaranteeing the safety, security and freedom of movement of United Nations personnel as well as associated personnel throughout the territory of Côte d'Ivoire.

By the end of 2004, the hostilities in Côte d'Ivoire had again flared up. By resolution 1572 of 15 November 2004, adopted under Chapter VII, the Council condemned as ceasefire violations the 6 November air strikes committed by the national armed forces of Côte d'Ivoire (FANCI) that left nine French peacekeepers and dozens of civilians dead. French reprisals destroyed the Ivorian airforce. It demanded that the government of Côte d'Ivoire as well as Forces Nouvelles fully comply with the ceasefire. The Council urged the Ivorian president and political leaders to begin resolutely implementing all the commitments they made under the Linas-Marcoussis and Accra III Agreements. It demanded that the Ivorian authorities stop all radio and television broadcasting inciting hatred, intolerance and violence, and requested UNOCI to strengthen its monitoring role in this regard. It decided that, for a 13 month period, all states should take the necessary measures to prevent the direct or indirect supply, sale or transfer to Côte d'Ivoire of arms or any related materiel, in particular military aircraft and equipment, whether or not originating in their territories, as well as the provision of any assistance, advice or training related to military activities. The Council decided to establish a Committee of the Security Council, consisting of all the members of the Council, whose tasks included the designation of individuals and entities subject to movement restrictions. All states should take the necessary measures, for a 12-month period, to prevent the entry into or transit through their territories of all persons designated by the Committee as constituting a threat to the peace and national reconciliation process in Côte d'Ivoire, any other person determined as responsible for serious violations of human rights and international humanitarian law in Côte d'Ivoire and any other person who incites publicly hatred and violence. States should, for the same period, freeze the funds, other financial assets and economic resources on their territories that are owned or controlled directly or indirectly by designated persons or entities. States should also ensure that any funds, financial assets or economic resources are prevented from being made available by their nationals or by any persons within their territories, to or for the benefit of such persons or entities.

8.1.1.5 Cyprus

By resolution 1548 of 11 June 2004 the Council reaffirmed all its relevant resolutions on Cyprus, in particular resolution 1251 of 29 June 1999, and decided to extend the mandate of the United Nations peacekeeping force in Cyprus (UNFICYP) for a further period ending 15 December 2004.

By resolution 1568 of 24 September 2004, the Council extended UNFICYP's mandate for a further period ending 15 June 2005. It endorsed the SG's recommendations for the amendment of the concept of operations and force level of UNFICYP, as outlined in his report of 24 September 2004.[76]

8.1.1.6 The Democratic Republic of the Congo

Security Council resolution 1522 of 15 January 2004 welcomed the efforts being made to establish the first integrated and unified brigade in Kisangani as a step towards the elaboration and implementation of a comprehensive program for the formation of a Congolese integrated national army. The Council urged the government of National Unity and Transition to take the appropriate measures for the restructuring and integration of the armed forces of the Democratic Republic of the Congo, including setting up a Supreme Defence Council and the elaboration of a national plan for DDR as well as the necessary legislative framework. Finally, it called on the international community to provide further assistance for the integration and restructuring of the armed forces of the Democratic Republic of the Congo, in accordance with Security Council resolution 1493 (2003).

In resolution 1533 of 12 March 2004 the Council returned to the subject of the exploitation of DRC's natural resources, which it had addressed in a number of previous resolutions (see resolution 1457 of 24 January 2003, 1493 of 28 July 2003 and 1499 of 13 August 2003[77]). Acting under Chapter VII, considering that the situation in DRC continued to constitute a threat to international peace and security in the region, the Security Council reaffirmed the demand, laid down in paragraph 20 of resolution 1493, that all states take the necessary measures to prevent the supply of arms and any related materiel or assistance to armed groups

---

76. Report of the UN Secretary-General on the United Nations Operation in Cyprus, S/2004/756, 24 September 2004.

77. See A. McDonald, 'The Year in Review', 6 *YIHL* (2003) pp. 270-273.

operating in North and South Kivu and in Ituri, and to groups not party to the Global and All-Inclusive agreement on the Transition in the Democratic Republic of the Congo (signed in Pretoria on 17 December 2002). It requested MONOC to continue to use all means within its capabilities to carry out the tasks outlined in paragraph 19 of resolution 1493, including spot inspections of aircraft cargo and any transport vehicle using the ports, airports, airfields, military bases and border crossings in North and South Kivu and in Ituri. It authorised MONUC to seize or collect, as appropriate, the arms and any related materiel whose presence in the territory of the DRC violated resolution 1493, and to dispose of such arms and related materiel as appropriate. It also reiterated the Council's condemnation of the continued exploitation of the natural resources in the Democratic Republic of the Congo, especially in the eastern part of the country, and reaffirmed the importance of bringing an end to these illegal activities, including by applying the necessary pressure on the armed groups, traffickers and all other actors involved.

Resolution 1552, adopted on 27 July 2004, was a response to the failure of the parties to comply with resolution 1493. It reaffirmed and renewed its demands and renewed the demands of that resolution and of resolution 1533. It decided that it would review those measures by 1 October 2004, and periodically thereafter. To this end, it requested the Secretary-General, in consultation with the Committee, to reestablish the Group of experts referred to in paragraph 10 of resolution 1533, within 30 days from the date of adoption of the resolution and for a period expiring on 31 January 2005. It requested the Group of Experts to report to the Council in writing before 15 December 2004, through the Committee, on the implementation of the measures imposed by paragraph 20 of resolution 1493, with recommendations in this regard, in particular regarding the lists provided for in resolution 1533.

By resolution 1555 of 29 July the Council extended MONUC's mandate until 1 October 2004 and requested the Secretary-General to submit a report to the Council, before 16 August, on the execution by MONUC of its mandate. It expressed its deep concern at the ongoing tensions and the continuation of hostilities in the Eastern part of the Democratic Republic of the Congo, particularly in the provinces of North and South Kivu, as well as in the Ituri district reiterated its full support to the government of National Unity and Transition of the Democratic Republic of the Congo and reaffirmed its readiness to support the peace and national reconciliation process, in particular through MONUC. It welcomed MONUC's readiness to take an active part in the joint verification mechanism whose creation was announced by the Presidents of the Democratic Republic of the Congo and of Rwanda in Abuja on 25 June 2004.

By resolution 1565 of 1 October 2004 the Council, deeply concerned at the continuation of hostilities in the eastern part of the country, particularly in the provinces of North and South Kivu and in the Ituri district, and by the grave violations of human rights and of humanitarian law that accompany them, extended the deployment of MONUC until 31 March 2005. Adopted under Chapter VII, the resolution requested the SG to arrange the rapid deployment of additional military capabilities for MONUC in accordance with the recommendation contained in his letter dated 3 September 2004, and to deploy as soon as possible in the provinces of North and South Kivu all the brigades and appropriate force enablers. It authorised an increase in MONUC's strength by 5,900 personnel, including up to 341 civilian police personnel, as well as the deployment of appropriate civilian personnel, appropriate and proportionate air mobility assets and other force enablers, and expressed its determination to keep MONUC's strength and structure under regular review, taking into account the evolution of the situation on the ground. The resolution also spelled out MONUCs mandate. It includes: deploying and maintaining a presence in key areas of potential volatility; ensuring the protection of civilians, including humanitarian personnel, under imminent threat of physical violence; ensuring the protection of United Nations personnel, facilities, installations and equipment; ensuring the security and freedom of movement of its personnel; establishing operational links with the United Nations Operation in Burundi (ONUB), and with the governments of the DRC and Burundi, in order to coordinate efforts towards monitoring and discouraging cross-border movements of combatants and arms between the two countries; and assisting with disarmament, demobilisation and reintegration of fighters.

The resolution also strongly condemned violence and other violations of international humanitarian law and human rights, in particular those perpetrated against civilians, and demanded that all parties and governments concerned in the region take without delay all necessary steps to bring to justice those responsible and to ensure respect for human rights and international humanitarian law. It also reaffirmed that all parties were obliged to comply fully IHL rules and principles concerning the protection of humanitarian and United Nations personnel, and urged all those concerned to allow immediate, full and unimpeded access by humanitarian personnel to all people in need of assistance. Recalling the link between the illegal exploitation of natural resources and armed conflict, the Council condemned categorically such exploitation and urged all states to take appropriate steps in order to end these illegal activities, including if necessary through judicial means. The Council also expressed grave concern at the allegations of sexual exploitation and misconduct by civilian and military personnel of MONUC and requested the SG to fully investigate them.

8.1.1.7 Eritrea/Ethiopia

By resolution 1531 of 12 March 2004 the Council extended the mandate of the United Nations Mission in Ethiopia and Eritrea (UNMEE) until 15 September 2004. It noted the Council's concern regarding the continuing impasse in the peace process, mainly due to the lack of progress in the demarcation of the border stemming from Ethiopia's rejection of significant parts of the Boundary Commission's decision, and its lack of cooperation with the Boundary Commission. It also rebuked Eritrea's refusal to engage with the Secretary-General's Special Envoy for Ethiopia and Eritrea, and emphasised that cooperation with the Special Envoy offered both parties a concrete opportunity to move the peace process forward. It called on the parties to cooperate fully and promptly with the Boundary Commission, and to create the necessary conditions for demarcation to proceed expeditiously, including through the unequivocal restating of Ethiopia's acceptance of the Boundary Commission's decision, the appointment by Ethiopia of field liaison officers, and the payment of its dues to the Boundary Commission.

Resolution 1560 of 14 September 2004 extended UNMEE's mandate until 15 March 2005 and approved adjustments to the mission, including its presence and operations, as recommended by the Secretary-General in his report in paragraph 13-18.[78] It called on both parties to cooperate fully and expeditiously with UNMEE, to ensure the security of its staff, and to remove all restrictions on and impediments to the mission's work and full and free movement. It expressed the Council's concern regarding the continuing lack of progress made in the border demarcation process and Ethiopia's ongoing rejection of significant parts of the Boundary Commission's decision, and its lack of cooperation with the Commission. It also expressed once again the Council's disappointment about Eritrea's continuing refusal to engage with the Secretary-General's Special Envoy. It called on both parties to cooperate fully and promptly with the Boundary Commission and to create the necessary conditions for demarcation to proceed expeditiously, including through the payment of Ethiopia's dues to the Boundary Commission and the appointment of field liaison officers.

8.1.1.8 Georgia

The Council once again vented its frustation over the lack of progress concerning the long-running conflict over Abkhazia in Resolution 1524 of 30 January 2004. With the Georgian and Abkhaz sides showing no sides of reaching a resolution of the territorial dispute (the Abkhazians are seeking their own state, with Sukhumi as the capital, while Georgia, backed by the SC and the international community are committed to keeping Abkhazia within its borders, albeit with some form of autonomy), the Council stressed its strong support for the document on 'Basic Principles for the Distribution of Competences between Tbilisi and Sukhumi' and its regret that the Abkhazians had refused to engage in a discussion on the substance of the document and its transmittal letter. It also expressed its regret concerning the lack of progress on the initiation of political status negotiations, and recalled, once again, that the purpose of these documents is to facilitate meaningful negotiations between the parties, under UN leadership, on the status of Abkhazia within the state of Georgia, and is not an attempt to impose or dictate any specific solution to the parties. *Inter alia*, it called again on the parties to ensure the necessary revitalisation of the peace process in all its major aspects, and reminded all concerned to refrain from any action that might impede it. It expressed the need for progress on the question of refugees and internally displaced persons (IDPs) and the unacceptability of the demographic changes resulting from the conflict and reaffirmed the inalienable right of all refugees and IDPs affected by the conflict to return to their homes in secure and dignified conditions, in accordance with international law. Resolution 1524 also extended the mandate of UNOMIG for a new period termi-

---

78. Progress Report of the Secretary-General on Ethiopia and Eritrea, S/2004/708, 2 September 2004.

nating on 31 July 2004, subject to a review as appropriate of its mandate by the Council in the event of changes in the mandate of the CIS peacekeeping force.

Resolution 1554 of 29 July 2004, reiterating most of the above still uncomplied with demands, extended UNOMIG's mandate for a new period terminating on 31 January 2005, subject to a review as appropriate of its mandate by the Council in the event of changes in the mandate of the CIS peacekeeping force.

8.1.1.9 Guinea Bissau

Following the mutiny of 6 October 2004 – which resulted in the assassinations of the Chief of General Staff, General Veríssimo Correia Seabra, and the armed forces spokesman, Colonel Domingos de Barros, the SC adopted resolution 1580 on 22 December 2004. The resolution extended the mandate of the United Nations Peace-Building Support Office (UNOGBIS) for one year from the date of adoption of the resolution and revised its mandate. The Council encouraged the authorities of Guinea-Bissau to enhance political dialogue and pursue constructive civil/military relations. It called upon the National Assembly of Guinea-Bissau, while addressing the issue of granting an amnesty for all those involved in military interventions since 1980, to take account of the principles of justice and fight against impunity. It strongly urged the government, together with military authorities and other concerned parties, to agree, as soon as possible, on a national plan for the reform of the security sector, in particular the military reform.

8.1.1.10 Haiti

Civil unrest broke out in Haiti in February 2004 as militias opposed to President Aristide attempted to forcibly overthrow his government.[79] On 29 February, matters came to a head when President Aristide left the country, first for the Central African Republic and then for Jamaica. According to himself he was forced to leave by US troops.[80] Resolution 1529 of 29 February 2004, adopted under Chapter VII, authorised the immediate deployment of a Multinational Interim Force (MIF) to Haiti for a period of not more than three months from adoption of the resolution with the following mandate: to contribute to a secure and stable environment in the Haitian capital and elsewhere in the country; to facilitate the provision of humanitarian assistance and the access of international humanitarian workers; and to facilitate the provision of international assistance to the Haitian police and the Haitian Coast Guard, *inter alia*.

Resolution 1529 also declared the Council's readiness to establish a follow-on United Nations stabilization force and requested the Secretary-General, in consultation with the Organization of American States, to submit to the Council recommendations for the size, structure and mandate of such a force, with a view to its

---

79. For background see International Politics and Haiti in 2004, Sourcewatch, <http://www.sourcewatch.org/index.php?title=International_Politics_and_Haiti_in_2004>.

80. 'Aristide says U.S. deposed him in 'coup d'etat'', CNN.com, 1 March 2004, <http://www.cnn.com/2004/WORLD/americas/03/01/aristide.claim/>.

deployment of the United Nations force not later than three months from adoption of the resolution.

By Resolution 1542 of 30 April 2004 the Council decided to establish the United Nations Stabilization Mission in Haiti (MINUSTAH) called for in resolution 1529 (2004) for an initial period of six months, with the intention to renew its mandate for further periods, and it requested that authority be transferred from the MIF to MINUSTAH on 1 June 2004. It authorised remaining elements of the MIF to continue carrying out its mandate under UNSCR 1529 (2004) for a transition period not exceeding 30 days from 1 June 2004. It requested the Secretary-General to appoint a Special Representative in Haiti who will have overall authority on the ground for the coordination and conduct of all the activities of the United Nations agencies, funds and programs in Haiti.

The Council decided that MINUSTAH would consist of a civilian and a military component, the former to include a maximum of 1,622 Civilian Police, including advisers and formed units and the latter to include and a military component to include up to 6,700 troops of all ranks. The military component should report directly to the Special Representative through the force commander.

MINUSTAH was given a robust Chapter VII mandate: (a) to ensure a secure and stable environment within which the constitutional and political process in Haiti could take place; (b) to assist the Transitional Government in monitoring, restructuring and reforming the Haitian National Police; (c) to assist the Transitional Government, particularly the Haitian National Police, with comprehensive and sustainable Disarmament, Demobilization and Reintegration (DDR) programs; (d) to assist with the restoration and maintenance of the rule of law, public safety and public order in Haiti through the provision, *inter alia*, of operational support to the Haitian National Police and the Haitian Coast Guard; (e) to protect United Nations personnel, facilities, installations and equipment and to ensure the security and freedom of movement of its personnel; and (f) to protect civilians under imminent threat of physical violence, within its capabilities and areas of deployment.

MINUSTAH was also mandated, though not under Chapter VII, to engage in other tasks, including supporting the constitutional and political process and assisting the Transitional Government in reconciliation efforts, in carrying out free and fair elections, and in promoting and protecting human rights. MINUSTAH in collaboration with other partners should also provide advice and assistance to the Transitional Government in the investigation of violations of human rights violations and international humanitarian law.

Resolution 1576 of 29 November 2004 extended MINUSTAH's mandate, until 1 June 2005, with the intention to renew for further periods.

8.1.1.11 Iraq

Resolution 1538 of 21 April 2004 established an independent high-level inquiry to investigate the administration and management of the UN Oil for Food Programme, which had for years been dogged by allegations of mismanagement and corruption. It called upon the Coalition Provisional Authority, which was administrating occupied Iraq, and all other UN Member States, including their national regulatory authorities, to cooperate fully by all appropriate means with the inquiry.

Security Council resolution 1546 of 8 June, adopted under Chapter VII, endorsed the formation of a sovereign Interim Government of Iraq on 1 June 2004, which by 30 June 2004 would assume full responsibility and authority for governing Iraq. It stated that on 30 June 2004 the occupation would end and the Coalition Provisional Authority would cease to exist, and that Iraq would regain its full sovereignty. It endorsed the proposed timetable for Iraq's political transition to democratic government, including the holding of direct democratic elections to a Transitional National Assembly by 31 December 2004 if possible, and in no case later than 31 January 2005. The Transitional National Assembly would, *inter alia*, have responsibility for forming a Transitional Government of Iraq and drafting a permanent constitution for Iraq leading to a constitutionally elected government by 31 December 2005. The Special Representative of the Secretary General in Iraq should play a leading role in the transitional process, as requested by the government of Iraq.

Resolution 1546 noted that the presence of the multinational force in Iraq was at the request of the incoming Interim Government of Iraq and therefore reaffirmed the authorisation for the multinational force under unified command established under resolution 1511 (2003). It decided that the multinational force shall have the authority to take all necessary measures to contribute to the maintenance of security and stability in Iraq, including by preventing and deterring terrorism. It requested Member States and international and regional organisations to contribute assistance to the multinational force, including military forces, as agreed with the government of Iraq, and to support the efforts of UNAMI.

The mandate for the multinational force would be reviewed at the request of the government of Iraq or twelve months from the date of the resolution, and would expire upon the completion of the political process or earlier if requested by the government of Iraq.

The resolution also condemned all acts of terrorism in Iraq and reaffirmed the obligations of Member States with respect, *inter alia*, to terrorist activities in and from Iraq or against its citizens, and specifically reiterated its call upon Member States to prevent the transit of terrorists to and from Iraq, arms for terrorists, and financing that would support terrorists, and reemphasised the importance of strengthening the cooperation of the countries of the region, particularly neighbours of Iraq, in this regard. It also addressed numerous other aspects of the transitional process, including financial assistance to Iraq, arms control, the reintegration of Iraqi veterans, and the Development Fund for Iraq.

Resolution 1557 of 12 August 2004 extended UNAMI's mandate for a period of 12 months from the date of the resolution.

8.1.1.12 Israel/Occupied Palestinian Territories

Resolution 1544 of 19 May 2004 was a rare expression of Security Council censure of Israel concerning the conditions in the Occupied Palestinian Territories. Adopted as a response to Israel's demolition of homes in the Rafah refugee camp during a week-long operation in the Gaza Strip in May, it called on Israel to respect its obligations under international humanitarian law, and insisted, in particular, on its obligation not to undertake demolition of homes contrary to that law. The resolution also expressed the Council's grave concern regarding the humanitarian situation of Palestinians made homeless in the Rafah area and called for the provision of emergency assistance to them. It called for the cessation of violence and for both parties to immediately implement their obligations under the Road Map. The resolution also condemned the killing of Palestinian civilians that took place in the Rafah area, and all acts of terror.

8.1.1.13 Lebanon

By resolution 1525 of 30 January 2004 the Council extended the mandate of the United Nations Interim Force in Lebanon (UNIFIL) until 31 July 2004. It urged the government of Lebanon to extend its efforts to ensure the return of its effective authority throughout the south, including through the deployment of Lebanese armed forces, and to do its utmost to ensure a calm environment, including along the Blue Line. It reiterated its call on the parties to fulfill their commitments to exercise utmost restraint and to cooperate fully with the United Nations and UNIFIL and expressed great concern about the serious continuing violations of the withdrawal line. It urged the parties to put an end to these violations, to refrain from any act or provocation that could further escalate the tension and to abide by their obligation to respect the safety of UNIFIL and other United Nations personnel.

Security Council resolution 1553 of 29 July 2004, endorsing the report of the Secretary-General on UNIFIL of 21 July 2004 (S/2004/572) and in particular its recommendation to renew the mandate of UNIFIL for a further period of six months, decided to extend the force's mandate until 31 January 2005.

Resolution 1559 of 2 September expressed the Council's concern regarding at the continued presence of armed militias in Lebanon, which prevented the Lebanese government from exercising its full sovereignty over all Lebanese territory, and called on all remaining foreign forces to withdraw from Lebanon and for the disbanding and disarmament of all Lebanese and non-Lebanese militias. It expressed the Council's support for the extension of the control of the government of Lebanon over the whole of the national territory.

8.1.1.14 Liberia

Resolution 1532 of 12 March 2004 was a response by the Security Council to the misappropriation of Liberian resources by former President Charles Taylor and their removal from the jurisdiction. Acting under Chapter VII, noting that the situation constituted a threat to international peace and security in West Africa, the Council ordered all states in which there were funds, other financial assets or economic resources owned or controlled by Taylor or his family to freeze them. The Committee established by paragraph 21 of resolution 1521 (22 December 2003) (the Committee) should identify individuals and entities associated with Taylor and promptly circulate to all states a list of the said individuals and entities, including by posting such a list on the Committee's website. The Committee should also assist states, where necessary, in tracing and freezing the funds, other financial assets and economic resources of such individuals and entities, and would also seek from states information regarding the actions taken by them in this regard.

By resolution 1549 of 17 June 2004 the Council decided to reestablish the Panel of Experts established by SC resolution 1408 of 6 May 2003[81] for a further period to commence no later than 30 June until 21 December 2004. It requested the Panel to provide a mid-term report to the Council for its review, through the Committee, no later than 30 September 2004 and to present a final report no later than 10 December 2004. The Panel should consist of no more than five experts appointed by the SG. The Council encouraged the National Transitional Government of Liberia (NTGL) to take urgent steps to establish an effective Certificate of Origin regime for trade in Liberian rough diamonds that is transparent and internationally verifiable, and urged the NTGL to establish its full authority and control over the timber producing areas.

Resolution 1561 of 17 September 2004 extended UNMIL's mandate until 19 September 2005. It called on all the parties to demonstrate their full commitment to the peace process and to work together to ensure that free, fair and transparent elections took place no later than October 2005. It also called upon the international community to respond to the continuing need for funds for the critically important rehabilitation and reintegration phase and to fulfill pledges made at the International Reconstruction Conference on Liberia held on 5 and 6 February 2004.

By resolution 1579 of 21 December 2004 the SC, acting under Chapter VII of the Charter, renewed the measures on arms and travel imposed by resolution 1521 (2003) for a further period of 12 months, renewed the measures on timber for a further period of 12 months and renewed the measures on diamonds for a further period of six months It reestablished the Panel of Experts for a further period until 21 June 2005.

8.1.1.15 Sierra Leone

Resolution 1537, adopted on 30 March 2004, extended the mandate of the United Nations Mission in Sierra Leone (UNAMSIL) for six more months until 30 September. It urged the government of Sierra Leone to intensify its efforts to develop an effective and sustainable police force, army, penal system and independent judiciary, to enable the government to rapidly take over from UNAMSIL full responsibility for maintaining law and order throughout Sierra Leone, and encouraged donors and UNAMSIL, in accordance with its mandate, to continue to assist the Government in this regard.

---

81. See 6 *YIHL* (2003) p. 300.

The resolution also stated that a residual UNAMSIL presence would remain in Sierra Leone, for an initial period of six months from 1 January 2005, reduced from the December 2004 level of 5,000 troops by 28 February 2005 to a new ceiling of 3,250 troops, 141 military observers and 80 United Nations civilian police personnel, and affirmed the Council's intention to confirm the precise tasks of the residual UNAMSIL presence, and the benchmarks for its duration, no later than 30 September 2004. It also urged the government of Sierra Leone to continue to strengthen its control over and regulation of diamond mining, including through the High Level Steering Committee.

Resolution 1537 also addressed several other areas, including the work of the Special Court for Sierra Leone, for which it expressed its appreciation. Noting the Court's precarious financial position, it urged all countries to make good on their financial commitments to it immediately.

Resolution 1562 adopted on 17 September 2004 extended UNAMSIL's mandate until 30 June 2005. It further enunciated the tasks of the residual UNAMSIL presence that would remain in Sierra Leone for an initial period of six months from 1 January 2005. It authorised the residual UNAMSIL presence to use all necessary means to carry out its mandate, within its capabilities and its areas of deployment. The Council also expressed its intention to regularly review the residual UNAMSIL presence.

8.1.1.16 Spain

On 11 March 2004, the same day as a series of bombs on the Madrid railway system killed 201 people, the Security Council issued resolution 1530, condemning the attacks in the strongest possible terms. The Council attributed the attacks to the Basque separatist organisation ETA, although it later transpired that the attacks were the work of Al Qaida.

The resolution urged all states, in accordance with their obligations under resolution 1373 (30 January 2001), to cooperate actively in efforts to find and bring to justice the perpetrators, organisers and sponsors of this terrorist attack, and expressed the Council's reinforced determination to combat all forms of terrorism.

8.1.1.17 Somalia

Resolution 1558 of 17 August 2004 addressed ongoing breaches of earlier SC resolutions, in particular resolution 733 of 23 January 1992, which established an embargo on all delivery of weapons and military equipment to Somalia, and resolution 1519 of 16 December 2003.

The Council condemned the continued flow of weapons and ammunition supplies to and through Somalia, in contravention of the arms embargo, and expressed its determination that violators should be held accountable. Acting under Chapter VII of the Charter, it stressed the obligation of all states to comply fully with the measures imposed by resolution 733. It took note of the report of the Monitoring Group dated 11 August 2004 (S/2004/604), and the observations and recommendations contained therein, and expressed its intention to give them due consideration in order to improve compliance with the measures imposed by resolution 733. It requested the SG, in consultation with the Committee established pursuant to resolution 751 of 24 April 1992, to reestablish, within 30 days from the date of the adoption of this resolution, and for a period of six months, the Monitoring Group referred to in paragraph 2 of resolution 1519. It stated that it expected the Committee, in accordance with its mandate, to recommend to the Council appropriate measures in response to violations of the arms embargo, by considering and developing, in close consultation with the Monitoring Group, specific proposals to improve compliance with the arms embargo.

8.1.1.18 Sudan

The year brought hope and despair to Sudan in equal measure, as one conflict on its territory appeared to have reached resolution while another one intensified, with catastrophic consequences for the civilian population. A ceasefire agreement signed by the parties to the conflict in Darfur – the government of Sudan, the Sudan Liberation Movement/Army and the Sudan Justice and Equality Movement – on 8 April in N'damena, Chad, failed to halt the fighting there or abuses of civilians.[82] On 25 May the Security Council addressed the situation in Darfur for the first time when its President issued a Statement which, *inter alia*, expressed the Council's deep concern at the continuing reports of large-scale violations of human rights and of international humanitarian law, including indiscriminate attacks on civilians, sexual violence, forced displacement and acts of violence, especially those with an ethnic dimension, and demanded that those responsible be held accountable.[83]

As the crisis continued in Darfur, the long-running conflict in southern Sudan appeared to be coming to an end. Following the signing on 5 June 2004 by the government of the Republic of the Sudan and the Sudan People's Liberation Movement/Sudan People's Liberation Army (SPLM/A) of the Nairobi Declaration on the Final Phase of Peace in the Sudan – in which the parties confirmed their agreement to the six protocols signed between the government and the SPLM/A, and reconfirmed their commitment to completing the remaining stages of negotiations – the Security Council adopted resolution 1547 on11 June 2004. Although mainly addressed to the peace process in southern Sudan it also made reference to the crisis in Darfur. As far as the former is concerned, it welcomed the signature of the Nairobi Declaration and reaffirmed the Council's support for the Machakos Protocol of 20 July 2002 and subsequent agreements based on this Protocol and its commitment to the sovereignty, independence and unity of Sudan. It condemned all acts of violence and violations of human rights and international humanitarian law by all parties and expressed its utmost concern at the consequences of the prolonged conflict for the civilian population of Sudan, including women,

82. Humanitarian Cease Fire Agreement on the Conflict in Darfur, N'djamena, 8 April 2004, <http://www.usip.org/library/pa/sudan/sudan_ceasefire_04082004.html>. See further the Sudan Report in Correspondents' Reports, this volume at p. 597.

83. S/PRST/2004/16, 25 May 2004.

children, refugees and internally displaced persons. It urged the two parties involved to conclude speedily a Comprehensive Peace Agreement and expressed its belief that the progress being made in the Naivasha Process, which began with the signing of the Machakos Protocol, would contribute to improved stability and peace in Sudan.

The resolution also welcomed the Secretary-General's report of 7 June 2004 (S/2004/453) in which he proposed to establish, for an initial period of three months under the authority of an SRSG, a United Nations advance team in Sudan as a special political mission dedicated to preparing for the international monitoring foreseen in the 25 September 2003 Naivasha Agreement on Security Arrangements. The task of the mission would be to facilitate contacts with the parties concerned and to prepare for the introduction of a peace support operation following the signing of a Comprehensive Peace Agreement. The Council declared its readiness to consider establishing a United Nations peace support operation to support the implementation of a Comprehensive Peace Agreement, and requested the Secretary-General to submit to the Council recommendations for the size, structure, and mandate of this operation, as soon as possible after the signing of a Comprehensive Peace Agreement. It requested the SG, in the interim, to take the necessary preparatory steps.

The Council also endorsed the SG's conclusions with regard to the situation in Sudan, in particular Darfur and the Upper Nile set out in paragraph 22 of his report, and called upon the parties to use their influence to bring an immediate halt to the fighting in the Darfur region, in the Upper Nile and elsewhere. It urged the parties to the Ndjamena Ceasefire Agreement of 8 April 2004 to conclude a political agreement without delay, welcomed the African Union efforts to that end, and called on the international community to be prepared for constant engagement, including extensive funding, in support of peace in Sudan.

Resolution 1556 of 30 July represented the Council's first serious engagement with the humanitarian crisis in Darfur, following the Statement by its President of 25 May and its brief allusion to the crisis in resolution 1547 of 11 June 2004 and resolution 1502 of 26 August 2003 on the access of humanitarian workers to populations in need. Adopted under Chapter VII, resolution 1556 called on the government of Sudan to immediately fulfill all of the commitments it made in its 3 July 2004 Communiqué, particularly by facilitating international relief for the humanitarian disaster by means of a moratorium on all restrictions that might hinder the provision of humanitarian assistance and access to the affected populations; by advancing independent investigation in cooperation with the UN of violations of human rights and international humanitarian law; by the establishment of credible security conditions for the protection of the civilian population and humanitarian actors; and by the resumption of political talks with dissident groups from the Darfur region, specifically the JEM and the SLM/A on Darfur.

The Council endorsed the deployment of international monitors, including the protection force envisioned by the African Union, to Darfur under AU leadership and urged the international community to continue to support and reinforce these efforts and the government of Sudan to facilitate them. It welcomed the work done by the High Commissioner for Human Rights to send human rights observers to

Sudan and called the government of Sudan to cooperate with the High Commissioner in the deployment of those observers. The Council urged the parties to the N'Djamena Ceasefire Agreement of 8 April 2004 to conclude a political agreement without delay, noted with regret the failure of senior rebel leaders to participate in the 15 July talks in Addis Ababa, Ethiopia and called for renewed talks under the sponsorship of the African Union. The Council also urged the rebels to observe the ceasefire and also demanded that the government of Sudan fulfill its commitments to disarm the Janjaweed militias and apprehend and bring to justice Janjaweed leaders and their associates who have incited and carried out human rights and international humanitarian law violations and other atrocities. The SG was requested to report to the Council within 30 days and thereafter monthly on the progress or lack thereof by the government of Sudan on this matter and expressed its intention to consider further actions in the event of non-compliance.

The Council decided that all states shall take the necessary measures to prevent the sale or supply, to all non-governmental entities and individuals, including the Janjaweed, operating in North Darfur, South Darfur and West Darfur, of arms and related materiel of all types. It urged the international community to make available assistance to mitigate the humanitarian catastrophe unfolding in the Darfur region and requested the Secretary-General to activate inter-agency humanitarian mechanisms to consider what additional measures were needed to avoid a humanitarian catastrophe. It encouraged the Secretary-General's Special Representative for Sudan and the independent expert of the Commission on Human Rights to work closely with the government of Sudan in supporting independent investigation of violations of human rights and international humanitarian law in the Darfur region. It extended the special political mission set out in resolution 1547 for an additional 90 days to 10 December 2004 and requested the Secretary-General to incorporate into the mission contingency planning for the Darfur region.

Resolution 1564, adopted by the Security Council on 18 September 2004 under Chapter VII, declared its grave concern that the government of Sudan has not fully met its obligations to improve the security of the civilian population of Darfur in the face of continued depredations which it attributed to the Janjaweed militia and the rebels but stopped at pointing the finger at Khartoum. The resolution deplored the ceasefire violations by all parties and welcomed and supported the intention of the African Union to enhance and augment its monitoring mission in Darfur. It encouraged the undertaking of proactive monitoring and urged Member States to support these initiatives. It called on the Sudanese government and the rebel groups to work together under the auspices of the African Union to reach a political solution in the negotiations then being held in Abuja under the leadership of President Obasanjo. It also urged the parties to the negotiations to sign and implement the humanitarian agreement immediately, and to conclude a protocol on security issues as soon as possible.

The Security Council reiterated its call on the government of Sudan to end the climate of impunity in Darfur by identifying and bringing to justice all those responsible for the widespread human rights abuses and violations of international humanitarian law and insisted that the government of Sudan take all appropriate steps to stop all violence and atrocities.

The Council demanded that Khartoum submit for verification to the African Union Mission concerning the names of Janjaweed militiamen disarmed and those arrested for human rights abuses and violations of international humanitarian law. It demanded that all armed groups, including rebel forces, cease all violence, cooperate with international humanitarian relief and monitoring efforts and ensure that their members comply with international humanitarian law, and facilitate the safety and security of humanitarian staff.

The Council also requested that the Secretary-General rapidly establish an international commission of inquiry in order to investigate reports of violations of international humanitarian law and human rights law in Darfur by all parties, to determine also whether or not acts of genocide have occurred, and to identify the perpetrators of such violations with a view to ensuring that those responsible are held accountable. It called on all parties to cooperate fully with such a commission.

By Resolution 1569 of 26 October 2004 the Council decided to hold meetings in Nairobi from 18-19 November 2004 with the agenda being the Reports of the Secretary-General on the Sudan.

On 19 November the Council issued resolution 1574 in which it urged a quick resolution of the conflict in southern Sudan pursuant to the ongoing peace process. It declared its strong support for the efforts of the government of Sudan and the Sudan People's Liberation Movement/Army to reach a Comprehensive Peace Agreement, welcomed the signing of the Memorandum of Understanding in Nairobi on 19 November 2004 entitled 'Declaration on the conclusion of IGAD negotiations on peace in the Sudan'. The Council declared its commitment, upon conclusion of a Comprehensive Peace Agreement, to assist the people of Sudan, on the understanding that the parties are fulfilling all their commitments, including those agreed in Abuja, Nigeria and Ndjamena, Chad. The Council again demanded that government and rebel forces and all other armed groups immediately cease all violence and attacks, including abduction, refrain from forcible relocation of civilians, cooperate with international humanitarian relief and monitoring efforts, ensure that their members comply with international humanitarian law, facilitate the safety and security of humanitarian staff, and reinforce throughout their ranks their agreements to allow unhindered access and passage by humanitarian agencies. It decided to monitor compliance by the parties with their obligations in that regard and, subject to a further decision of the Council, to take appropriate action against any party failing to fulfill its commitments.

8.1.1.19 Timor-Leste

By resolution 1543 of 14 May 2004 the Council extended the mandate of the United Nations Mission of Support in Timor-Leste (UNMISET) for a period of six months with a view to subsequently extending it for a further and final six months until 20 May 2005. It decided to reduce the size of UNMISET, to include up to 58 civilian advisers, 157 civilian police advisers, 42 military liaison officers, 310 formed troops and a 125-person International Response Unit. The Council also decided to revise its tasks to (i) support for the public administration and justice system of Timor-Leste and for justice in the area of serious crimes; (ii) support to the development of law enforcement in Timor-Leste; (iii) support for the security and stability of Timor-Leste.

The resolution also reaffirmed the need to fight against impunity and the importance for the international community to lend its support in this regard. It emphasised that the Serious Crimes Unit should complete all investigations by November 2004, and should conclude trials and other activities as soon as possible and no later than 20 May 2005.

By resolution 1573 of 16 November 2004 the Council extended UNMISET's mandate for a final period of six months until 20 May 2005. While it decided to maintain UNMISET's existing tasks, configuration and size in order to allow the mission to complete key tasks of its mandate and consolidate gains made, it requested UNMISET to focus increasingly on implementing its exit strategy. It urged the donor community to continue providing assistance to Timor-Leste, and the United Nations development and humanitarian agencies and multilateral financial institutions to start immediately planning for a smooth transition, in Timor-Leste, from a peacekeeping operation to a sustainable development assistance framework.

8.1.1.20 Western Sahara

By resolution 1523 of 30 January 2004 the Council extended the mandate of the United Nations Mission for the Referendum in Western Sahara (MINURSO) until 30 April 2004.

Resolution 1541 of 29 April reaffirmed the Council's support for the Peace Plan for Self-Determination of the People of Western Sahara as an optimum political solution. It also expressed the Security Council's support for the efforts of the Secretary-General and his Personal Envoy to achieve a mutually acceptable political solution to the dispute over Western Sahara, and called upon all the parties and the states of the region to cooperate fully with the Secretary-General and his Personal Envoy. Resolution 1541 also extended MINURSO's mandate until 31 October 2004 and requested the Secretary-General to provide a report on the situation before the end of the present mandate, including an evaluation of the mission size necessary for MINURSO to carry out its mandated tasks, with a view towards its possible reduction.

Resolution 1570, adopted on 28 October 2004, extended MINURSO's mandate until 30 April 2005. The Council requested the Secretary-General to provide a report on the situation before the end of the mandate period and an interim report, within three months from adoption of the resolution, on the evolution of the situation and on the mission's size and concept of operation.

8.1.2 *The Secretary-General*

8.1.2.1 Threats to international peace and security

On 1 December 2004 a High Level Panel on Threats, Challenges and Change established by the UN Secretary-General issued a powerful and cogent report entitled

'A more secure world: our shared responsibility'.[84] The report took an integrated and holistic approach to international peace and security by identifying all the major contemporary threats to peace and security and emphasising their interconnectedness. It proposed concrete reforms of the UN Organisation to enable it to better face old and new challenges, including changes to the composition of the Security Council.

The report stated that: 'The attacks of 11 September 2001 revealed that States, as well as collective security institutions, have failed to keep pace with changes in the nature of threats.'[85] The Panel noted that 'the biggest security threats we face now, and in the decades ahead, go far beyond States waging aggressive war. They extend to poverty, infectious disease and environmental degradation; war and violence within States; the spread and possible use of nuclear, radiological, chemical and biological weapons; terrorism; and transnational organized crime. The threats are from non-State actors as well as States, and to human security as well as State security.'

The report stressed the need for consensus among states and international actors of what constitute threats to international peace and security. It reiterated that states are the basic unit of the collective security system and that any event or process that leads to large-scale death or lessening of life chances and undermines states as the basic unit of the international system is a threat to international security. According to the Panel, the case for collective security rests on three pillars: the fact that threats are transnational and recognise no national boundaries; the fact that even the most powerful states are not invulnerable to today's threats; and the fact that it cannot be assumed that every state will be able or willing to meet its responsibility to protect its own peoples and not to harm its neighbours.

The Panel found that the UN Charter, including Article 51, is adequate to situations where force is used or required and needs neither extension nor restriction. The report also addressed the challenges of post-conflict environments, including the role of peacekeeping and peace building and the protection of civilians.

The report identified the underlying roots of conflict. 'Poverty (as measured by per capita gross domestic product (GDP)) is strongly associated with the outbreak of civil war (see figure II). Such diseases as malaria and HIV/AIDS continue to cause large numbers of deaths and reinforce poverty. Disease and poverty, in turn, are connected to environmental degradation; climate change exacerbates the occurrence of such infectious disease as malaria and dengue fever. Environmental stress, caused by large populations and shortages of land and other natural resources, can contribute to civil violence.'[86]

84. United Nations A/59/565, 2 December 2004.
85. Ibid., para. 16.
86. Ibid., para. 22.

8.1.2.2 The rule of law and transitional justice in conflict and post-conflict societies

The SC held a meeting on 26 January 2004 on 'Post conflict national reconciliation: the role of the United Nations'[87] At that meeting, the SC invited the SG to prepare a report which would give consideration to the views expressed during the meeting. Therefore, on 23 August 2004, the Secretary-General issued a Report on 'The rule of law and transitional justice in conflict and post-conflict societies'.[88] The objective of the report was to highlight key issues and lessons learned from the Organization's experiences in the promotion of justice and the rule of law in conflict and post-conflict societies.

The SG stated that: 'Our experience in the past decade has demonstrated clearly that the consolidation of peace in the immediate post-conflict period as well as the maintenance of peace in the long term, cannot be attained unless the population is confident that redress for grievances can be obtained through legitimate structures for the peaceful settlement of disputes and the fair administration of justice. At the same time, the heightened vulnerability of minorities, women, children, prisoners and detainees, displaced persons, refugees and others, which is evident in all conflict and post-conflict situations, brings an element of urgency to the imperative of restoration of the rule of law.'[89] He noted further that 'strategies for expediting a return to the rule of law must be integrated with plans to reintegrate both displaced civilians and former fighters. Disarmament, demobilization and reintegration processes are one of the keys to a transition out of conflict and back to normalcy. For populations traumatized by war, these processes are among the most visible signs of the gradual return of peace and security. Similarly, displaced persons must be the subject of dedicated programs to facilitate return. Carefully crafted amnesties can help in the return and reintegration of both groups and should be encouraged, although … these can never be permitted to excuse genocide, war crimes, crimes against humanity or gross violations of human rights.'[90] 'Finally, better safeguards must be established to ensure that the very interventions designed to protect vulnerable and victimized groups, including women and children, do not result in their further victimization … It is critically important that those who seek to abuse and exploit them are held accountable. Indeed, if the rule of law means anything at all, it means that no one, including peacekeepers, is above the law.'[91]

The report looked in depth at the role of a variety of transitional justice mechanisms, including international and internationalized courts and tribunals, and the role of victims in healing post-conflict societies and reestablishing the rule of law.

87. S/PRST/2004/2.

88. S/2004/616, 23 August 2004.

89. 'The rule of law and transitional justice in conflict and post-conflict societies', Report of the Secretary-General, United Nations Security Council, S/2004/616, 23 August, 2004, para. 2.

90. Ibid., para. 32.

91. Ibid., para. 33.

8.2 European Union

8.2.1 *EU Rapid Reaction Force*

On 22 November 2004 European Union defence ministers finally announced their agreement to establish a military rapid reaction force, a project that had been in the works since 1999. The first unit, consisting of about 1,500 troops, would be ready for deployment in 2005, and eight more by 2007.[92] France, the UK, Spain and Italy would each have their own units composed of their national troops, while other Member States would contribute to multinational units. The aim is to be able to deploy up to 60,000 troops to a situation for up to one year, drawing from a total force of up to 90,000.

The role of the force is to fulfill the so-called 'Petersberg Tasks', which include humanitarian tasks, rescue missions, peacekeeping and peace enforcement operations, including full combat.[93] UK Defence Secretary Geoff Hoon was reported as saying: 'They are particularly intended for situations where an early intervention with a highly capable battle group-size force could deal with an emerging crisis.'[94] It is supposed to work in close cooperation with NATO, but the real relationship between NATO and the EU Rapid Reaction Force has yet to be determined. It is complicated by the fact that NATO is in the process of establishing its own Rapid Reaction Force.

The rapid reaction force will not be a standing EU army but will be created on an ad hoc basis to address specific situations. Member States will decide on a case by case basis if they wish to contribute troops to an operation.[95]

8.2.2 *ECHO and EU Presidency meeting on humanitarian law and humanitarian principles*

On 25 and 26 March 2004, Ireland, as holder of the EU presidency, and ECHO, the humanitarian aid department of the European Commission, co-hosted an informal meeting on 'Humanitarian Action and Conflict: the Important Role of Humanitarian Principles', which explored the challenges to the upholding of international humanitarian law in today's crises. It was attended by senior representatives from humanitarian and civil protection/defence authorities from Member States, the European Commission, the International Committee of the Red Cross, the Irish Red Cross, the United Nations Office for the Co-ordination of Humanitarian Affairs (UNOCHA), Voluntary Organisations in Co-operation in Emergencies (VOICE), and the Overseas Development Institute (ODI).

The purpose of the meeting was to raise awareness about the importance of international humanitarian law, and in particular the principles of humanity, impar-

---

92. 'EU approves rapid reaction force', BBC News, 23 November 2004.

93. E. Cahen, 'European Union agrees on rapid reaction force', CNSNews.com, 25 November 2005.

94. EU approves rapid reaction force', BBC News, 23 November, 2004.

95. See Wikipedia, <http://en.wikipedia.org/wiki/European_Rapid_Reaction_Force>.

tiality, neutrality, independence and non-discrimination, and discuss among EU partners how they can better ensure that these principles are respected.[96]

8.3 African Union

On 25 May 2004 the Peace and Security Council of the African Union was inaugurated. Composed of 15 elected Member States, the Peace and Security Council is a permanent organ, intended to promote peace, security and stability in Africa, preventive diplomacy and restoration of peace. It will also deal with the management of disasters, humanitarian actions and post-conflict reconstruction.[97]

8.4 Organization of American States

A special meeting of the OAS's Committee on Juridical and Political Affairs on Promotion of and Respect for International Humanitarian Law was convened on 25 March 2004 in Washington DC Among the topics on the agenda were national application of the Rome Statute, with special guest speaker Luis Moreno Ocampo, the Prosecutor of the ICC, and the 1954 Cultural Convention.

At its 34th Regular Session, held in Quito, Ecuador from 6-8 June 2004, the OAS General Assembly adopted a number of resolutions of interest.

Resolution 2052 concerning Promotion of and Respect for International Humanitarian Law expressed the General Assembly's deep concern 'over persistent violations of international humanitarian law affecting the world's civilian populations, in particular children and women'. The Assembly resolved to urge the member states and all parties engaged in an armed conflict to honour their obligations under international humanitarian law, especially those that refer to protection of the civilian population and the treatment of prisoners of war, and urged all member states of the Organisation that are not already parties to the major IHL treaties to sign or ratify them. The US made a statement in which it stated that it could not support the resolution as it declared the OAS's support for the ICC.

A number of resolutions concerned small arms. Resolution 1995 concerned Support for the Program for Comprehensive Action against Antipersonnel Mines in Central America.[98] The resolution noted that Central America is now a region free of stockpiled antipersonnel mines and efforts are ongoing to complete mine clearance. Resolution 1997 addressed the Proliferation of and Illicit Trafficking in Small Arms and Light Weapons.[99] The General Assembly resolved to encourage member states to implement the United Nations Programme of Action to Prevent, Combat and Eradicate the Illicit Trade in Small Arms and Light Weapons in All Its

---

96. <http://ec.europa.eu/comm/echo/pdf_files/meeting_file.pdf>.

97. See African Union's Peace and Security Council Powerful Tool for Conflict Prevention, Secretary-General Says at Inauguration Ceremony', UN Press Release SG/SM/9327, AFR/944, 25 May 2004, <http://www.un.org/News/Press/docs/2004/sgsm9327.doc.htm>.

98. AG/RES. 1995 (XXXIV-O/04).

99. AG/RES. 1997 (XXXIV-O/04).

Aspects (UN Programme of Action). It would request the General Secretariat to present to the Permanent Council the report of the Seminar on Identification, Collection, Stockpile Management, and Destruction of Small Arms and Light Weapons, held in Managua, Nicaragua, on 12 and 13 May 2004, for consideration. It also resolved to request the Permanent Council to hold, at the level of the Committee on Hemispheric Security, an annual meeting on small arms and light weapons, which would review the status of implementation of national, regional and global elements of the UN Programme of Action. Resolution 2002 also addressed the Americas as an Antipersonnel-Land-Mine-Free Zone. Annexed to the resolution was a statement by the US Delegation which set out the US position on landmines. It alluded to its new landmine policy whose key elements are: 'a) a firm and fixed commitment to use no persistent (i.e., non-self-destructing or non-self-deactivating) landmine of any type after 2010; b) a firm commitment to use no non-detectable mine of any type by the end of this year; c) a 50% increase in US Department of State humanitarian mine action funding to $70 million per year, and d) the development of future landmines that incorporate enhanced self-destructing/self-deactivating and control mechanisms. The new policy also includes provisions to encourage international agreements to restrict the transfer of all persistent mines. The United States has not acceded to the "Ottawa Convention" and does not intend to do so.' The US delegation was critical of the OAS's 'landmine-free zone' policy, saying that 'it commits Member States and the OAS to an unnecessary action regardless of whether or not that mine generates any adverse impacts or poses a threat to civilians. Such an approach ignores the emerging global practice on the part of mine action practitioners to plan and manage mine action programs to achieve a "mine-impact free" or "mine safe" status. The "landmine free" approach also runs counter to funding trends on the part of most donor nations.' The statement concluded that for these and the other reasons given, 'the United States cannot in good faith join in the consensus on an OAS resolution that promotes an "anti-personnel landmine free hemisphere".'

Resolution 1999 addressed arms trafficking, specifically, the Inter-American Convention against the Illicit Manufacturing of and Trafficking in Firearms, Ammunition, Explosives and Other Related Materiels.[100]

In Resolution 2000 on The Americas as a Biological- and Chemical-Weapons-Free Region, the General Assembly resolved to 'concretely fulfill the shared commitment of member states to make the Americas a region free of biological and chemical weapons'.[101] In resolution 2008, entitled Inter-American Support for the Comprehensive Nuclear-Test-Ban Treaty, the General Assembly resolved 'to urge the states of the Hemisphere to implement the "Measures to Promote the Entry into Force of the Comprehensive Nuclear-Test-Ban Treaty (CTBT)," adopted at the Conference on Facilitating the Entry into Force of the Comprehensive Nuclear-Test-Ban Treaty (CTBT), held in Vienna, Austria, from September 3 to 5, 2003'. It entrusted the Permanent Council with holding, through its Committee on Hemi-

---

100. AG/RES. 1999 (XXXIV-O/04).
101. AG/RES. 2000 (XXXIV-O/04).

spheric Security, a special meeting, in 2005, on a worldwide comprehensive nuclear test ban. Resolution 2009 concerned Consolidation of the Regime Established in the Treaty for the Prohibition of Nuclear Weapons in Latin America and the Caribbean (Treaty of Tlatelolco).

By resolution 2010, the General Assembly amended the Statute of the Inter-American Committee Against Terrorism. G/RES. 2035 (XXXIV-O/04). In resolution 2035, entitled Protecting Human Rights and Fundamental Freedoms while Countering Terrorism, the General Assembly resolved to reaffirm 'that the fight against terrorism must be waged with full respect for the law, human rights, and democratic institutions, so as to preserve the rule of law and democratic freedoms and values in the Hemisphere'. It reaffirmed that 'all member states have a duty to ensure that all measures adopted to combat terrorism are in compliance with their obligations under international law, in particular international human rights law, international law on refugees, and international humanitarian law'.

Resolution 2039 concerned The Promotion of the International Criminal Court. In it the General Assembly resolved to urge those member states of the Organization that have not already done so to consider ratifying or acceding to the Rome Statute of the International Criminal Court. Even non-member states should participate as observers. Those states that are parties should implement the treaty into their domestic criminal law.

Annexed to the resolution was a Statement by the Delegation of the United States, in which it reiterated its commitment to international justice and its concerns about the International Criminal Court. In light of its opposition to the Court, the United States could not in good faith join in the consensus on an OAS resolution that promotes the Court.

Resolution 2051 expressed the General Assembly's Support for the Work of the Inter-American Committee against Terrorism (CICTE). The General Assembly resolved to reaffirm its commitment to continue strengthening hemispheric cooperation and implementing specific measures to prevent, combat and eliminate terrorism; to express its ongoing commitment to fight terrorism and the financing thereof with full respect for the rule of law and international law, including international humanitarian law, international human rights law, international refugee law, the Inter-American Convention against Terrorism, and United Nations Security Council resolution 1373 (2001). It urged CICTE to facilitate ongoing dialogue among member states with a view to undertaking preventive measures that anticipate and address emerging terrorist threats, whatever their origin, such as cybersecurity, bioterrorism, threats to critical infrastructure, and the possibility of access to and possession and use of weapons of mass destruction and related materiels and their means of delivery, by terrorists.

In Resolution 2055 concerning Internally Displaced Persons, the General Assembly urged member states to include, as appropriate, in their sectoral plans and programs the special needs of internally displaced persons, and appealed to member states to consider the Guiding Principles on Internal Displacement in designing public policy on this matter.

9. ARMS CONTROL AND DISARMAMENT

9.1 Landmines

The most significant event around mines was the convening from 29 November-3 December 2004 of the Nairobi Summit on a Mine-Free World, the title given to the first review conference of the Conference on the Prohibition of the Use, Stockpiling, Production and Transfer of Antipersonnel Mines and on Their Destruction. In the run up to the review conference, a series of preparatory meetings were held, on 13 February 2004 and from 28-29 June 2004. The number of states represented at the Review Conference was a testament to the success of the Landmines Treaty and its widespread acceptance. One hundred and nine states parties to the Landmines Treaty participated, and a further 26 states came as observers. In addition, a great many NGOs and IGOs sent representatives.

The work of the conference was divided into ten plenary sessions. The first three reviewed the general status and operation of the Landmines Treaty and concluded that to date the convention could be considered a success, although much work remains to be done. The question of further meetings of the states parties and related matters was considered at the third and fourth plenaries. At its fourth and fifth plenary meetings, the conference considered an eight-point plan of action for the period 2005-2009[102] to end once and for all the scourge of landmines and the suffering they cause. The sixth plenary discussed the report of the Director of the Geneva International Centre for Humanitarian Demining concerning the activities of the Implementation Support Unit. The seventh, eighth, ninth and tenth plenary meetings featured the conference high level segment, when 103 high level representatives of States Parties, observer states and observer organisations addressed the meeting. During its final plenary, the review conference adopted four key documents: Review of the operation and status of the Convention on the Prohibition of the Use, Stockpiling, Production and Transfer of Anti-Personnel Mines and on Their Destruction: 1999-2004; Ending the suffering caused by anti-personnel mines: Nairobi Action Plan 2005-2009; Towards a minefree world: the 2004 Nairobi Declaration; and Programme of meetings and related matters to facilitate implementation 2005-2009. All are annexed to the final report of the review conference.[103]

The States Parties decided to hold annual meetings of the States Parties to the Convention in the run up to the second review conference, to be held in 2009.

The First Conference of the States Party to the Inter-American Convention against the Illicit Manufacturing of and Trafficking in Firearms, Ammunition, Explosives, and Other Related CIFTA, held in Bogotá, Colombia, on 8 and 9 March 2004.

---

102. APLC/CONF/2004/L.4/Rev.1.

103. The Final Report of the First Review Conference of the States Parties to the Convention on the Prohibition of the Use, Stockpiling, Production and Transfer of Anti-Personnel Mines and on Their Destruction, APLC/CONF/2004/5, 9 February 2005, <http://www.reviewconference.org/fileadmin/pdf/review conference/documents/final_report/RC_Final_Report_en.pdf>.

9.2 Weapons of Mass Destruction

Security Council resolution 1540 of 28 April 2004 addressed the proliferation of weapons of mass destruction, namely nuclear, chemical and biological weapons, and their means of delivery. It noted the Council's grave concern 'by the threat of illicit trafficking in nuclear, chemical, or biological weapons and their means of delivery, and related materiels, which adds a new dimension to the issue of proliferation of such weapons and also poses a threat to international peace and security'. Adopted under Chapter VII, considering that the proliferation of WMD and particularly their acquisition by terrorists and other non-state actors constitutes a threat to international peace and security, it decided that 'all States shall refrain from providing any form of support to non-State actors that attempt to develop, acquire, manufacture, possess, transport, transfer or use nuclear, chemical or biological weapons and their means of delivery' and that 'all States, in accordance with their national procedures, shall adopt and enforce appropriate effective laws which prohibit any non-state actor to manufacture, acquire, possess, develop, transport, transfer or use nuclear, chemical or biological weapons and their means of delivery, in particular for terrorist purposes, as well as attempts to engage in any of the foregoing activities, participate in them as an accomplice, assist or finance them'. Resolution 1540 further decided that 'all States shall take and enforce effective measures to establish domestic controls to prevent the proliferation of nuclear, chemical, or biological weapons and their means of delivery, including by establishing appropriate controls over related materiels' and to this end should take a number of stipulated accounting, physical protection, border control, law enforcement, export and transshipment measures and controls.

By resolution 1540 the Security Council also established, for a period of no more than two years, a Committee of the Security Council, 'consisting of all members of the Council, which will, calling as appropriate on other expertise, report to the Security Council for its examination, on the implementation of this resolution'. States should present a first report no later than six months from the adoption of this resolution to the Committee on steps they have taken or intend to take to implement this resolution.

It also called upon states to develop national control lists at the earliest opportunity. The resolution invited states in a position to do so to provide assistance to states requiring it in implementing the provisions of this resolution within their territories.

INTERNATIONAL CRIMINAL COURTS ROUND-UP[1]

Olivia Swaak-Goldman and Maria Nybondas[2]

1. THE INTERNATIONAL CRIMINAL COURT

1.1 **The Chambers**

On 26 May 2004 the Judges adopted the Regulations of the Court.[3] The Regulations ensure the routine functioning of the International Criminal Court (ICC). The Regulations include, *inter alia*, provisions concerning the composition and administration of the Court, proceedings before the Court, victims' participation and reparations, and cooperation and enforcement.

1.2 **The Registry**

The Agreement on Privileges and Immunities of the International Criminal Court (APIC) came into force in July 2004 with its tenth ratification.[4] The APIC ensures that ICC officials can conduct their work without interference. It ensures access to territory, inviolability of archives and documents, facilities for communications and immunity of the funds and property of the ICC. The APIC also protects others involved with the work of the Court, including counsel and persons assisting counsel, victims, witnesses and experts, from obstruction by national authorities. The APIC is essential to the work of the ICC because, unlike the International Criminal Tribunal for the Former Yugoslavia (ICTY) and the International Criminal Tribunal for Rwanda (ICTR), the ICC is an independent organisation and therefore cannot depend on the privileges and immunities of UN bodies. The APIC remains open for accession by all states.

The Registry has developed regulations on conditions of detention to be used at the ICC's Detention Section. At least initially, the detention facility of the ICC will be located within a Dutch penitentiary.[5]

---

2. Olivia Swaak-Goldman is Senior Legal Advisor at the International Law Department, Ministry of Foreign Affairs of the Netherlands. Maria Nybondas is Researcher in International Humanitarian Law and International Criminal Law at the TMC Asser Institute for International Law, The Hague, Assistant Managing Editor of the *Yearbook of International Humanitarian Law*, and a Ph.D. candidate in international law at the University of Amsterdam.

3. Official documents of the International Criminal Court, ICC-BD/01-01-04, 26 May 2004.

4. ICC-ASP/1/3.

5. See International Criminal Court, ICC Newsletter No. 2, October 2004, at p. 3.

Yearbook of International Humanitarian Law
Volume 7 - 2004 - pp. 324-351 DOI 10.1017/S1389135904003241

1.3 The Office of the Prosecutor

The Cooperation Agreement between the Office of the Prosecutor (OTP) and Interpol was signed in December 2004.[6] The agreement established a framework for cooperation between the OTP and Interpol in the field of crime prevention and criminal justice, and will enable the OTP and Interpol to exchange police information and criminal analysis, and to cooperate in the search for fugitives and suspects. The Agreement also gives the OTP access to the Interpol telecommunications network and databases.[7]

1.4 The Assembly of State Parties

The Assembly of States Parties (ASP) held its third session in September 2004. While the first two sessions were held in New York, the third session was held in The Hague. The ASP – the management oversight and legislative body of the ICC – is composed of representatives of the states that have ratified the Court's Statute. To assist the ASP in the discharge of its duties, the ASP elected a Bureau consisting of a President, two Vice-Presidents and 18 members and established a permanent secretariat at the seat of the ICC.[8] In 2004 the ASP established a New York liaison office for the ICC and the secretariat of the ASP.[9]

At the third session, the ASP adopted the Court's 2005 program budget for almost 67 million euros and established a contingency fund of ten million euros.[10]

The ASP also adopted a Negotiated Relationship Agreement between the ICC and the United Nations.[11] The Agreement came into force upon the signature of President Kirsch and the Secretary General of the United Nations on 4 October 2004. The Agreement strengthens the cooperation between the ICC and the UN on matters of mutual interest relating to the exchange of information, judicial assistance, cooperation on infrastructure and technical matters. As a result of the Agreement, the ICC is entitled to participate in the General Assembly as an observer.[12] The Agreement also defines the mechanism of cooperation between the ICC and the Security Council concerning a referral of a situation to the ICC by the Security Council.[13] It also addresses the terms of cooperation between the OTP and the UN concerning investigations, exchange of information, conditions of confidentiality of information, protection of persons and security of any operation or activity of the UN.[14]

---

6. ICC Press Release, The Hague, 22 December 2004, <http://www.icc-cpi.int/press/pressreleases/.htm>.
7. Ibid.
8. The decision to create a permanent secretariat was made in September 2003; see ICC-ASP/2/L.5.
9. ICC-ASP/3/6.
10. ICC-ASP/3/Res. 4.
11. ICC-ASP/3/Res. 1.
12. Ibid., Art. 4(2).
13. Ibid., Art. 17.
14. Ibid., Art. 18.

The ASP elected Ms Fatou Bensouda of Gambia as Deputy Prosecutor. Ms Bensouda will manage the Prosecution Division of the OTP, which consists of the Prosecution Section and the Appeals Section.

Finally, the ASP adopted certain amendments to the procedures for the nomination and election of judges.[15] It also agreed on the establishment of a Secretariat for the Victims Trust Fund, enabling the Trust Fund to become operational.

1.5 **Cases**

1.5.1 *The Democratic Republic of Congo*

Since July 2003 the Office of the Prosecutor had been closely analysing the situation in the Democratic Republic of Congo (DRC), specifically the crimes committed in the Ituri region. In April 2004 the Prosecutor of the ICC announced that the DRC had asked him to investigate crimes that had allegedly taken place in the territory of the DRC since 1 July 2002. On 23 June the Prosecutor announced his decision to officially start an investigation, the ICC's first. The Presidency referred this situation to Pre-Trial Chamber I in July 2004.[16] In July the ICC made its first official visit to the DRC. The delegation, consisting of representatives of the Office of the Prosecutor and the Registry, held consultations concerning, *inter alia*, mechanisms of cooperation.

A provisional Memorandum of Understanding (MoU) on Privileges and Immunities of the Court was signed on 12 October 2004 between the Court and the Government of the DRC to facilitate the activities of the Court on Congolese territory while awaiting the ratification of the Agreement on Privileges and Immunities of the International Criminal Court (APIC) by the DRC. The MoU guarantees that the ICC will be able to carry out its activities in the field independently, safely and confidentially. Finally, from 6 through 11 December the ICC held a series of seminars and workshops in the DRC with the aim of promoting a better understanding of the ICC.[17]

1.5.2 *Uganda*

On 29 January 2004 the Prosecutor made public Uganda's referral of the situation concerning the Lord's Resistance Army to the ICC. On 29 July 2004 the Prosecutor announced that he had opened an investigation into crimes against humanity and war crimes committed in northern Uganda since 1 July 2002. The situation was assigned to Pre-Trial Chamber II in July 2004.[18] In August 2004 a delegation

---

15. ICC-ASP/3/Res. 6.

16. Decision Assigning the Situation in the Democratic Republic of Congo to Pre-Trial Chamber I, ICC-01/04, Presidency, 5 July 2004.

17. ICC Press Release, The Hague, 10 December 2004.

18. Decision Assigning the Situation in Uganda to Pre-Trial Chamber II, ICC-02/04, Presidency, 5 July 2004.

made up of representatives of the OTP and the Registry visited Uganda and signed an agreement setting out practical terms for cooperation.[19]

1.5.3 *Central African Republic*

In December 2004 a third situation was referred by the state concerned to the ICC: the situation in the Central African Republic (CAR). The government of the CAR asked the OTP to investigate crimes under the jurisdiction of the ICC that may have been committed since 1 July 2002 anywhere in the territory of the country. The Presidency assigned this situation to Pre-Trial Chamber III in January 2005.[20]

2. THE INTERNATIONAL CRIMINAL TRIBUNAL FOR THE FORMER YUGOSLAVIA

2.1 **Amendments to the Rules of Procedure and Evidence**

During 2004 the ICTY adopted internal reforms in order to comply with Security Council resolutions 1503 (2003) and 1534 (2004), mandating that the ICTY complete its investigations by the end of 2004, all trial activities in first instance by the end of 2008, and all of its work in 2010 (the completion strategy). On 6 April 2004 the judges adopted an amendment to Rule 28(A) of the Rules of Procedure and Evidence (RPE) to ensure that all indictments confirmed by the ICTY meet the Security Council's directive that the indictments *prima facie* concentrate on one or more of the most senior leaders suspected of being most responsible for crimes within the jurisdiction of the ICTY.[21] The judges also adopted an amendment to Rule 11*bis* of the RPE to facilitate the referral of cases involving intermediate and lower-level accused by increasing the jurisdictions available to receive its cases. The new amendment authorises trial chambers to refer a case to any jurisdiction in which the accused could be tried fairly and where the death penalty will not be imposed. Also on 6 April the judges adopted a revised Directive on the Assignment of Defense Counsel.[22] Finally, on 8 December 2004 the judges amended Rule 73(D), allowing for the withholding of fees associated with the production of motions that are found to be frivolous or an abuse of process, and Rule 98bis concerning judgements of acquittal.[23]

---

19. See ICC Newsletter No. 2, October 2004, at p. 5.

20. Decision Assigning the Situation in Darfur, Sudan to Pre-Trial Chamber II, ICC-01/05, Presidency, 21 April 2005.

21. 'Judges amend Rule 28 at extraordinary plenary', Press Release of the Plenary, JL/P.I.S./837e, The Hague, 8 April 2004.

22. 'Amendments to the Rules of Procedure and Evidence and Directive on Assignment of Defence Counsel', Press Advisory, P.I.S./PA189e, The Hague, 10 August 2004.

23. 'Judges amend Rules 73(D) and 98bis at plenary session', Press Release of the Plenary, CVO/P.I.S./925e, The Hague, 10 December 2004.

2.2 Election and appointment of judges

On 12 April 2004 the UN Secretary-General appointed Lord Bonomy from the United Kingdom as a judge of the ICTY, effective as of 1 June 2004.[24] Lord Bonomy was appointed to replace Judge Richard May, who retired because of ill-health.[25]

Two *ad litem* judges were sworn in on 21 September 2004: Judge Hans Henrik Brydensholt from Denmark and Judge Albin Eser from Germany.[26]

On 19 November 2004, after seven rounds of voting, the United Nations General Assembly elected the following 14 individuals as permanent judges of the ICTY for a term of four years, beginning on 17 November 2005 and ending in 2009: Carmel Agius (Malta); Jean-Claude Antonetti (France); Iain Bonomy (UK); O-gon Kwon (Republic of Korea); Liu Daqun (China); Theodor Meron (USA); Bakone Moloto (South Africa); Alphonsus Orie (Netherlands); Kevin Parker (Australia); Fausto Pocar (Italy), Patrick Robinson (Jamaica); Wolfgang Schomburg (Germany); Mohamed Shahabuddeen (Guyana); and Christine van den Wyngaert (Belgium).[27]

2.3 Office of the Prosecutor

In furtherance of the Prosecutor's commitment to complete the investigation of the remaining unindicted high-level targets, investigations were streamlined and made even more focused to concentrate on the highest-level political and military leaders responsible for having committed the gravest crimes.[28]

On 30 August 2004, Mr David Tolbert from the USA, formerly Deputy Registrar at the ICTY, took up his duties as Deputy Prosecutor.[29]

2.4 Enforcement of sentences

On 11 March 2004 the United Kingdom concluded an agreement for the enforcement of sentences with the ICTY, making it the tenth state to do so.[30]

---

24. 'Lord Bonomy appointed as Judge to the International Criminal Tribunal for the former Yugoslavia', Press Release of the Chambers, JP/P.I.S./838e, The Hague, 14 April 2004.

25. Ibid. Judge May subsequently passed away on 1 July 2004. 'Sir Richard May', Press Release of the Registry, JL/P.I.S./865-e, The Hague, 1 July 2004.

26. 'Judges Hans Henrik Brydensholt and Albin Eser sworn in as *ad litem* Judges of the International Criminal Tribunal for the former Yugoslavia', Press Release of the Chambers, CT/P.I.S./896e, The Hague, 21 September 2004.

27. 'Fourteen judges elected by the UN General Assembly', Press Release of the Registry, CT/P.I.S./913-e, The Hague, 22 November 2004.

28. See generally, Eleventh annual report of the International Tribunal for the Prosecution of Persons Responsible for Serious Violations of International Humanitarian Law Committed in the Territory of the Former Yugoslavia since 1991, UN Doc. A/59/215 – S/2004/627, 16 August 2004, at p. 66.

29. 'David Tolbert takes up his duties as Deputy Prosecutor', Press Release of the Office of the Prosecutor, JP/P.I.S./887e, The Hague, 30 August 2004.

30. 'The United Kingdom: the 10th state to sign an agreement on the enforcement of sentences with the ICTY', Press Release of the Registry, JL/P.I.S./830e, The Hague, 11 March 2004. The other

On 18 June 2004 Dragan Obrenović was transferred to Norway to serve his sentence.[31] Obrenović was sentenced on 10 December 2003 by Trial Chamber I to 17 years' imprisonment following his guilty plea to the charge of persecutions as a crime against humanity on 21 May 2003.

On 6 July 2004 Mitar Vasiljević was transferred to Austria to serve his 15 year sentence.[32] Vasiljević was sentenced to 20 years' imprisonment on 29 November 2002 by the Trial Chamber, but this sentence was reduced to 15 years by the Appeals Chamber on 25 February 2004.

On 23 November 2004 Darko Mrđa was transferred to Spain to serve his sentence.[33] On 31 March 2004 Mrđa had been sentenced to 17 years' imprisonment by Trial Chamber I following his plea of guilty to one count of a violation of the laws and customs of war and one count of a crime against humanity.[34]

Radislav Krstić was transferred to the United Kingdom to serve his sentence on 20 December 2004.[35] Krstić had been sentenced to 35 years' imprisonment following his conviction for aiding and abetting genocide at Srebrenica in July 1995.

2.5 Early release

On 29 July 2004 the President of the ICTY ordered that Anto Furundžija be granted early release, with effect from 17 August 2004.[36] Furundžija had been sentenced to ten years' imprisonment by the Trial Chamber on 10 December 1998 and his sentence was affirmed by the Appeals Chamber on 21 July 2000. On 29 July 2004 the President also ordered the early release of Tihomir Blaškić, whose Appeals Chamber Judgement was rendered on that date.[37]

On 3 November 2004 the President of the ICTY also ordered the release of Miroslav Tadić as early as was reasonably practicable.[38] Tadić had been found guilty of a crime against humanity (persecution) and sentenced to eight years' imprisonment on 17 October 2003.

---

states are Austria, Italy, Finland, Norway, Sweden, France, Spain, and Denmark, as well as Germany, which signed two *ad hoc* agreements regarding Duško Tadić and Dragoljub Kunarac.

31. 'Dragan Obrenovic transferred to Norway to serve his prison sentence', Press Release of the Registry, CT/P.I.S./859e, The Hague, 18 June 2004.

32. 'Mitar Vasiljevic transferred to Austria to serve his prison sentence', Press Release of the Registry, JP/P.I.S./868e, The Hague, 6 July 2004.

33. 'Darko Mrdja transferred to Spain to serve his sentence', Press Release of the Registry, CT/P.I. S./915e, The Hague, 23 November 2004.

34. See *infra*, p. 332.

35. 'Radislav Krstic transferred to the United Kingdom to serve his prison sentence', Press Release of the Registry, CT/P.I.S./915e, The Hague, 20 December 2004.

36. 'Anto Furundzija granted early release', Press Release of the President, CT/P.I.S./877e, The Hague, 30 July 2004.

37. 'Tihomir Blaskic granted early release', Press Release of the President, CT/P.I.S../876e, The Hague, 29 July 2004.

38. 'Miroslav Tadic granted early release', Press Release of the President, CT/P.I.S./908e, The Hague, 4 November 2004.

2.6 New indictments

On 20 May 2004 Judge Liu Daqun confirmed an indictment against Mirko Norac. Norac, a former Commander in the Croatian Army, is charged with individual responsibility and/or command responsibility for crimes against humanity (persecutions and murder) and violations of the laws and customs of war (murder; plunder of public or private property; and wanton destruction of cities, towns or villages) for his role in the attack on the Medak Pocket in the self-proclaimed 'Republika Srpska Krajina'.[39]

On 16 July 2004 Judge El Mahdi signed a decision making public the indictment against Goran Hadžić, the former President of the self-proclaimed 'Republic of Serbian Krajina' in Croatia.[40] The indictment, originally confirmed on 4 June 2004, charges Hadžić as a co-perpetrator in a joint criminal enterprise to permanently remove a majority of the Croat and other non-Serb population from approximately one-third of the territory of Croatia in order to make them part of a new Serb-dominated state. Specifically, Hadžić is charged under Article 7(1) with individual criminal responsibility for eight counts of crimes against humanity and six counts of violations of the laws or customs of war.

2.7 Judgements[41]

2.7.1 Prosecutor *v.* Mitar Vasiljević, *Judgement, Appeals Chamber, 25 February 2004*[42]

This case relates to events that took place in June 1992 in the municipality of Visegrad in south eastern Bosnia and Herzegovina. The Trial Chamber convicted Vasiljević, whom it found to have been associated with a Serb paramilitary group, of two of the ten counts charged by the prosecution, specifically: persecution as a crime against humanity for the underlying murder of five Muslim men and the infliction of inhumane acts on two others; and murder as a violation of the laws and customs of war for the murder of the same five Muslim men.[43] Vasiljević raised four grounds of appeal. The Appeals Chamber accepted some of these appeals and rejected others.

First, the Appeals Chamber dismissed Vasiljević's appeals based on factual errors relating to the general requirements of Articles 3 and 5 of the ICTY Sta-

39. 'Mirko Norac indicted by the ICTY for crimes against humanity and violations of the laws and customs of war', press release of the Registry, JP/P.I.S./851-3, The Hague, 25 May 2004.

40. 'Goran Hadzic indicted by the ICTY for crimes against humanity and violations of the laws and customs of war', Press Release of the Chambers, CT/P.I.S./869-e, The Hague, 16 July 2004.

41. The following case summaries are not intended to be comprehensive. The aim is to give a broad overview of the legal and factual findings, and to highlight any original jurisprudence and significant divergences from earlier cases.

42. *Prosecutor* v. *Mitar Vasiljević*, case No. IT-98-32-A, Judgement, Appeals Chamber, 25 February 2004.

43. Ibid., para. 2.

tute.[44] Second, it upheld some of Vasiljević's appeal based on alleged errors of fact concerning the shooting incident itself.[45] Third, concerning Vasiljević's participation in a joint criminal enterprise and his related criminal responsibility, it found that the Trial Chamber had erred in finding that the only reasonable inference from the evidence was that he shared the intent to kill all seven of the Muslim men, and that this error led to a miscarriage of justice. Without proof of an intent to kill, Vasiljević could not be found responsible as a co-perpetrator.[46] It did, however, find him responsible as an aider and abettor of the murders and persecution.[47] Finally, although it rejected Vasiljević's appeal of his sentence, the Appeals Chamber reduced it to 15 years' imprisonment as a result of its finding that he was responsible as an aider and abettor rather than a co-perpetrator.[48]

2.7.2 Prosecutor *v.* Miroslav Deronjić, *Sentencing Judgement, Trial Chamber II, 30 March 2004*[49]

In this Judgement the Trial Chamber affirmed the guilty plea of Miroslav Deronjić, a political leader in the municipality of Bratunac, Bosnia and Herzegovina, for the crime against humanity of persecution committed in the village of Glogova on 9 May 1992. In the Plea Agreement the prosecution recommended a term of imprisonment of ten years, while the defence recommended a sentence of not more than six years.[50]

The Trial Chamber confirmed the guilt of Deronjić for persecution as a crime against humanity, incorporating the attack on the village of Glogova and its destruction, the killing of Bosnian Muslim civilians and the forcible displacement of Bosnian Muslims civilians.[51] The Trial Chamber found that Deronjić committed these acts of persecution as a co-perpetrator in a joint criminal enterprise which had as its objective the permanent removal, by force if necessary, of Bosnian Muslim inhabitants from Glogova through the commission of persecution.[52] In sentencing Deronjić to ten years' imprisonment, the Trial Chamber balanced the extreme gravity of the crime – noting the Prosecution's assertion that this is precisely the type of crime about which the Security Council expressed its grave alarm in Resolution 808 (1993) in that it is a classic case of ethnic cleansing[53] – and Deronjić's senior position as a political leader in the municipality, with his guilty plea and his substantial cooperation.

---

44. Ibid., paras. 24-31.
45. Ibid., paras. 32-86.
46. Ibid., paras. 131-132, 141.
47. Ibid., paras. 135, 143.
48. Ibid., paras. 181-182.
49. *Prosecutor* v. *Miroslav Deronjić*, case No. IT-02-61-S, Sentencing Judgement, Trial Chamber II, 30 March 2004.
50. Ibid., paras. 277-278.
51. Ibid., para. 128.
52. Ibid., paras. 125-126.
53. Ibid., para. 179.

2.7.3 Prosecutor *v.* Darko Mrđa, *Sentencing Judgement, Trial Chamber I, 31 March 2004*[54]

On 31 March 2004 Trial Chamber I sentenced Mrđa to 17 years' imprisonment for his participation in the murder of approximately 200 civilians and attempted murder of 12 civilians at Koricanske Stijene in Bosnia and Herzegovina on 21 August 1992. Mrđa pleaded guilty to violations of the wars and customs of war and the crime of inhuman acts as a crime against humanity. As a result of the plea agreement, Mrđa, who was a member of the special police unit known as the 'Intervention Squad' which served under the Bosnian Serb authorities in Prijedor, admitted committing these crimes against the non-Serb population of Prijedor.

In determining the sentence of 17 years' imprisonment, the Trial Chamber noted that while Mrđa was not the 'architect' of the massacre and he was acting in furtherance of superior orders, he personally participated in the selection of the civilians who were going to be killed, and in the subsequent murder and attempted murder of 12 of them, knowing that a widespread and systematic attack against civilians was underway.[55]

2.7.4 Prosecutor *v.* Radislav Krstić, *Appeals Judgement, 19 April 2004*[56]

In this Judgement the Appeals Chamber unanimously confirmed that Bosnian Serb forces had committed genocide in Srebrenica in 1995 but reduced Krstic's liability from that of a participant in a joint criminal enterprise to commit it to an aider and abetter.

The Trial Chamber had found Krstić guilty of genocide; persecution for murder, cruel and inhumane treatment, terrorising the civilian population, forcible transfer and destruction of personal property of Bosnian Muslim civilians as crimes against humanity; and murder as a violation of the laws and customs of war and sentenced him to 46 years' imprisonment.[57] Both the prosecution and Krstić appealed the decision.

The prosecution had two grounds of appeal: (1) the Trial Chamber's conclusion on impermissibly cumulative convictions; and (2) the sentence imposed: it requested a life sentence with a minimum of 30 years' imprisonment. The defence had four grounds of appeal: (1) the conviction for genocide, alleging both factual and legal errors; (2) various disclosure practices of the prosecution which it alleged deprived Krstić of a fair trial; (3) other factual and legal errors; and (4) the sentence imposed.

The Appeals Chamber: (1) set aside Krstić's conviction as a participant in a joint criminal enterprise to commit genocide and found him guilty of aiding and abetting genocide; (2) concluded that the Trial Chamber had incorrectly disallowed

---

54. *Prosecutor* v. *Darko Mrđa*, case No. IT-02-59-S, Sentencing Judgement, Trial Chamber I, 31 March 2004.
55. Ibid., para. 31.
56. *Prosecutor* v. *Radislav Krstić*, case No. IT-98-33-A, Appeals Judgement, 19 April 2004.
57. *Prosecutor* v. *Radislav Krstić*, case No. IT-98-33-T, Judgement, 2 August 2001.

Krstić's conviction for extermination and persecution committed between 13 and 19 July 1995, but that his level of responsibility was that of an aider and abettor; (3) set aside Krstić's conviction for murder as a violation of the laws and customs of war committed between 13 and 19 July 1995 and found him guilty of aiding and abetting murder; (4) affirmed Krstić's convictions for murder as a violation of the laws and customs of war and persecution as a crime against humanity committed between 10 and 13 July 1995 in Potocari; and (5) dismissed the prosecution and defence appeals in all other respects and reduced his sentence from 46 to 35 years' imprisonment.

The case concerns the massacre of 7,000 to 8,000 Bosnian Muslim males in the UN 'safe haven' of Srebrencia in July 1995 by the Bosnian Serb army (VRS), of which Krstić was a General Major. Krstić was responsible for the Drina Corps, a sub-unit of the VRS in Srebrenica and he was connected to the VRS Main Staff. The Appeals Chamber unanimously upheld the Trial Chamber's finding that Bosnian Muslims of Srebrenica were targeted for genocide. The killings involved one demographic segment – males – of a part of the protected group of Bosnian Muslims living in Srebrenica. The Appeals Chamber held that in cases where a genocide conviction 'relies on the intent to destroy a protected group 'in part', the part must be a substantial part of that group'.[58] The Appeals Chamber enunciated some guidelines to help determine whether a part is substantial: the numeric size of the targeted part; the prominence of the targeted part within the overall group; and the area of the perpetrator's activity and control.[59] The Appeals Chamber confirmed the finding of the Trial Chamber that the Main Staff had the intent to destroy a substantial part of the Srebrenica Bosnian Muslim group.[60]

Despite its finding that the VRS Main Staff had genocidal intent, the Appeals Chamber overturned the Trial Chamber's finding that Krstić had the specific intent required to be convicted as a direct perpetrator of genocide. It found that his knowledge of the Srebrenica executions and his knowledge of the use of personnel and resources under his command to assist therein alone would not support the additional inference of genocidal intent.[61] In finding Krstić guilty of aiding and abetting genocide, the Appeals Chamber stated that Krstić knew that by allowing Drina Corps resources to be used he was making a substantial contribution to the execution of the Bosnian Muslim prisoners. Although he was not a supporter of the plan, as Commander of the Drina Corps he permitted the Main Staff to call upon Drina Corps and to employ their resources. The Appeals Chamber held that '[t]he conviction for aiding and abetting genocide upon proof that the defendant knew about the principal perpetrator's genocidal intent is permitted under the Statute and case law of the Tribunal.'[62] Further, the Appeals Chamber held that '[a] defen-

58. *Krstić*, Appeals Judgement, *supra* n. 56, para. 8.
59. Ibid., paras. 12-13.
60. Ibid., paras. 26-33.
61. Ibid., para. 129.
62. Ibid., para. 140.

dant may be convicted for having aided and abetted a crime which requires specific intent even where the principal perpetrators have not been tried or identified.'[63]

2.7.5 Prosecutor *v.* Milan Babić, *Sentencing Judgement, Trial Chamber I, 29 June 2004*[64]

This Judgement resulted from a plea agreement between Babić and the Prosecutor. Babić was one of the most influential Serb political leaders in the Krajina region of Croatia, having served as President of the self-proclaimed Republic of Serbian Krajina. He was indicted based on events which took place in the Krajina from August 1991 to February 1992. In exchange for a recommended sentence of no more than 11 years, Babić pleaded guilty to being a co-perpetrator of persecution as a crime against humanity committed by a joint criminal enterprise. The goal of the joint criminal enterprise was to forcibly remove Croat and other non-Serb populations from approximately one-third of Croatian territory in order to turn this territory into a Serb-dominated state through the commission of crimes. In rendering its Judgement, the Trial Chamber found that the suggested sentence of 11 years did not fit the gravity of the crime, whereby, *inter alia*, virtually the whole of the Croat and non-Serb population was expelled from the region by forcible removal or through fear of imminent attack.[65] As such, the Trial Chamber sentenced Babić to 13 years' imprisonment.

2.7.6 Prosecutor *v.* Tihomir Blaškić, *Appeals Judgement, 29 July 2004*[66]

On 29 July 2004 the Appeals Chamber rendered its Judgement in which it reduced Blaškić's sentence from 45 to nine years. Blaškić, the former commander of the armed forces of the Croatian Defense Council (HVO) in Central Bosnia, was convicted on 3 March 2000 by the Trial Chamber under Article 7(1) of the ICTY's Statute for ordering grave breaches, violations of the laws and customs of war and crimes against humanity during the conflict between the HVO and the Bosnian Muslim Army in Central Bosnia and Herzegovina from May 1992 until January 1994. The Trial Chamber also convicted him under Article 7(3) for failing to prevent or punish the commission of these crimes by his subordinates. Specifically, Blaškić was convicted of persecution as a crime against humanity; unlawful attacks on civilians, wilful killing and causing serious injury as violations of the laws and customs of war, grave breaches of the Geneva Conventions and crimes against humanity; the destruction and plunder of property, inhumane treatment, the taking of hostages and the use of human shields as violations of the laws and customs of war and grave breaches of the Geneva Conventions; and the destruction

---

63. Ibid., para. 143.
64. *Prosecutor* v. *Milan Babić*, case No. IT-03-72-S, Sentencing Judgement, Trial Chamber I, 29 June 2004.
65. Ibid., paras. 51, 101.
66. *Prosecutor* v. *Tihomir Blaškić*, case No. IT-95-14-A, Appeals Judgement, 29 July 2004.

of religious or educational institutions as a violation of the laws and customs of war. The Trial Chamber imposed a single sentence of 45 years.

On appeal, Blaškić argued, *inter alia*, that the Trial Chamber had erred in defining the criminal responsibility under Article 7(1) and 7(3) of the Statute and alleged legal errors concerning Articles 2 and 5. He also submitted additional evidence that had been unavailable during the trial but had become available with the opening of Croatia's archives upon the death of its former President Franjo Tudjman in December 1999. On this basis he challenged the factual findings of the Trial Chamber, alleging errors concerning his responsibility for crimes committed in Ahmici, other parts of the Vitez municipality, the Busovaca municipality, and the Kiseljak municipality, and for detention-related crimes. He also appealed against his sentence.

Concerning Article 7(1), the Trial Chamber had held that in ordering an act, knowledge of the risk that crimes may be committed and acceptance of this risk shows sufficient intent to incur responsibility for having ordered, planned or incited the commitment of the crimes. The Appeals Chamber, however, disagreed, finding that knowledge of any kind of risk is not sufficient for criminal responsibility. Rather, according to the Appeals Chamber, there must be a substantial risk that a crime will be committed in execution of that order.[67]

In relation to Article 7(3), Blaškić argued that the Trial Chamber had erred in its interpretation of the knowledge requirement. The Trial Chamber had held that commanders' role 'obliges them to be constantly informed of the way in which their subordinates carry out the tasks entrusted to them, and to take the necessary measures for this purpose'.[68] In response, the Appeals Chamber noted that the *Čelebići* Appeals Judgement establishes the standard for the 'had reason to know' issue, finding that 'a superior will be criminally responsible ... *only if information was available to him* which would have put him on notice of offenses committed by subordinates'.[69] The Appeals Chamber also found that the Trial Chamber had erred in finding a concurrent conviction under Articles 7(1) and 7(3) of the Statute in relation to the same counts based on the same facts.[70]

With regard to Article 5 of the Statute concerning crimes against humanity, the Appeals Chamber found that in order for the court to determine whether the presence of soldiers within a civilian population deprives the population of its civilian character, it needs to examine the number of soldiers as well as whether they are on leave. It concluded that the Trial Chamber erred when it found that the presence of soldiers within an intentionally targeted civilian population does not alter the civilian nature of the population.[71]

Turning to the alleged factual errors, the Appeals Chamber determined that the evidence available at trial did not support the Trial Chamber's finding that the

---

67. Ibid., para. 42.
68. Ibid., para. 61.
69. Ibid., para. 62.
70. Ibid., para. 92.
71. Ibid., paras. 115-116.

Bosnian Muslim forces were not preparing for combat in Ahmići.[72] Moreover, the Appeals Chamber found that additional evidence presented on appeal showed that there was a Muslim military presence in Ahmići and that Blaškić had reason to believe that an attack was intended. As such, the Appeals Chamber concluded that there was a military justification for Blaškić to order an attack. Additionally, the Appeals Chamber concluded on the basis of newly submitted evidence that certain attacks were not attributable to the HVO, as had been determined by the Trial Chamber.[73]

The Appeals Chamber also found that no reasonable trier of fact could conclude that Blaškić was responsible under Article 7(1) of the Statute for crimes committed in Kiseljak in April and June 1993, nor that he was responsible for hostage-taking.[74]

2.7.7 Prosecutor *v.* Radoslav Brđanin, *Judgement, Trial Chamber II, 1 September 2004*[75]

In this Judgement Trial Chamber II sentenced Brđanin, a former Bosnian Serb political leader, to 32 years' imprisonment for persecution as a crime against humanity; wilful killing and torture as grave breaches of the Geneva Conventions; wanton destruction of cities, towns and villages or devastation not justified by military necessity as a violation of the laws and customs of war; and destruction or wilful damage done to institutions dedicated to religion as a violation of the laws and customs of war. The Trial Chamber concluded that Brđanin was a leading political figure in the so-called Autonomous Region of Krajina and that he supported the 'Strategic Plan' of the Bosnian Serb leadership to link Serb-populated areas within Bosnia and Herzegovina, to gain control over these areas, to create a separate Bosnian Serb state, and to permanently remove most non-Serbs from this territory.

The Trial Chamber found that Brđanin knew that the Strategic Plan could only be implemented by the use of force and fear.[76] It also concluded that he made a substantial contribution to the implementation of the Strategic Plan, including through conducting a propaganda campaign against Bosnian Muslims and Bosnian Croats.[77] His comments incited Bosnian Serbs to commit crimes and contributed to creating a climate where the commission of crimes was tolerated. Further, the Trial Chamber was convinced that Brđanin had detailed knowledge that crimes were being committed in execution of the Strategic Plan.

Despite these conclusions, the Trial Chamber was not convinced that Brđanin had entered into an agreement with the relevant physical perpetrators to commit a

72. Ibid., para. 333.
73. Ibid., para. 339.
74. Ibid., paras. 557, 646.
75. *Prosecutor* v. *Radoslav Brđanin*, case No. IT-99-36-T, Judgement, Trial Chamber II, 1 September 2004.
76. Ibid., para. 305.
77. Ibid., para. 323.

crime, and found that joint criminal enterprise is not an appropriate mode of liability to describe the criminal liability of Brđanin given the extremely broad nature of the case.[78] The Trial Chamber also dismissed planning as a mode of liability under Article 7(1) because there was not sufficient evidence that he was involved in the immediate preparation of the crimes. Finally, the Trial Chamber found that Brđanin did not have effective control over members of the municipal authorities which would allow him to prevent or punish the commission of crimes by these individuals, thus dismissing superior responsibility under Article 7(3) as a possible mode of liability.

Rather, the Trial Chamber found Brđanin guilty under Article 7(1) of the Statute for aiding and abetting[79] the wilful killing and torture committed by the Bosnian Serb forces. It also found that he directly incited the deportation or forcible transfer of non-Serbs from the territory of the ARK and that he intended to induce the commission of these crimes. As a result, the Trial Chamber found that he instigated the forcible transfers and deportations and that he aided and abetted the execution of these crimes through, *inter alia*, his discriminatory and inflammatory public statements. The Trial Chamber found that Brđanin aided and abetted the destruction of cities, towns and villages committed by Bosnian Serb forces and the destruction or wilful damage done to religious institutions. Finally, the Trial Chamber found that he had aided and abetted persecution.

2.7.8 Prosecutor *v.* Slobodan Milošević

—Decision on the Assignment of Defense Counsel, Trial Chamber III, 2 September 2004;
—Decision on Interlocutory Appeal of the Trial Chamber's Decision on the Assignment of Defense Counsel, Appeals Chamber, 1 November 2004;
—Decision on Assigned Counsel's Motion for Withdrawal, Trial Chamber III, 7 December 2004.

These decisions concern the appointment of defence counsel for Slobodan Milošević, who is alleged to have committed genocide, crimes against humanity, war crimes and grave breaches of the Geneva Conventions while he was President of the Republic of Serbia and, subsequently, President of the Federal Republic of Yugoslavia.

Milošević has asserted his right to defend himself throughout his trial. After countless delays in the trial due to the defendant's ill-health, on 2 September 2004 the Trial Chamber gave an oral ruling in which it determined that it was both competent and appropriate to assign defence counsel to Milošević.[80] The justifications supporting this decision – in general that the right to represent oneself must yield when it is necessary to ensure that the trial is fair – were presented in writing on 22

78. Ibid., para. 355.
79. Ibid., para. 369.
80. *Prosecutor* v. *Slobodan Milošević*, case No. IT-02-54, Reasons for Decision on Assignment of Defense Counsel, Trial Chamber III, 22 September 2004, para. 1.

September.[81] Following the oral decision on 2 September, on 3 September the Deputy Registrar appointed Mr Steven Kay as lead counsel and Ms Gillian Higgins as co-counsel for Milošević, both of whom had been *amici curiae* in the case up until this point.[82] On the same day, the Trial Chamber issued an 'Order on the Modalities to be followed by Court Assigned Counsel', in which it defined how the court assigned counsel were to act. This Order provided that: (1) it is the duty of the court assigned counsel to determine how to present the case for Milošević; (2) Milošević may, with the leave of the Trial Chamber, continue to participate actively in the conduct of his case; (3) Milošević has the right to make a reasonable request to the Trial Chamber to consider allowing him to appoint counsel; and (4) court assigned counsel is authorised to seek such further orders from the Trial Chamber as they deem necessary to enable them to conduct the case.[83]

The decision to appoint counsel was the subject of an appeal by Milošević and on 1 November 2004 the Appeals Chamber affirmed the Trial Chamber's imposition of defence counsel, but reversed its order on modalities.[84] The Appeals Chamber ordered that the Trial Chamber on remand should develop a working regime that minimises the practical impact of the formal assignment of counsel, except to the extent required by the interests of justice. This requires, at a minimum, the default presumption that, when he is physically capable of doing so, Milošević will take the lead in presenting his case.[85]

Meanwhile, on 26 October 2004, subsequent to the hearing of the appeal but before its determination, the court assigned counsel wrote a letter to the Registrar requesting permission to withdraw as defence counsel.[86] On 27 October 2004 the Deputy Registrar issued a Decision referring the request to the Trial Chamber.[87] On 7 December 2004 Trial Chamber III denied the assigned counsels' request to withdraw.[88] In doing so, the Trial Chamber found that Milošević's refusal to communicate with or instruct counsel cannot be a basis for withdrawal.[89]

---

81. Ibid., para. 34.

82. 'Milosevic case: Steven Kay and Gillian Higgins "court assigned counsel"; Trial Chamber issues an order on the modalities by which they are to act', Press Release of the Registry, CC/P.I.S./890e, The Hague, 3 September 2004.

83. *Prosecutor* v. *Slobodan Milošević*, case No. IT-02-54, Order on the Modalities to be followed by Court Assigned Counsel, Trial Chamber III, 3 September 2004.

84. *Prosecutor* v. *Slobodan Milošević*, case No. IT-02-54-AR73.7, Decision on Interlocutory Appeal of The Trial Chamber's Decision on The Assignment of Defense Counsel, Appeals Chamber, 1 November 2004, para. 19.

85. Ibid.

86. *Prosecutor* v. *Slobodan Milošević*, case No. IT-02-54, Withdrawal of Assigned Counsel, 27 October 2004.

87. *Prosecutor* v. *Slobodan Milošević*, case No. IT-02-54, Referral of Request to Withdraw, Deputy Registrar, 27 October 2004.

88. *Prosecutor* v. *Slobodan Milošević*, case No. IT-02-54, Decision on Assigned Counsel's Motion for Withdrawal, Trial Chamber III, 7 December 2004, para. 35.

89. Ibid., para. 17.

2.7.9 Prosecutor *v.* Dario Kordić and Mario Čerkez, *Appeals Judgement, 17 December 2004*[90]

This case relates to the conflict between the Croatian Defense Council (HVO) and the Bosnian Muslim Army in the Lašva Valley region of Central Bosnia from 1992 to 1993. Of particular importance was the massacre committed in the village of Ahmići in April 1993.[91]

In this Judgement the Appeals Chamber affirmed that Kordić 'as the responsible regional politician planned and instigated the crimes which occurred in Ahmići on 16 April 1993 and its associated hamlets',[92] and upheld his sentence of 25 years. The Trial Chamber had convicted him on the basis of Article 7(1) of the ICTY Statute for planning, instigating and ordering persecution, unlawful attacks on civilians and civilian objects, murder, inhumane acts, imprisonment, wanton destruction not justified by military necessity, plunder and destruction or wilful damage to institutions dedicated to religion or education.

With regard to Čerkez, who was a military commander of the Viteška Brigade of the HVO, the Appeals Chamber upheld most of the grounds of his appeal and reduced his sentence from 15 to 6 years imprisonment. It also upheld the finding of the Trial Chamber that there was not sufficient evidence to find him responsible for the crimes committed in Ahmići.

The Trial Chamber had convicted Čerkez on the basis of Article 7(1) for committing persecution and pursuant to Article 7(1) and 7(3) for crimes including unlawful attacks on civilians and civilian objects, murder, inhuman acts, imprisonment, taking civilians as hostages, wanton destruction not justified by military necessity, plunder, and destruction or wilful damage to institutions dedicated to religion or education. The Appeals Chamber overturned most of his convictions, but found him guilty under Article 7(1) for persecution, imprisonment and unlawful confinement of civilians. The Appeals Chamber stated that 'the provisions of Article 7(1) and Article 7(3) of the Statute connote distinct categories of criminal responsibility. However, [...] in relation to a particular count, it is not appropriate to convict under both Article 7(1) and Article 7(3) of the Statute.'[93] The Appeals Chamber found that in such a situation the Trial Chamber should convict on the basis of Article 7(1) only and treat the superior position of Čerkez as an aggravating factor in sentencing.

Finally, the Appeals Chamber also affirmed the findings of the Trial Chamber that 'Croatia exercised overall control over the HVO at the relevant time'[94] and 'provided leadership in planning, coordination and organization of the HVO'[95]

---

90. *Prosecutor* v. *Dario Kordić and Mario Čerkez*, case No. IT-95-14/2-A, Appeals Judgement, Appeals Chamber, 17 December 2004.
91. Ibid., para. 1.
92. Ibid., para. 700.
93. Ibid., para. 34.
94. Ibid., para. 369.
95. Ibid., para. 371.

and that there was an international armed conflict between Croatia and Bosnia and Herzegovina.[96]

Čerkez was released from prison on 2 December 2004 because the new sentence determined by the Appeals Chamber was less than the time he had spent in the UN Detention Unit.[97]

3. THE INTERNATIONAL CRIMINAL TRIBUNAL FOR RWANDA

3.1 Registry

In its annual report covering the period 1 July 2003 to 30 June 2004,[98] the ICTR stated that it had increased cooperation with states, institutions and non-governmental organisations. In 2004 the ICTR signed agreements on enforcement of sentences with Italy and Sweden.[99] The cooperation between the ICTR and the ICTY was expanded to include the Special Court for Sierra Leone and the International Criminal Court.[100]

3.2 Office of the Prosecutor

In January 2004 an Appeals Section of the Office of the Prosecutor was established. Until the appointment of a separate Prosecutor for the ICTR in 2003,[101] the ICTY and the ICTR had shared a common Appeals Section.[102]

---

96. Ibid., para. 374.

97. 'Order to release Mario Cerkez', Press Release of the Appeals Chamber, CVO/P.I.S./919, The Hague, 2 December 2004.

98. Ninth annual report of the International Criminal Tribunal for the Prosecution of Persons Responsible for Genocide and Other Serious Violations of International Humanitarian Law Committed in the Territory of Rwanda and Rwandan Citizens Responsible for Genocide and Other Such Violations Committed in the Territory of Neighbouring States between 1 January and 31 December 1994, UN Doc. A/59/183-S/2004/601, 27 July 2004.

99. The agreement with Italy was signed on 17 March 2004 and with Sweden on 27 April 2004. Four other states, Mali (12 February 1999), Benin (18 August 1999), Swaziland (30 August 2000) and France (14 March 2003), have also signed enforcement agreements with the ICTR. See L. Munlo, 'Enforcement of Sentences in ICTR', Paper presented at the Colloquium of Prosecutors of International Criminal Tribunals, Arusha 25-27 November 2004, <www.ictr.org>.

100. See Annual Report, *supra* n. 98, para. 52.

101. See 6 *YIHL* (2003) at p. 310.

102. See Annual Report, *supra* n. 98, para. 47.

3.3 The Chambers

3.3.1 *Appointment of judges*

Judge Charles Michael Dennis Byron (St. Kitts and Nevis) was sworn in as a permanent judge on 23 June 2004.[103] On 3 August 2004 Judge Joseph Asoka Nihal de Silva (Sri Lanka) was appointed as a permanent judge. He replaced Judge Asoka de Zoysa Gunawardana who resigned from the Tribunal. Therefore, the appointment of Judge Asoka de Silva was to have effect for the remainder of Judge Gunawardana's term, which was to expire in 2007.[104]

In September 2004 four *ad litem* judges were appointed to serve at the ICTR. The new judges were Taghrid Hikmet (Jordan); Karin Hökborg (Sweden); Gberdao Gustave Kam (Burkina Faso) and Seon Ki Park (Republic of Korea). The appointment of four new judges made possible the commencement of two new trials in September 2004.[105]

3.3.2 *Arrests and new indictments*

A former senior officer of the Rwanda Armed Forces, Colonel Ephrem Setako, was arrested in the Netherlands on 25 February at the request of the ICTR. On 17 November he was transferred to Arusha to face charges in connection with the killing of Tutsi civilians in Ruhengeri and Kigali-ville prefectures in 1994. Setako allegedly committed the crimes in concert with others who were also facing charges before the ICTR: Théoneste Bagosora, Anatole Nsengiyumva, Joseph Nzirorera, Casmir Bizimungu, Augustin Bizimungu and Juvénal Kajelijeli.[106]

On 19 July the ICTR took custody of Gaspard Kanyarukiga, who was arrested in South Africa on 16 July 2004 on suspicion of genocide, complicity in genocide, conspiracy to commit genocide and extermination as a crime against humanity. Kanyarukiga was allegedly involved in the killing of about 2,000 Tutsi civilians at the Nyange Church in the Kivumu commune of Kibuye prefecture in April 1994. He allegedly supervised the massacres.[107]

---

103. 'Sir Dennis Byron sworn in as permanent ICTR judge', ICTR/INFO-9-2-393.EN, Arusha, 23 June 2004.

104. 'Secretary-General appoints new Sri Lankan judge', ICTR/INFO-9-2-400.EN, Arusha, 9 August 2004.

105. 'Four new *ad litem* judges appointed to the Tribunal', ICTR/INFO-9-2-402.EN, Arusha, 9 September 2004.

106. 'Colonel Setako transferred to Arusha to face charges', ICTR/INFO-9-2-409.EN, Arusha, 18 November 2004.

107. 'Genocide suspect arrested and to be transferred to Arusha', ICTR/INFO-9-2-397.EN, Arusha, 19 July 2004. 'Genocide suspect Gaspard Kanyarukiga transferred to Arusha', ICTR/INFO-9-2-398.EN, Arusha, 20 July 2004.

3.4 Judgements[108]

3.4.1 Prosecutor *v.* Jean de Dieu Kamuhanda, *Judgement, 22 January 2004*[109]

On 22 January 2004 Trial Chamber II convicted Jean de Dieu Kamuhanda of genocide and crimes against humanity (extermination) under Article 6(1) of the Statute. He was sentenced to imprisonment for the remainder of his life for each of these crimes, the sentences to run concurrently.

With regard to the charge of genocide, the Chamber found that the accused participated in the killings occurring in the Gikomero Parish Compound in the Kigali-Rural prefecture, which systematically targeted Tutsi civilians. The Chamber found it established that the accused had the specific intent to destroy the Tutsi ethnic group. Further, it was proved that the participation of the accused amounted to ordering and instigating others to carry out the killings and to aiding and abetting, through the distribution of weapons and by leading attackers to the place where the killings were to take place.[110]

The Chamber decided not to make a finding in relation to the charge of murder as a crime against humanity. The Chamber noted that insufficient distinction was made in the indictment between the crime of murder and the crime of extinction as crimes against humanity. No specification of the identities of the victims of the alleged crime of murder had been included in the indictment. Further, considering the evidence in the case, the Chamber found that the crimes could better be described as targeting of populations or groups of people for purposes of extermination, than specifying them as murder.[111]

During the period relevant to the case, the accused held the office of Minister of Higher Education and Scientific Research in the interim government. The prosecution attempted to demonstrate that the crimes of the accused, carried out within his position of authority within the administration of the country, were closely related to the hostilities or committed in conjunction with the armed conflict. The Chamber found that insufficient evidence had been brought forward in order to find such a nexus. Consequently, the accused was not guilty under Article 4 of the Statute, which requires that the crimes be committed in a non-international armed conflict and that there was a nexus between the acts and the armed conflict.[112]

Nevertheless, the position of the accused was brought up again in the context of the aggravating factors at the sentencing stage. The Chamber was of the opinion that the high position held by Kamuhanda aggravated the criminal acts. The accused 'was in the position to know and to appreciate the dignity and value of life,

---

108. The following case summaries are not intended to be comprehensive. The aim is to give a broad overview of the legal and factual findings, and to highlight any original jurisprudence and significant divergences from earlier cases.

109. *Prosecutor* v. *Jean de Dieu Kamuhanda*, case No. ICTR-95-54A-T, Judgement, Trial Chamber II, 22 January 2004.

110. Ibid., paras. 645-648.

111. Ibid., paras. 686-687.

112. Ibid., paras. 737-743.

and also the value and importance of a peaceful coexistence between communities. He was in the position to promote the value of tolerance. Instead of doing so, he blamed people who were living peacefully for not taking part in the campaign of violence. He instigated and led an attack to kill people who had taken shelter in a place universally recognised to be a sanctuary.'[113] Accordingly, the Chamber found the appropriate sentence to be life imprisonment.

Judge Maqutu's Separate and Concurring Opinion focused on some of the witness testimonies that had been heard. He doubted the credibility of some of the testimonies and disagreed with the acceptance of some of them by the majority. Judge Maqutu concurred with the majority of the Trial Chamber with regard to the final findings and the sentencing.[114]

3.4.2 Prosecutor *v.* André Ntagerura, Samuel Imanishimwe and Emmanuel Bagambiki (Cyangugu *case*), *Judgement and Sentence, 25 February 2004*[115]

On 25 February 2004 the Trial Chamber convicted Samuel Imanishimwe of genocide, crimes against humanity (extermination, murder, imprisonment and torture) and serious violations of common Article 3 of the Geneva Conventions (torture and cruel treatment). He was sentenced to 27 years' imprisonment. The two other accused in the same case, André Ntagerura and Emmanuel Bagambiki, were acquitted of all charges.

At the time of the crimes charged in the indictment, André Ntagerura served as Minister of Transport and Communications in the Rwandan interim government. Emmanuel Bagambiki was the prefect in the Cyangugu prefecture. Imanishimwe, on the other hand, was a lieutenant in the Rwandan Armed Forces and served as the acting commander of the Cyangugu military camp (also called Karmabo military camp).[116] All the accused were charged with genocide, crimes against humanity and serious violations of Article 3 common to the Geneva Conventions (Art. 4 (a) of the Statute) (hereinafter, serious violations of common Art. 3). While no evidence was submitted by the prosecution in support of some of the charges against Ntagerura, which were consequently not considered by the Chamber,[117] the rest of the charges against him and all charges against Bagambiki were found not to have been proven beyond a reasonable doubt at trial.

The Trial Chamber found that Imanishimwe, who himself gave a detailed description of the command structure within the Karmabo military camp, had effective control over his soldiers and the material ability to prevent or punish offences carried out by them. With regard to some charges of genocide, crimes against

113. Ibid., para. 764.

114. *Prosecutor* v. *Jean de Dieu Kamuhanda*, case No. ICTR-95-54A-T, Judge Maqutu's Separate and Concurring Opinion on the Verdict, 22 January 2004.

115. *Prosecutor* v. *André Ntagerura, Samuel Imanishimwe and Emmanuel Bagambiki*, case No. ICTR-99-46-T, Judgement and Sentence, 25 February 2004.

116. Ibid., paras. 5, 12-13.

117. Ibid., para. 40.

humanity and serious violations of common Article 3, the Chamber found that with regard to the massacre of Tutsi refugees at the Gashirabwoba football field, there was not sufficient evidence to show the participation of the accused himself in the attack, leading to responsibility under Article 6(1). However, the accused should have prevented the attack or punished his subordinates for their participation in the killings. By failing to do so the accused incurred responsibility under Article 6(3).[118]

It is worth noting that two dissenting opinions on the judgement were brought forward (Judges Williams and Dolenc). In brief, Judge Williams found that enough evidence was presented in order to find Emmanuel Bagambiki responsible for genocide, crimes against humanity and serious violations of common Article 3.[119] Judge Dolenc addressed the fact that Imanishimwe was found guilty of genocide, crimes against humanity and serious violations of common Article 3 in relation to the same events. According to Dolenc, this was a case of ideal concurrence of crimes based on the same facts. Accordingly, Dolenc would have found Imanishimwe guilty only of genocide in relation to the massacre at the Gashirabwoba football field and for crimes against humanity at the Karambo military camp.[120]

3.4.3 Prosecutor *v.* Sylvestre Gacumbitsi, *Judgement, 17 June 2004*[121]

On 17 June 2004 Sylvestre Gacumbitsi was convicted of genocide, crimes against humanity (extermination and rape) and acquitted him of complicity in genocide and a crime against humanity (murder). He was sentenced to 30 years imprisonment.[122]

At the time of the events addressed in the indictment, the accused held the position of *bourgmestre* of Rusumo commune, Kibungo prefecture. The Trial Chamber found that, in April 1994 the accused participated in meetings and instructed others to hold meetings to incite Hutus to massacre Tutsis. He also publicly incited people to attack Tutsis. Later that month the accused, among other things, participated in attacks against Tutsi refugees. With regard to these and other offences, the Trial Chamber found that the accused bore responsibility for planning, instigating, ordering, committing and aiding and abetting the commission of the crime of genocide. The accused was also found responsible for planning, instigating, ordering and aiding and abetting the extermination of Tutsis as a crime against humanity. With regard to the crime of rape as a crime against humanity, the accused was held responsible for instigation. The Chamber addressed the definition of rape, as defined in the *Akayesu* case and later in the *Kunarac* Appeals Judgement, and pointed out that although these definitions covered additional acts, all penetration

---

118. Ibid., paras. 652-654.

119. *Prosecutor* v. *André Ntagerura, Samuel Imanishimwe and Emmanuel Bagambiki* (*Cyangugu* case), case No. ICTR-99-46-T, Dissenting Opinion of Judge Williams, 25 February 2004.

120. *Prosecutor* v. *André Ntagerura, Samuel Imanishimwe and Emmanuel Bagambiki* (*Cyangugu* case), case No. ICTR-99-46-T, Separate and Dissenting Opinion of Judge Dolenc, 25 February 2004. See in particular paras. 70-71.

121. *Prosecutor* v. *Sylvestre Gacumbitsi*, case No. ICTR-2001-64-T, Judgement, 17 June 2004.

122. Ibid., para. 356.

of the victim's sexual organ by the sexual organ of the assailant or by any other object was certainly covered by the definition.[123] In the present case, Tutsi women and girls were raped by the assailants themselves and by the assailants inserting sticks into their vagina. The Chamber apparently considered it necessary to point out that the threats of the accused that in case of resistance the victims would be killed, in addition to the fact that the perpetrators were those persons that the victims were fleeing from, showed the victims' lack of consent to the rapes.[124] The accused was found criminally liable for instigating the rapes.[125]

The Trial Chamber did not find it necessary to consider the superior responsibility of the accused in relation to any of the crimes, but pointed out that his position and his influential personality constituted an aggravating circumstance at sentencing.[126] On the other hand, the earlier work of the accused as *bourgmestre* and his good character and good relations with the Tutsi prior to these events were considered in mitigation of the sentence.

3.4.4 Prosecutor *v.* Emmanuel Ndindabahizi, *Judgement, 15 July 2004*[127]

On 15 July 2004 Trial Chamber I unanimously convicted Emmanuel Ndindabahizi of genocide and crimes against humanity (extermination and murder) and sentenced him to imprisonment for the remainder of his life.[128]

At the time of the genocide, Ndindabahizi was the Minister of Finance of the Rwandan Interim Government.[129] He was charged with the crime of genocide in relation to the events at Gitwa Hill, a site where thousands of Tutsi refugees had gathered and which was encircled by a large number of mostly civilian attackers, and at roadblocks in Gitesi Commune, where Tutsis were killed. Two aspects in relation to the genocide charge are worth noting. The Chamber noted that the indictment charged the accused with genocide, without clearly setting out the mode of culpable participation of the accused. However, in its closing arguments, the prosecution specified that the accused should be held guilty of instigating, and of aiding and abetting, genocide.[130] In a footnote the Chamber pointed out that the submission by the prosecution in its closing arguments was not to add to, but to narrow, the prosecution case. Consequently, the Chamber found the accused guilty of instigating and aiding and abetting genocide in relation to the events at Gitwa Hill and in Gitesi Commune.

The second interesting finding concerned the killing of a certain person, known as Nors, at the Gaseke roadblock in Gitesi Commune. Nors was the only person in relation to whom enough evidence was gathered to prove a killing.[131] Accordingly,

123. Ibid., para. 321.
124. Ibid., para. 325.
125. Ibid., para. 330.
126. Ibid., para. 345.
127. *Prosecutor* v. *Emmanuel Ndindabahizi*, case No. ICTR-2001-71-T, Judgement, 15 July 2004.
128. Ibid., para. 511.
129. Ibid., para. 6.
130. Ibid., para. 455.
131. Ibid., para. 466.

the Chamber had to consider whether the killing of this one person constituted genocide. It found that the fact that a single person was killed 'does not negate the perpetrators' clear intent, which was to destroy the Tutsi population'.[132] However, the Chamber also had to determine that the targeting of Nors was based on his ethnicity. Based on a witness testimony, the Chamber found that Nors' father was German and his mother Rwandese. While normally in Rwandan culture, the ethnicity of the father determines the ethnic identity of the child, the situation in this case was different because the father was of an ethnicity entirely foreign to Rwanda. Testimony showed that Nors had physical traits of a Tutsi, and as these were an important indication of ethic identity in Rwanda at the time, the Chamber inferred that Nors was targeted because of his ethnic identity. Therefore, he was a victim of genocide.[133]

While the accused was charged with more than one criminal offence arising out of a single event, the Chamber held that genocide contains materially distinct elements from extermination and murder, and that therefore, it was appropriate to enter multiple convictions against the accused. The Chamber took the sentencing practice of the ICTR and the ICTY, as well as the general sentencing practice in Rwanda, into consideration, and found the appropriate punishment to be life imprisonment.[134]

3.4.5 Prosecutor *v.* Eliézer Niyitegeka, *Appeals Judgement, 9 July 2004*[135]

On 9 July 2004 the Appeals Chamber affirmed the trial judgement which Eliézer Niyitegeka had appealed. The Trial Chamber had convicted him of genocide, conspiracy to commit genocide, direct and public incitement to commit genocide, and crimes against humanity (murder, extermination and other inhumane acts) and sentenced him to imprisonment for the remainder of his life.

In his appeal brief, Niyitegeka presented 53 grounds of appeal challenging the decision by the Trial Chamber of 16 May 2003.[136] Regarding two grounds, concerning lack of sufficient notice of specific allegations in the indictment against the accused, the Appeals Chamber recognised that the Trial Chamber had erred in its judgement.[137] The error did not, however, invalidate its decision as the conviction on each of these counts rested on more facts than those in relation to which the Trial Chamber had erred. Accordingly, the Appeals Chamber dismissed the appeal in its entirety.

The discussion by the Appeals Chamber with regard to the ground of appeal concerning the definition of genocide deserves specific mention. The appellant submitted that the Trial Chamber in its interpretation of the definition failed to give the words 'as such' their true meaning. According to the appellant the term

---

132. Ibid., para. 471.
133. Ibid., paras. 467-469.
134. Ibid., paras. 510-511.
135. *Prosecutor* v. *Eliézer Niyitegeka*, case No. ICTR-96-14-A, Appeals Judgement, 9 July 2004.
136. Ibid., fn. 3.
137. Ibid., paras. 223 and 235.

'as such' should be understood as meaning 'solely'. From this followed that certain crimes would constitute genocide only where the acts were committed against a group '*solely because they were members of such a group*'.[138] The Appeals Chamber rejected this view and held that the words 'as such' have 'the *effet utile* of drawing a clear distinction between mass murder and crimes in which the perpetrator targets a specific group because of its nationality, race, ethnicity or religion'.[139] Thus it considered that the Trial Chamber was right in holding that the term meant that in order for acts to be considered as genocide they should be 'committed against the victims *because of* their membership in the protected group, but not *solely* because of such membership'.[140]

3.4.6 Prosecutor *v.* Elizaphan Ntakirutimana and Gérard Ntakirutimana, *Appeals Judgement, 13 December 2004*[141]

On 13 December 2004 the ICTR Appeals Chamber upheld the convictions and sentences of Elizaphan Ntakirutimana and his son, Dr Gérard Ntakirutimana. The Trial Chamber had concluded that Gérard Ntakirutimana had the requisite intent for genocide and, in the case of the killing of one victim, was individually criminally responsible for his death and thereby guilty of genocide. This same killing was the basis for his conviction for murder as a crime against humanity. He was sentenced to 25 years imprisonment. The Trial Chamber had found Elizaphan Ntakirutimana guilty of genocide for having 'conveyed armed attackers to the Mugonero Complex in his vehicle [...]', for which it sentenced him to 10 years imprisonment.

The Appellants appealed all the factual findings of the Trial Chamber and alleged several legal errors. Their principal contentions were that the indictments did not set forth the material facts with enough detail to inform them clearly of the charges against them and impaired their ability to prepare their defence. In this regard, the Appeals Chamber found that the indictment concerning the Mugonero Complex did not contain the victim's name or any of the circumstances surrounding his killing that were eventually found in the Judgement. It also found that the prosecution was in a position to plead specific material facts in the indictment regarding this killing but failed to do so. The Appeals Chamber found that this failure rendered the counts of genocide and murder as a crime against humanity against Gérard Ntakirutimana defective. However, the Appeals Chamber affirmed his conviction for genocide in relation to events which occurred at Bisesero, but found that his responsibility was that of an aider and abettor, and further quashed his conviction for murder as a crime against humanity under this indictment.

The Appeals Chamber also found that the Trial Chamber had erred in law in considering that an element of the crime of extermination is that the victims must be 'named or described' persons. It found that Gérard Ntakirutimana had incurred

---

138. Ibid., para. 47.
139. Ibid., para 53.
140. Ibid.
141. *Prosecutor* v. *Elizaphan Ntakirutimana and Gérard Ntakirutimana*, cases Nos. ICTR-96-10-A and ICTR-96-17-A, Appeals Judgement, 13 December 2004.

individual criminal responsibility for aiding and abetting extermination of the Tutsi as a crime against humanity.

The Appeals Chamber confirmed the conviction of Elizaphan Ntakirutimana for aiding and abetting genocide and entered a conviction for aiding and abetting extermination as a crime against humanity.

4. SPECIAL COURT FOR SIERRA LEONE

4.1 **Election and appointment of judges**

Judge Benjamin Mutanga Itoe of Cameroon was elected Presiding Judge of the Trial Chamber on 1 June 2004. He was elected for a renewable term of one year.[142] On 27 May 2004 Judge Emmanuel Ayoola of Nigeria was named the Presiding Judge of the Appeals Chamber. Thereby he also assumed the position of President of the Special Court for a period of one year.[143]

4.2 **Decisions**

4.2.1 Prosecutor *v.* Morris Kallon and Brima Bazzy Kamara, *Decision on Challenge to Jurisdiction, Lomé Accord Amnesty, 13 March 2004*[144]

The main argument of the motions submitted by the defence in these cases was that the Special Court should not exercise jurisdiction over crimes committed before July 1999, for which an amnesty was provided by the Lomé Accord.[145] The central question to be decided by the Chamber was whether the grant of an amnesty by virtue of the Lomé Accord deprived the Court of jurisdiction to try the crimes charged in the present case.[146] The Chamber found that the Lomé Accord brought an internal armed conflict to an end, but could not be considered an international instrument creating rights or obligations regulated by international law.[147] Whether the agreement was binding on the government of Sierra Leone was not a question to be answered by the Court, but the Chamber concluded that that question did not affect the jurisdiction of the Court to prosecute crimes contained in Articles 2 to 4 of its Statute. The Lomé Accord did not deprive 'an international court such as the Special Court' of its jurisdiction.[148]

---

142. 'Judge Itoe takes over as Presiding Judge of Trial Chamber', Press Release of the Special Court for Sierra Leone, 4 June 2004, <http://www.sc-sl.org/Press/pressrelease-060404.html>.

143. 'New President of the Special Court for Sierra Leone', Press Release of the Special Court for Sierra Leone, 27 May 2004, <http://www.sc-sl.org/Press/pressrelease-052704.html>.

144. *Prosecutor* v. *Morris Kallon and Brima Bazzy Kamara*, case Nos. SCSL-2004-15-AR72(E) and SCSL-2004-16-AR72(E), Decision on Challenge to Jurisdiction, Lomé Accord Amnesty, 13 March 2004.

145. Ibid., para. 1.

146. Ibid., para. 65.

147. Ibid., para. 42.

148. Ibid., paras. 86-90.

4.2.2 Prosecutor *v.* Moinina Fofana, *Decision on Preliminary Motion on Lack of Jurisdiction Materiae: Nature of the Armed Conflict, 25 May 2004*[149]

In a preliminary motion of 14 November 2003 the accused, Moinina Fofana, argued that Articles 3 and 4 of the Statute of the Special Court limit the jurisdiction of the Court to non-international armed conflicts only.[150] This was of relevance for the present case, as the defence argued that during the period for which the accused was indicted the armed conflict was international in character. According to the defence, the Court lacked subject matter jurisdiction in the case.[151] Both the prosecution and the defence agreed that the Statute of the Special Court was drawn up with a non-international armed conflict in mind.[152] However, the Appeals Chamber found that even if the drafting history of the Statute showed that the armed conflict in Sierra Leone had been considered as non-international, this did not necessarily mean that the Court lacked jurisdiction in relation to crimes committed in an international armed conflict.[153]

The Appeals Chamber considered the scope of applicability of Articles 3 and 4 of the Statute and noted that Article 3 (Violations of Article 3 common to the Geneva Conventions and of Additional Protocol II) was based on common Article 3 of the Geneva Conventions and Additional Protocol II. It found that common Article 3 constituted a minimum standard of protection that made part of the rules applicable to international armed conflicts also applicable in non-international armed conflict. The Chamber found support for this reasoning in the case law of the ICJ and the *ad hoc* tribunals.[154] It concluded that '[w]here the rules are identical in respect of both internal and international armed conflict it cannot follow that because the provision in the Statute is framed in terms of the treaty provision applicable to internal armed conflicts, the Court has no jurisdiction to apply the provision in the context of an international armed conflict'.[155]

With regard to Article 4 of the Statute (Other serious violations of international humanitarian law), the Chamber noted the fact that the wording of the article seemed to be borrowed from Article 8(2)(e) of the Statute of the ICC, which is applicable to non-international armed conflicts.[156] However, Article 4 did not contain any specific reference to the nature of the armed conflict. The Chamber considered that where the wording of a provision may have been borrowed from a certain treaty it did not follow that the context of applicability of the provision was incorporated. The Court thus found that there was no merit to the argument that the

---

149. *Prosecutor* v. *Moinina Fofana*, case No. SCSL-2004-14-AR72, Decision on Preliminary Motion on Lack of Jurisdiction *Materiae*: Nature of the Armed Conflict, 25 May 2004.

150. Ibid., para. 1.

151. Ibid., paras. 1-2.

152. Ibid., para. 18.

153. Ibid., para. 19.

154. Ibid., paras. 20-25.

155. Ibid., para. 26.

156. Ibid., para. 28.

Court's jurisdiction to apply Article 4 was restricted to non-international armed conflicts.[157]

Having decided that the applicability of Articles 3 and 4 of the Statute was not restricted by the nature of the armed conflict, the Appeals Chamber did not consider it necessary to make a factual decision regarding the nature of the conflict at a certain point in time. It noted that the Appeals Chamber was not a trier of fact and that, therefore, any legal questions that followed on the factual decision on the character of a specific conflict were not relevant at this stage.[158]

4.2.3 Prosecutor *v.* Sam Hinga Norman, *Decision on Preliminary Motion Based on Lack of Jurisdiction (Child Recruitment), 31 May 2004*[159]

The defence of the accused Sam Hinga Norman submitted that the Special Court did not have jurisdiction to try the accused for crimes under Article 4(c) of the Statute, which criminalises the recruitment of children under the age of 15 years into the armed forces. According to the defence, the application of this provision would violate the principle of *nullum crimen sine lege*, as no crime of child recruitment existed as part of customary international law at the time relevant to the case at hand. It was not disputed that there existed an obligation on states to refrain from recruiting child soldiers, but according to the defence, the obligation as laid down in international legal instruments did not criminalise this activity.[160]

The Chamber showed that child recruitment was prohibited both under conventional and customary international law and held that the central question to be considered was whether the act also gave rise to individual criminal responsibility at the time of the crimes allegedly committed by the accused.[161] The Chamber referred to legality discussions by the ICTY and the ICTR, according to which violations of the laws and customs of war entailed criminal responsibility. It also held that the criminalisation of child recruitment in the ICC Statute was recognised as a reflection of international customary law. As the first draft of the ICC Statute was produced in 1994, the criminalisation of war crimes predated the time of the crimes in the present case. To further support its findings, the Chamber noted that contrary to the allegation of the defence, several states had criminalised the recruitment of children under the age of 15 in their national legislation.[162] The Chamber considered there to be enough basis for concluding that child recruitment had become a crime entailing individual criminal responsibility under customary international law, i.e., even before it was explicitly set out as a crime in treaty law.[163]

---

157. Ibid., para. 30.

158. Ibid., paras. 31-32.

159. *Prosecutor* v. *Sam Hinga Norman*, case No. SCSL-2004-14-AR72(E), Decision on Preliminary Motion Based on Lack of Jurisdiction (Child Recruitment), 31 May 2004.

160. Ibid., para. 1.

161. Ibid., paras. 10-24. The crimes were allegedly committed after 30 November 1996. See *Prosecutor* v. *Samuel Hinga Norman, Moinina Fofana and Allieu Kondewa*, case No. SCSL-03-14-I, Indictment, 4 February 2004, para. 9.

162. See *Norman*, n. 159, at paras. 30-51.

163. Ibid., para. 53.

Judge Robertson appended his dissenting opinion to the decision, in which he held that child recruitment did not become an international crime until the signing of the Rome Statute for the ICC in July 1998. Accordingly, the accused in this case should not be prosecuted for the crime of child recruitment.[164]

164. Ibid., Dissenting Opinion of Justice Robertson, para. 47.

HEAD AGAINST THE WALL? ISRAEL'S REJECTION OF THE ADVISORY OPINION ON THE LEGAL CONSEQUENCE OF THE CONSTRUCTION OF A WALL IN THE OCCUPIED PALESTINIAN TERRITORIES[1]

Yuval Shany[2]

1. INTRODUCTION

In a concise order, issued on 19 August 2004, the Supreme Court of Israel (HCJ) ordered the Israeli government to respond to a new petition brought by a number of Palestinians and the Association for Civil Rights in Israel (ACRI) against the route of the West Bank separation barrier (or separation wall)[3] near the West Bank villages of Boudrous and Shukba.[4] Specifically, the order invited the government to refer to the recent advisory opinion of the International Court of Justice (ICJ) on the legality of the same barrier. On 23 February 2005 the Office of the Attorney General at the Ministry of Justice filed with the Court the state's response to the petition. More than half of the comprehensive 142-page memorandum submitted by the state addresses the implications of the ICJ advisory opinion on the *Wall* upon the case at hand. After an exhaustive review of the opinion, the written response concludes that the 'advisory opinion has no bearing upon the claims at hand, and the claims should be adjudicated in accordance with the factual and normative framework designed by the Supreme Court, as manifested in the *Beit*

2. Hersch Lauterpacht Chair in Public International Law, Faculty of Law, Hebrew University, Jerusalem. The author provided certain consultative services to the government of Israel in the context of the separation barrier litigation before the ICJ and the Israel Supreme Court. However, the views expressed here are his private views and do not reflect in any way upon the views of the government of Israel. The author would like to thank Dr Orna Ben-Naftali, Dr Moshe Hirsch and Ms Keren Michaeli for their useful comments to previous drafts of this note.

3. A controversy surrounds the proper terminology that should be used to describe the system of walls, ditches, fences, patrol roads etc. which Israel has been constructing in the West Bank since 2002. While Israel officially refers to the structure as the 'security fence', the ICJ, following the UN General Assembly, chose the term 'separation wall'. In contrast, the Secretary General's Report on the matter referred to the complex of fortifications as a 'separation barrier'. Report of the Secretary-General prepared pursuant to General Assembly resolution ES-10/13, 23 November 2003, UN Doc. A/ES 10/248 (2003). I will mostly use the term 'barrier', which I regard as most accurate (more than 90 percent of the wall/fence consists of barbed wire and non-wall-like structures) to address the aforementioned complex.

4. *Alian* v. *Prime Minister*, H.C.J. 4825/04, Order of 19 August 2004.

Yearbook of International Humanitarian Law
Volume 7 - 2004 - pp. 352-372 DOI 10.1017/S1389135904003526

Sourik case'.[5] Since the state's response represents the first comprehensive statement of the position of the state of Israel with relation to the ICJ advisory opinion, it is indicative of the degree of influence that the advisory opinion is likely to have upon Israel's future conduct in the Occupied Territories.

This short note seeks to critically analyse Israel's reaction to the ICJ advisory opinion in the context of the *Alian* litigation. While I accept the basic thrust of the Israeli position – that the deficient fact-finding and fact-analysis process undertaken by the ICJ renders the advisory opinion inapplicable to the specific facts of the *Alian* case – I argue that the HCJ decision in *Beit Sourik*, upon which the state relies in *Alian*, shares some of the deficiencies of the ICJ advisory opinion. In particular, I criticise the state's unwillingness to present a coherent legal theory on certain important aspects affecting the legality of the barrier and argue that this omission leaves in place regrettable legal ambiguities, which unduly complicate the legal situation in the Occupied Territories.

Chapter 2 of this note briefly recaptures the decisions of the HCJ in *Beit Sourik* and the ICJ in the *Wall* advisory opinion, and introduces the facts of the *Alian* case. Chapter 3 then describes the main points raised in the state's written response in *Alain*. Chapter 4 discusses some of the main problems common to the HCJ and ICJ decisions: artificial distinctions, controversial premises, and reluctance to fully elucidate the governing law. It also suggests that the state's response in *Alian* fails to remedy most of these problems. The concluding segment offers some general observations and speculates on the future direction of the separation barrier litigation in Israel.

2. BACKGROUND DEVELOPMENTS: *BEIT SOURIK*, THE HAGUE AND BEYOND

2.1 The *Beit Sourik* case

The decision of the government of Israel to construct a separation barrier in the West Bank, which was adopted on 23 June 2002 in the midst of an unprecedented wave of suicide bombing attacks against major population centres in Israel,[6] and the ensuing implementation of that decision, gave rise to numerous legal proceedings in Israel. These proceedings, brought by Palestinian individuals and organisations affected by the barrier (sometimes with the active support of Israeli NGOs) challenged both the authority to establish the separation barrier and the lawfulness

5. *Alian* v. *Prime Minister*, H.C.J. 4825/04, Written Response, 23 February 2005, para. 552 (unofficial translation). See *Beit Sourik Village Council* v. *Government of Israel*, H.C.J. 2056/04, 2004(2) *Takdin-Supreme* 3035 (hereafter, *Beit Sourik*). The decision of Israel to reject the relevance of the Advisory Opinion for domestic law purposes perhaps comes as no surprise to observers of Israel's ambivalent attitude towards international bodies. See J. Dugard, 'The implications for the legal profession of conflicts between international law and national law', 46 *South Texas LR* (2005) pp. 579-594, at p. 586.

6. Prime Minister's Office, Press Release, 24 June 2002, <http://www.pmo.gov.il/PMO/Archive/Spokesman/2002/יוני/Spokesman6892.htm> (in Hebrew).

of the route selected for that purpose. Specifically, it has been argued that the barrier's route was dictated by political considerations – i.e., the desire to solidify Israel's grasp on West Bank areas populated by Jewish settlements – and not by considerations of military necessity.[7]

Although some of the early petitions against the separation barrier were dismissed on technical grounds or settled out of court, the Supreme Court of Israel eventually rendered a comprehensive judgement, which outlined the main legal parameters that govern the lawfulness of the barrier: In *Beit Sourik Village Council* v. *Government of Israel* (decided on 30 June 2004) the Court held that while the military authorities were entitled to construct a separation barrier in the Occupied Territories for security reasons, the actual route of the barrier must adequately balance the state's security needs and the humanitarian interests of the local Palestinian population. Applying this criterion to the 40 km segment of the barrier reviewed in the *Beit Sourik* proceedings, the Court held that some 30 km of the route inflicted disproportional harm upon Palestinian residents and thus had to be rerouted.[8] In response to the Court's decision, the government announced some major changes in the route of the barrier – which included the removal of a few existing segments and redrawing of several plans for the remaining segments of the barrier, in a manner that runs more or less in proximity to the 1967 'Green Line'.[9]

2.2 The ICJ Advisory Opinion

In parallel to these developments within Israel, the ICJ was seized in December 2003 of a request for an advisory opinion on the legal consequences of the construction of the wall in the Palestinian Occupied Territories, referred to it by the UN General Assembly.[10] The Court's opinion, which was rendered on 9 July 2004, asserted that although an occupier may in principle take security measures which infringe upon the individual rights of an occupied population, the construction of the wall by Israel is linked indissolubly to the construction of the settlements in the Occupied Territories and to measures designed to strengthen Israel's exercise of sovereignty over East Jerusalem; hence, the wall might lead to the *de facto* annexation of parts of the West Bank.[11] In other words, the Court seemed to

---

7. See e.g., *Beit Sourik, supra* n. 5, at para. 10.

8. For discussion of the specific findings of the HCJ in *Beit Sourik*, see Y. Shany, 'Israel', Correspondents' Reports, in this volume at pp. 498-520.

9. *Alian*, Written Response, *supra* n. 5, at paras. 22 and 88-89. These changes have according to the Israeli authorities led to a significant reduction in the total area of the West Bank situated west of the barrier.

10. UN GA res. ES 10/14 (2003), UN Doc. A/ES-10/248 (2003).

11. *Legal Consequences of the Construction of a Wall in the Occupied Palestinians Territory* (hereafter *OPT Wall*), Advisory Opinion, 9 July 2004, at paras. 121-122, <http://www.icj-cij.org>. 'Whilst the Court notes the assurance given by Israel that the construction of the wall does not amount to annexation and that the wall is of a temporary nature (...), it nevertheless cannot remain indifferent to certain fears expressed to it that the route of the wall will prejudge the future frontier between Israel and Palestine, and the fear that Israel may integrate the settlements and their means of access.'

imply that the predominant goal or effect of the construction of the wall was political and not military.

In the same vein, the Court opined that Israel failed to show that the humanitarian law and human rights law violations caused by the wall were justified by military necessity or by general defences available under the law of state responsibility.[12] Having found that there was no justifiable claim of necessity which could sustain the lawfulness of the wall, the Court felt no need to review its proportionality. Consequently, it held that the construction of the wall was unlawful; it had to be dismantled and compensation had to be paid.[13]

It should be noted that Israel's cooperation with the ICJ proceedings had been very limited: Israel did not request the appointment of an *ad hoc* judge, as it arguably could have;[14] its written pleadings addressed only the jurisdictional aspects of the advisory procedure (although, on occasion, it alluded to some substantive arguments); and it declined to participate at the oral stage of the proceedings. This limited cooperation approach was designed to reconcile a few conflicting policies: the political futility of ignoring the proceedings altogether and the need to exercise damage control, on the one hand, and the reluctance to legitimate the outcome of the proceedings by way of active engagement, on the other hand.[15] However, the end result was that Israel's ability to influence the factual docket compiled by the ICJ and to sustain its arguments on the security justifications underlying the construction of the barrier were seriously impaired.

A comparative study of the *Beit Sourik* and *Wall* decisions suggests a closer degree of similarity in legal analysis than what might be initially perceived: Like its Hague counterpart, the HCJ opined that 'the military commander cannot order the construction of the separation fence if his reasons are political. The separation fence cannot be motivated by a desire to 'annex' territories to the State of Israel. The purpose of the separation fence cannot be to draw a political border.'[16] In other words, a 'political' barrier route would be unlawful according to both courts. Similarly, the two courts affirmed that the route of the barrier is subject to conditions of military necessity and proportionality.[17] So, the main difference between the two decisions – their inconsistent findings on the necessity of the route of the barrier –

---

12. Ibid., at paras. 135-140.

13. Ibid., at paras. 148-153.

14. See ibid., Separate Opinion of Judge Owade, at para. 19. Cf., *Western Sahara*, Advisory Opinion, *ICJ Rep.* (1975) p. 12.

15. Arguably, the ICJ itself contributed to Israel's strategy of incomplete cooperation by refusing to separate the hearings on jurisdiction from the merits of the case. *Legal Consequences of the Construction of a Wall in the Occupied Palestinian Territory*, Order of 19 December 2003, <http://icj-cij.org>. Since Israel argued in the jurisdictional phase of the proceedings that the Court does not have sufficient information to render the opinion, it was in an awkward position to provide detailed arguments on the merits before its jurisdictional objections were dismissed.

16. *Beit Sourik*, *supra* n. 5, at para. 27.

17. It may be noted that the discussion by the ICJ of other potential grounds of illegality – self determination and human rights – and other potential justifications – self-defense and state of necessity – that were not discussed by the HCJ seem to have had little effect on the ICJ's final conclusions (i.e., had the ICJ accepted Israel's military necessity plea, it would probably have rejected the other challenges against the route of the barrier).

seems to derive not from divergences in legal analysis, but rather from different fact assessment methodologies. As we shall see below, this last point was underlined by the state's response in *Alian.*

2.3 The *Alian* case

The petitioners in *Alian* challenged the lawfulness of the route of the separation barrier running in proximity to two West Bank Palestinian villages – Boudrous and Shukba (located roughly 20 km north-west of Ramallah). According to the petition, the construction of the barrier in this area will cut off the villages' agricultural land and deprive local residents of their source of livelihood. Hence, to the degree that the route deviates from the Green Line and traverses into the West Bank it is both unnecessary and disproportional. As indicated above, the HCJ required the state to respond to the petition, and present the military considerations which could justify infringement of the petitioners' rights. However, the Court also urged the state to address, in the context of the response, the potential implications for the proceedings of the ICJ advisory opinion.

3. THE STATE'S RESPONSE IN *ALIAN*: DISTINGUISHING AND DISCREDITING THE ICJ OPINION

The state's response in *Alian* may be divided into three parts. The first part lays out some general arguments supporting the legality of the barrier's route. The second part explains that the barrier's route near the villages of Boudrous and Shukba conforms to the legal parameters pronounced by the HCJ in *Beit Sourik.* The third and most significant part of the response discusses the relevance of the advisory opinion and urges the HCJ to refrain from applying the ICJ's findings to the case at hand.

3.1 General arguments on the legality of the barrier

According to the state, since the beginning of the second *intifada* (September 2000), the situation in the Occupied Territories has been one of an armed conflict, simultaneously governed by the laws of belligerent occupation and the laws of war.[18] Arguably, this does not present a serious problem of norm-coordination in the context of the separation barrier cases, because both branches of IHL facilitate the taking or requisitioning of private property for the purpose of constructing fortifications (such as the separation barrier), provided that conditions of necessity and proportionality are met.[19] Furthermore, the state undertook to apply the more

---

18. *Beit Sourik, supra* n. 5, at para. 170.

19. Geneva Convention Relative to the Protection of Civilian Persons in Time of War, 12 August 1949, Art. 53, 75 *UNTS* 287 (hereafter, Geneva IV); Hague Regulations Respecting the Laws and Customs of War, Arts. 23(g) and 54, 18 October 1907, 36 *Stat.* 2277; *TS* 539 (hereafter, Hague Regulations)

stringent conditions found in the laws of belligerent occupation, with regard to the availability of legal challenge proceedings and financial compensation.[20] Hence, the state maintained that the legality of the barrier could be defended under both branches of IHL, separately or cumulatively.

The state asserted that its decision to situate considerable parts of the separation barrier throughout the West Bank, and not on the Green Line, derived from pure military considerations; the need to protect Israeli security interests in the West Bank (including the lives of many Israeli citizens residing there); to overcome topographic conditions which would have rendered a barrier exclusively situated on the Green Line military indefensible; and to facilitate the better protection of Israeli towns and villages located on, or near, the Israeli side of the Green Line (e.g., prevent direct shooting at these localities or allow for the interception of infiltrators who manage to cross the barrier before they reach major Israeli population centres).[21] Allegedly, no political considerations relating to the permanent status of the Occupied Territories influenced the determination of the barrier's route.

The response also highlighted the overall effectiveness of these parts of the barrier that were already constructed, citing a more than 80 percent drop in terror casualties in areas protected by the barrier.[22]

3.2 Application of the tests of necessity and proportionality to Boudrous and Shukba

The second part of the state's response addresses the specific facts of the petitions against the route of the barrier near the villages of Boudrous and Shukba. First, the state explains that the barrier's incursion into the Occupied Territories near both villages is dictated by the topography of the area – the need to situate patrol roads running alongside the barrier up on the hill and not in the valley, where they can be targeted by hostile forces, and the need to provide patrolling soldiers with reasonable visibility.[23] Significantly, no Israeli settlements are situated in the area implicated in the petition; hence, questions relating to the permissibility of defending Israelis living in the Occupied Territories do not arise in *Alian*.

Second, the state argues that the harm caused to the local population in *Alian* is minimal: The barrier's intrusion into the West Bank is negligible; no Palestinians reside west of the barrier in that area; the harm to the villages' agricultural land is minor (the barrier affects only 0.04 square km of land belonging to Boudrous residents; and only some 0.6 square km of Shukba's lands; furthermore, the areas in question are sparsely cultivated, i.e., less than 300 trees are affected); and, in any event, full compensation was offered.[24] Hence, the state asserts that the construction of the barrier in the contested areas serves clear military needs and meets the conditions of proportionality established in *Beit Sourik*.

---

20. *Alian*, Written Response, *supra* n. 5, at paras. 215-216.
21. Ibid., at para. 64.
22. Ibid., at para. 77.
23. Ibid., at para. 232.
24. Ibid., at paras. 115-120, 142-150.

3.3 The relevance of the advisory opinion

The better part of the state's response addresses the relevance of the ICJ's advisory opinion to the *Alian* case. Although the response refers to the non-binding nature of ICJ advisory opinions,[25] it refrains from relying upon this formality in order to dismiss its legal significance altogether. Instead, it acknowledges that:

> 'The Court's stature attributes considerable weight to interpretations of international law it renders. Israel is committed to respect international law. Hence, even if the advisory opinion is non-binding, one should investigate the status of the legal findings it includes, as far as they interpret international law.'[26]

In other words, the response decides to tackle the advisory opinion head on, in an attempt to distinguish or discredit its actual conclusions on the basis of the applicable procedure and quality of analysis.[27]

The response then moves to discuss various deficiencies associated with the advisory opinion. It alleges that the opinions comprises four 'layers' of analysis – fact analysis, norm analysis, discussion of Israel's alleged violations and the consequences arising thereof.[28] The state argues that refutation of the factual conclusions reached by the Court would result in the collapse of the entire legal edifice the ICJ constructed thereupon.

The response criticises numerous aspects of the fact-finding and fact-analysis process undertaken by the ICJ. First, the Court's opinion and the individual opinions appended thereto suggest that the Court heavily relied upon the dossier of documents provided by the UN Secretary General.[29] However, the state alleges that these documents are typically one-sided and incomprehensive. Additionally, they do not adequately explain the military rationale of the barrier, from an Israeli perspective, and fail to reflect post-January 2004 alterations in the route of the barrier.[30] In particular, it is argued that the reports by the UN human rights rappor-

---

25. Ibid., at para. 261.

26. Ibid., at para. 266 (unofficial translation).

27. One possible explanation for the state's position on the effects of the Advisory Opinion is that declarative statements of customary law by the ICJ might be viewed by some Israeli judges as part of domestic Israeli law, entailing, as a result, binding consequences for the State regardless of the binding nature of the opinion itself. For a survey of the status of international law in Israeli law, see R. Lapidoth, 'International law within the Israeli legal system', 24 *Israel LR* (1990) p. 451.

28. *Alian*, Written Response, *supra* n. 5, at para. 343.

29. Dossier of Materials Compiled Pursuant to Art. 65(2) of the Statute of the International Court of Justice, 19 January 2004, <http://www.icj-cij.org/icjwww/idocket/imwp/imwppleadings/imwp_iIntroductoryNote_20040119.pdf>.

30. *Alian*, Written Response, *supra* n. 5, at para. 350.

teurs[31] which are cited by the Court are grossly exaggerated and biased.[32] According to the state, these flaws undercut the legitimacy of the Court's opinion: Since the Court had no specific information on the Israeli claim of necessity for constructing the barrier in the designated route, there was no factual basis upon which it could have reasonably concluded that the conditions of military necessity were not met.[33] Notably, the state refers to the dissenting opinion of Judge Buergenthal in support of the proposition that Israel was under no obligation to cooperate with the Court, and that, as a result, no adverse evidentiary conclusions should have been drawn against it.[34]

The state then identifies a second major deficiency in the Court's fact-analysis: the opinion fails to distinguish between different segments of the barrier (e.g., segments associated with Israeli settlements and segments designed exclusively to protect localities situated within Israel proper), and infers general conclusions, reflecting upon the legality of the barrier *in toto*, on the basis of information pertaining to a few specific sections.[35] The opinion thus arguably adopts excessively sweeping conclusions which are incompatible with its limited factual basis. This contrasts unfavourably with the case to case – essentially kilometre by kilometre – approach undertaken by the HCJ in the petitions relating to the route of the barrier it has reviewed so far.[36]

In addition to these deficiencies, the response maintains that recent developments have rendered the advisory opinion obsolete. The ICJ's opinion stated that the barrier will *de facto* annex 16.6 percent of the territory of the West Bank – home to 237,000 Palestinians – and will limit the movement of 160,000 additional Palestinians. At the same time, 320,000 Israeli settlers would be situated west of the barrier.[37] However, as a result of changes in the route of the barrier, introduced mainly after the decision of the HCJ in *Beit Sourik*, the swathe of West Bank land severed by the barrier has decreased to eight percent of the area, in which no more than 30,000 Palestinians reside (excluding East Jerusalem residents and territory). Furthermore, the military announced its intention to improve passage through the

---

31. Report of the Special Rapporteur of the Commission on Human Rights, John Dugard, on the situation of human rights in the Palestinian territories occupied by Israel since 1967, submitted in accordance with Commission resolution 1993/2 A. Question of the Violation of Human Rights in the Occupied Arab Territories, including Palestine, UN Doc. E/CN.4/2004/6 (2003); Report by the Special Rapporteur, Jean Ziegler, Commission on Human Rights on The right to food, Addendum – Mission to the Occupied Palestinian Territories, UN Doc. V E/CN.4/2004/10/Add.2 (2003).

32. For example, the state argues that the report of the Special Rapporteur for the Right to Food, on which the ICJ relied, alleges that a seven km section of the barrier, between the Jordan Valley and the city of Beit She'an might result in the annexation of half the West Bank, whereas the Secretary General's report finds the entire planned route may only affect 16.6 percent of the West Bank. Ibid., at para. 360.

33. Ibid., at paras. 379-381.

34. *OPT Wall*, Declaration of Judge Buergenthal, at para. 10.

35. *Alian*, Written Response, *supra* n. 5, at paras. 390-391.

36. Ibid., at para. 439. Until now, 51 petitions against the separation barrier had been filed with the HCJ.

37. *OPT Wall*, at paras. 84-85.

numerous gates spread along the route of the barrier.[38] Arguably, the significant changes in the route of the barrier and the improvements in the condition of the Palestinians adversely affected thereby render the advisory opinion, which addressed a considerably more intrusive route with far more serious humanitarian and territorial implications, irrelevant.

So, according to the state, the main problem associated with the ICJ advisory opinion lies with its factual layer. Indeed, the response emphasises that the legal analysis undertaken by the ICJ in relation to the laws of belligerent occupation was generally correct, or at least consistent with the state's *de facto*, if not *de jure*, positions. Hence, the state accepts that the lawfulness of the barrier should be reviewed in the light of the 1907 Hague Regulations and the 1949 Fourth Geneva Convention (whose humanitarian provisions Israel unilaterally undertook to apply in the Occupied Territories),[39] and, in particular, pursuant to the test of military necessity that these instruments embrace.

Following discussion of the adequacy and relevance of the ICJ's fact finding and fact analysis processes, the response proceeds to address some legal analysis problems concerning branches of international law other than the laws of belligerent occupation. First, the state criticises the ICJ's failure to address the legal significance of the Israeli-Palestinian 1995 Interim Agreement, in which the parties undertook to resolve the final status of the Israel settlements only in the course of the negotiations over the permanent status of the Occupied Territories.[40] In particular, the ICJ did not acknowledge Israel's obligation under the Interim Agreement (and, arguably, under international human rights law) to secure the lives of the Israeli settlers in the West Bank throughout the duration the Agreement.[41] Hence, inferring the unlawfulness of the barrier from the unlawfulness of the settlements under general international law might have been legally erroneous. Second, the state claims that the ICJ's refusal to accept at face value Israel's undertakings that the barrier is a temporary security measure, not designed to facilitate annexation of lands, stands in contrast with the long-established legal principle that bad faith on the part of sovereign states cannot be easily presumed.[42] Arguably, both of these observations undermine the validity of the ICJ's determinations concerning the political, not military rationale for the construction of the barrier.

Moreover, the state takes issue with some of the legal conclusions espoused by the ICJ, although it maintains that they have no bearing upon the outcome of the *Alian* case. For example, the state rejects the court's finding that the barrier vio-

---

38. Ibid., at paras. 88-93.

39. *Alian*, Written Response, *supra* n. 5, at paras. 476-480.

40. Ibid., at para. 466. See Interim Agreement on the West Bank and the Gaza Strip (Israel/PLO), 28 September 1995, Art. XXXI(5), 36 *ILM* (1997) p. 551.

41. Ibid., at para. 470. The responsibility for the protection of settlers was allocated to Israel under Article XII of the Interim Agreement. For relevant HCJ jurisprudence on the matter, see e.g., *Gossin* v. *IDF Gaza Strip Commander*, H.C.J. 4219/02, 56(4) P.D. 608; *Zindah* v. *IDF Gaza Scrip Commander*, H.C.J. 4363/02, 2002(2) *Takdin-Supreme* 1836.

42. *Alian*, Written Response, *supra* n. 5, at para. 467 (discussing the *Nuclear Tests* and *Lac Lanoux* cases). See also *Free Zones of the Upper Savoy and the District of Gex*, 1932 *PCIJ* (Series A/B) No. 46, at p. 167 ('[A]n abuse cannot be assumed by the Court').

lated the Palestinians' right to self-determination (but argues that the minuscule size of the land affected in *Alian* renders the question moot);[43] the state also challenges the ICJ's unsubstantiated assertion that only the laws of belligerent occupation (and not the laws of war) apply to the present *intifada*,[44] but claims that the laws of belligerent occupation provides a sufficient legal basis for constructing the barrier.[45] Similarly, the state questions the correctness of the ICJ's findings in relation to the applicability of human rights treaties to the Occupied Territories, but maintains that the existence of military necessity would have provided a valid defence under human rights law as well.[46] Finally, the state rejects the Court's conclusions as to the inapplicability of Article 51 of the UN Charter to armed attacks perpetrated by non-state entities, but accepts that the legality of the barrier is in essence a *jus in bello*, not a *jus ad bellum* issue.[47]

4. COMMON BUT DIFFERENTIATED MISCONCEPTIONS

Although I agree with much of the criticism levelled against the ICJ advisory opinion in the response,[48] the state's analysis ignores some parallel deficiencies associated with the decision of the HCJ in *Beit Sourik* (which the state now endorses). In this respect, I believe, the response is quite unsatisfactory.

4.1 The false dichotomy between the political and the professional

It seems that both the HCJ and ICJ accepted the proposition that a politically motivated separation barrier route, as opposed to one exclusively corresponding to military needs, is unlawful. The two courts differed, however, in their appraisal of Israel's true motives: while the HCJ accepted the veracity of the government's statement that the route of the barrier was dictated only by military considerations,[49] the ICJ rejected Israel's assertions on the temporary and military nature of the barrier, and expressed concern about the possible annexationist motives or effects of Israel's actions.[50] The state, in *Alian*, reaffirms this dichotomy, and supports the holding of the HCJ in *Beit Sourik*: 'The barrier's sole purpose is to obtain security (...) The barrier has no political purpose.'[51]

---

43. *Alian*, Written Response, *supra* n. 5, at paras. 473-475.

44. *OPT Wall*, at para. 124.

45. *Alian*, Written Response, *supra* n. 5, at paras. 493-495. For criticism of the ICJ's position on the inapplicability of the laws of warfare in the Occupied Territories, see D. Kretzmer, 'The advisory opinion: the light treatment of international humanitarian law', 99 *AJIL* (2005) pp. 88-102, at p. 96.

46. *Alian*, Written Response, *supra* n. 5, at paras. 508-528.

47. Ibid., at paras. 532-544.

48. See Y. Shany, 'Capacities and inadequacies: a look at the two separation barrier cases', 38 *Israel LR* (2005) pp. 230-246.

49. *Beit Sourik*, *supra* n. 5, at paras. 28-29 (relying on the text of the relevant government resolutions authorising the route and an affidavit by the IDF West Bank Military Commander).

50. *OPT Wall*, at paras. 121-122.

51. *Alian*, Written Response, *supra* n. 5, at para. 52.

However, the distinction between the derisively-termed 'political considerations' and professional 'security considerations' might be unreal, and obfuscating.[52] Law often introduces limiting side-constraints on the exercise of power.[53] Still, it does not normally exclude politics, and the two coexist side by side: law defines the outer parameters of legality and creates a space within which politics can apply. It thus follows that IHL seeks to introduce limits upon the methods and means of warfare and protect fundamental human values during times of conflict, and that, as a result, the relevant decision makers' strategic and tactical choices are not unlimited.[54] However, IHL does not prevent decision makers from considering broader policy considerations (i.e., political considerations) when selecting between the available lawful alternatives: e.g., which legitimate military targets to pursue, whether to provide services to population in occupied territories directly or indirectly (i.e., through international relief associations), whether to respond proportionally or under-react in the face of enemy provocations, etc. While the dominance of subjective political considerations might cast serious doubts on the *credibility* of certain legal arguments (raising fears that the delineation of the boundaries of legality had been manipulated to accommodate political needs),[55] the existence of political motives can hardly ever justify an automatic finding of objective illegality.

One caveat to the last proposition may be noted, however: under Israeli administrative law, administrative agencies (including the IDF) may not take improper considerations into account when exercising their legal authority.[56] However, the applicability of this general rule to IHL-type decisions is unclear. In the past, the HCJ affirmed the permissibility of considering broader policy considerations when choosing between lawful alternatives under IHL.[57] Furthermore, the reference by the HCJ in *Beit Sourik* to the impropriety of political considerations was made in the context of an analysis of the military commander's obligations under international law. Hence, it is questionable whether the HCJ intended to hold that domes-

52. For an important exposition on the relations between international law and politics, see D. Kennedy, 'When renewal repeats: thinking against the box', 32 *NY Univ. JIL & Pol.* (2000) p. 335.

53. For an influential theory of law as side constraints, see R. Nozick, *Anarchy, State and Utopia* (New York, Basic Books 1974) pp. 28-33.

54. Hague Regulations, Art. 22.

55. Cf., R.B. Bilder and D.F. Vagts, 'Speaking law to power: lawyers and torture', 98 *AJIL* (2004) pp. 689-695, at p. 693. '[T]here may be strong pressures on government lawyers to 'bend' or ignore the law in order to support policy decisions'.

56. See e.g., *Neiman* v. *Chairman of the Central Election Commission*, E.A. 2/84, 39(2) P.D. 225, 252.

57. See *Ajuri* v. *IDF West Bank Military Commander*, H.C.J. 7015/02, 56(6) P.D. 352, 374. 'May the military commander, when making a decision about assigned residence, take into account considerations of deterring others? As we have seen, what underlies the measure of assigned residence is the danger presented by the person himself if his place of residence is not assigned, and deterring that person himself by assigning his place of residence. The military commander may not, therefore, adopt a measure of assigned residence merely as a deterrent to others. Notwithstanding, when assigning a place of residence is justified because a person is dangerous, and the question is merely whether to exercise this authority, there is no defect in the military commander taking into account considerations of deterring others. Thus, for example, this consideration may be taken into account in choosing between internment and assigned residence.'

tic administrative law prohibits the weighing of political considerations. The HCJ's position on the matter is particularly confusing in the light of its own reluctance to review the legality of the settlements themselves (whose establishment is a clear political decision) under either Israeli administrative law or IHL.[58]

Applied to the separation barrier case, the question which should have been properly placed before the HCJ and ICJ is, then, whether the barrier can be justified in terms of military necessity. The policy makers' hidden or patent motives may reflect on the persuasiveness of Israel's military necessity arguments under IHL, but they cannot be determinative thereof. In other words, the clearly political nature of the decision to incorporate Israel's West Bank settlements within the barrier[59] does not prove *per se* that the route is unlawful from an IHL perspective (although, as will be discussed below, the link between the unlawful nature of the settlements and the barrier might lead to this very conclusion). In fact, one could argue that a decision not to incorporate the settlements would have been equally political.[60] Of course, the effects of the barrier, including its political effects (e.g., on the Palestinian right to self determination), might also be relevant to any assessment of proportionality, but they cannot be, in my mind, dispositive of the question of legality *per se*.[61]

When explored from this perspective, both the HCJ and the ICJ decisions are unsatisfactory. The HCJ judgement offers an unrealistic and unnecessary detachment between the political and the professional. The ICJ opinion is less explicit on the matter, but it seems to attribute excessive weight to the political implications of the barrier in rejecting Israel's military justifications thereof, without an independent investigation of the merits of such claims. The state's response in *Alian* also does little to clarify matters and to distinguish between the aforementioned subjective and objective legal and political elements. Instead, it advocates a rather unpersuasive general narrative of a professional decision making process, which allegedly governed determination of the route of the barrier. While this narrative might hold true for the route near Boudrous and Shukba, which has no clear political implications, it is far less probable in relation to more volatile sections of the barrier (e.g., in the Jerusalem, Ariel or Gush Ezion regions).[62]

---

58. See *infra* n. 63.

59. See e.g., Kretzmer, *supra* n. 45, at p. 92. 'The debate in Israel clearly demonstrates that the government did indeed have political intentions in setting the barrier's route.'

60. See e.g., the statement of Minister Tsippi Livni in F. Raday and Y. Shany, eds., *The Separation Area – An Interdisciplinary Look, Symposium Proceedings* (Rishon Le Zion, Concord Research Centre 2004) p. 20 (in Hebrew). 'To locate the fence on the Green Line is a mistake. First, because if there is something political on the ground – it is the Green Line. The rest is, seemingly, politically meaningless but based on security parameters of providing Israeli citizens with security' (unofficial translation). Cf., *Beit Sourik*, *supra* n. 5, at para. 30. 'The opposite is the case: it is the security perspective – and not the political one – which must examine the route on its security merits alone, without regard for the location of the Green Line.'

61. See Kretzmer, *supra* n. 45, at p. 92. 'If the premise that the sole purpose of the barrier is to prevent infiltration of terrorists into Israel remains unchallenged, why does the *potential* permanency of the barrier make it unlawful?'

62. Indeed, the state's representatives have recently admitted in the course of a public court session on another separation barrier, dealing with the route in East Jerusalem, that political consideration

4.2 Questionable premises: linking or de-linking the barrier and the settlements

Another problem common to both the HCJ and the ICJ decisions, which is not resolved by the response in *Alian*, is the inadequate handling of the link between the lawfulness of the Israeli settlements in the West Bank and that of the separation barrier. While the two decisions reach contrary findings on the matter, it seems that they share a methodological problem of reliance upon dubious legal premises. The *Beit Sourik* judgement evades the issue of legality of the settlements altogether and adopts an 'individual security' premise, which upholds the obligation of the IDF to provide security to all individuals residing in the Occupied Territories – Israelis and non-Israelis alike.[63] This premise is, however, questionable from a legal point of view, as it fails to acknowledge the legal import of Article 4 of the Fourth Geneva Convention, which excludes citizens of the occupying power from the Convention's scope of protection. It also runs contrary to the general principle *ex injuria jus non oritur*, which finds concrete expression in Article 25(2)(b) of the ILC Draft Articles on State Responsibility. This article seems to bar states who have contributed to the situation of illegality from invoking the defence of necessity. Hence, the construction of illegal settlements in the West Bank might bar the invocation of the defence of necessity in order to protect them.[64] The HCJ's problematic premise on the immateriality of the illegality of the settlements thus renders its judgement unsatisfactory from an international law point of view.

At the same time, the ICJ proceeded with an equally problematic premise – that the illegality of the settlements automatically renders unlawful any measure designed to protect the security of their residents.[65] This position overlooks the legal significance of the Oslo Accords, which deferred resolution of the final status of the settlements to future negotiations between the Israelis and Palestinians and

---

dictated in part the routing of the barrier in that area. Y. Yoaz, 'State Prosecution concedes political aim for Jerusalem fence', *Haaretz*, 21 June 2005, <http://www.haaretz.com/hasen/objects/pages/PrintArticleEn.jhtml?itemNo=590557>.

63. See e.g., *Beit Sourik*, *supra* n. 5, at para. 80. 'We also accept that "The Gazelles' Basin" is a part of Giv'at Ze'ev [a large West Bank settlement] and needs defense just like the rest of that town'. Cf., *Kawasme* v. *IDF West Bank Military Commander*, H.C.J. 7007/03, Judgment of 19 April 2005, at para. 7 (not yet published). 'There is no doubt that the respondent and the other regional commanders are responsible for the safety and security of the residents of "Hadassa House" [a Jewish outpost in Hebron] and that these organs may, and even must adopt measures to protect the "Hadassa House" residents' (unofficial translation). *Hess* v. *IDF West Bank Military Commander*, H.C.J. 10356/02, 58 (3) P.D. 443, 460-461. 'This obligation [to protect individual security] applies with regard to all residents without distinction – Jews, Arabs or foreigners. The question of the lawfulness of the residence of various population elements is not before us at present. Their mere presence in the area entails an obligation upon the regional commander to protect their lives and human rights.'

64. ILC Draft Articles on Responsibility of States for Internationally Wrongful Acts, UN Doc. A/CN.4/L.602/Rev.1 (2001).

65. See e.g., *OPT Wall*, at para. 122. 'In other terms, the route chosen for the wall gives expression *in loco* to the illegal measures taken by Israel with regard to Jerusalem and the settlements, as deplored by the Security Council.' Ibid., Declaration of Judge Buergenthal, at para. 9: ('segments of the wall being built by Israel to protect the settlements are *ipso facto* in violation of international humanitarian law').

authorised Israel to take security measures to protect the settlers during the life of the interim agreement.[66] Although the present legal status of the Oslo Accords is unclear,[67] and their ability to restrict the rights of protected persons in the Occupied Territories is debatable,[68] their existence seems to support the potential de-linking of the legality of the barrier and the settlements: the settlements might be unlawful, yet their residents might be entitled to protection pending a final negotiated agreement (which might ultimately allow some of the bigger settlements to remain in place).[69]

Furthermore, the ICJ did not discuss the material unfeasibility of dismantling the settlements and resettling the hundreds of thousands of Israeli citizens residing therein within a relatively short period of time. In other words, there might be a rather long interim period between an Israeli decision to evacuate the settlements and the actual execution of such a plan.[70] It is difficult to accept that in such an interim period Israel would not have the right of effectively protecting the settlers, by reason of the illegality of their settlements.[71]

Finally, it may be argued that the Court's uncompromising position on the matter of the settlements conflates assessing the legality of specific military measures (the barrier) with the general conditions of legality (the settlements or their underlying annexationist agenda)[72] in ways not dissimilar to the disavowed linkage

---

66. Interim Agreement on the West Bank and the Gaza Strip (Israel/PLO), 28 September 1995, Art. XII(1), 36 *ILM* (1997) p. 551. 'Israel shall continue to carry the responsibility for defense against external threats, including the responsibility for protecting the Egyptian and Jordanian borders, and for defense against external threats from the sea and from the air, as well as the responsibility for overall security of Israelis and Settlements, for the purpose of safeguarding their internal security and public order, and will have all the powers to take the steps necessary to meet this responsibility'; Ibid., Art. XXXI(5): 'It is understood that [the permanent status] negotiations shall cover remaining issues, including: Jerusalem, refugees, settlements, security arrangements, borders, relations and cooperation with other neighbors, and other issues of common interest.'

67. See e.g., G.R. Watson, 'The 'Wall' decisions in legal and political context', 99 *AJIL* (2005) pp. 6-26, at pp. 22-24 (discussing possible objections to the validity of the Oslo Accords).

68. See Geneva IV, Arts. 7, 8 and 47.

69. See e.g., Letter from President Bush to Prime Minister Sharon, 14 April 2004, <http://www.whitehouse.gov/news/releases/2004/04/20040414-3.html>: 'In light of new realities on the ground, including already existing major Israeli populations centers, it is unrealistic to expect that the outcome of final status negotiations will be a full and complete return to the armistice lines of 1949, and all previous efforts to negotiate a two-state solution have reached the same conclusion.'

70. The major political and legal difficulties and repetitive delays characterizing present attempts to evacuate the 8,000 Israeli residents of the Gaza Strip present a telling example in this regard.

71. See R. Wedgwood, 'The ICJ advisory opinion on the Israeli security fence and the limits of self-defense', 99 *AJIL* (2005) pp. 52-61, at p. 61. 'It is one thing for a judge to assume or conclude that a particular settlement, or indeed all settlements, on the West Bank are illegal. It is another matter to preclude any measure of interim protection while their status or removal is settled through diplomatic means.'

72. An analogous controversy surrounds the legitimacy of measures taken to suppress uprisings in unlawfully occupied territories. Cf., UN GA res. 3314 (XXIX) on the Definition of Aggression, Art. 7, GA res. 3314 (XXIX) (1974), reprinted in D.J. Djonovich, ed., *United Nations Resolutions*, Vol. 15 (New York, Oceana Publications 1984) pp. 392-393.

between *jus in bello* and *jus ad bellum*[73] or to the mostly defunct theory of reprisals (which removes IHL protections from parties acting unlawfully).[74] It also runs contrary to the Court's analysis regarding the applicability of human rights treaties to all individuals present in the Occupied Territories (which arguably encompasses the settler population as well).[75] Thus, Israel might be obliged to protect the settlers until it is able to extricate them from the Occupied Territories, or otherwise remedy the unlawfulness of their presence there (e.g., by way of a final status peace agreement). In my mind, the unlawfulness of the settlements is not by itself determinative of the matter.

A more persuasive legal position than the one taken by either the HCJ or the ICJ would be to assert that the unlawfulness of the settlements is an important factor in assessing the legality of the barrier, which has to be considered in the light of the legally and practically feasible policy alternatives available to the Israeli government (e.g., dismantling of settlements, constructing separate defensive structure for protecting settlements, etc.).[76] However, the illegality of the settlements is not the only relevant factor in determining the lawfulness of defensive measures designed to protect them as such a position might compromise, in certain situations, the obtainment of other important humanitarian and human rights objectives.

The state's response in *Alian* endorses the position of the HCJ relating to the irrelevance of the legal status of the settlements[77] and supports this position, *inter alia*, by reference to the Palestinian acquiescence to their continued existence under the Oslo Accords. The state's reluctance to develop a general theory which could justify the incorporation of the settlements within the barrier – despite their alleged illegality – is understandable, given the particular facts of *Alian*. Nevertheless, the response is disappointing from an international law perspective. One would expect that a response that seeks to expose the fallacy of the ICJ's premise on the link between the settlements and the barrier would develop a more coherent and convincing theory on that very link (even in the form of an *arguendo* type thesis). The end result is that neither the ICJ, nor the HCJ or the state's response offer a satisfactory theory on permissible military measures in situations of illegality. Arguably, such a theory should have introduced a nuanced temporal element, which is lacking in the current dichotomist approaches demonstrated by the two

---

73. For a classic rejection of the connection between *jus in bello* and *jus ad bellum*, see *United States* v. *List* (1948), 11 *Trials of War Criminals Before the Nuremberg Military Tribunals Under Control Council Law No. 10, October 1946-April 1949* (1949-1953) pp. 1230, 1247-1248.

74. See e.g., Protocol Additional to the Geneva Conventions of 12 August 1949, and Relating to the Protection of Victims of International Armed Conflicts (Protocol I), 8 June 1977, Art. 20, 1125 *UNTS* 3.

75. Cf., Kretzmer, *supra* n. 45, at p. 93. '[A] theory that posits that the fact that civilians are living in an illegal settlement should prevent a party to the conflict from taking any measures to protect them would seem to contradict fundamental notions of international humanitarian law'.

76. See ibid., at p. 94. '[O]ne of the factors that should have been taken into account is the illegality of the settlements, and the consequent duty of the occupying power to return its civilians in those settlements to its own territory'.

77. *Alian*, Written Response, *supra* n. 5, at paras. 469-475.

Courts, i.e., offer an interim regime of IHL protections until the more general conditions of illegality are resolved.

4.3 Partial legal framework: ignoring relevant norms

As already mentioned, the ICJ advisory opinion omits any meaningful reference to the Oslo Accords, which constitute the main body of agreements governing legal relations between the Israeli and the Palestinians.[78] Furthermore, the Court's treatment of the interplay between IHL and international human rights norms leaves much to be desired in terms of the Court's norm elucidating role.[79] At the same time, the HCJ's judgment also disregards several relevant international norms – most notably, the right to self determination of the Palestinian people, international human rights law and, also, the Oslo Accords.[80]

The state argues in its response in *Alian* that the omission of the HCJ to address self-determination and human rights did not affect the outcome of the separation barrier cases. If one were to dismiss the factual holdings of the ICJ on the non-availability of military necessity, then all other ICJ conclusions on Israel's violations of international law are unsustainable: 'With the collapse of the argument about the annexation, the second argument concerning the Palestinian right to self-determination falls too.' [81] In the same vein, the state argues that: '[E]ven if we accept the Court's position on the applicability of the [human rights] treaties, and analyze the construction of the barrier according to their provisions, the factual difficulty and the legal difficulty of the opinion will lead to different conclusions than the one which the Court reached, concerning the alleged violation of treaty provisions.'[82] In the alternative, the state's response argues that the ICJ misapplied the self-determination principle[83] and provided a poor analysis of the application of human rights in occupied territories.[84]

While the state's position might be sensible in the specific context of *Alian*, which has minor implications for the Palestinians' right to self-determination and their human rights (especially since IHL provides an alternative set of individual rights), it is once more disappointing that the state did not take up this opportunity

78. The Oslo Accords were only briefly mentioned in the context of the historical survey of the Israeli-Palestinian conflict and with respect to the Palestinian right to self determination. See *OPT Wall*, at paras. 77 and 118.

79. In particular, the ICJ failed to identify the implications that the *lex specialis* status of IHL might have upon the interpretation and application of human rights norms, and applied the two bodies of norms in cumulative, not integrative manner. For criticism, see O. Ben-Naftali and Y. Shany, 'Living in denial: the application of human rights in the Occupied Territories', 37 *Israel LR* (2003-2004) pp. 17-118, at pp. 116-117; M.J. Dennis, 'Application of human rights treaties extraterritorially in times of armed conflict and military occupation', 99 *AJIL* (2005) pp. 119-141, at p. 133.

80. See Watson, *supra* n. 65, at p. 22.

81. *Alian*, Written Response, *supra* n. 5, at para. 473 (unofficial translation).

82. Ibid., at para. 505 (unofficial translation).

83. Ibid., at para. 473. 'Without addressing the very existence of that right and its scope of application, it should be made clear that the barrier has no effect upon the political status of the Palestinians or the present or future status of the territories'(unofficial translation).

84. Ibid., at para. 505.

to develop a coherent theory on the link between the settlements project and the Palestinian right to self determination and on the co-application of IHL and human rights in the Occupied Territories[85] (although the state does explain why the barrier does not violate human rights treaties, if they are applicable).[86] This renders the Israeli legal discussion of the legality of the barrier, and its associated regime, once more, incomplete.

5. CONCLUSIONS

It may only be speculated why the HCJ selected the *Alian* case to tackle the ICJ advisory opinion (and not any of the other separation barrier cases pending before it). The particular circumstances of the case provide a possible explanation: the separation barrier's extension into the West Bank in *Alian* is relatively minor, and can be relatively easily justified on the basis of military necessity; most significantly, there are no Jewish settlements in the area. Arguably, these factors might help the Court, if it so chooses, to distinguish the *Alian* case from the advisory opinion, which attributed great importance to the size of the occupied territory cut off by the barrier and to the link between the route of the barrier and the spread of Israeli settlements. It thus seems reasonable to estimate that the separation barrier litigation in Israel will continue to take place in a piecemeal fashion, each case according to its particular circumstance (in conformity with the *Beit Sourik* methodology). The 'broad brush' approach of the ICJ is likely to be rejected; and the *Alian* case seemed to provide a convenient opportunity for justifying this judicial policy choice. Of course, replacing a 'broad brush' approach to the legality of the separation barrier with a microscopic review of distinct segments, without having sight of the entire barrier project and its implications, might be equally untenable.

Still, for its part, the state's response promotes a possible agenda of judicial distinction between the HCJ and ICJ jurisprudence: It presents effective criticism of the sweeping nature of the ICJ opinion, and encourages the HCJ to develop different jurisprudence on the matter. In this respect, it seems that the state has wisely chosen not to excessively rely on the formally non-binding status of the opinion; instead, it exposes the numerous fact-finding and fact-analysis shortcomings of the opinion, in a way which undermines the opinion´s credibility and potential applicability. However, the response itself fails to remedy some of the deficiencies which characterise the HCJ decision in *Beit Sourik*: a false dichotomy between political and professional discretion, a problematic legal premise relating to the status of the settlements and selective use of legal sources. This marks a problematic policy choice on the part of the government of Israel to perpetuate the legal ambiguities of the current situation in the Occupied Territories in a way which is less than conducive to the rule of international law.

---

85. For two conflicting positions on the matter, see Dennis, *supra* n. 79; Ben-Naftali and Shany, *supra* n. 79.

86. *Alian*, Written Response, *supra* n. 5, at paras. 506-527.

Finally, it may be observed that the state's response is unconvincing in its attempt to absolve Israel from responsibility for the ICJ's unsatisfactory performance in establishing the 'factual layer' of the opinion. As was mentioned above, Israel refrained from presenting before the Court a detailed and coherent explanation of the security considerations underlying the route of the barrier, and thus obstructed the fact-finding process. Although Israel was certainly within its right not to cooperate with non-contentious proceedings it considered to be improper,[87] one may question whether its criticism on the Court's factual conclusions – which it undermined through its non-cooperation – are consistent with its good faith obligations under the UN Charter.[88] Hence, although the ICJ advisory opinion certainly deserves criticism, the legal strategy adopted by the state of Israel in the course of the litigation before the ICJ also leaves much to be desired.

POSTSCRIPT

On 15 September 2005, after this note had been sent to print, a nine-member chamber of the HCJ has issued a unanimous judgment in one of the security barrier cases pending before it – *Mara'abe v. Prime Minister of Israel*,[89] which addressed the legality of a segment of the barrier running near the West Bank Jewish settlement of Alfei Menashe. In its judgment, the Court affirmed the legal parameters for review of the barrier's legality introduced in the *Beit Sourik* case and stroke down the reviewed segment by reason of the disproportional harm it inflicted upon the Palestinian villagers affected by the route.

Still, interestingly enough, the judgment addresses, *in extenso,* the weight that should be accorded to the ICJ's advisory opinion on the *Wall.* This discussion is based on the response submitted by the state in the *Alian* case and the reply issued by the petitioners in that case.[90] So, the submissions on the effect to be granted to the advisory opinion which were introduced in the course of the *Alian* litigation were eventually redirected to the *Mara'abe* case (which included, more or less, the same legal teams on both sides). The reasons for this change of course are not explained in the judgment, but it may be speculated that the Court belatedly realized that the specific facts of the *Alian* case (in particular, that no Palestinians or Israeli settlers reside west of the segment of the barrier reviewed there) render it

---

87. Ibid., at para. 293; *OPT Wall*, Declaration of Judge Buergenthal, at para. 10.

88. UN Charter, Art. 2(2). See also R.A. Falk, 'Toward authoritativeness: the ICJ ruling on Israel's Security Wall', 99 *AJIL* (2005) pp. 42-51, at pp. 46-47. 'As a member of the United Nations and a party to the Statute of the Court, Israel had some degree of responsibility to enable the Court to fulfill its role as principal judicial organ of the UN system. By exercising its undoubted legal right to refuse to participate on the merits, Israel can be regarded as having effectively forfeited the opportunity to present its security rationale for building the wall as it has done.'

89. H.C.J. 7957/04 *Mara'abe v. Prime Minister of Israel,* 2005(21) *Pador* 360.

90. *Alian* v. *Prime Minister*, H.C.J. 4825/04, Petitioners' Reply to the State's Response, 5 May 2005 (copy with author).

unsuitable for evaluating the impact of the advisory opinion upon many security barrier cases pending before the HCJ.

Writing for the Court in *Mara'abe*, President Barak first describes at length the chain of diplomatic events leading to the issuance of the advisory opinion by the ICJ and surveys its main findings.[91] He then moved on to assess the legal relevance of these findings for the work of the HCJ. Accepting the position specified in the state's position, Barak refused to rely on the non binding nature of ICJ advisory opinions as grounds for rejecting their relevance: '[T]he opinion of the International Court of Justice is an interpretation of international law, performed by the highest judicial body in international law [cite omitted]. The ICJ's interpretation of international law should be given its full appropriate weight.'[92] Furthermore, Barak emphasised the commonalities between the two advisory opinion and the *Beit Sourik* HCJ judgment – the applicability of the laws of belligerent occupation, acknowledgment of the harm caused by the barrier to the human rights of Palestinian residents and the theoretical possibility of invoking military necessity as a justification for restricting individual rights.[93] Yet, he also noted the difference in the final outcome reached by the two courts.

According to Barak, these divergent conclusions stem for different factual bases underlying the two decisions.[94] First, the record suggests that the ICJ had little information on the security considerations which have led Israel to construct the barrier: '[T]he reality is that the ICJ based its opinion on a factual basis regarding impingement of Palestinian residents' rights, without the factual basis regarding the security-military justification for this impingement. In contrast, in *The Beit Sourik* case, an expansive factual basis was laid before the court, both regarding the impingement upon the local residents' human rights and regarding the security-military needs.'[95] Second, the non-adversarial nature of the proceedings before the ICJ led the latter to accept in uncritical manner imprecise information which was presented to it by various UN officials.[96] In Barak's view, this deficient fact-gathering process prevented the ICJ from conducting a segment-by-segment review of the barrier, and led it to adopt of controversial sweeping statements on the legality of the entire barrier project.[97]

Consequently, Barak distinguished between the weight that should be given to the ICJ's legal and factual determinations: '[T]he Supreme Court of Israel shall give the full appropriate weight to the norms of international law, as developed

91. *Mara'abe*, *supra* n. 89, at paras. 37-55.

92. Ibid., at para. 56.

93. Ibid., at para. 57.

94. Ibid., at para. 61.

95. Ibid., at para. 65.

96. Ibid., at paras. 66-69. Interestingly enough, President Barak indirectly criticizes Israel's lack of cooperation with the ICJ and suggests that it shares the blame for the inadequate factual basis of the advisory opinion. Ibid., at para. 65.

97. Ibid., at para. 70-71. Judge Cheshin, who issued a separate opinion, used less sparing language. He wrote: 'The generality and lack of explanation which characterize the factual aspect of the opinion are not among the distinguishing marks worthy of appearing in a legal opinion or a judgment.' *Mara'abe*, *supra* n. 89, Separate Opinion of Judge Cheshin, at para. 4.

and interpreted by the ICJ in its Advisory Opinion. However, the ICJ's conclusion, based upon a factual basis different than the one before us, is not *res judicata*, and does not obligate the Supreme Court of Israel to rule that each and every segment of the fence violates international law. The Israeli Court shall continue to examine each of the segments of the fence, as they are brought for its decision and according to its customary model of proceedings; it shall ask itself, regarding each and every segment, whether it represents a proportional balance between the security-military need and the rights of the local population ... In doing so, the Court shall not ignore the entire picture; its decision will always regard each segment as a part of a whole.'[98] This last sentence is perhaps suggestive of the indirect influence that the advisory opinion had on the HCJ – unlike the *Beit Sourik* judgment, the *Mara'abe* decision displays increased sensitivity to the need to supplement the kilometer-by-kilometer review of the barrier undertaken by the HCJ with a broader perspective on the implications of the entire project.

In addition, Barak tackles in the judgement some of the legal analysis problems, which the state identified in the advisory opinion: He questions, in *obiter dicta*, the correctness of the ICJ's position on the inapplicability of the laws of warfare to the situation in the Occupied Territories;[99] and the appropriateness of the advisory opinion's conclusions on the non-availability of the right to self-defence to counter attacks emanating from occupied territories.[100] Two parts of the judgment, which deal with the legal analysis performed by the ICJ are particularly interesting. On the applicability of human rights treaties in occupied territories, Barak suggests that human rights standards should be read into the relevant IHL protections: '[I]n exercising his authority pursuant to the law of belligerent occupation, the military commander ... must consider, *on the one hand*, considerations of state security, security of the army, and the personal security of all who are present in the *area. On the other hand*, he must consider the human rights of the local Arab population.'[101] Hence, he was willing to assume, for the sake of argument, that human rights treaties apply in the Occupied Territories and also govern the legality of the separation barrier.

Furthermore, Barak touches upon the sensitive link between the alleged illegality of the settlements and the legality of the separation barrier. He asserts that IHL (in particular, Art. 43 of the 1907 Hauge Regulations), human rights principles and Israeli constitutional law oblige Israel to protect the lives of Israeli settlers residing in the Occupied Territories: 'Even if a person is located in the area illegally, he is not outlawed.'[102] The Oslo accords, which authorize Israel to protect the settlements, are cited as an additional factor supportive of the HCJ's conclusions.[103]

The *Mara'abe* judgment thus serves as an important indication in assessing Israel's reaction to the *Wall* advisory opinion. It suggests that the Israel's Supreme

---

98. *Mara'abe, supra* n. 89, at para. 74.
99. Ibid., at para. 17.
100. Ibid., at para. 23.
101. Ibid., at para. 28 [emphasis in original text].
102. Ibid., at para. 19.
103. Ibid., at para. 20.

Court essentially accepts the criticism raised by the state against the fact-finding and fact-analysis processes which took place before the ICJ. So, while the Court displays token deference towards the ICJ, it ultimately asserts its freedom to deviate from its conclusions. Hence, Israel's rejection of the advisory opinion primarily is primarily grounded upon the serious methodological deficiencies which underlie the fact-finding and fact-analysis processes before the ICJ. Arguably, these perceived deficiencies considerably limit the advisory opinion's persuasiveness in the eyes of the HCJ.

In addition, the HRC judgment partly rectifies some of the earlier deficiencies of the earlier *Beit Sourik* judgment: It discusses the implications of the possible illegality of the settlements upon the legality of the barrier, considers the effect of the Oslo Accords thereupon and raises the possibility that human rights treaties would also be applicable in the Occupied Territories. Still, there are institutional limits to the ability of the Court to tackle such issues – the HCJ does not contemplate that the state might be obliged to consider evacuating settlers in order to protect their lives (instead of protecting them while they remain in place); and refrains from explicitly applying human treaties, as this would be in direct opposition to the position taken by the executive branch before UN fora.[104] Furthermore, the *Mara'abe* judgment is open to criticism for reaffirming the false dichotomy between decisions based on military and political considerations.[105] On this last point, both Courts – the ICJ and HCJ – seem to adopt a shared unrealistic vision of international law as a-political body of law.

---

104. For discussion of these objections, see Ben-Naftali and Shany, *supra* n. 79.
105. *Mara'abe*, *supra* n. 89, at paras. 62, 71.

THE ICJ'S ADVISORY OPINION ON THE CONSEQUENCES OF ISRAEL'S CONSTRUCTION OF A SEPARATION BARRIER IN THE OCCUPIED PALESTINIAN TERRITORIES: A MOVE IN THE RIGHT DIRECTION OR AN IMPEDIMENT TO PEACE?[1]

Mustafa Mari[2]

1. INTRODUCTION

The issuance by the International Court of Justice (ICJ) of its Advisory Opinion on the consequences of Israel's construction of the separation barrier in the Occupied Palestinian Territories (OPT) raises myriad legal questions worth addressing. This paper leaves most of these issues to other scholars[3] and instead focuses on one of the key claims made by Israel and a number of other states since the request for an Advisory Opinion was brought before the Court: whether the involvement of the Court in the issue of the construction of the barrier constituted an obstacle to Israeli-Palestinian peace.

Palestinians have been accused, including by Palestinians themselves, of failing, in the course of their efforts to end Israeli occupation and work towards Israeli-Palestinian peace, to make use of international law and the assistance relevant institutions may provide in trying to bring to an end the Israeli occupation of the OPT.[4] Some authors have expressed a different view, including Shimon Shitreet,

---

2. Dr Mustafa Mari, Professor of Laws and Human Rights, School of Graduate Studies, Bir Zeit University, Bir Zeit, Palestine. The views expressed here are those of the author, and do not necessarily reflect those of the Bir Zeit University or any other group with which he is affiliated.

3. See S.M. Akram and J. Quigley, 'A reading of the International Court of Justice advisory opinion on the legality of Israel's wall in the Occupied Palestinian Territories', <http://www.palestinecen ter.org>; B. Claudie, *The Advisory Opinion of the International Court of Justice on the Construction of a Wall in the Occupied Palestinian Territory*, (The Palestinian Independent Commission for Citizen's Rights (PICCR) 2004); I. Scobbie, 'Smoke, mirrors and killer whales: the International Court's Opinion on the Israeli Barrier Wall', 5 *German LJ* (2004) pp. 1107-1131; P.H.F. Bekker, 'The World Court rules that Israel's West Bank barrier violates international law', *ASIL Insights* (July 2004) <http://www.asil.org>, and S. Verhoven, 'Advisory Opinion on the Legal Consequences of the Construction of a Wall in the Occupied Palestinian Territories', 6 *International Law FORUM du droit international* (2004) pp. 106-110.

4. See F.A. Boyle, 'Negotiating human rights in peace negotiations', 18 *HRQ* (1996) pp. 515-516; F.D. Gaer, 'UN-Anonymous: reflections on human rights in peace negotiations', 19 *HRQ* (1997) pp. 1-8; and J. Quigley, 'The role of law in a Palestinian-Israeli accommodation', 31 *Case Western Reserve JIL* (1999) pp. 351-381.

Yearbook of International Humanitarian Law
Volume 7 - 2004 - pp. 373-387 DOI 10.1017/S1389135904003733

who has argued that negotiations should determine the final shape of any Israeli-Palestinian settlement, away from any advice international law may offer.[5]

There have been a few attempts thus far to use international law in order to shed light on aspects of the conflict, and means of its resolution, but none, until 9 July 2004, has resulted in as clear a statement on as many legal aspects of the Israeli-Palestinian conflict as the Advisory Opinion of the ICJ. This failure to resort to international law was in part due to Palestinian acceptance of the 'conventional wisdom' that negotiations are one path, and international law is another.

The Palestinian government's support for the pursuit of the matter of the separation barrier before the ICJ, through the UN General Assembly (GA), represented a change in the Palestinian government's approach to the matter, but only time will tell if this change will be sustained, should negotiations between the parties resume. Regardless of what the future may bring however, the question remains: was the Advisory Opinion of the International Court of Justice on the consequences of Israel's construction of the Wall in the OPT a move in the right direction or an impediment to peace?

2. USE OF LAW IN THE COURSE OF THE ISRAELI-PALESTINIAN CONFLICT

The Palestine Question has been on the agenda of the international community and international organisations since before the establishment of Israel in 1948. The Palestine Question and the struggle for and about Palestine has also been the subject of numerous international law instruments, including UN Security Council (SC) and GA resolutions. In fact, it was a UN GA resolution that gave birth to Israel and an Arab state in Palestine in 1947, a unique occurrence.[6]

Several decades earlier, the League of Nations granted Britain a mandate over Palestine. The League of Nations and later its successor the United Nations were involved in attempts to find a resolution to the conflict over whose aspirations and rights in the territory of Palestine should be realised. But for much of the twentieth century, Palestinians and Jewish immigrants, and later the government of Israel, did not negotiate with one other. Rather, they sought the unilateral realisation of what each party believed to be their legitimate aspirations and rights.

Following the Gulf War of 1990 and the end of the Cold War, the parties to the conflict gave negotiations a chance to guide them to an agreed, negotiated resolution of the Palestinian-Israeli conflict. The Israeli-Palestinian negotiations resulted in a series of agreements, including the Declaration of Principles in 1993 and the

---

5. See S. Shitreet, 'Negotiations and Agreements are Better than Legal Resolutions: A response to Professor John Quigley', 32 *Case Western Reserve JIL* (2000) pp. 259-272. See also Anonymous, 'Human rights in peace negotiations', 18 *HRQ* (1996) pp. 249-258.

6. UN GA Res. 181 of November 1947 suggested partition of the country so as to create two states, one Jewish and one Arab. See UN GA Res. 181 (II), adopted on 29 November 1947.

Interim Agreement of 1998.[7] Subsequently, the Palestinian National Authority (PNA) was established, and a few years later, negotiations began on an Israeli-Palestinian settlement involving the issues that earlier agreements had failed to resolve.

Negotiations between the parties, with heavy US involvement, have failed thus far to result in agreement on the most important issues: the status of Jerusalem, refugees and the borders of the Arab Palestinian state. Since the failure of the Camp David Summit in 2000, in which the late President Arafat, Chairman of the PLO Executive Committee, is said to have refused what mainstream media, mainly in the US and Israel, described as a 'generous offer' made by the then Israeli Prime Minister Barak, meaningful negotiations between the two parties have yet to resume. Following the failure of the summit in 2000, the current Israeli Prime Minister Sharon made a visit to the Haram Al Sharif compound in Jerusalem, which resulted in the current *Intifada* – also called the Al Aqsa *Intifada*, after the holiest Muslim shrine in Jerusalem which the Haram Al Sharif compound houses.

2.1 The lack of reference to humanitarian law or human rights in peace negotiations and agreements

As noted, many commentators and human rights groups have criticised the Israeli and Palestinian parties for failing, during previous rounds of negotiations and in resulting agreements, to make use of, rely on and guarantee respect for minimum human rights law (HRL) and international humanitarian law (IHL) standards. Many have called on both parties to engage in 'principled' negotiations, with a view to ensuring that resulting agreements are based on, rather than violating, the applicable principles included in international instruments.[8] The parties have thus far failed to do so.

However, this is not to say that the Palestinian side has not shown any interest in making any use of the guidance that international law offers. Such an interest has even been professed in public. The Palestinian delegation to the Palestinian-Israeli

7. Agreements signed include: the Palestinian-Israeli Declaration of Principles on Self-Government Arrangements for Palestinians, signed 13 September 1993; Agreement on the Gaza Strip and the Jericho Area, signed 4 May 1994; Agreement on Preparatory Transfer of Powers and Responsibilities, 29 August 1994; Israeli-Palestinian Interim Agreement on the West Bank and the Gaza Strip, 28 September 1995; Protocol Concerning the Redeployment in Hebron, 17 January 1997; Agreement on Temporary International Presence in Hebron, 21 January 1997; Wye Plantation Memorandum, 23 October 1998; the Sharm el-Sheikh Memorandum on Implementation Timeline of Outstanding Commitments of Agreements Signed and the Resumption of Permanent Status Negotiations, 4 September 1999. Text of agreements <http://www.palestine-un.org/>.

8. See for example *Human Rights Neglected in Theory and Practice by All Involved in 'Peacemaking'*, (Amnesty International 23 December 1998); *An Analysis of the Wye River Memorandum* (Human Rights Watch November 1998); *Five years after Oslo, durable peace must be based on justice* (Amnesty International September 1998); *Developing a Human Rights Agenda for Peace* (Amnesty International 26 March 2001), and *Human Rights Should Not be Bargained Away in Road Map Negotiations* (Amnesty International 3 June 2003) <http://www.amnesty.org>. See also *Road Map Fails Rights Test* (Human Rights Watch 8 May 2003), and *The Road Map: Repeating Oslo's Human Rights Mistakes* (Human Rights Watch 8 May 2003) <http://www.hrw.org>.

negotiations held in 1991-1992 in Washington, led by Dr Haidar Abdu Shafi, made a serious effort to negotiate with the Israeli delegation using the international legal status of the OPT as a departure point.[9]

These negotiations took place at a time when 'secret'/back channel negotiations were taking place between a PLO delegation and an Israeli delegation. The Washington talks failed to produce results, as the Israeli delegation was not willing to accept the consequences of the status of Israel in the OPT as an occupying power, subject to IHL rules which provide some guidance on the way the occupied territory should be disposed of.[10]

The Declaration of Principles (DOP)[11] was the result of the Oslo 'secret' negotiations, concluded in August of 1993. In its more than 3,400 words, the DOP does not make a single reference to the 'human rights' of either Palestinians or Israelis. The Gaza-Jericho Agreement, reached in Cairo on 4 May 1994,[12] was the first of a series of Israeli-Palestinian agreements of a transitional nature, according to which the Israeli army redeployed in parts of the Gaza Strip and Jericho. It only includes a single, general sentence on human rights.[13]

The remaining provisions of the Agreement, however, put much emphasis on policing by the PNA, and set up Israeli-Palestinian structures for coordination, which left the Israeli occupation authority with wide powers in almost every aspect of the life of Palestinians, suggesting that the single provision on human rights was not meant to represent a serious commitment but to pay mere 'lip service' to these principles. Succeeding agreements were empty of even the single, vague, practically meaningless article mentioning human rights, although by 1996 human rights groups and ordinary citizens had expressed dismay at the deterioration of Palestinians' human rights as the peace process unfolded.[14]

Two years later, on 23 October 1998, the parties concluded the Wye River Memorandum.[15] The only reference to human rights in the Wye River Memorandum is weak and general and pertains only to actions of the Palestinian police:

> 'Pursuant to Article XI (1) of Annex I of the interim agreement, and without derogating from the above, the Palestinian police will exercise powers and responsibilities to imple-

---

9. See H. Abed Al-Shafi, 'A Political reading of the DOP', in *Challenges Facing Palestinian Society in the Interim Period* (Jerusalem, Palestinian Academic Society for the Study of International Affairs (PASSIA) 1994) pp. 11-18, and R. Shehadeh, 'A legal reading of the DOP', in ibid., pp. 19-26. See also R. Shehadeh, 'Al-madameen al-qanoniyah wal'amaliyah li'itifaqiyat al-qahira' [Legal and practical implications of the Cairo Agreement], 1 *Al-siyasa Al-falastiniyah* (1994) pp. 52-60 (Arabic).

10. See Shehadeh, 'A legal reading of the DOP', ibid., pp. 19-26. See also Shehadeh, 'Al-madameen al-qanoniyah wal'amaliyah li itifaqiyat al-qahira', ibid., pp. 52-60.

11. Palestinian-Israeli Declaration of Principles on Self-Government Arrangements for Palestinians, signed 13 September 1993, <http://www.palestine-un.org/peace/p_a.html>.

12. Agreement on the Gaza Strip and the Jericho Area, signed 4 May 1994, <http://www.palestine-un.org/peace/p_c.html>.

13. Art. XIV, Interim Agreement.

14. These include the Agreement on Temporary International Presence in the City of Hebron, signed 9 May 1996, and Protocol Concerning Redeployment in Hebron, concluded 15 January 1998.

15. Wye River Memorandum, 23 October 1998, <http://www.palestine-un.org/peace/p_k.html>.

ment this memorandum with due regard to internationally accepted norms of human rights and the rule of law, and will be guided by the need to protect the public, respect human dignity, and avoid harassment.'[16]

This provision not only fails to offer the minimum guarantees required in the complex situation prevailing in the OPTs, but it actually sent the wrong message to the parties and, more importantly, the people of the OPT, given the fact that Israel maintains extensive and in many areas and spheres exclusive control. The message the wording sends is that Israel's violations of the rights of Palestinians were beyond the scope of the Palestinian-Israeli negotiation process and agreements reached. In its analysis of the Memorandum, Human Rights Watch observed that:

> 'Instead of creating strong mechanisms to prevent such violations, many sections of the Wye River Memorandum can be read as encouraging them. Much of the document's language relating to security is broad and categorical, as in the requirement that the Palestinian side pursue a policy of "zero tolerance for terror and violence" and that both sides "take all measures necessary in order to prevent acts of terrorism, crime and hostilities". Without a countervailing emphasis on human rights, such language suggests that any and all measures, whether or not they accord with the parties' human rights obligations and the fundamental principles they have pledged to respect, are justified in the fight to eliminate armed attacks against civilians.'[17]

In later agreements, such as the Sharm el-Sheikh Memorandum, even this basic, vague text disappeared.[18] Thus, the many calls on both parties to address the numerous human rights issues and concerns so very present in the conflict unfortunately went unanswered.[19]

As violence in the OPTs rose to unprecedented levels,[20] in 2002 a quartet composed of representatives of the UN and the governments of the US, EU countries and Russia developed a 'Road Map for Peace in the Middle East'[21] as part of their efforts to revive the Israeli-Palestinian negotiation process. The Road Map is not a treaty but simply a performance-based list of sequential steps Israeli and Palestinian authorities could take with the backing of the quartet members. There is no

---

16. Art. C(4), Wye River Memorandum.

17. *An Analysis of the Wye River Memorandum* (Human Rights Watch, November 1998).

18. Sharm el Sheikh Memorandum, *supra* n. 7.

19. See *Five Years After The Oslo Agreement: Human Rights Sacrificed For 'Security'* (Amnesty International September 1998); *Human Rights Neglected*, *supra* n. 8, and *Developing a Human Rights Agenda for Peace*, *supra* n. 8.

20. In December 2000 and January 2001, just weeks before the Israeli elections of 6 February 2001, and while the Palestinian *Intifada* and violence continued throughout the OPTs, Israeli and Palestinian teams conducted negotiations in which progress was made, though no agreement was concluded on any of the issues discussed. See Israeli-Palestinian Joint Statement, issued at Taba, Egypt, 27 January 2001, *The Jerusalem Post*, 28 January 2001.

21. *A Performance-Based Road Map to a Permanent Two-State Solution to the Israeli-Palestinian Conflict*, released by the Office of the Spokesman of the US State Department on 30 April 2003, Press Statement No. 2003/451.

explicit reference to any provisions of international law in the Road Map, which is based on the premise that the parties will reach a negotiated settlement, without any stipulation that the outcome conform to international law.[22] This is not different or better than the Road Map's predecessors with regard to ensuring respect for or making use of human rights or international law generally.

Both Human Rights Watch and Amnesty International have studied the Road Map and, upon its release, made their positions clear. Human Rights Watch expressed its concern at 'the failure of the Road Map to incorporate into its provisions internationally recognized human rights and international humanitarian law (IHL) principles',[23] and concluded that: 'Other human rights and international humanitarian law standards are incorporated not as binding obligations but as political benchmarks subject to negotiation, political expediency, and performance by other parties.'[24] Amnesty International's position is similar: 'The failure of past agreements between Israel and the Palestinians has demonstrated that while a human rights agenda alone may not be the answer, it must be a central part of any solution. Only a just settlement, which respects the human rights of all parties, will endure.'[25]

Two further developments may shed more light on the parties' views or those of the international community with respect to the role respect for and enforcement of IHL rules may have in the course of conflict and its resolution. At the demand of the Palestine Liberation Organisation, the UN GA met on 17 March 1998, and recommended convening a Conference of High Contracting Parties to the Fourth Geneva Convention on 15 July 1999.[26] The Conference was indeed convened on the said date. After a brief, ceremonial session, a statement was issued.[27] Human rights organisations, who have for years criticised the parties for failure to make use of or respect international standards and rules in the search for a negotiated settlement, again criticised the parties for their repeated failure.[28] The statement only reiterated the duty to respect IHL, and is so general that it bears no significance for IHL enforcement or the search of peace. According to Amnesty International:

> 'Instead of studying ways to enforce compliance with the obligations of the Convention, the meeting was a simple procedural one and was concluded after 10 minutes. Even

---

22. See *The Road Map: Repeating Oslo's Human Rights Mistakes*, *supra* n. 8.
23. Ibid., at p. 1 of online version. Print version not available at any Palestinian law library to date.
24. Ibid., p. 1 of the online version. Same as above.
25. *Human Rights Should Not be Bargained Away in Road Map Negotiations*, *supra* n. 8, p. 1.
26. See GA Res. ES-10/5 (17 March 1998). This call was reiterated in GA Res. ES-10/6 (9 February 1999).
27. Conference of High Contracting Parties to the Fourth Geneva Convention, Statement, <http://www.palestine-un.org/news/jul99_statement.html>.
28. See *Fourth Geneva Convention meeting: an abdication of responsibility*, (Amnesty International, 15 July 1999) <http://web.amnesty.org/library/Index/ENGMDE150471999?open&of=ENG-ISR>. See also *U.S. Should Support Geneva Conventions Enforcement: International Law has Priority over Israel-PLO Political Negotiations* (Human Rights Watch, 12 July 1999) <http://hrw.org/english/docs/1999/07/12/isrlpa960_txt.htm>.

> worse, it set no date for a substantive discussion and decisions on enforcement measures, confining itself to the postponement of the meeting *sine die*.'[29]

Additionally, a Parallel Meeting of Human Rights organisations, held during 14-16 July 1999 in Geneva issued a statement in which the organisations stated:

> 'we deeply regret that the High Contracting Parties meeting here have not fulfilled and appeared to have repudiated the mandate they took upon themselves when they voted for the General Assembly resolution calling for this conference. By failing to hold a substantive conference to address pressing questions of enforcement of the Convention, the Parties have undermined and politicised the application of international humanitarian law, not only with regard to this conflict but other and future conflicts as well.'[30]

Another Conference of High Contracting Parties to the Fourth Geneva Convention convened on 5 December 2001.[31] The Conference was held upon the invitation of the government of Switzerland, the depository of the Geneva Conventions, following a call by the UN GA.[32] The Conference – which was boycotted by the US, Israel and Australia, under the pretext that it 'might undermine the delicate situation in the region'[33] – was attended by representatives of 114 states and delegates representing international and non-governmental organisations, including the UN and the International Committee of the Red Cross (ICRC).

The Conference, as with its predecessor, did not fully live up to expectations: while its aim was to discuss 'measures to enforce the Convention in the Occupied Palestinian Territory, including Jerusalem, and to ensure respect thereof in accordance with common article 1', it ended with a Declaration affirming its applicability to the OPTs, including East Jerusalem, without dealing with enforcement measures of any kind.[34] However, the 2001 Conference Declaration was more detailed than the 1999 Conference statement, and included new elements which were not included in the 1999 statement. Most importantly, paragraph 16 of the Declaration states:

---

29. *Fourth Geneva Convention meeting: an abdication of responsibility, supra* n. 28.

30. *Bad Precedent After Fifty Years* (Geneva, Parallel Meeting of Human Rights Organizations 15 July 1999) <http://www.pchrgaza.org/files/PressR/English/1999/15july.htm>.

31. See Conference of High Contracting Parties to the Fourth Geneva Convention, *Declaration,* 5 December 2001, <http://www.palestine-un.org/news/conference4GC.html>.

32. See 'Geneva Parley Delegates Blast Israel', *The Jerusalem Post*, 6 December 2001.

33. *Israel's reaction to the convening of the High Contracting Parties to the Fourth Geneva Convention,* Communicated by the Israeli Foreign Ministry Spokesperson, 6 December 2001, <http://www.israelemb.org/articles/2001/December/2001120602.html>. For reference to a number of statements by key US officials, including Vice-President Al Gore and Ambassador Martin Indyk, see *Letter to President Clinton* (Human Rights Watch, 7 July 1999) <http://hrw.org/english/docs/1999/07/07/isrlpa961.htm>.

34. *PCHR and LAW condemn High Contracting Parties farce* (PCHR and LAW – the Palestinian Society for the Protection of Human Rights and the Environment, 22 November 2001) <http://www.pchrgaza.org/files/PressR/English/2001/71-2001.htm>. See also *Declaration of the NGO parallel meeting concerning the Fourth Geneva Convention* (Geneva 5 December 2001) <http://www.reliefweb.int/w/Rwb.nsf/s/34D82A8C0B950F5B85256B1A005A76ED>.

'The participating High Contracting Parties stress that respect for the Fourth Geneva Convention and international humanitarian law in general is essential to improve the humanitarian situation in the field and to achieve a just and lasting peace.'

Despite this, States Parties to the Convention failed to take the Declaration they had adopted seriously. Major world powers, including the US, did not act to make use of the Declaration in bringing the parties closer to peaceful resolution of the conflict, and their search for peace in Palestine failed to avail of relevant international legal frameworks.

3. THE ADVISORY OPINION OF THE ICJ ON THE CONSEQUENCES OF THE CONSTRUCTION BY ISRAEL OF A WALL IN THE OPT

The most recent attempt at using international law in the course of attempting to resolve the Israeli-Palestinian conflict is represented in the Palestinian lobbying which resulted in the UN GA seeking an Advisory Opinion of the ICJ with respect to the separation barrier. Again, this Palestinian initiative took place during a period when Israeli-Palestinian negotiations had stalled.

First, however, what is the separation barrier? In 2002 the Israeli government approved a plan for the construction of a separation barrier, with its first segments lying in the northern part of the West Bank.[35] The Commander of the Israeli military in the West Bank issued orders to seize plots of land in various parts of the West Bank belonging to Palestinian residents of a large number of towns and villages.[36] The declared purpose of the seizure was the construction of a barrier or wall, a so-called 'obstacle', on the so-called 'seam' area, an area *in* the West Bank (including Jerusalem), whose 'boundary' is not defined but is adjacent to the 'Green Line'.[37] Due to the fact that the barrier is being built in the West Bank, if completed as planned it will surround over 16 percent of the territory of the West Bank.[38]

The construction of the barrier has since then begun, and it continued at the time of writing, resulting in severe limitations on the freedom of movement of Palestinians, both civilians and emergency crews alike, as well as causing serious damage

---

35. Details of the Israeli government's decisions pertaining to the construction of the barrier are available in *Beit Sourik Village Council* v. *The Government of Israel*, Israeli High Court of Justice, HCJ 2056/04, English translation of judgement, <http://www.nad-plo.org>. See the article by Y. Shany in this volume of the Yearbook for analysis of the decision.

36. Many orders have thus far been issued, many of which were the subject of appeals before the Israeli High Court. For details visit the website of the Negotiations Affairs Department, Palestine Liberation Organization, <http://www.nad-plo.org/listing.php?view=palisraeli_wall>.

37. See *Order Concerning Security Directives (Judea and Samaria) (number 378), 1970, Declaration Concerning the Closure of Area Number s/2/03 (Seam Area)* (Israeli Defense Forces 2 October 2003). English translation <http://www.nad-plo.org/inner.php?view=palisraeli_wall_primary_hborders3p>.

38. Statistics available at the website of the Israeli human rights organization, B'Tselem, <http://www.btselem.org/english/Separation_Barrier/Statistics.asp>.

to the fabric of Palestinian society and to the hopes for a viable Palestinian state in the OPT at the end of the Israeli occupation.

Realising the magnitude of the 'project' and the disaster it represents for the Palestinian people, and in the absence of a Palestinian-Israeli meaningful negotiation process – at a time when Israel had declared the elected Palestinian leadership as irrelevant – the PLO sought international assistance in trying to bring the construction of the barrier to an end. On 8 December 2003 the UN GA adopted a resolution seeking an ICJ Advisory Opinion on the legal consequences of the construction of a Wall in the Occupied Palestinian Territories.[39] The UN GA formulated its question as follows:

> 'What are the legal consequences arising from the construction of the wall being built by Israel, the occupying Power, in the Occupied Palestinian Territory, including in and around East Jerusalem, as described in the report of the Secretary-General, considering the rules and principles of international law, including the Fourth Geneva Convention of 1949, and relevant Security Council and General Assembly Resolutions?'[40]

On 23 February 2004 the Court began three-day hearings during which 15 states and organisations had the opportunity to present their views pertaining to the question the Court was asked to address.[41] Moreover, a total of 44 states, including the United States and Israel,[42] as well as the United Nations, the European Union, the Organization of the Islamic Conference, the League of Arab States and Palestine submitted written statements to the Court.

Before answering the question which the GA presented, the Court had first to decide on its jurisdiction and the appropriateness of giving an Advisory Opinion, especially given the many objections which Israel, the US and a number of other countries had raised, demanding that the Court should decline to render an Opinion. The grounds used for objecting to the Court's jurisdiction included: 'the active engagement of the Security Council with the situation in the Middle East';[43] 'the request concerns a contentious matter between Israel and Palestine, in respect of which Israel has not consented to the exercise of that jurisdiction',[44] 'an advisory opinion from the Court on the legality of the wall and the legal consequences of its construction could impede a political, negotiated solution to the Israeli-Palestinian conflict', and giving an Opinion 'could complicate the negotiations envisaged in the "Roadmap"'.[45]

The Court, having considered the above and other arguments, decided that it 'has jurisdiction to give an opinion on the question put to it by the General Assem-

---

39. UN GA Res. A/ES-10/14, adopted 8 December 2003, <http://www.icj-cij.org>.
40. Ibid.
41. *Legal Consequences of the Construction of a Wall in the Occupied Palestinian Territory*, ICJ Advisory Opinion, 9 July 2004, <http://www.icj-cij.org>.
42. Material available at the Court's website, <http://www.icj-cij.org>.
43. *Supra* n. 41, at para. 24.
44. Ibid., at para. 46.
45. Ibid., at para. 51.

bly', and 'also that there is no compelling reason for it to use its discretionary power not to give that opinion'.[46] On the issue of the possible impact the Opinion may have on Roadmap, the Court found that what influence the Court's opinion might have on those negotiations is not clear, and that it 'cannot regard this factor as a compelling reason to decline to exercise its jurisdiction'.[47]

The Court then moved to ruling on the Question put to it by the GA, and found, amongst other things, that 'the construction of the wall, and its associated regime, are contrary to international law'.[48] The Court further ruled that Israel must 'cease forthwith the works of construction of the wall being built in the Occupied Palestinian Territories, including in and around East Jerusalem',[49] must dismantle it, and compensate the Palestinian population for the damage and loss caused in and as a result of its construction.[50]

4. NEGOTIATING ON PRINCIPLE?

The 'Road Map'[51] has so far failed to guide the way to agreement on the most difficult issues deferred, in the framework of the Oslo negotiations process, to the final stage of the process: Jerusalem and the return of refugees. The failure to address these issues, and the violence, killing, loss and destruction which have followed, begs the question: why have the parties failed? For us, who live the current tragic reality, this is not a purely academic question, because our own children are growing up confined to 'ghettos' not of our choosing, and they, like their parents, will have to cross checkpoints from and to school, hospitals, etc., and because those of us destined to live here in this troubled land need, more than anything else, to find a solution to the current deadlock, and hopefully to the conflict altogether.

---

46. Ibid., at para. 65.
47. Ibid., at para. 53.
48. Ibid., at para. 142.
49. Ibid., at para. 151.
50. Ibid., at para. 152. The Israeli High Court was also asked by the Beit Sourik Village Council to decide on the route that certain segments of the Wall take in the OPTs. In a decision announced only days before the ICJ decision, the Israeli Court, on 30 June 2004, accepted the Israeli authorities' principal argument/assertion that the construction of the Wall is a security measure (part 28). The Court also accepted the Israeli government's argument that the Wall is a proportionate response to security realities Israeli authorities intend to deal with (part 47), but that with respect certain segments of the Wall, the High Court decided that the 'balance determined by the military commander is not proportionate' (parts 84 and 85). Having accepted the petition in part, the Court then ordered the Israeli authorities to reconsider the route that some segments of the Wall take (part 85). See *Beit Sourik Village Council* v. *The Government of Israel*, Israeli High Court of Justice, HCJ 2056/04. English translation of judgement at <http://www.nad-plo.org>.
51. *A Performance-Based Road Map*, *supra* n. 21. Although the Road Map was developed in 2002, it was only released following the creation by the Palestinian National Authority (PNA), on demand of the US, of the position of a Palestinian prime minister, and the swearing in, on April 2003, of the first Palestinian prime minister.

There is certainly more than a single reason why the parties have failed to reach a solution to their 'differences'. As a human rights lawyer, with training in the field of negotiation, however, my answers naturally come from these fields, not from the fields of economics, security or others – though these offer important and relevant guidance as well. Therefore, I shall, in this section, use both human rights standards and instruments, and negotiation theory to examine and identify relevant failures of the parties and make recommendations.

Palestinians and Israelis often imagine that the two people are engaged in a unique conflict, which warrants 'unique solutions'.[52] The study of other conflicts reveals similar assumptions.[53] But with many aspects of our life now subject to international standards, however weak or vague some of these may be, and given the many similarities amongst conflicts, comparisons are valid and offer valuable lessons.[54]

Generally, parties to a conflict negotiate with the same parties they fight, although the means and timing of negotiations vary from one conflict to another. Typically, negotiations take the form of political discussions, with some form or level of violence employed and seen as an integral part of such processes.

It is certainly true that the use of force has repercussions for those imposing it, as well as their targets. However, in situations where negotiating parties expect that the outcome of a negotiation process will largely, or even entirely, be shaped by the level of the parties' power, violence could be seen as a – or the only – means for disadvantaged groups to manipulate the balance of power prevailing at a certain point in time, in order to improve the position from which they negotiate. In 1977 Morton Deutsch had this to say:

> 'Is it not obvious that, with the great disparities in power and affluence within nations and between nations, there will be continuing pressure for social change? And is it not also obvious that the processes of social change will be disorderly and destructive unless

---

52. On this generally see E.E. Azar, 'Protracted International Conflicts: ten propositions', 12 *International Interactions* (1985) pp. 59-70; E. E. Azar, *The Management of Protracted Social Conflict* (Hampshire, Dartmouth Publishing 1990). See also D. Bar-Tal, 'Societal Beliefs in Times of Intractable Conflict: the Israeli case', 9 *The International Journal of Conflict Management* (1998) pp. 22-50, and J. McGarry, 'Political settlements in Northern Ireland and South Africa', XLVI *Political Studies* (1998) pp. 853-870.

53. Many authors have compared the Israeli-Palestinian conflict, or aspects thereof, with other conflicts. See for example T.G. Mitchell, *Native vs. Settler: Ethnic Conflict in Israel/Palestine, Northern Ireland, and South Africa* (Contributions in military studies, No. 200) (Westport CT, Greenwood Publishing Group 2000); D. Harman Akenson, *God's Peoples: Covenant and Land in South Africa, Israel, and Ulster* (Ithaca NY, Cornell University Press 1992). I have treated this issue in detail in my *Negotiating Human Rights in Peace Processes: The Lessons of South Africa, Northern Ireland and the Palestinian-Israeli Situations*, Ph.D. thesis submitted to the University of Ulster, Jordanstown, Northern Ireland, UK, 2001.

54. Among the obvious similarities of many world conflicts is the role played by the land/people nexus. A second common feature is the role of organized, political violence in the conflict, and the need to end the same. For more information on the settler vs. native origins of the Israeli-Palestinian, Northern Ireland and South Africa situations, see Mitchell and Akenson, ibid. See also P. Wallensteen and M. Sollenberg, 'Armed Conflicts, Conflict Termination and Peace Agreements, 1989-96'; 34 *Journal of Peace Research* (1997) pp. 339-358.

> those in power are able, or enabled, to lower their defensiveness and resistance to a change in their relative status?'[55]

Further, according to Thomas G. Mitchell, the first and perhaps most important stage of a negotiation process involves the search for a formula for reaching agreement.[56] Though each party may still try to ensure that its interpretation of the formula actually drives or shapes the ultimate outcome of a negotiation process, even this manoeuvring has to occur within the framework established by such agreed formula.

An international consensus on the universal nature of human rights has been developing for decades, with the international human rights and humanitarian law principles and the instruments pronouncing them clearly assuming much greater importance in international relations than ever before.[57] This increased role for human rights also extends to the management and resolution of conflicts.[58] This is evident in the many 'universally accepted' human rights and international law instruments, and in the repeated calls by human rights groups, activists and negotiation theorists alike for the use of these instruments and the principles included therein in conflict resolutions.[59]

The UN Secretary General in 2002 joined the many voices calling for a greater role for human rights in conflict resolution, stating in his Report on the Protection of Civilians in Armed Conflict that the 'effective protection of civilians is a critical element in laying the foundations of the peace process. The durability of peace is

---

55. M. Deutsch, *The Resolution of Conflict* (London, Yale University Press 1973) p. 400.

56. C. R. Mitchell, *The Structure of International Conflict* (London, MacMillan 1981) pp. 206-207.

57. Evidence of the strength of this trend is found in the overwhelming support given to the Rome Statute of the International Criminal Court and also in the British and Chilean judgments in the case of General Augusto Pinochet, the former Chilean dictator. See Rome Statute of the International Criminal Court, UN Doc. A/Conf.183/9, 17 July 1998; *Pinochet case: A landmark but rights group disappointed if no trial* (New York, Human Rights Watch 12 January 2000); *Regina* v. *Bow Street Metropolitan Stipendiary Magistrate and Others, Ex parte Pinochet Ugrate*, [1998] 3 W.L.R. 1456 (in which the House of Lords quashed the decision of the Divisional Court that invalidated the arrest warrants issued for Pinochet); *Regina* v. *Bow Street Metropolitan Stipendiary Magistrate and Others, Ex parte Pinochet Ugrate* (No. 2), [1999] 2 W.L.R. 272, and *Regina* v. *Bow Street Magistrate, Ex parte Pinochet* (No. 3), [1999] 2 W.L.R. 827 (in which the House of Lords finally decided to accept the appeal and quash the decision of the Divisional Court, thus permitting reinstatement of the arrest warrants against Pinochet). See also *Chile: Truth and justice must not be hindered*, AI Index AMR 22/009/2001 (London, Amnesty International 9 July 2001) and 'Chile's Pinochet unfit for trial, court says', Reuters, 10 July 2001.

58. See C. Campbell, 'Peace and the Laws of War: the Role of International Humanitarian Law in the Post-Conflict Environment', 82 *IRRC* (2000) pp. 627-651, especially pp. 628-631, and C. Bell, *Human Rights and Peace Agreements* (Oxford, Oxford University Press 2000) p. 4.

59. See for example *Human Rights Neglected*, *supra* n. 8; *An Analysis of the Wye River Memorandum*, *supra* n. 8; *Five years after Oslo*, *supra* n. 8; *Developing a Human Rights Agenda for Peace*, *supra* n. 8; *Road Map Fails Rights Test*, *supra* n. 8; *The Road Map: Repeating Oslo's Human Rights Mistakes*, *supra* n. 8; *Human Rights Should Not be Bargained Away in Road Map Negotiations*, *supra* n. 8; Boyle, *supra* n. 4; Gaer, *supra* n. 4; Quigley, *supra* n. 4, and Campbell, *supra* n. 58.

dependent on a commitment to the protection of civilians from its very inception.'[60]

A school in the field of negotiation theory has for decades been developing which emphasises the importance of making use of principle in negotiation processes. The proponents of the 'principled negotiation' theory believe that the use of principle in the making or design of the formula for agreement makes agreement possible, and at the same time provides a basis for outcomes that are 'durable'.[61]

Unlike the parties to the Israeli-Palestinian negotiation process, and contrary to submissions before the ICJ in the current case, the authors of principled negotiation theory argue that parties to a conflict cannot, and in fact do not have to, abandon principles to reach agreement.[62] This is not universally accepted, however. An exchange that occurred in 1996 and 1997 between an anonymous writer and Francis Boyle and Felice D. Gaer on the pages of *Human Rights Quarterly*, about the role of principle versus pragmatism in the search for peace, encapsulates the essence of the debate about the need to include human rights principles in peace negotiations.[63]

The place of principle in the Oslo process was debated more recently by US Professor John Quigley and Shimon Shitreet.[64] The views Mr Shitreet expressed in the pages of the *Case Western Reserve Journal of International Law* are of the kind the Israeli government used to try to prevent the ICJ from giving its Advisory Opinion in the present case, and later to reject calls to abide by it.[65] These views remain those of a minority and are contrary to the established trend in the fields of international law, human rights and peace studies.

5. CONCLUSIONS

In September 2003 the Special Rapporteur of the Commission on Human Rights, John Dugard, issued his Report on the situation of human rights in the Palestinian territories occupied by Israel since 1967. In his Report, the Special Rapporteur pointed to serious obstacles in the way of implementing the Road Map for Middle East Peace, released earlier in 2003. Of these, he said:

> 'Peace in the region cannot succeed without a return to the rule of law and respect for human rights and international humanitarian law. It is unfortunate that the road map, like the Oslo Accords, fails to give sufficient weight to this factor.'[66]

---

60. UN Secretary General Report on the Protection of Civilians in Armed Conflict, UN Doc. S/2002/1300.

61. R. Fisher, W. Ury, and B. Patton, *Getting to Yes: Negotiating Agreement Without Giving In,* 2nd edn. (Boston, Houghton Mifflin 1991) p 4.

62. Ibid.

63. See Anonymous, *supra* n. 5; Boyle, *supra* n. 4, at pp. 515-516, and Gaer, *supra* n. 4, pp. 1-8.

64. Quigley, *supra* n. 4, pp. 351-381.

65. Shitreet, *supra* n. 5, pp. 259-272.

66. *Report of the Special Rapporteur of the Commission on Human Rights, John Dugard, on the situation of human rights in the Palestinian territories occupied by Israel since 1967*, submitted in

A few months later, a long list of countries, including Israel and the US, 'petitioned' the ICJ to decline to give its Advisory Opinion on the consequences of the construction by Israel of the separation barrier or wall, using exactly the opposite argument. The arguments made against the issuance of the said Opinion were not all of a legal nature but largely were political, the essence of which is that efforts made towards reaching Palestinian-Israeli peace will not benefit from, but be jeopardised by, clarification of the legal status of an action of one of the parties. This suggested, again, that legal processes are alien to processes aimed at 'peacemaking' and should give way to negotiation.

The hopes of the two peoples of an end to the Israeli-Palestinian conflict will be dashed, again, by the failure of the parties to the conflict and influential world powers to learn from the mistakes of the past, through their continued failure to make use of the guidance that the applicable principles, including 'internationally-accepted' human rights and humanitarian law, offer. This sadly would indicate to the Palestinians, and others suffering the horrors of conflict for that matter, that the conventional wisdom remains that either the conflict continues or they, as the weaker party, agree to a 'solution' which offers them much less than international law provides for them.

Such failure will cast those in the international community opposed to the use of international law in the course of finding a solution to the conflict as accomplices to breaching the rights they advocate in other settings, and which they helped develop and declared as of 'universal' application.

The above should not, however, prevent us from shedding light on a few positive aspects of the current case.

First, the Court did not listen to the voices of sceptics and hypocrites. By rejecting their arguments, the Court actually sent a clear message that the existence of negotiations in and of itself does not constitute a compelling reason for abandoning the legal processes which the Court's deliberations and the issuance of its Opinion represented.[67]

Second, despite the pressures exerted by the US and Israel in order to prevent the issuance by the Court of its Opinion on the said Question, submissions to the ICJ generally supported the Request the GA made.[68] Though the behaviour of influential world powers, including the US, represents repeated failure to act in a manner which supports the premise that 'peace' building should be based on international law and result in improved enjoyment of equal rights by affected citizens, the position of states which supported the issuance of the Opinion gives hope of

---

accordance with Commission resolution 1993/2, UN Doc. AE/CN.4/2004/6 (8 September 2003) (Dugard Report).

67. *Supra* n. 41, at para. 53.

68. See for example written statement by the United States, France, Germany, and Japan, <http://www.icj-cij.org>. In the Written Statement by the United States, it is stated that: 'the United States believes that the giving of an advisory opinion in this matter risks undermining the peace process and politicizing the Court'. See *Written Statement of the United States of America*, 30 January 2004. In its Statement, Germany concurs: 'Such an opinion would be likely to hinder, rather than assist, the implementation of the Road Map.' See *Statement of the Government of the Federal Republic of Germany*, January 2004.

increased actual support in the world community for respect for the rule of law and its institutions on the international level. This is a welcome development, and must be supported and continued.

Third, the Israeli High Court, though it did not reach the same conclusion with respect to the legal consequences of the barrier, did not refrain from intervening in cases related to the same. This suggests that the position and arguments of the Israeli (and US) government was not accepted even by Israel's own judicial system. This is significant, especially given that Israel's courts have more often than not approved of other Israeli government actions, including the destruction of homes, deportations and other violations of international law.

Fourth, if the subsequent resumption of Israeli-Palestinian contacts and coordination with respect to the Israeli plan for disengagement from Gaza is of any relevance to this case, it serves to refute the argument that the Court's Opinion 'risks undermining the peace process'.[69]

And fifth, human rights organisations have increasingly become involved in advocating 'principled' solutions for conflicts, as shown by the many interventions human rights organisations made, referenced throughout this article. The upholding (or not) by parties to conflict of 'universal' human rights principles in peace negotiations and agreements resulting from such processes has become a yardstick against which human rights organisations measure and evaluate the outcome of peace processes. As Human Rights Watch rightly states: 'the legitimacy and sustainability of political processes are strengthened, not weakened, by including [international humanitarian law] and human rights standards. All conflict-related agreements should include and uphold human rights and international humanitarian law standards.'[70]

As shown above, there are some improvements in the world's view of the role of law in the context of conflict and the search for its resolution. But the fight for justice is far from over. Those who subscribe to universal human rights should not give up until the international community's declared support for international law, including human rights, is actually translated into support for using them as instruments and tools in the search for peace. Human rights activists and organisations, as well as people who endure the horrors of conflict, should keep up the pressure on all those involved in conflicts worldwide, and on the sponsors of processes established for conflict resolution, until humanitarian principles are accorded the status they deserve and the lessons of the past failures are taken seriously.

---

69. See *Written Statement of the United States of America, supra* n. 68.
70. See *The Road Map: Repeating Oslo's Human Rights Mistakes, supra* n. 8.

SOVIET GENOCIDE TRIALS IN THE BALTIC STATES: THE RELEVANCE OF INTERNATIONAL LAW[1]

Rytis Satkauskas[2]

1. INTRODUCTION

Soviet forces invaded Estonia, Latvia and Lithuania in 1940; after a brief German occupation, the Soviets retook them in 1944. Thousands of perceived Soviet enemies were deported to Siberia, where many died in the harsh conditions. Josef Stalin is blamed for killing a total of at least 15 million people and deporting another 40 million potential enemies during his reign.[3]

After regaining independence following the 1991 collapse of the Soviet Union, Lithuania, Latvia and Estonia vowed to prosecute those who took part in Soviet repressions. They have tried over a dozen ex-agents. Most have received suspended sentences, but several have been imprisoned. In turn, Moscow has sharply criticised the Baltic prosecutions, calling them revenge. Indeed, no other ex-Soviet republics have prosecuted Stalinist-era officials. But the Baltic States insist they are seeking long overdue justice and shedding light on some of the worst human rights abuses of the twentieth century.

To date, Baltic authorities have been investigating the suspects for more than ten years, interviewing deportees and combing Soviet secret police archives for evidence. In Lithuania alone, 91 proceedings have been initiated against the main perpetrators of the Soviet repressions during the post war period.[4] Similar figures

---

2. Rytis Satkauskas is a Doctoral Candidate at the Faculty of Law of the Universidad Autónoma, Madrid.

3. S. Courtois et al., *Le livre noir du communisme. Crimes, terreur, répression* (Paris, Laffont 1997) p. 37. See also N. Werth, 'The mechanism of a mass crime : the great terror in the Soviet Union' 1937-1938', in R. Gellately and B. Kiernan, eds., *The Spector of Genocide, Mass Murder in Historical Perspective* (Cambridge, Cambridge University Press 2003). See for an extensive collection of Soviet government orders, decrees, resolutions, reports, telegrams, and communications dealing with the deportation of Soviet citizens and others to special settlements. N.F. Bugai, ed., *Iosif Stalin – Laverentiiu Berii: 'Ikh nado deportirovat': dokumenty, fakty, kommentarii* [J. Stalin – L.Beria: 'They must be deported': documents, facts, commentary] (Moscow, Druzhba narodov 1992).

4. Figures from Report of the Prosecutor General of the Republic of Lithuania 'Activities of the Department of Special Investigations of the Prosecutor General Office 1992-2000', on file with author.

Yearbook of International Humanitarian Law
Volume 7 - 2004 - pp. 388-409

DOI 10.1017/S1389135904003885

appear in Latvia[5] and Estonia.[6] However, so far only a few judgments have appeared in these so-called 'Soviet genocide' cases and each of them has generated a certain amount of discussion in legal as well as in political circles.

Many factors influence the work of the lawyers dealing with the Soviet repressions. First of all are the usual difficulties related to the investigation of crimes committed more than half a century ago: the lack of documented evidence or credible testimony and, of course, the age of the accused[7] and the surviving victims and witnesses. In addition, some specific issues arise, namely those of the qualification of the Soviet repressions in international law and the consistency of national legislation with international norms. It is not surprising, therefore, that the decisions in these cases reveal a certain confusion over whether Soviet repressions must be qualified as war crimes, genocide or 'simply' as murder.

This paper is principally concerned with genocide as a legal norm. It seeks to address the question whether the indictments of the courts of the three Baltic republics for the crime of genocide, as it is described in their national statutes, correspond with the definition provided by international law. It avoids any qualification of the Soviet occupational regime; instead the emphasis is on the progress made by the legislators of the Baltic countries in defining the crime of genocide and the application of those definitions by the national courts.

2. HISTORICAL BACKGROUND

The military occupation of the three Baltic republics in June 1940 and their annexation in August 1940[8] was immediately followed by mass repression of their citizens, in particular of the so called 'hostile' elements or persons considered as potentially resistant to the Soviet regime. Arrests were mainly motivated as punishment for those persons perceived to be fighting against the revolutionary movement and the working class.[9] The definitions of 'fought against revolutionary movement' or 'the working class' were applied very broadly, including to persons who had served in the national army and the employees of the police and court systems. People were also often arrested for being 'members of counterrevolution-

---

5. For the Latvian perspective see more in Y.Nedyalkova, 'Latvia: The difference between Soviet and Nazi war criminals', 14 July 2000, Cyber-times News, <http://www.cyber-times.org>.

6. See more on the Estonian cases in L. Mälksoo, 'Soviet genocide?: Communist mass deportations in the Baltic States and international law', 14 *Leiden JIL* (2001) p. 782.

7. See ECHR Judgment in *Farbtuhs* v. *Latvia* case (application No. 4672/02) of 2 December 2004, where the Court found that, in view of his age (84), infirmity and condition, the applicant's continued detention was not appropriate. The situation in which he had been put was bound to cause him permanent anxiety and a sense of inferiority and humiliation so acute as to amount to degrading treatment within the meaning of Article 3.

8. See more on the qualification of the Soviet annexation in W.J.H. Hough, 'The annexation of the Baltic States and its effect on the development of law prohibiting forcible seizure of territory',6 *New York Law School Journal of International and Comparative Law* (1985) pp. 301-533.

9. See research by A. Anušauskas on the arrests and other forms of coercion carried out by Soviets in 1940-1941, <http://db.komisija.lt/Data/WEB6C.pdf>.

ary organisations', 'socially dangerous', and, less often, 'anti-Soviet elements'. The denomination 'counterrevolutionary' was particularly frequently used. It was attributed both to the political parties of the Baltic Republics, youth organisations, anti-Soviet leaflets and songs.[10]

Repression served to achieve both political and economic goals and manifested itself directly in arrests and administrative deportations as well as indirectly in dismissals and reprisals of an economic nature, etc. Often it was difficult to find a line of demarcation between them. Arrests and deportations were carried out along with the adjustment of the state apparatus to meet the requirements of the Soviet system: elimination of national movements, socialisation of the army, nationalisation of the large industrial companies and banks and land reform.[11]

According to the Soviet MVD (Ministry of State Security) reports, more than 17,500 people were deported from Lithuania[12] as a consequence of the Lithuanian Communist Party Bureau and the USSR Council of People's Commissars Resolution No. 1299-526 of 16 May 1941, 15,000 from Latvia[13] and almost 14,000 from Estonia.[14] It is estimated that another 10,000 conscripted Estonians died in Siberian 'work battalions' due to inhuman conditions and exterminations.[15]

A high number of deportees did not reach the place of destination: any attempt to escape or resist was suppressed by arms, and a great number of deaths was caused by the conditions of transportation when the people were transported in train cars intended for livestock, by the lack of fresh air, water, food and by the unsanitary conditions.

In 1941 the Nazi regime replaced that of the Soviets. However, after the reoccupation in 1945, the MVD troops, subordinate to the military security forces, the army of railway security and the internal troops, started their punitive operations against the participants of the armed resistance or any persons suspected of helping them. Repressions formally were directed against the supporters of German occupants. The most frequently used justification for arresting people was 'supporter of Germans', which, similarly to 'fought against revolutionary movement', was very widely applied. In fact, any person who during the German occupation lived in

---

10. R. Vīksne, 'Repressions Against Latvian Population in 1940/1941 -1944/1945: the Common and the Different', on Crimes Against the Humanity Latvian Site, <http://vip.latnet.lv/LPRA>.

11. See J. Pajaujis-Javis, *Soviet Genocide in Lithuania* (New York, Manyland Books 1980).

12. A. Anušauskas, 'Crimes of communism in Lithuania: historical-statistical survey', in *Anti-Communist Congress and the Proceedings of the International Public Tribunal in Vilnius: 'Evaluation of the Crimes of Communism', 2000* (Vilnius, Ramona 2002) p. 99.

13. Latvia's History Commission, 'Crimes against Humanity in the Territory of Latvia during the Soviet Occupation 1940-41', Progress Report of Latvia's History Commission *Crimes against Humanity Committed in the Territory of Latvia from 1940 to 1956 during the Occupations of the Soviet Union and National Socialist Germany*, at <http://vip.latnet.lv/lpra/1st_subcomission.htm#3>. See more in Latvian National Fund in the Scandinavian Countries, ed., *These Names Accuse, Nominal List of Latvians Deported to the Soviet Russia in 1940-41* (Stockholm, Latvian National Foundation 1951) p. 547.

14. L. Õispuu, ed., *Deportation from Estonia to Russia. 1941 & 1940-1953. Registers of Repressed Persons*. Book 6 (Tallinn, Argo TTP 2001) pp. 29-30.

15. J. Kahk, *World War II and Soviet Occupation in Estonia: a Damages Report* (Tallin, Perioodika 1991) p. 36.

Lithuania, Latvia and Estonia could be denounced as 'supporter of Germans' or 'collaborator of German occupants'. The first ones subjected to the reprisals were the persons who during the German occupation had served in self-defence units, auxiliary police and police battalions. Those who were employed in administrative positions during the occupation were likewise subject to arrests. In many cases, people were accused of using the labour of prisoners of war, not immigrating to the USSR upon the outbreak of the war, or, in case of Jews, of having survived the German occupation.

According to Dr Arvydas Anušauskas, Director of the Centre for the Investigation of Genocide and Resistance of the Lithuanian Population, out of 20,156 people who were killed during those operations, 5,000 were defenceless individuals.[16]

According to historians, there was no substantial difference between the repressions of 1940-1941 and 1944-1945; both were aimed at consolidation of power and ideology, elimination of active and passive resistance, and, at the same time, maintaining an atmosphere of fear. In most of the investigation cases, his membership of an organisation or the position held by a person was seen as being of more importance than his alleged offence.[17]

Out of 132,000 deported Lithuanian people, including those born in exile in 1945-1952, 28,000 died of disease, hunger and hard labour.[18] Personal cards of deportees (for 1941, 1949, 1951 and the years in between) in Estonian State Archives totalled 43,683.[19] According to the Estonian State Commission, Estonia lost nearly 121,000 people during both Soviet occupations approximately 18 percent of its population.[20] Soviet officials are also thought to have killed another 122,000 in Latvia.[21]

3. RECENT JUDICIAL DECISIONS IN ESTONIA, LATVIA AND LITHUANIA

Scholars writing on the Soviet mass deportations disagree over whether they should be considered as genocide. Some invoke the definition of the 1948 Genocide Convention,[22] others compare the scale of Soviet repression to that of Holo-

---

16. Anušauskas, *supra* n. 12, p. 96.
17. Vīksne, *supra* n. 10.
18. Anušauskas, *supra* n. 12, p. 95.
19. Museum's of Occupations of Estonia information, <http://www.okupatsioon.ee>.
20. A. Gunter, '"White Book" seeks to establish truth', *The Baltic Times*, No. 408 of 20-26 May 2004, pp. 1, 3.
21. Indictment of *Anti-Communist Congress, Anti-Communist Congress and the Proceedings of the International Public Tribunal in Vilnius: 'Evaluation of the Crimes of Communism'* (Vilnius, Ramona 2002, p. 927. See more in contributions to *Yearbook of the Occupation Museum of Latvia,* Rīga: Okupācijas muzeja fonds, from 2000, <http://www.occupationmuseum.lv/eng/Services/ gramatas. html>.
22. J. Otto Pohl, *Ethnic Cleansing in the USSR, 1937-1949* (Westport CT, Greenwood 1999) pp. 2-3.

caust.[23] In the Baltic States, however, the condemnation of the Soviet policies as 'genocide' has become almost axiomatic.[24]

The changes introduced in the Penal Codes of Estonia, Latvia and Lithuania during the years of regained independence signified their wish to prosecute the leaders of the Soviet terror and genocide of the population. This objective is also reflected in the court judgments that have been rendered to date.

3.1 Genocide in the Baltic context

The Law on the responsibility for the genocide of the population of Lithuania was adopted in 1992[25] to ensure that those who participated in the post war horror could not escape justice. Article 1 of the said Law introduces into the national law the definition of the crime of genocide. Article 2 provides that: 'Killing and torturing of the people of Lithuania, deportation of its population carried out during the years of Nazi and Soviet occupation and annexation of Lithuania, corresponds to the definition of the crime of genocide as it is described by international law.' The latter statement appears controversial even at first glance;[26] however, the Law was soon being applied.

On the basis of these provisions, in the *Kurakinas and others* case[27] three people were accused of participation in so called 'people's protection brigade', whose task was fighting the Lithuanian guerrillas opposed to the Soviet occupation, and executing two women, one of them nine months pregnant, and a child and burning the corpses in their house afterwards. The accused, except Kurakinas, admitted executing orders and participating in the operation.

All three accused were found guilty of committing the crime of genocide by participation in the destroyers' detachment, which was operating in Lithuania during the years of occupation with the object of carrying out the genocide of the population. The Court relied on the resolution of the Lithuanian Communist Party Central Committee of 24 July 1944 'On the formation of People's Protection Battalions on the territory of the Soviet Socialist Republic of Lithuania under liberation from German Fascist invaders,'[28] According to the Court, the objective of those punitive brigades was 'mass killing of Lithuanian population in the post-war

---

23. A. Lieven, *The Baltic Revolution, Estonia, Latvia and Lithuania and the Path to Independence* (New Heaven CT, Yale University Press 1993) p. 151.

24. On 19 December 2004 the Baltic Assembly, which unites parliaments of Lithuania, Latvia and Estonia, passed a resolution urging the governments of the three countries to start talks with Russia and Germany on compensation of damages caused by occupation. According to the resolution 'during the occupation, the totalitarian Soviet regime committed genocide against the native inhabitants by significantly altering the ethnic composition of the population of the Baltic States'. Text at <http://www3.lrs.lt/cgi-bin/preps2?Condition1=247378&Condition2=>. See also L. Mälksoo, 'Soviet genocide?: Communist mass deportations in the Baltic States and international law', 14 *Leiden JIL* (2001) p. 782.

25. Law on the responsibility for the genocide of the population of Lithuania, 9 April 1992, No. I-2477, *Valstybės žinios*, 1992, No.13-342.

26. See more in section 4.5 of this paper.

27. Judgments of Vilnius Regional Court, 21 January 1997 and 2 December 1998.

28. Proceedings of Anti-Communist Congress, *supra* n. 12, p. 639.

period'. The Court held that such an orientation of their activities is proven by the analysis made on 23 March 1945 by the Bureau of the Lithuanian Communist Party Central Committee 'On the strengthening of the fighting ability of destroyers' battalions of the Ministry of State Security' as well as the implementing resolutions of the Committee of 3 and 12 December 1944. Kirila Kurakinas, who was in charge of the brigade and executed the victims in person, was sentenced to seven years' imprisonment.[29]

In the *Preikšaitis and others* case[30] charges were brought against three former members of the Security forces for the killing of members of the Lithuanian resistance, the so-called 'forest brothers', in the post-war period. The accused Preikšaitis moved to dismiss on the ground that his participation in the Security forces was a necessity because he refused to become a member of the guerrilla fighters in 1948 and he knew another person who was killed after such a refusal. Besides, he agreed with the policy of the Ministry of State Security because the 'forest brothers' were killing innocent people. The crime of genocide was incriminated in this case with reference to Article 2 of the Law on the responsibility for the genocide of the population of Lithuania, but the accused were found not guilty, as their participation in alleged executions constituting the crime of genocide has not been proven. The Court also found that the mere participation in the arrests does not correspond to the crime incriminated. Therefore, despite the vague definition of genocide given by the legislator, the mere participation in the oppressive unit was not considered as the participation in the genocide of the population.

On the contrary, in some Latvian cases, the fact of signing the deportation order served as a ground to present charges of committing the genocide. Alfons Noviks, former Latvian people's commissar, who headed the security police during the second wave of deportations in 1949, died in prison in 1996 under a life sentence for the crimes committed, including genocide.[31] On 27 September 2000 Riga Regional Court sentenced[32] Mikhails Farbuths, the 83 year old local representative of the NKVD (State Security – the KGB predecessor) in Daugavpils for the murder of 31 people – members of local intelligentsia, Latvian national militia and others whose deportation to Siberia he supervised and who later died in transit or labour camps or were executed.[33] The Court rejected the appeal of the accused that his own life would have been in danger if he had failed to obey. On 4 December 2003 Kurzeme Regional Court also opened the case of *Nikolaj Tess*, 80, charged with

29. The same Court reexamined the case on 8 December 1998 after having analysed additional evidence, namely, the report of accused Kurakinas to the Bureau of Lithuanian Communist Party Central Committee in 1949. The punishment was increased.

30. Judgment of Vilnius Regional Court, 4 June 2002, reported in *Lietuvos Rytas*, 5 June 2002.

31. I. Ziemele, 'The application of international law in the Baltic States', 40 *GYIL* (1997) pp. 261 et seq.

32. Mihail Farbtuh had been sentenced to five years in prison for genocide and was freed in March 2002 by the Riga Regional Court on health grounds. International Helsinki Human Rights federation report on Latvia, <http://www.ihf-hr.org/viewbinary/viewdocument.php?doc_id=2256>.

33. See more in B. Smith, 'Soviet crimes in spotlight', *The Baltic Times*, 28 April-3 May 2000.

genocide on suspicion that he helped deport 138 people to Siberia in 1949. Evidence against Tess included deportation papers signed by him.[34]

In the majority of Estonian cases the charges for genocide have been connected with the preparation and carrying out of deportations.[35] In the *Beškov* case, on 10 March 1999 Pärnu Regional Court convicted Vasilii Beškov, an operative plenipotentiary of NKVD, for the 'intent to destroy in part a national group offering resistance to the occupation regime which was also a social group declared 'kulaks'.'[36]

The modified definition of the crime of genocide in the Lithuanian Penal Code has also been found to comprise acts directed towards the resisters of the regime.[37] In the *Viater and Kregždė* case,[38] proceedings were instituted against two former guerilla fighters who, after being arrested by State Security of Lithuanian SSR in 1951, agreed to collaborate. Working uncover for the State Security, they continued fighting as part of the resistance, and during this participated in the execution of several resistance fighters.

The Court stressed that the object of the activities of the Ministry of State Security was the elimination of a defined political group – those resisting the occupation regime. Therefore, the activities of the accused were qualified as genocide of this political group on the basis of Article 71 of the Penal Code in force. The charges were based *inter alia* on the reports of the accused and the correspondence of the State Security. However, the case was discontinued due to the poor health of both accused.

The intent of the accused to destroy in whole or in part a national, ethnical, racial or religious group, as such, the so called *dolus specialis* of the crime of genocide,[39] has been proven by the courts in the cases above by referring to the conscious execution of the orders, whose clear objective was to destroy the population group. Where the execution of the orders was not proven, the Supreme Court of Latvia decided on 25 April 2000 to release the former guerrilla fighter Vasily Kononov and ordered additional investigation as the case 'was investigated as a murder case and not as a war crime case'.[40]

In the *Paulov* case, the Estonian Regional court had found that it was impossible to conclude that Paulov's intention had been to destroy Estonians or to discrimi-

---

34. 'Latvia charges another Stalinist-era agent over Russian deportations', *Associated Press report,* AP WorldStream, 3 April 2001.

35. The judgements in the *Loginov, Beskov, Klaasepp* and *Neverovski* cases, cited in T. Kerikmäe and A. Parmas, 'Correspondents' reports on Estonia', 3 *YIHL* (2000) p. 485. The trial against Johannes Klaassepp was decided on 26 January 1999. The former NKVD operation officer, found guilty for being responsible for the deportations of 23 people, was sentenced for eight years imprisonment on probation for 'crimes against humanity.' *Eesti päevaleht* of 27 January 1999. Vassili Beskov, the former NKVD security employee, was given a sentence of eight years imprisonment on probation, and was ordered to pay 30,000 Estonian crowns legal expenses to the state. He was charged for signing an order for the deportation of 210 people. *Postimees* of 11 March 1999.

36. More on this case in L. Mälksoo, *supra* n. 6, pp. 774-775.

37. Art. 71, introduced on 21 April 1998, included social and political groups in the definition of the groups protected.

38. Judgment of Vilnius Regional Court, 4 June 2002, reported in *Lietuvos Rytas*, 5 June 2002.

39. See section 3.2 of this article.

40. A.Pridanova, 'Court releases war criminal Kononov', *The Baltic Times*, 28 April -3 May 2000.

nate against them. Based on the evidence,[41] the Court found that the accused had killed the forest brothers 'in order to save himself from repression, and for material gain' and therefore committed murder for the purpose of personal gain.[42] Later, the Supreme Court emphasised the fact that Paulov committed these murders in the interest of the occupation regime while knowing that he would not be held criminally liable for his actions.[43] In its judgement of 21 March 2000, the Supreme Court explained that the offender in the genocide cases 'acts in the name of other goals (such as ethnic cleansing) and the attacked goods – life, health, corporal integrity – are in the given context for him valueless'.[44]

3.2 Charges for genocide or crimes against humanity?

In other cases against the surviving executors of Soviet repression, Baltic courts failed or were unwilling to invoke the definition of the crime of genocide and used instead the notion of the crime against humanity.

Amendment of 9 November 1994 of the Estonian Criminal Code defined 'genocide', or, as it stated, 'crimes against humanity, including genocide' in Article 61 (1) as:

> 'deliberate acts whose aim it is to fully or partially eradicate a group, based on national, ethnic, racial or religious distinction, *which is resisting an occupation regime*, or any other social group; for the killing of a member of such a group or for causing him/her grave or very grave bodily injuries or mental dysfunction or for torturing him/her; for removal of his/her children by force; for deportation of the indigenous population or for banishment into exile once an armed invasion, occupation or annexation has occurred, and for depriving them of their economic, political and social human rights or for restriction of these rights.'[45]

This article caused some confusion in the qualification of the Soviet repression cases by Estonian judicial authorities.[46] Polva Regional Court's judgment of 26 October 1999 in the *Paulov* case states, for instance, that subsection 61(1) of the Criminal Code is broader than the definition of genocide given in the 1948 Genocide Convention, since the latter does not specify as a protected group one providing resistance to an occupation regime or any other social group. The Penal Chamber of the Estonian Supreme Court, on the contrary, emphasised when reviewing the same case, that under that norm, a group resisting occupation constitutes an

---

41. Reported by T. Kerikmäe and A. Parmas in 3 *YIHL*, *supra* n. 35, p. 489
42. Ibid., p. 488.
43. Ibid., p. 489.
44. Cited by L. Mälksoo, *supra* n. 6, p. 777.
45. Art. 61-1 of the Criminal Code. English translation on <http://www.preventgenocide.org/law/domestic/estonia.htm>. Para. 2 of the same article impose, that 'the representative of the state authorities, with whose approval the crimes mentioned in the first paragraph were committed, shall be punished due to his involvement as an accessory'. The new Criminal Code was adopted on 6 June 2001.
46. The same impression was mentioned by Mälksoo, *supra* n. 6, p. 779.

element of the crime of genocide and not the crime against humanity, and sent the case back to the Regional Court. Finally, on 29 June 2000, the Regional Court concluded in this case that the killings committed by Paulov met the elements of a crime against humanity as specified in the Nuremberg Charter and sentenced him to eight years in prison.[47]

As Lauri Mälksoo notes, in most deportation cases Estonian courts have restricted themselves to the pronouncement that the accused committed 'a crime under Article 61-1 of the Criminal Code' by their deliberate activities, 'the purpose of which was to destroy a [...] group'.[48] At the same time, none of these judgments explicitly uses the term 'genocide'.

For instance, in the Estonian case against *Mikhail Neverovski*, the charges were brought against a former operative plenipotentiary of the Soviet State Security service who participated in deportations in March 1949.[49] According to the indictment, he had 'caused, through his deliberate acts, the deportation of natives from the annexed Republic of Estonia with the purpose to destroy in part a national group which was offering resistance to the occupying power and a social group which was declared 'kulaks'.' According to the Pärnu Regional Court judgment of 30 July 1999, the defendant committed a crime under Article 61(1) of the Criminal Code.

The same was true in the *Nikolay Larionov* case, where a Latvian SSR Security Ministry senior operational executive was charged with compiling and signing decisions on deportation of persons to special domicile in the furthest northern areas of the USSR in 1949. The deportation decisions included elderly, women, small children and babies. Since in 1998 Latvia adopted legislation which declares the deportations as illegal, as well as rehabilitating repressed persons, the court aknowledged that Larionovs had committed a crime and was punishable in accordance with the Criminal Law of the Republic of Latvia, paragraph 68.1 – Crimes against Humanity, Genocide. In accordance with this paragraph the accused was sentenced to five years' imprisonment on 26 September 2003.[50]

In some other cases charges were presented exclusively for committing crimes against humanity. Thus, in the proceedings against *Idel Jakobson* (born in 1904) the indictment referred to the 'crimes against humanity' as they are defined in the Estonian Criminal Code. The case was started on the basis of the activities of this person in the Estonian State Security, where he allegedly signed orders of repression against at least 1,801 persons, including proposals to execute 621 persons. The investigation was closed due to the health conditions of the accused.[51]

Another qualification of similar acts was introduced by the amendment of 1998 to the Lithuanian Penal Code introducing a new chapter – 'war crimes'. Article 334 of this chapter defined 'Deportation of the civilian population of the occupied

---

47. See more in Kerikmäe and Parmas, *supra* n. 35, p. 489.
48. Mälksoo, *supra* n. 6, p. 779.
49. Ibid., p. 775.
50. A. Rodins, 'Vainīgs noziegumos pret cilvēci' [Guilty of crimes against humanity], *Diena* , 27 September 2003.
51. Ibid., p. 774.

country' as 'Deportation of the civilian population in the time of war, international armed conflict, occupation or annexing from the territory of occupied or annexed country to the territory of the occupying or annexing or third country'.

Under this provision, in the *Misiūnas* case Vincas Misiūnas, former officer of the Ministry of State Security of the puppet Government of the Lithuanian SSR, was sentenced by Vilnius Regional Court on 30 December 2002 for deportation of a Lithuanian 'kulak' family in 1951. The court found that by executing orders the accused had participated in the deportation of a Lithuanian farmer into Siberia and therefore committed a war crime – 'Deportation of the civilian population of the occupied country'.[52] It may be presumed that the accent on 'occupation' in this qualification emphasised the specific status of the occupied Baltic states in relation to the totalitarian practices in other parts of the Soviet Union, where mass repressions were not considered as war crimes.

Similar acts of the executioners of Stalin's atrocities in the Baltic states have thus been considered by the courts of the restored Lithuania, Latvia and Estonia as either genocide, crime against the humanity or war crimes. One of the reasons for such confusion may be found in the changing legislation of the restored states. The newly adopted Penal Codes of the three republics, however, provide no greater clarity for the courts.

3.3 Confusion in the revised Penal Codes

The criminal laws of the three Baltic Republics define separately the crimes of 'genocide', 'crimes against humanity' and 'war crimes'. However, the wording of the notion of the 'crime of genocide' in the criminal law of the three Baltic States continues to indicate the intention of the legislator to model the respective definitions according to their applicability to repressive acts committed during the Soviet occupation.

The Estonian Penal Code in particular refers to 'deportation of the indigenous population' and 'banishment into exile' 'once an armed invasion, occupation or annexation has occurred' and 'depriving them of their economic, political and social human rights or for restriction of these rights'. The Estonian Penal Code adopted in 2001 does not define 'genocide' but instead 'Crimes against humanity, including genocide'. This definition refers to and reproduces the definition given in the Rome Statute of the International Criminal Court. However, it also includes a 'group offering resistance to the occupant regime or other social group'.[53]

The current concept of genocide contained in Article 99 of the Penal Code of Lithuania, adopted in 2000, includes political as well as social groups in the list of protected groups; secondly, it adds two more inhumane acts: deportation and torture.[54] The Code also defines the war crime of 'Deportation of the civilian popula-

---

52. Reported in 5 *YIHL* (2002).

53. The Penal Code, entered into force on 1 September 2002. English translation at <http://www.legislationline.org/data/Documents/Estonia_CC.htm>.

54. The crime of genocide is defined in Art. 99 as acts 'with the intent to destroy all or part of people, belonging to any national, ethnical, racial, religious, social or political groups', in particular

tion of the occupied country or emplacement of the population of the occupying country'[55] as 'Deportation of the civilian population in the time of war, international armed conflict, occupation or annexing from the territory of occupied or annexed country to the territory of the occupying or annexing or third country'. Thus, the deportation without intent to destroy a group would be persecuted under this provision.

The Criminal Law of the Republic of Latvia also includes the 'social class' criteria and 'collective believe or faith' in the definition of the crime of genocide.[56] Even though the last part of the definition above addresses the deportation issue clearly enough, when committed in war deportation would be also qualified as a war crime on the basis of Article 74 of the Criminal Law.[57]

To summarise, the Penal Codes of Lithuania, Latvia and Estonia vary in determining the groups protected as well as in the acts constituting genocide. Do these regulations correspond to the norms of international humanitarian law, or do they only reveal the wish for political revenge at the turn of the regime? In order to answer this question we shall look into the doctrine and the court practice in similar cases. The legislative practices of different European countries will also be taken into account.

4. QUALIFICATION ACCORDING TO INTERNATIONAL LAW

The different definitions of the 'crime of genocide' have been discussed by Estonian lawyer Lauri Malksoo in an attempt to answer the question whether the general context of the Stalinist mass repressions in the Baltic States permits the qualification of the occupants' policy as 'genocide'. Having analysed the historical context of the Soviet repressions, Malksoo evokes the widespread misperception which restricts the communist repression to the destruction of hostile 'social' or 'political' groups but which has often proven to be a too simplistic answer. The

---

'organisation, direction or participation in their killings, torturing, mutilating, disturbing their mental development, deporting or otherwise creating conditions of living, which caused their destruction wholly or in part, limiting births within the groups or forcibly transferring children to the other groups' See the English translation on <http://www.preventgenocide.org/lt>. The similar illegal acts towards the civilian population in general shall be qualified as Treatment of persons prohibited by international law.

55. Art. 102 of the Penal Code of the Republic of Lithuania.

56. Art. 71 of the Criminal law of the Republic of Latvia, describes genocide as 'intentional acts for purposes of the destruction in whole or in part of any group of people identifiable as such by nationality, ethnic origin, race, social class or a defined collective belief or faith [as] killing members of the group, inflicting upon them physical injuries hazardous to life or health or causing them to become mentally ill, intentionally causing conditions of life for such people as result in their physical destruction in whole or in part'.

57. Art. 74 defines war crimes as 'violation of provisions and practices, in regard to prohibited conduct of war, comprised in international agreements binding upon the Republic of Latvia, as manifested in murder, torture, robbery, deportation or assignment to forced labour of civilians, hostages and prisoners of war of the occupied territory, or unjustifiable destruction of cities and other entities'.

attacks against political groups have often simultaneously had a 'hidden agenda', for instance, the subjugation of other ethnic or religious groups.[58]

However, as indicated by the recent court decisions of the International Criminal Tribunal for the former Yugoslavia (ICTY), the existence of a state plan or policy is not a legal ingredient of the crime of genocide,[59] even though in the context of proving the specific intent, the existence of a plan or policy may become an important factor in most cases.[60]

The present article is trying to put the question in a different manner. Leaving apart the theoretical considerations of what the real intent of the Stalinist policy in the Baltic States may have been,[61] it will try to find out whether those responsible for the repressions in Lithuania, Latvia and Estonia may be prosecuted for the crime of genocide, regardless of the existence of the relevant occupant state's plan to annihilate the entire population of the three Republics, i.e., whether their acts correspond with the other criteria of the crime of genocide.

4.1 Classical concept of the crime of genocide

All the different definitions of the genocide that emerged during the last century stressed more or less similar elements of this crime. Raphael Lemkin, who introduced this definition in the doctrine of international law, proposed the following definition:

> 'coordinated plan of different actions aiming at the destruction of essential foundations of the life of national groups, with the aim of annihilating the groups themselves. The objective of such a plan would be disintegration of the political and social institutions of culture, language, national feelings, religion, and the economic existence of national groups and the destruction of the personal security, liberty, health, dignity and even the lives of the individuals belonging to such groups.'[62]

As Schabas notes, Lemkin's definition was narrow, in that it addressed crimes directed against 'national groups' rather than against 'groups' in general. At the

---

58. Mälksoo, *supra* n. 6, p. 782. See also J. Verhoeven, 'Le crime de génocide, originalité et ambiguïté', 24 *Revue belge de droit international* (1991) where the author emphasises 'in many cases, ethnocide is merely the 'cultural' aspect of genocide proper, which should suffice in order for it to be punished', p. 16

59. *Prosecutor* v. *Jelisić*, Case No. IT-95-10-A, Judgement of 5 July 2001, para 48, see also *Prosecutor* v. *Kunarac* et al., Case No. IT-96-23, Judgement of 12 June 2002.

60. Ibid.

61. As Mr Ruhashyankiko stressed in his 1978 report: 'a number of allegations of genocide have been made since the adoption of the 1948 Convention. In the absence of a prompt investigation of these allegations by an impartial body, it has not been possible to determine whether they were well-founded. Either they have given rise to sterile controversy or, because of the political circumstances, nothing further has been heard about them Nicodème Ruhashyankiko, Special Rapporteur, 'Study of the question of the prevention and punishment of the crime of genocide', Sub-Commission on Prevention of Discrimination and Protection of Minorities, E/CN.4/Sub.2/416, 4 July 1978, para. 614.

62. R. Lemkin, *Axis Rule in Occupied Europe: Laws of Occupation, Analysis of Government, Proposals for Redress* (Washington, Carnegie Endowment for World Peace 1944) p. 79.

same time, it was broad, to the extent that it contemplated not only physical genocide but also acts aimed at destroying the culture and livelihood of the group.[63]

The crime of genocide was further addressed by the Nuremberg Trial of the Major War Criminals.[64] Although the final judgment of the International Military Tribunal of 30 September-1 October 1946[65] never used the term, the indictment described what was in fact a genocide.[66]

The prosecution of genocide was the subject of United Nations General Assembly resolution 96(I) of 11 December 1946. The resolution states, *inter alia*, that 'many instances of such crimes of genocide have occurred when racial, religious, political and other groups have been destroyed, entirely or in part'. But the Resolution spoke in the past tense, describing genocide as crimes which 'have occurred', besides which the binding force of the General Assembly's resolutions still may be questioned despite the affirmative position of the International Court of Justice.[67]

The standard setting of the notion of 'the crime of crimes' was completed with the 1948 adoption of the Convention on the Prevention and Punishment of the Crime of Genocide.[68]

Article II of the Convention defines genocide as an act committed: 'with intent to destroy, in whole or in part, a national, ethnical, racial or religious group, as such: (a) killing members of the group; (b) causing serious bodily or mental harm to members of the group; (c) deliberately inflicting on the group conditions of life calculated to bring about its physical destruction in whole or in part; (d) imposing measures intended to prevent births within the group; (e) forcibly transferring children of the group to another group'.

4.2 Elements of the definition of 1948

4.2.1 *Acts prohibited*

As Schabas notes, 'genocide' had a detailed and quite technical definition as a crime against the law of nations in the Genocide Convention. The material side of the crime described by the exhaustive list, includes killing or injuring the members

---

63. W.A. Schabas, *Genocide in International Law: The Crime of Crimes* (Cambridge, Cambridge University Press 2000) p. 25.

64. The Charter of the tribunal described the crime in its Art. 6(c). See Agreement for the Prosecution and punishment of Major War Criminals of the European Axis, and Establishing the Charter of the International Military Tribunal, 52 *UNTS* p. 279.

65. *Judgment of the International Military Tribunal for the Trial of German Major War Criminals*, 30 September and 1 October 1946, <http://www.yale.edu/lawweb/avalon/imt/proc/judcont.htm>.

66. As Schabas observes, the International Criminal Tribunal for Rwanda noted in 1998 that 'the crimes persecuted by the Nuremberg Tribunal (...), were very much constitutive of genocide but they could not be defined as such because the crime of genocide was not defined until later'. Schabas, *supra* n. 63, p. 38.

67. Advisory opinion concerning Legality of Threat or Use of Nuclear Weapons, *ICJ Rep* (1996) p. 226, para. 70. See also Schabas, affirming that the Resolution, 'imposes obligations and creates international law with respect to prevention and punishment of genocide'. Schabas, *supra* n. 63, p. 47.

68. Convention on the Prevention and Punishment of the Crime of Genocide, Adopted by the General Assembly of the United Nations on 9 December 1948, 78 *UNTS* p. 277.

of the group, inflicting on the group unsupportable conditions of life, preventing births and transferring children of the group.

As regards the critical question, in this context, of whether deportation can be considered as genocidal or a means of carrying out genocide, according to the International Law Commission,

> 'mass displacement of populations from one region to another (…) does not constitute genocide. It would, however, become genocide if the occupation were attended by such circumstances as to lead to the death of the whole or part of the displaced population (if, for example, people were driven from their homes and forced to travel long distances in a country where they were exposed to starvation, thirst, heat, cold and epidemics)'.[69]

Even though the unspoken reference was made principally to the mass displacement of Armenians within the Ottoman Empire in 1915, the dictum perfectly describes the situation of the Baltic deportees.

4.2.2 *Intent to destroy*

The Convention of 1948 also introduces a precise description of the subjective side of the crime. There can be no genocide without the 'intent to destroy, in whole or in part, a group [...], as such'. Where the specific intent is not established, the act remains punishable but not as genocide.[70] As Donnedieu de Vabres has noted, 'the theory of genocide [...] is therefore a derogation from ordinary law, because it encompasses the motive in the legal constitution of the offence'.[71] 'What matters', writes Joe Verhoeven, 'is the perpetrator of the crime rather than the number of victims'.[72] As the decisive factor is the intent to destroy a group in whole or in part, the number of victims is not an element constituting the offence.[73] Consequently, there is nothing to prohibit a crime being characterised as genocide, even if it has resulted in only a single victim, or at any rate very few victims.[74]

A faithful interpretation of the relevant instruments shows that what is required is not the destruction in whole or in part of a group, but 'the intent to destroy, in

---

69. UN Doc. E/447, p. 23.

70. Schabas, *supra* n. 63, p. 214. See also the *Djajić* case of the International Criminal Tribunal for the Former Yugoslavia, where the accused was acquitted of genocide 'because he lacked the necessary men's rea', proof of his intent was insufficient, and the court presumed in the accused's favour that he did not see the policy of 'ethnic cleansing' as the inderlying reason for his action', in C.J.M. Safferling, 'Public Prosecutor v. Djajić', 92 *AJIL* (1998) p. 528.

71. H. Donnedieu de Vabres, 'De la piraterie au génocide: les nouvelles modalités de la répression universelle', in H. Donnedieu de Vabres et al., eds., *Le droit privé français au milieu du XXe siècle: études offertes à Georges Ripert*; Vol. 1 (Paris, Pichon et Durand-Auzias 1950) p 245.

72. Verhoeven, *supra* n. 58, p.24.

73. Verhoeven, a proponent of this argument, explains that the number of victims is not without importance, especially in determining the penalty. Ibid., p. 24.

74. On this argument, ibid., p. 18; see also S. Glaser, *Droit international pénal conventionnel* (Bruxelles, Bruylant 1970) p. 112; A. Planzer, *Le crime de génocide* (St. Gallen, Schwald 1956) pp. 86 and 93.

whole or in part, a group [...] as such'.[75] Of course, such an intent will be difficult to prove. In practice, however, genocidal intent can often be proved through the material element. Genocide is usually expressed through acts (killings, disappearances, massacres, deportations, measures intended to prevent births within a group, rape, etc.) committed on so vast and so serious a scale as to make it possible to infer their perpetrators' intent.[76] The judgment of the International Criminal Tribunal for Rwanda in the *Akayesu* case refers to this aspect: 'the offender is culpable because he knew or should have known that the act committed would destroy, in whole or in part, a group'.[77] According to the International Law Commission, the necessary degree of knowledge and intent to commit genocide 'may be inferred from the nature of the order to commit the prohibited acts of destruction against individuals who belong to a particular group and are therefore singled out as the immediate victims of the massive criminal conducts'. Besides 'a subordinate is presumed to know the intentions of his superiors when he receives orders to commit the prohibited acts against individuals who belong to a particular group … the law does not permit an individual to shield himself from criminal responsibility by ignoring the obvious'.[78] Any additional motivation of a person implementing

---

75. See Rome Statute of the International Criminal Court, adopted in Rome on 17 July 1998, 2187 *UNTS.*

76. This is what the judgements of the International Criminal Tribunal for the Former Yugoslavia appear to indicate: in the *Nikolić* case (*Prosecutor* v. *Dragan Nikolić* aka 'Jenki', consideration of the bill of indictment in the framework of Art. 61 of the Rules of Procedure and Evidence, decision of the Trial Chamber, ICTY, Case No. IT-94-2-R-61, 20 October 1995), the Tribunal does not refer to a number of victims in particular, but cites the magnitude of the 'ethnic cleansing' conducted in the Vlasenica region; it indicates, precisely, that intent may be linked to the acts which fall within the purview of the 'ethnic cleansing' policy being conducted in the region, and may generally be inferred from this policy. The Tribunal states as follows: 'In the case at hand, this 'ethnic cleansing' policy took the form of extremely serious acts of discrimination, which would tend to indicate that it was of a genocidal nature.' See p. 21, para. 34.A/CONF.189/PC.1/7. Similarly, in the *Karadžić* and *Mladić* case, the Tribunal noted the link between the massively destructive effects of the acts before it and genocidal intent (case of 11 July 1996, No. IT-95-5-R-61, p. 61, para. 95). See also *Meakić et al.* case, 13 February 1995, Case No. IT-95-4-I, p. 5, paras. 18.1 to 18.3. In this case the judges tend to regard intent as taking precedence over the number of victims: 'the mere number of victims selected solely because of their membership in a group' could indicate genocidal intent. See p. 61, para. 94. In other cases, the Tribunal develops the same argument of the causal link between 'planned ethnic cleansing' or 'the serious nature of the ethnic cleansing involved' and 'genocidal intent' (Vukovar hospital and Srebrenica cases (*Mrksić, Radić, Sljivancanin and Dokmanović 'Vukovar hospital'*) case, decision of the Trial Chamber, ICTY, 3 April 1996, Case No. IT-95-13-R-61, p. 16, para. 35, *Karadžić* and *Mladić* ('Srebrenica') case, decision of 16 November 1995, Case No. IT-95-18-R-61, pp. 5-6 and of 11 July 1996 Case No. IT-95-5-R-61). However, in the *Karadžić* and *Mladić* case, the Tribunal developed the idea that genocidal intent may be either explicit or implicit. 'The specific intent to commit genocide does not have to be clearly expressed' and '… In the case at hand, the intent to destroy in whole or in part a national, ethnical, racial or religious group, which is specific to genocide, may be clearly inferred from the seriousness of the 'ethnic cleansing'', *Karadžić* and *Mladić* case, decision of 16 November 1995, pp. 5-6. It may even be inferred from acts which would not necessarily be listed in Art. 4(2) of its Statute.

77. *Prosecutor* v. *Akayesu*, Case No . ICTR-96-4-T, Judgement of 2 September 1998, para. 519.

78. Report of the International Law Commission on the Work of Its Forty-Eight Session, 6 May-26 July 1996, UN Doc. A/51/10, p. 90.

the genocidal policy or order may not therefore change the qualification of the crime as genocide.

4.2.3 *Groups protected*

Finally, genocide must be aimed at a group qualified by the relevant instruments as 'national, ethnical, racial or religious'. None of the texts defines these groups which should enjoy protection.[79] Although certain authors regard each of these concepts as having a different meaning,[80] it is difficult, as we have said, to distinguish definite boundaries between them.[81] However, the inclusion of political or social groups or groups resisting occupation as groups protected against genocide would definitely go beyond the limits of the Genocide Convention.

4.3 **State practice**

For the time being international law has retained the definition of the crime of genocide contained in the 1948 Convention. Article 4 of the Statute of the International Criminal Tribunal for the Former Yugoslavia, Article 2 of the International Criminal Tribunal for Rwanda, and Article 6 of the Statute of the International Criminal Court, reproduce this definition.

As concerns the practice of other European states, the definition of the crime of genocide from the Convention predominates in their criminal law. A classical example in Section 259 'Genocide' of the Criminal Code of the Czech Republic reads as follows:

> '(1) Whoever, with intent to annihilate, fully or partially, a national, racial or religious group,
> (a) causes the members of such group to live in conditions which will lead to their complete or partial physical extinction;
> (b) carries out measures designed to prevent the birth of children in such group;
> (c) forcibly transfers children from one such group to another;
> (d) causes severe injury to health, or death, to a member of such group, shall be sentenced to a term of imprisonment of from twelve to fifteen years or an exceptional term of imprisonment.'[82]

---

79. Legal writings are unanimous in excluding certain groups: political, sexual, linguistic, economic and social groups. Affirming this, in its Judgement of 6 December 1999 in *Prosecutor* v. *Rutaganda*, Case No. ICTR-96-3-T, the ICTR Trial Chamber recognised that 'it appears from reading of the travaux preparatoires of the Genocide Convention that certain groups, such as political and economic groups have been excluded from the protected groups, because they are considered to be 'mobile groups' which one joins through individual political commitment' (para. 58).

80. See Glaser, *supra* n. 74, p. 71.

81. Verhoeven, *supra* n. 58, p. 21. For this author, with some exceptions for the concept of 'religious' groups, it is impossible to define the others precisely.

82. Data on the domestic laws from Prevent Genocide International website <http://www.prevent genocide.org>.

The transformation of the Convention's definition, thus, is obvious in this formulation. In the similar way genocide is defined in the German Penal Code (A.220a), Spanish (A.607),[83] Russian (A.357), Austrian (A.321), Romanian (A.356), Portugal (A.239), Yugoslavian (A.141) Penal Codes, or in the Danish and Italian laws on genocide. In Ireland's law, the crime of genocide is simply defined by reference to the Convention.

4.4 Borderline between genocide and crime against humanity

Genocide can be defined as a qualified or aggravated case of the crime against humanity.[84] It differs from the latter essentially in two aspects: first, the criminal intent required to constitute the genocide is more restrictive: the crimes shall be committed with the intent to 'annihilate, fully or partially, a national, racial or religious group as such'. Second, only acts directed against the human life (in the large sense) may be qualified as genocide, while crime against humanity may have much broader definition.

In its customary meaning the crime against the humanity may be defined as a 'policy of atrocities and persecutions directed against the civilian population'.[85] The Hague Regulations of 1907 include a section concerning the treatment of civilian populations in occupied territories. The so called 'Martens clause' in the preamble of the four Conventions requires that 'the inhabitants and the belligerents remain under the protection and the rule of the principles of the law of nations, as they result from the usages established among civilized peoples, from the laws of humanity, and the dictates of the public conscience'.

However, contrary to the definition of the crime of genocide, international treaties provide no universal definition of 'crime against humanity', although this term is widely used in the international instruments.[86]

This common notion used for the first time in the Statute of the Nuremberg International Military Tribunal for the evaluation of atrocities committed by Nazis and their allies during World War II later appeared in the Tokyo Charter of the International Military Tribunal for the Far East,[87] in the United Nations General

---

83. Curiously Spain has changed the definition of the crime of genocide from 1971 on 25 June 1983 to correspond with its classical description.

84. Nicodeme Ruhashyankiko, Rapporteur special, Etude sur la question de la prevention et la repression du crime de genocide, Sous Commission de la lutte contre les measures discriminatoires et de la protection des minorities. Doc. UN E/CN.4/Sub.2/416 of 4 July 1978. Para. 393.

85. E. Zoller, 'La définition des crimes contre l'humanité', 12 *Journal du droit international* (1993) p. 551.

86. That may be the reason for the formulations found in certain national legislation. For instance, while Art. 1 of the Belgian Law relating to the repression of serious violations of international humanitarian law defines genocide by reference and in the words of the 1948 Convention, Art. 2 refers to the Statute of the International Criminal Court and includes in the notion of the crime against humanity '*persecution of any group or any identifiable community for reasons of a political* nature, *racial, national, ethnic, cultural, religious or sexist or according to other criteria universally recognized as inadmissible in international law, correlation with any act aimed in this article*'.

87. Charter of the International Military Tribunal for the Far East, text at <http://www.yale.edu/lawweb/avalon/imtfech.htm>

Assembly declaration concerning the prohibition of use of nuclear and thermonuclear weapons,[88] the United Nations Convention of 1973 concerning the elimination and repression of the crime of apartheid,[89] the Statutes of the International Criminal Tribunals for Rwanda and ex-Yugoslavia,[90] and of course in the Rome Statute of the International Criminal Court.[91]

For instance, Article 3 of the Statute of International Criminal Tribunal for Rwanda includes in the definition of the crime against the humanity crimes when committed as part of a widespread or systematic attack against any civilian population on national, political, ethnic, racial or religious grounds: murder; extermination; enslavement; deportation; imprisonment; torture; rape; persecutions on political, racial and religious grounds; and other inhumane acts.

Even though genocide is a subset of the crime against humanity, the recent case law of the *ad hoc* Tribunals has tended to insist upon the distinctions rather that the affinities between the two categories.[92]

The Soviet atrocities investigated by national courts in the Baltic States may certainly correspond to the meaning of the notion 'crimes against humanity' as it is used in international documents. But could they be qualified as genocide or prosecuted by the courts of third states by virtue of the principle of universal jurisdiction?

4.5 Expanding the limits of the concept?

Notwithstanding the general practice of incorporation of the definition contained in the Convention of 1948 into national law, several European states have introduced a broader definition of the crime of genocide in their criminal law, encompassing political groups or for that matter any group with a degree of permanence.

Article 118 of the Penal Code of Poland, for instance, includes in the definition 'political group or a group of persons with a definite philosophical conviction'.[93] In France, persecution of 'a group determined by other arbitrary criterion' would be also qualified as genocide.[94] Finland prosecutes for the crime of genocide in

---

88. United Nations General Assembly prohibition of use of nuclear and thermonuclear weaponshttp://daccess-ods.un.org/access.nsf/Get?Open

89. International Convention for the Suppression and Punishment of the Crime of Apartheid, opened for signature 30 November 1973, 1015 *UNTS* 243 (entered into force 18 July 1976)

90. Statute of the International Criminal Tribunal for the Former Yugoslavia, Arts. 7 and 23 (as amended through 2003) [Text ICTY web site], adopted by SC Res. 827, UN SCOR, 3217th meeting., UN Doc. S/RES/827 (1993); Statute of the International Criminal Tribunal for Rwanda, Arts. 6 and 22 (1994) [Text: ICTR web site], adopted by SCOR Res. 955, UN SCOR, 3453rd meeting., UN Doc. S/RES/955 (1994).

91. Rome Statute of the International Criminal Court, 17 July 1998, Art. 25, 2187 UNTS 3, 105 entered into force 1 July 2002)

92. W.A. Schabas, 'National courts finally begin to prosecute genocide, the 'crime of crimes'', 1 *Journal of international criminal justice* (2003) p. 52.

93. See *supra* n. 82.

94. Ibid.

respect of race or national, ethnic or religious group or another comparable group.[95]

The Genocide Convention introduced minimum requirements concerning the prosecution of those who committed the genocide as it is described in the Convention, i.e., the definition of 'genocide' in the 1948 Convention is given only for the purposes of the Convention and does not precludes evolution of this notion in international law. Therefore, the Crimes Against Humanity and War Crimes Act (2000), providing for the implementation of the Rome Statute of the International Criminal Court respecting genocide, crimes against humanity and war crimes in the United Kingdom, describes for the purposes of the act separately 'crime against humanity',[96] 'genocide' and 'war crime'. The crime of genocide here is defined by reference to international customary law at the time of the commission:

> '"genocide" means an act or omission committed with intent to destroy, in whole or in part, an identifiable group of persons, as such, that, at the time and in the place of its commission, constitutes genocide according to customary international law or conventional international law or by virtue of its being criminal according to the general principles of law recognized by the community of nations, whether or not it constitutes a contravention of the law in force at the time and in the place of its commission'.

It is presumed by the British legislator that the scope of the crime of genocide in international law may change in time and therefore it is not appropriate to give a precise meaning in national criminal law. A similar definition may be found in Canada's Crimes Against Humanity and War Crimes Act.

Despite the broader definitions in national law, only recently have more judgments under national penal codes appeared.[97] However, some of the proceedings, like the Romania's trial of the leaders of the Ceausescu regime in 1990 for mass killings[98] and Spain's indictment of Pinochet for genocide because of the killing of political prisoners in Chile,[99] are not recognised as genocide by many scholars. To quote Schabas, 'several national jurisdictions have prosecuted mass killings and

95. Ibid.

96. 'Crime against humanity' is described as 'murder, extermination, enslavement, deportation, imprisonment, torture, sexual violence, persecution or any other inhumane act or omission that is committed against any civilian population or any identifiable group and that, at the time and in the place of its commission, constitutes a crime against humanity according to customary international law or conventional international law or by virtue of its being criminal according to the general principles of law recognized by the community of nations, whether or not it constitutes a contravention of the law in force at the time and in the place of its commission' Crimes Against Humanity and War Crimes Bill, A.1(4), <http://www.parliament.the-stationery-office.co.uk/pa/cm199900/cmbills/166/00166–a.htm>

97. W.A. Schabas, 'Developments in the Law of Genocide', 5 *YIHL* (2002) p. 131.

98. J. Kifner, 'Army executes Ceausescu and wife for 'genocide' role, Bucharest says' *The New York Times*, 26 December 1989.

99. R. Brody and M. Ratner eds., *The Pinochet Papers: the case of Augusto Pinochet in Spain and Britain*, (The Hague, Kluwer Law International 2000) 520 pp.

atrocities under the label of genocide. In some cases, national law had changed the definition of genocide to give it a wider reach.'[100]

Nonetheless, the international legal order does not impede the wider use of the notion of the genocide. Jurisdiction is one of the expressions of the sovereignty of a state. It is understood as the possibility or the right to judge, that is, to exercise towards certain persons in relation to their certain acts one of the state's powers, submitting them, in the case of criminal law, to the *jus puniendi* imposed by the law. Taking account of the values of its specific society, traditions or history, the government may impose more severe punishments for the same crimes as compared to other states. It can also criminalise a specific act, or separate different categories of a single crime. As long as it acts in conformity with the norms of international law, a state may introduce its own notions or use the existing definitions in different context.

The latter argument is often used in defending the broader definition of the crime of genocide in national law. As Rimvydas Valentukevičius, Senior Prosecutor of the Special Investigations Department of the Attorney General's Office of the Republic of Lithuania, explains, 'such an expansion of genocide concept is totally valid and necessary, because the classical concept of the genocide established in international law is confined to four characteristics of the group destroyed that cannot be readily applied in the instance of mass destruction of the Lithuanian population'.[101] In his view, the Lithuanian lawmakers, '*have corrected the error*' in the definition contained in the Convention of 1948 by including two additional characteristics of genocide in the national criminal law.[102] Justinas Žilinskas also notes in his doctoral thesis that the extension of the definition has occurred 'due to the needs of Lithuania to cover all the cases of genocide of Lithuanian population'.[103]

It is doubtful whether the broader definition of the crime of genocide in the national laws constitutes a necessary *opinio juris* to manifest a changed customary international law. As yet, no international institution has pronounced to that effect. On the contrary, tribunals have expressed their position to consider the 1948 definition as being part of custom.[104] National lawmakers, however, feel less constrained by the terms of this international instrument.

100. Schabas, *supra* n. 63, pp. 391 and also 132-133.

101. R. Valentukevičius, 'The legal aspects of investigation and evaluation of the crimes of communism. Expansion of the concept of genocide', Proceedings of Anti-Communist Congress, *supra* n. 18, p. 639.

102. See also B. van Schaack, 'The crime of political genocide: repairing the Genocide Convention's blind spot', 106 *Yale LJ* (1997) pp. 2259-2291.

103. J. Žilinskas, Nusikaltimai žmoniškumui ir genocides tarptautinėje teisėje bei Lietuvos Respublikos teisėje, [Crimes against the humanity and genocide in the law of the Republic of Lithuania and the international law], Doctoral thesis, Lithuanian Law University (2002).

104. See *Prosecutor* v. *Rutaganda*, Case No. ICTR-96-3 (Trial Chamber), 6 December 1999, para. 46: 'The Genocide Convention is undeniably considered part of customary international law ...' See also *Prosecutor* v. *Musema*, Case No. ICTR-96-13-A (Trial Chamber), 27 January 2000, para. 15.

5. CONCLUSIONS

It may be argued whether the Soviet repressions in the Baltic states correspond with the international definition of genocide because of the narrow interpretation of the latter in the 1948 Genocide Convention. It is also true that an analysis of the constituent elements of the crime of genocide based on recent jurisprudence, in particular the groups protected or the element of intent, has revealed certain ambiguities.

From the point of view of international law, the characterisation of acts as genocide is important in order to apply the norms of the 1948 Convention, especially the ones concerning the compulsory jurisdiction of the International Court of Justice. But it seems that the central tension in the Baltic case is between the politics of compromise, the essence of which is to leave the past intact, and the radical notion of justice. Thus, the key dilemma facing the restored Baltic states is whether past violations should be forgotten or confronted, forgiven or prosecuted.[105] A society that does not investigate and reveal past crimes blurs the norms of right and wrong, which creates ambiguity and disrespect for prohibition and laws as the lies and denials are institutionalised and defended by the laws of the country.[106] Therefore, in the case against *Yavgeny Savenko*, the Latvian Regional Court of Kuzeme stressed that it was not 'a historical evaluation of the USSR and its politics but a stand against a monstrous crime whose relevance has no expiration date'.[107] On the other hand, the misuse of the term genocide, as it is defined by international law, could not only complicate the investigation of serious crimes but also lead to misunderstandings in inter-state relations. As a good example of this issue could be mentioned the lack of cooperation from the Russian side while investigating certain cases because the definition of the concept of genocide in the laws of Lithuania is broader than in the United Nations Convention.[108] The issues of terminology, periodization and coordinated research of the Communist totalitarian occupation of the Baltic countries from 1939 to 1991 have been the focus of many international conferences and research papers and will remain important research topics in the future. Meanwhile, trials are underway in Lithuania, Latvia and Estonia charging

---

105. G. Motzkin, 'The Memory of Crime and the Formation of Identity', in H. Dubiel and G. Motzkin, eds., *The Lesser Evil: Moral Approaches to Genocide Practices* (London, Routledge 2004) pp. 196-210.

106. See Report of the Secretary General of the United Nations, 'The rule of law and transitional justice in conflict and post-conflict societies', UN Doc. S/2004/616.

107. Y.Nedyalkova, 'Latvia: The Difference Between Soviet and Nazi War Criminals', 14 July 2000. Cyber-times news, <http:/www.cyber-times.org>.

108. R. Valentukevičius, 'The Legal aspects of Investigation and Evaluation of the Crimes of Communism. Expansion of the Concept of Genocide' in *Anti-Communist Congress and the Proceedings of the International Public Tribunal in Vilnius: 'Evaluation of the Crimes of Communism'*, Vilnius: Ramona 2002, p. 363. Russia has objected to the prosecutions of the former Soviet agents in many instances. In the declaration of the State Duma of the Russian Federation in connection with major violations of human rights and the rights of national minorities in the Latvian Republic of 14 October 2003 it was stressed that 'the fact that the laws adopted in Latvia in which the term 'Genocide' does not correspond to the one universally recognised are given the retroactive force constitute gross violation of human rights'. Translation at < http://www.russiaeu.org/duma_latv.htm>.

those responsible for the Soviet atrocities with genocide as defined in their penal codes. In this context it is important to stress that these are not the only countries introducing a broader definition in their legislation. A single ruling of a national court concerning the existence of the genocidal policy or practice – the necessary element of the crime of genocide – would hardly be binding on the other international actors. On the other hand, uniform state practice not only may qualify certain international acts but also influence the evolution of the customary notion of the crime of genocide, eventually creating the development of a new positive international law.

ENFORCING INTERNATIONAL HUMANITARIAN LAW AT THE NATIONAL LEVEL: THE *GACACA* JURISDICTIONS OF RWANDA[1]

Chiseche Mibenge[2]

'What Rwanda expects from the Gacaca Courts is to establish the truth about what happened, to expedite the backlog of Genocide cases, to eradicate the culture of impunity and to consolidate the unity of our people ... Furthermore, if the Gacaca Courts function as we anticipate, it will be an important contribution to the understanding and advancement of international law.'

Address to the nation by H.E. Paul Kagame President of the Republic of Rwanda on the eve of the *Gacaca* elections, 3 October 2001[3]

1. INTRODUCTION

Genocide was unleashed in Rwanda in April 1994. Within the first few hours, ten Belgian peacekeepers had been kidnapped and murdered and the leading moderate political leaders summarily and brutally executed. Approximately 100 days later, an estimated 800,000 people had been killed. Militias, armed forces, police officers and the ordinary man and woman on the street took part in the massacres.[4]

In the decade that has elapsed since the genocide, Rwanda has put transitional justice at the centre of its post-conflict reconstruction process. In September 1994 the United Nations Security Council, at the behest of the Rwandan government, passed a resolution creating the International Criminal Tribunal for Rwanda (ICTR), to adjudicate the crimes of genocide, war crimes and crimes against humanity committed in that country.[5] Subsequently, in September 1996 Rwanda's legislative body passed the Organic Law on the Organisation of Prosecutions for

---

2. Chiseche Mibenge is a Ph.D. researcher with the Netherlands Institute for Human Rights Research, University of Utrecht. The author expresses her gratitude to the Netherlands Organisation for Scientific Research (NWO) for the award of a WOTRO travel grant that facilitated a research visit to Rwanda and the study herein possible.

3. See <http://www.rwanda1.com/government/07_11_01_add.htm>.

4. For more information on the historical context as well as a descriptive account of the 1994 genocide see *Prosecutor* v. *Akayesu*, Judgment and Sentence, Case No. 96-4-T, T.Ch.I, 2 September 1998, in A. Klip and G. Sluiter, eds., *Annotated Leading Cases of International Criminal Tribunals, The International Criminal Tribunal for Rwanda 1994-1999*, Vol. 2 (Antwerp, Intersentia 2001) Commentaries-II-47-67.

5. SC Res. 955 (1994), UN Doc. S/RES/955 (1994), 8 November 1994.

Yearbook of International Humanitarian Law
Volume 7 - 2004 - pp. 410-424 DOI 10.1017/S1389135904004106

Offences Constituting the Crime of Genocide or Crimes Against Humanity (Organic Law).[6]

This law created specialised genocide chambers within the existing judicial system. Under the Organic Law, suspects were classified under four categories according to their degrees of culpability in the Rwandan genocide. Category one offenders included leaders and organisers of the genocide and perpetrators of sexual torture; category two offenders included perpetrators and accomplices of murders; category three included perpetrators of grave assaults against a victim not resulting in death; and the fourth category of offenders included those who committed offences against property, such as looting.[7] A punishment scale for each category of perpetrator was formulated, and the death penalty was reserved though not mandated for category one offenders. Category four offenders received no penal sanction but only the payment of restitution to the value of the damaged or looted property.[8] The Organic Law also introduced a confession and guilty plea procedure, which invited accused persons in categories two and three to confess to their crimes in exchange for greatly reduced sentences. This procedure is elaborated on in section 2.3 on sentencing.

The initial trials raised many concerns regarding the observance of international fair trial standards. It was suggested by some observers that false accusations were rife and that a large proportion of those detained in Rwanda's prisons were the victims of denunciations made by malicious neighbours or associates. Reportedly, the government accused political opponents of genocide and imprisoned them without cause.[9] At the outset, judicial staff and prosecutors received inadequate training and there was an absence of defence counsel. For about 100,000 prisoners awaiting trial, there were only 16 defence lawyers practising in Rwanda by mid 1997.[10]

Thus, by September 1996, two legal processes – one international and one national – were in operation, exercising concurrent jurisdiction over international crimes (Table I below illustrates the salient features of concurrent jurisdiction existing between the ICTR and the Specialised Chambers.). However, by the close of the century, justice remained indefinitely delayed, and indefinitely denied, for many victims and survivors, as well as detainees accused of gross violations of human rights and international humanitarian law. By January 2000 Rwanda's judiciary had tried approximately 2,500 people and over 120,000 were awaiting trial in

---

6. Organic Law No. 08/96 of 30 August 1996 on the Organisation of Prosecutions for Offences constituting the Crime of Genocide or Crimes against Humanity committed since 1 October 1990. Published in 1 *YIHL* (1998) p. 625.

7. Ibid., Art. 2.

8. Art. 14(d) provides that the acts committed by persons placed in Category 4 shall only give rise to civil damages determined by amicable agreement between the parties with the assistance of the community, failing which the rules pertaining to criminal proceedings and civil actions shall apply. If the accused is sentenced to a term of imprisonment, the sentence is suspended.

9. Organisation for African Unity, *Rwanda the Preventable Genocide* (June 2000) at p. 200.

10. Amnesty International, News Release, Grave Doubts about the Fairness of the First AI Index: AFR:47/13/97, 8 April 1997, <http://web.amnesty.org/library/Index/ENGAFR470131997?open&of=ENG-RWA>.

dangerously overpopulated prisons. The prosecution rate of the ICTR also remained modest. Seventy indictments have been brought since 1995, and by early 2000 nine trials had been completed resulting in eight convictions and one acquittal.

In response to the national judiciary's inability to make significant headway in the criminal prosecution of persons suspected of violating international law, the government of Rwanda began to seek alternative forms of justice which could operate concurrently with the ICTR as well as the ordinary criminal courts. There was an emphasis on establishing a model of justice that would embrace traditional Rwandan values by advocating restoration over retribution; a model that would expedite the process of justice, ease overcrowding in detention centres and uphold the rights of the accused while remaining palatable to the survivors of the genocide. *Gacaca* tribunals emerged as the only viable solution to the impasse in Rwanda's domestic transitional justice process.

Table I. Concurrent Jurisdiction between the International Criminal Tribunal for Rwanda and Domestic Specialised Chambers (1996 – 2000)

Tribunal	Temporal jurisdiction	Competence	Sentencing/Penalties		
			Maximum	Post trial confession	Pre-trial confession
International Criminal Tribunal for Rwanda	1 January 1994 to 31 December 1994	Category I Leaders and planners Genocide, war crimes, crimes against humanity	Life sentence	May mitigate	May mitigate
Specialised Chambers	1 October 1990-31 December 2004	Category 1 Leaders, planners and distinguished killers	Death sentence Loss of civil rights	N/A	N/A
		Category 2 Killers	Life sentence Loss of civil rights	12-15	7-11
		Category 3 Assault	Unspecified, but guided by Penal Code	1/3 reduction of normal sentence	½ reduction of normal sentence
		Category 4 Property crimes	Damages or restitution	N/A	N/A

2. WHAT IS *GACACA*?

The *gacaca* is a traditional community-based mechanism of dispute resolution, and a literal translation into English is 'lawn' or 'yard', referring to the fact that parties to a dispute as well as members of the *gacaca* sit on the grass whilst determining the dispute. Historically, it was a non-state or informal system used by indigenous

Rwandan families and communities for dispute resolution. Created on an *ad hoc* basis, it remained an unwritten law, and proceedings varied depending on the circumstances of the dispute.

Generally, the types of conflict dealt with by the *gacaca* were related to issues that struck at the core of social cohesion, tolerance and peaceful co-existence in Rwanda's densely populated rural communes. Disputes over property rights, livestock, marriage, succession, attacks on personal integrity, etc., were most often brought before the elders for mediation. *Gacaca* courts were not made obsolete by colonisation or independence; they remained active in regulating the lives of Rwandans and maintaining social harmony and justice in communities. Legal pluralism allowed *gacaca* to flourish generally unhindered and it remained active into the early 1990s, increasingly under minimum commune administration.

The 'new' *gacaca* is not an attempt by the government of Rwanda to duplicate the traditional *gacaca*. It is a unique process with similarities to the traditional mechanism but also incorporating a contemporary legislative framework derived from Rwanda's Penal Code, as well as international conventions to which Rwanda is a party, such as the 1949 Geneva Conventions and the 1948 Genocide Convention.

2.1 Establishing 'new' *gacaca* tribunals

The Transitional National Assembly of Rwanda formally adopted proposals for the introduction of modern *Gacaca* Tribunals on 12 October 2000. Rwanda's Constitutional Court declared the draft *Gacaca* Law constitutional on 18 January 2001. An amended *Gacaca* Law was enacted in June 2004 and where differences exist, the current Law will prevail.[11]

The *Gacaca* Law provides for the establishment of 11,000 *Gacaca* Tribunals throughout the country, from Rwanda's lowest political and administrative level of the cell to that of the sector. Each *gacaca* jurisdiction includes a general assembly, a seat (judges), and a coordinating committee. The general assembly of a cell is made up of all the cell's residents over the age of 18. This community elects from its members nine 'honest persons' constituting the seat and five deputies.[12] More than 90 percent of the Rwandan electorate participated in electing over 200,000 judges known as *les integres* in October 2001. Thirty five percent of those elected were women. This is notable, as historically *gacaca* courts were presided over by

---

11. Organic Law No.16/2004 of 19/6/2004 establishing the organisation, competence and functioning of *gacaca* courts charged with prosecuting and trying the perpetrators of the crime of genocide and other crimes against humanity, committed between 1 October 1990 and 31 December 1994.

12. Art. 14 provides that a judge must meet the following requirements: '(1) not have participated in genocide; (2) be free from sectarianism; (3) not to have been sentenced by a trial to a penalty of at least 6 months' imprisonment; (4) to be of high morals and conduct; (5) to be truthful; (6) to be honest; (7) to be characterised by a spirit of speech sharing.
Any person who meets these conditions and who has at least 21 years can be elected as a member of a *gacaca* tribunal without any discrimination of sex, origin, religion, opinion or social position.' Interestingly, Art. 15 prohibits lawyers, career magistrates, politicians, soldiers and policemen in active service, and civil servants from standing as judges of the *gacaca*.

male heads of families or communities. During the first round of elections at the cell level adults throughout the country were entrusted with the task of appointing candidates proposed by their representatives in *nyumba kumi* (ten households or smallest administrative level). This was done in public meetings where citizens were given the opportunity to step forward and voice their criticism against certain candidates or else endorse candidates by simply lining up behind them. Thereafter, the judges selected by each cell met to designate their representatives to the sector level and so on up to the district and province levels. The training of 781 trainers selected from magistrates and final year law students began in February 2002 and, subsequently, the training of 254,152 judges of *gacaca* began on 8 April 2002. In groups of around 80, judges received basic instruction in the principles of law, particularly the *gacaca* law, human rights, group management, conflict resolution, trauma, and financial management.

The sheer scale of the implementation of the *gacaca* process quickly overwhelmed the Rwandan government and the inauguration of the tribunals was repeatedly delayed. Finally, on 18 June 2002, President Kagame officially inaugurated a small sample of *gacaca* tribunals in order to test the efficiency and justness of the process. The government commenced the first and second phase of the *gacaca* mandate with pilot courts in select sectors.[13] *Gacaca* became operational only in 73 cells of the 12 sectors chosen for the pilot project. By the end of 2002 *gacaca* was operational in a total of 650 jurisdictions.[14]

In each community where *gacaca* had been set up, people held public meetings where residents detailed what happened in the neighbourhood during the massacre and identified the victims as well as culprits (phase 1).[15] Thereafter, *gacaca* judges would categorise the crimes alleged (phase 2).

During phase one and two of the pilot *gacaca*, an impressive 63,447 cases were recorded and, out of this number, approximately 38,896 were categorised and awaiting trial before the *gacaca* courts. The normal courts had compiled 56,763 cases.[16]

By early February 2005, 8,260 *gacaca* courts (3,000 less than first envisaged in 2001) at the cell level began carrying out genocide trials on a nationwide scale. The Rwandan government estimates that all pre-trial phase one and two activities will be completed by the end of June 2005. According to those estimates, the first trials in these courts would start on January 2006. Tentative projections made by the Ministry of Justice and Gacaca Department of the Supreme Court put the completion date of *gacaca* hearings at around five years.

Several other government bodies support the work of the *gacaca* jurisdictions. The election of judges is organised and conducted by the National Electoral Com-

---

13. Ibid.

14. Amnesty International, *Gacaca*: A question of justice (2002) AI Index: 470072002, <http://web.amnesty.org/library/index/engafr470072002>.

15. Reported by E. Karemera 'Kagame inaugurates *Gacaca* genocide trials', *The New Times* (Kigali) No. 551, 25-27 June 2004, at p. 1.

16. Reported by W. Kigabo, 'Elections fair – *Gacaca* official', *The New Times* (Kigali), No. 560, 19-20 July 2004, at p. 1.

mittee. Legal advice when required can be sought by the *gacaca* seat from legal experts appointed by the National Service, which is also responsible for the follow up, supervision and coordination of *gacaca* activities. It is also empowered to issue rules and regulations relating to the procedure of *gacaca*. The Ministry of Justice is responsible for the elaboration of all *gacaca*-related laws and decrees, while the Ministry of Interior Affairs is responsible for prisons and the transfer of detainees, and the Ministry of Finance controls and distributes the *gacaca* budget. The Office of the Prosecutor continues to receive denunciations and conducts investigations before transferring case files to the *gacaca* tribunals.

2.2 Jurisdiction of *gacaca* tribunals

The *Gacaca* Law categorises suspects according to the gravity of the crimes committed by them. It has slightly modified the categorisation first set down by the Organic Law of 1996, and reduces the categories from four to three. Category 1 offenders include: (1) The person whose criminal acts or criminal participation place him among planners, organisers and ringleaders of the genocide or crimes against humanity, together with his accomplices; (2) The person who, at the time, was in the organs of leadership, at the national level, at the level of prefecture, sub-prefecture, commune, political parties, army, gendarmerie, communal police, religious orders or in militia, has committed these offences or encouraged other people to commit them, together with his accomplices; (3) The well-known murderer who distinguishes himself because of the zeal which characterised him in killings or excessive wickedness with which they were carried out, together with his accomplices; (4) The person who committed acts of torture against others even though they did not result in death, together with his accomplices; (5) The person who committed acts of rape or torture against sexual organs, together with his accomplices; (7) The person who committed dehumanising acts on the dead body, together with his accomplices.[17]

With respect to the third (trial) phase, category 1 crimes fall outside the jurisdiction of *gacaca*, but investigations and categorisation of all case files is the responsibility of *gacaca*. Only once sufficient facts and evidence are adduced by the *gacaca* general assembly and a case is classified as category one by the seat of the *gacaca* tribunals will it be transferred to the ordinary courts for trial. This in effect means that victims and witnesses of sexual violence, torture and other class one offences have had to testify at the *gacaca* level during the first and second phase of *gacaca* in order that the allegations could be recorded, investigated and then categorised before transfer up to the ordinary courts for trial.

Gacaca courts therefore exercise jurisdiction over categories 2 and 3 offenders. Category 2 offenders are: (a) 'The person whose criminal acts or criminal participation places among authors, co-authors or accomplices of deliberate homicides or serious attacks against persons which caused death', and (b) 'The person who, with intention of giving death, has caused injuries or committed other serious viola-

17. Art. 51.

tions, but from which the victims have not died.'[18] The category 3 offender is: 'The person who only committed offences against property'.

The *gacaca* court of the cell deals at the first and final instance with Category 3 offenders.[19] The *gacaca* court at the sector deals at the first level with Category 2 offenders. Both *gacaca* at the cell and sector level have jurisdiction over community members accused of intimidating victims and witnesses of the *gacaca* courts as well as those victims and witnesses who commit perjury, refuse to participate in the proceedings or otherwise obstruct the course of justice.[20] The *gacaca* court at seat level has the power to hear appeals against judgments arising from the cell level regarding obstruction by witnesses and intimidation of witnesses. The *Gacaca* Court of Appeals deals with appeals against sentences pronounced at first instance at sector level.[21] Accused persons will be tried before the *gacaca* court in the area where the alleged crime was perpetrated.[22]

2.3 Sentencing

The *gacaca* justice system relies on the system of plea agreements established under the Organic Law. An important modification to this procedure is that reduced sentences are also applicable to category 1 offenders who take part in this process. A preset fixed reduction in the penalty that would otherwise be imposed for their crimes is available to all perpetrators in return for an accurate and complete confession, a plea of guilty to the crimes committed, and an apology to the victims.[23] A greater reduction in their sentence is made available to perpetrators who confess and plead guilty prior to prosecution than to perpetrators who come forward only after prosecution has begun.

The sentences provided under the *gacaca* legislation are as follows:

—Category 1 offenders, as categorised by *gacaca* courts and transferred and subsequently tried and convicted in the ordinary courts who refused to participate in the guilty and confession plea procedure or whose confession was rejected by the seat, are sentenced to death or life imprisonment whilst those who confess incur a sentence ranging from 25 to 30 years' imprisonment.

—Category 2 perpetrators who killed or had the intention of killing receive a sentence of 25 to 30 years if they refused to confess or had their confessions rejected by the Seat, and those who confessed during or after the trial incur a prison sentence ranging from 12 to 15 years, but out of this sentence half will be served in custody and the rest is commuted into community service on probation. Those who confess prior to the trial phase are sentenced to seven to 12 years, serving half in detention and half on community service. Category 2 offenders who committed assault are sentenced to a maximum of seven years and

18. Ibid.
19. Art. 41.
20. Art. 42.
21. Art. 43.
22. Art. 44.
23. Art. 54.

a minimum of one year, depending on their cooperation in the confession procedure. They are also entitled to have half of their sentence commuted into community service.

—All category 3 defendants convicted are liable only for civil reparations for damages caused to other people's property.[24]

Hundreds of children who were younger than 14 during the genocide, too young to be held criminally responsible, were incarcerated for years instead of benefiting from assistance for rehabilitation and reintegration into society.[25] Thousands more who were between the ages of 14 and 18 in 1994 have been held in prolonged pre-trial detention, often on unsubstantiated genocide charges.[26] Unlike the Organic Law, the *Gacaca* Law provides for lesser sentences for juvenile offenders who were 14 or older but less than 18 when they committed the crime. Sentences range from between six months to 20 years detention depending on the gravity of the crimes and cooperation with the guilty plea procedure.[27] Accused persons under the age of 14 at the time they committed the crime cannot be prosecuted and are released by *gacaca* and ordinary courts into solidarity camps created for the rehabilitation of juvenile delinquents.

The sentence reductions offered by the guilty plea procedure are drastic, and indeed the effect of this system will be that the majority of accused who confess will not serve a further day in Rwanda's prisons, as the system allows that category two and three offenders who plead guilty and are convicted can serve half of the sentence outside prison engaged in community work. So, for accused persons who have already served a substantial period in detention and who are guilty, a plea bargain is an attractive option. The guilty plea system requires a full and detailed confession, which may yield important evidentiary information, given that many crimes were committed in the context or under the cover of war where witnesses are few and survivors are often cowed by the fear of reprisals and desist from testifying. The guilty plea procedure has yielded impressive results: by June 2004, approximately 40,000 genocide suspects brought before the *gacaca* courts during the preliminary phases had admitted participating in the 1994 genocide, all 40,000 belonged to the 2nd category of offenders.[28]

In 2003 the prison population linked to genocide had climbed to 130,000. This marked the start of the government's policy to decongest prisons and to date the prison population has been almost halved. In 2005 alone approximately 40,000 prisoners were released provisionally under a Presidential Decree.[29] Some of these were released on grounds of poor health, old age or youth. The Justice Minister

---

24. Art. 71.

25. Human Rights Watch, Rwanda Lasting Wounds: Consequences of Genocide and War for Rwanda's Children, <http://hrw.org/reports/2003/rwanda0403/rwanda0403-09.htm>.

26. Ibid.

27. Art. 78.

28. Reported by M. Kembaga, '40,000 genocide suspects plead guilty', *The New Times* (Kigali) No. 560, 19-20 July 2004, at p. 4.

29. Rwanda: Release of thousands of prisoners begins, <http://www.irinnews.org/report.asp?ReportID=48373&SelectRegion=Great_Lakes>.

revealed that 7,000 of those released in the latest batch actually have no case to answer but remain subject to rearrest should evidence and fresh charges surface.[30] However, most of those conditionally released in August 2005 were released as a result of their full confession of guilt. In 2003 up to 24,000 inmates were released under a Presidential Decree and a further 4,000 were released the following year.[31] Again, the majority of those released participated in the confession and guilty plea procedure. Rwanda's chief Prosecutor has stated that the release is not an amnesty and that those who were accused would have to face charges before the *gacaca*.[32]

The release of prisoners pending *gacaca* trials has aroused strong opposition from many survivors. Documented cases in which survivors and potential witnesses have been intimidated, threatened, attacked or even killed by those on provisional release have increased insecurity amongst survivors.[33] Conversely, there has been reporting to the effect that hundreds of Rwandans have fled into neighbouring Burundi for fear of persecution or prosecution before *gacaca* courts.[34]

Table II below illustrates the *gacaca* court's jurisdiction and the effects of the guilty plea and confession procedure.

Table II. Gacaca Jurisdictions

Competence		Sentencing/Penalties		
		Maximum	Confession Post-trial	Confession Pre-trial
Category 1	Leaders, planners, rape Torture	Death penalty	30 Loss of civil rights	25 Loss of civil rights
Category 2	Murder	30 Loss of civil rights	12-15 Community service	7-12 Community service
	Category 2 Attempted murder	7	3-5	1-3
Category 2	Murder	10	6-7	3-6
Juvenile Offenders	Attempted murder	3	2	11/2
Category 3	Property crimes	N/A	N/A	Compensation

30. Reported by J. Munyaneza and M. Mazimpaka, 'Government, Ibuka clash over released suspects', *The New Times* (Kigali), posted at <http://www.allAfrica.com/stories/200508080233.html>.

31. Ibid.

32. Ibid.

33. Ibid.

34. IRIN News, Burundi-Rwanda: 'Hundreds flee Gacaca courts', 13 April, 2005, <http://www.irinnews.org/report.asp?ReportID=46614>.

2.4 **Reparations**

Increasingly, international conventions are coming equipped with provisions for punishment of perpetrators as well as reparation for victims, ranging from physical to psychosocial rehabilitation. The Declaration on the Elimination of Violence Against Women (the Women's Declaration), for example, provides that victims of gender-based violence have a right to a remedy, and the responsibility of the state to victims (and their children) is prescribed primarily in the form of reparational measures, including physical and psychological rehabilitation, assistance in child-care and maintenance, treatment, counselling, and health and social services.[35]

As the Gacaca Law 2004 includes sexual torture as well as torture as a Category 1 crime, one could also readily invoke the Convention Against Torture and Other Forms of Degrading and Inhuman Forms of Punishment (the Torture Convention) for guidance on state responsibility regarding the right to compensation for victims. The Torture Convention which, unlike the Women's Declaration, is *prima facie* binding on all states, provides that State Parties must ensure in their legal systems that victims of torture obtain redress and have an enforceable right to fair and adequate compensation, including the means for as full a rehabilitation as possible.[36] There is a growing consensus internationally that a remedy is incomplete without the concomitant award of reparations, compensation or restoration, in whatever shape or form the victim requires. A growing body of empirical research on the needs of victims of gross human rights violations reveals that the need for reparation routinely heads the wish list.[37]

Both the *Gacaca* Law of 2001 and the Organic Law of 1996 provided that victims could make civil claims in their own capacity or through legal representation.[38] Indeed, quite a number of the judgments of the Specialised Chambers included a criminal sanction as well as the payment of damages to the victim. The Belgian based NGO Lawyers without Borders conducted research on compensa-

---

35. The Declaration on the Elimination of Violence Against Women, GA Res. 2263(XXII) of 7 November 1967, Art. 4.

36. Art. 14 Convention against Torture and Other Cruel, Inhuman or Degrading Treatment or Punishment, UN Doc. A/RES/39/46, 10 December 1984. The Convention entered into force on 26 June 1987. See also Study concerning the right to restitution, compensation and rehabilitation for victims of gross violations of human rights and fundamental freedoms, Final Report submitted by T. van Boven, Special Rapporteur on the right to reparations for victims, UN Doc. E/CN.4/Sub.2/1993/8, 2 July 1993.

37. For qualitative research into the needs (rehabilitation, reparations, restitution, etc.) of victims of wartime violence, see D. Mazurana and K. Carlson, *From Combat to Community: Women and Girls of Sierra Leone* (January 2004), <http://www.peacewomen.org/resources/Peace_Negotiations/WWPSierraLeone.pdf>; Physicians for Human Rights, *War-related Sexual Violence in Sierra Leone – A Population based assessment 2002*, <http://www.phrusa.org/research/sierra_leone/report.html>; see also, The Draft Basic Principles and Guidelines on the Right to Remedy and Reparation for Victims of Violations of International Human Rights and Humanitarian Law, Human Rights Resolution 2005/35 Adopted 19 April 2005 and the Report of the independent expert on the right to restitution, compensation and rehabilitation for victims of grave violations of human rights and fundamental freedoms, Cherif Bassiouni, E/CN.4/1999/65 8 February 1999 submitted pursuant to Commission on Human Rights resolution 1998/43.

38. Art. 29.

tion awarded by Rwanda's specialised chambers. They used a selection of 159 (guilty) judgments pronounced between 1997 and 1999 and found that compensation had been awarded in only half of these cases. In 18 percent of these cases, the court decided that the civil and the penal aspects had to be treated separately.[39] Rombouts explains that this in effect meant that the civil parties should pursue their civil claim in civil procedures. Genocide victims have seldom done this because of their unfamiliarity with the procedures and because of the costs such a civil suit may entail.[40] However, it is unclear from the judgments perused whether enforcement of the damages was ever possible against the largely indigent detainees. And in those cases where government figures, and, in particular, members of the defence forces were implicated in genocide, the Specialised Chambers ordered that the Rwandan government had to compensate the victim.[41] The government has, however, consistently failed to pay damages awarded by the Specialised Chambers.[42] In effect, the award of damages has proven a symbolic act.

Further, the Organic Law provided that convicted persons whose acts place them within Categories 1 under 2 would be held jointly and severally liable for all damages caused in the country by their acts of criminal participation, regardless of where the offences were committed.[43] However, there was no attempt to enforce such a sweeping provision during the tenure of the Specialised Chambers.

The Gacaca Law of 2004 largely evades the question of damages or other forms of compensation and provides only that: 'Other forms of compensation the victims receive shall be determined by a particular law.'[44] This refers to the *Fonds d'Indemnisation* (FIND), which has been on the parliament's drafting board since 1996.

The Organic Law of 1996 referred to a Victims Compensation Fund 'whose creation and operation shall be determined by a separate law'.[45] Subsequently, the National Assembly passed a law establishing a National Assistance Fund under the Ministry of Social Affairs for needy victims of genocide (the Fund).[46] The Preamble acknowledged a state obligation to support victims in need based on the fact that 'the Government in place during genocide and massacres, and the administrative institutions played an essential role in the commission of these crimes …'.

In her comprehensive study on reparations politics in Rwanda, Heidy Rombouts clarifies that the government regards the Fund not as a form of reparation but as a

39. Avocats sans Frontiéres, Justice Pour Tous au Rwanda, Rapport Annuel 1999, p. 50, <http://www.asf.be/FR/Texte/Terrain/Rwanda/ASF.terrain.RWA.rapport%201999.pdf>.

40. H. Rombouts, *Victim Organisations and the politics of reparation: a case study on Rwanda* (Antwerp, Intersentia 2004) at p. 373

41. Francoise Digneffe and Jacques Fierens, eds., *Justice et gacaca: L'experience rwandaise et la genocide* (Namur, Presses universitaitres de Namur 2003) at p.103.

42. Ibid., at p. 103

43. Art. 30.

44. Art. 96.

45. Art. 32.

46. Law No. 02/98 of 22/01/1998 Establishing a national assistance fund for needy victims of genocide and massacres committed in Rwanda between 1 October 1990 and 31 December 1994.

form of assistance.[47] She explains that an earlier draft shows that the initial idea was to create one fund that would provide both assistance and compensation to genocide survivors and family members of genocide members.[48] According to this first draft, family members would receive only compensation, and assistance was reserved to survivors in need. Survivors in need were described as 'handicapped persons, physically weak persons, persons in need of assistance to meet their needs'. Whilst both elements of assistance and compensation were present in the first joint draft legislation, the 1998 law only retains 'assistance'. This could indicate a shift in the government's belief that it holds a positive obligation to compensate survivors of the state-sponsored genocide. Following the enactment of the Fund, the government organised a census of its target group and counted 282,804 needy survivors spread around the country.[49] The economic implications of meeting the needs of so many victims could not have been lost on the government.

The law provides that funds are to be obtained from a number of sources, including the government, which is to allocate an amount equal to five percent of the state's own domestic revenue of the budget.[50] Employed Rwandans must 'contribute' at least 100 Rwandan francs to the Fund annually and every Rwandan citizen over the age of 18 must contribute at least one percent of his annual salary annually. The assistance of the Fund targets particularly education, health and housing.[51]

The Fund remains an administrative challenge. The selection of the neediest survivors is not proceduralised by the Fund and it is a highly contentious and at times corrupt process. Administrators have been at the centre of allegations of fraud.[52] The payment of contributions falls terribly below target marks. To date, its main contribution has been to implement affirmative or preferential measures for child survivors or children of survivors with respect to higher education.

As mentioned earlier, the *Gacaca* Law 2004 provides that all Category 2 offenders are entitled to serve half of their sentence in custody while the rest is commuted into community services on a probationary basis. It has been explained by the government that community service would involve building and road construction, and growing vegetables for schools and prisons. And those paroled are to work three days a week while staying in their homes.[53] The Preamble of the *Gacaca* Law provides that the Law aims not only to provide punishment but also

---

47. Rombouts, *supra* n. 40 at p. 306.
48. Ibid.
49. Ibid., at p. 314.
50. In 1998, five percent of the domestic revenues of the budget was fixed at three billion eight hundred thirteen million one hundred thirty nine thousand one hundred twenty six Rwandan Francs (FRW 3,813,139,126). Figure taken from Law No. 11/98 of 02/11/1998 amending and completing the law No. 02/98 of 22/01/1998 establishing a national assistance fund for needy victims of genocide and massacres committed in Rwanda between 1 October 1990, and 31 December 1994, Art. 2.
51. Art. 14. The beneficiaries of the Fund assistance are survivors of genocide and massacres who are in need, especially orphans, widows, and handicapped persons. The assistance targets particularly education, health and housing.
52. Rombouts, *supra* n. 40, at p. 312.
53. Reported by Kembaga *supra* n. 28.

to reconstruct Rwandan society, to allow convicted persons to amend themselves and to favour their reintegration into the Rwandan society. Clearly, community service operates in this spirit. However, it would be erroneous to suggest that community service contributes to the government's fulfilment of its obligation to compensate victims of wartime sexual violence and other gross human rights violations.

2.5 International fair trial standards

It is apparent to even the most casual observer that the *gacaca* process conflicts in part with international fair trial standards. The right of all accused persons to be represented by counsel, and the right to a competent, independent and impartial tribunal immediately spring to mind. *Gacaca* does not provide for any form of legal representation, for either victims or perpetrators, and the government has argued that this is by default the best form of equality of arms: Rwanda's legal profession was decimated by the genocide and despite some recovery, it would be an impossible feat to provide all victims and perpetrators with legal representation. Advocates of restorative justice also suggest that the presence of legal counsel or active prosecutors in the *gacaca* process would 'steal' the responsibility for conflict resolution from the fractured community, and thereby retard reconciliation. Regarding the impartiality and competence of the *gacaca* judges, it has been argued that justice, in the traditional Rwandan sense, demands that stakeholders in the justice and reconciliation process, i.e., all those who were most closely affected by the dispute, in this case the genocide, are seen to be the principal actors in the *gacaca* process. Importing impartial judges from abroad would result in judgments that would lack recognition of the social, cultural and political undertones impacting Rwanda's process of transitional justice. Thus, an impartial judge violates the spirit of the *gacaca* process.

Accessibility is a crucial component of the fundamental right to a remedy. *Gacaca* is giving Rwandans the opportunity to access justice. The courts are brought to the people, judges are known to and elected by them, and the accused is brought home to defend himself. In this way, we are seeing accessibility to justice that the ordinary criminal courts and the ICTR based in Arusha can only ever dream of. In line with international fair trial standards, *gacaca* also promises to establish individual criminal responsibility without undue delay; again, its capacity to carry out expedient trials and determine questions of guilt or innocence far exceeds that of the ICTR and domestic courts.

3. CONCLUSIONS

Despite the best efforts of the Rwandan government to reconstruct the judiciary, very few prosecutions occurred between 1996 and 2000. The process moved at a snail's place and violations of basic international fair trial standards were frequently reported.

Gacaca, as a mechanism to expedite genocide trials, cannot be underestimated. The impact on the case load of the ordinary courts can only be welcomed. Finally, there is a real opportunity to prosecute international crimes before (decongested) domestic courts. Due to extensive restructuring and professionalisation of the judiciary, Rwanda's domestic courts are increasingly capable of dispensing justice, as professional ethics and a human rights culture are increasingly evident. A shared caseload is a reduced caseload, and the achievements of the national courts will hopefully be more visible as the prosecution rate for Category 1 offences such as rape and genocide increases.

The innovative aspect of the *gacaca* must surely be welcomed in a region of Africa (Great Lakes) that has been plagued by chronic internal and cross border conflict characterised by gross violations of human rights. *Gacaca* is a model of justice that responds to the conundrum of how to establish individual criminal responsibility for state-sponsored violence committed on a mass scale by the masses.

The introduction of plea agreements to Rwanda's traditionally civil law system is illustrative of the government's desire to innovate and meet the demands of prosecuting well over 100,000 accused persons in an expedient manner. Due to the passage of time and defects in the reporting and investigation procedures during wartime and post-conflict conditions, it was clear that many allegations of violations of humanitarian law and genocide would not withstand the strict evidentiary requirements of criminal procedure. If effectively employed, the guilty plea procedure will assist the prosecution greatly with regard to the strict evidentiary requirements under the domestic Penal Code. *Gacaca* is useful as an investigative process, as the jurisdictions are empowered to conduct investigations into alleged crimes. For many victims of the conflict, and for many suspects, this will be their first opportunity since the conflict in 1994 to see criminal dockets containing witness testimony and perhaps even full and detailed confessions of perpetrators opened with charges supported by evidence.

Gacaca's powers are extensive. They have the power to summon witnesses, to order and carry out searches of premises, issue severe sentences, attach property of accused persons, summon the Public Prosecutor to provide information on case files, and even order parole of detained persons required as witnesses. The extent of these powers does demand that the government must meet minimum norms of fair trial. At present, international fair trial standards as they are tabled in international conventions are selectively and sparingly observed by the *gacaca* process. It is unlikely that the *gacaca* courts will ever prioritise the full observance of these norms in the administration of their version of restorative justice. It is a system operating in a hugely under-resourced legal and judicial system, and the reality is that post conflict reconstruction is a slow and tedious process. It can only be hoped that the huge reductions in sentences and, in some cases, immediate release of prisoners who confess to their crimes will slightly mitigate the gross abuse of process suffered by accused persons whilst in detention.

The lack of enforcement mechanisms against the state and individuals for civil damages awarded to victims has had an adverse impact on the willingness of victims to participate in the *gacaca* process. At present, measures such as the 'assistance' fund for the neediest or community service by prisoners fall short of international obligations to rehabilitate or compensate victims of human rights violations. However, increasing efficiency in the administration of the Victims Fund may go some way to relieving survivors of the physical and psychosocial consequences of the conflict. In particular, the Victims Fund promises to focus on basic economic and social human rights, such as the right to housing, the right to health and the right to education. It is unfortunate, however, that the Fund benefits only a limited number of survivors. Before the Rwandan government can fulfil its human rights obligations regarding compensation of victims of gross human rights violations, the FIND must be enacted and implemented. Victims have a right to compensation and not only assistance or charity.

The process of transitional justice in Rwanda has been three-tiered to date. The establishment of the ICTR, the ordinary courts and the *gacaca* tribunals illustrate the challenges existing in a post conflict society attempting to redress gross human rights violations. The three models of justice, and their establishment, show the dynamism and evolution in justice models that can occur in a mere decade after the end of a conflict. While all three mechanisms of accountability have faced a barrage of criticism from observers, relating mainly to issues of fair trial observance such as impartiality and undue delays, one cannot but admire the commitment of the international community and the Rwandan government to establish international criminal responsibility for gross human rights violations and war crimes. The concurrent jurisdiction existing between these tribunals is an important step towards establishing international law at the domestic level and ensuring the participation of Rwandan society in the prosecution of international crimes.

THE USE AND ABUSE OF MILITARY MANUALS[1]

Charles Garraway[2]

1. INTRODUCTION

In July of 2004, at a conference at St Anthony's College, Oxford University, the Attorney General, Lord Goldsmith, formally launched the new United Kingdom Manual of the Law of Armed Conflict.[3] This long-awaited publication was designed to replace the earlier 1958 Manual on the Law of War on Land,[4] written by Sir Hersch Lauterpacht[5] with the assistance of Colonel (later Professor) Gerald Draper.[6] Much had happened since the last amendment to the 1958 Manual in 1969 but although work had been in progress on a new Manual for some time, decisions on publication were held up, first by the delay in the United Kingdom decision to ratify the Additional Protocols to the Geneva Conventions of 1977[7] and then by concern over the appropriate timing for publication of such a Manual, which would inevitably be seen as an authoritative statement of the United Kingdom's position on international law.

---

2. Professor Charles Garraway served as the Stockton Professor of International Law at the United States Naval War College for 2004-2005. He previously served for 30 years as an officer in the United Kingdom Army Legal Services and was himself involved in the drafting of the new United Kingdom Manual of the Law of Armed Conflict. The author is writing in his personal capacity and his views should not be taken as necessarily representing those of any organisation or government. He would like to thank, W. Hays Parks of the Office of General Counsel, United States Department of Defense, and Professor George Walker of Wake Forest University School of Law (both previous Stockton Professors) for making available unpublished material which greatly assisted in the writing of this article.

3. UK Ministry of Defence, *The Manual of the Law of Armed Conflict* (Oxford, Oxford University Press 2004) (hereinafter, UK Manual).

4. The Law of War on Land, being Part III of the Manual of Military Law (London, HMSO 1958).

5. Sir Hersch Lauterpacht QC 1897-1960, Whewall Professor of International Law, Cambridge University 1937-1955, Judge of the International Court of Justice 1955-1960.

6. Professor Colonel Gerald Draper OBE (1914-1989) was regarded as the foremost specialist in the law of armed conflict of his generation in the United Kingdom. During his army career, he was a Military Prosecutor in the war crimes trials in Germany after the Second World War and, following his retirement, took up the post of Professor of Law at the University of Sussex.

7. Protocol Additional to the 12 August 1949 Geneva Conventions and Relating to the Protection of Victims of International Armed Conflicts (hereafter, Additional Protocol I), and Protocol Additional to the Geneva Conventions of 12 August 1949, and Relating to the Protection of Victims of Non-International Armed Conflicts (hereinafter, Additional Protocol II), both dated 8 June 1977, reprinted in A. Roberts and R. Guelff, eds., *Documents on the Law of War*, 3rd edn. (Oxford, Oxford University Press 2000) pp. 422 and 483, respectively. The United Kingdom ratified both Protocols on 28 January 1998.

Yearbook of International Humanitarian Law
Volume 7 - 2004 - pp. 425-440
DOI 10.1017/S1389135904004258

The increased tempo of military operations in the 1990s, and the pressure that was imposed on previously accepted legal principles by the military response to the terrorist attacks on New York and Washington on 11 September 2001, engendered a renewed interest in the law of armed conflict. The law had been developing quickly through new treaties, such as the Additional Protocols to the 1980 Conventional Weapons Convention[8] and also, for the first time since the end of the Second World War, through judicial decisions, of the *ad hoc* Tribunals established for the Former Yugoslavia and Rwanda.[9] A further complicating factor was the seemingly increasing gulf between the United States and its allies in the North Atlantic Treaty Organization (NATO) on a number of key issues. The United States, which is not a Party to 1977 Additional Protocol I to the 1949 Geneva Conventions,[10] walked out of the negotiations that led to the 1997 Ottawa Convention on anti-personnel landmines[11] and is strongly opposed to the new International Criminal Court.[12] Was this the time to publish a Manual stating United Kingdom positions that might increase the divide with our major ally?

Whatever, the delaying factors, the Manual has indeed now been published and its 16 chapters and seven appendices provide a comprehensive view of the law as seen by the United Kingdom. Unlike its predecessor, this Manual is designed to apply across all Services and thus contains chapters on maritime and air operations as well as land. However, when considering its effect, it is important to note both its scope and its intended audience. In the words of the Preface:

> 'This Manual is a reference work for members of the United Kingdom's Armed Forces and officials within the Ministry of Defence and other departments of Her Majesty's Government. It is intended to enable all concerned to apply the law of armed conflict when conducting operations and when training or planning for them.'[13]

---

8. The 1980 Convention on Prohibitions or Restrictions on the Use of Certain Conventional Weapons Which May be Deemed to be Excessively Injurious or to Have Indiscriminate Effects, reprinted in Roberts and Guelff, ibid., at p. 515. The Convention originally had three Protocols attached on Non-Detectable Fragments (hereinafter, Protocol I), Mines, Booby Traps and Other Devices (hereinafter, Protocol II) and Incendiary Weapons (hereinafter, Protocol III). An Amended Protocol on Mines, Booby Traps and Other Devices was adopted in 1996 (hereinafter, Amended Protocol II), as were later additional Protocols on Blinding Laser Weapons (1995) (hereinafter, Protocol IV) and Explosive Remnants of War (2003) (hereinafter, Protocol V).

9. The International Criminal Tribunal for the Former Yugoslavia (hereinafter, ICTY), established under Security Council resolution 827/93 of 25 May 1993, and the International Criminal Tribunal for Rwanda (hereinafter, ICTR), established under Security Council resolution 955/94 on 8 November 1994.

10. See *supra* n. 7.

11. Convention on the Prohibition of the Use, Stockpiling, Production and Transfer of Anti-Personnel Mines and on Their Destruction of 18 September 1997, reprinted in Roberts and Guelff, *supra* n. 7, at p. 645.

12. See Rome Statute of the International Criminal Court, adopted on 17 July 1998, reprinted in D. Schindler and J. Toman, eds., *The Laws of Armed Conflicts*, 4th edn. (Dordrecht, Martinus Nijhoff Publishers 2004) p. 1309.

13. UK Manual, *supra* n. 3, at p. vii.

It is essentially a handbook for practitioners dealing with the law of armed conflict. It is not designed as an academic treatise – though its academic credentials are far from minimal – nor does it purport to deal in any more than cursory detail with the law regulating 'the circumstances in which states may use armed force (traditionally termed '*jus ad bellum*')'.[14]

The United Kingdom Manual follows in a long tradition of manuals of many different types and from many different countries. In order to assess its possible impact, it is necessary to look back at that tradition and to examine where this new manual fits in the greater scheme. Manuals are essentially a mode of dissemination. However, the word 'manual' has been used to cover a multitude of different types of publication. The three main types of manuals are those of an international nature, such as the San Remo Manual on International Law Applicable to Armed Conflicts at Sea,[15] national Manuals, such as the new United Kingdom Manual of the Law of Armed Conflict[16] and internal manuals (often referred to as 'handbooks'), such as the Operational Law Handbook produced by the International and Operational Law Department of the United States Army Judge Advocate General's Legal Center and School.[17] Each type has a different purpose and needs to be examined separately.

2. INTERNATIONAL MANUALS

In the early days of the development of treaty law governing the law of armed conflict, it was recognised, for example in such pronouncements as the Martens Clause,[18] that not all the law was codified and that there remained a large body of customary law that underpinned the conduct of operations.[19]

---

14. Ibid., para. 1.2, at p. 1.

15. L. Doswald Beck, ed., *San Remo Manual on International Law Applicable to Armed Conflicts at Sea* (hereinafter, San Remo Manual) (Cambridge, Cambridge University Press 1995).

16. See *supra* n. 3.

17. Operational Law Handbook (2005), <https://www.jagcnet.army.mil/jagcnetintranet/databases/operational+law/clamo.nsf/(JAGCNetDocID)/C7719006CE434DF385256F3B006E39EA/$FILE/OpLaw%20Handbook%2005%20PDF.pdf>.

18. Named after Feodor Martens 1845-1909, Russian diplomat and authority on international law. He became an official in the foreign ministry in 1868 and was professor of international law at the University of St. Petersburg from 1873 to 1907. He was a representative at many international conferences, including The Hague Conferences of 1899 and 1907, for which he helped lay the foundation. His decisions as arbitrator and his many books contributed much to international law, and his efforts toward international understanding earned him the Nobel Peace Prize in 1902.

19. The Martens Clause, as found in the Preamble to the 1899 and 1907 Fourth Convention on the Laws and Customs of War on Land, states: 'It has not, however, been possible to agree forthwith on provisions embracing all the circumstances which occur in practice. On the other hand, it could not be intended by the High Contracting Parties that the cases not provided for should, for want of a written provision, be left to the arbitrary judgment of the military commanders. Until a more complete code of the laws of war is issued, the High Contracting Parties think it right to declare that in cases not included in the Regulations adopted by them, populations and belligerents remain under the protection and empire of the principles of international law, as they result from the usages established between civilized nations, from the laws of humanity, and the requirements of the public conscience.' Conven-

As the process of codification continued, so did attempts by scholars to fill the gaps. Even before 1899 the Institute of International Law had adopted the Oxford Manual on 9 September 1880.[20] This followed the Brussels Conference of 1874 where 15 European States had tried to formulate an international agreement dealing with the laws and customs of war. However, the final Protocol was never ratified and it was in an attempt to move the process forward that the International Institute acted. In the words of the preface:

> 'The Institute, too, does not propose an international treaty, which might perhaps be premature or at least very difficult to obtain; but, being bound by its by-laws to work, among other things, for the observation of the laws of war, it believes it is fulfilling a duty in offering to the governments a 'Manual' suitable as the basis for national legislation in each State, and in accord with both the progress of juridical science and the needs of civilized armies. Rash and extreme rules will not, furthermore, be found therein. The Institute has not sought innovations in drawing up the 'Manual'; it has contented itself with stating clearly and codifying the accepted ideas of our age so far as this has appeared allowable and practicable.'[21]

It was recognised that such a Manual was not binding but it was intended to be authoritative and to be in a form 'from which the text of a law may be easily secured when desired'.[22] The aspirations of the drafters were indeed met when the 1899 and 1907 Hague Peace Conferences agreed Conventions which owed much of their substance to the Oxford Manual.

At the 1907 Conference, in the Final Act, the Parties stated that:

> 'The Conference expresses the opinion that the preparation of regulations relative to the laws and customs of naval war should figure in the programme of the next Conference, and that in any case the Powers may apply, as far as possible, to war by sea the principles of the Convention relative to the laws and customs of war on land.'[23]

The initiative was again taken up by the Institute of International Law, which in 1913 published the Oxford Manual of Naval War.[24] Unfortunately, developments in treaty law were then interrupted by the First World War and no 'next confer-

---

tion (IV) with Respect to the Laws and Customs of War on Land and its Annex: Regulations Respecting the Laws and Customs of War on Land, signed at The Hague, 29 July 1899, reprinted in Schindler and Toman, *supra* n. 12, at p. 7. Similar wording is to be found in the Preface to the 1907 Convention IV printed on the same page.

20. *The Laws of War on Land*, Manual Published by the Institute of International Law (Oxford Manual), reprinted in Schindler and Toman, *supra* n. 12, at p. 29.

21. Ibid., at p. 30.

22. Ibid., Preface, at p. 31.

23. Final Act of the Second International Peace Conference, signed at The Hague, 18 October 1907, reprinted in Schindler and Toman, *supra* n. 12, at p. 47.

24. *The Laws of Naval War Governing the Relations between Belligerents*, Manual Adopted by the Institute of International Law (Oxford Manual of Naval War), Schindler and Toman, *supra* n. 12, at p. 1123.

ence' in The Hague series was ever held. Despite attempts to deal with specific subjects such as submarine warfare,[25] to this day there has been no concerted effort to produce a treaty containing a list of codified rules on naval warfare.

This gap was acknowledged by the International Institute of Humanitarian Law in San Remo, Italy, which, in 1987, began a series of meetings involving academics, military experts and government representatives, all acting in their private capacities. The result of these efforts was the 1994 San Remo Manual on International Law Applicable to Armed Conflicts at Sea.[26] In the words of the Foreword:

> 'This document is a contemporary restatement of the law, together with some progressive development, which takes into account recent State practice, technological developments and the effect of related areas of the law, in particular, the United Nations Charter, the 1982 Law of the Sea Convention, air law and environmental law. The last restatement of the law of armed conflict at sea was undertaken by the Institute of International Law in 1913. Developments in the law since that date have for the most part not been incorporated into treaty law, with the exception of the Second Geneva Convention which is essentially limited to the protection of the wounded, sick and shipwrecked at sea, and does not address the whole question of the law on the conduct of hostilities at sea. The Manual and the related Explanation represent a unique effort of experts from different parts of the world to establish the present state of the law based on State practice and treaty law of continuing validity.'[27]

Unlike the Oxford Manuals, which sought to provide impetus for a future codification, the aim of the San Remo Manual was more modest. The drafters recognised the difficulty in reaching agreement on codification today in a world of over 190 countries and therefore sought to restate the existing law as they found it through treaty law, customary law and state practice. They admitted that, on occasions, there has been 'some progressive development' but this has been limited and on most issues, a conservative view has been taken.

The Manual is not legally binding but, through the authoritative nature of its drafters and the increasing acceptance of its text amongst nations, it is exercising a considerable influence both as to the existing state of the law and as to its future development. A number of states have adopted it verbatim as their 'national' text and even the new United Kingdom Manual's provisions on maritime warfare are 'based substantially' on the text of the San Remo Manual.[28] On the other hand, states are free to differ from the view espoused by the Manual, as do both the United Kingdom Manual[29] and, to a greater extent, the United States Manual

25. See Art. 22 of the Treaty for the Limitation and Reduction of Naval Armaments The Treaty of London, signed on 22 April 1930 and the *Procès-Verbal* relating to the Rules of Submarine Warfare set forth in Part IV of the Treaty of London, signed on 6 November 1936, reprinted in Schindler and Toman, *supra* n. 12, at pp. 1143 and 1145, respectively.

26. See *supra* n. 15.

27. Ibid., at p. ix.

28. UK Manual, *supra* n. 3, Chapter 13, at p. 347.

29. Ibid., para. 13.2.

NWP 1-14M, the Commander's Handbook on the Law of Naval Operations with its Annotated Supplement.[30]

A similar project is currently underway in relation to Air Warfare under the auspices of the Harvard Program on Humanitarian Policy and Conflict Research. There is little treaty law applicable to air and missile warfare and the Rules of Aerial Warfare drafted in The Hague in 1923 were never adopted in legally binding form. A series of expert meetings are being held with a view to elaborating a manual along the lines of the San Remo Manual, which can be used as a benchmark.[31]

It will be seen from this short analysis that the purpose of these international manuals is to seek to clarify the law and, in some cases, act as a catalyst for developments in the law. An example of the latter can be taken from the San Remo Manual. Article 34(2) of the Second Geneva Convention states in unambiguous terms that:

> '... hospital ships may not possess or use a secret code for their wireless or other means of communication.'[32]

However, such a provision is now impracticable in the age of modern communications. As the Explanation points out:

> 'Technology has changed since the adoption of the Geneva Conventions. All messages to and from warships, including unclassified messages, are nowadays automatically encrypted when sent and decrypted when received by communication equipment that organically includes the crypto function. Hospital ships, therefore, should have the same type of communication equipment to avoid delays in receiving vital information caused by having separate and outdated radio equipment that does not have the integral crypto function.'[33]

The San Remo Manual itself thus states:

> 'In order to fulfil most effectively their humanitarian mission, hospital ships should be permitted to use cryptographic equipment. The equipment shall not be used in any circumstances to transmit intelligence data nor in any other way to acquire any military advantage.'[34]

---

30. See R. Thomas and J. Duncan, eds., 'Annotated Supplement to the Commander's Handbook on the Law of Naval Operations', 73 *International Law Studies* (1999). At para. 8.1.1, at p. 402, the authors use a wider definition of 'military objective' than that contained in either Additional Protocol I or the San Remo Manual, whilst referring to both sources for comparison.

31. See the website of the Program on Humanitarian Policy and Conflict Research at Harvard University, at <http://www.hsph.harvard.edu/hpcr/ihl_research.htm>.

32. Art. 34(2), Geneva Convention for the Amelioration of the Condition of the Condition of Wounded, Sick and Shipwrecked Members of Armed Forces at Sea of August 12, 1949 (Geneva Convention II), reprinted in Roberts and Guelff, *supra* n. 7, at p. 233.

33. See San Remo Manual, *supra* n. 15, para. 171.3 at p. 236.

34. Ibid., para. 171.

The 'should be permitted' indicates that the participants were encouraging a change in the law. They had no power to override treaty provisions but they could indicate where the law had perhaps become out of touch with reality. In such a way, they could contribute to the development of the law.

3. NATIONAL MANUALS

National manuals fulfil a different function. Whereas international manuals seek to provide an agreed version of the law, national manuals provide evidence of state practice and *opinio juris* in relation to the states by which they are issued. Whilst such manuals will of course look at contentious areas, their aim is not to reach a consensus agreement but to reflect the position adopted by the state concerned. They do not form law, as of themselves, but inevitably will be cited as example of 'international custom, as evidence of a general practice accepted as law'.[35]

One of the first national 'Manuals' was perhaps the Lieber Code prepared by Dr. Francis Lieber in 1863 during the American Civil War and designed to govern the conduct of the Union forces in the field.[36] This was published as a Presidential Executive Order, and though more commonly described as a 'Code'[37] it certainly purported to lay out the position of the Government. Interestingly, it appeared during what would now be described as a 'non-international' armed conflict though it stated that:

> 'Public war is a state of armed hostility between sovereign nations or governments.'[38]

Only in Section X was there explicit reference to 'Insurrection – Civil War – Rebellion'. The text was clearly designed to extend far beyond the immediate circumstances in which it was issued.

At this time, of course, the development of the law of armed conflict in its modern form was in its infancy. One of the roles that the Lieber Code had was as a model for future multilateral agreements. As the codification of the law began to evolve, so the major powers saw the need to ensure that their views were cogently expressed. In this way they could influence that development.

The first official British Manual was published in 1914 as Chapter XIV to the sixth edition of the Manual of Military Law which had itself been first published in 1884. The Manual itself dealt with many topics, in particular, military justice, but Chapter XIV was designed specifically to deal with the law of armed conflict, or

---

35. Art. 38(1)(b), Statute of the International Court of Justice, reprinted in I. Brownlie, ed., *Basic Documents in International Law*, 5th edn. (Oxford, Oxford University Press 2002) p. 319.

36. Instructions for the Government of Armies of the United States in the Field, prepared by Francis Lieber, promulgated as General Orders No. 100 by President Lincoln on 24 April 1863, reprinted in Schindler and Toman, *supra* n. 12, at p. 3.

37. See L. Green, *The Contemporary Law of Armed Conflict*, 2nd edn., (Manchester, Manchester University Press 2000) pp. 29-30.

38. Art. 20, Lieber Code, Schindler and Toman, *supra* n. 12, at p. 4.

'law of war' as it was then known. The authors were Professor Oppenheim and Colonel J.E. Edmonds C.B., a combination of military and academic expertise that was to set the pattern for all future iterations right up to the present day.[39] The 1914 Chapter survived until after the Second World War with revisions, including a major revision in 1936.[40]

Neither the Royal Air Force nor the Royal Navy has, in the past, published equivalent Manuals although both have dealt with the law of armed conflict in other publications.[41] The Air Force approach was heavily influenced by the writings of J.M. Spaight,[42] whose *Air Power and Air Rights*, published in three editions in 1924, 1933 and 1947, fulfilled much of the requirements of a Manual.[43] Spaight was himself a Government employee, in the Air Ministry, and it can be assumed therefore that his work carried at least some form of official approval.

The 2004 United Kingdom Manual was the product of a multitude of minds, including military personnel, civil servants and academics, such as Professors Christopher Greenwood,[44] Vaughan Lowe[45] and Sir Adam Roberts.[46] Unusually, for a government publication, many of the Government personnel involved are identified in the Preface.

The United States has also published a number of Manuals. The first official army Manual was dated 1914[47] and was revised or updated in 1917, 1940 and 1944. The current Manual dates from 1956,[48] with amendments made in 1976,[49] but plans have been underway for many years to produce a new Joint Service Manual on similar lines to the United Kingdom Manual.

In the United States Navy, the 'Blue Book' series published by the Naval War College has been a rich source on international law aspects of naval operations. Captain Charles H. Stockton, then President of the Naval War College, published a 'United States Naval War Code' in 1900,[50] although this was officially withdrawn in 1904. Stockton went on to be a delegate to the 1907 Hague Peace Conference and later published his own 'Manual of International Law for the Use of

39. See UK Manual, *supra* n. 3, Preface, at p. vii.

40. See Foreword by Sir Hersch Lauterpacht to the 1958 Manual of Military Law, the Law of War on Land, *supra* n. 4. For example, citations are made to the 1944 version of the Chapter in The Almelo Trial, Law Reports of Trials of War Criminals, The United Nations War Crimes Commission, Vol. I, (London, HMSO 1949) at p. 35.

41. The Air Force in Part II of their Manual of Air Force Law and the Navy primarily through the Handbook on the Law of Maritime Operations (BR-3012).

42. 1877-1968.

43. The original edition was published by Longman Green in London in 1924.

44. Professor of International Law, London School of Economics.

45. Chichele Professor of International Law, University of Oxford.

46. Montague Burton Professor of International Relations, University of Oxford.

47. Rules of Land Warfare, 1914, United States War Department.

48. The Law of Land Warfare, FM 27-10, Department of the Army, July 1956. This superseded FM 27-10 of 1 October 1940 with Change 1 of 15 November 1944.

49. Change 1, 15 July 1976.

50. See J.H. Doyle, Jr., 'International Law and Naval Operations', in M. Schmitt, ed., *The Law of Military Operations: Liber Amicorum Professor Jack Grunawalt*, – Newport RI, Naval War College Press 1998) p. 18.

Naval Officers'. In June 1917 the Navy Department published 'Instructions for the Navy of the United States Governing Maritime Warfare'. This was followed by a draft 'Instruction' prepared in 1933, revised in 1939/40 and then published to the Fleet with the caveat that 'In the event of emergency these instructions may be supplemented by additional instructions made necessary by circumstances then existing.'[51] The first official Manual, as such, on the 'Law of Naval Warfare' (NWP 10-2) was published in 1955, the work of the then Stockton Professor at the Naval War College, Robert Tucker. This was followed in 1987 by NWP 9A, 'The Commander's Handbook on the Law of Naval Operations', authored primarily by Professor Jack Grunawalt, then the Stockton Professor.[52] This in turn has been revised and updated with the latest iteration being NWP 1-14M, also entitled 'The Commander's Handbook on the Law of Naval Operations', published with an Annotated Supplement for lawyers in 1997.[53] This publication goes well beyond the law of armed conflict, dealing with the whole spectrum of naval operations, including large sections on the law of the sea. It is thus much more of an 'operational law manual' rather than a law of armed conflict manual and this indeed fits better with the maritime environment.

The United States Air Force issued a Manual in 1976 in the form of AFP 110-31.[54] However, plans to develop a single 'Joint Manual' have meant that Single Service Manuals in the Army and the Air Force have not been updated.

A number of other countries have also produced national 'Manuals'.[55] Some are original works, such as the Canadian Manual prepared originally by Professor Leslie Green.[56] Others are copied more or less verbatim from other publications such as the San Remo Manual. Germany published the 'Humanitarian Law in Armed Conflicts – Manual' in August 1992[57] and followed this up with a Commentary in the form of 'The Handbook of Humanitarian Law in Armed Conflicts'.[58]

One of the difficulties with drafting Manuals of this type is to decide on the 'target audience'. Fundamentally, with the exception of the naval manuals, these are not 'operational manuals'. They would be of little use to the ordinary soldier in

---

51. See W. Hays Parks, 'Making Law of War Treaties: Lessons from Submarine Warfare Regulation', in M. Schmitt, ed., *International Law across the Spectrum of Conflict: Essays in Honour of Professor L.C. Green on the Occasion of his Eightieth Birthday*, (Newport RI, Naval War College Press 2000) p. 362.

52. For a full account of the writing of this publication, see Doyle, *supra* n. 50, at p. 21.

53. See *supra* n. 30.

54. AFP 110-31, International Law-The Conduct of Armed Conflict and Air Operations, November 1976.

55. These include the People's Republic of China (Basis of International Law for Modern Soldiers, 1996) and Turkey (Guide to the Law of Armed Conflict of Armed Forces, Partnership for Peace Training Center Command, 2001).

56. Professor Emeritus at the University of Alberta. The current iteration is 'The Law of Armed Conflict at the Operational and Tactical Level', B-GG-005-027/AF-021 (2004).

57. *Humanitarian Law in Armed Conflicts*, edited by The Federal Ministry of Defence of the Federal Republic of Germany, VR II 3, DSK VV207320067, August 1992.

58. Dieter Fleck, ed., *The Handbook of Humanitarian Law in Armed Conflicts* (Oxford, Oxford University Press 1995).

the field. Their purpose is to lay out a national view of the legal constraints accepted by the particular state. Beneath them, there will need to be a subset of 'manuals' and operational instructions translating the rather esoteric legal language into operational concepts. It is these 'Manuals' that will be studied in the third section.

As international law has become more contentious, states have become reluctant to take firm positions on issues of international law for fear that their position may need to change in the case of new circumstances. It is because of the seeming authoritative nature of national manuals that they are often so feared by politicians. In the past, states were proud to state their views and to be 'world leaders'. The 1958 Lauterpacht Manual[59] of the United Kingdom was used all over the world both within the British Commonwealth and outside. However, international law is a remarkably flexible animal, particularly in this area, and the law is under continuous development, rarely more so than in the current times. The United Kingdom Manual states in its foreword, written jointly by the Chief of the Defence Staff and the Permanent Under Secretary, Ministry of Defence, that:

> 'In this fast moving world, some issues cannot of necessity be stated in absolute terms. What follows is, however, a clear articulation of the UK's approach to the Law of Armed Conflict [...]. The publication of this Manual should be seen as another step in stating publicly the UK's interpretation of what the Law of Armed Conflict requires'.[60]

To ensure that the point is made further, the Preface states:

> '[The Manual] does not commit Her Majesty's Government to any particular interpretation of the law. Every effort has been made to ensure the accuracy of the Manual at this date [1 July 2004] but it must be read in the light of subsequent developments in the law.'[61]

This would seem to give to the United Kingdom a degree of 'plausible deniability'. The increasing tendency to cite national manuals as evidence before international tribunals[62] and the use made of them in the Customary Law Study of the International Committee of the Red Cross[63] has led to a degree of reserve. The new United Kingdom Manual was delayed both in its preparation and in publication by the need to ensure that, not only were military lawyers and the Ministry of Defence happy with the text but also the Foreign Office Legal Advisers and Ministers. In

---

59. See *supra* n. 4.
60. UK Manual, *supra* n. 3, at p. v.
61. Ibid., at p. x.
62. See for example, the reference made to both the US Manual FM 27-10 and to the 1958 UK Manual in relation to the definition of command responsibility in the Judgement of the Trial Chamber in the *Čelebići* case before the ICTY Trial Chamber, Case No. IT-96-21-T, 16 November 1998, at p. 358.
63. J.-M. Henckaerts and L. Doswald Beck, eds., *Customary International Humanitarian Law*, ICRC, (Cambridge, Cambridge University Press 2005). There are numerous references in the footnotes to military manuals.

some of the most controversial areas, the Manual says little or nothing[64] and it is not too much of an assumption that this is because of the reluctance of the United Kingdom to take an 'official' position on such points. However, for the practitioner, there is no such relief. If the problem arises in reality on the ground, he has to take a decision and that is where the operational manuals cut in. However, as will be seen, similar difficulties are now beginning to appear with operational manuals due to their increased accessibility.

A similar problem arises in relation to military alliances. It is obviously unhelpful if Manuals of allied states take diametrically opposed views of the law. This cannot assist interoperability. And yet, as has been apparent in recent years, states do often have opposing – or at least differing – views on a range of topics. Those who carry out detailed studies of the United Kingdom Manual, together with its Australian and Canadian counterparts, will find a certain degree of similarity amidst the differences. This is largely due to an unofficial 'Working Group' made up of United States, United Kingdom, Canadian, Australian and New Zealand legal officers, who have been meeting on an irregular basis since the late 1970s to try to iron out friction. These meetings have, over the years, not only helped to clarify some difficult issues but also lead to firm friendships between participants that have been invaluable in operational environments. Amongst those who have taken part are Major General Tony Rogers, the Editor of the United Kingdom Manual, Hays Parks, who is producing the United States Manual, and Bill Fenrick, recently retired from the ICTY but for many years the Canadian 'point man' for their Manual. Differences remain but at least they have been kept to a minimum and the various authors have worked hard to ensure that that is so.[65]

The participants in these meetings followed in a rich heritage. Similar meetings had been held in Cambridge in May 1953 between United States and British officials and academics prior to the production of the 1956 US Army Field Manual 27-10 and the 1958 Lauterpacht Manual.[66] However, the two Manuals eventually adopted different styles largely because of different time constraints. FM 27-10 consisted primarily of a statement of the law, reflecting the recent entry into force for the United States of the Geneva Conventions of 1949.[67] Lauterpacht was able to be more expansive and was aided by his own editorship of Volume II of *Oppenheim's International Law* (Disputes, War and Neutrality)[68] from the text of which he was able to borrow. It follows that his United Kingdom Manual is much more discursive and heavily footnoted.

---

64. The chapter in the 1958 Manual on the 'Rights and Duties of Neutral States and Persons' has been omitted and there is little discussion in Chapter 8 on 'Prisoners of War' of some of the contentious status issues that have arisen out of Afghanistan and the 'Global War on Terror'.

65. The author himself took part in several of these meetings.

66. Participants were Brigadier General CB Micklewait, US Army, Assistant Judge Advocate General of the Army, Professor Hersch Lauterpacht, Miss J.A.C. Gutteridge, Assistant Legal Adviser, Foreign Office, Lieutenant Colonel G.I.A.D. Draper, Directorate of Army Legal Services and Major Richard Baxter, US Army, Office of the Judge Advocate General of the Army.

67. These entered into force for the United States on 2 February 1956.

68. H. Lauterpacht, *Oppenheim's International Law*, Vol. II, 'Disputes, War and Neutrality', 7th edn. (London, Longman 1952).

4. INTERNAL MANUALS

The 1899 Hague Convention II, dealing with the laws and customs of war on land, required in Article 1 that:

> 'The High Contracting Parties shall issue instructions to their armed land forces, which shall be in conformity with the 'Regulations respecting the laws and customs of war on land' annexed to the present Convention.'[69]

This provision was repeated without any substantial change in Article 1 of Hague Convention IV in 1907.[70]

Whilst National Manuals are an element in the fulfillment of this requirement, they form only a small part. The requirement is for 'instructions' to be issued which are 'in conformity' with the law. To the ordinary soldier, a manual dealing with esoteric points of law is worse than useless. He needs simple and clear instructions. Similarly, even at lower levels of command, something more 'operational' is required.

In the United Kingdom, the Manual is seen as only the top tier of a series of publications, some of which are already in existence. At the lowest level, the soldier, when deploying on operations, is issued with a small 'LOAC' card which contains the key 'dos and don'ts'. It is drafted in simple language and designed for easy reference. It supplements, of course, the more detailed Rules of Engagement which contain the operational and political instructions. Again for the soldier, these are reduced to simple terms – often also to a card.

At the next level, the United Kingdom has for some years published 'A Soldier's Guide to the Law of Armed Conflict' (Army Code 71130).[71] Despite its title, this small booklet of some 40 pages is designed for senior non-commissioned officers and junior officers. It is updated every year and contains a 'potted' version of the law of armed conflict with references to the appropriate Conventions, etc. This booklet has been in great demand and one Commanding Officer in Bosnia when serving as part of the British contingent to UNPROFOR stated that he carried it everywhere – even if only to answer press questions![72]

Above that, it is envisaged that each Service will have a 'Commander's Handbook'. This will seek to distil the legal text of the Manual into operational guidance for the Commander. The Royal Navy has long had such a publication in the form of BR 3012 – Handbook on the Law of Maritime Operations.[73] This is the British equivalent to NWP 1-14M, published by the United States Navy.[74]

---

69. Convention (II) with Respect to the Laws and Customs of War on Land, signed at The Hague, 29 July 1899, Schindler and Toman, *supra* n. 12, at p. 62.

70. Convention (IV) Respecting the Laws and Customs of War on Land, signed at The Hague, 18 October 1907, Reprinted in Schindler and Toman, *supra* n. 12, at p. 62.

71. This is published by the Directorate General of Development and Doctrine (Army).

72. Based on a conversation with the author.

73. See also *supra* n. 41.

74. See *supra* n. 30.

'Manuals' or 'Handbooks' of this nature are usually drafted at a much lower level and do not have the same degree of status as more 'official' publications. However, most are unclassified and thus open to public scrutiny. This can cause difficulties in that it is often necessary to take operational positions on controversial areas where governments may wish to reserve their position. An example of this tension can be found in the Operational Law Handbook issued by the International and Operational Law Department of the Judge Advocate General's Legal Center and School, US Army.[75] It is described as 'a "how to" guide for Judge Advocates practicing operational law.'[76] Although it covers a wide field of 'operational law', including fiscal and administrative law, it also covers 'the law of war'. For many years, there has been much debate on the official position of the United States Government in relation to Additional Protocol I to the 1949 Geneva Conventions,[77] a treaty that the United States signed but has not ratified. President Reagan, in recommending to the Senate that the United States should not ratify the Protocol, stated that, whilst it had 'certain meritorious elements', it was 'fundamentally and irreconcilably flawed'.[78] The problem has always been to assess which parts are accepted by the United States as customary law, and thus binding, and which are not. For many years, academics and operators have relied upon an article published by Michael Matheson, then Deputy Legal Adviser at the Department of State, as the authority for the United States position on particular articles.[79] This is reflected in the text of the 2005 Operational Law Handbook.[80] However, the authors were forced to publish an 'Errata Sheet' which states 'This information was taken from an article written by Michael Matheson in 1986. It takes an overly broad view of the US position and as a result may cause some confusion as to US policy.[81] That is fine as a statement but does not help the judge advocate in the field in that it makes no attempt to replace the Matheson view with anything at all. The confusion therefore remains – and indeed is probably now greater. Judge advocates in the field will now have to make up their own minds as to the effect of Additional Protocol I with no guidance whatsoever.

This illustrates the increasing difficulty in producing publications of this sort. The more that they are cited as evidence of state practice, the harder it will be to obtain approval for them. Already attempts to rewrite the US Air Force Manual, published in 1976,[82] have been thwarted by the need to ensure that it is compatible

75. See *supra* n. 17.

76. Preface, at p. ii.

77. See *supra* n. 7.

78. See Letter of Transmittal dated 29 January 1987, printed in 81 *AJIL* (1987) p. 911.

79. M.J Matheson, 'The United States Position on the Relation of Customary International Law to the 1977 Protocols Additional to the 1949 Geneva Conventions', 2 *Amer. Univ .JIL & Pol.* (1987) p. 419.

80. Operational Law Handbook (2005), *supra* n. 17, at pp. 15-16.

81. Errata Sheet to Operational Law Handbook (2005), accessed at <https://www.jagcnet.army.mil/jagcnetintranet/databases/operational+law/clamo.nsf/(JAGCNetDocID)/71395D6C2324A3D785256F1F006BA45F/$FILE/CLAMO%20OpLaw%20Handbook%2005%20ERRATA%20SHEET.doc>.

82. See *supra* n. 54.

with the new Joint Manual being written in the Pentagon. A redraft of NWP 1-14M,[83] currently being prepared by the International Law Department of the US Naval War College, may suffer the same fate. This unfortunate state of affairs leaves lawyers – and operators – in the field with minimum (and often outdated) guidance. One solution suggested is to classify all publications of this nature so that they cannot be cited. Many already contain statements similar to that found in the Royal Australian Navy Publication 'Australian Maritime Doctrine':

> 'All Defence information, whether classified or not, is protected from unauthorized disclosure under the Crimes Act 1914. Defence information may only be released in accordance with the Defence Protective Security Manual (SECMAN 4) and/or Defence Instruction (General) OPS 13-4 – Release of Classified Defence Information to Other Countries, as appropriate.'[84]

Even the UK Manual, in its loose leaf version,[85] issued within the Services states:

> 'The information in this manual is Crown copyright and the intellectual property rights for this publication belong exclusively to the Ministry of Defence (MOD). No material or information contained in this publication should be reproduced, stored in a retrieval system or transmitted in any form outside MOD establishments except as authorized by both the sponsor and the MOD where appropriate. This information is released by the United Kingdom Government to a recipient Government for defence purposes only. It may be disclosed only within the Defence Department of a recipient Government, except as otherwise authorized by the MOD. This information may be subject to privately owned rights.'

This seems particularly strange when the hardback version is on public sale through Oxford University Press and obviously contains only the standard copyright caveats! The contents are identical and amendments to the loose leaf version will be available on the MOD website.

However, any attempt to curtail public access to these documents would be most unsatisfactory. There is a need for many of these publications to be in the public domain. Apart from anything else, they are an encouragement to those states who do not take their obligations in this area as seriously, as well as a stimulus to debate.

---

83. See *supra* n. 30.

84. Royal Australian Navy, Australian Maritime Doctrine, RAN Doctrine 1 (2000) at p. ii. As this publication is now available on the internet at <http://www.navy.gov.au/spc/amd/html/chapt1.htm>, the provision seems even more esoteric.

85. JSP 383, The Joint Service Manual of the Law of Armed Conflict, 2004 edn, title page.

5. CONCLUSION

It will be seen from the above that the new United Kingdom Manual fits squarely into the category of 'national manuals'. It does not seek to clarify the law as an international manual would seek to do, nor does it seek to be a tactical guide for implementation. Instead, it seeks to expound a particular position on the law, which it will then be for others to translate into operational and tactical guidance.

The style is generally conservative and areas of controversy are for the most part avoided. For example, Chapter 8 on Prisoners of War sets out the traditional law contained in the Third Geneva Convention without seeking to comment on the disputed interpretations that have arisen out of the 'Global War on Terror', particularly of Article 5, requiring a 'competent tribunal' to rule on status in cases of doubt. Indeed, there is no reference to the 'Global War on Terror' at all in the Manual.[86] Where the United Kingdom holds a distinctive national position, such as in its reservation to Additional Protocol I to the Geneva Conventions on reprisals, that position is made clear.[87] However, the reasons for the position taken are not outlined and for that it is necessary to consult other academic writings. Thus, those who look for a detailed justification of the legal positions taken will be disappointed.

At the same time, no attempt has been made to 'dumb down' the document to make it accessible to the lowest ranks. This task will be carried out through doctrine manuals,[88] the regularly updated Soldier's Guide[89] and other similar publications. Much of this has already been done over recent years as the Manual was in preparation. It will also be necessary for the Manual itself – in its loose-leaf version – to be continually updated. Indeed, Amendment 1 has already been issued.[90]

Manuals, of all sorts, are a vital tool in the dissemination of the law. However, they go further than that. At one extreme, they provide evidence of 'state practice' which can be used in the development of the law. At the other, they form the basis for the more detailed operational instructions that will need to be relayed down to the soldier, sailor or airman at the eye of the storm. These two extremes often contradict in that, in such a fast moving area, guidance and instructions may have to be given at field level to enable decisions to be taken. However, the state itself may not want to take an official 'position' on the point in question for fear of compromising its freedom of action at a later date in similar (though perhaps not identical) circumstances. Operators do not have the benefit of time and often have to take fast decisions in response to problems arising on the ground. The Secretary of State for Defence declined to answer questions in the House of Commons as to

---

86. See *supra* n. 64.

87. See UK Manual, *supra* n. 3, para.16.19.1, at p. 420.

88. See for example, JWP 1-10, Prisoners of War Handling, accessed through the website of the Ministry of Defence, Joint Doctrine and Concepts Centre at <www.mod.uk/linked_files/jdcc/publications>

89. See *supra* n. 71.

90. The Manual of the Law of Armed Conflict – Amended Text 01/04, accessed at: <http://www.mod.uk/issues/laws_and_regs/lawmanual/amended_text01-04.htm>

the guidance given to United Kingdom forces in relation to persons captured in Afghanistan.[91] Although the ground cited was national security, it is perhaps more likely that the United Kingdom did not wish to take an official line in the light of the controversy over the treatment of detainees by the United States. However, those in the field – and those advising them – would have had to have reached a decision, and that there was a policy there can be no doubt!

Those who look at Manuals must never forget the real purpose:

> 'Manuals are not an end in themselves. They are an instrument for achieving an end: the prescription and application of a law of armed conflict which tempers the harshness and cruelty of combat and confines human and material destruction to targets of military necessity and utility.'[92]

Looked at as tools, they can serve many purposes but care must be taken not to expect too much from them or to place too heavy a burden on their authors. That way lies chaos as states become more and more reluctant to publish manuals for fear that they will be used against them. Manuals can indeed be used as part of the lawmaking process but their evidential value should not be overstated. Their purpose is ultimately practical – to assist the soldiers, sailors and airman on the front line to 'temper the harshness and cruelty of combat' by abiding by the law.

---

91. Written answer to Ann Clywd MP, 12 February 2002, Hansard, Column 174W, accessed at <http://www.parliament.the-stationery-office.co.uk/pa/cm200102/cmhansrd/vo020212/text/20212w09.htm>

92. M. Reisman and W. Lietzau, 'Moving International Law from Theory to Practice: the Role of Military Manuals in Effectuating the Law of Armed Conflict', 64 *International Law Studies* (1991) p. 12.

CORRESPONDENTS' REPORTS

CORRESPONDENTS' REPORTS*

A guide to state practice in the field of international humanitarian law

* Correspondents' Reports is compiled and edited by Avril McDonald, primarily from information provided to the *YIHL* by its correspondents but also drawing on other sources. The research assistance of Jacob Ramer is very gratefully acknowledged. The section does not purport to be a fully inclusive compilation of all international humanitarian law-related developments in every state, reporting in this volume mainly developments since the beginning of 2004 until the end of 2004 that have come to the Yearbook's attention. Developments from early-2005 that are part of a sequence of events starting in 2004 or earlier are noted in brief. Legal developments from early 2004 that were noted in volume 6 of the *YIHL* are not repeated here. Readers are thus advised to consult this section in conjunction with Correspondents' Reports in volume 6. We apologise for this inconvenience. Further, some 2003 humanitarian law-related developments came to our attention after volume 6 went to press and which could not be noted there. For the sake of completeness we have included them here. Reference is also included to a number of legal developments which are not strictly-speaking related to IHL but which are nonetheless interesting and relevant for our readers, in particular, relating to justice issues, jurisdictional questions, *jus ad bellum*, state security, human rights, refugee law and terrorism. Presentation of subject matter roughly follows the sequence in the Classification of Documents at pp. XXX, with the exception that all cases are grouped together at the end of each report, followed by news of pending developments. Where citations or dates or other details have not been provided, they were not available or obtainable. Where not otherwise specified, comments are prepared by Avril McDonald, mainly based on reports of NGOs and IGOs and news media, *inter alia*. The *YIHL* is actively seeking new correspondents, particularly in Africa, Asia and Latin America. Interested persons and anyone who is willing to contribute information should contact the Managing Editor at A.McDonald@asser.nl.

Yearbook of International Humanitarian Law
Volume 7 - 2004 - pp. 443-638 DOI 10.1017/S138913590400443X

ALGERIA[1]

Amnesties

☛ Creation of National Committee for General Amnesty, 2 December 2004

Since the end of the internal armed conflict which took place in Algeria from the beginning of the nineties to the eve of the twenty-first century, Algerian military forces have been engaged in the use of force to reduce and stop violent action carried out by armed Islamic groups to terrorise the civilian population. After the first election in April 1999 of President A. Bouteflika,[2] who pledged to bring peace to the country, violence was reduced but not eradicated. The President was re-elected in April 2004[3] and promised the people of Algeria a return to peace and security by way of national reconciliation, as he called it in various national and international speeches.[4] No indications were given as to the exact content of the term 'national reconciliation', however. Still, the subject was considered at length, at the political level, by civil society and by the media. The debate on national reconciliation in Algeria produced another lengthy discussion related to the use of a legal instrument to make reconciliation possible. The president himself referred to a law on amnesty and pledged that a decision on such a law would be made after consulting with the people by way of a referendum.[5]

On 2 December 2004 a National Committee for General Amnesty was formed. This spontaneously created open association has no legal basis.[6] It was set up by a political elite close to the President of the Algerian Democratic and Popular Republic.[7] At the time of its foundation, the association was headed by the former and first President of Algeria Ahmed B. Enbella. The Association has structures covering the national territory of Algeria.[8] It has set as objectives the raising of awareness about the necessity of national reconciliation and the adoption of a law on amnesty.

According to the National Committee the law on amnesty will provide:

— An end to all penal cases against those living in or outside Algeria and involved in the national tragedy;
— Annulment of all judicial decision taken against person convicted in relation to the national tragedy;
— Rehabilitation of all the victims;
— Fiscal amnesty for persons financially victimised by the national tragedy.[9]

---

1. Information and commentaries by Kamel Filali, Law Lecturer at the University of Constantine.

2. See Cornell University's 'Algeria: 1999 Presidential Election in the Press', <www.library.cornell.edu/colldev/mideast/ele99pr.htm>.

3. See Algerian presidential election, 2004, Wikipedia, <http://en.wikipedia.org/wiki/Algerian_-presidential_election>,_2004; 'Butaflika to gain second term of office', ArabicNew.com, 9 April 2004, <http://www.arabicnews.com/ansub/Daily/Day/040409/2004040915.html>; 'Algeria press aghast at election result', BBC News, 10 April 2004, <http://news.bbc.co.uk/2/hi/africa/3616461.stm>.

4. A. Mammeri, 'Campagne pour la reconciliation nationale: le Président arrête son programme, *L'Expression*, 22 February 2005, p. 3.

5. 'Bouteflika veut un Referendum', *El Watan*, 4 May 2005, <www.elwatan.com>.

6. 'Le CNAG au creux de la vague', *Liberte*, 21 June 2005, <www.liberté-algerie.com>.

7. 'Le CNAG se met sous l'egide du FLN', *L'Expression*, 12 March 2005, <www.lexpressiondz.com>.

8. 'CNAG reunion d'evaluation', *El Watan*, 6 February 2005.

9. Ibid.

The Disappeared

- Presidential Decree No. 03-299 on the Establishment of an *ad hoc* Committee on the Disappeared (Formation A disparitions en Algerie). Adopted on 11 September 2003 and entered into force on the day of its publication in the *Journal officiel* of the Algerian Republic. Published in the *Journal officiel* of the Algerian Republic on 14 September 2003, No. 55

KAMEL FILALI

ARGENTINA

National Information Bureau

- Decree 1430/20041 creating the 'National Information Bureau'. Adopted 19 October 2004, published on 21 October 2004 and entered into force on 29 October 2004, eight days after its publication

'According to the Decree, the Legal Department of the Ministry of Foreign Relations, International Trade and Worship of the Argentine Republic will act as National Information Bureau upon the outbreak of an armed conflict, as foreseen under article 122 of the Third Geneva Convention of 1949 relative to the Treatment of Prisoners of War. The Ministry will propose measures, actions and reforms to comply with its obligations under article 122 of the Third Convention and may gather any useful information from official bodies, in order to accomplish its duties.'[10]

ARMENIA

International Criminal Court

- Decision of the Constitutional Court of Armenia on the issue of compatibility of the provisions stipulated by the Statute of the International Criminal Court signed in Rome on 17 July 1998 with the Constitution of the Republic of Armenia, Yerevan, 13 August 2004[11]

AUSTRALIA[12]

Internment

- International Transfer of Prisoners Amendment Act 2004 No. 19 (Cth), Assented to on 23 March 2004 <www.austlii.edu.au>
- Parliamentary debate about the status of Australian citizens detained in Guantánamo Bay

In 2004 David Hicks and Mamdouh Habib, both Australian citizens, continued to be detained by American Forces at Guantánamo Bay. Habib, whose detention commenced in

---

10. Source: 'National Implementation of International Humanitarian Law, Biannual update on national legislation and case law', July-December 2004, 87 *IRRC* (March 2005) p. 217.

11. Ibid., p. 224.

12. This entry was prepared by Anita Coles, Purnika Dharmadasa, Alison Duxbury and Cecelia Klein on behalf of the Australian Red Cross International Humanitarian Law Advisory Committee (Victorian Division).

early 2002, was released from Guantánamo Bay in early 2005 and returned to Australia. In contrast, Hicks, who has been detained since November 2001, was charged in June 2004 by the United States Military Commission with:

a) conspiracy to commit murder, attack civilians and civilian objects and terrorism;
b) attempted murder by an unprivileged belligerent; and
c) aiding the enemy.

According to these charges, the Commission alleged that Hicks undertook military training with terrorist groups, including al Qaeda, in Pakistan and Afghanistan.[13]

The Australian Parliament enacted the International Transfer of Prisoners Amendment Act 2004 No. 19 (Cth) on 23 March 2004. This Act amends the International Transfer of Prisoners Amendment Act 1997 No. 75 (Cth) ('the Act') 'to facilitate the transfer back to Australia of Australian citizens detained at Guantánamo Bay who may subsequently be convicted, found guilty and sentenced to a term of imprisonment by a military commission of the United States of America'.[14] The Act widens the meaning of 'transfer country' to include certain regions in a foreign country and specifies that a military commission of the US 'is taken to be a court or tribunal' of the US.

In the parliamentary debates introducing this Act, the Attorney-General Philip Ruddock stated that the Bill provides for 'a statutory basis for returning Mr Hicks and Mr Habib to Australia' if the circumstances described arise. He stated that the amendments would address 'an anomaly' where a region or area, such as Guantánamo Bay or previously Hong Kong, that is not a sovereign country in its own right, does not fall under the definition of a 'transfer country' under the Act.

During the parliamentary debates the opposition, the Australian Labor Party, moved a statement condemning the government for 'acquiescing in the use of US military commissions to try Australian citizens [and] failing to explore all options for the two Australians currently being detained by US authorities in Guantánamo Bay, to be tried in Australia'.[15] Reference was made to the fact that the US government maintained that the detainees at Guantánamo Bay were not entitled to the status of prisoners of war and to a comment made by the US Secretary of Defense that even if people held in Guantánamo Bay were acquitted they may continue to be detained.

In addition, during these debates a member of a minor party, the Australian Democrats, stated that the US government had created a new category of detainee, the 'unlawful combatant', to avoid obligations under the Geneva Conventions concerning prisoners of war, with the result that detainees are being held in 'legal limbo'. The Australian Democrats stated that the argument that military commissions represent a recognised way of trying people have who have committed offences against the laws of war ignores the fact that the Guantánamo Bay detainees have been denied classification as prisoners of war.[16]

---

13. *United States* v. *David Matthew Hicks*, <http://www.defenselink.mil/news/Jun2004/d20040610cs.pdf>.

14. Explanatory Memorandum, International Transfer of Prisoners Bill 2004 (Cth).

15. Commonwealth, *Parliamentary Debates,* Senate, 8 March 2004, 20928 (Joseph Ludwig, Senator, Australian Labor Party, Queensland Party), <http://www.aph.gov.au/hansard/senate/dailys/ds080304.pdf>.

16. Commonwealth, *Parliamentary Debates*, Senate, 8 March 2004, 20932, Second Reading of the International Transfer of Prisoners Amendment Bill 2004 (Cth), <http://www.aph.gov.au/hansard/senate/dailys/ds080304.pdf>.

During the parliamentary process, in response to a question as to which country David Hicks had committed an offence against the Attorney General explained that the jurisdiction of the US Military Commission extends to offenders that, by statute or the law of armed conflict, may be tried by a military commission. This, in turn, was defined by the executive in US President George W Bush's Military Order of 13 November 2001. The Attorney General also stated that Hicks and Habib may have committed an offence against the laws of the United States[17] and therefore the US military commission was a proper authority to try them.[18] The Minister for Foreign Affairs and Trade also stated that the government believed that a military commission should try these two Australian citizens, 'given the state of Australian law at the time they were training with al Qaeda'.[19]

In contrast, Peter King, a member of the government, in a speech in the House of Representatives concerning the military detention of Australian citizens, discussed the applicability of the Third Geneva Convention and the International Covenant on Civil and Political Rights to David Hicks' situation.[20] He contended that David Hicks met the definition of a prisoner of war in the Third Geneva Convention,[21] as he was a member of an organised military force which displayed a distinctive ensign. Further, he contended that to arrest combatants in Afghanistan and detain them for an indefinite period was against international law.[22]

In a joint media release, the Foreign Minister and the Attorney-General discussed improvements to the Guantánamo Bay military commission process after Australian officials had observed the preliminary hearings for David Hicks on 25 August 2004.[23] Concerning procedural fairness, the Foreign Minister stated that 'it is important that Mr Hicks and Mr Habib face justice as quickly as possible, consistent with a fair trial', and that the Australian government had queried the US government about the delays in the trial process. He also said that the Australian government would continue to request the appointment of defence counsel for Mamdouh Habib, who has since been released.[24]

---

17. Commonwealth, *Parliamentary Debates*, House of Representatives, 1 March 2004, 25510, <http://www.aph.gov.au/hansard/reps/dailys/dr010304.pdf>.

18. Commonwealth, *Parliamentary Debates*, House of Representatives, 1 June 2004, 29644, <http://www.aph.gov.au/hansard/reps/dailys/dr010604.pdf>.

19. Commonwealth, *Parliamentary Debates*, House of Representatives, 24 May 2004, <http://www.aph.gov.au/hansard/reps/dailys/dr240504.pdf>.

20. Commonwealth, *Parliamentary Debates*, House of Representatives, 9 August 2004, p. 32543, <http://www.aph.gov.au/hansard/reps/dailys/dr090804.pdf>. The speech concerned the military detention of Australian citizens.

21. Commonwealth, *Parliamentary Debates*, House of Representatives, 9 August 2004, p. 32544, <http://www.aph.gov.au/hansard/reps/dailys/dr090804.pdf>.

22. The reference here made by Peter King was to Art. 14(3) of the International Covenant on Civil and Political Rights and the right to be tried in a timely manner and know the nature of the alleged crime.

23. Attorney-General's Department, 'Government to discuss improvements on Guantanamo Bay military commission process' (Joint Media Release, 5 September 2004).

24. Attorney-General's Department, 'Statement on Mamdouh Habib' (Joint Media Release, 11 January 2005), <http://www.ag.gov.au/agd/WWW/MinisterRuddockHome.nsf/Page/Media_Releases_2005_First_Quarter_11_January_2005_-_Statement_on_Mamdouh_Habib_-_0062005>.

☛ Parliamentary debates regarding Australia's status in Iraq

Against the backdrop of controversy concerning the abuse of prisoners of war at the Abu Ghraib prison in Iraq, a parliamentary debate took place on the subject of Australia's precise legal status in Iraq. The uncertainty arose due to the Australian Defence Force's lack of control of any designated physical territory in Iraq. Article 12 of Geneva Convention III provides that the 'detaining power' is responsible for the treatment of prisoners of war, and that prisoners of war may only be transferred by the detaining power to another power (the so-called accepting power) after the detaining power is satisfied of the accepting power's willingness and ability to apply the Convention. Responsibility then rests on the accepting or protecting power, but if this power fails to comply with Geneva Convention III in any important respect, the original detaining power must take measures to correct the situation or request the return of the prisoners.

As part of the US-led 'Coalition of the Willing', the Australian Defence Force ('ADF') contributed to a number of efforts and operations in Iraq throughout 2004. On 23 March 2003 the Australian government entered into 'An Arrangement for the Transfer of Prisoners of War, Civilian Internees, and Civilian Detainees Between the Forces of the United States of America, the United Kingdom of Great Britain and Northern Ireland and Australia' ('the Arrangement').[25] The reason for the Arrangement, as the ADF explained, was for the allies to clarify their treaty obligations, particularly those obligations under Geneva Convention III.[26] The Arrangement sought to 'establish procedures in the event of the transfer from custody of either the US, UK, or Australian forces to the custody of any of the other parties, any Prisoners of War, Civilian Internees and Civilian Detainees taken during operations against Iraq'.

In 2004 questions arose regarding Australia's arrangements for the detention of prisoners[27] and whether or not Australia was an occupying power in Iraq prior to the handover of sovereignty on 30 June 2004 to the Iraqi Interim Government. Indeed, in 2003 Prime Minister John Howard stated that Australia has 'the obligation of an occupying power under the Geneva Conventions. We, along with the Americans and the British have responsibilities, certainly, and we won't neglect those responsibilities.'[28]

However, United Nations Security Council Resolution 1483 ('Resolution 1483'), which was adopted on 22 May 2003,[29] expressly recognised only the US and the UK as occupying powers in Iraq, noting 'the letter of 8 May 2003 from the Permanent Representatives of the US, UK and Northern Ireland to the President of the Security Council (S/2003/538), and

---

25. See M. Kingston, 'Avoiding the Geneva Conventions: How Australia does the job', *The Sydney Morning Herald*, 3 June 2004, <http://www.smh.com.au/articles/2004/06/03/1086203552597.html>.

26. Commonwealth of Australia, *Foreign Affairs, Defence and Trade Legislation Committee – Consideration of Budget Estimates*, Senate, 4 June 2003, p. 387, <http://www.aph.gov.au/hansard/senate/commttee/S6484.pdf>

27. Commonwealth of Australia, *Foreign Affairs, Defence and Trade Legislation Committee – Consideration of Budget Estimates*, Senate, 1 June 2004, p. 19, <http://www.aph.gov.au/hansard/senate/commttee/S7647.pdf>.

28. P. Murray, Interview with John Howard, Prime Minister of Australia (Radio Interview, 17 April 2003), <http://www.pm.gov.au/news/interviews/Interview312.html>. See also Commonwealth of Australia, *Parliamentary Debate,* House of Representatives, 13 May 2004, p. 28672.

29. Resolution 1483, SC Res 1483, UN SCOR, 4761st mtg, UN Doc S/RES/1483 (2003). <http://daccessdds.un.org/doc/UNDOC/GEN/N03/368/53/PDF/N0336853.pdf?OpenElement>.

recognising the specific authorities, responsibilities and obligations under applicable international law of these states as occupying powers under unified command'.[30]

In May 2004 Shadow Foreign Minister Kevin Rudd proposed that a matter of importance be submitted to the House of Representatives for discussion, namely, '[t]he failure of the Howard Government as an Occupying Power in Iraq to honour its obligations under the Geneva Conventions for the humane treatment of Iraqi prisoners.'[31] Rudd argued that occupying power status did not cease with the adoption of Resolution 1483, for the following reasons:

a) Australia's status as an occupying power was defined by the fact of the invasion in Iraq and the continued military presence;
b) The Australian government is unable to 'simply legislate away [the] occupying power responsibilities' by relying on a Security Council resolution;
c) Resolution 1483 is not an exhaustive list of occupying powers, as it makes specific mention only of those states from which the Security Council received correspondence; and
d) the reference to an 'authority' as an occupying power was apparently to the CPA, in which Australia was represented.

More specifically, he stated that even within the narrow interpretation of the period of occupation (from March 2003 to May 2003), Australia had conjoint responsibility with the US and the UK for the protection of prisoners of war and the civilian population. Indeed, as was confirmed in June 2004, Australian forces assisted in the capture of around 120 Iraqis during the combat phase of the war. However, it was claimed that the detaining force in each case was the US.[32] The question was then raised as to when the Australian government became aware of the allegations of prisoner abuse at Abu Ghraib and whether this was during the period for which it was an occupying power. The relevant question was whether Australia had put in place protective measures to ensure that its legal obligations were fulfilled, namely, whether it had made certain that a regime for the proper treatment of prisoners of war was established.

There was debate that, even taking a conservative interpretation of SC Resolution 1483, this omission to follow an obligation may have occurred before May 2003, during a period when the Australian government agreed it had conjoint authority prior to the passing of Resolution 1483.[33]

The response of the Minister for Foreign Affairs to questioning in the Commonwealth Parliament was that the Department of Foreign Affairs and Trade had advised that there was uncertainty as to whether Australia was an occupying power in the earlier stages of involvement in Iraq. This was due to the fact that Australia did not control territory.[34] Furthermore,

30. Ibid.

31. Commonwealth of Australia, *Parliamentary Debate,* House of Representatives, 13 May 2004, p. 28670, <http://www.aph.gov.au/hansard/reps/dailys/dr130504.pdf>.

32. Commonwealth of Australia, *Parliamentary Debate,* Senate, 16 June 2004, <http://www.aph.gov.au/hansard/senate/dailys/ds160604.pdf>.

33. Reference was made in the debate to the Red Cross report which was leaked in February 2004. See Commonwealth of Australia, *Parliamentary Debate,* House of Representatives, 13 May 2004, pp. 28673 – 28764, <http://www.aph.gov.au/hansard/reps/dailys/dr130504.pdf>.

34. Commonwealth of Australia, *Parliamentary Debate,* House of Representatives, 13 May 2004, p. 28677, <http://www.aph.gov.au/hansard/reps/dailys/dr130504.pdf>. The requirement that '[t]erri-

Australia no longer bore legal responsibility for Iraq as an occupying force under international law due to the fact that the Security Council had specifically identified the US and the UK as occupying powers in Resolution 1483.[35] The argument was that Australia was one of the 'other States that are *not* occupying powers [that] are working now or in the future may work under the Authority' as mentioned in the Resolution.[36]

The Minister for Foreign Affairs claimed that neither ADF personnel nor Australian civilian personnel had been involved in the abuse of prisoners. Relying on his department's advice, he argued that Australia was not a 'detaining power' as on each of the occasions that Australian troops had contact with prisoners during the period of occupation an American officer was present and was technically the person responsible for the prisoners.[37]

As a counterpoint to the allegation that Australia did not take enough measures to ensure that prisoners were properly protected, Senator Hill stated that an Australian officer posted to the Office of General Counsel in the CPA in 2003 contributed to improving detention conditions in Abu Ghraib and facilitated the work of the Red Cross in the prison.[38] However, there was also debate as to whether the Australian government knew about the prisoner abuse at Abu Ghraib as early as October 2003, with an ICRC report into the conditions at the prison having been delivered to an Australian military lawyer in October 2003.

In June 2004 the Shadow Minister for Foreign Affairs released a legal opinion he had requested regarding Australia's status as an occupying power in Iraq. The advice concluded that Australia has a legal responsibility to all detained persons as a joint occupying force in Iraq and as a member of the CPA, and that these obligations were not altered by Resolution 1483, 'in the absence of express termination of its status in relation to future acts'.[39] It stated that the Security Council probably does not have the legal capacity to change the characterisation of a state as an occupying power. On that view the letter from the US and the UK referred to in the Resolution was not determinative of Australia's status as an occupying power.

Cases (Application of Article 1F of the Refugee Convention)

- *SRDDDD and Minister for Immigration and Multicultural and Indigenous Affairs* [2004] AATA 150 (13 February 2004) <http://www.austlii.edu.au/au/cases/cth/aat/2004/150.html>

---

tory is considered occupied when it is actually placed under the authority of the hostile army' is located in Art. 42 of Hague Convention IV of 1907.

35. Commonwealth of Australia, *Parliamentary Debate,* House of Representatives, 13 May 2004, p. 28677, <http://www.aph.gov.au/hansard/reps/dailys/dr130504.pdf>. See also B. Nicholson, 'Australia "not liable" for Iraq', *The Age (Melbourne)*, 3 May 2004, <http://www.theage.com.au/articles/2004/05/02/1083436474211.html>.

36. Resolution 1483, SC Res 1483, UN SCOR, 4761st mtg, UN Doc S/RES/1483 (2003), <http://daccessdds.un.org/doc/UNDOC/GEN/N03/368/53/PDF/N0336853.pdf?OpenElement>.

37. Commonwealth of Australia, *Parliamentary Debate,* House of Representatives, 13 May 2004, p. 28677, <http://www.aph.gov.au/hansard/reps/dailys/dr130504.pdf>.

38. Commonwealth of Australia, *Parliamentary Debate,* Senate, Wednesday 16 June 2004, 23940 <http://www.aph.gov.au/hansard/senate/dailys/ds160604.pdf>.

39. K. Rudd, 'Legal Opinion on Iraq' (Media Release, 4 June 2004), <http://www.ilals.unsw.edu.au/Triggs-Opinion-Torture.DOC>.

As was the case in earlier years,[40] in 2004 the Commonwealth Administrative Appeals Tribunal ('AAT') considered an application to set aside a decision in which a protection visa had been denied to the Applicant on the basis that there were serious grounds for believing that he had been complicit in committing war crimes and crimes against humanity.

SRDDDD (not the applicant's real name) is a Nepalese citizen who was active in the Maoist movement. Due to his fear of arrest for terrorist activities he left Nepal in 1999, travelled to India and then entered Australia on a false passport.[41] The Refugee Review Tribunal found that the applicant satisfied the criteria in Article 1A(2) of the Convention Relating to the Status of Refugees, but his application for a protection visa in Australia was denied by the minister's delegate on the basis of Article 1F. Pursuant to Article 1F, the protective regime in the Refugee Convention does not apply to a person if there are serious reasons for considering that they have committed a war crime, a crime against humanity or a serious non-political crime (amongst other offences).

In order to determine whether the Applicant had committed a crime within the ambit of Article 1F, the AAT referred to the definitions in the Rome Statute of the International Criminal Court (ICC) for crimes against humanity (Art. 7), war crimes (Art. 8) and individual criminal responsibility (Art. 25). In analysing the situation in Nepal, the Tribunal relied upon a number of sources, including excerpts of the applicant's interview by the Refugee Review Tribunal, country information contained in Jane's Intelligence Review, an ICRC Annual Report, the US State Department Country Reports on human rights practices, as well as news sources. On the basis of this information, the minister's delegate found that the applicant had been involved in some violence and had gathered information to be used in an attack on a police station.[42]

In determining whether a crime against humanity could have been committed, the applicant's submission that the police force was not part of the civilian population by reason of the role that it played in maintaining order was rejected by the Tribunal.[43] In addition, the Tribunal pointed to evidence that the applicant was involved in other acts of violence against the Nepalese civilian population, such as landowners and bureaucrats.[44] Similar evidence was used to find that the Applicant had engaged in acts that could constitute war crimes on the basis that there was an armed conflict in Nepal between the Maoists, the King and governmental authorities during which civilians were intentionally attacked.[45] When dealing with both crimes the Tribunal drew upon the definitions in the Rome Statute.

In conclusion, the AAT was satisfied that there were 'serious reasons for considering that the Applicant did commit and, within the meaning of the Rome Statute, was criminally responsible for, committing crimes against humanity and war crimes'.[46] SRDDDD's submission that the political motivation relevant in determining whether a serious non-political crime had been committed should be taken into account in determining whether the offences of war crimes and crimes against humanity were committed was firmly rejected by

40. See for example, 6 *YIHL* (2003) pp. 453-461.
41. At para. 12 of the decision.
42. Ibid., para. 16.
43. Ibid., para. 41.
44. Ibid., para. 41.
45. Ibid., para. 45.
46. Ibid., para. 58.

the Tribunal. The fact that the applicant's involvement in the activities was politically motivated was not a defence to the commission of war crimes and crimes against humanity.[47]

☛ *WAKN* v. *Minister for Immigration and Multicultural and Indigenous Affairs*, [2004] FCA 1245 (23 September 2004) <http://www.austlii.edu.au/au/cases/cth/federal_ct/2004/1245.html>

In 2004 the Federal Court of Australia heard an application concerning Article 1F of the Refugee Convention.

The applicant, WAKN, was born in Afghanistan and arrived in Australia by boat in 1999. In 2000 he was granted a temporary protection visa but was refused a permanent protection visa in 2003 on the basis of Article 1F.

A delegate of the Minister for Immigration and Multicultural and Ethnic Affairs found that, while in Afghanistan, WAKN had been a high ranking officer in the Wahdat Party Army. The delegate considered both the applicant's statements about his involvement with Hezb-i-Wahdat, a political and military movement in Afghanistan, and a report by the Council of the European Union on human rights violations by that movement in Afghanistan. Due to WAKN's position within Hezb-i-Wahdat, the delegate concluded that 'he would have been expressly involved in decision making and security questions and as a consequence would have had specific knowledge of human rights violations'.[48] On behalf of the applicant it was submitted that the report was insufficiently specific about those in the same position as the applicant and that he had a reputation for assisting non-governmental organisations. In addition, the applicant had already been found to have been a refugee by virtue of the grant of the temporary protection visa in 2000.[49]

WAKN applied to the AAT for review of the decision to deny him a permanent visa. However, after a preliminary ruling from the Tribunal to the effect that it would consider whether Article 1F applied in this case, the applicant applied to the Federal Court for the writs of certiorari, mandamus and prohibition. The Applicant presented a number of arguments on the basis that the Tribunal had misconstrued the law.

French J. in the Federal Court rejected WAKN's application as there was nothing preventing the reconsideration of the Article 1F issue if facts came to light after a temporary protection visa had been granted. He also rejected WAKN's arguments that the Tribunal had erred on the law. In the course of his judgment, French J. commented on the inquiry required by Article 1F. He suggested that it was 'debatable' that the approach of the delegate in relying upon a report of human rights violations by the Wahdat Army and extending the contents of that report to the WAKN by inference would meet the necessary standard of inquiry.[50] French J. referred to previous jurisprudence in Australia which indicated that 'serious reasons for considering that [...]' does not require a positive finding that an applicant has engaged in war crimes and crimes against humanity.[51] However, although this requirement could not be equated with a civil or criminal standard of proof, there was still a need for a 'meticulous investigation and solid grounds' in order to meet the 'serious reasons'

47. Ibid., para. 59.
48. Ibid., paras. 7, 14-15.
49. Ibid., para. 12.
50. Ibid., para. 53.
51. Ibid., para. 51.

standard.[52] In conclusion, as no error had been committed in the course of the Tribunal's proceedings, no relief was granted against its preliminary ruling that Article IF would be considered in this case.

ANITA COLES, PURNIKA DHARMADASA, ALISON DUXBURY and CECELIA KLEIN

AUSTRIA[53]

Cultural Property

☛ Second Protocol to the Hague Convention of 1954 for the Protection of Cultural Property in the Event of Armed Conflict [Zweites Protokoll zur Haager Konvention von 1954 zum Schutz von Kulturgut bei bewaffneten Konflikten]. Austria signed this Protocol on 17 May 1999 and the Austrian Parliament approved it (on 21 November 2001 the Austrian National Council and on 20 December 2001 the Federal Council).[54] According to its Article 43(1), this Protocol entered into force for Austria on 9 March 2004. Published in *BGBl* III Nr. 113/2004

On the occasion of the deposit of its instrument of ratification of the Second Protocol with the Director-General of UNESCO on 1 March 2002, Austria made the following Interpretative Declarations. Concerning Article 15(1)(c):

> 'The Republic of Austria considers that the term "appropriation" refers to the offence of (grave) theft as set forth in §§ 127 and 128 sub-paragraph 1 (3) of the Austrian Criminal Code (österreichisches Strafgesetzbuch – StGB).'

Concerning Article 16(1)(c)

> 'The Republic of Austria considers with regard to the provision of Article 17 paragraph 1 that the obligation under Article 16 sub-paragaph 1 (c) to establish jurisdiction over the serious violations set forth in Article 15 sub-paragraphs (a) to (c) only applies to such cases where the alleged offender cannot be extradited (aut dedere aut judicare).'

Reparations and War Damages

☛ Federal Law amending the Federal Law on the Reconciliation Fund [Bundesgesetz, mit dem das Versöhnungsfonds-Gesetz geändert wird]. Adopted on 9 July by the Austrian National Council and on 22 July by the Federal Council and entered into force on 11 August 2004. Published in *BGBl* I Nr. 109/2004

The law was initiated by all four parties represented in the Austrian Parliament. It extends the period for which the Fund is established until 31 December 2005. [55]

---

52. Ibid., para. 52.

53. Information and commentaries by Dr Thomas Desch, Federal Ministry of Defence, Vienna, and Mag. Peter Kustor, Federal Chancellery, Vienna.

54. For the draft text and the Explanatory Memorandum see *RV [Regierungsvorlage] 752 BlgNR* 21. *GP.* For the contents of this Protocol see T. Desch in 2 *YIHL* (1999) p. 63.

55. For the draft text and the Explanatory Memorandum see *IA [Initiativantrag]* 421/A *BlgNR [Beilagen zu den Stenographischen Protokollen des Nationalrates]* 22. *GP [Gesetzgebungsperiode]*. Parliamentary documents are also available at <http://www.parlament.gv.at>.

- Federal Law amending the General Settlement Fund Law [Bundesgesetz, mit dem das Entschädigungsfondsgesetz geändert wird]. Adopted on 9 July 2004 by the Austrian National Council and on 22 July 2004 by the Federal Council and entered into force on 11 August 2004. Published in *BGBl* I Nr. 108/2004

The law was initiated by all four parties represented in the Austrian Parliament. It extends the period for which applications for in rem restitutions may be filed with the Arbitration Panel until 31 December 2004.[56]

Torture

- Response of the Federal Minister of Foreign Affairs to a parliamentary request concerning 'Anti-Torture-Measures' [Antwort der Bundesministerin für auswärtige Angelegenheiten auf die Anfrage der Abgeordneten Mag. Walter Posch, Kolleginnen und Kollegen betreffend 'Anti-Folter-Maßnahmen'] (6 September 2004). Published in 1963 *AB* [*Anfragebeantwortung*] 22. *GP*

The response dealt, *inter alia,* with the torture incidents in Iraqi prisons. The Federal Minister of Foreign Affairs reported that she had discussed those incidents with the US Ambassador in Vienna on 14 May 2004 and had made it clear that Austria objects to these violations of human rights in Iraqi prisons. Furthermore, the response reported that on 17 May 2004 the Council of Ministers of the EU, upon a proposal *inter alia* of the Austrian Federal Minister of Foreign Affairs, condemned this mistreatment of prisoners in Iraq and welcomed the commitment of the US Government to put on trial those responsible for this mistreatment and to take measures against the non-compliance with international humanitarian law.

International Criminal Tribunals

- Memorandum of Understanding between the Federal Government of Austria and the United Nations on the Extension and Amendment of the Memorandum of Understanding between the Federal Government of Austria and the United Nations for the Loan of Prison Staff to the International Criminal Tribunal for the former Yugoslavia[57] [Vereinbarung zwischen der Österreichischen Bundesregierung und den Vereinten Nationen über die Verlängerung und Abänderung der Vereinbarung zwischen der Österreichischen Bundesregierung und den Vereinten Nationen zur leihweisen Beistellung von Gefängnispersonal an den Internationalen Strafgerichtshof für das ehemalige Jugoslawien]. This Memorandum entered into force on 1 June 2004. The Agreement is laid up for insight at the Federal Ministry for Foreign Affairs, cf. Austrian Federal Law Gazette, *BGBl. [Bundesgesetzblatt]* [58] III Nr. 82/2004

As in the previous years, this Agreement extends the period of loan of prison staff to the International Criminal Tribunal for the former Yugoslavia for a further year and adjusts the payments to the said personnel.

THOMAS DESCH and PETER KUSTOR

---

56. For the draft text and the Explanatory Memorandum see *IA* 420/A *BlgNR* 22. *GP.*
57. For the original version of the agreement cf. 3 *YIHL* (2000) p. 422.
58. The Federal Law Gazette is also available via Internet, <http://www.ris.bka.gv.at>.

BELGIUM[59]

International Criminal Court

☛ Law of 29 March 2004 relating to cooperation with the International Criminal Court and the International Criminal Tribunals. Entered into force on 1 April and published in *Moniteur belge* (Belgian official journal) on 1 April 2004[60]

The law replaces the law of 22 March 1996 relating to the recognition of the ICTY and the ICTR and cooperation with these Tribunals.[61] Title II of the law specifically addresses cooperation with the ICC whereas Title III takes up the provisions of the 1996 law relating to the cooperation with the international criminal tribunals. It was planned that the law would be amended in 2005 or 2006 in order to enable cooperation with other international criminal jurisdictions, such as the Special Court for Sierra Leone and the Extraordinary Chambers for Cambodia.

Concerning cooperation with the ICC, the main features of the law are the following:

— the Ministry of Justice is the competent authority to receive requests for cooperation (Art. 5);[62]

— the Belgian judicial authorities can themselves request cooperation from the ICC (Art. 7);

— the Ministry of Justice can refer a situation to the ICC according to Article 14 of the Statute (Art. 8(1);

— the Ministry of Justice can also refer to the court a crime of international humanitarian law provided for by the Belgian penal code when the crime has been submitted to the Belgian judge and if the federal prosecutor considers that the ICC would be a better forum to take cognisance of the case (Art. 8(2) combined with Art. 10(1) *bis*, 3rd paragraph, no. 4 and Art. 12 *bis*, 3rd paragraph, no. 4 of the Preliminary Title of the Code of Criminal Proceedings). This could be the case when the accused is protected by immunity from criminal process (Art. 10, 1 *bis*, 5th paragraph, and Art. 12 *bis*, 5th paragraph of the Preliminary Title of the Code of Criminal Proceedings). If the ICC does not take up the case referred by Belgium, the Belgian courts are again competent (Art. 8(2) 3rd paragraph);

— when a case is submitted to the ICC according to Article 13 of the Statute, the Ministry of Justice can claim Belgium's jurisdiction according to Articles 1 and 17-19 of the Statute (Art. 9);

— the Ministry of Justice can, *ex officio*, transmit to the ICC information and elements of evidence relating to relevant cases for the ICC (Art. 10);

— the ICC's requests for arrest and surrender of a person are implemented by the *chambre du conseil* of the place where the accused is found. The latter has a right of appeal to the *chambre des mises en accusation* (Indictments Chamber). The request will be accepted if there is no mistake about the identity of the person and if the request fulfils the conditions provided for by Article 91 of the ICC Statute. When the judicial decision is final,

59. Information and commentaries by Eric David, Professeur ordinaire, Free University of Brussels.

60. For a commentary of the law, see *La Belgique et la Cour pénale internationale: Complémentarité et coopération*, actes du Colloque du 17 mai 2004 (Bruxelles, SPF Justice et Bruylant 2005).

61. Ibid., 27 April 1996.

62. Unless otherwise indicated, the articles refer to the 2004 law.

the Ministry of Justice and the Registrar of the ICC will organise, by agreement, the surrender of the person (Arts. 13-20);

— the Ministry of Justice cooperates with the ICC in other ways. More especially, it will seize or freeze assets and instruments which are linked to the crimes provided for in the Statute (Art. 22, no. 12);
— the Belgian law requires that a request of cooperation from the ICC fulfil a number of formal conditions in order to be implemented: a statement of the purpose of the request, the legal basis, detailed information about the person and his or her whereabouts, etc. (Art. 23); these conditions are provided for in Article 96 of the ICC Statute. The Ministry of Justice will check that these conditions are respected (Art. 24);
— searches and seizures are executed according to Belgian law (Art. 26);
— requests for cooperation can be refused or postponed in cases provided for by Articles 93(4), 94 and 95 of the ICC Statute (Arts. 30-31);
— if the Prosecutor of the ICC wishes to carry out some acts in Belgium according to Article 99(4) of the ICC Statute, the Ministry of Justice can refuse if these acts can be executed within the same time limits by Belgian authorities (Art. 32);
— the law sets out the procedure for the enforcement of sentences delivered by the ICC if Belgium agrees to be on the list of the states which accept sentenced persons (Art. 33 ff.);
— jail and pecuniary penalties have been provided for offences against the administration of justice by the ICC, according to Article 70 of the Statute (Art. 41);
— the nomination of a candidate for election to the ICC follows the procedure for the nomination of candidates for appointment to the highest judicial offices in Belgium, i. e., by a proposal from the Superior Council of Justice, an organ established by the Belgian Constitution in order to propose nominations of judges (Art. 151; *code judiciaire*, Art. 259*ter* ff.); the final decision is taken by the Council of Ministers (Art. 42).

Cases

☛ Aung Maw Zin, Aung Thu, Ko Aung – alias Aung Kyaw Soe – *and* Myint Hlaing *v.* TotalFinaElf, Cour de cassation, *5 May 2004*[63]

In 2002 four Burmese refugees in Belgium lodged a complaint against the oil company TotalFinaElf and its chairman and managing director, Thierry Desmarest, for complicity in crimes against humanity committed in Myanmar by the Burmese military authorities. They accused the firm of having financed and equipped armed battalions of the Burmese army to protect the Yadana gas pipeline, knowing that these battalions (locally called 'Total Battalions') obliged the local population to work for its construction, torturing, raping and killing people who refused.[64]

Concerning the company itself, the case was submitted to the investigating judge on the basis of Article 5 of the Penal Code, which provides for the criminal responsibility of legal

63. <www.juridat.be/juris/jucf.htm>.
64. For more details, <www.birmanie.net/birma/ab111.html>.

persons, combined with the 1993/1999 law which provided for universal jurisdiction for crimes of international humanitarian law.[65]

In the meantime, the law was the basis of a large number of other complaints lodged in Belgium against leaders and members of foreign governments.[66] Facing serious diplomatic difficulties, Belgium decided in 2003 to abrogate the law and to replace it by less extensive provisions in the Preliminary Title of the Code of Criminal Proceedings (Law of 5 August 2003), which will not been recalled here.[67]

Article 29(3) – a transitory provision – of the new law provided that the pending cases which were under investigation by a Belgian judge and which had no link with Belgium (crimes committed abroad against a foreigner by a foreigner who was not in Belgium) should be dismissed by the *Cour de cassation* on application from the General Prosecutor.

Such an application was submitted in the *TotalFinaElf* case. In its judgement of 5 May 2004, the *Cour de cassation* observed that there was no link between the case and Belgium since:

— there was no Belgian complainant;
— the headquarters of TotalFinaElf were not located in Belgium;
— a TotalFinaElf coordination centre was based in Belgium, but this centre had a distinct legal personality from the eponymous transnational group and could not, legally, be confused with the latter;
— the chairman and managing director of TotalFinaElf had no residence in Belgium, even if he could be found in Belgium from time to time.

However, the court agreed to ask the *Cour d'arbitrage*[68] for a preliminary ruling in order to discover whether Article 29(3) of the new law introduced an element of discrimination contrary to Articles 10, 11 and 192 of the Constitution by prohibiting the removal of an IHL case brought by a Belgian citizen and allowing the removal of a similar case brought by a foreign refugee.[69]

ERIC DAVID

BELIZE

Landmines

☛ Anti-personnel Mines Act, Act No. 24 of 2003. Assented to on 5 January and published on 10 January 2004

---

65. Act of 16 June 1993 on the punishment of serious violations of the international Conventions of Geneva of 12 August 1949 and to the Protocols I and II of 8 June 1977, additional to these Conventions) and Act of 10 February 1999 relating to the repression of serious violations of international humanitarian law, 10 February 1999. Reprinted in 2 *YIHL* (1999) at pp. 541 and 539, respectively.

66. See 3 *YIHL* (2000) pp. 430-431; 4 *YIHL* (2001) pp. 454-455.

67. See 6 *YIHL* (2003) pp. 466-468.

68. The *Cour d'arbitrage* was established in 1989 in order to settle (by way of cancellation or interpretation) questions relating to laws and decrees which would have been adopted either in violation of the rules governing the competencies of the federated powers in Belgium or in violation of the fundamental rights and liberties provided for in the Constitution (Law of 6 January 1989, Arts. 1 and 26).

69. <www.juridat.be/cgi_juris/jurf.pl> The answer of the *Cour d'arbitrage* was given on 13 April 2005 <www.arbitrage.be/fr/common/home.html> and the final judgement of the *Cour de cassation* was given on 29 June 2005. These decisions will be dealt with in the 2005 correspondent's report.

The Act implements the Convention on the Prohibition of the Use, Stockpiling, Production and Transfer of Anti-personnel Mines and on their Destruction (the 1997 Ottawa Convention).[70]

BENIN

The Emblem

- The Law No. 2004-06 on the use and protection of the emblem and name of the Red Cross and Red Crescent in the Republic of Benin. Adopted by the National Assembly on 11 May 2004

'This Law lays down the terms and conditions governing the use of, and the rules of protection for, the emblem and name of the Red Cross and Red Crescent in peacetime and in times of armed conflict.'[71]

BOSNIA AND HERZEGOVINA[72]

The Emblem

- The Law on the Red Cross Society of Bosnia and Herzegovina. Adopted on 21 October 2004, published on 2 November and entered into force on 10 November 2004, the eighth day following the date of publication

'This Law establishes the Red Cross Society of Bosnia and Herzegovina and regulates its legal status, structure, competence and other related matters, and allows for the use by the National Society of the Red Cross emblem.'[73]

Missing Persons

- Law on Missing Persons of Bosnia and Herzegovina. Adopted on 21 October, published on 9 November and entered into force on 17 November 2004, the eighth day after its publication

'Its purpose is to revise the definition of a missing person, to improve the process of tracing of missing persons, the exchange of information, the keeping of central records and the realization of social and other rights of family members, as well as to address other issues related to missing persons in Bosnia and Herzegovina. The Law furthermore establishes the Institute for Missing Persons of Bosnia and Herzegovina, which is assigned the task of tracing missing persons in and from Bosnia and Herzegovina. The Law also creates the Central Records of Missing Persons, stipulating that the latter shall include all records of missing persons kept at local and entity levels by associations of families of missing per-

---

70. Source and for further information, National Implementation of International Humanitarian Law, ICRC National Advisory Service, Biannual Update on National Legislation and Case Law, January-June 2004, 86 *IRRC* (2004) pp. 694 at 695.

71. *Supra* n. 10, pp. 217 at 217-218.

72. Information and commentaries by Jacob Ramer, Chicago-Kent College of Law, and Avril McDonald.

73. *Supra* n. 10, pp. 217-218.

sons, by other associations of citizens and by the Tracing Agencies of the Red Cross Society of Bosnia and Herzegovina, in accordance with their respective mandates.'[74]

Srebrenica Commission

- 'The Events in and around Srebrenica between 10 and 19 July 1995', The Commission for Investigation of the Events in and around Srebrenica between 10th and 19th July 1995, 11 June 2004 <http://www.vladars.net/pdf/srebrenicajun2004engl.pdf>
- Addendum to the Report of the 11 June 2004 on the Events in and around Srebrenica between 10 and 19 July 1995, 15 October 2004 <http://www.vladars.net/pdf/srebr_final_e.pdf>

The Republika Sprska (RS) established the Srebrenica Commission on 15 December 2003 in response to 7 March 2003 decisions of Bosnia and Herzegovina's (BiH) Human Rights Chamber that ordered the RS to investigate the events of Srebrenica in July 1995 and to provide victims' families with information on their missing kin.[75] The seven-person Commission, including five Serbs, one victims' representative and one international representative, requested and received information from RS and BiH institutions, international organisations and institutions, and individuals involved in the event.

In its report issued on 11 June 2004, the Commission 'established that between 10 and 19 July 1995, several thousands of Bosnians were liquidated, in a manner that represents severe violation of International Humanitarian Law and that the perpetrators, among the others, undertook measures to cover up the crime by reallocating the bodies'.[76]

The Commission also established and provided evidence of the 'participation of military and police units, including special units of the RS Ministry of Internal Affairs';[77] the first time this was admitted by a government entity. The Commission concluded by stating:

> 'Accepting and facing the fact that certain members of the Serb people committed crimes in Srebrenica in July 1995, could favorably influence creation of the conditions for the investigation of all other crimes committed in the area of BiH as well as for the punishment of the perpetrator.'[78]

An addendum to the report, issued on 15 October 2004, included the location of 32 mass graves, including 11 that were previously unknown,[79] and found that there were 7,806 confirmed victims. A previous report by the RS's Office for the Investigation of War Crimes had concluded in September 2002 that over a thousand soldiers died in Srebrenica while fighting, but stated that there was no evidence of a massacre or any other crime.

---

74. Ibid., pp. 218-219.
75. On 7 March 2004, the Human Rights Chamber delivered five Decisions on Admissibility and Merits and one Decision on Further Remedies, in cases involving 49 applications concerning Srebrenica. See <www.hrc.ba/ENGLISH/press_eng/pressEng/march03.pdf>.
76. 'The Events in and around Srebrenica between 10 and 19 July 1995', p. 32.
77. Ibid.
78. Ibid., p. 33.
79. OHR Press Release, 'High Representative Briefs Solana and De Hoop Scheffer on RS Srebrenica Report', 11 June 2004, <http://www.ohr.int/ohr-dept/presso/pressr/default.asp?content_id=32657>.

After seeing the preliminary report, on 22 June 2004 the president of the Serb Democratic Party, Dragan Cavić, was the first RS politician to publicly accept that a massacre had occurred at Srebrenica, calling it 'a dark page of Serb history' and adding that Serbs must face 'the truth … which, although not complete, still is frightening'.[80]

On 10 November 2004 the RS publicly acknowledged the Srebrenica massacre and issued an official apology to the victims' families, stating: 'The government of the RS commiserates with the pain of the relatives of [the victims] of Srebrenica, and truly regrets and apologises for the tragedy they experienced', and that the 'report doubtlessly demonstrates that, in the area of Srebrenica in July 1995, crimes of huge extent were committed by means of rude violation of the international humanitarian law. The government of the RS is committed to, and it assumes decisive measures to, bring to the justice all persons who committed war crimes.'[81]

Criminal Court Reform

THE COURT OF BOSNIA AND HERZEGOVINA AND THE WAR CRIMES CHAMBER

- Decision Enacting the Law re-amending the Law on Court of Bosnia and Herzegovina. Enacted by the High Representative on 24 January 2003 and entered into force immediately. The Law, which formed an integral part of the Decision, entered into force on 1 February 2003 pursuant to its Article 13 <http://www.ohr.int/decisions/judicialrdec/default.asp?content_id=29080>
- Decision Enacting the Law on further re-amending the Law on Court of BiH. Enacted by the High Representative on 28 October 2003 and entered into force immediately. The law, which formed an integral part of the Decision, entered into force on 29 October 2003 <http://www.ohr.int/decisions/judicialrdec/default.asp?content_id=31098>
- Decision Enacting the Law on the Amendments to the Law on Court of Bosnia and Herzegovina. Enacted by the High Representative on 6 February 2004 and entered into force on the same date, as did the Law, which formed an integral part of the decision <http://www.ohr.int/decisions/judicialrdec/default.asp?content_id=31835>
- Agreement Between The High Representative For Bosnia And Herzegovina and Bosnia and Herzegovina on the Establishment of the Registry for Section I for War Crimes and Section II for Organised Crime, Economic Crime and Corruption of the Criminal and Appellate Divisions of the court of Bosnia and Herzegovina and the Special Department for War Crimes and the Special Department for Organised Crime, Economic Crime and Corruption of the Prosecutor's Office of Bosnia And Herzegovina. Signed by the Presidency of Bosnia and Herzegovina and the High Representative on 1 December 2004
- Decision on Appointment of the International Registrar to the Registry for Section I for War Crimes and Section II for Organized Crime, Economic Crime and Corruption of the Criminal and Appellate Divisions of the court of Bosnia and Herzegovina. Enacted by the High Representative on 17 December 2004 and came into force immediately as did

80. I. Gajić, 'Bosnian Serb president expresses regrets for a wartime massacre of Muslims,' Associated Press, 22 June 2004.

81. Antonio Prlenda, 'Despite Apology, RS War Crimes Co-operation Still Falls Short,' 2 December 2004, Southeast European Times, <http://www.setimes.com/cocoon/setimes/xhtml/en_GB/features/setimes/features/2004/12/02/feature-02>.

the appointment of the Registrar, Michael Johnson <http://www.ohr.int/decisions/war-crimes-decs/default.asp?content_id=33830>

- Decision Enacting the Law on Protection of Witnesses under Threat and Vulnerable Witnesses. Enacted by the High Representative on 24 January 2004 and entered into force immediately <http://www.ohr.int/decisions/judicialrdec/default.asp?content_id=29116>
- Law on Protection of Witnesses under Threat and Vulnerable Witnesses. Enacted pursuant to the above decision and entered into force on 1 March 2003<http://www.ohr.int/decisions/judicialrdec/doc/HiRep-dec-102-law-witness-protection-bih.doc>

THE STATE INVESTIGATION AND PROTECTION AGENCY

- Law on the State Investigation and Protection Agency, 15 June 2004

The Law on the State Investigation and Protection Agency gives the State Investigation and Protection Agency executive authority to investigate serious crimes, including terrorism, trafficking, narcotics, organised crime, war crimes and money laundering.[82]

THE PROSECUTOR'S OFFICE

- Decision Enacting the Law on Amendments to the Law on Prosecutor's Office of Bosnia and Herzegovina. Enacted by the High Representative on 24 January 2003 and entered into force immediately. The Law, which formed an integral part of the Decision, entered into force on 1 February 2003 <http://www.ohr.int/decisions/judicialrdec/default.asp?content_id=29093>
- Decision Enacting the Law Re-amending the Law on the Prosecutor's Office of BiH. Enacted by the High Representative on 28 October 2003 and entered into force immediately. The law, which formed an integral part of the decision, entered into force on 29 October 2003 <http://www.ohr.int/decisions/judicialrdec/default.asp?content_id=31102>

CRIMINAL LAW REFORM

- Decision Enacting the Criminal Procedure Code of Bosnia and Herzegovina. Enacted by the High Representative on 24 January and entered into force immediately <http://www.ohr.int/decisions/judicialrdec/default.asp?content_id=29094>
- Criminal Procedure Code of Bosnia and Herzegovina. Enacted pursuant to the above decision and entered into force on 1 March 2003, as provided for in Article 451 of the Code <http://www.ohr.int/decisions/judicialrdec/doc/HiRep-dec-100-law-cpc-bih.doc>
- Decision Enacting the Criminal Code of Bosnia and Herzegovina, issued on 24 January 2003 and entered into force immediately <http://www.ohr.int/decisions/judicialrdec/default.asp?content_id=29095>
- Criminal Code of Bosnia and Herzegovina. Enacted pursuant to the above decision and entered into force on 1 March 2003 pursuant to Article 252, on an interim basis until adoption by the Bosnian Parliamentary Assembly <http://www.ohr.int/decisions/judicialrdec/doc/HiRep-dec-101-law-crim-code-bih.doc>

---

82. 2004 Country Report on Human Rights Practices in Bosnia and Herzegovina, US State Department, <http://www.state.gov/g/drl/rls/hrrpt/2004/41673.htm>.

- Decision Enacting the Law on Amendment to the Criminal Code of BiH. Enacted by the High Representative on 26 November 2004 and entered into force immediately, as did the Law, which was attached to and formed an integral part of the Decision <http://www.ohr.int/decisions/judicialrdec/default.asp?content_id=33595>
- Decision Enacting the Law on Amendments to the Criminal Procedure Code of Bosnia and Herzegovina. Enacted by the High Representative on 16 December 2004 and came into force immediately, as did the Law, which formed was attached to and formed an integral part of the Decision <http://www.ohr.int/decisions/judicialrdec/default.asp?content_id=33791>

ICTY

- Resolution of Republika Srpska Parliament regarding cooperation with ICTY, 20 July 2004

On 20 July 2004 the RS parliament publicly called on war crimes suspects to surrender to authorities to stand trial before the ICTY. The parliament passed a resolution that stated: 'We call on all indictees to immediately ... surrender to the police and courts of the Serb Republic because otherwise they risk arrest by the police.'[83] The parliament was to step up the hunt for war crime suspects, including Radovan Karadžić and around 20 others. Earlier in the year, in April, the RS parliament called on local authorities to cooperate with the ICTY authorities in trying to apprehend war crimes suspects.[84]

Repatriation of Detainees

In October 2004 the Bosnian government sought the return of six individuals suspected of plotting to blow up the American and British embassies in Sarajevo who were handed over to the US in January 2002 after charges against them were dropped by the Federal Supreme Court on 17 January for lack of evidence. All six were Algerians, although four of them had Bosnian citizenship (but it was revoked after they were expelled from the country). They were sent to Guantánamo Bay, Cuba and subsequently classified by the US as enemy combatants. In July 2004 the cases of two of the men were included in a petition for a writ of *habeas corpus* by the New York-based Center for Constitutional Rights seeking to challenge the lawfulness of their detention.[85]

Red Cross Society

- Law on the Red Cross Society of Bosnia and Herzegovina. Adopted on 21 October 2004 and entered into force on 10 November 2004. Published in the *Official Gazette of Bosnia and Herzegovina*, No. 49/04, of 2 November 2004

---

83. D. Dardić 'Bosnian Serb parliament urges Karadzic to surrender', Reuters, 20 July 2004, <http://www.reuters.com/newsArticle.jhtml?type=worldNews&storyID=5722465>.
84. 'Bosnian Serb lawmakers urge government to cooperate with UN court', Agence France-Presse, 22 April 2004.
85. N. Wood, 'For Bosnia, getting 6 freed from Guantánamo is a balancing act', *The New York Times*, 21 October 2004.

The Law establishes the Red Cross Society of Bosnia and Herzegovina and provides for its legal status, structure and competence. The Law abolishes the Law on the Status and Authorities of the Red Cross of the Republic of Bosnia and Herzegovina.[86]

Missing Persons

- Law on Missing Persons of Bosnia and Herzegovina. Adopted on 21 October 2004 and entered into force on 17 November 2004. Published in the *Official Gazette of Bosnia and Herzegovina*, No. 50, of 9 November 2004

The Law on Missing Persons redefines what constitutes a missing person, and improves the systems of tracing, information exchange and record keeping, *inter alia*. The Law also provides for the establishment of an Institute for Missing Persons of Bosnia and Herzegovina, with responsibility for tracing persons missing both in and from Bosnia and Herzegovina, and establishes the Central Records of Missing Persons.

Arms Control

- Law on Changes to the Criminal Code of Bosnia and Herzegovina. Adopted on 30 September 2004, entered into force on 6 January 2005, published in the *Official Gazette of Bosnia and Herzegovina*, No. 61/04, on 29 December 2004

The Law on Changes to the Criminal Code of Bosnia and Herzegovina introduces a new Article 193a into the Criminal Code entitled 'Prohibited Weapons and Other Combat Means', which prohibits all use, production, stockpiling or transfer or any weapons prohibited by international law.[87]

Cases

- Mostar 4 *case (*Zeljko Dzidić, Erhad Poznić, Ivan Skutor *and* Mate Anicić*), Mostar Cantonal Court, 30 January 2004*

In April 2001 the Mostar Cantonal Court acquitted the four Croat defendants of war crimes relating to their alleged involvement in the killing of Bosnian Muslim civilians and prisoners of war held at the Faculty of Mechanical Engineering in Mostar between May and July 1993. The Federation of Bosnia and Herzegovina Supreme Court ordered a retrial, stating that additional evidence needed to be heard. During the retrial, which began on 17 February 2003 and ended in January 2004, several witnesses changed the testimonies they had given at the investigative stages in favour of the defendants. On 30 January 2004 the Mostar Cantonal Court again acquitted all four defendants. On 4 November 2004 the FBiH Supreme Court ordered a second trial after the prosecutor's appeal on various grounds.[88]

---

86. Official Gazette of the Republic of Bosnia and Herzegovina, No. 21/92 I 13/94.
87. Ibid.
88. OSCE, 'War Crimes Trials Before the Domestic Courts of Bosnia and Herzegovina', March 2005 <http://www.oscebih.org/documents/1407-eng.pdf>.

☛ *Jovo Torbica* case, Sarajevo Cantonal Court, 11 March 2004

On 11 March 2004 Jovo Torbica, a Bosnian Serb, was acquitted by the Sarajevo Cantonal Court of war crimes charges for lack of evidence. He had been charged, under Article 154 of the FBiH Criminal Code, with pillaging the property and livestock of Bosnian Muslims following an attack on the village of Ahatovići. The prosecutor filed an appeal on 29 April 2004.[89]

☛ *Duško Tadić* case, Sarajevo Cantonal Court, 31 March 2004

Tadić, a Serb, was charged under Article 154 of the FBiH Criminal Code (war crimes against civilians) with unlawfully detaining Bosnian Muslims in Cajnice in April 1992 and acquitted by the Sarajevo Cantonal Court. The prosecutor appealed the decision on 4 May 2004.[90]

☛ *Ivan Baković* case, Livno Cantonal Court, 7 April 2004

On 7 April 2004 the Livno Cantonal Court found Baković, a General in the Croatian Defense Counsel (HVO), guilty of war crimes against civilians and sentenced him to 15 years' imprisonment. He was accused of killing nine Bosnian Muslims in August 1993 in Mokronoge, Tomislavgrad Municipality. The Zagreb County Court had previously convicted him of murder in relation to the same charges but the Croatian Supreme Court overturned the verdict and ordered a retrial. He failed to appear for the retrial and was arrested in Livno in 2001. The FBiH Supreme Court confirmed the conviction.[91]

☛ *Romeo Blazević* case, Mostar Cantonal Court, 26 April 2004

Blazević, a Croatian soldier in the HVO, was found guilty of war crimes against civilians and prisoners of war under Articles 142 and 144 of the SFRY Criminal Code and sentenced to two years' imprisonment. He was accused of 'being involved in inhuman treatment of the BiH Army prisoners of war captured in the Vranica building in Mostar and held in the HVO police station of Siroki Brijeg. … [and] of inhumane treatment and intimidation of a Bosniak female civilian detained in Heliodrom and other detainees'. On 16 December 2004 the FBiH Supreme Court increased the sentence from two years to three years.[92]

☛ *Konjić 7* case (*Jasmin Guska*, *Muharem Hujdur*, *Sadat Sarajlić*, *Safet Sarajlić*, *Muhamed Sarjlić*, *Senad Begluk* and *Miralem Salihović*), Mostar Cantonal Court, 29 June 2004

Seven Bosnian Muslims were acquitted on charges of unlawfully detaining, torturing and murdering two Serbs in Konjić in May 1992. Guska, Head of Konjić Police Administration and a member of the Konjić War Presidency, allegedly ordered his co-defendants to arrest

---

89. Ibid.
90. Ibid.
91. Ibid.
92. Ibid.

the two Serbs and torture them. The other defendants, all members of the Territorial Defence of the Republic of BiH, allegedly beat the prisoners to death.[93] Guska was found guilty of command responsibility because he was aware of the torture and failed to prevent the crimes or punish the perpetrators. The ICTY had approved the beginning of the trial under the Rules of Road.[94]

☛ *Vlastimir Pusara* case, Sarajevo Cantonal Court, 29 June 2004

Pusara, a member of the Bosnian Serb army, was found guilty of four counts of war crimes against civilians (ethnic cleansing in the Hadžići Municipality) under Article 154 of the FBiH Criminal Code. He was found to have taken part in the shelling of civilian targets in the Musići village near Hadžići, which was followed by an infantry attack when three civilians from Musići lost their lives and 13 were imprisoned, tortured and abused, and some also killed. Pusara was also convicted of illegal imprisonment and psychological and physical abuse of Bosniak civilians in Hadžići.[95] He received a ten year sentence of imprisonment. The defence appealed the decision on 2 September 2004. On 8 December 2004 the FBiH Supreme Court reduced the sentence to seven years' imprisonment.[96]

☛ *Zvonko Trlin* case, Mostar Cantonal Court, 29 June 2004

The Mostar Cantonal Court found Trlin, a Croat, guilty of war crimes against civilians, namely, 'for torture and inhumane treatment, inflicting grave sufferings and bodily harm to civilian detainees at the military barracks in Grabovina, Capljina municipality', and sentenced him to 18 months in prison. He was acquitted on the charge of murder.[97]

☛ *Milorad Rodić* case, Sarajevo Cantonal Court, 9 July 2004

Rodić, a Serbian soldier of the RS Army, pleaded guilty to war crimes against the civilian population under Article 142 of the SFRY Criminal Code on 6 July 2004. He threatened civilians with a knife on 13 July 1992 after entering their apartment in Grbavica, and on 13 January 1993 he raped a female after entering her apartment in Grbavica. On 9 July 2004 he was sentenced to five years' imprisonment.[98]

☛ *Mario Matić* case, Mostar Cantonal Court, 6 July 2004

Matić, a Croatian member of the HVO Military Police, was accused of inhumane treatment to unlawfully arrested Bosnian Muslim civilians and BiH Army prisoners of war while they were transported to the prison 'Plocara' in Gornje Zabrde, Konjic Municipality. The crimes

---

93. Ibid.
94. 'War crimes trial of seven Bosnian Muslims opens', Deutsche Presse-Agentur, 10 May 2004.
95. 'Sarajevo court sentences Bosnian Serb to ten years in prison for war crimes', BBC Monitoring International Reports (citing BHTV1, Sarajevo from 29 June 2004, 30 June 2004.
96. OSCE, 'War Crimes Trials Before the Domestic Courts of Bosnia and Herzegovina', March 2005 <http://www.oscebih.org/documents/1407-eng.pdf>
97. Ibid.
98. Ibid.

were said to have been carried out in April 1993 during the conflict between the HVO and the BiH Army. He was also accused of killing a detained Bosnian Muslim civilian.

On 6 July the Mostar Cantonal Court sentenced Matić to six years in prison and ordered him to pay 200 convertible marks for the killing of Ismet Kovacević and the physical and verbal assault on Vejsil Hajduk, both Bosniak civilians, in 1993.[99] Both were found to be war crimes.

☛ *Dragan Bunoza* case, Mostar Cantonal Court, 12 July 2004

Bunoza, a Croat member of the HVO, was found guilty of war crimes against the civilian population under Article 142 of the SFRY Criminal Code and sentenced to nine years in prison. He was charged with and found guilty of forcing Bosnian Muslims from their village of Pjesivac, Stolac Municipality on 30 June 1993 and 13 July 1993 and for their illegal detention, as well as for murdering a civilian.[100]

☛ *Ratko Gasović* case, Sarajevo Cantonal Court, 9 February 2004; Supreme Court, 6 October 2004

Pursuant to Article 154 of the FBiH Criminal Code the Cantonal Court in Sarajevo on 9 February 2004 had sentenced Ratko Gasović, a member of a Bosnian Serb paramilitary group, to ten years in jail for war crimes, namely, forced labour, inhuman treatment, and the raping and beating of two Muslim sisters detained in the Sarajevo suburb of Hadžići in 1992.[101]

On 6 October 2004 the FBiH Supreme Court reduced the sentence to eight years.

☛ *Dragan* Palameta case, Mostar Cantonal Court, 29 October 2004

After an 18-month trial the Mostar Cantonal Court acquitted Palameta, a Croat, of war crimes against the civilian population, punishable under Article 142 of the SFRY Criminal Code. 'About 20 witnesses were heard, and the trial recommenced several times because of long adjournments between hearings partly due to serious problems with summoning the witnesses, their appearance in court and the reappointment process.'[102]

☛ *Ostoja Sando* case, Sarajevo Cantonal Court, 22 November 2004

Sando, a Serb, was charged with war crimes against wounded prisoners under Article 143 of the SFRY Criminal Code, specifically, shooting and killing wounded members of the BiH Army. The trial began in January 2004 and he was acquitted on 22 November 2004.[103]

---

99. 'Bosnia: War crimes suspect sentenced to six years in prison', BBC Worldwide Monitoring, 6 July 2004.

100. OSCE, 'War Crimes Trials before the Domestic Courts of Bosnia and Herzegovina', March 2005 <http://www.oscebih.org/documents/1407-eng.pdf>.

101. 'Sarajevo Court sentences Bosnian Serb to ten years for war crimes', Agence France-Presse, 9 February 2004.

102. OSCE, 'War Crimes Trials before the Domestic Courts of Bosnia and Herzegovina', March 2005, <http://www.oscebih.org/documents/1407-eng.pdf>.

103. Ibid.

The prosecution stated that it would appeal to the Bosnia and Herzegovina Federation Supreme Court.

☛ *Zoran Knežević* case, Sarajevo Cantonal Court, 8 December 2004

Knežević, a Serb, was sentenced to ten years in prison after being found guilty of war crimes against civilians under Article 142 of the SFRY Criminal Code. The court established that Knežević, as a member of the RS Army, had raped female Bosnian Muslim civilians in Grbavica during the war.[104]

Ongoing Cases

☛ Ranko Jakovljević, Miroslav Cadjo, Mile Rodić, Drazen Raković, Rade Savić, Gojko Kesić, Zoran Banović, Miroslav Zec, Djordje Jelcić, Zoran Milojica *and* Slobodan Muzgonja *case*

On 18 May 2004 the Banja Luka District Court began the trial of 11 former police officers from Prijedor charged with the abduction and murder of Father Tomislav Matanović, a Roman Catholic priest, and his parents in 1995. This was the first war crimes trial in Republika Srpska.

☛ *Dominik Ilijasević* case

In June 2004 the trial against Dominik Ilijasević resumed before the Zenica Cantonal Court. Ilijasević, a former Bosnian Croat military commander, is accused of war crimes committed against Bosniak civilians in Stupni Do in central Bosnia during the war.[105]

Pending Cases

☛ Abdul Maktouf *case, 13 September 2004*

On 13 September 2004 Bosnia's state prosecutor charged Abdul Maktouf, an Iraqi-born Bosnian citizen, with war crimes allegedly committed during the Bosnian war against Bosnian Serb and Bosnian Croat civilians. The indictment alleged that he abducted five civilians, including four Bosnian Croats and one Bosnian Serb, from the Bosnian town of Travnik in October 1993, and then transported them to a mujahedin camp where they all were beaten and the Serb was beheaded. He is also alleged to have been a 'facilitator' between a group of mujahedin fighters, known as El-Mujahed, and the third corps of the Bosnian army commanded by Enver Hadzihasanović, who is currently in The Hague standing trial.[106]

---

104. Ibid.

105. Country Report 2005, Bosnia and Herzegovina, Amnesty International, <http://web.amnesty.org/report2005/bih-summary-eng>.

106. B. Kampschror, 'Bosnia Charges Alleged Mujahedin', Tribunal Update TU No 373, 17 September 2004, Institute for War and Peace Reporting, <http://iwpr.gn.apc.org/?s=f&o=164224&apc_state=henitri2004>.

☛ *Miroslv Vjestica* case

On 24 December 2004 the Bihac Cantonal Court ordered a 30-day detention for war crimes suspect Miroslav Vjestica after he was arrested by the Banja Luka police force on the basis of an arrest warrant issued from the Bihac court. He was suspected of, *inter alia*, organising and ordering an attack on Bosanska Krupa in 1992 and expelling the local non-Serb population. He was the first war crimes suspect to be arrested by the Bosnian Serb police.

☛ Svetko Novaković, Jovan Skobo, Momir Glisić, Dragoje Radanović, Momir Skakavac, Zeljko Mitrović, Veselin Cancar *and* Goran Vasić *case*

On 15 November 2004 the police of the Republika Sprska arrested eight war crimes suspects in Foča, Pale and Lukavica following an order by the Sarajevo Cantonal Court.[107] The suspects were handed over to the Sarajevo Cantonal Court. [108] The charges against them include genocide, war crimes against civilians and war crimes against prisoners of war. This was the first cooperative operation between the Bosnian Serb police and the Bosnian Muslim-Croat courts.[109]

JACOB RAMER

CAMBODIA[110]

International Criminal Court

☛ Agreement between the Royal Government of Cambodia and the Government of the United States of America Regarding the non-surrender of Persons to the International Criminal Court, 27 June 2003

On 27 June 2003 the Royal Government of Cambodia and the Government of the United States of America signed a bilateral agreement excluding surrender of nationals of the other party to the ICC without the latter's consent.

By the end of 2004 there had been no progress towards adoption of implementation legislation for the ICC Statute or ratification of the Agreement with the United States.

Extraordinary Chambers for Cambodia

☛ Khmer Rouge trials, UNGA Res. 57/228 B, 13 May 2003 <http://www.un.org/Depts/dhl/resguide/r57.htm>

☛ Agreement between the United Nations and the Royal Government of Cambodia concerning the prosecution under Cambodian Law of crimes committed during the period of Democratic Kampuchea, 6 June 2003 <http://www.cambodia.gov.kh/krt/pdfs/Agreement%20between%20UN%20and%20RGC.pdf>

---

107. 'Republika Srpska: apology for Srebrenica', Transitions Online (Prague), 18 November 2004.

108. 'Bosnian Serb police detain eight war crimes suspects', Deutsche Presse-Agentur, 15 November 2004.

109. Ibid.

110. Information and commentaries by David Boyle, Solicitor admitted to the Bar of the New South Wales Supreme Court, Australia; instructor at the Paris Law Clinic in international criminal law, University of Paris I; Doctoral candidate, University of Paris II.

- Law Approving the Agreement Between the United Nations and the Royal Government of Cambodia Concerning the Prosecution under Cambodian Law of Crimes Committed During the Period of Democratic Kampuchea, Kram NS/RKM/1004/004, 19 October 2004 <http://www.cambodia.gov.kh/krt/pdfs/Kram%20promulgating%20Agreement%2019%20October%202004-En.pdf>
- Law on the Amendments to the Law on the Establishment of the Extraordinary Chambers in the courts of Cambodia for the Prosecution of Crimes Committed during the Period of Democratic Kampuchea, Kram NS/RKM/1004/006, 27 October 2004 <http://www.cambodia.gov.kh/krt/pdfs/Kram%20and%20KR%20Law%20amendments%2027%20Oct%202004%20–%20Eng.pdf>

On 17 March 2003 UN and Cambodian negotiators adopted the draft international Agreement concerning the Khmer Rouge trials. The text was accepted, as negotiated, by the Cambodian government on 28 March and by the UN General Assembly on 13 May 2003, then officially signed by both parties in Phnom Penh on 6 June 2003. However, the Agreement was only ratified by Cambodia on 19 October 2004, after the formation of a new government. The 2001 Law on the Establishment of the Extraordinary Chambers was then amended, on 27 October 2004, to bring Cambodian law into conformity with the international Agreement. However, the UN indicated that the Agreement would not come into force until the budget for the Chambers had been secured. A donors conference was planned for early 2005.

The main changes introduced by the 2003 Agreement are: simplification of the Extraordinary Chambers structure to allow only one degree of appeal (Arts. 9 and 36); strengthened provisions relating to respect for international standards (Art. 33); recognition of the 'unconditional' entitlement of suspects to counsel of their own choosing (Art. 24); extension of the statute of limitations for certain serious crimes under Cambodian law by 30 years (Art. 3); a compromise provision authorising the Chambers to decide on the validity of previous amnesties and pardons (Art. 40); Khmer, English and French given equal status as official working languages (Art. 45); recognition of the UN Secretary General's right to provide further judges for the Chambers, if necessary (Art. 46); and giving the Agreement itself international treaty status (Art. 47).

Cases
- *Sam Bith* case, Phnom Penh Municipal Court, 23 December 2002 (written Judgment, 24 February 2003)
- Chhouk Rin *case, Cambodian Court of Appeal (Second Appeal), Phnom Penh, 27 October 2003 (written Judgment, 5 November 2003)*

On 24 February 2003, in continuing developments in cases involving the kidnapping and murder of three western backpackers by the Khmer Rouge in July 1994, the Phnom Penh Municipal Court handed down its written judgment concerning the 23 December 2002 conviction of Sam Bith, the officer in command of the zone where the train was ambushed, for command responsibility in a range of crimes, including murder, hostage-taking and terrorism. Sam Bith's appeal to the court of Appeal was scheduled for hearing in 2005.

On 27 October 2003 the Cambodian Court of Appeals confirmed its 6 September 2002 *in absentia* decision overturning the acquittal of another rebel officer, Colonel Chhouk Rin. The written judgment, handed down on 5 November 2003, confirmed that the amnesty law passed three weeks before the attack did not apply to crimes committed after it came into force. Chhouk Rin's appeal to the Supreme Court was scheduled for hearing in 2005.

DAVID BOYLE

CANADA[111]

War Crimes/Immigration and Asylum

- Seventh Annual Report, Canada's War Crimes Programme, Activities for the Period of 1 April 2002 to 31 March 2003
  <http://www.cbsa-asfc.gc.ca/general/enforcement/annual/annual7-e.html#P65_1784>

If a person who has been involved in war crimes or crimes against humanity manages to enter Canada, Canadian officials may take action against that person whether they are in the refugee stream, the immigration process, the citizenship process, or if they have already become a Canadian citizen but they hid their war crimes activities when they originally immigrated to Canada.

On the immigration side, a major change in the organisational structure of the department responsible for the administration of the immigration process, Citizenship and Immigration Canada (CIC), occurred in that its intelligence and enforcement functions were transferred to a new agency, the Canadian Border Services Agency (CBSA) on 12 December 2003. The immigration war crimes programme was transferred to this new agency, a process which was completed in 2004. CBSA continues to work closely with CIC in upholding the objectives of the Immigration and Refugee Protection Act (IRPA), by preventing persons involved in war crimes or crimes against humanity from coming to Canada and by taking enforcement action against those who arrive or remain in Canada.

During the fiscal year 2003-2004, visa officials prevented a total of 242 persons from coming to Canada because of allegations of war crimes or crimes against humanity. This includes those refused specifically for possible involvement in war crimes or crimes against humanity, those who withdrew when asked for more information and those who were investigated for allegations of war crimes but were refused for other reasons. Canadian missions abroad investigated a total of 2,300 potential war crimes cases, resulting in the refusal or withdrawal of more than ten percent. Visa offices identify potential war crimes cases through security screening and refer many of them to CBSA's Modern War Crimes Unit. Analysts with geographic expertise provide analysis and recommendations on immigration cases. Visa officers abroad concluded the review of 331 immigrant applicants for possible involvement in war crimes or crimes against humanity. As a result, 44 persons considered involved in war crimes or atrocities were refused visas to immigrate to Canada or withdrew their applications. Temporary resident applications from countries where conflict or human rights abuses are a concern are sent to the unit's Visitor Information Transmission (VIT) analysts. In fiscal year 2003-2004 the VIT section handled 1,969 temporary resident applications (including student and temporary worker applications), over 50 percent more than the previous year. During the year, 198 alleged war criminals were refused temporary resident visas or withdrew their applications.

---

111. Information and commentaries by Joseph Rikhof, Senior Counsel, Manager of the Law, Crimes against Humanity and War Crimes Section, Department of Justice and part-time Professor, International Criminal Law, University of Ottawa.

If a potential war criminal manages to enter Canada or is identified as already living in Canada, CBSA officials take the appropriate enforcement action. Persons claiming refugee protection must first complete a Personal Information Form (PIF). After 11 September 2001, a decision was made to begin front-end screening of refugee claimants, by screening all PIFs for security concerns as well as for possible war crimes or crimes against humanity. Those PIFs which raise concerns about possible war crimes are referred for a second, in depth, review. The increased screening, combined with a surge in refugee protection claims leading up to the implementation of IRPA in June 2002, resulted in an increased investigative workload in the following year. During 2003-2004, a total of 2,680 refugee claimant cases were reviewed for possible war crimes or crimes against humanity, leaving an inventory of 883 claims under investigation at the end of March 2004. During the fiscal year, CBSA hearings officers filed 387 interventions before the Refugee Protection Division (RPD) of the Immigration and Refugee Board (IRB) based on allegations of war crimes. During the same period, CBSA received a total of 308 decisions from the RPD in cases where CBSA had intervened to seek exclusion based on war crimes concerns. These included: exclusions of 63 refugee claimants for war crimes; 107 decisions to refuse refugee status, although the persons were not excluded for war crimes; rulings that 61 individuals, where there was an allegation of involvement in war crimes or crimes against humanity, had withdrawn or abandoned their claims; and, finally, granting of refugee status to 77 persons. In 2003-2004, 44 persons considered war criminals were removed from Canada. Removal may be delayed for a number of reasons, including court proceedings, problems obtaining a travel document, or a moratorium on removals to that country because of war or serious civil conflict. As of 31 March 2004 there were 145 unexecuted removal orders, down from the previous year's cumulative total of 183.[112]

Cases (Application of Article 1(F) of the Refugee Convention)

- *Abbas* case, IMM-6488-02, 9 January 2004 (Federal Court Trial Division)
- *Mukumba* case, IMM-3088-03, 22 January 2004 (FCTD)
- *Alwan* case, IMM-8204-03, 2 June 2004 (FCTD)
- *Omar* case (Djama), IMM-2452-03, 17 June 2004 (FCTD)
- *Saftarov* case, IMM-4718-03, 21 July 2004 (FCTD)

The Federal Court issued five judgments in 2003 in which decisions of the Refugee Protection Division of the Immigration and Refugee Board pertaining to the exclusion clause 1F (a) (crimes against peace, war crimes and crimes against humanity) of the Refugee Convention were examined as part of judicial review proceedings. This number is significantly down from previous years, most likely because of the fact that cases are refused leave to be heard since they do not disclose a serious legal issue as a result of the well established exclusion case law in Canada. All cases dealt with the parameters of complicity[113] of persons involved in crimes against humanity and covered situations in places as varied as Iraq, the Republic of the Congo, Lebanon, Djibouti and Azerbaijan.

In the *Mukumba* case, the court upheld a decision of the Refugee Protection Division (RPD) – the successor of the Convention Refugee Determination Division (CRDD), a division of the Immigration and Refugee Board), since 28 July 2002 – to exclude a person who

112. Ibid.

113. See 3 *YIHL* (2000) p. 443 for an overview of the case law in this area.

worked for the CSE (Comité de Securité de l'Etat) in the Republic of Congo in the late 1990s. Her job involved listening incognito to conversations of individuals in public places and reporting back to the CSE on their opinions. The court was of the view that factually the activities of the CSE amounted to crimes against humanity. The CSE was described as one of the institutions responsible for the arrest and detention of political opponents and journalists. Once arrested, the evidence suggested, individuals are routinely beaten and tortured and many are tried and executed without due process. The court also found that the activities of the claimant amounted to complicity.

The *Alwan* case was another example of the trend in the Federal case law to find persons with an association with the South Lebanese Army (SLA) guilty of crimes against humanity;[114] in this case, the person was an informer for the SLA.

In the case of *Saftarov*, the Federal Court Trial Division overruled the RPD decision to exclude a person who was a member of the police force in the city of Baku based on the grounds that the police in Azerbaijan and in Baku were known to be responsible for serious violations of human rights, although there was no information that *Saftarov* himself participated in them. The court was of the view that there was no evidence that the claimant was a knowing participant in crimes against humanity. Since the RPD concluded that the Baku police was not a limited, brutal purpose organisation in which mere membership could lead to complicity, exclusion based on his long-time low-ranking membership in the police was found not to be sufficient. Some evidence of knowing participation is required.

The *Abbas* and *Omar* cases raise the issue of imputing complicity to high officials who have no direct part in decision making with respect to human rights violations. It is clear that the inspiration for this type of complicity comes from the unique provision in the Immigration and Refugee Protection Act (IRPA) whereby senior officials of a regime involved in atrocities are deemed to be inadmissible.[115] However, that provision has a safeguard that before a person can be found to be a senior official in a certain regime that regime first has to be designated by the Minister of Citizenship and Immigration (usually in consultation with Foreign Affairs Canada).[116] Unless a person from such a regime enters the refugee

---

114. See 6 *YIHL* (2003) pp. 475-476 for an overview of the case law in this area.

115. Section 35(1)(b) of *IRPA* in combination with IRPA Regulation 16, which deems ambassadors and other senior diplomats, among other functionaries, to be senior officials.

116. As a result of the government reorganisation in December 2003, the designation of regimes was transferred from the Minister of Citizenship and Immigration to the Minister of Public Safety and Emergency Preparedness Canada. Nine regimes have been designated since 1993, namely:
– the Bosnian Serb regime from 27 March 1992 until 10 October 1996: designated 16 June 1993;
– the Siad Barré regime in Somalia between 1969 and 1991: designated 12 October 1993;
– the former military governments in Haiti between 1971 and 1986 and between 1991 and 1994, except the period August - December 1993: designated 8 April 1994;
– the former Marxist regimes of Afghanistan between 1978 and 1992: designated 21 October 1994;
– the governments of Ahmed Hassan Al-Bakr and Saddam Hussein in power since 1968: designated 3 September 1996;
– the government of Rwanda under President Habyarimana between October 1990 and April 1994, as well as the interim government in power between April 1994 and July 1994: designated 27 April 1998;
– the governments of the Federal Republic of Yugoslavia and the Republic of Serbia (Milosevic) between 28 February 1998, and 7 October 2000: designated 30 June 1999, amended 14 March 2001;
– the Taliban regime in Afghanistan from 27 September 1996: designated 14 March 2001;
– the government of Ethiopia under Mengistu Haile Mariam for the period of 12 September 1974 to 21 May 1991; designated 21 November 2003.

stream, as was the case with Abbas – who had been a diplomat in the Saddam Hussein government – or unless there is overwhelming evidence that would allow a finding that an entire government can be considered a brutal regime,[117] such a transposition from a finely calibrated provision in the immigration context into the refugee sphere should be used with caution.[118]

As a starting point, it should be remembered that the Federal Court of Appeal had already made a statement with respect to complicity of senior functionaries in an organisation in the *Sivakumar* decision of November 1993, where it found that 'the closer one is to a position of leadership or command within an organization, the easier it will be to draw an inference of awareness of the crimes and participation in the plan to commit the crimes'.[119]

The *Imama* case[120] built on this statement in exclusion law by finding that a person is complicit if that person holds a high position in a government which is involved in violations of human rights and that person is aware of such government action. Mr Imama had been a senior diplomat and senior official in the Mobutu regime of Zaire between 1963 and 1998, during which time the regime was involved in widespread deliberate human rights violations; Mr Imama had acknowledged during his asylum hearing before the CRDD that he knew that such activities took place while he was in the government. While no mention was made of this by the judge, the CRDD relied on the inadmissibility provisions of section 19(1)(l) of the Immigration Act (now section 35(1)(b) of IRPA) to come to a decision to exclude for 1F(a) related activities.

The situation of complicity of government officials was addressed again a year later in the *Sungu* decision.[121] This case involved an individual who, between 1982 and 1987, served as a member of parliament or deputy of the Mobutu government, after which he worked as an analyst in the president's political strategy planning office until 1990, when he started a reform movement. In 1992 he left the Mobutu government. The court was of the view that while Mr Sungu was aware of the international crimes committed by the Mobutu government, neither this of itself nor his function were sufficient to impute complicity. Since the CRDD had made no finding that the Mobutu government was a brutal, limited purpose organisation, mere membership of that regime could not lead complicity and instead specific activities carried out by Mr Sungu which would show a common purpose with the regime needed to be established. The evidence showed the opposite, especially since Mr Sungu had started a reform movement. Incidentally, this case does refer to section 35(1)(b) of IRPA but in an unusual manner; this section was raised by Mr Sungu to argue that he should not be excluded since members of parliament were not mentioned in IRPA Regulation 16.

The next case dealing with senior officials is the *Abbas* case, decided in January 2004. Mr Abbas held positions of trust, including diplomatic posts (although this last fact is not mentioned in the decision), within the government of Saddam Hussein for 22 years, a government which in the view of the court had a brutal purpose based on the fact that the 'Iraqi regime under Saddam Hussein and the Baath party was founded on a forced arabisation policy which brought about the genocide of some ethnic communities in Iraq'. Mr Abbas

---

117. Such a finding had not been made in either the *Imama* or *Omar* cases.

118. See the *Aden* ([1994] 1 F.C. 625 (fn. 141) and *Wajid*, IMM-1706-99, 25 May 2000, cases for a similar approach.

119. [1994] 1 F.C. 433.

120. IMM-118-01, 6 November 2001.

121. IMM-1020-01, 22 November 2002.

was also aware of the crimes against humanity committed by the Hussein government and had never taken any measures to disengage himself from this regime. While this decision does not mention section 35(1)(b) of IRPA, it is worthwhile noting that the Saddam Hussein regime had been designated as a regime under that provision at the time that this case was decided.

The last case in this area is the *Omar* case, decided on 17 June 2004. The RPD's decision to exclude an individual who was a former ambassador of the Djibouti government at a time when this government was involved in crimes against humanity was upheld by the court based on the traditional jurisprudence of the Federal Court, while also relying on the cases of *Sivakumar* and *Sungu* for jurisprudence involving officials occupying high positions in a repressive regime. It is not clear from the juxtaposition of the conclusion and the case law whether this conclusion was based on the reasoning in *Abbas*, where the Saddam Hussein regime was considered a brutal organisation, or on the *Imama* case, which derived its conclusion from analogous reasoning to the immigration-designated regime approach, since neither case was mentioned in the decision.

Cases (Application of section 35(1)(a) of the Immigration and Refugee Protection Act)
☛ *Zazai* case, IMM-377-02, 1 October 2004 (Federal Court, Trial Division)

Mr Zazai had served as a member of the 5th Directorate of the KHAD in Afghanistan which, according to the documents before the CRDD, was a 'secret intelligence organization with the purpose of eliminating anti-government activity, and which engaged in crimes, which could be characterized as crimes against humanity'. As a result, the CRDD had found that he fell within Article 1F(a) of the Refugee Convention and was not entitled to refugee status. Subsequently, he applied for immigrant status in Canada but became the subject of an immigration hearing and a deportation order based on another provision, section 35(1)(a) of the Immigration and Refugee Protection Act (IRPA), which makes immigrants inadmissible if they are suspected of involvement in genocide, war crimes and crimes against humanity. Unlike the exclusion provision for asylum seekers, which makes a direct connection between exclusion and international criminal law, the IRPA makes this connection in an indirect fashion by referring to the criminal statute which regulates this area of international law, the Crimes against Humanity and War Crimes Act,[122] which in turn refers to international criminal law. This statute states in section 6(1.1): 'Every person who conspires or attempts to commit, is an accessory after the fact in relation to, or counsels in relation to, an offence referred to in subsection (1) is guilty of an indictable offence.' Mr Zazai argued that since this provision does not make a reference to complicity or aiding and abetting, section 35(1)(a) of *IRPA* had dispensed with the notion of complicity, as a result of which a finding of complicity in the exclusion context cannot be carried over to the immigration context, meaning that Mr Zazai should be allowed to stay in Canada.

This argument was rejected by the court for two reasons. The first one was based on legislative interpretation:

> 'In my view, it is inconceivable that Parliament intended to exclude an individual who – but for the existence of serious grounds for considering that the individual had committed international crimes – may otherwise be entitled to Convention refugee status

122. <http://laws.justice.gc.ca/en/C-45.9/index.html>.

> and, in the same breath, permit that individual to apply for and be granted permanent resident status – notwithstanding the inadmissibility provision – on the basis that the jurisprudence in relation to the exclusion provision does not apply to the inadmissibility provision. Despite their different purposes, it defies logic that one provision could collide so incongruously with the other.'[123]

Secondly, the judge pointed out that the offences set out in section 6(1.1) which are inchoate offences, are not modalities of other offences such as aiding and abetting but offences in their own right and for that reason needed to be regulated specifically in a statute which regulates criminal offences outside the general Criminal Code of Canada.[124] The relationship between special criminal statutes and the Criminal Code, including the notion of parties to an offence, is set out, according to the judgment, in the Interpretation Act.[125] The case is under appeal to the Federal Court of Appeal.

Apart from the *Zazai* case, inchoate offences as related to genocide, war crimes or crimes against humanity have not been considered in Canadian law as of yet, unlike in international criminal law. The inchoate offences of conspiracy, attempt and incitement have received different treatments depending on the type of substantive offence. Conspiracy, incitement and attempt can only occur in relation to the crime of genocide, according to the ICTY and ICTR Statutes,[126] while the ICC Statutes extends the notion of attempt to all three crimes, retains incitement for genocide only and does not mention conspiracy at all.

Cases (hostage-taking)
- *Ribić* case, Decision of the Federal Government, 1 April 2004
- *Ribić* case, Decision of the Ontario Superior Court of Justice, 16 June 2004[127]

On 1 April 2004, the Federal government laid new charges against Nicholas Nikola Ribić, the Canadian of Serb descent who, while a member of the Bosnian Serb Army during the Bosnia war, took a fellow Canadian hostage and threatened to use him as a human shield.[128] A few days later, Ribić applied to stay the proceedings on the basis that there has been an unreasonable delay in bringing him to trial, as charges were first laid on 17 February 1999. This motion was denied by the Ontario Superior Court of Justice on 16 June 2004. In determining the balancing factors inherent in the right of the accused to a speedy trial, the judge was of the view that a delay of five years between laying charges and starting a trial which would normally have been sufficient to grant the motion was outweighed in this case as a result of national and international considerations:

---

123. Para. 43 of the decision.
124. Para. 48.
125. Section 34(2) of the *Interpretation Act*; see para. 47 of the judgement.
126. Arts. 4.3(b),(c) and (d) and 2.3(b), (c) and (d), respectively. The Decision on Dragoljub Ojdanić's Motion Challenging Jurisdiction – *Joint Criminal Enterprise*' (Appeals Chamber, 21 May 2003) in the *Milutinović et al* case (Case No. IT-99-37-AR72) indicates that conspiracy might not be necessarily be excluded from the ICTY Statute.
127. Court file Number: 99-G10018.
128. For earlier developments in the case see 3 *YIHL* (2000) pp. 445-446; 5 *YIHL* (2002) p. 466; *6 YIHL* (2003) pp. 477-478.

'Although no one died as a direct result of the alleged hostage-taking, the threat or risk of death was very real. Such an offence strikes at the core of the safety and security of United Nations personnel in every outbreak of hostilities into which they are sent. The taking hostage of United Nations personnel, unarmed ones at that, strikes at the very heart of the capacity of this international body to be effective in intervening and bringing about, enforcing and maintaining peace in the world's war zones. In a figurative sense I think it can be said that the eyes of the community of nations are on this case and on Canada's capacity to bring it to trial. Canada's armed forces including Captain Rechner, who participate in United Nations peace-making and peace-keeping efforts around the globe, and the armed forces of the Czech Republic, from whose ranks Captain Zidlik came, and the armed services of all of the member states of the United Nations have a very real interest in trial of this case and in its outcome because of the its potential implications for United Nations forces deployed in war zones in future times.'

Cases (torture/civil remedies)

- *Bouzari* case, Decision of Ontario Court of Appeal, 30 June 2004[129]

The decision, denying Bouzari's appeal, agreed with the first instance judge both in analysis and result.[130] The Supreme Court of Canada denied leave to appeal on 28 January 2005.

JOSEPH RIKHOF

CHILE[131]

Cases

- Appeals and Supreme Courts, 5 January and 17 November 2004, regarding the conviction of two military officers, Miguel Krassnoff and Fernando Lauriani, with regard to the kidnapping and/or forced disappearance of Miguel Ángel Sandoval

On 5 January 2004 Santiago's Court of Appeals, with a divided verdict, rejected an annulment recourse (Recurso de Casación) pleaded by two former Chilean military officers, Miguel Krassnoff and Fernando Lauriani, against a sentence of that same Court of Appeals, which convicted the first plaintiff as an author of grave kidnapping against Miguel Ángel Sandoval, and the second as an accomplice of the same offence against Mr Sandoval.

The decision considered as an important part of its justification strong arguments of international humanitarian law and its prevalence beyond national legislation, as it is granted constitutional rank in Article 5(2) of the Chilean Constitution, which provides for the legal supremacy of international humanitarian law treaties.

It is significant that the judgment of the court determined that the kidnapping, which is a continuing crime (an offence considered by Art. 141 of the Chilean Criminal Code), is also classified as a crime in Article II of the Inter-American Convention on Forced Disappearances, signed on 9 June 1994, in Belem de Pará, Brazil and which entered into force on 29

129. Court File Number: C38295.

130. For the earlier decision of the Ontario Superior Court of Justice see 6 *YIHL* (2003) p. 478.

131. Information and commentaries by Hernan Salinas Burgos, Professor of Public International Law, Catholic University of Chile.

March 1996, despite the fact that the Convention had not yet been been ratified by Chile. As of the date of this award, the Convention was before the Chilean Congress.

This sentence establishes that, in fact, Article II of the aforementioned statute declares that for the purposes of this convention, 'a forced disappearance is considered to be the act of depriving a person or persons of his or their freedom, in whatever way, perpetrated by agents of the state or by persons or groups of persons acting with the authorization, support, or acquiescence of the state, followed by an absence of information or a refusal to acknowledge that deprivation of freedom or to give information on the whereabouts of that person, thereby impeding his or her recourse to the applicable legal remedies and procedural guarantees'.

The court said that Article III provides for the extreme gravity of this offence and its continuous or permanent character as long as the fate or whereabouts of the victim has not been determined. Chile, being a signatory of that Convention if not yet a party, is obligated, under Article 18 of the Vienna Convention on the Law of the Treaties – an instrument that has already been incorporated to the Chilean legal system – not to frustrate the object and purpose of any convention signed but not enacted. In consequence, if the situation described by the said Article II was left unpunished in Chile, it would constitute such a breach. Furthermore, the presidential message included in the bill sent to congress in order to approve this convention stated that 'the practice of forced disappearances of persons constitutes one of the worst violations to human rights ever imaginable and that this Convention, will support the political will of the American continent in order to completely eradicate such an abominable way of violation of the human dignity'.[132]

On 17 November 2004 the Supreme Court rejected a second petition against the Court of Appeals decision of 5 January, stating that it could not proceed, because the reference to the Inter-American Convention on Forced Disappearances was intended only as an illustration of the crimes committed by the plaintiffs, who were ultimately convicted under Article 141 of the Chilean Criminal Code.

HERNAN SALINAS BURGOS

COLOMBIA[133]

The Emblem

- Law No. 875 of 2 January 2004 'by means of which is regulated the use of the Red Cross emblem and the Red Crescent and other emblems' [Ley 875 de 2004 (enero 2) 'por la cual se regula el uso del emblema de la Cruz Roja y de la Media Luna Roja y otros emblemas']. Published in *Diario Oficial* (D.O.) No. 45418 of 2 January 2004, p. 12
- Implemented by Decree No. 138 of 25 January 2005 implementing Law No. 875 of 2 January 2004 [por el cual se reglamentan los artículos 5º, 6º, 14 y 18 de la Ley 875 de 2004 y se dictan otras disposiciones]. Published in *D.O.* No. 45804 of 27 January 2005, p. 42
- Ministerial Bulletin No. 072 of September 2004

132. Translated from the Spanish by the authors.

133. Information and commentaries by Rafael A. Prieto Sanjuán, Professor of Public International Law at Pontifical Xaverian University and Andes University of Bogotá.

Thanks to a combined effort of the Presidency of the Republic, the Ministry of Defence, the ICCR, the Colombian Red Cross and the Ministry of Social Protection, Decree 138/2005 was adopted which implements Law 875/2004 concerning the use of the Red Cross emblem by humanitarian (civil and military) personnel.

The law recognises that respect for the emblem and those it protects is an international right of humanitarian personnel but moreover an obligation of the parties. This is because the non-international armed conflict in Colombia has always affected medical missions using the Red Cross emblem. In particular, non-state or irregular actors have attacked ambulances or hospitals where they presume their adversary to be. Indeed, humanitarian personnel qualify as one of the eight 'risk groups' identified by the government. According to the Ministry of Social Protection, 46 attacks were registered against medical missions in 2004, which resulted in 43 victims. Such attacks may force humanitarian personnel to abandon their work, with a resulting reduction in the accessibility to health services of the civilian population.[134] Such attacks are grave breaches of humanitarian law.

As part of the National Health Programme, the Ministry of Social Protection, with the support of the Pan-American Health Organisation, constantly updates the information regarding violations of IHL involving medical missions. For 2004 it developed a new methodology for disseminating IHL norms concerning health and medical services in times of armed conflict. In an effort to disseminate and to promote respect for the emblem, on 3 December 2004, the third National Day for respect of the Medical Mission in Colombia was celebrated. In the same vein, with the support of the World Health Organization (WHO), 10,000 copies of the new *Manual of Protection to the Medical Mission* were published and distributed. Furthermore, pursuant to Ministerial Bulletin No. 072 of September 2004, an authorisation format for the use of the Emblem was disseminated as well as the format to record infractions of its use. Finally, it must be noted that all this work has been undertaken pursuant to Resolution No. 13 of the 55th World Health Assembly, concerning 'Protection of medical missions during armed conflict',[135] which was promoted by Colombia.

The Peace Process

- Decree No. 2767 of 31 August 2004 'by means of which is set down the Law 418 of 1997, prorogued and modified by Law 548 of 1999 and Law 782 de 2002 in matter of reintegration to civil life [por el cual se reglamenta la Ley 418 de 1997, prorrogada y modificada por la Ley 548 de 1999 y la Ley 782 de 2002 en materia de reincorporación a la vida civil]. Published in *D.O.* No. 45657 of 31 August 2004, p. 43

In 2004 the government engaged in peace negotiations with paramilitary groups. An initial result of this process was the first demobilisation in late 2004 of approximately 3,000 members of the Cacique Nutibara and a discreet OAS-monitored ceasefire.[136] But the demobili-

---

134. Republic of Colombia. Vice-presidency, Presidential Programme on HR and IHL. *Informe Anual de Derechos Humanos, 2004*, p.19.

135. Doc. WHA55.13, Ninth plenary meeting, 18 May 2002 – Committee A, second report.

136. In February 2004 the Government entered into an agreement with the Organization of American States (OAS) regarding the opening of a mission to support the peace process in Colombia (MAPP-OEA), with the principal tasks of verifying eventual agreements between the government and the illegal armed groups relating to a ceasefire, their demobilisation and their reintegration into society, in accordance 'with the obligations of its Member States with respect to fully comply with

sation process was faulted for its lack of legal framework and insufficient safeguards and for failing to ensure that paramilitaries responsible for the commission of crimes are brought to justice.

A draft bill initially proposed by the administration of President Alvaro Uribe in 2003 was modified by a new version proposed in April 2004, which had not yet been passed as the year closed. Thus, the legal framework for regulating the demobilisation of the paramilitaries in 2004 continued to be the so-called Public Order Law (Law 782 of 2002). The only improvement in 2004 was Decree 2761 concerning some economic benefits in case of individual and voluntary demobilisation or by virtue of delivering information and war material.

In the meantime, most of the negotiation attempts with the guerrilla groups (ELN and FARC) were unsuccessful; in particular, it was very difficult to secure a 'humanitarian exchange' in order to liberate the persons kidnapped by these groups, despite the good offices of representatives of the Catholic Church and states like Mexico and France. On the contrary, those groups continued their hostile activities. The Colombian Armed Forces was hardly able to develop the 'Patriot Plan' against the guerrillas[137] in the south of the country with the technical and economic support of the US. Repeated statements by high-level officials denied the existence of the armed conflict and referred to Colombia as just having a 'terrorist threat'.

Criminal Law

- Law No. 906 of 31 August 2004 by which is issued the criminal procedural code [*Ley 906 de 2004 (agosto 31) por la cual se expide el código de procedimiento penal*]. Published in *D.O.* no. 45658 of 1 September 2004, p. 1

As part of the Project of Fight against Impunity, headed by the Human Rights and IHL Presidential Programme and supported by the Dutch Government,[138] the so-called Inter-institutional Administration and Coordination System [*Sistema de Gestión y Coordinación Interinstitucional*] was created. It establishes a Special Committee of Impulse to the Investigations [*Comité Especial de Impulso a las Investigaciones*], which works from two main directions: on one side is the Prosecutor's Office, with responsibility for criminal prosecution, and on the other side is the Attorney's Office or Public Ministry, which is charged with disciplinary investigations of officials and guaranteeing the rule of law.

Certain positive actions in the struggle against impunity by the Special Committee on the investigation of human rights violations and breaches of international humanitarian law can be noted, mainly through judicial procedures leading to arrests and indictments. Nevertheless, major measures and greater commitment, sustained over time, is required. For that

---

human rights and international humanitarian law'. See <http://www.oas.org/documents/eng/colombia.asp>.

137. On the Plan Patriot see R. Van Dongen, 'Plan puts Colombia on offensive', *The Christian Science Monitor*, 22 June 2004, <http://csmonitor.com/2004/0622/p06s02-woam.html>; R. Van Dongen, 'Quietly, the war on drugs gains ground', *The Christian Science Monitor*, 22 November 2004, <http://csmonitor.com/2004/1122/p01s02-woam.html>.

138. See description of the Project of Fight against Impunity, in the Agreement signed between Colombia and Netherlands's Governments, of July 2003, <http://www.derechoshumanos.gov.co/observatorio/tematico/impunidad.pdf>.

reason, the Congress approved Law No. 906 of 2004 adopting the new Criminal Procedure Code, which will progressively come into effect in 2005.

This law – implementing the oral and adversarial principles – responds to Constitutional Reform *(Acto Legislativo)* no. 003 of 2002 and a government initiative, which were publicly debated.

Fight against Impunity

- National General Prosecutor's Office, Resolution No. 4117 of 30 August 2004, 'By which it regulates the functions of the National General Prosecutor's Office in the Special Committee of Impulse to the investigations of human rights violations' [Fiscalía General de la Nación, Resolución No. 4117 del 30 de agosto de 2004, 'Mediante la cual se reglamentan las funciones de la Fiscalía General de la Nación en el Comité Especial de Impulso a las investigaciones de violaciones a los Derechos Humanos']. On file with author
- National General Attorney's Office, Resolution No. 327 of 24 August 2004, 'By which measures are implemented within the National General Attorney's Office, based on Presidential Decree No. 2429 of 1998, by means of which it was created the Special Committee of Impulse to the Investigations of Human Rights Violations' [Procuraduría General de la Nación, Resolución No. 327 del 24 de agosto de 2004, 'Por la cual se implementan las medidas al interior de la Procuraduría General de la Nación, con fundamento en el Decreto Presidencial No. 2429 de 1998, mediante el cual se creó el Comité Especial de Impulso a las investigaciones por violación de Derechos Humanos'] <websql.procuraduria.gov.co/relatoriaweb/Btipodocumento.htm>

RAFAEL PRIETO SANJUÁN

COSTA RICA

Implementation

- Decree creating a National Commission for International Humanitarian Law, adopted on 21 May 2004. Published on 4 November 2004, entered into force on the day of its publication[139]

DENMARK[140]

Military Penal Code

- Government Commission Report on the Military Penal Code, the Military Administration of Justice Code and the Military Disciplinary Code (report No. 1435, January 2004 <www.fmn.dk> (Danish version only; the report does not include a summary in English)

139. Source and for further information: National Implementation of International Humanitarian Law, Biannual update on national legislation and case law, July-December 2004, 87 *IRRC* (March 2005) pp. 222-223.

140. Information provided by Peter Otken, LL.M., Special Assistant for International & Operational Law to the Judge Advocate General, Copenhagen.

The Danish Military Penal Code and the Military Administration of Justice Code both date from 1973. As reported in Volume 3 of the Yearbook, in 1999 the Minister of Defence directed a commission to conduct a complete review of this legislation.[141] The report of the commission was published in January 2004 and included drafts for revised Military Penal and Military Administration of Justice Codes as well as a completely new Military Disciplinary Code.

The report included a description of the military penal legislation currently in force in Denmark (chapter 6-7). The commission stated that since the last review of Danish military penal legislation in 1973, the Danish Armed Forces have been providing military forces for international missions at an increasing rate. Such international service is generally characterised by situations where increased attention is necessary and by situations which may develop into direct military confrontation. Service and training in Denmark must take place under circumstances which enable military personnel to participate in international missions in the said situations. The majority of the commission (all members except one) thus proposed that provisions describing important military duties must be upheld and that the authorities must be able to sanction the violation of such duties during basic service and education in peacetime in Denmark (chapter 11, pp. 249-50). The commission also made reference to the obligation under international humanitarian law (e.g., Art. 43 of 1977 Additional Protocol I to the Geneva Conventions) to establish an internal disciplinary system for military forces and opined that this obligation already exists in peacetime (p. 251). However, the commission proposed a number of amendments to the existing legislation.

Concerning the applicability of certain rules only applicable during armed conflict, the commission proposed that the use of the word 'wartime' in the existing Military Penal Code be changed to 'armed conflict' in order to better resemble modern international law terminology (chapter 13, p. 285). The commission also proposed to uphold and amend the current provision banning violations of both conventional as well as customary international humanitarian law (pp. 286-290) and providing for penal sanctions.

The Government submitted all three proposals to Parliament in the autumn of 2004 but the proposals did not become law as a consequence of the general election in February 2005. It was expected that the proposals would become law following their resubmission to Parliament following the general election.

Jus ad Bellum

- Parliamentary hearing on the legality of the military intervention in Iraq in 2003, 24 March 2004

As a consequence of the public debate following the decision of the Danish government and parliament to contribute Danish military forces to the coalition intervening in Iraq in March 2003, a parliamentary hearing was held on 24 March 2004. Among the speakers was the Prime Minister, Mrs Anders Fogh Rasmussen, who stressed that the legal rationale for the government's decision to participate in the intervention was to be found in Saddam Hussein's non-compliance with UN Security Council resolutions. Christopher Greenwood, Professor of International Law at the London School of Economics, examined the legal basis for the use of force in Iraq and found it to be legally justified, based on an interpretation of a number of Security Council resolutions – among them 678, 687 and 1141 – passed

141. See 3 *YIHL* (2000) p. 470.

since the Iraqi invasion of Kuwait in August 1990. On the other hand, Jens Elo Rytter, Associate Professor at University of Copenhagen, expressed his doubts about this interpretation and submitted that the use of force in Iraq was in violation of international law because the Security Council could not be considered to have authorised the intervention.

Cases

- Trial of a Ugandan charged with murder in a non-international armed conflict. Judgement by the City Court of Aalborg, 27 May 2004 (Case SS No. 8.1209/2004. The judgement has not been made public)

A Ugandan refugee living in Denmark was charged with two counts of robbery of a specifically dangerous character, two counts of manslaughter and one count of illegal detention, all committed in 1995 in Uganda when he was the leader of an organisation called the National Democratic Alliance. The two murdered persons were a regional chief of police and a policeman, both killed with an axe, according to the indictment. One of two detained persons was the then-Ugandan Minister of Health. The defendant pleaded not guilty to the counts of robbery and manslaughter but pleaded guilty to the count of illegal detention. He did not contest that the conditions in common Article 3 of the Geneva Conventions and/or Additional Protocol II for considering the acts committed as part of a non-international armed conflict were met in the present case. Following medical examination, the defendant was found to be suffering from severe mental illness, likely to be schizophrenia. For that reason, the recommendation of the prosecution was not punishment but treatment at a mental hospital under supervision from the Danish Prison Authority.

During the investigation a number of witnesses had been questioned in a court outside Denmark, presumably in Uganda, but these witnesses were not questioned again by the Danish court. In general, the court accepted that the events described in the indictment had taken place and that they had been carried out by members of the National Democratic Alliance, of which the defendant was the leader. The question for the court was whether the defendant could be considered personally responsible for the said acts.

As the defendant pleaded guilty to the charge of illegal detention, the court found him guilty on this charge. Concerning the two counts of robbery, the court found him guilty after a careful examination of the statement submitted to the court by a witness questioned by another jurisdiction. Concerning the two counts of manslaughter, the court did not find it proven beyond reasonable doubt that the defendant had committed the murders and the defendant was acquitted on both counts. The court expressed doubt as to the validity of the statements by some of the witnesses heard outside Denmark. A major reason appears to have been the fact that one of the witnesses had been questioned as a suspect by the Ugandan police at the time of the killings and said that he was beaten during this questioning. However, he had later been acquitted for participation in the manslaughter. Nevertheless, the City Court of Aalborg found that the circumstances concerning the original questioning and the witness' possible interest then as well as now in connecting the defendant with the murders affected the credibility of his statement.

The court must be commended for taking a careful approach when examining the statements of witnesses not heard directly by the court. On the other hand, the case shows the difficulties – generic to both national and international prosecutions – of bringing persons responsible for international atrocities to court many years after and thousands of kilometres from where the events took place.

PETER OTKEN

FRANCE[142]

Mercenaries

- Law No. 2003-340 of 14 April 2003 on punishment of mercenaries' activities. Published in the Official Gazette of the French Republic [*Journal officiel de la République française*], No. 89, 15 April 2003, p. 6636

The Law introduces a new Chapter into the Criminal Code concerning participation in mercenary activities. These activities include taking part in an armed conflict or *coup* and are punishable by five years' imprisonment and a 75,000 euro fine. Recruiting and organising groups for recruiting, equipping and training of mercenaries is punishable by seven years' imprisonment and a 100,000 euro fine. French law applies even for activities conducted abroad. Companies are also criminally responsible for recruiting activities.

The Law was first discussed and adopted by the Senate on 5 February 2003 (Bill No. 287 [2001-2002]; Report by Mr. Michel Pelchat, in the name of the Commission for Foreign Affairs) and then by the National Assembly on 3 April 2003 (Bill, as adopted by the Senate, No. 607; Report of Mr Marc Joulaud, in the name of the Defence Commission, No. 671).

Torture

- National Advisory Commission on Human Rights. Opinion on France's third periodic report to the United Nations Committee against Torture [Commission nationale consultative des droits de l'homme (CNCDH): Avis sur le troisième rapport périodique de la France au Comité des Nations Unies contre la torture]. Adopted on 22 January 2004

The National Advisory Commission's Opinion on France's third periodic report to the UN Committee against Torture noted that it was very pleased about its consultations with the government during the drafting process. It expressed its hope that France would soon ratify the 2002 Optional Protocol to the Convention against Torture and other Cruel, Inhuman or Degrading Treatment or Punishment. It regretted that the report was a purely technical one and failed to mention what is at stake, politically, legally and ethically in French society as far as the crime of torture is concerned. It recommended that special attention be paid to places like prisons and detention zones and to the training of personnel. It stressed the need to introduce in French law the crime against humanity of torture and the war crime of torture.

- National Advisory Commission on Human Rights. Opinion on the 2002 Optional Protocol to the United Nations Convention against Torture [Commission nationale consultative des droits de l'homme (CNCDH): Avis relatif au Protocole facultatif à la Convention des Nations Unies contre la torture]. Adopted 17 June 2004

This Opinion followed from the previous one (see above). It recommended that France sign the Optional Protocol to the Torture Convention as soon as possible and undertake the preparations for the creation and installation of an independent national body and mechanism, as foreseen in Article 18(4) of the Protocol. The existence of the European Committee for

142. Information and commentaries provided by Professor Paul Tavernier, Professor Paris-Sud University, Director, Centre de Recherches et d'Etudes sur les droits de l'Homme et le droit humanitaire (CREDHO).

the Prevention of Torture (ECPT) must not be considered as an excuse for delaying the creation of a national mechanism, as both national and international mechanism are complementary. France will have to campaign against torture and cruel, inhuman or degrading treatment or punishment, especially in the framework of the Organisation of Francophone States (Francophonie). Finally, it stated that the prohibition of torture is absolute, even in the fight against terrorism in time of war or of international crises.

Crimes against Internationally Protected Persons

- Law No. 2003-556 of 26 June 2003 authorising adhesion to the Convention on the Prevention and Punishment of Crimes against Internationally Protected Persons, including Diplomatic Agents [Loi no. 2003-556 du 26 juin 2003 autorisant l'adhésion à la convention sur la prévention et la répression des infractions contre les personnes jouissant d'une protection internationale, y compris les agents diplomatiques]. Published in the Official Gazette of the French Republic [*Journal officiel de la République française*] n° 147, 27 June 2003, p. 10792
- Decree No. 2003-974 of 8 October 2003 publishing the Convention on the Prevention and Punishment of Crimes against Internationally Protected Persons, including Diplomatic Agents [décret no. 2003-974 du 8 octobre 2003 portant publication de la convention sur la prévention et la répression des infractions contre les personnes jouissant d'une protection internationale, y compris les agents diplomatiques]. Published in the Official Gazette of the French Republic [*Journal officiel de la République française*] n° 240, 16 October 2003, p. 17597

The Convention on the Prevention and Punishment of Crimes against Internationally Protected Persons, including Diplomatic Agents, was adopted in New York on 14 December 1973 and came into force on 20 February 1977 (25 September 2003 for France, after her accession). Article 3 provides for application of the principle *aut dedere aut persequi* and for universal jurisdiction. France does not exercise universal jurisdiction without a convention or law clause, hence the need for the adoption of this law and decree implementing the Convention in French law. France's accession to the Convention should be seen in the context of post-11 September priorities and the fight against terrorism.

International Criminal Tribunals

- Decree No. 2004-267 of 23 March 2004 publishing the Agreement between the Government of the French Republic and the United Nations Organisation concerning the accomplishment of punishment decided by the International Tribunal for the former Yugoslavia [Décret no. 2004-267 du 23 mars 2004 portant publication de l'accord entre le Gouvernement de la République française et l'Organisation des Nations unies concernant l'exécution des peines prononcées par le Tribunal pénal international pour l'ex-Yougoslavie]. Published in the *Official* Gazette of the French Republic [*Journal officiel de la République française*] No. 73 of 26 March 2004, p. 5778

The Agreement was signed in The Hague on 25 February 2000 and came into force on 21 October 2003.

- Law No. 2004-495 of 7 June 2004 authorising approval of the Agreement between the Government of the French Republic and the United Nations Organisation concerning the accomplishment of punishment decided by the International Crimminal Tribunal for

Rwanda [Loi no. 2004-495 du 7 juin 2004 autorisant l'approbation de l'accord entre le Gouvernement de la République française et l'Organisation des Nations unies concernant l'exécution des peines prononcées par le Tribunal pénal international pour le Rwanda]. Published in the Official Gazette of the French Republic [*Journal officiel de la République française*] No. 131 of 8 June 2004, p. 10113

The Agreement was signed in Arusha (Tanzania) on 14 March 2003 and came into force on 25 June 2004; publication in the Official Gazette of the French Republic would follow. This Agreement is similar to the Agreement concerning the International Criminal Tribunal for former Yugoslavia (see *supra*). Similar Agreements have been concluded with Mali, Benin and Swaziland and more recently with Italy (March 2004) and Sweden (April 2004).

The Bill was firstly discussed and adopted by the National Assembly on 6 January 2004 (Bill No. 1149; report of M. Christian Philip, in the name of the Commission for Foreign Affairs, No. 1296) and then by the Senate on 27 May 2004 (Bill No. 137, as adopted by the National Assembly [2003-2004]; report of Mrs Maryse Bergé-Lavigne, in the name of the Commission for Foreign Affairs, No. 220 [2003-2004]).

International Criminal Court

☛ National Advisory Commission on Human Rights. Opinion on International Criminal Court [Commission nationale consultative des droits de l'homme (CNCDH): Avis concernant la Cour pénale internationale]. Adopted 3 March 2003

In a letter sent to the Minister of Foreign Affairs, the President of the National Advisory Commission wrote that the Commission is satisfied with the election of Judge Claude Jorda as a judge of the International Criminal Court but is concerned about the procedure for submitting French candidates for election to international criminal courts and tribunals, referring to Article 36 of the Rome Statute. The President of the National Advisory Commission also recalled its previous opinion concerning the necessity to adopt a law introducing into French law the crimes provided for in the Rome Statute and to abandon the declaration made under Article 124 of the Rome Statute (transitional opt-out from Art. 8).

☛ National Advisory Commission on Human Rights. Opinion on the preliminary draft Bill adapting French legislation to the Statute of the International Criminal Court [Commission nationale consultative des droits de l'homme (CNCDH): Avis sur l'avant-projet de loi portant adaptation de la législation française au Statut de la Cour pénale internationale]. Adopted 15 May 2003

A preliminary draft Bill adapting French legislation to the Statute of the International Criminal was prepared by the Ministry of Justice and put before the National Advisory Commission.

In its opinion the Commission expressed its satisfaction that significant progress was reflected in the draft bill, especially concerning the specific inclusion of war crimes in French law, which indicates France's will to fulfill her international obligations. Nevertheless, the Commission regretted that the French government did not take the opportunity to include in a more comprehensive manner the punishment of grave breaches of the 1949 Geneva Conventions and Additional Protocol I, as well as war crimes committed during non-international armed conflicts.

The Commission also noted that the Bill does not implement Article 27 of the Rome Statute on the question of 'official capacity', and that there are *lacunae* in this respect. Moreover, some of the definitions contained in the Bill are not adequate or adapted to those included in the Rome Statute; the consequence would be some difficulty in applying the complementarity principle. The National Advisory Commission recalled that the Rome Treaty does not make any distinction between crimes categories, all of them being treated on the same legal footing, that is, equally serious international crimes giving rise to individual criminal responsibility. It profoundly regretted that the French Bill created a special legal régime for war crimes, including them in a separate Chapter of the Penal Code, different from the chapter dedicated to Genocide and Crimes against Humanity. As a result, prescription would be possible for war crimes and indeed some of them could be considered as minor offences ('délits'). The Commission also expressed its concern regarding the legal position of the victims. Under the Bill, only the Public Prosecutor could activate prosecution for crimes committed abroad. That is contrary to French policy, which favours victims in the ICC system. The Opinion also examined the clauses of the draft Bill in detail and proposed some amendments.

☛ Law No. 2003-1367 of 31 December 2003 authorising Approval of Agreement on Privileges and Immunities of the International Criminal Court [Loi no. 2003-1367 du 31 décembre 2003 autorisant l'approbation de l'accord sur les privilèges et immunités de la Cour pénale internationale]. Published in the Official Gazette of the French Republic [*Journal officiel de la République française*] No. 1 of 1 January 2004, p. 1515

☛ Decree No. 2004-707 of 13 July 2004 publishing the Agreement [Décret de publication no. 2004-707 du 13 juillet 2004]. Published in the Official Gazette of the French Republic [*Journal officiel de la République française*] No. 1 of 13 July 2004, p. 1515

ICRC

☛ Law No. 2003-475 of 4 June 2003 on privileges and immunities of the International Committee of the Red Cross delegation in France (Loi no. 2003-475 du 4 juin 2003 relative aux privilèges et immunités de la délégation du Comité international de la Croix-Rouge en France). Published in the Official Gazette of the French Republic [*Journal officiel de la République française*] no. 129 of 5 June 2003, p. 9561

The law is quite short and contains only one brief clause. Pursuant to this law, the International Committee of the Red Cross and its personnel will enjoy the same privileges and immunities in France as the United Nations Organisation and its personnel, except for salaries and wages, which will be subject to income tax. The law does not take up a position on the controversial question whether the ICRC is a true international organisation or an non-governmental organisation.

Humanitarian/Military Operations

☛ National Advisory Commission on Human Rights. Opinion on relations between humanitarian and military operations [Commission nationale consultative des droits de l'homme (CNCDH): Avis concernant des réflexions sur les relations humanitaires/militaires]. Adopted 8 December 2003

The National Advisory Commission expresses its concern about the Draft European Constitution, some clauses of that text being unclear or vague, in its view. It recalled that humanitarian operations must always be based on the recipient population's needs and conducted in conformity with principles of international humanitarian law, especially the principles of independence and impartiality. The relationship between politics, diplomacy and humanitarian action have to be clarified and any confusion between them must be avoided. The National Advisory Commission recalled that it had previously examined the sensitive question of the relationship between humanitarian and military personnel and the role of ECHO.

Cases (crimes against humanity)

☛ Mouvement contre le Racisme et pour l'Amitié entre les Peuples (MRAP) [Movement against Racism and for Friendship between Peoples; *Aussaresses* case], Cour de Cassation, Case No. 02-80719, 17 June 2003. Published in *Bulletin criminel* 2003 No. 122, p. 465

The MRAP (Movement against Racism and for Friendship between Peoples) is a 'partie civile' ('civil party') in the *Aussaresses* case, although the complaint was lodged against an unnamed person and General Aussaresses is not specifically mentioned in the court's decision. During the Algerian Independence War (1954-1962), this French General was involved in cases of torture and indeed admitted to personal involvement in both torture and summary execution in a recently published book.[143]

The French Cour de Cassation [Court of Cassation] dismissed the MRAP's claim in a short and concise decision. First of all, the Supreme Court recalled that the provisions of the 1964 Law on Imprescriptibility and of the Statute of the Nuremberg Military Tribunal which were invoked by the complainants are not applicable because these instruments only apply to crimes committed against the nationals of European Axis States. Furthermore, the court pointed out that Article 212(1) of the Criminal Code, introducing the crime against humanity into French law, only applies to crimes committed after 1 March 1994 and therefore could not apply in this case in accordance with the legality and non-retroactivity principles in criminal matters (Art. 8 of the French Bill of Rights of 1789, Art. 7(1) European Convention on Human Rights, Art. 15(1) International Covenant on Civil and Political Rights, Arts. 111(3) and 112(1) Criminal Code). Last but not least, international customary law could not fill the gap and serve as a solution for the lack of a legal provision in both national and international law. That point provokes disagreement amongst jurists.[144]

PAUL TAVERNIER

Pending Cases

☛ In November 2004 survivors (on behalf of 329 survivors and victims' relatives) of Srebrenica filed a lawsuit against the United Nations in a French court, alleging that UN troops abandoned the victims of the massacre. They are demanding financial compensation for allegedly failing to prevent the atrocity from occurring, which according to the claimants, were under an international legal obligation to do so. Earlier in the year the

---

143. P. Aussaresses, *The Battle of the Casbah: Terrorism and Counterterrorism in Algeria 1955-1957* (New York, Enigma Books 2002).

144. See J.-F. Roulot, 'Commentary', in *La semaine juridique*, edn. générale, No. 38, 2003-09-17, Jurisprudence, II, 10146, p. 1628-1632 and F. Poirat in *Revue générale de droit international Public* (2004) pp. 754-762.

claimants had proposed to the Dutch government an out-of-court settlement in the amount of 2 billion euros, but it was not settled. The case was filed in the Administrative Tribunal in Paris.

GERMANY[145]

Civilians Generally

- Statement by Federal Foreign Minister Joschka Fischer on the situation in the Sudan, Federal Foreign Office, Press Release, 24 April 2004 <http://www.auswaertiges-amt.de/www/en/ausgabe_archiv?archiv_id=5728>

On 24 April 2004 Federal Foreign Minister Fischer stated with regard to the situation in Darfur (Sudan):

> 'The humanitarian and human rights situation in the Darfur region in western Sudan is extremely worrying. Fighting between rebel groups and the Sudanese Government have apparently led to thousands of people losing their lives as well as brutal attacks on the civilian population and caused up to one million people, mainly women, children and the elderly, to flee their homes. Militia seem to have committed the most serious violations of human rights. (…) An urgent call goes out to the Sudanese Government to ensure that the militia attacks on the civilian population are halted immediately.'

- Statement by Ambassador Wolfgang Trautwein at the UN Security Council on Protection of Civilians in Armed Conflicts, Permanent Mission of Germany to the United Nation, Press Release, 14 June 2004 <http://www.germany-un.org/archive/speeches/2004/sp_06_14_04.html>

In a debate at the United Nations Security Council on 'Protection of Civilians in Armed Conflict', the German representative stressed that:

> 'combatants violating the principles of humanitarian law, be it by acts directed against civilians or against humanitarian personnel, need to know that they are acting against fundamental principles of humanity and their acts eventually will come under the judicial scrutiny of the ICC or a regional tribunal. (…) Perpetrators of serious crimes against civilians must be brought to justice. (…) National sovereignty can and should not be an excuse when thousands of innocent, vulnerable civilians are threatened.'

- German Explanation of Vote on the occasion of the adoption of UN Security Council Resolution 1556 regarding the situation in the Sudan, Permanent Mission of Germany to the United Nations, Press Release, 30 July 2004 <http://www.germany-un.org/archive/press/2004/pr_07_30_04.html>

---

145. Information and commentaries provided by Gregor Schotten, Desk Officer in the Political Department of the Federal Foreign Office, Berlin. The views expressed in these commentaries are those of the author alone.

Germany made an explanation of vote on the occasion of the adoption of UN Security Council Resolution 1556 regarding Sudan. It stated, *inter alia*:

> 'The Government of Sudan must now act rapidly and decisively for the sake of its very own population, which it has the obligation – as the Secretary-General rightly put it: the "sacred obligation" –to protect. Otherwise, paragraph 6 of the resolution would apply, and further Council deliberations may lead to the imposition of sanctions. (…) Our goal is to stop the suffering and killing of innocent civilians. We expect all parties, the rebel side as much as the Government of Sudan, to fulfill their obligations.'

☛ Statement by Ambassador Dr Gunter Pleuger at the Security Council's Open Debate on the Protection of Civilians in Armed Conflict, Permanent Mission of Germany to the United Nation, Press Release, 14 December 2004 <http://www.germany-un.org/archive/speeches/2004/sp_12_14_04.html>

In the December debate of the UN Security Council on the protection of civilians in armed conflict, the German representative emphasised that:

> 'the protection of civilians in armed conflict is one of the priorities in the Millennium Declaration, citing the need to expand and strengthen the protection of civilians in complex emergencies and crises in conformity with international humanitarian law. (…) Impunity is one of the worst root causes of the violation of the integrity of civilians. Parties to armed conflict need to comply with international humanitarian law, in particular the four Geneva Conventions and its two additional protocols. (…) Combatants who violate the principles of humanitarian law, be it by acts directed against the civilian population or against humanitarian personnel, need to know that they are acting against fundamental principles of humanity and that their acts eventually will come under the close scrutiny of the ICC or a regional tribunal.'

Women

☛ Statement by Ambassador Wolfgang Trautwein at the UN Security Council's Debate on Resolution 1325, Permanent Mission of Germany to the United Nations, Press Release, 28 October 2004 <http://www.germany-un.org/archive/speeches/2004/sp_10_28_04.html>

In the UN Security Council's debate on resolution 1325 the German representative underlined that:

> 'violence against women is an issue of utmost priority because of its human, political, social and economic dimensions. (…) We strongly believe in the need for accountability for war-time violence against women and in the necessity to end impunity. (…) The ICC certainly has a key role to play with regard to the investigation and prosecution of gender-based crimes. However, its efforts must be supplemented by national legal mechanisms.'

☛ Statement by Ambassador Dr Gunter Pleuger at the Security Council's Open Debate on the Protection of Civilians in Armed Conflict, Permanent Mission of Germany to the

United Nation, Press Release, 14 December 2004 <http://www.germany-un.org/archive/speeches/2004/sp_12_14_04.html>

In the December debate of the UN Security Council on the protection of civilians in armed conflict, the German representative stated that:

> 'the importance of reversing the strengthening cycle of violence against women and children during and after conflict cannot be overstated. (...) Women and children are also to an unprecedented extent victims of atrocious sexual violence. Worse still, sexual or gender violence is intentionally and systematically used as weapon of warfare. We must undertake special efforts and study this phenomenon as diligently as possible to come to a swift determination on how to stop this practice.'

Refugees

☛ Statement by Federal Foreign Minister Fischer on the massacre in Gatumba refugee camp, Burundi, Federal Foreign Office, Press Release, 15 August 2005 <http://www.germany-info.org/relaunch/politics/news/pol_burundi_8_2004.html>

Against the backdrop of the massacre ina refugee camp in Gatumba, Burundi, in which by UN accounts, at least 160 people were killed, Federal Foreign Minister Fischer stated on August 15:

> 'The German Government condemns in the sharpest manner the barbaric massacre which occurred in a UNHCR refugee camp in Burundi. This abominable bloody deed must be vigorously investigated, the perpetrators brought to justice, and further assaults against refugees and the civilian population stopped. (...) The German Government urgently calls on the states in the region and all those responsible to work closely together with the United Nations to ensure a full investigation of the massacre and to guarantee the protection of the civilian population.'

War Crimes

☛ Statement by Federal Foreign Minister Joschka Fischer on the situation in the Sudan, Federal Foreign Office, Press Release, 24 April 2004 <http://www.auswaertiges-amt.de/www/en/ausgabe_archiv?archiv_id=5728>

In his statement on the situation in Sudan (Darfur), the German Foreign Minister stressed that 'the perpetrators of these most serious violations of human rights have to be prosecuted with the full force of the law. Ten years after the genocide in Rwanda everything has to be done to prevent genocide, rapes and expulsions from happening again.'

☛ Speech by the Minister of State at the Federal Foreign Office, Kerstin Müller, at the Stockholm International Forum on Preventing Genocide, 26 January 2004, Federal Foreign Office, Press Release, 26 January 2004 <http://www.auswaertiges-amt.de/www/en/archiv_print?archiv_id=5310>

Humanitarian Assistance

☛ Statement by Ambassador Wolfgang Trautwein at the UN Security Council on Protection of Civilians in Armed Conflicts, Permanent Mission of Germany to the United

Nation, Press Release, 14 June 2004 <http://www.germany-un.org/archive/speeches/2004/sp_06_14_04.html>

At the UN Security Council, the German representative stated: 'Germany supported the efforts aimed at enlarging the scope of protection of the Convention on the Safety of United Nations and Associated Personnel. Measures taken to ensure sufficient security for humanitarian personnel would lead to better humanitarian access and thus to a better protection of civilians.'

- German Explanation of Vote on the occasion of the adoption of UN Security Council Resolution 1556 regarding the situation in the Sudan, Permanent Mission of Germany to the United Nations, Press Release, 30 July 2004 <http://www.germany-un.org/archive/press/2004/pr_07_30_04.html>

The explanation stresses that 'we hold the Government of Sudan responsible for the security of all 1.5 million people at risk in Darfur and for the unhindered delivery of humanitarian aid'.

Peacekeeping

- Statement by Ambassador Wolfgang Trautwein at the UN Security Council on Protection of Civilians in Armed Conflicts, Permanent Mission of Germany to the United Nation, Press Release, 14 June 2004 <http://www.germany-un.org/archive/speeches/2004/sp_06_14_04.html>

The German representative emphasised that:

> 'We have to seek protection of civilians from exploitation by peacekeepers. As the members of UN peace keeping missions do not fall under UN jurisdiction, we must find a way to ensure that every country that provides peace keepers establishes and applies its own laws that peace keepers who commit crimes against the local population are to be sued and convicted. It is not acceptable if there were pockets of impunity left for UN peace keepers.'

Explosive Remnants of War

- Ratification by Germany of the Protocol on Explosive Remnants of War, Federal Foreign Office, Press Release, 4 March 2005 <http://www.auswaertiges-amt.de/www/en/ausgabe_archiv?archiv_id=6952>

On 4 March 2005 Germany became the fifth state to deposit, with the UN Secretary General, its Instrument of Acceptance to the Protocol on Explosive Remnants of War (Protocol V to the 1980 Convention on Certain Conventional Weapons).

Human rights in armed conflict

- Speech by Federal Foreign Minister Joschka Fischer at the UN Commission on Human Rights, Geneva, 22 March 2005, Federal Foreign Office, Press Release, 22 March 2005 <http://www.auswaertiges-amt.de/www/en/archiv_print?archiv_id=6983>

At the UN Commission on Human Rights, Federal Foreign Minister Fischer spoke about human rights and terrorism. He underlined 'that terrorism can only be combated successfully with human rights – not without or even against them. (...) Human rights norms must retain their full validity. This is true above all of the ban on torture which is absolute and must on no account be watered down.'

☛ Speech by Minister of State at the Federal Foreign Office, Kerstin Müller, at the opening of the International Commission of Jurists Biennial Conference on Human Rights and Counter Terrorism in Berlin, 27 August 2004, Federal Foreign Office, Press Release, 27 August 2004 <http://www.auswaertiges-amt.de/www/en/archiv_print?archiv-id=6058>

Minister of State, Kerstin Müller, emphasised that:

> 'the state has a duty to maintain international standards with respect to human rights and fundamental freedoms, especially in times of emergency. Democracies must live up to their own standards even when fighting against terrorism. (...) By preventing the emergence of "extra-legal areas", we show that our value system will not falter in face of the new security threats.'

GREGOR SCHOTTEN

GREECE

National Implementation and Dissementation

☛ The Greek Committee for the Implementation and Dissemination of International Humanitarian Law. Established by Ministerial Decree No. 2/53482/2002 issued on 24 December 2003 and published on 16 January 2004. The Decree came into force on the date of its official publication[146]

ICELAND[147]

The Geneva Conventions

☛ Publication of Icelandic translation of the Geneva Conventions <http://www.redcross.is/book/>

In 2004 the Icelandic Red Cross and the Ministry for Foreign Affairs published *Genfar Samningarnir* [Geneva Conventions] containing the conventions in Icelandic translation. The publication had been in preparation for many years. The translation is available at the website of the Icelandic Red Cross.

Peacekeeping

☛ Establishment of Icelandic Crisis Response Unit

---

146. *Supra* n. 70, pp. 694 at 701-702.
147. Information and commentaries by Thordis Ingadottir, Lecturer, University of Iceland.

Iceland has recently increased its activities in the field of peacekeeping operations. In 2001 the Icelandic Crisis Response Unit (ICRU) was established, which is entirely civilian based as Iceland has no military forces. The ICRU has deployed medical professionals and police officers on peacekeeping missions in the Balkans, Sri Lanka and Afghanistan. Before deployment, members of the ICRU receive briefing in IHL. The Ministry of Foreign Affairs is currently preparing a Code of Conduct for ICRU members, largely based on the UN Code of Conduct for Law Enforcement Officials, the UN Code of Conduct on sexual exploitation and sexual abuse, and the OSCE Code of Conduct.

International Criminal Court

☛ Iceland ratified the Agreement on the Privileges and Immunities of the International Criminal Court on 1 December 2003

THORDIS INGADOTTIR

INDIA[148]

Peacekeeping

☛ Increase in the size of the Indian contingent to MONUC

The Indian contingent of the UN peacekeeping operation in the Democratic Republic of the Congo was strengthened during 2004 to over 3,000 personnel, including 19 helicopters.

Terrorism

☛ Repeal of the Prevention of Terrorism Act 2002

This law was repealed by the President of India on 21 September 2004 amidst political and media criticism about its misuse and the extraordinary powers that it provided to police officials.

☛ Sixth meeting of the Indo-US Joint Working Group on counter-terrorism, 31 August-1 September 2004, New Delhi

The two sides exchanged information on the law enforcement, legislative, financial and other measures in the field of counter-terrorism.

Refugees

☛ First meeting of the Expert Committee on Refugees, 9 March 2004

The Expert Committee on Refugees, constituted by the National Human Rights Commission, met for the first time on 9 March 2004 to render its opinion on the Model National Law on Refugees.

NILENDRA KUMAR

148. Information and commentaries by Major General Nilendra Kumar, Judge Advocate General of the Indian Army.

IRELAND[149]

Counter-Terrorism/Criminal Law

- Criminal Justice (Joint Investigation Teams) Act, 2004, No. 20/2004. Adopted 23 June 2004, entered into force 30 June 2004 <http://www.oireachtas.ie/documents/bills28/acts/2004/2004.pdf>

The Criminal Justice (Joint Investigation Teams) Act was one of the many acts introduced in the Irish Parliament after the September 11th 2001 attacks in the United States. This extensive legislation, including the Criminal Justice (Terrorist Offences) Act 2005 and the Maritime Security Act 2004, sought to create a statutory, EU-wide, anti-terrorism response.[150] Much of this legislation was advanced by the European Council's framework decision on Combating Terrorism.[151] This decision calls on each member state to implement certain legislation to respond to and protect against international terrorism. Article 13 of the Convention on Mutual Assistance in Criminal Matters includes a provision for the creation of joint investigation teams between EU member states.[152]

The purpose of the Act is to enable effect to be given in Irish law to the EU Council Framework Decision of 13 June 2002 on Joint Investigations Teams. Joint investigation teams may be set up for a specific purpose and limited period by mutual agreement of two or more Member States in order to carry out criminal investigations with a cross border dimension in one or more of the member states setting up the team. The Council of Europe meeting held in Tampere in 1999 called for joint investigation teams, as foreseen in Article 30 of the Treaty on European Union, to be set up to combat trafficking in drugs and human beings as well as terrorism. Following the events of 11 September 2001 the Council of Europe considered that such teams should be set up to combat offences committed by terrorists and organised crime generally and that a specific and legally binding instrument on joint investigation teams should be adopted as soon as possible.

Section 3(1) provides that the Irish Competent Authority may agree to establish a joint investigation team to investigate certain conduct if it is satisfied that:

i) either conduct which would be an offence if it occurred in the State has occurred, or that there are reasonable grounds for suspecting that such conduct has occurred, in another Member State or States, and the investigation of the conduct has links with the State or that conduct which would constitute an offence if it had occurred in the State has occurred partly in the State and partly in another member State, and
ii) there are reasonable grounds for believing that it is in the public interest to agree to the establishment of a joint investigation team because, or it is anticipated that, some part of the investigation will be conducted in the State and the investigation requires co-ordinated and concerted action by the State and those other Member States concerned.

Section 3(2) specifies the information which should be included in a request to establish a joint investigation team. It gives effect to Article 1.2 of the Framework Decision. The in-

---

149. Information and commentaries by Ray Murphy, Irish Centre for Human Rights, School of Law, National University of Ireland.

150. *Dáil Debates* Vol. 578 p. 167, 22 January 2004, <http://debates.oireachtas.ie/Xml/29/DAL20040122.pdf>.

151. 2002/475/JHA, Adopted on 13 June 2002.

152. *Seanad Debates* para. 7, 14 May 2003, <http://www.irlgov.ie/debates-03/s14May/Sect3.htm#8>.

formation required is as follows: the competent authority making the request, the purpose of the request, the conduct to be investigated, the identity and nationality of the person(s) whose conduct is to be investigated, proposed membership of the team and the period for which the team is required.

Section 6 deals with a joint investigation team's membership and the terms and conditions of membership, including renumeration and allowances.

Section 7 gives effect to Article 1.3 of the Framework Decision and provides for the operation of a joint investigation team. Subsection (1) provides that where a joint investigation team or a part of it is operating in the state, it will perform its functions in accordance with the law of the state. A team will operate under the control and general superintendence of the Commissioner of An Garda Síochána (the police), who will make the necessary organisational arrangements for it, including the appointment of a team leader.

Though generally accepted by the members of Parliament as an effective and necessary response to the levels of contemporary international crime, a few aspects of the Act were questioned and criticised in the Seanad (upper house) and Dáil (lower house) debates. The most common criticism was that the Act lacked time restraints on investigations.[153] Many members of Parliament were concerned that investigations could continue indefinitely, draining resources and time from an already over-worked state police force.

Concerns about potential human rights abuses were also raised. In the Seanad, Senator David Norris raised concerns about the suggestion to create an international police school. He sought specific assurance that such a school would not be limited to education on policing techniques but would also include information on interfacing with the public, recognising and respecting human rights, and would create severe penalties for civil rights violations of individuals in police custody. His second concern was with the scope of the offences that could be investigated by the joint teams. By allowing for broad inclusion of criminal offences within the Act, the legislation could run the risk of incorporating minor offences which could be used by states, for example, 'for the purpose of political harassment of figures in other member states'.[154]

Though there were a number of concerns raised during the Parliamentary debates, particularly with respect to the feasibility of funding for the teams, the primary human rights concern was that raised by Deputy Ó Snodaigh in the Dáil debates, regarding the Minister's refusal to seek any review of the legislation from the Irish Human Rights Commission (IHRC), the Irish Council of Civil Liberties or Amnesty International. Section 8 of the Human Rights Commission Act establishes that it is the responsibility of the IHRC to 'review the adequacy and effectiveness of law and practice in [Ireland] relating to the protection of human rights' and to 'examine any legislative proposal and report [the Commission's] views on any implications of such proposal for human rights'.[155] Specifically, the Deputy asserted that the Act 'is flawed in its presumption that all EU police and intelligence forces are democratically sound and can be trusted not to violate human rights'.[156] Ó Snodaigh proposed that specific regulations be added to the Act to curtail potential abuses. An independent ombudsman's office and a civilian policing board should be established to

153. See *supra* n. 152, para. 34.
154. See *supra* n. 152, para. 89.
155. Human Rights Commission Act 2000. p. 6, <http://www.irlgov.ie/bills28/acts/2000/a900.pdf>.
156. See *supra* n. 151, p. 167.

create investigation mechanisms for complaints.[157] Furthermore, he called for greater elaboration in the Act on the 'conditions under which foreign police forces will be invited to participate in a joint investigation team and the conditions under which the consent to participation of gardai on joint investigations teams based elsewhere will be withheld on the basis of human rights concerns'.[158]

☛ Maritime Security Act 2004, No. 29/2004. Adopted on 8 July 2004 and entered into force on 17 July 2004 <http://www.oireachtas.ie/documents/bills28/acts/2004/A2904.pdf>

Immediately following the 2001 terrorist attacks on the US, the United Nations adopted Resolution 1373, calling on all UN member states to become parties to 12 international conventions and protocols created to prevent and suppress terrorism. In response to this mandate, multiple bills were introduced into the Dail (parliament). This Maritime Security Act gives effect to two of the 12 conventions: the 1988 United Nations Convention for the Suppression of Unlawful Acts against the Safety of Maritime Navigation and the 1988 Protocol to that Convention for the Suppression of Unlawful Acts against the Safety of Fixed Platforms on the Continental Shelf.[159] Its specific purpose is to protect Irish waters and coasts and to prevent terrorist activities from originating in or coming into the territory.

Introduced as a 'technical measure'[160] by the Minister of State at the Department of Communications, Marine and Natural Resources (Deputy J. Browne), the Act creates offences constituting terrorist activity, grants powers to designated authorities to prevent and prosecute these offences and establishes safeguards to protect civil liberties. The Act creates specific offences against the safety of Irish ships and other ships which are in Irish territorial waters and against fixed platforms on the Continental Shelf (subject to imprisonment for life on conviction on indictment), and consequentially provides for extraterritorial jurisdiction to cover offences committed outside the state in breach of the Convention or Protocol, the apprehension and detention of alleged offenders and handing them over to the appropriate authorities. It also covers extradition, bail, avoidance of double jeopardy and other necessary matters, on the model of provisions of the Criminal Justice (Terrorist Offences) Act 2005, and makes necessary provision in relation to four other international conventions against terrorism.

The Act is modelled heavily after the Criminal Justice (Terrorist Offences) Act 2005, which gives effect to four of the 12 UN conventions.[161] Though civil liberty and human rights concerns were raised repeatedly by a minority of Deputies, the Act was enacted without substantial changes from the original draft. Furthermore, neither Amnesty International Ireland, the Irish Council for Civil Liberties, nor the Irish Human Rights Commission issued any statement or acknowledgement of the Act before or after it became law. Lauded by almost every Deputy in the Parliament as a long overdue implementation of the Conven-

---

157. See *supra* n. 151, p. 168.

158. Ibid.

159. *Seanad Debate* Vol. 176 p. 29, 31 March 2004, <http://debates.oireachtas.ie/Xml/29/SEN20040331.pdf>; *Dáil Debate* Vol. 585 p. 850, 13 May 2004, <http://debates.oireachtas.ie/Xml/29/DAL20040513.pdf>.

160. Ibid.

161. *Seanad Debate* Vol. 176 p. 29, 31 March 2004, <http://debates.oireachtas.ie/Xml/29/SEN20040331.pdf>.

tion and Protocol, the Act passed into law after spending about eight months moving through the Dáil and Seanad.

- Ombudsman (Defence forces) Act 2004. Adopted 10 November 2004 and entered into force 1 December 2005. The 31st day of August 2005 was appointed as the day on which sections 1, 2, 3, 14, 16, 17, 18 and 19 of the Act came into operation <http://www.oireachtas.ie/viewdoc.asp?fn=/documents/bills28/acts/2004/a3604.pdf>

The purpose of the Act is to establish the office of Ombudsman for the Defence Forces and to provide for the appointment, functions and staff of the Ombudsman. The need for such an office arose from a lack of confidence among Defence Force personnel in grievance procedures in existence following a survey of perception of and experiences of unacceptable workplace practices.[162]

Section 2 provides for the establishment of the office of the Defence Forces ombudsman and for the appointment of an individual to that office by the President upon the recommendation of the government.

Section 4 provides for the functions of the Ombudsman and sets out the nature of the complaints that may be investigated by him or her when it appears that the complaint is not likely to be resolved by the military authorities by way of the redress procedures prescribed in the Defence Act 1954.

The Act defines the functions of the ombudsman and sets out the general right of Defence Forces personnel to make a complaint to the ombudsman. The Act also sets out the limited circumstances in which the ombudsman shall not investigate particularly defined types of complaint.

The Bill provides the ombudsman with considerable independence and autonomy in the discharge of his or her statutory functions and in the conduct of investigations. Military personnel are assured of complete independence from the Minister, the Department of Defence and the military authorities in the investigation of complaints.

RAY MURPHY

ISRAEL[163]

The Armed Forces-Discipline

- Knesset Committee for Constitutional, Legislative and Legal Affairs, Protocol No. 157, agenda item: Protecting Human Rights during the War on Terror (Session of 3 February 2004)[164]

---

162. Minister of Defence, Dáil Debates, 6 October 2004, Cols. 131-132.

163. Information and commentaries by Dr Yuval Shany, Hersch Lauterpacht Chair in Public International Law, Faculty of Law, Hebrew University, Israel. The reporter would like to thank the Research Foundation of the Law School of the Academic College of Management for their financial support of this research. Additional thanks are due to Mr Ron Avital, who assisted in the research for this report, and to Mr Rotem Giladi (ICRC Tel Aviv Delegation) and Capt. Joshua Gortler (IDF Legal Corps International Law Division) for their comments on previous drafts. Responsibility for errors remains with the reporter.

164. Knesset Committee for Constitutional, Legislative and Legal Affairs, Protocol no. 157, 4 February 2004, Knesset Doc. Protocols/Constitution Committee/7814.

- Knesset Committee for Constitutional, Legislative and Legal Affairs, Protocol No. 291, agenda item: Protecting Human Rights during the War on Terror (Session of 18 August 2004)

The IDF Military Advocate-General (MAG) reported to the Knesset Committee for Constitutional, Legislative and Legal Affairs that since the beginning of the second *intifada* his office received more than 1,600 complaints concerning the conduct of IDF service members in the Occupied Territories. At that time, more than 470 criminal investigations had been initiated (more than 190 of these cases involved complaints of violent conduct, and some 170 complaints of harm to property). The investigation led so far to some 65 indictments, which led, in turn, to 40 convictions entailing prison time (less than a year, in all cases). According to the MAG, no manslaughter cases have yet been concluded, although several such cases are pending.

In August 2004 the IDF MAG updated the Knesset Committee for Constitutional, Legislative and Legal Affairs. More than 120 new criminal investigations against IDF soldiers were opened since his previous report to the Committee, and 30 new indictments were served.

Extrajudicial Killing

- Knesset Proceedings, Agenda Motions 3161, 4444, 4447, 4455, 4479, 4483, 4495, 4499, 4515: Shooting of 'Kassem' Rockets at Sderot; IDF Military Activities in Gaza; Inquiry into the Death of the Girl in Rafah, 13 October 2004[165]

The Deputy Minister of Defense announced in the Knesset that an initial inquiry into the death of a 13-year-old Palestinian girl in Rafah indicated that she entered a military outpost by mistake and that soldiers shot and killed her, mistaking her for a terrorist. However, a military police investigation showed that the outpost's commander continued to shoot at the girl's body from close range, while she lay down on the ground, citing fears of possible explosives on her body. Pursuant to the investigation, the commander was suspended from active duty and the prosecuting authorities are considering putting him on trial for a prohibited 'killing confirmation' act.[166]

Administrative Detention

- Knesset Committee for Constitutional, Legislative and Legal Affairs, Protocol no. 157, agenda item: Protecting Human Rights during the War on Terror (Session of 3 February 2004)[167]

The IDF Military Advocate-General (MAG) reported to the Knesset Committee for Constitutional, Legislative and Legal Affairs that during 2003 some 2,600 administrative detention orders issued against Palestinian individuals were reviewed by military courts. This review led to the revocation of 200 orders and to the shortening of some 1,400 detention

---

165. *Knesset Proceedings,* 16th Knesset, 168th Sess., 13 October 2004 (item 15)(Jerusalem).

166. The Officer in question was subsequently tried. He was acquitted of all charges on 15 November 2005, after the court found the testimony of his subordinate soldiers concerning the alleged 'killing confirmation' to be untrustworthy.

167. Knesset Committee for Constitutional, Legislative and Legal Affairs, Protocol No. 157, 4 February 2004, Knesset Doc. Protocols/Constitution Committee/7814.

periods. The MAG also stated that hundreds of criminal trials of Palestinians on terror-related murder charges are pending before military courts in the Occupied Territories, yet only five such trials are taking place in Israel proper before ordinary courts.

Release of Detainees

☛ Prime Minister of Israel's Office, Press Release of 24 January 2004

A governmental press release announced that an agreement was reached between Israel and the Hezbollah to return to Israel one Israeli civilian and three dead IDF soldiers held by the Hezbollah, in return for the release of prisoners and detainees held in Israel[168] and the return to Lebanon of the bodies of dead Lebanese citizens. The government also noted that the fate of a senior Lebanese prisoner imprisoned for life in Israel for murder and terror-related crimes (Samir Kuntar) is tied to the supply of additional information on the whereabouts of the Israeli missing in action serviceman, Lt. Col. Ron Arad. The government of Israel thanked the German government for its assistance in facilitating the said agreement.

Disengagement

☛ Government of Israel, Decision of 6 June 2004 <http://www.pmo.gov.il/NR/rdonlyres/AFB8AC38-9B35-446E-AB96-09B34540CE56/0/2510מזכיר.rtf> (in Hebrew)

The Government adopted the Prime Minister's disengagement plan under which Israel is to withdraw all Israeli settlements and military presence from the Gaza Strip and evacuate four West Bank settlements (located in Northern Samaria). The Annexes to the decision proclaim that Israel intends to keep control over major Jewish population centres in the West Bank under a future negotiated settlement; that the complete evacuation of Gaza will release Israel from all legal responsibility to the local population residing there; that Israel preserves its right to self-defence and may forcefully counter future threats emanating from evacuated areas; and that Israel views favourably the continued activities of international agencies in the evacuated areas.

Financing of Terrorism

☛ Knesset Proceedings, Agenda Motion 3160, 3161: Return of Funds Seized in Ramallah Banks, 17 March 2004[169]

A plenary Knesset session debated the consequences of an IDF operation in Ramallah (executed on 25 February 2004), in which several bank safes were raided, and some 40 million dollars, allegedly used for funding terrorism, confiscated. A government minister reported that hearings designed to address ownership claims of private individuals and foreign governments over the seized funds are being held. The fate of the seized funds is therefore still unclear.

---

168. More than 400 prisoners, mostly Palestinians, were released pursuant to the agreement between Israel and Hezbollah.

169. *Knesset Proceedings,* 16th Knesset, 120th Sess., 17 March 2004 (item 33)(Jerusalem).

- Prohibition on the Financing of Terrorism Law, 200. Adopted by the Knesset on 29 December 2004 and entered into force on 1 August 2005. Published in *Official Gazette* vol. 1973, p. 76 (Jewish Year 5765) (Hok Issur Mimun Terror, 5765, 2005)

The legislation seeks to give effect to Israel's obligations under the International Convention for the Suppression of the Financing of Terrorism (ratified by Israel on 19 December 2002).[170] It penalises the funding of terrorist activities and transactions involving assets belonging to domestic or international terror organisations, and introduces upon financial institutions a duty to report suspicious fund transfers. The law also authorises a government commission to designate individuals or groups as terrorists or terror groups, after consulting with an expert committee. Such a designation, which is subject to periodic review, could facilitate the seizing of terror-related assets pursuant to criminal law or administrative law procedures (including the introduction of provisional measures in order to frustrate ongoing terror operations).

Cases

1. Humanitarian conditions in Rafah

- *Physicians for Human Rights* v. *IDF Gaza Strip Military Commander*, Supreme Court of Israel, H.C.J. 4764/04, Judgement of 30 May 2004, 48(5) *P.D.* 385.[171] For an English version <http://62.90.71.124/files_eng/04/640/047/a03/04047640.a03.htm>

The petition, which was brought by four Israeli NGOs, requested the court to instruct the IDF to facilitate the delivery of health services and supplies, food, water and electricity to several neighbourhoods of Rafah (in the southern tip of the Gaza Strip), while the IDF conducted large-scale military operations which adversely affected the conditions of the local residents there. In addition, the petitioners requested the investigation of an incident that took place on 19 May 2004 in which several civilians were killed by IDF tank shells, and asked the court to instruct the IDF to refrain from shelling civilians, even if armed individuals are within their midst (provided that they present no immediate threat). During the course of litigation, matters relating to burial of the dead were also brought before the court.

In its judgment, the court confirmed its power of judicial review over ongoing military operations. Although it acknowledged that such review imposes certain constraints on the work of the judiciary (stemming especially from acknowledgment of the military commanders' ultimate responsibility for the lives of their troops and the success of their mission), the court held that it may nonetheless review the legality of the operations.

The court then reaffirmed the applicability of the 1907 Hague Regulations and the Fourth Geneva Convention to the situation in Rafah (in addition to Israeli administrative law), and emphasised the importance of the right to humane treatment (Art. 27 of the Fourth Geneva Convention; Art. 46 of the Hague Regulations). According to the court, this right imposes upon the acting commander two types of obligations:

---

170. International Convention for the Suppression of the Financing of Terrorism, 9 December 1999, 39 (2000) 270.

171. Law Reports or Judicial Decisions.

'First, he must refrain from operations that may cause harm to the civilian population. This duty is formulated in the negative. Second, he must take all measures required to ensure the safety of civilians. This latter duty calls for positive action [cite omitted]. Both these duties – which are not always easily distinguishable – should be reasonably and proportionately implemented given considerations of time and place.'

In addition, the court held that other IHL rights, which constitute specific expressions of the right to humane treatment, are relevant to the case at hand: the right to receive medical and food supplies (Arts. 55, 59 and 23 of the Fourth Geneva Convention) and the right to medical treatment (Arts. 56, 20 and 63 of the Fourth Geneva Convention).

After laying out the normative framework, the judgment proceeded to address the specific humanitarian problems which arose during the Rafah operations:

— *Water shortages*: The court introduced the following standard:

'It is the responsibility of the military commander to ensure the provision of water in the area of combat activities. This includes not only the responsibility to ensure that no damage is caused to the sources of water, but also the positive obligation to provide water in areas of shortage. Everything should be done in order to ensure the provision of water; sources of water must be repaired with due speed. Water tankers should be provided if no running water is available.'

The court noted with satisfaction that the water shortage problem had been resolved after the military placed several water tankers in the relevant neighborhoods and moved quickly to repair the water infrastructure which had been damaged during the fighting.

— *Electricity*: The court accepted that repairing the electric service infrastructure which was damaged in the fighting entails several complexities and would take some time (e. g., special equipment needed to be brought from Israel). It noted that electricity had been restored in most of Rafah. It thus declined to intervene in this aspect of the respondent's humanitarian work.

— *Medical supplies*: Again, the court set a high standard of performance:

'It is the duty of the military commander to ensure that there is enough medical equipment in the combat zone. This is surely his obligation towards his soldiers; but his obligation is also towards the civilian population under his control. In the framework of the preparation for a military operation, this issue – which is always to be expected – must be taken into account. In this regard, both the local medical system as well as the ability of local hospitals to give reasonable medical care during combat must be examined in advance. Medical equipment must be prepared in advance in case of shortage; provision of medical equipment from different sources must be allowed in order to relieve the shortage; contact must be maintained, to the extent possible, with the local medical services. The obligation is that of the military commander, and the receipt of assistance from external sources does not release him from that obligation. *Cf.* the Fourth Geneva Convention, § 60. However, such external assistance is likely to lead to the fulfilment of the obligation, *de facto*.'

Moving on to apply this standard, the court held that, on the basis of the information provided to it, all of the logistical medical problems had been resolved. Thus, it saw no need for intervention on these grounds.

— *Food*: The court noted that 'it is prohibited for combat [sic] to cause the starvation of local residents under the control of the army.' It also stressed the military's duty to make adequate advance plans for provision of food during military operations. Still, under the ruling circumstances, the court found that all problems relating to food provision had been satisfactorily resolved.

— *Evacuation of the wounded*: The court reaffirmed that: 'The army must do all possible, subject to the current state of the combat, to allow the evacuation of local residents wounded during combat activities.' It held that this obligation appeared to have been met during the Rafah operation. It did offer two additional observations – that the IDF's policy of seeking to identify the wounded before their transfer between hospitals is not unlawful, provided that identification is not being made a condition to the evacuation of the wounded, and it accepts the IDF's explanation that an incident in which shots were fired at a Palestinian ambulance was exceptional and in clear violation of the existing IDF instructions.

— *Burial of the dead*: The court noted that: 'Our assumption is that the fundamental principle that the dignity of local residents must be protected, as enshrined in section 27 of the Fourth Geneva Convention, encompasses not only local residents who are living, but also the dead... The military commander is duty-bound to search for and locate dead bodies [cite omitted]. After bodies are found [sic], he is obligated to ensure that they are accorded a dignified burial.' Applying this standard, the court opined that the IDF's preparations in this respect were lacking, noting in particular its failure to promptly negotiate proper burial arrangements with the local authorities.

— *Shelling civilians*: The court held that it would be premature to rule on the legal aspects of a specific shelling incident in which several Palestinian civilian demonstrators were killed, which was still being investigated by the military authorities. The court stated, however, that 'the army must employ all possible caution in order to avoid harming a civilian population, even one that is protesting against it'.

— *Entry of NGO medical teams*: The court accepted the position of the IDF that NGO delegations may freely enter the area, but that, for reasons of personal safety, no Israeli citizens would be allowed into Rafah. The judgment concluded with a few general observations: 'First, that the rules of conduct be taught to, and that they be internalized by, all combat soldiers, from the Chief of General Staff down to new recruits [cite omitted]. Second, that procedures be drawn up that allow implementation of these rules, and which allow them to be put into practice during combat.' Although the court commended the respondent for great progress in adopting such procedures (e.g., the appointment of humanitarian officers, the establishment of humanitarian hotlines, etc.) – especially when compared to previous large scale operations reviewed by the court in 2002 – it opined that some room for future improvement remained (especially better coordination between various units and better flow of information between the IDF and humanitarian NGOs).

The *Rafah* judgment is perhaps indicative of the growing willingness of the Supreme Court to ensure compliance of the state of Israel with its IHL obligations. Several aspects of the decisions are particularly notable: a) an unconditional acceptance of the Fourth Geneva Convention as a governing source of law for review of the legality of measures taken by Israel in the Occupied Territories; b) elaboration of a comprehensive body of negative as well as positive obligations that the law of occupation imposes upon the occupying power and that the laws of armed conflict seem to impose upon combatants *vis-à-vis* civilians in combat zones; and c) remarkable readiness on the part of the court to exercise judicial oversight during the course of active hostilities, transforming the court from an *ex post facto* examiner of legality into a managerial actor involved in the 'real time' enforcement of legal standards.

2. Administrative detention

- *Al-Ahmar* v. *IDF West Bank Military Commander,* H.C.J. 1139/04, Judgment of 26 February 2004, 2004(2) *Takdin-Supreme* 1998

The court affirmed the continued detention of an administrative detainee after reviewing the evidence compiled against him *ex parte.* The court noted that there is no necessity to produce new evidence in each periodic review of the detention, and that the decision whether to prolong the detention on the basis of the old evidence ought to be taken on a case by case basis. It also noted that the petitioner declined to consider the state's offer to substitute detention with an agreed upon exile for a number of years.

- *Tail Muhammad Salim Uda* v. *Ofer Camp Military Court Judge,* H.C.J. 6585/04, Supreme

Court of Israel, Judgment of 28 July 2004, 2004(3) *Takdin-Supreme* 1110

The court affirmed the continued detention of a Palestinian engaged in currency-exchange activities, who allegedly provided funds for terror groups. The court, however, recommended that after expiration of the current detention period, the IDF explore alternative restrictions (i.e., other than detention) that could be imposed upon the petitioner to ensure discontinuation of his involvement with terrorism.

3. The separation barrier[172]

- *Beit Sourik Village Council* v. *The Government of Israel,* H.C.J. 2056/04 Supreme Court of Israel, Judgment of 30 June 2004, 48(5) *P.D.* 807. For an English version <http://elyon1.court.gov.il/files_eng/04/560/020/a28/04020560.a28.HTM>

The case concerned the petition of a Palestinian village council against the seizure of lands belonging to various West Bank villages located North West of Jerusalem for the purpose of constructing a separation barrier designed to curb terror attacks against Israeli citizens. According to the petitioner, the 40 km barrier stretch challenged in the proceedings will span four km2 and would bar the villagers' access to 37 km2 of agricultural land. The barrier is also expected to hinder movement between the villages and East Jerusalem and create numerous other hardships. The petitioner claimed that the construction of the barrier is unlawful since it is designed to protect Israel's interests, and not the interests of the local population or those of the occupation forces themselves. It also alleged that the route of the barrier had no military justification but was rather intended to annex West Bank lands to Israel; that the seizure procedures suffered from various irregularities; and that the harm to Palestinian interests was disproportionate to any military benefits that might appertain to the barrier. An Israeli NGO – the Council for Peace and Security – joined the proceedings, as did several residents of the Israeli town of Mevaseret Zion (situated within Israel proper, in proximity to the route of the barrier).

---

172. Also see *infra* p. 515 under NGOs.

The court's judgment, which was rendered only ten days before the issuing of the ICJ Advisory Opinion on the separation barrier,[173] confirmed the applicability of the laws of belligerent occupation found in the 1907 Hague Regulations and 1949 Fourth Geneva Convention (whose humanitarian rules Israel undertook to apply to the Occupied Territories, notwithstanding its arguments regarding the Convention's formal applicability) to questions concerning the legality of the barrier, alongside Israeli administrative law. According to these bodies of law, the court held that the military commander may, in principle, erect a security barrier in occupied territories, but his authority is limited:

> 'the military commander of territory held in belligerent occupation must balance between the needs of the army on one hand, and the needs of the local inhabitants on the other. In the framework of this delicate balance, there is no room for an additional system of considerations, whether they be political considerations, the annexation of territory, or the establishment of the permanent borders of the state. This Court has emphasized time and time again that the authority of the military commander is inherently temporary, as belligerent occupation is inherently temporary. Permanent arrangements are not the affair of the military commander. True, the belligerent occupation of the area has gone on for many years. This fact affects the scope of the military commander's authority [cite omitted]. The passage of time, however, cannot extend the authority of the military commander and allow him to take into account considerations beyond the proper administration of the area under belligerent occupation.'

Since the court accepted the evidence presented by the Israeli military that the barrier's route was exclusively dictated by military considerations, it declined to strike down the barrier *in toto*: 'Indeed, the obstacle is intended to take the place of combat military operations, by physically blocking terrorist infiltration into Israeli population centres.'

The court held, however, that the barrier's route must balance between security needs and the rights of the local population (mainly provided for in Article 46 of the Hague Regulations and Article 27 of the Fourth Geneva Convention), and that the general principle of international law and Israeli administrative law governing that balancing act is the proportionality principle. This test comprises, according to the court, several sub-tests: a rational link between means and objectives, a least injurious alternative, and proportionality in the 'narrow sense', i.e., relations of proportionality between harm and benefits. This last sub-test is to be applied in a relative manner, in the light of existing alternatives which might produce better harm-benefit ratios. In applying these standards, the court noted that the military authorities are entitled to deference by virtue of their expertise and ultimate responsible for security.

Moving on to review the specific land seizure decree, the court nullified seven seizure orders (out of the eight orders reviewed) relating to some 30 km of the reviewed 40 km of the barrier, by reason of their disproportionate injury upon the rights of the Palestinian villagers in the area. In reaching that conclusion, the court emphasised that alternative barrier routes exist offering slightly lesser security protection but considerably reducing hu-

173. Legal Consequences of the Construction of a Wall in the Occupied Palestinian Territory, International Court of Justice, Advisory Opinion of 9 July 2004.

manitarian harm. It thus instructed the military authorities to reroute the barrier in the light of the proportionality requirements introduced in the judgment.[174]

☛ *Alian* v. *Prime Minister*, H.C.J. 4825/04, Supreme Court of Israel, Decision of 19 August 2004, not published

The court instructed the state, in an interim decision, to respond to a petition against the route of the separation barrier in the proximity of two Palestinian villages (Bidu and Shukba). Furthermore, it asked the respondents to address the implications of the 2004 ICJ Advisory Opinion on the legality of the wall upon the present case.

4. Destruction of property

☛ *Yoav Hess* v. *IDF West Bank Military Commander*, H.C.J. 10356/02, Supreme Court of Israel, Judgment of 4 March 2004, 58(3) *P.D.* 443

The petitioners, Israeli leftist political activists, the municipality of Hebron, a Palestinian historical preservation society and Palestinian individual landowners, challenged the lawfulness of a land seizure order issued by the IDF in order to facilitate the destruction of 13 properties owned by Palestinians. The order was issued as part of a plan to widen a 730-metre long and narrow road leading from the Jewish Settlement of Kiryat Arba to the Tomb of the Patriarchs in Hebron. The road, which serves thousands of Jewish worshippers that march to the Tomb on Sabbath and holidays, has been the site of several terror attacks, and the IDF sought its expansion in order to improve the prevailing security arrangements (primarily, to allow the unimpeded movement of emergency vehicles). Following preliminary court hearings, the IDF revised its plans and decided to seek the destruction of only two Palestinian abandoned houses and the partial destruction of a third house.

The court upheld in its judgment the IDF's authority to infringe upon the right of property of local residents of the Occupied Territories if this is demanded by military exigencies (Art. 23(g) and 52 of the 1907 Hague Regulations and Art. 53 of the Fourth Geneva Convention). However, it noted that such harm must be proportionate to the benefits the measure in question seeks to obtain. Since it was not shown that the IDF commanders considered any inappropriate considerations in issuing the order, the court accepted the reasonableness of the security needs they invoked (especially in the light of past attacks on the aforementioned road). It did, however, examine whether an adequate balance had been struck between the conflicting interests – the Palestinians' right to property and the cultural heritage status of the targeted houses (under the 1954 Hague Convention for the Protection of Cultural Property in the Event of Armed Conflict), on the one hand, and the settlers' right to personal safety, worship and freedom of movement, on the other hand. According to the court, the balancing made by the IDF authorities under the revised plan meets the conditions of legality, as it does not require removal of individuals from their houses and involves full compensation and supervision of the demolition operation by expert preservationists. It may be noted that the judgment contains an additional interesting aspect: In reaching its conclusions, the court held that both the Israeli settlers and the local Palestinian population of Hebron enjoy rights under the 1907 Hague Regulations and under Israeli

---

174. For a more in depth discussion of this case, see in this volume Y. Shany at p. 352.

constitutional law. Little reasoning is, however, offered for these two assertions (both of which might be described as controversial under international law and Israeli law).

- *Taib Ali Faraj* v. *IDF West Bank Military Commander,* H.C.J. 893/04, Supreme Court of Israel, Judgment of 4 March 2004, 2004 (1) *Takdin-Supreme* 2123

The court affirmed an order to demolish part of a housing complex in which a senior terrorist, allegedly responsible for launching a series of deadly suicide attacks, resided. The order was issued pursuant to the law in force in the West Bank (Art. 119 of the Defense (Emergency) Regulations, 1945), which permits punitive house demolitions for reasons of deterrence. The court noted that the initial order was amended so to exclude another structure in the complex in which some other family members resided, and that the balance struck between the general public's interest and that of the petitioners was not unlawful.

- *Hassan Abed Al-Karim Alzar* v. *IDF Gaza Strip Military Commander,* H.C.J. 4103/04 Supreme Court of Israel, Judgment of 3 May 2004, 2004 (2) *Takdin-Supreme* 1030
- *Muhammad Al-Bassiouni* v. *IDF Gaza Strip Military Commander*, H.C.J. 4573/04, Supreme Court of Israel, Judgment of 16 May 2004, 2004 (2) *Takdin-Supreme* 1580
- *Zaber Muhammad Abu-Dayer* v. *IDF Gaza Strip Military Commander,* H.C.J. 4372/04, Supreme Court of Israel, Judgment of 10 May 2004, 2004 (2) *Takdin-Supreme* 1606
- *Abed Al-Karim Al-Rahman Shkapat* v. *IDF Gaza Strip Military Commander*, H.C.J. 4585/04-B, Supreme Court of Israel, Judgment of 16 May 2004, 2004 (2) *Takdin-Supreme* 1284
- *Ismail Abed Al-Aziz Salem Abu-Atra* v. *IDF Gaza Strip Military Commander,* H.C.J. 4694/04-A, Supreme Court of Israel, Judgment of 18 May 2004, 2004 (2) *Takdin-Supreme* 1645

All petitions seeking to prevent potential IDF house demolitions in the Gaza Strip were withdrawn or rejected following an undertaking by the state not to resort, at this stage, to punitive house demolitions in relation to the specific events giving rise to the petitions (a terror attack on a major Gaza Strip road and active fighting in the Philadelphi Route in southern Rafah).[175] According to the state, any house demolition operation which already took place was justified by immediate operational needs and was not punitive or deterrent in nature. The state also undertook to give prior notice to the relevant homeowners before future house demolition operations, unless barred by considerations of immediate operational necessity, soldier safety or the need not to frustrate the demolition mission.

Still, in *Abu Atra* the court noted that the right to prior hearing is often non-feasible under the circumstances in the Gaza Strip. It also expressed some concern at the high number of house demolitions near the Philadelphi Route. However, the court found no legal grounds for judicial intervention and rejected the petition.

It may also be noted that in the *Zaber* case a subsequent shooting incident led to the destruction of seven out of the eight houses implicated in the petition in the course of a military operation designed to apprehend the shooters.

---

175. It may be noted that in February 2005 a military commission recommended to the military authority the suspension of all punitive house demolitions in the Occupied Territories. The recommendation was adopted by the IDF Chief of Staff and by the Minster of Defence.

- *Fahria Rabah Ali Mahtsab* v. *IDF West Bank Military Commander,* H.C.J. 9704/02 Supreme Court of Israel, Judgment of 9 February 2004, 2004 (1) *Takdin-Supreme* 1404
- *Muhammad Ibrahim Hassin Asrawi* v. *IDF West Bank Military Commander,* H.C.J. 9566/02, Supreme Court of Israel, Judgment of 9 November 2004, 2004 (4) *Takdin-Supreme* 790

Petitions against possible house demolition operations were withdrawn or rejected after the state undertook to notify the petitioners if and when it decides to demolish their property – unless special considerations relating to the security of IDF servicemen or the non-frustration of the operation would prevent such notification. In the *Mahtsab* case, it was agreed by the parties that any special considerations justifying demolition without prior notice would be recorded on a proper document.

- *Jawad Naji Awad Barri* v. *IDF West Bank Military Commander,* H.C.J. 1321/04 Supreme Court of Israel, Judgment of 1 March 2004, 2004 (1) *Takdin-Supreme* 2394

A petition against the trimming of trees situated in an orchard from which shots were fired at IDF vehicles was withdrawn after the state agreed to reduce the number of affected trees from 50 to 20 and to consider compensating the orchard owner.

5. Removal of outposts

- *Amana – Gush Emunim Settlement Movement* v. *IDF West Bank Military Commander,* H.C.J. 548/04 Supreme Court of Israel, Judgment of 26 February 2004, 58(3) P.D. 373

The petition challenged the legality of two military decrees designed to facilitate the removal of unauthorised Jewish outposts in the West Bank. The decrees authorise military commanders to bar the presence of individuals in areas containing unauthorised buildings and to clear all unauthorised structures. According to the petitioners, the decrees are discriminatory (i.e., directed only against Jewish settlers) and are in breach of the duties of the military commander under Article 43 of the 1907 Hague Regulations to refrain from altering local legislation. The court rejected the petition and held that the distinction between Israelis and Palestinians is permissible in the light of the different nature of their respective violations of building and zoning laws and the differences in the applicability of Israeli law to their conduct (Israeli law has been applied to several aspects of the settlers' lives; hence, they are already subject to a different legal regime than the Palestinians in the area). As for Article 43, the court noted that the commander may resort to new legislation if he is prevented from restoring law and order on the basis of the pre-existing law in the territories.

- *The Center for the Land of Israel – Haifa and the North* v. *Supreme Planning Council for Judea and Samaria,* H.C.J. 10912/03, Supreme Court of Israel, Judgment of 8 January 2004, 2004 (1) *Takdin-Supreme* 75
- *Amana – Gush Emunim Settlement Movement* v. *IDF West Bank Military Commander,* H.C.J. 7938/04 Supreme Court of Israel, Judgment of 26 February 2004, 2004 (3) *Takdin-Supreme* 3313
- *Ofra – A Cooperative Settlement Village Ltd.* v. *IDF West Bank Military Commander,* H.C.J. 4715/04, Supreme Court of Israel, Judgment of 18 May 2004, 2004 (1) *Takdin-Supreme* 75

☛ *Avital Atlas.* v. *IDF West Bank Military Commander,* H.C.J. 9087/04, Supreme Court of Israel, Judgment of 12 October 2004, 2004 (4) *Takdin-Supreme* 372

The court declined to prohibit the removal of outposts located near the settlements of Yitzhar Ofra and Beit El. In the *Center for the Land of Israel*, the court noted that the petitioner, who represents the residents of the outpost, failed, when given the opportunity, to demonstrate any legal title over the land in question, and had therefore exhausted his right to a prior hearing. In the *Ofra* and *Amana* cases, the court held that failure to establish legal title over the land in question bars intervention by the court in IDF attempts to evacuate the outpost. Finally, in *Atlas,* the court rejected the petitioners' claim that their presence in the unauthorised outposts contributes to, rather than undermines, law and order in the West Bank. The court noted that the IDF has discretion in determining how to uphold law and order and that it is hard to see how the construction of unauthorised outposts can be conducive to the rule of law in the Occupied Territories.

6. Human shields/cooperation by enemy civilians

☛ *Adalah – The Legal Center for Arab Minority Rights in Israel* v. *IDF West Bank Military Commander,* H.C.J. 3799/02, Supreme Court of Israel, Decision of 5 September 2004, 2003 (1) *Pador* 91

This case, which was originally filed with the court in 2002, challenged the IDF practice of requesting the assistance of local Palestinians during military operations, and alleged that they amount to a violation of the prohibition against using civilians as human shields or hostages.[176] Pursuant to an interim order barring the use of human shields in military operations issued by the Supreme Court in 2003, the IDF issued a new directive – an 'early warning operation directive' – which authorised IDF soldiers to receive voluntary assistance by Palestinian civilians in circumstances where no danger to their lives exists (and subject to a number of additional limitations). However, the petitioner claimed that the new directive was also unlawful, and that it was being exploited to contravene the court's interim order. As a result, it requested the court to issue a new interim order to bar any use of Palestinians during military operations.

In its procedural decision of 5 September, the Supreme Court decided to allow the state to respond to the new request for an interim order.[177]

7. Compensation

☛ *Osama Hamed* v. *State of Israel,* C.A. 5604/94, Supreme Court of Israel, Judgment of 12 January 2004 58(2) *P.D.* 498

The court reversed a lower court's decision which exempted the state from liability for injuries inflicted upon an 11-year old Palestinian boy by rubber coated metal bullets shot at him by IDF soldiers during a riot control operation which took place in Jenin in 1990. The court held that the soldiers had no justification to open fire while chasing rioters since they were not subject to any particular threat. In addition, the state was not entitled to invoke the

---

176. See the reports on Israel in 5 *YIHL* (2002) p. 541 and 6 *YIHL* (2003) p. 516.

177. On 6 October 2005, the Supreme Court issued its judgment in the case in which it invalidated the 'early warning procedure' promulgated by the IDF.

'combat situation' immunity from tort claims (established by the Supreme Court's decision in *Benni Udah*[178]), since the operation was predominantly one of policing and not active fighting. The case was thus sent on remand to the District Court to set the sum of compensatory damages.

- *Morad Fathi Jamjum* v. *State of Israel,* C.C. 923/98, Haifa District Court, Judgment of 18 August 2004, 2004 (3) *Takdin-District* 3106

The court accepted a claim for damages brought by a Palestinian who was seriously injured in Hebron in 1997 (at the age of 14) by a rubber coated metal bullet shot by IDF soldiers during a riot control operation. According to the court, there was clear evidence that the soldiers were negligent in firing rubber coated metal bullets at a road used by both rioters and innocent pedestrians and that combat-situation conditions which might give rise to state immunity from tort action were absent. However, the court ruled that there was contributory negligence on the part of the claimant, who failed to distance himself from the rioting zone. As a result, it instructed the state to pay the claimant 565,791 NIS (about US$ 130,000) in compensatory damages.

- *Azam Abu-Turkey* v. *State of Israel,* C.C. 7923/99 (Jer.), Jerusalem Justice of the Peace (First Instance Court), Judgment of 2 February 2004, 2004 (1) *Takdin-Peace* 3729

The court rejected a claim for damages brought by a Palestinian who was injured after being shot by undercover plain-clothed IDF soldiers in Hebron in 1992. The court found that the claimant's version of the events lacked credibility and preferred the soldiers' account, according to which the claimant was part of a three-member group of masked individuals who confronted the soldiers with axes and then escaped. Under these circumstances, the court held that shooting in the direction of the escaping militants, after they had been warned to stop, was not unlawful. Furthermore, the court opined that the life-threatening situation in which the soldiers found themselves probably entitled the state to invoke the 'combat situation' immunity from tort claims.

- *Abu-Taima Fatma* v. *State of Israel,* C.C. 1873/00 (Ramla.) Ramla Justice of the Peace

(First Instance Court), Judgment of 12 May 2004, 2004 (2) *Tadkin-Peace* 3713

The court rejected a claim for damages brought by the parents of a 13 year-old Palestinian killed in 1993 in the Gaza Strip by IDF soldier who shot him with a rubber coated metal bullet. According to the court, it had been proven that the deceased led a group of violent demonstrators who threw stones at IDF soldiers on patrol and put them in a life-threatening situation. In these circumstances, the firing of rubber-coated bullet at the lower part of the deceased's body, using a gun equipped with telescopic lenses, was not negligent despite the deadly consequences that ensued. In any event, the court held that the state was entitled to invoke the combat situation immunity and, alternatively, a self-endangerment defence from liability.

178. See the report on Israel in 5 *YIHL* (2002) pp. 534-535.

☛ *Fatma Ashak* v. *State of Israel,* C.C. 24148/97 (Jer.) Jerusalem Justice of the Peace (First Instance Court), Judgment of 5 September 2004, 2004 (3) *Takdin-Peace* 9410

The court rejected a damages claim brought by a Palestinian woman who claimed she had been injured in 1997 by a random bullet shot by IDF soldiers during a riot control operation near Bethlehem. According to the court, the state showed that on the relevant date there were violent clashes in Bethlehem between IDF soldiers and Palestinian militants, involving the use of firearms on both sides. Since the claimant failed to establish that it was an IDF bullet, and not a Palestinian bullet, which had struck her, the case was not proven. In any event, the state was entitled to invoke its combat situation immunity from tort claims.

8. Criminal law

☛ *State of Israel* v. *Barghouti,* Cr. C. 1158/02, Tel Aviv District Court of Israel, Judgment of 20 May 2004, 2004 (4) *Pador* 664.

Marwan Barghouti, head of the *Fattah* political movement in the West Bank and two of its military offshoots – the *Tanzim* and the *Al Aqsa Brigades* – and a member of the Palestinian Parliament, was charged in an Israeli court with murder and responsibility for numerous terrorist acts.

In its judgment, the Tel Aviv District Court reaffirmed that the defendant is not entitled to any immunity under international law, either as a parliament member or as member of an armed group (since he failed to meet the conditions specified in the Third Geneva Convention and violated the laws of war), and held that the defendant's involvement in terrorism – especially in military operations targeting civilians – cannot be justified under the laws of war. It further held that Barghouti is generally responsible for the activities of the *Tanzim* and *Al Aqsa Brigades,* as he was regarded by their own members as their leader, provided them with funds and weapons, encouraged these groups to execute terror attacks, issued specific instructions to some militant factions, and received regular reports from members of these militant groups. As a result, the court convicted him for the crime of membership and activity in a terror organisation. Still, the court decided to convict Barghouti only for four attacks in which five civilians were killed (out of the 37 attacks specified in the indictment) in which his personal involvement was proven. For these acts, the defendant was convicted for murder, attempted murder and conspiracy to commit a crime. Notably, the court refrained from invoking a 'command responsibility' legal construction with relation to the other attacks executed by *Tanzim* and *Al Aqsa Brigades* that were mentioned in the indictment, claiming that Israeli law, as it stood at the time of the acts in question, did not contain such a basis for criminal responsibility.

On 6 June 2004 Barghouti was sentenced to five consecutive life imprisonment sentences and two additional 20 year sentences.[179]

---

179. Cr. C. 1158/02 *State of Israel* v. *Barghouti,* sentencing decision, 6 June 2004, 2004(24) *Pador* 493.

9. Habeas corpus

- *Muhammad Abed-Al-Rahim Muhammad Al-Shaf'i* v. *IDF West Bank Military Commander,* H.C.J. 7862/02, Registrar of the Supreme Court of Israel, Decision of 2 February 2004 (1) *Takdin-Supreme* 972

Given the one week delay on the part of the IDF authorities in providing family members of Palestinian detainees with details on their whereabouts, the court ordered the state to pay the petitioners 5,000 NIS in legal costs.

- *The Center for Defense of the Individual* v. *State of Israel,* H.C.J. 9733/03, Registrar of the Supreme Court of Israel, Decision of 14 November 2004, 2004 (4) *Takdin-Supreme* 842

In a procedural decision, the court instructed the state to provide some information to the petitioners concerning the reasons for designating 'detention facility 1391' as a secret facility, the exact location of which is undisclosed. Specifically, the state was required to report on the number of detainees in the facility since the time of its establishment and the duration of their dentition, and to explain whether conditions of detention in the facility are identical to conditions in all other military facilities.

10. Movement restrictions

- *Muhammad Mousa Al-Razi* v. *IDF Gaza Strip Military Commander,* H.C.J. 7960/04, Supreme Court of Israel, Judgment of 29 September 2004, 2004 (3) *Takdin-Supreme* 3384

The petition challenged the refusal on the part of the IDF to permit the travel of ten young Palestinians from Gaza to Bethlehem for university studies, on the basis of the argument that their 'risk profile' renders them probable candidates for recruitment by Gaza-based terror groups (in addition, there existed specific information implicating four of the ten petitioners in security-compromising activities). The court declined to intervene in the discretion of the military authorities, noting the significant danger to security of the public in Israel and in the Occupied Territories that movement between Gaza and the West Bank entails at the present time. The court also noted that the IDF is willing to allow the petitioners to travel to study abroad.

- *Osama Sakker Abu-Nada* v. *IDF Gaza Strip Military Commander,* H.C.J. 4566/04 Supreme Court of Israel, Judgment of 21 June 2004, 2004 (2) *Takdin-Supreme* 2964

The court rejected a petition against restrictions imposed by the IDF upon passage through the Rafah Terminal, connecting the Gaza Strip and Egypt. The court accepted that the closure of the terminal on some dates by virtue of active fighting in its vicinity renders the petition of some petitioners – doctors who wished to attend a conference in Beirut, which already took place – irrelevant, and that the arguments brought by the petitioners against the general policy of not allowing Palestinians younger than 35 to cross the terminal is too broad to facilitate judicial intervention at this stage. Still, the court noted that the IDF is reviewing the procedures for crossing the Rafah Terminal, and that the petitioners may challenge in the future any decision adopted pursuant to the review process.

11. Family reunifications

- *Uda Nancy* v. *IDF West Bank Military Commander,* H.C.J. 4332/02, Supreme Court of Israel, Judgment of 2 February 2004, 2004 (2) *Takdin-Supreme* 1656
- *Osama Abed Al-Rahim Hader* v. *IDF West Bank Military Commander,* H.C.J. 7835/02, Supreme Court of Israel, Judgment of 1 September 2004, 2004 (3) *Takdin-Supreme* 2123

The court rejected these two petitions against the deportation from the West Bank of Jordanian citizens who married local Palestinian women. The court held in *Nancy* that since no request for family reunification was presented to the Israeli authorities by their Palestinian counterparts – as is required by the Oslo Accords (Article 28(11) to the First Annex of the 1995 Israeli-Palestinian Interim Agreement) – there is no basis upon which the Israeli authorities could have approved the request.

- *Isdaher Mahmud Muhammad Kassem* v. *IDF West Bank Military Commander,* District Court of Jerusalem, A.C.A. 757/03, Decision of 9 June 2004, 2004 (2) *Takdin-District* 4760

The court rejected an appeal against the decision of the Israeli authorities not to allow the petitioner, who is a West Bank resident, to reside in East Jerusalem by virtue of her husband's residency. The court noted that the petition has several procedural flaws, but that, in any event, the fact that the husband is serving 35 life sentences in an Israeli prison for his involvement in mass terror activities defeats the rationale of family reunification.

12. Deportation of aliens

- *Anonymous* v. *Israeli Police,* H.C.J. 4914/04, Supreme Court of Israel, Judgment of 18 July 2004, (3) *Takdin-Supreme* 721

The court rejected the petition of a Palestinian unlawfully present in Israel against his deportation to the Gaza Strip, noting that several courts have already rejected past attempts on the part of the petitioner to legalise his stay in Israel and that his claim of expected life-threatening persecution in Gaza is unsubstantiated.

13. Freedom of the press

- *Ahmed Sayif* v. *Governmental Press Office,* H.C.J. 5627/02, Supreme Court of Israel, Judgment of 25 April 2004, 2004 (2) *Takdin-Supreme* 448

The petitioner challenged the new policy of the Israel Governmental Press Office to refuse issuing press cards to Palestinian journalists, citing primarily security concerns. The court held that the sweeping nature of the new policy and the refusal on the part of the government to examine requests for press cards on a case by case basis unduly infringes upon freedom of the press, and is therefore unlawful.

Pending Legislation (disengagement)

- Implementation of the Disengagement Plan Draft Law 2004, *Official Gazette for Draft Legislation,* Vol. 130, p. 2 <Haza'at Hok Yisum Tochnit Ha'Hitnatkut, 764, 2004>

The draft bill is designed to implement the government's decision to remove all Israeli settlements and military presence from the Gaza Strip (with the possible exception of the Philadelphi Route along the Gaza Strip/Egyptian border, which was designed at the time to temporarily remain under IDF control) and evacuate four northern West Bank settlements. It comprises exclusive compensatory arrangements for the settlers and prohibits, by way of criminal law provisions, the presence of Israeli citizens after a certain date in areas designated as 'evacuation areas'.

Pending Legislation (Geneva law)

- Geneva Convention Draft Law, 2004, Knesset Doc. P/2189 (2004), submitted to the Knesset on 24 March 2004

This private bill (i.e., not sponsored by the Israeli government) seeks to incorporate the four 1949 Geneva Conventions into Israeli law and accord their grave breach provisions explicit status under Israeli penal law. Two similar draft laws were voted down by the Knesset on 28 January 2004.

Pending Legislation (financing of terrorism)

- Prohibition of Fund Transfers to the Palestinian Authority Draft Law, 2004, Knesset Doc. P/2514 (2004), submitted to the Knesset on 26 July 2004

This private bill aims to prohibit the transfer of funds from Israel to the Palestinian Authority (such funds have been mainly transferred pursuant to the Oslo Accords tax and custom arrangements), in response to the latter's alleged involvement in terrorism. The bill authorises the government to deviate from the conditions set therein, if it finds that the Palestinian Authority had, in good faith, engaged in efforts to curb terror for a period of no less than 18 consecutive months. A similar draft bill was voted down by the Knesset on 3 March 2004.

Pending Cases (*targeted killings*)

- *The Public Committee Against Torture in Israel* v. *Government of the State of Israel,* H. C.J. 769/02, pending before the Supreme Court of Israel

On 21 January 2004 the state submitted its additional pleadings on the lawfulness of its policy of targeted killing. The 118-page document seeks to address the claimant's submissions and, in particular, the assertions made in the expert opinion of Professor Antonio Cassese, which the claimants submitted to the court in 2003.[180] The state's additional pleadings allege that since September 2000 Israel has been the target of numerous armed attacks by Palestinian groups, which give rise to the application of the laws of warfare governing armed conflicts. Killing of individuals taking direct part in hostilities is lawful, regardless of the precise classification of the armed conflict (international armed conflict, non-international armed conflict, or a *sui generic* 'war on terror') and the status of targeted Palestinians is equivalent to that of 'unprivileged combatants' – they are legitimate military targets, yet ineligible for POW status. The pleadings also allege that Article 51(3) of the First Additional Protocol (to which Israel is not party) – a provision that restricts the ability to target

---

180. See the report on Israel in 6 *YIHL* (2003) p. 517.

civilians taking a direct part in hostilities only to times in which they take a direct part in hostilities – does not reflect customary law. The state also argues that the term 'taking a direct part in hostilities' should, in any event, be broadly construed so to encompass leaders and planers of terrorist acts. Additionally, it submits that the term 'for such times as they take a direct part' should be liberally read so to cover the relevant individual's entire duration of active membership in terror groups. Finally, the pleadings highlight the ambiguities associated with the application of the principle of proportionality under IHL and maintain that the IDF meets international standards in that regard.

The claimants submitted later that year a written response, in which they argued *inter alia* that numerous legal authorities support the customary status of Article 51(3) and its restrictive interpretation. The response also alleges that the Israeli-Palestinian conflict should be defined as an international armed conflict and that Israel's targeted killing practices produce disproportional harm upon civilian populations not taking part in hostilities.

The court has not rendered, to date, its judgment in the case.[181] It may be noted that throughout 2004 targeted killing was used by the IDF on several occasions, including in some high profile cases (the killing of Hamas leaders Yassin and Rantisi).

NGO Reports

1. The separation barrier

- Amnesty International, *Israel and the Occupied Territories: The place of the fence/wall in international law* (London 2004) <http://web.amnesty.org/library/Index/ENGMDE150162004?open&of=ENG-ISR>

The report criticises the construction of the barrier in the Occupied Territories and identifies numerous violations of IHL and international human rights law that the barrier entails. In particular, the barrier will impede freedom of movement, result in extensive seizures and destruction of property and result in serious deterioration of the economic and social condition in the Occupied Territories.

- B'Tselem, Facing the Abyss: The Isolation of Sheikh Sa'ad Village – Before and After the Separation Barrier (Jerusalem 2004) <http://www.btselem.org/Download/200402_Sheikh_Saed_Eng.doc>

The report chronicles the numerous hardships imposed upon the Palestinian village of Sheikh Sa'ad, located in the outskirts of Jerusalem, as a result of the construction of the separation barrier. It argues that the harm to the village is particularly grave given its total dependence on East Jerusalem, from which it has now been detached, for health, education, burial services, commerce and the like. According to B'Tselem, the movement restrictions caused by Israel violate a number of internationally recognised human rights and humanitarian law norms, including Article 43 of the 1907 Hague Regulations. In response, an IDF

181. On 16 February 2005 the state informed the court that following the Sharm El-Sheikh cease-fire declaration (8 February 2005), it indefinitely suspende all targeted killing operations, though it reserves the right to resort to such operations in extreme 'ticking bomb' circumstances. The court has not decided, to date, whether the proceedings in the case should be continued in the light of the state's new position. However, since the state resumed in late 2005 its policy of targeted killings, in response to new terror attacks, the case will probably continue.

spokesperson issued a statement indicating that the military is exploring ways to improve access of Sheikh Sa'ad residents to the West Bank, and a police spokesperson stated that access of permit holders to Jerusalem will be improved in the foreseeable future. The Jerusalem Municipality General Director responded by stating that the responsibility for the provision of municipal services to Sheikh Sa'ad lies with the Palestinian Authority.

☛ B'Tselem, *Not All it Seems: Preventing Palestinians Access to their Lands West of the Separation Barrier in the Tulkarm-Qalqiliya Area* (Jerusalem 2004) <http://www.btselem.org/Download/200406_Qalqiliya_Tulkarm_Barrier_Eng.pd>

The report describes the various impediments introduced by the separation barrier and its associated regime upon the ability of Palestinian farmers to access their lands located west of the barrier. It identifies a number of human rights and humanitarian law violations that the situation entails (e.g., violation of Article 39 of the Fourth Geneva Convention).

☛ ICRC Press Release, West Bank Barrier Causes Serious Humanitarian and Legal Problems 17 February 2004 <http://www.icrc.org/web/eng/siteeng0.nsf/iwpList74/F06BB484D900B227C1256E3E00324D96>

The ICRC stated that to the extent that the barrier deviates from the 'Green Line' it is unlawful under IHL, as it causes disproportionate harm to the humanitarian interests of the local Palestinian population in the Occupied Territories.

2. Movement restrictions

☛ B'Tselem, *Forbidden Roads: Israel's Discriminatory Road Regime in the West Bank* (Jerusalem 2004) <http://www.btselem.org/download/200408_Forbidden_Roads_Eng.pdf>

The report surveys Israel's policy of restricting the access of Palestinians to some main roads in the West Bank. It criticises the questionable legal basis of the policy – it is based not on legislative acts but rather on verbal order of military commanders – and the security rationale underlying such a sweeping restriction. Instead, the policy arguably serves, in the main, the needs of Israeli settlements in the West Bank. At the same time, the policy adversely affects numerous aspects of day-to-day Palestinian life, e.g., in the fields of health, education, the economy, etc. According to B'Tselem, the road regime in the West Bank violates fundamental human rights and a number of international humanitarian law standards, including the prohibition against discrimination (Article 27 of the Fourth Geneva Convention) and against collective punishment (Article 33 of the Fourth Geneva Convention).

An IDF spokesperson responded to the report by confirming the general authority of military commanders to impose temporary restrictions on movement in order to curb terror activity, but stated that the report exaggerated the scope of the actual restrictions in place.

3. House demolitions

☛ Amnesty International, *Israel and the Occupied Territories: Under the rubble: House demolition and destruction of land and property* (London 2004) <http://web.amnesty.org/library/Index/ENGMDE150332004?open&of=ENG-ISR>

The report surveys the house demolition practices of Israel in the Occupied Territories and in the Arab sector in Israel proper since the beginning of the second *intifada.* These operations are conducted on the basis of alleged military needs – including punitive and operational house demolitions – or for the enforcement of planning and zoning laws (mainly in Israel proper and in East Jerusalem).

The report asserts that more than 3,000 Palestinian buildings and commercial properties have been destroyed in the Occupied Territories in the preceding 3.5 years and that thousands of other properties have been damaged beyond repair – resulting in tens of thousands of Palestinians becoming homeless or unemployed. The report also criticises the lack of warning which typically characterises house demolition operations in the Occupied Territories and highlights the illegality of demolitions designed to facilitate the development of nearby Israeli settlements (e.g., construction of bypass roads).

According to the report, Israeli house demolition practices violate IHL and international human rights law, and may amount to war crimes.

☛ Human Rights Watch, Razing Rafah: Mass Home Demolitions in the Gaza Strip (New York 2004) <http://hrw.org/reports/2004/rafah1004/>

The report documents the widespread demolition of houses in Rafah during the second *intifada* and questions the authenticity of Israel's security justification for such operations.

☛ B'Tselem, *Through No Fault of Their Own: Israel's Punitive House Demolitions in the al-Aqsa Intifada* (Jerusalem 2004) <http://www.btselem.org/download/200411_Punitive_House_Demolitions_Eng.pdf>

The report describes Israel's policy of punitive house demolitions, since the beginning of the second *intifada.* It chronicles 628 cases of punitive house demolition, and alleges that, as a result, more than 3,000 Palestinians lost their homes. It further alleges that in the vast majority of cases no prior warning was given to dwellers before demolition operations, and criticises the role of the Supreme Court in eroding the administrative law-based right to be heard. According to B'Tselem, punitive house demolitions are unlawful under IHL, and constitute war crimes – in particular, demolitions violate the Fourth Geneva Convention's prohibition against wanton destruction of property and collective punishment.

An IDF spokesperson responded to the report by citing the deterrent value of punitive house demolitions, especially in relation to would-be suicide bombers, and noted that the Supreme Court approved this policy, subject to several conditions, which the IDF strictly applies. He also noted that the authority to execute punitive house demolitions is sparsely used, in cases where the residency of a terrorist in the house in question or its use for hostile activities has been proven.

4. Family reunification

☛ Committee on the Elimination of All Forms of Racial Discrimination, *Prevention of Racial Discrimination, including early warning measures and urgent action procedures: Israel,* Decision of 20 August 2004[182]

The Committee reiterated its call to Israel to revoke the Citizenship and Entry to Israel Law (Provisional Order) 2003,[183] which bars the Minister of the Interior from naturalising or granting temporary permits to Palestinians residing in the Occupied Territories, even if they are married to Israeli citizens. According to the Committee, the law – whose validity was extended by the Knesset until early 2005 – raises serious questions under the Convention on the Elimination of All Forms of Racial Discrimination.

☛ Amnesty International, *Israel and the Occupied Territories: Torn Apart: Families split by discriminatory policies* (London 2004) <http://web.amnesty.org/library/Index/ENGMDE150632004?open&of=ENG-ISR>

The report criticises the 2003 amendment to the Citizenship and Entry to Israel Law. The amended law was enacted in response to the alleged involvement in terrorism of some 23 Palestinians carrying Israeli residence permits. However, according to the report, it is discriminatory and violates a number of international human rights. It also runs contrary to Israel's duty to respect the family rights of individuals in occupied territories provided for in Article 27 of the Fourth Geneva Convention and Article 46 of the 1907 Hague Regulations.

☛ B'Tselem, *Forbidden Families: Family Unification and Child Registration in East Jerusalem* (Jerusalem 2004) <http://www.btselem.org/Download/200401_Forbidden_Families_Eng.pdf>

The report describes the effects of the 2003 amendment to Israel's Citizenship and Entry to Israel Law upon the family lives of Palestinians residing in East Jerusalem. The new temporary law, which essentially freezes the family reunification process of Palestinian Jerusalemites, causes numerous hardships to local Palestinians, and is, according to the report, unlawful under IHL and international human rights law. The report also describes the legal challenges against the constitutionality of the amended law before Israeli courts and criticises the security justification underlying this piece of legislation.

The second part of the report criticises the refusal of the Israeli authorities to register Palestinian children born in the Occupied Territories to Palestinian residents of East Jerusalem as Israelis residents. This new policy also adversely affects Palestinian family unification processes, as it bars the residence of Palestinian children with their Jerusalemite families and is also allegedly unlawful under international law.

182. Committee on the Elimination of All Forms of Racial Discrimination, *Prevention of Racial Discrimination, including early warning measures and urgent action procedures: Israel,* UN Doc. CERD/C/65/Dec.2 (2004).

183. See report on Israel, 6 *YIHL* (2003) pp. 503-504.

5. Protection of civilians

☛ Amnesty International, *Israel and the Occupied Territories: Israeli settlers wage campaign of intimidation on Palestinians and internationals alike* (London 2004) <http://web.amnesty.org/library/Index/ENGMDE150992004?open&of=ENG-ISR>

The report alleges that Israeli settlers in the Occupied Territories have been waging a campaign of violence against Palestinians and non-Palestinian NGO activists and that the Israeli authorities have been ineffective in preventing these attacks and in bringing to justice their perpetrators.

6. Removal of settlements from the Gaza Strip

☛ Harvard Programme on Humanitarian Policy and Conflict Research – International Humanitarian Law Research Initiative, *Legal Aspects of Israel's Disengagement Plan under International Humanitarian Law: A Policy Brief* (Cambridge, MA 2004)

The brief discussed the legal situation which would result from Israel's planned disengagement from the Gaza Strip in 2005. It concluded that in the absence of a contrary determination by an authoritative international organisation, the situation is likely to remain one of occupation, by reason of Israel's continued control over numerous aspects of Palestinian life within the Gaza Strip, its military control over the perimeters of the Strip, and, at the same time, the Palestinian Authority's limited control over the same area.

7. General conditions in the Occupied Territories

☛ Report of the Special Rapporteur of the Commission on Human Rights on the situation of human rights in the Palestinian territories occupied by Israel since 1967, UN Doc. E/CN.4/2005/29 (2004)

The report criticised IDF military operations in the Gaza Strip, which took place in 2004, in which some 150 Palestinians were killed and some 500 houses demolished or rendered uninhabitable. Such wanton destruction is indicative, according to the special rapporteur, of punitive actions which probably amount to war crimes under the Fourth Geneva Convention. In addition, the report criticises the continued construction of the separation wall, in contravention of the ICJ Advisory Opinion, and not in full conformity with the Israeli Supreme Court judgment in *Beit Sourik*[184] (the Israeli government allegedly refused to apply the *Beit Sourik* test of proportionality with regard to the 200 km of the wall constructed prior to the court's judgment). These actions seriously hinder Palestinians' freedom of movement, entail considerable hardships in almost every aspect of their life and could result in the forced exodus eastwards of Palestinians residing west of the wall. The Special Rapporteur also pointed to special difficulties resulting from the route of the wall in East Jerusalem. Finally, the report submitted that Israel's expected withdrawal from the Gaza Strip in 2005 would not relieve it of its obligations as an occupier by reason of the continued control it will exert over Strip's external perimeters, air space and sea ports.

---

184. H.C.J. 2056/04..

☛ The US State Department, *Israel and the occupied territories: Country Reports on Human Rights Practices* (Washington 2004)

The report reviewed the human rights situation in the Occupied Territories during 2004. It indicated that arbitrary or unlawful killings by Israeli and Palestinian forces and by Israeli settlers and Palestinian militants continued to occur (including 'excessive collateral damage' –killing of Palestinians civilians during IDF military operations); that on a few occasions IDF forces fired at Palestinian ambulances and journalists; that several Palestinian detainees were beaten or otherwise maltreated during their interrogation or detention; that some detention facilities, used for the detainment of Palestinians, were 'austere' and overcrowded; that the number of Palestinian detainees suspect of security-related offences has arisen significantly during 2004; that Israel holds some 960 Palestinians in administrative detention, but refrained in 2004 from transferring Palestinians from the West Bank to the Gaza Strip (and allowed the return of one individual transferred in 2002).

The report also discussed the Israeli military trial system, which applies to Palestinian criminal defendants; house demolitions undertaken by Israel in the Occupied Territories; and the effects on movement restrictions in the Occupied Territories (including the construction of the separation barrier) on Palestinian access to academic, health and religious facilities, and on other aspects of their daily lives. It addressed, in addition, the various impediments upon the ability of Palestinians to move out of the Occupied Territories, and documented several incidents of settler violence against Palestinians and foreigners in the Occupied Territories.

YUVAL SHANY

ITALY[185]

Conventional Weapons

☛ Law No. 131 of 28 April 2004, 'Ratification and Execution of the Amendment (21 December 2001) to Article 1 of the Convention on Prohibition or Restrictions on the use of Certain Conventional Weapons Which May Be Deemed to be Excessively Injurious or to Have Indiscriminate Effects' (Geneva, 10 October 1980). Published in the *Official Journal* No. 121 of 25 May 2004 and entered into force on 26 May 2004 [Legge 28 Aprile 2004 no. 131 'Ratifica ed esecuzione dell'Emendamento all'articolo 1 della Convenzione sulla proibizione o limitazione di alcune armi convenzionali che possono essere considerate eccessivamente dannose o aventi effetti indiscriminate' (CCW) del 10 ottobre 1980, adottato a Ginevra il 21 dicembre 2001, pubblicata nella *Gazzetta Ufficiale* no. 121 del 25 maggio 2004]

By Law No. 131 of 28 April 2004 the Italian Parliament authorised the ratification of the amendment (21 December 2001) to Article 1 of the Convention on Prohibition or Restrictions on the Use of Certain Conventional Weapons (CCW) which May Be deemed to be Excessively Injurious or to Have Indiscriminate Effects (Geneva, 10 October 1980). The

185. Information and commentaries provided by Valeria Eboli, Valentina della Fina, Ornella Ferrajolo and Giovanni Carlo Bruno of the Institute for International Legal Studies of the National Research Council (CNR).

amendment extends the scope of application of the CCW to armed conflicts not of an international character as referred to in Article 3 common to the four Geneva Conventions.

By ratifying the amendment, states bind themselves to apply the Convention in case of internal armed conflicts occurring on their own territory (Article 1(3) amended).

The equalisation of international and internal armed conflicts as far as restrictions and prohibitions on the use of certain conventional weapons is concerned is a consequence of the evolution of international humanitarian law applicable to conflicts not of an international character in the last decade.[186] The admission of the fact that the same kinds of weapons were equally available in both categories of conflicts determined this legal change. By ratifying the amendment, Italy demonstrates its approval of this evolving trend in IHL. The support of the Italian Government for the extension of some of the norms applicable to international armed conflicts to internal armed conflict was already apparent with its ratification of the Second Protocol to the CCW[187] (as amended in 1996), which already applied to non-international armed conflicts.

VALERIA EBOLI[188]

Chemical Weapons

- Law No. 196 of 19 July 2004, 'Ratification and Execution of the Additional Protocol to the Moscow Agreement (20 January 2000) between the Italian Government and the Russian Federation Government for the Italian Assistance regarding the Destruction of Chemical Weapons' stocks in the Russian Federation, done in Rome on April 17th 2003'. Published in the *Official Journal* No. 182 of 5 August 2004 and entered into force on 6 August 2004 [Legge 19 luglio 204 n. 196 'Ratifica ed esecuzione del Protocollo aggiuntivo all'Accordo di Mosca del 20 gennaio 2000 tra il Governo della Repubblica italiana ed il Governo della Federazione russa per l'assistenza italiana nella distruzione degli stock di armi chimiche nella Federazione russa', fatto a Roma il 17 aprile 2003, pubblicato nella *Gazzetta Ufficiale* no. 182 del 5 agosto 2004]

---

186. The jurisprudence of the *ad hoc* Tribunals for the Former Yugoslavia (ICTY) and for Rwanda (ICTR) has particularly contributed to the evolution of IHL in this direction. The ICTY Appeals Chamber decision on the Defence Motion for Interlocutory Appeal on Jurisdiction in the case of Tadić (Decision of 2 October 1995 in Case No. IT-94_1_AR72) at para. 199 ff., affirmed the consolidation of a good set of customary law norms applicable to internal armed conflict. See D. Momtaz, 'Le droit international humanitaire applicable aux conflits armés non internationaux', in *Recueil des Cous de l'Académie de droit international de La Haye*, 2001, tome 292 (The Hague/Boston/London) pp. 11-145.

187. Italy ratified it on 20 January 1995 and, as amended, on 13 January 1999.

188. Valeria Eboli, Ph. D in International Law, University 'La Sapienza' of Rome, is a consultant at the Institute for International Legal Studies of the National Research Council (CNR), Rome. She is National Instructor of IHL of the Italian Red Cross and a Qualified Adviser of the Italian Armed Forces on IHL.

By Law No. 196 of 19 July 2004 the Italian Parliament authorised the Head of State[189] to ratify the Protocol[190] annexed to the Moscow Agreement[191] (20 January 2000) between the Italian government and the Russian Federation government for Italian Assistance regarding the Destruction of Chemical Weapons Stocks in the Russian Federation (Rome, 17 April 2003).

The Protocol sets out the programme of cooperation between the Italian Republic and the Russian Federation established in the framework of the Kananaskis G8 Meeting.[192] The Moscow Agreement aimed to contribute to armaments control, as provided for in the Convention on the Prohibition of the Development, Production, Stockpiling and Use of Chemical Weapons and on their Destruction (Paris, 10 January 1993), to which both Italy[193] and the Russian Federation are High Contracting Parties. So, the Protocol is explicitly related to the accomplishment of previous international engagements of the governments.

In the bilateral Agreement, the Parties reaffirmed their wish to protect humankind and the environment through the destruction of chemical weapons' stocks. Italy bound itself to financially assist the Russian Federation and the latter engaged itself to realise an installation for the destruction of chemical weapons in Kizner (Republic of Uzmurtia), through an Italian enterprise.

The Additional Protocol provides for further financial support by Italy to the Russian Federation (5 millions euros) in order to realise the installation for the destruction of chemical weapons in Schuch'ye (region of Kurgan) and, in particular (Art. 2), to build a system for the distribution of natural gas. The modalities of the use of the fund by the Russian Federation are dealt with in the previous Agreement, of which the Protocol is an integral part (Art. 4).

As did the original Agreement, the Protocol indicates which governmental authorities within the two states are responsible to implement its dispositions. For Italy, it is the Ministry for Foreign Affairs, while for Russia it is the Russian Agency for Munitions.[194] In case of controversies between the Parties concerning the Protocol, Article 12 of the Agreement of 20 January 2000 applies. It provides for the solution of every controversy by diplomatic channels or, in any case, by peaceful means.

---

189. Art. 80 of the Italian Constitution requires the previous authorisation of the Chambers to the Head of State for the ratification of certain kinds of international treaties, among which are those involving financial engagement.

190. It was signed in Rome on 17 April 2003 by the Italian Under-Secretary of State Roberto Antonione and the Vice-Director of the Russian Agency for Munitions Viaceslav Nicolaevitch Kuliebiakin.

191. This Agreement was ratified by Italy by Law No. 34 of 17 February 2001, published in the *Official Journal* No. 54 of 6 March 2001 and entered into force on 7 March 2001.

192. In the framework of the '*Global Partnership*' provided for at the Kananaskis' G8 Meeting, two important bilateral agreements on disarmament matters were signed: one concerned the destruction of Russian submarines and the other concerned chemical weapons. This aim was reaffirmed in the framework of a bilateral meeting that took place in Rome on 5 November 2003, where Italy and the Russian Federation recalled the previous agreements and expressed the will to continue in the path of cooperation in order to let Russia able to join the European Union as soon as possible. See Joint Declaration on bilateral cooperation between the Italian Republic and the Russian Federation, <http://www.governo.it/GovernoInforma/Dossier/vertice_italia_russia_05112003/dichiarazione.html>.

193. Italy ratified the Convention on 8 December 1995.

194. In the Agreement the appointed authorities were the following: for the Italian Government, the Ministry for the Foreign Affairs; for the Russian Federation, the Ministry of Defence (Art. 4).

The Italian Law concerning the Protocol contributes to effectively realising the aims of the Kananaskis G8 Meeting, which included, among others, prevention of the diffusion of all weapons and materials of mass destruction.[195]

VALERIA EBOLI[196]

Peacekeeping

☛ Law No. 68 of 12 March 2004, 'Conversion in law, with modifications, of Decree No. 9 of 20 January 2004, concerning the extension of Italian participation in international operations. Dispositions in favour of military and civilian victims of terrorist attacks abroad' [Legge 12 marzo 2004, no. 68 'Conversione in legge, con modificazioni, del decreto-legge 20 gennaio 2004, n. 9, recante proroga della partecipazione italiana a operazioni internazionali. Disposizioni in favore delle vittime militari e civili di attentati terroristici all'estero']. Entered into force on 19 March 2004. Published in the Italian Official Journal No. 65 of 18 March 2004 <http://www.parlamento.it/parlam/leggi/04068l.htm>

☛ Law No. 208 of 30 July 2004, 'Extension of Italian participation in international operations' <Legge 30 luglio 2004, no. 208 'Proroga della partecipazione italiana a missioni internazionali'>. Entered into force on 13 August 2004. Published in the Italian Official Journal, No. 188 of 12 August 2004 <http://www.parlamento.it/parlam/leggi/04208l.htm>

Italy is one of the European countries most involved in peacekeeping and enforcement operations. Currently, about 9,000 Italian soldiers participate in 25 international operations in 18 countries.[197] Notwithstanding this engagement at the international level, it is noteworthy that the Italian legal system lacks a comprehensive law regulating all aspects of overseas missions. For this reason, the Italian legislature needs to adopt *ad hoc* acts authorising military and civilian staff to take part in new international missions or to continue their participation in current operations. The need for general rules concerning the missions of Italian military contingents abroad was underlined by the Chamber of Deputies during debate on the adoption of Law No. 68 of 12 March 2004.[198]

Law No. 68 extends the duration of some Italian military missions abroad until 30 June 2004 and, in the meantime, contains some dispositions on criminal law and staff pay. Articles 1 and 2 continue the humanitarian and reconstruction mission in Iraq (Operation 'Antica Babilonia'[199]) until 30 June 2004, authorising the expenditure of 11,627,450 euros for the organisation of the mission and its equipment and of 209,017,084 euros for military staff during 2004.

---

195. See Communication by the Ministry of Foreign Affairs of 17 April 2003, <http://ww.esteri.it/ita/6_38_90_01.asp?id=71&mod=6&min=0>.

196. Valeria Eboli, Ph. D in International Law, University 'La Sapienza' of Rome, is a consultant at the Institute for International Legal Studies of the National Research Council (CNR), Rome. She is National Instructor of IHL of the Italian Red Cross and Qualified Adviser of the Italian Armed Forces for IHL.

197. See <http://www.difesa.it/NR/exeres/6F1D2705-009F-40BC-97E7-C0695FF351BC.htm>.

198. See Parliamentary Acts, Chamber of Deputies, XIV Legislature, draft Bill No. 4725-A. Published at <http://www. parlamento.it>.

199. On this Operation see V. Della Fina in 6 *YIHL* (2003) pp. 525-526.

Article 3 provides for the extension, until 30 June 2004, of a series of international missions authorising the participation of the Italian military and civilian staff in the following operations: Joint Force and Over the Horizon Force in Bosnia; Multinational Specialised Unit (MSU) in Bosnia and in Kosovo; Joint Guardian in Kosovo and the Former Yugoslav Republic of Macedonia (FYROM); NATO Headquarters Skopje (NATO HQS) in FYROM; United Nations Mission in Kosovo (UNMIK) and Criminal Intelligence Unit (CIU) in Kosovo; Albit, Albania 2 and NATO Headquarters Tirana (NATO HQT) in Albania; Temporary International Presence in Hebron (TIPH 2); and United Nations Mission in Ethiopia and Eritrea (UNMEE). Furthermore, the same article extends, for the same period, Italian participation in Operation Enduring Freedom, in the missions Active Endeavour and Resolute Behaviour and in the International Security Assistance Force-ISAF in Afghanistan; in the monitoring mission of the European Union in the former Yugoslavia-EUMM and in the peace processes in Somalia and Sudan.

Article 4 concerns the participation of the Italian Police and Carabinieri (paramilitary police) in some UN and EU missions in the Balkans. In particular, it authorises the Italian Police to take part in the United Nations Mission in Kosovo (UNMIK) and to develop programmemes of cooperation with Albania[200] and other countries of the Balkan region. The personnel of the Police and Carabinieri can also participate in the EU Missions in Bosnia and Herzegovina and in Macedonia, respectively named EUPM and EUPOL Proxima.[201]

With regard to criminal law, Article 12 of Law No. 68 reaffirms that the Military Penal Code of War, as amended in conformity with international humanitarian law,[202] applies only to military personnel engaged in Iraq (Operation 'Antica Babilonia') and Afghanistan (Enduring Freedom, Active Endeavour and Resolute Behaviour, International Security Assistance Force-ISAF), where the operations are characterised by the use of armed force. For the military staff participating in other missions mentioned in the Law, which are principally humanitarian, the Military Penal Code of Peace applies. The choice between the two Codes is based on the different nature of the operations and is made on a case by case basis.[203]

The same article establishes the primacy of Italian jurisdiction over crimes committed in Iraq and Afghanistan by foreigners to the prejudice of the Italian state or citizens employed in the missions. It prescribes their punishment at the request of the Italian Minister of Justice, while for offences against military staff consultation with the Italian Minister of Defense is also necessary. The Tribunal of Rome has competence regarding these crimes.

Following the suspicious deaths of Italian soldiers participating in NATO operations in Bosnia and Kosovo, Article 13-*ter* of Law No. 68 authorises scientific research in order to verify the level of uranium or other toxic substances in soldiers involved in international missions.[204]

---

200. Article 11 of the Law No. 68 authorizes the expenditure of 5.165.000 euros for supplying the Albanian army with equipment and telecommunication services.

201. On these missions see also V. Eboli 6 *YIHL* (2003) p. 528.

202. On these modifications and on the Italian practice about the application of the Military Penal Codes of War and of Peace see V. Della Fina 4 *YIHL* (2001) pp. 563-565.

203. See the observations of V. Eboli 6 *YIHL* (2003) at pp. 524-525.

204. On the enquiries made in Italy to verify the link between depleted uranium and tumoral pathologies see G. Salberini, 4 *YIHL* (2001) pp. 558-559.

Law No. 208 of 30 July 2004 is closely linked with Law No. 68 because it extends Italian participation in international missions mentioned in the latter until 31 December 2004 (with the exception of the mission in Iraq[205]), and reaffirms the same principles concerning the implementation of criminal law and the primacy of Italian jurisdiction over offences committed abroad against the Italian state or citizens.

VALENTINA DELLA FINA[206]

☛ Law No. 207 of 30 July 2004, 'Conversion in law, with modifications, of Decree No. 160 of 24 June 2004 concerning the extension of Italian participation in international missions' [Legge 30 luglio 2004, n° 207, 'Conversione in legge, con modificazioni, del decreto-legge 24 giugno 2004, n. 160 recante proroga della partecipazione italiana a missioni internazionali']. Entered into force on 13 August 2004. Published in the Italian Official Journal No. 188 of 12 August 2004 <http://www.parlamento.it/parlam/leggi/04207l.htm>

By Decree No. 160 of 24 June 2004 the Italian government authorised the continuation of Italian participation in a number of international missions and also provided new funding.[207] The authorisation included the extension of the duration of the missions in Iraq established by Law No. 219 of 1 August 2003, namely, the humanitarian and reconstruction mission in accordance with Security Council resolution 1483 of 22 May 2003 and the military operation 'Antica Babilonia', aimed at contributing, in the context of the Anglo-American operation 'Iraqi Freedom', to the country's stabilisation and guaranteeing secure preconditions for humanitarian intervention.[208]

Decree No. 160/2004 was adopted under Article 77 of the Italian Constitution, as a matter of urgent necessity. On the same day as its entry into force (25 June 2004), a draft bill on the conversion into law of the Decree was introduced by the government in the Chamber of Deputies.[209] Pending parliamentary debate, the discussion concentrated principally on the extension of the missions in Iraq.[210] At the request of the opposition, which announced its intention to vote against the continuation of Operation 'Antica Babilonia', the draft bill's provisions concerning the participation of Italy in other international (UN and EU) missions – not a controversial issue – were eliminated from the text and inserted in another draft bill, later approved as Law No. 208 of 30 July 2004.[211] In consequence, Decree No. 160/2004, as modified by Law No. 207 of 30 July 2004, only deals with the

205. The exception of the Mission in Iraq has been decided by Law No. 207 of 30 July 2004, see O. Ferrajolo, in this volume.

206. Valentina Della Fina is a researcher at the Institute for International Legal Studies of the National Research Council (CNR), Rome.

207. Decree No. 160/2004 is published in the Italian Official Journal No. 147 of 25 June 2004. The text amended by Law No. 207/2004 is annexed to the latter.

208. See V. Della Fina's contribution in 6 *YIHL* (2003) pp. 525-526.

209. See Parliamentary Acts, Chamber of Deputies, XIV Legislature, draft Bill No. 5088, <http://www. camera.it>. Under Art. 77 of the Italian Constitution, a provisional decree adopted by the government in case of urgent necessity has immediately to be presented to the Parliament for conversion into law; it ceases to have any legal effect if not converted into law within 60 days of its publication.

210. Cf., Proceedings of the Chamber of Deputies, Assembly's Meetings No. 488 of 12 July and No. 489 of 13 July 2004, <http://www.camera.it>.

211. See *supra*.

Italian missions in Iraq.[212] It should be said, regarding these missions, that some modifications with respect to previous legislation were needed to bring the Italian intervention into line with Security Council resolution 1546 of 8 June 2004, which was followed, on 28 June, by the transferral of the powers of the CPA to the new Iraqi interim government. By resolution 1546 the Security Council requested UN member states to 'contribute assistance to the multinational force, including military forces, as agreed with the government of Iraq' and 'to help meet the needs of the Iraqi people for security and stability, humanitarian and reconstruction assistance'.[213] It also invited member states to respond in support of requests by the Iraqi government to provide technical and expert assistance in the rebuilding of administrative capacity, and to strengthen their efforts for the reconstruction and development of the country's economy.[214] Accordingly, Decree No. 160, converted into Law No. 207/2004, partially modified the mandate of the Italian humanitarian mission for the stabilisation and reconstruction of Iraq (Chapter One), while providing (in Chapter Two) for the continuation of the military operation 'Antica Babilonia' as a contribution to the multinational force that is now operating in Iraq on the basis of the consent of the interim government and in coordination with it.[215]

Regarding the humanitarian mission, Article 1(1) of Decree No. 160 authorised an expenditure of 20,925,066 euros until 31 December 2004 for the purposes of a mission aimed at 'supporting the Iraqi government in the reconstruction of the country and in assistance to the Iraqi people'. To this end, it added to the mission's operational activities, enumerated in Law No. 219/2003, the implementation of those further initiatives that will be agreed with the government of Iraq, 'within the objectives and the aims of Security Council resolution 1546'. These initiatives specifically include: a) support in the sector of health, to contribute to the assistance of the Iraqi people; b) institutional and technical assistance; c) support for small and medium sized enterprises, in particular in the South of Iraq; and d) support for local communications (Art. 1(2)). Moreover, Italian military experts will cooperate with the local authorities for the reorganisation of the Iraqi Ministry of Defence and in the training of Iraqi military personnel, with a further expenditure of 556,788 euros (Art. 6(2)).

The intervention shall be carried out giving 'any contribution to guarantee the respect for human rights' (Art. 1(2)*bis*). Given the reestablishment of diplomatic relations between Italy and Iraq, the Head of the Italian representation in Baghdad has been entrusted with the direction of the mission's activities *in loco* (Art. 2).

Chapter Two of Decree No. 160, dealing with the military operation, authorised an expenditure of 284,984,563 euros during 2004, in order to guarantee the continued presence of Italian military staff in the multinational force (Art. 4). The commander of the Italian contingent was authorised an eventual additional expenditure of a maximum of 4,000,000 euros, to meet 'indispensable and urgent needs of local people, including restoration of essential services' (Art. 6(1)).

Regarding criminal law, the Decree confirmed the relevant clauses of Law No. 219/2003. Article 10 states, in fact, that the Military Penal Code of War and Article 9 of Decree No.

---

212. The opposition maintained its decision to vote against approval in both the Chamber of Deputies and in the Senate. Cf., Parliamentary Acts, Chamber of Deputies, Assembly's Meeting No. 489, quoted at n. 210 and Senate, Meeting No. 647 of 27 July 2004, <http://www.senato.it>.

213. S/RES/1546, 8 June 2004, para. 15.

214. Ibid., paras. 19 and 20.

215. Cf., the letter of the Prime Minister of the Iraqi Interim Government to the President of the Security Council of 5 June 2004, annexed to SC res. 1546.

421 of 1 December 2001, converted into Law No. 6 of 31 January 2002, apply to Italian military staff participating in the multinational force; the same norms apply to the Italian military experts who collaborate in the reorganisation of the Iraqi Ministry of Defence and military forces (para. 1). Crimes committed by foreigners in the territory of Iraq to the prejudice of Italy or of Italian citizens employed in the missions are punishable at the request of the Italian Minister of Justice; the latter has to request the opinion of the Minister of Defence as regards crimes committed to the prejudice of the military staff (para. 2). Finally, under Article 10(3), the competence for prosecuting all said crimes lies with the Tribunal of Rome.

ORNELLA FERRAJOLO[216]

Cases (mercenaries)

☛ *Nerozzi and others* case. Court of Cassation (*Corte di Cassazione*) (VI Section - *Penale*), Judgment, 1 July 2003. Published in *Foro italiano*, 2004, II, 217 et seq..

In this case the applicants, Nerozzi, Leva and Ghedini, challenged the Order of arrest before trial of the judge for preliminary examination (*Giudice per le indagini preliminari*) of the *Tribunale* of Verona of 3 December 2002, confirmed by the Review Tribunal (*Tribunale del riesame*) of Venice on 19 December 2002, and the Order of the *Tribunale* of Verona of 16 January 2003.

The facts were related to the activities carried out by the applicants, together with other accomplices, for recruiting personnel and financing activities with the aim of subverting the constitutional order of a foreign country – in particular of the Federal and Islamic Republic of the Comoros.

The applicants had been charged with a violation of Article 4 of Law No. 210 of 12 May 1995, punishing the recruitment, use, financing and training of mercenaries for activities against a foreign state. Against the arguments of the lower courts, the applicants argued that the word 'recruitment' (*reclutamento*) under Article 4 of the above mentioned Law was synonymous with the word 'enlistment' (*arruolamento*) used in Article 244 of the Italian Criminal Code, under which conduct of enlisting personnel in military structures to carry out acts of hostility against a foreign state is punished. Their responsibility could not be proven, since there had been neither conscription nor direct action against the Comoros.

In the opinion of the court of Cassation, the wording of Law No. 210/1995, ratifying and executing the United Nations Convention against the Recruitment, Use, Financing and Training of Mercenaries – adopted by the United Nations General Assembly on 4 December 1989 (A/RES/44/34) – has to be interpreted according to the international obligations provided for in Article 2 of the Convention, under which 'any person who recruits, uses, finances or trains mercenaries ... commits an offence for the purposes of the Convention'.

The applicants had been also charged with the crime of terrorist or subversive association against the democratic order (*Associazioni con finalità di terrorismo anche internazionale o di eversione dell'ordine democratico*). As provided for in the Italian Criminal Code (Art. 270 *bis*), 'anyone promoting, instituting, organising, managing or financing organisations whose purpose is to propose acts of violence for the purposes of terrorism or for subverting the democratic order shall be liable for a term of imprisonment of between seven and fifteen

---

216. Ornella Ferrajolo is a senior researcher at the Institute for International Legal Studies of the National Research Council (CNR), Rome.

years. Anyone participating in the aforementioned organisations shall be liable for a term of imprisonment of between five and ten years. Under criminal law, the pursuit of terrorism shall also apply when the acts of violence are directed against a foreign state, or an international organisation or institution.' The *Corte di Cassazione* did not share the reasoning followed by the Tribunals of Venice and Verona. In particular, it had been maintained that the activities of 'subversion of democratic order' of a foreign state were covered by Article 270 *bis*. According to the court of Cassation, only 'acts of terrorism' carried out against a foreign state fall within the sphere of application of the above-mentioned Article. Activities aimed at 'subverting the democratic order' may be punished only if they are directed against the Italian Constitutional order, since Article 270 *bis* has to be interpreted following the settled jurisprudence of the same *Corte di Cassazione* on this topic. Consequently, the *Corte di Cassazione* quashed the three Orders asking for a new examination of the cases.

GIOVANNI CARLO BRUNO[217]

JAPAN[218]

Laws to Implement the Geneva Conventions

- Law Concerning Measures to Ensure National Independence and Security in Situations of Armed Attack, Law No. 79 of 13 June 2003. Published in Japanese Official Gazette Extra Edition [*Kanpou gougai*], No. 131 of 13 June 2003, pp. 8-11
- Law concerning Measures for Protection of the Civilian Population in Armed Attack Situations (Civil Protection Law). Adopted on 14 June and published on 18 June 2004. Entered into force on 17 September 2004
- Law Concerning Penal Sanctions against Grave Breaches of the International Humanitarian Law. Adopted on 14 June and published on 18 June 2004. Entered into force on 28 February 2005
- Law Concerning the Restriction of Maritime Transportation of Foreign Military Supplies etc. in Armed Attack Situations. Adopted on 14 June 2004 and published on 18 June. Entered into force on 28 February 2005
- Law Concerning the Treatment of Prisoners of War etc. in Armed Attack Situations. Adopted on 14 June and published on 18 June 2004. Entered into force on 28 February 2005

In June 2003 during the 156th ordinary session of the Diet, Japan enacted into law three emergency bills under which Japan can respond to attacks by a foreign enemy. These laws are the first legislation for war contingencies since the end of World War II. Among them, the Law concerning Measures to Ensure National Independence and Security in a Situation of Armed Attack, which establishes a posture for responding to situations of armed attack against Japan and situations where armed attack is predicted, prescribes the legal framework of national emergency. As they were only a part of emergency legislation, the government planned to enact separate laws within one year: (a) to ensure the protection of the

217. Giovanni Carlo Bruno is a researcher at the Institute for International Legal Studies of the National Research Council (CNR), Naples.

218. Information and commentaries provided by Professor Hideyuki Kasutani, Professor of International Law, Setsunan University, Japan, and Seigo Iwamoto, Professor of International Law, Kyoto Sangyo University, Japan.

lives, bodies and property of the nation; to facilitate the SDF's effective execution of its mission; and to facilitate actions by US forces taken in connection with the defence of Japan in the situation of an armed attack.

Therefore, in June 2004 during the 159th ordinary session of the Diet, Japan approved seven emergency bills and three treaties concerning response to armed attack situations. The following bills and treaties relate to international humanitarian law: 1) Law concerning Measures for Protection of the Civilian Population in Armed Attack Situations (Civil Protection Law; 2) Law Concerning Penal Sanctions against Grave Breaches of the International Humanitarian Law; 3) Law Concerning the Restriction of Maritime Transportation of Foreign Military Supplies etc., in Armed Attack Situation; 4) Law Concerning the Treatment of Prisoners of War etc. in Armed Attack Situation; 5) Additional Protocol to the Geneva Conventions to Protection of Victims of International Armed Conflicts (Protocol I); 6) Additional Protocol to the Geneva Conventions to Protection of Victims of Non-International Armed Conflicts (Protocol II)

Humanitarian Assistance

☛ Law Concerning Special Measures on Humanitarian and Reconstruction Assistance in Iraq, Law No. 137 of 1 August 2003. Published in Japanese Official Gazette Extra Edition [*Kanpou gougai*], No. 178 of 1 August 2003, pp. 23-25

On 20 March 2003, when US-led coalition forces initiated military operations against Iraq, Japan supported the use of force. Since May 2004, when major combat operations in Iraq ended, Japan has provided various types of reconstruction assistance to Iraq, in an effort to contribute to international peace and security.

Firstly, from 17 July to 12 August 2004, shuttling between Jordan and Italy, where the World Food Programme (WFP) has a supply base, Air Self Defense Force (two C-130 transport aircrafts) transported relief goods to Iraq under the International Peace Cooperation Law (Law No. 79 of 19 June 1992), following a request by the WFP.

Secondly, the Iraqi Special Measures Law of 2003 allows for SDF personnel to be dispatched to non-combat areas in Iraq. It stipulates that they are to engage in activities for humanitarian and reconstruction assistance and support activities for ensuring security. The legislation expires in four years, but can be extended.

This is the first legislation allowing the SDF to embark on an overseas mission without the imprimatur of the United Nations. Japan's decision to enact this Law was heavily influenced by a US desire to see Japanese 'boots on the ground' in Iraq.

Where Japan dispatches SDF personnel to Iraq under the Law, Kuwait is the transport base. Therefore, on 22 December 2003, Japan concluded an exchange of notes with Kuwait concerning the legal status of dispatched SDF personnel, which provided them with immunity from criminal, civil and administrative jurisdiction in the receiving state.

Since January 2004 Japanese Ground Self-Defense Forces (about 600 members) have engaged in humanitarian/reconstruction support activities in Samawah, province of Muthanna, including medical services, water supply and reconstruction of public facilities.

Arms Control

- Since May 2003, Japan Defense Agency and the SDF have participated actively in Proliferation Security Initiative (PSI). In October 2004 Japan sponsored an exercise for maritime interdiction operations to improve interdiction skills by participating countries.

Antipersonnel landmines

- Destruction of Japanese landmines stockpiles

Japan signed the international treaty banning anti-personnel landmines in Ottawa on 3 December 1997 and ratified it on 30 September 1998. Since 1 March 1999, when the Treaty took effect, Japan began to eliminate antipersonnel landmines stockpiled by the Self-Defense Forces. By 8 February 2003 it had destroyed about 1 million mines. Fifteen thousand mines were retained for the purposes of clearance training and research.

Missile Defence

- Approval of the introduction of a Ballistic Missiles Defence system

Japan started to conduct joint research on Ballistic Missiles Defence (BMD) technologies with the United States in 1999. On 19 December 2003, the Japan Cabinet approved the introduction of a BMD system from the United States (Sea-based midcourse system and Ground-based midcourse system). Japan considers BMD as an inherently defensive capacity which meets Japan's exclusively defence-oriented policy.

Cases (World War II compensation)

1. Forced labour

- Kyoto District Court, Judgment of 15 January 2003, *Hanrei Jiho*, No. 1822, pp. 83-117

On 15 January 2003 the Kyoto District Court rejected a suit brought by former wartime Chinese labourers and the family of a former labourer now deceased. The plaintiffs, who were said to have been forced to work at a nickel factory in Kyoto after being forcibly brought from China, were demanding compensation for damages as well as an apology from the government and the firm. The suit was filed in August 1998 and the court had recommended a settlement in July 2001. The government and the firm refused it, citing the expired statute of limitations.

Although the court acknowledged that the government and the firm had acted illegally, it rejected the plaintiffs' demand for compensation on the grounds that their right to claim for compensation had expired under a 20-year statute of limitations of the Civil Code.[219] The plaintiffs argued that they had the right to claim compensation under international law, especially Article 3 of the 1907 Hague Convention respecting the Laws and Customs of War on Land, in addition to the right under the Civil Code. However the court rejected the plaintiffs' argument, saying that Article 3 provides that while contracting parties can be responsible for damages to individuals in case of violation of the rules, they are not responsible directly to individuals but to the contracting parties. The court also stated that the

219. Art. 724 of Japanese Civil Code (*Minpo*).

Article was not relevant to this case, because forcibly taking labourers and putting them to work was done by the former Japanese Military during war, but was neither an act of war nor or occupation.

☛ Tokyo District Court, Judgment of 11 March 2003, *Shomu Geppou*, Vol. 50, No. 2, pp. 439-812

On 11 March 2003 the Tokyo District Court dismissed the lawsuit filed by 42 Chinese people who were forcibly brought to Japan and made to work at ten companies under harsh conditions during World War II. The suit, filed against the Japanese government and the companies in September 1997, sought damages and unpaid wages, as well as an apology printed in newspapers in Japan and China.

The plaintiffs based their claims against the government on two main grounds,[220] one of which was conventional and customary international law. They grounded their claims especially in Article 3 of the 1907 Hague Convention respecting the Laws and Customs of War on Land, the ILO Convention concerning Forced or Compulsory Labour (1930), the League of Nations Convention to Suppress the Slave Trade and Slavery (1926) and Article 5(c) of the Statue of the International Military Tribunal for the Far East. However, the court rejected all of them as grounds for the claims, because none of the cited treaties or international customary laws supported the claim that individuals have the right to claim compensation directly from a state. It found that the plaintiffs would have had to refer to concrete provisions that may give individuals the right to claim against the government, because international law is basically expected to apply between states. Specifically, as to Article 3 of the 1907 Hague Convention, after examining its drafting history and subsequent practice in detail, the court concluded that it didn't seem to give the individuals the right to claim against states whose military personnel violated the Hague regulations. The court also decided that Article 5(c) of the International Military Tribunal for the Far East only provided that persons accused of the crimes against humanity should be punished, but did not give the victims the right to claim against the states to which the accused belonged.

The court also rejected the plaintiffs' demand for compensation on the basis of statutory limitations. The plaintiffs lost their right to demand compensation when 20 years had passed since the illegal act, in the same way as in the above case.

☛ Supreme Court, Judgment of 30 March 2004, *Kyodo Tsushin* (*Kyodo News*), 30 March 2004

On 30 March 2004, in its first ruling concerning former allied prisoners of war (POWs) seeking compensation from the Japanese Government, the Supreme Court rejected two appeals by former Australian and allied prisoners of war demanding compensation for suffering inflicted during internment by Japan during World War II.

One was filed by seven former POWs from Australia, Britain, the US and New Zealand and the other by six former Dutch POWs. The former POWs claimed they suffered abuse by guards and underwent forced labour during internment in Japanese-occupied South-East Asia. They said the abuse violated conventional international humanitarian law, especially

---

220. The plaintiffs also argued that the 1930 Chinese Civil Code should be an applicable law for the illegal act of government officials. However the court rejected it.

the 1907 Hague Convention respecting the Laws and Customs of War on Land and the 1929 Geneva Convention, and international customary law, and demanded compensation from Japan. Earlier, the District and High Courts had ruled that individuals do not have the right to sue a state for compensation under Article 3 of the Hague Convention or international law.[221]

2. 'Ex-comfort women' or wartime sex slaves cases

☛ Tokyo District Court, Judgment of 24 April 2003, *Hanrei Jiho*, No. 1823, pp. 61-82

On 24 April 2003 the Tokyo District Court rejected a suit filed by seven Chinese women and families of three deceased women who were repeatedly raped by Japanese soldiers during World War II. The plaintiff filed the damages suit in October 1998, based on international law and Chinese and Japanese civil law.

Following the logic of similar cases,[222] the court rejected the plaintiffs' argument that victims have the right to claim against a defendant state under Article 3 of the 1907 Hague Convention respecting the Laws and Customs of War on Land, and pursuant to a responsibility theory which admits the possibility that states are directly responsible to individuals in the case of a violation of international law. The court backed the government's argument that there was no law at the time requiring it to pay compensation and that the plaintiffs' right to claim damages under the Civil Code expired 20 years after the rapes occurred.

However the court recognised that the actions of the Japanese soldiers were abnormal, contemptible and barbaric, even if they were carried out in wartime, and that the state failed to maintain discipline among the military. The court then suggested that both sides settle out of court, which the plaintiffs accepted, in order to provide relief for the aging victims, but the government rejected. It was the first time that a court called for a legislative or administrative settlement in such a lawsuit.

☛ Tokyo High Court, Judgment of 22 July 2003, *Hanrei Jiho*, No. 1843, pp. 32-68

☛ Supreme Court, 29 November 2004, *Hanrei Jiho*, No. 1879, pp. 58-62

On 22 July 2003 the Tokyo High Court dismissed the appeal filed by 35 Korean plaintiffs who were members of the Japanese Army and families of deceased members as well as ex-comfort women during World War II. The appellants sought damages for their intolerable suffering caused by acts of the Japanese Army during World War II.

The court acknowledged that it might be possible to enact a law to compensate the appellants as the acts of the Japanese Army, especially *vis-à-vis* the ex-comfort women plaintiffs, could be violations of the ILO Convention concerning Forced or Compulsory Labour of 1930 and the International Convention for the Suppression of the White Slave Traffic of 1910. However the court judged that the legislature didn't have the obligation to enact a law under the Constitution because it would be within the government's discretion to decide what kind of measures it would take to meet its obligations.

The court also rejected the right of individuals to claim against the government under treaties like the 1907 Hague Convention respecting the Laws and Customs of War on Land, the ILO Convention concerning Forced or Compulsory Labour (1930), the League

221. See 2 *YIHL* (1999) pp. 389-390, 4 *YIHL* (2001) p. 571 and 5 *YIHL* (2002) pp. 560-561.
222. For example, see 2 *YIHL* (1999) pp. 389-390 and 3 *YIHL* (2000) pp. 543-544.

of Nations Convention to Suppress the Slave Trade and Slavery of 1926, the International Military Tribunal for the Far East, or international customary law.

This case went to the Supreme Court. However, on 29 November 2004 the Supreme Court also rejected the appeal without considering the details of the case on the grounds that the argument of the plaintiffs could not be based on the Constitution.[223]

☛ Supreme Court, Decision of 25 December 2003, *The Japan Times Online*, 26 December 2003

On 25 December 2003 the Supreme Court rejected a 920 million yen damages suit filed by Filipino women forced into sexual slavery for the Japanese military during World War II. The plaintiffs include 81 former 'comfort women' and relatives of those from the Philippines who died.

It was the third decision by the Supreme Court in a total of ten pending appeals filed by mostly Asian women who were taken to frontline brothels to serve Japanese troops before and during World War II. The plaintiffs lost in the two other cases.[224] While avoiding the question of whether the women had suffered as alleged, the lower courts ruled that international laws didn't allow individuals to directly sue a foreign country for damages.

☛ Tokyo High Court, Judgment of 9 February 2004. Not published but see <http://www.jca.apc.org/taiwan-ianfu-support/kousai/04_2_9hanketu_kousai.htm>

On 9 February 2004 the Tokyo High Court rejected the appeal by seven women from Taiwan for an official apology from the government and a total of 70 million yen in damages for being forced to provide sex for the Japanese military before and during World War II.

The plaintiffs had asked for compensation because they claimed that the acts of the Japanese Military in forcing Taiwanese women to provide sex violated the ILO Convention concerning Forced or Compulsory Labour of 1930 and the League of Nations Convention to Suppress the Slave Trade and Slavery of 1926, and could be war crimes or crimes against humanity. However, the Tokyo High Court rejected the appeal for essentially the same reasons as in first instance hearing of the case by the Tokyo District Court on 15 October 2002.[225] The High Court judged that you have to refer to the concrete provisions of special treaties or international customary law which may give individuals the right to claim directly against the government if you want to do so, as international law is basically expected to apply between states.

☛ Tokyo High Court, Judgment of 15 December 2004. Not published but see <http://www.suopei.org/saiban/ianfu/kousai-hanketsuyoushi.html>

---

223. See also the home page for the Supreme Court, <http://courtdomino2.courts.go.jp/home.nsf?OpenDatabase>.

224. *Kanpu* case (Korean ex-'comfort women' case), Supreme Court, Decision of 25 March 2003 and *So Shinto* case, Supreme Court, Decision of 28 March 2003.

225. See *Hanrei Taimuzu*, No. 1162, pp. 154-166.

On 15 December 2004 the Tokyo High Court dismissed an appeal by four Chinese women who were forced to serve as sex slaves for Japanese soldiers during World War II. The plaintiffs had demanded 23 million yen each and an official apology.

This case was first referred to the Tokyo District Court, but the court rejected the plaintiffs' claim on 30 May 2001.[226] The court found that there was no Japanese law that existed during the war requiring the government to pay compensation, and that the Civil Code, which secures the plaintiffs' right to claim compensation, expired 20 years after the damage had occurred. The court also refused the plaintiffs' argument that victims can have the right to claim directly against a government under Article 3 of the 1907 Hague Convention respecting the Laws and Customs of War on Land.

The High Court adopted the same reasoning as earlier cases that individuals cannot have the right to claim against the government unless specific treaty provisions or international customary law provide for it.

Cases (abandoned chemical weapons)

☛ Tokyo District Court, Judgment of 15 May 2003, *Shomu Geppou*, Vol. 50, No. 11, pp. 3146-3303

On 15 May 2003 the Tokyo District Court rejected the compensation claims for health damage caused by chemical weapons left behind in China by the Imperial Japanese Army after World War II. Five Chinese plaintiffs filed the lawsuit in 1997 seeking a total of 80 million yen from the Japanese government for health problems they suffered after being exposed to poison gas agents.

Plaintiffs argued that the defendant should be responsible to the damage because the defendant violated international law, such as the Hague Convention respecting the Laws and Customs of War on Land of 1907 and its annexed Regulations, the Protocol for the Prohibition of the Use in War of Asphyxiating, Poisonous or Other Gases, and of Bacteriological Methods of Warfare of 1925, the Convention on the Prohibition of the Development, Production, Stockpiling and Use of Chemical Weapons and on their Destruction of 1993, the International Covenant on Civil and Political Rights of 1966, as well as domestic laws.

After acknowledging that the plaintiffs suffered from exposure to the chemical weapons produced and left behind by the Japanese Army, the court ruled that it was an illegal act for the Army to abandon the chemical weapons. The court also judged that the use of poison gas agents had been prohibited by international customary law at the time that the Hague Convention respecting the Laws and Customs of War on Land and the annexed Regulations were enacted. However, it concluded that Article 3 of 1907 Hague Convention could not be interpreted to give an individual a right to claim against states after examining the Article in view of the object or purpose, ordinary meaning, subsequent practice and preparatory work of the Convention.

☛ Tokyo District Court, Judgment of 29 September 2003, *Hanrei Jiho*, No. 1843, pp. 90-118

---

226. See *Hanrei Taimuzu*, No. 1138, pp. 167-191.

On 29 September 2003 the Tokyo District Court ordered the Japanese government to pay a total of 190 million yen to 13 Chinese plaintiffs who lost relatives or suffered health problems due to weapons abandoned by the Imperial Japanese Army at the end of World War II. Filed in 1996 by the 13 plaintiffs, the case concerned three incidents in China's Heilongjiang Province. It was the first time that a Japanese court recognised the government's responsibility for wartime poison gas agents abandoned in China.

The court applied Article 1[227] of the Nation Compensation Law to this case, exempting it from the 20-year statute of limitations, as it found that applying the statute of limitations in this case would be contrary to the principles of justice and fairness. The court also rejected the government's argument that Beijing renounced wartime repatriation from Japan when it signed the 1972 Japan-China Joint Communiqué, for the reason that the communiqué renounced only wartime repatriation relating to wartime acts. It insisted that the plaintiffs retained the right to claim damages, as the government's inaction in not providing sufficient information regarding abandoned weapons to China, which had continued after each incident[228] since the communiqué, was not a wartime act.

The plaintiffs partly grounded their claims in international law, such as the Hague Convention respecting the Laws and Customs of War on Land of 1907 and the Hague Regulations annexed thereto, the Protocol for the Prohibition of the Use in War of Asphyxiating, Poisonous or Other Gases and of Bacteriological Methods of Warfare of 1925, the Convention on the Prohibition of the Development, Production, Stockpiling and Use of Chemical Weapons and on their Destruction of 1993 and the International Covenant on Civil and Political Rights of 1966.

The court refrained from examining the argument that the plaintiffs as individuals could claim compensation under international law as it based its decision on the Nation Compensation Law. The court only referred to the fact that the 1907 Hague Convention and the Hague Regulations[229] as well as the 1925 Geneva Gas Protocol[230] already prohibited the use of poison gas weapons at the time that the Japanese Army tried to hide and abandon them.

Moot Court

☛ Mock trial of George W. Bush for attack on Afghanistan, March 2004

On 13 March 2004 a mock court, known as the International Criminal Tribunal for Afghanistan (ICTA), rendered its decision in the 'trial' of US President George W. Bush for crimes committed as part of the US armed attack on Afghanistan after the September 11 2001 terrorist attacks.[231]

The citizens' tribunal, sitting in Tokyo, judged that President Bush was guilty of aggression, crimes against humanity and war crimes for attacking civilians with indiscriminate weapons during the US-led antiterrorism operation in Afghanistan in 2001. The Tribunal

---

227. *Kokka Baisho Ho*, 1 Jyo, which stipulates that the government or a public corporation bears responsibility for the illegal act of their officials.

228. Each incident happened in 1974, 1982 and 1995 after the 1972 Japan-China Joint Communiqué was signed.

229. Japan ratified it in 1911.

230. Japan was an original member, but ratified it in 1970.

231. See <http://afghan-tribunal.3005.net/japanese/english-top.htm>, and as to the judgment, see <http://afghan-tribunal.3005.net/japanese/pdf/judgement.pdf>.

also issued some recommendations for banning what it considered to be indiscriminate weapons, such as depleted uranium shells, for compensating the victims in Afghanistan, and for reforming the United Nations in light of its failure to stop the US-led operation there.

The Tribunal spent two years examining Bush's role as the chief commander in the war, and held nearly 20 public hearings.

Organisers said the Tribunal on Afghanistan was the latest attempt by citizens to try a head of state. Such citizens' tribunals date back to the 1960s when the British philosopher Bertrand Russell and others tried to examine the acts of the US government during the Vietnam War.

HIDEYUKI KASUTANI and SEIGO IWAMOTO

KENYA[232]

Mines

☛ Nairobi Summit on Mines, December 2004

In December 2004 Kenya hosted the Nairobi Summit on a Mine Free World. The Summit, attended by heads of state, ministers and senior government officials from over 130 countries, brought together the State Parties to the 1997 Ottawa Convention Prohibiting Anti personnel Landmines for the treaty's first review conference.[233]

Pending Legislation

☛ Geneva Conventions Bill

The Geneva Conventions Bill has been prepared by the National Committee on the Implementation of International Humanitarian Law (hereafter, the 'Committee') to replace the Geneva Conventions Act (chapter 198, laws of Kenya).

☛ Draft Bill on Conventional Weapons

In conjunction with the ICRC, the Committee has drafted a Bill to introduce in Kenya the Convention on Conventional Weapons (1980) and its five Protocols. These two bills are expected to be forwarded to Cabinet for approval before discussion in Parliament prior to enactment.

☛ National Museums and Heritage (Amendment) Bill

The Ministry of Gender, Sports, Culture and Social Services of the Republic of Kenya has drafted a National Museums and Heritage (Amendment) Bill. If enacted, the Bill would incorporate into Kenyan law the provisions of the 1954 Hague Convention on the Protection of Cultural Property in Time of War and its two protocols.

---

232. Dr. Kithure Kindiki, Lecturer in Law, University of Nairobi, P.O. Box 30197 00100, Nairobi, Kenya.

233. For further information, see in this volume The Year in Review at p.322.

☛ International Crimes Bill

The International Crimes Bill is at the final stages of drafting. It seeks to introduce into Kenya the Rome Statute of the ICC, which Kenya has ratified.

Pending (training and education)

☛ Training Manual on IHL

The National Committee on the Implementation of International Humanitarian Law is working with the Faculty of Law, University of Nairobi, to develop a training manual for IHL.

KITHURE KINDIKI

LITHUANIA[234]

Reparations and Compensation

- ☛ Resolution on Normalisation of Relations between the Baltic States and Russia, urging Moscow to pay for Soviet occupation damages. Adopted on 17 June 2004 and entered into force on 17 June 2004. Published in *Valstybės žinios* 2004 No. 103-3759 <http://www3.lrs.lt/cgi-bin/preps2?Condition1=236314
- ☛ Interview with President Valdas Adamkus, *Nezavisimaya Gazeta*, 18 August 2004
- ☛ Statement of Minister of Foreign Affairs, Antanas Valionis, 19 August 2004
- ☛ Resolution of the Baltic Assembly regarding Accusations by the State Duma of the Russian Federation, 19 December 2004. English text at <http://www3.lrs.lt/cgi-bin/preps2?Condition1=247380&Condition2=>
- ☛ Statement of Ministry of Foreign Affairs of the Republic of Lithuania, 23 February 2005 <www.urm.lt>

In 2004 Lithuania, together with Estonia and Latvia, continued to urge Russia to recognise the fact of occupation of the three states in 1940 and pay compensation. Since 2000, when Lithuania adopted a law obliging the government to talk with Russia regarding compensation, estimated at about $20 billion,[235] it has been trying to enter negotiations with the Russian government, but so far to no avail. It is worth mentioning that Russia accepted the obligation to provide compensation for the persons deported from the Baltic States and their families when it became a member of the Council of Europe.[236]

Lithuania also supports the efforts of its Baltic neighbours to obtain compensation. On 17 June 2004 the Lithuanian parliament adopted a resolution on normalisation of relations between the Baltic States and Russia which supported 'the aspiration of the Estonian parliament to defend human rights violated by the Soviet occupation and normalize the relations

234. Information and commentaries provided by Rytis Satkauskas, Doctoral candidate at Universidad Autónoma de Madrid.

235. See report on Lithuania in 4 *YIHL* (2001) at p. 577.

236. See on Russia's request for membership of the Council of Europe in Council of Europe Document OPI 193 (1996), <http://assembly.coe.int/Documents/AdoptedText/ta96/EOPI193.htm>.

with Russia after it compensates for the damages caused by the rule of 1940-1941 and 1944-1991'.[237]

However, Lithuania shall not resort to international institutions to advance its demands for damages for the half-century Soviet occupation. This statement was made by President Valdas Adamkus in an interview to the Russian daily *Nezavisimaya Gazeta* on 18 August 2004.[238] On 19 August, the Lithuanian Foreign Minister Antanas Valionis noted that in the talks with Russia over compensation for damage caused by the Soviet occupation, Lithuania will not only consult with other Baltic States but will also consider the stance of Central and Eastern European countries, first of all Poland.[239]

On 23 February 2005 the Lithuanian Foreign Ministry declared that it failed to understand the evaluation of the Molotov-Ribbentrop Pact made by Russian President Vladimir Putin in an interview on 22 February 2005.[240] In the interview, the Russian President claimed that the Soviet Union signed the so-called Molotov-Ribbentrop Pact in order to 'safeguard its interests and security of its western borders'. However, the protection of one's interests may not serve as an excuse for annexation of another sovereign country, according to the declaration. The Ministry recalled that the Congress of the People's Deputies of the USSR gave its political and legal evaluation of this notorious pact on 24 December 1989,[241] whereby the Congress condemned the secret protocols and declared them void.

The Lithuanian Foreign Ministry stressed in its declaration that present intergovernmental relations between the Republic of Lithuania and the Russian Federation are based on the treaty of 1991,[242] whereby both parties acknowledged the fact of the annexation of Lithuania by the USSR and Russia committed itself to eliminate the consequences of annexation.

The Russian reaction may have been provoked by the resolution of the Baltic Assembly – which unites the parliaments of Lithuania, Latvia and Estonia – passed on 19 December 2004,[243] urging the governments of the three countries to start talks with Russia and Germany on compensation for damage caused by occupation.[244]

Landmines

☛ Seminar on implementation of the Ottawa Convention in northern and eastern Europe, Vilnius, 7-9 June 2004

---

237. Lithuanian Parliament Adopts Conservatives' resolution on compensation for Soviet occupation damages, *BNS* report of 17 June 2004.

238. E. Jurkeviciute, 'Valdas Adamkus: 'Paying of compensation is Russia's moral obligation', *Nezavisimaya Gazeta*, 18 August 2004.

239. Lithuania expects a broad front in talks with Moscow over compensation of Soviet damages, BNS report of 19 August 2004.

240. Statement of Ministry of Foreign Affairs of the Republic of Lithuania of 23 February 2005, <www.urm.lt>.

241. French translation at <http://www.letton.ch/lvriben2.htm>.

242. Treaty on the foundations of inter-state relations. Signed at Moscow on 29 July 1991. Came into force on 4 May 1992. *United Nations Treaty Series*, No. I-31051, Vol. 1787, 1994, pp. 20-26.

243. English text at <http://www3.lrs.lt/cgi-bin/preps2?Condition1=247378&Condition2=>.

244. The Estonian state commission reported its conclusions on the effects of the occupation in May 2004. According to the report, during the first Soviet occupation from 1940 to 1941, Estonia lost about 48,000 people. During the second Soviet occupation which lasted from 1944 to 1994, Estonia lost nearly 121,000 people, approximately 18 percent of its population. The second Soviet occupation of Estonia caused $100 billion in losses to the economy, and the Soviet army caused $4 billion in environmental damage. A.Gunter, 'White Book' seeks to establish truth', *The Baltic Times*, No. 408 of 20-26 May 2004, pp. 1, 3.

☛ Destruction and conversion of stockpiled Lithuanian mines

After becoming a party to the 1997 Convention on the Prohibition of the Use, Stockpiling, Production and Transfer of Anti-Personnel Mines and on their Destruction on 1 November 2003, Lithuania held a seminar in Vilnius from 7-9 June 2004 on implementation of the Ottawa Convention in northern and eastern Europe.[245] The seminar was hosted by the Lithuanian Foreign Ministry and was attended by diplomats and NGOs. Following Estonia's accession to the Ottawa Convention on 12 May 2004, five countries in the region remain outside the treaty: Finland, Latvia, Poland, Russia and Ukraine.

Lithuania's deadline for destroying its stockpiled mines, as required by Article 4 of the 1997 Ottawa Convention, is 1 November 2007. During 2004 Lithuania destroyed a total of over 4,000 mines out of a total stockpile of 8,091 antipersonnel mines, including 3,975 PMN mines (a type of pressure mine), and converted others (409 MON-100 and 3,703 OZM-72s) to command-detonated munitions. Furthermore, Lithuania destroyed its remaining 340 PMN antipersonnel mines on 7 June 2004, thus taking the lead in the region with no mines retained.[246]

Cases (genocide)

☛ Vasiliauskas and Žukaitienė *case, Judgment of Kaunas Regional Court, 4 February 2004*[247]

This case concerned two former Soviet State Security agents who in 2001 were charged with genocide for their part in executing two Lithuanian guerrilla fighters resisting the Soviet occupation in 1953. The State Security Agents were charged on the basis of Article 71 of the Penal Code in force at that time,[248] which included 'political group' among the groups protected.

The court considered the case on the basis of Article 99 of the newly adopted criminal code,[249] which defines genocide as acts 'with the intent to destroy all or part of people, belonging to any national, ethnical, racial, religious, social or political groups', in particular 'organisation, direction or participation in their killings, torturing, mutilating, disturbing their mental development, deporting or otherwise creating conditions of living which caused their destruction wholly or in part, limiting births within the groups or forcibly transferring children to the other groups'. It stressed that the objective of the activities of the Ministry of State Security was the elimination of a defined political group – those resist-

---

245. See <http://www.reviewconference.org/466.0.html>.

246. S. Brigot, 'Lithuania retains no mines', *International Campaign to Ban Landmines Report*, 8 June 2004, <www.icbl.org/news/archive/old/498>.

247. Reported in A. Endriukaitis, '2004, <http://www.slaptai.lt/Lie_papulkininkis-0719.htm>.

248. Art. 71 'Genocide' of the Lithuania Penal Code provided at that time that actions by means of which one attempts to destroy all or part of the population belonging to a certain national, ethnic, racial, religious, social or political group, and which are manifested by brutal torture, heavy bodily injuries, impediment of the mental development of the members of the said groups; by purposeful creation of such living conditions by means of which one attempts to destroy all or part of such a group of people; by a coercive shift of children from these groups into the other or by use of means by which one attempts to restrict birth. Such actions are punishable by imprisonment from five to 20 years.

249. English translation at <http://www.preventgenocide.org/lt>.

ing the occupational regime. Therefore, the activities of the accused were qualified as genocide of this political group. Both accused were found guilty. However, no real imprisonment penalties were imposed taking into account the age and the health of the accused.

- *Vilčinskas* case, Indictment of 30 December 2004, Judgment of Vilnius Regional Court, 15 February 2005.[250] Reported in 'Generalinė prokuratūra perdavė teismui bylą dėl Molėtų rajone gyvenusios Tiškevičių šeimos trėmimo į Krasnojarsko kraštą 1951 metais', Press release of the Prosecutor's General Office of 30 December 2004 <http://www.elta.lt/zinute_pr.php?inf_id=393016>

This case concerned another Ministry of State Security officer who was accused of the participation in 'deportation of the civilian population in the time of war, international armed conflict, occupation or annexing from the territory of occupied or annexed country to the territory of the occupying or annexing or third country' in accordance with Article 102 of the New Penal Code. Aleksandras Vilčinskas, 78, in compliance with the decree of the Ministry of State Security of the puppet Lithuanian government of 29 September 1951,[251] forced a family to leave home and expedited them to a train station from where they were transported to Krasnoyarsk region, Soviet Russia. For his participation in the deportation of the family, he was sentenced to two years' personal freedom limitation penalty.

RYTIS SATKAUSKAS

MAURITIUS

Biological Weapons

- The Biological and Toxin Weapons Convention Act of 2004, Act No. 2 of 2004. Passed by the National Assembly of Mauritius on 13 March 2004 and assented to on 6 April 2004

The Act implements the Convention on the Prohibition of the Development, Production and Stockpiling of Bacteriological (Biological) and Toxin Weapons and on their Destruction.[252]

NAMIBIA

Geneva Law

- Geneva Conventions Act of 2003, No. 15 of 2003. Promulgated on 28 November 2003, published on 18 December 2003 and entered into force on the same day

---

250. Reported in 'Generalinė prokuratūra perdavė teismui bylą dėl Molėtų rajone gyvenusios Tiškevičių šeimos trėmimo į Krasnojarsko kraštą 1951 metais', Press release of the Prosecutor's General Office of 30 December 2004, <http://www.elta.lt/zinute_pr.php?inf_id=393016>.

251. Published in Lithuanian in *Anti-Communist Congress and the Proceedings of the International Public Tribunal in Vilnius: Evaluation of the Crimes of Communism* (Vilnius, Ramona 2002) pp. 652-653.

252. For further information see *supra* n. 70, pp. 694 at 696-697.

'The Act gives effect to the Geneva Conventions of 1949 and to Protocol I additional to these Conventions. It contains provisions on the punishment of grave breaches of the four Geneva Conventions and Additional Protocol I and establishes universal jurisdiction with regard to these crimes. The Act also provides for the jurisdiction of the High Court of Namibia for the purpose of determining the prisoner-of-war status of persons who have taken part in hostilities, in accordance with Article 45, paragraphs 1 and 2 of Protocol I additional to the Geneva Conventions. The Act sets out the obligation to serve notice of trial of protected prisoners of war and internees on the protecting power or the accused or prisoner's representative, and contains provisions on the legal representation of prisoners of war, on appeal by protected prisoners of war and internees and on reduction of sentence and custody. Finally, the Act provides for the prevention of misuse of the red cross emblem and other emblems, signs, signals, identity cards, insignia and uniforms as prescribed for the purpose of giving effect to Additional Protocol I of 1977.'[253]

THE NETHERLANDS[254]

Cases (torture/universal jurisdiction)

- *Prosecutor* v. *N.*, Rotterdam District Court, 7 April 2004, LJN:AO7287 (Translation in English in 439 *NILR* (2004) pp. 444-449

On 7 April 2004 the Rotterdam District Court convicted Sebastien N. of one count of torture committed in the Democratic Republic of Congo (then Zaire) in 1996. The conviction of Sebastien N. is the first successful prosecution on the basis of universal jurisdiction in the Netherlands.[255]

The court found that the defendant, while serving as colonel of the *Garde Civile* in the province of Bas-Zaire, had assaulted and threatened a prisoner in a manner that amounted to co-perpetration ('medeplegen') of torture.[256] The court acquitted N. for lack of proof on two other counts of torture. N. received a prison sentence of two and a half years, half of the prison term requested by the prosecutor. In determining the sentence, the court took into account that the defendant had been convicted in his home country in 1997 for abuse of authority and other relevant crimes. The court held that the fact that the defendant's reputation in the *Garde Civile* had earned him the nickname '*Roi des bêtes*' (king of beasts) 'would seem to indicate that the facts that are now proved were not isolated facts'.[257] Since neither side appealed, the judgment is final.

---

253. Ibid., pp. 694 at 697-698.

254. Information and commentaries by Professor Emeritus Nico Keijzer, Justice Extraordinary, Supreme Court of the Netherlands and Dr Elies van Sliedregt, Associate Professor of Criminal Law, Leiden University.

255. See further W. Ferdinandusse, *Direct Application of International Criminal Law in National Courts* (The Hague, TMC Asser Press 2005).

256. In the English translation of this case, 'medeplegen' is translated as 'complicity' rather than 'co-perpetration'. Complicity differs from co-perpetration in that the liability of an accomplice rests on that of the principal who carries out the *actus reus* whereas co-perpetrators are thought to have *both* contributed (in an equal manner) to the *actus reus*. Complicity liability and co-perpetration differ in the attribution stage but in the sentencing stage they can lead to the same result.

257. 51 *NILR* (2004) p. 448.

The Dutch Torture Convention Implementation Act[258] (TCIA) granted the court universal jurisdiction over the defendant, a Congolese who was accused of having committed torture in his home country. In *re Bouterse*[259] the Dutch Supreme Court held that universal jurisdiction under the TCIA was not unlimited; it could only be exercised in cases where there was a link to the Netherlands, such as the presence of the suspect on Dutch soil. The legislator adopted this approach when it drafted the International Crimes Act (ICA), which replaced the TCIA from 1 October 2003 onwards.[260] In the present case, the defendant was present on Dutch territory. N. had fled to the Netherlands in 1998 after the fall of the Mobutu regime. He was later recognised by one of his victims, who reported him to the police. This victim had formerly worked in the Matadi harbour as a clearer.

While serving as a commander of the *Garde Civile*, N. had ordered his subordinates or bodyguards to inflict grievous bodily harm on the victim. The purpose of the torture was, according to the court, '[t]o punish the victim because he had refused to clear the car of one the accused's friends, who did not want to pay the shipping costs due, and to force the victim to release the car as yet.'[261]

The court addressed the nature of the crime of torture. It held that:

> '[t]he seriousness of the torture is to be found in the fact that it was carried out by the authorities, or by a civil servant, causing the victim to believe, whether or not justified, that there was nothing he could do about it, because if he wanted to file a complaint or report a crime, he would have to turn to those same authorities. In addition to the emotional and physical pain he has suffered, this caused feeling of powerlessness and a feeling that one is completely in the power of the torturer.'[262]

It is generally held that the definition of the crime of torture encapsulates three elements: the severity of pain or the suffering of the victim, the official capacity of the perpetrator and the purpose of the act of torture.[263] The definition of the Torture Convention (CAT), contains these three elements. Article 1 of the CAT provides:

> '[T]orture means any act by which severe pain or suffering, whether physical or mental, is intentionally inflicted on a person for such purposes as obtaining from him or a third person information or a confession, punishing him for an act he or a third person has committed or is suspected of having committed, or intimidating or coercing him or a third person, or for any reason based on discrimination of any kind, when such pain or

---

258. Act for the implementation of the Convention against Torture and Other Cruel Inhuman or Degrading Treatment or Punishment, Act of 29 September 1988, *Stb.* (Staatsblad: Bulletin of Acts, Orders and Decrees) 1988, p. 478.

259. Dutch Supreme Court, 18 September 2001, *NJ* 2002, p. 559 (English translation in 32 *NYIL* (2001) pp. 282-296.

260. International Crimes Acts, 19 June 2003, *Stb.* 2003, p. 270. English translation available at <www.iicnow.org/resourcestools/ratimptoolkit/nationalregionaltools/legislationdebates/NL.Int.CrAct.doc>. See also 6 *YIHL* (2003) pp. 545-547.

261. Rotterdam District Court, 7 April 2004, No. LJN:AO7287, p. 5, <www.rechtspraak.nl>.

262. Ibid., pp. 4-5.

263. See *Prosecutor* v. *Delalić et al.,* Judgement, Case No. IT-92-21, 16 November 1998, paras. 452-473.

suffering is inflicted by or at the instigation of or with the consent or acquiescence of a public official or other person acting in an official capacity'.

The purpose element has always been subject to much debate.[264] Nowadays, there seems to be consensus that it should be interpreted in conjunction with the official capacity element.[265] This means that acts aimed at punishment, intimidation or coercion for purely private purposes, even when committed by a state official, do not amount to torture as defined by the CAT and implemented in the Netherlands by the TCIA.

The Rotterdam District Court did not address the purpose element in conjunction with the defendant's official capacity. Instead, it linked the official capacity element to the position of the victim. The court held that the distinctive nature of torture lies in the element of state involvement as an abuse of power, leaving the victim in a state of helplessness. This way the court brought tortuous acts committed for private purposes under the CAT regime. The District Court's interpretation is in conformity with the text of the CAT as 'intimidating or coercing' the victim 'with the consent of a public official'. This broader interpretation of the torture definition has been described as a 'commendable approach'.[266] Only violent acts committed by a state official in a purely private capacity should be excluded from the torture definition.[267] It means that acts of torture committed by state officials for private purposes in governmental facilities such as prisons would fall under the CAT regime. Bearing in mind recent events at the Abu Ghraib prison in Baghdad and at a UK military base in Basra, demonstrating that violence towards prisoners is not necessarily committed for purely public purposes such as extracting information, the interpretation of torture in this case may well be welcomed.

Cases (extradition)
☛ *Kesbir* v. *The Netherlands*, The Hague District Court, 8 November 2004, LJN:AR5322

In summary proceedings, Mrs N. Kesbir challenged the decision of the Dutch Minister of Justice to extradite her to Turkey to be prosecuted for membership of the Partiya Karkeren Kurdistan (PKK). Kesbir, who came to the Netherlands in 2001, was a member of the Presidential Council of the PKK and had been engaged in the struggle for Kurdish independence for some ten years. According to the Turkish authorities, Kesbir was a member of a criminal organisation and as such was responsible for 25 assaults in the period 1993-1995 in which 150 people died.

The District Court in The Hague prohibited Kesbir's extradition to Turkey in its decision of 8 November 2004. The assurances given by the Turkish Embassy that Turkey would live up to its international obligations under the European Convention for Human Rights (ECHR) and the Convention Against Torture (CAT) were not deemed to be sufficiently clear.

The decision was an important victory for Kesbir. Earlier, on 10 December 2002, the Amsterdam District Court determined that Kesbir's extradition was inadmissible because it

---

264. See J. H. Burgers and H. Danelius, *The United Nations Convention Against Torture: A Handbook on the Convention against Torture and Other Cruel, Inhuman or Degrading Treatment or Punishment* (Dordrecht, Nijhoff 1988) pp. 46-47.

265. Ibid., pp. 118-119; *Delalić* judgement, *supra* n. 263, paras. 470-471.

266. W. Ferdinandusse, 'Case Note "Prosecutor v. N"', 99 *AJIL* (2005) pp. 686, 686-690.

267. Ibid.

was impossible to determine whether the requirement of double criminality pursuant to Article 2(1) of the European Extradition Convention had been met. However, in a decision rendered in June 2003, the Supreme Court quashed the decision of the Amsterdam District Court and held that the extradition request fulfilled the requirement of double criminality; membership of a criminal organisation was also a crime under the Dutch Penal Code (DPC).[268] Defence counsel for Kesbir argued that the offences with which his client was charged concerned lawful belligerent acts committed during an internal armed conflict pursuant to common Article 3 of the Geneva Conventions. Therefore, the acts should be brought under the International Crimes Act (ICA, particularly Art. 6) rather than the DPC. The Supreme Court rejected this argument. It held that even if the acts for which extradition was sought could be qualified as lawful acts of belligerency this would not preclude a double criminality test under the DPC. After all, Article 3 of the Geneva Conventions contains minimum norms and is not the only law that would apply in situations of internal armed conflict; the DPC remains applicable during situations of internal armed conflict. Bearing in mind the marginal test of double criminality in extradition procedures, where possible defences cannot play a role in determining whether a certain crime is punishable, the Supreme Court's decision is not surprising.[269]

The Supreme Court, in deciding whether there was a real risk that Kesbir upon return would face torture and an unfair trial, i.e., that extradition by the Netherlands would violate, respectively, Articles 3 and 6 of the ECHR, found that there was insufficient ground to refuse extradition. However, it did urge the Minister of Justice to request from the Turkish authorities guarantees that Kesbir would be treated according to the norms laid down in the ECHR. The Minister complied with the Supreme Court's suggestion and asked for diplomatic guarantees. Having been assured by the Turkish Embassy that Kesbir would receive a fair trial according to Article 6 of the ECHR, he decided to allow extradition on 7 September 2004.

Kesbir then applied for an injunction forbidding execution of the Minister's decision. In deciding whether the Minister had acted unlawfully in granting extradition, the District Court in The Hague noted that the diplomatic guarantees given by the Turkish authorities were unreliable. This finding was based on country reports submitted by Amnesty International and Human Rights Watch and was endorsed by the Special Rapporteur on Torture at the United Nations, Theo van Boven. The latter had sent an 'urgent appeal' to the Dutch Minister of Foreign Affairs on 28 May 2004 expressing his concern regarding the extradition of Kesbir. The Minister of Justice had not addressed any of the concerns expressed in the country reports, nor had he asked the Turkish authorities for additional or special guarantees as suggested by the Special Rapporteur. The Hague District Court considered the Minister's reluctance to react to the alarming information against the background of the Supreme Court's advice, and ruled that extradition of Kesbir could not be reasonably permitted.

The Minister of Justice appealed this decision of the District Court. At the end of 2004, the appeal was still pending.

ELIES VAN SLIEDREGT

---

268. Dutch Supreme Court, 17 June 2003, LJN: AF6988, pp. 31-33, <www.rechtspraak.nl>.

269. See further N. Keijzer, 'The Double Criminality Requirement' in R. Blekxtoon et al., eds., *Handbook on the European Arrest Warrant* (The Hague: TMC Asser Press 2004) pp. 137-164.

Cases (military trial)

☛ *Eric O.* case (the *civilian casualty* case), Arnhem District Court, 18 October 2004, LJN: AR4029, *Militair Rechtelijk Tijdschrift* 2004, p. 443-459

Eric O., a sergeant-major of the Netherlands Marines serving in the Dutch battalion on a peace mission in southern Iraq, was involved in a shooting incident that resulted in the death of an Iraqi civilian on 27 December 2003.

A container (force property) had to be recovered from a road that was located in an area known for the activities of criminal gangs. Eric O., with a small unit (Quick Reaction Force), was charged with protecting the container, putting it on a trailer and transporting it to the base. During this operation, a group of Iraqis approached, apparently interested in the contents of the container. Then, one of the Iraqi was hit, probably by a shot fired by Eric O.

After a preliminary investigation by the Royal Netherlands Military Constabulary, Eric O. was arrested on 31 December 2003 on suspicion of either premeditated murder or voluntary or involuntary manslaughter. He was transported to the Netherlands, where he was taken into police custody on 1 January 2004. On 6 January 2004 he was released, after the Arnhem District Court Magistrate denied an application for his remand custody.

Later, after further investigations, Eric O. was committed for trial in the Arnhem District Court. This is the competent court in military cases. These are tried by a panel of three judges, one of whom (not the presiding judge) is a military lawyer.

Eric O. was charged with the crime of intentional non-compliance with official instructions (Art. 136 Military Penal Code), the applicable instructions for the use of force, by firing in the direction of persons in a situation not justifying such violence, which resulted in the death of one of those persons. Alternatively, he was charged with the crime of involuntary manslaughter (Art. 307 Dutch Penal Code).

After having rejected the argument of counsel that because of serious violations of due process the case had to be dismissed, the District Court rendered an acquittal.

As to the facts, the court took the position that it had to believe the version given by Eric O. himself, the testimony given by other persons only deviating from it in minor details. Accordingly, the court established that when the Iraqis approached, Eric O. had first conspicuously loaded his firearm, and next given a warning shot in the air. When the Iraqis continued to approach him, and thereby put into jeopardy the communication possibilities between himself and his men and consequently the safety of the unit, Eric O. had fired a second shot, aimed at a spot in the mud between him and the closest group of Iraqis, at his left side before that group. When he looked again, he saw that one of them had been hit.

Although finding that there had not been an immediate danger that would have justified the application of intentional deadly force, the court considered the situation to have been of a potential threat to the accomplishment of the mission, calling for the application of proportionate non-lethal force. Under the applicable rules of engagement, in the court's view, warning shots were permitted in such situations. Eric O. had, by the court's judgement, in the absence of other possibilities of averting the danger, respected the principles of subsidiarity and proportionality. Accordingly, the applicable instructions for the use of force had not been violated.

As concerns the charge of involuntary manslaughter, the court found that Eric O's conduct had not met the threshold of gross negligence, a required element of that crime.

The public prosecutor appealed against this acquittal. At the end of 2004, the appeal was still pending.

NICO KEIJZER

NEW ZEALAND[270]

Mercenaries

- Mercenary Activities (Prohibition) Act 2004. Received Royal Assent on 6 July 2004 and entered into force on 7 July 2004 <www.legislation.govt.nz>
- Parliamentary Debates, pp. 12827-12834 (11 May 2004) and pp. 14235-14271 (29 June 2004) <www.clerk.parliament.govt.nz/hansard/Hansard.aspx>

New Zealand acceded to the Mercenaries Convention on 24 September 2004. The purpose of the Mercenary Activities (Prohibition) Act is to implement the treaty in New Zealand.[271] To that end, the legislation prohibits the recruitment, use, financing or training of mercenaries.[272] The legislation also asserts extraterritorial jurisdiction in respect of these activities[273] and institutes a system of international cooperation as envisaged by the treaty.[274]

In the course of vigorous parliamentary debate, it became clear that there were a number of concerns regarding the definition of mercenaries in the legislation (the definition in the Act is based on and not materially different to the Convention definition). Opposition was based on concerns that the definition as set out in the original Bill would capture legitimate activities, for example, professional soldiers who were acting as private consultants. Some amendments were made to take account of these concerns, including a stipulation that the motivation of 'private gain' need only be one of the purposes, rather than the primary purpose of the activity in question.[275] The Act also specifically excludes certain categories of persons, such as persons taking part in peace support missions, mine clearances and deactivation, delivery of humanitarian aid or domestic policing duties.[276]

Conventional Weapons

- Report of the Health Committee, *Inquiry into the exposure of New Zealand defence personnel to Agent Orange and other defoliant chemicals during the Vietnam War and any health effects of that exposure, and transcripts of evidence*, October 2004 (I.6E) <http://www.clerk.parliament.govt.nz/Publications/CommitteeReport>

In 2003, following new evidence that came to light about the use of Agent Orange in Vietnam where New Zealand defence personnel had been stationed, the Health Committee commenced an inquiry into that evidence and to the health effects of that exposure. The Committee heard evidence from November 2003 to May 2004 and released its report in October 2004.

The Committee concluded that it was 'beyond doubt that New Zealand defence personnel were exposed to Agent Orange and other herbicides during their service in Vietnam' and that 'photographic evidence and the map documentation confirm that New Zealand defence personnel served in defoliated areas'.[277] It recommended that the New Zealand

270. Information and commentaries by Treasa Dunworth, Senior Lecturer, Faculty of Law, University of Auckland.
271. Section 3.
272. Sections 7-12.
273. Section 13.
274. Sections 14-23.
275. Section 5.
276. Section 5(3)(a)-(d).
277. At p. 20 of the report.

government accept that New Zealand's Vietnam veterans were exposed to a toxic environment during their service and publicly acknowledge that successive governments have failed to recognise this fact.[278]

International Criminal Court

- Diplomatic Privileges and Immunities Amendment Act 2004. Received Royal Assent on 1 March 2004 and entered into force on 2 March 2004 <www.legislation.govt.nz>
- Diplomatic Privileges (International Criminal Court) Order SR79/2004. Adopted by Order in Council on 29 March 2004 and entered into force on 1 July 2004
- *Parliamentary Debates*, pp. 11175-11185 (19 February 2004) and pp. 11342-11352 (25 February 2004) <www.clerk.parliament.govt.nz/hansard/Hansard.aspx>

The Diplomatic Privileges and Immunities Amendment Bill, which had been introduced to Parliament in 2003,[279] progressed through its Second and Third Readings in February 2004.[280] As explained in the previous report, the key feature of the amendment, for present purposes, was to elaborate the privileges and immunities of the International Criminal Court in New Zealand law. The Bill passed into law on 2 March 2004 and the Diplomatic Privileges (International Criminal Court) Order 2004, which elaborates the detail of the privileges and immunities, came into force from 1 July 2004.

Essentially, the Act introduces ss10D and 10E into the existing legislation (Diplomatic Privileges and Immunities Act 1968), which, together with the regulations, grant the ICC itself, the judges and staff of the court, and persons attending a meeting of the Assembly of States Parties diplomatic protections, as required by the Agreement on Privileges and Immunities.[281] Witnesses, experts and victims also acquire certain protections under the regulations, as provided for in the International Agreement.

New Zealand deposited its instrument of ratification of the Agreement on Privileges and Immunities of the International Criminal Court on 14 April 2004, thus becoming a State Party to the Agreement in July 2004 on its entry into force.

Overseas Operations

- Crimes and Misconduct (Overseas Operations) Act 2004. Received Royal Assent on 5 April 2004 and entered into force 24 July 2003 <www.legislation.govt.nz>
- Special Reference by the Morobe Provincial Executive Pursuant to Section 19 Constitution, Supreme Court of Justice, Papua New Guinea, SCR No. 2 of 2004

The Bill, introduced to Parliament in July 2003, received Royal Assent on 5 April 2004 although its provisions have retrospective effect to 24 July 2003, the date on which the original deployment of police personnel took place to the Solomon Islands.[282]

---

278. Ibid.

279. See 6 *YIHL* (2003) pp. 552-553.

280. *New Zealand Parliamentary Debates*, Vol. 615, p. 11175 (2nd Reading) and p. 11342 (3rd Reading).

281. Agreement on the Privileges and Immunities of the International Criminal Court, ICC-ASP/1/3, opened for signature 10 September 2002, entered into force 1 July 2004, <www.un.org/law/icc/apic/apic(e).pdf>.

282. See 6 *YIHL* (2003) p. 553 for the background to the legislation and its effect.

A similar deployment scheduled for Bouganville did not take place due to a constitutional challenge in the Supreme Court of Justice of Papua New Guinea to its domestic legislation allowing the deployment, in particular, the immunity provisions.[283] While the Relief Assistance Mission to the Solomon Islands is open to a similar challenge, thus far the Mission has continued to operate.

Visiting Forces

- Visiting Forces Act 2004. Received Royal Assent on 1 July 2004 and entered into force on 1 July 2004 <www.legislation.govt.nz>
- Parliamentary Debates, pp. 12813-12827 (11 May 2004) and pp. 14092-14100 (29 June 2004) <www.clerk.parliament.govt.nz/hansard/Hansard.aspx>

This Act, which replaces the Visiting Forces Act 1939, amends and updates the law relating to the status of visiting forces in New Zealand. The main deficiencies of the 1939 legislation, highlighted in the course of negotiations with Australia for a Status of Forces Agreement, were that it limited visiting forces to the exercise of disciplinary jurisdiction and had no provisions to resolve issues of concurrent jurisdiction. The 1939 Act also only applied to other Commonwealth countries – an aspect thought to be inappropriate in the light of modern international practice. The new legislation applies to all states, not simply other Commonwealth states. The key feature of the Act is that jurisdiction of visiting forces now can extend to criminal, not simply disciplinary, jurisdiction, as provided for in a relevant Status of Forces Agreement (SOFA). Where there is no SOFA in place, the visiting force may still exercise criminal jurisdiction where New Zealand persons or property are not involved. The Act also provides for some protections, such as prohibitions on the death penalty and torture. The Act came into force on 1 July 2004.

Arms Control

- Report of the Law and Order Committee, International treaty examination of the Protocol against the Illicit Manufacturing of and Trafficking in Firearms, their Parts, Components and Ammunition, supplementing the United Nations Convention against Transnational Organised Crime <www.clerk.parliament.govt.nz/Publications/Committee Report>

A party to the Convention against Transnational Organized Crime and its two Protocols,[284] New Zealand has now started considering acceding to the Firearms Protocol. To that end, a National Interest Analysis was prepared by the Ministry of Foreign Affairs and Trade (as required by Standing Orders of Parliament), setting out the advantages, disadvantages and obligations involved in acceding to the Protocol.[285] The National Interest Analysis was presented to Parliament in early 2004 and was subsequently referred to the Law and Order Select Committee for examination. That Committee met on 7 April, 12 and 19 June, 28

---

283. The case had been heard but a decision was still pending at the end of 2004.

284. Protocol to Prevent, Suppress and Punish Trafficking in Persons, Especially Women and Children, UN Doc. A/55/383, opened for signature 15 November 2001, entered into force 25 December 2003, and Protocol Against the Smuggling of Migrants by Land, Sea and Air, UN Doc A/55/383, opened for signature 15 November 2001, entered into force 28 January 2004.

285. The National Interest Analysis is reproduced in Appendix B of the Law and Order Select Committee Report.

July, 4, 11 and 25 August and 1 September 2004 to consider the Protocol but could not reach agreement on whether to recommend that New Zealand accede to it.[286] Those opposing (all members of the Opposition) raised a number of concerns including compliance costs for the taxpayer and firearms dealers and owners; the lack of evidence of any existing problem with illicit supply of weapons through New Zealand; the belief that New Zealand's current laws and border controls are sufficient to deal with any issue which might arise; and the fact that Australia, UK, Canada and the USA had not ratified the Protocol.

To comply with the Protocol, New Zealand would need to make significant amendments to its Arms Act 1983. In addition, new regulatory and administrative measures will be needed to implement the Protocol. By late 2004 a Bill was being prepared but had not yet been presented to the House for consideration.

TREASA DUNWORTH

NIGER

Penal Law

- Law No. 2003-025 of 13 June 2003 modifying Law No. 61-27 of 15 July 1961 introducing the Penal Code
- Law No. 2003-026 of 13 June 2003 modifying Law No. 61-33 of 14 August 1961 introducing the Code of Penal Procedure. Both came into force and were published in the official gazette of the Republic of Niger on 7 April 2004

'Law No. 2003-025 introduces, among other things, into Part III of Book II of the Penal Code, a preliminary chapter entitled "Crimes against humanity and war crimes" comprising four sections: genocide, crimes against humanity, war crimes and common principles. … Law No. 2003-026 introduces, among other things, the following modifications to the Code of Penal Procedure: separation of civil action from public action, right to counsel for anyone brought before the Attorney General (Procureur de la République) and for anyone after the first 24 hours of detention, and separation of minors from adults in places of detention.'[287]

Landmines

- Law No. 2004-044 implementing the Convention on the Prohibition of the Use, Stockpiling, Production and Transfer of Anti-Personnel Mines and on their Destruction. Adopted on 8 June 2004 and promulgated by the President of the Republic on the same day. Published on 15 June 2004

'The Law implements Article 9 of the Ottawa Convention of 3 December 1997 and foresees prison sentences and fines in the event of violation of the Act ratifying that Convention.[288]

286. The New Zealand Parliament, and thus its Select Committees, does not have the power to approve or disapprove of ratification of an international treaty. For the relationship between the Executive and Parliament in the context of international treaties, see T. Dunworth, 'Public International Law', *NZ Law Review* (2000) pp. 217-221; *NZ Law Review* (2002) pp. 255-261, and *NZ Law Review* (2004) pp. 411-415.

287. *Supra* n. 70, pp. 694 at 698.

288. *Supra* n. 10, p. 220.

OCCUPIED PALESTINIAN TERRITORIES[289]

During 2004 Israel continued policies and practices violating IHL principles, and rules in the OPT, including the placement of hundreds of Palestinian civilians, by order of its military, in administrative detention without charge or trial, the moving of its citizens (settlers) into the OPT, the carrying out of extrajudicial killings, and the imposition of collective punishment, to name but a few. Moreover, use and imposition of these and other policies and practices intensified during the year, with numerous accounts of violations of the rights of Palestinians.

During the year, the Israeli government and the Knesset adopted the so-called Gaza 'disengagement' plan, while movement by Palestinian armed groups towards a ceasefire with the Israeli occupation authorities was again on the horizon.

Direct and Indiscriminate Attacks

At least 811 Palestinian civilians were reported killed by Israeli authorities during 2004, including 175 children.[290] Of these, 43 Palestinians were killed/assassinated by Israel, mainly through the use of air-to-surface missiles, 25 were the intended targets of Israeli assassination operations, and 18 were bystanders, including children.[291]

Collective Punishment

During the year, the Israeli authorities intensified the destruction of Palestinian civilians' homes and other property. Human rights organisations and other sources reported the demolition of 1,356 homes in 2004, compared with 219 in 2003, which were not necessarily owned by persons whom the Israeli authorities suspected of involvement in anti-Israeli activities.[292] In addition to the above, the Israeli authorities demolished 184 homes as a form of punishment for involvement or suspected involvement by tenants, owners or their relatives in anti-Israeli activities, an increase from 142 in the preceding year.[293]

Cases (land seizure/the separation barrier)

☛ *Beit Sourik Village Council* v. *The Government of Israel*, Israeli High Court of Justice 2056/04

The Commander of the Israeli army in the West Bank issued orders to seize plots of land in those areas belonging to Palestinian residents of a number of villages in the Jerusalem governorate. The declared purpose of the seizure was the construction of a wall in the Occupied Territory.

The question petitioners asked the Israeli High Court to answer was whether orders issued for the seizure of land for the said purpose were legal. This the court divided into two questions: first, whether the Israeli military commander was authorised to order the

---

289. Information and commentaries by Dr Mustafa Mari, Professor of Laws and Human Rights, School of Graduate Studies, Bir Zeit University, Bir Zeit, Palestine.

290. Statistics available at <http://www.btselem.org/english/Statistics/Index.asp>.

291. See *Country Reports on Human Rights Practices -2004*, Israel and the Occupied Territories entry, <http://www.state.gov/g/drl/rls/hrrpt/2004/41723.htm>.

292. Statistics available at <http://www.btselem.org/english/Statistics/Index.asp>.

293. Ibid.

construction of the wall, and, if so, second, where could a wall be constructed within the parameters of applicable law.[294]

The court made reference to international law, including international humanitarian law, in its judgment,[295] and it also referred to Israeli administrative law. The court concluded, based on the arguments petitioners submitted and the facts brought before it, that 'the fence is motivated by security concerns'.[296]

The court decided that the construction of the wall and the seizure of property for this purpose was within the power of the military commander, as vested in him in accordance with the provisions of international humanitarian law. It rejected the argument petitioners made to the effect that the construction of the wall was politically motivated. It found that should the construction of a 'barrier'/wall be needed for security reasons, the military commander could indeed do so.[297]

After rejecting the argument against the construction of the wall in the Occupied Territory, the court went into the second sub-question: whether the route of the wall takes all necessary considerations into account, including the welfare and interests of the local Palestinian population. The court reviewed the status and circumstances of each segment of the wall in the area North West of Jerusalem and received updates on alterations to the 'original' route which the military commander suggested during the proceedings. Based on this, the court rejected the appeal with respect to certain segments where changes, however minor, were made,[298] accepted it with respect to others (thereby ordering the military commander to propose alternative route(s),[299] and refrained from making a final determination with respect to a third group of segments.[300]

The court accepted that the Wall does massive damage to Palestinian civilians and stated that they 'are of the opinion that the balance determined by the military commander is not proportionate', and that in order to rectify this 'a renewed examination of the route of the [wall], according to the standards of proportionality' which the court has set is needed.[301]

Despite this ruling, the construction of the wall continues, and damage to the 'fabric of life of the entire population'[302] continues to be inflicted unhindered.

MUSTAFA MARI

PARAGUAY

The Emblem

☛ Law No. 2.365 prohibiting the misuse of the name, distinctive signs and emblems of the Red Cross [Ley no 2.365 que modifica la Ley no 993 del 6 de agosto de 1928, 'Que prohibe el uso del nombre, signos distintivos y emblemas de la cruz roja']. Promulgated on 23 April 2004, published on 29 April 2004 and entered into force on 9 May 2004

294. *Beit Sourik Village Council* v. *The Government of Israel*, Israeli High Court of Justice 2056/04, para. 25. English translation available at <www.hamoked.org> and <www.plo-nad.org>.
295. Ibid., para. 23.
296. Ibid., para. 28.
297. Ibid., para. 10.
298. Ibid., para. 50.
299. Ibid., para. 71.
300. Ibid., para. 67.
301. Ibid., para. 85.
302. Ibid., para. 84.

'It sets out rules on the use of the emblem as a protective device by medical personnel, units and vehicles in times of armed conflict, and by armed forces medical personnel, units and vehicles, by civilian or military religious personnel, and, with the authorization of the Ministry of National Defence, by Paraguayan Red Cross medical personnel, units and vehicles, and by civilian medical personnel and hospitals and other civilian medical units or vehicles. The Law also sets out rules on the use of the emblem as an indicative device by the Paraguayan Red Cross and foreign Red Cross and Red Crescent Societies. The use of the emblem by the ICRC and the International Federation of Red Cross and Red Crescent Societies is also provided for.'[303]

PERU

International Criminal Court

- Decree No. 957, adopting the new Criminal Procedure Code. Adopted on 22 July 2004 and published on 29 July 2004

'Book 7 entitled "International Judicial Cooperation" contains Section VII on "Cooperation with the International Criminal Court", which covers in particular "Arrest and surrender of persons and provisional arrest", "Other forms of cooperation" and "Enforcement of sentences". Section VII of Book 7 will enter into force on 1 February 2006, and will allow Peru to cooperate with the ICC in accordance with Part 9 of the Rome Statute.' [304]

THE PHILIPPINES[305]

Non-State Actors

- Central Committee, Communist Party of the Philippines, 'Fight for national liberation, democracy and peace through protracted people's war,' 29 March 2004

This was the 35th anniversary statement of the New People's Army. In it is one sentence relevant to IHL: 'We must treat captives leniently in accordance with the Geneva Convention and Protocol I and demonstrate that we treat well those who surrender or are rendered incapable of fighting in the course of combat.'

Ceasefire and Peace Agreements

- 'Oslo Joint Statement' of the peace panels of the Government of the Republic of the Philippines and the National Democratic Front of the Philippines (NDFP) on 14 February 2004 in Oslo, Norway on their resumed formal talks

This was a major breakthrough in the actual resumption of formal talks on 10-14 February 2004, since being suspended in June 2001. Among the significant IHL-related agreements

---

303. *Supra* n. 70, pp. 694 at 698-699.

304. *Supra* n. 10, p. 221.

305. Information and commentaries by Atty. Soliman M. Santos, Jr., LL.B., LL.M., Filipino lawyer, legislative consultant and legal scholar based in Quezon City, Philippines. He is the Vice-Chair for NGOs of the Philippine National Red Cross (PNRC) IHL National Committee. He would like to acknowledge the research assistance of law student Monica S. Ramos, IHL Bill Project Officer of the Committee.

in the 'Oslo Joint Statement' were: (1) the parties' reaffirmation of their Comprehensive Agreement on Respect for Human Rights and International Humanitarian Law (CARH-RIHL) of 16 March 1998 as part of the framework and foundation of the talks; (2) resolving the outstanding issue of the 'terrorist' listing of the CPP/NPA and the NDFP Chief Political Consultant Jose Maria Sison; (3) formation of the Joint Monitoring Committee (JMC) as an interim body to monitor implementation of the CARHRIHL; (4) indemnification of victims of human rights violations under the Marcos regime; and (5) release of prisoners and detainees. Incidentally, unlike with the Moro Islamic Liberation Front (MILF), there is no interim ceasefire arrangement with the CPP-NPA-NDFP.

The CARHRIHL is one of several Philippine examples of how non-state armed groups have some role in shaping the state practice on human rights and IHL.

☛ 'Terms of Reference of the International Monitoring Team,' signed by representatives of the GRP Peace Panel, the MILF Peace Panel and the Government of Malaysia on 8 September 2004 in Kuala Lumpur

The objective of the International Monitoring Team (IMT) is to monitor the implementation of the Agreement on Peace between the GRP and the MILF of 22 June 2001 (Tripoli Peace Agreement) and its Implementing Guidelines on the Security Aspect of 7 August 2001 and Implementing Guidelines on the Humanitarian, Rehabilitation and Development Aspects of 7 May 2002. The latter in particular contains references to IHL. The main team of the IMT, which is similar to a peacekeeping force, was deployed in Central Mindanao starting October 2004.

Dissemination

☛ Policy statements for the observance of IHL Day, 12 August 2004, by the Department for Foreign Affairs (DFA) through the Secretary of Foreign Affairs, Delia D. Albert, and Assistant Secretary for the Office of the United Nations and International Organizations (UNIO), Maria Lourdes V. Ramiro-Lopez

In the Statement of Foreign Affairs Secretary Albert for IHL Day, she said: 'We rededicate ourselves to the task of promoting greater public consciousness in the ideals of international humanitarian law as well as their significance to us as a nation and as a people.' She emphasised the crucial importance of public awareness and education in the successful implementation of IHL and its treaties.

At a Round Table Conference on IHL held on 12 August 2004, Assistant Secretary Ramiro-Lopez referred to the fact that the Philippines has historically been at the forefront of the international struggle for the promotion of IHL, including through its accession to various IHL treaties. She announced that the Department for Foreign Affairs was working for the ratification of three important IHL treaties: 1977 Protocol I to the 1949 Geneva Conventions, the 1954 Hague Convention for the Protection of Cultural Property, and the 1998 Rome Statute of the International Criminal Court.

Small Arms and Light Weapons

☛ Statement by Philippine Permanent Representative Lauro L. Baja, Jr. at the Open Meeting of the UN Security Council on Small Arms on 19 January 2004

In his 19 January 2004 statement at the Security Council, Ambassador Baja described the problem of illicit trade in SALW as a 'menace to international security, a factor that protracts and complicates armed conflicts and fuels the rise of terrorism and organized crime', underscoring the importance of the diagnostic phase of identification and appreciation of the gravity and complexity of the problem by the international community. As for the prescriptive stage, he focused on two important points: 1) the value of the complementarity between two organs of the UN, i.e., the General Assembly for universal norm-setting and rule-making and the Security Council for practical measures; and 2) the importance of regional or sub-regional cooperative arrangements.

Landmines

☛ Philippine Report dated 15 February 2004 submitted to the UN Secretary-General under Article 7 of the Convention on the Prohibition of the Use, Stockpiling, Production and Transfer of Anti-Personnel Mines and on their Destruction

The report covers the period 8 September 2003 to 15 February 2004. The report mentioned one pre-2003 legislative bill on landmines but failed to mention the two bills filed in 2003, as reported in the 2003 Yearbook.[306] There has been not much other data to report since there is 'presently, no Anti-Personnel Mine in the AFP inventory'. The report noted that the Armed Forces of the Philippines (AFP) conduct, on an annual basis, Explosive Ordnance Disposal Training and Bomb Threat Prevention Seminars for military and civilians as part of the AFP's sustainable Mine Awareness Education Programme, but the number of courses given in the reporting period was not indicated, unlike in the previous report. The AFP has deployed seven detachments of explosives experts nationwide that have played an instrumental role in educating as well as protecting civilians and soldiers alike from the threat of improvised explosive devices/mines. The latter have been used mainly by rebel groups.[307]

☛ Philippine Statement at the First Review Conference of the States Parties to the Convention on the Prohibition of the Use, Stockpiling, Production and Transfer of Anti-Personnel Mines and on their Destruction, 2 December 2004, United Nations Headquarters, Nairobi, Kenya

The statement, delivered by the Head of the Philippine Delegation, Ambassador to Kenya Rosalinda Valenton-Tirona, mainly highlighted principles, policies and measures in the pending national legislation on landmines (see below under pending legislation). The Philippines affirmed the need to support and develop approaches that would commit armed non-state actors to a mine ban and mine action. These approaches could include securing commitments through ceasefire and peace agreements and other conflict-resolution measures that include specific mine ban and mine action provisions, or unilateral commitments

---

306. 6 *YIHL* (2003) p. 567.

307. See the country report on the Philippines (pp. 669-75) in *Landmine Monitor Report 2004: Toward a Mine-Free World*, published annually by the International Campaign to Ban Landmines since 1999.

that will stop more mines from being planted and enable mine clearance and rehabilitation of affected communities to take place.

The statement acknowledged the importance of the work of the International Campaign to Ban Landmines' (ICBL) Non-State Actors Working Group, co-chaired by the Philippine Campaign to Ban Landmines (PCBL). The Philippines supports the efforts of such country campaigns and acknowledged the courage and sensitivity required in working in conflict areas. It called on other states to likewise continue to provide the enabling environment to achieve the work of universalisation by supporting the ICBL, civil society groups working on the ground and NGO initiatives to get all stakeholders into the mine ban regime.

Terrorism

- Mindanao Truth Commission, Initiatives for Peace in Mindanao (InPEACE Mindanao), Executive Summary Progress Report June 2003-March 2004, Independent Fact Finding Mission on the Davao Bombings and Human Rights Violations, 3 March 2004
- The Report of the Presidential Commission on the Davao City Bombings (Pursuant to Administrative Order No. 84), 4 March 2004

These inquiries pertain mainly to two terrorist bombings, on 4 March 2003 in Davao City at the old Davao International Airport and on 2 April 2003 at the Philippine Port Authority passenger terminal, both resulting in numerous civilian casualties. This was followed a day later by explosions in three mosques in the city. The bombings were blamed on the rebel Moro Islamic Liberation Front (MILF). Then, during the 'Oakwood Mutiny' several months later,[308] the mutinous officers charged that the Davao bombings were part of a secret plot of the government to discredit the MILF. This led to several inquiries, including one by a Presidential Commission, also known as the Maniwang Commission after its Chairman Fr. Pedro B. Maniwang, assistant parish priest of the city. The main conclusions of the Commission were:

— The so-called 'Oplan Greenbase' (alleged government plot) documents were fake.
— There was no evidence linking the defence secretary and intelligence chief to the wharf bombing.
— The Commission was not convinced that Muntazer Sudang (himself killed in the airport bombing) was the bomber with MILF links, as tagged by the police.
— There was no evidence that the mosque bombings were carried out by the military or the MILF.
— There was no reliable evidence to support the claim of one mutinous officer that he was ordered to bomb the mosques.
— The resources of the law enforcement authorities during the airport bombing incident were inadequate.

On the other hand, the non-governmental Mindanao Truth Commission of InPEACE Mindanao, had this summary of initial findings in relation to several entities suspected of the bombings

— The State's case against the MILF was not based on or supported by solid legal evidence.

---

308. See 6 *YIHL* (2003) pp. 561-564 and *infra* in this report at pp. 557-558:

— The Commission took notice of allegations that the state may have had knowledge of the existence of a so-called 'Third Force' and that the state believed it to be behind the bombings.
— The Commission took cognisance of serious allegations by the Oakwood mutineers about state-sponsored terrorism. It found suspicious the hasty clean-up of the airport bombing scene of the crime. It found substantial evidence that the military ordered a special operation to lob grenades at mosques.
— The Commission took notice of the reported admission by the Abu Sayyaf armed opposition group regarding the airport bombing. It found that the state had inexplicably rejected sweepingly this admission and has not made efforts to prosecute responsible operatives of this group.
— The Commission found substantial evidence for the probably culpability of Michael Terrence Meiring, believed to be a US Central Intelligence Agency (CIA) agent, for some bombings in Mindanao and that his surreptitious flight from Davao, allegedly with the aid of US Federal Bureau of Investigation (FBI) agents, could be taken as an indication of guilt.

☛ Department of Justice Resolution in I.S. No. 03-C-1955 (*Philippine National Police, etc.* v. *Terso Sudang, et al.)* and I.S. No. 03-D-2818 (*P/Insp. Jordine Crisostomo A. Maribojo, et al.* v. *Esmael Mamalangkas, et al.*), 17 August 2004

This Resolution dismissed on reinvestigation the criminal cases filed for the Davao bombings against about 190 suspects, mostly leaders and members of the MILF, except four suspects who are actually in detention. The indictment of the 190 MILF leaders and members was found to be flawed because the evidence on record bears nothing material and relevant to link each and every one of them to the bombings by conspiracy, except for the bare say-so that some of the perpetrators were MILF members. The subject bombings were not shown to be in furtherance of the MILF's political purpose and appear to be the independent acts of the actual perpetrators. Their membership in the MILF, even if true, is not an overt act sufficient and relevant to prove conspiracy in the commission of the bombings. The assumed or say-so intimacy of some of the perpetrators with the MILF is of no legal bearing in order to implicate the 190 or so MILF leaders and members by conspiracy. The alleged pronouncement of the MILF leadership of their intent to conduct bombings, even if true, cannot be the basis to link the 190 to the bombings by conspiracy because this would be inadmissible in evidence to prove conspiracy in the bombings for being violative of the res inter alios acta doctrine under the Rules of Court.[309]

This Resolution is a good example of political will in support of the then-stalled peace process with the MILF, which had posed the dropping of criminal charges against MILF leaders for the Davao bombings as a condition for the resumption of suspended peace negotiations.

Cases (military rebellion)

☛ *Sanklakas and Partido ng Manggagawa* v. *Executive Secretary, et al.*), Supreme Court Decision in Case G.R. No. 159085, 3 February 2004

309. *Rules of Court*, Rule 130, Section 28: 'The rights of a party cannot be prejudiced by an act, declaration, or omission of another, except as hereinafter provided.'

During the 'Oakwood Mutiny' of military rebels on 27 July 2003, President Gloria Macapagal-Arroyo issued Proclamation No. 427, which 'confirm(ed) the existence of an actual and ongoing rebellion, compelling me to declare a state of rebellion', and General Order No. 4, which called upon the Armed Forces of the Philippines (AFP) and the Philippine National Police (PNP) to suppress and quell the rebellion 'with due regard to constitutional rights'. Several petitions were filed in the Supreme Court challenging the validity of these presidential issuances on the ground that the Philippine Constitution does not provide for a presidential power to declare a state of rebellion.

In its Decision, the Supreme Court upheld the validity of the Proclamation and the Order by voting 11-2 to dismiss the petitions. The majority opinion of the court, drawing much from US constitutional history and jurisprudence, ruled that: 'The President, in declaring a state of rebellion and in calling out the armed forces, was merely exercising a wedding of her Chief Executive and Commander-in-Chief powers. These are purely executive powers…' At the same time, the court pointed out that:

> '…in calling out the armed forces, a declaration of a state of rebellion is an utter superfluity. At most, it only gives notice to the nation that such a state exists and that the armed forces may be called upon to prevent or suppress it. Perhaps the declaration may wreak emotional effects upon the perceived enemies of the State, even on the entire nation. But this Court's mandate is to probe only into the legal consequences of the declaration. This Court finds that such a declaration is devoid of any legal significance. For all intents, the declaration is deemed not written.'

The court apparently did not consider the legal significance or consequences of such a declaration when it comes to the application of IHL, where a 'state of rebellion' connotes at least a common Article 3, if not a Protocol II, situation. However, significantly, the Decision clarified that 'the mere declaration of a state of rebellion cannot diminish or violate constitutionally protected rights'.

☛ *Gregorio B. Honasan II* v. *The Panel of Investigating Prosecutors, et al.*, Supreme Court Decision in Case G.R. No. 159747, 13 April 2004

This case dealt with the proper jurisdictional body in the preliminary investigation of a Philippine senator who was implicated in the 'Oakwood Mutiny' and charged with the felony of *coup d'etat* (Revised Penal Code, Art. 134-A). The main issue was whether jurisdiction lay with the Department of Justice (DOJ), which was already conducting the investigation, or with another body, the Office of the Ombudsman, which Senator Honasan contended was the proper jurisdictional body. He based this on the exclusive original jurisdiction of the *Sandiganbayan* court for public officials over the trial of felonies committed by public officers 'in relation to their office', in which case the Ombudsman has primary jurisdiction in preliminary investigation and can take over from the DOJ.

The Supreme Court ruled that the DOJ has concurrent jurisdiction with the Ombudsman and is not precluded in the investigation of offences involving public officers though the Ombudsman may in the exercise of its primary jurisdiction take over cases exclusively cognisable by the *Sandiganbayan*. But the court did not resolve the question whether the felony of *coup d'etat* was committed by Senator Honasan in relation to his office, so as not to preempt the result of the investigation being conducted by the DOJ. There were several dissenting opinions in the court, all of which were of the view that the charge of *coup d'etat* against Senator Honasan was committed in relation to his office and therefore under the exclusive jurisdiction of the *Sandiganbayan* to try and the primary jurisdiction of the Ombudsman to investigate.

- *Roberto Rafael 'Roel' Pulido* v. *Gen. Narciso Abaya, et al.* and *Lt. Julius R. Navales, et al.* v. *Gen. Narciso Abaya, et al.*, Supreme Court Decision in Case G.R. No. 162318 and Case No. 162341, 25 October 2004

This case involved 321 soldiers from the 'Oakwood Mutiny' who were initially charged with the felony of *coup d'etat* before a regular civilian Regional Trial Court (RTC). But as a result of a preliminary investigation, the charges were amended to include only 31 of the original accused, dropping the other 290. These 290 were, however, subsequently charged with violations of the Articles of War (Commonwealth Act No. 408) before the General Court-Martial, while the other 31 accused were not included in the charge sheets there. Then, the RTC issued an order declaring that all charges before the court-martial against the accused were 'not service connected, but rather absorbed and in furtherance to the alleged crime of *coup d'etat*'. On this basis, the 290 charged before the court-martial contended that it had no jurisdiction to try them, jurisdiction for *coup d'etat* being with the RTC, and that whatever violations of the Articles of War were absorbed in the *coup d'etat* charges against them had been dismissed by the RTC.

The Supreme Court ruled that the sweeping declaration made by the RTC could not be given effect for being, among others, in violation of Republic Act No. 7055 (An Act to Strengthen Civilian Supremacy Over the Military by Returning to the Civil Courts the Jurisdiction Over Certain Offenses Involving Members of the Armed Forces of the Philippines). This law clearly provides that members of the Armed Forces who commit crimes or offences penalised under the Revised Penal Code, other special penal laws, or local government ordinances shall be tried by the proper civil court 'except when the offense, as determined before arraignment by the civil court, is service-connected, in which case the offense shall be tried by court-martial … service-connected crimes or offenses shall be limited to those defined in Articles 54 to 70, Articles 72 to 92, and Articles 95 to 97 of Commonwealth Act No. 408, as amended'. In view of this, the RTC cannot divest the General Court-Martial of its jurisdiction over the 290 charged with violations of the Articles of War. Neither was there any factual or legal basis for the RTC to rule that such violations were committed in furtherance of *coup d'etat* and, as such, absorbed by the latter crime.[310]

Cases (right to bear arms)

- *Francisco I. Chavez* v. *Hon. Alberto G. Romulo, et al.*, Supreme Court Decision in Case G.R. No. 157036, 9 June 2004[311]

---

310. There are at least two other similar cases of Oakwood mutineers pending decision in the Supreme Court but these will not be reported in the Yearbook until the decisions are promulgated: G. R. No. 159201 (*Homobono Adaza and Roberto Rafael [Roel] Pulido* v. *Gen. Pedro Cabuay, et al.*) for habeas corpus filed on 11 August 2003, and G.R. No. 160792 (*Homobono Adaza and Roberto Rafael [Roel] Pulido* v. *Gen. Pedro Cabuay, et al.*) for review on certiorari filed on 4 December 2003.

311. This and other Philippine Supreme Court decisions may be accessed through <www.supreme-court.gov.ph> and <www.lawphil.net> .

This case involved the validity of 'Guidelines in the Implementation of the Ban on the Carrying of Firearms Outside of Residence' issued by the Chief of the Philippine National Police (PNP) in early 2003. Among the issues raised by the petitioner, who is a licensed gun owner, was that the ban violated the people's right to carry firearms, which is also intertwined with the people's inherent right to life and to protect life, in short a constitutionally protected right. This he mainly based on various American authorities, particularly the Second Amendment to the US Constitution, which reads: 'A well regulated militia, being necessary for the security of the state, the right of the people to keep and bear arms shall not be infringed.'

In rebutting the petitioner, the Supreme Court examined the historical background of the US provision to show that it pertains to citizens' 'collective right' to take up arms in defence of the state, not to citizens' 'individual right' to own and possess arms. The setting under which the right was contemplated has a profound connection with the keeping and maintenance of a militia or an armed citizenry. With more reason, the right to bear arms cannot be classified as fundamental under the 1987 Philippine Constitution, which contains no provision similar to the Second Amendment. The right to bear arms is a mere statutory privilege (currently under Presidential Decree No. 1866 as amended by Republic Act No. 8294), not a constitutional right. It cannot be considered an inalienable or absolute right. It is subject to regulation pursuant to the constitutional duties of the state to maintain peace and order and to protect the people against violence. It is to be construed in connection and in harmony with these constitutional duties.

The Supreme Court in this Decision did not make use of or reference to relevant international legal instruments, such as the UN Programme of Action to Prevent, Combat and Eradicate the Illicit Trade in Small Arms and Light Weapons in All Its Aspects, which the Philippines adheres to.

Pending Legislation (reparations and compensation)

☛ House Bill No. 3315, 'An Act Providing Compensation to Victims of Human Rights Violations During the Marcos Regime, Documentation of Said Violations, Appropriating Funds Therefore and for Other Purposes,' per Committee Report No. 117. Submitted by the Committee on Human Rights on 19 November 2004

This is the latest version of a human rights compensation bill, a consolidated one, in the House of Representatives. It seeks 'to restore the dignity and honor of victims of summary execution, torture, involuntary disappearance and other gross human rights violations committed by agents of the State during the struggle against the regime of former President Ferdinand Marcos including the victims of the Muslim insurrection in the period from January 1, 1969 to February 25, 1986.'

The principal source of funds for the compensation will be those transferred through the 10 December 1997 Order of the Swiss Federal Supreme Court and presently held in escrow in the Philippines in connection with Civil Case No. 141. From the aforesaid judgment amounting to US$ 682 million, the amount of PhP 8 billion would be set aside and appropriated to fund this compensation act. To implement this act, a Board of Compensation for Victims of Human Rights Violations under the Marcos Regime would be created.

Unfortunately, the phrase in the Bill 'including the victims of the Muslim insurrection' has the unfortunate effect of putting the blame on the Muslim struggle rather than the Marcos regime. The bill's definitions of human rights violations and torture have the element of commission by agents of the state; thus, it should be made clear that these definitions are only for the purposes of the Act and not necessarily for other acts, like an anti-torture law. The bill's enumerated acts or omissions do not expressly mention several particular forms of human rights violations prevalent during the Marcos regime, namely, salvaging or summary extrajudicial execution, massacres and forced evacuation/internal displacement, including hamletting.

Pending Legislation (criminalising IHL violations and other serious crimes)

- House Bill No. 2557, 'An Act Defining and Penalizing Crimes Against International Humanitarian Law and Other Serious International Crimes, Adopting Corresponding Principles of Criminal Responsibility, Operationalizing Universal Jurisdiction, Designating Special Courts, and for Related Purposes'. Introduced by Representative Antonio V. Cuenco in the House of Representatives on 23 August 2004, pending on 1st reading

This bill is the version for the new 13th Congress (parliament) of the Philippines, as the previously reported House Bill No. 6298 lapsed without being enacted into law with the close of the 12th Congress in June 2004.[312] This new pending legislation, if passed, shall be known as the 'Philippine Statute on Crimes Against International Humanitarian Law and Other Serious International Crimes'. It covers the most serious crimes of international concern, namely genocide, crimes against humanity and war crimes, and also other crimes against IHL, namely, misuse and abuse of the Red Cross emblem, violations against cultural property and places of worship, and the involvement of children in armed conflict. Much of the bill uses the Rome Statute as a model or source but the Bill's Explanatory Note says it should not be treated per se as the national legislation for the implementation of the Rome Statute. Though the Philippines has not yet ratified the Rome Statute, this does not bar Congress (the national legislature) from adopting certain provisions thereof and of other IHL treaties as part of national legislation in the exercise of plenary legislative power. The other IHL treaty references of the bill are to the 1949 Geneva Conventions and its 1977 Additional Protocol I, the 1954 Hague Convention for the Protection of Cultural Property and its 1999 Second Protocol and the 2000 Optional Protocol to the 1989 Convention on the Rights of the Child on the involvement of children in armed conflict.

The research, consultation for and drafting of the bill were done under the auspices of the Philippine National Red Cross IHL National Committee, with assistance from the International Committee of the Red Cross (ICRC) Manila delegation. No counterpart Senate bill had been introduced in the Philippine bicameral Congress by year's end.

Pending Legislation (terrorism)

- Senate Bill No. 735, 'An Act to Define and Penalise Acts of Terrorism and for Other Purposes,' as lead bill pending
- House Bill No. 309, 'An Act Defining Terrorism, Providing Penalties Therefor, and for Other Purposes,' as lead bill pending

The Senate bills address the five major themes considered as indispensable for effective anti-terrorism legislation: (1) criminalisation of terrorism, (2) enhancement of law enforcement capabilities, (3) establishment of institutional mechanisms to fight terrorism, (4) protection of human rights, and (5) international cooperation.

---

312. See 6 *YIHL* (2003) p. 577.

The police-oriented Philippine Center for Transnational Crime (PCTC), while fully supporting these bills, has noted the following needs: (a) to define terrorism, (b) to consolidate all acts of terrorism, (c) to repackage the acts of terrorism to preclude ambiguity, (d) to repackage and group similar preparatory acts of terrorism, (e) to expand the coverage of anti-wire tapping orders, (f) to rationalise the Anti-Terrorism Council, (g) for a detention period of at least 30 days, and (h) to rationalise the penalties.[313]

As for the different issues and points raised against the pending bills both in the Senate and the House of Representatives, these may be summarised as: (1) a broad, vague and loose definition of terrorism and its various aspects, (2) unconstitutionality in terms of violation of due process and other basic rights and proneness to abuse and misinterpretation, (3) adverse implications against particular groups of people like Muslims, revolutionary forces and even legitimate NGOs and people's organisations, and (4) unnecessary legislation.[314]

These pending laws have not yet been passed because of controversy and opposition, including from various advocates of human rights, a tradition which counterveils the anti-terrorism trend.

Pending Legislation (internal displacement)

- House Bill No. 3334, 'An Act Improving Philippine Commitment to Human Rights Promotion and Protection by Providing the Necessary Mechanisms for the Prevention of the Occurrence and Protection from the Adverse Effects of Internal Displacement and for Other Purposes'. Introduced by AKBAYAN Party-List Representative Loretta Ann P. Rosales, et al. in the House of Representatives on 23 November 2004, pending on 1st reading

This pending legislation for an 'Internal Displacement Act' is described as a localisation of the 1998 UN Guiding Principles on Internal Displacement (UNGPID). The bill contains provisions on prohibition against/protection from arbitrary displacement; protection during displacement; addressing the continuing needs of displaced communities; assistance during the return, resettlement or local integration of displaced persons; penalties; liability of concerned law enforcement agencies; appropriations; and monitoring of compliance. It aims to install a mechanism of support to victims of internal displacement so that damage and injury may be minimised in cases where they cannot be prevented. A Monitoring Group tasked to periodically monitor and check compliance with this Act shall be headed by the Chairperson of the Commission on Human Rights with the following members: a representative each from the Department of Social Welfare and Development (DSWD), Department of National Defense (DND), Department of the Interior and Local Government (DILG), National Disaster Coordinating Council (NDCC), and at least two representatives from human rights NGOs working with internally displaced persons. One such NGO is the Balay Rehabilitation Center, which was the prime mover of this Bill.

---

313. P/Supt. Reynold E. Osia, Director, Plans and Policies, PCTC, 'Briefing on the Anti-Terror Bills Filed in the Senate' (n.d.).

314. Ma. Araceli B. Habaradas, 'Issues and Discussion Points on the Anti-Terrorism Bills', Munidabao Consultation-Workshop on Anti-Terrorism Legislation, 27-28 January 2005.

Pending Legislation (landmines)

- House Bill No. 2675 and Senate Bill No. 2064, 'An Act Providing for a Total Ban on Anti-Personnel Landmines, for Other Prohibitions or Restrictions on the Use of Landmines, Booby-Traps and Other Devices, for Creation of a Philippine Coordinating Committee on Landmines, and for Related Purposes'. Introduced by Akbayan Representatives Mario 'Mayong' Joyo Aguja, Ana Theresia Hontiveros-Baraquel and Loretta Ann P. Rosales in the House of Representatives on 31 August 2004 and by Senator Juan M. Flavier in the Senate on 24 November 2004, both pending on 1st reading

These bills are the versions for the 13th Congress to consider, as the previously reported House Bill No. 6043 and Senate Bill No. 2064[315] lapsed without being enacted into law with the close of the 12th Congress.

This pending legislation for a 'Philippine Comprehensive Law on Landmines' would implement and reconcile the implementation of two IHL treaties which the Philippines has ratified, namely the 1997 Convention on the Prohibition of the Use, Stockpiling, Production and Transfer of Anti-Personnel Mines and on Their Destruction, and the 1996 Amended Protocol on Prohibitions or Restrictions on the Use of Mines, Booby-Traps and Other Devices annexed to the 1980 Convention on Prohibitions or Restrictions on the Use of Certain Conventional Weapons which May be Deemed to be Excessively Injurious or to Have Indiscriminate Effects.

The bill resolves any conflict in the implementation and application of both treaties in favour of a total ban on antipersonnel mines, as represented by the Ottawa Treaty which is improved on in several ways (such as redefinition of antipersonnel mines based on impact or effect, not just design). But it also adopts important aspects of Amended Protocol II (like coverage of and rules for anti-vehicle mines) not found in the Ottawa Treaty. The draft bill was prepared by the Philippine Campaign to Ban Landmines.

Pending Cases (International Criminal Court)

- *Sen. Aquilino Pimentel, Jr., et al.* v. *Office of the Executive Secretary, et al.*, Supreme Court G.R. No. 158088

This pending litigation is a 2003 case for mandamus to compel the Office of the Executive Secretary and the Department of Foreign Affairs to transmit the Philippine-signed copy of the 1998 Rome Statute of the International Criminal Court (ICC) – which is in the process of ratification – to the Senate as a ministerial act under Executive Order No. 459, series of 1997. This is to enable the Senate to express its concurrence or non-concurrence with the treaty since the assertion is that discretionary power to ratify lies with the Senate. Both parties filed their respective Memoranda in April 2004, and the decision had not yet been rendered as 2004 closed.

In the petitioners' Memorandum, they pose as substantive issues the following: (1) The Executive Branch, under international and constitutional law, has a ministerial duty to transmit the Rome Statute for the ratification of the Philippine Senate on the theory that it is the latter alone which has the discretionary power to ratify; and (2) Under treaty law and customary international law, the Philippines has a duty to ratify the Rome Statute. Petitioners call particular attention to two landmark Philippine Supreme Court decisions, *Yama-*

---

315. See 6 *YIHL* (2003) pp. 576-577.

shita v. *Styer*[316] and *Kuroda* v. *Jalandoni*,[317] which were two full decades ahead of the *North Sea Continental Shelf* cases[318] in recognising that customary international law may exist contemporaneously with treaty law and that treaty law may embody long-held norms and principles of customary international law.

In the respondents' Memorandum, they reiterate their arguments that the Executive Department has no duty to transmit the Rome State to the Senate for concurrence because the President has yet to ratify it, a function that solely belongs to her and in her discretion. They argue that under international law, states have no obligation to ratify treaties that they have signed.

Pending Cases (ex-'comfort women'/reparations and compensation)

☛ *Isabelita C. Vinuya, et al.* v. *The Honorable Executive Secretary et al.*, filed on 8 March 2004, Supreme Court Case G.R. No. 162230, pending decision

In this case, according to counsel for petitioners, the 'Malaya Lolas' (literally 'Free Grandmothers'), a group of Filipino women victims of rapes committed by Japanese soldiers during World War II, are compelling the Philippine government to sponsor their claims for reparation under international law. The petition assails the waiver of the Philippine government of its right to claim reparations against Japan (in the Treaty of Peace with Japan) and its consequent refusal to espouse the claims of Filipino ex-'comfort women' against Japan. The respondents, in their Comment, argue that the treaty's waiver clause is valid and hence the Philippines must comply therewith pursuant to the international law principle of *pacta sunt servanda*. Further, that the formal apology of Japan and the reparation it provides through the Asian Women's Fund (AWF) are sufficient to recompense petitioners for their loss and sufferings. Petitioners replied that *erga omnes* obligations not to provide impunity for rape, sexual slavery, torture and other forms of sexual violence constituting crimes against humanity and war crimes – acts violative of *jus cogens* norms – are not subject to a waiver, nor can these obligations be sacrificed in the name of the principle of *pacta sunt servanda* under both treaty and customary international law. In their view, the formal apology of Japan and the establishment of the AWF, as well as the reparations agreement between the Philippines and Japan, do not constitute adequate reparations for the sufferings of the victims of the comfort women system under international law.

Sol Santos

POLAND

Implementation and Dissemination

☛ The Polish Commission for International Humanitarian Law Affairs, established by Prime Minister's Regulation No. 51 of 20 May 2004. Published on 27 May 2004 and entered into force on the same day[319]

---

316. 75 Phil. 563 [1945].
317. 83 Phil. 171 [1949].
318. 1969 *ICJ Reps*. 3.
319. *Supra* n. 70, pp. 694 at 702-703.

PORTUGAL

International Criminal Court

☛ Law adapting Portuguese criminal legislation to the Statute of the International Criminal Court, defining Conduct constituting Crimes against International Humanitarian Law. Adopted on 22 July 2004 and published on the same day. The Law provides for its entry into force 30 days after its publication, except for Article 3, revoking certain articles of the Criminal Code, which entered into force on 14 September 2004[320]

RWANDA[321]

Gacaca Courts

☛ Organic Law No. 16/2004 establishing the organisation, competence and functioning of Gacaca Courts charged with prosecuting and trying the perpetrators of the crime of genocide and other crimes against humanity, committed between 1 October 1990 and 31 December 1994 (Gacaca Law of 2004). Adopted and published on 19 June 2004 and entered into force on the same day

The Gacaca Law of 2004 amended several provisions of the first Gacaca Law, enacted in 2001, and streamlined the trial process. Under the Gacaca Law of 2004 the number of gacaca courts been reduced from the 258,209 provided by the earlier Law to 169,400. The number of judges per court has gone from 19 to nine and the highest two levels of courts have been removed.

By June 2004 about 40,000 genocide suspects brought before the pilot gacaca courts had admitted to participating in the 1994 genocide. All of these reportedly fell into the second category and were eligible to have their sentences reduced by half and to carry out community service in place of detention. Community service would involve building and road construction as well as planting food for schools and prisons.

An estimated 20,000 prisoners accused of genocide who confessed to their crimes before 15 March 2004 in accordance with the plea bargaining system established under the Gacaca Law of 2001 were released provisionally until the commencement of nation wide gacaca trials. This release was timed to mark the tenth anniversary of the genocide on 7 April 2004.

Mediation

☛ Establishment of mediation committees

In order to further relieve the caseload of the ordinary court system and permit it to focus on prosecuting genocide cases, the government established mediation committees, known locally as Abunzi. These have jurisdiction over both criminal cases and civil suits involving claims of less than three million Rwandan francs ($5,200). On 12 July 2004 local communities elected 18,540 local judges, who will serve two-year terms. They do not have jurisdiction to deal with genocide cases. Such committees were a common feature of Rwandan life prior to Belgian colonial rule.

CHISECHE MIBENGE

---

320. *Supra* n. 10, pp. 221-222.

321. Information and comments by Chiseche Mibenge, Researcher with the Netherlands Institute for Human Rights Research.

SENEGAL

Implementation and Dissemination

☛ Decree No. 2004-657 relating to the Creation, the Organisation and the Functions of the High Commission for Human Rights and the Promotion of Peace, adopted on 2 June 2004

'The Commission has competence in relation to human rights and international humanitarian law. It is attached to the Presidency of the Republic and its main responsibilities are to receive and conduct investigations into complaints made by corporate bodies, persons and organisations working in the field of human rights and international humanitarian law; to promote the reception, integration and implementation into domestic law of international treaties relating to human rights law or international humanitarian law and to contribute to the dissemination of these bodies of law.'[322]

SERBIA AND MONTENEGRO

1. Serbia

Implementation and Dissemination

☛ Commission for International Humanitarian Law of Serbia and Montenegro. Established by Decision of the Council of Ministers of Serbia and Montenegro on 9 September 2004, which was published in the Official Gazette No. 43/2004 the following day and came into force the eighth day after publication

'Its mandate is to follow the development and implementation of international humanitarian law and to propose measures for its national implementation, to promote dissemination and training, as well as to cooperate with the ICRC and other bodies. It is required to submit reports to the Council of Ministers.'[323]

2. Kosovo[324]

Criminal Law

☛ Regulation 2003/25, On the Provisional Criminal Code of Kosovo. Adopted 6 July 2003 and entered into force 6 April 2004 <www.unmikonline.org> under 'Publications' subdirectory of the UNMIK 'Official Gazette'

☛ Regulation 2003/26, On the Provisional Criminal Procedure Code of Kosovo. Adopted 6 July 2003 and entered into force 6 April 2004 <www.unmikonline.org> under 'Publications' subdirectory of the UNMIK 'Official Gazette'

---

322. *Supra* n. 10, p. 223.
323. Source ibid., pp. 223-224.
324. Information and commentaries by Michael E. Hartmann, former International Prosecutor February 2000-July 2005, Office of the Public Prosecutor of Kosovo (before the Supreme Court, hereinafter, OPPK), currently Advisor to the Attorney General of Afghanistan for the Justice Sector Support Program of the US State Dept./Bureau INL. His email is intprosecutor@yahoo.com. This report has been written in his private capacity, and does not reflect the opinion of the Kosovo OPPK or UNMIK, or the Afghan Attorney General or US government.

- UNMIK Regulation 2004/8, The Juvenile Justice Code of Kosovo. Adopted and entered into force on 20 April 2004 <www.unmikonline.org> under 'Publications' subdirectory of the UNMIK 'Official Gazette'

On 6 July 2003 UNMIK adopted through Regulations 2003/25 and 2003/26 a new substantive criminal law (penal code) and criminal procedure,[325] respectively.[326] These new procedures and laws did not become effective until 6 April 2004.

Regulation 2003/25 introduced wide-ranging changes necessary to modernise Kosovo's definitions of war crimes and crimes against humanity in line with current trends in international humanitarian law. While the new criminal procedure code changed the procedures for investigation and trial of war crimes cases, the new penal code in fact had very little effect upon substantive war crimes and IHL applied in Kosovo in 2004.

Regulation 2003/26, the new Provisional[327] Criminal Procedure Code of Kosovo [PCPCK], abolished a half-century's use of an investigating judge. Instead, it established the prosecutor as the investigating officer.[328] The role of a pretrial judge is limited to protecting the basic freedoms and human rights[329] of the suspect by conducting hearings as to detention and allowing witnesses to testify anonymously, by deciding whether to order covert and technical measures of investigation, such as surveillance and monitoring of conversations,[330] and by determining whether to 'immunise' or reduce punishment for cooperating suspects and defendants who agree to testify.[331] In addition, the right of the accused to be present during the investigation was curtailed, with the prosecutor being given the option of taking witness statements without the defendant being present.[332] However, such evidence at trial could not be exclusively relied upon to support conviction.[333] The result is a code allowing the prosecutor to investigate and take statements personally or through directing judicial police, with the option of not alerting the defendant until the very end of an investigation.[334]

The procedure for evidence presentation during the main trial morphed toward an adversarial model, with the inculpatory witnesses proposed by the prosecution testifying first

325. Regulation 2003/25.

326. Regulation 2003/26.

327. So called because it was adopted by regulation rather than the nascent Kosovo Parliament, due to the UNMIK Interim Administration's reserving for itself legislative powers regarding security and law enforcement.

328. PCPCK Arts. 220-222.

329. PCPCK Arts. 9(3), 21(2). I.e., the European Convention of Human Rights Arts. 5 (detention), 6 (fair trial) and 8 (privacy).

330. E.g., PCPCK Arts. 168 et seq. (anonymous witness procedures) and Arts. 256 et seq. (covert and technical measures of investigations).

331. PCPCK Arts. 298 et seq.

332. PCPCK Art. 237(4) (the prosecutor 'may invite' defence counsel and the defendant 'to be present at the examination of the witness'. Emphasis supplied). Moreover, Art. 156(2) requires that such a witness must testify at trial subject to examination of the defence if the defence was not present during that witness' investigation testimony.

333. PCPCK Art. 157(1). This limitation also applies to the trial court's use of the defendant's admissions/confession to police or prosecutor, Art. 157(2); of testimony from a single anonymous witness, Art. 157(3); and testimony from a witness or accused whose cooperation resulted in a reduced sentence or immunity, Art. 157(4).

334. 'The defendant shall be examined, at the latest, prior to the conclusion of the investigation unless the proceedings result in termination.' PCPCK Art. 298.

under examination by the prosecutor, followed by questions by the defence.[335] The defence witnesses follow. Whereas the previous Kosovo and Yugoslav procedure gave the defendant the opportunity to address the court before all the other witnesses, the new procedure provides this opportunity only after the defendant has heard those witnesses testify.[336] However, the new procedure retains the requirement that co-accused are not allowed to hear the testimony of the first accused but are instead sequestered, to be then brought in one-by-one to give their statements.[337]

As for the new Provisional Criminal (Penal) Code of Kosovo [PCCK], while it could have done so, it did not in any way change the law applicable to current and future prosecutions of the war crimes and genocide committed during the Kosovo armed conflict, which ended in June 1999. The PCCK replaced the existing penal definitions of genocide (Art. 141)[338] and war crimes (Art. 142) in the Federal Republic of Yugoslavia Criminal Code (FRY CC)[339] with modern definitions following the Rome Statute of the International Criminal Court and by any measure was a far superior codification of international humanitarian law.[340] Yet none of those newly codified penal measures can be used in cases involv-

---

335. PCPCK Art. 360(3): 'Evidence shall be presented in the sequence determined by the presiding judge. As a rule, evidence proposed by the prosecution shall be presented first, followed by evidence proposed by the defence counsel or the defendant and finally the evidence which the trial panel has ordered to be collected *ex officio* . The testimony of the injured party as a witness shall be presented before the testimony of other witnesses.'

336. PCPCK Art. 371(1).

337. PCPCK Art. 373. After each co-accused gives a statement, should s/he chose to waive the right to silence, s/he is then informed of the other co-accused's statement and allowed to comment: 'After each question [sic – meaning a co-accused examination in court] the person being examined shall be informed of the testimony of the co-accused examined previously and shall be asked whether he or she has any comments thereon. The accused who has been examined previously shall be asked whether he or she has any comments on the testimony of the co-accused subsequently examined. Each accused shall be entitled to address questions to the other co-accused who have been examined.'

338. 'Whoever, with the intention of destroying a national, ethnic, racial or religious group in whole or in part, orders the commission of killings or the inflicting of serious bodily injuries or serious disturbance of physical or mental health of the group members, or a forcible dislocation of the population, or that the group be inflicted conditions of life calculated to bring about its physical destruction in whole or in part, or that measures be imposed intended to prevent births within the group, or that children of the group be forcibly transferred to another group, or whoever with the same intent commits one of the foregoing acts, shall be punished by imprisonment for not less than five years or by the death penalty.'

339. 'Whoever in violation of rules of international law effective at the time of war, armed conflict or occupation, orders that the civilian population be subject to killings, torture, inhuman treatment, biological experiments, immense suffering or violation of bodily integrity or health; dislocation or displacement or forcible conversion to another nationality or religion; forcible prostitution or rape; application of measures of intimidation and terror, taking hostages, imposing collective punishment, unlawful bringing in concentration camps and other illegal arrests and detention, deprivation of rights to fair and impartial trial; forcible service in the armed forces of the enemy's army or in its intelligence service or administration; forcible labour, starvation of the population, property confiscation, pillaging, illegal and self-willed destruction and stealing on a large scale of a property that is not justified by military needs, taking an illegal and disproportionate contribution or requisition, devaluation of domestic currency or the unlawful issuance of currency, or who commits one of the foregoing acts, shall be punished by imprisonment for not less than five years or by the death penalty.'

340. I.e., PCCK Arts. 116 (Genocide; cf., SFRY CC 141), 117 (Crimes Against Humanity, not present in the previous SFRY CC), 118 (War Crimes in Grave Breach of the Geneva Conventions; cf., SFRY CC Art. 142), 119 (War Crimes in Serious Violation of Laws and Customs Applicable in Inter-

ing the Kosovo conflict because UNMIK decided not to make these new (PCCK) IHL and war crime definitions and bases of personal liability retroactive and applicable, even though it could have done so. The principle of *nullum crimen nulla poena sine lege* (no crime or no penalty without statute) does not apply to IHL crimes, which are customary in nature.[341] Thus, Kosovo war crimes prosecutions continue to be based upon criminal codes that do not reflect modern IHL treaty and customary law, which has meant that Kosovo courts have not been able to adjudicate any crimes against humanity except for genocide (Art. 141), and can only adjudicate some of the crimes of war (primarily those previously recognised in Articles 142 and 145 of the FRY CC[342]). Moreover, command responsibility, as provided in the prospectively-based PCCK Article 129,[343] cannot be used as a means of attaching liability in any of the pending investigations or cases.[344]

2004 saw UNMIK promulgate a regulation 2004/8 establishing separate juvenile justice provisions which replace and supplement the applicable criminal procedure and penal codes.

---

national Armed Conflict; cf., SFRY CC Art. 142), 120 (War Crimes in Serious Violation of Article 3 Common to the Geneva Conventions), 121 (War Crimes in Serious Violation of Laws and Customs Applicable in Armed Conflict Not of an International Character), 122 (Attacks in Armed Conflicts Not of an International Character Against Installations Containing Dangerous Forces), 128 (Organization of Groups to Commit Genocide, Crimes Against Humanity and War Crimes; cf. SFRY CC Art. 145 for partial coverage), and critically, 129 (Command Responsibility; no SFRY CC counterpart). Where the SFRY had only two paragraphs, at Arts. 141 and 142, and had a total of less than three pages on IHL and War Crimes, the PCCK provides over ten pages on the same.

341. See, e.g., European Convention on Human Rights, Art. 7, at para. 2.

(1) No one shall be held guilty of any criminal offence on account of any act or omission which did not constitute a criminal offence under national or international law at the time when it was committed. Nor shall a heavier penalty be imposed than the one that was applicable at the time the criminal offence was committed.

(2) This article shall not prejudice the trial and punishment of any person for any act or omission which, at the time when it was committed, was criminal according the general principles of law recognized by civilized nations.

342. Art. 145 (Organizing a group and instigating the commission of genocide and war crimes)

'(1) Whoever organizes a group for the purpose of committing criminal acts referred to in Articles 141 to 144 of this law, shall be punished by imprisonment for not less than five years.

(2) Whoever becomes a member of a group referred to in Paragraph 1 of this Article, shall be punished by imprisonment for not less than one year.

(3) A member of a group referred to in Paragraph 1 of this Article who exposes the group before he has committed a criminal act in its ranks or on its account, shall be punished by imprisonment for a term not exceeding three years, but the court may also refrain from imposing a punishment on him.

(4) Whoever calls on or instigates the commission of criminal acts referred to in Articles 141 to 144 of this law, shall be punished by imprisonment for a term exceeding one year but not exceeding 10 years.'

343. PCCK 129(1): 'A military commander or person effectively acting as a military commander shall be criminally liable for the crimes referred to in Articles 116 – 124 of the present Code committed by forces under his or her effective command and control, or effective authority and control, as a result of his or her failure to exercise control properly over such forces, where:

1) That military commander or person either knew or, owing to the circumstances at the time, should have known that the forces were committing or about to commit such crimes; and

2) That military commander or person failed to take all necessary and reasonable measures within his or her power to prevent or repress their commission or to submit the matter to the competent authorities for investigation and prosecution.

(2) With respect to superior and subordinate relationships not described in paragraph 1 of the present

Cases[345]

- *Andjelko Kolasinac* case, Case No. AP-KZ 230/2003, Supreme Court of Kosovo, Decision of 9 January 2004 overturning the verdict of 31 January 2003 by the District Court of Prizren, P. No. 226/2001, and remanding the case for retrial

This lengthy and comprehensive Supreme Court decision,[346] by a three international judge panel,[347] broke new ground by providing detailed and unprecedented analysis on (1) the nature of the armed conflict in Kosovo and whether the protections of the law applicable in international or internal conflict, or both, applied to the KLA-Serbian forces in conflict with each other; (2) whether customary IHL may be directly applied in Kosovo courts; (3) the scope of protection of civilians and protected persons under IHL, (i.e., the Geneva Conventions and their Additional Protocols I and II) and how it affects criminal liability under FRY CC Article 142; and (4) whether Article 142 and general individual criminal responsibility principles under Kosovo law permit application of the doctrine of command responsibility that exists as part of customary IHL.

On the nature of the armed conflict in Kosovo and whether the protections of the law applicable in international or internal conflict, or both, applied to the KLA-Serbian forces which were in conflict with each other, the Supreme Court rejected the District Court's approach that since both an international and internal armed conflict existed during the period of the indictment further analysis of the differences 'is not necessary'.[348] According to the Supreme Court:

---

article, a superior shall be criminally liable for the crimes referred to in Articles 116 - 127 of the present Code committed by subordinates under his or her effective authority and control, as a result of his or her failure to exercise control properly over such subordinates, where:
1) The superior either knew, or consciously disregarded information which clearly indicated, that the subordinates were committing or about to commit such crimes;
2) The crimes concerned activities that were within the effective responsibility and control of the superior; and
3) The superior failed to take all necessary and reasonable measures within his or her power to prevent or repress their commission or to submit the matter to the competent authorities for investigation and prosecution.'

344. Cf. the Kosovo Supreme Court's decision in *Kolasinac*, discussed *infra*.

345. This report concerns only that small minority of war crimes cases that reached a court trial or had investigations conducted after arrests and judicial remand of the suspects, and thus were public knowledge. In 2004 many more cases were under investigation by the Complex Criminal Investigative Unit of the UNMIK Police, with guidance from International Prosecutors, and other cases were selected by international prosecutors and judges at the judicial investigation stage and resulted in no indictment being filed. E.g., at the end of 2004, 34 war crimes cases received priority and active investigation by the UNMIK Police War Crimes Unit [WCU] of the Central Criminal Investigations Unit, with direction or supervision by international prosecutors, in addition to the ones commented upon here. Moreover, the WCU had hundreds more such cases in its files, to be investigated as limited resources permitted.

346. Fifty-five single-spaced pages.

347. Presiding Judge Agnieszka Klonowiecka-Milart (of Poland), author of the decision (written reasoning), and Judges Gustin Reichbach (US) and Edward Wilson (US).

348. *Kolasinac* Supreme Court decision (hereinafter, Supreme Court decision) at p. 15, fn. 8, cited the District Court as stating 'further analysis of the differences is not necessary. Instead, to the extent required, the international law related to both international and internal armed conflict will be referenced with respect to the relevant war crimes charges against Kolasinac.' The court went on to cite the

> 'The critical issue is the impact of the NATO intervention on the character of the on-going armed conflict in Kosovo, assuming [as accepted by the District Court] that the hostilities between the FRY and KLA reached the requisite level of intensity, prior to the NATO intervention in March 1999, to render this conflict internal in character. The conflict between NATO States involved in the Operation *Allied Force* and the FRY was *par excellence* international.
>
> [...]
>
> The question relevant for this case is whether the NATO intervention from March 1999 onwards transformed the character of that conflict into an international one, or whether there remained two concurrent armed conflicts different in character. A finding to the effect that there were two concurrent conflicts raises a question whether the emergence of an international armed conflict could affect the legal situation of the internal armed conflict, i.e., entail the applicability of the legal regime pertinent to international conflicts in relation to both. The Supreme Court holds that in the context of the Kosovo conflict it is justified to speak about an international conflict along an internal one, and that each of the conflicts fell under the legal regime pertinent to its character.'[349]

The Supreme Court then proceeded to review in detail various tests and standards supporting the position that foreign intervention changes the legal character of a conflict. It referred to the ICTY jurisprudence, in particular to the interlocutory decision on jurisdiction in of the Appeals Chamber in the *Tadić case*, which found that 'an internal conflict may be deemed international if "another State intervenes in that conflict through its troops or [...] some of the participants in the internal armed conflict act on behalf of that other State".'[350] In developing this standard, the ICTY Appeals Chamber found that, depending on the nature of the entity involved, one of three tests could be used to demonstrate that participants in an internal armed conflict acted on behalf of another state: (1) the instructions/approval test, (2) the overall control test, and (3) private individuals acting for the state test.[351] The Supreme Court then concluded that 'for the present case, the relevant test would be the overall control test'.[352] Still, this did not answer the question of what IHL applies when there is an international armed conflict existing concurrently with a non-international armed conflict:

> 'The classic solution is to employ the theory of pairings, enabling the application of different legal regimes between various parties according to their relationship with each other. This approach was taken by the International Court of Justice in the *Nicaragua* Case, where it was held that the connection between the *Contras* and the United States

---

District Court as also concluding that 'an armed conflict of both an internal and international character existed during the relevant time period, as required by Article 142 of the CCY'.

349. Supreme Court decision at pp. 15-16.

350. The Supreme Court here cited the Judgement of the ICTY Appeals Chamber in the *Tadić* case, 15 July 1999, para. 84.

351. Supreme Court decision, p. 16.

352. The Supreme Court here cited the ICTY's Judgment in the *Blaškić* case, 3 March 2002, Declaration of Judge Shahabuddeen.

> was not of such character that the *Contras* were acting on behalf of the United States. Fighting between the Contras and the Nicaraguan Government was accordingly non-international and subject to Common Article 3. The involvement of the United States itself, however, as regards its relation with Nicaragua, attracted the regulation applicable to international armed conflicts, i.e., Geneva Conventions as a whole.[353]
>
> The aforementioned double characterization of the conflict is logically unimpeachable, but it entails as a consequence that certain rules and protections granted under international humanitarian law in the context of the international conflict do not directly extend over relations pertinent to the internal component of the conflict. Furthermore, although it might be seen as undesirable for the purpose of prosecuting atrocities, the pairing theory imposes additional evidentiary requirements resulting from the need to differentiate the internal aspects of armed conflicts from the international ones, a process that in the practice of international tribunals has proven convoluted and imprecise; moreover, relations pertinent to internal armed conflict have obviously less detailed conventional protection and might require onerous proving of the contents of the customary law.'[354]

The Supreme Court then reviewed the 'global view',[355] which held that a foreign state's intervention changes the overall nature of an existing internal conflict, 'resulting in one single international conflict in the entire territory that contains multiple conflicts of international and internal origin, as to which the full body of international humanitarian law applies'.[356] The Supreme Court went on to characterise this approach as one of 'practicality over legality'[357] and chose to apply the pairings theory instead:

> 'Arguments invoking practical and humanitarian concerns were certainly well made in the face of several conflicts concurrently breaking out on the territory where one State, the SFRY, was falling apart and new States have risen. The Supreme Court notes that nevertheless the prevailing doctrine, at least in relation to conflicts whose segment are practically discernible, remains the pairing theory, as more faithful to the terms of Geneva Conventions, more consistent theoretically and based in actual practice of the States and international organisations.[358]

---

353. The Supreme Court here cited *Nicaragua* v. *US*, Merits, 76 *ILR* p. 5, para 219.

354. Supreme Court decision at p. 19.

355. The Supreme Court decision at p. 19, fn. 31: 'From Judges Li and Rodrigues dissenting opinion in ICTY case-law (respectively *Tadic Jurisdiction Appeal* and *Prosecutor v. Alekovski, Judgement*, 25 June 1999), the ICTY *Nikolic* and *Mladic* decisions, the United Nations Commission of Experts (*Final Report* 4-27 May 1994, Section II. A), the United States government (Prosecutor v. Tadic, *Amicus Curiae Brief*, 25 July 1995), to several academic scholars, see T. Meron: "*Classification of armed conflict in the former Yugoslavia: Nicaragua's fallout*", American Journal of International Law, Vol. 92, 1998, p. 238.'

356. Supreme Court decision at p. 19.

357. Supreme Court decision at p. 20, quoting G.H. Aldrich: 'This [Tadic Jurisdiction Appeal] first decision by the appeals chamber is unfortunate in that it complicates unnecessarily the further work of the Tribunal by suggesting that each prosecution will have to involve arguments and decisions as to the characterization of the armed conflict in which the alleged offenses occurred.' Comment, "Jurisdiction of the International Criminal Tribunal for the Former Yugoslavia",' 90 *AJIL* (1996) p. 64.

358. The Supreme Court decision at p. 19, fn. 31: 'See: Lindsay Moir, *Ibidem,* p. 47: 'Given the reluctance of States to accept openly even the limited measure of protection contained in common

The Supreme Court notes that it is understandable and in accordance with the purpose and the mandate of the ICTY that in the context of the pre-Dayton conflicts in former Yugoslavia efforts are made to seek such interpretations and functional adaptations of international humanitarian law as to encompass under the jurisdiction of the Tribunal a possibly wide range of human rights abuses. Yet, the Tribunal refused to adopt a quasi-legislative judicial process and never explicitly rejected the dichotomy between the international and internal armed conflict; rather it chose to deal with the tension between the established legal doctrine and evidentiary difficulties by resolving the relevant issues on a case-by case basis. By the same virtue, the Supreme Court considers that it would be illegitimate and inappropriate for a domestic court, which operates within a complete statutory system, and which is bound to uphold international standards of protection of individuals *inter alia* in criminal process, to accept a practice based in legal views that are not yet clearly articulated and firmly accepted under the international law. The Supreme Court considers that challenges of practical nature should not anyway lead to court practice that is not justified; the court notes, however, that the Kosovo conflict, unlike the pre-Dayton conflicts in former Yugoslavia, appears to have distinct features of dichotomy, which from both theoretical and practical angles supports the application of the theory of pairings.'[359]

Applying the pairings and overall control tests to the 1999 Kosovo conflict, the Supreme Court then held that the legal regime is one of an internal armed conflict:

'In this case before the Supreme Court, in order to qualify the FRY–KLA conflict as internationalized in keeping with ICTY *Tadic* Appeal approach, it would be necessary to establish a link between KLA and NATO forces, specifically, it would have to be demonstrated that the KLA acted as an agent of the ten NATO countries involved in Operation *Allied Force* by being under the "overall control" of NATO, i.e., control going beyond financing, training and equipping or providing operational support to that group.[360] Based on the information available to the Supreme Court upon the record before us and notorious facts known, there is no evidence that during the NATO inter-

---

Article 3, it seems unlikely that outside interference on behalf of the insurgents would persuade the authorities to be any more charitable and implement the entire *ius in bello* against enemies within the State.' The author gives the example of the Iraqi invasion in Kuwait in 1991 where applicable legal regime between various parties of the conflict was dependent upon whether or not those particular states were parties to the Additional Protocol I. Further, in the conflict in Afghanistan where the Soviet Union intervened on behalf of the Government against *mujahadin* groups, the ICRC continued to treat the conflict as internal, which must be correct where two states are not actually in conflict with each other. Also, according to the declaration adopted by the ICRC following the NATO intervention, the conflict between FRY forces and the KLA remained internal, see: J-F. Oeguiner, 'Dix ans après la creation du Tribunal penal international pour l'ex Yugoslavie […],' in *International Review of the Red Cross*, No 850, p. 288. Ibid., see J.G. Stewart: 'Although the global view is positive from a practical and humanitarian perspective, it is contradicted by the international community's rejection of the ICTR's attempts to adopt an explicit provision in Additional Protocol I making the whole body of international law applicable to a civil war if foreign troops intervened [in support of both sides].' p. 335.'

359. Supreme Court decision at p. 20.

360. The Supreme Court here cited S. Boelaert-Suominen, 'The International Criminal Tribunal for the Former Yugoslavia and the Kosovo conflict', *International Review of the Red Cross* No 837, and also the *Tadić* Appeal Judgement, *supra* n. 351, para 137.

vention in the armed conflict in Kosovo there was such a link between NATO and the KLA that would allow considering the KLA an agent of NATO, even applying the most lax "overall control" test. Hence the Supreme Court accepts that the armed conflict in Kosovo between March 24 1999 and June 1999 consisted of an international conflict [i.e., FRY-NATO] alongside an internal one [i.e., FRY-KLA]. Accordingly, the trial court's finding to this effect, albeit not explained as to its basis, was correct.'[361]

Moving to the issue of whether customary IHL may be directly applied in Kosovo courts, the Supreme Court held that 'in the application of Article 142 CL FRY it would not be legitimate to resort to international customary law in such areas as defining prohibited conduct, defining basis of individual responsibility and the punishment'.[362] The court reasoned that because Article 142 requires that an act of war crime must also be in violation of international law, it is the international law 'applicable to Kosovo in 1989, pursuant to UNMIK Regulation 1999/24'.[363] The Supreme Court disagreed with the finding of the District Court that ratified treaties were directly applicable, and that the Geneva Conventions 'have become customary international law and applicable to FRY'. It stated:

'the District Court overlooked two aspects of the applicability of the legal regime as defined by UNMIK Regulation 1999/24. First, the applicability of the regime as of 22 March 1989 in Kosovo recognises only one derogation: in any individual criminal proceedings, any subsequent law to the law of the SFRY before 23 March 1989 will be dispositive of the issue, if it is more lenient to the accused. Second, the applicable law in force on 22 March 1989 results in the *prima facie* reference to the constitutional principle of legality as established in two articles of the SFRY 1974 Constitution:

Art. 181: '*No one shall be punished for any act, which before its commission was not defined as a punishable offence by law or a legal provision based on law, or for which no penalty was envisaged. Criminal offences and criminal sanctions may only be determined by statutes.*'

Art. 210: '*International treaties shall be applied as of the day they enter into force, unless otherwise specified by the instrument of ratification or by an agreement of the competent bodies. International treaties, which have been promulgated shall be directly applied by the courts.*'

Accordingly, the constitutional principle of legality presupposes that criminal offences and punishments must be provided for in specific domestic legislation. The principle of legality in criminal matters laid down by Art. 181 SFRY Constitution does constitute *lex specialis* in relation to Art. 210. As a result, international treaties, which have been ratified and promulgated, are a constituent part of the internal legal order; however, direct application of international treaty law is not allowed in domestic criminal pro-

---

361. Supreme Court decision at p. 21.
362. Ibid., p. 23.
363. While 1999/24 was amended by 2000/59, the applicable Section 1.4 benefiting the accused, remained unchanged.

ceedings unless the provisions of international law do correspond with the domestic criminal law in terms of their contents.'[364]

The Supreme Court also explained that the 1992 FRY Constitution did not change its conclusion that customary IHL and the IHL treaty provisions cannot be directly applied in Kosovo but must be applied through the filter of Article 142 of the 1989 FRY CC.[365]

As to the scope of protection of civilians and protected persons under IHL (i.e., the Geneva Conventions and their Additional Protocols I and II) and how it affects criminal liability under Article 142 FRY CC, the court first discussed customary international law applicable to internal armed conflicts, which 'in the legal system of Kosovo ... can only be relevant for the interpretation of concrete prohibitions contained in both conventional instruments'.[366] The court reviewed the *Tadić* Interloctutory Decision on Jurisdiction where it referred to common Article 3,[367] and emphasised that:

> 'the Appeals Chambers was nevertheless careful to point out that the emergence of the above-mentioned general principles governing internal armed conflicts does not mean that they are regulated by general international law in all its aspects. Two limitations were particularly spelled out:
> [i] only a number of rules and principles governing international armed conflicts have gradually been extended to apply to internal armed conflicts; and

---

364. At p. 22 of the judgement.

365. At pp. 22-23 of the judgement: 'The 1992 FRY Constitution did not change the fundamental relationship between principle of legality in criminal matters and the principle of direct applicability of the international law in the internal legal order, as *lex specialis* derogating provisions of a general nature.'

Art. 16: '[1]The Federal Republic of Yugoslavia shall fulfill in good faith the obligations contained in international treaties to which it is a contracting party. [2] International treaties which have been ratified and promulgated in conformity with the present Constitution and generally accepted rules of international law shall be a constituent part of the international legal order.

Art. 27: 'No one may be punished for an act which did not constitute a penal offence under law or by law at the time it was committed, nor may punishment be inflicted which was not envisaged for the offence in question. Criminal offences and criminal sanctions shall be determined by statute.'

Notably, after the promulgation of the FRY 1992 Constitution, international customary law became a constituent part of the national legal system, in addition to ratified international treaties. Nevertheless, only in theory this could have an impact on the prosecution of war crimes in UN-administered Kosovo, since conduct set out in Article 142 CL FRY constitutes a war crime pursuant to that Article only if it at the same time constitutes a violation of international law effective at the relevant time. Hence, taking into account that the SFRY provisions are *prima facie* dispositive in criminal matters pursuant to Regulation No. 1999/24, and that subsequent provisions can be applied only if more favorable to the accused, in practice the conduct set out in Article 142 of the Criminal Law [CL] of FRY constitutes a war crime only if it constitutes a violation of the relevant ratified treaties. Any developments in international humanitarian customary law to support war crimes prosecution instead of prosecution for ordinary crimes cannot be considered applicable in domestic courts of Kosovo for the implementation of Article 142 CL FRY because the guarantees contained in Art. 210 SFRY Constitution are to be applied, as they are more favorable to the accused.'

366. Supreme Court Decision, p. 23.

367. The Supreme Court here cited the ICTY Appeals Chamber's Decision on the Defence Motion for Interlocutory Appeal on Jurisdiction, 2 October 1995, at para. 126.

[ii] this extension has not taken place in the form of a full and mechanical transplant of those rules to internal armed conflicts, rather, the general essence of those rules, and not the detailed regulation they may contain, has become applicable to internal conflicts.'[368]

The Supreme Court also reviewed the Rome Statute of the ICC Article 8(2)(c) and (e), and held that its list of war crimes:

'is likely to represent these serious violations of international humanitarian law committed in internal armed conflict, to which individual criminal responsibility can attach under customary international law. Accordingly, it is likely to set boundaries within which customary interpretation of prohibitions contained in Common Article 3 and Additional Protocol II can be considered.'[369]

The court also examined the Fourth Geneva Convention, noting that 'save Common Article 3 – [it] does not cover explicitly the category of protected persons afforded protection in the case before the trial court, i.e., Kosovo Albanians who were Yugoslav nationals and resided on the territory controlled by Yugoslav government'.[370]

The Supreme Court then focused upon the District Court's following of ICTY jurisprudence[371] and the District Court's finding that 'in the complexity of present-day international armed conflicts that are inter-ethnic armed conflicts, like the one in former Yugoslavia, ethnicity rather than nationality may become determinative of national allegiance'. The Supreme Court noted that:

'the District Court appears to derive from that statement that injured parties in their relation with FRY Government had protected status from Geneva Convention IV and both Additional Protocols, despite having been nationals of FRY. The Supreme Court finds that in the light of evidence adduced in the main trial such conclusion was neither factually supported nor sufficiently legally explained.'[372]

The Supreme Court expressly cautioned:

'Given especially the fact that there is yet no final ICTY jurisprudence relating specifically to the Kosovo conflict, it is particularly important that the courts verify whether ICTY's views and findings expressed on the ground of the conflict in Bosnia are of such universal applicability that they can be extrapolated on the circumstances of the cases in Kosovo. In the instant case, the Supreme Court finds that the trial court was not right to take the above-quoted ICTY's statement out of its context and use it as basis to automatically import the whole of Geneva Convention's protection of non-combatants to the facts of this case.'[373]

---

368. Supreme Court Decision, p. 24.
369. Ibid.
370. Supreme Court Decision, p. 25.
371. The Supreme Court here cited the District Court's reliance upon, *inter alia*, the *Tadić* Appeals Judgment of 15 July 1999 at paras. 164-9 and the *Čelebići* Appeals Judgment of 20 February 2001 at paras. 54-59,
372. Supreme Court Decision, p. 25.
373. Ibid.

The Supreme Court set out a two-pronged requirement that would have to be met before applying the Fourth Geneva Convention to Kosovo Albanians residing in the territory controlled by the Yugoslav government. First, the issue must be relevant to the international conflict, that is, that the protected status is based on bonds linking the protected persons with another party to the international conflict.[374] Second, the ethnicity criterion may only be used 'when the *substance* of the relations indicate that they do not owe allegiance to, and do not receive diplomatic protection of, the party in whose hands they find themselves, instead, there is an effective connection to another adverse party'.[375]

Applying that test to the District Court's reasoning, the Supreme Court held that it was insufficient to simply find that the victims and their captors were ethnicities representing opposing parties in an internal conflict, even a conflict existing alongside an international conflict.

> 'Rather, the court would need to establish whether between the victims and the party who had control over that group the allegiance based on nationality did not effectively exist, and that, instead, there was an effective allegiance to an adverse party to the international conflict, ethnicity being a possible decisive for the issue of allegiance. Alternatively, it might be considered whether a lack of an effective bond with the party of whom the victims were formally nationals could result in such a situation that the victims who found themselves in the midst of an international conflict were *in substance* treated as stateless persons and therefore, for the purpose of protected status, should be regarded as such.'[376]

The Supreme Court then advised future trial courts that:

> 'In the determination of the effective allegiance the following factual elements, subject to proof, could be relevant: (1) whether in the relevant period the Yugoslav government ceased offering protection to the Kosovo Albanian civilian population as a whole or to the specific group seeking protection, whereupon they acquired a status of *de facto* stateless persons; (2) whether NATO intervened on behalf of Kosovo Albanian civilian

374. Citing the decision of the ICTY Appeals Chamber in the *Tadić* case, Case No. IT-94-1-A, 15 July 1999 (which first overturned the Trial Chamber's finding of the internal character of the conflict and held instead that it was international), and in the *Čelebići* case, Case No. IT-96-21-A, 20 February 2001, at paras. 26 and 83. The Supreme Court cited *Čelebići's* statement that 'Article 4 of the Geneva Convention IV is to be interpreted as intending to protect civilians who find themselves in the midst of an international, or internationalized, conflict to the maximum extent possible [...]. In today's ethnic conflicts the victims may be [assimilated] to the external State involved in the conflict, even if they formally have the same nationality as their captors.' Ibid., at para. 83.

375. The Supreme Court here stated: 'that this [was the] approach taken in *Tadic*: 'In granting its protection Article 4 intends to look to the substance of relations, not their legal characterization as such', para 168, was confirmed in *Aleksovski*, Appeal Judgment paras. 151-152 and in the *Čelebići* Appeal Judgment which stated that 'formal nationality may not be regarded as determinative in this context, whereas ethnicity may reflect more appropriately the reality of the bonds [...]'. At para. 83. Likewise, the Trial Chamber in the more recent *Naletilić* Judgment held: 'The Chamber abides by the consistent jurisprudence on this issue and will review, on a case by case basis, the effective allegiance of the victims rather than their formal nationality'. At para. 207.' The Supreme Court also cited the ICJ in *Nottebohm, ICJ Rep.* 1955, pp. 22-23.

376. Supreme Court Decision, p. 26.

population thus alienating them in their relations with the Government, whereupon members of this population gained a status of *de facto* stateless persons or aliens in the territory of the adverse party; [and] (3) whether the specific group in question was denied protection and renounced allegiance to Yugoslav Government.'[377]

Once the Supreme Court had held that customary IHL was not directly applicable, it necessarily applied this to the doctrine of command responsibility that had been used to find Kolasinac individually criminally responsible. The District Court had assumed that Article 86 of Additional Protocol I was applicable to Kosovo trials because FRY had ratified that protocol in 1977, and in its trial verdict concluded that Kolasinac 'knew or should have known that the property was being destroyed and looted by his subordinates'.[378]

The Supreme Court, after lengthy historical and legal analysis,[379] concluded that Article 142 of FRY CC and general individual criminal responsibility principles under Kosovo law do not permit application of the doctrine of command responsibility that exists as part of customary IHL as to the forms of liability resulting in a superior's criminal liability for either negligence ('should have known' that crimes were being committed), or for *post facto* failure to report, discipline, or punish upon discovery after the fact of the war crime committed by subordinates.[380]

The Supreme Court first contrasted the ability of international tribunals to find commanders liable for their omissions – even if such omission was not a cause of the particular war crime at issue, e.g., when a commander fails to punish or report subordinates after they commit a war crime of which the commander was then not aware – with Kosovo's general criminal liability principles on acts and omissions.[381] After a historical review of the growth and development of the doctrine, the court noted that:

> 'Additional Protocol I to the Geneva Conventions, and the customary international humanitarian law, impose an obligation on States to either hold violators liable directly, under the language of the Protocol, or to enact domestic legislation to enable liability for the proscribed command responsibility behaviour. The Supreme Court notes, however, that the mode of the implementation of the Protocol as well as the question whether it should be a criminal liability or disciplinary liability was left to the States. The FRY did meet its obligation in that regard through domestic legislation, by providing for criminal liability as defined in article 142 CL FRY and also by providing for the system of disciplinary liability for proscribed command responsibility behavior.'[382]

After reviewing the SFRY (armed forces disciplinary) Regulations, which laid out the provisions of Additional Protocol I on command responsibility, and indeed required the superiors to report and discipline the perpetrators of war crimes or be held liable, the court then

---

377. Ibid., p. 27.

378. Ibid., p. 28, citing District Court Verdict p. 43.

379. Supreme Court Decision, pp. 28-36.

380. Ibid., p. 29.

381. FRY CC Art. 30 allows criminal liability for an omission only if the offender 'abstained from performing an act which he was obligated to perform'. Moreover, Art. 11 allows negligence ('should have known') to result in criminal liability only if the specific penal article expressly allows it, and Art. 142 does not.

382. Supreme Court Decision, p. 30.

reviewed UNMIK Regulation 1999/24, with its provision that the defendant gains the benefit of the most favourable provision of criminal laws in force in Kosovo between 1989 and 2000.[383] The court noted that its holding that customary law does not apply directly to Kosovo courts will not allow direct application of customary law command responsibility as a basis for criminal liability. Thus, Article 30 of FRY CC must be applied. In doing so, the court held:

> 'Accordingly, a superior's failure to report or discipline subordinates for committing war crimes may constitute an omission which is criminalized, but that crime of non-reporting or non-disciplining does not under domestic criminal law result in the superior's being guilty of those war crimes. A *mens rea* in case of negligence ("should have known") cannot result in criminal liability under Article 142 because Article 11 only allows negligence to be the basis for criminal liability if the crime explicitly allows liability due to negligence, and Article 142 does not refer to negligence.
> Furthermore, for a criminal conviction because of an omission, it is indispensable that the causality due to that omission be established. In the case of Article 142, the evidence must prove that the failure of the superior to act resulted in the occurrence of the criminal act of war crimes as a consequence of that omission. Thus, the conviction may be based on an omission only if the accused superior was not only in a *de jure* but also in a *de facto* position to prevent the commission of the war crime, and failed to act with direct or indirect intention [*dolus directus or dolus eventualis*].[384] If these elements are not met, the superior may have committed other crimes that are criminalized by the military justice system or other penal statutes [*e.g.,* failure to report a crime, CL FRY Art. 199(1), aiding the perpetrator after the commission of the crime, CL Kosovo Art. 174] but the superior would not have committed a war crime under domestic Kosovo law as tried in Kosovo courts. It follows from this discussion that the concept of command responsibility liability under Additional Protocol I cannot entirely be transferred to Kosovo domestic criminal law, as not every type of command responsibility that is encompassed by that term is cognizable under Kosovo's criminal law principles of liability.'[385]

In addition to the four legal issues in the case discussed above which are of general concern to all war crimes prosecutions, the Kosovo Supreme Court also addressed a practical legal issue of concern to prosecutors: the question of singularity of a war crime, that is, whether

383. Ibid., p. 32; Reg. 1999/24 was amended by 2000/59 in October 2000, but this Section 1.4 remained unchanged.

384. The Supreme Court here quoted L. Lazarević, *Commentary of the CCY* (art. 30) (Belgrade 1999): 'If a general idea of a criminal act is accepted in its objective and subjective subject matter, the non-acting [omission] itself also represents a wilful and conscious undertaking of a perpetrator. It can be manifested either in a totally passive attitude of the perpetrator towards a particular obligation, as a result of which a consequence of the criminal act occurred, or in undertaking of some other activity that is contrary to the actions that a person in question supposed to undertake as a result of an obligatory norm.'

385. The Supreme Court here stated: 'It may be possible to prove with concrete facts that a superior, by not disciplining for, or reporting, a war crime committed by subordinates, has the requisite *mens rea* or *dolus* if there are sufficient facts to show the superior did know that the subordinates would commit more war crimes due to the superior's failure to discipline or punish.'

multiple criminal acts, each defined within Article 142 as war crimes, are considered as one or more war crimes for the purpose of allegation in the indictment. The court held that:

> 'the singularity or plurality of a war crime against the civilian population, being connected to the element of criminal intention as well as to the objective element [*actus reus*], is a factual circumstance subject to proof, directly or conclusively. The Supreme Court appreciates that repeated acts of underlying offences, especially when committed in the same opportunity, would often justify a conclusion about a single intent, whereas circumstances indicating separate acts of war crime can practically be rare. However, once established as a single act of war crime, such charge is subsequently indivisible in the procedural sense, one of the consequences of it being that the proceedings can only result in one decision in relation to the charge as a whole, irrespective of differences in findings pertaining to specific underlying events. Accordingly, when the results of the main trial confirm only some of the underlying acts, averments that were found not proven must not result in acquittal of these parts of the charge; rather, the court should explain in its opinion which specific facts have been found to be unsupported.'[386]

It concluded in *Kolasinac* that:

> 'the acts alleged as well the acts attributed to the accused were dated as April/May 1999, *i.e.*, in close time proximity to one another and causally related. Moreover, as stated in the Amended Indictment and endorsed by the first instance Verdict, acts charged had been allegedly committed with the unity of criminal intent and opportunity.'[387]

The decision also analysed the facts and findings of law under which the District Court found Kolasinac guilty of the Article 142 war crimes of (1) being an accomplice in forced 'displacement and deportations' by carrying out registration of the Kosovo Albanians in Rahovec after the District Court found that this registration was an essential tool in the deportations;[388] (2) being an accomplice in the 'forced labour'[389] of Kosovo Albanians who were required to work two days pruning vineyards and to clean up roads by removing the household goods and vehicles blocking and littering them; and (3) failing to prevent, as Commander of the headquarters of the Civil Defence, the looting, pillaging and destruction of the abandoned property of Kosovo Albanians who had been displaced and deported.[390] The Supreme Court found error in each of the three categories.

First, the Supreme Court found that the District Court 'did not sufficiently discern the notions of deportation and other displacement. Article 17 of Additional Protocol II covers both situations'. Second, the Supreme Court examined the law applicable in Kosovo as to the charge of forced labour, as this case was the first to put this alleged war crime at issue, and concluded that 'the District Court's findings with regard to the prohibition of forced labour were incorrect in both aspects referred to by Article 142 CL FRY, that of interna-

---

386. Supreme Court decision, pp. 7-8.

387. Ibid., p. 8.

388. FRY CC Art. 142 includes as acts of war crimes '...a forcible dislocation of the population...'.

389. An act included in Art. 142's acts of war crimes.

390. FRY CC Art. 142 includes as acts of war crimes '...pillaging, illegal and self-willed destruction and stealing on large scale of a property that is not justified by military needs...'.

tional law and that of domestic law'.[391] Third, the District Court's finding of Kolasinac's guilt in failing to prevent the looting, pillaging and destruction of the abandoned property of Kosovo Albanians who were displaced and deported was reversed, because 'the verdict on that charge was internally contradictory; moreover, the facts have not been sufficiently established as concerns objective and subjective elements of crime'.[392]

In sum, the *Kolasinac* decision was the first attempt, in the four-year history of UNMIK jurisprudence, to sort out legal issues relevant to war crimes adjudication. The Supreme Court's decision to adopt the theory of pairings, i.e., that there were two parallel conflicts in Kosovo (internal and international), each governed by a different IHL regime, is legalistic but well founded on the factual circumstances of Kosovo, where indeed the conflicted pairs were by far more discernable than in the conflicts in Bosnia.

Most significant in this decision, however, is the Supreme Court's analysis of the legal framework applicable to Kosovo war crimes prosecutions. The court rightly acknowledged that internationalised court panels operating in Kosovo were exercising the function of the domestic courts, and as such the internationalised panels were restricted to adjudication on the basis of domestic laws, i.e., UNMIK regulations and statutes. Among these, in particular UNMIK Regulation 1999/24, which granted the accused the benefit of the most favourable law from March 1989 and December 1999, had the effect of retaining all Yugoslav constitutional protections shielding the accused from the direct application of international criminal law, especially that of a customary nature.

While this Supreme Court holding does not render the prosecution of war crimes easier, its legal logic is impeccable and compelling.

☛ *Veselin Besović* case, Case No. AP-KZ 80/2004, Supreme Court of Kosovo, Decision of 27 May 2004, overturning the verdict of 26 June 2003 by the District Court of Pejë/Pec, C/P 136/2001, and remanding the case for retrial

This Supreme Court decision, by a three international judge panel,[393] was decided upon appeals by both the defence and prosecution against an Article 142 war crimes trial verdict in which the District Court had found the defendant not guilty of war crimes alleged in counts 3 through 19 of the indictment, and found him guilty of war crimes in counts 20-26. Besović had been found guilty of war crimes against the civilian population on 14 May 1999 in Zahaq[394] and in Qyshk[395] villages, both in the Municipality of Pejë/Peć, in violation of Article 142 FRY CC.

The Supreme Court upheld most of the acquittals, but reversed the acquittals for counts 12-13 and 15-19. The court reversed all convictions (counts 20-26) and remanded the case back for retrial. Counts 20 and 21 were considered by the District Court as one single criminal transaction, as were counts 22-26.

There were two independent grounds for reversal of the convictions, with the first being the most important: (1) contradiction between the enacting clause announced at the closing session of the trial, and the enacting clause of the written Verdict (reasons) filed later, and

---

391. Supreme Court decision, p. 8.

392. Ibid.

393. Presiding Judge Agnieszka Klonowiecka-Milart (of Poland), author of the decision (written reasoning), and Judges Martin Karopkin (US) and David Doyscher (US).

394. The Serbian spelling is Zahac.

395. The Serbian spelling is Cusk.

(2) insufficient reasoning and fact-finding due to a lack of complete and critical evaluation of witness testimony. The Supreme Court also felt it necessary to address the application of the substantive criminal law *ex officio* to prevent erroneous application of the law in a possible retrial, but admitted that given the unreliability of the fact-finding, any legal discussion would be abstract.

The announced enacting clause, in relation to counts 20-21, had found that Besović, 'in association with a group of paramilitaries and police, committed acts of torture, attempted murder of an injured party, robbery of possessions and burned houses; a number of people were killed and others were expelled by force. These acts were qualified as a war crime under Article 142 as read with Articles 22 (complicity[396]) and 26 (criminal association[397])' of the FRY CC. In relation to counts 22 to 26, the announced enacting clause had found that Besović, 'in association with a group of paramilitaries committed acts of torture, with some people being killed, and attempted murder of 5 injured parties, for the purpose of expelling Kosovo Albanians from Kosovo. Similarly, these acts were qualified as a war crime under Article 142 as read with Articles 22 and 26' of the FRY CC. In contrast, the enacting clause in the written Verdict, in relation to counts 20-21, found that Besović 'committed war crimes of torture, displacement of the civilian population and pillaging in violation of Article 142 in connection with Article 26 CL FRY (in criminal association) with regard to Counts 20-21',[398] and stated the same as to counts 22 to 26.[399] The Supreme Court described the contradictions:

> 'In the enacting clause of the written verdict the court did not include murder and attempted murder, which contradicts the findings it made in the announcement of the Verdict. Moreover, in the reasoning part of the Verdict the District Court specifically stated that it did not hold the accused accountable for the killings alleged in these Counts of the indictment. This contradiction clearly violates the requirements of Article 357 of the LCP, which states that the written Verdict "must fully correspond with the verdict which was announced.'[400]

The Supreme Court also found the enacting clause of the written verdict flawed because it failed to specify the elements of the acts attributed to Besović. The written verdict merely referenced the counts of the indictment, thus implying that the trial court had endorsed those allegations in their entirety – which was then denied later on in the written reasoning, particularly as to the factual question of acting in criminal association.

The Supreme Court emphasised that this 'discrepancy between the two enacting clauses as well as the contradictions within the reasoning are not purely a formal matter; the sub-

---

396. Art. 22, Complicity: 'If several persons jointly commit a criminal act by participating in the act of commission or in some other way, each of them shall be punished as prescribed for the act.'

397. Art. 26, Criminal Responsibility of Organizers and Leaders of Criminal Associations: 'Anybody creating or making use of an organization, gang, cabal, group or any other association for the purpose of committing criminal acts is criminally responsible for all criminal acts resulting from the criminal design of these associations and shall be punished as if he himself has committed them, irrespective of whether and in what manner he himself directly participated in the commission of any of those acts.'

398. Supreme Court Decision, *supra*.

399. Ibid.

400. Ibid.

stantive disparity, particularly on the issue of murder, raises the possibility that the Verdict had not been completely resolved at the time of the announcement'.[401] This alone required retrial; indeed, the Supreme Court noted that 'in the face of major internal contradictions apparent in the enacting clauses and the reasoning parts of the Verdict as to what the trial court has actually decided, the issue of correct fact finding becomes a secondary matter'.[402] However, the court proceeded to discuss the fact finding 'because it is concerned about the patent inadequacy of the trial court's approach to evidence, which must be avoided in the re-trial'.[403] The court then discussed the factual findings as to the counts the District Court had found to be not proven, finding the written verdict flawed because its findings, though voluminous, were incomplete.[404]

The Supreme Court also found that the findings of guilt on counts 20-26 were not properly established because the written verdict 'failed to give sufficient reasons to support its findings, as there is a lack of complete and critical evaluation of the testimonies of the witnesses' as to identification of the accused at the scene of the crimes for which he was found guilty'.[405] The Supreme Court discussed the legal standards for evaluation of witness testimony and generic flaws and concrete examples of insufficient analysis.[406]

It emphasised that the mere fact that witness testimony contains contradictions will not automatically render it unreliable. However, a trial court must examine and evaluate witness testimony in detail, in light of defence claims and the surrounding circumstances, in relation to the thesis the testimony is offered to prove.[407]

The Supreme Court discussed two substantive legal issues of interest: (1) the singularity of the crime of war crimes against the civilian population, and (2) the applicability of international humanitarian law to Kosovo war crimes proceedings.[408] As to the singularity, the reasoning in *Besović*[409] followed that in the *Kolasinac* case, discussed *supra*, and concluded that:

> 'Relatively narrow time span, territorial unity and similar *modus operandi* of the alleged offences would indicate that the offences should be treated as a single war crime. In any case, however, in relation to each underlying offence, the trial court would need to determine whether the nature of the alleged offence places it within the ambit of prohibited conduct defined in Article 142 CL FRY, whether the alleged underlying offence was committed in the period of armed conflict and whether in that period the accused could be considered a party to the armed conflict.'[410]

401. Ibid., p. 6.
402. Ibid., p. 9.
403. Ibid.
404. Ibid., pp. 6-8.
405. Ibid., p. 9.
406. Ibid., pp. 9-15.
407. Ibid., pp. 13-14.
408. The court noted it was addressing these issues *ex officio*, 'as it appears that somewhat vague position expressed by the District Court may potentially lead to a violation of the criminal law to the detriment of the accused'. Ibid., p. 16.
409. Ibid., pp. 15-18.
410. Ibid., p. 18.

As to the direct applicability of international humanitarian law treaties in the Kosovo criminal justice system, the Supreme Court also repeated the reasoning of *Kolasinac,* discussed *supra.*[411] The Supreme Court concluded by explaining:

> 'in the application of Article 142 CL FRY it would not be legitimate to resort to international customary law in such an areas as primarily defining prohibited conduct, defining the basis of individual criminal responsibility and punishment. International custom as well as the jurisprudence of international tribunals can however be used for the purpose of lending assistance to the interpretation of the concrete prohibitions contained in Article 142 CL FRY and relevant international treaties applicable in times of war, armed conflict or occupation. This was for example, correctly done by the District Court in relation to the notion of "torture".'[412]

The Supreme Court concluded by cautioning Kosovo courts that they should not simply follow ICTY and ICTR sentencing practices, in particular the length of imprisonment terms, because the appropriate sentencing factors in Kosovo law may not track those in the tribunals:

> 'the length of punishments imposed by international tribunals ... could only constitute a point of reference where the [Kosovo] court evaluates decisive factors in these cases in comparison with the case before it. However, a reference to the judgments of the international tribunals cannot simply replace a [Kosovo court's] substantive discussion of the gravity of the crime, including the specific elements of the acts attributed to the accused, the concerns of prevention and specifics of mitigating and aggravating circumstances, when such are present.'[413]

In sum, in *Besović* the Supreme Court reiterated its position taken in *Kolasinac* that the legal framework of the Kosovo justice system does not allow the importing of international customary law to define crimes, modes of criminal responsibility and punishment. The Supreme Court, however, seemingly being aware of the importance of the developments in international customary law, recommended that such may lend assistance to the Kosovo judiciary in interpreting the underlying offences of Article 142. *Besović* also exemplifies a common phenomenon in Kosovo war crimes cases, witness testimony that contradicts prior statements, or recantation, and the Supreme Court criticised the District Court for its 'nonchalance' in accepting without any explanatory analysis such 'inconsistencies or obvious contradictions'.[414] This issue of inconsistency and the need for serious analysis and comparison among witness testimony is also reaffirmed in the *Vucković* case (below).

☛ *Miroslav Vucković* case, Case No. AP-KZ 186/2003, Supreme Court of Kosovo, Decision of 15 July 2004, overturning the verdict of 25 October 2002 by the District Court of Mitrovica, P. No. 48/2001, and remanding the case for retrial

---

411. Ibid., pp. 18-19.
412. Ibid., p. 19.
413. Ibid., p. 20.
414. Ibid., p. 12.

This Supreme Court decision, by a three international judge panel,[415] reversed Vucković's conviction for committing war crimes against the civilian population, in violation of Article 142 FRY CC, in complicity with others under Article 22, and remanded the case back for retrial. Vucković had been found guilty of various war crimes against the civilian population between September 1998 and 10 May 1999 for the following three acts: (1) illegal and self-willed destruction of property as encompassed by Article 147 of the Fourth Geneva Convention of 1949; (2) stealing on a large scale of property, as encompassed by Article 4 (2)(g) of Additional Protocol II; and (3) application of measures of intimidation and terror and endangering the safety of other persons, as encompassed by Common Article 3 (1)(a) of the Geneva Conventions of 1949, and Article 4(2)(a) of Additional Protocol II.

The Supreme Court reversed the conviction because it was 'based on an incorrect and an incomplete evaluation of the evidence with the implicit inaccurate establishment of facts'.[416] In making this determination, the Supreme Court considered numerous discrepancies and inconsistencies found in the incriminating evidence relied upon by the trial court, which undermined the overall factual foundation of the charges. Accordingly, it decided that the verdict should be quashed and the case returned for retrial.[417] In what the common law system would call *dicta, Vucković* also followed *Kolasinac* in its discussion of the direct applicability of IHL in Kosovo courts.

The Supreme Court held that the District Court's application of stealing property on a large scale in violation of Additional Protocol II,[418] and measures of intimidation and terror in violation of common Article 3 and Additional Protocol II,[419] were applicable under Article 142 FRY CC, because they applied to internal armed conflicts. However, the Supreme Court held that the District Court erroneously applied Article 147 of the Fourth Geneva Convention concerning the illegal and self-willed destruction of property not justified by military necessity.[420] The Supreme Court stated: 'the applicability of this Article is limited to situations of belligerent occupation in the course of an international armed conflict, which was not the issue in the instant case. In this regard we refer to ICTY's decision in *Prosecutor v. Dario Kordic and Mario Cerkez*.'[421]

Finally, the Supreme Court noted that the sentencing approach taken by the District Court:

> 'in treating the lack of remorse as an aggravating factor in deciding the punishment contradicted the presumption of innocence. The presumption of innocence includes the right to remain silent and freedom from self-incrimination. Remorse of an accused who pleads guilty, when genuine, may constitute a mitigating factor. It would however be inappropriate to reverse the rule and hold against the accused who pleads innocent that

---

415. Presiding Judge Agnieszka Klonowiecka-Milart (of Poland), author of the decision (written reasoning), and Judges Tudor Pantiru (Moldova) and Christine Lindemann-Proetel (Germany).

416. This is a ground for reversal and remand under FRY Law on Criminal Procedure [LCP] Art. 366.

417. Supreme Court Decision, p. 10.

418. Art. 4(2)(g).

419. Para. 1(a) of common Art. 3 and Art. 4(2)(a) of Additional Protocol II.

420. At p. 25 of the Judgement.

421. The Supreme Court here cites *Prosecutor* v. *Dario Kordić and Mario Cerkez*, Case No. IT-95-14/2-T, Judgment, 26 February 2001, paras. 330-347.

he is not showing remorse. Such approach would, in effect, attach negative consequence to the plea of innocence.'[422]

Ongoing Cases

- *Ejup Runjeva et al.*, P. No. 215/04, *District Court of Pristina*, upon an Amended Indictment dated 1 June 2004

On 5 October 2004 a three-judge international panel[423] of the District Court of Pristina began a trial that continued through to 2005 of Rrustem Dema, Enver Axhami, Ejup Runjeva (nickname 'Era'), Bujar Tafili and Nuhi Provoliu, charged with the criminal act of War Crimes against the Civilian Population as defined by Article 142 FRY CC, as read with Articles 22 (complicity), 24 (aiding),[424] 26 (criminal association) and 30 (commission by act or omission). The indictment alleged that between 27 February and 21 March 1999 the defendants and others in KLA/UCK uniforms kidnapped, unlawfully detained, inflicted serious bodily injuries upon and murdered a number of Kosovo Albanian civilians. This occurred during a period of time prior to the NATO bombings, when armed conflict came to Kacanik region, an area of Kosovo just north of the Macedonian border.

The indictment accuses the five defendants, former KLA members, of the kidnap and torture of five fellow Kosovo-Albanians who were believed to have collaborated with the Serbian authorities. They are also charged with the murder of four of them. The principal witness is one of the victims who escaped. The indictment alleges and investigation evidence states that the victims along with about ten others were abducted from their homes and taken prisoner.

MICHAEL E. HARTMANN

SEYCHELLES

Antipersonnel Mines

- The Anti-Personnel Mines (Prohibition) Act. Passed by the National Assembly on 30 March 2004, received presidential assent and came into force on 8 April 2004. Published in the Official Gazette on 12 April 2004

'The Act gives effect to the Convention on the Prohibition of the Use, Stockpiling, Production and Transfer of Anti-personnel Mines and on their Destruction.'[425]

---

422. At p. 27 of the judgement.

423. Presiding Judge Martin Karopkin (of US) with Judges Annunziata Ciaravolo (Italy) and Linn Slattengren (US).

424. '(1) Anybody who intentionally aids another in the commission of a criminal act shall be punished as if he himself had committed it, but his punishment may also be reduced.
(2) The following, in particular, shall be considered as aiding: the giving of instructions or counseling about how to commit a criminal act, the supply of tools and resources for the crime, the removal of obstacles to the commission of a crime, as well as the promise, prior to the commission of the act, to conceal the existence of the criminal act, to hide the offender, the means to commit the crime, its traces, or goods gained through the commission of a criminal act.'

425. *Supra* n. 70, pp. 699-700.

SIERRA LEONE

Truth and Reconciliation

- Final Report of the Sierra Leone Truth and Reconciliation Commission. Transmitted to the President of Sierra Leone on 5 October 2004 and presented to the UN Security Council on 27 October 2004[426]

The Commission found that 'the central cause of the war was endemic greed, corruption and nepotism that deprived the nation of its dignity and reduced most people to a state of poverty'.[427] In addition to making specific findings on a range of aspects of the armed conflict, the Commission in its report considered other relevant issues, such as exploitation of Sierra Leone's mineral wealth as a contributing factor. In this respect, it found that 'the exploitation of diamonds did not cause the conflict in Sierra Leone, but different fighting factions did target diamond areas for purposes of supporting their war efforts'.[428] 'During the conflict period, the global diamond industry deliberately chose not to determine the origin of diamonds, thereby promoting the trade in conflict diamonds, which, in turn, prolonged local wars.'[429]

As far as violations of IHL and human rights are concerned, the Commission found 'the leadership of the RUF,[430] the AFRC,[431] the SLA[432] and the CDF[433] to be responsible for either authorising or instigating human rights violations against civilians; alternatively for failing to stop such practices or to speak out against them; and for failing to acknowledge the atrocities committed by their followers or members'.[434] The Commission pointed to many specific violations of IHL by the RUF,[435] AFRC[436] and CDF.[437]

The TRC was critical of the UN and Sierra Leone's decision to overturn the amnesty they had agreed to in the Lomé Peace Agreement, finding that 'both the Government of Sierra Leone and the RUF committed breaches of the Lomé Peace Agreement which culminated in its collapse in May 2000'. Significantly, the Commission found that 'in repudiating the amnesty clause in the Lomé Peace Agreement, both the United Nations and the Government of Sierra Leone may have sent an unfortunate message to combatants in future wars that they cannot trust peace agreements that contain amnesty clauses. The Commission subscribes to the general proposition that there will be circumstances where a trade of peace for amnesty represents the least bad of the available alternatives.'[438]

Sierra Leone was the first laboratory for the simultaneous working of both a court established to prosecute war crimes and other international crimes and a truth commission, but not a very successful one, according to the TRC's report. The report found 'insufficient

---

426. The report is partly available online at the website of the US Institute for Peace, <http://www.usip.org/library/tc/tc_regions/tc_sl.html#rep>.
427. Vol. 2, Ch. 3, Findings, para. 13.
428. Ibid., paras. 502, 509.
429. Ibid., para. 506.
430. Revolutionary United Front.
431. Armed Forces Revolutionary Council.
432. Sierra Leone Army.
433. Civil Defense Forces.
434. Vol. 2, Ch. 3, Findings, para. 27.
435. Ibid., paras. 127, 154, 474.
436. Ibid., para. 252.
437. Ibid., para. 479.
438. Ibid., paras. 562, 553.

consideration was given to the laying down of guidelines for the simultaneous conduct of the Commission and the Special Court'. In particular, the Commission found that 'the United Nations and the Government of Sierra Leone should have enshrined the right of detainees and prisoners in the custody of the Special Court to participate in the truth and reconciliation process.'[439] 'The failure to establish policy which would set out clearly the nature of the relationship between the two bodies led to a great deal of confusion in the minds of the public. As a result, many Sierra Leoneans stayed away from the Commission for fear that their information may be turned over to the Special Court.'[440]

As far as the right to truth itself is concerned, the Commission found that there is one and that its realisation is 'an essential component of the universally recognised "right to an effective remedy".'[441] Courts are limited in their ability to discover the full truth. Truth commissions, on the other hand, are designed for this purpose.[442] According to the Commission: 'Truth and Reconciliation Commissions represent one of the most viable means of securing a sustainable peace.'[443]

Human Rights

☛ The Human Rights Commission of Sierra Leone Act 2004 <http://www.sierra-leone.org/Laws/humanrightscommissionact2004.pdf>

SOUTH AFRICA[444]

Peacekeeping

☛ Participation of the South African National Defence Force (SANDF) in the UN Operation in Burundi (ONUB)

In January 2003 the African Union (AU) authorised the deployment of forces to supervise the ceasefire agreements concluded between the Transitional Government of Burundi and the Armed Movements. The mandate of the mission was to provide security for the cantonment of combatants and assist with the demobilisation, disarmament and reintegration of armed groups. The AU Mission in Burundi (AMIB) was to be composed of forces from Ethiopia, Mozambique and South Africa as the lead nation. South Africa has provided a neutral protection force to ensure the security of returning exiled leaders and political figures (South African Protection and Support Detachment (SAPSD)) since October 2001. The mandate for the mission was given until 2 April 2004 but on request of the United Nations (UN) it was extended until 2 July 2004.

Following an assessment report by the UN Secretary-General, the UN Security Council adopted UN SC Resolution 1545 on 21 May 2004 authorising and mandating the takeover of AMIB by the UN as recommended by the UN Secretary-General. The mandate of the United Nations Mission in Burundi (ONUB) came into effect from 1 June 2004 for an

439. Ibid., paras. 554, 564.
440. Ibid., para. 555.
441. Ibid., para. 575.
442. Ibid., para. 577.
443. Ibid., para. 578.
444. Information and commentaries provided by Dr Phenyo Rakate, LL.D. (UNISA), Directorate Research and Analysis, Defence Secretariat, Department of Defence, Pretoria, Republic of South Africa.

initial period of six months, with the intention to renew it for further periods. South Africa was requested by the United Nations Department Peacekeeping Operations (UNDPKO) to provide personnel and associated equipment for the mission. In August 2004 a Memorandum of Understanding (MOU) for South Africa's contribution was negotiated and signed in which South Africa, amongst others, agreed to contribute a maximum of 1,099 SANDF personnel and associated equipment for the UN mission. The post of Force Commander was also offered to South Africa.

Cases (crimes committee abroad)

☛ *S.* v. *Basson*, Constitutional Court, 10 March 2004. Published in 2004 (6) BCLR 620 (CC)

Dr Wouter Basson, a Captain in the former South African Defence Force (SADF), who headed the SADF chemical and biological warfare program (known as 'Project Coast') during the apartheid era was originally charged in the Pretoria High Court on 67 counts of fraud, murder, conspiracy to commit crimes abroad, drug offences and possession of classified information relating to apartheid era crimes.[445] His trial commenced on 4 October 1999. Just over a week into the trial, the presiding judge, Judge Harzenberg, quashed six counts in the original indictment, including the killing of 200 South West African People's Organisation (SWAPO) cadres in Namibia and conspiracy to commit crimes abroad in terms of the Riotous Assemblies Act,[446] on the basis of the amnesty granted by the former Administrator-General of Namibia, Louis Pienaar, in the 1991 Amnesty Proclamation. During the course of the trial, the remaining charges were reduced from 61 to 46. On 11 April 2002 Judge Harzenberg ruled that all remaining 46 counts against Basson must be dropped and that he should be granted indemnity from prosecution.

The state applied for the recusal of the presiding judge on the ground that there was a reasonable perception that he was biased. When Judge Harzenberg refused to recuse himself, the state appealed to the Supreme Court of Appeal, which on 3 June 2003 ruled in favour of Judge Harzenberg[447] and refused to order a retrial of Basson, saying that the state did not have the right to appeal.

Basson's acquittal was met with mixed reactions by South African society generally, and by human rights organisations and politicians in particular; some viewed it as a 'travesty of justice' and 'a shameful day for truth and justice in post-apartheid South Africa'.[448] The then-Namibian Minister of Foreign Affairs, Mr Theo-Ben Gurirab, reported that Namibia would apply for Basson's extradition to face the charge of killing 200 SWAPO cadres which had been expunged from the original South African indictment.[449]

In November 2003 the state filed for special leave to appeal before the Constitutional Court against the decision of the Supreme Court of Appeal and the refusal of the High

---

445. *S* v. *Basson* 2000 (3) All SA 59(T).

446. Section 18(2) of Act 17 of 1956.

447. *S* v. *Basson*, 2004 (6) BCLR 620 (CC).

448. M. Tsele, 'A General Amnesty is not the Way to Heal the Wounds of Apartheid', *The Sunday Times*, 23 March 2003, p. 18; J. Battersby, 'De Klerk Adds Voice to Call for Wide-Ranging Amnesty', *The Star*, 21 May 2002, p. 5.

449. 'Basson may be Extradited to Face Trial in Namibia', *The Namibian*, 16 September 2003, p. 7.

Court to remove the presiding judge.[450] The state argued that South African common law was applicable to Namibia at the time of the commission of the offences, which are crimes under South African law, including conspiracy to murder which was criminalised by the Riotous Assemblies Act.[451] At the time of the commission of the offence, the 1957 Defence Act[452] and the Military Discipline Supplementary Measures Act[453] applied to members of the former South African Defence Force (SADF) beyond the borders of the country, and those who breached these laws were accordingly held accountable.

On 10 March 2004 the majority of the Constitutional Court, while rejecting the state's request to overturn the acquittal of Basson, held that the quashing of the charges and the refusal of the presiding judge to recuse himself raised constitutional and international law issues, thus opening a way for the state to retry Basson on the six charges originally quashed by Harzenberg.[454] The court held that the question of whether Basson would be exposed to double jeopardy did not arise in this matter because the charges had been quashed, and, as such, the question of the interests of justice raised by section 35(3)(d) of the Constitution, which provides that accused persons are entitled to be tried without unreasonable delay, had not been triggered.[455] As the court stated: '[the] accused did not plead to the charges that were subsequently quashed and was therefore never in jeopardy of conviction upon them'.[456]

According to Sachs J, the case raised three fundamental constitutional matters, namely, (1) whether the charges constitute war crimes, and if so, (2) whether that imposed a constitutional obligation on the state to prosecute, and (3) whether the quashing of the charges constituted a failure to give effect to South Africa's international law obligation to prosecute under the constitution.[457] Sachs J concluded that the consequences of the High Court's decision to quash the charges, and the subsequent refusal of the Supreme Court of Appeal to entertain the appeal by the state, had a direct impact 'on the legal order as envisaged by the Constitution, particularly insofar as war crimes may be involved'.[458]

On the first question, Sachs J concluded that if the material facts in the charge sheet (counts 31 and 61), subsequently quashed by the trial judge – namely, that in 1989 Basson furnished cholera bacteria to poison the water supply of a SWAPO refugee camp in order to manipulate the outcome of the elections in Namibia – were proved to be correct, such actions would constitute war crimes.[459] Secondly, if it were proved that war crimes had been committed, should consideration be given to South Africa's international law obligations? Sachs J concluded that indeed the rules of humanitarian law, including customary international law, constitute an integral part of our constitution and therefore there is a duty on the state to impose penal sanctions on persons involved in grave breaches of international humanitarian law.[460] Finally, Sachs J concluded that failure by the Supreme Court of

---

450. *S* v. *Wouter Basson*, 2004 (6) BCLR 620 (CC).
451. Section 18(2) of the Riotous Assemblies Act 17 of 1956.
452. The Act has been repealed by the Defence Act 42 of 2002.
453. Section 47 of Act 16 of 1999.
454. *S* v. *Wouter Basson,* 2004 (6) BCLR 620 (CC), paras. 17-38.
455. Ibid., paras. 61-69.
456. Ibid., para. 67.
457. Ibid., paras. 110-126.
458. Ibid., para. 115.
459. *S* v. *Wouter Basson* 2004 (6) BCLR 620 (CC), paras. 117-120.
460. Ibid., paras. 121-123.

Appeal to take into account South Africa's international law obligations raised constitutional questions that were within the competence of the Constitutional Court.[461]

The decision of the court raises two important issues. Firstly, the net effect of the court's ruling is that the amnesty granted by the last Administrator-General of Namibia for crimes committed in Namibia, which was the basis for the trial court to quash some of the charges against Basson, is invalid and has no extraterritorial effect. Secondly, the Namibian prosecuting authorities have a right to apply for Basson's extradition to face trial in Namibia for the murder of 200 SWAPO prisoners of war. Although South Africa and Namibia do not have a formal extradition agreement, the latter is one of the designated countries for the purposes of extradition in terms of section 2(1)(b) of the Extradition Act 67 of 1962.[462]

Pending

☛ Establishment of a National Inter-Departmental Committee on the Implementation of International Humanitarian Law

Given the growing number of conventions relating to international humanitarian law (IHL), the International Committee of the Red Cross has been advocating and facilitating the creation by states of IHL Committees in order to coordinate national measures relating to the implementation of the law. This is largely because the implementation of the rules of international humanitarian law often requires coordination and cooperation of relevant line-function government departments and institutions. The function of such national committees is to advise, guide and assist governments in their implementation and dissemination of IHL. So far, countries in the SADC region which have already created IHL committees include Zimbabwe, Namibia, Malawi, Lesotho, Mauritius, Seychelles and Comoros.

In November 2004 the Department of Foreign Affairs recommended to Cabinet that it approve the establishment of a National Inter-Departmental Committee on the implementation of IHL. It is envisaged that the Committee will consist of representatives of the Departments of Defence, the South African Police Service, Justice, Education, Home Affairs, Arts and Culture and Foreign Affairs. The Committee will have the power to co-opt members of civil society.

PHENYO RAKATE

SPAIN[463]

Cases (genocide, terrorism and torture)

Brady case

☛ Central Investigating Court number 5, National Court (Audiencia Nacional). Madrid. Summary of Proceedings 19/1997, Order of 9 May 2001 giving leave to proceed in the charge against Hernán Julio Brady Roche for the crimes of genocide, terrorism and torture, issuing an arrest warrant for his extradition and ordering his preventive detention

461. Ibid., paras. 124-126.

462. See *Government Gazette* No. 18663, 13 February 1998.

463. Information and commentaries by Antoni Pigrau, Professor of International Law at the Rovira I Virgili University, Tarragona.

- Central Investigating Court number 5, National Court (Audiencia Nacional). Madrid. Summary of Proceedings 19/1997, Order of 30 May 2001 dismissing the Appeal for Amendment filed by the Prosecutor against the Order of 9 May 2001
- Criminal Division, Third Section, National Court (Audiencia Nacional). Madrid. Court records 19/97 – L. Central Investigating Court number 5. Order of 31 May 2002 allowing the Prosecutor's appeal against the Order of 30 May 2001 and overruling the orders and the international arrest warrant
- Supreme Court. Criminal Division. Appeal for Cassation No. 1812/2002. Ruling No. 319/2004 of 8 March 2004, which partially allows the appeals for cassation brought by the plaintiffs
- Supreme Court. Criminal Division. Appeal for Cassation No. 1812/2002. Ruling No. 319/2004 of 8 March 2004, which grants leave to proceed

In the framework of the proceedings underway at the Spanish National Court against the military dictatorship that came to power in Chile on 11 September 1973, the Central Investigating Court No. 5 issued a Court Order on 9 May 2001 granting leave to proceed in the charge brought, among others, by the family of the Spanish civil servant, Carmelo Soria, murdered in Santiago, and by Izquierda Unida against Hernán Julio Brady Roche, Major General and Commander-in-Chief of the II Division; Military Chief of Santiago de Chili during the *coup d'etat* of 1973 and later Minister of Defense of Chile, for the alleged crimes of genocide, terrorism and torture. The order stated that the Chilean general be remanded in unconditional custody. The same order issued an international arrest warrant for extradition purposes, particularly for Germany, because it seemed that he was residing temporarily in Hamburg under a false name.

The Prosecutor filed an appeal for amendment against this resolution, which was dismissed by the Order of 30 May 2001, against which, in turn, the Prosecutor filed an appeal.

The ruling of the Criminal Chamber of the National Court of 31 May 2002 allowed the Prosecutor's appeal because Spain had no jurisdiction over the events that were the subject of the action. It overruled the court orders and, therefore, also the international arrest warrant. To reach this conclusion, the National Court justified the fact that it used different criteria from its ruling of 4 November 1998,[464] in which it stated its competence regarding the events that took place in Chile, which were initially qualified as constituting the crimes of genocide, terrorism and torture in the 'novel criteria' of the Second Chamber of the Supreme Court, 'which are contained in the Order of 23rd May 2002, issued during the so-called Otegui case'.[465]

The plaintiffs appealed to the Supreme Court to annul this ruling. They considered that the Spanish courts were competent to judge the events of which General Brady was accused by virtue of the principle of universal jurisdiction enunciated in Article 23 of the Organic Law of the Judiciary 1985.

The Supreme Court's ruling of 8 March 2004 reflects the criteria established by the National Court in 1998 and discounts the relevance of the order of 23 May 2002 in the Otegui case as a precedent for the *Brady* case.

---

464. Decision of National Court, Criminal Division, Plenary Session, Appeal record 84/98, Summary of Proceedings 19/97, Central Investigating Court number 5, Madrid, 4 November 1998. See 2 *YIHL* (1999), p. 411.

465. Supreme Court, Criminal Division, Order of 23 May 2002.

According to the Supreme Court:

> 'the order issued by this Court in the "Otegui case" did not specifically examine the scope of Spanish jurisdiction to have cognisance of events that have taken place abroad and which are susceptible of being qualified as crimes of terrorism, genocide or torture. The order did not accept that the Spanish courts were competent to judge the charge against a member of the Basque parliament who had allegedly shouted "Gora Euskadi ta Atkatasuna" at the end of his speech at the Jai Alai *pelota* court in the French city of San Juan de Luz. Because this constituted generic public defence of terrorism—a crime of opinion—it could not be considered to be a crime of terrorism, in the sense in which the crime is defined in the international arena by the respective Treaties. And it is these Treaties that must be taken into account when defining whether Spanish jurisdiction is entitled to have cognisance of this sort of crime committed outside national territory, without detriment, logically, to how this sort of behaviour is specified domestically by the Penal Code.'

On the other hand, the Supreme Court confirmed the criteria enunciated in its ruling of 25 February 2003 In the case of *Guatemala*.[466] It considered that the appeal for cassation should be accepted, the order appealed against should be annulled and that it should be stated that:

> 'the Spanish courts have jurisdiction to have cognisance of the events that are the object of the criminal action brought against the Chilean general Hernán Julio Brady Roche, logically in accordance with the doctrine laid down by the Plenary Session of this Court in the ruling on the "Guatemala case". To this effect, we should state that, among the events in which—according to the plaintiff—the mentioned general is involved are those pertaining to two Spanish priests and the death of the Spanish diplomat Carmelo Soria.'

As a result of this ruling, the Supreme Court issued a second ruling on the same date by which it granted leave to proceed with the action brought against General Hernán Brady.

Perú case

- Central Investigating Court number 1, National Court. Madrid. Order of 15 June 2001 rejecting the competence of the court
- Central Investigating Court number 1, National Court. Madrid. Order of 20 September 2001 dismissing the Appeal for Amendment filed by the plaintiffs against the Order of 15 July 2001
- Criminal Chamber, National Court. Madrid. Order of 21 January 2002 dismissing the appeal filed by the plaintiffs
- Supreme Court. Criminal Division. Ruling No. 712/2003 of 20 May 2003. Appeal for cassation

---

466. Supreme Court. Criminal Division. Sentence nº 327/2003, of 25/02/2003. Appeal for cassation nº 803/2001. See 6 *YIHL* (2003) pp. 618-627.

In its ruling in the *Guatemala* case of 25 February 2003,[467] the Criminal Division of the Supreme Court made a restrictive interpretation of the scope of the principle of universal jurisdiction in Spain by requiring some connection between the events being judged and Spain's interests: for instance, the perpetrators of the crime must be on Spanish soil or the crime must have been committed against Spanish nationals or against other Spanish interests. For this reason, it limited the competence of the Spanish courts to the crimes committed in Guatemala against Spanish nationals.

The seven magistrates who subscribed to the dissenting vote[468] disagreed with the majority because they considered that Spanish legislation required no connection with Spanish interests. The dissenting magistrates accepted a criterion of subsidiarity in the case of competing jurisdictions. They even spoke of the 'principle of the need for jurisdictional intervention', derived from the very nature and purpose of universal jurisdiction, which 'determines the priority of competences when territorial jurisdiction coincides with jurisdiction based on the principle of Universal Justice'.

The present *Perú* case goes back to the action brought by the 'Committee for Solidarity with Peru in Catalonia' in 2001. The action was based on the principle of universal jurisdiction and referred to events that had taken place in Perú 'between 1986 and the present' during the political repression carried out by the ex-Presidents Alan García and Alberto Fujimori, by Vladimiro Montesinos and by other high-ranking civilians and military officers. The events were qualified as crimes of genocide, terrorism, torture and illegal detention. On 15 June 2001 an Order was issued by the Central Investigating Court number 1 rejecting the competence of the court to have cognisance of the events alleged in the charge sheet. The plaintiffs filed an appeal for amendment and a subsidiary remedy of appeal. By means of a court order issued on 20 September 2001, the Central Investigating Court number 1 dismissed the appeal for amendment and referred the case to the National Court to solve the remedy of appeal. The Full Session of the Criminal Division of the National Court resolved, through the Order of 21 January 2002, to dismiss the remedy of appeal on the grounds that Spanish jurisdiction was subsidiary to Peruvian jurisdiction.

The 'Committee for Solidarity with Peru in Catalonia' filed an appeal for cassation with the Supreme Court for a variety of reasons provided for in Spanish legislation. Of particular interest for our purposes here is that the Supreme Court explicitly accepted the criterion put forward by the dissenting magistrates in the case of Guatemala:

> 'SIXTH. However, it must be accepted that the need for jurisdictional intervention in accordance with the principle of Universal Justice is excluded when the territorial jurisdiction is effectively pursuing the universal crime committed in its own country. In this respect, there may be a principle of the need for jurisdictional intervention, which is derived from the very nature and purpose of universal jurisdiction.
>
> The application of this principle determines the priority of competences when territorial jurisdiction coincides with jurisdiction based on the principle of Universal Justice.
>
> This criterion does not make it possible to use the provisions of article 23.4 of the LOPJ (Organic Law of the Judiciary) as if they established that, for a universal jurisdiction action to be admitted, the criminal prosecution by the territorial jurisdiction need to be

467. Supreme Court. Criminal Division. Sentence no. 327/2003, of 25/02/2003. Appeal for cassation no. 803/2001. See 6 *YIHL* (2003) pp. 618-627.

468. Supreme Court, Criminal Division, Dissenting Vote in the Appeal for cassation nº 803/2001.

> proven to be inactive or ineffective. This requisite would effectively annul the principle of universal prosecution, because this proof is practically impossible to obtain, and would necessitate an extremely delicate assessment at this premature moment in the legal procedure.
> For the action to be admitted, the requirements are the same as for events that supposedly constitute a universal crime. Serious and reasonable evidence must be provided that the grave crimes reported have not been effectively pursued by the territorial jurisdiction, for whatever reason, without this casting aspersions on any of the political, social or material influences that have been involved in such "de facto" impunity.
> However, in the present case, the facts, as the dismissed order succinctly expresses, suggest that the political change in Peru was instrumental in the initiation of criminal procedures against several of the accused, some of whom are or have been in prison while other leading figures have absconded. Therefore, it cannot be accepted that at the present moment there is a need for Spanish jurisdiction to intervene in virtue of the principle of universal jurisdiction and the appeal must consequently be dismissed.'

Despite the dismissal of the appeal for cassation, the present ruling qualifies the jurisprudence laid down in the ruling of 23 February 2003 on the issue of Guatemala because the Supreme Court accepted here the criteria of the dissenting minority with reference to the application of 'a principle of the need for jurisdictional intervention'.

☛ *Scilingo* case, Second Criminal Division, Supreme Court, Ruling no. 1362/2004 of 15 November 2004 dismissing appeal no. 945/2003 filed by Adolfo Scilingo

On 27 June 2003 the Criminal Division of the National Court issued an Order confirming the end of the pre-trial proceedings and initiating the oral proceedings against Adolfo Francisco Scilingo Manzorro, charged in case 19/97 in relation to the crimes committed by the military governments in Argentina between 1976 and 1983.[469] On 1 July 2003, the Prosecutor filed an appeal against the Order of 27 June 2003, which was dismissed by the Order of 28 July 2003 of the Criminal Division of the National Court, resolving a question of prior decision in the *Scilingo* case. As expected, the Prosecutor and the counsel for the accused filed an appeal for cassation with the Second Criminal Division of the Supreme Court. Subsequently, in 2004, the Prosecutor dropped the appeal.[470]

Of all the grounds for cassation rejected by the Supreme Court, the ruling deals most extensively with the one that is based on the violation of the right to the judge predetermined by law, a formula that, for the court, is equivalent to that of Article 14 of the International Covenant on Civil and Political Rights: everyone shall be entitled to a fair and public hearing by a competent, independent and impartial tribunal established by law. The appeal states that the Spanish courts have no authority because exactly the same charges have been brought against the defendant in Argentina and a procedure has been initiated in which the defendant has been charged, and it adds that as well as violating the constitutional princi-

469. See precedents and the commentary in 6 *YIHL* (2003) pp. 629-633.

470. After the general election of 14 March 2004, which was to put the Socialist Party into power, Cándido Conde-Pumpido Tourón, who had until then been a Supreme Court magistrate and one of the minority in the ruling of 25 February 2003 in the *Guatemala* case, was appointed as the new Attorney-general. This led to a change in policy and the prosecutor's office no longer opposed the practice of universal jurisdiction by the Spanish courts.

ples of the ordinary judge and access to justice they would also be violating the principle of non bis in idem.

With reference to the violation of the right to a judge predetermined by law, the court pointed out that, in accordance with its previous jurisprudence – coinciding with that of the Constitutional Court – this right 'requires, first of all, that the judicial body has been legally created, that it was invested with jurisdiction and authority prior to the event that motivated the charge or the legal proceedings, and that its organizational and procedural regulations do not qualify it as a special or exceptional body'. The ruling considers that the court that issued the Order that has been appealed against was invested with authority by the law prior to its intervention in the events being tried.

In relation to the allegation of lack of authority of the Spanish courts, the Supreme Court recalled and reiterated the ruling of 8 March 2004 in the *Brady* case,[471] which, in turn, referred to the *Guatemala* case.[472]

Finally, as far as the mentioned violation of the 'non bis in idem' principle was concerned, the court referred to its ruling in the *Perú* case[473] of 20 May 2003 in stating that:

> 'the need for jurisdictional intervention in accordance with the principle of universal justice is excluded when the territorial jurisdiction is effectively pursuing the universal crime committed in its own country. In this respect, there may be a principle of the need for jurisdictional intervention, which is derived from the very nature and purpose of universal jurisdiction.
>
> The application of this principle determines the priority of competences when territorial jurisdiction coincides with jurisdiction based on the principle of universal justice.
>
> This criterion does not make it possible to use the provisions of Article 23.4 of the LOPJ (Organic Law of the Judiciary) as if they established that, for a universal jurisdiction action to be admitted, the criminal prosecution by the territorial jurisdiction would need be proven to be inactive or ineffective. This requisite would effectively annul the principle of universal prosecution, because this proof is practically impossible to obtain, and would necessitate an extremely delicate assessment at this premature moment in the legal procedure.
>
> For the action to be admitted, the requirements are the same as for events that supposedly constitute a universal crime. Serious and reasonable evidence must be provided that the grave crimes reported have not been effectively pursued by the territorial jurisdiction, for whatever reason, without this casting aspersions on any of the political, social or material influences that have been involved in such *de facto* impunity.'

The doctrine of the Supreme Court with reference to the crimes of which Scilingo has been charged is summarised in the paragraph below:

> 'Applying the jurisprudential doctrine that has been expressed and on the basis of what is provided for in Article 23.4, g) of the LOPJ, Spanish jurisdiction will be competent to have cognisance of events that have occurred outside the national territory and which

---

471. See the commentary in this volume of the *YIHL*, p. 590.

472. Supreme Court. Criminal Division. Sentence nº 327/2003, of 25/02/2003. Appeal for cassation nº 803/2001. See 6 *YIHL* (2003) pp. 618-627.

473. See the commentary in this volume of the *YIHL* at p. 592.

> are statutory offences whenever, according to international treaties or agreements, they must be pursued in Spain. Considering that the Vienna Convention on the Law of Treatises stipulates that the agreements of treaties "cannot be altered or breached by the regulations of the internal legislation of each State"; and considering the Convention for the prevention and punishment of the crime of genocide, on 9th December 1948, to which Spain acceded on 13th September 1968 (see BOE of 8th February 1969) and which added the crime of genocide to our criminal legislation by Law 44/1971 of 15th November and included it in the Penal Code in force at that time among the crimes against law of nations, and in which the contracting parties confirm that genocide is a crime against international law that they agree to prevent and to punish; and considering the Convention against torture and other cruel, inhuman or degrading treatment or punishment of 10th December 1984 (BOE of 9th November 1987)); and considering the European convention for the repression of terrorism of 21st January 1977 (BOE of 28th October 1980), and although none of these Treaties expressly establish universal jurisdiction, there arises, however, the obligation to bring alleged guilty parties to justice when they are in their territory and the extradition requested by one of the other States that have been obliged by the respective Convention to claim their jurisdiction has not been granted. Finally, to supplement the aforementioned principles, the jurisprudence of this Division acknowledges the relevance that a link with a national interest could have as a legitimating element, in the framework of the principle of universal justice, although this should respond to criteria of rationality and respect the principle of non-intervention.'

For all these reasons, the crimes of which Scilingo is accused are

> 'compatible with the demands of the international order because the crimes of genocide, torture and terrorism affect rights that the International Community is interested in protecting. We should also add that the alleged guilty party is in Spanish territory, that there is a direct link with national interests because some victims are of Spanish nationality and that there is no evidence to show that he is being prosecuted for the same crimes in Argentina, which are all reasons expressed in the order that was appealed against, so it is not an issue of litis pendencia or of "non bis in idem", because the specific serious crimes that are the object of the accusation, according to the proceedings, are not being pursued by the territorial jurisdiction.'

To sum up, the Supreme Court dismissed the appeal for cassation filed by Adolfo Francisco Scilingo Manzorro, which means that the oral proceedings, set for the beginning of January 2005, can begin.

ANTONI PIGRAU

SUDAN

The Peace Process

- Framework Agreement on Wealth Sharing Between the Government of the Sudan (GOS) and the Sudan People's Liberation Movement/Sudan People's Liberation Army (SPLM/A). Signed on 7 January 2004 <http://www.usip.org/library/pa/sudan/wealth_-sharing_01072004.pdf>

- Humanitarian Cease Fire Agreement on the Conflict in Darfur. Signed in N'Djamena, Chad, on 8 April 2004 <http://www.usip.org/library/pa/sudan/sudan_ceasefire_04082004.html>
- Protocol Between the Government of the Sudan (GOS) and the Sudan People's Liberation Movement/Army (SPLM/A) on the Resolution of Abyei Conflict. Adopted on 26 May 2004 <http://www.usip.org/library/pa/sudan/abyei_05262004.pdf>
- Protocol Between the Government of the Sudan (GOS) and the Sudan People's Liberation Movement (SPLM) on the Resolution of Conflict in Southern Kordofan/Nuba Mountains and Blue Nile States. Adopted on 26 May 2004 <http://www.usip.org/library/pa/sudan/nuba_bnile_05262004.pdf>
- Protocol Between the Government of the Sudan (GOS) and the Sudan People's Liberation Movement (SPLM) on Power Sharing. Adopted on 26 May 2004 <http://www.usip.org/library/pa/sudan/pa_sudan.html>
- The Nairobi Declaration on the Final Phase of Peace in the Sudan. Signed on 5 June 2004 <http://www.usip.org/library/pa/sudan/nairobi_06052004.pdf
- The Comprehensive Peace Agreement between the Government of the Republic of the Sudan and the Sudan People's Liberation Movement/Sudan People's Liberation Army. Agreed to on 31 December 2004 and signed on 5 January 2005 <http://www.reliefweb.int/rw/rwb.nsf/db900SID/EVIU-6AZBDB?OpenDocument>. The Comprehensive Agreement consists of a series of agreements
- Agreement between the Government of Sudan (GOS) and the Sudan People's Liberation Movement/Sudan People's Liberation Army (SPLM/A) on Implementation Modalities of the Protocols and Agreements. Agreed to on 31 December 2004 <http://www.usip.org/library/pa/sudan/cpa01092005/implementation_coversheet.pdf>
- Agreement on Implementation Modalities of the Protocols and Agreements. Agreed to on 31 December 2004 <http://www.usip.org/library/pa/sudan/cpa01092005/implementation_agreement.pdf>
- Agreement on Permanent Ceasefire and Security Arrangements Implementation Modalities between the Government of the Sudan (GOS) and the Sudan People's Liberation Movement/Sudan People's Liberation Army (SPLM/SPLA) during the pre-interim and interim periods. Agreed to on 31 December 2004 <http://www.usip.org/library/pa/sudan/cpa01092005/ceasefire_agreement.pdf>

On 31 December 2004 the government of Sudan and the rebels it has been fighting for over a 20 years in southern Sudan agreed to a Comprehensive Peace Agreement at Naivasha, Kenya. The Agreement was formally signed on 5 January 2005.

SWEDEN[474]

Computer Network Attack

- Conference in Stockholm on computer network attack, November 2004

Following a pledge by the Swedish Government, together with the Swedish Red Cross, during the 28th International Red Cross and Red Crescent conference in December 2003 in Geneva, an International Expert Conference on Computer Network Attacks and the Applic-

474. Information and commentaries by Dr Ola Ingdahl, Swedish National Defence College.

ability of International Humanitarian Law was held in Stockholm from 17-19 November 2004.[475]

There was a shared understanding among participants at the conference, at which more than 20 states were represented, that international humanitarian law applies to computer network attacks (CNA) in an ongoing international armed conflict. It was noted that the emergence of CNA was a new phenomenon requiring further discussion on what this entails more concretely. Such attacks, however, were not regarded as inherently indiscriminate. They should not and could not be outlawed as such, but certain CNAs would be illegal under existing international humanitarian law. This would mainly be against the background of the principles of distinction, proportionality and feasible precautions, all of which required further analysis.

The participants identified several issues in relation to CNA requiring further clarification and discussion. These topics include: the concept of military objectives; the definition of attacks and the so-called effects doctrine; the protection or non-protection of dual-use objects, such as banking systems; the question of actors (state employees, other civilians, hackers, terrorists) and attributability; combatant status for civilian technicians; the issue of civilian direct participation in hostilities (where the ICRC and the TMC Asser Instituut already have a clarification process going on); the reverberating effects of CNA in relation to the principle of proportionality; the direction of CNAs against civilians and civilian objects not causing death or destruction, but serious inconvenience; and perfidy and improper use of protected signals.

The participants agreed that a basis now existed for further work on these issues. Continued interaction between lawyers, practitioners and technical experts was of fundamental importance. The next meeting shall be held in Switzerland in the autumn of 2005. It is proposed that, at that meeting, an expert group will discuss a prepared written document with suggested interpretations of relevant principles.

OLA ENGDAHL

SYRIAN ARAB REPUBLIC

Implementation and Dissemination

- National Committee on International Humanitarian Law in the Syrian Arab Republic. Established by Decree No. 2,989 of 2 June 2004 ,which entered into force on 3 June 2004[476]

UNITED KINGDOM[477]

Training and Dissemination

- United Kingdom Ministry of Defence, *The Manual of The Law of Armed Conflict*, Oxford University Press, 2004

---

475. A report on the conference can be ordered from the Swedish National Defence College. The following remarks are based upon that report.

476. *Supra* n. 71, pp. 694 at 703.

477. Information provided by A.P.V. Rogers, Yorke Distinguished Visiting Fellow, Faculty of Law, and Fellow, Lauterpacht Centre for International Law, University of Cambridge.

The United Kingdom manual, which was published in July 2004, is intended to be a reference work for members of all three services of the armed forces and government officials to enable them to apply the law of armed conflict when conducting operations and when training and planning for them.

The need for a new manual became apparent when the Additional Protocols of 1977 to the Geneva Conventions of 1949 were adopted, and drafting started in 1979.

Following the ratification of the Protocols by the United Kingdom on 28 January 1998, the draft was revised for publication. This work was done under the supervision, and with the active assistance, of an Editorial Board, listed alphabetically as follows: Commodore Jeffrey Blackett, Royal Navy, Chief Naval Judge Advocate; Group Captain William Boothby, Royal Air Force Legal Services; Colonel Charles Garraway CBE, Army Legal Services; Professor Christopher Greenwood CMG, QC, London School of Economics (Academic Consultant); Commander Steven Haines, Royal Navy, Joint Doctrine and Concepts Centre (Ministry of Defence Central Staff Sponsor and Chairman, Editorial Board); John Hudson Esq., Ministry of Defence Legal Adviser; Miss Ruma Mandal, Foreign and Commonwealth Office (FCO) Legal Adviser; and Major General (retired) Anthony Rogers OBE, Fellow of the Lauterpacht Research Centre for International Law, University of Cambridge (General Editor).

The Editorial Board received great assistance from Martin Eaton Esq CMG, FCO Legal Adviser; Professor Vaughan Lowe, Chichele Professor of Public International Law at the University of Oxford; Professor Sir Adam Roberts KCMG FBA, Fellow of Balliol College, Oxford; Michael Meyer Esq OBE of the British Red Cross Society; and Miss Elizabeth Wilmshurst CMG. The full text was read by Sir Michael Wood KCMG (FCO Legal Adviser) and Martin Hemming Esq CB (MOD Legal Adviser) prior to its formal adoption on 1 July 2004 as the United Kingdom's official manual on the subject.

In the manual, each legal rule or proposition is set out in a numbered and headed paragraph, followed in sub-paragraphs by any necessary definitions, explanations or examples. The manual does not, generally, contain treaty texts, since these can be found elsewhere, for example, in A. Roberts and R. Guelff, *Documents on the Laws of Armed Conflict* (Oxford, 2000), but the appendix to the manual contains documents that are not to be found in Roberts and Guelff.

The substantive chapters of the manual are as follows:

Chapter 1 – Historical and General Background
Chapter 2 – Basic Principles of the Law of Armed Conflict
Chapter 3 – The Applicability of the Law of Armed Conflict
Chapter 4 – The Armed Forces of the Belligerents
Chapter 5 – The Conduct of Hostilities
Chapter 6 – Weapons
Chapter 7 – The Wounded, Sick and Dead and Medical Services
Chapter 8 – Prisoners of War
Chapter 9 – Protection of Civilians in the Hands of a Party to the Conflict
Chapter 10 – Negotiations between Belligerents
Chapter 11 – Occupied Territory
Chapter 12 – Air Operations
Chapter 13 – Maritime Warfare
Chapter 14 – Application of the Law of Armed Conflict during Peace Support Operations
Chapter 15 – Internal Armed Conflict
Chapter 16 – Enforcement of the Law of Armed Conflict

The manual was formally launched at a conference on United Kingdom Perspectives on the Law of Armed Conflict held at St Antony's College, Oxford, from 30 June to 2 July 2004. Amendments to the manual will be published from time to time at <www.mod.uk>.

Cases (extraterritorial effect of human rights obligations)

- *The Queen – on the Application of – Mazin Jumaa Gatteh Al Skeini and others* v. *The Secretary of State for Defence*, [2004] EWHC 2911 (Admin) 14 December 2004, before Rix LJ and Forbes J

The Divisional Court dealt with applications for judicial review under Articles 2 and 3 of the European Convention of Human Rights, by virtue of the Human Rights Act 1998. The claims were brought by relatives of six Iraqi citizens who died in provinces of Iraq at a time when the United Kingdom was the occupying power, that is, between 1 May 2003 and 28 June 2004.

The judgment was concerned with two preliminary issues: (1) whether the deaths took place within the jurisdiction of the United Kingdom so as to fall within the scope of the Convention and the Act and, if so, (2) whether there had been a breach of the requirements of Articles 2 and 3 of the Convention regarding an adequate inquiry into those deaths.

The Secretary of State accepted that at the time of the deaths the United Kingdom was in the position of an occupying power under the Hague Regulations 1907 and the Fourth Geneva Convention of 1949 in the provinces of Al Basrah and Maysan; that in four cases the deceased had been shot and killed by British troops; that in one case the deceased was killed in the course of an exchange of fire between British troops and Iraqi gunmen; and that in the sixth case, that of Baha Mousa, the deceased died while in the custody of British troops.

In four of the cases, a report had been submitted by the unit to a higher military authority who decided that the soldiers concerned had acted in accordance with their rules of engagement and that no further investigation was necessary. In two cases, the Special Investigation Branch (SIB) of the Royal Military Police carried out an investigation. In one case this was still ongoing. In the case of Baha Mousa, the SIB had submitted a report to the unit's chain of command in April 2004, but at the time of the Divisional Court hearing the outcome was unknown.

The court first considered the question of jurisdiction under Article 1 of the European Convention of Human Rights, which requires States Parties to secure the Convention rights 'to everyone within their jurisdiction'. Having exhaustively considered the Strasbourg jurisprudence as well as domestic cases, the court concluded that, while application of Article 1 was primarily limited to the territory of a contracting state (para. 245), there were two exceptions to the territoriality principle: (a) cases of effective control of an area within the regional sphere of the convention (para. 277) and (b) exceptional and limited cases, to be found in specific instances recognised in international law,[478] of extraterritorial personal jurisdiction arising from the exercise of authority by state agents of party states (para. 269). Applying those conclusions to the facts of the cases before it, the court decided that exception (a) did not apply to Iraq as it was outside the regional sphere of the Convention (para. 281); that the five deaths resulting from military operations in the field did not

478. These exceptions are cases such as embassies, consulates, vessels and aircraft.

fall within exception (b) (para. 284); but that the case of the death of Baha Mousa in a British military prison did fall within exception (b) (para. 287).

Applying Articles 2 and 3 of the convention to the case of Baha Mousa, the court considered that the articles implied a procedural obligation of a proper and adequate investigation into loss of life or torture or inhuman or degrading treatment or punishment (para. 319). A proper investigation must be 'official, i.e., initiated by the state; timely, i.e., in both intention and completion; independent, i.e., both formally and practically, from those implicated in the events; open, i.e., to a sufficient element of public scrutiny as well as to the involvement of the next-of-kin; and effective, i.e., capable of achieving objective accountability of the state agents and thus of leading as appropriate, to conclusions about all the circumstances, including the background issues leading to the death, as well as about responsibility for it, and the identification and punishment of those responsible' (para. 322).

The court concluded that there had been a breach of the procedural investigative obligation in this case (para. 336).

As it is to be the subject of an appeal to the court of Appeal, comment on the case would be inappropriate at this stage.

A.P.V. ROGERS

☛ *A and Others* v. *The Secretary of State for the Home Department*, UK Court of Appeals, 11 August 2004

On 11 August the UK Court of Appeals ruled that evidence obtained by torture could be admitted into evidence in UK cases, except where it had been directly procured by UK agents or in whose procurement UK agents had connived. The court of Appeal dismissed the appeals of ten foreign nationals interned without charge or trial under the Anti-terrorism, Crime and Security Act 2001 (ATCSA).[479]

UNITED STATES OF AMERICA[480]

Status of Detainees

- ☛ Order establishing 'Combatant Status Review Tribunal', 7 July 2004
- ☛ *United States of America* v. *Ibrahim Ahmed Mahmoud Al Qosi*, charges
- ☛ United States of America *v.* Ali Hamza Ahmad Sulayman Al Bahlul, *charges*
- ☛ *United States of America* v. *Salim Ahmed Hamdan*, charges
- ☛ *United States of America v. David Matthew Hicks*, charges

On 7 July 2004 the Department of Defense issued an order establishing a 'Combatant Status Review Tribunal', consisting of three military officers, to review the cases of all persons held as enemy combatants at the Guantánamo Bay Naval Base in Cuba. The new Tribunal will determine, by majority vote, whether each detainee 'is properly detained as an enemy combatant'.

---

479. See 'UK court rules to use evidence obtained by torture' ABC News, 12 August 2004, <http://www.abc.net.au/news/newsitems/200408/s1174584.htm>: 'UK: Court of Appeal gives green light to torture', Amnesty International Press Release, AI Index: EUR 45/019/2004, 11 August 2004.

480. Information and commentaries by Burrus N. Carnahan, Professorial Lecturer in Law, the George Washington University, Washington, D.C., and Jacob Ramer, Chicago-Kent College of Law.

Under the order, the term 'enemy combatant' is broadly defined. It includes 'any person who has committed a belligerent act or has directly supported hostilities in support of enemy armed forces'. This part of the definition closely tracks the language in Article 51 (3) of Protocol I Additional to the Geneva Conventions, under which civilians lose their immunity from attack if 'they take a direct part in hostilities'. The order also provides, however, that any person may be found to be an enemy combatant 'who was part of, or supporting, Taliban or al Qaeda forces, or associated forces' engaged in hostilities against the United States and its cobelligerents.

This formulation implies that an individual who had not taken a direct part in hostilities could be found to be an 'enemy combatant' based solely on non-combat support work for Taliban and al Qaeda forces. This part of the definition may have been adopted by analogy to Article 4A(4) of the Third Geneva Convention (Prisoners of War), which provides that civilian persons accompanying an armed force in the field, such as 'supply contractors, members of labour units or of services responsible for the welfare of the armed forces', are to be treated as prisoners of war. The United States regards Taliban and al Qaeda fighters as unlawful 'enemy combatants', not entitled to be prisoners of war under Article 4A(1) or (2) of the Third Convention. Individuals who accompany and support these unlawful combatants are also classified as enemy combatants, by analogy to Article 4A(4).

It is interesting to compare this approach to the Military Commission charges filed against four detainees held at Guantánamo. The basic charge in each case is conspiracy to commit war crimes (attacks on civilians) and unlawful belligerency (murder by an unlawful belligerent). However, almost all of the other acts alleged against each of the accused are non-combat support activities for al Qaeda (creation of training materials and propaganda, providing food, shelter and clothing to al Qaeda members, etc.). The same activities that would establish that a detainee is an enemy combatant would also, in the view of the United States, constitute evidence of a punishable conspiracy to support unlawful belligerent acts.

The civilian nationals of a state at war frequently engage in similar activities in support of their national armed forces. In that situation, no one would argue that the enemy could lawfully punish civilians for providing support to their own armed forces. For example, Article 70 of the Fourth Geneva Convention specifically forbids an occupying power from punishing the inhabitants of occupied territory 'for acts committed or for opinions expressed before the occupation'. The prosecution of these four detainees appears to be based in part on the theory that since al Qaeda is an unlawful belligerent, non-combat acts in support of that belligerency are punishable by the states that are the targets of al Qaeda's hostilities.

The Combatant Status Tribunal and its procedures are patterned after the administrative tribunals used by the United States armed forces in Vietnam and later conflicts to determine prisoner of war status in accordance with Article 5 of the 1949 Geneva Convention on Prisoners of War. It is important to note, however, that the Combatant Status Review Tribunal is not a 'competent tribunal' under Article 5 since it has no power to decide whether a detainee is entitled to prisoner of war status under Article 4 of the Convention.

According to information released by the Defense Department in May 2005, during the first eight months of operation (August 2004 through March 2005), 558 Tribunal hearings were held. In 38 of those cases the detainee was found not to have been an enemy combatant and was then released.

BURRUS CARNAHAN

- Memorandum for Distribution from the Secretary of the Navy Gordon H. England, on Implementation of Combatant Status Review Tribunal Procedures for Enemy Combatants detained at Guantánamo Bay Naval Base, Cuba, 29 July 2004

The Order Establishing Combatant Status Review Tribunals, issued by Deputy Defense Secretary Paul Wolfowitz on 7 July 2004 (see *supra*), grants each 'enemy combatant' the opportunity to personally present his case before a board of three military officers. The Memorandum on Implementation of Combatant Status Review Tribunal Procedures for Enemy Combatants detained at Guantánamo Bay Naval Base, Cuba of 29 July 2004, fleshes out various aspects of the Order. With the assistance of a military officer, the detainee may call witnesses and introduce evidence, including written submissions from the detainee's family and his national government. The assisting military officer is not a lawyer. The detainee, when presenting evidence, may call witnesses if reasonably available and question witnesses called by the military tribunal. The decision is made on a preponderance of evidence, with a rebuttable presumption in favour of the government's evidence. If the Tribunal determines that the detainee should be released, the detainee will be released through the coordination of the Secretary of Defense and Secretary of State.

After assessing all of the information, including submissions by other US government agencies, the review board will recommend to a 'high-level Department of Defense official' selected by the Secretary of Defense whether the detainee should be released, which will then make the final determination. Those determined not to be an enemy combatant will be transferred to their country of citizenship or other country in accordance with US foreign policy and legal obligations.

The Combatant Status Review Tribunal will provide detainees with the basis for their detention. They will provide notice and an opportunity to be heard. But, importantly, these proceedings will not preclude them from seeking additional review in federal court.

The first Combatant Status Review Tribunal was held on 30 July 2004.

Treatment of Detainees

- Memorandum to the Chairman of the Joint Chiefs of Staff from Secretary of Defense Donald Rumsfeld, on the Status of Taliban and Al Qaida. Dated 19 January 2002, released by Department of Defense on 22 June 2004. Press Release, No. 596-04, 'DoD Provides Details on Interrogation Process' <http://www.defenselink.mil/releases/2004/nr20040622-0930.html>
- Memorandum for Commander, US Southern Command from Major General Michael Dunlavey. Dated 11 October 2002, released by Department of Defense on 22 June 2004. Press Release, No. 596-04, 'DoD Provides Details on Interrogation Process' <http://www.defenselink.mil/releases/2004/nr20040622-0930.html>
- Memorandum to the Chairman of the Joint Chiefs of Staff from General James T. Hill, on Counter-Resistance Techniques, 25 October 2002
- Memorandum to the Secretary of Defense from General Counsel William J. Haynes II, on Counter-Resistance Techniques. Dated 27 November 2002, released by Department of Defense on 22 June 2004. Press Release, No. 596-04, 'DoD Provides Details on Interrogation Process' <http://www.defenselink.mil/releases/2004/nr20040622-0930.html>
- Memorandum for Commander USSOUTHCOM from Secretary of Defense Donald Rumsfeld, on Counter-Resistance Techniques. Dated 15 January 2003, released by Department of Defense on 22 June 2004. Press Release, No. 596-04, DoD Provides Details

on Interrogation Process <http://www.defenselink.mil/releases/2004/nr20040622-0930.html>

- Working Group Report on Detainee Interrogations in the Global War on Terrorism: Assessment of Legal, Historical, Policy, and Operational Considerations. Submitted to Secretary of Defense Donald Rumsfeld on 4 April 2003, released by Department of Defense on 22 June 2004. Press Release, No. 596-04, 'DoD Provides Details on Interrogation Process', <http://www.defenselink.mil/releases/2004/nr20040622-0930.html>
- Memorandum to the Commander, US Southern Command from the Secretary of Defense Donald Rumsfeld, on Counter-Resistance Techniques in the War on Terrorism, 16 April 2003, released by Department of Defense on 22 June 2004, Press Release, No. 596-04, 'DoD Provides Details on Interrogation Process' <http://www.defenselink.mil/releases/2004/nr20040622-0930.html>

In a brief memorandum to the Chairman of the Joint Chiefs of Staff dated 19 January 2002 and released in June 2004, Secretary of Defense Donald Rumsfeld stated:

> 'The United States has determined that Al Qaida and Taliban individuals under the control of the Department of Defense are not entitled to prisoner of war status for purposes of the Geneva Conventions of 1949', but that the 'Combatant Commanders shall ... treat them humanely and, to the extent appropriate and consistent with military necessity, in a manner consistent with the principles of the Geneva Conventions of 1949.'

This designation was subsequently relayed by the Chairman of the Joint Chiefs of Staff to the Unified Commands and Services in a Memorandum to the Commander of US Southern Command from the Secretary of Defense Donald Rumsfeld on Counter-Resistance Techniques in the War on Terrorism dated 16 April 2003.

On 11 October 2002 the commander of Task Force 170, Major General Michael Dunlavey, requested from the Commander of the US Southern Command that additional methods of interrogation be approved for Guantánamo Bay, Cuba, noting that although the current methods had 'resulted in significant exploitable intelligence, the same methods have become less effective over time'. The memo included a legal assessment from a Department of Defense lawyer, Staff Judge Advocate, LTC Diane E. Beaver, that stated the strategies 'do not violate applicable federal law'.

Acknowledging that current interrogation techniques were not producing intelligence on certain detainees, on 25 October 2002 General James Hill sent a memo to the Chairman of the Joint Chiefs of Staff requesting assistance in identifying new techniques of interrogation, noting that 'some detainees have tenaciously resisted our current interrogation methods'. He expressed concern with the legality, under US law, of certain techniques requested by Major General Dunlavey, 'given the absence of judicial interpretation of the US torture statute'. He also expressed concern with the use of threats against detainees or their families, but noted that he wished to have as many options available as possible.

In a memo dated 27 November 2002 to the Secretary of Defense Rumsfeld, General Counsel William J. Haynes recommended (and Rumsfeld approvingly signed on 2 December 2002) that the first two categories[481] be approved but that only one technique of cate-

---

481. Category I methods included: yelling; techniques of deception, such as multiple interrogator techniques and interrogator identity. Category II methods including: stress positions, such as standing,

gory III –i.e., 'use of mild, non-injurious physical contact such as grabbing, poking in the chest with the finger, and light pushing' – be approved, even though he determined the other techniques 'may be legally available'. He disagreed with the use of Category III techniques 'as a matter of policy', not necessarily from a legal standpoint. He said that the techniques were 'not warranted at this time', and noted that US Armed Forces 'are trained to a standard of interrogation that reflects a tradition of restraint'. Rumsfeld wrote a question on the memo, asking, 'I stand for 8-10 hours a day. Why is standing limited to 4 hours?'

Then, on 15 January 2003, Rumsfeld rescinded his 2 December 2002 official approval for the use of all Category II techniques and the one Category III technique in Guantánamo Bay. However, the commander of US SOUTHCOM could request use of these techniques on a case by case basis, explaining in such a request the reasons and exact methods to be employed. On the same day, Rumsfeld also established a team to assess the legal and policy issues concerning the interrogation techniques used on detainees held in the war on terrorism. In its report of 4 April 2003, the Working Group on Detainee Interrogations in the Global War on Terrorism reported favourably 35 techniques and rejected others.[482] On 16 April 2003 the Secretary of Defense subsequently approved 24 of these techniques for use at Guantánamo Bay. Specific techniques that were approved (again stressing that the detainees should be treated 'humanely and, to the extent appropriate and consistent with military necessity, in a manner consistent with the principles of Geneva Conventions'), which were highlighted in the memo as being potentially contentious with other states' interpretation of the Geneva Conventions, include, providing and removing an incentive; attacking or insulting the detainee's ego; intimidating the detainee; environmental manipulation; and isolation. The memo provided several procedural safeguards, such as requiring supervision by medical personnel and specially trained interrogators.

Jacob Ramer

- Report of Independent Panel to Review Department of Defense Detention Operations. August 2004, pp. 79-88
- The Inspector General, US Army, 'Detainee Operations Inspection'. Report dated 21 July 2004, Annex E, p. E-106 (excerpts)
- AR 15-6 Investigation of the Abu Ghraib detention facility and 205th military intelligence brigade (u) Major General George R. Fay Investigating Officer. August 2004 (excerpts)

United States practice in 2004 was dominated by a series of scandals involving criminal mistreatment of detainees in occupied Iraq and the publication of classified documents

---

for maximum of four hours; use of falsified documents; isolation for up to 30 days; questioning outside standard interrogation booth; deprivation of light and auditory stimuli; use of hood during transport and questioning; 20-hour interrogations; removal of comfort items such as religious items; removal of clothing; switching from hot to cold rations; forced grooming including shaving facial hair; using fear to induce stress such as fear of dogs. Category III methods included: 'use of scenarios designed to convince the detainee that death or severely painful consequences are imminent for him and/or his family;' 'exposure to cold weather or water (with appropriate medical monitoring); 'use of a wet towel and dripping water to induce the misperception of suffocation;' 'use of mild, noninjurious physical contact such as grabbing, poking in the chest with the finger, and light pushing.'

482. <http://ww.antiwar.com/sperry/?articleid=2786>

that, some believed, authorised inhumane treatment and even torture of other detainees. Numerous official investigations were conducted. Three of the investigative reports reflect significant practice in international humanitarian law – the August 2004 report to the Secretary of Defense by the Independent Panel to Review Department of Defense Detention Operations; the 21 July 2004 report of the US Army Inspector General; and the investigation ordered by US Central Command, conducted by Army Major General George Fay.

The Independent Panel was composed of eminent former officials, chaired by former Defense Secretary James Schlesinger. The Panel report's chapter on the law of war summarises the debate within the US government, at the beginning of the conflict in Afghanistan, on whether Taliban and al Qaeda combatants would be treated as prisoners of war under the Third Geneva Convention. After it was decided that they would be regarded as unlawful combatants, commanders in the field were instructed that captured persons were to be treated 'humanely and, to the extent appropriate and consistent with military necessity, in a manner consistent with the principles of the Geneva Conventions of 1949'. (The pertinent part of the message from the chairman of the Joint Chiefs of Staff is quoted in the Army Inspector General's report).

Under this order, the Third Geneva Convention would be applied to unlawful combatants as a matter of policy and only when consistent with military necessity. Regardless of military necessity, however, an obligation was recognised to accord captured combatants a certain minimum level of humane treatment. The ICRC's study of customary international humanitarian law, published in 2005, agrees that humane treatment is the basic standard for persons not protected by one of the Geneva Convention's; Rule 87 of the study provides that 'persons *hors de combat* must be treated humanely'.

The chief practical problem with the Joint Chiefs of Staff directive, a problem that directly contributed to the abuses that occurred, was that it lacked specific guidance as to what constituted humane treatment or how to determine when a military necessity existed to depart from Geneva standards.

In 2004 the US Army Inspector General, faced with the task of determining whether certain acts violated the order to treat enemy combatants humanely, turned to Common Article 3 of the Geneva Conventions to flesh out the 'humane treatment' standard for unlawful combatants and to provide a 'floor measure of humane treatment and corresponding training', in the words of the report. By its strict terms, of course, common Article 3 was not applicable to the US intervention in Afghanistan which was, the report notes, an international armed conflict. It makes sense, however, to apply Common Article 3 by analogy to define the minimum international standard for the treatment of unlawful combatants in international armed conflict. The States Parties to the Geneva Conventions have all accepted this Article as defining the minimum standard of treatment for rebel forces in internal conflicts, and rebels are the classic examples of unlawful combatants, in the view of most governments. Rule 90 of the ICRC's study of customary international humanitarian law also draws on the language of common Article 3 to clarify the meaning of humane treatment: 'Torture, cruel or inhuman treatment and outrages upon personal dignity, in particular humiliating or degrading treatment, are prohibited.'

The ICRC has rejected the US government's position that Taliban and al Qaeda fighters are unlawful combatants, outside the protection of the Third Geneva Convention. The Independent Panel reviewed this dispute in its chapter on the role of the law of war, and essentially concluded that the United States position was correct.

> 'The Panel accepts the proposition that these terrorists are not combatants entitled to the protections of Geneva Convention III. … As a matter of logic, there should be a category of persons who do not comply with the specified conditions and thus fall outside the category of persons entitled to EPW [enemy prisoner of war] status. Although there is not a particular label for this category in law of war conventions, the concept of "unlawful combatant" or "unprivileged belligerent" is a part of the law of war.'

The Panel found that interrogation of the detainees was a major point of dispute between the United States and the ICRC. Since the ICRC regarded the Taliban and al Qaeda detainees as protected by the Third Convention, it objected to any intelligence interrogation of them. Opposition to interrogation of prisoners of war is a long-standing position of the ICRC. This position is based on Article 17 of the Third Geneva Convention, which provides that prisoners of war should not suffer any 'unpleasant' consequences if they refuse to answer questions. Pictet's Commentary on that Article concludes that the 'Detaining Power may not, therefore, exert any pressure on prisoners to obtain information'.[483]

The United States Department of Defense, on the other hand, approved (at the highest level) the use of specific stress techniques (e.g., sleep deprivation and forced standing in uncomfortable positions) in the questioning of Taliban and al Qaeda detainees from Afghanistan. These would not be consistent with Article 17 of the Third Geneva Convention, but presumably the Secretary of Defense believed they did not constitute inhumane treatment. While the Independent Panel did not expressly approve this practice, it approved it in principle by concluding that ceasing interrogations 'would deprive the U.S. of an indispensable source of intelligence in the war on terrorism'.

The main issue raised by this approach is whether it is even possible to deliberately induce stress in a detained combatant without inflicting 'humiliating or degrading treatment' in violation of customary international law. The degree of humiliation involved must be weighed against the importance of the goal to be achieved. In some cultures, fingerprinting is considered humiliating, and in other cultures photographing a woman's unveiled face is regarded as degrading. Yet forcing a person to submit to both activities is generally considered lawful if a legitimate government interest (accurate identification) will be served. Many of the stress-inducing techniques proposed by the Department of Defense for use in intelligence interrogations – inducing exhaustion, standing in uncomfortable positions, loud, disturbing noise – are routinely used in military training to prepare soldiers for the stress of combat. Because of their legitimate purposes, few would argue that these governmental actions rise to the level of an outrage on human dignity.

The danger in officially recognising that inducing a certain level of stress is a legitimate interrogation tool is that intelligence teams in the field might begin to bend the rules. Gradually, more and more stressful and coercive practices might be used that would not fit within any reasonable definition of 'humane treatment'. That is exactly what happened at the Abu Ghraib prison in occupied Iraq. Investigating the abuses there, Major General Fay found that what started as 'stress and physical training (exercise), carried over into sexual and physical assaults by a small group of morally corrupt and unsupervised soldiers and civilians'.

---

483. <http://www.icrc.org/ihl.nsf/COM/375-590022?OpenDocument>

Detainee Release

- Department of Defense, Order on Administrative Review Procedures for Enemy Combatants in the Control of the Department of Defense at Guantánamo Bay Naval Base, 11 May 2004

On 11 May 2004 the Department of Defense issued an order on 'Administrative Review Procedures for Enemy Combatants in the Control of the Department of Defense at Guantánamo Bay Naval Base, Cuba'. This order affords each detainee at Guantánamo an annual opportunity to appear before a board of officers to 'explain why he is no longer a threat to the United States and its allies in the ongoing armed conflict against al Qaida and its affiliates and supporters or to explain why his release would otherwise be appropriate'. The order notes that '[t]he law of war permits the detention of enemy combatants until the end of an armed conflict', and that '[i]t does not require the use of a review process to support continued detention'. In the view of the United States government, the review process is an act of grace, not required by international law. By way of contrast, in the case of civilian internees, Articles 43 and 78 of the Fourth Geneva Convention require that the reasons for their continued internment be reviewed periodically, 'if possible every six months' (Art. 78).

The order codifies the standard for release from Guantánamo adopted by the United States in previous years – 'whether there is reason to believe that the enemy combatant poses a threat to the United States or its allies in the ongoing armed conflict against al Qaida and its affiliates and supporters'. It should be noted that the Third Geneva Convention does not accord prisoners of war any similar right to release if they are found to no longer be a threat to the detaining power. Articles 112 and 113 encourage, but do not require, the repatriation of sick and wounded prisoners of war. For all others, Article 118 allows the detaining power to retain prisoners of war until the 'the cessation of active hostilities'.

The 'cessation of active hostilities' standard has proven inadequate to protect prisoners of war in the unconventional wars, with shadowy termination dates, that have marked the 50 years since the end of World War II. As an example, the Polisario Liberation Front has held some Moroccan soldiers as prisoners of war for decades. The conflict between the United States and al Qaeda and its affiliates and supporters is just such a shadowy, unconventional war. The review process established by the 11 May order thus meets a real humanitarian need.

Perhaps the 'continued threat' standard for release should also be applied to prisoners of war under the Third Geneva Convention, particularly in unconventional conflicts with indeterminate beginning and end dates. Where the positive rules of the law of war are inadequate, the Martens Clause of Hague Convention IV suggests that governments look to 'the principles of the law of nations, as they result from the usages established among civilized peoples, from the laws of humanity, and the dictates of the public conscience'. In long drawn out conflicts, where Article 118 provides an inadequate standard for release, the general principles of humanitarian law may demand the adoption of a more appropriate standard, such as that embodied in the 11 May 2004 order.

BURRUS CARNAHAN

- Memorandum for Distribution from Designated Civilian Official for Administrative Review of the Detention of Enemy Combatants at U.S. Naval Base Guantánamo Bay, Cuba, on the Implementation of Administrative Review Procedures for Enemy Combatants Detained at U.S. Naval Base Guantánamo Bay, Cuba, 14 September 2004 <http://www.defenselink.mil/news/Sep2004/d20040914adminreview.pdf>

On 14 September 2004 the Secretary of the Navy, Gordon R. England, formally issued guidance on the administrative review board, consisting of three military officers, that would make annual assessments as to whether each 'enemy combatant' held in Guantánamo Bay should remain detained. These procedures are similar to the Combatant Status Review Tribunal (see above), i.e., with the assistance of an assigned military officer, the detainee has the opportunity to personally appear before and present information to the board, including written submissions from the detainee's family and national government. Based on the submissions, the board will then recommend to the designated civilian official to release, transfer or further detain the individual. This annual review differs from the Combatant Status Review Tribunal in that the latter is a one-time proceeding to challenge the detainee's designation as an 'enemy combatant'. All enemy combatants held in Guantánamo Bay are eligible for the annual review process, except those who are pending trial by military commissions.

JACOB RAMER

POWs

☛ Gerry J. Gilmore, 'Saddam Is a POW, But Status Could Change', American Forces Press Service, 10 January 2004

On 10 January 2004 the Coalition Provisional Authority announced that Saddam Hussein, the former president of Iraq who had been captured in late 2003, would be considered a prisoner of war under the Third Geneva Convention. While Saddam Hussein had clearly controlled the Iraqi armed forces, both as head of government and as chief of the Baath Party, he does not fit easily into any of the categories of persons entitled to prisoner of war status in Article 4 of the Convention. As a matter of custom, however, heads of government of an enemy state have often been treated as prisoners of war. Dr Francis Lieber, in his 1863 codification of the law of war as it existed at that time (General Order #100.), observed that the 'monarch and members of the hostile reigning family, male or female, the chief, and chief officers of the hostile government' could be held as prisoners of war (Article 50). More recently, in December 1989 Manuel Noriega, the *de facto* head of government in Panama, was held as a prisoner of war after his surrender to US forces there.

Occupation

☛ AR 15-6 Investigation of the Abu Ghraib detention facility and 205th military intelligence brigade (u) Major General George R. Fay Investigating Officer (Excerpts), August 2004

In his investigation of abuses at the Abu Ghraib prison in Iraq, Major General George Fay concluded that all Iraqis held in the prison were civilian internees protected by the Fourth Geneva Convention. His report explored, in detail, specific acts of abuse that he determined were violations of the Convention, such as threatening internees with attack dogs.

BURRUS CARNAHAN

Landmines

☛ Landmine Policy White Paper, Bureau of Political-Military Affairs, 27 February 2004 <www.state.gov/t/pm/rls/fs/30047.htm>

Citing humanitarian concerns, specifically the risk to civilians long after a conflict, on 27 February 2004 the US announced a new policy on landmines, declaring that it would stop using persistent landmines of any type, both anti-personnel and anti-vehicle, after the year 2010, and that it would stop using non-detectable mines, both anti-personnel and anti-vehicle, within one year.[484] The US will only use mines that are in accordance with the specifications for self-destruction and self-deactivation set forth in the Amended Mines Protocol to the Convention on Conventional Weapons. The US stated that it would seek an international ban on the sale and export of all persistent landmines, both anti-personnel and anti-vehicle, and later called on the Conference on Disarmament to help.[485] Current US self-destructing mines destroy themselves between four hours and 15 days, well within the mandate of the Amended Mines Protocol, and the US stated that it will continue to meet or go beyond this standard. Additionally, the US stated that all of its mines after 2010 will not only be self-destructing but also self-deactivating in the event of a faulty self-destructing mine. The self-deactivating feature is a result of the limited battery lifespan of 90 days, and thus ensures that the mine will be destroyed within a reasonable amount of time. Notably, the US also reiterated that it would not join the Ottawa Convention because 'its terms would have required us to give up a needed capability'.[486]

Jacob Ramer

☛ White House Press Release, 2 March 2004

In a statement issued on 2 March 2004 the President announced the new United States policy on landmines (see above). If not carefully used, landmines can pose a unique threat to civilian populations years or even decades after the end of the conflict in which they were emplaced. Under the new policy, the United States is now committed to stockpiling and using only mines that self-destruct after a period of time ('non-persistent mines'). This policy applies to both antipersonnel and anti-vehicle mines. As in earlier policy statements on landmines, an exception was reserved for the continued use of persistent mines in the Demilitarized Zone between North and South Korea.

Civilian Objects

☛ 'Terrorists Use Mosque To Fire Upon Forces', CENTCOM Release Number: 04-11-33, 10 November 2004

---

484. The US expressly reserved the right to use non-persistent and detectable antipersonnel and anti-vehicle mines. For more general information, see L.P. Bloomfield, Jr., Assistant Secretary for Political-Military Affairs, On-The-Record Briefing on New Developments in the U.S. Approach to Landmines, Washington, D.C., 27 February 2004, <http://www.state.gov/t/pm/rls/rm/29976.htm>.

485. Remarks to 59th UN General Assembly First Committee, Stephen G. Rademaker, Assistant Secretary of State for Arms Control, New York City, October 8, 2004, <http://www.state.gov/t/ac/rls/rm/2004/44816.htm>.

486. New United States Policy on Landmines: Reducing Humanitarian Risk and Saving Lives of United States Soldiers, Fact Sheet, Bureau of Political-Military Affairs, 27 February 2004, <http://www.state.gov/t/pm/rls/fs/30044.htm>.

- 'Significant Weapons Cache Discovered At Mosque', CENTCOM Release Number: 04-11-87, 25 November 2004

During 2004 official Central Command (CENTCOM) press releases on combat activities of United States forces in Iraq provided valuable insights into US practice. Journalism has often been described as producing a first, rough draft of history, and historians may later correct the factual accounts in these releases. Regardless of the factual accuracy of these accounts, such releases are themselves important evidence of state practice because they reflect the US military's understanding of the legal obligations within which they must operate.

For example, two accounts of minor actions in Fallajah in November stress that the US military regards mosques and other religious site as 'protected under international law', (cf. 1907 Hague Regulations Article 27) and that they lose protection against attack 'when used as fighting positions or for other military operations'. The second press release describes military equipment found stored in a mosque, and indicates that this use would also deprive it of protected status. The releases also accuse the enemy of perfidy by deliberately taking unlawful advantage of the protected status of mosques.

Precaution

- 'Bradley fighting vehicle destroyed in attack', CENTCOM News Release Number: 04-09-36, 12 September 2004
- 'Terrorists use mosque to fire upon forces', CENTCOM Release Number: 04-11-33, 10 November 2004
- 'Significant weapons cache discovered at mosque', CENTCOM Release Number: 04-11-87, 25 November 2004

The United States recognises that customary international law requires that incidental civilian losses or damage be minimised to the extent feasible. An example of how this principle might be applied in practice may be found in a 10 November 2004 CENTCOM press release describing an attack against enemy forces firing on US Marines from a mosque in Fallujah. The release stresses that US commanders concluded that in light of the tactical situation there was no alternative to attacking the enemy while in the mosque, and that precision munitions were used to minimise damage to the religious building. While a minaret was destroyed in the attack, CENTCOM argued that its forces 'used only enough force to remove the threat'.

Another example is found in a 12 September 2004 release. A US Army Bradley Fighting Vehicle was attacked by a car bomb in Baghdad and enemy forces fired on the soldiers exiting the damaged vehicle. An armed helicopter called in to provide support was also fired on and returned the fire. As the situation developed, however, a crowd of civilians gathered around the damaged Bradley, and the helicopter crew ceased firing because the 'air crew could not discriminate between armed insurgents and civilians on the ground'.

Authorities on the law of armed conflict generally agree that an attack should be called off or halted if expected civilian casualties would be excessive or disproportionate to the expected military advantage. There are, however, few historical examples of this principle being applied in practice. The action of the helicopter crew in this incident appears to be one of those rare examples.

Humanitarian Assistance

- 'Coalition Suspends Offensive Operations in Fallujah for Humanitarian Reasons', Coalition Provisional Authority press statement, Baghdad, Iraq, 9 April 2004

During the fighting in Fallujah in spring of 2004 the US authorities announced a unilateral ceasefire, in part to allow relief supplies to enter the city and the wounded to be collected and cared for. The Geneva Conventions have several provisions encouraging the parties to a conflict to collect the sick and wounded and permit passage of relief supplies for civilians. These provisions are weak and the obligations they impose are subject to significant qualifications. Article 30 of the Fourth Convention thus requires an occupying power to 'facilitate, *as much as possible*, visits to protected persons' by relief organisations. During sieges, parties are merely required to '*endeavour to conclude* local agreements ... for the passage of ministers of all religions, medical personnel and medical equipment on their way to such areas' (Art. 17). (Emphasis added.) The collection of civilian wounded is governed by Article 16, which only requires parties to 'facilitate' the search for killed and wounded, '[a]s far as military considerations allow'.

Role of the ICRC

- Report of Independent Panel to Review Department of Defense Detention Operations, August 2004, pp. 79-88
- AR 15-6 Investigation of the Abu Ghraib detention facility and 205th military intelligence brigade (u) Major General George R. Fay Investigating Officer (Excerpts), August 2004
- Kathleen T. Rhem, 'All Red Cross reports now to go through Miller', American Forces Press Service [Department of Defense], 20 May 2004
- Samantha L. Quigley, 'DoD creates Office of Detainee Affairs', American Forces Press Service [Department of Defense], 16 July 2004

The 2004 investigations of detainee abuse noted that early warnings of that abuse from the International Committee of the Red Cross had not been properly handled by the US government. ICRC reports to lower level military officials were ignored or responded to inadequately. As a result, the United States command in Iraq directed that all future ICRC reports be referred to a single point of contact, the Deputy Commander for Detainee Operations. The Department of Defense also responded by creating a central office in the Department's headquarters to receive and act on all ICRC reports. The creation of this new office was praised by the Independent Panel to Review Department of Defense Detention Operations, which also strongly backed continued access to the ICRC by all persons detained by the Defense Department.

BURRUS CARNAHAN

Genocide

- Resolution of the US Congress on Darfur, 22 July 2004

On 22 July 2004 both houses of the US Congress passed a resolution that used the term genocide in relation to the events in Darfur in western Sudan, and which urged the Security Council to impose sanctions on Sudan.

International Criminal Court

- 'Nethercutt Amendment' (Sec. 574, Limitation on Economic Support Fund Assistance for Certain Foreign Governments that are Parties to the International Criminal Court. Adopted as part of the Foreign Operations, Export Financing, and Related Programs Appropriations Act, 2005. Located within the Consolidated Appropriations Act, 2005) <http://www.gpoaccess.gov/serialset/creports/appropriations05.html>

On 8 December 2004 the US Congress adopted and President Bush subsequently signed the $338 billion government appropriations bill for 2005, which included the so-called 'Nethercutt Amendment' to the Foreign Operations, Export Financing, and Related Programs Appropriations Act, 2005, H.R. 4818. The provision, introduced by US Representative George Nethercutt (Republican – State of Washington) in the House of Representatives on 15 July 2004, cuts Economic Support Fund ('ESF') assistance for the year 2005 to State Parties to the ICC that have not signed a bilateral immunity agreement (or Article 98 agreement) with the US. According to the United States Agency for International Development, the ESF 'supports the economic and political foreign policy interests of the United States', focusing on the war on terrorism by 'providing assistance to front-line states and building new relationships as the campaign against global terrorism widens'.[487] The ESF, with a budget of nearly $2.5 billion, funds various programmes that promote civil society, rule of law, human rights, democracy, and economic growth, as well as programmes that combat terrorism, drug trafficking, and regional instability.[488]

The provision contains two exceptions. If the President determines that 'it is important to the national security interests of the United States to waive such prohibition', he may do so: a) if the state is a member of NATO or a 'major non-NATO ally (including Australia, Egypt, Israel, Japan, Jordan, Argentina, the Republic of Korea, and New Zealand), or Taiwan'; or b) if the state subsequently signs an Article 98 agreement with the United States. Additionally, under the terms of the Amendment, it does not apply to countries receiving economic assistance under the Millennium Challenge Act of 2003. This Act, through the Millennium Challenge Account and the Millennium Challenge Corporation, provides funds to developing countries that adopt appropriate governance, health, education, and economic policies that stimulate economic growth. These exceptions to the Amendment came after the US Department of State expressed concern that the mandatory spending cuts would jeopardise US foreign policy through the continuation of its numerous programmes.[489]

The Nethercutt Amendment differs from the American Servicemembers' Protection Act of 2002[490] in that the former targets all foreign governance programmes funded by the US,

---

487. USAID, Congressional Budget Justification FY 2005 – Statement of the Administrator, <http://www.usaid.gov/policy/budget/cbj2005/summary.html>.

488. USAID, Congressional Budget Justification FY 2005 – Statement of the Administrator, <http://www.usaid.gov/policy/budget/cbj2005/summary.html>.

489. C. Lynch, 'Congress seeks to curb international court', *The Washington Post*, 26 November 2004.

490. American Servicemembers' Protection Act of 2002. Adopted as part of the 2000 Supplemental Appropriations Act for further recovery from and response to terrorist attacks on the United States for the fiscal year ending 30 September 2002, and for other purposes), Public Law 107-206. Signed by President George W. Bush on 2 August 2002 http://www.usaforicc.org/ASPA.htm. See 5 *YIHL* (2002) p. 621.

whereas the latter only concerns military aid. According to Citizens for Global Solutions, over 50 states could be affected by the Amendment in 2005.[491] Concerning the American Servicemembers' Protection Act, Human Rights Watch reported that the US suspended military aid to more than 20 countries in 2004.[492]

- The First Bush-Kerry Presidential Debate, 30 September 2004, Commission on Presidential Debates, 2004 Debate Transcripts <http://www.debates.org/pages/debtrans.html>

The 2004 US Presidential election pitted incumbent President George Bush against Democratic Senator John Kerry from Massachusetts. Both candidates discussed the International Criminal Court throughout the campaign, and it was even mentioned by President Bush during two of the three presidential debates in September and October 2004.[493] President Bush frequently cited his position against the court as an example where he and Kerry differed; however, Kerry generally gave vague responses and it is unclear whether the US position on the court would be different had Kerry won the election. In the first presidential debate, Bush unequivocally stated: 'I wouldn't join the International Criminal Court. It's a body based in The Hague where unaccountable judges and prosecutors can pull our troops up for trial'.[494] But Kerry, who four years earlier had joined with 17 other Senators in urging President Clinton to sign the Rome Statute,[495] never declared his outright support for the ICC, stating that he would not sign the Rome Statute within its current framework.[496] In a written statement, Kerry vaguely stated: 'My administration will carefully consider the full range of U.S. interests at stake with respect to the court as we review our policy and fashion a more constructive approach.'[497]

- Explanation of Position on Article 98 Agreements by Eric Rosand, Legal Advisor for the United States Mission to the United Nations, on the Adoption of Resolution concerning the Report of the International Criminal Court, in the Sixth Committee, 19 November 2004, United States Mission to the United Nations Press Release #257(04) <http://www.un.int/usa/04_257.htm>

By the end of 2004 the US Department of State had secured almost 100 Article 98 agreements, but those states with which the US had not reached agreements represented approximately two-thirds of States Parties to the Rome Statute, including 45 states that publicly

491. Citizens for Global Solutions, 'U.S. sanctions key allies over ICC participation: cuts support for over 50 countries, including anti-terror initiatives', Press Release, 8 December 2004.

492. Human Rights Watch, 'U.S.: Congress tries to undermine war crimes court, 8 December 2004, <http://hrw.org/english/docs/2004/12/08/usint9794_txt.htm>.

493. Commission on Presidential Debates, 2004 Debate Transcripts, http://www.debates.org/pages/debtrans.html.

494. The First Bush-Kerry Presidential Debate, 30 September 2004, Commission on Presidential Debates, 2004 Debate Transcripts, <http://www.debates.org/pages/debtrans.html>.

495. Letter by 18 Senators urging President Clinton to sign the Rome Statute, December 20, 2000, <http://www.amicc.org/usinfo/congress_general.html>.

496. J. Lauria, 'Kerry opposes role in tribunal', 5 October 2004, <http://www.boston.com/news/nation/articles/2004/10/05/kerry_opposes_role_in_tribunal/>.

497. J. Podgers, 'Bush, Kerry spar over International Criminal Court', ABA Journal E-Report, 24 September 2004, <http://www.amicc.org/docs/ABA%20Journal.pdf>.

announced their refusal to enter into such an agreement.[498] However, according to the US, there was:

> 'a growing consensus that Article 98 Agreements are an important mechanism to protect states not parties to the Rome Statute from the ICC's claims of jurisdiction. Indeed, just as many nations—97 including the United States—have signed Article 98 agreements as have taken the final step to join the ICC. While we continue to respect the right of States to become parties to the Rome Statute, at the same time, we continue to ask that our decision not to be a party also be respected.'[499]

☛ Attempted Renewal of United Nations Security Council Resolutions 1422 and 1487, May 2004

In May 2004 the US pushed for a resolution renewing Security Council resolutions 1422 and 1487. The proposed resolution would have granted a third consecutive one-year exemption from the ICC to military and civilian personnel from non-States Parties serving in UN peacekeeping missions or 'related to a UN-authorized operation', and would have applied to all UN countries, even those that had not yet ratified the Rome Statute. But in late June 2004, after recognising the unlikelihood of passing the resolution, the US dropped its campaign to secure the renewal. It encountered strong opposition from Security Council members, especially coming in the wake of the Iraqi prisoner abuse scandal and UN Secretary-General Kofi Annan's public criticism of the resolution.[500] Thus, after 30 June 2004, US personnel no longer enjoyed absolute immunity from the ICC. UN S-G Kofi Annan declared that 'the decision by the United States not to pursue a resolution on this matter will help maintain the unity of the Security Council at a time when it faces difficult challenges'.

As a result of the failed resolution, in early July 2004 the US announced that it would withdraw a seven-person team serving in an Ethiopia/Eritrea UN peacekeeping mission and two Americans from the UN mission in Kosovo. A Pentagon spokesman further indicated that all peacekeeping missions involving American personnel would be reviewed.[501]

The Security Council resolution extending the UN operation in Burundi exemplified the differences held between the US and other states. In supporting the mission (noting that it was still US policy to seek exemption from ICC jurisdiction but that there were no Americans serving in the Burundi mission), the US specified that its support for the mission must not be construed as support for the ICC. However, because Burundi had discussed referring

498. Explanation of Position by Eric Rosand, Legal Advisor, on the Adoption of Resolution concerning the Report of the International Criminal Court, in the Sixth Committee, 19 November 2004. United States Mission to the United Nations Press Release #257(04), <http://www.un.int/usa/04_257.htm>.

499. Ibid.

500. 'Resolution to shield U.S. troops from war crimes prosecution dropped', USA Today, 23 June 2004, <http://www.usatoday.com/news/world/2004-06-23-us-un-resolution_x.htm>.

501. 'U.S. pulls some forces from two U.N. missions over war crimes tribunal', Associated Press, 1 July 2004, <http://www.boston.com/dailynews/183/wash/U_S_pulls_some_forces_from_two:.shtml>.

certain crimes to the ICC, Europeans interpreted the same resolution as supporting the ICC's role in providing international judicial assistance.[502]

Cases (habeas corpus for enemy combatants)

☛ *Hamdi* v. *Rumsfeld*, Supreme Court of the United States, 542 U.S. 507, No. 03-6696, 28 June 2004 <http://a257.g.akamaitech.net/7/257/2422/28june20041215/www.supremecourtus.gov/opinions/03pdf/03-6696.pdf>

☛ *Rumsfeld* v. *Padilla*, Supreme Court of the United States, 542 U.S. 426, No. 03-1027, 28 June 2004 <http://a257.g.akamaitech.net/7/257/2422/28june20041215/www.supremecourtus.gov/opinions/03pdf/03-1027.pdf>

☛ *Rasul* v. *Bush*, Supreme Court of the United States, 542 U.S. 466, Nos. 03-334, 03-343, 28 June 2004 <http://a257.g.akamaitech.net/7/257/2422/28june20041215/www.supremecourtus.gov/opinions/03pdf/03-334.pdf>

On 28 June 2004 the Supreme Court of the United States decided three cases concerning 'enemy combatants'.

In the first case, *Hamdi* v. *Rumsfeld*, Yaser Esam Hamdi, an American citizen, was seized by the Northern Alliance (an ally of the United States) in a combat zone in Afghanistan in late 2001 and later turned over to American forces. The US first interrogated and then transferred Hamdi to Guantánamo Bay in January 2002. Upon learning in April 2002 that Hamdi was an American citizen, the US transferred him first to Norfolk, Virginia and later to Charleston, South Carolina. The government asserted that he had taken up arms with the Taliban against American armed forces, making him an 'enemy combatant', and thus, he could be held indefinitely without formal charges or further proceedings. However, Hamdi's father, in his petition for a writ of *habeas corpus* on behalf of his son filed in June 2002 in the United States District Court for the Eastern District of Virginia, maintained that Hamdi went to Afghanistan to do relief work and had only arrived in Afghanistan before the conflict. The petition stated that for a year and a half Hamdi did not have access to counsel or the right to send or receive communication from beyond the prison.

The District Court appointed a federal public defender for Hamdi and ordered the Government to provide Hamdi with access to his counsel. The United States Court of Appeals for the Fourth Circuit reversed the order and held that the District Court failed to appropriately defer to the government's national security and intelligence interests. The Fourth Circuit found that 'because it was 'undisputed that Hamdi was captured in a zone of active combat in a foreign theater of conflict, no factual inquiry or evidentiary hearing allowing Hamdi to be heard or to rebut the government's assertions was necessary or proper'. The Fourth Circuit further considered the detention to be lawful.

The government filed a motion to dismiss, and included, as its only evidence, a declaration from Michael Mobbs, Special Advisor to the Under Secretary of Defense for Policy. Mobbs asserted that he was familiar with Hamdi's case, as well as the government's overall policy concerning detention of unlawful combatants, and that the government had good reason to designate Hamdi as an 'enemy combatant'. Indefinite detention was therefore appropriate. The government never released its criteria regarding who may be designated as an 'enemy combatant,' but 'for purposes of this case' the government said that an

---

502. UN Press Release SC/8258, Security Council Extends UN Operation in Burundi Until 1 June 2005, Unanimously Adopting Resolution 1577 (2004), 1 December 2004.

'enemy combatant' is one who is "part of or supporting forces hostile to the United States or coalition partners" in Afghanistan and who "engaged in an armed conflict against the United States" there'.

Justice O'Connor wrote the four-person judgment of the court, in which Justices Rehnquist, Kennedy and Breyer joined. The court considered whether the Government can designate American citizens as 'enemy combatants' and detain them on American soil, and if so, what process is due to the person who wishes to challenge such status. O'Connor wrote that 'although Congress authorized the detention of combatants in the narrow circumstances alleged here, due process demands that a citizen held in the United States as an enemy combatant be given a meaningful opportunity to contest the factual basis for that detention before a neutral decisionmaker.'

The threshold question in this case was whether the Executive has authority to detain citizens who are designated as 'enemy combatants'. The court only addressed whether the government is authorised to detain a US citizen who falls within that definition. In assessing whether the Executive had authority O'Connor stated: 'Because detention to prevent a combatant's return to the battlefield is a fundamental incident of waging war, in permitting the use of "necessary and appropriate force," Congress has clearly and unmistakably authorized detention in the narrow circumstances considered here.' Explicit language in the statute permitting these detentions was deemed not necessary; 'necessary and appropriate force' implicitly included the authority.

Hamdi also objected to the possibility of indefinite detention, and argued that, even if Congress did authorise such detention, Congress did not authorise indefinite detentions. O'Connor acknowledged the dangers involved and stated: 'We recognize that the national security underpinnings of the "war on terror," although crucially important, are broad and malleable,' especially after considering the government's position that 'given its unconventional nature, the current conflict is unlikely to end with a formal cease-fire agreement'. O'Connor recognised that the Government's position, when taken to its logical conclusions, would be tantamount to unconditional authority to detain American citizens for an indefinite period, possibly lasting many years. O'Connor cautioned that '[i]f the Government does not consider this unconventional war won for two generations, and if it maintains during that time that Hamdi might, if released, rejoin forces fighting against the United States, then the position it has taken throughout the litigation of this case suggests that Hamdi's detention could last for the rest of his life.' O'Connor then cited Article 118 of Geneva Convention III and stated: 'It is a clearly established principle of the law of war that detention may last no longer than active hostilities.' O'Connor concluded that the AUMF did not authorise indefinite detention, but noted that '[i]f the record establishes that United States troops are still involved in active combat in Afghanistan, those detentions are part of the exercise of "necessary and appropriate," and therefore are authorized by the AMUF.' The court also stressed that the location of the detainee does not matter; otherwise, there would be a 'perverse incentive' to hold individuals outside the US where they would not be entitled to process.

After addressing whether the detention of enemy combatants was legally authorised, O'Connor next examined what process is due such persons who wish to dispute their status as an enemy combatant. To do so the court looked at the statute of the writ of habeas corpus and the Due Process Clause of the Constitution. Regarding the writ of habeas corpus, both parties agreed that 'absent suspension, the writ of habeas corpus remains available to every individual detained within the United States'. ('The Privilege of the Writ of Habeas Corpus shall not be suspended, unless when in Cases of Rebellion or Invasion the public Safety may require it.' Article I, § 9, cl. 2.) Because all parties agreed that the writ had not been suspended, 'it is undisputed that Hamdi was properly before an Article III court to challenge his detention under 28 U.S.C. § 2241'. Furthermore, the court stressed that the writ is a check on the Executive, 'ensuring that it does not detain individuals except in accordance with law'.

The Government gave two reasons as to how the Mobbs Declaration satisfied the required factual requirement of the procedural protections of the habeas statute. First, because everyone agreed that Hamdi was captured in a combat zone, he is presumed to be an 'enemy combatant' and no other fact-finding or hearing is necessary, and second, further process and factual exploration in individual cases would interfere with the Executive's military decision-making.

The court rejected both of these arguments, stating that Hamdi disputed the circumstances surrounding his capture but was not given the opportunity to refute the claim that he was part of the anti-American combat forces, and that the separation of powers involves deference but does not necessarily preclude courts from addressing constitutional concerns. Concerning the process due, O'Connor, using the test espoused in *Mathews* v. *Eldridge*,[503] balanced Hamdi's interests at stake against the government's interests and burdens in providing greater process, while considering the benefits of providing and the risks in not providing additional procedural safeguards. O'Connor concluded that governmental interests in ensuring that those released do not return to fighting, and the dangerous distractions to military commanders of litigation and potential exposure of sensitive secrets, do not outweigh the most fundamental constitutional rights of American citizens. O'Connor wrote: 'We therefore hold that a citizen-detainee seeking to challenge his classification as an enemy combatant must receive notice of the factual basis for his classification, and a fair opportunity to rebut the government's factual assertions before a neutral decisionmaker.' Additionally, these rights must be granted 'at a meaningful time and in a meaningful manner'. In dictum, O'Connor suggested what such proceedings may look like, stating:

> 'the exigencies of the circumstances may demand that, aside from these core elements, enemy combatant proceedings may be tailored to alleviate their uncommon potential to burden the Executive at a time of ongoing military conflict. Hearsay, for example, may need to be accepted as the most reliable available evidence from the Government in such a proceeding. Likewise, the Constitution would not be offended by a presumption in favour of the government's evidence, so long as the presumption remained a rebuttable one and fair opportunity for rebuttal were provided.'

Thus, once the government puts forth credible evidence that the habeas petitioner meets the enemy-combatant criteria, the onus could shift to the petitioner to rebut that evidence with more persuasive evidence that he falls outside the criteria. A burden-shifting scheme of this sort would meet the goal of ensuring that the errant tourist, embedded journalist, or local aid worker has a chance to prove military error while giving due regard to the Executive once it has put forth meaningful support for its conclusion that the detainee is in fact an enemy combatant.' (Note: The court's assessment of this came from the Constitution; it did not address whether any treaty guaranteed such process.) This process is due only when the

503. 424 U.S. 319 (1976).

government wishes to continue a detention, not when the Government initially captures an individual on the battlefield.

The court rejected the government's view of a limited role for the courts in the adjudication of individual cases, and stated that 'unless Congress acts to suspend it, the Great Writ of habeas corpus allows the Judicial Branch to play a necessary role in maintaining this delicate balance of governance, serving as an important judicial check on the Executive's discretion in the realm of detentions'. Thus, a 'process in which the Executive's factual assertions go wholly unchallenged or are simply presumed correct without any opportunity for the alleged combatant to demonstrate otherwise falls constitutionally short'. The government's 'screening' processes and the interrogations that Hamdi received did not constitute adequate process afforded under the Due Process Clause of the Constitution, despite the Government's assertion that Hamdi had the opportunity to contest his enemy-combatant status. The court did not specify the exact process due individuals detained by the Government, but stated:

> '[t]here remains the possibility that the standards we have articulated could be met by an appropriately authorized and properly constituted military tribunal. Indeed, it is notable that military regulations already provide for such process in related instances, dictating that tribunals be made available to determine the status of enemy detainees who assert prisoner-of-war status under the Geneva Convention.'

O'Connor concluded that a court should take into consideration the government's case against an alleged enemy combatant, but the individual must be able to rebut the evidence against him in front of an impartial adjudicator. O'Connor wrote:

> 'We anticipate that a District Court would proceed with the caution that we have indicated is necessary in this setting, engaging in a factfinding process that is both prudent and incremental. We have no reason to doubt that courts faced with these sensitive matters will pay proper heed both to the matters of national security that might arise in an individual case and to the constitutional limitations safeguarding essential liberties that remain vibrant even in times of security concerns.'

Justice Souter, joined by Justice Ginsburg, wrote a separate opinion, concurring in part and dissenting in part, and concurring in the judgment. Souter disagreed with the majority's contention that the AUMF authorises Hamdi's detention. Souter stated that Congress intended for the habeas statute to apply to military wartime detentions as well as those in peace and that the AUMF does not authorise such detentions. Souter also cited the Third Geneva Convention, stating that detaining Hamdi's incommunicado detention violates the prisoner of war status to which he is entitled. Souter also stated that the President does not have authority under his constitutional powers as commander-in-chief to detain citizens in this manner. Because he found no evidence of congressional authority, inherent presidential powers or any law of war authorising these detentions, thus making Hamdi's detention unlawful, Souter refrained from positing what level of process is due individuals in this situation. As such, Souter stated that he would 'vacate the judgment of the Court of Appeals and remand for proceedings consistent with this view'. Because Souter declined to address the constitutional issues of process, he refrained from adopting the majority's discussion on due process. However, he stated that he would not necessarily disagree with the minimum protections of having notice of the charges, the opportunity to rebut the evidence before a neutral decision-maker and the right to counsel. But Souter also suggested that he may not agree with allowing an evidentiary presumption in favour of the government, or that a military tribunal may be sufficient.

Justice Scalia, with Justice Stevens joining, wrote a dissenting opinion. Scalia stated that Hamdi should be released immediately unless either the government pursues criminal proceedings against him or Congress has suspended the writ of habeas corpus. He stated: 'A suspension of the writ could, of course, lay down conditions for continued detention, similar to those that today's opinion prescribes under the Due Process Clause.' Scalia wrote that American citizens, even if taking up arms, have historically been treated as traitors and tried through the criminal process, but he also noted that military exigency has sometimes rendered this process impracticable. However, when this has occurred the writ has been suspended, and Scalia argued that the writ has not been suspended in this case.

Justice Thomas dissented and stated that the courts do not have authority to challenge and second-guess the President's determination to detain 'enemy combatants'. Citing what he deemed explicit congressional approval and the presidential powers of the Constitution, Thomas stated that the courts must defer to the President's decisions on the detention of individuals considered to be 'enemy combatants'.

The second case heard by the Supreme Court on 28 June 2004 was *Rumsfeld* v. *Padilla*. After disembarking a flight from Pakistan to Chicago on 8 May 2002, Jose Padilla, an American citizen, was 'apprehended by federal agents executing a material witness warrant issued by the United States District Court for the Southern District of New York (Southern District) in connection with its grand jury investigation into the September 11th terrorist attacks'. He was subsequently transported to New York and held in federal criminal custody. Padilla's appointed counsel moved to vacate the material witness warrant, and while the motion was pending, on 9 June 2002 the President, acting pursuant to his authority under the AUMF, 'issued an order to Secretary of Defense Donald H. Rumsfeld designating Padilla an "enemy combatant" and directing the Secretary to detain him in military custody'. Department of Defense officials then took him into custody and transferred him to a naval brig in Charleston, South Carolina, where he was detained until this case. [Note: On the same day of the order of 9 June, the Government withdrew its grand jury subpoena of Padilla and asked the court to vacate the warrant.]

Padilla filed a petition for a writ of *habeas corpus*, challenging his detention as an 'enemy combatant' and alleging that his detention violated the United States Constitution. Padilla named as respondents President George W. Bush, Secretary of Defense Donald Rumsfeld, and Melanie A. Marr, Commander of the Consolidated Naval Brig. The District Court ruled that Rumsfeld's 'personal involvement' in the detention made him a proper respondent and that New York could assert jurisdiction through its long-arm statute. On the merits, it ruled ruled that the President had the authority to detain Padilla on American soil as an 'enemy combatant'. The United States Court of Appeals for the Second Circuit reversed on the merits, holding that neither the President's constitutional powers as commander-in-chief nor the AUMF authorises military detentions of Americans captured on American soil. On the jurisdictional issue, the Court of Appeals stated that Rumsfeld was a proper respondent because he had 'the legal reality of control' over Padilla.

Chief Justice Rehnquist delivered the 5-4 opinion of the Supreme Court, which held that the commander of the naval brig where Padilla was held was the only proper respondent, and that the District Court for the Southern District of New York did not have jurisdiction over the commander. The Supreme Court concluded that 'there is generally only one proper respondent to a given prisoner's habeas petition' and that person is the one 'with the ability to produce the prisoner's body before the habeas court'. Therefore, the court stated that 'the immediate custodian, not a supervisory official who exercises legal control, is the proper respondent'. In this case the immediate custodian was Commander Marr because she exercised day-to-day control over Padilla. The court disagreed with the 'legal reality of control' argument, because 'identification of the party exercising legal control only comes into play when there is no immediate physical custodian with respect to the challenged 'custody'. Thus, petitions must name as respondents the warden or immediate custodian, and be filed in the district of confinement. Notably, the court did acknowledge that in the past it has recognised exceptions to this general rule, where the American citizen is detained outside the United States and thus outside the territorial jurisdiction of any federal district court. Because it found that the District Court lacked jurisdiction to hear the petition, the Supreme Court did not answer the question whether the President has authority to detain Padilla militarily.

The third case, *Rasul* v. *Bush*, was brought by two Australian and 12 Kuwaiti citizens captured abroad during hostilities between the United States and the Taliban in Afghanistan, and who have been held since early 2002 by the United States military at the Guantánamo Bay Naval Base, Cuba. Approximately 640 other non-Americans were detained at this facility at the time of this case. The detainees filed petitions for writs of *habeas corpus*, challenging their detention and asserting that they had never fought against the United States or committed acts of terrorism. Some petitioners stated that they had been providing humanitarian aid in Afghanistan and Pakistan when they were captured by local bounty hunters and later turned over to American forces. According to the petitions, they had not been provided access to counsel, charged with any crime or granted access to any competent tribunal.

The United States District Court for the District of Columbia dismissed, and the Court of Appeals affirmed, all the petitions for writs of habeas corpus for lack of jurisdiction, holding that the Supreme Court's opinion in *Johnson* v. *Eisentrager*[504] precluded foreign nationals detained outside the United States from invoking a petition for a writ of habeas corpus.

In an opinion written by Justice Stevens and joined by Justices O'Connor, Souter, Ginsburg and Breyer, the Supreme Court reversed and remanded the case back to the District Court to consider the merits, holding that federal district courts can exercise jurisdiction over writs of habeas corpus filed by non-Americans captured during hostilities and detained at Guantánamo Bay Naval Base, Cuba. Habeas jurisdiction extended to aliens held in territory under 'plenary and exclusive jurisdiction' but not under the 'ultimate sovereignty' of the United States. The court noted that the habeas statute[505] does not distinguish between Americans and aliens held in federal custody, and concluded that both may seek habeas relief in federal courts. Section 2241 grants jurisdiction to federal courts once it is established that the petitioner has alleged he is being held in federal custody in violation of United States law, and that the District Court exercises jurisdiction over the petitioner's custodian; nothing more is required. Therefore, the location of the prisoner is not dispositive. The habeas statute does not require the detainee to be within the territorial jurisdiction of the federal court before that court may exercise jurisdiction over a petition for writ of habeas corpus. Instead, 'because 'the writ of habeas corpus does not act upon the prisoner

504. 399 U.S. 763 (1950).
505. 28 U.S.C. § 2241.

who seeks relief, but upon the person who holds him in what is alleged to be unlawful custody', a District Court acts 'within [its] respective jurisdiction' within the meaning of § 2241 as long as 'the custodian can be reached by service of process'. The court focused on, and ultimately found, a statutory entitlement to habeas review, and not on whether the aliens had a constitutional entitlement to it.

The court also held that federal courts have jurisdiction over the petitioners' other claims, specifically, the Alien Tort Claims Act (28 U.S.C. § 1350) and the federal question statute.[506] The court stated: '[t]he fact that petitioners in these cases are being held in military custody is immaterial to the question of the District Court's jurisdiction over their nonhabeas statutory claims'.

☛ *Gherebi v. Bush*, United States Court of Appeals, Ninth Circuit, 374 F.3d 727, No. 03-55785, 8 July 2004

The issue in this case was whether the executive branch has the authority to detain foreign citizens indefinitely held in territory under the 'complete jurisdiction and control' of the United States, while providing no legal means to challenge their detention, either in American or foreign courts. In January 2002 the US began transferring detainees captured during the Afghanistan military campaign of late 2001 to Guantánamo Bay, Cuba, a naval base leased by the United States. The detainees were classified as 'enemy combatants' and provided no access to challenge their detention. The government did not file charges, provide counsel or afford them the opportunity to challenge their detention through any means. Top US officials, including Secretary of Defense Donald Rumsfeld, had indicated earlier that the government had authority to hold individuals in the same manner until the war on terror came to an end.

In February 2003 Belaid Gherebi filed a petition for a writ of *habeas corpus* on behalf of his brother Faren, alleging that President Bush, Secretary Rumsfeld, and other military officials had violated the US Constitution and the Third Geneva Convention of 1949. The petition claimed that Guantánamo Bay Naval Base was 'under the exclusive and complete jurisdiction' of the respondents. The US District Court for the Central District of California dismissed Gherebi's petition for lack of jurisdiction, holding that case precedent 'foreclosed jurisdiction over Gherebi's petition in any federal court because Guantánamo 'is not within sovereign U.S. territory'.

The Court of Appeals for the Ninth Circuit agreed with Gherebi, holding that the District Court had erred in finding that neither it nor any other federal court had jurisdiction over the claim. The threshold question was the legal status of the Guantánamo Bay naval base. The government acknowledged that if the base was American soil, then federal district courts could exercise jurisdiction. But according to the government, the base was not American territory and under the ultimate sovereignty of Cuba, and therefore 'in the case of alien enemies habeas is not available when their acts and the situs of their trial and detention all lie outside of this nation's territorial jurisdiction'.

The government argued that the question of jurisdiction turns on 'sovereignty', not 'territorial jurisdiction'. However, the Court of Appeals held that territorial jurisdiction is enough; sovereignty is not required. Furthermore, the United States exercised 'complete

506. 28 U.S.C. § 1331.

jurisdiction and control' over the land for over one hundred years, and '[w]here a nation exercises "exclusive jurisdiction" over a territory, territorial jurisdiction lies.'

Having established that the US has territorial jurisdiction over the base, the Court of Appeals ruled that the federal courts can hear habeas petitions from Guantánamo detainees. But the court stressed that its analysis only pertained to the legal status of the base. It did not address any potential constitutional or international law issues surrounding the detentions, or whether 'enemy combatants' are even able to file habeas petitions. These two issues were not before the Court of Appeals in this case.

However, the court did state in a footnote, that 'the government's position here is at odds with the United States' longtime role as a leader in international efforts to codify and safeguard the rights of prisoners in wartime. It is also at odds with one of the most important achievements of these efforts – the 1949 Geneva Conventions, which require that a competent tribunal determine the status of captured prisoners.' The Court of Appeals rejected the government's position that the 'Executive Branch possesses the unchecked authority to imprison indefinitely any persons, foreign citizens included, on territory under the sole jurisdiction and control of the United States, without permitting such prisoners recourse of any kind to any judicial forum, or even access to counsel, regardless of the length or manner of their confinement.' The court continued, 'the government's position is inconsistent with fundamental tenets of American jurisprudence and raises most serious concerns under international law'. During oral argument the government stated that it would retain the same position even if the claims included alleged acts of torture or summary execution of detainees. The Court of Appeals was strongly against a legal blackhole as that espoused by the government.

The Court then remanded the case to the District Court of Washington DC. The Court noted in the *Padilla* case, that 'the Supreme Court held that an American citizen detained within the United States must name his immediate custodian as the respondent in a habeas petition and must file in the district of confinement'. But there was an exception noted by the court in that case (regarding the district of confinement and immediate custodian rules) 'where an American citizen is detained outside the territorial jurisdiction of any district court', and this Court noted that this applies to foreign nationals detained at Guantánamo. The Court ruled that the claim should be heard in Washington, DC

☛ *Hamdan* v. *Rumsfeld*, United States District Court for the District of Columbia, 344 F. Supp.2d 152, No. CIV.A.04-1519 JR., 8 November 2004

Before Judge James Robertson of the US District Court for the District of Columbia, Salim Ahmed Hamdan had petitioned for a writ of habeas corpus, 'challenging the lawfulness of the Secretary of Defense's plan to try him for alleged war crimes before a military commission convened under special orders issued by the President of the United States, rather than before a court-martial convened under the Uniform Code of Military Justice'. Hamdan, a former driver of Osama bin Laden, was captured in Afghanistan by American forces in late 2001 and transferred the following year to a detention centre at Guantánamo Bay Naval Base, Cuba. President Bush, in accordance with the Military Order issued on 13 November 2001, declared on 3 July 2003 that Hamdan would be tried by military commission. Hamdan was assigned military counsel on 18 December 2003, who later requested a speedy trial and notice of the charges as provided under the Uniform Code of Military Justice (UCMJ). On 23 February 2004, however, the government determined that the UCMJ did not apply to Hamdan's case. Hamdan was later charged with conspiracy to commit several offences, including attacking civilians and civilian objects, murder and destruction of property by unprivileged belligerent, and acts of terrorism.

Judge James Robertson, writing the opinion, determined that only three facts were relevant to the disposition of the petition for writ of habeas corpus: 1) Hamdan was captured in Afghanistan during hostilities; 2) Hamdan claimed he was entitled to prisoner of war status; and 3) the government had not provided a competent tribunal to determine Hamdan's status as a prisoner-of-war or enemy combatant.

Judge Robertson discussed the lack of a 'proper determination' showing that Hamdan could be tried by a military commission under the law of war. After discussing prior case law, including *Quirin* and *Yamashita*, the court concluded that the power to create military tribunals comes from the Articles of War and its successor (i.e., UCMJ), which are both congressionally-granted authority. Therefore, contrary to the government's assertion, the power to create military tribunals is not inherent in the president's powers as commander-in-chief or under Article II of the Constitution. There must be positive congressional approval of the 'historical, traditional, non-statutory military commission'.

Judge Robertson next concluded that the law of war, which includes the Third Geneva Convention, requires trial by court-martial when the status of the detainee is in doubt. The government agreed that prisoners of war must be tried by court-martial, but it asserted that Hamdan was not a POW because he was captured in a 'separate' conflict with Al Qaeda, which is not a state. The court rejected this argument and stated that the Geneva Conventions 'are triggered by the place of the conflict, and not by what particular faction a fighter is associated with.' The court determined that the Third Geneva Convention, whether in its entirety or only Common Article 3, 'applies to all persons detained in Afghanistan during the hostilities there'. The government further contended that Al Qaeda members are not entitled to protection under the Geneva Convention because they do not carry their weapons openly or operate in accordance with the law of war. Hamdan was unable to challenge the government's findings of fact pertaining to these elements, and the court rejected the government's assertion that its designation as such, even without evidence, be given 'extraordinary deference'. The court disagreed with the government's contention that Hamdan's status was in doubt and that he had been afforded a proper hearing. Hamdan had appeared before the Combatant Status Review Tribunal, but the court found this insufficient because the Tribunal was not established for the purpose of determining the status of detainees under the Geneva Conventions, but rather for the purpose of assessing whether a detainee is an 'enemy combatant' subject to continued detention. The court gave little weight to the Tribunal's decision and the presidential determination of Hamdan's status as an Al Qaeda member. Neither action, according to the court, was a 'competent tribunal', and until Hamdan had presented his case before such a tribunal, he must be afforded the full protections provided POWs under the Geneva Conventions.

The court also rejected the government's contention that common Article 3 only applies to non-international conflicts. Citing the International Court of Justice in *Nicaragua* v. *US*, the court stated that common Article 3 provides a 'minimum yardstick' as to the rules of both international and non-international conflicts. The court also concluded that the Geneva Conventions, contrary to the Government's position, are self-executing treaties, and that Hamdan was entitled to protection under them until he was determined not to be a prisoner of war.

The court then concluded that although most of the procedures of the military commission are adequate,[507] some features are 'fatally contrary to or inconsistent with' the procedures of the UCMJ. The court strongly questioned the appropriateness of the power of the military commission to 'exclude the accused from hearings and deny him access to evidence presented against him' – a power not granted in a court-martial convened under the UCMJ. The UCMJ provides for the right to be present at all proceedings. The court cited the ICCPR, Article 14(d)(3); Protocol I, Article 75(4)(e); and case law from the European Court of Human Rights, and stated: 'It is also apparent that the right to trial "in one's presence" is established as a matter of international humanitarian and human rights law.'

The court did not rule on Hamdan's claim of unlawful and inhumane detention because his transfer out of isolation before the case rendered the issue moot. The court also refrained from ruling on his claim to a speedy trial and claim to equal protection under the Constitution.

In his order accompanying the opinion, Judge Robertson provided that Hamdan could only be tried by court-martial convened under the UCMJ, rather than a military commission, unless and until a 'competent tribunal' found him to be not entitled to the protections afforded POWs under the Geneva Conventions, and that a military commission that permits the withholding of evidence and exclusion from proceedings would be unlawful.

☛ *Abu Ali* v. *Ashcroft*, United States District Court for the District of Columbia, 350 F. Supp.2d 28, No. CIV.A. 04-1258JDB, 16 December 2004

Abu Ali, a citizen of the United States detained in the Kingdom of Saudi Arabia since June 2003, filed a petition for a writ of habeas corpus against American officials, alleging that they requested and supervised his detention. Ali was arrested by Saudi officers on 11 June 2003 while taking an exam at the Islamic University of Medina in Saudi Arabia, and he had been detained ever since without charges or access to counsel. Three other Americans were arrested around the same time but were sent to the US weeks later and charged in Northern Virginia with 'undertaking paramilitary training to wage a terrorist jihad on behalf of Muslims'. Abu Ali was the only one surrounding these events not extradited to the US and charged with a crime. The complaint alleged that FBI agents visited Ali's prison five days after his arrest and watched his interrogation by Saudi officials, and that in September 2003 several FBI agents went to Saudi Arabia and interrogated him for at least four days.

The government filed a motion to dismiss, which the District Court denied. It ordered the parties to meet and discuss the scope and process of jurisdictional discovery. The government argued that the identity and location of Ali's detaining authority was dispositive (i.e., the 'immediate custodian' and 'district of confinement' rules), because a federal court 'simply lacks jurisdiction to grant habeas relief where the prisoner seeking the writ is being held by a foreign custodian, even where the United States allegedly has been involved in

---

507. The procedures cited are the following rights: to appointed military counsel; to replace military counsel; to get civilian attorney if affordable; to receive a copy of the charges in an understandable language; to be presumed innocent until proven guilty; to proof beyond a reasonable doubt; to be presented with the prosecution's evidence used against the accused and any exculpatory evidence known by the prosecution; to choose not to testify without adverse consequences or inferences; to obtain and present witnesses and documents for his defence; to cross-examine witnesses; and to be free from double jeopardy.

the prisoner's incarceration in the first place'. The District Court emphasised the dangerous lack of limits involved in such a proposition, by stating that:

> 'the position would permit the United States, at its discretion and without judicial review, to arrest a citizen of the United States and transfer her to the custody of allies overseas in order to avoid constitutional scrutiny; to arrest a citizen of the United States through the intermediary of a foreign ally and ask the ally to hold the citizen at a foreign location indefinitely at the direction of the United States; or even to deliver American citizens to foreign governments to obtain information through the use of torture. In short, the United States is in effect arguing for nothing less than the unreviewable power to separate an American citizen from the most fundamental of his constitutional rights merely by choosing where he will be detained or who will detain him.'

The District Court concluded that the broad language of the habeas statute, combined with consistent case law, confirms that physical custody (of Americans detained abroad) is not necessary, 'constructive' custody is enough. When an American is detained abroad he 'may name as respondents any of his custodians (not just the immediate custodians) and may file the claim in the court that has jurisdiction over those respondents'. Habeas jurisdiction has been found where the detainee has been under the physical control of a foreign sovereign or even not under the physical control of any entity at all but where 'the respondent was responsible for significant restraints on the petitioner's liberty'. The District Court stated that 'the United States may not avoid the habeas jurisdiction of the federal courts by enlisting a foreign ally as an intermediary to detain the citizen'.

The District Court found against the government's position on the text of the habeas statute and controlling precedent, and the government then cited, alternatively, the act of state, separation of powers, and political question doctrines. But the court said that 'none, however, extinguishes the fundamental right of a citizen to challenge his detention colorably alleged to be at the behest of the executive'.

The District Court found the act of state doctrine to be inapplicable because it precludes US courts from examining the validity of public acts committed by foreign states within their own territory, whereas this case involves the acts of US officials, albeit committed abroad, but nevertheless within the jurisdiction of federal courts. The issue was not the validity of Saudi officials' actions, but rather whether US officials violated Ali's constitutional rights by '"obtaining" the detention from the Saudis'.

The District Court also concluded that the separation of powers and political question doctrines, despite giving due deference, must not be used to eliminate the basic constitutional right to be free from unlawful detention. Finally, the Hostage Act[508] does not proscribe to the President a mandatory or enforceable duty to demand that the Saudi government release Ali.

Cases (terrorism)

- *United States* v. *Koubriti*, United States District Court for the Eastern District of Michigan, 336 F.Supp.2d 676, No. 01-CR-80778, 2 September 2004

---

508. 22 U.S.C. § 1732.

In one of the first post-9/11 terrorism prosecutions, after securing a conviction against Abdel-Ihah Elhardoudi and Karim Koubriti, both Moroccan immigrants, on charges of conspiracy to provide material support and resources to terrorists, conspiracy to engage in document fraud and engaging in document fraud, the government moved to dismiss the charge related to terrorism and to agree to the defendants' motion for a new trial as to the document charges, acknowledging that it had failed to produce critical documents and information to the defence and to the court, including exculpatory evidence. The court characterised these omissions as 'not sporadic or isolated' but rather:

> 'they were of such a magnitude, and were so prevalent and pervasive as to constitute a pattern of conduct, that when all of the withheld evidence is viewed collectively, it is an inescapable conclusion that the Defendants' due process, confrontation and fair trial rights were violated and that the jury's verdict was infected to the point that the Court believes there is at least a reasonable probability that the jury's verdict would have been different had constitutional standards been met'.

The District Court held that the government's failure to produce the documents required dismissal of the terrorism-related charge and a new trial on the document charges, but praised the government's cooperation and diligence in the nine-month post-trial review of document production. Ultimately, the government realised its prosecution of the case was erroneous and moved for dismissal of the terrorism-related charge.

☛ *United States* v. *Moussaoui*, United States Court of Appeals, Fourth Circuit, 382 F.3d 453, No. 03-4792, 13 September 2004

Zacarias Moussaoui, a foreign national arrested in mid August 2001 on immigration violations, was charged with conspiracy related to the 11 September 2001 terrorist attacks. Moussaoui wished to depose witnesses who had been captured by the United States in the course of its investigations and military operations in relation to the terrorist attacks and al-Qaeda. The United States District Court for the Eastern District of Virginia ordered production of the enemy combatant witnesses but the government, asserting national security concerns, stated that it would not produce them for purposes of deposition, and it did not do so.

The Court of Appeals held that the District Court had process power over enemy combatant witnesses who were foreign nationals being held in military custody outside the territory of the United States (because their ultimate custodian was the Secretary of Defense), and that ordering production of such witnesses in relation to a case involving the prosecution for conspiring to commit international terrorism did not unduly infringe upon the Executive's warmaking authority.

The Court of Appeals stated that an indictment is usually dismissed when the government refuses to produce witnesses but held that substitutes were available and therefore 'no punitive sanction is warranted here because the Government has rightfully exercised its prerogative to protect national security interests by refusing the produce the witnesses'. The Court of Appeals reversed the District Court's ruling that any substitute for witness testimony was inadequate, holding that the available substitutes do not unfairly disadvantage the defendant or penalise the government for protecting national security interests. The Court of Appeals left the ultimate decision as to the nature of the substitutes to the District Court but suggested that witness summaries would be adequate.

Cases (Foreign Sovereign Immunities Act)

☛ Acree *v.* Republic of Iraq, et al., *United States Court of Appeals, District of Columbia Circuit, 370 F.3d 41, No. 03-5232, 4 June 2004*

Seventeen American soldiers serving in the Gulf War following the Iraqi invasion of Kuwait were captured and held as prisoners of war by the Iraqi government between January and March 1991. They brought suit in the United States District Court for the District of Columbia and named as defendants the Republic of Iraq, the Iraqi Intelligence Service, and Saddam Hussein, citing the terrorism exception to the Foreign Sovereign Immunities Act ('FSIA'), 28 U.S.C. § 1605(a)(7). They sought compensatory and punitive damages for torture and injuries endured during captivity. Iraq failed to respond to the complaint, and the District Court subsequently awarded damages in the amount of over $959 million after looking at the plaintiffs' evidentiary submissions. Two weeks after the court's decision, the United States government filed a motion to intervene to challenge the District Court's subject matter jurisdiction but the court denied the motion as being untimely.

The Court of Appeals held that the District Court had erred in finding the government's motion to intervene as untimely because the case and entry of default judgment involved 'weighty foreign policy interests' that must given due deference. Therefore, the government was a proper party to this case and could appeal the judgment. The Court of Appeals further held that the District Court was proper in exercising jurisdiction over the suit, but that the judgment must be vacated because the plaintiffs' lawsuit failed to state a proper cause of action.

The government argued that an appropriations bill passed in April 2003 contained a provision that gave the President the authority to make the FSIA's terrorism exception inapplicable to Iraq, which he then exercised and implemented by a presidential declaration on 7 May 2003. Doing so, argued the government, barred the District Court from having jurisdiction.

The Court of Appeals held otherwise, stating that the appropriations bill, including the provision cited by the government, was 'aimed at legal provisions that present obstacles to assistance and funding for the new Iraqi Government and was not intended to alter the jurisdiction of the federal courts under the FSIA', in addition to 'appropriat[ing] additional funding for military operations in Iraq, homeland security efforts in the United States, and bilateral economic assistance to America's allies in the war in Iraq'.

The Court of Appeals concluded that the District Court did properly find jurisdiction over the case, but found that the plaintiffs failed to state a cause of action. The District Court based its finding of liability on the FSIA, but the Court of Appeals stated that this law only serves as a vehicle for liability; it does not create a substantive claim against foreign states. No party raised the non-jurisdictional issue but the Court of Appeals cited 'exceptional circumstances', specifically the extraordinary nature of the nearly-billion dollar judgment against 'a foreign government whose present and future stability has become a central preoccupation of the United States' foreign policy'. The Court of Appeals held that the District Court's judgment should be vacated and dismissed for failure to state a cause of action.

☛ *Republic of Austria* v. *Altmann*, Supreme Court of the United States, 541 U.S. 677, No. 03-13, 7 June 2004

The plaintiff alleged that the Austrian Gallery, an instrument of the Republic of Austria, had wrongfully acquired several paintings belonging to the plaintiff's uncle. The complaint stated that the artworks had either 'been seized by the Nazis or expropriated by the Austrian Republic after World War II'. The defendants, the Republic of Austria and the gallery, claimed sovereign immunity and filed a motion to dismiss, which was denied by the United States District Court for the Central District of California and upheld by the Court of Appeals for the Ninth Circuit.

The Supreme Court held that the Foreign Sovereign Immunities Act (FSIA), 28 U.S.C. § 1602 et seq., and its 'expropriation exception' (which expressly exempts certain conduct from immunity involving 'rights in property taken in violation of international law'), applied to conduct prior to its enactment in 1976. The court also held that the alleged conduct could be litigated against even if it occurred during the pre-1952 policy of absolute immunity. In 1952 the United States endorsed restrictive immunity, essentially restricting the sovereign's public acts but not private acts. The court held that the FSIA can be retroactively applied but expressly stated that this was a narrow decision; it only determined that the FSIA applied retroactively, it did not decide as to whether the 'expropriation exception' applied to the facts of this case. This decision allows for the litigation of claims occurring before 1976 that fall into an exception to immunity under the FSIA. The court did not explore other issues, including the presence of a 'suggestion of immunity', the political question or act of state doctrines.

☛ *Ye* v. *Zemin*, United States Court of Appeals, Seventh Circuit, 383 F.3d 620, No. 03-3989, 8 September 2004

The plaintiffs were members of Falun Gong, a spiritual movement banned in China. They filed a claim against the President of China, Jiang Zemin, and a government office, the Falun Gong Control Office, within the Chinese Communist Party that is responsible for monitoring and allegedly suppressing Falun Gong. The complaint, filed on 18 October 2002 in the United States District Court for the Northern District of Illinois, was based on the Alien Tort Claims Act and alleged, *inter alia*, torture, genocide, arbitrary arrest and imprisonment, and claims against the freedom of movement and religion. Jiang was President of China from March 1993 to March 2003.

While President Jiang was meeting with President Bush in Chicago, the plaintiffs served process on United States security agents assigned to Jiang, which a previously issued court order had deemed effective service. The Chinese government, including Jiang, did not respond and the plaintiffs moved for an entry of default. The United States government intervened and entered a 'suggestion of immunity', claiming that service of process was inadequate, and alternatively, President Jiang was entitled to head of state immunity for claims against him and could not be served in any capacity because he was personally inviolable, and thus, service could not be served on the Falun Gong Control Office through serving Jiang.

The District Court dismissed both claims, holding that Jiang could not be sued in his official capacity due to his head of state immunity, and that process on the Control Office through process on Jiang was improper because the plaintiffs had not established that Jiang was indeed an agent of that government entity. But the District Court rejected the government's assertion that Jiang was personally inviolable from service of process in acting as an agent of the government office.

The Court of Appeals concluded that the Foreign Sovereign Immunities Act pertains to foreign states but does not specifically address the immunity of foreign heads of state, and thus, this is an issue left to the Executive Branch not subject to judicial inquiry. The court determined that federal courts must grant appropriate deference to the Executive in issues of foreign policy and must respect the Executive's decisions with respect to the granting of immunity. Where the Executive has not provided exceptions to the blanket head of state immunity, especially where the Executive has argued strongly in favor of immunity, the courts are not free to disregard the Executive's position, regardless of the alleged violations.

The Court of Appeals also stated that process had not been properly served on the Control Office because Jiang was personally inviolable due to the Executive designation of immunity. However, the Court of Appeals stated that its opinion only applies to cases where the Executive has designated a head of state as immune. In dictum the Court of Appeals suggested that process on a head of state might be allowable when the Executive chooses not to recognise the immunity of a head of state visiting the United States. The court further suggested that service of process might reach the head of state himself as well as the third party of which he is affiliated.

☛ *Tachiona* v. *U.S.*, United States Court of Appeals, Second Circuit, 386 F.3d 205, No. 03-6033(L), 03-6043(XAP), 6 October 2004

The plaintiffs filed a complaint against the Zimbabwe African National Union Patriotic Front ('ZANU-PF'); Robert Mugabe, President of Zimbabwe and President and First Secretary of ZANU-PF; and Stan Mudenge, Foreign Minister of Zimbabwe and a ZANU-PF official. The complaint alleged that ZANU-PF, under the orders of its officials, including Mugabe and Mudenge, had committed, *inter alia*, torture, assault, and execution, which are violations of the Alien Tort Claims Act, the Torture Victim Protection Act and international human rights norms.

Mugabe and Mudenge were sued in their individual capacities and served with process in New York City while attending the United Nations Millennium Summit in September 2000. Mudenge was served outside the Zimbabwe Mission building and Mugabe was served outside a local church after attending a private political rally for ZANU-PF. Mugabe received two copies of the complaint, one in relation to his personal capacity and the other on behalf of his political party, ZANU-PF.

After no response from the defendants, and despite the filing of a 'suggestion of immunity' by the United States government, the United States District Court for the Southern District of New York entered a default judgment against ZANU-PF on 19 December 2002, finding it liable for over $20 million in compensatory damages and $51 million in punitive damages. The District Court determined that service of process on foreign officials may constitute service on foreign private entities with which the officials are affiliated. The District Court dismissed the claims against Mugabe and Mudenge, holding that they were entitled to head of state and diplomatic immunity.

The plaintiffs appealed the dismissal of the claims against Mugabe and Mudenge. The US government, through intervention, appealed the judgment against ZANU-PF, arguing that the claims should be dismissed on grounds of head of state immunity, because of their position in government, and diplomatic immunity, because, as representatives of Zimbabwe at the UN conference, the Vienna Convention on Diplomatic Relations and the Convention on Privileges and Immunities of the United Nations provided immunity. The government further contended that the claims against ZANU-PF should be dismissed because 'under both the head of state and diplomatic immunity doctrines, [Mugabe and Mudenge] had 'personal inviolability' and could not be served with legal process in any capacity, including on behalf of ZANU-PF'.

The Court of Appeals upheld the dismissal of the claims against Mugabe and Mudenge, citing diplomatic immunity, and reversed the District Court's judgment against ZANU-PF. The court concluded that the Foreign Sovereign Immunities Act did not permit service on diplomatic and consular representatives 'even as agents for private, non-immune entities'. The court also stated that the Vienna Convention prohibited such affronts to personal dignity, which would interfere with diplomats' official duties.

☛ *Price* v. *Socialist People's Libyan Arab Jamahiriya*, United States Court of Appeals, District of Columbia Circuit, 389 F.3d 192, No. 03-7095, 23 November 2004

Two American citizens, arrested and detained in Libya in 1980 for taking photographs for an illegal purpose, sued the government of Libya for alleged torture and hostage-taking and sought $40 million in damages. The United States District Court for the District of Columbia denied Libya's motion to dismiss based on sovereign immunity. The District Court held, and the Court of Appeals affirmed, that Libya had failed to satisfy its burden of proving that the acts in question fell outside the terrorism exception to the Foreign Sovereign Immunities Act ('FSIA'), and therefore Libya was divested of its sovereign immunity.

The court ruled that Libya had failed to show that the action fell outside the terrorism exception to immunity under the FSIA, but did not rule on whether the complaint failed to state a cause of action, which Libya had argued.

Cases (Alien Tort Claims Act/Torture Victims Protection Act/Federal Tort Claims Act)

☛ *Bowoto, et al.* v. *Chevron Texaco Corp.*, et al. and Moes 1-50, United States District Court for the Northern District of California, 312 F.Supp.2d 1229, No. C 99-2506 SI, 22 March 2004

Five Nigerian citizens filed this action in 1999 alleging that ChevronTexaco Corporation ('Chevron') and a subsidiary corporation, ChevronTexaco Overseas Petroleum, Inc. ('CTOP'), were involved in the commission of human rights abuses in Nigeria. The complaint alleged that, on 28 May 1998, Chevron Nigeria Limited ('CNL'), a company owned by CTOP, 'acting in concert with defendants, recruited the Nigerian military and police to fire weapons at Nigerians staging a protest on one of Chevron's oil platforms', where two protesters were killed. One of the leaders of the protest was later detained and tortured by CNL's management and security forces. Two other incidents occurred on 4 January 1999, when a helicopter being flown by Chevron pilots, while transporting Nigerian military and/or police, flew over the community of Opia and began firing on the villagers, which resulted in the killing of one person and the injuring of others. The helicopter later fired upon the community of Ikeynan, killing one and injuring others. '[T]hirty minutes later, CNL sea trucks containing CNL personnel and Nigerian military approached Opia and opened fire on the villagers, killing several people', and then the 'soldiers disembarked from the sea trucks and set fire to buildings and livestock, killing one person'.

The plaintiffs alleged that Chevron and CTOP were liable both directly and indirectly for the actions of CNL. Because there was no evidence of their direct participation in the commission of the acts, the court granted summary judgment in favour of the defendants with respect to the theory of direct liability. But the court found that the plaintiffs had alleged sufficient facts to survive the motion for summary judgment concerning indirect liability, meaning that 'plaintiffs have presented facts, which, if accepted by a jury, could warrant finding defendants liable for CNL's actions on an agency theory or based on aiding and abetting or ratification'.

The plaintiffs asserted several theories for finding liability, i.e., agency, alter-ego, aiding and abetting and ratification. Concerning the agency theory, the court found that the evidence presented by the plaintiffs 'reflects not that defendants made decisions during the attacks, but that there was an extraordinarily close relationship between the parents and the subsidiary prior to, during and after the attacks', including 'regular communications [between the defendants and CNL] regarding security measures before and after the attacks'. The defendants' close monitoring of CNL, the common management of the two business entities, and the 'more than usual degree of direction and control which a parent exercises over its subsidiary' led the court to conclude that the agency relationship could support a finding of liability. The same evidence might also support a finding of liability based on aiding and abetting. Finally, the defendants' media statements that attempted to 'cover up' CNL's actions might constitute acceptance and ratification, and thus, attach liability to the defendants. Liability based on the alter-ego theory failed because there was insufficient evidence to support such a finding. As such, the court denied the defendants' motion for summary judgment.

☛ *Van Tu* v. *Koster*, United States Court of Appeals, Tenth Circuit, 364 F.3d 1196, No. 02-4209, 16 April 2004

The plaintiffs, residents of the Republic of Vietnam, brought a claim against American soldiers who had served during the Vietnam War, alleging violations of the law of war, including murder and attacks against the civilian population arising from the My Lai Massacre of 16 March 1968. The plaintiffs, all survivors or relatives of victims of the incident, filed the complaint in the United States District Court for the District of Utah on 12 October 2000 against several soldiers, including Lt. William Calley.

The Court of Appeals affirmed the District Court's holding that the Alien Tort Claims Act (ATCA) has a ten year statute of limitations, even though the ATCA does not contain a statute-of-limitations within the statute itself. The District Court, as affirmed by the Court of Appeals, borrowed the ten year statute of limitations from the Torture Victim Protection Act. Under the government principle cited by both courts, a court can look to a closely analogous statute to determine the statute of limitations. The plaintiffs argued that there was no statute of limitations in Vietnam, but the Court of Appeals disregarded the laws of the state of Vietnam as being influential on domestic rulings on statutes of limitations.

The Court of Appeals also affirmed the District Court's dismissal of the claim based on 42 U.S.C. § 1983 because the 'activities of the United States military were not taken under the color of state law', and because the statute of limitations was four years, which began to run on the date of the My Lai Massacre.

☛ *Sosa* v. *Alvarez-Machain*, Supreme Court of the United States, 542 U.S. 692, Nos. 03-339, 03-485, 29 June 2004

Humberto Alvarez-Machain, a citizen of Mexico, brought an action under the Alien Tort Statute and the Federal Tort Claims Act against the United States, four agents of the United States Drug Enforcement Agency ('DEA'), and former Mexican policemen and civilians, for their alleged participation in his abduction from Mexico to stand trial in the United States for the 1985 torture and murder of a DEA agent in Mexico. A federal grand jury had indicted Alvarez for the crimes and the United States District Court for the Central District of California issued an arrest warrant in 1990.

After failed attempts to secure Mexico's cooperation, the DEA approved a plan to hire Mexican nationals, including Sosa, to capture Alvarez and bring him to the United States. The hired group then abducted Alvarez from his home and transported him to Texas aboard a private plane. He was then turned over to and arrested by United States federal agents. He was acquitted in 1992 of the charges and brought suit the following year alleging false arrest by the United States (under the Federal Tort Claims Act (FTCA)) and a violation of the law of nations by Sosa (under the Alien Tort Claims Act (ATCA)).

The District Court granted the government's motion to dismiss the FTCA claim but granted summary judgment to Alvarez based on the ATCA claim. On appeal, the United States Court of Appeals for the Ninth Circuit affirmed the ATCA judgment but reversed the dismissal of the FTCA claim.

The government and Sosa argued that the ATCA only granted jurisdiction to federal courts and did not create private causes of action, and thus, further congressional action was required. However, in an opinion written by Justice Souter, the Supreme Court concluded that the First Congress, which enacted the ATCA, not only granted jurisdiction but also created causes of a 'relatively modest set of actions alleging violations of the law of nations', as they were recognised at the time of enactment of the statute more than 200 years ago, most notably including Blackstone's three primary offences (acts of piracy, offences against ambassadors, and violations of safe conduct). The Supreme Court attempted to set standards and stated that 'courts should require any claim based on the present-day law of nations to rest on a norm of international character accepted by the civilized world and defined with a specificity comparable to the features of the 18th-century paradigms we have recognized', or more specifically, the alleged violation of the law of nations should be 'definable, universal and obligatory norms'. The court cautioned future courts against taking a liberal interpretation of those violations that are proper causes of action, and stated: '[j]udicial power should be exercised on the understanding that the door is still ajar subject to vigilant doorkeeping, and thus open to a narrow class of international norms today'.

Regarding Alvarez's claim, the Supreme Court concluded: '[i]t is enough to hold that a single illegal detention of less than a day, followed by the transfer of custody to lawful authorities and a prompt arraignment, violates no norm of customary international law so well defined as to support the creation of a federal remedy.' However, regarding the FTCA claim against the United States, the court found that an exception to waiver of sovereign immunity applied. The exception precludes claims 'arising in a foreign country'.[509] Because this claim originated in Mexico and the United States had not waived its sovereign immunity, the court dismissed this claim. The Court of Appeals had relied on the 'headquarters doctrine' to find that because the planning of the abduction had taken place in the United States, the District Court had jurisdiction. The Supreme Court held otherwise, stating that the 'FTCA's foreign country exception bars all claims based on any injury suffered in a foreign country, regardless of where the tortuous act or omission occurred'.

509. 28 U.S.C. § 2680(k).

☛ *Doe* v. *Rafael Saravia*, United States District Court for the Eastern District of California, 348 F.Supp.2d 1112, No. CIV-F-03-6249, 24 November 2004

Plaintiff brought suit against Alvaro Rafael Saravia, the former chief of security for an organiser of El Salvadoran paramilitary groups, for coordinating and planning the 1980 assassination of El Salvadoran Archbishop Oscar Romero, including the equipping, transporting, and paying of the assassin. The claims were brought under the Alien Tort Claims Act and the Torture Victim Protection Act. Saravia, residing in Modesto, California at the time the action commenced, failed to respond to the complaint and the District Court entered a default judgment and awarded $5 million in compensatory damages and $5 million in punitive damages.

The District Court determined that Saravia had acted under apparent authority and colour of law of the government of El Salvador, and found him liable as a direct participant, conspirator, accomplice and aider and abettor for the claim of extrajudicial killing under the Torture Victim Protection Act, and for the claims of extrajudicial killing and crimes against humanity under the Alien Tort Claims Act ('ATCA'). Significantly, the court held that the assassination constituted a crime against humanity actionable under the ATCA because it was part of a widespread and systematic attack against a civilian population by the ruling military regime. After examining case law from the United States and international tribunals, the District Court concluded that 'crimes against humanity constitute a specific, universal, and obligatory norm … actionable under the ATCA'. This decision marked the first time that anyone had been held responsible for the assassination of Archbishop Romero.

☛ *In re South African Apartheid Litigation*, United States District Court for the Southern District of New York, 346 F.Supp.2d 538, 29 November 2004

The plaintiffs suffered damages resulting from crimes committed during the South Africa apartheid regime and brought suit against numerous multinational corporations that had done business with and in South Africa. The complaint alleged that the corporations violated international law through their business dealings with the repressive regime and could be sued under the Alien Tort Claims Act (ATCA) in federal district court. The United States District Court for the Southern District of New York held that the corporations did not engage in state action and did not violate international law, which could support federal district court's jurisdiction under ATCA.

The complaint alleged, *inter alia*, forced labour, genocide, torture, unlawful detention, war crimes, racial discrimination and sexual assault. The plaintiffs asserted that the corporations had 'supplied resources, such as technology, money, and oil, to the South African government or to entities controlled by the government', which were subsequently used to support its repression – e.g., 'the military kept its machines in working order with oil supplied by Shell'; the 'government received needed capital and favorable terms of repayment of loans from defendant banks'; and the 'South African police shot demonstrators 'from cars driven by Daimler-Benz engines'.

The plaintiffs linked the defendant corporations to the violations of international law in three ways: a) the corporations were 'engaged in state action by acting under colour of law in perpetrating these international law violations'; b) the corporations 'aided and abetted the apartheid regime in the commission of these violations'; c) the corporations' 'business activities alone are sufficient to make out an international law violation'.

The District Court held that the plaintiffs had not asserted sufficient evidence to establish state action by acting under colour of law. The corporations 'benefitted from the unlawful state action of the apartheid government', but there were no other actions or relationships that might constitute state action. In not finding state action, the District Court refrained from deciding whether the apartheid regime had violated the law of nations, thus conferring jurisdiction over this case under the ATCA. Regarding the aiding and abetting allegation, the District Court stated that the plaintiffs failed to establish that 'aiding and abetting international law violations is itself an international law violation that is universally accepted as a legal obligation'. Under the District Court's reading of the ATCA, it does not provide for aider and abettor liability.

Finally, the District Court held that doing business with an apartheid regime is not a violation of the law of nations. In dictum, the court stated that it would be 'extremely cautious' in allowing such suits against politically and economically unpopular regimes 'especially since the consequences of such an approach could have significant, if not disastrous, effects on international commerce'. The court also noted that the United States Congress had even supported and encouraged business investment in South Africa during this time period. As a result, the District Court found that it had no jurisdiction over the ATCA claims and dismissed them. The court also dismissed the claim under the Torture Victim Protection Act because it did not find sufficient evidence to support the state action requirement of the statute.

Cases (Holocaust reparations)

☛ *Ungaro-Benages v. Dresdner Bank AG*, United States Court of Appeals, Eleventh Circuit, 379 F.3d 1227, No. 03-11880, 3 August 2004

The Plaintiff brought this claim against two German banks to recover assets that were allegedly stolen from her family's estate during the Nazi-era. The complaint alleged that the banks were involved in and profited from the process of 'Aryanisation', including the ousting of the plaintiffs' relatives from their board positions and the stealing of their stock.

The United States District Court for the Southern District of Florida granted summary judgment for the defendants, asserting the political question doctrine, international comity, statute of limitations and the failure to state an actionable claim. The plaintiffs appealed the dismissal.

The Court of Appeals concluded that the political question doctrine did not prohibit the action because it would not interfere with foreign policy or disrespect the Executive's powers in foreign affairs. However, the court decided to abstain based on international comity due to the strength of the United States' and Germany's interests in using the Foundation (see *In re Nazi Era Cases* below) and the adequacy of the Foundation as an appropriate forum to hear the case.

☛ *In re Nazi Era Cases Against German Defendants Litigation*, United States District Court for the District of New Jersey, 334 F.Supp.2d 690, 10 September 2004 (*Simon Rozenkier, Plaintiff* v. *Schering AG & Bayer AG, Defendants*. No. Civ. 03-3413(WGB))

The plaintiff, Simon Rozenkier, was a prisoner during World War II in the Auschwitz-Birkenau concentration camps where he endured Nazi-camp horrors, including numerous experiments on his genitalia. After his liberation from the camp he emigrated from Poland to the United States where he married in 1952 but was unable to have children. The cause of his infertility remained inconclusive until 1999 when he learned that it was the result of a Nazi 'medical experiment'. He filed a complaint in the Eastern District of New York (where it was ordered to be transferred to New Jersey and consolidated with other Nazi-era cases) against defendants Schering AG and Bayer AG, alleging that they violated international law by complying with the Nazi regime, specifically, by participating in secret experiments 'to evaluate the efficacy of "mass sterilization" drugs manufactured by Defendants'. Rozenkier sought 'full disclosure of the chemical substance used to sterilize him' in addition to compensatory and punitive damages. Defendants moved to dismiss the complaint, arguing that the issue was non-justiciable.

The court dismissed the complaint on the ground that the issue was a political question:

> 'On July 17, 2000 an agreement (the 'Joint Statement') was signed between interested federal governments including those of Germany and the United States, German corporations ('German Industry') and attorneys of various plaintiffs, who agreed to dismiss their lawsuits against German Industry in exchange for the creation of the German Foundation 'Remembrance, Responsibility and the Future' (the 'Foundation'). Concurrently, the Governments of Germany and United States signed an executive agreement (the 'Executive Agreement') that reflected the commitments of the two governments to the Foundation. The Foundation's funding was to be shared equally by the German Government and German Industry in the amount of DM 10 billion.'

The Joint Statement stated as its common objective that German Industry 'receive all embracing and enduring legal peace' stemming from involvement in Nazi-era atrocities, which was agreed to and reinforced by the United States in its Executive Agreement with the German Government. The Executive Agreement stated:

> '[T]he United States will timely file a Statement of Interest and accompanying formal foreign policy statement of the Secretary of State and Declaration of Deputy Treasury Secretary Stuart E. Eizenstat in all pending and future cases, regardless of whether the plaintiff(s) consent(s) to dismissal, in which the United States is notified that a claim has been asserted against German companies arising from the National Socialist era and World War II.'

Rozenkier applied for relief from the Foundation but also brought this action seeking additional relief. The court dismissed Rozenkier's claim and stated that a 'private individual tort action for damages against private corporate defendants falls squarely within the estimable bounds of litigation anticipated by the Executive Agreement', and as such, 'the Court is restrained from adjudicating the merits of the Complaint due to foreign policy considerations'. The court agreed with the United States' Statement of Interest that, in accordance with foreign policy interests, the Foundation is the desired and only appropriate mechanism to provide relief, not the courts. The court cited cases where the judicial branch has respected the Executive's position that claims related to World War II should be resolved through government-to-government negotiations, not through private action. The Executive Agreement further confirms this position. In sum: 'The history of foreign policy commitments devoted to the resolution of Holocaust-era claims, coupled with the relatively recent creation of the Foundation, renders such claims non-justiciable in this Court. Instead, the proper forum for restitution or compensation for Holocaust survivors and other victims of the Nazi era is the Foundation.'

☛ *In re Assicurazioni Generali S.P.A. Holocaust Insurance Litigation*, United States District Court for the Southern District of New York, 340 F.Supp.2d 494, No. MDL 1374, No. M21-89MBM, 14 October 2004

Plaintiffs sued the Italian insurer Assicurazioni Generali, S.P.A. for failing to pay claims that resulted from the Holocaust, namely, life insurance and property damage benefits. The District Court granted the motion to dismiss because 'the laws supporting litigation of plaintiffs' benefits claims are preempted by a federal Executive Branch policy favoring voluntary resolution of Holocaust-era insurance claims through ICHEIC'. The International Commission on Holocaust Era Insurance Claims is 'a private commission established by several European insurance companies (including Generali), certain nongovernmental Jewish organizations, the State of Israel, and domestic state insurance regulators, to resolve unpaid Holocaust-era insurance claims'.

Pending Cases (extraordinary rendition)
☛ *Arar* v. *Ashcroft*, United States District Court for the Eastern District of New York, No. 04-CV-0249-DGT-VVP

Maher Arar, a Canadian citizen, sued the United States Government for deporting him to Syria in late 2002 where he was allegedly tortured during his ten-month detention. The complaint alleges that the United States transported him to a country known for state-sponsored torture in an effort to allow methods of interrogation prohibited under United States law. Citing the Torture Victims Protection Act, he seeks financial compensation and an official declaration from the government that it acted illegally. Arar filed his lawsuit in the United States District Court for the Eastern District of New York, and named several officials, including Attorney General John Ashcroft, Secretary of Homeland Security Tom Ridge and FBI Director Robert Mueller, as well as other individuals that took part in the detention and interrogation in the United States.

Pending Cases (ATCA)
☛ *Sami Abbas Al Rawi, et al.* v. *Titan Corp.*, filed in the United States District Court for the Southern District of California on 9 June 2004

Former Iraqi prisoners held in US custody in Iraq sued two private security companies for allegedly abusing and torturing them during interrogation. The class-action lawsuit alleges that prospects of future government contracts enticed Titan Corporation of San Diego, California and CACI International of Arlington, Virginia to conspire with US officials to 'humiliate, torture and abuse persons' detained by American forces in Iraq. The complaint, filed in the United States District Court for the Southern District of California, also named as defendants CACI's subsidiary companies and three workers, and alleges violations of, *inter alia*, the Alien Tort Claims Act, Geneva Conventions, and US Constitution. The complaint alleges that the companies used torture as a business strategy, in that it was used to extract information from detainees to show their productiveness, in order to secure future government contracts.

Pending Cases (rape as a ground for asylum)
☛ *Garcia-Martinez* v. *Ashcroft*, United States Court of Appeals, Ninth Circuit, 371 F.3d 1066, No. 02-74068, filed on 14 June 2004

The United States Court of Appeals for the Ninth Circuit held that evidence of rape was a ground for asylum. The court did not dismiss it as merely a random or isolated criminal act, but rather as a form of political persecution.

Reina Izabel Garcia-Martinez was gang-raped by three soldiers in 1993 in her Guatemalan village. She later fled to the United States, fearing that they would return to her village. In 2001 an immigration judge denied her request for asylum, holding that she had 'failed to show ... that her attack had anything to do with ... her political opinion, her race, religion, her political affiliation or membership in a particular social group', which are the grounds on which asylum may be granted.

The government argued that the rape was an isolated incident and was unconnected to any political goal. But Garcia-Martinez argued that the soldiers continuously returned to the village and raped women because they believed the village supported the guerrillas at war with the government. The guerrillas had forcibly conscripted men, including her brother, into their ranks, and the soldiers sought reprisal for such support. Significantly, the court ruled that rape may be used as a political weapon, and therefore, it may constitute persecution that would support a finding in favour of a refugee seeking to stay within the United States.

JACOB RAMER

UZBEKISTAN

The Emblem

- The Law on use and protection of the red crescent and red cross emblems (No. 615-II). Promulgated on 29 April 2004, published on 22 May 2004 and entered into force on the same day[510]

ZAMBIA

Antipersonnel Mines

- The Prohibition of Anti-personnel Mines Act No. 16 of 2003. Assented to on 11 December 2003

'The Act implements the Convention on the Prohibition of the Use, Stockpiling, Production and Transfer of Antipersonnel Mines and on their Destruction (the 1997 Ottawa Convention).'[511]

510. *Supra* n. 70, pp. 694 at 700.
511. Ibid., at pp. 700-701.

DOCUMENTATION

CLASSIFICATION SCHEME

Part Zero	International humanitarian law in general
Part One	Sources and general principles
Part Two	Conflicts, armed forces and combatants
Part Three	Protected persons
Part Four	Methods, means and types of warfare
Part Five	Termination of armed conflicts
Part Six	International criminal law
Part Seven	Implementation of IHL
Part Eight	The law of neutrality
Part Nine	International organisations and international actions
Part Ten	Regional organisations and actions
Part Eleven	Arms control and disarmament
Part Twelve	Conflict prevention and resolution
Part Thirteen	Related fields

Yearbook of International Humanitarian Law
Volume 7 - 2004 - pp. 641-638 DOI 10.1017/S1389135904006415

0.	**Zero:**	**INTERNATIONAL HUMANITARIAN LAW IN GENERAL**
1.	**One:**	**SOURCES AND GENERAL PRINCIPLES**
1.1	I	SOURCES
1.11		A. Pre-Hague
1.12		B. Hague Law
1.13		C. Geneva Law
1.14		D. Post-1977 Developments
1.15		E. Customary Law
1.2	II	GENERAL PRINCIPLES
1.21		A. Martens Clause
1.22		B. Superfluous Injury and Unnecessary Suffering
1.23		C. Principle of Distinction
1.24		D. Prohibition of Indiscriminate Attacks
1.25		E. Principle of Proportionality
1.26		F. Principle of Precaution
1.27		G. Military Necessity
2.	**Two:**	**CONFLICTS, ARMED FORCES AND COMBATANTS**
2.1	I	TYPES OF CONFLICTS
2.11		A. International
2.12		B. Non-international
2.13		C. Other
2.2	II	TYPES OF ACTOR(S)
2.21		A. Armed Forces and Combatant Status
2.22		B. Non-State Actors
2.23		C. Specific Groups
2.231		1. Mercenaries
2.232		2. Spies
2.233		3. Other
3.	**Three:**	**PROTECTED PERSONS**
3.1	I	TYPES OF PROTECTED PERSONS
3.11		A. Wounded, Sick and Shipwrecked
3.12		B. Prisoners of War
3.13		C. Civilian Population
3.131		1. Civilians Generally
3.132		2. Women and Children
3.133		3. Medical and Religious Personnel
3.134		4. Journalists
3.135		5. Other
3.2	II	SPECIFIC SITUATIONS AND PROHIBITIONS
3.21		A. Internment
3.22		B. Occupation
3.23		C. Prohibition of Collective Punishment
3.24		D. Prohibition of Deportation and Transfer
3.25		E. Reprisals

4.	**Four:**	**METHODS, MEANS AND TYPES OF WARFARE**
4.1	I	METHODS AND MEANS OF WARFARE
4.11		A. Basic Rules
4.111		1. Existing Weapons
4.1111		a. Conventional Weapons
4.11111		i. Mines
4.11112		ii. Small weapons and others
4.1112		b. Weapons of Mass Destruction
4.11121		i. Nuclear weapons
4.11122		ii. Chemical and biological weapons
4.112		2. New Weapons
4.113		3. Prohibition of Perfidy
4.114		4. Emblems and Safeguards of Persons hors de combat
4.12		B. Direct and Indiscriminate Attacks
4.13		C. Precautionary Measures
4.14		D. Protection of Civilian and Other Specified Objects
4.141		1. Specifically Protected Objects
4.142		2. Cultural Property and Places of Worship
4.143		3. Works and Installations Containing Dangerous Forces
4.144		4. The Natural Environment
4.145		5. Localities and Zones
4.146		6. Civil Defence
4.15		E. Medical Assistance
4.16		F. Humanitarian Assistance Operations
4.2	II	SPECIFIC TYPES OF WARFARE
4.21		A. Land Warfare
4.22		B. Air and Missile Warfare
4.23		C. Naval Warfare
5.	**Five:**	**TERMINATION OF ARMED CONFLICTS**
5.1	I	CEASEFIRE, ARMISTICES AND PEACE AGREEMENTS
5.2	II	WAR CRIMES COMMISSIONS
5.3	III	AMNESTIES, TRUTH AND RECONCILIATION COMMISSIONS
5.4	IV	REPARATIONS/COMPENSATION
5.5	V	MILITARY COMMISSIONS AND TRIBUNALS
6.	**Six:**	**INTERNATIONAL CRIMINAL LAW**
6.1	I	THE CRIMES
6.11		A. War Crimes
6.12		B. Genocide
6.13		C. Crimes Against Humanity
6.14		D. Aggression
6.15		E. Terrorism
6.16		F. Other
6.2	II	GENERAL PRINCIPLES, INCLUDING DEFENCES
6.21		A. Nullum Crimen Sine Lege and Nulla Poena Sine Lege
6.22		B. Individual Criminal Responsibility

6.23		C. Superior/Command Responsibility
6.24		D. Irrelevance of Official Capacity
6.25		E. Non-Retroactivity of Criminal Law
6.26		F. Non-Applicability of Statutory Limitations
6.27		G. Grounds for Excluding Criminal Responsibility
6.3	III	REPRESSION OF BREACHES
6.31		A. International and Internationalised Courts
6.311		1. Nuremberg and Tokyo
6.312		2. International Criminal Tribunal for the former Yugoslavia
6.313		3. International Criminal Tribunal for Rwanda
6.314		4. International Criminal Court
6.315		5. East Timor's Special Panels for Serious Crimes
6.316		6. Kosovo's Internationalised Courts
6.317		7. Special Court for Sierra Leone
6.318		8. Extraordinary Chambers for Cambodia
6.319		9. Iraqi Special Tribunal
6.32		B. National Courts
7.	**Seven:**	**IMPLEMENTATION OF IHL**
7.1	I	NATIONAL POLICY STATEMENTS
7.2	II	NATIONAL LAW
7.21		A. Legislation to Implement IHL Treaties
7.22		B. Legislation to Implement Obligations vis-à-vis the International Criminal Court and International Criminal Tribunals
7.23		C. Military Manuals/National Instructions/Codes of Conduct
7.24		D. Role of Defence Force Legal Advisers
7.3	III	PROTECTING POWERS
7.4	IV	ICRC
7.5	V	FACT-FINDING, INCLUDING THE INTERNATIONAL FACT-FINDING COMMISSION
7.6	VI	DISSEMINATION
8.	**Eight:**	**THE LAW OF NEUTRALITY**
8.1	I	THE RIGHTS AND DUTIES OF NATIONALS
8.2	II	WAR ON LAND
8.3	III	NAVAL WARFARE
8.4	IV	AERIAL WARFARE
9.	**Nine:**	**INTERNATIONAL ORGANISATIONS AND INTERNATIONAL ACTIONS**
9.1	I	INTERNATIONAL ORGANISATIONS
9.11		A. United Nations Organisation
9.12		B. Other
9.2	II	INTERNATIONAL ACTIONS
9.21		A. Peacekeeping
9.22		B. Peace Enforcement and Peace Building
9.23		C. Fact-Finding and Monitoring

9.24		D. Humanitarian and Other Interventions
9.25		E. Sanctions
10.	**Ten:**	**REGIONAL ORGANISATIONS AND ACTIONS**
10.1	I	EUROPEAN
10.2	II	AMERICAN
10.3	III	ASIAN
10.4	IV	AFRICAN
11.	**Eleven:**	**ARMS CONTROL AND DISARMAMENT**
11.1	I	CONVENTIONAL WEAPONS
11.11		A. Mines
11.12		B. Small Weapons and Others
11.13		C. Production and Transfer
11.2	II	WEAPONS OF MASS DESTRUCTION
11.21		A. Nuclear Weapons
11.22		B. Chemical and Biological Weapons
11.23		C. New Types
12.	**Twelve:**	**CONFLICT PREVENTION AND RESOLUTION**
12.1	I	CONFLICT PREVENTION
12.2	II	CONFLICT RESOLUTION
12.3	III	THE PEACE MOVEMENT
13.	**Thirteen:**	**RELATED FIELDS**
13.1	I	JUS AD BELLUM
13.2	II	THE LAW RELATING TO TERRORISM AND COUNTER-TERRORISM
13.3	III	MILITARY LAW
13.4	IV	HUMAN RIGHTS LAW
13.5	V	REFUGEE LAW

DOCUMENTS 2003-2004[1]

NOTE: Many international and national documents related to international humanitarian law are available on the Internet through an online access to the ICRC IHL database (ICRC website: http://www.icrc.org). This database now contains almost 100 treaties and texts on the conduct of hostilities and the protection of victims of war (dating from 1856 to the present); the commentaries on the four Geneva Conventions and their Additional Protocols; an up-to-date list of signatures, ratifications, accessions or successions to IHL treaties; and, the full text of reservations. Constantly updated, this data is also regularly replicated on a CD-ROM that can be obtained from the ICRC (Public Information Division, 19, av. de la Paix, CH-1202 GENEVA; e-mail: webmaster.gva@icrc.org; Fax: ++ 41 22 733 20 57; CHF 49.- or USD 39,-). National implementing legislation (Geneva Conventions Acts, extracts from Penal Codes, laws related to the protection of the emblem, laws on cooperation with the international tribunals, etc.) and jurisprudence are also available for an increasing number of countries.

1. The Documentation Section has been prepared by Avril McDonald, Managing Editor of the YIHL. This year, a greatly reduced section is provided, solely concerning developments noted in the US report in the Correspondents' Reports Section, in preparation for the section's abolition, effective

Yearbook of International Humanitarian Law
Volume 7 - 2004 - pp. 647-660

DOI 10.1017/S1389135904006476

3.21 Internment

☛ USA: The Inspector General, US Army, 'Detainee Operations Inspection', report dated 21 July 2004, Annex E, p. E-106 (excerpts)

(2) Standard: Training on standard of treatment for detainees in Operation Enduring Freedom (OEF): Guidance was provided stating that members of the Taliban militia and members of Al Qaida under the control of U.S. Forces would be treated humanely and, to the extent appropriate and consistent with military necessity, in a manner consistent with the principles of the Geneva Conventions of 1949. The DAIG [Department of the Army Inspector General] has therefore used the provisions of the Geneva Conventions as a benchmark against which to measure the treatment provided to detainees by U.S. Forces to determine if detainees were treated humanely and if the corresponding training was consistent with this obligation. The use of these standards as benchmarks does not state or imply a position for the United States or U.S. Army on the legal status of its operations in OEF.
Chairman, Joint Chiefs of Staff (CJCS) Message dated 2119 332 JAN 02, provides the determination regarding the humane treatment of Al Qaida and Taliban detainees. Convention Relative to the Treatment of Prisoners of War of August 12, 1949 (GPW) is the international treaty that governs the treatment of prisoners of war), and Geneva Convention Relative to the Protection of Civilian Persons in Time of War (GC), August 12, 1949, is the international treaty that governs the treatment of civilian persons in time of war.
As the guidance did not define 'humane treatment' but did state that the U.S. would treat members of the Taliban militia and Al Qaida in a manner consistent with the Geneva Conventions, the DAIG determined that it would use Common Article 3 of the GCs as its floor measure of humane treatment and corresponding training, but would also include provisions of the Geneva Convention on the Treatment of Prisoners of War (GPW) and Geneva Convention Relative to the Protection of Civilian Persons in Time of War (GC) as other relevant indicia of 'humane treatment'. The use of this standard does not state or imply a position for the United States or U.S. Army on the legal status of its operations in OEF.

Standard of treatment for detainees in Operation Iraqi Freedom (OIF): OIF was an international armed conflict and therefore the provisions of the Geneva Conventions applied.

The minimum treatment provided by Common Article 3 of the Geneva Conventions is: (1) No adverse distinction based upon race, religion, sex, etc.; (2) No violence to life or person; (3) No taking hostages; (4) No degrading treatment; (5) No passing of sentences in absence of fair trial, and; (6) The wounded and sick must be cared for.

The specific language in the CJCS Message for OEF and the GP W/GC and H.IV follows:

CJCS Message dated 2119332 JAN 02, 'Paragraph 3. The combatant commanders shall, in detaining Al Qaida and Taliban individuals under the control of the Department of Defense, treat them humanely and, to the extent appropriate and consistent with military necessity, in a manner consistent with the principles of the Geneva Conventions of 1949.'

☛ USA: Report of Independent Panel to Review Department of Defense Detention Operations, August 2004, pp.

Laws of war/Geneva Conventions

American military culture, training, and operations are steeped in a long held commitment to the tenets of military and international law as traditionally codified by the world community. Department of Defense Directive 5100.77, DoD Law of War Program, describes the law of war as:

> That part of international law that regulates the conduct of armed hostilities. It is often called the law of armed conflict. The law of war encompasses all international law for the conduct of hostilities binding on the United States or its individual citizens, including treaties and international agreements to which the United States is a party, and applicable customary international law.

The law of war includes, among other agreements, the Geneva Conventions of 1949. The Geneva Conventions set forth the rights and obligations which govern the treatment of civilians and combatants during periods of armed conflict. Specifically, Geneva Convention III addresses the treatment of prisoners of war; and Geneva Convention IV addresses the treatment of civilians.

Chairman of the Joint Chiefs of Staff Instruction 5810.01 B, Implementation of the DoD Law of War Program, reiterates U.S. policy concerning the law of war: 'The Armed Forces of the United States will comply with the law of war during all armed conflicts, however such conflicts are characterized …'

The United States became engaged in two distinct conflicts, Operation Enduring Freedom (OEF) in Afghanistan and Operation Iraqi Freedom (OIF) in Iraq. As a result of a Presidential determination, the Geneva Conventions did not apply to Al Qaida and Taliban combatants. Nevertheless, these traditional standards were put into effect for OIF and remain in effect at this writing. Some would argue this is a departure from the traditional view of the law of war as espoused by the ICRC and others in the international community.

Operation Enduring Freedom

On October 17, 2001, pursuant to the commencement of combat operations in OEF, the Commander, CENTCOM, issued an order instructing the Geneva Conventions were to be applied to all captured individuals in accordance with their traditional interpretation. Belligerents would be screened to determine whether or not they were entitled to prisoner of war status. If an individual was entitled to prisoner of war status, the protections of Geneva Convention III would apply. If armed forces personnel were in doubt as to a detained individual's status, Geneva Convention III rights would be accorded to the detainee until a Geneva Convention III Article 5 tribunal made a definitive status determination. If the individual was found not to be entitled to Geneva Convention III protections, he or she might be detained and processed under U.S. criminal code, a procedure consistent with Geneva Convention IV.

A policy debate concerning the application of treaties and laws to al Qaeda and Taliban detainees then began taking shape. The Department of Justice Office of Legal Counsel (OLC) provided opinions to Counsel to the President and Department of Defense General Counsel concluding the Geneva Conventions did not protect members of the al Qaeda organization, and the President could decide that Geneva Conventions did not protect Taliban militia. Counsel to the President and the Attorney General so advised the President.

On February 7, 2002 the President issued a memorandum stating, in part,

> '… the war against terrorism ushers in a new paradigm … Our nation recognizes that this new paradigm ushered in not by us, but by terrorists requires new thinking in the law of war, but thinking that should nevertheless be consistent with the principles of Geneva.'

Upon this premise, the President determined the Geneva Conventions did not apply to the U.S. conflict with al Qaeda, and that Taliban detainees did not qualify for prisoner of war status. Removed from the protections of the Geneva Conventions, al Qaeda and Taliban detainees have been classified variously as 'unlawful combatants', 'enemy combatants', and 'unprivileged belligerents'.

The enemy in the Global War on Terror is one neither the United States nor the community of nations has ever before engaged on such an extensive scale. These far-reaching, well resourced, organized, and trained terrorists are attempting to achieve their own ends. Such terrorists are not of a nation state such as those who are party to the agreements which comprise the law of war. Neither do they conform their actions to the letter or spirit of the law of war.

The Panel accepts the proposition that these terrorists are not combatants entitled to the protections of Geneva Convention III. Furthermore, the Panel accepts the conclusion the Geneva Convention IV and the provisions of domestic criminal law are not sufficiently robust and adequate to provide for the appropriate detention of captured terrorists.

The Panel notes the President qualified his determination, directing that United States policy would be 'consistent with the principles of Geneva'. Among other things, the Geneva Conventions adhere to a standard calling for a delineation of rights for all persons, and humane treatment for all persons. They suggest that no person is 'outlaw', that is, outside the laws of some legal entity.

The Panel finds the details of the current policy vague and lacking. Justice Sandra Day O'Connnor, writing for the majority in *Hamdi v Rumsfeld,* June 28, 2004 points out 'the Government has never provided any court with the full criteria that it uses in classifying individuals as [enemy combatants]'. Justice O'Connor cites several authorities to support the proposition that detention 'is a clearly established principle of the law of war', but also states there is no precept of law, domestic or international, which would permit the indefinite detention of any combatant.

As a matter of logic, there should be a category of persons who do not comply with the specified conditions and thus fall outside the category of persons entitled to EPW status.

Although there is not a particular label for this category in law of war conventions, the concept of 'unlawful combatant' or 'unprivileged belligerent' is a part of the law of war.

Operation Iraqi Freedom

Operation Iraqi Freedom is wholly different from Operation Enduring Freedom. It is an operation that clearly falls within the boundaries of the Geneva Conventions and the traditional law of war. From the very beginning of the campaign, none of the senior leadership or command considered any possibility other than that the Geneva Conventions applied.

The message in the field, or the assumptions made in the field, at times lost sight of this underpinning. Personnel familiar with the law of war determinations for OEF in Afghanistan tended to factor those determinations into their decision-making for military actions in Iraq. Law of war policy and decisions germane to OEF migrated, often quite innocently, into decision matrices for OIF. We noted earlier the migration of interrogation techniques from Afghanistan to Iraq. Those interrogation techniques were authorized only for OEF. More important, their authorization in Afghanistan and Guantanamo was possible only because the President had determined that individuals subjected to these interrogation techniques fell outside the strict protections of the Geneva Conventions.

One of the more telling examples of this migration centers around CJTF-7's [Combined Joint Task Force 7 – the U.S. military command in Iraq] determination that some of the detainees held in Iraq were to be categorized as unlawful combatants. 'Unlawful combatants' was a category set out in the President's February 7, 2002 memorandum. Despite lacking specific authorization to operate beyond the confines of the Geneva Conventions, CJTF 7 nonetheless determined it was within their command discretion to classify, as unlawful combatants, individuals captured during OIF. CJTF-7 concluded it had individuals in custody who met the criteria for unlawful combatants set out by the President and extended it in Iraq to those who were not protected as combatants under the Geneva Conventions, based on the OLC opinions. While CJTF-7's reasoning is understandable in respect to unlawful combatants, nonetheless, they understood there was no authorization to suspend application of the Geneva Conventions, in letter and spirit, to all military actions of Operation Iraqi Freedom. In addition, CJTF-7 had no means of discriminating detainees among the various categories of those protected under the Geneva Conventions and those unlawful combatants who were not.

The Role of the International Committee of the Red Cross

Since December 2001, the International Committee of the Red Cross (ICRC) has visited U. S. detention operations in Guantanamo, Iraq, and Afghanistan numerous times. Various ICRC inspection teams have delivered working papers and reports of findings to U.S. military leaders at different levels. While the ICRC has acknowledged U.S. attempts to improve the conditions of detainees, major differences over detainee status as well as application of specific provisions of Geneva Conventions III and IV remain. If we were to follow the ICRC's interpretations, interrogation operations would not be allowed. This would deprive the U.S. of an indispensable source of intelligence in the war on terrorism.

The ICRC is an independent agency whose activities include observing and reporting on conditions in wartime detention camps and facilities. During visits, it attempts to register all prisoners, inspect facilities, and conduct private interviews with detainees to discuss any problems concerning detainee treatment or conditions; it also provides a means for detainees to contact their families. While the ICRC has no enforcing authority and its reports are supposedly confidential, any public revelation regarding standards of detainee treatment can have a substantial effect on international opinion.

The ICRC seeks to handle problems at the lowest level possible. When a team conducts an inspection, it provides a briefing, and sometimes a report, to the local commander. Discrepancies and issues are presented to the detaining authorities, and follow-up visits are made to monitor compliance with recommendations. The commander may or may not implement the recommendations based on either resource constraint or his interpretation of applicable law. These constraints can make complete implementation of ICRC recommendations either difficult or inappropriate. If recommendations are not implemented, the ICRC may address the issue with higher authorities. The ICRC does not expect to receive, nor does the DoD have a policy of providing, a written response to ICRC reports. However, DoD elements do attempt to implement as many of the recommendations as practicable, given security and resource constraints.

One important difference in approach between the U.S. and the ICRC is the interpretation of the legal status of terrorists. According to a Panel interview with CJTF-7 legal counsel, the ICRC sent a report to the State Department and the Coalition Provisional Authority in February 2003 citing lack of compliance with Protocol 1. But the U.S. has specifically rejected Protocol 1 stating that certain elements in the protocol, that provide legal protection for terrorists, make it plainly unacceptable. Still the U.S. has worked to preserve the positive elements of Protocol I. In 1985, the Secretary of Defense noted that 'certain provisions of Protocol 1 reflect customary international law, and others appear to be positive new developments. We therefore intend to work with our allies and others to develop a common understanding or declaration of principles incorporating these positive aspects, with the intention they shall, in time, win recognition as customary international law'. In 1986 the ICRC acknowledged that it and the U.S. government had "agreed to disagree" on the applicability of Protocol 1. Nevertheless, the ICRC continues to presume the United States should adhere to this standard under the guise of customary international law.

This would grant legal protections to terrorists equivalent to the protections accorded to prisoners of war as required by the Geneva Conventions of 1949 despite the fact terrorists do not wear uniforms and are otherwise indistinguishable from noncombatants. To do so would undermine the prohibition on terrorists blending in with the civilian population, a situation which makes it impossible to attack terrorists without placing noncombatants at risk. For this and other reasons, the U.S. has specifically rejected this additional protocol.

The ICRC also considers the U.S. policy of categorizing some detainees as 'unlawful combatants' to be a violation of their interpretation of international humanitarian law. It contends that Geneva Conventions III and IV, which the U.S. has ratified, allow for only two categories of detainees: (1) civilian detainees who must be charged with a crime and tried and (2) enemy combatants who must be released at the cessation of hostilities. In the ICRC's view, the category of 'unlawful combatant' deprives the detainees of certain human rights. It argues that lack of information regarding the reasons for detention and the conditions for release are major sources of stress for detainees.

However, the 1949 Geneva Conventions specify conditions to qualify for protected status. By logic, then, if detainees do not meet the specific requirements of privileged status, there clearly must be a category for those lacking in such privileges. The ICRC does not acknowledge such a category of 'unprivileged belligerents', and argues that it is not consistent with its interpretation of the Geneva Conventions.

Regarding the application of current international humanitarian law, including Geneva Conventions III and IV, the ICRC has three concerns: (1) gaining access to and ascertaining the status of all detainees in U.S. custody; (2) its belief that linking detention with interrogations should not be allowed which follows from its refusal to recognize the category of unprivileged combatants and (3) they also worry about losing their effectiveness.

Although the ICRC found U.S. forces generally cooperative, it has cited occasions when the forces did not grant adequate access to detainees, both in Iraq and Afghanistan. Of particular concern to the ICRC, however, has been the existence of 'ghost detainees', detainees who were kept from ICRC inspectors. While the Panel has not been able to ascertain the number of ghost detainees in the overall detainee population, several investigations cite their existence. Both the Taguba and Jones/Fay reports cite instances of ghost detainees at Abu Ghraib. Secretary Rumsfeld publicly declared he directed one detainee be held secretly at the request of the Director of Central Intelligence.

On balance, the Panel concludes there is value in the relationship the Department of Defense historically has had with the ICRC. The ICRC should serve as an early warning indicator of possible abuse. Commanders should be alert to ICRC observations in their reports and take corrective actions as appropriate. The Panel also believes the ICRC, no less than the Defense Department, needs to adapt itself to the new realities of conflict, which are far different from the Western European environment from which the ICRC's interpretation of Geneva Conventions was drawn. The Department of Defense has established an office of detainee affairs and should continue to reshape its operational relationship with the ICRC.

☛ USA: AR 15-6 Investigation of the Abu Ghraib Detention Facility and 205th Military Intelligence Brigade (U), Major General George R. Fay Investigating Officer, (Excerpts)

P. 9 - (1) (U) Physical and sexual abuses of detainees at Abu Ghraib were by far the most serious. The abuses spanned from direct physical assault, such as delivering head blows rendering detainees unconscious, to sexual posing and forced participation in group masturbation. At the extremes were the death of a detainee in OGA [Other U.S. Government Agency] custody, an alleged rape committed by a US translator and observed by a female Soldier, and the alleged sexual assault of a female detainee. These abuses are, without question, criminal. They were perpetrated or witnessed by individuals or small groups. Such abuse cannot be directly tied to a systemic US approach to torture or approved treatment of detainees. The MPs being prosecuted claim their actions came at the direction of MI. Although self-serving, these claims do have some basis in fact. The environment created at Abu Ghraib contributed to the occurrence of such abuse and the fact that it remained undiscovered by higher authority for a long period of time. What started as nakedness and humiliation, stress and physical training (exercise), carried over into sexual and physical assaults by a small group of morally corrupt and unsupervised Soldiers and civilians.

P. 12 - [2] (U) Civilian Internee. Using Geneva Convention IV (GC IV), Article 78, as further defined by AR [Army Regulation] 190-8, a 'Civilian Internee' is someone who is interned during armed conflict or occupation for security reasons or for protection or because he has committed an offense against the detaining power. ... The overwhelming evidence in this investigation shows that all 'detainees' at Abu Ghraib were civilian internees. Within the confinement facility, however, there were further sub-classifications that were used, to include criminal detainee, security internee, and MI Hold.

[a] (U) Criminal Detainee. A person detained because he/she is reasonably suspected of having committed a crime against Iraqi Nationals or Iraqi property or a crime not related to the coalition force mission (Reference Annex H, Appendix 1, FRAGO 749 to CJTF-7OPORD 03-036).

[b] (U) Security Internee. Civilians interned during conflict or occupation for their own protection or because they pose a threat to the security of coalition forces, or its mission, or are of intelligence value. This includes persons detained for committing offenses (including attempts) against coalition forces (or previous coalition forces), members of the Provisional Government, Non-Government Organizations, state infrastructure, or any person accused of committing war crimes or crimes against humanity. Security internees are a subset of civilian internees ....

[c] (U) MI Hold. A directive to hold and not release a detainee/internee in the custody of the Coalition Forces, issued by a member or agent of a US Military Intelligence Organization ....

[d] (U) Most detainees located within Abu Ghraib, ... were Civilian Internees and therefore, entitled to protections under GC IV. In addition to applicable international laws, ARs, and the FMs [Army Field Manuals] on Intelligence Interrogations further clarify US Policy regarding the protections afforded Civilian Internees.

(f) (U) Geneva Convention Relative to the Protection of Civilians in Time of War.

GC IV provides protections for civilians in time of war. The US is bound by the Geneva Conventions; therefore, any individual acting on behalf of the US during an armed conflict is also bound by Geneva Conventions. This includes not only members of the armed forces, but also civilians who accompany or work with the US Armed Forces.

...

P. 68 - 5. Summary of Abuses at Abu Ghraib

a. (U) Several types of detainee abuse were identified in this investigation: physical and sexual abuse; improper use of military working dogs; humiliating and degrading treatments; and improper use of isolation.

(1) (U) Physical Abuse. Several Soldiers reported that they witnessed physical abuse of detainees. Some examples include slapping, kicking, twisting the hands of a detainee who was hand-cuffed to cause pain, throwing balls at restrained internees, placing gloved hand over the nose and mouth of an internee to restrict breathing, 'poking' at an internee's in-

jured leg, and forcing an internee to stand while handcuffed in such a way as to dislocate his shoulder. These actions are clearly in violation of applicable laws and regulations.
(2) (U) Use of Dogs. The use of military working dogs in a confinement facility can be effective and permissible under AR 190-12 as a means of controlling the internee population. When dogs are used to threaten and terrify detainees, there is a clear violation of applicable laws and regulations. One such impermissible practice was an alleged contest between the two Army dog handlers to see who could make the internees urinate or defecate in the presence of the dogs. An incident of clearly abusive use of the dogs occurred when a dog was allowed in the cell of two male juveniles and allowed to go 'nuts'. Both juveniles were screaming and crying with the youngest and smallest trying to hide behind the other juvenile.
(3) (U) Humiliating and Degrading Treatments. Actions that are intended to degrade or humiliate a detainee are prohibited by GC IV, Army policy and the UCMJ. The following are examples of such behavior that occurred at Abu Ghraib, which violate applicable laws and regulations.
(4) (U) Nakedness. Numerous statements, as well as the ICRC report, discuss the seemingly common practice of keeping detainees in a state of undress. A number of statements indicate that clothing was taken away as a punishment for either not cooperating with interrogators or with MPs. In addition, male internees were naked in the presence of female Soldiers. Many of the Soldiers who witnessed the nakedness were told that this was an accepted practice. Under the circumstances, however, the nakedness was clearly degrading and humiliating.
(5) (U) Photographs. A multitude of photographs show detainees in various states of undress, often in degrading positions.
P. 69 - (6) (U) Simulated Sexual Positions. A number of Soldiers describe incidents where detainees were placed in simulated sexual positions with other internees. Many of these incidents were also photographed.
(7) (U) Improper Use of Isolation. There are some legitimate purposes for the segregation (or isolation) of detainees, specifically to prevent them from sharing interrogation tactics with other detainees or other sensitive information. Article 5 of Geneva Convention IV supports this position by stating that certain individuals can lose their rights of communication, but only when absolute military security requires. The use of isolation at Abu Ghraib was often done as punishment, either for a disciplinary infraction or for failure to cooperate with an interrogation. These are improper uses of isolation and depending on the circumstances amounted to violation of applicable laws and regulations. Isolation could properly be a sanction for a disciplinary infraction if applied through the proper process set out in AR 190-8 and the Geneva Conventions.
(8) (U) Failure to Safeguard Detainees. The Geneva Conventions and Army Regulations require that detainees be 'protected against all acts of violence and threats thereof and against insults and public curiosity'. Geneva Convention IV, Article 27 and AR 190-8, paragraph 5-1(a)(2). The duty to protect imposes an obligation on an individual who witnesses an abusive act to intervene and stop the abuse. Failure to do so may be a violation of applicable laws and regulations.
(9) (U) Failure to Report Detainee Abuse. The duty to report detainee abuse is closely tied to the duty to protect. The failure to report an abusive incident could result in additional abuse. Soldiers who witness these offenses have an obligation to report the violations under the provision of Article 92, UCMJ. Soldiers who are informed of such abuses also have a duty to report violations. Depending on their position and their assigned duties, the failure

to report detainee abuse could support a charge of dereliction of duty, a violation of the UCMJ. Civilian contractors employed as interrogators and translators would also have a duty to report such offenses as they are also bound by the Geneva Conventions and are charged with protecting the internees.

...

P. 109 - 6. (U) Findings and Recommendations.

a. (U) Major Finding: From 25 July 2003 to 6 February 2004, twenty-seven (27) 205 MI BDE personnel allegedly:
— Requested, encouraged, condoned, or solicited MP personnel to abuse detainees or;
— Participated in detainee abuse or;
— Violated established interrogation procedures and applicable laws and regulations as preparation for interrogation operations at Abu Ghraib.

(U) Explanation: Some MI personnel encouraged, condoned, participated in, or ignored abuse. In a few instances, MI personnel acted alone in abusing detainees. MI abuse and MI solicitation of MP abuse included the use of isolation with sensory deprivation ('the Hole'), removal of clothing and humiliation, the use of dogs to "fear up" detainees, and on one occasion, the condoned twisting of a detainee's cuffed wrists and the smothering of this detainee with a cupped hand in MI's presence. Some MI personnel violated established interrogation practices, regulations, and conventions which resulted in the abuse of detainees. While Interrogation and Counter-Resistance Policies (ICRP) were poorly defined and changed several times, in most cases of detainee abuse the MI personnel involved knew or should have known what they were doing was outside the bounds of their authority. Ineffective leadership at the JIDC failed to detect violations and discipline those responsible. Likewise, leaders failed to provide adequate training to ensure Soldiers understood the rules and complied.
(U) Recommendation: The Army needs to re-emphasize Soldier and leader responsibilities in interrogation and detention operations and retrain them to perform in accordance with law, regulations, and Army values and to live up to the responsibilities of their rank and position. Leaders must also provide adequate training to ensure Soldiers understand their authorities. The Army must ensure that future interrogation policies are simple, direct and include safeguards against abuse. Organizations such as the JIDC must possess a functioning chain of command capable of directing interrogation operations.

b. (U) Other Findings and Recommendations.

....

P. 111 - (4) (U) Finding: Selecting Abu Ghraib as a detention facility placed soldiers and detainees at an unnecessary force protection risk.
(U) Explanation: Failure adequately to protect and house detainees is a violation of the Third and Fourth Geneva Conventions and AR 190-8. Therefore, the selection of Abu Ghraib as a detention facility was inappropriate because of its inherent indefensibility and poor condition. The selection of Abu Ghraib as a detention center was dictated by the Coalition Provisional Authority officials despite concerns that the Iraqi people would look ne-

gatively on Americans interning detainees in a facility associated with torture. Abu Ghraib was in poor physical condition with buildings and sections of the perimeter wall having been destroyed, resulting in completely inadequate living conditions. Force protection must be a major consideration in selecting any facility as a detention facility. Abu Ghraib was located in the middle of the Sunni Triangle, an area known to be very hostile to coalition forces. Further, being surrounded by civilian housing and open fields and encircled by a network of roads and highways, its defense presented formidable force protection challenges. Even though the force protection posture at Abu Ghraib was compromised from the start due to its location and poor condition, coalition personnel still had a duty and responsibility to undertake appropriate defensive measures. However, the poor security posture at Abu Ghraib resulted in the deaths and wounding of both coalition forces and detainees.

(U) Recommendations:

— Detention centers must be established in accordance with AR 190-8 to ensure safety and compliance with the Geneva Conventions. (DoD/DA/CJTF-7).
— As a matter of policy, force protection concerns must be applicable to any detention facility and all detention operations. (DoD/DA/CJTF-7)
— Protect detainees in accordance with Geneva Convention IV by providing adequate force protection. (DoD/DA/CJTF-7)

...

Pp. 114-115 - (12) (U) Finding: Interrogator training in the Laws of Land Warfare and the Geneva Conventions is ineffective.

(U) Explanation: The US Army Intelligence Center and follow on unit training provided interrogators with what appears to be adequate curriculum, practical exercises and man-hours in Law of Land Warfare and Geneva Conventions training. Soldiers at Abu Ghraib, however, remained uncertain about what interrogation procedures were authorized and what proper reporting procedures were required. This indicates that Initial Entry Training for interrogators was not sufficient or was not reinforced properly by additional unit training or leadership.

(U) Recommendation: More training emphasis needs to be placed on Soldier and leader responsibilities concerning the identification and reporting of detainee abuse incidents or concerns up through the chain of command, or to other offices such as CID, IG or SJA. This training should not just address the rules, but address case studies from recent and past detainee and interrogation operations to address likely issues interrogators and their supervisors will encounter. Soldiers and leaders need to be taught to integrate Army values and ethical decision- making to deal with interrogation issues that are not clearly prohibited or allowed. Furthermore, it should be stressed that methods employed by US Army interrogators will represent US values.

P. 115 - (13) (U) Finding: MI, MP, and Medical Corps personnel observed and failed to report instances of Abuse at Abu Ghraib. Likewise, several reports indicated that capturing units did not always treat detainees IAW the Geneva Convention.

(U) Recommendation: DoD should improve training provided to all personnel in
Geneva Conventions, detainee operations, and the responsibilities of reporting detainee abuse.

P. 118 - (22) (U) Finding: Other Government Agency (OGA) interrogation practices led to a loss of accountability at Abu Ghraib.

(U) Explanation: While the FBI, JTF-121, Criminal Investigative Task Force, Iraq Survey Group, and the CIA were all present at Abu Ghraib, the acronym 'Other Government Agency' referred almost exclusively to the CIA. Lack of military control over OGA interrogator actions or lack of systemic accountability for detainees plagued detainee operations in Abu Ghraib almost from the start. Army allowed CIA to house 'Ghost Detainees' who were unidentified and unaccounted for in Abu Ghraib. This procedure created confusion and uncertainty concerning their classification and subsequent DoD reporting requirements under the Geneva Conventions. Additionally, the treatment and interrogation of OGA detainees occurred under different practices and procedures which were absent any DoD visibility, control, or oversight. This separate grouping of OGA detainees added to the confusion over proper treatment of detainees and created a perception that OGA techniques and practices were suitable and authorized for DoD operations. No memorandum of understanding on detainee accountability or interrogation practices between the CIA and CJTF-7 was created.
(U) Recommendation: DoD must enforce adherence by OGA with established DoD practices and procedures while conducting detainee interrogation operations at DoD facilities.

(23) (U) Finding: There was neither a defined procedure nor specific responsibility within CJTF-7 for dealing with ICRC visits. ICRC recommendations were ignored by MI, MP and CJTF-7 personnel.

(U) Explanation: Within this investigation's timeframe, 16 September 2003 through 31 January 2004, the ICRC visited Abu Ghraib three times, notifying CJTF-7 twice of their visit results, describing serious violations of international Humanitarian Law and of the Geneva Conventions. In spite of the ICRC's role as independent observers, there seemed to be a consensus among personnel at Abu Ghraib that the allegations were not true. Neither the leadership, nor CJTF-7 made any attempt to verify the allegations.

(U) Recommendation: DoD should review current policy concerning ICRC visits and establish procedures whereby findings and recommendations made by the ICRC are investigated. Investigation should not be done by the units responsible for the facility in question. Specific procedures and responsibilities should be developed for ICRC visits, reports, and responses. There also needs to be specific inquiries made into ICRC allegations of abuse or maltreatment by an independent entity to ensure that an unbiased review has occurred.

4.13 Precautionary Measures

☛ USA: CENTCOM Release Number: 04-11-33, November 10, 2004

Terrorists Use Mosque To Fire Upon Forces

BAGHDAD, Iraq – In Fallujah today, Multi-National Force-Iraq struck terrorists illegally using a mosque to fire upon Iraqi and coalition troops. Anti-Iraqi forces in Fallujah have made extensive use of mosques as bases of operations, storage sites for weapons and explosives, and as safe havens. Throughout Iraq, insurgents and terrorists continue to operate from mosques and other protected sites in clear violation of international law as well as religious and moral standards.

On two separate occasions, Iraqi and coalition forces came under fire from insurgents in the Khulafah Al Rashid mosque. Using small arms fire, the combined forces could not remove the threat. Insurgents had effective control of the area and a tactical advantage, leaving no alternative other than to engage them while they remained inside the mosque. The mosque was struck by coalition aerial assets at approximately 9:25 a.m. with three precision-guided munitions and then again at 1:38 p.m. with another precision-guided munition, which destroyed the minaret. The combined forces used only enough force to remove the threat.

During periods of armed conflict, religious sites are protected under international law. However, they lose their protected status when used as fighting positions or for other military operations.

Foreign fighters continue to use mosques, hospitals, schools and other protected sites to stage and plan their attacks on innocent civilians and security forces. These actions by the terrorists and foreign fighters display once again their complete disregard and disrespect for Islam as well as international law. …

☛ USA: CENTCOM Release Number: 04-11-87, November 25, 2004

Significant Weapons Cache Discovered At Mosque

FALLUJAH, Iraq – Iraqi Security Forces supported by Marines of the 1st Marine Division of the I Marine Expeditionary Force discovered the largest weapons cache to date in the city of Fallujah. It was found in and around the Sa'ad Abi Bin Waqas Mosque in the Hey Al Shorta District here yesterday. … The complex had … been suspected to be a safe house and logistics node for insurgents and their activities. Iraqi Security Forces and Marines also discovered a vendor's truck in the mosque's compound that contained various explosive compounds, RPG's, grenades, mortar rounds, and rockets as well as miscellaneous IED [improvised explosive device]-making materials. Initial assessments indicate the truck may have been a mobile IED factory. The mosque itself is a multi-building complex that is situated within a larger compound and surrounded by a ten-foot high concrete wall. The main-prayer building … was heavily laden with small arms, artillery shells, heavy machine guns, and anti-tank mines. Other buildings within the compound had mortar systems, rocket propelled grenades, launchers, recoilless rifles and parts of surface to air weapons systems. Marines also found the barrel of an anti-aircraft gun outside one of the buildings. … Just outside the rectory door, they found a large bag of rockets. In a small shed adjacent to the rectory, used to house the mosque's air conditioning unit, Marines found a room packed with ordnance and weapons that had been rigged to explode. The insurgents have used mosques as safe havens and took advantage of Multi-National Force-Iraq's respect for these sites. Mosques are granted protective status unless they are being used for militant purposes. Many mosques in Fallujah lost their protective status as places of religious worship when insurgents fired from minarets of these mosques at Multi-National Forces personnel.

☛ USA: CENTCOM News Release Number: 04-09-36, September 12, 2004

Bradley Fighting Vehicle Destroyed In Attack

BAGHDAD, Iraq – A Multi-National Force Bradley Fighting Vehicle was destroyed during an attack this morning at approximately 6:50 on Hayfa Street near the International Zone in Baghdad.

The Bradley and its crew were en route to assist a small unit under fire when it was hit by a car bomb and was rendered inoperable.

Two of the Bradley crewmen were wounded in the attack.

While evacuating the vehicle, the crewmembers came under attack by hand grenades, rocket propelled grenades and small-arms fire, further wounding four more Soldiers.

Soldiers kept an eye on the vehicle from a safe distance ensuring that sensitive equipment and weapons were not taken.

Air support was called, and as the helicopters flew over the burning Bradley they received small-arms fire from the insurgents in vicinity of the vehicle. Clearly within the rules of engagement, the helicopters returned fire destroying some anti-Iraqi forces in the vicinity of the Bradley.

Air assets fired upon the anti-Iraqi forces and the Bradley preventing the loss of sensitive equipment and weapons.

As the helicopters made their final pass, the Bradley Fighting Vehicle was on fire and a crowd was gathering around the vehicle. The air crew could not discriminate between armed insurgents and civilians on the ground and did not reengage. U.S. forces did not engage the crowd of civilians that gathered around the vehicle.

An unknown number of insurgents and Iraq civilians were wounded or killed in the incident. The incident is currently under investigation.

☛ **USA: Coalition Provisional Authority press statement: Coalition Suspends Offensive Operations in Fallujah for Humanitarian Reasons, Baghdad, Iraq, April 9, 2004**

Ambassador Bremer today issued the following statement:

Today at 1200, Coalition Forces initiated a unilateral suspension of offensive operations in Fallujah in order to hold a meeting between members of the Interim Governing Council, Fallujah leadership and leaders of the anti-coalition forces, to allow delivery of additional supplies provided by the Iraqi Government, and to allow residents of Fallujah to tend to wounded and dead.

During this suspension period, Coalition Forces retain the inherent right of self defense, and will remain fully prepared to resume offensive operations unless significant progress in these discussions occurs.

BIBLIOGRAPHY 2003-2004[1]

0. INTERNATIONAL HUMANITARIAN LAW IN GENERAL

Books

- Bill, Brian J., *Law of War Workshop Deskbook* (Buffalo, Hein 2004) 278 pp.
- Carey, John, William B. Dunlap and R. John Pritchard, eds., *International Humanitarian Law*, Vol. 2 Challenges (Ardsley, Transnational Publishers 2004) 367 pp.
- Cassese, Antonio, *Man's Inhumanity to Man: Essays on International Law in Honour of Antonio Cassese* (The Hague, Kluwer Law International 2003) 1032 pp.
- David, Eric, *Code de droit international humanitaire: textes réunis au 1er août 2004, 2e éd. à jour au 1er août 2004* (Bruxelles, Bruylant 2004) 860 pp.
- Ishøy, Rikke, *Handbook on the Practical Use of International Humanitarian Law* (Copenhagen, Danish Red Cross 2004) 100 pp.
- Lijnzaad, Liesbeth, Johanna van Sambeek and Bahia Tahzib-Lie, *Making the Voice of Humanity Heard: Essays on Humanitarian Assistance and International Humanitarian Law in Honour of HRH Princess Margriet of the Netherlands* (Leiden, Nijhoff 2004) 546 pp.
- Rogers, A.P.V., *Law on the Battlefield*, 2nd edn. (Manchester, Manchester University Press/Huntington, Juris Publishing 2004) 269 pp.
- Sanajaoba, Naorem, *A Manual of International Humanitarian Laws* (New Delhi, Regency Publications 2004) 776 pp.
- Sassòli, Marco, *Un droit dans la guerre?* Vol. I pt. 1: *Présentation du droit international humanitaire* (Comité International de la Croix-Rouge 2003) 396 pp.
- Sassòli, Marco, *Un droit dans la guerre?* Vol. II pt. 2: *Cas et documents.* pt. 3: *Plans de cours* (Geneva, Comité International de la Croix-Rouge 2003) pp. 401-2084
- Schindler, Dietrich and Jirí Toman, *The Laws of Armed Conflicts: a Collection of Conventions, Resolutions and Other Documents,* 4th rev. and completed edn. (Leiden, Nijhoff 2004) 1493 pp.
- 6 *Yearbook of International Humanitarian Law* (2003) (The Hague, T.M.C. Asser Press 2005) 874 pp.

Articles

- De Mulinen, F., 'Essentials of the law of war', in Naorem Sanajaoba, ed., *A Manual of International Humanitarian Laws* (New Dehli, Regency Publications 2004) pp. 89- 105
- Fleck, Dieter, 'International humanitarian law after September 11: challenges and the need to respond', 6 *YIHL* (2003) pp. 41-72
- Gasser, Hans-Peter, 'International humanitarian law', in Naorem Sanajaoba, ed., *A Manual of International Humanitarian Laws* (New Dehli, Regency Publications 2004)
- Herrmann, Philipp, 'Aktueller Fall: Recht auf Leben nicht einklagbar?: das Varvarin-Urteil des Landgerichts Bonn vom 10. Dezember 2003,'17 *Humanitäres Völkerrecht* (2004) pp. 79-86

 DOI 10.1017/S1389135904006610

– 'International humanitarian law and the challenges of contemporary armed conflicts: excerpt of the report prepared by the International Committee of the Red Cross for the 28th International Conference of the Red Cross and the Red Crescent Geneva', December 2003, 86 *IRRC* (2004) pp. 213-244
– Johann, Christian, 'Amtshaftung und humanitäres Völkerrecht: zur Möglichkeit eines Anspruches auf Schadenersatz bei Verstößen gegen das humanitäre Völkerrecht nach § 839 BGB i.V.m. Art. 34 GG', 17 *Humanitäres Völkerrecht* (2004) pp. 86-92
– Lavoyer, Jean-Philippe, 'International humanitarian law: should it be reaffirmed, clarified or developed?', 34 *Israel YB HR* (2004) pp. 35-58
– Mani, V.S., 'International humanitarian law: an Indo-Asian perspective', in Naorem Sanajaoba, ed., *A Manual of International Humanitarian Laws* (New Dehli, Regency Publications 2004) pp. 728-743
– Mani, V.S., 'International humanitarian law: challenges in the twenty-first century', 4 *ISIL Year Book of International Humanitarian and Refugee Law* (2004) pp. 1-10
– McDonald, Avril, 'The year in review', 6 *YIHL* (2003) pp. 239-291
– Otto, Ralf, 'Kann die humanitäre Hilfe für Binnenvertriebene durch die Schaffung von vorgefassten Kategorien verbessert werden?', 17 *Humanitäres Völkerrecht* (2004) pp. 98-104
– Sandoz, Yves, 'International humanitarian law in the twenty-first century', 6 *YIHL* (2003) pp. 3-40
– Sandoz, Yves, 'Is there a "droit d'ingérence" in the sphere of information?: the right to information from the standpoint of international humanitarian law', in Naorem Sanajaoba, ed., *A Manual of International Humanitarian Laws* (New Dehli, Regency Publications 2004) pp. 627-637

1.13 Geneva Law

Articles

– Arnold, Roberta, 'The Abu Ghraib misdeeds: will there be justice in the name of the Geneva Conventions', 2 *Journal of International Criminal Justice* (2004) pp. 999-1006
– Bosch, Shannon, 'Geneva under siege', *37 The Comparative and ILJ of Southern Africa* (2004) pp. 294-311
– Condorelli, Luigi and Yasmin Naqvi, 'The war against terrorism and jus in bello: are the Geneva Conventions out of date?', in Andrea Bianchi, ed., *Enforcing International Law Norms against Terrorism* (Oxford, Hart 2004) pp. 25-37
– Fastenrath, Ulrich, 'Berichterstattung oder Entwürdigung?: die Genfer Konvention', in Kai Ambos and Jörg Arnold, eds., *Der Irak-Krieg und das Völkerrecht* (Berlin, Berliner Wissenschafts-Verlag 2004) pp. 435-436
– Forsythe, David, '1949 and 1999: Making the Geneva Conventions relevant after the cold war', in Naorem Sanajaoba, ed., *A Manual of International Humanitarian Laws* (New Dehli, Regency Publications 2004) pp. 56-67
– Happold, Matthew, 'The conference of high contracting parties to the fourth Geneva Convention', 4 *YIHL* (2004) pp. 389-405
– Ingram, John Dwight, 'The Geneva Convention is woefully outdated', 23 *Penn. State ILR* (2004) pp. 79-88

– Jinks, Derek and David Sloss, 'Is the President bound by the Geneva Conventions?', 89 *Cornell LR* (2004) pp. 97-202
– Kosirnik, René, 'The 1977 Protocols: a landmark in the development of international humanitarian law', in Naorem Sanajaoba, ed., *A Manual of International Humanitarian Laws* (New Dehli, Regency Publications 2004) pp. 69-88
– Nolte, Georg, 'Guantanamo und Genfer Konventionen: eine Frage der "lex lata" oder "de lege ferenda"?', in Horst Fischer, ed., *Krisensicherung und humanitärer Schutz: Festschrift für Dieter Fleck* (Berlin, Berliner Wissenschafts-Verlag 2004) pp. 393-404
– Salomons, Machiel and Constantin Hruschka, 'Zur Auslegung und Inhalt des Art. 1 C (5) 1 der Genfer Flüchtlingskonvention', 24 *Zeitschrift für Ausländerrecht und Ausländerpolitik* (2004) pp. 386-392
– Schindler, Dietrich, 'Significance of the Geneva Conventions for the contemporary world', in Naorem Sanajaoba, ed., *A Manual of International Humanitarian Laws* (New Dehli, Regency Publications 2004) pp. 42-55
– Yoo, John C., 'The status of soldiers and terrorists under the Geneva Conventions', 3 *Chinese JIL* (2004) pp. 135-150

1.15 Customary Law

Articles

– Heinegg, Wolff Heintzel von, 'Criminal international law and customary international law', in Andreas Zimmermann, ed., *International Criminal Law and the Current Development of Public International Law* (2003) pp. 27-47
– Kammerhofer, Jörg, 'Uncertainty in the formal sources of international law: customary international law and some of its problems', 15 *EJIL* (2004) pp. 523-553
– Vagts, Detlev F., 'International relations looks at customary international law: a traditionalist's defence', 15 *EJIL* (2004) pp. 1031-1040

1.21 The Martens Clause

Articles

– Ticehurst, Rupert, 'The Martens clause and the laws of armed conflict', in Naorem Sanajaoba, *A Manual of International Humanitarian Laws* (New Dehli, Regency Publications 2004) pp. 312-322

1.22 Superfluous Injury or Unnecessary Suffering

Articles

– Clark, Roger S., 'The Rome Statute of the International Criminal Court and weapons of a nature to cause superfluous injury or unnecessary suffering, or which are inherently indiscriminate', in John Carey, ed., *International Humanitarian Law,* Vol. 2 (Ardsley, Transnational Publishers 2004) pp. 259-281

1.23 Principle of Distinction

Articles

- Ferrell, William H., 'No shirt, no shoes, no status: uniforms, distinction, and special operations in international armed conflict', 178 *Mil. LR* (2003) pp. 94-140
- Pfanner, Toni, 'Military uniforms and the law of war', *86 IRRC* (2004) pp. 93-130

1.24 Principle of Proportionality

Books

- Gardam, Judith, *Necessity, Proportionality and the Use of Force by States* (Cambridge, Cambridge University Press 2004) 259 pp.

1.25 Military Necessity

Articles

- Jaworski, Eric, '"Military necessity" and "civilian immunity": where is the balance?', in Sienho Yee, 2 *International Crime and Punishment: Selected Issues* (2004) pp. 87-127

2.11 International

Books

- Ambos, Kai, *Der Irak-Krieg und das Völkerrecht* (Berlin, Berliner Wissenschafts-Verlag 2004) 530 pp.
- American Society of International Law, *Future Implications of the Iraq Conflict: January 2004* (Washington, American Society of International Law 2004) 216 pp.
- Braams, Karin, *Wasser als völkerrechtlicher Regelungsgegenstand im bewaffneten Konflikt* (Aachen, Shaker 2004) 283 pp.
- Potter, Lawrence G., *Iran, Iraq, and the Legacies of War* (New York, Palgrave Macmillan 2004) 224 pp.
- Tomuschat, Christian, *Völkerrechtliche Aspekte bewaffneter Konflikte* (Heidelberg, Müller 2004) 28 pp.

Articles

- Abtahi, Hirad, 'Le conflit armé du printemps 2003 en Irak et le sort du patrimoine culturel mésopatamien', in Karine Bannelier, ed., *L'intervention en Irak et le droit international* (Paris, Pedone 2004) pp. 195-219
- Downes, Chris, '"Targeted killings" in an age of terror: the legality of the Yemen strike', 9 *Journal of Conflict and Security Law* (2004) pp. 277-294
- Guiora, Amos, 'Targeted killing as active self-defense', 36 *Case Western Reserve JIL* (2004) pp. 319-334
- Genugten, W.J.M. van, 'De oorlog in Irak als bijdrage aan het hervormingsdebat binnen de VN', 97 *Militair rechtelijk tijdschrift* (2004) pp. 185-191

- Hallo de Wolf, A., 'Wordt oorlog geprivatiseerd?: het inzetten van particuliere militaire bedrijven in Irak in het licht van internationaal recht en de rechten van de mens', 79 *Nederlands Juristenblad* (2004) pp. 1687-1695
- Nolte, Georg, 'Vorbeugende Gewaltanwendung und gezielte Tötungen: der Weg in eine andere Rechtsordnung', in Kai Ambos and Jörg Arnold, eds., *Der Irak-Krieg und das Völkerrecht* (Berlin, Berliner Wissenschafts-Verlag 2004) pp. 303-321
- Pokempner, Dinah, Marc Garlasco and Bonnie Docherty, '*Off Target* on the Iraq campaign: a response to Professor Schmitt', 6 *YIHL* (2003) pp. 111-126
- Schmitt, Michael N., 'The conduct of hostilities during Operation Iraqi Freedom: an international humanitarian law assessment', 6 *YIHL* (2003) pp. 73-110

2.12 Non-International

Books

- Mitchell, Neil J., *Agents of Atrocity: Leaders, Followers, and the Violation of Human Rights in Civil War* (New York, Palgrave Macmillan 2004) 228 pp.

Articles

- Bugnion, Francois, 'Jus ad bellum, jus in bello and non-international armed conflicts', 6 *YIHL* (2003) pp. 167-198
- Canestaro, Nathan A., '"Small wars" and the law: options for prosecuting the insurgents in Iraq', 43 *Columbia JTL* (2004) pp. 73-140
- Cuadra Lacayo, Joaquín, 'International humanitarian law and irregular warfare: Latin America', in Naorem Sanajaoba, ed., *A Manual of International Humanitarian Laws* (New Dehli, Regency Publications 2004) pp. 137-146
- Hadden, Tom and Colin Harvey, 'The law of internal crisis and conflict', in Naorem Sanajaoba, *A Manual of International Humanitarian Laws* (New Dehli, Regency Publications 2004) pp. 147-162
- Lacina, Bethany, 'From side show to centre stage: civil conflict after the cold war', 5 *Security Dialogue* (2004) pp. 191-205
- Metz, Steven, 'Insurgency and counterinsurgency in Iraq', in Alexander T.J. Lennon and Camille Eiss, eds., *Reshaping Rogue States: Preemption, Regime Change, and U.S. Policy toward Iran, Iraq, and North Korea* (Cambridge, MIT Press 2004) pp. 303-316
- Plattner, Denise, 'The penal repression of violations of international humanitarian law applicable in non-international armed conflicts', in Naorem Sanajaoba, ed., *A Manual of International Humanitarian Laws* (New Dehli, Regency Publications 2004) pp. 397-409
- Ross, Michael L., 'How do natural resources influence civil war? Evidence from thirteen cases', 58 *International Organization* (2004) pp. 35-67
- Schwabach, Aaron, 'Ecocide and genocide in Iraq: international law, the Marsh Arabs, and environmental damage in non-international conflicts', 15 *Colorado Jl Eviron. L & Pol.* (2004) pp. 1-28
- Waldmann, Peter, 'The asymmetry between the dynamics of violence and the dynamics of peace: the case of civil wars', in Andreas Wimmer, ed., *Facing Ethnic Conflicts: toward a New Realism* (Lanham, Rowman & Littlefield 2004) pp. 96-110

2.13 Other

Articles

- Newman, Edward, 'The "new wars" debate: a historical perspective is needed', 35 *Security Dialogue* (2004) pp. 173-189
- Münkler, Herfried, 'Was ist neu and den neuen Kriegen?', in Helmut König and Manfred Sicking, eds., *Der Irak-Krieg und die Zukunft Europas* (Bielefeld, Transcript 2004) pp. 101-115
- Münkler, Herfried, 'The wars of the 21st century', in Naorem Sanajaoba, ed., *A Manual of International Humanitarian Laws* (New Dehli, Regency Publications 2004) pp. 744-761

2.21 Armed Forces and Combatant Status

Books

- Rouillard, Louis-Philippe F., *Precise of the Laws of Armed Conflicts: With Essays Concerning the Combattant Status of the Guantanamo Detainees and the Statute of the Iraqi Special Tribunal* (New York, Universe 2004) 321 pp.

Articles

- Abbott, Kirby, 'Terrorists: criminals, combatants or ... ?: the questions of combatancy', *in The Measure of International Law: Effectiveness, Fairness and Validity: Proceedings of the 31st Annual Conference of the Canadian Council on International Law, Ottawa, October 24-26, 2002* (The Hague, Kluwer Law International 2004) pp. 366-385
- Callen, Jason, 'Unlawful combatants and the Geneva Conventions', 44 *Virginia JIL* (2004) pp. 1025-1072
- Franck, Thomas M., 'Criminals, combatants, or what? an examination of the role of law in responding to the threat of terror', 98 *AJIL* (2004) pp. 686-688
- Martinez, Jenny S., 'Availability of U.S. courts to review decision to hold U.S. citizens as enemy combatants: executive power in war on terror', 98 *AJIL* (2004) pp. 782-788
- Paust, Jordan J., 'Post-9/11 overreaction and fallacies regarding war and defense, Guantanamo, the status of persons, treatment, judicial review of detention, and due process in military commissions', 79 *Notre Dame Law Review* (2004) pp. 1335-1364
- Peterke, Sven, 'Die Umgehung rechtsstaatlicher Garantien durch Bestimmung Terrorverdächtiger zu "feindlichen Kombattanten": zur Entscheidung des New Yorker Bundesberufungsgerichts in der Sache "Padilla v. Rumsfeld"', 17 *Humanitäres Völkerrecht* (2004) pp. 39-46
- Préfontaine, Daniel C., 'Under international law is there a category of prisoner in armed conflicts known as an "unlawful or unprivileged or enemy combatant"?', in Canadian Council on International Law, *The Measure of International Law: Effectiveness, Fairness and Validity: Proceedings of the 31st Annual Conference of the Canadian Council on International Law, Ottawa, October 24-26, 2002* (The Hague, Kluwer Law International 2004) pp. 386-395
- Raven-Hansen, Peter, 'Detaining combatants by law or by order?: the rule of lawmaking in the war on terrorists', 64 *Louisiana LR* (2004) pp. 831-850

- Sassòli, Marco, 'The status of persons held in Guantánamo under international humanitarian law', 2 *Journal of International Criminal Justice* (2004) pp. 96-106
- Shi, J. Stephen, 'The legal status of foreign military and civilian personnel following the transfer of power to the Iraqi interim government', 33 *Georgia JL & Comp. L* (2004) pp. 245-260
- Stumpf, Juliet, 'Citizens of an enemy land: enemy combatants, aliens, and the constitutional rights of the pseudo-citizen', 38 *University of California Davis LR* (2004) pp. 79-140
- Tarin, Danielle, 'Will an attack on America justify an attack on Americans? congressional and constitutional prohibitions on the executive's power to detain U.S. citizens as enemy combatants', 44 *Virginia JIL* (2004) pp. 1145-1196
- Wuerth, Ingrid Brunk, 'The President's power to detain "enemy combatants": modern lessons from Mr. Madison's forgotten war', 98 *Northwestern University LR* (2004) pp. 1567-1615
- Vierucci, Luisa, 'Is the Geneva Convention on prisoners of war obsolete?: the views of the counsel to the US President on the application of international law to the Afghan conflict', 2 *Journal of International Criminal Justice* (2004) pp. 866-871
- Wallach, Evan J., 'The logical nexus between the decision to deny application of the third Geneva Convention to the Taliban and Al Qaeda and the mistreatment of prisoners in Abu Ghraib', 36 *Case Western Reserve JIL* (2004) pp. 541-638

2.22 Non-State Actors

Books

- Heere, Wybo P., *From Government to Governance: the Growing Impact of Non-State Actors on the International and European Legal System: Proceedings of the Sixth Hague Joint Conference Held in The Hague, the Netherlands, 3-5 July 2003* (The Hague, T.M.C. Asser Press 2004) 533 pp.
- Huggins, Peter Watson, *Trans-State Actors and the Law of War: a Just War Argument* (S.I., s.n. 2004) 283 pp.

Articles

- Franco, Andrés, 'Armed nonstate actors', in David M. Malone, ed., *The UN Security Council: From the Cold War to the 21st Century* (Boulder, Rienner 2004) pp. 117-130
- Kinley, David and Junko Tadaki, 'From talk to walk: the emergence of human rights responsibilities for corporations at international law', 44 *Virginia JIL* (2004) pp. 931-1023
- Singer, P.W., 'War, profits, and the vacuum of law: privatized military firms and international law', 42 *Columbia JTL* (2004) pp. 521-549

2.231 Mercenaries

Articles

- Behnsen, Alexander, 'The status of mercenaries and other illegal combatants under international humanitarian law', 46 *German YIL* (2004) pp. 494-536

– O'Meara Barrie, Bernard, 'Private military firms and mercenaries: potential for liabilty under international law', 12 *Tilburg Foreign Law Review* (2004) pp. 324-347

3.12 Prisoners of War

Books

– Landas, Marc, *The Fallen: a True Story of American POWs and Japanese Wartime Atrocities* (Hoboken, John Wiley 2004) 289 pp.

Articles

– Hillman, Elizabeth Lutes, 'Disloyalty among "men in arms": Korean War POWs at court-martial', 82 *North Carolina LR* (2004) pp. 1629-1659
– Jinks, Derek, 'The declining significance of POW status', 45 *Harvard ILJ* (2004) pp. 367-442
– Liegl-Paul, Charlotte M., 'Civilian prisoners of war: a proposed citizen code of conduct', 182 *Mil. LR* (2004) pp. 106-151
– Noone, Gregory P., 'Prisoners of war in the 21st century: issues in modern warfare', 50 *Naval LR* (2004) pp. 1-69
– Tokudome, Kinue and Azusa K. Tokudome, 'Individuals claims: are the positions of the U.S. and Japanese governments in agreement in the American POW forced labor cases?', 21 *UCLA Pacific Basin LJ* (2003) pp. 1-28
– Winter, Michael, 'Der völkerrechtliche Schutz Kriegsgefangener vor Abbildungen ihrer Person in den Medien', 42 *Archiv des Völkerrechts* (2004) pp. 425-444

3.131 Civilians Generally

Articles

– Bellamy, Alex J., 'Supreme emergencies and the protection of non-combatants in war', 80 *International Affairs* (2004) pp. 829-850
– Kravetz, Daniela, 'The protection of civilians in war: the ICTY's Galić Case', 17 *Leiden JIL* (2004) pp. 521-536
– Liegl-Paul, Charlotte M., 'Civilian prisoners of war: a proposed citizen code of conduct', 182 *Mil. LR* (2004) pp. 106-151

3.132 Women and Children

Books

– Harvey, Rachel, *Children and Armed Conflict: a Short Guide to International Law and Developments* (Colchester, Children's Legal Centre 2003) 8 pp.

Articles

– Cohn, Ilene, 'Progress and hurdles on the road to preventing the use of children as soldiers and ensuring their rehabilitation and reintegration', 37 *Cornell ILJ* (2004) pp. 531-540

– Kadam, Umesh , 'Protection of women in times of armed conflicts and work of the International Committee of the Red Cross', in R.K. Dixit and C. Jayaraj, eds., *Dynamics of International Law in the New Millennium* (New Dehli, Indian Society of International Law 2004) pp. 197-205
– Li, Fiona Ang Chun, 'Kinderen en gewapende conflicten: een mensenrechtelijke benadering', 13 *Zoeklicht* (2004) pp. 11-15
– Maxted, Julia, 'The International Criminal Court and the prohibition of the use of children in armed conflict', in Ramesh Thakur and Peter Malcontent, eds., *From Sovereign Impunity to International Accountability: the Search for Justice in a World of States* (New York, United Nations University Press 2004) pp. 253-263
– Wells, Sarah L., 'Crimes against child soldiers in armed conflict situations: application and limits of international humanitarian law', 12 *Tulane Jl & Comp. L* (2004) pp. 287-306

3.132 Religious Personnel

Books

– Lunze, Stefan, *The Protection of Religious Personnel in Armed Conflict* (Frankfurt am Main, Peter Lang 2004) 219 pp.

Articles

– Lunze, Stefan, 'Serving God and Ceasar: religious personnel and their protection in armed conflict', 86 *IRRC* (2004) pp. 69-91

3.134 Journalists

Articles

– Buchanan, Kelly, 'Freedom of expression and international criminal law: an analysis of the decision to create a testimonial privilege for journalists', 35 *Victoria University of Wellington Law Review* (2004) pp. 609-655
– Fairlie, Megan A., 'Evidentiary privilege of journalists reporting in areas of armed conflict – evidence in war crimes trials – rule-making process of ICTY', 98 *AJIL* (2004) pp. 805-809
– Gasser, Hans-Peter, 'The journalist's right to information in time of war and on dangerous missions', 6 *YIHL* (2003) pp. 366-388
– Obote Odora, Alex, 'Criminal responsibility of journalists under international criminal law: the ICTR experience', 73 *Nordic JIL* (2004) pp. 307-323

3.22 Occupation

Books

– Benvenisti, Eyal, *The International Law of Occupation* (Princeton, Princeton University Press 2004) 241 pp.

– Henriot, Christian, *In the Shadow of the Rising Sun: Shanghai under Japanese Occupation* (Cambridge, Cambridge University Press 2004) 392 pp.

Articles

– Benchikh, Madjid, 'L'occupation de l'Iraq: aspects juridiques et politiques', 5 *Annuaire français de relations internationals* (2004) pp. 297-311
– Benvenisti, Eyal, 'Water conflicts during the occupation of Iraq', in American Society of International Law, *Future Implications of the Iraq Conflict: January 2004* (Washington, American Society of International Law 2004) pp. 148-160
– Cardona Llorens, Jorge, 'Liberation ou occupation? les droits et devoirs de l'état vainqueur', in Karine Bannelier, ed., *L'intervention en Irak et le droit international* (Paris, Pedone 2004) pp. 221-250
– Deiwert, Brian, 'A new trusteeship for world peace and security: can an old League of Nations idea be applied to a twenty-first century Iraq', 14 *Indiana International & Comparative Law Review* (2004) pp. 771-806
– Diamond, Larry, 'What went wrong in Iraq', 83 *Foreign Affairs* (2004) pp. 34-56
– Dopagne, Frédéric and Pierre Klein, 'L'attitude des états tiers et de l'ONU à l'égard de l'occupation de l'Irak', in Karine Bannelier, ed., *L'intervention en Irak et le droit international* (Paris, Pedone 2004) pp. 325-341
– Gathii, James Thuo, 'Foreign and other economic rights upon conquest and under occupation: Iraq in comparative and historical context', 25 *University of Pennsylvania Journal of International Economic Law* (2005) pp. 491-556
– Gill, T.D., 'Iraq: occupation, stabilization and transition', 22 *Merkourios* (2004) pp. 4-6
– Gill, T.D., 'Iraq: occupation, stabilization and transition', 97 *Militair-rechtelijk tijdschrift* (2004) pp. 192-195
– Hmoud, Mahmoud, 'The use of force against Iraq: occupation and Security Council resolution 1483', 36 *Cornell ILJ* (2004) pp. 435-453
– Horvat, Stanislas, 'The extension of jurisdiction of a state to the territory of another state in its effective control: the Al-Skeini judgment of the England and Wales High Court of Justice', 43 *Revue de droit militaire et de droit de la guerre* (2004) pp. 155-192
– Hudson, Walter M., 'The U.S. military government and the establishment of democratic reform, federalism, and constitutionalism during the occupation of Bavaria, 1945-47', 180 *Mil. LR* (2004) pp. 115-154
– Joosten, Veronique, 'De toepassing van het internationaal humanitair recht in de door Israël bezette gebieden', 13 *Zoeklicht* (2004) pp. 24-27
– Kelly, Michael J., 'Iraq and the law of occupation: new tests for an old law', 6 *YIHL* (2003) pp. 127-166
– Kolb, Robert, 'Etude sur l'occupation et sur l'article 47 de la IVeme Convention de Genève du 12 aout 1949 relative à la protection des personnes civiles en temps de guerre: le degré d'intangibilité des droits en territoire occupé', 10 *African YbIL* (2004) pp. 267-321
– Murphy, Melissa A., 'A world occupation" of the Iraqi economy?: how order 39 will create a semi-sovereign state', 19 *Connecticut JIL* (2004) pp. 445-464
– O'Connell, Mary Ellen, 'Occupation failures and the legality of armed conflict: the case of Iraqi cultural property', 9 *Art, Antiquity and Law* (2004) pp. 323-362
– Perez, Antonio F., 'Legal frameworks for economic transition in Iraq: occupation under the law of war vs. global governance under the law of peace', 18 *The Transnational Lawyer* (2004) pp. 53-69

- Rabinowitz, Richard W., 'Staying on: reminiscences of early post-occupation Japan', 9 *Zeitschrift für japanisches Recht* (2004) pp. 157-182
- Rivkin, David B. and Darin R. Bartram, 'Military occupation: legally ensuring a lasting peace', in Alexander T.J. Lennon and Camille Eiss, eds., *Reshaping Rogue States: Preemption, Regime Change, and U.S. Policy toward Iran, Iraq, and North Korea* (Cambridge, MIT Press 2004) pp. 121-140
- Scheffer, David J., 'Beyond occupation law', in American Society of International Law, *Future Implications of the Iraq Conflict: January 2004* (Washington, American Society of International Law 2004) pp. 130-148
- Simon, Reeva Spector, 'The view from Bagdad', in Reeva Spector Simon and Eleanor H. Tejirian, eds., *The Creation of Iraq, 1914-1921* (New York, Columbia University Press 2004) pp. 36-49
- Stad, Jeroen M., 'Creating a safe and secure environment during stabilisation missions: Iraq: occupation, stabilisation and transition', 22 *Merkourios* (2004) pp. 7-11
- Starita, Massimo, 'L'occupation de l'Iraq: le Conseil de sécurité, le droit de la guerre et le droit des peuples a disposer d'eux-mêmes', 108 *Revue générale de droit international public* (2004) pp. 883-916
- Tripp, Charles, 'The United States and state-building in Iraq', 30 *Review of International Studies* (2004) pp. 545-558
- Vité, Sylvain, 'L'applicabilité du droit international de l'occupation militaire aux activités des organisations internationales', 86 *IRRC* (2004) pp. 9-35
- Yaphe, Judith S., 'The view from Basra: southern Iraq's reaction to war and occupation, 1915-1925', in Reeva Spector Simon and Eleanor H. Tejirian, eds., *The Creation of Iraq, 1914-1921* (New York, Columbia University Press 2004) pp. 19-35
- Zwanenburg, Marten, 'Existentialism in Iraq: Security Council resolution 1483 and the law of occupation', 86 *IRRC* (2004) pp. 745-769

3.24 Prohibition of Deportation and Transfer

Articles

- Grimm, Simone, 'The return of illegal refugees and deportation practice in the Federal Republic of Germany', 42 *AWR bulletin* (2004) pp. 15-36
- Grimm, Simone, 'The return of illegal refugees and deportation practice in the Federal Republic of Germany', 42 *AWR bulletin* (2004) pp. 24-44
- Hing, Eric Jeffrey Ong, 'Deportation into chaos: the questionable removal of Somali regugees', 38 *Univ.Calif.Davis LR* (2004) pp. 309-342

3.25 Reprisals

Books

- Hebenstreit, Johannes, *Repressalien im humanitären Völkerrecht* (Baden-Baden, Nomos 2004) 210 pp.

Articles

- Kalshoven, Frits, 'Reprisals and the protection of civilians: two recent decisions of the Yugoslav Trinunal', in Lal Chand Vohrah, ed., *Man's inhumanity to man* (The Hague, Kluwer Law International 2003) pp. 481-509

4.11111 Mines

Articles

- Price, Richard, 'Emerging customary norms and anti-personnel landmines', in Christian Reus-Smit, ed., *The Politics of International Law* (Cambridge, Cambridge University Press 2004) pp. 106-130
- Torres Nachón, Claudio, 'The environmental impacts of landmines', in Richard A., Bryan Matthew, Bryan McDonald, and Kenneth R. Rutherford, eds., *Landmines and Human Security: International Politics and War's Hidden Legacy* (Albany, State University of New York Press 2004) pp. 191-207

4.11112 Small Weapons and Others

Articles

- Frey, Barbara A., 'Small arms and light weapons: the tools used to violate human rights', 3 *Disarmament Forum* (2004) pp. 37-46

4.11121 Nuclear Weapons

Articles

- Fujita, Hisakazu, 'The advisory opinion of the International Court of Justice on the legality of nuclear weapons', in Naorem Sanajaoba, ed., *A Manual of International Humanitarian Laws* (New Dehli, Regency Publications 2004) pp. 617-626
- Gowlland-Debbas, Vera, 'The relevance of paragraph 25 of the ICJ's advisory opinion on nuclear weapons', 98 *Proceedings of the Annual Meeting* (2004) pp. 358-363
- Moxley, Charles J., 'The sword in the mirror: the lawfulness of North Korea's use and threat of use of nuclear weapons based on the United States' legitimization of nuclear weapons', 27 *Fordham ILJ* (2004) pp. 1379-1489

4.11122 Chemical and Biological Weapons

Books

- Zammit Borda, Aldo, *The Threat and Use of Chemical and Biological Weapons Under International Law* (Valetta, University of Malta 2003) 264 pp.

Articles

- Pinson, Robert D., 'Is nanotechnology prohibited by the Biological and Chemical Weapons Conventions?', 22 *Berkeley JIL* (2004) pp. 279-309

4.112 New Weapons

Articles
- Beckett, Jason A., 'Interim legality: a mistaken assumption? an analysis of depleted uranium munitions under contemporary international humanitarian law', 3 *Chinese JIL* (2004) pp. 43-86
- Daoust, Isabelle, and Coupland, Robin and Ishoey, Rikke, 'New wars, new weapons?: the obligation of states to assess the legality of means and methods of warfare', in Naorem Sanajaoba, ed., *A Manual of International Humanitarian Laws* (New Delhi, Regency Publications 2004) pp. 546-563

4.142 Cultural Property and Places of Worship

Books
- Chamberlain, Kevin, *War and Cultural Heritage: an Analysis of the 1954 Convention for the Protection of Cultural Property in the Event of Armed Conflicts and its Two Protocols* (Leicester, Institute of Art and Law 2004) 333 pp.
- Syssoeva, Elena, *Kunst im Krieg: eine völkerrechtliche Betrachtung der deutsch-russischen Kontroverse um kriegsbedingt verbrachte Kulturgüter* (Berlin, Duncker & Humblot 2004) 431 pp.

Articles
- Bugnion, François, 'La genèse de la protection juridique des biens culturels en cas de conflit armé', 86 *IRRC* (2004) pp. 313-324
- Dixit, R.K., 'Saving cultural property holocaust during armed conflicts', in R.K. Dixit and C. Jayaraj, eds., *Dynamics of International Law in the New Millennium* (New Dehli, Indian Society of International Law 2004) pp. 183-196
- Hladik, Jan, 'Marking of cultural property with the distinctive emblem of the 1954 Hague Convention for the Protection of Cultural Property in the Event of Armed Conflict', 86 *IRRC* (2004) pp. 379-387
- Hladik, Jan, 'The control system under the Hague Convention for the Protection of Cultural Property in the Event of Armed Conflict 1954 and its Second Protocol', 4 *YIHL* (2004) pp. 419-431
- Hladik, Jan, 'The UNESCO Declaration concerning the intentional destruction of cultural heritage: a new instrument to protect cultural heritage', 9 *Art, Antiquity and Law* (2004) pp. 215-236
- O'Connell, Mary Ellen, 'Occupation failures and the legality of armed conflict: the case of Iraqi cultural property', 9 *Art, Antiquity and Law* (2004) pp. 323-362
- Paroff, Sasha P., 'Another victim of the war in Iraq: the looting of the national museum in Baghdad and the inadequacies of international protection of cultural property', 53 *Emory Law Journal* (2004) pp. 2021-2054
- Phuong, Catherine, 'The protection of Iraqi cultural property', 53 *The International and Comparative Law Quarterly* (2004) pp. 985-998
- Picavet, Sofie, 'De bescherming van culturele goederen in gewapende conflicten: recente ontwikkelingen', 13 *Zoeklicht* (2004) pp. 4-8

4.143 Works and Installations Containing Dangerous Forces

Articles
- Lamm, Vanda, 'Protection of civilian nuclear installations in time of armed conflict', 72/a2 *Nuclear Law Bulletin* (2003) pp. 29-38

4.144 The Natural Environment

Books
- Al-Duaij, Nada Y., *Environmental Law of Armed Conflict* (Ardsley, Transnational Publishers 2004) 521 pp.

Articles
- Antoine, Philippe, 'International humanitarian law and the protection of the environment in time of armed conflict', in Naorem Sanajaoba, ed., *A Manual of International Humanitarian Laws* (New Delhi, Regency Publications 2004) pp. 184-203
- Costa, Kathryn H., 'The status of toxins in 2003: how toxins affect human health and the environment during war', *Colorado JL Environ. L & Pol.* (2004) pp. 75-85
- Jensen, Eric Talbot, 'The international law of environmental warfare: active and passive damage during armed conflict', 38 *Vanderbilt JTL* (2005) pp. 145-185
- Kreike, Emmanuel, 'War and the environmental effects of displacement in Southern Africa (1970s-1990s)', in William G. Moseley and B. Ikubolajeh Logan, eds., *African Environment and Development: Rhetoric, Programs, Realities* (Burlington VT, Ashgate 2004) pp. 89-110
- Schwabach, Aaron, 'Ecocide and genocide in Iraq: international law, the Marsh Arabs, and environmental damage in non-international conflicts', 15 *Colorado Jl Environ. L & Pol.* (2004) pp. 1-28
- Torres Nachón, Claudio, 'The environmental impacts of landmines', in Richard A. Matthew, Bryan McDonald and Kenneth R. Rutherford, eds., *Landmines and Human Security: International Politics and War's Hidden Legacy* (Albany, State University of New York Press 2004) pp. 191-207

4.16 Humanitarian Assistance Operations

Books
- Dijkzeul, Dennis, 'Mapping international humanitarian organisations', 17 *Humanitäres Völkerrecht* (2004) pp. 216-225
- Fischer, Horst and Dieter Fleck, *Krisensicherung und humanitärer Schutz: Festschrift für Dieter Fleck* (Berlin, Berliner Wissenschafts-Verlag 2004) 734 pp.
- Lijnzaad, Liesbeth, *Making the Voice of Humanity Heard: Essays on Humanitarian Assistance and International Humanitarian Law in Honour of HRH Princess Margriet of the Netherlands* (Leiden, Nijhoff 2004) 546 pp.
- Rudd, Gordon W., *Humanitarian Intervention: Assisting the Iraqi Kurds in Operation Provide Comfort, 1991* (Washington, Department of the Army 2004) 280 pp.

- Torroja Mateu, Helena, *La asistencia humanitaria en la Organización de las Naciones Unidas: fundamentos y perspectivas actuales* (Barcelona, Atelier 2004) 382 pp.
- United Nations, Office for the Coordination of Humanitarian Affairs, *The Humanitarian Decade: Challenges for Humanitarian Assistance in the Last Decade and into the Future* (New York, United Nations 2004) 2dl.
- United Nations, Office for the Coordination of Humanitarian Affairs, *The Humanitarian Decade: Challenges for Humanitarian Assistance in the Last Decade and into the Future,* Vol. I *Panel Discussion on the Occasion of the Tenth Anniversary of General Assembly Resolution 46/182: Dag Hammarskjöld Library Auditorium, United Nations, New York, Wednesday 17 July 2002* (New York, United Nations 2004) 73 pp.
- United Nations, Office for the Coordination of Humanitarian Affairs, *The Humanitarian Decade: Challenges for Humanitarian Assistance in the Last Decade and into the Future,* Vol. II *General Assembly Resolution 46/182: the Development of Practice, Principles and the Humanitarian Framework* (New York, United Nations 2004) 222 pp.

Articles
- Cornillon, Lisa, 'Certain human rights standards as a condition for humanitarian and development assistance', in Tobias Gries and Ralf Alleweldt, eds., *Human Rights Within the European Union* (Berlin, Berliner Wissenschafts-Verlag 2004) pp. 77-85
- Forsythe, David P., 'The International Committee of the Red Cross and humanitarian assistance: a policy analysis', in Naorem Sanajaoba, ed., *A Manual of International Humanitarian Laws* (New Dehli, Regency Publications 2004) pp. 664-685
- Graduate Institute of International Studies Geneva, 'Humanitarian assistance in armed conflict: conference of the Luxemburg Group 24-25 May 2004', 86 *IRRC* (2004) pp. 879-916
- Grünfeld, Fred, 'Conflictpreventie en soevereiniteit', in Duco Hellema and Hilde Reiding, eds., *Humanitaire interventie en soevereiniteit: de geschiedenis van een tegenstelling* (Amsterdam, Boom 2004) pp. 159-173
- Kassa, Michel, 'Humanitarian assistance in the DRC', in Mark Malan and João Gomes Porto, eds., *Challenges of Peace Implementation: the UN Mission in the Democratic Republic of the Congo* (Pretoria, Institute for Security Studies 2004) pp. 81-95
- Schmitz, Peter, 'Quality and accountability in humanitarian assistance: how to put it into practice?', 17 *Humanitäres Völkerrecht* (2004) pp. 28-30

4.21 Land Warfare

Books
- Dinstein, Yoram, *The Conduct of Hostilities Under the Law of International Armed Conflict* (Cambridge, Cambridge University Press 2004) 275 pp.
- Rogers, A.P.V., *Law on the Battlefield*, 2nd edn. (Manchester, Manchester University Press/Huntington, Juris Publishing 2004) 269 pp.

Articles
- Levie, Howard S., 'Humanitarian law and the law of war on land', in John Carey, William V. Dunlap and R. John Pritchard, eds., *International Humanitarian Law* (Ardsley, Transnational Publishers 2003) pp. 181-189

4.22 Air and Missile Warfare

Articles

- Canestaro, Nathan A., 'Legal and policy constraints on the conduct of aerial precision warfare', 37 *Vanderbilt JTL* (2004) pp. 431-484
- Guisández Gómez, Javier, 'The law of air warfare', in Naorem Sanajaoba, ed., *A Manual of International Humanitarian Laws* (New Dehli, Regency Publications 2004) pp. 106-123

4.23 Naval Warfare

Articles

- Doswald-Beck, Louise, 'San Remo manual on international law applicable to armed conflict at sea', in Naorem Sanajaoba, ed., *A Manual of International Humanitarian Laws* (New Dehli, Regency Publications 2004) pp. 124-135
- Heintschel v. Heinegg, Wolff, 'Maritime interception/interdiction operations within the framework of operation enduring freedom', in Société Française pour le Droit International, *Les nouvelles menaces contre la paix et la sécurité internationales: journée franco-allemande* (Paris, Pedone 2004) pp. 149-164
- Roach, J. Ashley, 'Initiatives to enhance maritime security at sea', 28 *Marine Policy* (2004) pp. 41-66

5.1 CEASEFIRE, ARMISTICES AND PEACE AGREEMENTS

Books

- Fortna, Virginia Page, *PeaceTime: Cease-fire Agreements and the Durability of Peace* (Princeton, Princeton University Press 2004) 243 pp.

Articles

- Deng, Biong Kuol, 'The legal implications of the Sudan peace process: interpretation of the texts of the agreements', in Korwa G. Adar, John G. Nyuot Yoh and Eddy Maloka, eds., *Sudan Peace Process: Challenges and Future Prospects* (Pretoria, Africa Institute of South Africa 2004) pp. 102-127

5.3 AMNESTIES, TRUTH AND RECONCILIATION COMMISSIONS

Books

- Gilligan, George P., *Crime, Truth and Justice: Official Inquiry, Discourse, Knowledge* (Cullompton, Willan 2004) 285 pp.
- Phelps, Teresa Godwin, *Shattered Voices: Language, Violence, and the Work of Truth Commissions* (Philadelphia, University of Pennsylvania Press 2004) 180 pp.

Articles

- Attafuah, Ken Agyemang, 'An overview of Ghana's national reconciliation commission and its relationship with the courts', 15 *Criminal LR* (2004) pp. 125-134
- Brown, David, 'Royal commissions and criminal justice: behind the ideal', in George Gilligan and John Pratt, eds., *Crime, Truth and Justice: Official Inquiry, Discourse, Knowledge* (Cullompton, Willan 2004) pp. 26-45
- Burgess, Patrick, 'Justice and reconciliation in East Timor: the relationship between the Commission for Reception, Truth and Reconciliation and the courts', 15 *Criminal LR* (2004) pp. 135-158
- Burton, Mary, 'Custodians of memory: South Africa's truth and reconciliation commission', 32 *International Journal of Legal Information* (2004) pp. 417-425
- Cottereau, Gilles, 'Une Licorne en Côte d'Ivoire au service de la paix: avant Marcoussis et jusqu'à la réconciliation?', 49 *Annuaire français de droit international* (2004) pp. 176-206
- Du Plessis, Willemien, 'The South African truth and reconciliation commission: "the truth will set you free"', in Marie-Claire Foblets and Trutz von Trotha, eds., *Healing the Wounds: Essays on the Reconstruction of Societies After War* (Oxford, Hart 2004) pp. 169-200
- Fombad, Charles Manga, 'Prospects for peace building through truth commissions', in Alfred G. Nhema, ed., *The Quest for Peace in Africa: Transformations, Democracy and Public Policy* (Utrecht, International Books 2004) pp. 189-219
- Gibson, James L., 'Truth, reconciliation, and the creation of a human rights culture in Siouth Africa', 38 *Law and Society Review* (2004) pp. 5-40
- González Cueva, Eduardo, 'The contribution of the Peruvian truth and reconciliation commission to prosecutions', 15 *Criminal LR* (2004) pp. 55-66
- Gross, Aeyal M., 'The constitution, reconciliation, and transitional justice: lessons from South Africa and Israel', 40 *Stanford JIL* (2004) pp. 47-104
- Hansotte, Majo and Paul-Henri Content, 'La réconciliation', *Université de Paix, Promouvoir la paix* (Brussels, De Boeck 2004) pp. 139-153
- Josephs, Hilary K., 'The remedy of apology in comparative and international law: self-healing and reconciliation', 18 *Emory ILR* (2004) pp. 53-84
- Leman-Langlois, Stéphane and Clifford D. Shearing, 'Repairing the future: the South African truth and reconciliation commission at work', in George Gilligan and John Pratt, eds., *Crime, Truth and Justice: Official Inquiry, Discourse, Knowledge* (Cullompton, Willan 2004) pp. 222-242
- Lyons, Beth S., 'Getting untrapped, struggling for truths: the Commission for Reception, Truth and Reconciliation (CAVR) in East Timor', in Cesare P.R. Romano, André Nollkaemper and Jann K. Kleffner, eds., *Internationalized Criminal Courts and Tribunals: Sierra Leone, East Timor, Kosovo, and Cambodia* (Oxford, Oxford University Press 2004) pp. 99-124
- Maclellan, Nic, 'Creating peace in the pacific: conflict resolution, reconciliation and restorative justice: regional introduction', in Annelies Heijmans, Nicola Simmonds and Hans van de Veen, eds., *Searching for Peace in Asia Pacific: an Overview of Conflict Prevention and Peacebuilding Activities* (Boulder, Rienner 2004) pp. 526-542
- Owen, David, 'Justice and reconciliation: the contribution of war crimes tribunals and truth and reconciliation commissions', in Kevin M. Cahill, ed., *Human Security for All: A Tribute to Sergio Vieira de Mello* (New York, Fordham University Press 2004) pp. 190-214

– Pedain, Antje, 'Was amnesty a lottery? An empiral study of the decisions of the truth and reconciliation commission's committee on amnesty', 121 *South African Law Journal* (2004) pp. 785-828
– Sadat, Leila Nadya, 'Universal jurisdiction, national amnesties and truth commissions: reconciling the irreconcilable', in Stephen Macedo, ed., *Universal Jurisdiction National Courts and the Prosecution of Serious Crimes under International Law* (Pennsylvania, University of Pennsylvania Press 2004) pp. 193-213
– Sarkin, Jeremy and Erin Daly, 'Too many questions, too few answers: reconciliation in transitional societies', 35 *Columbia HRLR* (2004) pp. 661-728
– Schabas, William A., 'A synergistic relationship: the Sierra Leone Truth and Reconciliation Commission and the Special Court for Sierra Leone', 15 *Criminal LR* (2004) pp. 3-54
– Schabas, William A., 'Conjoined twins of transitional justice? The Sierra Leone Truth and Reconciliation Commission and the Special Court', 2 *Journal of International Criminal Justice* (2004) pp.1082-1099
– Schabas, William A., 'Truth commissions and courts working in parallel: the Sierra Leone experience', 98 *Proceedings of the Annual Meeting* (2004) pp. 189-192
– Seibert-Fohr, Anja, 'The relevance of the Rome Statute of the International Criminal Court for amnesties and truth commissions', 7 *MPYIL*(2004) pp.553-590

5.4 REPARATIONS/COMPENSATION

Books

– Bottigliero, Ilaria, *Redress for Victims of Crimes Under International Law* (Leiden, Nijhoff 2004) 304 pp.
– Boisson de Chazournes, Laurence*, Crimes de l'histoire et réparations: les réponses du droit et de la justice* (Brussels, Bruylant 2004) 401 pp.
– Rathkolb, Oliver, *Revisiting the National Socialist Legacy: Coming to Terms with Forced Labor, Expropriation, Compensation, and Restitution* (New Brunswick, Transaction 2004) 480 pp.

Articles

– Eizenstat, Stuart E., 'Imperfect justice: looted assets, slave labor, and the unfinished business of World War II', 37 *Vanderbilt JTL* (2004) pp. 333-351
– Levmore, Saul, 'Privatizing reparations', 84 *Boston University Law Review* (2004) pp. 1291-1318
– Levush, Ruth, 'Compensation for victims of terrorist actions: Israel as a case study', 32 *International Journal of Legal Information* (2004) pp. 582-592
– Logue, Kyle D., 'Reparations as redistribution', 84 *Boston University Law Review* (2004) pp. 1319-1374
– Palmer, Michael G., 'Compensation for Vietnam's Agent Orange victims', 8 *International Journal of Human Rights* (2004) pp. 1-15
– Wühler, Norbert, 'German compensation for World War II slave and forced labour', in Laurence Boisson de Chazournes, Jean-François Quéguiner and Santiago Villalpando, eds., *Crimes de l'histoire et réparations: les réponses du droit et de la justice* (Brussels, Bruylant 2004) pp. 163-175

5.5 MILITARY COMMISSIONS AND TRIBUNALS

Books

- Hook, Gordon, 'US military commissions and international law', *New Zealand Law Journal* (2004) pp. 468

Articles

- Finnin, Sarah, 'The proposed trials by the UN Military Commission', 6 *YIHL* (2003) (The Hague, Asser Press 2005) pp. 409-423
- Locy, Toni, 'The trials of Al Qaeda: Federal Court vs. Military Commission', 36 *Case Western Reserve JIL* (2004) pp. 507-512
- Noone, Gregory P., Noone, Diana C., 'The military commissions: a possible strength giving way to possible weakness: and the required fix', 36 *Case Western Reserve JIL* (2004) pp. 523-527

6. INTERNATIONAL CRIMINAL LAW

Books

- Buruma, Ybo and Verrest, P.A.M., *Introductie internationaal strafrecht*, 2e dr. (Nijmegen, Ars Aequi Libri 2004) 128 pp.
- Donnedieu de Vabres, Henri, *Les principes modernes du droit pénal international* (Paris, Editions Panthéon-Assas, L.G.D.J. Diffuseur 2004) 470 pp.
- International Conference of the ISISC, *International Criminal Law: Quo Vadis?: Proceedings of the International Conference Held in Siracusa, Italy, 28 November - 3 December 2002, of ISISC* (Romonville Saint-Agne, Erès 2004) 575 pp.
- Knoops, Geert-Jan Alexander, *The Prosecution and Defense of Peacekeepers Under International Criminal Law* (Ardsley, Transnational Publishers 2004) 368 pp.
- Podgor, Ellen S., *Understanding International Criminal Law* (Newark, LexisNexis 2004) Onreg. gep
- Simbeye, Yitiha, *Immunity and International Criminal Law* (Aldershot, Ashgate 2004) 173 pp.
- Vogel, Joachim und Grotz, Michael, *Perspektiven des internationalen Strafprozessrechts* (Heidelberg, Müller 2004) 71 pp.
- Yee, Sienho, *International Crime and Punishment: Selected Issues*, Vol. 2 (Lanham, University Press of America 2004) 267 pp.

Articles

- Bantekas, Ilias, 'Defences in international criminal law', in Dominic McGoldrick, Peter Rowe and Eric Donnelly, eds., *The Permanent International Criminal Court* (Oxford, Hart 2004) pp. 263-284
- Bassiouni, Cherif, 'The "indirect enforcement system": modalities of international cooperation in penal matters', in International Conference of the ISISC, *International Criminal Law: Quo Vadis?: Proceedings of the International Conference Held in Siracusa, Italy, 28 November - 3 December 2002, of ISISC* (Romonville Saint-Agne, Erès 2004) pp. 79-155

– Cedarbaum, Jonathan G., 'Restrictions on U.S. attorneys practicing before international criminal tribunals', 98 *AJIL* (2004) pp. 141-149
– Cryer, Robert, 'The boundaries of liability in international criminal law, or "selectivity by stealth", in Gerry Simpson, ed., *War Crimes Law*, Vol. 1 (Aldershot, Ashgate 2004) pp. 59-87
– Delmas-Marty, Mireille, 'Criminal law as ethics of globalisation', 17 *Humanitäres Völkerrecht* (2004) pp. 4-9
– Defeis, Elizabeth F., 'The evolution of international criminal law', in Yassin El-Ayouty, ed., *Perspectives on 9/11* (Westport, Praeger 2004) pp. 39-50
– Etcheberry, Alfredo, 'The principles of legality and non bis in idem', in International Conference of the ISISC, *International Criminal Law: Quo Vadis? Proceedings of the International Conference Held in Siracusa, Italy, 28 November - 3 December 2002, of ISISC* (Romonville Saint-Agne, Erès 2004) pp. 337-344
– Gattini, Andrea, 'Kelsen's contribution to international criminal law', 2 *Journal of International Criminal Justice* (2004) pp. 795-809
– Joyce, Daniel, 'The historical function of international criminal trials: re-thinking international criminal law', 73 *Nordic JIL* (2004) pp. 461-484
– Koskenniemi, Marrti, 'Hersch Lauterpacht and the development of international criminal law', 2 *Journal of International Criminal Justice* (2004) pp. 810-825
– Kalshoven, Frits, 'From international humanitarian law to international criminal law', 3 *Chinese JIL* (2004) pp. 151-161
– Ling Yan, 'The Beijing symposium on the comparative study of international criminal law', 3 *Chinese JIL* (2004) pp. 305-318
– Log, Sure, 'The practical applications of ne bis in idem in international criminal law', in Sienho Yee, ed., *International Crime and Punishment: Selected Issues* (University Press of America 2004) pp. 169-204
– Nemitz, Jan Christoph, 'The law of sentencing in international criminal law: the purpose of sentencing and the applicable method for the determination of the sentence', 4 *YIHL* (2004) pp. 87-127
– Obote Odora, Alex, 'Criminal responsibility of journalists under international criminal law: the ICTR experience', 73 *Nordic JIL* (2004) pp. 307-323
– Ottenhof, Reynald, 'Les droits des victimes en droit pénal international', in International Conference of the ISISC, *International Criminal Law: Quo Vadis?: Proceedings of the International Conference Held in Siracusa, Italy, 28 November - 3 December 2002, of ISISC* (Romonville Saint-Agne, Erès 2004) pp. 519-523
– Piragoff, Donald K. and Paula Clarke, 'The emergence of common standards of "due process" in international and national criminal proceedings', in International Conference of the ISISC, *International Criminal Law: Quo Vadis?: Proceedings of the International Conference Held in Siracusa, Italy, 28 November - 3 December 2002, of ISISC* (Romonville Saint-Agne, Erès 2004) pp.*of ISISC* (Romonville Saint-Agne, Erès 2004) pp. 363-395
– Sluiter, Göran, 'Kroniek internationaal strafrecht'(deel II), 29 *NJCM-bulletin* (2004) pp. 475-484
– Schwarzenberger, Georg, 'The problem of an international criminal law', in Gerry Simpson, ed., *War Crimes Law*, Vol. 1 (Aldershot, Ashgate 2004) pp. 5-38
– Ratner, Steven R., The schizophrenias of international criminal law', in Gerry Simpson, ed., *War Crimes Law*, Vol. 1 (Aldershot, Ashgate 2004) pp. 39-58

– Stephens, Tim, 'International criminal law and the response to international terrorism', 27 *University of New South Wales Law Journal* (2004) pp. 454-481
– Yee, Sienho, 'The "tu quoque" argument as a defence to international crimes, prosecution or punishment', 3 *Chinese JIL* (2004) pp. 87-133
– Zolo, Danilo, 'Peace through criminal law?', 2 *Journal of International Criminal Justice* (2004) pp. 727-734

6.1 THE CRIMES

Articles

– Ambos, Kai, 'Selected issues regarding the "core crimes" in International Criminal Law', in International Conference of the ISISC, *International Criminal Law: Quo Vadis?: Proceedings of the International Conference Held in Siracusa, Italy, 28 November - 3 December 2002, of ISISC* (Romonville Saint-Agne, Erès 2004) pp. 219-282
– Alvarez, José E., 'Crimes of states, crimes of hate: lessons from Rwanda', in Gerry Simpson, ed., *War Crimes Law*, Vol. 1 (Aldershot, Ashgate-Dartmouth 2004) pp. 147-265
– 'Elements of crimes', in Elin Hilwig, Relinde van Laar, Willem-Jan van der Wolf, eds., *International Courts and Tribunals: Selected Documents and Materials* (Nijmegen, Wolf Legal Publishers 2004) pp. 439-475

6.11 War Crimes

Books

– Chuter, David, *War Crimes: Confronting Atrocity in the Modern World* (Boulder, Rienner 2003) 299 pp.
– Drakulić, Slavenka, *They Would Never Hurt a Fly: War Criminals on Trial in The Hague* (New York, Viking 2004) 209 pp.
– Hagan, John, *Justice in the Balkans: Prosecuting War Crimes in The Hague Tribunal* (Chicago, University of Chicago Press 2003) 274 pp.
– Hilton, Fern Overbey, *The Dachau Defendants: Life Stories From Testimony and Documents of the War Crimes Prosecutions* (Jefferson, McFarland 2004) 201 pp.
– Ivanisevic, Bogdan, *Justice At Risk: War Crimes Trials in Croatia, Bosnia and Herzegovina, and Serbia and Montenegro* (New York, Human Rights Watch 2004) 31 pp.
– Jones, Adam, *Genocide, War Crimes and the West: History and Complicity* (London, Zed Books 2004) 424 pp.
– Maogoto, Jackson Nyamuya, *War Crimes and Realpolitik: International Justice From World War I to the 21st Century* (Boulder, Lynne Rienner 2004) 267 pp.
– Pritz, Pál, *The War Crimes Trial of Hungarian Prime Minister László Bárdossy* (Boulder, Social Science Monographs 2004) 221 pp.
– Ratner, Steven R., *International War Crimes Trials: Making a Difference? Proceedings of an Interdisciplinary Conference at the University of Texas School of Law, Austin, Texas, November 6-7, 2003* (Austin, Texas, University of Texas, Austin School of Law 2004) 160 pp.
– Simpson, Gerry, *War Crimes Law*, Vol. I (Aldershot, Ashgate 2004) 444 pp.

– Simpson, Gerry, *War Crimes Law*, Vol. II (Aldershot, Ashgate 2004) 484 pp.
– Trahan, Jennifer, Adela Mall and Widney Brown, *Genocide, War Crimes, and Crimes Against Humanity: Topical Digests of the Case Law of the International Criminal Tribunal for Rwanda and the International Criminal Tribunal for the Former Yugoslavia* (New York, Human Rights Watch 2004) 277 pp.
– Weindling, Paul Julian, *Nazi Medicine and the Nuremberg Trials: From Medical War Crimes to Informed Consent* (Basingstoke, Palgrave Macmillan 2004) 482 pp.

Articles

– Borgwardt-Kopelman, Elizabeth S., 'Ideology and international law: the dissent of the Indian justice at the Tokyo war crimes trial', in Gerry Simpson, ed., *War Crimes Law*, Vol. II (Aldershot, Ashgate 2004) pp. 145-213
– Dixon, Rosalind, 'Rape as a crime in international humanitarian law: where to go from here?', in Gerry Simpson, ed., *War Crimes Law*, Vol. I (Aldershot, Ashgate 2004) pp. 267-289
– Dörmann, Knut, 'War crimes under the Rome Statute of the International Criminal Court, with a special focus on the negotiations on the elements of crimes,' 7 *MPYIL* (2004) pp. 341-407
– Ellis, Mark S., 'Coming to terms with its past: Serbia's new court for the prosecution of war crimes', 22 *Berkeley JIL* (2004) pp. 165-194
– Ilgner, Claudia, 'Besonderheiten und Problemstellungen bei Strafverfolgungsmaßnahmen und kriminalpolizeilichen Ermittlungen wegen Völkermordes, Verbrechen gegen die Menschlichkeit und Kriegsverbrechen,' in Gunnar Theissen and Martin Nagler, eds., *Der Internationale Strafgerichtshof: fünf Jahre nach Rom: Tagungsdokumentation Berlin, 27.-28. Juni 2003* (Berlin, Deutsches Institut für Menschenrechte 2004) pp. 53-56
– La Haye, Eve, 'The elaboration of the elements of war crimes', in Flavia Lattanzi and William A. Schabas, eds., *Essays on the Rome Statute of the International Criminal Court* (Ripa Fagnano Alto, Sirente 2004) pp.305-331
– Meron, Theodor, 'War crimes law comes of age', in John Carey, William V. Dunlap and R. John Pritchard, eds., *International Humanitarian Law*, Vol. II (Transnational Publishers 2004) pp. 27-32
– Panovsky, Damjan, 'Some war crimes are not better than others: the failure of the International Criminal Tribunal for the Former Yugoslavia to prosecute war crimes in Macedonia', 98 *Northwestern University Law Review* (2004) pp. 623-655
– Prévost, Ann Marie, 'Race and war crimes: the 1945 war crimes trial of General Tomoyuki Yamashita', in Gerry Simpson, ed., *War Crimes Law*, Vol. II (Aldershot, Ashgate 2004) pp. 215-250
– 'Report of the Inquiry into the Alleged Commission of War Crimes by Coalition Forces in the Iraq War during 2003', 44 *Indian JIL* (2004) pp. 382-418
– Rowe, Peter, 'War crimes', in Dominic McGoldrick, Peter Rowe and Eric Donnelly, eds., *The Permanent International Criminial Court* (2004) pp. 203-230
– Salter, Michael, 'Intelligence agencies and war crimes prosecution: Allen Dulles' involvement in witness testimony', 2 *Journal of International Criminal Justice* (2004) pp. 826-854
– Simonović, Ivan, 'Attitudes and types of reaction toward past war crimes and human rights abuses', 29 *Yale JIL* (2004) pp. 343-361

- Simpson, Gerry J., 'Didactic and dissident histories in war crimes trials', in Gerry Simpson, ed., *War Crimes Law*, Vol. I (Aldershot, Ashgate 2004) pp. 401-439
- Simonović, Ivan, 'Dealing with the legacy of past war crimes and human rights abuses: experiences and trends', 2 *Journal of International Criminal Justice* (2004) pp. 701-710
- Simonović, Ivan, 'Attitudes and types of reaction toward past war crimes and human rights abuses', 29 *Yale JIL* (2004) pp. 343-361
- Wald, Patricia M., 'Accountability for war crimes: what roles for national, international and hybrid tribunals?', 98 *Proceedings of the Annual Meeting* (2004) pp. 192-195

6.12 Genocide

Books

- Akçam, Taner, *From Empire to Republic: Turkish Nationalism and the Armenian Genocide* (London, Zed Books 2004) 273 pp.
- Dubiel, Helmut, *The Lesser Evil: Moral Approaches to Genocide Practices* (London, Routledge 2004) 232 pp.
- Fawthrop, Tom and Helen Jarvis, *Getting Away With Genocide? Elusive Justice and the Khmer Rouge Tribunal* (London, Pluto Press 2004) 327 pp.
- Fisanick, Christina, *The Rwanda Genocide* (San Diego, Greenhaven Press 2004) 141 pp.
- Frey, Robert S., *The Genocidal Temptation: Auschwitz, Hiroshima, Rwanda, and Beyond* (Dallas, University Press of America 2004) 267 pp.
- Jones, Adam, *Genocide, War Crimes and the West: History and Complicity* (London, Zed Books 2004) 424 pp.
- Jones, Adam, *Gendercide and Genocide* (Nashville, Vanderbilt University Press 2004) 302 pp.
- Koff, Clea, *The Bone Woman: Among the Dead in Rwanda, Bosnia, Croatia and Kosovo* (London, Atlantic Books 2004) 321 pp.
- Lugan, Bernard, *Rwanda: le génocide, l'Église et la démocratie*, (Lonrai, Editions du Rocher 2004) 234 pp.
- Melvern, Linda, *Conspiracy to Murder: the Rwandan Genocide* (London, Verso 2004) 358 pp.
- Mujawayo, Esther, *SurVivantes: Rwanda, dix ans après le génocide: suivi de Entretien croisé entre Simone Veil et Esther Mujawayo* (La Tour d'Aigues, Aube 2004) 303 pp.
- Rittner, Carol, *Genocide in Rwanda: Complicity of the Churches?* (St. Paul, Paragon House) 319 pp.
- Shelton, Dinah, *Encyclopedia of Genocide and Crimes Against Humanity* (Detroit, Thomson/Gale 2004) 1458 pp.
- Totten, Samuel, *Century of Genocide: Critical Essays and Eyewitness Accounts*, 2nd edn. (London, Routledge 2004) 507 pp.
- Trahan, Jennifer, Adela Mall, and Widney Brown, *Genocide, War Crimes, and Crimes Against Humanity: Topical Digests of the Case Law of the International Criminal Tribunal for Rwanda and the International Criminal Tribunal for the Former Yugoslavia* (New York, Human Rights Watch 2004) 277 pp.
- Valentino, Benjamin A., *Final Solutions: Mass Killing and Genocide in the Twentieth Century* (Ithaca, Cornell University Press 2004) 317 pp.

– Veil, Simone, *Genocide and Accountability: Three Public Lectures* (Amsterdam, Vossiuspers UvA 2004) 52 pp.
– Waugh, Colin M., *Paul Kagame and Rwanda: Power, Genocide and the Rwandan Patriotic Front* (Jefferson, McFarland 2004) 254 pp.
– Yürükel, Sefa M., *The History of Genocide* (Nicosia, Near East Publishing 2004)
– Zawati, Hilmi M., *A Selected Socio-Legal Bibliography on Ethnic Cleansing, Wartime Rape, and Genocide in the Former Yugoslavia and Rwanda* (Lewiston, Edwin Mellen Press 2004) 587 pp.

Articles

– Adalian, Rouben Paul, 'The Armenian genocide', in Samual Totten, ed., *Century of Genocide: Critical Essays and Eyewitness Accounts*, 2nd edn. (New York Routledge 2004) pp. 53-90
– Aschheim, Steven E., 'Imagining the absolute: mapping Western conceptions of evil', in Helmut Dubiel and Gabriel Motzkin, eds., *The Lesser Evil: Moral Approaches to Genocide Practices* (London, Routledge 2004) pp. 73-84
– Bibliowicksz, M., 'The Armenian genocide: legacies and challenges of a silenced past', 16 *Sri Lanka JIL* (2004) pp. 27-64
– Boraine, Alexander, 'Retributive justice and restorative justice: contradictory or complimentary?', in Simone Veil, Geoffrey Nice and Alex Boraine, eds., *Genocide and Accountability: Three Public Lectures* (Amsterdam, Vossiuspers UvA 2004) pp. 39-52
– Bowen, Roger W., 'Genocide in Rwanda 1994: an Anglican perspective', in Carol Rittner, ed., *Genocide in Rwanda: Complicity of the Churches?* (St. Paul, Paragon House 2004) pp. 37-48
– Bridgman, John and Leslie J. Worley, eds., 'Genocide of the hereros', in Samual Totten, *Century of Genocide: Critical Essays and Eyewitness Accounts*, 2nd edn. (New York, Routledge 2004) pp. 15-51
– Buchanan, David, 'Gendercide and human rights', in Adam Jones, ed., *Gendercide and Genocide* (Nashville, Vanderbilt University Press 2004) pp. 138-156
– Budrytė, Dovilė, '"We call it genocide": Soviet deportations and repression in the memory of Lithuanians', in Robert S. Frey, ed., *The Genocidal Temptation: Auschwitz, Hiroshima, Rwanda, and Beyond* (Dallas, University Press of America 2004) pp. 79-95
– Burkhalter, Holly, 'Preventing genocide and crimes against humanity', 98 *Proceedings of the Annual Meeting* (2004) pp. 41-47
– Byron, Christine, 'The crime of genocide', in Dominic McGoldrick, Peter Rowe and Eric Donnelly, eds., *The Permanent International Criminal Court: Legal and Policy Issues* (Oxford, Hart 2004) pp. 143-177
– Cribb, Robert, 'The Indonesian massacres', in Samual Totten, ed., *Century of Genocide: Critical Essays and Eyewitness Accounts*, 2nd edn. (New York, Routledge 2004) pp. 233-260
– Des Forges, Alison and Timothy Longman, 'Legal responses to genocide in Rwanda', in Eric Stover and Harvey M. Weinstein, eds., *My Neighbor, My Enemy: Justice and Community in the Aftermath of Mass Atrocity* (Cambridge, Cambridge University Press 2004) pp. 49-68
– Dunn, James, 'Genocide in East Timor', in Samual Totten, ed., *Century of Genocide: Critical Essays and Eyewitness Accounts*, 2nd edn. (New York, Routledge 2004) pp. 263-293

– Etcheson, Craig, 'The politics of genocide justice in Cambodia', in Cesare P.R. Romano, André Nollkaemper and Jann K. Kleffner, eds., *Internationalized Criminal Courts and Tribunals: Sierra Leone, East Timor, Kosovo, and Cambodia* (Oxford, Oxford University Press 2004) pp. 181-205
– Felman, Shoshana, 'Theaters of justice: Arendt in Jerusalem, the Eichmann trial and the redefinition of legal meaning in the wake of the holocaust', in Gerry Simpson, ed., *War Crimes Law*, Vol. II (Aldershot, Ashgate 2004) pp. 271-308
– Fowler, Jerry, 'Out of that darkness: responding to genocide in the 21st century', in Samual Totten, ed., *Century of Genocide: Critical Essays and Eyewitness Accounts*, 2nd edn. (London, Routledge 2004) pp. 455-468
– Gallagher, Hugh Gregory, 'Holocaust: the genocide of disabled peoples', in Samual Totten, ed., *Century of Genocide: Critical Essays and Eyewitness Accounts*, 2nd edn. (New York, Routledge 2004) pp. 205-230
– Halliday, Dennis J., 'US Policy and Iraq: a case of genocide?', in Adam Jones, ed., *Genocide, War Crimes and the West: History and Complicity* (London, Zed Books 2004) pp. 264-269
– Herik, Larisse van den and Elies van Sliedregt, 'Ten years later, the Rwanda Tribunal still faces legal complexities: some comments on the vagueness of the indictment, complicity in genocide, and the nexus requirement for war crimes', 17 *Leiden JIL* (2004) pp. 537-557
– Holter, Øystein Gullvåg, 'A theory of gendercide', in Adam Jones, ed., *Gendercide and Genocide* (Nashville, Vanderbilt University Press 2004) pp. 62-97
– Huttenbach, Henry R., 'More than genocide: Rwanda revisited (before and after 1994)', in Robert S. Frey, ed., *The Genocidal Temptation: Auschwitz, Hiroshima, Rwanda, and Beyond* (Dallas, University Press of America 2004) pp. 57-65
– Huttenbach, Henry R., 'The genocide factor in the Yugoslav wars of dismemberment', in Jeffrey S. Morton, ed., *Reflections on the Balkan Wars: Ten Years After the Break Up of Yugoslavia* (New York, Palgrave Macmillan 2004) pp. 23-34
– Ilgner, Claudia, 'Besonderheiten und Problemstellungen bei Strafverfolgungsmaßnahmen und kriminalpolizeilichen Ermittlungen wegen Völkermordes, Verbrechen gegen die Menschlichkeit und Kriegsverbrechen', *Der Internationale Strafgerichtshof: fünf Jahre nach Rom: Tagungsdokumentation Berlin, 27.-28. Juni 2003* (Berlin, Deutsches Institut für Menschenrechte 2004) pp. 53-56
– Jacobs, Steven Leonard, 'Afraid to Call Genocide Genocide? Reflections on Rwanda and Beyond', in Robert S. Frey, ed., *The Genocidal Temptation: Auschwitz, Hiroshima, Rwanda, and beyond* (Dallas, University Press of America 2004) pp. 67-78
– Jahan, Rounaq, 'Genocide in Bangladesh', in Samual Totten, ed., *Century of Genocide: Critical Essays and Eyewitness Accounts*, 2nd edn. (New York, Routledge 2004) pp. 295-319
– Jefremovas, Villia, 'Socioeconomic conditions, not ethnic hatred, led to the genocide', in Christina Fisanick, ed., *The Rwanda Genocide* (San Diego, Greenhaven Press 2004) pp. 29-39
– Jones, Adam, 'Afghanistan and beyond', in Adam Jones, ed., *Genocide, War Crimes and the West: History and Complicity* (London, Zed Books 2004) pp. 383-403
– Jones, Adam, 'Gender and genocide in Rwanda', in Adam Jones, ed., *Gendercide and Genocide* (Nashville, Vanderbilt University Press 2004) pp. 98-138
– Jones, Adam, 'Gendercide and genocide', in Adam Jones, ed., *Gendercide and Genocide* (Nashville, Vanderbilt University Press 2004) pp. 1-38

– Khan, Shaharyar M., 'The United Nations dismissed the warning signs and failed to stop the genocide', in Christina Fisanick, ed., *The Rwanda Genocide* (San Diego, Greenhaven Press 2004) pp. 58-67
– Kamanzi, Stanislas, 'Preventing genocide: the role of the United Nations', 10 *ILSA Jl & CL ILSA* (2004) pp. 329-333
– Karekezi, Urusaro Alice, Alphonse Nshimiyimana and Beth Mutamba, 'Localizing justice: Gacaca courts in post-genocide Rwanda', in Eric Stover and Harvey M. Weinstein, eds., *My Neighbor, My Enemy: Justice and Community in the Aftermath of Mass Atrocity* (Cambridge, Cambridge University Press 2004) pp. 69-84
– Keane, Fergal, 'President Habyarimana's government was responsible for the genocide', in Christina Fisanick, ed., *The Rwanda Genocide* (San Diego, Greenhaven Press 2004) pp. 17-28
– Kiernan, Ben, 'The Cambodian genocide: 1975-1979', in Samual Totten, ed., *Century of Genocide: Critical Essays and Eyewitness Accounts*, 2nd edn. (New York, Routledge 2004) pp. 339-373
– Lagsub, Archelle F., 'On bloodshed, national healing and the rule of law: the Genocide Convention and its progress, problems and prospects', 48 *Ateneo Law Journal* (2004) pp. 1301-1378
– Leezenberg, Michiel, 'The Anfal operations in Iraqi Kurdistan', in Samual Totten, ed., *Century of Genocide: Critical Essays and Eyewitness Accounts*, 2nd edn. (New York, Routledge 2004) pp. 375-393
– Lemarchand, René, 'The Burundi genocide', in Samual Totten, ed., *Century of Genocide: Critical Essays and Eyewitness Accounts*, 2nd edn. (New York, Routledge 2004) pp. 321-337
– Lemarchand, René, 'The Rwanda genocide', in Samual Totten, ed., *Century of Genocide: Critical Essays and Eyewitness Accounts*, 2nd edn. (New York, Routledge 2004) pp. 395-412
– Locke, Hubert G., 'Religion and the Rwandan genocide: some preliminary considerations', in Carol Rittner, ed., *Genocide in Rwanda: Complicity of the Churches?* (St. Paul, Paragon House) pp. 27-36
– Mace, James E., 'Soviet man-made famine in Ukraine', in Samual Totten, ed., *Century of Genocide: Critical Essays and Eyewitness Accounts*, 2nd edn. (New York, Routledge 2004) pp. 93-124
– Melvern, Linda R., 'The Security Council: behind the scenes in the Rwanda genocide', in Adam Jones, ed., *Genocide, War Crimes and the West: History and Complicity* (London, Zed Books 2004) pp. 260-263
– Mennecke, Martin and Eric Markusen., 'Genocide in Bosnia and Herzegovina', in Samual Totten, ed., *Century of Genocide: Critical Essays and Eyewitness Accounts*, 2nd edn. (New York, Routledge 2004) pp. 415-447
– Mennecke, Martin, 'Genocide in Kosovo?', in Samual Totten, ed., *Century of Genocide: Critical Essays and Eyewitness Accounts*, 2nd edn. (New York, Routledge 2004) pp. 449-454
– Milton, Sybil, 'Holocaust: the gypsies', in Samual Totten, ed., *Century of Genocide: Critical Essays and Eyewitness Accounts*, 2nd edn. (New York, Routledge 2004) pp. 161-202
– Molier, Gelijn, 'Genocide in Soedan: een juridische plicht tot ingrijpen?', *Jaarboek vrede en veiligheid* (2004) pp. 50-88

- Nice, Geoffrey, 'The reality of the modern war crimes trial', in Simone Veil, Geoffrey Nice and Alex Boraine, eds., *Genocide and Accountability: Three Public Lectures* (Amsterdam, Vossiuspers UvA 2004) pp. 23-38
- Niewyk, Donald L., 'Holocaust: the genocide of the Jews', in Samual Totten, ed., *Century of Genocide: Critical Essays and Eyewitness Accounts*, 2nd edn.(New York, Routledge 2004) pp. 127-159
- Olendzki, Krzysztof, 'Memory and responsibility: a few remarks on Raphael Lemkin's views on genocide', in Hans-Joachim Giessmann, Roman Kúzniar and Zdzislaw Lachowski, eds., *International Security in a Time of Change: Threats, Concepts, Institutions: Festschrift for Adam Daniel Rotfeld* (Baden-Baden, Nomos 2004) pp. 100-113
- Paech, Norman, 'Saddam könnte nicht wegen Völkermord angeklagt werden: Interview der Frankfurter Rundschau mit Norman Paech', *Der Internationale Strafgerichtshof: fünf Jahre nach Rom: Tagungsdokumentation Berlin, 27.-28. Juni 2003* (Berlin, Deutsches Institut für Menschenrechte 2004) pp. 475-477
- Power, Samantha, 'Bystanders to genocide. Why the United States let the Rwandan tragedy happen', in Christina Fisanick, ed., *The Rwanda Genocide* (San Diego, Greenhaven Press 2004) pp. 78-87
- Power, Samantha, 'Bystanders to genocide', in Karen Mingst and Jack Snyder, eds., *Essential Readings in World Politics* (New York, Norton 2004) pp. 233-253
- Riza, Igbal, 'The disaster in Somalia influenced the United Nations to delay intervention in Rwanda', in Christina Fisanick, ed., *The Rwanda Genocide* (San Diego, Greenhaven Press 2004) pp. 68-77
- Ronayne, Peter V., 'The United States and the "G-word": genocide and denial before and beyond Rwanda', in Robert S. Frey, ed., *The Genocidal Temptation: Auschwitz, Hiroshima, Rwanda, and Beyond* (Dallas, University Press of America 2004) pp. 101-114
- Salzman, Todd, 'Tutsi favoritism by the catholic church contributed to the genocide', in Christina Fisanick, ed., *The Rwanda Genocide* (San Diego, Greenhaven Press 2004) pp. 40-46
- Scheirs, Tom L.W, 'Genocide in Srebenica', 13 *Zoeklicht* (2004) pp. 19-20
- Schwabach, Aaron, 'Ecocide and genocide in Iraq: international law, the Marsh Arabs, and environmental damage in non-international conflicts', 15 *Colorado Jl Environ. L & Pol.* (2004) pp. 1-28
- Schwarzenberger, Georg, 'The Eichmann Judgment: an essay in censorial jurisprudence', in Gerry Simpson, ed., *War Crimes Law*, Vol. II (Aldershot, Ashgate 2004) pp. 253-270
- Tetzlaff, Rainer, 'Genozid in Afrika: Darfur: fernbleiben oder sich einmischen?', 59 *Internationale Politik* (2004) pp. 87-94
- Totten, Samuel, 'The Intervention and prevention of genocide: where there is the political will, there is a way', in Samual Totten, ed., *Century of Genocide: Critical Essays and Eyewitness Accounts*, 2nd edn. (London, Routledge 2004) pp. 469-490
- Ugirashebuja, Octave, 'The church and the genocide in Rwanda', in Carol Rittner, John K. Roth, Wendy Whitworth, eds., *Genocide in Rwanda: Complicity of the Churches?* (St. Paul, Paragon House 2004) pp. 49-63
- Uvin, Peter, 'Rwanda's lack of resources and extreme poverty provided the breeding grounds for genocide', in Christina Fisanick, ed., *The Rwanda Genocide* (San Diego, Greenhaven Press 2004) pp. 47-56

– Valentino, Benjamin and Paul Huth and Dylan Balch-Lindsay, eds., '"Draining the sea": mass killing and guerrilla warfare', 58 *International Organization* (2004) pp. 375-407
– Verdeja, Ernesto, 'Institutional responses to genocide and mass atrocity', in Adam Jones, ed., *Genocide, War Crimes and the West: History and Complicity* (London, Zed Books 2004) pp. 327-345
– Wohlfarth, Irving, 'Worstward Ho: on comparing totalitarianisms', in Helmut Dubiel and Gabriel Motzkin, eds., *The Lesser Evil: Moral Approaches to Genocide Practices* (London, Routledge 2004) pp. 35-72

6.13 Crimes Against Humanity

Books

– Meseke, Stephan, *Der Tatbestand der Verbrechen gegen die Menschheit nach dem Römischen Statut des Internationalen Strafgerichtshofes: eine völkerstrafrechtliche Analyse* (Berlin, Berliner Wissenschafts-Verlag 2004) 371 pp.
– Shelton, Dinah, *Encyclopedia of Genocide and Crimes Against Humanity,* 4 Vols. (Detroit, Thomson/Gale 2004) 1458 pp.
– Trahan, Jennifer, Adela Mall, and Widney Brown, eds., *Genocide, War Crimes, and Crimes Against Humanity: Topical Digests of the Case Law of the International Criminal Tribunal for Rwanda and the International Criminal Tribunal for the Former Yugoslavia* (New York, Human Rights Watch 2004) 277 pp.

Articles

– Blakesley, Christopher L., 'The modern blood-feud: thoughts on the philosophy of crimes against humanity and the proper response', in John Carey, William V. Dunlap and R. John Pritchard, eds., *International Humanitarian Law*, Vol. 2 (Ardsley Transnational Publishers 2004) pp. 89-121
– Burkhalter, Holly, 'Preventing genocide and crimes against humanity', 98 *Proceedings of the Annual Meeting* (2004) pp. 41-47
– Day, Adam, 'Crimes against humanity as a nexus of individual and state responsibility: why the ICJ got Belgium v. Congo wrong', 22 *Berkeley JIL* (2004) pp. 489-512
– Finney, John W., 'Media limitations in reporting crimes against humanity', in John Carey, William V. Dunlap and R. John Pritchard, eds., *International Humanitarian Law,* Vol. 2 (Ardsley, Transnational Publishers 2004) pp. 1-15
– Guesnier, Francine, 'Acts of terrorism as crimes against humanity under the Rome Statute', in Sienho Yee, ed., *International Crime and Punishment: Selected Issues*, Vol. 2 (Lanham, University Press of America 2004) pp. 55-86
– Ilgner, Claudia, 'Besonderheiten und Problemstellungen bei Strafverfolgungsmaßnahmen und kriminalpolizeilichen Ermittlungen wegen Völkermordes, Verbrechen gegen die Menschlichkeit und Kriegsverbrechen' in Gunnar Theissen and Martin Nagler, eds., *Der Internationale Strafgerichtshof: fünf Jahre nach Rom: Tagungsdokumentation Berlin, 27.-28. Juni 2003* (Berlin, Deutsches Institut für Menschenrechte 2004) pp. 53-56
– Lelieur-Fischer, Juliette, 'Prosecuting the crimes against humanity committed during the Algerian war: an impossible endeavour?: the 2003 decision of the French Court of Cassation in Aussaresses', 2 *Journal of International Criminal Justice* (2004) pp. 231-244

- Luban, David, 'A theory of crimes against humanity', 29 *Yale JIL* (2004) pp. 85-167
- MacCormack, Timothy L.H, 'Crimes against humanity', in Dominic McGoldrick, Peter Rowe and Eric Donnelly, eds., *The Permanent International Criminial Court* (Oxford, Hart) pp. 179-202
- MacKinnon, Catharine A., 'Prosecutor v. Nahimana, Barayagwiza, & Ngeze: case no. ICTR 99-52-T: International Criminal Tribunal for Rwanda, December 3, 2003: ICTR judgment and sentence on crimes against humanity and incitement to genocide through broadcast and press outlets', 98 *AJIL* (2004) pp. 325-330
- Proux, Vincent-Joël, 'Rethinking the jurisdiction of the International Criminal Court in the Post-September 11th era: should acts of terrorism qualify as crimes against humanity?', 19 *Amer. Univ. ILR* (2004) pp.1009-1089
- Schabas, William A, 'Is terrorism a crime against humanity?', 8 *International Peacekeeping* (2004) pp. 255-261
- Stoett, Peter, 'Shades of complicity: towards a typology of transnational crimes against humanity', in Adam Jones, ed., *Genocide, War Crimes and the West: History and Complicity* (London, Zed Books 2004) pp. 3-30
- Wiethoff, Jan, 'Folter: ein zulässiges Mittel einer effektiven Terrorismus Bekämpfung?: die tickende Zeitbombe in der Großstadt', 17 *Humanitäres Völkerrecht* (2004) pp. 104-108

6.14 Aggression

Books

- Politi, Mauro and Giuseppe Nesi, eds., *The International Criminal Court and the Crime of Aggression* (Aldershot, Ashgate 2004) pp. 193 pp.

Articles

- Dascalopoulou-Livada, Phani, 'Aggression and the ICC: views on certain ideas and their potential for a solution', in Mauro Politi and Giuseppe Nesi, eds., *The International Criminal Court and the Crime of Aggression* (Aldershot, Ashgate 2004) pp. 79-85
- Escaramela, Paula, 'The ICC and the Security Council on aggression: overlapping competencies?', in Mauro Politi and Giuseppe Nesi, eds., *The International Criminal Court and the Crime of Aggression* (Aldershot, Ashgate 2004) pp. 133-143
- Gaja, Giorgio, 'The respective roles of the ICC and the Security Council in determining the existence of an aggression', in Mauro Politi and Giuseppe Nesi, eds., *The International Criminal Court and the Crime of Aggression* (Aldershot, Ashgate 2004) pp. 121-124
- Gommaa, Mohammed M., 'The definition of the crime of aggression and the ICC jurisdiction over that crime', in Mauro Politi and Giuseppe Nesi, eds., *The International Criminal Court and the Crime of Aggression* (Aldershot, Ashgate 2004) pp. 55-77
- Kaul, Hans-Peter, 'The crime of aggression: definitional options for the way forward', in Mauro Politi and Giuseppe Nesi, eds., *The International Criminal Court and the Crime of Aggression* (Aldershot, Ashgate 2004) pp. 97-108
- Khan, Daniel-Erasmus, 'Die individuelle (völker-)strafrechtliche Verantwortlichkeit für eine völkerrechtswidrige militärische Aggression gegen den Irak', in Kai Ambos and

Jörg Arnold, eds., *Der Irak-Krieg und das Völkerrecht* (Berlin, Berliner Wissenschafts-Verlag 2004) pp. 449-470
- Kress, Claus, 'The Iraqi Special Tribunal and the crime of aggression', 2 *Journal of International Criminal Justice* (2004) pp. 347-352
- Kress, Claus, 'The German Chief Federal Prosecutor's decision not to investigate the alleged crime of preparing aggression against Iraq', 2 *Journal of International Criminal Justice* (2004) pp. 245-264
- Lehto, Marja, 'The ICC and the Security Council: about the argument of politization', in Mauro Politi and Giuseppe Nesi, eds., *The International Criminal Court and the Crime of Aggression* (Aldershot, Ashgate 2004) pp. 145-149
- Paulus, Andreas L., 'Peace through justice? The future of the crime of aggression in a time of crisis', 50 *Wayne Law Review* (2004) pp. 1-35
- Politi, Mauro , 'The debate within the Preparatory Commission for the International
- Criminal Court', in Mauro Politi and Giuseppe Nesi, eds., *The International Criminal Court and the Crime of Aggression* (Aldershot, Ashgate 2004) pp. 43-51
- Schabas, William A., 'Origins of the criminalization of aggression: how crimes against peace became the "supreme international crime"', in Mauro Politi and Giuseppe Nesi, eds., *The International Criminal Court and the Crime of Aggression* (Aldershot, Ashgate 2004) pp. 17-32
- Schweisfurth, Theodor, 'Aggression', in Kai Ambos and Jörg Arnold, eds., *Der Irak-Krieg und das Völkerrecht* (Berlin, Berliner Wissenschafts-Verlag 2004) pp. 359-365
- Shukri, Muhammad Aziz, 'Will aggressors ever be tried before the ICC?', in Mauro Politi and Giuseppe Nesi, eds., *The International Criminal Court and the Crime of Aggression* (Aldershot, Ashgate 2004) pp. 33-42
- Stancu, Ioana Gabriela, 'Defining the crime of aggression or redefining aggression?', in Mauro Politi and Giuseppe Nesi, eds., *The International Criminal Court and the Crime of Aggression* (Aldershot, Ashgate 2004) pp. 87-91
- Wilmshurst, Elizabeth, 'Definition of the crime of aggression: state responsibility or individual criminal responsibility?', in Mauro Politi and Giuseppe Nesi, eds., *The International Criminal Court and the Crime of Aggression* (Aldershot, Ashgate 2004) pp. 93-96
- Yáñez-Barnuevo, Antonio, 'The exercise of the International Criminal Courts' jurisdiction over the crime of aggression: short term and long term proposals', in Mauro Politi and Giuseppe Nesi, eds., *The International Criminal Court and the Crime of Aggression* (Aldershot, Ashgate 2004) pp. 109-117
- Yengejeh, Saeid Mirzaee, 'Reflections on the role of the Security Council in determining an act of aggression', in Mauro Politi and Giuseppe Nesi, eds., *The International Criminal Court and the Crime of Aggression* (Aldershot, Ashgate 2004) pp. 125-132

6.15 Torture

Books

- Levinson, Sanford, *Torture: a Collection* (New York, Oxford University Press 2004) 319 pp.
- Benvenisti, Meron, *Abu Ghraib: the Politics of Torture* (Berkeley, North Atlantic Books 2004) 144 pp.

– Baldauf, Dieter, *Die Folter: eine deutsche Rechtsgeschichte* (Köln, Böhlau 2004) 235 pp.

Articles

– Alvanou, Maria, 'Combating terrorism and human rights protection: the ticking bomb theories and torture', 8 *Mediterranean Journal of Human Rights* (2004) pp. 33-52
– Bilder, Richard B. and Detlev F. Vagts, 'Speaking law to power: lawyers and torture', 98 *AJIL* (2004) pp. 689-695
– Boven, Theo van, 'Urgent appeals on behalf of torture victims', in Luigi Condorelli and Gérard Cohen-Jonathan, eds., *Libertés, justice, tolérance: mélanges en hommage au doyen Gérard Cohen-Jonathan*, Vol. 2 (Brussels, Bruylant 2004) pp. 1651-1666
– Branche, Raphaëlle, 'Torture and other violations of the law by the French Army during the Algerian war', in Adam Jones, ed., *Genocide, War Crimes and the West: History and Complicity* (London, Zed Books 2004) pp. 134-145
– Brouwer, Charles H., 'The lives of animals, the lives of prisoners, and the revelations of Abu Ghraib', 37 *Vanderbilt JTL* (2004) pp. 1353-1388
– Cassese, Antonio, 'Are international human rights treaties and customary rules on torture binding upon US troops in Iraq?', 2 *Journal of International Criminal Justice* (2004) pp. 872-878
– De Wet, Erika, 'The prohibition of torture as an international norm of jus cogens and its implications for national and customary law', 15 *EJIL* (2004) pp. 97-121
– Dershowitz, Alan M., 'Should the ticking bomb terrorist be tortured?: a case study in how a democracy should make tragic choices', in M. Katherine B. Darmer, Robert M. Baird and Stuart E. Rosenbaum, eds., *Civil Liberties vs. National Security in a Post-9/11 World* (Amherst, Prometheus Books 2004) pp. 189-214
– Dershowitz, Alan M., 'The torture warrant: a response to Professor Strauss', 48 *New York Law School Law Review* (2004) pp. 275-294
– Dershowitz, Alan, 'Tortured reasoning', in Sanford Levinson, ed., *Torture: a Collection* (New York, Oxford University Press 2004) pp. 257-280
– Elshtain, Jean Bethke, 'Reflection on the problem of "dirty hands"', in Sanford Levinson, ed., *Torture: a Collection* (New York, Oxford University Press 2004) pp. 77-89
– Gaeta, Paola, 'May necessity be available as a defence for torture in the interrogation of suspected terrorist?', 2 *Journal of International Criminal Justice* (2004) pp. 785-794
– Gill, Ryan, 'The federalization of the crime of torture: an analysis of the constitutional and international law issues', in Sienho Yee, ed., *International Crime and Punishment: Selected Issues*, Vol. 2 (Lanham, University Press of America 2004) pp. 205-251
– Gross, Michael L., 'Torture, assassination and blackmail: violating human rights to fight terror', 8 *Mediterranean Journal of Human Rights* (2004) pp. 185-209
– Gur-Arye, Miriam, 'Can the war against terror justify the use of force in interrogations? Reflections in light of the Israeli experience', in Sanford Levinson, ed., *Torture: a Collection* (New York, Oxford University Press 2004) pp. 183-198
– Haeck, Yves and Valentina Staelens, 'Verbod van foltering en onmenselijke of vernederende behandeling of straffen', Handboek EVRM. Dl. 2: artikelsgewijze commentaar, Vol. 1 (Antwerp, Intersentia 2004) pp. 123-229
– Hathaway, Oona A., 'The promise and limits of the international law of torture', in Sanford Levinson, ed., *Torture: a Collection* (New York, Oxford University Press 2004) pp. 199-212
– Hope, David, 'Torture', 53 *ICLQ* (2004) pp. 807-832

– Kamminga, Menno T., 'First conviction under the universal jurisdiction provisions of the UN convention against torture: Rotterdam District Court, 7 April 2004, Sebastien N.', 51 *NILR* (2004) pp. 439-449
– Keller, Linda M., 'Is truth serum torture?', 20 *Amer. Univ. ILR* (2004) pp. 521-612
– Langbein, John H., 'The legal history of torture', in Sanford Levinson, ed., *Torture: a Collection* (New York, Oxford University Press 2004) pp. 93-103
– Lanzi, Alessio and Tullio Scovazzi, 'Una dubbia repressione della tortura e di altri gravi crimini di guerra', 87 *Rivista di diritto internazionale* (2004) pp. 685-694
– La Violette, Nicole, 'La loi sur l'immigration et la protection des réfugiés et la définition internationale de la torture', 34 *Revue générale de droit* (2004) pp. 587-610
– Levinson, Sanford, 'Contemplating torture: an introduction', in Sanford Levinson, ed., *Torture: a Collection* (New York, Oxford University Press 2004) pp. 23-43
– Marks, Susan, 'Apologising for torture', 73 *Nordic JIL* (2004) pp. 365-385
– Nessel, Lori A., '"Willful blindness" to gender-based violence abroad: United States' implementation of article three of the United Nations Convention against torture', 89 *Minnesota Law Review* (2004) pp. 71-162
– Ní Aoláin, Fionnuala, 'The European Convention on Human Rights and its prohibition on torture', in Sanford Levinson, ed., *Torture: a Collection* (New York, Oxford University Press 2004) pp. 213-227
– Ochoa Ruiz, Natalia, 'La jurisprudencia del Comité de las Naciones Unidas contra la Tortura', 20 *Anuario de derecho internacional* (2004) pp. 521-565
– Osiel, Mark, 'The mental state of torturers: Argentina's dirty war', in Sanford Levinson, ed., *Torture: a Collection* (New York, Oxford University Press 2004) pp.129-141
– Parry, John T., White, Welsh S., 'Interrogating suspected terrorists: should torture be an option?', in M. Katherine B. Darmer, Robert M. Baird and Stuart E. Rosenbaum, eds., *Civil Liberties vs. National Security in a Post-9/11 World* (Amherst, Prometheus Books 2004) pp. 229-247
– Parry, John T., 'Escalation and necessity: defining torture at home and abroad', in Sanford Levinson, ed., *Torture: a Collection* (New York, Oxford University Press 2004) pp. 145-164
– Posner, Richard A., 'Torture, terrorism, and interrogation', in Sanford Levinson, ed., *Torture: a Collection* (New York, Oxford University Press 2004) pp. 291-298
– Supreme Court of Israel, 'Judgment concerning the legality of the general security service's interrogation methods (September 6, 1999)', in Sanford Levinson, ed., *Torture: a Collection* (New York, Oxford University Press 2004) pp.165-181
– Press, Eyal, 'In torture we trust?', in M. Katherine B. Darmer, Robert M. Baird, and Stuart E. Rosenbaum, eds., *Civil Liberties vs. National Security in a Post-9/11 World* (Amherst, Prometheus Books 2004) pp. 219-228
– Scarry, Elaine, 'Five errors in the reasoning of Alan Dershowitz', in Sanford Levinson, ed., *Torture: a Collection* (New York, Oxford University Press 2004) pp. 281-290
– Shue, Henry, 'Torture', in Sanford Levinson, ed., *Torture: a Collection* (New York, Oxford University Press 2004) pp. 47-60
– Skolnick, Jerome H., 'American interrogation: from torture to trickery', in Sanford Levinson, ed., *Torture: a Collection* (New York, Oxford University Press 2004) pp. 105-127
– Soler, Christopher, 'Why is freedom from torture an absolute right? A multi-disciplinary analysis', 8 *Mediterranean Journal of Human Rights* (2004) pp. 369-380

- Sørensen, Bent and Paul Dalton, 'The Convention against Torture and Other Cruel, Inhuman or Degrading Treatment or Punishment: limitations, restrictions and reservations', in Ineta Ziemele, ed., *Reservations to Human Rights Treaties and the Vienna Convention Regime: Conflict, Harmony or Reconciliation* (Leiden, Nijhoff 2004) pp. 79-93
- Strauss, Marcy, 'Torture', 48 *New York Law School Law Review* (2004) pp. 201-274
- Weisberg, Richard H., 'Loose professionalism, or why lawyers take the lead on torture', in Sanford Levinson, ed., *Torture: a Collection* (New York, Oxford University Press 2004) pp. 299-305
- Yoo, John C., 'A crucial look at torture law', in M. Katherine B. Darmer, Robert M. Baird, and Stuart E. Rosenbaum, eds., *Civil Liberties vs. National Security in a Post-9/11 World* (Amherst, Prometheus Books 2004) pp. 321-323

6.2 GENERAL PRINCIPLES, INCLUDING DEFENCES

Articles

- Cryer, Robert, 'General principles of liability in international criminal law', in Dominic McGoldrick, Peter Rowe and Eric Donnelly, eds., *The Permanent International Criminial Court* (Oxford, Hart 2004) pp. 233-262

6.22 Individual Criminal Responsibility

Articles

- Greppi, Edoardo, 'The evolution of individual criminal responsibility under international law', in Naorem Sanajaoba, ed., *A Manual of International Humanitarian Laws* (New Dehli, Regency Publications 2004) pp. 410-433
- Levinson, Sanford, 'Responsibility for crimes of war', in Gerry Simpson, ed., *War Crimes Law*, Vol. I (Aldershot, Ashgate 2004) pp. 369-398
- Plattner, Denise, 'The penal repression of violations of international humanitarian law applicable in non-international armed conflicts', in Naorem Sanajaoba, ed., *A Manual of International Humanitarian Laws* (New Dehli, Regency Publications 2004) pp. 397-409
- Sellers, Patricia Viseur, 'Individual(s') liability for collective sexual violence', in Karen Knop, ed., *Gender and Human Rights* (Oxford, Oxford University Press 2004) pp. 153-194

6.23 Superior/Command Responsibility

Books

- Air Force Judge Advocate of the General School, *The Military Commander and the Law* (Honolulu, University Press of the Pacific 2004) 629 pp.

Articles

- Hingorani, R.C., 'Chain of Command and War Crimes: Yamashita revisited', 4 *ISIL Year Book of International Humanitarian and Refugee Law* (2004) pp. 131-135

- Jia, Bing Bing, 'The doctrine of command responsibility revisited', 3 *Chinese JIL* (2004) pp. 1-42
- Mundis, Daryl A., 'Crimes of the commander: superior responsibility under article 7(3) of the ICTY statute', in Gideon Boas and William A. Schabas, eds., *International Criminal Law Developments in the Case Law of the ICTY* (Leiden, Nijhoff 2003) pp. 239-275
- Olaneff, Jared, 'Holding a head of state liable for war crimes: command responsibility and the Milosevic trial', 27 *Suffolk Transnational Law Review* (2004) pp. 327-355
- O'Reilly, Arthur Thomas, 'Command responsibility: a call to realign doctrine with principles', 20 *American University International Law Review* (2004) pp. 71-107
- Perkins, Sarah, 'The failure to protect: expanding the scope of command responsibility to the United Nations at Srebrenica', 62 *University of Toronto Faculty of Law Review* (2004) pp. 193-212
- Triffterer, Otto, 'Command responsibility, Article 28 Rome Statute, an extension of individual criminal responsibility for crimes within the jurisdiction of the court: compatible with Article 22, nullum crimen sine lege?', in Otto Triffterer, ed., *Gedächtnisschrift für Theo Vogler* (Heidelberg, Müller 2004) pp. 213-262

6.31 International and Internationalised Courts

Books

- Hilwig, Elin, *International Courts and Tribunals: Selected Documents and Materials* (Nijmegen,Wolf Legal Publishers 2004) 639 pp.
- Romano, Cesare P.R. André Nollkaemper and Jann K. Kleffner, *Internationalized Criminal Courts and Tribunals: Sierra Leone, East Timor, Kosovo, and Cambodia* (Oxford, Oxford University Press 2004) 491 pp.

Articles

- Biddiss, Michael D., 'From the Nuremberg Charter to the Rome Statute: a historical analysis of the limits of international criminal accountability', in Ramesh Thakur and Jørgensen, Nina H.B., eds., 'The right of the accused to self-representation before International Criminal Tribunals', 98 *AJIL* (2004) pp. 711-744
- Malcontent, Peter, *From Sovereign Impunity to International Accountability: the Search for Justice in a World of States* (Tokyo, United Nations University Press 2004) pp. 42-60
- Schabas, William A., 'Internationalized Courts and their relationship with alternative accountability mechanisms: the case of Sierra Leone', in Cesare P.R. Romano, André Nollkaemper and Jann K. Kleffner, eds., *Internationalized Criminal Courts and Tribunals: Sierra Leone, East Timor, Kosovo, and Cambodia* (Oxford, Oxford University Press 2004) pp. 157-180

6.311 Nuremberg and Tokyo

Books

- Freyhofer, Horst H., *The Nuremberg Medical Trial: the Holocaust and the Origin of the Nuremberg Medical Code* (New York, Lang 2004) 209 pp.

– Goldensohn, Leon and Robert Gellately, *The Nuremberg Interviews* (New York, Knopf 2004) 490 pp.
– Kahn, Robert A., *Holocaust Denial and the Law: a Comparative Study* (New York, Palgrave Macmillan 2004) 207 pp.
– Pätzold, Kurt, *Stufen zum Galgen: Lebenswege vor den Nürnberger Urteilen* (Leipzig, Militzke 2004) 480pp.
– Schmidt, Ulf, *Justice at Nuremberg: Leo Alexander and the Nazi Doctors' Trial* (Basingstoke, Palgrave Macmillan 2004) 386 pp.
– Ushimura Kei, *Beyond the "Judgment of Civilization": the Intellectual Legacy of the Japanese War Crimes Trials*, 1946-194 (Tokyo, International House of Japan 2003) 336 pp.

Articles

– Borgwardt-Kopelman, Elizabeth S., 'Ideology and International Law: the Dissent of the Indian Justice at the Tokyo War Crimes Trial', in Gerry Simpson, ed., *War Crimes Law*, Vol. 2 (Aldershot, Ashgate-Dartmouth 2004) pp. 145-213
– Bryson, Brady O., 'Remembering Robert H. Jackson at Nuremberg Decades Ago', 68 *Albany Law Review* (2004) pp. 9-12
– Ferencz, Benjamin B., 'Tribute to Nuremberg Prosecutor Jackson', 16 *Pace International Law Review* (2004) pp. 365-375
– Fuchs, Moritz, 'Robert H. Jackson at the Nuremberg Trials, 1945-1946 as Rembered by his Personal Bodyguard', 68 *Albany Law Review* (2004) pp. 13-17
– Jescheck, Hans-Heinreich, 'The general principles of international criminal law set out in Nuremberg, as mirrored in the ICC Statute', 2 *Journal of International Criminal Justice* (2004) pp. 38-55
– Luban, David, 'The legacies of Nuremberg', in Gerry Simpson, ed., *War Crimes Law*, Vol. 2 (Aldershot, Ashgate-Dartmouth 2004) pp. 5-55
– Lüder, Sascha Rolf, 'Die Geschichte der Verfolgung von Kriegsverbrechen', in Horst Fischer und Dieter Fleck, eds., *Krisensicherung und humanitärer Schutz* (Berlin, Berliner Wissenschafts-Verlag 2004) pp. 365-382
– Meltzer, Bernard D., 'Robert H. Jackson: Nuremberg's Architect and Advocate', 68 *Albany Law Review* (2004) pp. 55-65
– Weindling, Paul Julian, *Nazi Medicine and the Nuremberg Trials: from Medical War Crimes to Informed Consent* (Basingstoke, Palgrave Macmillan 2004) 482 pp.

6.312 International Criminal Tribunal for the Former Yugoslavia

Books

– Barratt Brown, Michael, Edward S. Herman and and David Peterson, *The Trial of Slobodan Milosevic* (Nottingham, Spokesman 2004) 78 pp.
– Calvetti, Gianmaria, *Dal Tribunale per la Ex-Iugoslavia alla Corte Penale Internazionale* (Milano, Giuffrè 2004) 445 pp.
– Drakulić, Slavenka, *They Would Never Hurt a Fly: War Criminals on Trial in The Hague* (New York, Viking 2004) 209 pp.

- Hazan, Pierre, *Justice in a Time of War: the True Story Behind the International Criminal Tribunal for the Former Yugoslavia* (College Station, Texas A & M University Press 2004) 248 pp.
- Kerr, Rachel, *The International Criminal Tribunal for the Former Yugoslavia: an Exercise in Law, Politics, and Diplomacy* (Oxford, Oxford University Press 2004) 239 pp.
- Trahan, Jennifer, *Genocide, War Crimes, and Crimes against Humanity: Topical Digests of the Case Law of the International Criminal Tribunal for Rwanda and the International Criminal Tribunal for the Former Yugoslavia* (New York, Human Rights Watch 2004) 277 pp.
- Stephen, Chris, *Judgement day: the Trial of Slobodan Milosević* (London, Atlantic Books 2004) 258 pp.

Articles

- Bohlander, Michael, 'The influence of academic research on the jurisprudence of the International Criminal Tribunal for the Former Yugoslavia: a first overview', 1 *The Global Community* (Dobbs Ferry, Oceana 2004) pp. 195-209
- Carcano, Andrea, 'The International Criminal Tribunal for the Former Yugoslavia: Activities in 2003', 3 *Chinese JIL* (2004) pp. 267-290
- Darcy, Shane, 'An effective measure of bringing justice? The joint criminal enterprise doctrine of the International Criminal Tribunal for the Former Yugoslavia', 20 *Amer. Univ. ILR* (2004) pp. 153-191
- Dingwall, Joanna, 'Unlawful confinement as a war crime: the jurisprudence of the Yugoslav Tribunal and the common core of international humanitarian law applicable to contemporary armed conflicts', 9 *Journal of Conflict and Security Law* (2004) pp. 133-179
- Epstein, Melissa J.and Richard Butler, 'The customary origins and elements of select conduct of hostilities charges before the International Criminal Tribunal for the Former Yugoslavia: a potential model for use by military commissions', 179 *Mil. LR* (2004) pp. 68-127
- Fairlie, Megan A., 'Evidentiary privilege of journalists reporting in areas of armed conflict - evidence in war crimes trials - rule-making process of ICTY', 98 *AJIL* (2004) pp. 805-809
- Fairlie, Megan A., 'Rulesmaking from the bench: a place for minimalism at the ICTY', 39 *Texas ILJ* (2004) pp. 257-285
- Gall, Liza, 'Introductory note to ICTY: Prosecutor v. Galić: Cite as 43 ILM 789 (2004)', 43 *ILM* (2004) pp. 789-877
- Gaparayi, Idi, 'The Milosevic trial at the halfway stage: judgement on the motion for acquittal', 17 *Leiden JIL* (2004) pp. 737-766
- Grosscup, Scott, 'The trial of Slobodan Milosevic: the demise of head of state immunity and the specter of victor's justice', 32 *Denver JIL and Pol.* (2004) pp. 355-381
- Jötten, Sara, Schütze, Julia, 'Die Rechtsprechung des Internationalen Strafgerichtshofes für das ehemalige Jugoslawien im Jahre 2003', 46 *German YIL* (2004) pp. 635-674
- Kravetz, Daniela, 'The protection of civilians in war: the ICTY's Galić case', 17 *Leiden JIL* (2004) pp. 521-536
- Lobwein, Wendy, 'The work of the victims and witness section of the International Criminal Tribunal for the Former Yugoslavia', in Gunnar Theissen, Martin Nagler, eds., *Der Internationale Strafgerichtshof: fünf Jahre nach Rom: Tagungsdokumentation*

Berlin, 27.-28. Juni 2003 (Berlin, Deutsches Institut für Menschenrechte 2004) pp. 67-70
- Meernik, James D., King, Kimi L., 'Crimes and punishments: how the International Criminal Tribunal for the Former Yugoslavia distinguishes among massive human rights violations', in Sabine C. Carey and Steven C. Poe, eds., *Understanding Human Rights Violations: New Systematic Studies* (Aldershot, Ashgate 2004) pp. 147-161
- Mladjenovic, Lepa, 'The ICTY: the validation of the experiences of survivors', in Steven R. Ratner and James L. Bischoff, eds., *International War Crimes Trials: Making a Difference?: Proceedings of an interdisciplinary Conference at the University of Texas School of Law, Austin, Texas, November 6-7, 2003* (Austin, Austin School of Law 2004) pp. 59-65
- Mutua, Makau, 'Never again: questioning the Yugoslav and Rwanda tribunals', in Gerry Simpson, ed., *War Crimes Law*, Vol. II (Aldershot, Ashgate 2004) pp. 355-375
- Nieto-Navia, Rafael, 'The International Criminal Tribunal for the Former Yugoslavia in 2002', 1 *The Global Community* (2004) pp. 593-612
- Panovsky, Damjan, 'Some war crimes are not better than others: the failure of the International Criminal Tribunal for the Former Yugoslavia to prosecute war crimes in Macedonia', 98 *Northwestern University LR* (2004) pp. 623-655
- Rubin, Alfred P., 'An International Criminal Tribunal for Former Yugoslavia', in Gerry Simpson, ed., *War Crimes Law* Vol. 2 (Aldershot, Ashgate-Dartmouth 2004) pp. 343-353
- Statute of the International Criminal Tribunal for the Former Yugoslavia: Version of 19 May 2003, in Elin Hilwig, Relinde van Laar and Willem-Jan van der Wolf, eds., *International Courts and Tribunals: Selected Documents and Materials* (Nijmegen, Wolf Legal Publishers 2004) pp. 153-164
- Wald, Patricia MacGowan, 'The Omarska trial: a war crimes tribunal close-up', 57 *SMU Law Review* (2004) pp. 271-291
- Weigend, Thomas, 'The Harmonization of General Principles of Criminal Law: the Statutes and Jurisprudence of the ICTY, ICTR, and the ICC: an Overview', *International Criminal Law:Quo Vadis?: Proceedings of the International Conference Held in Siracusa, Italy, 28 November - 3 December 2002, of ISISC* (Romonville Saint-Agne, Erès 2004) pp. 319-335
- Wilkitzki, Peter, 'Deutsche Vollstreckungshilfe für den Internationalen Jugoslawien-Gerichtshof oder: Gedanken zur Lernfähigkeit des Gesetzgebers', in Otto Triffterer, ed., *Gedächtnisschrift für Theo Vogler* (Heidelberg, Müller 2004) pp. 263-273

6.313 International Criminal Tribunal for Rwanda

Books

- Torres Pérez, María, *La contribución del Tribunal Internacional Penal para Ruanda a la configuración jurídica de los crímenes internacionales* (Valencia, Tirant lo Blanch 2004) 486 pp.
- Trahan, Jennifer, *Genocide, War Crimes, and Crimes Against Humanity: Topical Digests of the Case Law of the International Criminal Tribunal for Rwanda and the International Criminal Tribunal for the Former Yugoslavia* (New York, Human Rights Watch 2004) 277 pp.

- United Nations Organization (UNO), *International Criminal Tribunal for Rwanda: Reports of Orders, Decisions and Judgements 1999: Recueil des ordonnances, décisions, jugements et arrêts 1999* (Brussels, Bruylant/New York, UNO 2004) 2042 pp.
- United Nations Organization (UNO), *International Criminal Tribunal for Rwanda: reports of orders, decisions and judgements 1999: recueil des ordonnances, décisions, jugements et arrêts 1999*, Vol. I (Brussels, Bruylant/New York, UNO 2004) 816 pp.
- United Nations Organization (UNO), International Criminal Tribunal for Rwanda: reports of orders, decisions and judgements 1999: recueil des ordonnances, décisions, jugements et arrêts 1999, Vol. II (Brussels, Bruylant/New York, UNO 2004) pp. 820-2042

Articles

- Adjovi, Roland, Mazeron, Florent, 'Chronique de la jurisprudence du Tribunal penal international pour le Rwanda (1995-2002)', 10 *African YIL* (2004) pp. 493-591
- Askin, Kelly Dawn, 'The International Criminal Tribunal for Rwanda and its treatment of crimes against women', in John Carey, William V. Dunlap and R. John Pritchard, eds., *International Humanitarian Law*, Vol. 2 (Ardsley, Transnational Publishers 2004) pp. 33-88
- Carcano, Andrea, 'Requests for review in the practice of the International Criminal Tribunals for the Former Yugoslavia and for Rwanda', 17 *Leiden JIL* (2004) pp. 103-119
- Côté, Luc, 'Compliance with the laws of war: the role of the International Criminal Tribunal for Rwanda', in Edward C. Luck and Michael W. Doyle, eds., *International Law and Organization: Closing the Compliance Gap* (Lanham, Rowman & Littlefield 2004) pp. 153-183
- Davidson, H. Ron, 'The International Criminal Tribunal for Rwanda's decision in the prosecutor v. Ferdinand Nahimana et al.: the past, present and future of International incitement law', 17 *Leiden JIL* (2004) pp. 505-519
- Habimana, Aloys, 'Judicial responses to mass violence: is the International Criminal Tribunal for Rwanda making a difference towards reconciliation in Rwanda?', in Steven R. Ratner and James L. Bischoff, eds., *International War Crimes Trials: Making a Difference?: Proceedings of an Interdisciplinary Conference at the University of Texas School of Law, Austin, Texas, November 6-7, 2003* (Austin, University of Texas 2004) pp. 83-90
- Henzelin, Marc, 'Les "raisons de savoir" du supérieur hiérarchique qu'un crime va être commis ou a été commis par un subordonné: examen de la jurisprudence des tribunaux pénaux internationaux pour l'ex-Yougoslavie et le Rwanda', in Paul Tavernier, ed., *Actualité de la jurisprudence pénale internationale: à l'heure de la mise en place de la Cour pénale internationale* (Brussels, Bruylant 2004) pp. 81-125
- Herik, Larissa van den and Elies van Sliedregt, 'Ten years later, the Rwanda tribunal still faces legal complexities: some comments on the vagueness of the indictment, complicity in genocide, and the nexus requirement for war crimes', 17 *Leiden JIL* (2004) pp. 537-557
- Jackson Nyamuya Maogoto, 'The International Criminal Tribunal for Rwanda: a paper umbrella in the rain?: 'pittfalls and brighter prospects', 73 *Nordic JIL* (2004) pp. 187-221
- Koenig, Dorean Marguerite, 'Two transformations of sexual assault: the first in domestic law and the second in the United Nations International Criminal Courts for Yugoslavia & Rwanda & the ICC treaty', 50 *Wayne LR* (2004) pp. 185-199

- Ling Yan, 'The International Criminal Tribunal for Rwanda: achievements and activities in 2003', 3 *Chinese JIL* (2004) pp. 291-304
- Maogoto, Jackson Nyamuya, 'The International Criminal Tribunal for Rwanda: a paper umbrella in the rain? Initial pitfalls and brighter prospects', 73 *Nordic JIL* (2004) pp. 187-221
- MacKinnon, Catharine A., 'Prosecutor v. Nahimana, Barayagwiza, & Ngeze: Case No. ICTR 99-52-T: International Criminal Tribunal for Rwanda, December 3, 2003: ICTR judgment and sentence on crimes against humanity and incitement to genocide through broadcast and press outlets', 98 *AJIL* (2004) pp. 325-330
- Mutua, Makau, 'Never again: questioning the Yugoslav and Rwanda Tribunals', in Gerry Simpson, *War Crimes Law* Vol. 2 (Aldershot, Ashgate-Dartmouth 2004) pp. 355-375
- Rabkin, Jeremy, 'The U.N. criminal tribunals for Yugoslavia and Rwanda: international justice or show of justice? Hearing before the committee on international relations, U.S. House of Representatives, February 28, 2002: Testimony', in William Driscoll, Joseph Zompetti and Suzette Zompetti, eds., *The International Criminal Court: Global Politics and the Quest for Justice* (New York, International Debate Education Association 2004) pp. 73-80
- Sluiter, Göran, 'Kroniek van het internationale strafrecht 2003: deel 1: de ad hoc tribunalen voor het voormalige Joegoslavië en voor Rwanda', 29 *NJCM-bulletin* (2004) pp. 329-341
- 'Statute of the International Tribunal for Rwanda', in Elin Hilwig, Relinde van Laar and Willem-Jan van der Wolf, eds., *International Courts and Tribunals: Selected Documents and Materials* (Nijmegen, Wolf Legal Publishers 2004) pp. 3-14
- Stockman, Farah, 'The anatomy of a court: the International Criminal Tribunal for Rwanda', in John Carey, William V. Dunlap and R. John Pritchard, eds., *International Humanitarian Law*, Vol. 2 (Ardsley, Transnational Publishers 2004) pp. 283-306
- Tavernier, Paul, 'The experience of the International Criminal Tribunals for the Former Yugoslavia for Rwanda', in Naorem Sanajaoba, ed., *A Manual of International Humanitarian Laws* (Regency Publications 2004) pp. 454-472

6.314 International Criminal Court

Books

- Aksar, Yusuf, *Implementing International Humanitarian Law: From the Ad Hoc Tribunals to a Permanent International Criminal Court* (London, Routledge 2004) 314 pp.
- Arnold, Roberta, *The ICC As a New Instrument for Repressing Terrorism* (Ardsley, Transnational Publishers 2004) 382 pp.
- Bekou, Olympia, *The International Criminal Court* (Aldershot, Ashgate-Dartmouth 2004) 524 pp.
- Driscoll, William, *The International Criminal Court: Global Politics and the Quest for Justice* (New York, International Debate Education Association 2004) 285 pp.
- Escudero Espinosa, Juan Francisco, *La Corte Penal Internacional y el Consejo de Seguridad: hacia la paz por la justicia* (Madrid, Ed. Dilex 2004) 229 pp.
- Biegi, Mandana, *Die humanitäre Herausforderung: der International Criminal Court und die USA* (Baden-Baden, Nomos 2004) 264 pp.

- García Ramírez, Sergio, *La Corte Penal Internacional*, 2nd edn. (México, Instituto Nacional de Ciencias Penales 2004) 304 pp.
- Kemper, Gregor, *Der Weg nach Rom: die Entwicklung völkerrechtlicher Strafgerichtsbarkeit und die Errichtung des Ständigen Internationalen Strafgerichtshofs* (Frankfurt am Main, Lang 2004) 320 pp.
- Lattanzi, Flavia and William A. Schabas and Valeria Santori, *Essays on the Rome Statute of the International Criminal Court*, Vol. II (Ripa Fagnano Alto, Sirente 2004) 337 pp.
- Lüders, Barbara, *Die Strafbarkeit von Völkermord nach dem Römischen Statut für den Internationalen Strafgerichtshof* (Berlin, Berliner Wissenschafts-Verlag 2004) 314 pp.
- Meseke, Stephan, *Der Tatbestand der Verbrechen gegen die Menschheit nach dem Römischen Statut des Internationalen Strafgerichtshofes: eine völkerstrafrechtliche Analyse* (Berlin, Berliner Wissenschafts-Verlag 2004) 371 pp.
- Politi, Mauro and Nesi, Giuseppe, *The International Criminal Court and the Crime of Aggression* (Aldershot, Ashgate 2004) 193 pp.
- Schabas, William A., *An Introduction to the International Criminal Court*, 2nd edn. (Cambridge, Cambridge University Press 2004) 481 pp.
- Theissen, Gunnar, *Internationale Strafgerichtshof: fünf Jahre nach Rom: Tagungsdokumentation Berlin, 27.-28. Juni 2003* (Berlin, Deutsches Institut für Menschenrechte 2004) 84 pp.

Articles

- Akande, Dapo, 'International law immunities and the International Criminal Court', 98 *AJIL* (2004) pp. 407-433
- Benzing, Markus, 'The complementarity regime of the International Criminal Court: international criminal justice between state sovereignty and the fight against impunity', 7 *MPYIL* (2004) pp. 591-632
- Cryer, Robert and Nigel D. White, 'The Security Council and the International Criminal Court: who's feeling threatened?', 8 *International Peacekeeping* (2004) pp. 143-170
- Dörmann, Knut, 'War crimes under the Rome Statute of the International Criminal Court, with a special focus on the negotiations on the elements of crimes', 7 *MPYIL* (2004) pp. 341-407
- Grammer, Christoph, 'The Rome Statute regime as a mainspring of international criminal law: the success of the Rome Statute in Latin America and the opposition of the USA', 64 *ZaöRV* (2004) pp. 1059-1076
- Hall, Christopher Keith, 'The powers and role of the prosecutor of the International Criminal Court in the global fight against impunity', 17 *Leiden JIL* (2004) pp. 121-139
- Jescheck, Hans-Heinreich, 'The general principles of international criminal law set out in Nuremberg, as mirrored in the ICC Statute', 2 *Journal of International Criminal Justice* (2004) pp. 38-55
- Jeu, Cassandra, 'A successful, permanent International Criminal Court ... "isn't it pretty to think so?"', 26 *Houston JIL* (2004) pp. 411-448
- Keen, Peter Carmichael, 'Tempered adversariality: the judicial role and trial theory in the International Criminal Tribunals', 17 *Leiden JIL* (2004) pp. 767-814
- MacKay, Fiona, 'U.S. unilateralism and international crimes: the International Criminal Court and terrorism', 36 *Cornell ILJ* (2004) pp. 455-471

- Mégret, Frédéric, 'Three dangers for the International Criminal Court: a critical look at a consensual project', in Gerry Simpson, *War Crimes Law*, Vol. 2 (Aldershot, Ashgate 2004) pp. 425-479
- Muller, Sam, 'Establishing an effective International Criminal Court', in Steven R. Ratner and James L. Bischoff, eds., *International War Crimes Trials: Making a Difference?: Proceedings of an Interdisciplinary Conference at the University of Texas School of Law, Austin, Texas, November 6-7, 2003* (Austin, University of Texas, Austin School of Law 2004) pp. 132-146
- Nissel, Alan, 'Continuing crimes in the Rome Statute', 25 *Michigan JIL* (2004) pp. 653-689
- Oosterveld, Valerie, 'Sexual slavery and the International Criminal Court: advancing international law', 25 *Michigan Journal of International Law* (2004) pp. 605-651
- Philipp, Christiane E., 'The International Criminal Court: a brief introduction', 7 *MPYIL* (2004) pp. 331-339
- Röben, Völker, 'The procedure of the ICC: status and function of the prosecutor', 7 *MPYIL* (2004) pp. 513-552
- Robertson, Helen, 'Looking forward: prospects for the International Criminal Court', in Steven R. Ratner and James L. Bischoff, eds., *International War Crimes Trials: Making a Difference?: Proceedings of an Interdisciplinary Conference at the University of Texas School of Law, Austin, Texas, November 6-7, 2003* (Austin, University of Texas, Austin School of Law 2004) pp. 147-154
- Schabas, William A., 'United States Hostility to the International Criminal Court: it's all about the Security Council', 15 *EJIL* (2004) pp. 701-720
- Seibert-Fohr, Anja, 'The relevance of the Rome Statute of the International Criminal Court for amnesties and truth commissions', 7 *MPYIL* (2004) pp. 553-590
- Struett, Michael J., 'NGOs, the International Criminal Court and the politics of writing international law', in Ige F. Dekker and Wouter G. Werner, eds., *Governance and International Legal Theory* (Leiden, Nijhoff 2004) pp. 321-353
- Vandermeersch, Damien, 'The ICC Statute and Belgian law', 2 *Journal of International Criminal Justice* (2004) pp. 133-157
- Wagner, Markus, 'The ICC and its jurisdiction: myths, misperceptions and realities', 7 *MPYIL* (2004) pp. 409-512

6.315 East Timor's Special Panels for Serious Crimes

Books

- Romano, Cesare P.R., André Nollkaemper and Jann K. Kleffner, eds., *Internationalized Criminal Courts and Tribunals: Sierra Leone, East Timor, Kosovo, and Cambodia* (Oxford, Oxford University Press 2004) 491 pp.

Articles

- Bowman, Herbert D., 'Letting the big fish get away: the United Nations justice effort in East Timor', 18 *Emory ILR* (2004) pp. 371-400
- Burgess, Patrick, 'Justice and reconciliation in East Timor: the relationship between the commission for reception, truth and reconciliation and the courts', 15 *Criminal LF* (2004) pp. 135-158

- De Bertodano, Sylvia, 'East Timor: trials and tribulations', in Cesare P.R. Romano, André Nollkaemper and Jann K. Kleffner, eds., *Internationalized Criminal Courts and Tribunals: Sierra Leone, East Timor, Kosovo, and Cambodia* (Oxford, Oxford University Press 2004) pp. 79-97
- Ishizuka, Katsumi, 'Australia's policy towards East Timor', 93 *Round Table* (2004) pp. 271-285
- Linton, Suzannah and Caitlin Reiger, 'The evolving jurisprudence and practice of East Timor's special panel for serious crimes on admissions of guilt, duress and superior orders', 4 *YIHL* (2004) pp. 167-212
- Linton, Suzannah, 'Unraveling the first three trials at Indonesia's ad hoc court for human rights violations in East Timor', 17 *Leiden JIL* (2004) pp. 303-361

6.316 Kosovo's Internationalised Courts

Books

- Romano, Cesare P.R., André Nollkaemper and Jann K. Kleffner, eds., *Internationalized Criminal Courts and Tribunals: Sierra Leone, East Timor, Kosovo, and Cambodia* (Oxford, Oxford University Press 2004) 491 pp.

6.317 Special Court for Sierra Leone

Books

- Romano, Cesare P.R., André Nollkaemper and Jann K. Kleffner, eds., *Internationalized Criminal Courts and Tribunals: Sierra Leone, East Timor, Kosovo, and Cambodia* (Oxford, Oxford University Press 2004) 491 pp.

Articles

- 'Agreement between the United Nations and the government of Sierra Leone on the establishment of the Special Court for Sierra Leone: 16 January 2002', in Elin Hilwig, Relinde van Laar, Willem-Jan van der Wolf, eds., *International Courts and Tribunals: Selected Documents and Materials* (Nijmegen, Wolf Legal Publishers 2004) pp. 67-73
- Cassese, Antonio, 'The Special Court and International Law: the decision concerning the Lomé agreement amnesty', 2 *Journal of International Criminal Justice* (2004) pp. 1130-1140
- Cockayne, James, 'Special Court for Sierra Leone: decisions on the refusal of judges Robertson and Winter', 2 *Journal of International Criminal Justice* (2004) pp. 1154-1162
- Damgaard, Ciara, 'The Special Court for Sierra Leone: challenging the tradition of impunity for gender-based crimes?', 73 *Nordic JIL* (2004) pp. 485-503
- Dougherty, Beth K., 'Right-sizing international criminal justice: the hybrid experiment at the Special Court for Sierra Leone', 80 *International Affairs* (2004) pp. 311-328
- Elagab, Omer Yousif, 'The Special Court for Sierra Leone: some constraints', 8 *International Journal of Human Rights* (2004) pp. 249-273
- Evenson, Elizabeth M., 'Truth and justice in Sierra Leone: coordination between commission and court', 104 *Columbia Law Review* (2004) pp. 730-767

- 'Headquarters agreement between the Republic of Sierra Leone and the Special Court for Sierra Leone', in Elin Hilwig, Relinde van Laar, Willem-Jan van der Wolf, eds., *International Courts and Tribunals: Selected Documents and Materials* (Nijmegen, Wolf Legal Publishers 2004) pp. 139-150
- Jones, John R.W.D., 'The Special Court for Sierra Leone: a defence perspective', 2 *Journal of International Criminal Justice* (2004) pp. 211-230
- Kanu, Allieu I. and Giorgia Tortora, 'The legal basis of the Special Court for Sierra Leone', 3 *Chinese JIL* (2004) pp. 515-552
- Klingberg, Vanesa, '(Former) Heads of state before international(ized) criminal courts: the case of Charles Taylor before the Special Court for Sierra Leone', 46 *German YIL* (2004) pp. 537-564
- Meisenberg, Simon M., 'Die Anklage und der Haftbefehl gegen Charles Ghankay Taylor durch den Sondergerichtshof für Sierra Leone', 17 *Humanitäres Völkerrecht* (2004) pp. 30-39
- Meisenberg, Simon M., 'Legality of amnesties in international humanitarian law: the Lomé Amnesty Decision of the Special Court for Sierra Leone', 86 *IRRC* (2004) pp. 837-851
- Mochochoko, Phakiso and Giorgia Tortora, 'The Management Committee for the Special Court for Sierra Leone', in Cesare P.R. Romano, André Nollkaemper, and Jann K. Kleffner, eds., *Internationalized Criminal Courts and Tribunals: Sierra Leone, East Timor, Kosovo, and Cambodia* (Oxford, Oxford University Press 2004) pp. 141-156
- Schabas, William A., 'Internationalized Courts and their relationship with alternative accountability mechanisms: the case of Sierra Leone', in Cesare P.R. Romano, André Nollkaemper and Jann K. Kleffner, eds., *Internationalized Criminal Courts and Tribunals: Sierra Leone, East Timor, Kosovo, and Cambodia* (Oxford, Oxford University Press 2004) pp. 157-180
- Schabas, William A., 'A synergistic relationship: the Sierra Leone Truth and Reconciliation Commission and the Special Court for Sierra Leone', 15 *Criminal Law Forum* (2004) pp. 3-54
- Schabas, William A., 'Conjoined twins of transitional justice? The Sierra Leone Truth and Reconciliation Commission and the Special Court', 2 *Journal of International Criminal Justice* (2004) pp. 1082-1099
- Smith, Alison, 'Sierra Leone: the intersection of law, policy, and practice', in Cesare P. R. Romano, André Nollkaemper and Jann K. Kleffner, eds., *Internationalized Criminal Courts and Tribunals: Sierra Leone, East Timor, Kosovo, and Cambodia* (Oxford, Oxford University Press 2004) pp. 125-139
- Smith, Alison, 'Child recruitment and the Special Court for Sierra Leone', 2 *Journal of International Criminal Justice* (2004) pp. 1141-1153
- Special Court for Sierra Leone: Prosecutor v. Sam Hinga Norman: Case No. SCSL-2003-08-PT, 15 *Criminal Law Forum* (2004) pp. 247-272
- 'Special Court for Sierra Leone: Prosecutor v. Sam Hinga Norman (May 31, 2004)', 43 *ILM* (2004) pp. 1129-1165
- 'Statute of the Special Court for Sierra Leone', in Elin Hilwig, Relinde van Laar, Willem-Jan van der Wolf, eds., *International Courts and Tribunals: Selected Documents and Materials* (Nijmegen, Wolf Legal Publishers 2004) pp. 75-82

6.318 Extraordinary Chambers for Cambodia

Books

- Romano, Cesare P.R., André Nollkaemper and Jann K. Kleffner, eds., *Internationalized Criminal Courts and Tribunals: Sierra Leone, East Timor, Kosovo, and Cambodia* (Oxford, Oxford University Press 2004) 491 pp.

Articles

- Etcheson, Craig, 'The politics of genocide justice in Cambodia', in Cesare P.R. Romano, André Nollkaemper and Jann K. Kleffner, eds., *Internationalized Criminal Courts and Tribunals: Sierra Leone, East Timor, Kosovo, and Cambodia* (Oxford, Oxford University Press 2004) pp. 181-205
- Luftglass, Scott, 'Crossroads in Cambodia: the United Nation's responsibility to withdraw involvement from the establishment of a Cambodian tribunal to prosecute the Khmer Rouge', 90 *Virginia LR* (2004) pp. 893-964
- Meijer, Ernestine E., 'The Extraordinary Chambers in the Courts of Cambodia for prosecuting crimes committed by the Khmer Rouge: jurisdiction, organization, and procedure of an internationalized national tribunal', in Cesare P.R. Romano, André Nollkaemper, and Jann K. Kleffner, eds., *Internationalized Criminal Courts and Tribunals: Sierra Leone, East Timor, Kosovo, and Cambodia* (Oxford, Oxford University Press 2004) pp. 207-232

6.319 Iraqi Special Tibunal

Books

- Rouillard, Louis-Philippe F., *Precise of the Laws of Armed Conflicts: With Essays Concerning the Combattant Status of the Guantanamo Detainees and the Statute of the Iraqi Special Tribunal* (New York, Universe 2004) 321 pp.

Articles

- Bantekas, Ilias, 'The Iraqi Special Tribunal for Crimes against Humanity', 54 *The International and Comparative Law Quarterly* (2005) pp. 237-253
- Gersh, David M., 'Poor judgement: why the Iraqi Special Tribunal is the wrong mechanism for trying Saddam Hussein on charges of genocide, human rights abuses, and other violations of international law', 33 *Georgia Journal of International and Comparative Law* (2004) pp. 273-302
- Goldstone, Richard, 'The trial of Saddam Hussein: what kind of court should prosecute Saddam Hussein and others for human rights abuses?', 27 *Fordham ILJ* (2004) pp. 1490-1508
- Kress, Claus, 'The Iraqi Special Tribunal and the crime of aggression', 2 *Journal of International Criminal Justice* (2004) pp. 347-352
- Scharf, Michael P., 'Is it international enough? A critique of the Iraqi Special Tribunal in light of the goals of international justice', 2 *Journal of International Criminal Justice* (2004) pp. 330-337

- Shany, Yuval, 'Does one size fit all?: reading the jurisdictional provisions of the new Iraqi Special Tribunal statute in the light of the statutes of international criminal tribunals', 2 *Journal of International Criminal Justice* (2004) pp. 338-346
- Zappalà, Salvatore, 'The Iraqi Special Tribunal's draft rules of procedure and evidence: neither fish nor fowl?', 2 *Journal of International Criminal Justice* (2004) pp. 855-865
- Zolo, Danilo, 'The Iraqi Special Tribunal: back to the Nuremberg paradigm?', 2 *Journal of International Criminal Justice* (2004) pp. 313-318

6.32 National Courts

Books

- Macedo, Stephen, *Universal Jurisdiction: National Courts and the Prosecution of Serious Crimes Under International Law* (Philadelphia, University of Pennsylvania Press 2004) 383 pp.

Articles

- Benvenisti, Eyal, 'National courts and the "war on terrorism"', in Andrea Bianchi, ed., *Enforcing International Law Norms against Terrorism* (Oxford, Hart 2004) pp. 307-329
- Ellis, Mark S., 'Coming to terms with its Past: Serbia's new court for the prosecution of war crimes', 22 *Berkeley JIL* (2004) pp. 165-194
- Sarkin, Jeremy, 'Reparation for past wrongs: using domestic courts around the world, especially the United States, to pursue African human rights claims', 32 *International Journal of Legal Information* (2004) pp. 426-460
- Schmahl, Stefanie, 'Specific methods of prosecuting terrorists in national law', in Christian Walter, ed., *Terrorism as a Challenge for National and International Law: Security Versus Liberty?* (Berlin, Springer 2004) pp. 81-118
- Steinhardt, Ralph G., 'International humanitarian law in the courts of the United States: Yamashita, Filartiga, and 911', 36 *George Washington International Law Review* (2004) pp. 1-46

6.4 VICTIMS OF CRIMES

Articles

- Dembour, Marie-Bénédicte and Haslam, Emily, 'Silencing hearings? Victim-witnesses at war crimes trials', 15 *EJIL* (2004) pp. 151-177
- Fak, Glenna L., 'The victim assistance provision of the mine ban treaty', in Richard A. Matthew, Bryan McDonald, and Kenneth R. Rutherford, eds., *Landmines and Human Security: International Politics and War's Hidden Legacy* (Albany, State University of New York Press 2004) pp. 179-190
- Schabas, William A., 'The place of victims in international criminal law', in International Conference of ISISC, Anniversary of ISISC (28-11-2002, Siracusa), *International Criminal Law: quo vadis?: Proceedings of the International Conference Held in Siracusa, Italy, 28 November - 3 December 2002, of ISISC Anniversary of ISISC* (Romonville Saint-Agne, Erès 2004) pp. 505-517

– Willerman, Raquel, 'Victim assistance: landmine survivors' perspectives', in Richard A. Matthew, Bryan McDonald and Kenneth R. Rutherford, eds., *Landmines and Human Security: International Politics and War's Hidden Legacy* (Albany, State University of New York Press 2004) pp. 103-114

7. IMPLEMENTATION

Articles

– Fleck, Dieter, 'Implementing international humanitarian law: problems and priorities', in Naorem Sanajaoba, *A Manual of International Humanitarian Laws* (New Dehli, Regency Publications 2004) pp. 348-362
– Kadam, Umesh, 'Implementation of international humanitarian law: problems and prospects', in Naorem Sanajaoba, ed., *A Manual of International Humanitarian Laws* (New Dehli, Regency Publications 2004) pp. 379-396

7.21 Legislation to Implement IHL Treaties

Books

– Aksar, Yusuf, *Implementing International Humanitarian Law: From the Ad Hoc Tribunals to a Permanent International Criminal Court* (London, Routledge 2004) 314 pp.

Articles

– Kadam, Umesh, 'Implementation of international humanitarian law: problems and prospects', in Naorem Sanajaoba, *A Manual of International Humanitarian Laws* (New Dehli, Regency Publications 2004) pp. 379-396
– Lavoyer, Jean-Philippe, 'Implementation of international humanitarian law and the role of the International Committee of the Red Cross', in John Carey, William V. Dunlap and R. John Pritchard, eds., *International Humanitarian Law,* Vol. 2 (Ardsley, Transnational Publishers 2004) pp. 213-225
– Tolstykh, V.L., 'International humanitarian law in Russia (1850-1917) in Russian Academy of Legal Sciences', in *Russian Law: Theory and Practice*, Journal of the Russian Academy of Legal Sciences (London, Simmonds & Hill 2004) pp. 67-83
– Vashakmadse, Mindia, 'Durchsetzung des humanitären Völkerrechts in Georgien', 17 *Humanitäres Völkerrecht* (2004) pp. 234-241
– Weissbrodt, David, and Peggy L. Hicks, 'Implementation of human rights and humanitarian law in situations of armed conflict', in Naorem Sanajaoba, ed., *A Manual of International Humanitarian Laws* (New Dehli, Regency Publications 2004) pp. 325-347

7.22 Legislation to Implement Obligations vis-à-vis the International Criminal Court and International Criminal Tribunals

Articles

- Boas, Gideon, 'An overview of implementation by Australia of the Statute of the International Criminal Court', 2 *Journal of International Criminal Justice* (2004) pp. 179-190
- Sluiter, Göran, 'Implementation of the ICC Statute in the Dutch legal order', 2 *Journal of International Criminal Justice* (2004) pp. 158-178
- Symposium on national implementation of the ICC Statute, 2 *Journal of International Criminal Justice* (2004) pp. 133-210
- Turns, David, 'Aspects of national implementation of the Rome Statute: the United Kingdom and selected other states', in Dominic McGoldrick, Peter Rowe and Eric Donnelly, eds., *The Permanent International Criminial Court* (2004) pp. 337-387
- Vandermeersch, Damien, 'The ICC Statute and Belgian law', 2 *Journal of International Criminal Justice* (2004) pp. 133-157

7.23 Military Manuals/National Instructions/Codes of Conduct

Books

- Ministry of Defence, *The Manual of the Law of Armed Conflict* (Oxford, Oxford University Press 2004) 611 pp.

7.24 Role of Defence Force Legal Advisers

Books

- Borch, Frederic L., *Judge Advocates in Combat: Army Lawyers in Military Operations From Vietnam to Haiti* (Honolulu, University Press of the Pacific 2004) 413 pp.

7.4 ICRC

Articles

- Forsythe, David P., 'The International Committee of the Red Cross and humanitarian assistance: a policy analysis', in Naorem Sanajaoba, ed., *A Manual of International Humanitarian Laws* (New Dehli, Regency Publications 2004) pp. 664-685
- Harrof-Tavel, Marion, 'Do wars ever end? The work of the International Committee of the Red Cross when the guns fall silent', 85 *IRRC* (2003) pp. 465-496
- 'International humanitarian law and the challenges of contemporary armed conflicts: excerpt of the report prepared by the International Committee of the Red Cross for the 28th International Conference of the Red Cross and the Red Crescent Geneva, December 2003', 86 *IRRC* (2004) pp. 213-244
- Kolanowski, Stéphane, 'Preventing conflict: a EU-International Committee of the Red Cross common interest,' in Vincent Kronenberger and Jan Wouters, eds., *The European*

Union and Conflict Prevention: Policy and Legal Aspects (The Hague, T.M.C. Asser Press 2004) pp. 501-509
- Krähenbühl, Pierre, 'The ICRC's approach to contemporary security challenges: a future for independent and neutral humanitarion action', 86 *IRRC* (2004) pp. 505-514
- Lavoyer, Jean-Philippe, 'Implementation of international humanitarian law and the role of the International Committee of the Red Cross', in John Carey, William V. Dunlap and R. John Pritchard, eds., *International Humanitarian Law,* Vol. 2 (Ardsley,Transnational Publishers 2004) pp. 213-225
- Lavoyer, Jean-Philippe, 'Refugees and internally displaced persons: international humanitarian law and the role of the ICRC', in Naorem Sanajaoba, ed., *A Manual of International Humanitarian Laws* (New Dehli, Regency Publications 2004) pp. 163-183
- MacDowell, Joshua, 'The International Committee of the Red Cross as a witness before International Criminal Tribunals', in Sienho Yee, ed., *International Crime and Punishment* (Lanham, University Press of America 2003) pp. 1-33
- Roberts, David Lloyd, 'Training the armed forces to respect international humanitarian law: the perspective of the ICRC delegate to the armed and security forces of South Asia', in Naorem Sanajaoba, ed., *A Manual of International Humanitarian Laws* (New Dehli, Regency Publications 2004) pp. 363-378
- Studer, Meinrad, 'The ICRC and civil-military relations in armed conflict', in Naorem Sanajaoba, ed., *A Manual of International Humanitarian Laws* (New Dehli, Regency Publications 2004) pp. 686-709
- Umesh Kadam, 'Protection of women in times of armed conflicts and work of the International Committee of the Red Cross', in R.K. Dixit and C. Jayaraj, eds., *Dynamics of International Law in the New Millennium* (New Dehli, Indian Society of International Law 2004) pp. 197-205

7.5 Fact-finding, including the International Fact-finding Commission

Articles

- Roach, J. Ashley, 'The International Fact Finding Commission: Article 90 of Protocol I additional to the 1949 Geneva Conventions', in Naorem Sanajaoba, ed., *A Manual of International Humanitarian Laws* (New Dehli, Regency Publications 2004) pp. 638-663

7.6 Dissemination

Articles

- Dunlap, William V., 'Dissemination and international humanitarian law in modern social conflict', in John Carey, William V. Dunlap, R. John Pritchard, eds., *International Humanitarian Law* (Ardsley, Transnational Publishers 2004) pp. 15-26

7.7 Training and Education

Articles

- Roberts, David Lloyd, 'Training the armed forces to respect international humanitarian law: the perspective of the ICRC delegate to the armed and security forces of South Asia', in Naorem Sanajaoba, ed., *A Manual of International Humanitarian Laws* (New Dehli, Regency Publications 2004) pp. 363-378

8. THE LAW OF NEUTRALITY

Articles

- Heintschel von Heinegg, Wolff, 'Current legal issues in maritime operations: maritime interception operations in the global war on terrorism, exclusion zones, hospital ships and maritime neutrality', 34 *Israel YB HR* (2004) pp. 151-178
- Ku, Charlotte, Cáceres Brun, Joaquín, 'Neutrality and the ICRC contribution to contemporary humanitarian operations', 10 *International Peacekeeping* (2003) pp. 56-72

9.11 United Nations Organisation

Books

- Abass, Ademola, *Regional Organisations and the Development of Collective Security: Beyond Chapter VIII of the UN Charter* (Oxford, Hart 2004) 239 pp.
- Boulden, Jane, *Terrorism and the UN: Before and After September 11* (Bloomington, Indiana University Press 2004) 256 pp.
- Bowles, Newton R., *The Diplomacy of Hope: the United Nations Since the Cold War* (London, Tauris 2004) 207 pp.
- Bucherer, Jeanine, *Die Vereinbarkeit von Militärgerichten mit dem Recht auf ein faires Verfahren gemäss Art.6 Abs. 1 EMRK, Art. 8 Abs. 1 AMRK und Art. 14 Abs. 1 des UN-Paktes über bürgerliche und politische Rechte* (Berlin, Springer 2004) 307 pp.
- Chesterman, Simon, *You, the People: the United Nations, Transitional Administration, and State-building* (Oxford, Oxford University Press 2004) 296 pp.
- De Wet, Erika, *The Chapter VII Powers of the United Nations Security Council* (Oxford, Hart 2004) 413 pp.
- Del Valle, Alexandre, *La Turquie dans l'Europe: un cheval de Troie islamiste?* (Paris, Éd. des Syrtes 2004) 457 pp.
- Fenton, Neil, *Understanding the UN Security Council: Coercion or Consent?* (Aldershot, Ashgate 2004) 246 pp.
- Friedrich, Alexander G., *Public-private Partnership within the United Nations System: Now and Then* (Bielefeld, Bertelsmann 2004) 147 pp.
- Gold, Dore, *Tower of Babble: How the United Nations Has Fueled Global Chaos* (New York, Crown Forum 2004) 308 pp.
- Gowlland-Debbas, Vera, *National Implementation of United Nations Sanctions: A Comparative Study* (Leiden, Nijhoff 2004) 671 pp.
- Hill, Stephen M., *United Nations Disarmament in Intra-state Conflict* (Basingstoke, Palgrave Macmillan 2004) 303 pp.

– Jolly, Richard, *UN Contributions to Development Thinking and Practice* (Bloomington, Indiana University Press 2004) 387 pp.
– Kirton, John J., *The G8, the United Nations, and Conflict Prevention* (Aldershot, Ashgate 2004) 334 pp.
– Koechler, Hans, *The Iraq Crisis and the United Nations: Power Politics vs. the International Rule of Law: Memoranda and Declarations of the International Progress Organization* (1990-2003) (Vienna, International Progress Organization 2004) 105 pp.
– Krasno, Jean E., *The United Nations: Confronting the Challenges of a Global Society* (Boulder, Lynne Rienner 2004) 443 pp.
– Malone, David M., *The UN Security Council: From the Cold War to the 21st Century* (Boulder, Rienner 2004) 746 pp.
– Pajunk, Inken, *Möglichkeiten und Grenzen der Prävention gewaltsamer Konflikte durch die Vereinten Nationen: eine an Konfliktstudien orientierte Untersuchung multilateraler Konfliktverhütung nach Ende des Kalten Krieges* (Münster, LIT 2004) 306 pp.
– Price, Richard M., *The United Nations and Global Security* (Basingstoke, Palgrave Macmillan 2004) 288 pp.
– Weiss, Thomas G., *The United Nations and Changing World Politics,* 4th ed. (Boulder, Westview Press 2004) 392 pp.

Articles

– Anderson, Kenneth, 'Humanitarian inviolability in crisis: the meaning of impartiality and neutrality for U.N. and NGO agencies following the 2003-2004 Afghanistan and Iraq conflicts', 17 *Harvard Human Rights Journal* (2004) pp. 41-74
– Fassbender, Bardo, 'All illusions shattered? Looking back on a decade of failed attempts to reform the UN Security Council', 7 *MPYIL* (2004) pp. 183-218
– Jonah, James O.C., 'The United Nations', in Adekeye Adebajo and Ismail Rashid, eds., *West Africa's Security Challenges: Building Peace in a Troubled Region* (Boulder, Rienner 2004) pp. 319-347
– Kamanzi, Stanislas, 'Preventing genocide: the role of the United Nations', 10 *ILSA Journal of International and Comparative Law* (2004) pp. 329-333
– Pauwels, Ann, 'De Verenigde Naties en het internationaal humanitair recht: recente ontwikkelingen', 13 *Zoeklicht* (2004) pp.17-20
– White, Nigel D., 'The will and authority of the Security Council after Iraq', 17 *Leiden JIL* (2004) pp. 645-672

9.12 North Atlantic Treaty Organisation

Articles

– Antonopoulos, Constantino, 'Some thoughts on the NATO position in relation to the Iraqi crisis', 17 *Leiden JIL* (2004) pp. 177-183

9.21 Peacekeeping

Books

– Bellamy, Alex J., *Understanding Peacekeeping* (Cambridge, Polity Press 2004) 325 pp.

– Briscoe, Neil, *Britain and UN Peacekeeping, 1948-67* (Basingstoke Palgrave Macmillan 2003) 294 pp.
– Cassidy, Robert M., *Peacekeeping in the Abyss: British and American Peacekeeping Doctrine and Practice After the Cold War* (Westport, Praeger 2004) 284 pp.
– Dobson, Hugo, *Japan and United Nations Peacekeeping: New Pressures, New Responses* (London Routledge Curzon 2003) 188 pp.
– Henn, Francis, *A Business of Some Heat: the United Nations Force in Cyprus Before and During the 1974 Turkish Invasion* (Barnsley, Pen & Sword Military 2004) 550 pp.
– Higate, Paul, *Gender and Peacekeeping: Case Studies: the Democratic Republic of the Congo and Sierra Leone* (Pretoria, Institute for Security Studies 2004) 65 pp.
– Ishizuka, Katsumi, *Ireland and International Peacekeeping Operations 1960-2000: A Study of Irish Motivation* (London, Cass 2004) 234 pp.
– Keeley, James F., *Commercial Satellite Imagery and United Nations Peacekeeping: A View From Above* (Aldershot, Ashgate 2004) 251 pp.
– Lüder, Sascha Rolf, *Völkerrechtliche Verantwortlichkeit bei Teilnahme an "Peace-keeping"-Missionen der Vereinten Nationen* (Berlin, Berliner Wissenschafts-Verlag 2004) 234 pp.
– Malan, Mark, *Challenges of Peace Implementation: the UN Mission in the Democratic Republic of the Congo* (Pretoria, Institute for Security Studies 2004) 277 pp.
– Mays, Terry M., *Historical Dictionary of Multinational Peacekeeping*, 2nd edn. (Lanham, Scarecrow Press 2004) 319 pp.
– Polman, Linda, *We Did Nothing: Why the Truth Doesn't Always Come Out When the UN Goes in* (London, Penguin Books 2004) 234 pp.
– Razack, Sherene H., *Dark Threats and White Knights: the Somalia Affair, Peacekeeping, and the New Imperialism* (Toronto, University of Toronto Press 2004) 236 pp.
– United Nations, *United Nations Peacekeeping: Meeting New Challenges: Frequently Asked Questions* (New York, United Nations 2004) 16 pp.
– Welin, Gustaf, *The U.N. in Cyprus: the Swedish Peace Keeping Operations 1964-1993* (Oxford, Hurst 2004) 274 pp.
– Whitworth, Sandra, *Men, Militarism, and UN Peacekeeping: A Gendered Analysis* (Boulder, Lynne Rienner 2004) 225 pp.

Articles

– Bernath, Clifford and Sayre Nyce, 'A peacekeeping success: lessons learned from UNAMSIL', 8 *International Peacekeeping* (2004) pp. 119-142
– Caplan, Richard, 'Partner or patron? International civil administration and local capacity-building', 11 *International Peacekeeping* (2004) pp. 229-247
– Durch, William J., 'The Brahimi report at thirty (months): reviewing the UN's record of implementation', 8 *International Peacekeeping* (2004) pp. 1-32
– Katahara, Eiichi, 'Japan as a civilian peacekeeper', in Lorraine Elliott and Graeme Cheeseman, eds., *Forces for Good: Cosmopolitan Militaries in the Twenty-First Century* (Manchester, Manchester University Press 2004) pp. 263-275
– Krasno, Jean E., 'To end the scourge of war: the story of UN peacekeeping', in Jean E. Krasno, ed., *The United Nations: Confronting the Challenges of a Global Society* (Boulder, Lynne Rienner 2004) pp. 225-268
– Levin, Scott A., 'Sexual exploitation of refugee children by U.N. peacekeepers', 19 *New York Law School Journal of Human Rights* (2003) pp. 833-842

– MacMullin, Jaremey, 'Reintegration of combatants: were the right lessons learned in Mozambique?', 11 *International Peacekeeping* (2004) pp. 625-643
– Morrison, Alex, 'Peacekeeping and intelligence: single or double bed?', in James F. Keeley, Rob Huebert, eds., *Commercial Satellite Imagery and United Nations Peacekeeping: a View from above* (Aldershot, Ashgate 2004) pp. 113-121
– Oliver, George F., 'The other side of peacekeeping: peace enforcement and who should do it?', 8 *International Peacekeeping* (2004) pp. 99-117
– Oswald, Bruce M., 'Model codes for criminal justice and peace operations: some legal issues', 9 *Journal of Conflict and Security Law* (2004) pp. 253-275
– Oswald, Bruce M., The rule of law on peace operations: a cornerstone of effective peace operations, 8 *International Peacekeeping* (2004) pp. 291-299
– Sens, Allen G., 'From peace-keeping to peace-building: the United Nations and the challenge of intrastate war', in Richard M. Price and Mark W. Zacher, eds., *The United Nations and Global Security* (New York, Palgrave Macmillan 2004) pp. 141-160
– Soeters, Joseph, 'Turkish-Dutch encounters in peace operations', 11 *International Peacekeeping* (2004) pp. 354-392
– Stephan, Maria J., 'The case for peacekeeping in the occupied Palestinian territories', 11 *International Peacekeeping* (2004) pp. 248-270
– Talmon, Stefan, 'Impediments to peacekeeping: the case of Cyprus', 8 *International Peacekeeping* (2004) pp. 33-63

9.22 Peace Enforcement and Peace Building

Books

– Batchelor, Peter, *Demilitarisation and Peace-Building in Southern Africa;* Vol. I, *Concepts and Processes* (Aldershot, Ashgate 2004) 173 pp.
– Batchelor, Peter, *Demilitarisation and Peace-Building in Southern Africa;* Vol. II, *National and Regional Experiences* (Aldershot, Ashgate 2004) 273 pp.
– Batchelor, Peter, *Demilitarisation and Peace-Building in Southern Africa;* Vol. III, *The Role of the Military in State Formation and Nation-Building* (Aldershot, Ashgate 2004) 150 pp.
– Coleman, Katharina Pichler, *States, International Organisations and Legitimacy: the Role of International Organisations in Contemporary Peace Enforcement Operations* (Ann Arbor, University Microfilms International 2004) 148 pp.
– Heijmans, Annelies, *Searching for Peace in Asia Pacific: an Overview of Conflict Prevention and Peacebuilding Activities* (Boulder, Lynne Rienner 2004) 848 pp.
– Keating, Thomas F., *Building Sustainable Peace* (Tokyo, United Nations University Press 2004) pp. 439
– Kemp, Graham, *Keeping the Peace: Conflict Resolution and Peaceful Societies Around the World* (New York, Routledge 2004) 231 pp.
– Lesaffer, Randall, *Peace Treaties and International Law in European History: From the Late Middle Ages to World War One* (Cambridge, Cambridge University Press 2004) 481 pp.
– Malan, Mark, *Challenges of Peace Implementation: the UN Mission in the Democratic Republic of the Congo*, (Pretoria, Institute for Security Studies 2004) 277 pp.

- Meijer, Guus, *From Military Peace to Social Justice? The Angolan Peace Process*, (London, Conciliation Resources 2004) 100 pp.
- Sriram, Chandra Lekha, *Confronting Past Human Rights Violations: Justice vs. Peace in Times of Transition* (London, Cass 2004) pp. 229
- Tardy, Thierry, *Peace Operations After 11 September 2001* (London, Cass 2004) pp. 204

Articles

- Adam, Hussein M., 'Somalia: international versus local attempts at peacebuilding', in Taisier M. Ali and Robert O. Matthews, eds., *Durable Peace: Challenges for Peace-building in Africa* (Toronto, University of Toronto 2004) pp. 253-281
- Adebajo, Adekeye, 'Pax West Africana?: regional security mechanisms', in Adekeye Adebajo and Ismail Rashid, eds., *West Africa's Security Challenges: Building Peace in a Troubled Region* (Boulder, Rienner 2004) pp. 291-318
- Adebajo, Adekeye, 'West Africa's tragic twins: building peace in Liberia and Sierra Leone', in Tom Keating and W. Andy Knight, eds., *Building Sustainable Peace* (Tokyo, United Nations University Press 2004) pp. 167-188
- Adedeji, Adebayo, 'ECOWAS: a retrospective journey', in Adekeye Adebajo and Ismail Rashid, eds., *West Africa's Security Challenges: Building Peace in a Troubled Region* (Boulder, Rienner 2004) pp. 21-49
- Ankersen, Christopher P., 'Praxis versus policy: peacebuilding and the military', in Tom Keating and W. Andy Knight, eds., *Building Sustainable Peace* (Tokyo, United Nations University Press 2004) pp. 71-92
- Benjamin, Barnaba Marial, 'The Sudan People's Liberation Movement/Army (SPLM/A) and the peace process', in Korwa G. Adar, John G. Nyuot Yoh and Eddy Maloka, eds., *Sudan Peace Process: Challenges and Future Prospects* (Pretoria, Africa Institute of South Africa 2004) pp. 37-57
- Böge, Volker and Lorraine Garasu, 'Papua New Guinea: a success story of postconflict peacebuilding in Bougainville', in Annelies Heijmans, Nicola Simmonds and Hans van de Veen, eds., *Searching for Peace in Asia Pacific: an Overview of Conflict Prevention and Peacebuilding Activities* (Boulder, Rienner 2004) pp. 564-580
- Chandler, David, 'Imposing the 'rule of law': the lessons of BiH for peacebuilding in Iraq', 11 *International Peacekeeping* (2004) pp. 312-333
- Kelly, Michael, 'Transitional justice in peace operations: shaping the twilight zone in Somalia and East Timor', 4 *YIHL* (2004) pp. 213-251
- Kühne, Winrich, 'Peace operations and governance: lessons learned and perspectives', in Thierry Tardy, ed., *Peace Operations after 11 September 2001* (London, Cass 2004) pp. 101-124
- Robert O. Matthews, *Durable Peace: Challenges for Peacebuilding in Africa* (Toronto, University of Toronto 2004) pp. 61-85
- Oliver, George F., 'The other side of peacekeeping: peace enforcement and who should do it?', 8 *International Peacekeeping* (2004) pp. 99-117
- Oswald, Bruce M., 'Model codes for criminal justice and peace operations: some legal issues', 9 *Journal of Conflict and Security Law* (2004) pp. 253-275
- Oswald, Bruce M., 'The rule of law on peace operations: a cornerstone of effective peace operations', 8 *International Peacekeeping* (2004) pp. 291-299
- Reinhart, A. Kevin, 'Reconstruction and constitution building in Iraq', 37 *Vanderbilt JTL* (2004) pp. 765-790

– Sens, Allen G., 'From peace-keeping to peace-building: the United Nations and the challenge of intrastate war', in Richard M. Price and Mark W. Zacher, eds., *The United Nations and Global Security* (New York, Pargrave Machmillan) pp. 141-160

9.24 Humanitarian and Other Interventions

Books

– Liberia Deme, Mourtada, *Law, Morality and International Armed Intervention: the United Nations and ECOWAS* (S.l., s.n. 2004) 225 pp.
– Liebach, Ingo, Die *unilaterale humanitäre Intervention im "zerfallenen Staat" ("failed state")* (Cologne, Heymann 2004) 331 pp.
– Orford, Anne, *Reading Humanitarian Intervention: Human Rights and the Use of Force in International Law* (Cambridge, Cambridge University Press 2003) 243 pp.
– Rudd, Gordon W., *Humanitarian Intervention: Assisting the Iraqi Kurds in Operation Provide Comfort, 1991* (Washington, Department of the Army 2004) 280 pp.
– Welsh, Jennifer M., *Humanitarian Intervention and International Relations* (Oxford, Oxford University Press 2004) 229 pp.

Articles

– Baehr, Peter and Flinterman, Cees, 'Humanitaire interventie: de huidige stand van zaken', in Duco Hellema and Hilde Reiding, eds., *Humanitaire interventie en soevereiniteit: de geschiedenis van een tegenstelling* (Amsterdam, Boom 2004) pp. 125-133
– Baudet, Floribert, 'Soevereiniteit en humanitaire interventie: theorie en praktijk in de Koude Oorlog', in Duco Hellema and Hilde Reiding, eds., *Humanitaire interventie en soevereiniteit: de geschiedenis van een tegenstelling* (Amsterdam, Boom 2004) pp. 105-122
– Chesterman, Simon, 'Humanitarian intervention and Afghanistan', in Jennifer M. Welsh, ed., *Humanitarian Intervention and International Relations* (Oxford, Oxford University Press 2004) pp. 163-175
– Daudelin, Jean, 'Rethinking humanitarian intervention', in Tom Keating and W. Andy Knight, eds., *Building Sustainable Peace* (United Nations University Press 2004) pp. 1-22
– Evans, Gareth, 'The responsibility to protect: rethinking humanitarian intervention', 98 *Proceedings of the Annual Meeting* (2004) pp. 78-89
– Eysink, Simone, 'Een omstreden interventie: de casus van Kosovo', in Duco Hellema and Hilde Reiding, eds., *Humanitaire interventie en soevereiniteit: de geschiedenis van een tegenstelling* (Amsterdam, Boom 2004) pp. 217-234
– Finnemore, Martha, 'Constructing norms of humanitarian intervention', in Karen Mingst and Jack Snyder, eds., *Essential Readings in World Politics* (New York, Norton 2004) pp. 102-118
– Glasius, Marlies, 'De interventie in Oost-Timor: "soevereiniteit" en goede relaties versus zelfbeschikkingsrecht en solidariteit', in Duco Hellema and Hilde Reiding, eds., *Humanitaire interventie en soevereiniteit: de geschiedenis van een tegenstelling* (Amsterdam, Boom 2004) pp. 253-269

- Goor, Jur van, 'Kolonialisme en humanitaire interventies: de Lombok-expeditie van 1894', in Duco Hellema and Hilde Reiding, eds., *Humanitaire interventie en soevereiniteit: de geschiedenis van een tegenstelling* (Amsterdam, Boom 2004) pp. 235-252
- Heinze, Eric A., 'Humanitarian intervention: morality and international law on intolerable violations of human rights', 8 *International Journal of Human Rights* (2004) pp. 471-490
- Hellema, Duco, 'Humanitaire interventie en de verbreiding van democratie' in Duco Hellema and Hilde Reiding, eds., *Humanitaire interventie en soevereiniteit: de geschiedenis van een tegenstelling* (Amsterdam, Boom 2004) pp. 175-186
- Lietzau, William K., 'The role of military force in foreign relations, humanitarian intervention and the Security Council', 64 *ZaöRV* (2004) pp. 281-304
- Malcontent, Peter, 'De CNN-factor: humanitaire interventie en de macht van de massamedia', in Duco Hellema and Hilde Reiding, eds., *Humanitaire interventie en soevereiniteit: de geschiedenis van een tegenstelling* (Amsterdam, Boom 2004) pp. 135-157
- Marks, Jonathan H., 'Mending the web: universal jurisdiction, humanitarian intervention and the abrogation of immunity by the Security Council', 42 *Columbia JTL* (2004) pp. 445-490
- Martin, Ian, 'International intervention in East Timor', in Jennifer M. Welsh, ed., *Humanitarian Intervention and International Relations* (Oxford, Oxford University Press 2004) pp. 142-162
- Mayall, James, 'Humanitarian intervention and international society: lessons from Africa', in Jennifer M. Welsh, ed., *Humanitarian Intervention and International Relations* (Oxford, Oxford University Press 2004) pp. 120-141
- Morris, Nicholas, 'Humanitarian intervention in the Balkans', in Jennifer M. Welsh, ed., *Humanitarian Intervention and International Relations* (Oxford, Oxford University Press 2004) pp. 98-119
- Nincic, Miroslav and Donna Nincic, 'Humanitarian intervention and paradoxes of moral authority: lessons from the Balkans', 8 *International Journal of Human Rights* (2004) pp. 45-64
- Roberts, Adam, 'The United Nations and humanitarian intervention' in Jennifer M. Welsh, ed., *Humanitarian Intervention and International Relations* (Oxford, Oxford University Press 2004) pp. 71-97
- Shue, Henry, 'Limiting sovereignty', in Jennifer M. Welsh, ed., *Humanitarian Intervention and International Relations* (Oxford, Oxford University Press 2004) pp. 11-28
- Schmitz, Peter, 'Quality and accountability in humanitarian assistance: how to put it into practise?', 17 *Humanitäres Völkerrecht* (2004) pp. 28-30
- Schweizer, Beat, 'Moral dilemmas for humanitarianism in the era of "humanitarian" military interventions', 86 *IRRC* (2004) pp. 547-564
- Stoffels, Ruth Abril, 'Legal regulation of humanitarian assistance in armed conflict: achievements and gaps', 86 *IRRC* (2004) pp. 515-546
- Vuurde, Rob van, '"Humanitaire interventies" tijdens de opkomst van de natiestaat, 1800-1870', in Duco Hellema and Hilde Reiding, eds., *Humanitaire interventie en soevereiniteit: de geschiedenis van een tegenstelling* (Amsterdam, Boom 2004) pp. 57-81
- Waart, Paul de, 'Humanitaire interventie rechtmatig of niet?', 17 *VN Forum* (2004) pp. 28-35
- Weiss, Thomas G., 'The sunset of humanitarian intervention? The responsibility to protect in a unipolar era', 35 *Security Dialogue* (2004) pp. 135-153

- Welsh, Jennifer M., 'Authorizing humanitarian intervention', in Richard M. Price and Mark W. Zacher, eds., *The United Nations and Global Security* (2004) pp. 177-192
- Welsh, Jennifer M., 'Taking consequences seriously: objections to humanitarian intervention', in Jennifer M. Welsh, ed., *Humanitarian Intervention and International Relations* (Oxford, Oxford University Press 2004) pp. 52-68
- Wheeler, Nicholas J., 'The humanitarian responsibilities of sovereignty: explaining the development of a new norm of military intervention for humanitarian purposes in international society', in Jennifer M. Welsh, ed., *Humanitarian Intervention and International Relations* (Oxford, Oxford University Press 2004) pp. 29-51
- Zaghari-Mask, Danette, Sabine Tomshinsky and Tosha Fernandez, 'The United Nations and humanitarian intervention: building legitimacy by confronting our past: an open letter', 16 *Florida JIL* (2004) pp. 483-528

11. ARMS CONTROL AND DISARMAMENT

Books

- Frieman, Wendy, *China, Arms Control, and Non-Proliferation* (London, Routledge-Curzon 2004) 228 pp.
- Hill, Stephen M., *United Nations Disarmament in Intra-State Conflict* (Basingstoke,Palgrave Macmillan 2004) 303 pp.
- Maslen, Stuart, *Commentaries on Arms Control Treaties,* Vol. I (Oxford, Oxford University Press 2004) 522 pp.
- Organización para la Prohibición de las Armes Químicas, *Fundamentos del desarme químico*, 4e edn. (The Hague, Organización para la Prohibición de las Armes Químicas 2004) 36 pp.

Articles

- Ahlström, Christer, 'Arrows for India? Technology transfers for ballestic missile defence and the missile technology control regime', 9 *Journal of Conflict and Security Law* (2004) 1p
- Anthony, Ian, 'Arms control in a new international environment', in Hans-Joachim Giessmann, Roman Kúzniar and Zdzislaw Lachowski, eds., *International Security in a Time of Change: Threats, Concepts, Institutions: Festschrift for Adam Daniel Rotfeld* (Baden-Baden, Nomos 2004) pp. 476-483
- Bailes, Alyson J.K., 'Thoughts on the integrity of arms control', in Hans-Joachim Giessmann, Roman Kúzniar and Zdzislaw Lachowski, eds., *International Security in a Time of Change: Threats, Concepts, Institutions: Festschrift for Adam Daniel Rotfeld* (Baden-Baden, Nomos 2004) pp. 435-443
- Boothby, Derek, 'Disarmament: success and failures', in Jean E. Krasno, ed., *The United Nations: Confronting the Challenges of a Global Society* (Boulder, Lynne Rienner 2004) pp. 193-223
- Dutra, Michael, 'Strategic myopia: the United States, cruise missiles, and the missile technology control regime', 14 *Journal of Transnational Law and Policy* (2004) pp. 1-36
- Harrington, John, 'Arms control and national security', 38 *The International Lawyer* (2004) pp. 391-404

– Mian, Zia, 'The American problem: the United States and noncompliance in the world of arms control and nonproliferation', in Edward C. Luck and Michael W. Doyle, eds., *International Law and Organization: Closing the Compliance Gap* (Lanham, Rowman & Littlefield 2004) pp. 247-302

11.1 Conventional Weapons

Articles

– Angelet, Damien, 'Het protocol over explosieve oorlogsresten: een vijfde protocol bij de conventie over onmenselijke wapens', 13 *Zoeklicht* (2004) pp. 21-23
– Husbands, Jo L., 'The proliferation of conventional weapons and technologies', in Michael E. Brown, ed., *Grave New World: Security Challenges in the 21st Century* (Washington, Georgetown University Press 2003) pp. 62-90
– Huynen, Paul, 'Bijna een kwarteeuw Conventie Inhumane Wapens, een flexibel en dynamisch instrument, in staat om antwoorden te geven op moderne uitdagingen', 13 *Zoeklicht* (2004) pp. 8-12
– Lachowski, Zdzislaw, 'The Future of conventional arms control', in Hans-Joachim Giessmann, Roman Kúzniar and Zdzislaw Lachowski, eds., *International Security in a Time of Change: Threats, Concepts, Institutions: Festschrift for Adam Daniel Rotfeld* (Baden-Baden, Nomos 2004) pp. 459-467
– Lawson, Rick, 'A farewell to arms', 97 *Militair-rechtelijk tijdschrift* (2004) pp. 217-222
– Maresca, Louis, 'A new protocol on explosive remnants of war: the history and negotiation of Protocol V to the 1980 Covention on Certain Conventional Weapons', 86 *IRRC* (2004) pp. 815-835
– Mathews, Robert J., 'The second review conference of the 1980 Convention on Certain Conventional Weapons', 4 *YIHL* (2001) pp. 406-418
– Sidhu, Waheguru Pal Singh, 'A languid but lethal arms race', *Disarmament Forum* (2004) pp. 7-19

11.11 Mines

Books

– Matthew, Richard A., *Landmines and Human Security: International Politics and War's Hidden Legacy* (Albany, State University of New York Press 2004) 294 pp.

Articles

– Goose, Stephen and Jody William, 'The campaign to ban antipersonnel landmines: potential lessons', in Richard A. Matthew, Bryan McDonald and Kenneth R. Rutherford, eds., *Landmines and Human Security: International Politics and War's Hidden Legacy* (Albany, State University of New York Press 2004) pp. 239-249
– Hubert, Don, '"New" humanitarian advocacy? Civil society and the landmines ban', in Paul Gready, ed., *Fighting for Human Rights* (London, Routledge 2004) pp. 78-103
– MacDonald, Bryan, 'The global landmine crisis in the 1990s', in Richard A. Matthew, Bryan McDonald and Kenneth R. Rutherford, eds., *Landmines and Human Security:*

International Politics and War's Hidden Legacy (Albany, State University of New York Press 2004) pp. 21-33.
- Marques-Gross, Isabelle, 'Le dilemme des mines antipersonnel: le retour vers le futur', 5 *Annuaire français de relations internationales* (2004) pp. 782-800
- Matthew, Richard A., 'Human security and the mine ban movement I: introduction', in Richard A. Matthew, Bryan McDonald and Kenneth R. Rutherford, eds., *Landmines and Human Security: International Politics and War's Hidden Legacy* (Albany, State University of New York Press 2004) pp. 3-19
- Price, Richard, 'Emerging customary norms and anti-personnel landmines', in Christian Reus-Smit, ed., *The Politics of International Law* (Cambridge, Cambridge University Press 2004) pp. 106-130
- Torres Nachón, Claudio, 'The environmental impacts of landmines', in Richard A., Bryan Matthew, Bryan McDonald and Kenneth R. Rutherford, eds., *Landmines and Human Security: International Politics and War's Hidden Legacy* (Albany, State University of New York Press 2004) pp. 191-207
- Wapner, Paul, 'The campaign to ban antipersonnel landmines and global civil society', in Richard A. Matthew, Bryan McDonald and Kenneth R. Rutherford, eds., *Landmines and Human Security: International Politics and War's Hidden Legacy* (Albany, State University of New York Press 2004) pp. 251-268

11.12 Small Weapons and Others

Articles

- Capie, David, 'Regional introduction: missing the target: the human cost of small-arms proliferation and misuse in Southeast Asia', in Annelies Heijmans, Nicola Simmonds and Hans van de Veen, eds., *Searching for Peace in Asia Pacific: an Overview of Conflict Prevention and Peacebuilding Activities* (Boulder, Rienner 2004) pp. 294-312
- Ero, Comfort and Angela Ndinga-Muvumba, 'Small arms, light weapons', in Adekeye Adebajo and Ismail Rashid, eds., *West Africa's Security Challenges Building Peace in a Troubled Region* (Boulder, Rienner 2004) pp. 223-243
- Frey, Barbara A., 'Small arms and light weapons: the tools used to violate human rights', *Disarmament Forum* (2004) pp. 37-46
- Hillman, Elizabeth Lutes, Disloyalty among "men in arms": Korean war POWs at court-martial, 82 *North Carolina LR* (2004) pp. 1629-1659
- Lloyd, Carolyn Elizabeth , 'Prospects for the emergence of a global small arms regime', in Tom Keating and W. Andy Knight, eds., *Building Sustainable Peace* (Tokyo, United Nations University Press 2004) pp. 281-302
- Vugt, G.A.J.M. van, 'Juridische aspecten van niet-letale wapens', 97 *Militair-rechtelijk tijdschrift* (2004) pp. 246-253
- Wairagu, Francis K., 'The proliferation of small arms and their role in the escalating conflicts in East Africa', in Alfred G. Nhema, ed., *The Quest for Peace in Africa: Transformations, Democracy and Public Policy* (Utrecht, International Books 2004) pp. 107-121

11.2 Weapons of Mass Destruction

Books

- Blix, Hans, *Disarming Iraq: the Search for Weapons of Mass Destruction* (London, Bloomsbury 2004) 285 pp.
- Graham, Thomas, *Common Sense on Weapons of Mass Destruction* (Seattle, University of Washington Press 2004) 206 pp.
- Krömer, Katrin, *Massenvernichtungswaffen und die NATO: die Bedrohung durch die Proliferation von Massenvernichtungswaffen als Kooperationsproblem der transatlantischen Allianz* (Baden-Baden, Nomos 2003) 420 pp.

Articles

- Ekeus, Rolf, 'Reassessment: the IISS strategic dossier on Iraq's weapons of mass destruction', 46 *Survival* (2004) pp. 73-87
- Fidler, David P., 'International law and weapons of mass destruction: end of the arms control approach?', 14 *Duke JC & IL* (2004) pp. 39-88
- Flibbert, Andrew, 'After Saddam: regional insecurity, weapons of mass destruction, and proliferation pressures in postwar Iraq', in Demetrios James Caraley, ed., *American Hegemony: Preventive War, Iraq, and Imposing Democracy* (New York, Academy of Political Science 2004) pp. 51-80
- Gottemoeller, Rose, 'Voluntary action in the fight against weapons of mass destruction', 4 *Disarmament Forum* (2004) pp. 51-56
- Mani, V.S., 'Future strategies in the war against terrorism and proliferation of weapons of mass destruction: an Indian perception', 44 *Indian JIL* (2004) pp. 221-259
- Mantels, Valère, 'How to control weapons of mass destruction', in Yassin El-Ayouty, ed., *Perspectives on 9/11* (Westport, Praeger 2004) pp. 185-196
- Neuneck, Götz, 'Die Proliferation von Massenvernichtungswaffen als Herausforderung für die EU', in Hans-Georg Ehrhart and Burkard Schmitt, eds., *Die Sicherheitspolitik der EU im Werden: Bedrohungen, Aktivitäten, Fähigkeiten* (Baden-Baden, Nomos 2004) pp. 32-44
- Norov, Vladimir, 'Strategien im Kampf gegen den Terrorismus und die Weiterverbreitung von Massenvernichtungswaffen', in Bernhard Vogel, Rudolf Dolzer and Mathias Herdegen, eds., *Die Zukunft der UNO und des Völkerrechts: Beiträge und Thesen einer internationalen Konferenz* (Freiburg im Breisgau, Herder 2004) pp. 85-97
- Schaller, Christian, 'Massenvernichtungswaffen und Präventivkrieg: Möglichkeiten der Rechtfertigung einer militärischen Intervention im Irak aus völkerrechtlicher Sicht', in Kai Ambos and Jörg Arnold, eds., *Der Irak-Krieg und das Völkerrecht* (Berlin, Berliner Wissenschafts-Verlag 2004) pp. 329-358
- Silva, Pascal Teixeira da, 'Weapons of mass destruction: the Iraqi case', in David M. Malone, ed., *The UN Security Council* (Boulder, Rienner 2004) pp. 205-218
- Sur, Serge, 'La Resolution 1540 du Conseil de sécurité (28 avril 2004): entre la prolifération des armes de destruction massive, le terrorisme et les acteurs non etatiques', 108 *Revue générale de droit international public* (2004) pp. 855-882
- Tannenwald, Nina, 'The UN and debates over weapons of mass destruction', in Richard M. Price and Mark W. Zacher, eds., *The United Nations and Global Security* (New York, Palgrave Macmillan 2004) pp. 3-20

11.21 Nuclear Weapons

Articles

- Cohen, Stephen P., 'Nuclear weapons and nuclear war in South Asia: unknowable futures', in Ramesh Thakur and Oddny Wiggen, eds., *South Asia in the World: Problem-Solving Perspectives on Security, Sustainable Development, and Good Governance* (Tokyo, United Nations University Press 2004) pp. 39-57
- Fujita, Hisakazu, 'The advisory opinion of the International Court of Justice on the legality of nuclear weapons', in Naorem Sanajaoba, ed., *A Manual of International Humanitarian Laws* (New Dehli, Regency Publications 2004) pp. 617-626
- Gowlland-Debbas, Vera, 'The relevance of paragraph 25 of the ICJ's advisory opinion on nuclear weapons', 98 *Proceedings of the Annual Meeting* (2004) pp. 358-363
- Moxley, Charles J., 'The sword in the mirror: the lawfulness of North Korea's use and threat of use of nuclear weapons based on the United States' legitimization of nuclear weapons', 27 *Fordham ILJ* (2004) pp. 1379-1489
- Mueller, John, 'The essential irrelevance of nuclear weapons: stability in the postwar world', in Karen Mingst and Jack Snyder, eds., *Essential Readings in World Politics* (New York, Norton 2004) pp. 341-347
- Sagan, Scott D. and Kenneth N Waltz, 'Indian and Pakistani nuclear weapons: for better or worse?', in Karen Mingst and Jack Snyder, eds., *Essential Readings in World Politics* (New York, Norton 2004) pp. 322-341

11.22 Chemical and Biological Weapons

Books

- Chevrier, Marie Isabelle, *The Implementation of Legally Binding Measures to Strengthen the Biological and Toxin Weapons Convention* (Dordrecht, Kluwer Academic Publishers 2004) 299 pp.
- Zammit Borda, Aldo, *The Threat and Use of Chemical and Biological Weapons Under International Law* (Valetta, University of Malta 2003) 264 pp.

Articles

- Kelle, Alexander and Pamela Mills, 'The Chemical Weapons Convention regime and its evolution', in Marie Isabelle Chevrier, ed., *The Implementation of Legally Binding Measures to Strengthen the Biological and Toxin Weapons Convention* (Dordrecht, Kluwer Academic Publishers 2004) pp. 79-102
- Pinson, Robert D., 'Is nanotechnology prohibited by the Biological and Chemical Weapons Conventions?', 22 *Berkeley JIL* (2004) pp. 279-309
- Sutherland, Ronald G., 'The resurgence of chemical and biological weapons', in Hans-Joachim Giessmann, Roman Kúzniar and Zdzislaw Lachowski, eds., *International Security in a Time of Change: Threats, Concepts, Institutions: Festschrift for Adam Daniel Rotfeld* (Baden-Baden, Nomos 2004) pp. 78-94
- Wheelis, Mark, 'A short history of biological warfare and weapons', in Marie Isabelle Chevrier, ed., *The Implementation of Legally Binding Measures to Strengthen the Biological and Toxin Weapons Convention* (Dordrecht, Kluwer Academic Publishers 2004) pp. 15-31

12.1 CONFLICT PREVENTION

Books

- Carment, David, *Conflict Prevention from Rhetoric to Reality,* Vol. II, *Opportunities and Innovations* (Lanham, Lexington Books 2004) 444 pp.
- Heijmans, Annelies, *Searching for Peace in Asia Pacific: An Overview of Conflict Prevention and Peacebuilding Activities* (Boulder, Lynne Rienner 2004) 848 pp.
- Kirton, John J., *The G8, the United Nations, and Conflict Prevention*, (Aldershot, Ashgate 2004) 334 pp.
- Schnabel, Albrecht, *Conflict Prevention from Rhetoric to Reality* (Lanham, Lexington Books 2004) 2 dl.
- Sriram, Chandra Lekha, *Exploring Subregional Conflict: Opportunities for Conflict Prevention* (Boulder, Rienner 2004) 209 pp.

Articles

- Blagescu, Monica, 'Conflict prevention through peace education: a debate', in Albrecht Schnabel and David Carment, eds., *Conflict Prevention from Rhetoric to Reality,* Vol. 2 (Lanham, Lexington Books 2004) pp. 199-226
- Boothby, Derek and George D'Angelo, 'Building capacity within the United Nations: cooperation on the prevention of violent conflicts', in David Carment and Albrecht Schnabel, eds., *Conflict Prevention from Rhetoric to Reality,* Vol. 2 (Lanham, Lexington Books 2004) pp. 251-271
- Kolanowski, Stéphane, 'Preventing conflict: a EU-International Committee of the Red Cross common interest', in Vincent Kronenberger and Jan Wouters, eds., *The European Union and Conflict Prevention: Policy and Legal Aspects* (The Hague, T.M.C. Asser Press 2004) pp. 501-509
- Mani, Rama, 'The root causes of terrorism and conflict prevention', in Jane Boulden and Thomas G. Weiss, eds., *Terrorism and the UN* (Bloomington, Indiana University Press 2004) pp. 219-241
- Mezoui, Hanifa, 'The United Nations' view on the role of NGOs with consultative status in the conflict prevention, peace building and development', 43 *Revue de droit militaire et de droit de la guerre* (2004) pp. 155-164
- Szapiro, Manuel, 'Organisations' cooperation in the field of conflict prevention', in Vincent Kronenberger and Jan Wouters, eds., *The European Union and Conflict Prevention: Policy and Legal Aspects* (The Hague, T.M.C. Asser Press 2004) pp. 347-368
- Tanner, Fred, 'Conflict prevention and conflict resolution: limits of multilateralism', in Naorem Sanajaoba, ed., *A Manual of International Humanitarian Laws* (New Dehli, Regency Publications 2004) pp. 710-727

12.2 CONFLICT RESOLUTION

Books

- Kemp, Graham, *Keeping the Peace: Conflict Resolution and Peaceful Societies Around the World* (New York, Routledge) 231 pp.

- Maoz, Zeev, *Multiple Paths to Knowledge in International Relations: Methodology in the Study of Conflict Management and Conflict Resolution* (Lanham, Lexington Books 2004) 373 pp.
- Schneckener, Ulrich, *Managing and Settling Ethnic Conflicts: Perspectives on Successes and Failures in Europe, Africa and Asia* (London, Hurst 2004) 291 pp.

Articles

- Hanne, Gottfried, 'The role and activities of the OSCE mission to Moldova in the process of Transdniestrian conflict resolution', 2 *European Yearbook of Minority Issues* (2004) pp. 31-51
- Lundin, Ira Baptista, 'Reflections on conflict resolution and "provention": the state and citizens in Mozambique', in Peter Batchelor, ed., *Demilitarisation and Peace-building in Southern Africa*, Vol. 2 (Aldershot, Ashgate 2004) pp. 19-45
- Rösel, Jakob, 'Democracy and ethnic conflicts: the politics of ethnicity and conflict resolution in South Asia', in Marie-Claire Foblets and Trutz von Trotha, eds., *Healing the Wounds: Essays on the Reconstruction of Societies After War* (Oxford, Hart 2004) pp. 203-220
- Tanner, Fred, 'Conflict prevention and conflict resolution: limits of multilateralism', in Naorem Sanajaoba, ed., *A Manual of International Humanitarian Laws* (New Dehli, Regency Publications 2004) pp. 710-727
- Williams, Paul R., and Karen Heymann, 'Earned sovereignty: an emerging conflict resolution approach', 10 *ILSA Jl & CL ILSA* (2004) pp. 437-445
- Youngs, Richard, 'Democratic institution-building and conflict resolution: emerging EU approaches', 11 *International Peacekeeping* (2004) pp. 526-543

13.1 JUS AD BELLUM

Books

- Frostad, Magne, *Jus in Bello After September 11, 2001: the Relationship Between Jus Ad Bellum and Jus in Bello and the Requirements for Status As Prisoner of War* (Baden-Baden, Nomos 2004) 212 pp.
- Karoubi, Mohammad Taghi, *Just or Unjust War? International Law and Unilateral Use of Armed Force by States at the Turn of the 20th Century* (Aldershot, Ashgate 2004) 267 pp.
- Roscher, Bernhard, *Der Briand-Kellogg-Pakt von 1928: der "Verzicht auf den Krieg als Mittel nationaler Politik" im völkerrechtlichen Denken der Zwischenkriegszeit* (Baden-Baden, Nomos 2004) 344 pp.

Articles

- Andreopoulos, George J., 'Violations of human rights and humanitarian law and threats to international peace and security', in Ramesh Thakur and Peter Malcontent, eds., *From Sovereign Impunity to International Accountability: the Search for Justice in a World of States* (Tokyo, United Nations University Press 2004) pp. 80-99
- Brunnée, Jutta and Stephen J. Toope, 'Slouching towards new "just" wars: international law and the use of force after September 11th', 51 *Netherlands International Law Review* (2004) pp. 363-392

- Gaja, Giorgio, 'Combating terrorism: issues of jus ad bellum and jus in bello: the case of Afghanistan', in Wolfgang Benedek and Alice Yotopoulos-Marangopoulos, eds., *Anti-terrorist Measures and Human Rights* (Leiden, Nijhoff 2004) pp. 161-170
- Gill, Terry D., 'The war in Iraq and the contemporary jus ad bellum', 22 *Merkourios* (2004) pp. 50-54
- Heintschel von Heinegg, Wolff, 'Irak-Krieg und ius in bello', 41 *Archiv des Völkerrechts* (2003) pp. 272-294
- Laursen, Andreas, 'The use of force and (the state of) necessity', 37 *Vanderbilt JTL* (2004) pp. 485-526
- Lippman, Matthew, 'The history, development and decline of crimes against peace', 36 *George Washington International Law Review* (2004) pp. 957-1056
- Pedigo, Jason, 'Rogue states, weapons of mass destruction, and terrorism: was Security Council approval necessary for the invasion of Iraq?', 32 *Georgia JL & Comp. L* (2004) pp. 199-229
- Pellet, Alain and Tzankov, Vladimir, 'Can a state victim of a terror act have recourse to armed force?', 17 *Humanitäres Völkerrecht* (2004) pp. 68-72
- Pierson, Charles, 'Preemptive self-defense in an age of weapons of mass destruction: Operation Iraqi Freedom', 33 *Denver JIL & Pol.* (2004) pp. 150-178
- Preiser, Simone, '"Operation Enduring Freedom" and the UN Charter: the terrorist attack of 11 September 2001 and the subsequent military response', 8 *International Peacekeeping* (2004) pp. 213-240
- Strydom, Hennie, 'Jus ad bellum and jus in bello in the South African constitution', 29 *South African YIL* (2004) pp. 78-104
- Weisburd, A. Mark, 'The war in Iraq and the dilemma of controlling the international use of force', 39 *Texas ILJ* (2004) pp. 522-560
- Wolfrum, Rüdiger, 'The attack of September 11, 2001, the wars against the Taliban and Iraq: is there a need to reconsider international law on the recourse to force and the rules in armed conflict?', 7 *MPYIL* (2004) pp. 1-78

13.2 THE LAW RELATING TO TERRORISM AND COUNTER-TERRORISM

Books

- Bianchi, Andrea, *Enforcing International Law Norms Against Terrorism* (Oxford, Hart Publishing 2004) 549 pp.
- Biegi, Mandana, *Die humanitäre Herausforderung: der International Criminal Court und die USA* (Baden-Baden, Nomos 2004) 264 pp.
- Boulden, Jane, *Terrorism and the UN: Before and After September 11* Bloomington, Indiana University Press 2004) 256 pp.
- Cassel, Elaine, *The War on Civil Liberties: How Bush and Ashcroft Have Dismantled the Bill of Rights* (Chicago, Lawrence Hill Books 2004) 204 pp.
- Chaliand, Gérard, *Histoire du terrorisme: de l'Antiquité à Al Qaida* (Paris, Bayard 2004) 667 pp.
- Christian Walter, *Terrorism as a Challenge for National and International Law: Security Versus Liberty?* (Berlin, Springer 2004) 1484 pp.

- Cohen, David B., *American National Security and Civil Liberties in an Era of Terrorism* (New York, Palgrave Macmillan 2004) 248 pp.
- Council of Europe, *"Apologie du terrorisme" and "incitement to terrorism"* (Strasbourg, Council of Europe Publishing 2004) 205 pp.
- Council of Europe, *The Fight Against Terrorism: Council of Europe Standards*, 2nd edn. (Strasbourg, Council of Europe Publishing 2004)
- Foot, Rosemary, *Human Rights and Counter-Terrorism in America's Asia Policy* (Oxford, Oxford University Press 2004) 94 pp.
- Gareau, Frederick H., *State Terrorism and the United States: from Counterinsurgency to the War on Terrorism* (Atlanta, Clarity Press/London, Zed Books 2004) 254 pp.
- Garfinkle, Adam, *A Practical Guide to Winning the War on Terrorism* (Stanford, Hoover Institution Press 2004) 230 pp.
- Gilmore, William C., *Dirty Money: the Evolution of International Measures to Counter Money Laundering and the Financing of Terrorism*, 3rd edn., (Strasbourg, Council of Europe Publishing 2004) 347 pp.
- Klein, Eckart, *Der Terror, der Staat und das Recht* (Berlin, Duncker & Humblot 2004) 108 pp.
- *La lutte contre le terrorisme: les normes du Conseil de l'Europe* (Strasbourg, Conseil de l'Europe 2004) 430 pp.
- Moore, John Norton, *Civil Litigation Against Terrorism* (Durham, Carolina Academic Press 2004) 294 pp.
- Pearlstein, Richard M., *Fatal Future? Transnational Terrorism and the New Global Disorder* (Austin, University of Texas Press 2004) 198 pp.
- Richardson, Michael, *A Time Bomb for Global Trade: Maritime-Related Terrorism in an Age of Weapons of Mass Destruction* (Singapore, Institute of Southeast Asian Studies 2004) 155 pp.
- Schaller, Christian, *Das Friedenssicherungsrecht im Kampf gegen den Terrorismus: Gewaltverbot, kollektive Sicherheit, Selbstverteidigung und Präemption* (Berlin, Deutsches Institut für Internationale Politik und Sicherheit 2004) 23 pp.
- *Terrorism: Documents of International and Local Control*, Vol. 42 U.S. Perspectives (Dobbs Ferry, Oceana 2004) 426 pp.
- *Terrorism: Documents of International and Local Control*, Vol. 43 U.S. Perspectives (Dobbs Ferry, Oceana 2004) 517 pp.
- *Terrorism: Documents of International and Local Control*, Vol. 44 U.S. Perspectives (Dobbs Ferry, Oceana 2004) 485 pp.
- *Terrorism: Documents of International and Local Control*, Vol. 45 U.S. Perspectives (Dobbs Ferry, Oceana 2004) 477 pp.
- *Terrorism: Documents of International and Local Control*, Vol. 46 U.S. Perspectives (Dobbs Ferry, Oceana 2004) 474 pp.
- *Terrorism: Documents of International and Local Control*, Vol. 49 U.S. Perspectives (Dobbs Ferry, Oceana 2004) 438 pp.
- *Terrorism: Documents of International and Local Control*, Vol. 50 U.S. Perspectives (Dobbs Ferry, Oceana 2004) 445 pp.
- Thévenoz, Luc BF, *Blanchiment: réglementation et autoréglementation de la lutte contre le blanchiment et le financement du terrorisme en Suisse* (Zürich, Schulthess 2004) Onreg. gep

– Vöneky, Silja, 'The Fight Against Terrorism and the Rules of the Law of Warfare', in Christian Walter, *Terrorism As a Challenge for National and International Law: Security Versus Liberty?* (Berlin, Springer 2004) pp. 925-949

Articles

– Ascensio, Hervé, 'Terrorisme et juridictions internationales', in Société Française pour le Droit International, *Les nouvelles menaces contre la paix et la sécurité internationales: journée franco-allemande* (Paris, Pedone 2004) pp. 271-285
– Bachus, Alison S., 'From drugs to terrorism: the focus shifts in the international fight against money laundering after September 11, 2001', 21 *Arizona Jl & CL* (2004) pp. 834-872
– Baldwin, Fletcher N., 'The rule of law, terrorism, and countermeasures including the USA Patriot Act of 2001', 16 *Florida JIL* (2004) pp. 43-87
– Beyries, Pierre, 'Le terrorisme en mer', in Société Française pour le Droit International, *Les nouvelles menaces contre la paix et la sécurité internationales: journée franco-allemande* (Paris, Pedone 2004) pp. 140-147
– Biderman, Michael Hayes, 'A potentially dubious new front in the war on terrorism: state-sponsored civil suits and the Omagh Bombing', 14 *Transn. L & Contemp. Probs.* (2004) pp. 803-829
– Bothe, Michael, 'The international community and terrorism', in Société Française pour le Droit International, *Les nouvelles menaces contre la paix et la sécurité internationales: journée franco-allemande* (Paris, Pedone 2004) pp. 47-62
– Cumin, David, 'Tentative de définition du terrorisme à partir du jus in bello', in Université de Paris, Institut de Criminologie, *Revue de science criminelle et de droit pénal comparé* (Paris, Sirey 2004) pp. 11-30
– Dederer, Hans-Georg, 'Krieg gegen Terror', 59 *Juristenzeitung* (2004) pp. 421-431
– De Kerchove, Gilles, 'L' action de l'Union européenne en matière de lutte contre le terrorisme', 480 *Revue du marché commun* (2004) pp. 421-424
– Dupuy, Pierre-Marie, 'La Communauté internationale et le terrorisme', in Société Française pour le Droit International, *Les nouvelles menaces contre la paix et la sécurité internationales: journée franco-allemande* (Paris, Pedone 2004) pp. 35-45
– Dupuy, Pierre-Marie, 'State sponsors of terrorism: issues of international responsibility', in Andrea Bianchi, ed., *Enforcing International Law Norms against Terrorism* (Oxford, Hart 2004) pp. 3-16
– Gardella, Anna, 'The fight against the financing of terrorism between judicial and regulatory cooperation', in Andrea Bianchi, ed., *Enforcing International Law Norms against Terrorism* (Oxford, Hart 2004) pp. 415-452
– Gasser, Hans-Peter, 'International humanitarian law, the prohibition of terrorist acts and the fight against terrorism', 4 *YIHL* (2004) pp. 329-347
– Gehr, Walter, 'The Counter-Terrorism Committee and Security Council resolution 1373 (2001)', in Wolfgang Benedek, ed., *Anti-terrorist Measures and Human Rights* (Leiden, Nijhoff 2004) pp. 41-44
– Goldstone, Richard J., 'Der Schutz der Menschenrechte und Grundfreiheiten im Zeiten des "Kriegs gegen den Terrorismus"', in Bernhard Vogel, Rudolf Dolzer und Mathias Herdegen, eds., *Die Zukunft der UNO und des Völkerrechts: Beiträge und Thesen einer internationalen Konferenz* (Freiburg im Breisgau, Herder 2004) pp. 79-84

- Grabenwarter, Christoph, 'Right to fair trial and terrorism', in Société Française pour le Droit International, *Les nouvelles menaces contre la paix et la sécurité internationales: journée franco-allemande* (Paris, Pedone 2004) pp. 211-236
- Grzeszick, Bernd, 'Staat und Terrorismus: ein staatstheoretische Überlegung in praktischer Absicht', in Eckart Klein, Christian Hacke and Bernd Grzeszick, eds., *Der Terror, der Staat und das Recht* (Berlin, Duncker & Humblot 2004) pp. 55-81
- Hoss, Cristina and Christiane E. Philipp, 'The Islamic world and the fight against terrorism', in Christian Walter, ed., *Terrorism as a Challenge for National and International Law: Security Versus Liberty?* (Berlin, Springer 2004) pp. 363-379
- Jekewitz, Jürgen, 'The action of the European Union to combat terrorism', in Société Française pour le Droit International, *Les nouvelles menaces contre la paix et la sécurité internationales: journée franco-allemande* (Paris, Pedone 2004) pp. 77-94
- Jordán, Javier, 'El terrorismo y la transformación de la guerra: consideraciones sobre la lucha global de Al-Qaida', 20 *Anuario de derecho internacional* (2004) pp. 409-424
- Jörg, N. and J.S. Holthuis, 'Toetsing van het Nederlandse voorbehoud bij het Europese Terrorisme Verdrag (ETV)', 97 *Militair-rechtelijk tijdschrift* (2004) pp. 196-203
- Joseph, Sarah, 'Australian counter-terrorism legislation and the international human rights framework', 27 *University of New South Wales Law Journal* (2004) pp. 428-453
- Klein, Eckart, 'Die Herausforderung durch den internationalen Terrorismus: hört hier das Völkerrecht auf?', in Eckart Klein, Christian Hacke and Bernd Grzeszick, eds., *Der Terror, der Staat und das Recht* (Berlin, Duncker & Humblot 2004) pp. 9-39
- MacKay, Fiona, 'U.S. unilateralism and international crimes: the International Criminal Court and terrorism', 36 *Cornell ILJ* (2004) pp. 455-471
- Malloy, Michael P., 'Was bedeutet "Terrorismus?"', 17 *Transnational Lawyer* (2004) pp. 39-50
- Meessen, Karl M., 'Selbstverteidigung gegen den internationalen Terrorismus als werdendes Völkergewohnheitsrecht', in Kai Ambos and Jörg Arnold, eds., *Der Irak-Krieg und das Völkerrecht* (Berlin, Berliner Wissenschafts-Verlag 2004) pp. 276-281
- Millard, George, 'Post-September 11 terrorism measures', 16 *Florida JIL* (2004) pp. 97-105
- Morris, Madeline, 'Terrorism and unilateralism: criminal jurisdiction and international relations', 36 *Cornell ILJ* (2004) pp. 473-489
- Münkler, Herfried, 'Terrorismus heute: die Asymmetrisierung des Krieges', 59 *Internationale Politik* (2004) pp. 1-11
- Neuhold, Hanspeter, 'Post-Cold war terrorism: systemic background, phenomenology and definitions', in Société Française pour le Droit International, *Les nouvelles menaces contre la paix et la sécurité internationales: journée franco-allemande* (Paris, Pedone 2004) pp. 13-34
- Neuman, Gerald L., 'Comment, counter-terrorist operations and the rule of law', 15 *EJIL* (2004) pp. 1019-1029
- Oeter, Stefan, 'Terrorism and laws of war', in Société Française pour le Droit International, *Les nouvelles menaces contre la paix et la sécurité internationales: journée franco-allemande* (Paris, Pedone 2004) pp. 183-210
- Olivier, Clémentine, 'Human rights law and the international fight against terrorism: how do Security Council resolutions impact on states' obligations under international human rights law?', 73 *Nordic JIL* (2004) pp. 399-419
- Pellet, Alain and Vladimir Tzankov, 'L'état victime d'un acte terroriste peut-il recourir à la force armée?', in Société Française pour le Droit International, *Les nouvelles menaces*

contre la paix et la sécurité internationales: journée franco-allemande (Paris, Pedone 2004) pp. 95-107

- Pingel, Isabelle, 'L'action de l'Union européene face au terrorisme', in Société Française pour le Droit International, *Les nouvelles menaces contre la paix et la sécurité internationales: journée franco-allemande* (Paris, Pedone 2004) pp. 63-75
- Rosand, Eric, 'The Security Council's efforts to monitor the implementation of Al Qaeda/Taliban sanctions', 98 *AJIL* (2004) pp. 745-763
- Roth, Kenneth, 'The fight against terrorism: the Bush administration's dangerous neglect of human rights', in Thomas G. Weiss, Margaret E. Crahan and John Gering, eds., *Wars on Terrorism and Iraq: Human Rights, Unilateralism, and U.S. Foreign Policy* (New York, Routledge 2004) pp. 113-131
- Sadat, Leila Nadya, 'Do all Arabs really look alike? Prejudice and the U.S. "war" on terror', 50 *Wayne LR* (2004) pp. 69-78
- Schabas, William A., 'Is terrorism a crime against humanity?', 8 *International Peacekeeping* (2004) pp. 255-261
- Scharf, Michael P., 'Defining terrorism as the peacetime equivalent of war crimes: problems and prospects', 36 *Case Western Reserve Journal of International Law* (2004) pp. 359-374
- Sloss, David L., 'Availability of U.S. courts to detainees at Guantánamo Bay naval base - reach of habeus corpus – executive power in war on terror', 98 *AJIL* (2004) pp. 788-798
- Sossai, Mirko, 'La cooperazione multilaterale nella lotta al terrorismo internazionale: il Comitato contro il terrorismo del Consiglio di sicurezza delle Nazioni Unite', 1 *Pace diritti umani* (2004) pp. 79-90
- Stephens, Tim, 'International criminal law and the response to international terrorism', 27 *University of New South Wales Law Journal* (2004) pp. 454-481
- Stephenson, Evan, 'Does United Nations war prevention encourage state-sponsorship of international terrorism? An economic analysis', 44 *Virginia JIL* 2004) pp. 1197-1230
- Tavernier, Paul, 'Competence universelle et terrorisme', in Société Française pour le Droit International, *Les nouvelles menaces contre la paix et la sécurité internationales: journée franco-allemande* (Paris, Pedone 2004) pp. 237-256
- Tomuschat, Christian, 'Universal jurisdiction and terrorism', in Société Française pour le Droit International, *Les nouvelles menaces contre la paix et la sécurité internationales: journée franco-allemande* (Paris, Pedone 2004) pp. 257-270
- Vöneky, Silja, 'The fight against terrorism and the rules of the law of warfare', in Christian Walter, ed., *Terrorism as a Challenge for National and International Law: Security Versus Liberty?* (Berlin, Springer 2004) pp. 925-949
- Weckel, Philippe, 'Terrorisme et droit de la guerre: le droit de la "guerre contre le terrorisme", in Société Française pour le Droit International, *Les nouvelles menaces contre la paix et la sécurité internationales: journée franco-allemande* (Paris, Pedone 2004) pp. 165-182
- Wiethoff, Jan, 'Folter: ein zulässiges Mittel einer effektiven Terrorismus Bekämpfung?: die tickende Zeitbombe in der Großstadt', 17 *Humanitäres Völkerrecht* (2004) pp. 104-108
- Wolfrum, Rüdiger, 'The attack of September 11, 2001, the wars against the Taliban and Iraq: is there a need to reconsider international law on the recourse to force and the rules in armed conflict?', 7 *MPYBUNL* (2004) pp. 1-78

– Zeidan, Sami, 'Desperately seeking definition: the international community's quest for identifying the specter of terrorism', 36 *Cornell ILJ* (2004) pp. 491-496

13.3 MILITARY LAW

Books

– Schlueter, David A., *Military Criminal Justice: Practice and Procedure*, 6th edn. (San Francisco, LexisNexis/Bender 2004) 1429 pp.

13.4 HUMAN RIGHTS

Articles

– Ateneo de Manila University, 'Ushering a new age for humanity: the interface of public international law with human rights and humanitarian laws', 48 *Ateneo LJ* (2004) pp. 902-1378
– 'Ushering a new age for humanity: the interface of public international law with human rights and humanitarian laws', 48 *Ateneo Law Journal* (2005) pp. 902-1378
– Warbrick, Colin, 'The European response to terrorism in an age of human rights', 15 *EJIL* (2004) pp. 989-1018
– Watkin, Kenneth, 'Controlling the use of force: a role for human rights norms in contemporary armed conflict', 98 *AJIL* (2004) pp. 1-34

13.5 REFUGEE LAW/IDPs

Articles

– Funke, Daniela, 'Internal displacement in Georgia: a humanitarian or a political Issue?', 17 *Humanitäres Völkerrecht* (2004) pp. 241-247
– Kumar Sinha, Manoj, 'The Afghan refugees post- 9/11: dilemmas and prospects', 4 *ISIL Year Book of International Humanitarian and Refugee Law* (2004) pp. 89-102
– Kumar, S.Y. Surendra, 'The Afghan refugees post- 9/11: dilemmas and prospects', 4 *ISIL Year Book of International Humanitarian and Refugee Law* (2004) pp. 79-88
– Lavoyer, Jean-Philippe, 'Refugees and internally displaced persons: international humanitarian law and the role of the ICRC', in Naorem Sanajaoba, ed., *A Manual of International Humanitarian Laws* (New Dehli, Regency Publications 2004) pp. 163-183
– Saideman, Lewis, 'Do Palestinian refugees have a right of return to Israel? An examination of the scope of and limitations on the right of return', 44 *Virginia JIL* (2004) pp. 830-877
– Shoyele, Olugbenga, 'Armed conflicts and Canadian refugee law and policy', 16 *International Journal of Refugee Law* (2004) pp. 547-583
– Suryanarayan, V., 'Outcasts in their own country: internally displaced people in Sri Lanka', 4 *ISIL Year Book of International Humanitarian and Refugee Law* (2004) pp. 136-142

TABLE OF CASES*

INTERNATIONAL

* The Table of cases was compiled by Mrs B.M. Hall, Elie, UK

 DOI 10.1017/S1389135904007299

NATIONAL

INDEX

The index contains references to all matters of substance dealt with in the text of the articles. Detailed references to cases dealt with will be found in the accompanying Table of Cases. Multilateral agreements are indexed under Agreements, multilateral, classified by subject. The section on Correspondents' Reports is also indexed, but for information on the practice of individual states regarding detailed aspects of international humanitarian law the reader should consult the index under the states concerned. The index does contain, however, references to material from this section and the Documentation section which relate to the major topics of discussion in the present volume. Footnotes containing substantive material are also indexed, as are references to the work of scholars the first time such work is listed.

The index was compiled by Mrs B.M. Hall, Elie, UK

Abbreviations frequently used

g.r.	general references
ICC	International Criminal Court
ICJ	International Court of Justice
ICTR	International Criminal Tribunal for Rwanda
ICTY	International Criminal Tribunal for the Former Yugoslavia
IHL	International humanitarian law
p.a.r.	parties, accessions, ratifications
UN	United Nations Organisation
US	United States of America

Yearbook of International Humanitarian Law
Volume 7 - 2004 - pp. 739-787 DOI 10.1017/S1389135904007391